The Cumulative Standardized Normal Distribution (Continued)

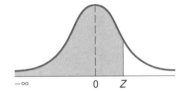

Entry represents area under the stadardized normal distribution from $-\infty$ to Z

Z	0.00	0.01	0.02	0.03	0.04	0.05	0.06	0.07	0.08	0.09
0.0	0.5000	0.5040	0.5080	0.5120	0.5160	0.5199	0.5239	0.5279	0.5319	0.5359
0.1	0.5398	0.5438	0.5478	0.5517	0.5557	0.5596	0.5636	0.5675	0.5714	0.5753
0.2	0.5793	0.5832	0.5871	0.5910	0.5948	0.5987	0.6026	0.6064	0.6103	0.6141
0.3	0.6179	0.6217	0.6255	0.6293	0.6331	0.6368	0.6406	0.6443	0.6480	0.6517
0.4	0.6554	0.6591	0.6628	0.6664	0.6700	0.6736	0.6772	0.6808	0.6844	0.6879
0.5	0.6915	0.6950	0.6985	0.7019	0.7054	0.7088	0.7123	0.7157	0.7190	0.7224
0.6	0.7257	0.7291	0.7324	0.7357	0.7389	0.7422	0.7454	0.7486	0.7518	0.7549
0.7	0.7580	0.7612	0.7642	0.7673	0.7704	0.7734	0.7764	0.7794	0.7823	0.7852
0.8	0.7881	0.7910	0.7939	0.7967	0.7995	0.8023	0.8051	0.8078	0.8106	0.8133
0.9	0.8159	0.8186	0.8212	0.8238	0.8264	0.8289	0.8315	0.8340	0.8365	0.8389
1.0	0.8413	0.8438	0.8461	0.8485	0.8508	0.8531	0.8554	0.8577	0.8599	0.8621
1.1	0.8643	0.8665	0.8686	0.8708	0.8729	0.8749	0.8770	0.8790	0.8810	0.8830
1.2	0.8849	0.8869	0.8888	0.8907	0.8925	0.8944	0.8962	0.8980	0.8997	0.9015
1.3	0.9032	0.9049	0.9066	0.9082	0.9099	0.9115	0.9131	0.9147	0.9162	0.9177
1.4	0.9192	0.9207	0.9222	0.9236	0.9251	0.9265	0.9279	0.9292	0.9306	0.9319
1.5	0.9332	0.9345	0.9357	0.9370	0.9382	0.9394	0.9406	0.9418	0.9429	0.9441
1.6	0.9452	0.9463	0.9474	0.9484	0.9495	0.9505	0.9515	0.9525	0.9535	0.9545
1.7	0.9554	0.9564	0.9573	0.9582	0.9591	0.9599	0.9608	0.9616	0.9625	0.9633
1.8	0.9641	0.9649	0.9656	0.9664	0.9671	0.9678	0.9686	0.9693	0.9699	0.9706
1.9	0.9713	0.9719	0.9726	0.9732	0.9738	0.9744	0.9750	0.9756	0.9761	0.9767
2.0	0.9772	0.9778	0.9783	0.9788	0.9793	0.9798	0.9803	0.9808	0.9812	0.9817
2.1	0.9821	0.9826	0.9830	0.9834	0.9838	0.9842	0.9846	0.9850	0.9854	0.9857
2.2	0.9861	0.9864	0.9868	0.9871	0.9875	0.9878	0.9881	0.9884	0.9887	0.9890
2.3	0.9893	0.9896	0.9898	0.9901	0.9904	0.9906	0.9909	0.9911	0.9913	0.9916
2.4	0.9918	0.9920	0.9922	0.9925	0.9927	0.9929	0.9931	0.9932	0.9934	0.9936
2.5	0.9938	0.9940	0.9941	0.9943	0.9945	0.9946	0.9948	0.9949	0.9951	0.9952
2.6	0.9953	0.9955	0.9956	0.9957	0.9959	0.9960	0.9960	0.9962	0.9963	0.9964
2.7	0.9965	0.9966	0.9967	0.9968	0.9969	0.9970	0.9971	0.9972	0.9973	0.9974
2.8	0.9974	0.9975	0.9976	0.9977	0.9977	0.9978	0.9979	0.9979	0.9980	0.9981
2.9	0.9981	0.9982	0.9982	0.9983	0.9984	0.9984	0.9985	0.9985	0.9986	0.9986
3.0	0.99865	0.99869	0.99874	0.99878	0.99882	0.99886	0.99889	0.99893	0.99897	0.99900
3.1	0.99903	0.99906	0.99910	0.99913	0.99916	0.99918	0.99921	0.99924	0.99926	0.99929
3.2	0.99931	0.99934	0.99936	0.99938	0.99940	0.99942	0.99944	0.99946	0.99948	0.99950
3.3	0.99952	0.99953	0.99955	0.99957	0.99958	0.99960	0.99961	0.99962	0.99964	0.99965
3.4	0.99966	0.99968	0.99969	0.99970	0.99971	0.99972	0.99973	0.99974	0.99975	0.99976
3.5	0.99977	0.99978	0.99978	0.99979	0.99980	0.99981	0.99981	0.99982	0.99983	0.99983
3.6	0.99984	0.99985	0.99985	0.99986	0.99986	0.99987	0.99987	0.99988	0.99988	0.99989
3.7	0.99989	0.99990	0.99990	0.99990	0.99991	0.99991	0.99992	0.99992	0.99992	0.99992
3.8	0.99993	0.99993	0.99993	0.99994	0.99994	0.99994	0.99994	0.99995	0.99995	0.99995
3.9	0.99995	0.99995	0.99996	0.99996	0.99996	0.99996	0.99996	0.99996	0.99997	0.99997
4.0	0.99996832									
4.5	0.99999660									
5.0	0.99999971									
5.5	0.99999998									
6.0	0.99999999									

A ROADMAP FOR SELECTING A STATISTICAL METHOD

Type of Analysis	TYPE OF DATA	
	Numerical	**Categorical**
Describing a Group or Several Groups	Ordered array, stem-and-leaf display, frequency distribution, relative frequency distribution, percentage distribution, cumulative percentage distribution, histogram, polygon, cumulative percentage polygon **(Sections 2.2 and 2.3)** Mean, median, mode, quartiles, geometric mean, range, interquartile range, standard deviation, variance, coefficient of variation, Z scores, box-and-whisker plot **(Sections 3.1–3.4)** Index numbers **(Section 16.8)**	Summary table, bar chart, pie chart, Pareto diagram **(Section 2.1)**
Inference about One Group	Confidence Interval Estimate of the Mean **(Sections 8.1 and 8.2)** Z Test of Hypothesis for the Mean **(Section 9.2)** t Test of Hypothesis for the Mean **(Section 9.4)**	Confidence Interval Estimate for the Proportion **(Section 8.3)** Z Test of Hypothesis for the Proportion **(Section 9.5)**
Comparing Two Groups	Z and t Tests for the Difference in the Means of Two Independent Populations **(Section 10.1)** Paired t Test **(Section 10.2)** F Test for the Differences in Two Variances **(Section 10.4)** Wilcoxon Rank Sum Test **(Section 12.5)**	Z Test for the Difference between Two Proportions **(Section 10.3)** Chi-Square Test for the Difference between Two Proportions **(Section 12.1)** McNemar Test for Two Related Samples **(Section 12.4)**
Comparing More than Two Groups	One-Way Analysis of Variance **(Section 11.1)** Two-Way Analysis of Variance **(Section 11.2)** Kruskal-Wallis Test **(Section 12.6)**	Chi-Square Test for Differences among More than Two Proportions **(Section 12.2)**
Analyzing the Relationship between Two Variables	Scatter Plot, Time-Series Plot **(Section 2.5)** Covariance, Coefficient of Correlation **(Section 3.5)** Simple Linear Regression **(Chapter 13)** t Test of Correlation **(Section 13.7)**	Contingency Table, Side-by-Side Bar Chart **(Section 2.4**) Chi-Square Test of Independence **(Section 12.3)**
Analyzing the Relationship between Two or More Variables	Multiple Regression **(Chapters 14 and 15)** Time-Series Forecasting **(Chapter 16)**	

HAVE YOU THOUGHT ABOUT
Customizing THIS BOOK?

THE PRENTICE HALL JUST-IN-TIME PROGRAM IN DECISION SCIENCE

You can combine chapters from this book with chapters from any of the Prentice Hall titles listed on the following page to create a text tailored to your specific course needs. You can add your own material or cases from our extensive case collection. By taking a few minutes to look at what is sitting on your bookshelf and the content available on our Web site, you can create your ideal textbook.

The Just-In-Time program offers:

➡ **Quality of Material to Choose From**—In addition to the books listed, you also have the option to include any of the cases from Prentice Hall Custom Business Resources, which gives you access to cases (and teaching notes where available) from Darden, Harvard, Ivey, NACRA, and Thunderbird. Most cases can be viewed online at our Web site.

➡ **Flexibility**—Choose only the material you want, either from one title or several titles (plus cases) and sequence it in whatever way you wish.

➡ **Instructional Support**—You have access to the text-specific CD-ROM that accompanies the traditional textbook and desk copies of your JIT book.

➡ **Outside Materials**—There is also the option to include up to 20% of the text from materials outside of Prentice Hall Custom Business Resources.

➡ **Cost Savings**—Students pay only for material you choose. The base price is $6.00, plus $2.00 for case material, plus $.09 per page. The text can be shrink-wrapped with other Pearson textbooks for a 10% discount. Outside material is priced at $.10 per page plus permission fees.

➡ **Quality of Finished Product**—Custom cover and title page—including your name, school, department, course title, and section number. Paperback, perfect bound, black-and-white printed text. Customized table of contents. Sequential pagination throughout the text.

Visit our Web site at www.prenhall.com/custombusiness and create your

custom text on our bookbuildsite or download order forms online.

THE PRENTICE HALL
Just-In-Time program

YOU CAN CUSTOMIZE YOUR TEXTBOOK WITH CHAPTERS FROM ANY OF THE FOLLOWING PRENTICE HALL TITLES: *

BUSINESS STATISTICS

- Berenson/Levine/Krehbiel, BASIC BUSINESS STATISTICS, 10/e
- Groebner/Shannon/Fry/Smith, BUSINESS STATISTICS: A DECISION-MAKING APPROACH, 6/e
- Levine/Stephan/Krehbiel/Berenson, STATISTICS FOR MANAGERS USING MICROSOFT EXCEL, 5/e
- Levine/Krehbiel/Berenson, BUSINESS STATISTICS: A FIRST COURSE, 4/e
- Newbold/Carlson/Thorne, STATISTICS FOR BUSINESS AND ECONOMICS, 5/e
- Groebner/Shannon/Fry/Smith, A COURSE IN BUSINESS STATISTICS, 4/e

PRODUCTION/OPERATIONS MANAGEMENT

- Anupindi/Chopra/Deshmukh/Van Mieghem/Zemel, MANAGING BUSINESS PROCESS FLOWS, 2e
- Bozarth/Handfield, INTRODUCTION TO OPERATIONS AND SUPPLY CHAIN MANAGEMENT
- Chopra/Meindl, SUPPLY CHAIN MANAGEMENT, 3/e
- Foster, MANAGING QUALITY: INTERPRETING THE SUPPLY CHAIN, 3/e
- Handfield/Nichols, Jr., SUPPLY CHAIN MANAGEMENT
- Heineke/Meile, GAMES AND EXERCISES IN OPERATIONS MANAGEMENT
- Heizer/Render, OPERATIONS MANAGEMENT, 8/e
- Krajewski/Ritzman/Malhotra, OPERATIONS MANAGEMENT, 8/e
- Latona/Nathan, CASES AND READINGS IN PRODUCTION AND OPERATIONS MANAGEMENT
- Ritzman/Krajewski, FOUNDATIONS OF OPERATIONS MANAGEMENT
- Schmenner, PLANT AND SERVICE TOURS IN OPERATIONS MANAGEMENT, 5/e

MANAGEMENT SCIENCE/SPREADSHEET MODELING

- Render/Stair/Hanna, QUANTITATIVE ANALYSIS FOR MANAGEMENT, 9/e
- Balakrishnan/Render/Stair, MANAGERIAL DECISION MODELING WITH SPREADSHEETS, 2/e
- Render/Greenberg/Stair, CASES AND READINGS IN MANAGEMENT SCIENCE, 2e
- Taylor, INTRODUCTION TO MANAGEMENT SCIENCE, 9/e

For more information, or to speak to a customer service representative, contact us at 1-800-777-6872.

www.prenhall.com/custombusiness

* Selection of titles on the JIT program is subject to change

Just-In-Time

STATISTICS FOR MANAGERS

Using Microsoft® Excel

FIFTH EDITION

DAVID M. LEVINE
Department of Statistics and Computer Information Systems
Zicklin School of Business, Baruch College, City University of New York

DAVID F. STEPHAN
Department of Statistics and Computer Information Systems
Zicklin School of Business, Baruch College, City University of New York

TIMOTHY C. KREHBIEL
Department of Decision Sciences and Management Information Systems
Richard T. Farmer School of Business, Miami University

MARK L. BERENSON
Department of Management and Information Systems
School of Business, Montclair State University

PEARSON

Prentice
Hall

Upper Saddle River, New Jersey 07458

Library of Congress Cataloging-in-Publication Data

Statistics for managers using Microsoft Excel / David M. Levine . . . [et al.].—5th ed.
    p. cm.
  Includes bibliographical references and index.
  ISBN 978-0-13-229545-1
  1. Microsoft Excel (Computer file) 2. Management—Statistical methods. 3. Commercial
statistics. 4. Electronic spreadsheets. 5. Management—Statistical methods—Computer
programs. 6. Commercial statistics—Computer programs. I. Levine, David M., 1946–
    HD30.215.S73 2008
    519.50285′554—dc22   2006101531

AVP/Executive Editor: Mark Pfaltzgraff
VP/Editorial Director: Jeff Shelstad
Manager, Product Development: Pamela Hersperger
Assistant Editor: Barbara Whitmer
Editorial Assistant: Kelly Loftus
Product Development Manager, Media: Nancy Welcher
AVP/Director of Marketing: Eric Frank
Marketing Assistant: Laura Cirigliano
Associate Director, Production Editorial: Judy Leale
Senior Managing Editor: Cynthia Zonneveld
Senior Production Editor: Anne Graydon
Permissions Coordinator: Charles Morris
Associate Director, Manufacturing: Vinnie Scelta

Manufacturing Manager: Arnold Vila
Creative Director: Christy Mahon
Composition Liaison: Susanne Duda
Art Director: Pat Smythe
Cover Design: Kevin Kall
Cover Illustration/Photo: Getty Images
Illustration (Interior)/Composition: GGS Book Services
Image Permission Coordinator: Angelique Sharps
Composition: GGS Book Services
Full-Service Project Management:
    Heidi Allgair/GGS Book Services
Printer/Binder: Courier/Kendallville
Typeface: 10.5/12 Times NewRoman

Photo Credits: frontmatter, page iv, Rudy Krehbiel; Chapter 1, page 4, Chuck Savage;
Chapter 2, page 32, Ed Young/Science Photo Library/Photo Researchers, Inc.; Chapter 3,
page 96, Susan Van Ettan Lawson/PhotoEdit Inc.; Chapter 4, page 148, Michael
Newman/PhotoEdit Inc.; Chapter 7, page 252, Chuck Mason/ImageState/International Stock
Photography Ltd.; Chapter 8, page 284, Spencer Grant/PhotoEdit Inc.; Chapter 9, page 328,
Mark Richards/PhotoEdit Inc.; Chapter 10, page 370, Greg Mancuso/Stock Boston; Chapter
11, page 422, Edith G. Haun/Stock Boston; Chapter 12, page 462, Jeff Greenberg/Stock
Boston; Chapter 13, page 512, Jack Star/Getty Images, Inc.—PhotoDisc; Chapter 14, page
572, Courtesy of David Levine; Chapter 15, page 614, Rob Crandall/Stock Boston; Chapter
16, page 646, Will & Deni McIntyre/Photo Researchers, Inc.; Chapter 17, page 706, Rick
Gayle/Corbis/Stock Market; Chapter 18, page 734, Jeff Greenberg/PhotoEdit Inc.

Credits and acknowledgments borrowed from other sources and reproduced, with permission,
in this textbook appear on appropriate page within the text.

Microsoft® and Windows® are registered trademarks of the Microsoft Corporation in the
U.S.A. and other countries. Screen shots and icons reprinted with permission from the
Microsoft Corporation. This book is not sponsored or endorsed by or affiliated with the
Microsoft Corporation.

Pearson Prentice Hall™ is a trademark of Pearson Education, Inc.
Pearson® is a registered trademark of Pearson plc
Prentice Hall® is a registered trademark of Pearson Education, Inc.

Pearson Education LTD.
Pearson Education Singapore, Pte. Ltd
Pearson Education, Canada, Ltd
Pearson Education–Japan

Pearson Education Australia PTY, Limited
Pearson Education North Asia Ltd
Pearson Educación de Mexico, S.A. de C.V.
Pearson Education Malaysia, Pte. Ltd.

10 9 8 7 6 5 4 3 2 1

ISBN-13: 978-0-13-229545-1
ISBN-10: 0-13-229545-8

To our wives,
Marilyn L., Mary N., Patti K., and Rhoda B.,

and to our children
Sharyn, Mark, Ed, Rudy, Rhonda, Kathy, and Lori

ABOUT THE AUTHORS

The textbook authors meet to discuss statistics at Shea Stadium for a Mets v. Phillies game. Shown left to right, Mark Berenson, David Stephan, David Levine, Tim Krehbiel.

David M. Levine is Professor Emeritus of Statistics and Computer Information Systems at Bernard M. Baruch College (City University of New York). He received B.B.A. and M.B.A. degrees in Statistics from City College of New York and a Ph.D. degree from New York University in Industrial Engineering and Operations Research. He is nationally recognized as a leading innovator in statistics education and is the co-author of 14 books including such best selling statistics textbooks as *Statistics for Managers using Microsoft Excel, Basic Business Statistics: Concepts and Applications, Business Statistics: A First Course*, and *Applied Statistics for Engineers and Scientists using Microsoft Excel and Minitab*.

He also recently wrote *Even You Can Learn Statistics* and *Statistics for Six Sigma Green Belts* published by Financial Times-Prentice-Hall. He is coauthor of *Six Sigma for Green Belts and Champions* and *Design for Six Sigma for Green Belts and Champions*, also published by Financial Times-Prentice-Hall, and *Quality Management Third Ed.*, McGraw-Hill-Irwin (2005). He is also the author of *Video Review of Statistics* and *Video Review of Probability*, both published by Video Aided Instruction. He has published articles in various journals including *Psychometrika, The American Statistician, Communications in Statistics, Multivariate Behavioral Research, Journal of Systems Management, Quality Progress*, and *The American Anthropologist* and given numerous talks at Decision Sciences, American Statistical Association, and Making Statistics More Effective in Schools of Business conferences. While at Baruch College, Dr. Levine received several awards for outstanding teaching and curriculum development.

David F. Stephan is an instructional designer and lecturer who pioneered the teaching of spreadsheet applications to business school students in the 1980's. He has over 20 years experience teaching at Baruch College, where he developed the first personal computing lab to support statistics and information systems studies and was twice nominated for his excellence in teaching. He is also proud to have been the lead designer and assistant project director of a U.S. Department of Education FIPSE project that brought interactive, multimedia learning to Baruch College.

Today, David focuses on developing materials that help users make better use of the information analysis tools on their computer desktops and is a co-author, with David M. Levine, of *Even You Can Learn Statistics*.

Timothy C. Krehbiel is Professor of Decision Sciences and Management Information Systems at the Richard T. Farmer School of Business at Miami University in Oxford, Ohio. He teaches undergraduate and graduate courses in business statistics. In 1996 he received the prestigious Instructional Innovation Award from the Decision Sciences Institute. In 2000 he received the Richard T. Farmer School of Business Administration Effective Educator Award. He also received a Teaching Excellence Award from the MBA class of 2000.

Krehbiel's research interests span many areas of business and applied statistics. His work appears in numerous journals including *Quality Management Journal, Ecological Economics, International Journal of Production Research, Journal of Marketing Management, Communications in Statistics, Decision Sciences Journal of Innovative Education, Journal of Education for Business, Marketing Education Review*, and *Teaching Statistics*. He is a co-author of three statistics textbooks published by Prentice Hall: *Business Statistics: A First Course, Basic Business Statistics*, and *Statistics for Managers Using Microsoft Excel*. Krehbiel is also a co-author of the book *Sustainability Perspectives in Business and Resources*.

Krehbiel graduated *summa cum laude* with a B.A. in history from McPherson College in 1983, and earned an M.S. (1987) and Ph.D. (1990) in statistics from the University of Wyoming.

Mark L. Berenson is Professor of Management and Information Systems at Montclair State University (Montclair, New Jersey) and also Professor Emeritus of Statistics and Computer Information Systems at Bernard M. Baruch College (City University of New York). He currently teaches graduate and undergraduate courses in statistics and in operations management in the School of Business and an undergraduate course in international justice and human rights that he co-developed in the College of Humanities and Social Sciences.

Berenson received a B.A. in economic statistics and an M.B.A. in business statistics from City College of New York and a Ph.D. in business from the City University of New York.

Berenson's research has been published in *Decision Sciences Journal of Innovative Education, Review of Business Research, The American Statistician, Communications in Statistics, Psychometrika, Educational and Psychological Measurement, Journal of Management Sciences and Applied Cybernetics, Research Quarterly, Stats Magazine, The New York Statistician, Journal of Health Administration Education, Journal of Behavioral Medicine*, and *Journal of Surgical Oncology*. His invited articles have appeared in *The Encyclopedia of Measurement & Statistics* and in *Encyclopedia of Statistical Sciences*. He is co-author of 11 statistics texts published by Prentice Hall, including *Statistics for Managers using Microsoft Excel, Basic Business Statistics: Concepts and Applications*, and *Business Statistics: A First Course*.

Over the years, Berenson has received several awards for teaching and for innovative contributions to statistics education. In 2005 he was the first recipient of The Catherine A. Becker Service for Educational Excellence Award at Montclair State University.

BRIEF CONTENTS

CONTENTS

PREFACE

Educational Philosophy

In our many years of teaching business statistics, we have continually searched for ways to improve the teaching of these courses. Our active participation in a series of Making Statistics More Effective in Schools and Business (MSMESB), Decision Sciences Institute (DSI), and American Statistical Association conferences as well as the reality of serving a diverse group of students at large universities have shaped our vision for teaching these courses. Over the years, our vision has come to include these key principles:

1. **Students need to be shown the relevance of statistics.**
   - Students need a frame of reference when learning statistics, especially when statistics is not their major. That frame of reference for business students should be the functional areas of business—that is, accounting, finance, information systems, management, and marketing. Each statistical topic needs to be presented in an applied context related to at least one of these functional areas.
   - The focus in teaching each topic should be on its application in business, the interpretation of results, the presentation of assumptions, the evaluation of the assumptions, and the discussion of what should be done if the assumptions are violated.
2. **Students need to be familiar with the software used in the business world.**
   - Integrating spreadsheet software into all aspects of an introductory statistics course allows the course to focus on interpretation of results instead of computations.
   - Introductory business statistics courses should recognize that in business, spreadsheet software is typically available on a decision maker's desktop.
3. **Students need to be given sufficient guidance on using software.**
   - Textbooks should provide enough instructions so that students can effectively use the software integrated with the study of statistics, without having the software instruction dominate the course.
4. **Students need ample practice in order to understand how statistics is used in business.**
   - Both classroom examples and homework exercises should involve actual or realistic data as much as possible.
   - Students should work with data sets, both small and large, and be encouraged to look beyond the statistical analysis of data to the interpretation of results in a managerial context.

New to This Edition: Statistics Coverage

This new fifth edition of *Statistics for Managers Using Microsoft Excel* enhances the statistical coverage of previous editions in a number of ways:

- Every chapter has been rewritten to use a more engaging, conversational writing style that students will appreciate. Complex topics are discussed in simple, straightforward sentences.
- "From the Authors' Desktop" essays provide greater background for the topic just covered and raise important issues.
- This edition includes many more examples from everyday life. Notable examples include what you would do with $1,000 (Chapter 2), time to get ready in the morning (Chapter 3), and waiting time at a fast-food restaurant (Chapter 9).
- Many new applied examples and exercises with data from *The Wall Street Journal, USA Today, Consumer Reports*, and other sources have been added to the book.
- Many problems have been restructured to contain no more than four parts, allowing students to break down the concepts and apply the material more easily.
- A "Key Equations" list at the end of each chapter lists the equations used in the chapter.
- Worked-out solutions to self-test questions are provided at the back of the book.

- A roadmap for selecting the proper statistical method is included at the front of the text to help students select the proper technique and to make connections between topics.
- Student surveys are included as an integrating theme for exercises across many chapters.

New to This Edition: Excel Coverage

This new fifth edition of *Statistics for Managers Using Microsoft Excel* enhances the Excel coverage of previous editions in a number of ways:

- Totally rewritten Excel sections have been organized into end-of-chapter Excel Companions for easy reference.
- Wherever possible, Excel Companions present step-by-step instructions and Excel command sequences that are compatible across all current versions of Excel, including Excel 2007.
- Clearly marked separate Excel 97–2003 and Excel 2007 instructions are provided for those Excel techniques that are fundamentally different in Excel 2007.
- "Basic Excel" sections allow the use of Excel without any outside enhancement, and "PHStat2" sections describe the use of the PHStat2 add-in included on the student CD-ROM.
- Margin notes link worksheet and chart illustrations to the instructions of Excel Companion sections.
- Worksheet illustrations, like the following example, display underlying cell formulas that show how results are computed:

	A	B	
1	**Estimate for the Mean Sales Invoice Amount**		
2			
3	**Data**		
4	**Sample Standard Deviation**	28.95	
5	**Sample Mean**	110.27	
6	**Sample Size**	100	
7	**Confidence Level**	95%	
8			
9	Intermediate Calculations		
10	Standard Error of the Mean	2.8950	=B4/SQRT(B6)
11	Degrees of Freedom	99	=B6 - 1
12	*t* Value	1.9842	=TINV(1 - B7, B11)
13	Interval Half Width	5.7443	=B12 * B10
14			
15	**Confidence Interval**		
16	**Interval Lower Limit**	104.53	=B5 - B13
17	**Interval Upper Limit**	116.01	=B5 + B13

Chapter-by-Chapter Changes in the Fifth Edition

Each chapter includes a new opening page that displays the chapter sections and subsections. Accompanying each chapter is an Excel Companion that discusses how to apply Microsoft Excel to the statistical techniques of the chapter. In addition, the Excel Companion includes completely new material for using Excel in most chapters. The following changes have been made to this fifth edition:

- *Chapter 1* has rewritten Sections 1.1 (Why Learn Statistics), 1.2 (Statistics for Managers), and 1.3 (Basic Vocabulary of Statistics) and a completely new Section 1.6 (Microsoft Excel Worksheets). The sections on survey sampling have been moved to Chapter 7.
- *Chapter 2* includes a new data set concerning mutual fund returns for 2001–2005. Graphs for a single variable are covered prior to graphs for two variables. Graphs for categorical variables are covered prior to graphs for numerical variables. The examples in this chapter refer to what to do with $1,000 and the cost of restaurant meals in addition to mutual fund returns.
- *Chapter 3* includes a new data set concerning mutual fund returns for 2001–2005. The examples in this chapter refer to the time to get ready in the morning as well as mutual fund

returns. Z scores for detecting outliers are now included. The sample covariance is now included, as is the coefficient of correlation.

- *Chapter 4* now includes additional examples.
- *Chapter 5* covers the Poisson distribution prior to the hypergeometric distribution.
- *Chapter 6* has a simplified section on the normal probability plot. Coverage of sampling distributions has been moved to a new Chapter 7.
- *Chapter 7* now covers sampling distributions along with types of survey sampling methods and survey worthiness.
- *Chapter 8* (formerly Chapter 7) has 28 new problems.
- *Chapter 9* (formerly Chapter 8) uses a simple, six-step method to perform hypothesis tests using the critical value approach and a straightforward five-step method to perform hypothesis tests using the *p*-value.
- *Chapter 10* (formerly Chapter 9) includes a new example for the paired *t* test and additional examples.
- *Chapter 11* (formerly Chapter 10) includes a new example for understanding interaction.
- *Chapter 12* (formerly Chapter 11) now includes the McNemar test.
- *Chapter 13* (formerly Chapter 12) now includes computations for the regression coefficients and sum of squares in chapter examples.
- *Chapter 14* (formerly Chapter 13) now covers R^2, and adjusted R^2 prior to residual analysis.
- *Chapter 15* (formerly Chapter 14) provides additional coverage of model building.
- *Chapter 16* (formerly Chapter 15) has new and updated data sets throughout the chapter.
- *Chapter 17* (formerly Chapter 16) maintains its previous content strengths.
- *Chapter 18* (formerly Chapter 17) includes more coverage of Six Sigma management.

Hallmark Features

We have continued many of the traditions of past editions and have highlighted some of those features below:

- **Using Statistics business scenarios**—Each chapter begins with a Using Statistics example that shows how statistics is used in accounting, finance, information systems, management, or marketing. Each scenario is used throughout the chapter to provide an applied context for the concepts.
- **Emphasis on data analysis and interpretation of Excel results**—We believe that the use of computer software is an integral part of learning statistics. Our focus emphasizes analyzing data by interpreting the results from Microsoft Excel while reducing emphasis on doing computations. For example, in the coverage of tables and charts in Chapter 2, the focus is on the interpretation of various charts, not on their construction by hand. In our coverage of hypothesis testing in Chapters 9 through 12, extensive computer results have been included so that the *p*-value approach can be emphasized.
- **Pedagogical aides**—An active writing style, boxed numbered equations, set-off examples to provide reinforcement for learning concepts, problems divided into "Learning the Basics" and "Applying the Concepts," key equations, and key terms are included.
- **Answers**—Most answers to the even-numbered exercises are provided in an appendix at the end of the book.
- **PHStat2**—This add-in, which is included on the student CD-ROM, extends the statistical capabilities of Microsoft Excel and executes the low-level menu selection and worksheet entry tasks associated with implementing statistical analysis in Excel. When combined with the Analysis ToolPak add-in, virtually all statistical methods taught in an introductory statistics course can be demonstrated using Microsoft Excel.
- **Web Cases**—A chapter-ending Web Case is included for each of the first 17 chapters. By visiting Web sites related to the companies and researching the issues raised in the Using Statistics scenarios that start each chapter, students learn to identify misuses of statistical information. The Web Cases require students to sift through claims and assorted information in order to discover the data most relevant to the case. Students then determine whether the conclusions and claims are supported by the data. (Instructional tips for using

the Web Cases and solutions to the Web Cases are included in the Instructor's Solutions Manual.)

- **Case studies and team projects**—Detailed case studies are included in numerous chapters. A *Springville Herald* case is included at the end of most chapters as an integrating theme. A team project relating to mutual funds is included in many chapters as an integrating theme.
- **Visual Explorations**—Microsoft Excel add-in workbook that allows students to interactively explore important statistical concepts in descriptive statistics, the normal distribution, sampling distributions, and regression analysis. For example, in descriptive statistics, students observe the effect of changes in the data on the mean, median, quartiles, and standard deviation. With the normal distribution, students see the effect of changes in the mean and standard deviation on the areas under the normal curve. In sampling distributions, students use simulation to explore the effect of sample size on a sampling distribution. In regression analysis, students have the opportunity of fitting a line and observing how changes in the slope and intercept affect the goodness of fit.

Supplement Package

The supplement package that accompanies this text includes the following:

- **Instructor's Solutions Manual**—This manual includes solutions for end-of-section and end-of-chapter problems, answers to case questions, where applicable, and teaching tips for each chapter. Electronic solutions are provided in Excel and Word formats.
- **Student Solutions Manual**—This manual provides detailed solutions to virtually all the even-numbered exercises and worked-out solutions to the self-test problems.
- **Test Item File**—The Test Item File contains true/false, multiple-choice, fill-in, and problem-solving questions based on the definitions, concepts, and ideas developed in each chapter of the text.
- **TestGen software**—A test bank has been designed for use with the TestGen test-generating software. This computerized package allows instructors to custom design, save, and generate classroom tests. The test program permits instructors to edit, add, or delete questions from the test bank; edit existing graphics and create new graphics; analyze test results; and organize a database of tests and student results. This software allows for flexibility and ease of use. It provides many options for organizing and displaying tests, along with a search and sort feature. The program is available on the instructor's CD-ROM, and associated conversion files can be found online at the Instructor's Resource Center.
- **Instructor's Resource Center**—The Instructor's Resource Center contains the electronic files for the complete Instructor's Solutions Manual, the Test Item File, and Lecture PowerPoint presentations (**www.prenhall.com/levine**).
- **Course and Homework Management Tools**
  - **Prentice Hall's OneKey**—This tool offers the best teaching and learning resources, all in one place. OneKey for *Statistics for Managers Using Microsoft Excel*, is all an instructor needs to plan and administer a course and is all students need for anytime, anywhere access to course materials. Conveniently organized by textbook chapter, the compiled resources include links to quizzes, PowerPoint presentations, data files, links to Web Cases, a PHStat2 download, a Visual Explorations download, the Student Solutions Manual, and additional instructor resources.
  - **WebCT and Blackboard**—With a local installation of either course management system, Prentice Hall provides content designed especially for this textbook to create a complete course suite, tightly integrated with the system's course management tools.
  - **PH GradeAssist**—This online homework and assessment system allows the instructor to assign problems for student practice, homework, or quizzes. The problems, taken directly from the text, are algorithmically generated, so each student gets a slightly different problem with a different answer. This feature allows students multiple attempts for more practice and improved competency. PH GradeAssist grades the results and can export them to Microsoft Excel worksheets.

- **Companion Web site—www.prenhall.com/levine** contains the following:
  - An online study guide with true/false, multiple-choice, and essay questions designed to test students' comprehension of chapter topics
  - PowerPoint presentation files with chapter outlines and key equations
  - Student data files for text problems in Excel
- **PHStat2 Web site—**PHStat2 has a home page at **www.prenhall.com/phstat**.
- **Index page Web site—**An index page for the supporting material for all the Web Cases included in the text can be found at **www.prenhall.com/Springville/ SpringvilleSFM5e.htm**.

Acknowledgments

We are extremely grateful to the Biometrika Trustees, American Cyanimid Company, the RAND Corporation, the American Society for Testing and Materials for their kind permission to publish various tables in Appendix E and the American Statistical Association for its permission to publish diagrams from the *American Statistician*. Also, we are grateful to Professors George A. Johnson and Joanne Tokle of Idaho State University and Ed Conn, Mountain States Potato Company, for their kind permission to incorporate parts of their work as our Mountain States Potato Company case in Chapter 15.

A Note of Thanks

We would like to thank John Beyers, University of Maryland, University College; Ephrem Eyob, Virginia State University; Mickey Hepner, University of Central Oklahoma; Bill Jedicka, Harper College; Morgan Jones, University of North Carolina; Michael Lewis, West Virginia State University; Susan Pariseau, Merrimack College; Rupert Rhodd, Florida Atlantic University; Jim Robison, Sonoma State University; Abdulhamid Sukar, Cameron University; and Gary Tikriti, University of South Florida, St. Petersburg, for their comments, which have made this a better book.

We would especially like to thank Mark Pfaltzgraff, Jeff Shelstad, Eric Frank, Anne Graydon, Cynthia Zonneveld, Nancy Welcher, Ashley Lulling, Barbara Witmer, Kelly Loftus, and Laura Cirigliano of the editorial, marketing, and production teams at Prentice Hall. We would like to thank our statistical reader and accuracy checker Annie Puciloski for her diligence in checking our work; Kitty Jarrett for her copyediting; Julie Kennedy for her proofreading; and Heidi Allgair, Sandra Krausman, and Cindy Miller of GGS Book Services, for their work in the production of this text.

Finally, we would like to thank our parents, wives, and children for their patience, understanding, love, and assistance in making this book a reality. It is to them that we dedicate this book.

Concluding Remarks

We have gone to great lengths to make this text both pedagogically sound and error free. If you have any suggestions or require clarification about any of the material, or if you find any errors, please contact us at **David_Levine@baruch.cuny.edu** or **KREHBITC@muohio.edu**. Include the phrase "SMUME edition 5" in the subject line of your email. For more information about using PHStat2, see Appendix F, review the PHStat2 readme file on the student CD-ROM, and visit the PHStat2 Web site, at **www.prenhall.com/phstat**.

David M. Levine
David F. Stephan
Timothy C. Krehbiel
Mark L. Berenson

CHAPTER 1

Introduction and Data Collection

LEARNING OBJECTIVES

This chapter will help you learn:

- How statistics is used in business
- The sources of data used in business
- The types of data used in business
- The basics of Microsoft Excel

1.1   WHY LEARN STATISTICS

The reality TV series *The Apprentice* stars the real estate developer Donald Trump. When it premiered several years ago, Trump assigned two teams of contestants the task of setting up and running a lemonade stand. At the time, a number of businesspeople criticized that task as not being a *realistic* business task. They saw the task of selling lemonade as a simple act of salesmanship that was more dependent on the persuasive skills of the seller than anything else.

If you have ever sold lemonade or held other childhood jobs such as selling cookies or delivering daily newspapers, you know your task was fairly simple. For example, to deliver newspapers, you need only to keep track of a list of addresses and perhaps record the weekly or monthly payments. In contrast, sales and marketing managers of the newspaper need to keep track of much more data—including the incomes, education levels, lifestyles, and buying preferences of their subscribers—in order to make appropriate decisions about increasing circulation and attracting advertisers. But unless that newspaper has a tiny circulation, those managers are probably not looking at data directly. Instead, they are looking at summaries, such as the percentage of subscribers who attended at least some college, or trying to uncover useful patterns, such as whether more subscriptions are delivered to single-family homes in areas associated with heavy sales of luxury automobiles. That is to say, the managers at the newspaper are using statistics, the subject of this text.

Statistics is the branch of mathematics that transforms data into useful information for decision makers. These transformations often require complex calculations that are practical only if done by computer, so using statistics usually means also using computers. This is especially true when dealing with the large volumes of data that a typical business collects. Attempting to do statistics using manual calculations for such data would be too time-consuming to benefit a business.

When you learn statistics, you learn a set of methods and the conditions under which it is appropriate for you to use those methods. And because so many statistical methods are practical only when you use computers, learning statistics also means learning more about using computer programs that perform statistical analyses.

1.2   STATISTICS FOR MANAGERS

Today, statistics plays an ever increasing important role for business managers. These decision makers use statistics to:

- Present and describe business data and information properly
- Draw conclusions about large populations, using information collected from samples[1]
- Make reliable forecasts about a business activity
- Improve business processes

"Statistics for managers" means knowing more than just how to perform these tasks. Managers need a conceptual understanding of the principles behind each statistical analysis they undertake in order to have confidence that the information produced is correct and appropriate for a decision-making situation.

To help you master these necessary skills, every chapter of *Statistics for Managers Using Microsoft Excel* has a *Using Statistics* scenario. While the scenarios are fictional, they represent realistic situations in which you will be asked to make decisions while using Microsoft Excel to transform data into statistical information. For example, in one chapter, you will be asked to decide the location in a supermarket that best enhances sales of a cola drink, and in another chapter, you will be asked to forecast sales for a clothing store. (You will not be asked, as the television apprentices were asked, to decide how best to sell lemonade on a New York City street corner.)

[1]*The statistical terms* population *and* sample *are formally defined in Section 1.3, on page 5.*

How This Text Is Organized

Table 1.1 shows the chapters of *Statistics for Managers Using Microsoft Excel* organized according to the four activities for which decision makers use statistics.

TABLE 1.1

Organization of This Text

Presenting and Describing Information

Data Collection (Chapter 1)
Presenting Data in Tables and Charts (Chapter 2)
Numerical Descriptive Measures (Chapter 3)

Drawing Conclusions About Populations Using Sample Information

Basic Probability (Chapter 4), a prerequisite for the rest of the chapters of this group
Some Important Discrete Probability Distributions (Chapter 5)
The Normal Distribution and Other Continuous Distributions (Chapter 6) and Sampling and Sampling Distributions (Chapter 7), which lead to Confidence Interval Estimation (Chapter 8) and Hypothesis Testing (Chapters 9–12)
Decision Making (Chapter 17)

Making Reliable Forecasts

Simple Linear Regression (Chapter 13)
Introduction to Multiple Regression (Chapter 14)
Multiple Regression Model Building (Chapter 15)
Time-Series Forecasting and Index Numbers (Chapter 16)

Improving Business Processes

Statistical Applications in Quality and Productivity Management (Chapter 18)

Methods presented in the Chapters 1–3 are all examples of **descriptive statistics**, the branch of statistics that collects, summarizes, and presents data. Methods discussed in Chapters 7 through 12 are examples of **inferential statistics**, the branch of statistics that uses sample data to draw conclusions about an entire population. (Chapters 4–6 provide the foundation in probability and probability distributions needed for Chapters 7–12.) The definition of inferential statistics uses the terms *sample* and *population,* the second time you have encountered these words in this section. You can probably figure out that you cannot learn much about statistics until you learn the basic vocabulary of statistics. Continue now with the first Using Statistics scenario, which will help introduce you to several important terms used in statistics.

USING STATISTICS @ Good Tunes

Good Tunes, a growing four-store home entertainment systems retailer, seeks to double their number of stores within the next three years. The managers have decided to approach local area banks for the cash needed to underwrite this expansion. They need to prepare an electronic slide show and a formal prospectus that will argue that Good Tunes is a thriving business that is a good candidate for expansion.

You have been asked to assist in the process of preparing the slide show and prospectus. What data would you include that will convince bankers to extend the credit it needs to Good Tunes? How would you present that data?

In this scenario, you need to identify the most relevant data for the bankers. Because Good Tunes is an ongoing business, you can start by reviewing the company's records, which show both its current and recent past status. Because Good Tunes is a retailer, presenting data about the company's sales seems a reasonable thing to do. You could include the details of every sales transaction that has occurred for the past few years as a way of demonstrating that Good Tunes is a thriving business.

However, presenting the bankers with the thousands of transactions would overwhelm them and not be very useful. As mentioned in Section 1.1, you need to transform the transactions data into information by summarizing the details of each transaction in some useful way that would allow the bankers to (perhaps) uncover a favorable pattern about the sales over time.

One piece of information that the bankers would presumably want to see is the dollar sales totals by year. Tallying and totaling sales is a common process of transforming data into information and a very common statistical analysis. When you tally sales—or any other relevant data about Good Tunes you choose to use—you follow normal business practice and tally by a business period such as by month, quarter, or year. When you do so, you end up with multiple values: sales for this year, sales for last year, sales for the year before that, and so on. How best to refer to these multiple values requires learning the basic vocabulary of statistics.

1.3   BASIC VOCABULARY OF STATISTICS

Variables are characteristics of items or individuals and are what you analyze when you use a statistical method. For the Good Tunes scenario, sales, expenses by year, and net profit by year are variables that the bankers would want to analyze.

> **VARIABLE**
>
> A **variable** is a characteristic of an item or individual.

When used as an adjective in everyday speech, *variable* suggests that something changes or varies, and you would expect the sales, expenses, and net profit to have different values from year to year. These different values are the **data** associated with a variable, and more simply, the "data" to be analyzed. In later sections, you will be sometimes asked to enter the cell range of a variable in Excel. When you see such an instruction, you should enter the cell range of the different values that collectively are the data to be analzyed. (Section 1.6 on page 11 explains what a cell range is and further discusses how to enter data in Excel.)

Variables can differ for reasons other than time. For example, if you conducted an analysis of the composition of a large lecture class, you would probably want to include the variables class standing, gender, and major field of study. Those variables would vary, too, because each student in the class is different. One student might be a freshman male Economics major, while another may be a sophomore female Finance major.

You also need to remember that values are meaningless unless their variables have **operational definitions.** These definitions are universally accepted meanings that are clear to all associated with an analysis. While the operational definition for sales per year might seem clear, miscommunication could occur if one person was referring to sales per year for the entire chain of stores and another to sales per year per store. Even individual values for variables sometimes need definition—for the class standing variable, for example, what *exactly* is meant by the words *sophomore* and *junior*? (Perhaps the most famous example of vague definitions was the definition of a valid vote in the state of Florida during the 2000 U.S. presidential election. Vagueness about the operational definitions there ultimately required a U.S. Supreme Court ruling.)

Understanding the distinction between variables and their values helps in learning four other basic vocabulary terms, two of which you have already encountered in previous sections.

POPULATION

A **population** consists of all the items or individuals about which you want to draw a conclusion.

SAMPLE

A **sample** is the portion of a population selected for analysis.

PARAMETER

A **parameter** is a numerical measure that describes a characteristic of a population.

STATISTIC

A **statistic** is a numerical measure that describes a characteristic of a sample.

All the Good Tunes sales transactions for a specific year, all the customers who shopped at Good Tunes this weekend, all the full-time students enrolled in a college, and all the registered voters in Ohio are examples of populations. Examples of samples from these four populations would be 200 Good Tunes sales transactions randomly selected by an auditor for study, 30 Good Tunes customers asked to complete a customer satisfaction survey, 50 full-time students selected for a marketing study, and 500 registered voters in Ohio contacted via telephone for a political poll. In each sample, the transactions or people in the sample represent a portion of the items or individuals that make up the population.

"The average amount spent by all customers who shopped at Good Tunes this weekend" is an example of a parameter because the amount spent in the entire population is needed. In contrast, "the average amount spent by the 30 customers completing the customer satisfaction survey" is an example of a statistic because the amount spent from only the sample of 30 people is required.

Using and Learning Microsoft Excel

From the Authors' Desktop

Although we have talked a lot about statistics to this point, we haven't mentioned much about using Microsoft Excel. Using any computer program is a two-step process that begins with learning to operate the program and then advances to mastering how to apply the program to a decision-making task—and Excel is no exception.

The Excel Companion to this chapter will help you become familiar with operating Excel. In writing that Companion, we have assumed that you have operated a personal computer in the past to do something such as surf the Web, send an instant message, play music or games, or write homework assignments. If you have never used a personal computer for any of these or similar activities, you should ask a friend to introduce you to personal computers before you read the Companion for this chapter. While this Companion was primarily written for novices, experienced Excel users will benefit from learning the words used to describe the Excel operations in this book.

The Excel Companion to Chapter 2 and those for later chapters will help you understand how you can apply the statistical methods discussed in this book by using Microsoft Excel. For each method discussed, you will typically learn two ways that you can use Excel. One way, labeled **Basic Excel**, uses Excel without any outside enhancements to the program. The other way, labeled **PHStat2**, uses the free PHStat2 statistics add-in* that is included on this book's CD.

These two ways are truly interchangeable. The Excel solutions you create using either way will be identical (or nearly so) to each other and the example worksheets and charts you see in this book. You can switch between the two ways at any time as you use this text without losing any comprehension of the Excel material. That this book includes two complementary ways of learning Microsoft Excel is a distinctive feature of the book.

Which way is best for you?

Unless your instructor requires you to use one way, you may want to choose a way that best suits how you like to learn. Do you like to learn by building things from scratch, one step at a time? If so, using the Basic Excel way would be the best way for you. Do you worry about the time it takes to build things and the typing errors you might make? Or do you like to learn by closely examining a solution to discover its details, a discovery process some call reverse engineering? In either of these cases, using PHStat2 would be your best choice.

For a few statistical methods, you will not find either a Basic Excel way or a PHStat2 way, due to the limitations of Excel. For such methods, you will find Excel workbook files on the book's CD that you can open and use as a template for creating your own solutions. (Actually, you will find files that contain template examples for every statistical method discussed in the Excel Companions and for every Excel worksheet or chart illustrated in this book. A good starting point for these examples are the Excel workbook files named for the chapters of this text, such as Chapter 2.xls.)

Regardless of the way you use and learn Microsoft Excel, you are invited to go online and explore the Web site for this book. There, you will find supplementary material about using Excel, including discussions of Excel techniques that the authors were not able to include in the book because of space limitations.

Postscript: Isn't Using an Add-in a Bad Thing?

If you are an experienced Microsoft Excel user, you may have concerns about using an add-in such as PHStat2. You may be concerned that you will become dependent on something you would not be able to use in business or think that using PHStat2 somehow means that you are not really using and learning Microsoft Excel.

Both of these concerns are unfounded. PHStat2 is a learning tool whose sole purpose is to help you understand how Excel can be used to support specific statistical methods. PHStat2 is designed to make using Microsoft Excel more convenient, by doing the "busy work" activities of creating an Excel solution, such as cell formatting, for you. When you read the Excel Companions, you will understand what PHStat2 is doing for you in a generalized way as well as what it is doing specifically for a problem (following the Basic Excel instructions).

It is true that other add-ins, including add-ins for other introductory business statistics textbooks, can obscure Microsoft Excel by not building an Excel-based solution and only reporting outcomes and statistical information that the add-in has internally (and invisibly) computed. Using such add-ins would not be truly "learning" Microsoft Excel, and using such add-ins would leave you dependent on their use. In contrast, PHStat2 creates model Excel solutions that you can examine and incorporate into your own Excel solutions.

*Section E1.6 that begins on page 28 explains what an add-in is.

1.4 DATA COLLECTION

The managers at Good Tunes believe that they will have a stronger argument for expansion if they can show the bankers that the customers of Good Tunes are highly satisfied with the service they received. How could the managers demonstrate that good service was the typical customer experience at Good Tunes?

Unlike the earlier Good Tunes scenario, in which sales per year was automatically collected as part of normal business activities, the managers now face the twin challenges to first identify relevant variables for a customer satisfaction study and then devise a method for *data collection*—that is, collecting the values for those variables.

Many different types of circumstances, such as the following, require data collection:

- A marketing research analyst needs to assess the effectiveness of a new television advertisement.
- A pharmaceutical manufacturer needs to determine whether a new drug is more effective than those currently in use.
- An operations manager wants to monitor a manufacturing process to find out whether the quality of product being manufactured is conforming to company standards.
- An auditor wants to review the financial transactions of a company in order to determine whether the company is in compliance with generally accepted accounting principles.

In each of these examples, and for the Good Tunes managers as well, collecting data from every item or individual in the population would be too difficult or too time-consuming. Because this is the typical case, data collection almost always involves collecting data from a sample. (Chapter 7 discusses methods of sample selection.)

Unlike the Good Tunes example that begins this section, the source of the data to be collected is not always obvious. Data sources are classified as being either **primary sources** or **secondary sources**. When the data collector is the one using the data for analysis, the source is primary. When the person performing the statistical analysis is not the data collector, the source is secondary. Sources of data fall into one of four categories:

- Data distributed by an organization or an individual
- A designed experiment
- A survey
- An observational study

Organizations and individuals that collect and publish data typically use that data as a primary source and then let others use it as a secondary source. For example, the United States federal government collects and distributes data in this way for both public and private purposes. The Bureau of Labor Statistics collects data on employment and also distributes the monthly consumer price index. The Census Bureau oversees a variety of ongoing surveys regarding population, housing, and manufacturing and undertakes special studies on topics such as crime, travel, and health care.

Market research firms and trade associations also distribute data pertaining to specific industries or markets. Investment services such as Mergent's provide financial data on a company-by-company basis. Syndicated services such as AC Nielsen provide clients with data that enables the comparison of client products with those of their competitors. Daily newspapers are filled with numerical information regarding stock prices, weather conditions, and sports statistics.

Outcomes of a designed experiment are another data source. These outcomes are the results of an experiment, such as a test of several laundry detergents to compare how well each detergent removes a certain type of stain. Developing proper experimental designs is a subject mostly beyond the scope of this text because such designs often involve sophisticated statistical procedures. However, some of the fundamental experimental design concepts are discussed in Chapters 11 and 12.

Conducting a survey is a third type of data source. People being surveyed are asked questions about their beliefs, attitudes, behaviors, and other characteristics. For example, people could be asked their opinion about which laundry detergent best removes a certain type of stain. (This could lead to a result different from a designed experiment seeking the same answer.)

Conducting an observational study is the fourth important data source. A researcher collects data by directly observing a behavior, usually in a natural or neutral setting. Observational studies are a common tool for data collection in business. Market researchers use *focus groups* to elicit unstructured responses to open-ended questions posed by a moderator to a target audience. Other, more structured types of studies involve group dynamics and consensus building. Observational study techniques are also used in situations in which enhancing teamwork or improving the quality of products and service is a management goal.

Identifying the most appropriate source is a critical task because if biases, ambiguities, or other types of errors flaw the data being collected, even the most sophisticated statistical methods will not produce useful information. For the Good Tunes example, variables relevant to the customer experience could take the form of survey questions related to various aspects of the customer experience, examples of which are shown in Figure 1.1.

FIGURE 1.1

Questions about the Good Tunes customer experience

1. How many days did it take from the time you ordered your merchandise to the time you received it?_____

2. Did you buy any merchandise that was featured in the Good Tunes Sunday newspaper sales flyer for the week of your purchase? Yes _____ No_____

3. Was this your first purchase at Good Tunes? Yes _____ No_____

4. Are you likely to buy additional merchandise from Good Tunes in the next 12 months? Yes _____ No_____

5. How much money (in U.S.dollars) do you expect to spend on stereo and consumer electronics equipment in the next 12 months?_____

6. How do you rate the overall service provided by Good Tunes with respect to your recent purchase?

Excellent ☐　　Very good ☐　　Fair ☐　　Poor ☐

7. How do you rate the selection of products offered by Good Tunes with respect to other retailers of home entertainment systems?

Excellent ☐　　Very good ☐　　Fair ☐　　Poor ☐

8. How do you rate the quality of the items you recently purchased from Good Tunes?

Excellent ☐　　Very good ☐　　Fair ☐　　Poor ☐

The survey might also ask questions that seek to classify customers into groups for later analysis.

One good way for Good Tunes to avoid data-collection flaws would be to distribute the questionnaire to a random sample of customers (as discussed in Chapter 7). A poor way would be to rely on a business rating Web site that allows online visitors to rate a merchant. Such Web sites cannot provide assurance that those who do the rating are customers.

Web Surveys

From the Authors' Desktop

Web-based surveys and ratings seem to be of growing importance for many marketers. Their use and misuse raise many concerns. By coincidence, while writing Section 1.4, one of us received an email requesting that he rate the Marriott Rewards travel loyalty program a perfect "10" in the voting for the InsideFlyer Freddie Awards. The author had never heard of those awards, but soon he received other emails from various other travel loyalty programs, also asking that the same high rating be submitted. He even got an email for a program for which he had just signed up in the prior month (and for a travel company of which he was not yet a customer).

At the same time, another one of us found an article in *The New York Times* that reported

that Internet travel sites had to closely monitor submitted reviews to avoid fraudulent claims (C. Elliott, "Hotel Reviews Online: In Bed with Hope, Half-Truths and Hype," *The New York Times*, February 7, 2006, pp. C1, C8). The article also reported that a hotel in Key West, Florida, offered its guests a 10% discount if they published a rave review of that hotel on a particular travel Web site! Our co-author with all the "Freddie" emails felt cheated.

Have you ever received an email asking you to rate an online merchant? Many of us have, especially when we have just purchased something from an online merchant. Often, such emails come with an incentive, not unlike the Key West hotel's discount. Would an incentive cause you to rate the merchant? Would the incentive affect your opinion?

What would you say about a ratings Web site that accepts advertising from merchants that are rated on the site? What would you say about a ratings Web site that gets paid a commission if a visitor first views a rating and then clicks on a link for the merchant? These are among the several practices that may raise ethical concerns for some.

If you do use a ratings Web site, be sure to check out the "fine print" on your next visit. Although you will find a privacy statement that explains how the Web site uses data that can personally identify you, most likely you will not find a "data collection statement" that explains the methods the Web site uses to collect its data. Perhaps you should find such a statement.

1.5 TYPES OF VARIABLES

Statisticians classify **variables** as either being categorical or numerical and further classify numerical variables as having either discrete or continuous values. Figure 1.2 shows the relationships and provides examples of each type of variable.

FIGURE 1.2

Types of variables

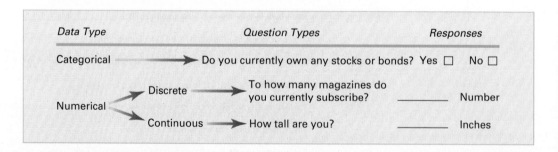

Categorical variables (also known as **qualitative variables**) have values that can only be placed into categories, such as "yes" and "no". Questions 2–4 in Figure 1.1 are examples of categorical variables, all of which have "yes" or "no" as their values. Categorical variables can also result in more than two possible responses. An example of this type of variable is asking customers to indicate the day of the week on which they made their purchases. Questions 6–8 result in one of four possible responses.

Numerical variables (also known as **quantitative variables**) have values that represent quantities. For example, Questions 1 and 5 in Figure 1.1 are numerical variables. Numerical variables are further subdivided as discrete or continuous variables.

Discrete variables have numerical values that arise from a counting process. "The number of magazines subscribed to" is an example of a discrete numerical variable because the response is one of a finite number of integers. You subscribe to zero, one, two, and so on magazines. The number of days it takes from the time you ordered your merchandise to the time you receive it is a discrete numerical variable because you are counting the number of days.

Continuous variables produce numerical responses that arise from a measuring process. The time you wait for teller service at a bank is an example of a continuous numerical variable because the response takes on any value within a *continuum*, or interval, depending on the precision of the measuring instrument. For example, your waiting time could be 1 minute, 1.1 minutes, 1.11 minutes, or 1.113 minutes, depending on the precision of the measuring device you use.

Theoretically, with sufficient precision of measurement, no two continuous values will be identical. As a practical matter, however, most measuring devices are not precise enough to detect small differences, and tied values for a continuous variable (i.e., two or more items or individuals with the same value) are often found in experimental or survey data.

Levels of Measurement and Measurement Scales

Using levels of measurement is another way of classifying data. There are four widely recognized levels of measurement: nominal, ordinal, interval, and ratio scales.

Nominal and Ordinal Scales Data from a categorical variable are measured on a nominal scale or on an ordinal scale. A **nominal scale** (see Figure 1.3) classifies data into distinct categories in which no ranking is implied. In the Good Tunes customer satisfaction survey, the answer to the question "Are you likely to buy additional merchandise from Good Tunes in the next 12 months?" is an example of a nominal scaled variable, as are your favorite soft drink, your political party affiliation, and your gender. Nominal scaling is the weakest form of measurement because you cannot specify any ranking across the various categories.

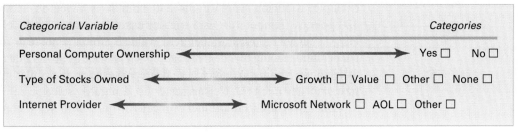

FIGURE 1.3 Examples of nominal scales

An **ordinal scale** classifies data into distinct categories in which ranking is implied. In the Good Tunes survey, the answers to the question "How do you rate the overall service provided by Good Tunes with respect to your recent purchase?" represent an ordinal scaled variable because the responses "excellent, very good, fair, and poor" are ranked in order of satisfaction level. Figure 1.4 lists other examples of ordinal scaled variables.

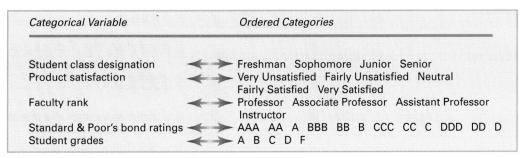

FIGURE 1.4 Examples of ordinal scales

Ordinal scaling is a stronger form of measurement than nominal scaling because an observed value classified into one category possesses more of a property than does an observed value classified into another category. However, ordinal scaling is still a relatively weak form of measurement because the scale does not account for the amount of the differences *between* the categories. The ordering implies only *which* category is "greater," "better," or "more preferred"— not by *how much.*

Interval and Ratio Scales Data from a numerical variable are measured on an interval or a ratio scale. An **interval scale** (see Figure 1.5) is an ordered scale in which the difference between measurements is a meaningful quantity but does not involve a true zero point. For example, a noontime temperature reading of 67 degrees Fahrenheit is 2 degrees warmer than a noontime reading of 65 degrees. In addition, the 2 degrees Fahrenheit difference in the noontime temperature readings is the same as if the two noontime temperature readings were 74 and 76 degrees Fahrenheit because the difference has the same meaning anywhere on the scale.

FIGURE 1.5

Examples of interval and ratio scales

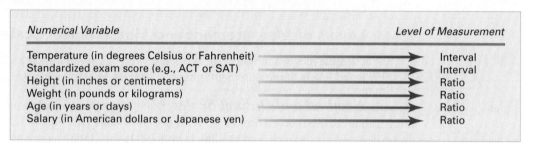

Numerical Variable	Level of Measurement
Temperature (in degrees Celsius or Fahrenheit)	Interval
Standardized exam score (e.g., ACT or SAT)	Interval
Height (in inches or centimeters)	Ratio
Weight (in pounds or kilograms)	Ratio
Age (in years or days)	Ratio
Salary (in American dollars or Japanese yen)	Ratio

A **ratio scale** is an ordered scale in which the difference between the measurements involves a true zero point, as in height, weight, age, or salary measurements. In the Good Tunes customer satisfaction survey, the amount of money (in U.S. dollars) you expect to spend on stereo equipment in the next 12 months is an example of a ratio scaled variable. As another example, a person who weighs 240 pounds is twice as heavy as someone who weighs 120 pounds. Temperature is a trickier case: Fahrenheit and Celsius (centigrade) scales are interval but not ratio scales; the "zero" value is arbitrary, not real. You cannot say that a noontime temperature reading of 4 degrees Fahrenheit is twice as hot as 2 degrees Fahrenheit. But a Kelvin temperature reading, in which zero degrees means no molecular motion, is ratio scaled. In contrast, the Fahrenheit and Celsius scales use arbitrarily selected zero-degree beginning points.

Data measured on an interval scale or on a ratio scale constitute the highest levels of measurement. They are stronger forms of measurement than an ordinal scale because you can determine not only which observed value is the largest but also by how much.

PROBLEMS FOR SECTION 1.5

Learning the Basics

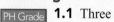
1.1 Three different beverages are sold at a fast-food restaurant—soft drinks, tea, and coffee.
a. Explain why the type of beverage sold is an example of a categorical variable.
b. Explain why the type of beverage sold is an example of a nominal scaled variable.

1.2 Soft drinks are sold in three sizes at a fast-food restaurant—small, medium, and large. Explain why the size of the soft drink is an example of an ordinal scaled variable.

1.3 Suppose that you measure the time it takes to download an MP3 file from the Internet.

a. Explain why the download time is a continuous numerical variable.
b. Explain why the download time is a ratio scaled variable.

Applying the Concepts

1.4 For each of the following variables, determine whether the variable is categorical or numerical. If the variable is numerical, determine whether the variable is discrete or continuous. In addition, determine the level of measurement for each of the following.
a. Number of telephones per household
b. Length (in minutes) of the longest long-distance call made per month

c. Whether someone in the household owns a cell phone
d. Whether there is a high-speed Internet connection in the household

 1.5 The following information is collected from students upon exiting the campus bookstore during the first week of classes:
a. Amount of time spent shopping in the bookstore
b. Number of textbooks purchased
c. Academic major
d. Gender

Classify each of these variables as categorical or numerical. If the variable is numerical, determine whether the variable is discrete or continuous. In addition, determine the level of measurement for these variables.

 1.6 For each of the following variables, determine whether the variable is categorical or numerical. If the variable is numerical, determine whether the variable is discrete or continuous. In addition, determine the level of measurement for each of the following.
a. Name of Internet provider
b. Amount of time spent surfing the Internet per week
c. Number of emails received in a week
d. Number of online purchases made in a month

1.7 For each of the following variables, determine whether the variable is categorical or numerical. If the variable is numerical, determine whether the variable is discrete or continuous. In addition, determine the level of measurement for each of the following.
a. Amount of money spent on clothing in the past month
b. Favorite department store
c. Most likely time period during which shopping for clothing takes place (weekday, weeknight, or weekend)
d. Number of pairs of winter gloves owned

1.8 Suppose the following information is collected from Robert Keeler on his application for a home mortgage loan at the Metro County Savings and Loan Association:
a. Monthly payments: $1,427
b. Number of jobs in past 10 years: 1
c. Annual family income: $86,000
d. Marital status: Married

Classify each of the responses by type of data and level of measurement.

1.9 One of the variables most often included in surveys is income. Sometimes the question is phrased "What is your income (in thousands of dollars)?" In other surveys, the respondent is asked to "Place an X in the circle corresponding to your income level" and given a number of income ranges to choose from.
a. In the first format, explain why income might be considered either discrete or continuous.
b. Which of these two formats would you prefer to use if you were conducting a survey? Why?
c. Which of these two formats would likely bring you a greater rate of response? Why?

 1.10 If two students score a 90 on the same examination, what arguments could be used to show that the underlying variable—test score—is continuous?

1.11 The director of market research at a large department store chain wanted to conduct a survey throughout a metropolitan area to determine the amount of time working women spend shopping for clothing in a typical month.
a. Describe both the population and the sample of interest, and indicate the type of data the director might want to collect.
b. Develop a first draft of the questionnaire needed in (a) by writing a series of three categorical questions and three numerical questions that you feel would be appropriate for this survey.

1.6 MICROSOFT EXCEL WORKSHEETS

When you use Microsoft Excel, you place the data you have collected in **worksheets**. Worksheets appear as pages containing gridlines that separate individually lettered columns from numbered rows. While worksheets look like the simple tables you can create in a word processing program, worksheets have special features that are particularly suited to data analysis. Understanding the special features of worksheets will help you to better understand the interplay of data and results in Microsoft Excel.

Worksheet Cells

The intersections of the columns and rows of worksheets form boxes called **cells.** You refer to a cell by its column letter and row number. For example, you refer to the cell in the first column and second row as cell A2 and the cell in the fifth column and first row as cell E1. You enter in a cell a single value or an expression that can include a reference to another cell. This flexibility, as explained further in Section E1.3 of the Excel Companion to this chapter, is one of the special features that makes Microsoft Excel more than just a fancy table-oriented word processor.

You can refer to more than one cell in a cell reference. If you want to refer to a group of cells that forms a contiguous rectangular area, you can use a **cell range** in which references to the upper leftmost cell and the lower rightmost cell are joined with a colon. For example, the cell range A1:C2 refers to the six cells found in the first two rows and three columns of a worksheet. Excel also allows ranges such as A:A or 4:4, as a shorthand way of referring to all the cells in a column or a row. Later in this text, you will see cell ranges such as D1:D8,F1:F8 that refer to cells from two non-adjacent area of a worksheet.

Worksheets exist inside a **workbook**, a collection of worksheets and other types of sheets, including **chart sheets** that help visualize data. Usually, you will use only one sheet at any given time and open to a worksheet by clicking its sheet tab (see Section E1.1). If someone says that they are opening an "Excel file," they are most likely opening a workbook file. All versions of Excel can open workbook files saved using the **.xls** file format (and all Excel files on the Student CD are in this format). Excel 2007 can also open workbooks saved in the newer **.xlsx** format discussed in Appendix F.

Designing Effective Worksheets

Because thousands of cells are available on individual worksheets, you will never have to worry about running out of cells to use. This spaciousness of worksheets invites careless use and causes some to ignore the important process of effectively arranging worksheet data. Poor arrangements can increase the chance of user errors, create confusing results, lead to unattractive printouts, or worse.

To be consistent with standard business usage, you should associate column cell ranges with variables. In this arrangement, you use the first (row 1) cell of a column for a name label for a variable and place the data for the variable in the subsequent cells of the column. You do not skip any rows as you enter data, so column cell ranges will never contain any empty cells. (Empty cells can interfere with Excel ability's to process your data and can lead to inaccurate results.)

This standard practice is always used in this text and in all of the Excel files on the student CD. Because all of the Excel instructions assume this data arrangement, you should never deviate from this practice when you use this book.

Another good practice is to place all the variables on a worksheet that is *separate* from the worksheet containing the results. Such separation will increase the reusability of your results worksheet and minimize the chance of inadvertent changes to the values of your variables as you construct your results. In the workbooks found on the book's CD as well as the workbooks produced by PHStat2, you will generally find a Results worksheet showing the results separate from the worksheet containing the variables.

Sometimes, worksheets used in this book require only the values of certain parameters or statistics and not the values associated with a variable. For such worksheets, good practice is to place the parameters and statistics at the top of the worksheet so that a user can easily perform what-if analyses, changing values to see their effects on the results. In this book, these values always appear in bold, in cells tinted a shade Excel calls light turquoise and under the heading Data. When you see such tinted cells, you know that you can change the values in those cells to perform what-if analyses and solve other, similar problems.

Another good design practice is to allow the user to be able to explicitly see the chain of calculations from the starting data, through any intermediate calculations, to the results. This practice is particularly advantageous when preparing statistical worksheets because most "intermediate calculations" are statistics themselves. Showing the chain of calculations helps you review your worksheet for errors and helps others better understand what your worksheet does.

In the worksheets of this book, intermediate calculations appear under the heading Intermediate Calculations and are in a cell range that immediately precedes the cell range containing the results. The results appear in cells that are tinted a light yellow and contain boldfaced text. There is also a heading over the results cells that varies with the type of statistical analysis performed.

Whether you use the worksheet design of this book or your own design, do not overlook the importance of skipping rows or columns to create white space to separate different regions of the worksheet that present results. In this book, worksheets tend to skip only a single row or a single column. This choice is due more to making all illustrations compact than any hard or fast rule. You should experiment with your own worksheets with an eye to making them easy to follow on both the display screen and the printed page. Do not hesitate to create two copies of your worksheets—one optimized for the screen, the other for the printer, if you have anything but the simplest worksheet to produce.

When to Excel

From the Authors' Desktop

Perhaps you have heard from some people that Microsoft Excel shouldn't be used for statistics or you have searched the Internet and discovered that statistics educators have had a long-running discussion over the use of Excel in the classroom.

As authors of a text whose title includes the phrase *Using Microsoft Excel*, we believe that Microsoft Excel provides a good way to introduce you to basic statistical methods and demonstrate how to apply these methods in business decision making. Many managers, noting the prevalence of Microsoft Excel on the computers in their businesses, have similarly considered using Excel, rather than a specialized statistical program, for statistical analysis. Microsoft Excel seems like an attractive choice because:

- Using Excel means not having to incur the extra costs of using specialized statistical programs.
- Most business users already have some familiarity with Excel.
- Excel is easy to use and easy to learn, at least for casual users.
- Excel graphical and statistical functions can use the same worksheet-based data that users have created for other business purposes.
- Some Excel graphical functions produce more vivid visual outputs than some specialized statistical programs.

While these traits are attractive, those who have chosen Microsoft Excel have not necessarily considered the accuracy and completeness of the statistical results that Excel produces. Unfortunately, some investigators have determined that certain Microsoft Excel statistical capabilities contain flaws that can lead to invalid results, especially when data sets are very large or have unusual statistical properties (see reference 1, 2, and 4). Even using Microsoft Excel with small data sets to produce the relatively simple descriptive statistics can lead to nonstandard results. (As an example, see the discussion for creating histograms in the Excel Companion to chapter 2 on page 86.) Clearly, when you use Microsoft Excel, you must be careful about the data and the method you are using. Whether this complication outweighs the benefits of Excel's attractive features is still an unanswered question in business today.

SUMMARY

In this chapter, you have been introduced to the role of statistics in turning data into information and the importance of using computer programs such as Microsoft Excel. In addition, you have studied data collection and the various types of data used in business. In conjunction with the Using Statistics scenario, you were asked to review the customer survey used by the Good Tunes company (see page 7). The first and fifth questions of the survey shown will produce numerical data. Questions 2, 3, and 4 will produce nominal categorical data. Questions 6–8 will produce ordinal categorical data. The responses to the first question (number of days) are discrete, and the responses to the fifth question (amount of money spent) are continuous. In the next two chapters, tables and charts and a variety of descriptive numerical measures that are useful for data analysis are developed.

KEY TERMS

categorical variable   8
cell   11
cell range   12
chart sheet   12
continuous variable   9
data   4
descriptive statistics   3
discrete variable   9
inferential statistics   3

interval scale   10
nominal scale   9
numerical variable   8
operational definition   4
ordinal scale   9
parameter   5
population   5
primary source   6
qualitative variable   8

quantitative variable   8
ratio scale   10
sample   5
secondary source   6
statistic   5
statistics   2
variable   4
workbook   12
worksheet   11

CHAPTER REVIEW PROBLEMS

Checking Your Understanding

 1.12 What is the difference between a sample and a population?

 1.13 What is the difference between a statistic and a parameter?

 1.14 What is the difference between descriptive and inferential statistics?

 1.15 What is the difference between a categorical variable and a numerical variable?

1.16 What is the difference between a discrete variable and a continuous variable?

1.17 What is an operational definition and why is it so important?

1.18 What are the four levels of measurement scales?

Applying the Concepts

1.19 The Data and Story Library, **lib.stat.cmu.edu/ DASL**, is an online library of data files and stories that illustrate the use of basic statistical methods. The stories are classified by method and by topic. Go to this site and click on **List all topics**. Pick a story and summarize how statistics were used in the story.

1.20 Go to the official Microsoft Excel Web site, **www.microsoft.com/office/excel**. Explain how you think Microsoft Excel could be useful in the field of statistics.

1.21 The Gallup organization releases the results of recent polls at its Web site, **www.galluppoll.com**. Go to this site and read today's top analysis.
a. Give an example of a categorical variable found in the poll.
b. Give an example of a numerical variable found in the poll.
c. Is the variable you selected in (b) discrete or continuous?

1.22 The U.S. Census Bureau site, **www.census.gov**, contains survey information on people, business, geography, and other topics. Go to the site and click on **Housing** in the "People and Households" section. Then click on **American Housing Survey**.
a. Briefly describe the American Housing Survey.
b. Give an example of a categorical variable found in this survey.
c. Give an example of a numerical variable found in this survey.
d. Is the variable you selected in (c) discrete or continuous?

1.23 On the U.S. Census Bureau site, **www.census.gov**, click on **Survey of Business Owners** in the "Business & Industry" section and read about The Survey of Business Owners. Click on **Sample SBO-1 Form** to view a survey form.
a. Give an example of a categorical variable found in this survey.
b. Give an example of a numerical variable found in this survey.
c. Is the variable you selected in (b) discrete or continuous?

1.24 An online survey of almost 53,000 people (N. Hellmich, "Americans Go for the Quick Fix for Dinner," *USA Today*, February 14, 2005, p. B1) indicated that 37% decide what to make for dinner at home at the last minute and that the amount of time to prepare dinner averages 12 minutes, while the amount of time to cook dinner averages 28 minutes.
a. Which of the four categories of data sources listed in Section 1.4 on page 6 do you think were used in this study?
b. Name a categorical variable discussed in this article.
c. Name a numerical variable discussed in this article.

1.25 According to a Harris Interactive survey of 502 senior human resource executives, 58% responded that referrals were one of the methods for finding the best candidates. ("USA Snapshots," *USA Today*, February 9, 2006, p. A1).
a. Describe the population for the Harris Interactive survey.
b. Is a response to the question "By which methods do you feel you find the best candidates?" categorical or numerical?
c. Fourteen percent of the senior human resources executives polled indicated that professional associations were one of the methods for finding the best candidates. Is this a parameter or a statistic?

1.26 A manufacturer of cat food was planning to survey households in the United States to determine purchasing habits of cat owners. Among the questions to be included are those that relate to
　　1. where cat food is primarily purchased.
　　2. whether dry or moist cat food is purchased.
　　3. the number of cats living in the household.
　　4. whether the cat is pedigreed.
a. Describe the population.
b. For each of the four items listed, indicate whether the variable is categorical or numerical. If it is numerical, is it discrete or continuous?
c. Develop five categorical questions for the survey.
d. Develop five numerical questions for the survey.

Student Survey Data Base

1.27 A sample of 50 undergraduate students answered the following survey.
1. What is your gender?   Female___   Male___
2. What is your age (*as of last birthday*)?___
3. What is your height (*in inches*)?___
4. What is your current registered class designation?
Freshman___ Sophomore___ Junior___ Senior___
5. What is your major area of study?
Accounting___   Economics/Finance___
Information Systems___ International Business___
Management___ Marketing/Retailing___ Other___
Undecided___
6. At the present time, do you plan to attend graduate school?
Yes___   No___   Not sure___
7. What is your current cumulative grade point average?___
8. What would you expect your starting annual salary (*in $000*) to be if you were to seek employment immediately after obtaining your bachelor's degree?___
9. What do you anticipate your salary to be (*in $000*) after five years of full-time work experience?___
10. What is your current employment status?
Full-time___   Part-time___   Unemployed___
11. How many clubs, groups, organizations, or teams are you currently affiliated with on campus?
12. How satisfied are you with the student advisement services on campus?___
Extremely 1 2 3 4 5 6 7 Extremely
unsatisfied   Neutral   satisfied
13. About how much money did you spend this semester for textbooks and supplies?___

The results of the survey are in the file undergradsurvey.xls.
a. Which variables in the survey are categorical?
b. Which variables in the survey are numerical?
c. Which variables are discrete numerical variables?

1.28 A sample of 50 MBA students answered the following survey:

1. What is your gender?   Female___   Male___
2. What is your age (*as of last birthday*)?___
3. What is your height (*in inches*)?___
4. What is your current major area of study?
Accounting ___   Economics/Finance___
Information Systems___ International Business___
Management___ Marketing/Retailing___ Other___
Undecided___
5. What is your graduate cumulative grade point index?___
6. What was your undergraduate area of specialization?
Biological Sciences___ Business Administration___
Computers or Math___ Education___
Engineering___ Humanities___ Performing Arts___
Physical Sciences___ Social Sciences___
Other___
7. What was your undergraduate cumulative grade point average?___
8. What was your GMAT score?___
9. What is your current employment status?___
Full-time___   Part-time___   Unemployed___
10. How many different full-time jobs have you held in the past 10 years?___
11. What do you expect your annual salary (*in $000*) to be immediately after completion of the MBA program?___
12. What do you anticipate your salary to be (*in $000*) after five years of full-time work experience following the completion of the MBA program?___
13. How satisfied are you with the student advisement services on campus?
Extremely 1 2 3 4 5 6 7 Extremely
unsatisfied   Neutral   satisfied
14. About how much money did you spend this semester for textbooks and supplies?___

The results of the survey are in the file gradsurvey.xls.
a. Which variables in the survey are categorical?
b. Which variables in the survey are numerical?
c. Which variables are discrete numerical variables?

End-of-Chapter Cases

At the end of most chapters, you will find a continuing case study that allows you to apply statistics to problems faced by the management of the *Springville Herald*, a daily newspaper. Complementing this case are a series of Web Cases that extend many of the Using Statistics scenarios that begin each chapter.

Learning with the Web Cases

People use statistical techniques to help communicate and present important information to others both inside and outside their businesses. Every day, as in these examples, people misuse these techniques:

- A sales manager working with an "easy-to-use" charting program chooses an inappropriate chart that obscures data relationships.
- The editor of an annual report presents a chart of revenues with an abridged *Y*-axis that creates the false impression of greatly rising revenues.
- An analyst generates meaningless statistics about a set of categorical data, using analyses designed for numerical data.

Identifying and preventing misuses of statistics, whether intentional or not, is an important responsibility for all managers. The Web Cases help you develop the skills necessary for this important task.

Web Cases send you to Web sites that are related to the Using Statistics scenarios that begin each chapter. You review internal documents as well as publicly stated claims, seeking to identify and correct the misuses of statistics. Unlike a traditional case study, but much like real-world situations, not all of the information you encounter will be relevant to your task, and you may occasionally discover conflicting information that you need to resolve before continuing with the case.

To assist your learning, the Web Case for each chapter begins with the learning objective and a summary of the problem or issue at hand. Each case directs you to one or more Web pages where you can discover information to answer case questions that help guide your exploration. If you prefer, you can view these pages by opening corresponding HTML files that can be found on this **Web Case** folder on the Student CD. You can find an index of all files/pages by opening the **SpringvilleCC.htm** file in the **Web Case** folder or by visiting the Springville Chamber of Commerce page, at **www.prenhall.com/ Springville/SpringvilleCC.htm**.

Web Case Example

To illustrate how to learn from a Web Case, open a Web browser and link to **www.prenhall.com/Springville/ Good_Tunes.htm**, or open the **Good_Tunes.htm** file in the **WebCase** folder on the book's CD. This Web page represents the home page of Good Tunes, the online retailer mentioned in the Using Statistics scenario in this chapter. Recall that the privately held Good Tunes is seeking financing to expand its business by opening retail locations. Since it is in management's interest to show that Good Tunes is a thriving business, it is not too surprising to discover the "our best sales year ever" claim in the "Good Times at Good Tunes" entry at the top of their home page.

The claim is also a hyperlink, so click on **our best sales year ever** to display the page that supports the claim. How would you support such a claim? with a table of numbers? a chart? remarks attributed to a knowledgeable source? Good Tunes has used a chart to present "two years ago" and "latest twelve months" sales data by category. Are there any problems with the choices made on this Web page? *Absolutely!*

First, note that there are no scales for the symbols used, so it is impossible to know what the actual sales volumes are. In fact, as you will learn in Section 2.6, charts that incorporate symbols in this way are considered examples of *chartjunk* and would never be used by people seeking to properly use graphs.

This important point aside, another question that arises is whether the sales data represent the number of units sold or something else. The use of the symbols creates the impression that unit sales data are being presented. If the data are unit sales, does such data best support the claim being made—or would something else, such as dollar volumes—be a better indicator of sales at Good Tunes?

Then there are those curious chart labels. "Latest twelve months" is ambiguous; it could include months from the current year as well as months from one year ago and therefore may not be an equivalent time period to "two years ago." Since the business was established in 1997, and the claim being made is "best sales year ever," why hasn't management included sales figures for *every* year?

Is Good Tunes management hiding something, or are they just unaware of the proper use of statistics? Either way, they have failed to properly communicate a vital aspect of their story.

In subsequent Web Cases, you will be asked to provide this type of analysis, using the open-ended questions of the case as your guide. Not all the cases are as straightforward as this sample, and some cases include perfectly appropriate applications of statistics.

REFERENCES

1. McCullough, B. D., and B. Wilson, "On the Accuracy of Statistical Procedures in Microsoft Excel 97," *Computational Statistics and Data Analysis*, 31 (1999), 27–37.
2. McCullough, B. D. and B. Wilson, "On the Accuracy of Statistical Proucedures in Microsoft Excel 2003," *Computational Statistics and Data Analysis*, 49, (2005), 1244–1252.
3. *Microsoft Excel 2007* (Redmond, WA: Microsoft Corporation, 2007).
4. Nash, J. C., "Spreadsheets in Statistical Practice— Another Look," *The American Statistician*, 60, (2006), 287–289.

Excel Companion
to Chapter 1

This Excel Companion serves as a primer for Microsoft Excel, helping you become familiar with the concepts and commands that everyday use of Microsoft Excel requires. Before you intensely study this Companion, you should first consider how you plan to use Excel as you learn statistics. If you skipped reading the "From the Authors' Desktop: Using and Learning Microsoft Excel" on page 5, you may want to review it now so that you have a better understanding of the choices you have in using Excel with this text.

How you plan to use Excel will affect which Excel skills you *immediately* need to know. If you plan to use the Basic Excel instructions in later companions, you should know, or at least have some awareness of, just about every skill discussed in the rest of this Companion. If you plan to use PHStat2, you will have a less immediate need for the skills related to worksheet entries and formulas discussed in Sections E1.3, E1.4, and E1.5. (You can master such skills later, as you read through this book.)

The rest of this companion presents skills in an increasing order of difficulty. Make sure you have mastered the skills presented in the first sections before going on to the later sections. If you consider yourself an experienced Excel user, you might want to take the time to scan this companion if only to become familiar with the terms used throughout the book to describe Excel objects and operations.

E1.1 PRELIMINARIES: BASIC COMPUTING SKILLS

If you have ever surfed the Web, sent an instant message, played music or games, or written word-processed assignments, you have already mastered the skills necessary in order to use Microsoft Excel. However, if you are new to computing, you should use the following countdown of skills—on your mark, get ready, get set, go—to master the basic computing skills needed with this book. (If you are an experienced computer user, you will want to skim this section and note the definitions of the boldfaced terms.)

On Your Mark!

Like many other programs, Microsoft Excel makes frequent use of a keyboard and a mouse-type pointing device. Microsoft Excel expects your pointing device to have two buttons: a primary button (typically the left button) and a secondary button (typically the right). You move your pointing device and use one of the buttons to execute one of these six basic operations[1]:

Click Move the mouse pointer over an object and press the primary button. You click links on a Web page and many of the user interface elements identified in the "Get Set!" part of this section. The book also uses the verb **clear** when telling you to click on a check box to remove its check mark.

Select Similar to click, but when you press the primary button, another list of menu commands or choices appear. You click the Microsoft Windows Start menu and then select Programs or All Programs (depending on the version) to display a list of programs and program folders installed on your system.

Double-click Move the **mouse pointer** over an object and click the primary button twice in rapid succession. You double-click Desktop program icons to open programs, and you double-click the icons that represent files to open and use those files.

Right-click Move the mouse pointer over an object and click the secondary button. You typically right-click an object to reveal a **shortcut menu** of commands that apply to that object.

Drag A multipart mouse operation. First, you move the mouse pointer over an object and then, while pressing and holding down the primary button, you move the mouse pointer somewhere else on the screen and release the primary button. You use drag to resize windows and, in Microsoft Excel, to select a group of adjacent worksheet cells.

Drag-and-drop A multipart mouse operation. First, you move the mouse pointer over an object and then, while pressing and holding down the primary button, you move the mouse pointer over another onscreen object and release the primary button. Drag-and-drop has many applications, but in this text, you mostly use this operation when defining PivotTables (discussed in the Excel Companion to Chapter 2).

---

[1]*Alternate methods of interaction, such as using speech recognition input, are possible on suitably equipped systems. If you are using an alternate method, make sure you know the equivalents to the mouse operations defined in this section.*

If these operations are new to you, you can practice them by opening the Mousing Practice.xls file on the Student CD. (If you do not know how to open a file, ask a friend or use the instructions available in Section E1.2.) Otherwise, you are ready to advance to the "Get Ready!" stage.

Get Ready!

When you start Microsoft Excel, you see a window that contains the Excel user interface and a workspace area that displays open workbooks. If you start any Excel version other than 2007, you will see a window very much like the one shown in Figure E1.1, the actual window for Excel 2003. If you start Excel 2007, you will see the very different-looking window, similar to the one shown in Figure E1.2 on page 20.

In designing Excel 2007, Microsoft tried to minimize the find-and-seek process that many users of earlier versions experience trying to find a particular command or Excel feature. Generally, Excel 2007 displays all relevant commands for a particular task at the top of the window. If you are new to Microsoft Excel and have a choice of using Excel 2007 or an earlier version, you will most likely benefit from choosing Excel 2007 because displaying all relevant commands lessens the initial training you need. However, Excel 2007 is functionally equivalent to earlier Excel versions, and every Excel activity in this text can be done with any version of Excel, starting with Excel 97, although sometimes there are special instructions specific to Excel 2007.

Get Set!

To get started using Microsoft Excel, you need to be familiar with the objects you will commonly see when using

Excel. When opening Excel, you see a window that is either similar to Figure E1.1 if you use Excel 97, 2000, 2002, or 2003[2] or Figure E1.2 if you use Excel 2007. (Should your Excel window not contain some of the elements shown in the figure appropriate for the Excel version you use, see the "Microsoft Excel FAQs" section in Appendix F. As you begin using Excel, you will encounter dialog boxes, special windows that display messages to allow you to make entries or selections. Because you will be frequently interacting with dialog boxes, you should be familiar with the objects you will commonly see in these special windows (see Figure E1.3 on page 20).

The rest of this section defines the objects labeled in Figures E1.1, E1.2, and E1.3. You should be familiar with the objects that apply to the Excel version you use before continuing to the next section.

Excel Window Elements (all versions)

Minimize, resize, and close buttons minimize (that is, hide without closing), resize, and close windows. When you click the sets of labeled buttons in Figures E1.1 and E1.2, you affect the Excel window itself; other, similar buttons operate on other elements in the Excel window, such as the currently opened workbook.

Workspace area displays the currently opened workbook or workbooks. (Although you will not need to open more than one workbook at a time when using this text, you can open multiple workbooks and view all of them by resizing them to fit in the workspace area.)

---

[2]*In the remainder of the book, the labels "Excel 97–2003" or "97–2003" are used when collectively referring to one of these Excel versions.*

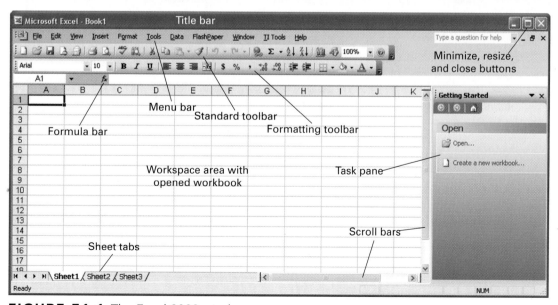

FIGURE E1.1 The Excel 2003 window

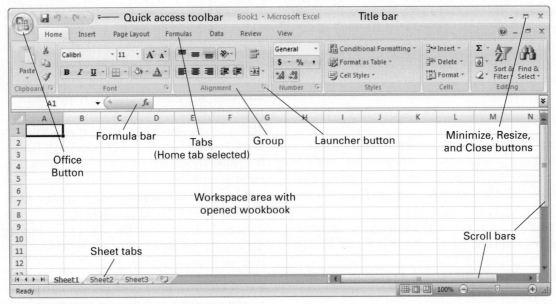

FIGURE E1.2 The Excel 2007 window

Formula bar shows the name of the currently selected worksheet cell (see Section E1.3) and the current contents of that cell.

Sheet tabs display the name of each sheet in the opened workbook. You click a sheet tab to select a sheet and make it the currently active sheet. You double-click a sheet tab to rename the sheet.

Scroll bars allow you to travel horizontally or vertically through parts of a worksheet that are offscreen (for example, row 100 or column T in Figures E1.1 or E1.2).

Title bar displays the name of the currently active workbook and contains the minimize, resize, and close buttons for the Excel window. You drag the title bar to reposition the Excel window on your screen.

Additional Window Objects (Excel 97–2003)

Menu Bar The horizontal list of words at the top of the window that represent sets of commands. You click a menu bar word and pull down lists of command choices, some of which lead to further menu choices.

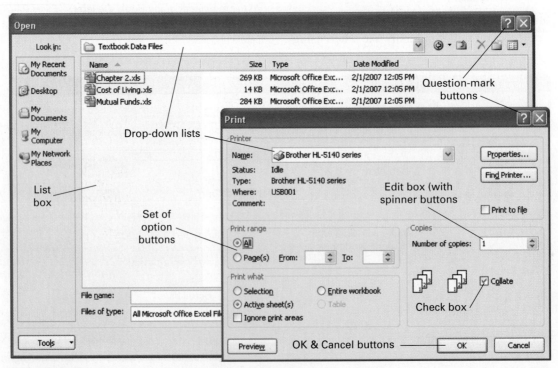

FIGURE E1.3 Commonly encountered elements

Standard Toolbar The toolbar that contains shortcuts to many file-oriented commands, including the common workbook operations discussed in Section E1.4.

Formatting Toolbar The toolbar that contains shortcuts to many common worksheet cell formatting commands (see Section E1.4).

Task Pane A closable window that contains clickable links that represent shortcuts to menu and toolbar operations (Excel 2002 and 2003 only).

Additional Windows Objects Excel 2007

Office Button displays a menu of commonly issued commands similar to the File menu in Excel 97–2003. The Office Button also gives you access to many Excel options settings.

Quick Access Toolbar (to the right of the office button) Displays buttons that are shortcuts to commonly used commands. When you first see Excel 2007, the **Save**, **Undo**, and **Redo** buttons are displayed, but you can add or remove buttons in this toolbar (see "Microsoft Excel 2007-Specific FAQs" in Appendix F to add or remove buttons.)

Tabs Displays groups of commands and features associated with a single type of Excel task. The **Home Tab** (seen in Figure E1.2) displays all commands and features associated with making worksheet cell entries.

Tab Groups Display named collections of related commands and features. Some tab groups, such as the Font, Alignment, and Number groups shown in Figure E1.2 contain **launcher buttons** that open related dialog boxes or task panes.

Contextual Tabs Additional tabs that appear only when you are doing a specific task (that is, working in a specific "context"), such as creating charts. Contextual tabs are displayed with a title (for example, "Chart Tools") that appears in the title bar.

Ribbon is the collective name for the tab-and-group user interface exclusive to Excel 2007. (See "Microsoft Excel 2007-Specific FAQs" in Appendix F if your Excel 2007 window does not display the ribbon.)

Common Dialog Box Objects

List boxes Display lists of choices available to you. Should a list exceed the dimensions of a list box, you will see **scroll buttons** and a **slider** that you can click in order to see the other choices available.

Drop-down lists Display lists of commands or choices when you click over them. Many drop-downs in Excel 2007 display **galleries**, which are illustrated (and sometimes annotated) sets of choices.

Edit boxes Areas into which you type entries. Some edit boxes also contain drop-down lists or **spinner buttons** that you can use to complete the entry. Cell range edit boxes typically include a button that allows you to point to a cell range instead of typing the range.

Option buttons Present a set of mutually exclusive choices. When you click one option button, all the other option buttons in the set are cleared.

Check boxes Present optional actions that are not mutually exclusive choices. Unlike with option buttons, clicking a check box does not affect the status of other check boxes, and more than one check box can be checked at a time. If you click an already checked check box, you clear the check from the box.

OK buttons (in dialog boxes) Allow you to execute tasks using the current values and settings of the currently displayed dialog box. Sometimes the "OK button" will have a different legend, such as Finish, Create, Open, or Save.

Cancel buttons Close dialog boxes and cancel operations represented by the dialog boxes. In most contexts, clicking the Cancel button is equivalent to clicking the Close button in the title bar of the dialog box.

Question-mark buttons Display Excel help messages. Many dialog boxes contain a button with the legend **Help** that also displays help messages.

Go!

To start using Microsoft Excel, you need to understand the conventions used in Excel menus and be familiar with commonly used special keys and keystroke combinations.

Excel menus use these conventions (labeled in Figure E1.4):

- An underlined letter in a menu choice represents an **accelerator key**, a keystroke that is equivalent to selecting the choice with your mouse.
- An **ellipsis** indicates that when you select a menu choice, a dialog box will appear.
- A triangle marker indicates that when you select that menu choice, you will see either another menu of choices or a gallery of choices.

You can execute a number of frequently used menu choices or Excel operations by using a **combination keystroke**—that is, holding down one or more keys while pressing another key. In Excel versions other than Excel 2007, many of these combinations appear next to the menu choices they represent. You can print your currently active worksheet by pressing the combination **Ctrl+P** (that is, while holding down the **Ctrl** key, press the **P** key) and save your currently active workbook by pressing **Ctrl+S**. You can copy (or cut) and paste worksheet cell entries by pressing **Ctrl+C** (or **Ctrl+X**) and **Ctrl+V**.

You can use some of the special keys to execute frequently used operations. When you type an entry, pressing the **Escape** key usually cancels that entry. Pressing the **Backspace** key when typing an entry erases typed characters

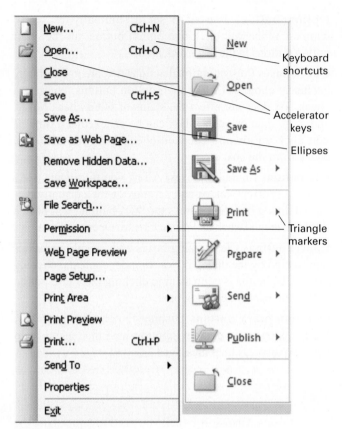

FIGURE E1.4 Excel menu conventions

to the left of the cursor, one character at a time. Pressing the **Delete** key when typing erases characters to the right of the cursor, one character at a time. Pressing either the **Enter** or **Tab** keys finalizes a typed worksheet cell entry.

When viewing a dialog box, pressing **Escape** usually cancels its operation. After clicking a workbook object such as a chart, pressing **Delete** deletes that object. If you get stuck while using Excel, you can move the mouse pointer over an object and then pause to see if Excel displays a **Tool Tip**, a pop-up help message, about the object. At any time, you can also press the **F1** key to display either a help message or help search box.

Textbook Conventions

In this book, dialog box objects are usually referred to by their names or labels. You will find instructions such as "Click **Labels**" or "Click **OK**" when referring to check boxes and command buttons. You will find instructions such as "Select the **Lower-Tail** option" when referring to option boxes or drop-down lists. When object names or labels can vary due to context, the book uses italics, as in "Select *variable name*."

To describe a sequence of menu (Excel 97–2003) or ribbon (Excel 2007) choices, the book uses an arrow sym-

bol to link selections. For example, in Excel versions other than 2007, "select **Tools → Data Analysis**" means that you would first select **Tools** from the Excel menu bar and then select **Data Analysis** from the submenu of choices that appears after you select **Tools**. The equivalent Excel 2007 sequence "select **Data → Data Analysis**" means select the Formulas tab and then select **Data Analysis** (from the Solutions group).

E1.2   BASIC WORKBOOK OPERATIONS

As you work with Microsoft Excel, you will need to open workbooks to use data and results created by you or others at an earlier time. You will also need to save workbooks to ensure their future availability and to protect yourself against any computer system failures that might occur as you work with Excel. You may also need to create new workbooks and may want to print out individual sheets for your workbooks for later study or use in projects and assignments.

In all Excel versions, including Excel 2007, these operations involve dialog boxes that differ only in minor ways. While the dialog box of the version you are using may subtly differ from the ones shown in Figure E1.3 (see page 21), the instructions in this section apply to all Excel versions, except when otherwise noted.

Opening and Saving Workbooks

You open and save workbooks by selecting the storage folder to use and then specifying the file name of the workbook. You begin the process by selecting **File** from the Excel menu bar in Excel 97–2003 or by clicking the **Office Button** in Excel 2007. In either case, a menu of commands appears, as partially shown in Figure E1.4. While the contents of the menus differ (the Excel 2007 menu is on the right in Figure E1.4), they both have **Open** and **Save As** choices. These choices lead to similar dialog boxes, shown in Figure E1.3 and Figure E1.5.

You select the storage folder using the drop-down list at the top of these dialog boxes. You enter (or select from the list box) a file name for the workbook in the **File name** box. You click **Open** (obscured in Figure E1.3) or **Save** to complete the task.

Sometimes when saving files, you will want to change the file type before you click **Save**. If you use Excel 2007 and want to save your workbook in the format used by earlier Excel versions, you select **Excel 97-2003 Workbook (*.xls)** from the **Save as type** drop-down list before you click **Save** (shown in Figure E1.5). If you use any version of Excel and want to save data in a form that can be opened by programs that cannot open Excel workbooks, you might select either **Text (Tab delimited) (*.txt)** or **CSV (Comma delimited) (*.csv)** as the save type.

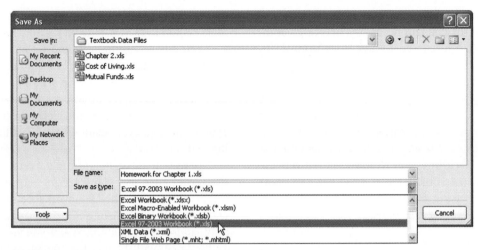

FIGURE E1.5 Save As dialog box (Excel 2007 version)

Likewise, if you are opening a data file that is not an Excel workbook format, you can change the file type (labeled as **File of type** in Figure E1.3). If you cannot find a file that you are sure is in the current Look in folder, changing the file type to **All Files (*.*)** can reveal an inadvertent misspelling or missing file extension (the part of the file name after the period) that otherwise prevents the file from being displayed.

Although all versions of Microsoft Excel include a **Save** command, you should avoid this choice until you gain experience. Using Save makes it too easy for you to inadvertently overwrite your work, and in Excel 2007, it saves your workbook in the new **.xlsx** workbook format that cannot be used by Excel 97–2003. In contrast, using **Save As** always presents you with an opportunity to name your file and choose its file type, and using Save As is also the simplest way you can create a backup copy of your workbook as you work.

If you open a workbook from a nonmodifiable source, such as a CD-ROM, Excel marks the workbook "read-only." You must use Save As to save a modified version of such a workbook, which is another good reason for always using this command.

Creating New Workbooks

You create a new workbook through a straightforward process that varies depending on the version of Excel you are using. In Excel 97 or 2000, you select **File → New**. In Excel 2002 (also known as Excel XP) or 2003, you select **File → New** and then click **Blank workbook** in the New Workbook task pane. In Excel 2007, you click **Office button → New** and in the New Workbook dialog box, you first click **Blank workbook** and then **Create**.

New workbooks are created with a fixed number of worksheets. You can delete extra worksheets or insert more sheets by right-clicking a sheet tab and clicking either **Delete** or **Insert**.

Printing Worksheets

When you want to print the contents of a workbook, you should print one sheet at a time to get the best results. You print sheets by first previewing their printed form onscreen and then making any adjustments to the worksheet and/or to the print setup settings.

To print a specific worksheet, you first click on the sheet tab of that worksheet to make the worksheet the currently active one. Then you display the Print Preview window. If you use a version of Excel other than 2007, select **File → Print Preview**. If you use Excel 2007, click **Office Button**, move the mouse pointer over **Print** (do not click) and select **Print Preview** from the Preview and Print gallery.

The Print Preview windows for all Excel versions are similar to one another. Figure E1.6 shows a partial window for Excel 2003 (top) and Excel 2007 (bottom). If the preview contains errors or displays the worksheet in an unde-

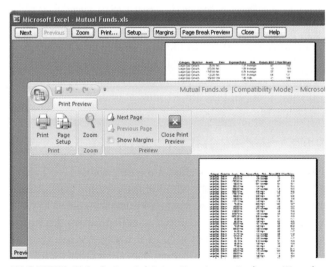

FIGURE E1.6 Partial Print Preview windows (Excel 2003 and 2007 versions)

sirable manner, click **Close** (or **Close Print Preview** in Excel 2007), make the changes necessary, and reselect the preview command. You can customize your printout by clicking **Setup** (or **Page Setup**) and making the appropriate entries in the Page Setup dialog box, which is similar for all Excel versions. For example, to print your worksheet with grid lines and numbered row and lettered column headings (similar to the appearance of the worksheet onscreen), you click the **Sheet** tab in the Page Setup dialog box and then click **Gridlines** and **Row and column headings** and click **OK** (see Figure E1.7). (You can find more information about using Page Setup in Section F4 of Appendix F.)

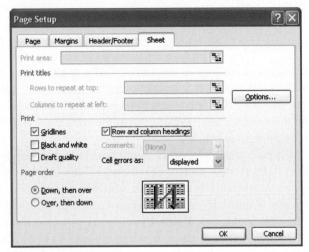

FIGURE E1.7

Sheet tab of the Page Setup dialog box (Excel 2003 version)

When you are ready to print, you can click **Print** in the Print Preview window, but to gain maximum control over your printout, click **Close** (or **Close Print Preview**) and then select **File → Print** (Excel 97–2003) or **Office Button → Print** (Excel 2007). In the Print dialog box that appears (see Figure E1.3 on page 20), you can select the printer to use, make sure you are printing only the currently active worksheet, or print multiple copies at once.

E1.3 WORKSHEET ENTRIES

As first discussed in Section 1.6 (see page 11), you make entries into worksheet cells, the intersections of lettered columns and numbered rows. You use the cursor keys or your pointing device to move a **cell pointer** through a worksheet and to select a cell for entry. As you type an entry, it appears in the formula bar (see Figures E1.1 and E1.2 on pages 19 and 20), and you place that entry into the

cell by either pressing **Tab** or **Enter** or clicking the checkmark button in the formula bar.

You enter individual numeric and label (sometimes called text) values into cells. You can also enter **formulas**, which are instructions to perform a calculation or some other task. Usually, formulas use values found in other cells to produce a displayed result. Formulas can automatically change the displayed result when the values in the supporting cells change.

To refer to a cell in a formula, you use a cell address in the form *Sheetname!ColumnRow*. For example, Data!A2 refers to the cell in the Data worksheet that is in column A and row 2. You can also use just the *ColumnRow* portion of a full address, for example A2, if you are referring to a cell on the same worksheet as the one into which you are entering a formula.

Sometimes you need to refer to a group of cells, called a **cell range**. If the group of cells forms a rectangular area—for example, a group composed of cells from two adjacent columns—you use an address in the form *Sheetname!Upperleftcell:Lowerrightcell*. For example, Data!A1:B10 refers to the 20 cells that are in rows 1 through 10 in columns A and B of the Data worksheet. If your group forms two or more rectangular areas, you enter the range as a list of rectangular areas separated by commas, for example, Data!A1:A10,Data!C1:C10. If the name of the sheet contains spaces or special characters, such as "City Data" or "Figure-1.2", you must enclose the sheet name in a pair of single quotes, as in 'City Data'!A1:A10 or 'Figure-1.2'!A1:A10.[3]

(Because you use names of sheets in formulas, you may want to rename sheets from their default names. As mentioned in Section E1.1, you can rename a sheet by double-clicking the **sheet tab** for the sheet, typing a new, more descriptive name, and then pressing **Enter**.)

Entering Formulas

You enter formulas by typing the equal sign (=) followed by some combination of mathematical or other data processing operations. For simple formulas, the symbols +, −, *, /, and ^ are used for the operations addition, subtraction, multiplication, division, and exponentiation (a number raised to a power), respectively. For example, the

---

[3]For cases in which you need to distinguish between two similarly located cells on two similarly named worksheets in two different workbooks, you use an address in the form '[Workbookname]Sheetname'!ColumnRow. For example, you use '[Chapter1]Data'!A1 to refer to the first cell on the Data worksheet in the Chapter1 workbook.

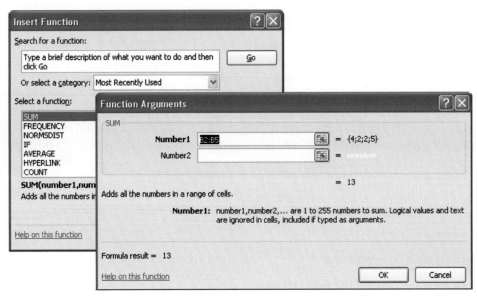

FIGURE E1.8 Insert Function dialog box of the Function Wizard

formula =**Data!B2** + **Data!B3** + **Data!B4** + **Data!B5** adds the contents of cells B2, B3, B4, and B5 of the Data worksheet and displays the sum as the value of the cell containing the formula. You can also use **worksheet functions** to simplify formulas. For example, the formula =**SUM(Data!B2:B5)** uses the worksheet **SUM** function to create a shorter equivalent to the example in this paragraph.

When you are using worksheet functions, you can use the Function Wizard to minimize your typing. To use this wizard, which is similar in all Excel versions, you select **Insert → Function** (Excel 97–2003) or **Formulas → Function Wizard** (Excel 2007) and then make entries and selections in one or more dialog boxes. For example, to enter the formula =**SUM(Data!B2:B5)** using this wizard, you select the function SUM and click **OK** in the Insert Function dialog box (obscured in Figure E1.8). You then type or point to the cell range **B2:B5** in the **Number1** box and click **OK** in the Function Argument dialog box (also shown in Figure E1.8). The wizard then enters the completed formulas in the currently active cell.

As Figure E1.8 shows, the Function Wizard also previews the results of the SUM function (13) and displays the contents of the range B2:B5 (4, 2, 2, and 5).

Verifying Formulas

Whether you enter formulas on your own in a new worksheet, open a workbook that contains formulas, or use commands that add formulas to worksheets, you should review and verify formulas before you use their results. To view the formulas in a worksheet, press **Ctrl+`** (backtick key).

To restore the original view, the results of the formulas, press **Ctrl+** a second time.

As you create and use more complicated worksheets, you may want to visually examine the relationships among a formula and the cells it uses (called the precedents) and the cells that use the results of the formula (the dependents). To display arrows that show these relationships, use the formula auditing feature of Excel. For Excel 97 or 2000, select **Tools → Auditing** and for Excel 2002–2003, select **Tools → Formula Auditing**. Then select one of the choices on the **auditing** submenu. To use this feature In Excel 2007, select **Formulas** and then select one of the choices from the **Formula Auditing** group. The **Remove All Arrows** choice restores your display by removing all auditing arrows when you are finished auditing the formulas.

E1.4 WORKSHEET FORMATTING

You can use various formatting commands to enhance the appearance of your worksheets. If you use Excel 97–2003, you will find many of the common formatting operations on the Formatting Toolbar (see Figures E1.1 and E1.9) and the rest inside the Format Cells dialog box (select **Format → Cells** to view this dialog box). If you use Excel 2007, most formatting operations are visible on the Home tab (see Figures E1.2 and E1.9), and the rest are available through the launcher buttons of several groups or the **Format** choice of the Cells group.

Use Figure E1.9 as a visual guide for locating the common formatting operations.

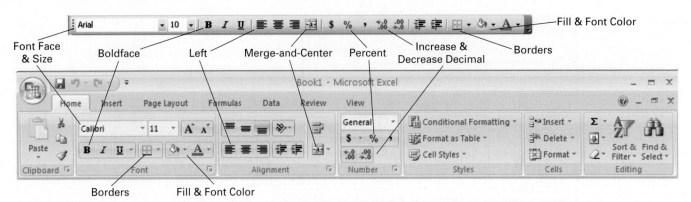

FIGURE E1.9 Formatting Toolbar (Excel 97–2003) and Home tab groups (Excel 2007)

Common Formatting Operations

Font Face & Size Drop-down lists set the font face and font size for the currently selected cells. You will get best results if you select entire rows before changing the font face or size.

Boldface Displays the values of the currently selected cells, using boldface type. Consider using this for cells that contain titles, column headings, or important results. You can also use the **Italic** and **Underline** buttons to the immediate right of Boldface for additional type effects.

Left Displays the values of the currently selected cells left-justified in their cells. The **Center** and **Right** buttons next to Left, center, and right-justify values, respectively. In a worksheet with many filled columns, using Center for the values of categorical variables can sometimes improve readability.

Merge-and-Center Combines the currently selected cells, merges them into one, and displays the value in the first cell of the group, centered across the merged cells. Consider using this for a worksheet title or a title that applies to several contiguous rows or columns.

Percent Displays numeric values in the currently selected cells as percentages. The value 0.01 displays as 1%, the value 1 as 100%, and the value 100 as 10000%.

Increase Decimal and Decrease Decimal Increases/decreases the number of decimal places that will be used to display numeric values in the currently selected cells. Particularly useful to align the decimal points in a column of numeric values.

Borders Drops down a gallery of border effects from which you can choose to change the borders for the currently selected cells. Many worksheet examples in this text use one or more of these border effects: **All Borders**, **Outside Borders**, and **Top Border**.

Fill Color and Font Color Drop down a gallery from which you can choose to change the cell background color and the type color for the currently selected cells. Many

worksheet examples in this text use the color "Light Turquoise" to tint areas that contain user-changable data values and the color "Light Yellow" to tint areas that contain results. These colors are available in the Excel 2002–2003 galleries and by clicking **More Colors** in the Excel 2007 gallery.

In addition to these operations, you may want to adjust the width of a worksheet column so that its column heading and all its values are clearly visible. To do this, select the entire column and then select **Format →Column → AutoFit Selection** (Excel 97–2003) or **Home → Format** (in the Cells group) → **AutoFit Selection** (Excel 2007).

E1.5   COPY-AND-PASTE OPERATIONS

There will be times that you will want to copy cell entries to another part of the same worksheet or to another worksheet as well as copy an entire worksheet for insertion into another workbook. Copying and pasting cell entries entirely composed of numeric or text values is fairly straightforward. You select the cells to be copied, press **Ctrl+C**, move to the first cell of the range in which you want to paste the copy, and press **Ctrl+V.** However, often you will copy cells that contain one or more formulas. Copying cells that contain formulas is not necessarily as straightforward as you might expect. Likewise, copying cells or entire worksheets between workbooks raises some issues you need to understand in order to get the best results possible.

Copying Formulas

Copying entries that contain formulas requires extra attention because exact duplicates may or may not result, depending on how you have entered cell addresses. If you entered addresses using the *Sheetname!ColumnRow* or *ColumnRow* form, as introduced in Section E1.3, Excel considers them **relative references** that will change to reflect the difference, or offset, between the original (source) cell and the cell into which you are pasting the formula (the target cell). For example, when you copy the formula =A2 + B2 in cell C2 down to cell C3, an offset of one row, Excel pastes the formula =A3 + B3 in C3 to reflect that one-row offset. Cell ranges also get changed, so if you copy the formula =SUM(A1:A4) from cell A5 to cell B5, the formula is changed to =SUM(B1:B4).

You typically want Excel to make these changes when you are copying a formula down a column or across a row. This allows you to enter the formula once and then use copy-and-paste to fill in the similar formulas in the column or row. Sometimes, especially in cases in which you want to copy and paste a single formula, you may not want Excel to make a change. You can stop Excel from making changes in the column or row offset by inserting a dollar sign ($) before either the column letter or row number (or both) of a cell address. Addresses written with inserted dollar signs, such as $A$2, are called **absolute references** and do not change during a copy operation. For example, if you copy the formula from one cell to another, the formula that appears in the target cell will be the same, =$A$2 + $B$2. You can also use addresses such as $A2 or A$2, if you want Excel to change only the row or column, respectively. For example, when you copy the cell C2 formula =A2/B$10 to cell C3, the formula that appears in C3 is =A3/B$10. However, if you copy the cell C2 formula to cell D3, the formula that would appear is =B3/C$10.

Do not confuse the use of the dollar sign with formatting cell values for currency display. To format cell values for currency display (in dollars and cents, in the U.S. version of Microsoft Excel), you use the **Currency ($)** format button, located to the left of the Percent button in either the Formatting toolbar or the Home tab group (see Figure E1.9).

Copying Formulas Between Worksheets

When you copy and paste formulas between worksheets, you generally want to make sure that all cell addresses contain a worksheet name and are absolute references—for example, Data!$A$1:$A$12—in order to ensure consistent results.

If you only need to transfer the calculated results from one sheet to another (for example, to create your own summary or report worksheet), you should consider using one of two methods to transfer information between worksheets. If you need to transfer only one or a few cells' worth of information, consider entering formulas in the form =*Sourcesheetname!Cellreference* to transfer the information into the second worksheet. For example, if you want to transfer the results of a formula found in cell B10 of the worksheet named Results to cell A5 in the worksheet named Summary, you can enter the formula =Results!B10 in cell A5 of the Summary sheet instead of copying the original formula. You can also use this technique to transfer column headings or other labeling information between worksheets in order to maintain consistency across worksheets.

If you need to transfer information from a large range of cells, you should consider using the Paste Special command. To use this command, you first select the cell range to be copied and press **Ctrl+C**. Then select the first cell of the cell range in the second worksheet that is your target and right-click. Next, select **Paste Special** from the shortcut menu that appears. In the Excel Paste Special dialog box (similar for all Excel versions; Figure E1.10 shows the Excel 2003 dialog box), you select the **Values and number formats** option and click **OK**. Selecting this option places the current values of all formulas in the second worksheet, so if you change the underlying data, you need to repeat this procedure to update the values shown on the second worksheet.

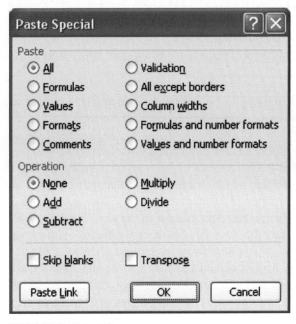

FIGURE E1.10
Paste Special dialog box (Excel 2003 version)

Copying Worksheets

You can copy worksheets to a new workbook or to any opened workbook, including the source of the copy. To copy a worksheet to a new workbook, you first select the worksheet by clicking its sheet tab. Then you right-click the tab and select **Move or Copy** from the shortcut menu that appears. In the Move or Copy dialog box (similar for all Excel versions; Figure E1.11 shows the Excel 2007 dialog box), select **(new book)** from the **To book** drop-down, click **Create a copy**, and click **OK**.

FIGURE E1.11

Move or Copy dialog box (Excel 2007 version)

You use the same procedure, changing only your selection in the To book drop-down list, to copy a worksheet to any opened workbook, including the source of the copy. (You may want to duplicate a worksheet in the same workbook so that you can have a copy that shows the formulas contained in the worksheet or that presents the same information in an alternate format.) When you make a copy of a worksheet and place it in the same workbook, Excel assigns the copied worksheet the name of the original sheet, plus a number, in parentheses. For example, if you copy a sheet named Calculations, the copied sheet will be named Calculations (2). (You can and should consider renaming copied worksheets to give them more descriptive names.)

E1.6   ADD-INS: MAKING THINGS EASIER FOR YOU

Add-ins can simplify the task of creating something to add to a workbook. Add-ins are programming components not included in the main Excel program and may need to be **installed**, or added, to your computer system separately. Add-ins are not always available for you to use because they can be disabled by other users or system security set-

tings. However, the little extra effort you need to ensure that the right add-ins are installed and enabled is well worth the features that add-ins bring to Excel.

In this book, you use the **Analysis ToolPak** add-in that is included with Microsoft Excel. You may make use of **PHStat2**, a Prentice Hall add-in that is included on the Student CD. The Analysis ToolPak add-in (which the book simply calls the "ToolPak" from this point forward) adds statistical procedures to Excel, but creates worksheets that contain only text and numbers and no formulas. This means that the results you create using the ToolPak will not change if you change the underlying data. (To get updated results, you would have to use the ToolPak a second time. This is in contrast to worksheets that contain formulas which update themselves automatically when data are changed.)

PHStat2 adds a PHStat menu of procedures to the Excel menu bar (Excel 97–2003) or the Add-ins tab (Excel 2007). Unlike the ToolPak, PHStat2 usually creates worksheets that contain formulas and that will produce new results as the underlying data changes. Sometimes, though, PHStat2 asks the ToolPak to create sheets on its behalf, and the resulting sheets are similar to the no-formulas sheets that the ToolPak creates. In many such cases, PHStat2 enhances the sheets it asks the ToolPak to create, correcting errors the ToolPak makes or adding new formula-based calculations.

Before you continue, you should check to see if the ToolPak is already installed and active in your copy of Microsoft Excel. If you are using an Excel version other than Excel 2007, select **Tools** and then see if **Data Analysis** appears on the **Tools** menu. If you see Data Analysis, the ToolPak is installed and enabled. If you are using Excel 2007, the best way to check the ToolPak status is to click the **Office Button** and then click **Excel Options** in the Office menu. Finally, you click **Add-Ins** in the Excel Options dialog box. If Analysis ToolPak appears in the **Active Applications Add-Ins** list, the ToolPak is installed and enabled.

If the ToolPak is not installed and enabled, you may need to use your original Microsoft Office or Excel CD or DVD and go through the Microsoft Office setup process to add the ToolPak add-in to your copy of Excel. If you plan to use the PHStat2 add in, you should review the appropriate part of Appendix F and read the PHStat2 readme file on the book's CD.

How to Use the ToolPak Add-in

Once you have determined that the ToolPak add-in is properly installed and active, you use the ToolPak by selecting **Tools → Data Analysis** (Excel 97–2003) or **Formulas → Data Analysis** (Excel 2007). In either case, you will see a Data Analysis dialog box similar to the one shown in Figure E1.12.

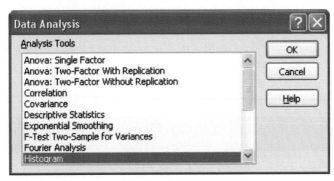

FIGURE E1.12 Data Analysis dialog box

To use a ToolPak procedure, you select the name of the procedure that you want to use from the **Analysis Tools** list and then click **OK**. (The **Histogram** procedure has been selected in Figure E1.12.) A second dialog box then appears, in which you make entries and selections appropriate for the selected procedure. Click **OK** in this second dialog box to execute the procedure.

Macro Security Issues

In all Excel versions other than Excel 97, all add-ins that you open will be screened by Microsoft Office security components. If you use Excel 2000, 2002, or 2003, you can review and change the security settings by selecting **Tools → Macros → Security** to display a Security dialog box (similar to the one shown in Figure E1.13 for Excel 2003). To use an add-in such as PHStat2 that is "not signed," select the **Medium** option and click **OK**.

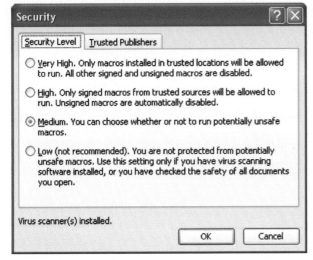

FIGURE E1.13 Security dialog box (Excel 2003 version)

If you use Excel 2007, click the **Office Button**, then click **Excel Options** in the Office menu. In the Excel Options dialog box (see Figure E1.14) click **Trust Center** in the left pane to display information about security

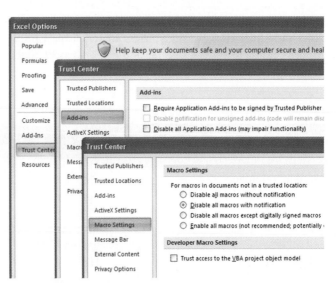

FIGURE E1.14 Excel Options and Trust Center panes (Excel 2007)

issues. Then click **Trust Center Settings** (obscured in Figure E1.14) to display the Trust Center dialog box. To use an add-in such as PHStat2 that is not signed, click Add-Ins in the left pane and then clear all checkboxes in the right pane (see Figure E1.15). Then click **Macro Settings** in the left pane and click **Disable all macros with notification** in the right pane (see Figure E1.14). (On some systems, you may also have to click **Trusted Locations** in the left pane and add the file location of the add-in.)

With the Security screen set to an appropriate level, you will see a macro virus warning dialog box when you open

FIGURE E1.15 Macro warning dialog boxes (Excel 2003 and 2007)

an add-in such as PHStat2. Figure E1.15 shows the Excel 2003 and Excel 2007 warning boxes. You click the **Enable Macros** button to allow virus-free add-ins, such as PHStat2, to be opened and used.

Forum: Click the SETUP AND INSTALLATION ISSUES link if you need additional information setting up and using the add-ins.

KEY TERMS

absolute reference   27
accelerator key   21
add-in   28
Cancel button   21
cell   26
cell pointer   24
cell range   24
check box   21
clear   18
click   18
combination keystroke 21
contextual tabs   21
dialog box   21
double-click   18
drag   18
drag-and-drop   18
drop-down list   21
edit box   21

ellipsis   21
Formatting toolbar   21
formula   24
formula bar   20
gallery   21
Help   21
Home tab   21
launch button   21
list box   21
menu bar   20
minimize, resize, and close buttons   19
mouse pointer   18
Office Button   21
OK button   21
option buttons   21
question-mark button   21
quick access tool bar   21
relative reference   27

ribbon   21
right-click   18
scroll bars   20
select   18
sheet tab   20
shortcut menus   18
slider   21
spinner button   21
Standard toolbar   21
tab   21
tab groups   21
task pane   21
title bar   20
Tool Tip   22
workbook   22
worksheet   24
workspace area   19

CHAPTER 2

Presenting Data in Tables and Charts

USING STATISTICS @ Choice Is Yours, Part I

LEARNING OBJECTIVES

In this chapter, you learn:
- To develop tables and charts for categorical data
- To develop tables and charts for numerical data
- The principles of properly presenting graphs

USING STATISTICS @ Choice Is Yours, Part I

Choice Is Yours is a service that helps customers make wise investment choices. You've been hired to assist investors interested in mutual funds, a market basket of securities. According to investopedia.com, "A mutual fund is nothing more than a collection of stocks and/or bonds. You can think of a mutual fund as a company that brings together a group of people and invests their money in stocks, bonds, and other securities. Each investor owns shares, which represent a portion of the holdings of the fund." (You can learn more about mutual funds at **www.investopedia.com/ university/mutualfunds/**.)

The Choice Is Yours company previously selected a sample of 838 mutual funds that it believes might be of interest to its customers. You have been asked to present data about these funds in a way that will help customers make good investment choices. What facts about each mutual fund would you collect to help customers compare and contrast the many funds?

A good starting point would be to collect data that would help customers classify mutual funds into various categories. You could research such things as the amount of risk involved in a fund's investment strategy and whether the fund focuses on growth securities, those companies that are expected to grow quickly in the next year, or, on value securities, those companies whose stock prices are currently considered undervalued. You might also investigate whether a mutual fund specializes in a certain size of company and whether the fund charges management fees that would reduce the percentage return earned by an investor.

Of course, you would want to know how well the fund performed in the past. You would also want to supply the customer with several measures of each fund's past performance. While past performance is no assurance of future performance, past data could give customers insight into how well each mutual fund has been managed.

As you further think about your task, you realize that all these data for all 838 mutual funds would be a lot for anyone to review. How could you "get your hands around" such data and explore them in a comprehensible manner?

To get your hands around the data described in this chapter's Using Statistics scenario, you need to use methods of descriptive statistics, defined in Chapter 1 as the branch of statistics that collects, summarizes, and presents data. In this scenario, you need to use descriptive techniques for both categorical variables (to help investors classify the mutual funds) and numerical variables (to help show the return each fund has achieved). Reading this chapter will help you to prepare tables and charts that are appropriate for both types of variables. You'll also learn techniques to help answer questions that require two variables, such as "Do growth-oriented mutual funds have lower returns than 'value' mutual funds?" and "Do growth funds tend to be riskier investments than value funds?"

Many examples in this chapter use a sample of 838 real mutual funds, the data for which you can find in the Data worksheet of the Mutual Funds.xls *file on the Student CD-ROM.*

2.1 TABLES AND CHARTS FOR CATEGORICAL DATA

When you have categorical data, you tally responses into categories and then present the frequency or percentage in each category in tables and charts.

The Summary Table

A **summary table** indicates the frequency, amount, or percentage of items in a set of categories so that you can see differences between categories. A summary table lists the categories in one column and the frequency, amount, or percentage in a different column or columns. Table 2.1 illustrates a summary table based on a recent survey that asked people what they would do if they had an extra $1,000 to spend ("If You Had an Extra $1,000 to Spend, What Would You Do with the Money?" *USA Today*, January 11, 2006, p. A1). In Table 2.1, the most common choices are saving and paying debt, followed by buying a luxury item, vacation, or gift and spending on essentials. Very few respondents mentioned giving to charity or other uses.

TABLE 2.1

What People Would Do with an Extra $1,000

What You Would Do with the Money	Percentage (%)
Buy a luxury item, vacation, or gift	20
Give it to charity	2
Pay debt	24
Save	31
Spend on essentials	16
Other	7

EXAMPLE 2.1

SUMMARY TABLE OF LEVELS OF RISK OF MUTUAL FUNDS

The 838 mutual funds that are part of the Using Statistics scenario (see page 32) are classified according to their risk level, categorized as low, average, and high. Construct a summary table of the mutual funds, categorized by risk.

SOLUTION The mutual funds are fairly evenly divided by risk (see Table 2.2). There are more high-risk funds (346, or 41%) than low-risk or average-risk funds. There are about the same number of average-risk funds as low-risk funds (29%).

TABLE 2.2

Frequency and Percentage Summary Table Pertaining to Risk Level for 838 Mutual Funds

Fund Risk Level	Number of Funds	Percentage of Funds (%)
Low	247	29.47
Average	245	29.24
High	346	41.29
Total	838	100.00

The Bar Chart

In a **bar chart**, a bar shows each category, the length of which represents the amount, frequency, or percentage of values falling into a category. Figure 2.1 on page 34 displays the bar chart for spending an extra $1,000 presented in Table 2.1.

Bar charts allow you to compare percentages in different categories. In Figure 2.1, respondents are most likely to save or pay debt, followed by buy a luxury item, vacation, or gift and spend on essentials. Very few respondents mentioned giving to charity or other uses.

FIGURE 2.1

Microsoft Excel bar chart for spending an extra $1,000

See Sections E2.2 and E2.3 to create this.

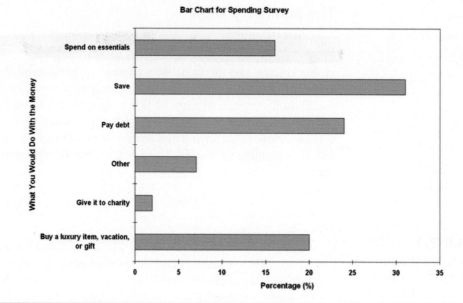

EXAMPLE 2.2

BAR CHART OF LEVELS OF RISK OF MUTUAL FUNDS

Construct a bar chart for the levels of risk of mutual funds (based on the information in Table 2.2) and interpret the results.

SOLUTION   The mutual funds are fairly evenly divided by risk (see Figure 2.2 on page 33). There are more high-risk funds (346, or 41%) than low-risk or average-risk funds. There are about the same number of average-risk funds as low-risk funds (29%).

FIGURE 2.2

Microsoft Excel bar chart of the levels of risk of mutual funds

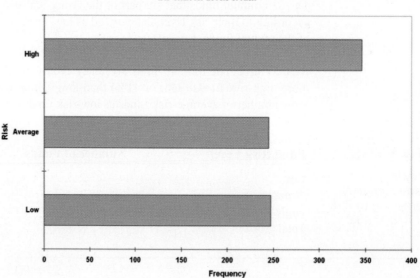

The Pie Chart

The **pie chart** is a circle broken up into slices that represent categories. The size of each slice of the pie varies according to the percentage in each category. In Table 2.1 on page 33, for example, 31% of the respondents stated that they would save the $1,000. Thus, in constructing the pie chart, the 360 degrees that makes up a circle is multiplied by 0.31, resulting in a slice of the pie that takes up 111.6 degrees of the 360 degrees of the circle. From Figure 2.3, you can see that the pie chart lets you visualize the portion of the entire pie that is in each category. In this figure, saving takes 31% of the pie and giving to charity takes only 2%.

FIGURE 2.3

Microsoft Excel pie chart for spending an extra $1,000

See Sections E2.2 and E2.3 to create this.

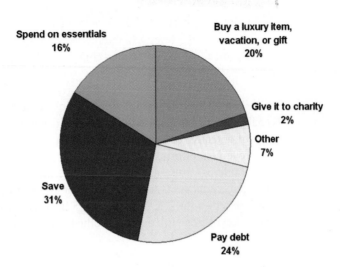

Pie Chart for Spending Survey

Spend on essentials 16%

Buy a luxury item, vacation, or gift 20%

Give it to charity 2%

Other 7%

Save 31%

Pay debt 24%

Which chart should you use—a bar chart or a pie chart? The selection of a particular chart often depends on your intention. If a comparison of categories is most important, you should use a bar chart. If observing the portion of the whole that is in a particular category is most important, you should use a pie chart.

EXAMPLE 2.3

PIE CHART OF LEVELS OF RISK OF MUTUAL FUNDS

Construct a pie chart for the levels of risk of mutual funds (see Table 2.2 on page 33) and interpret the results.

SOLUTION (See Figure 2.4.) The mutual funds are fairly evenly divided by risk. There are more high-risk funds (346, or 41%) than low-risk or average-risk funds. There are about the same number of average-risk funds as low-risk funds (29%).

FIGURE 2.4

Microsoft Excel pie chart of the levels of risk of mutual funds

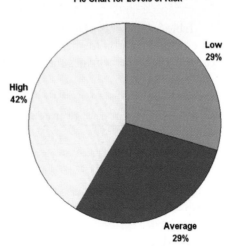

Pie Chart for Levels of Risk

Low 29%

High 42%

Average 29%

The Pareto Diagram

In a **Pareto diagram**, the categorized responses are plotted in descending order, according to their frequencies, and are combined with a cumulative percentage line on the same chart. The Pareto diagram can identify situations in which the Pareto principle occurs.

PARETO PRINCIPLE

The **Pareto principle** exists when the majority of items in a set of data occur in a small number of categories and the few remaining items are spread out over a large number of categories. These two groups are often referred to as the "vital few" and the "trivial many."

The Pareto diagram has the ability to separate the "vital few" from the "trivial many," enabling you to focus on the important categories. In situations in which the data involved consist of defective or nonconforming items, the Pareto diagram is a powerful tool for prioritizing improvement efforts.

Table 2.3 presents data for a large injection-molding company that manufactures plastic molded components used in computer keyboards, washing machines, automobiles, and television sets (see the keyboarddefects.xls file). The data presented in Table 2.3 consist of all computer keyboards with defects produced during a three-month period.

TABLE 2.3

Summary Table of Causes of Defects in Computer Keyboards in a Three-Month Period

Cause	Frequency	Percentage
Black spot	413	6.53
Damage	1,039	16.43
Jetting	258	4.08
Pin mark	834	13.19
Scratches	442	6.99
Shot mold	275	4.35
Silver streak	413	6.53
Sink mark	371	5.87
Spray mark	292	4.62
Warpage	1,987	31.42
Total	6,324	100.01*

Result differs slightly from 100.00 due to rounding.
Source: Extracted from U. H. Acharya and C. Mahesh, "Winning Back the Customer's Confidence: A Case Study on the Application of Design of Experiments to an Injection-Molding Process," Quality Engineering, 11, 1999, pp. 357–363.

Table 2.4 presents a summary table for the computer keyboard data in which the categories are ordered based on the percentage of defects present (rather than arranged alphabetically). The cumulative percentages for the ordered categories are also included as part of the table.

TABLE 2.4

Ordered Summary Table of Causes of Defects in Computer Keyboards in a Three-Month Period

Cause	Frequency	Percentage	Cumulative Percentage
Warpage	1,987	31.42	31.42
Damage	1,039	16.43	47.85
Pin mark	834	13.19	61.04
Scratches	442	6.99	68.03
Black spot	413	6.53	74.56
Silver streak	413	6.53	81.09
Sink mark	371	5.87	86.96
Spray mark	292	4.62	91.58
Shot mold	275	4.35	95.93
Jetting	258	4.08	100.00
Total	6,324	100.01*	

Result differs slightly from 100.00 due to rounding.

In Table 2.4, the first category listed is warpage (with 31.42% of the defects), followed by damage (with 16.43%), followed by pin mark (with 13.19%). The two most frequently occurring categories—warpage and damage—account for 47.85% of the defects; the three most frequently occurring categories—warpage, damage, and pin mark—account for 61.04% of the defects, and so on. Figure 2.5 is a Pareto diagram based on the results displayed in Table 2.4.

FIGURE 2.5

Microsoft Excel Pareto diagram for the keyboard defects data

See Sections E2.2 and E2.4 to create this.

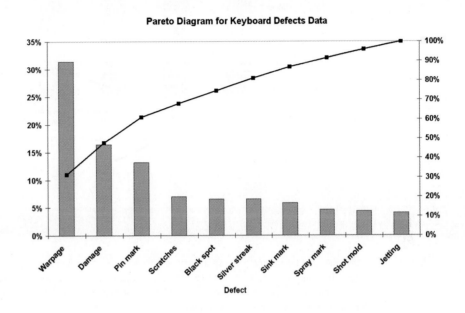

Figure 2.5 presents the bars vertically, along with a cumulative percentage line. The cumulative line is plotted at the midpoint of each bar, at a height equal to the cumulative percentage. If you follow the line, you see that these first three categories account for about 60% of the defects. Because the categories in the Pareto diagram are ordered by the frequency of occurrences, decision makers can see where to concentrate efforts to improve the process. Attempts to reduce defects due to warpage, damage, and pin marks should produce the greatest payoff. Then efforts can be made to reduce scratches, black spots, and silver streaks.

In order for a Pareto diagram to include all categories, even those with few defects, in some situations you need to include a category labeled *Other* or *Miscellaneous*. In these situations, the bar representing these categories is placed to the right of the other bars.

EXAMPLE 2.4

PARETO DIAGRAM OF SPENDING AN EXTRA $1,000

Construct a Pareto diagram of what respondents would do with an extra $1,000 (see Table 2.1 on page 33).

SOLUTION In Figure 2.6, saving and paying debt account for 55% of what respondents would do with the extra $1,000; 91% of the respondents would save; pay debt; buy a luxury item, vacation, or gift; or spend on essentials.

FIGURE 2.6

Microsoft Excel Pareto diagram for spending an extra $1,000

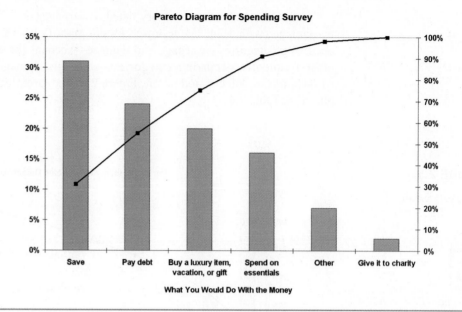

Pareto Diagram for Spending Survey

Using Microsoft Excel *Properly*

Usually when you learn something, there is eventually some sort of feedback. Providing feedback is one reason instructors give tests. When you get the results of a test, you can reflect on how well you have properly learned the subject matter. Unfortunately, feedback opportunities are rare when you are learning to use a computer program such as Microsoft Excel as you study statistics. You either get the worksheet to calculate what you want or get a worksheet with misleading or inaccurate results. This good/bad, pass/fail type of feedback cannot help you refine your Microsoft Excel skills. We hope the following list will.

You are using Microsoft Excel *properly* if you can:

1. Understand how to operate the program. Understanding how to operate the program does not mean that you need to know everything about Microsoft Excel. Don't waste your time teaching yourself every command or trying to memorize every function. Use the Excel Companion to Chapter 1 as your guide for what you need to know to get started using Excel effectively. Learn about additional features only just-in-time—when you need to use the feature. Excel features that you learn but don't immediately use are features that you will soon forget. However, if you learn an Excel feature when you need to

use it, such as discovering that you can use Data → Sort to sort data in Excel 97–2003, you are more likely to remember the proper command.

2. Understand the underlying statistical concepts. Make sure you understand what a worksheet is doing as it produces its information. As a minimum, be informed about what each function you use calculates, or returns, as its value. Knowing this information will minimize your confusion and help you avoid making mistakes such as using the NORMSDIST function described in Chapter 6 when you meant to use the similar looking but different NORMDIST function.

3. Understand how to format and present information in a worksheet. Section 1.6 on page 11 has already discussed how to organize your worksheets. With that as a starting point, you should plan how you are going to use the rows and columns of a worksheet to enhance the contents of your worksheets. For almost every worksheet illustrated in this text, the authors changed column widths, book font characteristics, and background tints of selected cells and added borders to highlight various cell ranges. Use the author's techniques (reviewed in the Excel Companion to Chapter 1) or invent your own, but always remember to have a plan that will present information effectively.

4. Know how to review formulas for errors. Never assume that any worksheet you create or that was created for you is free of error. Always examine all formulas that have been entered into a worksheet. (See the Excel Companion to Chapter 1 for one way to do this.) You need to do this even if you use worksheets created by PHStat2 or retrieved from the Student CD-ROM.

5. Take control of your copy of Microsoft Excel. Customize the settings of Microsoft Excel (and Microsoft Windows) to best suit your style, abilities, and needs. For example, many overlook increasing the default 10-point Arial font to a more readable size when examining the contents of a worksheet. If you own or control the computer on which you use Excel, you can make such customizations permanent so that they are automatically available to you every time you use Microsoft Excel.

In addition, if you own or control your own computer, you should regularly apply the security updates to Microsoft Office that Microsoft puts on its Web site. And if you plan to use PHStat2 on your own computer, you should read all the technical documentation including the PHStat readme file on the Student CD-ROM.

Forum > *Visit the online forum to continue this discussion online.* <<<

PROBLEMS FOR SECTION 2.1

Learning the Basics

2.1 A categorical variable has three categories with the following frequencies of occurrence:

Category	Frequency
A	13
B	28
C	9

a. Compute the percentage of values in each category.
b. Construct a bar chart.
c. Construct a pie chart.
d. Construct a Pareto diagram.

2.2 A categorical variable has four categories with the following percentages of occurrence:

Category	Percentage	Category	Percentage
A	12	C	35
B	29	D	24

a. Construct a bar chart.
b. Construct a pie chart.
c. Construct a Pareto diagram.

Applying the Concepts

2.3 A survey of 705 workers asked how much they used the Internet at work. The results (*USA Today Snapshots*, March 21, 2006) were as follows:

Use of the Internet at Work	%
Too much	5
More than I should	4
Within limits	60
Very little	5
Do not use	26

a. Construct a bar chart, a pie chart, and a Pareto diagram.
b. Which graphical method do you think is best to portray these data?
c. Based on this survey, what conclusions can you reach about the use of the Internet at work?

2.4 An article (R. Richmond, "Anatomy of a Threat," *The Wall Street Journal*, February 13, 2006, pp. R5, R6) discussed the costs companies face in defending their networks from attack. The following table provides the breakdown in costs:

Cost	Percentage (%)
Consulting	7.6
Hardware tools	8.2
Labor	25.9
Lost business/revenue	23.6
Nonproductive employee time	15.5
Software tools	14.2
Other	5.0

a. Construct a bar chart, a pie chart, and a Pareto diagram.
b. Which graphical method do you think is best to portray these data?
c. What conclusions can you reach concerning the costs companies face in defending their networks from attack?

2.5 When do Americans decide what to make for dinner? An online survey (N. Hellmich, Americans Go for the Quick Fix for Dinner," *USA Today*, February 14, 2005, p. 1B) indicated the following:

When Americans Decide What to Make for Dinner	%
At the last minute	37
Plan in advance	25
That day	37
Don't know	1

a. Construct a bar chart, a pie chart, and a Pareto diagram.
b. Which graphical method do you think is best to portray these data?

2.6 The following table represents the U.S. sources of electric energy in a recent year:

Source	%
Coal	51
Hydropower	6
Natural gas	16
Nuclear	21
Petroleum	3
Oil	3

Source: U.S. Department of Energy.

a. Construct a Pareto diagram.
b. What percentage of electricity is derived from either coal, nuclear energy, or natural gas?
c. Construct a pie chart.
d. Which chart do you prefer to use for these data—the Pareto diagram or the pie chart? Why?

2.7 An article (P. Kitchen, "Retirement Plan: To Keep Working," *Newsday*, September 24, 2003) discussed the results of a sample of 2,001 Americans ages 50 to 70 who were employed full time or part time. The following table represents their plans for retirement:

Plans	Percentage (%)
Not work for pay at all	29
Start own business	10
Work full time	7
Work part time	46
Don't know	3
Other	5

a. Construct a bar chart and a pie chart.
b. Which graphical method do you think is best to portray these data?

2.8 U.S. companies spent more than $250 billion in advertising in 2005 (K. Delaney, "In Latest Deal, Google Steps Further into World of Old Media," *The Wall Street Journal*, January 18, 2006, pp. A1, A6). The spending was as follows:

Media	Amount ($billions)	Percentage (%)
Cinema	0.4	0.16
Direct mail	44.5	17.35
Internet	10.0	3.90
Magazines	23.9	9.32
Newspapers	50.2	19.57
Outdoor	5.7	2.22
Radio	20.6	8.03
TV	55.4	21.60
Other	45.8	17.86

a. Construct a bar chart and a pie chart.
b. Which graphical method do you think is best to portray these data?

2.9 Medication errors are a serious problem in hospitals. The following data represent the root causes of pharmacy errors at a hospital during a recent time period:

Reason for Failure	Frequency
Additional instructions	16
Dose	23
Drug	14
Duplicate order entry	22
Frequency	47
Omission	21
Order not discontinued when received	12
Order not received	52
Patient	5
Route	4
Other	8

a. Construct a Pareto diagram.
b. Discuss the "vital few" and "trivial many" reasons for the root causes of pharmacy errors.

2.10 The following data represent complaints about hotel rooms:

Reason	Number
Room dirty	32
Room not stocked	17
Room not ready	12
Room too noisy	10
Room needs maintenance	17
Room has too few beds	9
Room doesn't have promised features	7
No special accommodations	2

a. Construct a Pareto diagram.
b. What reasons for complaints do you think the hotel should focus on if it wants to reduce the number of complaints? Explain.

2.2 ORGANIZING NUMERICAL DATA

When the number of data values is large, you can organize numerical data into an ordered array or a stem-and-leaf display to help understand the information you have. Suppose you decide to undertake a study that compares the cost for a restaurant meal in a major city to the cost of a similar meal in the suburbs outside the city. The data file restaurants.xls contains the data for 50 city restaurants and 50 suburban restaurants, as shown in Table 2.5. The data are not arranged in order from lowest to highest. This arrangement makes it difficult to make conclusions about the price of meals in the two geographical areas.

TABLE 2.5

Price per Person at 50 City Restaurants and 50 Suburban Restaurants

City

50	38	43	56	51	36	25	33	41	44
34	39	49	37	40	50	50	35	22	45
44	38	14	44	51	27	44	39	50	35
31	34	48	48	30	42	26	35	32	63
36	38	53	23	39	45	37	31	39	53

Suburban

37	37	29	38	37	38	39	29	36	38
44	27	24	34	44	23	30	32	25	29
43	31	26	34	23	41	32	30	28	33
26	51	26	48	39	55	24	38	31	30
51	30	27	38	26	28	33	38	32	25

The Ordered Array

An **ordered array** is a sequence of data, in rank order, from the smallest value to the largest value. Table 2.6 contains ordered arrays for the price of meals at city restaurants and suburban restaurants. From Table 2.6 you can see that the price of a meal at the city restaurants is between $14 and $63 and the price of a meal at the suburban restaurants is between $23 and $55.

TABLE 2.6

Ordered Array of Price per Person at 50 City Restaurants and 50 Suburban Restaurants

City

14	22	23	25	26	27	30	31	31	32
33	34	34	35	35	35	36	36	37	37
38	38	38	39	39	39	39	40	41	42
43	44	44	44	44	45	45	48	48	49
50	50	50	50	51	51	53	53	56	63

Suburban

23	23	24	24	25	25	26	26	26	26
27	27	28	28	29	29	29	30	30	30
30	31	31	32	32	32	33	33	34	34
36	37	37	37	38	38	38	38	38	38
39	39	41	43	44	44	48	51	51	55

The Stem-and-Leaf Display

A **stem-and-leaf display** organizes data into groups (called stems) so that the values within each group (the leaves) branch out to the right on each row. The resulting display allows you to see how the data are distributed and where concentrations of data exist. To see how to construct a stem-and-leaf display, suppose that 15 students from your class eat lunch at a fast-food restaurant. The following data are the amounts spent for lunch:

5.40 4.30 4.80 5.50 7.30 8.50 6.10 4.80 4.90 4.90 5.50 3.50 5.90 6.30 6.60

To form the stem-and-leaf display, you use the units as the stems and round the decimals (the leaves) to one decimal place. For example, the first value is 5.40. Its stem (row) is 5, and its leaf is 4. The second value, is 4.30. Its stem (row) is 4, and its leaf is 3. You continue with the remainder of the 15 values and then reorder the leaves within each stem as follows;

3	5
4	38899
5	4559
6	136
7	3
8	5

EXAMPLE 2.5

STEM-AND-LEAF DISPLAY OF THE THREE-YEAR ANNUALIZED RETURN OF MUTUAL FUNDS

In this chapter's Using Statistics scenario, you are interested in studying the past performance of mutual funds. One measure of past performance is the three-year annualized return (2003–2005)—that is, the average percentage return over the past three years. Construct a stem-and-leaf display of the three-year annualized returns.

SOLUTION From Figure 2.7, you can conclude that:

- The lowest three-year annualized return was 6.7.
- The highest three-year annualized return was 42.3.
- The three-year annualized returns were concentrated between 11 and 23.
- Only six mutual funds had three-year annualized returns below 8, and only two mutual funds had three-year annualized returns above 40.

FIGURE 2.7

Microsoft Excel stem-and-leaf display of the three-year annualized returns (2003–2005)

See Section E2.6 to create this.

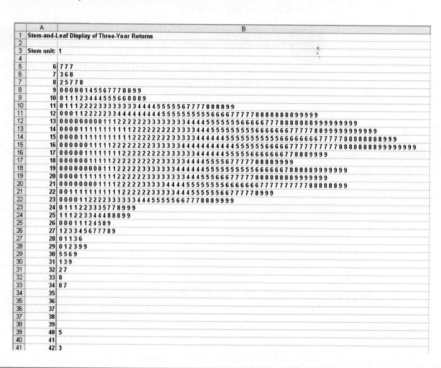

PROBLEMS FOR SECTION 2.2

Learning the Basics

 2.11 Form an ordered array, given the following data from a sample of $n = 7$ midterm exam scores in accounting:

68 94 63 75 71 88 64

 2.12 Form a stem-and-leaf display, given the following data from a sample of $n = 7$ midterm exam scores in finance:

80 54 69 98 93 53 74

2.13 Form an ordered array, given the following data from a sample of $n = 7$ midterm exam scores in marketing:

88   78   78   73   91   78   85

 2.14 Form an ordered array, given the following stem-and-leaf display from a sample of $n = 7$ midterm exam scores in information systems:

```
5 | 0
6 |
7 | 446
8 | 19
9 | 2
```

Applying the Concepts

 2.15 The following is a stem-and-leaf display representing the amount of gasoline purchased, in gallons (with leaves in tenths of gallons), for a sample of 25 cars that use a particular service station on the New Jersey Turnpike:

```
 9 | 147
10 | 02238
11 | 125566777
12 | 223489
13 | 02
```

a. Place the data into an ordered array.
b. Which of these two displays seems to provide more information? Discuss.
c. What amount of gasoline (in gallons) is most likely to be purchased?
d. Is there a concentration of the purchase amounts in the center of the distribution?

2.16 The data in the file **bankcost1.xls** contains the bounced check fees, in dollars, for a sample of 23 banks for direct-deposit customers who maintain a $100 balance:

26   28   20   20   21   22   25   25   18   25   15   20
18   20   25   25   22   30   30   30   15   20   29

Source: Extracted from The New Face of Banking, *June 2000 Copyright © 2000 by Consumers Union of U.S., Inc., Yonkers, NY 10703–1057.*

a. Place the data into an ordered array.
b. Construct a stem-and-leaf display for these data.
c. Which of these two displays seems to provide more information? Discuss.
d. Around what value, if any, are the bounced check fees concentrated? Explain.

2.17 The file **movieprices.xls** contains data on the price for two tickets, with online service charges, large popcorn, and two medium soft drinks at a sample of six theater chains:

$36.15 $31.00 $35.05 $40.25 $33.75 $43.00

Source: Extracted from K. Kelly, "The Multiplex Under Siege," The Wall Street Journal, *December 24–25, 2005, pp. P1, P5.*

a. Place the data into an ordered array.
b. Construct a stem-and-leaf display for these data.
c. Which of these two displays seems to provide more information? Discuss.
d. Around what value, if any, are the movie prices concentrated? Explain.

 2.18 The file **chicken.xls** contains data on the total fat, in grams per serving, for a sample of 20 chicken sandwiches from fast-food chains. The data are as follows:

7   8   4   5   16   20   20   24   19   30
23   30   25   19   29   29   30   30   40   56

Source: Extracted from "Fast food: Adding Health to the Menu," Consumer Reports, *September 2004, pp. 28–31.*

a. Place the data into an ordered array.
b. Construct a stem-and-leaf display.
c. Does the ordered array or the stem-and-leaf display provide more information? Discuss.

2.19 The data in the file **batterylife.xls** represent the battery life, in shots, for three pixel digital cameras:

300   180   85   170   380   460   260   35   380   120   110   240

Source: Extracted from "Cameras: More Features in the Mix," Consumer Reports, *July 2005, pp. 14–18.*

a. Place the data into an ordered array.
b. Construct a stem-and-leaf display.
c. Does the ordered array or the stem-and-leaf display provide more information? Discuss.
d. Around what value, if any, is the battery life concentrated? Explain.

2.3 TABLES AND CHARTS FOR NUMERICAL DATA

When you have a data set that contains a large number of values, reaching conclusions from an ordered array or a stem-and-leaf display can be difficult. In such circumstances, you need to use tables and charts. There are many types of tables and charts that you can use to visually present numerical data. These include the frequency and percentage distributions, histogram, polygon, and cumulative percentage polygon (ogive).

The Frequency Distribution

The **frequency distribution** is a summary table in which the data are arranged into numerically ordered class groupings. In constructing a frequency distribution, you must give attention to selecting the appropriate *number* of **class groupings** for the table, determining a suitable *width* of a class grouping, and establishing the *boundaries* of each class grouping to avoid overlapping.

The number of class groupings you use depends on the number of values in the data. Larger numbers of values allow for a larger number of class groupings. In general, the frequency distribution should have at least 5 class groupings but no more than 15. Having too few or too many class groupings provides little new information.

When developing a frequency distribution, you define each class grouping by class intervals of equal width. To determine the **width of a class interval**, you divide the **range** (highest value – lowest value) of the data by the number of class groupings desired.

DETERMINING THE WIDTH OF A CLASS INTERVAL

$$\text{Width of interval} = \frac{\text{Range}}{\text{Number of desired class groupings}} \qquad \textbf{(2.1)}$$

Because the city restaurant data consist of a sample of 50 restaurants, 10 class groupings are acceptable. From the ordered array in Table 2.6 on page 41, the range of the data is $63 – 14 = $49. Using Equation (2.1), you approximate the width of the class interval as follows:

$$\text{Width of interval} = \frac{49}{10} = 4.9$$

You should choose an interval width that simplifies reading and interpretation. Therefore, instead of using an interval width of $4.90, you should select an interval width of $5.00.

To construct the frequency distribution table, you should establish clearly defined **class boundaries** for each class grouping so that the values can be properly tallied into the classes. You place each value in one and only one class. You must avoid overlapping of classes.

Because you have set the width of each class interval for the restaurant data at $5, you need to establish the boundaries of the various class groupings so as to include the entire range of values. Whenever possible, you should choose these boundaries to simplify reading and interpretation. Thus, for the city restaurants, because the cost ranges from $14 to $63, the first class interval ranges from $10 to less than $15, the second from $15 to less than $20, and so on, until they have been tallied into 11 classes. Each class has an interval width of $5, without overlapping. The center of each class, the **class midpoint**, is halfway between the lower boundary of the class and the upper boundary of the class. Thus, the class midpoint for the class from $10 to under $15 is $12.50, the class midpoint for the class from $15 to under $20 is $17.50, and so on. Table 2.7 is a frequency distribution of the cost per meal for the 50 city restaurants and the 50 suburban restaurants.

TABLE 2.7

Frequency Distribution of the Cost per Meal for 50 City Restaurants and 50 Suburban Restaurants

Cost per Meal ($)	City Frequency	Suburban Frequency
10 but less than 15	1	0
15 but less than 20	0	0
20 but less than 25	2	4
25 but less than 30	3	13
30 but less than 35	7	13
35 but less than 40	14	12
40 but less than 45	8	4
45 but less than 50	5	1
50 but less than 55	8	2
55 but less than 60	1	1
60 but less than 65	1	0
Total	50	50

The frequency distribution allows you to draw conclusions about the major characteristics of the data. For example, Table 2.7 shows that the cost of meals at city restaurants is concentrated between $30 and $55, and the cost of meals at suburban restaurants is clustered between $25 and $40.

If the data set does not contain many values, one set of class boundaries may provide a different picture than another set. For example, for the restaurant cost data, using a class-interval width of 4.0 instead of 5.0 (as was used in Table 2.7) may cause shifts in the way the values distribute among the classes.

You can also get shifts in data concentration when you choose different lower and upper class boundaries. Fortunately, as the sample size increases, alterations in the selection of class boundaries affect the concentration of data less and less.

EXAMPLE 2.6

FREQUENCY DISTRIBUTION OF THE THREE-YEAR ANNUALIZED RETURN FOR GROWTH AND VALUE MUTUAL FUNDS

In the Using Statistics scenario, you are interested in comparing the three-year annualized return (2003–2005) of growth and value mutual funds. Construct frequency distributions for the growth funds and the value funds.

SOLUTION The three-year annualized returns of the growth funds and the value funds are highly concentrated between 10 and 25 (see Table 2.8). You should not directly compare the frequencies of the growth funds and the value funds because there are 480 growth funds and 358 value funds in the sample. On page 47, relative frequencies and percentages are introduced.

TABLE 2.8

Frequency Distribution of the Three-Year Annualized Return for Growth and Value Mutual Funds

Three-Year Annualized Return	Growth Frequency	Value Frequency
5 but less than 10	21	7
10 but less than 15	148	85
15 but less than 20	172	132
20 but less than 25	113	97
25 but less than 30	21	28
30 but less than 35	5	7
35 but less than 40	0	0
40 but less than 45	0	2
Total	480	358

The Relative Frequency Distribution and the Percentage Distribution

Because you usually want to know the proportion or the percentage of the total that is in each group, the relative frequency distribution or the percentage distribution is preferred to the frequency distribution. When you are comparing two or more groups that differ in sample size, you must use either a relative frequency distribution or a percentage distribution.

You form the **relative frequency distribution** by dividing the frequencies in each class of the frequency distribution (see Table 2.7 on page 45) by the total number of values. You form the **percentage distribution** by multiplying each relative frequency by 100%. Thus, the relative frequency of meals at city restaurants that cost between $30 and $35 is 7 divided by 50, or 0.14, and the percentage is 14%. Table 2.9 presents the relative frequency distribution and percentage distribution of the cost of restaurant meals at city and suburban restaurants.

TABLE 2.9

Relative Frequency Distribution and Percentage Distribution of the Cost of Restaurant Meals at City and Suburban Restaurants

Cost per Meal ($)	City Relative Frequency	City Percentage	Suburban Relative Frequency	Suburban Percentage
10 but less than 15	0.02	2.0	0.00	0.0
15 but less than 20	0.00	0.0	0.00	0.0
20 but less than 25	0.04	4.0	0.08	8.0
25 but less than 30	0.06	6.0	0.26	26.0
30 but less than 35	0.14	14.0	0.26	26.0
35 but less than 40	0.28	28.0	0.24	24.0
40 but less than 45	0.16	16.0	0.08	8.0
45 but less than 50	0.10	10.0	0.02	2.0
50 but less than 55	0.16	16.0	0.04	4.0
55 but less than 60	0.02	2.0	0.02	2.0
60 but less than 65	0.02	2.0	0.00	0.0
Total	1.00	100.0	1.00	100.0

From Table 2.9, you conclude that meals cost more at city restaurants than at suburban restaurants—16% of the meals at city restaurants cost between $40 and $45 as compared to 8% of the suburban restaurants; 16% of the meals at city restaurants cost between $50 and $55 as compared to 4% of the suburban restaurants; and only 6% of the meals at city restaurants cost between $25 and $30 as compared to 26% of the suburban restaurants.

EXAMPLE 2.7

RELATIVE FREQUENCY DISTRIBUTION AND PERCENTAGE DISTRIBUTION OF THE THREE-YEAR ANNUALIZED RETURN FOR GROWTH AND VALUE MUTUAL FUNDS

In the Using Statistics scenario, you are interested in comparing the three-year annualized return (2003–2005) for growth and value mutual funds. Construct relative frequency distributions and percentage distributions for the growth funds and the value funds.

SOLUTION You conclude (see Table 2.10) that the three-year annualized return (2003–2005) for the growth funds is slightly lower than for the value funds. 4.38% of growth funds have returns below 10, while only 1.96% of value funds have returns below 10. Of the growth funds, 30.83% have returns between 10 and 15 as compared to 23.74% of the value funds. Also, more of the value funds have higher returns. For example, 34.91% of the value funds made between 20 and 30, while 27.92% of the growth funds made between 20 and 30.

TABLE 2.10

Relative Frequency Distribution and Percentage Distribution of the Three-Year Annualized Return (2003–2005) for Growth and Value Mutual Funds

Three-Year Annualized Return	Growth		Value	
	Proportion	Percentage	Proportion	Percentage
5 but less than 10	0.0438	4.38	0.0196	1.96
10 but less than 15	0.3083	30.83	0.2374	23.74
15 but less than 20	0.3583	35.83	0.3687	36.87
20 but less than 25	0.2354	23.54	0.2709	27.09
25 but less than 30	0.0438	4.38	0.0782	7.82
30 but less than 35	0.0104	1.04	0.0196	1.96
35 but less than 40	0.0000	0.00	0.0000	0.00
40 but less than 45	0.0000	0.00	0.0056	0.56
Total	1.0000	100.00	1.0000	100.00

The Cumulative Distribution

The **cumulative percentage distribution** provides a way of presenting information about the percentage of items that are less than a certain value. For example, you might want to know what percentage of the city restaurant meals cost less than $20, less than $30, less than $50, and so on. The percentage distribution is used to form the cumulative percentage distribution. Table 2.11 illustrates how to develop the cumulative percentage distribution for the cost of meals at city restaurants. 0.00% of the meals cost less than $10, 2% cost less than $15, 2% also cost less than $20 (because none of the meals cost between $15 and $20), 6% (2% + 4%) cost less than $25, and so on, until all 100% of the meals cost less than $65.

TABLE 2.11

Developing the Cumulative Percentage Distribution for the Cost of Meals at City Restaurants

Cost per Meal ($)	Percentage	Percentage of Meals Less Than Lower Boundary of Class Interval
10 but less than 15	2	0
15 but less than 20	0	2
20 but less than 25	4	2 = 2 + 0
25 but less than 30	6	6 = 2 + 0 + 4
30 but less than 35	14	12 = 2 + 0 + 4 + 6
35 but less than 40	28	26 = 2 + 0 + 4 + 6 + 14
40 but less than 45	16	54 = 2 + 0 + 4 + 6 + 14 + 28
45 but less than 50	10	70 = 2 + 0 + 4 + 6 + 14 + 28 + 16
50 but less than 55	16	80 = 2 + 0 + 4 + 6 + 14 + 28 + 16 + 10
55 but less than 60	2	96 = 2 + 0 + 4 + 6 + 14 + 28 + 16 + 10 + 16
60 but less than 65	2	98 = 2 + 0 + 4 + 6 + 14 + 28 + 16 + 10 + 16 + 2
65 but less than 70	0	100 = 2 + 0 + 4 + 6 + 14 + 28 + 16 + 10 + 16 + 2 + 2

Table 2.12 on page 48 summarizes the cumulative percentages of the cost of city and suburban restaurant meals. The cumulative distribution clearly shows that the cost of meals is lower in suburban restaurants than in city restaurants—34% of the suburban restaurants cost less than $30 as compared to only 12% of the city restaurants; 60% of the suburban restaurants cost less than $35 as compared to only 26% of the city restaurants; 84% of the suburban restaurants cost less than $40 as compared to only 54% of the city restaurants.

TABLE 2.12

Cumulative Percentage Distributions of the Cost of City and Suburban Restaurant Meals

Cost ($)	City Percentage of Restaurants Less Than Indicated Value	Suburban Percentage of Restaurants Less Than Indicated Value
10	0	0
15	2	0
20	2	0
25	6	8
30	12	34
35	26	60
40	54	84
45	70	92
50	80	94
55	96	98
60	98	100
65	100	100

EXAMPLE 2.8

CUMULATIVE PERCENTAGE DISTRIBUTION OF THE THREE-YEAR ANNUALIZED RETURN FOR GROWTH AND VALUE MUTUAL FUNDS

In the Using Statistics scenario, you are interested in comparing the three-year annualized return (2003–2005) of growth and value mutual funds. Construct cumulative percentage distributions for the growth funds and the value funds.

SOLUTION The cumulative distribution in Table 2.13 indicates that more of the growth funds have lower returns than the value funds—35.21% of the growth funds have returns below 15 as compared to 25.70% of the value funds; 71.04% of the growth funds have returns below 20 as compared to 62.57% of the value funds; 94.58% of the growth funds have returns below 25 as compared to 89.66% of the value funds.

TABLE 2.13

Cumulative Percentage Distributions of the Three-Year Annualized Return for Growth and Value Funds

Annual Return	Growth Fund Percentage Less Than Indicated Value	Value Fund Percentage Less Than Indicated Value
5	0.00	0.00
10	4.38	1.96
15	35.21	25.70
20	71.04	62.57
25	94.58	89.66
30	98.96	97.48
35	100.00	99.44
40	100.00	99.44
45	100.00	100.00

The Histogram

A **histogram** is a bar chart for grouped numerical data in which the frequencies or percentages of each group of numerical data are represented as individual vertical bars. In a histogram, there are no gaps between adjacent bars as there are in a bar chart of categorical data. You display the variable of interest along the horizontal (X) axis. The vertical (Y) axis represents either the frequency or the percentage of values per class interval.

Figure 2.8 displays a Microsoft Excel frequency histogram for the cost of restaurant meals at city restaurants. The histogram indicates that the cost of restaurant meals at city restaurants is concentrated between approximately $30 and $50. Very few meals cost less than $20 or more than $60.

FIGURE 2.8

Microsoft Excel histogram for the cost of restaurant meals at city restaurants

See Sections E2.7 and E2.8 to create this.

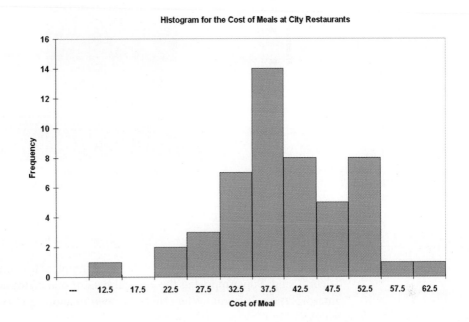

EXAMPLE 2.9

HISTOGRAM OF THE THREE-YEAR ANNUALIZED RETURN FOR GROWTH AND VALUE MUTUAL FUNDS

In the Using Statistics scenario, you are interested in comparing the three-year annualized return (2003–2005) of growth and value mutual funds. Construct histograms for the growth funds and the value funds.

SOLUTION Figure 2.9 shows that the distribution of the growth funds (shown below) has more low returns as compared to the value funds (shown on p. 50), which have more high returns.

FIGURE 2.9

Histogram of the three-year annualized return (2003–2005) (Panel A—growth funds and Panel B—value funds)

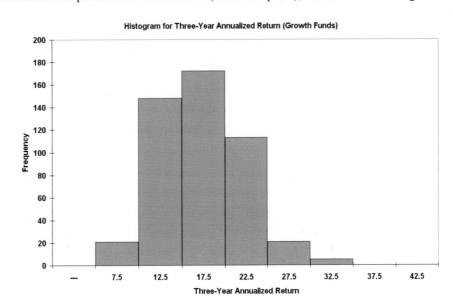

Panel A

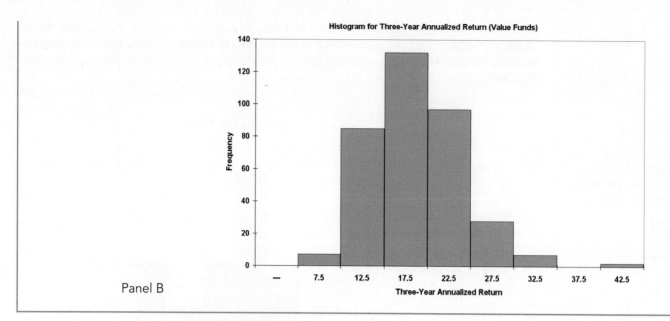

Panel B

The Polygon

Constructing multiple histograms on the same graph when comparing two or more sets of data is confusing. Superimposing the vertical bars of one histogram on another histogram makes interpretation difficult. When there are two or more groups, you should use a percentage polygon.

PERCENTAGE POLYGON

A **percentage polygon** is formed by having the midpoint of each class represent the data in that class and then connecting the sequence of midpoints at their respective class percentages.

Figure 2.10 displays percentage polygons for the cost of restaurant meals for city and suburban restaurants. The polygon for the suburban restaurants is concentrated to the left of (corresponding to lower cost) the polygon for city restaurants. The highest percentages of cost for the suburban restaurants are for class midpoints of $27.50 and $32.50, while the highest percentages of cost for the city restaurants are for a class midpoint of $37.50.

FIGURE 2.10

Microsoft Excel percentage polygons of the cost of restaurant meals for city and suburban restaurants

See Section E2.9 to create this.

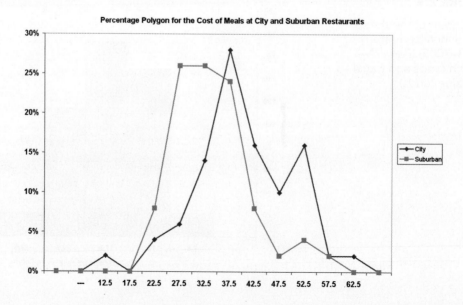

The polygons in Figure 2.10 have points whose values on the X axis represent the midpoint of the class interval. For example, look at the points plotted on the Y axis at 22.5 ($22.50). The point for the suburban restaurants (the higher one) represents the fact that 8% of these restaurants have meal costs between $20 and $25. The point for the city restaurants (the lower one) represents the fact that 4% of these restaurants have meal costs between $20 and $25.

When you construct polygons or histograms, the vertical (Y) axis should show the true zero, or "origin," so as not to distort the character of the data. The horizontal (X) axis does not need to show the zero point for the variable of interest, although the range of the variable should constitute the major portion of the axis.

EXAMPLE 2.10

PERCENTAGE POLYGONS OF THE THREE-YEAR ANNUALIZED RETURN (2003–2005) FOR GROWTH AND VALUE MUTUAL FUNDS

In the Using Statistics scenario, you are interested in comparing the three-year annualized return (2003–2005) of growth and value mutual funds. Construct percentage polygons for the growth funds and the value funds.

SOLUTION Figure 2.11 shows that the distribution of the growth funds has slightly more low returns as compared to the distribution of value funds, which has more high returns.

FIGURE 2.11

Microsoft Excel percentage polygons of the three-year annualized return

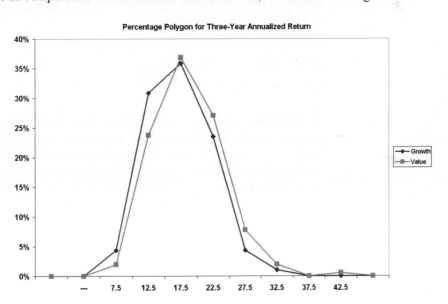

The Cumulative Percentage Polygon (Ogive)

The **cumulative percentage polygon**, or **ogive**, displays the variable of interest along the X axis, and the cumulative percentages along the Y axis.

Figure 2.12 illustrates the Microsoft Excel cumulative percentage polygons of the cost of restaurant meals at city and suburban restaurants. Most of the curve for the city restaurants is located to the right of the curve for the suburban restaurants. This indicates that the city restaurants have fewer meals that cost below a particular value. For example, 12% of the city restaurant meals cost less than $30 as compared to 34% of the suburban restaurant meals.

FIGURE 2.12

Microsoft Excel
cumulative percentage
polygons of the cost of
restaurant meals at city
and suburban
restaurants

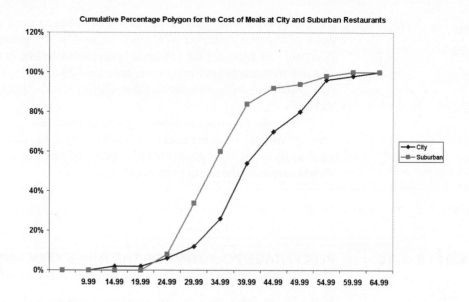

EXAMPLE 2.11

CUMULATIVE PERCENTAGE POLYGONS OF THE THREE-YEAR ANNUALIZED RETURN (2003–2005) FOR GROWTH AND VALUE MUTUAL FUNDS

In the Using Statistics scenario, you are interested in comparing the three-year annualized return (2003–2005) of growth and value mutual funds. Construct cumulative percentage polygons for the growth funds and the value funds.

SOLUTION Figure 2.13 illustrates the Microsoft Excel cumulative percentage polygons of the three-year annualized return for growth and value funds. The curve for the value funds is located slightly to the right of the curve for the growth funds. This indicates that the value funds have fewer returns below a particular value. For example, 62.57% of the value funds have returns less than 20 as compared to 71.04% of the growth funds.

FIGURE 2.13

Microsoft Excel
cumulative percentage
polygons of the three-
year annualized return

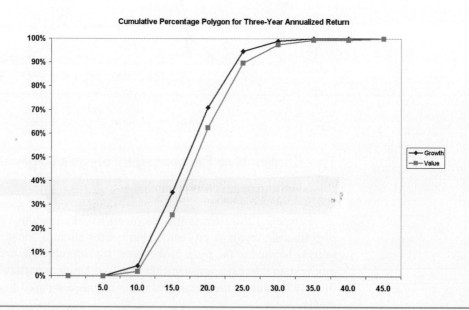

PROBLEMS FOR SECTION 2.3

Learning the Basics

 2.20 The values for a set of data vary from 11.6 to 97.8.

    a. If these values are grouped into nine classes, indicate the class boundaries.

b. What class-interval width did you choose?

c. What are the nine class midpoints?

 2.21 The GMAT scores from a sample of 50 applicants to an MBA program indicate that none of the applicants scored below 450. A frequency distribution was formed by choosing class intervals 450 to 499, 500 to 549, and so on, with the last class grouping being 700 to 749. Two applicants scored in the interval 450 to 499, and 16 applicants scored in the interval 500 to 549. Construct a cumulative percentage polygon.

a. What percentage of applicants scored below 500?

b. What percentage of applicants scored between 500 and 549?

c. What percentage of applicants scored below 550?

d. What percentage of applicants scored below 750?

Applying the Concepts

 2.22 The following data (contained in the file utility.xls) represent the cost of electricity during July 2006 for a random sample of 50 one-bedroom apartments in a large city:

Raw Data on Utility Charges ($)

96	171	202	178	147	102	153	197	127	82
157	185	90	116	172	111	148	213	130	165
141	149	206	175	123	128	144	168	109	167
95	163	150	154	130	143	187	166	139	149
108	119	183	151	114	135	191	137	129	158

a. Form a frequency distribution and a percentage distribution that have class intervals with the upper class limits $99, $119, and so on.

b. Construct a histogram and a percentage polygon.

c. Form a cumulative percentage distribution and plot a cumulative percentage polygon.

d. Around what amount does the monthly electricity cost seem to be concentrated?

2.23 One operation of a mill is to cut pieces of steel into parts that will later be used as the frame for front seats in an automobile. The steel is cut with a diamond saw and requires the resulting parts to be within ±0.005 inch of the length specified by the automobile company. The following table (contained in the file steel.xls) comes from a sample of 100 steel parts. The measurement reported is the difference in inches between the actual length of the steel part, as measured by a laser measurement device, and the specified length of the steel part. For example, the first value, −0.002, represents a steel part that is 0.002 inch shorter than the specified length.

−0.002	0.002	0.0005	−0.0015	−0.001
0.0005	0.001	0.001	−0.0005	−0.001
0.0025	0.001	0.0005	−0.0015	0.0005
0.001	0.001	0.001	−0.0005	−0.0025
0.002	−0.002	0.0025	−0.0005	0.0025
0.001	−0.003	0.001	−0.001	0.002
0.005	−0.0015	0	−0.0015	0.0025
−0.002	−0.0005	−0.0025	0.0025	−0.002
0	0	−0.001	0.001	0
0.001	−0.0025	0.0035	0.0005	−0.0005
−0.0025	−0.003	0	0	−0.001
−0.003	−0.001	−0.003	0.002	0
0.001	0.002	−0.002	−0.0005	−0.002
−0.0005	−0.001	−0.001	0.0005	0
0	0	−0.0015	0.0005	0
−0.003	0.003	−0.0015	0	0.002
−0.001	0.0015	−0.002	−0.0005	−0.003
0.0005	0	0.001	0.002	−0.0005
0.0025	0	−0.0025	0.001	−0.002
−0.0025	−0.0025	−0.0005	−0.0015	−0.002

a. Construct a frequency distribution and a percentage distribution.

b. Construct a histogram and a percentage polygon.

c. Plot a cumulative percentage polygon.

d. Is the steel mill doing a good job in meeting the requirements set by the automobile company? Explain.

 2.24 A manufacturing company produces steel housings for electrical equipment. The main component part of the housing is a steel trough that is made out of a 14-gauge steel coil. It is produced using a 250-ton progressive punch press with a wipe-down operation that puts two 90-degree forms in the flat steel to make the trough. The distance from one side of the form to the other is critical because of weatherproofing in outdoor applications. The company requires that the width of the trough be between 8.31 inches and 8.61 inches. The following (contained in the file **trough.xls**) are the widths of the troughs, in inches, for a sample of 49 troughs.

8.312 8.343 8.317 8.383 8.348 8.410 8.351 8.373

8.481 8.422 8.476 8.382 8.484 8.403 8.414 8.419

8.385 8.465 8.498 8.447 8.436 8.413 8.489 8.414

8.481 8.415 8.479 8.429 8.458 8.462 8.460 8.444

8.429 8.460 8.412 8.420 8.410 8.405 8.323 8.420

8.396 8.447 8.405 8.439 8.411 8.427 8.420 8.498

8.409

a. Construct a frequency distribution and a percentage distribution.
b. Construct a histogram and a percentage polygon.
c. Plot a cumulative percentage polygon.
d. What can you conclude about the number of troughs that will meet the company's requirements of troughs being between 8.31 and 8.61 inches wide?

2.25 The manufacturing company in Problem 2.24 also produces electric insulators. If the insulators break when in use, a short circuit is likely to occur. To test the strength of the insulators, destructive testing in high-powered labs is carried out to determine how much *force* is required to break the insulators. Force is measured by observing how many pounds must be applied to the insulator before it breaks. The strengths of 30 insulators (contained in the file **force.xls**) are as follows:

1,870 1,728 1,656 1,610 1,634 1,784 1,522 1,696

1,592 1,662 1,866 1,764 1,734 1,662 1,734 1,774

1,550 1,756 1,762 1,866 1,820 1,744 1,788 1,688

1,810 1,752 1,680 1,810 1,652 1,736

a. Construct a frequency distribution and a percentage distribution.
b. Construct a histogram and a percentage polygon.
c. Plot a cumulative percentage polygon.
d. What can you conclude about the strength of the insulators if the company requires a force measurement of at least 1,500 pounds before breaking?

2.26 The ordered arrays in the accompanying table (and contained in the file **bulbs.xls**) deal with the life (in hours) of a sample of 40 100-watt light bulbs produced by Manufacturer A and a sample of 40 100-watt light bulbs produced by Manufacturer B.

Manufacturer A					Manufacturer B				
684	697	720	773	821	819	836	888	897	903
831	835	848	852	852	907	912	918	942	943
859	860	868	870	876	952	959	962	986	992
893	899	905	909	911	994	1,004	1,005	1,007	1,015
922	924	926	926	938	1,016	1,018	1,020	1,022	1,034
939	943	946	954	971	1,038	1,072	1,077	1,077	1,082
972	977	984	1,005	1,014	1,096	1,100	1,113	1,113	1,116
1,016	1,041	1,052	1,080	1,093	1,153	1,154	1,174	1,188	1,230

a. Form a frequency distribution and a percentage distribution for each manufacturer, using the following class-interval widths for each distribution:
   1. Manufacturer A: 650 but less than 750, 750 but less than 850, and so on.
   2. Manufacturer B: 750 but less than 850, 850 but less than 950, and so on.
b. Construct percentage histograms on separate graphs and plot the percentage polygons on one graph.
c. Form cumulative percentage distributions and plot cumulative percentage polygons on one graph.
d. Which manufacturer has bulbs with a longer life— Manufacturer A or Manufacturer B? Explain.

2.27 The following data (contained in the file **drink.xls**) represent the amount of soft drink in a sample of 50 2-liter bottles:

2.109 2.086 2.066 2.075 2.065 2.057 2.052 2.044

2.036 2.038 2.031 2.029 2.025 2.029 2.023 2.020

2.015 2.014 2.013 2.014 2.012 2.012 2.012 2.010

2.005 2.003 1.999 1.996 1.997 1.992 1.994 1.986

1.984 1.981 1.973 1.975 1.971 1.969 1.966 1.967

1.963 1.957 1.951 1.951 1.947 1.941 1.941 1.938

1.908 1.894

a. Construct a frequency distribution and a percentage distribution.
b. Construct a histogram and a percentage polygon.
c. Form a cumulative percentage distribution and plot a cumulative percentage polygon.
d. On the basis of the results of (a) through (c), does the amount of soft drink filled in the bottles concentrate around specific values?

2.4 CROSS TABULATIONS

The study of patterns that may exist between two or more categorical variables is common in business. These patterns are explained by cross-tabulating the data. You can present **cross tabulations** in tabular form (contingency tables) or graphical form (side-by-side charts).

The Contingency Table

A **contingency table** presents the results of two categorical variables. The joint responses are classified so that the categories of one variable are located in the rows and the categories of the other variable are located in the columns. The values located at the intersections of the rows and columns are called **cells**. Depending on the type of contingency table constructed, the cells for each row–column combination contain the frequency, the percentage of the overall total, the percentage of the row total, or the percentage of the column total.

Suppose that in the Using Statistics scenario, you want to examine whether there is any pattern or relationship between the level of risk and the objective of the mutual fund (growth versus value). Table 2.14 summarizes this information for all 838 mutual funds.

TABLE 2.14

Contingency Table Displaying Fund Objective and Fund Risk

See Section E2.10 to create this.

	RISK LEVEL			
OBJECTIVE	High	Average	Low	Total
Growth	332	132	16	480
Value	14	113	231	358
Total	346	245	247	838

You construct this contingency table by tallying the joint responses for each of the 838 mutual funds with respect to objective and risk into one of the six possible cells in the table. The first fund listed in the Mutual Funds.xls file is classified as a growth fund with an average risk. Thus, you tally this joint response into the cell that is the intersection of the first row and second column. The remaining 837 joint responses are recorded in a similar manner. Each cell contains the frequency for the row–column combination.

In order to further explore any possible pattern or relationship between objective and fund risk, you can construct contingency tables based on percentages. You first convert these results into percentages based on the following three totals:

1. The overall total (i.e., the 838 mutual funds)
2. The row totals (i.e., 480 growth funds and 358 value funds)
3. The column totals (i.e., 346 high, 245 average, and 247 low)

Tables 2.15, 2.16, and 2.17 summarize these percentages.

TABLE 2.15

Contingency Table Displaying Fund Objective and Fund Risk, Based on Percentage of Overall Total

	RISK LEVEL			
OBJECTIVE	High	Average	Low	Total
Growth	39.62	15.75	1.91	57.28
Value	1.67	13.48	27.57	42.72
Total	41.29	29.23	29.48	100.00

TABLE 2.16

Contingency Table Displaying Fund Objective and Fund Risk, Based on Percentage of Row Total

	RISK LEVEL			
OBJECTIVE	High	Average	Low	Total
Growth	69.17	27.50	3.33	100.00
Value	3.91	31.56	64.53	100.00
Total	29.24	41.29	29.47	100.00

TABLE 2.17

Contingency Table Displaying Fund Objective and Fund Risk, Based on Percentage of Column Total

	RISK LEVEL			
OBJECTIVE	**High**	**Average**	**Low**	**Total**
Growth	95.95	53.88	6.48	57.28
Value	4.05	46.12	93.52	42.72
Total	100.00	100.00	100.00	100.00

Table 2.15 shows that 41.29% of the mutual funds sampled are high risk, 57.28% are growth funds, and 39.62% are high-risk funds that are growth funds. Table 2.16 shows that 69.17% of the growth funds are high risk and 3.33% are low risk. Table 2.17 shows that 95.95% of the high-risk funds and only 6.48% of the low-risk funds are growth funds. The tables reveal that growth funds are more likely to be high risk, while value funds are more likely to be low risk.

The Side-by-Side Bar Chart

A useful way to visually display the results of cross-classification data is by constructing a **side-by-side bar chart**. Figure 2.14, which uses the data from Table 2.14, is a Microsoft Excel side-by-side bar chart that compares the three fund risk levels, based on their objectives. An examination of Figure 2.14 reveals results consistent with those of Tables 2.15, 2.16, and 2.17: Growth funds are more likely to be high risk, while value funds are more likely to be low risk.

FIGURE 2.14

Microsoft Excel side-by-side bar chart for fund objective and risk

See Section E2.11 to create this.

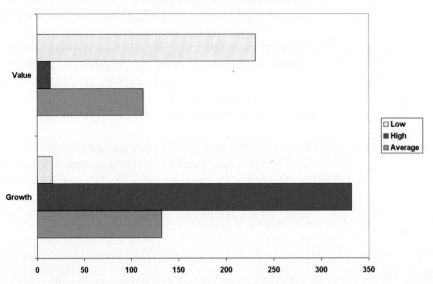

Side-By-Side Chart for Fund Objective and Risk

PROBLEMS FOR SECTION 2.4

Learning the Basics

PH Grade ASSIST **2.28** The following data represent the responses to two questions asked in a survey of 40 college students majoring in business—What is your gender? (male = M; female = F) and What is your major? (accounting = A; computer information systems = C; marketing = M):

Gender:	M	M	M	F	M	F	F	M	F	M	F	M	M	M	M	F	F	M	F	F
Major:	A	C	C	M	A	C	A	A	C	C	A	A	A	M	C	M	A	A	A	C
Gender:	M	M	M	M	F	M	F	F	M	F	M	M	M	M	M	F	M	F	M	M
Major:	C	C	A	A	M	M	C	A	A	A	C	C	A	A	A	A	C	C	A	C

a. Tally the data into a contingency table where the two rows represent the gender categories and the three columns represent the academic-major categories.

b. Form contingency tables based on percentages of all 40 student responses, based on row percentages and based on column percentages.

c. Using the results from (a), construct a side-by-side bar chart of gender based on student major.

 2.29 Given the following contingency table, construct a side-by-side bar chart comparing *A* and *B* for each of the three-column categories:

	1	2	3	Total
A	20	40	40	100
B	80	80	40	200

Applying the Concepts

 2.30 The results of a study made as part of a yield improvement effort at a semiconductor manufacturing facility provided defect data for a sample of 450 wafers. The following table presents a summary of the responses to two questions: Was a particle found on the die that produced the wafer? and Is the wafer good or bad?

	CONDITION OF DIE		
QUALITY OF WAFER	No Particles	Particles	Totals
Good	320	14	334
Bad	80	36	116
Totals	400	50	450

Source: Extracted from S. W. Hall, "Analysis of Defectivity of Semiconductor Wafers by Contingency Table," Proceedings Institute of Environmental Sciences, *Vol. 1 (1994), pp. 177–183.*

a. Construct contingency tables based on total percentages, row percentages, and column percentages.

b. Construct a side-by-side bar chart of quality of wafers based on condition of die.

c. What conclusions do you draw from these analyses?

 2.31 Each day at a large hospital, several hundred laboratory tests are performed. The rate at which these tests are done improperly (and therefore need to be redone) seems steady, at about 4%. In an effort to get to the root cause of these nonconformances (that is, tests that need to be redone), the director of the lab decided to keep records over a period of one week. The laboratory tests were subdivided by the shift of workers who performed the lab tests. The results are as follows:

	SHIFT		
LAB TESTS PERFORMED	Day	Evening	Total
Nonconforming	16	24	40
Conforming	654	306	960
Total	670	330	1,000

a. Construct contingency tables based on total percentages, row percentages, and column percentages.

b. Which type of percentage—row, column, or total—do you think is most informative for these data? Explain.

c. What conclusions concerning the pattern of nonconforming laboratory tests can the laboratory director reach?

 2.32 A sample of 500 shoppers was selected in a large metropolitan area to determine various information concerning consumer behavior. Among the questions asked was "Do you enjoy shopping for clothing?" The results are summarized in the following cross-classification table:

	GENDER		
ENJOY SHOPPING FOR CLOTHING	Male	Female	Total
Yes	136	224	360
No	104	36	140
Total	240	260	500

a. Construct contingency tables based on total percentages, row percentages, and column percentages.

b. Construct a side-by-side bar chart of enjoying shopping for clothing based on gender.

c. What conclusions do you draw from these analyses?

2.33 As more Americans use cell phones, they question where it is okay to talk on cell phones. The following is a table of results, in percentages, for 2000 and 2006 (extracted from W. Koch, "Business Put a Lid on Chatterboxes," *USA Today*, February 7, 2006, p. 3A):

	YEAR	
OK TO TALK ON A CELL PHONE IN A RESTAURANT	2000	2006
Yes	31	21
No	69	79
Total	100	100

a. Construct a side-by-side bar chart.

b. Discuss the changes in attitude concerning the use of cell phones in restaurants between 2000 and 2006.

2.34 An experiment was conducted by James Choi, David Labson, and Brigitte Madrian to study the choices made in fund selection. When presented with four S&P 500 index funds that were identical except for their fees, undergraduate and MBA students chose the funds as follows (in percentages):

| | Student Group | |
Fund	Undergraduate	MBA
Lowest-cost fund	19	19
Second-lowest-cost fund	37	40
Third-lowest-cost fund	17	23
Highest-cost fund	27	18

Source: Extracted from J. Choi, D. Laibson, and B. Madrian, Why Does the Law of One Practice Fail? An Experiment on Mutual Funds *www.som.yale.edu/faculty/jjc83/fees.pdf*.

a. Construct a side-by-side bar chart for the two student groups.

b. What do these results tell you about the differences between undergraduate and MBA students in their ability to choose S&P 500 index funds?

2.35 Where people turn to for news is different for various age groups. A study indicated where different age groups primarily get their news.

| | Age Group | | |
Media	Under 36	36–50	50+
Local TV	107	119	133
National TV	73	102	127
Radio	75	97	109
Local newspaper	52	79	107
Internet	95	83	76

a. Construct a side-by-side bar chart for the three age groups.

b. What differences are there in the age groups?

2.5 SCATTER PLOTS AND TIME-SERIES PLOTS

When analyzing a single numerical variable such as the cost of a restaurant meal or the three-year annualized return, you use histograms, polygons, and cumulative percentage polygons, developed in Section 2.3. This section discusses scatter plots and time series plots, which are used when you have two numerical variables.

The Scatter Plot

You use a **scatter plot** to examine possible relationships between two numerical variables. For each observation, you plot one variable on the X axis and the other variable on the vertical Y axis. For example, a marketing analyst could study the effectiveness of advertising by comparing weekly sales volumes and weekly advertising expenditures. Or a human resources director interested in the salary structure of the company could compare the employees' years of experience with their current salaries.

To demonstrate a scatter plot, you can examine the relationship between the cost of different items in various cities (extracted from K. Spors, "Keeping Up with . . . Yourself," *The Wall Street Journal*, April 11, 2005, p. R4). Table 2.18 provides the cost of a fast-food hamburger meal and the cost of two movie tickets in 10 cities around the world. The data file Cost of Living.xls contains the complete data set.

TABLE 2.18

Cost of a Fast-Food Hamburger Meal and Cost of Two Movie Tickets in 10 Cities

City	Hamburger	Movie Tickets
Tokyo	5.99	32.66
London	7.62	28.41
New York	5.75	20.00
Sydney	4.45	20.71
Chicago	4.99	18.00
San Francisco	5.29	19.50
Boston	4.39	18.00
Atlanta	3.70	16.00
Toronto	4.62	18.05
Rio de Janeiro	2.99	9.90

For each city, you plot the cost of a fast-food hamburger meal on the X axis, and the cost of two movie tickets on the Y axis. Figure 2.15 presents a Microsoft Excel scatter plot for these two variables.

FIGURE 2.15

Microsoft Excel scatter plot of the cost of a fast-food hamburger meal and the cost of two movie tickets

See Section E2.12 to create this.

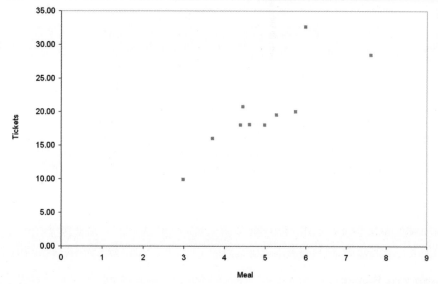

Although there is some variation, there appears to be a clearly increasing (positive) relationship between the cost of a fast-food hamburger meal and the cost of two movie tickets. In other words, cities in which the cost of a fast-food hamburger meal is low seem to also have a low cost of two movie tickets. Other pairs of variables may have a decreasing (negative) relationship in which one variable decreases as the other increases. The scatter plot will be studied again in Chapter 3, when the coefficient of correlation and the covariance are presented, and in Chapter 13, when regression analysis is developed.

The Time-Series Plot

A **time-series plot** is used to study patterns in the values of a numerical variable over time. Each value is plotted as a point in two dimensions with the time period on the horizontal X axis and the variable of interest on the Y axis.

To demonstrate a time-series plot, you can examine the yearly movie attendance, in billions, from 1999 to 2005 (extracted from C. Passy, "Good Night and Good Luck," *Palm Beach Post*, February 5, 2006, p. 1J). Table 2.19 presents the data for the yearly movie attendance (see the file movies.xls). Figure 2.16 is a time-series plot of the movie attendance (in billions) from 1999 to 2005. You can see that although movie attendance increased from 1999 to 2002, it has declined since then. Attendance in 2005 was below attendance in 1999.

TABLE 2.19

Movie Attendance, in Billions, from 1999 to 2005

Year	Attendance
1999	1.47
2000	1.42
2001	1.49
2002	1.63
2003	1.57
2004	1.53
2005	1.41

FIGURE 2.16

Microsoft Excel time-series plot of movie attendance from 1999 to 2005

See Section E2.13 to create this.

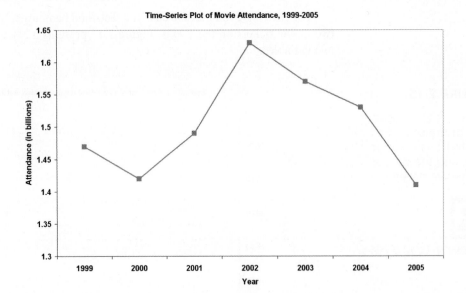

PROBLEMS FOR SECTION 2.5

Learning the Basics

 2.36 The following is a set of data from a sample of $n = 11$ items:

X	7	5	8	3	6	10	12	4	9	15	18
Y	21	15	24	9	18	30	36	12	27	45	54

a. Construct a scatter plot.
b. Is there a relationship between X and Y? Explain.

 2.37 The following is a series of annual sales (in millions of dollars) over an 11-year period (1996 to 2006):

Year	1996	1997	1998	1999	2000	2001	2002	2003	2004	2005	2006
Sales	13.0	17.0	19.0	20.0	20.5	20.5	20.5	20.0	19.0	17.0	13.0

a. Construct a time-series plot.
b. Does there appear to be any change in real annual sales over time? Explain.

Applying the Concepts

 2.38 There are several methods for calculating fuel economy. The following table (contained in the file mileage.xls) indicates the mileage as calculated by owners and by current government standards:

Car	Owner	Government
2005 Ford F-150	14.3	16.8
2005 Chevrolet Silverado	15.0	17.8
2002 Honda Accord LX	27.8	26.2
2002 Honda Civic	27.9	34.2
2004 Honda Civic Hybrid	48.8	47.6
2002 Ford Explorer	16.8	18.3
2005 Toyota Camry	23.7	28.5
2003 Toyota Corolla	32.8	33.1
2005 Toyota Prius	37.3	56.0

a. Construct a scatter plot with owner mileage on the X axis and current government standards mileage on the Y axis.
b. Does there appear to be a relationship between owner and current government standards mileage? If so, is the relationship positive or negative?

2.39 The file chicken.xls contains data on the calories and total fat, in grams per serving, for a sample of 20 chicken sandwiches from fast-food chains:

Sandwich	Calories	Fat
Wendy's Ultimate Chicken Grill	360	7
Baja Fresh Original Baja Taco with Charbroiled Chicken	370	8
Burger King Smoky BBQ Fire Grilled Chicken Baguette	380	4
Quiznos Sub Honey Bourbon Chicken on wheat bread	400	5
McDonald's Chicken McGrill	400	16
Blimpie Grilled Chicken Hot Sub	470	20
Subway Oven Roasted Chicken Breast	470	20
Blimpie Buffalo Chicken Hot Sub	500	24
Wendy's Spicy Chicken Fillet	510	19

(continued)

Sandwich	Calories	Fat
Taco Bell Ranchero Chicken Soft Taco (two tacos)	540	30
KFC Oven Roasted Chicken Tender Wrap	550	23
Subway Buffalo Chicken Sub	550	30
Burger King Chicken Whopper	570	25
Au Bon Pain Arizona Chicken	580	19
Boston Market Rotisserie Chicken Carver	640	29
Chipolte Soft Tacos with Chicken (three tacos)	660	29
Cosi Grilled Chicken with Tomato, Basil, and Mozzarella	720	30
Atlanta Bread Company Chargrilled Chicken Pesto Panini	740	30
Corner Bakery Café Chicken Pomodori Panini	910	40
Panera Bread Tuscan Chicken on Rosemary & Onion Focaccia	950	56

Source: Extracted from "Fast food: Adding Health to the Menu," Consumer Reports, *September 2004, pp. 28–31.*

a. Construct a scatter plot with calories on the X axis and total fat on the Y axis.

b. What conclusions can you reach about the relationship between the calories and total fat in chicken sandwiches?

2.40 College basketball is big business, with coaches' salaries, revenues, and expenses in millions of dollars. The data file colleges-basketball.xls contains the coaches' salary and revenue for college basketball at selected schools in a recent year (extracted from R. Adams, "Pay for Playoffs," *The Wall Street Journal*, March 11–12, 2006, pp. P1, P8).

a. Construct a scatter plot with coaches' salaries on the X axis and revenue on the Y axis.

b. What conclusions can you reach about the relationship between the coach's salary and the revenue?

c. You would expect a school with a higher revenue to have a higher coach's salary? Is this borne out by the data?

2.41 College football players trying out for the NFL are given the Wonderlic standardized intelligence test. The data file wonderlic.xls contains the average Wonderlic scores of football players trying out for the NFL and the graduation rate for football players at selected schools (extracted from S. Walker, "The NFL's Smartest Team," *The Wall Street Journal*, September 30, 2005, pp. W1, W10).

a. Construct a scatter plot with average Wonderlic score on the X axis and graduation rate on the Y axis.

b. What conclusions can you reach about the relationship between the average Wonderlic score and graduation rate?

2.42 The U.S. Bureau of Labor Statistics compiles data on a wide variety of workforce issues. The following table (contained in the file unemploy.xls) gives the monthly seasonally adjusted civilian unemployment rate for the United States from 2000 to 2005:

Month	2000	2001	2002	2003	2004	2005
January	4.0	4.2	5.7	5.8	5.7	5.2
February	4.1	4.2	5.7	5.9	5.6	5.4
March	4.0	4.3	5.7	5.9	5.7	5.1
April	3.8	4.4	5.9	6.0	5.5	5.1
May	4.0	4.3	5.8	6.1	5.6	5.1
June	4.0	4.5	5.8	6.3	5.6	5.0
July	4.0	4.6	5.8	6.2	5.5	5.0
August	4.1	4.9	5.7	6.1	5.4	4.9
September	3.9	5.0	5.7	6.1	5.4	5.1
October	3.9	5.3	5.7	6.0	5.4	4.9
November	3.9	5.5	5.9	5.9	5.4	5.0
December	3.9	5.7	6.0	5.7	5.4	4.9

*Source: U.S. Bureau of Labor Statistics, **www.bls.gov**, Sept. 19, 2006.*

a. Construct a time-series plot of the U.S. unemployment rate.

b. Does there appear to be any pattern?

2.43 In 2005, five million people in the United States subscribed to online dating services. The subscribers spent, on average, $99 for the services provided, thus generating nearly $500 million for the online dating companies. The following table (contained in the file dating.xls) gives the number of subscribers (in millions) to U.S. dating Web sites from 2000 to 2005:

Year	Number of Subscribers (millions)
2000	0.7
2001	1.6
2002	2.8
2003	4.3
2004	4.7
2005	5.0

Source: Extracted from "Making an E-Match," National Geographic, February, 2006, p. 128.

a. Construct a time-series plot.

b. Do you think the number of subscribers is increasing or decreasing? Do you think the *rate* of growth is increasing or decreasing? Explain.

 2.44 The following table contained in the file prescriptions.xls (extracted from "Price of Sickness

Rising," *USA Today*, April 7, 2006, p. A1), shows the average price of prescription drugs from 2000 to 2004:

Year	Price ($)
2000	46
2001	50
2002	55
2003	60
2004	64

a. Construct a time-series plot for the average price of prescription drugs from 2000 to 2004.
b. What pattern, if any, is present in the data?
c. If you had to make a prediction of the average price of prescription drugs in 2005, what would you predict?

2.45 The following data, contained in the file `deals.xls`, provide the number of mergers and acquisitions made during January 1 through January 11 of each year from 1995 to 2006 (extracted from "Back of the Envelope," *The New York Times*, January 13, 2006, p. C7):

Year	Deals
1995	715
1996	865
1997	708
1998	861
1999	931
2000	939
2001	1,031
2002	893
2003	735
2004	759
2005	1,013
2006	622

a. Construct a time-series plot.
b. What pattern, if any, is present in the data?
c. If you had to make a prediction of the mergers and acquisitions made during January 1 through January 11, 2007, what would you predict?

2.6 MISUSING GRAPHS AND ETHICAL ISSUES

Good graphical displays reveal what the data convey. Unfortunately, many graphs presented in newspapers and magazines as well as graphs that can be developed using the Chart Wizard of Microsoft Excel either are incorrect, misleading, or so unnecessarily complicated that they should never be used. To illustrate the misuse of graphs, the graph presented in Figure 2.17 is similar to one that was printed in *Time* magazine as part of an article on increasing exports of wine from Australia to the United States.

FIGURE 2.17

"Improper" display of Australian wine exports to the United States, in millions of gallons

Source: Adapted from S. Watterson, "Liquid Gold—Australians Are Changing the World of Wine. Even the French Seem Grateful," Time, November 22, 1999, p. 68.

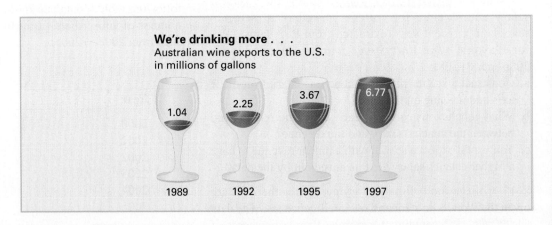

In Figure 2.17, the wineglass icon representing the 6.77 million gallons for 1997 does not appear to be almost twice the size of the wineglass icon representing the 3.67 million gallons for 1995, nor does the wineglass icon representing the 2.25 million gallons for 1992 appear to be twice the size of the wineglass icon representing the 1.04 million gallons for 1989. Part of the reason for this is that the three-dimensional wineglass icon is used to represent the two dimensions of exports and time. Although the wineglass presentation may catch the eye, the data should instead be presented in a summary table or a time-series plot.

In addition to the type of distortion created by the wineglass icons in the *Time* magazine graph displayed in Figure 2.17, improper use of the vertical and horizontal axes leads to distortions. Figure 2.18 presents another graph used in the same *Time* magazine article.

FIGURE 2.18

"Improper" display of amount of land planted with grapes for the wine industry

Source: Adapted from S. Watterson, "Liquid Gold—Australians Are Changing the World of Wine. Even the French Seem Grateful," Time, November 22, 1999, pp. 68–69.

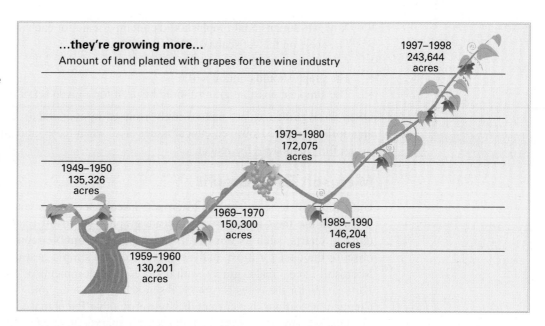

There are several problems in this graph. First, there is no zero point on the vertical axis. Second, the acreage of 135,326 for 1949 to 1950 is plotted above the acreage of 150,300 for 1969 to 1970. Third, it is not obvious that the difference between 1979 to 1980 and 1997 to 1998 (71,569 acres) is approximately 3.5 times the difference between 1979–1980 and 1969–1970 (21,775 acres). Fourth, there are no scale values on the horizontal axis. Years are plotted next to the acreage totals, not on the horizontal axis. Fifth, the values for the time dimension are not properly spaced along the horizontal axis. The value for 1979–1980 is much closer to 1989–1990 than it is to 1969–1970.

Other types of eye-catching displays that you typically see in magazines and newspapers often include information that is not necessary and just adds excessive clutter. Figure 2.19 represents one such display. The graph in Figure 2.19 shows those products with the largest market share for soft drinks in 1999. The graph suffers from too much clutter, although it is designed to show the differences in market share among the soft drinks. The display of the fizz for each soft drink takes up too much of the graph relative to the data. The same information could have been conveyed with a bar chart or pie chart.

FIGURE 2.19

Plot of market share of soft drinks in 1999

Source: Adapted from Anne B. Carey and Sam Ward, "Coke Still Has Most Fizz," USA Today, May 10, 2000, p. 1B.

Some guidelines for developing good graphs are as follows:

- The graph should not distort the data.
- The graph should not contain unnecessary adornments (sometimes referred to as **chartjunk**).

- Any two-dimensional graph should contain a scale for each axis.
- The scale on the vertical axis should begin at zero.
- All axes should be properly labeled.
- The graph should contain a title.
- The simplest possible graph should be used for a given set of data.

Often these guidelines are unknowingly violated by individuals unaware of how to construct appropriate graphs. However, ethical issues arise when these guidelines are purposely violated in an effort to mislead the reader.

Microsoft Excel Graphs

Unfortunately, to some extent, Microsoft Excel encourages you to violate these guidelines when you use the Chart feature to create graphs. Microsoft Excel offers you many types of unusual charts, such as doughnut, radar, surface, bubble, cone, and pyramid charts, that obscure the data for most analyses. Even for the simple graphs discussed in this chapter, Microsoft Excel creates graphs with unnecessary adornments or other examples of poor style. Fortunately, for the types of graphs discussed in this text, you will find instructions in Excel Companion sections that correct the style errors that Excel makes.

Oddly, many of the sample graphs used in marketing or educational materials by Microsoft for Microsoft Excel 2007, feature "three-dimensional" charts, such as the 3-D pie chart shown in Figure 2.20. Although you may see many examples of such "3-D" charts in Microsoft-supplied materials, you should avoid creating this type of chart as the prospective of the faked third dimension serves only to distort the relative proportions of each category shown on the chart.

FIGURE 2.20

"Poor-style" 3-D pie chart

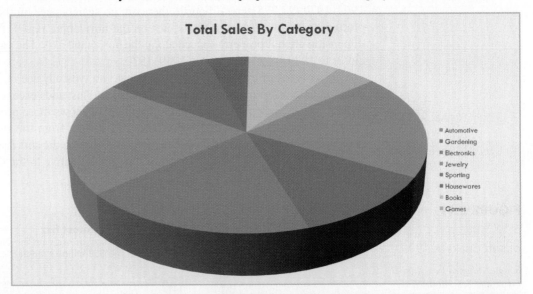

PROBLEMS FOR SECTION 2.6

Applying the Concepts

2.46 (Student Project) Bring to class a chart from a newspaper or magazine that you believe to be a poorly drawn representation of a numerical variable. Be prepared to submit the chart to the instructor with comments as to why you believe it is inappropriate. Do you believe that the intent of the chart is to purposely mislead the reader? Also, be prepared to present and comment on this in class.

2.47 (Student Project) Bring to class a chart from a newspaper or magazine that you believe to be a poorly

drawn representation of a categorical variable. Be prepared to submit the chart to the instructor with comments as to why you consider it inappropriate. Do you believe that the intent of the chart is to purposely mislead the reader? Also, be prepared to present and comment on this in class.

2.48 (Student Project) Bring to class a chart from a newspaper or magazine that you believe to contain too many unnecessary adornments (i.e., chartjunk) that may cloud the message given by the data. Be prepared to submit the chart to the instructor with comments about why you think it is inappropriate. Also, be prepared to present and comment on this in class.

2.49 The following visual display contains an overembellished chart similar to one that appeared in *USA Today*, dealing with the number of deaths from lightning strikes in the United States:

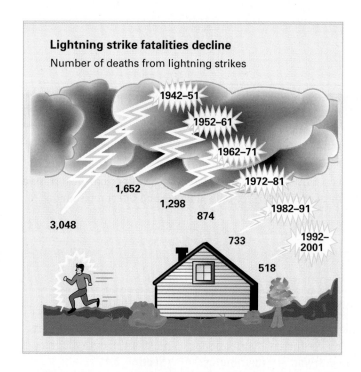

Lightning strike fatalities decline
Number of deaths from lightning strikes

1942–51
1952–61
1962–71
1972–81
1,652
1,298
1982–91
874
3,048
733
1992–2001
518

a. Describe at least one good feature of this visual display.
b. Describe at least one bad feature of this visual display.
c. Redraw the graph, using the guidelines given on pages 63 and 64.

2.50 The following visual display is similar to one that appeared in *USA Today* concerning the relative size of police departments in major U.S. cities:

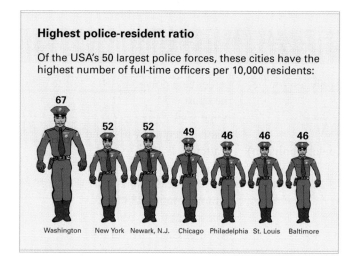

Highest police-resident ratio

Of the USA's 50 largest police forces, these cities have the highest number of full-time officers per 10,000 residents:

67
52
52
49
46
46
46

Washington   New York   Newark, N.J.   Chicago   Philadelphia   St. Louis   Baltimore

a. Indicate a feature of this chart that violates the principles of good graphs.
b. Set up an alternative graph for the data provided in this figure.

2.51 The following visual display concerning where the United States gets its electricity is similar to one that appeared in *USA Today*:

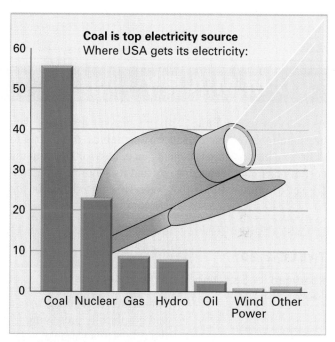

Coal is top electricity source
Where USA gets its electricity:

Coal   Nuclear   Gas   Hydro   Oil   Wind Power   Other

a. Describe at least one good feature of this visual display.
b. Describe at least one bad feature of this visual display.
c. Redraw the graph, using the guidelines given on pages 63 and 64.

2.52 An article in *The New York Times* (Donna Rosato, "Worried About the Numbers? How About the Charts?" *The New York Times*, September 15, 2002, p. B7) reported on research done on annual reports of corporations by Professor Deanna Oxender Burgess of Florida Gulf Coast University. Professor Burgess found that even slight distortions in a chart changed readers' perception of the information. The article displayed sales information from the annual report of Zale Corporation and showed how results were exaggerated.

Go to the World Wide Web or the library and study the most recent annual report of a selected corporation. Find at least one chart in the report that you think needs improvement and develop an improved version of the chart. Explain why you believe the improved chart is better than the one included in the annual report.

2.53 Figures 2.1, 2.3, and 2.6 consist of a bar chart, a pie chart, and a Pareto diagram for how respondents would spend $1,000.

a. Use the Chart Wizard of Microsoft Excel to construct a doughnut chart, a cone chart, and a pyramid chart for how respondents spend $1,000.

b. Which graphs do you prefer—the bar chart, pie chart, and Pareto diagram or the doughnut chart, cone chart, and pyramid chart? Explain.

2.54 Figures 2.2 and 2.4 consist of a bar chart and a pie chart for the risk level for the mutual fund data.

a. Use the Chart Wizard of Microsoft Excel to develop a doughnut chart, a cone chart, and a pyramid chart for the risk level of the mutual funds.

b. Which graphs do you prefer—the bar chart and pie chart or the doughnut chart, cone chart, and pyramid chart? Explain.

SUMMARY

As you can see in Table 2.20, this chapter discusses data presentation. You have used various tables and charts to draw conclusions about spending an extra $1,000, about the cost of restaurant meals in a city and its suburbs, and about the set of mutual funds that were first introduced in the Using Statistics scenario at the beginning of the chapter. Now that you have studied tables and charts, in Chapter 3 you will learn about a variety of numerical descriptive measures useful for data analysis and interpretation.

TABLE 2.20

Roadmap for Selecting Tables and Charts

Type of Analysis	Type of Data	
	Numerical	**Categorical**
Tabulating, organizing, and graphically presenting the values of a variable	Ordered array, stem-and-leaf display, frequency distribution, relative frequency distribution, percentage distribution, cumulative percentage distribution, histogram, polygon, cumulative percentage polygon **(Sections 2.2 and 2.3)**	Summary table, bar chart, pie chart, Pareto diagram **(Section 2.1)**
Graphically presenting the relationship between two variables	Scatter plot, time-series plot **(Section 2.5)**	Contingency table, side-by-side bar chart **(Section 2.4)**

KEY TERMS

bar chart   33
cells   55
chartjunk   63
class boundaries   44
class grouping   44
class midpoint   44
contingency table   55
cross tabulations   54
cumulative percentage distribution   47

cumulative percentage polygon (ogive)   51
frequency distribution   44
histogram   48
ogive (cumulative percentage polygon)   51
ordered array   41
Pareto diagram   35
Pareto principle   36
percentage distribution   46

percentage polygon   50
pie chart   34
range   44
relative frequency distribution   46
scatter plot   58
side-by-side bar chart   56
stem-and-leaf display   41
summary table   33
time-series plot   59
width of class interval   44

CHAPTER REVIEW PROBLEMS

Checking Your Understanding

PH Grade ASSIST **2.55** How do histograms and polygons differ in terms of construction and use?

PH Grade ASSIST **2.56** Why would you construct a summary table?

PH Grade ASSIST **2.57** What are the advantages and/or disadvantages of using a bar chart, a pie chart, or a Pareto diagram?

PH Grade ASSIST **2.58** Compare and contrast the bar chart for categorical data with the histogram for numerical data.

2.59 What is the difference between a time-series plot and a scatter plot?

PH Grade ASSIST **2.60** Why is it said that the main feature of the Pareto diagram is its ability to separate the "vital few" from the "trivial many"? Discuss.

PH Grade ASSIST **2.61** What are the three different ways to break down the percentages in a contingency table?

Applying the Concepts

2.62 The following data represent the breakdown of the price of a new college textbook:

Revenue Categories	Percentage	
Publisher	64.8	
Manufacturing costs		32.3
Marketing and promotion		15.4
Administrative costs and taxes		10.0
After-tax profit		7.1
Bookstore	22.4	
Employee salaries and benefits		11.3
Operations		6.6
Pretax profit		4.5
Author	11.6	
Freight	1.2	

Source: Extracted from T. Lewin, "When Books Break the Bank," The New York Times, *September 16, 2003, pp. B1, B4.*

a. Using the four categories publisher, bookstore, author, and freight, construct a bar chart, a pie chart, and a Pareto diagram.

b. Using the four subcategories of publisher and three subcategories of bookstore along with the author and freight categories, construct a Pareto diagram.

c. Based on the results of (a) and (b), what conclusions can you reach concerning who gets the revenue from the sales of new college textbooks? Do any of these results surprise you? Explain.

2.63 The following data represent the global market share for plasma TVs and LCD TVs in the fourth quarter of 2005:

Company	Plasma TVs (%)	Company	LCD TVs (%)
Hitachi	7.3	LGE	6.5
LGE	15.4	Phillips/Magnavox	14.2
Panasonic	26.0	Samsung	11.6
Phillips	13.3	Sharp	13.6
Samsung	14.4	Sony	14.6
Others	23.6	Others	39.5

Source: Extracted from Y. Kkageyama, "Flat-Panel TVs Proving Savior of Japanese Electronics Makers," The Palm Beach Post, *April 23, 2006, p. F3.*

a. For plasma TVs and LCD TVs, separately construct a bar chart, a pie chart, and a Pareto diagram.

b. Based on the results of (a), explain how the market share of plasma TVs differs from the market share of LCD TVs.

2.64 The following data represent energy consumption and renewable energy consumption in the United States in 2005:

Energy Source	%*	Renewable Energy Source	%*
Coal	23.0	Ethanol	10.1
Hydroelectric power	2.7	Geothermal	10.8
Natural gas	22.2	Solar	1.9
Nuclear electric power	8.1	Waste	17.1
Petroleum	40.5	Wind	4.5
Renewable fuels	3.3	Wood	55.5

*Percentages do not add to 100% due to rounding.
Source: Energy Information Administration, 2006.

*Percentages do not add to 100% due to rounding.
Source: Energy Information Administration, 2006.

a. For energy consumption and renewable energy consumption, separately construct a bar chart, a pie chart, and a Pareto diagram.

b. Based on the results of (a), what conclusions can you reach about energy consumption and renewable energy consumption in the United States in 2005?

2.65 The data on page 68 represent proven conventional oil reserves, in billions of barrels, subdivided by region and country:

Region and Country	Proven Conventional Reserves (Billions of Barrels)
North America	54.8
Mexico	28.3
U.S.	21.8
Canada	4.7
Central and South America	95.2
Venezuela	76.9
Brazil	8.1
Other Central and South America	10.2
Western Europe	17.2
Norway	9.5
Britain	5.0
Other Western Europe	2.7
Africa	74.9
Libya	29.5
Nigeria	22.5
Algeria	9.2
Angola	5.4
Other Africa	8.3
Middle East	683.6
Saudi Arabia	259.2
Iraq	112.5
United Arab Emirates	97.8
Kuwait	94.0
Iran	89.7
Qatar	13.2
Oman	5.5
Other Middle East	11.7
Far East and Oceania	44.0
China	24.0
Indonesia	5.0
India	4.7
Other Far East and Oceania	10.3
Eastern Europe and Former USSR	59.0
Russia	48.6
Kazakhstan	5.4
Other Eastern Europe and Former USSR	5.0

Source: U.S. Department of Energy.

a. Using the set of countries, construct a bar chart, a pie chart, and a Pareto diagram.

b. Using the set of regions, construct a bar chart, a pie chart, and a Pareto diagram.

c. Which graphical method do you think is best to portray these data?

d. Based on the results of (a) and (b), what conclusions can you make concerning the proven conventional oil reserves for the different countries and regions?

2.66 In the aftermath of the attacks of September 11, 2001, statisticians at the National Center for Health Statistics became more concerned with their ability to track and classify victims of terrorism (E. Weinstein, "Tracking Terror's Rising Toll," *The Wall Street Journal*, January 25, 2002, p. A13). The following data represents deaths due to terrorism on U.S. soil from 1990 to 2001 and also the deaths in the United States in 2000 due to various causes:

Year	Deaths Due to Terrorism in the United States
1990	0
1991	0
1992	0
1993	6
1994	1
1995	169
1996	2
1997	0
1998	1
1999	3
2000	0
2001	2,717

Cause	Deaths, in Thousands
Smoke and fire	3.3
Accidental drowning	3.3
Alcohol-induced deaths	18.5
Alzheimer's disease	49.0
Assault by firearms	10.4
Assault by non-firearms	5.7
Asthma	4.4
Cancer	551.8
Strokes and related diseases	166.0
Emphysema	16.9
Diabetes	68.7
Heart disease	710.0
Falls	12.0
HIV	14.4
Influenza and pneumonia	67.0
Injuries at work	5.3
Motor vehicle accidents	41.8
Suicide	28.3
Drug-related deaths	15.9

Source: Federal Bureau of Criminal Justice Statistics, National Center for Health Statistics, National Highway Transportation Safety Administration, Department of Defense.

a. Construct a time-series plot of deaths due to terrorism on U.S. soil. Is there any pattern to the deaths due to terrorism on U.S. soil between 1990 and 2001?

b. For the deaths, in thousands, due to different causes, construct a bar chart, a pie chart, and a Pareto diagram.

c. Which graphical method do you think is best to portray these data?

d. Based on the results of (c), what conclusions can you make concerning the deaths in the United States in 2000 due to various causes?

2.67 The owner of a restaurant serving Continental-style entrées is interested in studying patterns of patron demand for the Friday-to-Sunday weekend time period. Records are maintained that indicate the type of entrée ordered. The data are as follows:

Type of Entrée	Number Served
Beef	187
Chicken	103
Duck	25
Fish	122
Pasta	63
Shellfish	74
Veal	26

a. Construct a percentage summary table for the types of entrées ordered.

b. Construct a bar chart, a pie chart, and a Pareto diagram for the types of entrées ordered.

c. Do you prefer a Pareto diagram or a pie chart for these data? Why?

d. What conclusions can the restaurant owner draw concerning demand for different types of entrées?

2.68 Suppose that the owner of the restaurant in Problem 2.67 is also interested in studying the demand for dessert during the same time period. She decided that two other variables, along with whether a dessert was ordered, are to be studied: the gender of the individual and whether a beef entrée is ordered. The results are as follows:

	GENDER		
DESSERT ORDERED	Male	Female	Total
Yes	96	40	136
No	224	240	464
Total	320	280	600

	BEEF ENTRÉE		
DESSERT ORDERED	Yes	No	Total
Yes	71	65	136
No	116	348	464
Total	187	413	600

a. For each of the two contingency tables, construct a contingency table of row percentages, column percentages, and total percentages.

b. Which type of percentage (row, column, or total) do you think is most informative for each gender? for beef entrée? Explain.

c. What conclusions concerning the pattern of dessert ordering can the owner of the restaurant reach?

2.69 An article in *The New York Times* (William McNulty and Hugh K. Truslow, "How It Looked Inside the Booth," *The New York Times*, November 6, 2002) provided the following data on the method for recording votes in 1980, 2000, and 2002, broken down by percentage of counties in the United States using each method and the percentage of registered voters using each method. The results are as follows:

Percentage of Counties Using Method	1980	2000	2002
Punch cards	18.5	18.5	15.5
Lever machines	36.7	14.4	10.6
Paper ballots	40.7	11.9	10.5
Optical scan	0.8	41.5	43.0
Electronic	0.2	9.3	16.3
Mixed	3.1	4.4	4.1

Percentage of Registered Voters Using Method	1980	2000	2002
Punch cards	31.7	31.4	22.6
Lever machines	42.9	17.4	15.5
Paper ballots	10.5	1.5	1.3
Optical scan	2.1	30.8	31.8
Electronic	0.7	12.2	19.6
Mixed	12.0	6.7	9.3

a. Construct separate pie charts for each year for the percentage of counties and the percentage of registered voters using the various methods.

b. Construct side-by-side bar charts, by year, for the percentage of counties and the percentage of registered voters using the various methods.

c. Which type of graphical display is more helpful in depicting the data? Explain.

d. What differences are there in the results for the counties and the registered voters?

2.70 In summer 2000, a growing number of warranty claims on Firestone tires sold on Ford SUVs prompted Firestone and Ford to issue a major recall. An analysis of warranty-claims data helped identify which models to recall. A breakdown of 2,504 warranty claims based on tire size is given in the following table:

Tire Size	Warranty Claims
23575R15	2,030
311050R15	137
30950R15	82
23570R16	81
331250R15	58
25570R16	54
Others	62

Source: Extracted from Robert L. Simison, "Ford Steps Up Recall Without Firestone," The Wall Street Journal, August 14, 2000, p. A3.

The 2,030 warranty claims for the 23575R15 tires can be categorized into ATX models and Wilderness models. The type of incident leading to a warranty claim, by model type, is summarized in the following table:

Incident	ATX Model Warranty Claims	Wilderness Warranty Claims
Tread separation	1,365	59
Blowout	77	41
Other/unknown	422	66
Total	1,864	166

Source: Extracted from Robert L. Simison, "Ford Steps Up Recall Without Firestone," The Wall Street Journal, August 14, 2000, p. A3.

a. Construct a Pareto diagram for the number of warranty claims by tire size. What tire size accounts for most of the claims?

b. Construct a pie chart to display the percentage of the total number of warranty claims for the 23575R15 tires that come from the ATX model and Wilderness model. Interpret the chart.

c. Construct a Pareto diagram for the type of incident causing the warranty claim for the ATX model. Does a certain type of incident account for most of the claims?

d. Construct a Pareto diagram for the type of incident causing the warranty claim for the Wilderness model. Does a certain type of incident account for most of the claims?

2.71 One of the major measures of the quality of service provided by any organization is the speed with which the organization responds to customer complaints. A large family-held department store selling furniture and flooring, including carpet, had undergone a major expansion in the past several years. In particular, the flooring department had expanded from 2 installation crews to an installation supervisor, a measurer, and 15 installation crews. During a recent year, the company got 50 complaints concerning carpet installation. The following data (contained in the file furniture.xls) represent the number of days between the receipt of the complaint and the resolution of the complaint:

54	5	35	137	31	27	152	2	123	81	74	27
11	19	126	110	110	29	61	35	94	31	26	5
12	4	165	32	29	28	29	26	25	1	14	13
13	10	5	27	4	52	30	22	36	26	20	23
33	68										

a. Construct a frequency distribution and a percentage distribution.

b. Construct a histogram and a percentage polygon.

c. Form a cumulative percentage distribution and plot a cumulative percentage polygon (ogive).

d. On the basis of the results of (a) through (c), if you had to tell the president of the company how long a customer should expect to wait to have a complaint resolved, what would you say? Explain.

2.72 Data concerning 58 of the best-selling domestic beers in the United States are located in the file domesticbeer.xls. The values for three variables are included: percentage alcohol, number of calories per 12 ounces, and number of carbohydrates (in grams) per 12 ounces.

Source: Extracted from www.Beer100.com, March 31, 2006.

a. Construct a histogram for each of the three variables.

b. Construct three scatter plots: percentage alcohol versus calories, percentage alcohol versus carbohydrates, and calories versus carbohydrates.

c. Discuss the information you learned from studying the graphs in (a) and (b).

2.73 The data in the file spending.xls are the per-capita spending, in thousands of dollars, for each state in 2004.

a. Develop an ordered array.

b. Construct a frequency distribution and a percentage distribution.

c. Plot a percentage histogram.

d. What conclusions can you reach about the differences in federal per-capita spending between the states?

2.74 The data in the file savings.xls are the yields for a money market account, a one-year certificate of deposit (CD), and a five-year CD for 40 banks in south Florida, as of December 20, 2005 (extracted from Bankrate.com, December 20, 2005).

a. Construct a histogram for each of the three variables.

b. Construct three scatter plots: money market account versus one-year CD, money market account versus five-year CD, and one-year CD versus five-year CD.

c. Discuss the information you learned from studying the graphs in (a) and (b).

2.75 The data in the file **ceo.xls** represent the total compensation (in $millions) of CEOs of the 100 largest companies, by revenue (extracted from "Special Report: Executive Compensation," *USA Today*, April 10, 2006, pp. 3B, 4B).
a. Construct a frequency distribution and a percentage distribution.
b. Construct a histogram and a percentage polygon.
c. Construct a cumulative percentage distribution and plot a cumulative percentage polygon (ogive).
d. Based on (a) through (c), what conclusions can you reach concerning CEO compensation in 2005?

2.76 Studies conducted by a manufacturer of "Boston" and "Vermont" asphalt shingles have shown product weight to be a major factor in customers' perception of quality. Moreover, the weight represents the amount of raw materials being used and is therefore very important to the company from a cost standpoint. The last stage of the assembly line packages the shingles before the packages are placed on wooden pallets. When a pallet is full (a pallet for most brands holds 16 squares of shingles), it is weighed, and the measurement is recorded. The company expects pallets of its "Boston" brand-name shingles to weigh at least 3,050 pounds but less than 3,260 pounds. For the company's "Vermont" brand-name shingles, pallets should weigh at least 3,600 pounds but less than 3,800. The data file **pallet.xls** contains the weights (in pounds) from a sample of 368 pallets of "Boston" shingles and 330 pallets of "Vermont" shingles.
a. For the "Boston" shingles, construct a frequency distribution and a percentage distribution having eight class intervals, using 3,015, 3,050, 3,085, 3,120, 3,155, 3,190, 3,225, 3,260, and 3,295 as the class boundaries.
b. For the "Vermont" shingles, construct a frequency distribution and a percentage distribution having seven class intervals, using 3,550, 3,600, 3,650, 3,700, 3,750, 3,800, 3,850, and 3,900 as the class boundaries.
c. Construct histograms for the "Boston" shingles and for the "Vermont" shingles.
d. Comment on the distribution of pallet weights for the "Boston" and "Vermont" shingles. Be sure to identify the percentage of pallets that are underweight and overweight.

2.77 Do marketing promotions, such as bobble-head give-aways, increase attendance at Major League Baseball games? An article in *Sport Marketing Quarterly* reported on the effectiveness of marketing promotions (extracted from T. C. Boyd and T. C. Krehbiel, "An Analysis of the Effects of Specific Promotion Types on Attendance at Major League Baseball Games," *Mid-American Journal*

of Business, Vol. 21, 2006, pp. 21–32). The data file **royals.xls** includes the following variables for the Kansas City Royals during the 2002 baseball season:
GAME = Home games in the order they were played
ATTENDANCE = Paid attendance for the game
PROMOTION 1 = If a promotion was held; 0 = if no promotion was held
a. Construct a percentage histogram for the attendance variable. Interpret the histogram.
b. Construct a percentage polygon for the attendance variable. Interpret the polygon.
c. Which graphical display do you prefer, the one in (a) or (b)? Explain.
d. Construct a graphical display containing two percentage polygons for attendance—one for the 43 games with promotions and the second for the 37 games without promotions. Compare the two attendance distributions.

2.78 The data in the file **protein.xls** indicate fat and cholesterol information concerning popular protein foods (fresh red meats, poultry, and fish).
Source: U.S. Department of Agriculture.

For the data relating to the number of calories and the amount of cholesterol for the popular protein foods:
a. Construct a frequency distribution and a percentage distribution.
b. Construct a histogram and a percentage polygon.
c. Form a cumulative percentage distribution and plot a cumulative percentage polygon.
d. What conclusions can you draw from these analyses?

2.79 The data in the file **states.xls** represent the results of the American Community Survey, a sampling of households taken in all states during the 2000 U.S. Census. For each of the variables average travel-to-work time in minutes, percentage of homes with eight or more rooms, median household income, and percentage of mortgage-paying homeowners whose housing costs exceed 30% of income:
a. Construct a frequency distribution and a percentage distribution.
b. Construct a histogram and a percentage polygon.
c. Construct a cumulative percentage distribution and plot a cumulative percentage polygon.
d. What conclusions about these four variables can you make based on the results of (a) through (c)?

2.80 The economics of baseball has caused a great deal of controversy, with owners arguing that they are losing money, players arguing that owners are making money, and fans complaining about how expensive it is to attend a game and watch games on cable television. In addition to data related to team statistics for the 2001 season, the file **bb2001.xls** contains team-by-team statistics on ticket prices;

the fan cost index; regular-season gate receipts; local television, radio, and cable receipts; all other operating revenue; player compensation and benefits; national and other local expenses; and income from baseball operations. For each of these variables,

a. Construct a frequency distribution and a percentage distribution.

b. Construct a histogram and a percentage polygon.

c. Construct a cumulative percentage distribution and plot a cumulative percentage polygon.

d. Construct a scatter plot to predict the number of wins on the Y axis from the player compensation and benefits on the X axis. What conclusions can you reach based on this scatter plot?

e. What conclusions about these variables can you reach based on the results of (a) through (d)?

2.81 In Section 2.5 on page 59, a scatter plot of the relationship between the cost of a fast-food hamburger meal and the cost of movie tickets in 10 different cities was constructed. The data file Cost of Living.xls also includes the overall cost index, the monthly rent for a two-bedroom apartment, the cost of a cup of coffee with service, the cost of dry cleaning a men's blazer, and the cost of toothpaste.

a. Construct six separate scatter plots. For each, use the overall cost index as the Y axis. Use the monthly rent for a two-bedroom apartment, the costs of a cup of coffee with service, a fast-food hamburger meal, dry cleaning a men's blazer, toothpaste, and movie tickets as the X axis.

b. What conclusions can you reach about the relationship of the overall cost index to these six variables?

2.82 In Problem 2.39 on page 60, using the data set chicken.xls, you constructed a scatter plot of calories with the total fat content of chicken sandwiches.

a. Construct a scatter plot of calories on the Y axis and carbohydrates on the X axis.

b. Construct a scatter plot of calories on the Y axis and sodium on the X axis.

c. Which variable (total fat, carbohydrates, or sodium) seems to be most closely related to calories? Explain.

2.83 The data file gas.xls contains the weekly average price of gasoline in the United States from March 1, 2004, to March 6, 2006. Prices are in dollars per gallon.

Source: U.S. Department of Energy, www.eia.doe.gov.

a. Construct a time-series plot.

b. What pattern, if any, is present in the data?

2.84 The data contained in the file drink.xls represent the amount of soft drink filled in a sample of 50 consecutive 2-liter bottles. The results are listed horizontally in the order of being filled:

2.109 2.086 2.066 2.075 2.065 2.057 2.052 2.044 2.036 2.038

2.031 2.029 2.025 2.029 2.023 2.020 2.015 2.014 2.013 2.014

2.012 2.012 2.012 2.010 2.005 2.003 1.999 1.996 1.997 1.992

1.994 1.986 1.984 1.981 1.973 1.975 1.971 1.969 1.966 1.967

1.963 1.957 1.951 1.951 1.947 1.941 1.941 1.938 1.908 1.894

a. Construct a time-series plot for the amount of soft drink on the Y axis and the bottle number (going consecutively from 1 to 50) on the X axis.

b. What pattern, if any, is present in these data?

c. If you had to make a prediction of the amount of soft drink filled in the next bottle, what would you predict?

d. Based on the results of (a) through (c), explain why it is important to construct a time-series plot and not just a histogram, as was done in Problem 2.27 on page 54.

2.85 The S&P 500 Index tracks the overall movement of the stock market by considering the stock prices of 500 large corporations. The data file stocks2005.xls contains weekly data for this index as well as the weekly closing stock price for three companies during 2005. The variables included are:

WEEK —Week ending on date given
S&P —Weekly closing value for the S&P 500 Index
SEARS —Weekly closing stock price for Sears
TARGET —Weekly closing stock price for the Target
SARA LEE —Weekly closing stock price for the Sara Lee

Source: Extracted from finance.yahoo.com.

a. Construct a time-series plot for the weekly closing values of the S&P 500 Index, Sears, Target, and Sara Lee.

b. Explain any patterns present in the plots.

c. Write a short summary of your findings.

2.86 (Class Project) Let each student in the class respond to the question "Which carbonated soft drink do you most prefer?" so that the teacher can tally the results into a summary table.

a. Convert the data to percentages and construct a Pareto diagram.

b. Analyze the findings.

2.87 (Class Project) Let each student in the class be cross-classified on the basis of gender (male, female) and current employment status (yes, no) so that the teacher can tally the results.

a. Construct a table with either row or column percentages, depending on which you think is more informative.

b. What would you conclude from this study?

c. What other variables would you want to know regarding employment in order to enhance your findings?

Report Writing Exercises

2.88 Referring to the results from Problem 2.76 on page 71 concerning the weight of "Boston" and "Vermont" shingles, write a report that evaluates whether the weight of the pallets of the two types of shingles are what the company expects. Be sure to incorporate tables and charts into the report.

2.89 Referring to the results from Problem 2.70 on page 69 concerning the warranty claims on Firestone tires, write a report that evaluates warranty claims on Firestone tires sold on Ford SUVs. Be sure to incorporate tables and charts into the report.

Team Project

The data file Mutual Funds.xls contains information regarding nine variables from a sample of 838 mutual funds. The variables are:

Category—Type of stocks comprising the mutual fund (small cap, mid cap, large cap)
Objective—Objective of stocks comprising the mutual fund (growth or value)
Assets—In millions of dollars
Fees—Sales charges (no or yes)
Expense ratio—Ratio of expenses to net assets in percentage
2005 return—Twelve-month return in 2005
Three-year return—Annualized return, 2003–2005
Five-year return—Annualized return, 2001–2005
Risk—Risk-of-loss factor of the mutual fund (low, average, or high)

2.90 For the expense ratio:
a. Construct a histogram.
b. Plot percentage polygons of the expense ratio for mutual funds that have fees and mutual funds that do not have fees on the same graph.
c. What conclusions about the expense ratio can you reach based on the results of (a) and (b)?

2.91 For the five-year annualized return from 2001 to 2005:
a. Construct a histogram.
b. Plot percentage polygons of the five-year annualized return from 2001 to 2005 for growth mutual funds and value mutual funds on the same graph.

c. What conclusions about the five-year annualized return from 2001 to 2005 can you reach based on the results of (a) and (b)?

2.92 For the return in 2005:
a. Construct a histogram.
b. Plot percentage polygons of the return in 2005 for growth mutual funds and value mutual funds on the same graph.
c. What conclusions about the return in 2005 can you reach based on the results of (a) and (b)?

Student Survey Database

2.93 Problem 1.27 on page 15 describes a survey of 50 undergraduate students (see the file undergradsurvey.xls). For these data, construct all the appropriate tables and charts and write a report summarizing your conclusions.

2.94 Problem 1.27 on page 15 describes a survey of 50 undergraduate students (see the file undergradsurvey.xls).
a. Select a sample of 50 undergraduate students at your school and conduct a similar survey for those students.
b. For the data collected in (a), construct all the appropriate tables and charts and write a report summarizing your conclusions.
c. Compare the results of (b) to those of Problem 2.93.

2.95 Problem 1.28 on page 15 describes a survey of 50 MBA students (see the file gradsurvey.xls). For these data, construct all appropriate tables and charts and write a report summarizing your conclusions.

2.96 Problem 1.28 on page 15 describes a survey of 50 MBA students (see the file gradsurvey.xls).
a. Select a sample of 50 MBA students in your MBA program and conduct a similar survey for those students.
b. For the data collected in (a), construct all the appropriate tables and charts and write a report summarizing your conclusions.
c. Compare the results of (b) to those of Problem 2.93.

Managing the *Springville Herald*

Advertising fees are an important source of revenue for any newspaper. In an attempt to boost these revenues and to minimize costly errors, the management of the *Herald* has established a task force charged with improving customer service in the advertising department. Open a Web browser and link to **www.prenhall.com/HeraldCase/Ad_Errors.htm** (or open the **Ad_Errors.htm** file in the Student CD-ROM's **HeraldCase** folder) to review the task force's data collec-

tion. Identify the data that are important in describing the customer service problems. For each set of data you identify, construct the graphical presentation you think is most appropriate for the data and explain your choice. Also, suggest what other information concerning the different types of errors would be useful to examine. Offer possible courses of action for either the task force or management to take that would support the goal of improving customer service.

Web Case

In the Using Statistics scenario, you were asked to gather information to help make wise investment choices. Sources for such information include brokerage firms and investment counselors. Apply your knowledge about the proper use of tables and charts in this Web Case about the claims of foresight and excellence by a Springville financial services firm.

Visit the EndRun Financial Services Web site at **www. prenhall.com/Springville/EndRun.htm** (or open the **EndRun.htm** file in the Student CD-ROM's **WebCase** folder). Review the company's investment claims and supporting data and then answer the following.

1. How does the presentation of the general information about EndRun on its home page affect your perception of the business?

2. Is EndRun's claim about having more winners than losers a fair and accurate reflection of the quality of its investment service? If you do not think that the claim is a fair and accurate one, provide an alternate presentation that you think is fair and accurate.

3. EndRun's "Big Eight" mutual funds are part of the sample found in the Mutual Funds.xls workbook. Is there any other relevant data from that file that could have been included in the Big Eight table? How would that new data alter your perception of EndRun's claims?

4. EndRun is proud that all Big Eight funds have gained in value over the past five years. Do you agree that EndRun should be proud of its selections? Why or why not?

REFERENCES

1. Huff, D., *How to Lie with Statistics* (New York: Norton, 1954).
2. *Microsoft Excel 2007* (Redmond, WA: Microsoft Corporation, 2007).
3. Tufte, E. R., *Envisioning Information* (Cheshire, CT: Graphics Press, 1990).
4. Tufte, E. R., *The Visual Display of Quantitative Information*, 2nd ed. (Cheshire, CT: Graphics Press, 2002).
5. Tufte, E. R., *Visual Explanations* (Cheshire, CT: Graphics Press, 1997).
6. Wainer, H., *Visual Revelations: Graphical Tales of Fate and Deception from Napoleon Bonaparte to Ross Perot* (New York: Copernicus/Springer-Verlag, 1997).

Excel Companion
to Chapter 2

Introduction

From this point forward, the Excel Companions discuss Excel techniques that support specific statistical methods. For most statistical methods, you will be able to choose between two ways of using Excel—Basic Excel, which uses Excel without any outside enhancements, and PHStat2, which uses the free PHStat2 add-in that is included on this Student CD-ROM. If you haven't already reviewed the From the Authors' Desktop: *Using and Learning Microsoft Excel* feature on page 5, you should do so now in order to decide whether the Basic Excel or PHStat2 approach better suits your learning goals.

Many of the Excel techniques discussed are illustrated with examples based on worksheets you see in the chapter. For most examples, you will have your choice of step-by-step Basic Excel *or* PHStat2 instructions for creating a solution. An added complication in this Excel Companion is that many of the Excel features you would use to present data in tables and charts have been greatly altered in Microsoft Excel 2007. These changes, in turn, necessitate having a special set of Basic Excel instructions for Excel 2007. When this occurs, you will see two labels, (97–2003) and (2007), to distinguish material appropriate for either Excel 97, 2000, 2002, or 2003 (97–2003), from material appropriate only for Excel 2007. (PHStat2 instructions are the same for all versions of Microsoft Excel, other than having to click the **Add-Ins** tab in Excel 2007 in order to see the PHStat2 menu.)

Because the Excel 2007 changes do not affect *most* of the statistical methods discussed in later chapters, you will not see the (97–2003) and (2007) labels as frequently in later Companions. However, when you do see these labels, you should read only the passages that apply to the Excel version you use.

E2.1   CREATING SUMMARY TABLES

You create a summary table from unsummarized data by creating PivotTables. (If your data are already summarized in table form, you can simply type that table into a blank worksheet and skip creating a PivotTable.) PivotTables are worksheet areas that act as if you had entered formulas to summarize data. PivotTables have many uses beyond those discussed in this book, including giving Excel users the capability to drill down, or look at the unsummarized, detailed data from which the summarized data are derived.

You create a PivotTable by dragging variable names into a form or template. Because the exact process is different for Excel 2007, this section includes passages specific to Excel 97–2003 and Excel 2007.

Using the PHStat2 One-Way Tables & Charts procedure, you can create a PivotTable, and finish the summary table, and optionally add the entries needed for a bar chart, pie chart, or Pareto diagram, using the instructions discussed later in this section.

Starting a PivotTable (97–2003)

To start a PivotTable in Excel 97–2003, open to the worksheet that contains your unsummarized data and select **Data → PivotTable Report** (Excel 97) or select **Data → PivotTable and PivotChart Report** (Excel 2000–2003). Selecting these commands begins the PivotTable Wizard, a sequence of three dialog boxes (four in Excel 97) that step you through the process of creating a PivotTable. Figure E2.1 shows the dialog boxes for Excel 2003. (Other versions have similar dialog boxes; Excel 97 uses four dialog boxes, breaking the third box into two.)

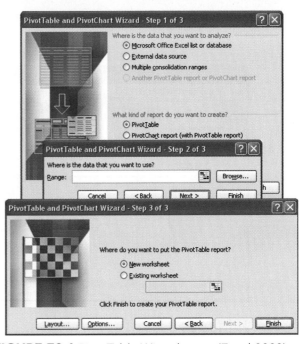

FIGURE E2.1 PivotTable Wizard steps (Excel 2003)

You step through these dialog boxes by clicking **Next** to advance to the next dialog box or **Back** to move back to a previous one. At any point, you can click **Cancel** to stop creating a PivotTable or click **Finish** to end the wizard and create a PivotTable. To create a summary table, you make the following entries in the dialog boxes:

Step 1 Click **Microsoft Excel list or database** as the source and **PivotTable** as the report type. (You do not select a report type in Microsoft Excel 97; PivotTable is assumed.)

Step 2 Enter the cell range of the data to be summarized in the PivotTable. This cell range must contain variable labels (column headings) in the first row of the range because the wizard, in Step 3, will use the cells in the first row as the names for your variables.

Step 3 First click the **New worksheet** option as the location for your PivotTable. Then click **Layout** to display the Layout dialog box (see Figure E2.2).[1] Design your table using the instructions in the next paragraph and then click **OK** to return to the Step 3 box. Then click **Options** to display the PivotTable Options dialog box (see Figure E2.2). Enter **0** as the **For empty cells, show** value and click **OK** to return to the Step 3 dialog box. Then click **Finish** to create the PivotTable.

---

[1]*If you use Excel 97, the Layout dialog box appears as the Step 3 dialog box. When you click **Next** in this box, you then see a Step 4 dialog box that contains location options. There is no **Options** button in either the Step 3 or Step 4 dialog boxes in Excel 97.*

In the Layout dialog box of Step 3, drag the label of the variable to be summarized and drop it in the ROW area. Drag a second copy of this same label and drop it in the DATA area. (This second label changes to **Count of variable name** to indicate that the PivotTable will be counting, or tallying, the occurrences of each category of the variable.)

Starting a PivotTable (2007)

To start a PivotTable in Excel 2007, open to the worksheet that contains your unsummarized data and select **Insert → PivotTable**. In the Create PivotTable dialog box (see Figure E2.3), leave selected the **Select a table or range** option and verify and change, if necessary, the **Table/Range** cell range. (In Figure E2.3, the cell range of the mutual funds data of the **Data** worksheet of Mutual Funds.xls is shown.) Select the **New Worksheet** option and click **OK**.

In the PivotTable Field List task pane, drag the label of the variable to be summarized and drop it in the **Row Labels** area. Drag a second copy of this same label and drop it in the Σ **Values** area. (This second label changes to **Count of variable name** to indicate that the PivotTable will be counting, or tallying, the occurrences of each category of the variable.)

Right-click the PivotTable and click **Table Options** in the shortcut menu that appears. In the PivotTable Options dialog box (a reorganized version of the older one shown in Figure E2.2), click the **Layout & Format** tab, check **For empty cells show**, enter **0** as its value, and click **OK**.

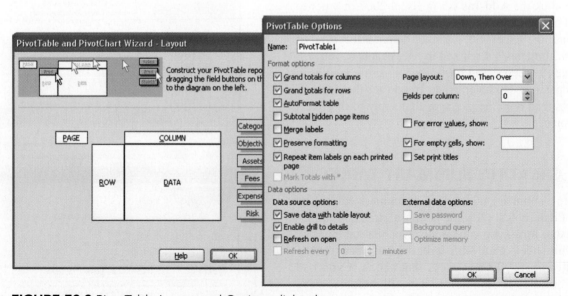

FIGURE E2.2 PivotTable Layout and Options dialog boxes

FIGURE E2.3 Create PivotTable dialog box and PivotTable Field List task pane (Excel 2007)

EXAMPLE Table 2.2 Summary Table

To start a PivotTable version of the Table 2.2 summary table on page 33, similar to the PivotTable shown below, open the Mutual Funds.xls workbook to the **Data** worksheet and use the appropriate set of instructions.

Count of Risk		
Risk ▾	Total	Percentage
Low	247	29.47%
Average	245	29.24%
High	346	41.29%
Grand Total	838	

Basic Excel 97–2003 Begin the PivotTable Wizard and follow the instructions for "Starting a PivotTable 97–2003" in Section E2.1. In Step 2, enter **F1:F839** as the **Range**. In the Layout dialog box of Step 3, drag the **Risk** variable label twice, once to the ROW area and a second time to the DATA area. (This second label changes to **Count of Risk** when you drop it in the DATA area.) After you click **Finish** to create the PivotTable, continue with "Finish the

PivotTable" instructions that follow this example to complete a PivotTable version of Table 2.2.

Basic Excel 2007 Select **Insert → PivotTable**. In the PivotTable Field List task pane, drag the **Risk** variable label twice, once to the **Row Labels** area and a second time to the **Σ Values** area. (This second label changes to **Count of Risk** when you drop it in the **Σ Values** area.) Continue with "Finish the PivotTable" instructions that follow this example to complete a PivotTable version of Table 2.2.

PHStat2 Select **PHStat → Descriptive Statistics → One-Way Tables & Charts**. In the dialog box for this procedure (shown below), click the **Raw Categorical Data** option and enter **F1:F839** as the **Raw Data Cell Range**. Click **First cell contains label** and enter a **Title**. Click **Percentage Column** and **Pareto Diagram** and click **OK**. The worksheet PHStat2 creates columns for percentage frequency and cumulative percentage. (You can safely delete the chart sheet that contains the Pareto diagram if you do not want this chart.) If you want to create charts from the summary table that PHStat2 creates, you can also click **Bar Chart** and/or **Pie Chart** before you click **OK**.

Finish the PivotTable

After Excel creates the PivotTable, close any floating PivotTable toolbar windows (97–2003) or the PivotTable Field List task pane (2007). Enter a title in cell A1 of the new worksheet that contains your PivotTable. Also, rename the new worksheet, using a descriptive name. Then in cell C4, enter **Percentage** and in cell C5, enter the formula in the form **=B5/B$n**, in which **n** is the row that contains the Grand Total. For example, if the Grand Total row is row 8, enter **=B5/B$8**. (If you do not know the significance of the $ (dollar sign) symbol, review Section E1.5.) Copy this formula down through all the category rows of the summary table. Format the cell range that contains these formulas for percentage display. Adjust the number of decimals displayed and the width of column C, as necessary, and add borders around the percentage column cells. (If necessary, review the instructions for doing these things presented in the Excel Companion to Chapter 1.)

If you use PHStat2, these finishing touches are done for you if you select the Percentage Column output option.

Cell Entries for a Pareto Diagram

If you plan to create a Pareto diagram, enter the heading **Cumulative Pctage** in cell D4 and enter the formula **=C5** in cell D5. Enter the formula **=C6+D5** in cell D6 and copy this formula down through all the category rows of the summary table. Format the column D cell range that contains formulas for percentage display. Adjust the number of decimals displayed and the width of column D as necessary.

If you use Excel 2007, click cell B5 (the first frequency) and select **Home → Sort & Filter** (in the Editing group) **→ Sort Largest to Smallest**. If you are not using Excel 2007, right-click cell A4 and click **Field Settings** in the shortcut menu (**Field**, if using Microsoft Excel 97). In the PivotTable Field dialog box that appears (see Figure E2.4), click **Advanced**. In the PivotTable Field Advanced

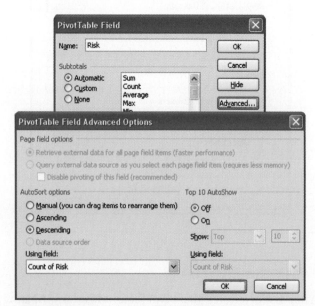

FIGURE E2.4 PivotTable Field and PivotTable Field Advanced Options dialog boxes (Excel 97–2003)

Options dialog box that appears (also see Figure E2.4), select the **Descending** option and **Count of *variable*** from the **Using field** drop-down list. Click **OK** to return to the PivotTable Field dialog box and then click **OK** in that dialog box to return to the worksheet. (These last steps reorder the category rows in the table in descending order.)

If you use PHStat2, these additional entries are done for you if you select the Pareto Diagram output option.

> **Forum** Click the Alternate Techniques link to learn how the COUNTIF function can also be used to selectively count occurrences of individual categories.

E2.2   CREATING CHARTS

You create charts by associating worksheet data with a chart type, which you then customize. To create a chart, you must specify the cell range of the worksheet data, choose the chart type and its subtype, set formatting details such as titles and axis legends, and choose whether to put the chart on its own chart sheet or to embed the chart on a worksheet. Because the process is different for Excel 2007, this section includes passages specific to Excel 97–2003 and Excel 2007.

Many PHStat2 procedures, including One-Way Tables & Charts, include output options that create charts for you.

Creating Charts (97–2003)

To create a chart in Excel versions other than 2007, open to the worksheet containing your unsummarized data and select **Insert → Chart**. This begins the Chart Wizard, a sequence of four dialog boxes that step you through the process of creating a chart. Figure E2.5 shows these dialog boxes for Excel 2003. (Other versions have similar dialog boxes.) To create a chart, make the following entries and choices in the Step dialog boxes.

Step 1   Choose the chart type from either the **Standard Types** or **Custom Types** tab. Most of the charts you create in this text are chart types found in the Standard Types tab.

Step 2   Enter the cell range of the data to be graphed in the **Data Range** tab.[2] For some types of charts, you also enter the cell range or ranges that contain chart labeling information in the **Series** tab. Cell ranges in the Series tab must always be entered with their worksheet names as a formula, in the form =*SheetName*!*CellRange*.

---

[2]*In some rare situations, with older versions of Excel, if you type a simple cell range, you get an error. In those cases, either retype the range using the SheetName/CellRange form discussed in Section E1.3 or point to the cell range.*

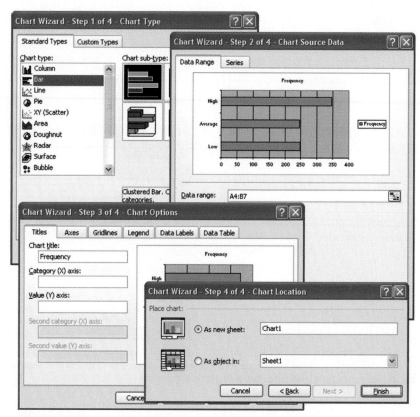

FIGURE E2.5 Chart Wizard dialog boxes (Excel 2003)

Step 3   Enter titles and select customizing options for your chart. Unless overridden specifically in later instructions, use the following settings (for a given chart type, some of these tabs may not be available).

In the **Titles** tab, enter a title and enter axis labels, if appropriate.

In the **Axes** tab, check both the (X) axis and (Y) axis check boxes and select the **Automatic** option under the (X) axis check box.

In the **Gridlines** tab, clear all the check boxes.

In the **Legend** tab, clear the **Show legend** check box.

In the **Data Labels** tab, click the **None** option under the **Data labels** heading.

In the **Data Table** tab, clear the **Show data table** check box.

Step 4   Click the **As new sheet** option to place the chart on its own chart sheet. (This choice creates a better-scaled and better-looking chart that can be more easily printed separately.) Then click **Finish** to create the chart.[3]

If you discover a mistake in your chart after your chart is created, right-click the chart and select **Chart Type, Source Data, Chart Options,** or **Location** to return to versions of the Step 1, Step 2, Step 3, or Step 4 dialog boxes, respectively.

Creating Charts (2007)

To create a chart in Excel 2007, open to the worksheet that contains your unsummarized data. Select the cell range of the data to be charted.[4] If your cell range contains two non-adjacent areas, hold down the Ctrl key as you drag and select each area. Select **Insert** and in the Charts group, click the chart type. From the drop-down gallery that appears, click the chart sub-type you want. To help distinguish sub-types, move the mouse pointer over a sub-type and wait for the sub-type description to appear. In Figure E2.6, the description for the bar chart "clustered bar" sub-type has appeared.

---

[3]*Because the Step 4 dialog box instructions never vary, they are not explicitly listed in the later charting instructions. You should, of course, always click **As New Sheet** and **Finish** in the Step 4 dialog box for every chart you create in Excel 97–2003.*

[4]*If you fail to select a cell range, Excel may try to construct a chart using all the data in your worksheet. For a worksheet such as **Data** in* Mutual Funds.xls, *not selecting a range would lead to a very complex—and worthless—chart that could slow down or even disrupt the operation of your computer.*

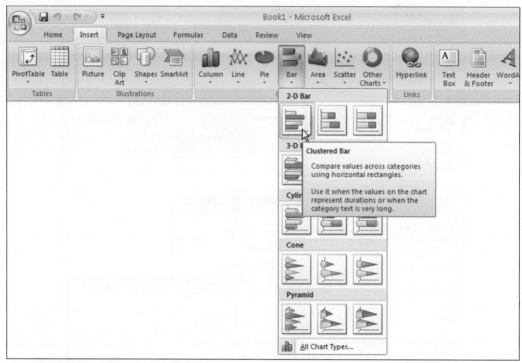

FIGURE E2.6 Selecting a chart sub-type (Excel 2007)

Customize your chart by clicking the chart and selecting the Layout tab of the Chart Tools ribbon group (or PivotChart Tools, if the chart is based on a PivotTable). Review the settings for the members of the Labels and Axes groups in this tab. Unless overridden specifically in later instructions, use the following settings for these items (for a given chart type, some of these items may be disabled and not available):

Chart Title Choose either **Centered Overlay Title** or **Above Chart**.

Axes Titles For the **Primary Horizontal Axis Title**, select **Title Below Axis**. For the **Primary Vertical Axis Title**, select **Rotated Title**. Some charts have secondary axes; for such charts, select **Title Below Axis** as the **Secondary Horizontal Axis Title** and **None** as the **Secondary Vertical Axis Title**.

Data Labels Select **None**.

Data Table Select **None**.

Axes For the **Primary Horizontal Axis Title**, select **Show Left to Right Axis**. For the **Primary Vertical Axis Title**, select **Show Default Axis**. Some charts have secondary axes; for such charts, select **None** as the **Secondary Horizontal Axis Title** and **Show Default Axis** as the **Secondary Vertical Axis Title**.

Gridlines Select **None** for both the **Primary Horizontal Gridlines** and **Primary Vertical Gridlines**. Also select **None** for secondary gridlines, if the chart contains those as well.

Excel 2007 creates charts on worksheets. To move a newly created chart to its own chart sheet (recommended), right-click the chart frame and click **Move Chart** in the shortcut menu that appears. In the Move Chart dialog box that appears, select the **New sheet** option and click **OK**.

Additional Chart Tips

Many charts, especially those created in Excel 97-2003, contain colored backgrounds (typically gray) that you may want to remove if you plan either to print charts or display them through a video projector or on an LCD-type device. To remove the background in an Excel 97-2003 chart, right-click the background and click **Format Plot Area** in the shortcut menu. In the dialog box that appears, click the **None** option of the **Area** group and click **OK**. (This was done for all the charts shown in this book.) To remove the background in Excel 2007, right-click the chart background and select **Layout → Plot Area** and select **None** in the Plot Area gallery.

Occasionally, you may open to a chart sheet and see only part of a (too-large) chart or see a (too-small) chart surrounded by a too-large frame mat. To display an optimally sized chart in Excel 97–2003, open to the chart sheet and press **Esc**. Select **View → Zoom** and then, in the Zoom dialog box, select the **Fit selection** option and click **OK**. To display an optimally sized chart in Excel 2007, use the Zoom slider on the lower right of the Excel window frame or click the chart and then select **Format** and use the items in the Size group.

Finally, if the symbols, captions, and/or legends and titles prove too big or too small for you, you can usually change these elements by right-clicking over them and clicking the shortcut menu choice that contains the word **Format**. For labeling elements, you can use a simpler procedure: Click the element and use the formatting features described in Section E1.4 to change such things as the type size and style. (Most of the charts shown in this text have such elements set to 12 point, boldfaced type.)

E2.3 CREATING BAR AND PIE CHARTS FROM SUMMARY TABLES

You create bar and pie charts from summary tables (not unsummarized data), using Excel charting features. Because this process is different for Excel 2007, this section includes passages specific to Excel 97–2003 and Excel 2007, as well as passages that apply to all versions.

The PHStat2 One-Way Tables & Charts procedure can create bar and pie charts for you and can use either a summary table or unsummarized data.

Creating Bar and Pie Charts (97–2003)

Open to the worksheet that contains your summary table. If your summary table is a PivotTable (like the ones created in Section E2.2), click a cell that is outside your PivotTable.[5] Begin the Chart Wizard and make these entries:

[5]*If you forget to click outside the PivotTable, the Chart Wizard will instantly create a (wrong type of) chart. If this occurs, you can press* **Ctrl+Z** *to undo the chart.*

Step 1 Click the **Standard Types** tab. For a bar chart, click **Bar** as the **Chart type** and then click the first **Chart sub-type** choice, labeled **Clustered Bar** when selected. For a pie chart, click **Pie** as the **Chart type** and then click the first **Chart sub-type** choice, labeled **Pie** when selected.

Step 2 Click the **Data Range** tab and enter the cell range of the category labels and the frequency counts as the **Data range**. If you used the instructions in Section E2.2 to create your summary table, this range will always start with cell A4 and end with a cell in column B. (You do not include the column C cells that contain the percentages.) Click the **Columns** option if it is visible. In some versions of Excel, the model chart shown in the dialog box contains additional boxed labels that you can ignore for now.

Step 3 Click the **Titles** tab. Enter a title as the **Chart title** and, if you are creating a bar chart, enter appropriate values for the **Category (X) axis** and **Value (Y) axis** titles. For a bar chart, click, in turn, the **Axes**, **Gridlines**, **Legend**, **Data Labels**, and **Data Table** tabs and adjust the settings, as discussed in the "Creating Charts (97–2003)" part of Section E2.2 on page 78. For a pie chart, click the **Legend** tab and clear **Show legend** and then click the **Data Labels** tab. If you are using Excel 97 or Excel 2000, click the **Show label and percent** option; otherwise, click **Category name** and **Percentage**.

If the chart created contains the additional boxed labels, such as "Drop Page Fields Here," that you ignored in the Step 2 dialog box, right-click the category drop-down list on the chart sheet (**Risk** in Figure E2.7) and click **Hide PivotChart Field Buttons**. This eliminates the clutter and makes your chart look more like the one shown in Figure 2.4 on page 35.

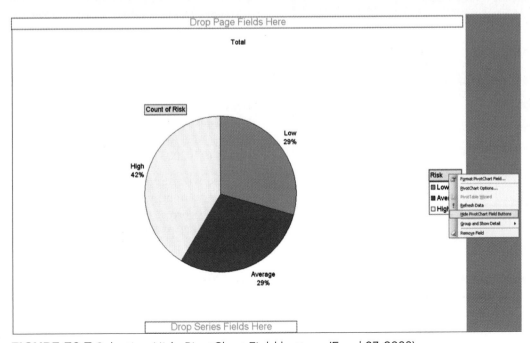

FIGURE E2.7 Selecting Hide PivotChart Field buttons (Excel 97-2003)

EXAMPLE Figure 2.4 Pie Chart for Levels of Risk

To create your own Figure 2.4 pie chart for levels of risk (see page 35), open the Chapter 2.xls workbook to the **Table 2.2** worksheet, click cell D1 (a cell outside the PivotTable), and use the appropriate set of instructions.

Basic Excel 97–2003 Follow the "Creating Bar & Pie Charts (97–2003)" instructions. In **Step 1**, click **Pie** as the **Chart Type** and then click the first chart sub-type choice, labeled as **Pie** when selected. In **Step 2**, enter the cell range **A4:B7** as the **Data Range** in the Step 2 dialog box.

Basic Excel 2007 Follow the "Creating Bar & Pie Charts 2007" instructions, clicking cell A5 before you select **Insert**.

PHStat2 Select **PHStat → Descriptive Statistics → One-Way Tables & Charts**. Click the **Table of Frequencies** option, enter **A4:B7** as the **Freq. Table Cell Range**, and click **First row of table contains labels**. Enter a **Title** and click **Pie Chart**. (You can also click **Bar Chart** and **Pareto Diagram** to create those charts at the same time.)

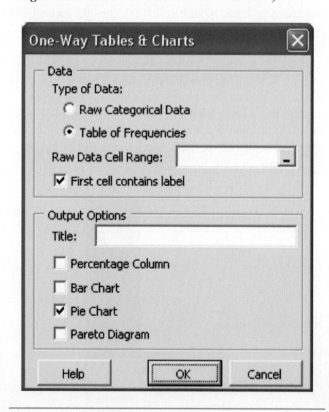

Creating Bar & Pie Charts (2007)

Open to the worksheet that contains your summary table. Click a cell inside your table and then select **Insert**. For a bar chart, click **Column** in the Charts group, and then click **Clustered Column** in the chart gallery. For a pie chart, click **Pie** in the Charts group, and then click **Pie** in the chart

gallery. Adjust chart settings as discussed in the "Creating Charts (2007)" part of Section E2.2 on page 79.

E2.4 CREATING PARETO DIAGRAMS FROM SUMMARY TABLES

You create a Pareto diagram from a summary table by using Excel charting features. To begin, open to the worksheet that contains your summary table. Enter, if necessary, the entries discussed in the "Cell Entries for a Pareto Diagram" part of Section E2.1 (see page 78). Because creating charts differs for Excel 2007, this section includes passages specific to Excel 97–2003 and Excel 2007.

The PHStat2 One-Way Tables & Charts procedure can create a Pareto diagram for you when you select the One-Way Tables & Charts procedure.

Creating a Pareto Diagram (97–2003)

If your worksheet contains a PivotTable summary table (like the ones created in Section E2.2), click a cell that is outside your PivotTable.[6] Begin the Chart Wizard (by selecting **Insert → Chart**) and make these entries:

Step 1 Click the **Custom Types** tab. Click the **Built-in option** and then select **Line - Column on 2 Axes** as the **Chart type**.

Step 2 Click the **Data Range** tab. Enter the cell range of the percentage and cumulative percentage frequencies, without their column headings, in the **Data range** edit box. This range will always start with cell C4 and end with a cell in column D. Click the **Columns** option in the **Series in** group and then click the **Series** tab. Enter as a **formula** the column A cell range that contains the category labels as the **Category (X) axis labels**. Leave the **Second category (X) axis labels** box blank, if it appears.

Step 3 Click the **Titles** tab. Enter a title as the **Chart title**, the name of the variable in the **Category (X) axis** edit box, and **Percentage** in the **Value (Y) axis** edit box. Leave the other two boxes blank. Click, in turn, the **Gridlines**, **Legend**, **Data Labels**, and **Data Table** tabs and use the formatting settings given in the "Creating Charts (97–2003)" part of Section E2.2 on page 78.

The wizard creates a Pareto diagram that contains a secondary (right) y-axis scale that improperly extends past 100%. To correct this error, right-click that axis (you will see the ToolTip[7] **Secondary Value Axis** when your mouse is properly positioned) and click **Format Axis** in the short-

---

[6]*If you forget to click outside the PivotTable, the Chart Wizard instantly creates a chart of the wrong type. If this occurs, you can press* **Ctrl+Z** *to undo the chart.*

[7]*ToolTips are pop-up balloons that display informational messages about onscreen objects.*

cut menu. In the **Scale** tab of the Format Axis dialog box, change the **Maximum** value to **1** and click **OK**.

The Pareto Diagram output option of the PHStat2 One-Way Tables & Charts procedure makes this correction for you.

Creating a Pareto Diagram (2007)

Select the cell range of the data to be charted. (This range will begin with cell C4, if you used the "Cell Entries for a Pareto Diagram" instructions in Section E2.1.) Select **Insert → Column** (in the Charts group) and select the first sub-type, identified as **Clustered Column** when you move the mouse pointer over that sub-type and pause. Select **Format** and select the cumulative percentage series from the drop-down in the Current Selection group. Then select **Format Selection** (from the same group) and in the Format Data Series dialog box select the **Secondary Axis** in the Series Options panel and click **Close**. With the cumulative percentage series still selected in the Current Selection group, select **Design → Change Chart Type**, and in the Change Chart Type gallery, select the line chart identified as **Line with Markers** and click **OK**.

If your chart contains extraneous plots—for example, a plot of percentage frequencies—delete this plot one series at a time by doing the following: Select **Format** and then select an extraneous series from the drop-down in the Current Selection group. Select **Design → Select Data**. In the Select Data Source dialog box (see Figure E2.8), select the extraneous **Legend Entries** series (**Percentage** in Figure E2.8) and click **Remove** and then **OK**.

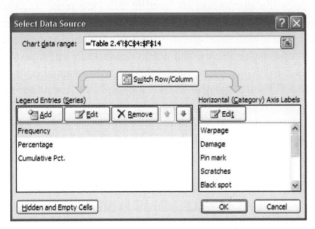

FIGURE E2.8 The Select Data Source dialog box (Excel 2007)

Relocate your chart to a chart sheet and customize your chart, using the instructions in "Creating a Chart (Excel 2007)" in Section E.2.2. If your chart has a secondary (right) y-axis scale that improperly extends past 100%, right-click the axis and click **Format Axis** in the shortcut menu. In the **Scale** tab of the Format Axis dialog box, change the value in the **Maximum** edit box to **1** and click **Close**.

EXAMPLE Figure 2.5 Pareto Diagram

To create your own Figure 2.5 Pareto diagram (see page 37) from the Table 2.4 keyboard defects summary table on page 36, first open the `Chapter 2.xls` workbook to the **Table 2.4** worksheet, a PivotTable version of Table 2.4. Click cell D2 (a cell outside the PivotTable) and use the appropriate set of instructions.

Basic Excel 97–2003 Use the instructions of the preceding "Creating a Pareto Diagram (97–2003)" section. In Step 2 of the Chart Wizard, enter **C4:D14** as the **Data Range** in the Data Range tab and enter the formula **=ParetoData!A5:A14** in the **Category (X) axis labels** box in the Series tab.

Basic Excel 2007 Select the cell range **C4:F14**. (Although this range includes columns you do not need, this helps Excel make a good guess about the type of chart you want.) Follow the instructions of the preceding "Creating a Pareto Diagram (2007)" section. Because your chart range includes the percentage frequency column, you will have to delete this series using the process discussed in those instructions.

PHStat2 Select **PHStat → Descriptive Statistics → One-Way Tables & Charts**. Click the **Table of Frequencies** option, enter **A4:B14** as the **Freq. Table Cell Range**, and click **First row of table contains labels**. Enter a **Title** and click **Pareto Diagram**. (You can also click **Bar Chart** and **Pie Chart** to create those charts at the same time.)

E2.5   CREATING AN ORDERED ARRAY

You create an ordered array by using Excel sorting features. Because this process differs for Excel 2007, this section includes passages specific to Excel 97–2003 and Excel 2007.

Creating an Ordered Array (97–2003)

Select the data to be sorted and then select **Data → Sort**. (In the Sort dialog box (shown below, similar for all versions, but enhanced in Excel 2007), select the column by which to sort from the **Sort by** drop-down list and click either the first **Ascending** or **Descending** option button. (In the dialog box, a column named Price has been selected as an example.) You then click the **Header row** option and **OK** button to complete the sort.

Creating an Ordered Array (2007)

Select the data to be sorted and then select **Home → Sort & Filter** (in the Editing group) → **Sort Smallest to Largest**.

E2.6   CREATING STEM-AND-LEAF DISPLAYS

You create stem-and-leaf displays by using the PHStat2 Stem-and-Leaf Display procedure or by manually creating the stems and leaves in worksheet cells. If you choose to manually create a stem-and-leaf display, you will find that sorting your data to create an ordered array (see previous section) will simplify your task.

Using PHStat2 Stem-and-Leaf Display

Open to the worksheet containing the data to be plotted. Select **PHStat → Descriptive Statistics → Stem-and-Leaf Display**. Enter the cell range of the data to be plotted as the **Variable Cell Range**. Click **Select the First cell contains label**. *Always* select the **Autocalculate stem unit** option, enter a **Title**, and click **OK**. (**Summary Statistics** is automatically checked for you.)

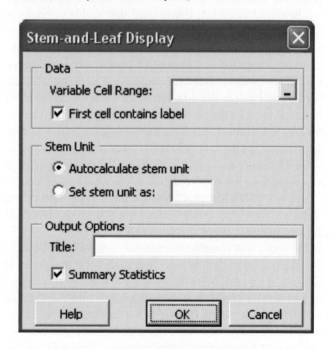

Manually Creating Stems and Leaves

Apply the discussion of Section 2.2 (see page 41) that describes the manual process of creating stems and leaves. Use a new worksheet and use two columns, one for the stems and one for the leaves. You need to enter each leaf as a label value. To do this, begin your cell entry with an apostrophe (') and follow that apostrophe with the digits that form the leaf. As you enter each digit, you may also want to add a space after each digit for greater readability. For example, to enter a leaf that contains 2, 2, 3, and 7, enter **'2 2 3 7**.

E2.7   CREATING FREQUENCY DISTRIBUTIONS AND HISTOGRAMS

You create frequency distributions and histograms from unsummarized data by using the ToolPak Histogram procedure or the PHStat2 Histogram & Polygons procedure. Both procedures require that you first translate your class groupings into what Excel calls bins (explained later in this section).

Unlike the frequency distribution discussion in Chapter 2, you typically include frequency, percentage frequency, and cumulative percentage frequencies as columns of one table and not as separate tables, as shown in Tables 2.8, 2.10, and 2.13 on pages 45, 47, and 48. Also, unlike what is done in Chapter 2, in Excel, you create frequency distributions for individual categories, one at a time (growth funds *or* value funds, for example) and not frequency distributions that contain two categories (for example, growth *and* value funds). To create multiple category tables, such as Tables 2.8, 2.10, and 2.13, you must combine columns from the individual tables using copy and paste operations.

If you use the ToolPak procedure, you face a final complication of having to correct several errors that the procedure makes in the frequency distribution and histogram. If you have data already summarized in a frequency distribution, you should skip ahead to Section E2.8, which explains how to create a histogram from that frequency distribution, using Excel charting features.

Translating Class Grouping into Bins

When summarizing numerical data in Microsoft Excel, you use bins which have implied ranges of values, and not class groupings, which have well-defined boundary values. A **bin** is the set of values that are less than or equal to the current bin value and that are greater than the previous bin value, which must be a lesser value. To create a frequency distribution, you must translate your class groupings into a set of bin values and enter those bin values on the same worksheet as your unsummarized data.

In Chapter 2, Table 2.7 (and Tables 2.8 through 2.11) uses class groupings in a form that enables you to make the translation from class to bin. When you express class groupings in the Table 2.7 form *valueA but less than valueB*, you can create nearly equivalent bins, as Table E2.1 illustrates.

TABLE E2.1 Class Grouping and Bins

Table 2.7 Classes	The Nearly Equivalent Bins
0 but less than 5	4.99
5 but less than 10	9.99
10 but less than 15	14.99
15 but less than 20	19.99
20 but less than 25	24.99
25 but less than 30	29.99
30 but less than 35	34.99
35 but less than 40	39.99
40 but less than 45	44.99

The first bin value always represents a grouping with no explicit lower boundary (other than negative infinity). Thus, the first bin can never have a midpoint. (You may have noticed in this chapter that in the charts in which mid-

points are used as labels, the first bin is labeled with — and not with a midpoint.)

Sometimes you work with class groupings in the form "all values from *valueA* to *valueB*," as in this set of classes: 0.0 through 4.9, 5.0 through 9.9, 10.0 through 14.9, and 15.0 through 19.9. In such cases, you can approximate each class grouping by choosing a bin value just above the *valueB* value for the class groupings. For example, the numbers 4.99, 9.99, 14.99, and 19.99 would create bins that approximate the four class groupings, assuming that all data values were measured in units no smaller than tenths. (While the last digit of the bin values could be any digit other than zero, using 9 as the last digit is a standard practice.)

When you have defined your set of bin values, enter them into a new column of the worksheet that contains your unsummarized data. Make sure the first cell in that column contains the column heading "Bins."

Using the ToolPak Histogram Procedure

To create a frequency distribution and histogram, open to the worksheet that contains the unsummarized data and verify that bin values have been placed in their own column. Begin the Analysis ToolPak add-in and select **Histogram** from the **Analysis Tools** list and then click **OK**. In the Histogram dialog box (see Figure E2.9), enter the cell range of the data to be summarized as the **Input Range**. Enter the cell range of the bin values (including the cell containing the heading "Bins") as the **Bin Range**.[8] Click **Labels** to indicate that the first cells of the Input Range and Bin Range contain a label. Select the **New Worksheet Ply** option, click **Cumulative Percentage**, and click **Chart Output** to create a histogram and click **OK**.

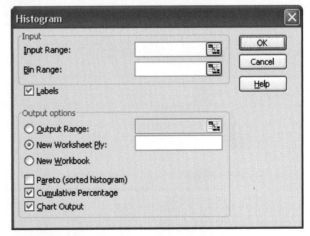

FIGURE E2.9 The Data Analysis Histogram dialog box

---

[8]*If you leave the **Bin Range** blank, the procedure creates a set of bin values for you. However, the better practice is to supply your set of bin values as these instructions require you to do.*

The procedure creates a frequency distribution and histogram together on a new worksheet.

Editing and Enhancing the Frequency Distribution

The frequency distribution you create will improperly contain an open-ended bin labeled "More" and contain some errors in column heading formatting. To eliminate the "More" class, first manually add the More frequency count to the count of the preceding class and set the cumulative percentage of the preceding class to 100%. Then, select the entire row containing the "More" row, select **Edit → Delete**, and in the Delete dialog box, select the **Shift cells up** option and click **OK**.

Next, enhance your frequency distribution. Select a cell in row 1 and then select **Insert → Rows**. In the "new" row 1, enter a title for the frequency distribution. Then add a column for the percentage frequency by selecting column C and then selecting **Insert → Columns**. In the new column C, enter the heading **Percentage** in cell C2. Enter the formula =**B3/SUM(B:B)** in cell C3 and copy the formula down the column through the rest of the frequency distribution. Format column C for percentage display to complete the column. Finally, add a column for midpoints. Select cell E2 and enter the heading **Midpoints**. Then use the cells in column E, starting with cell E3, to enter your midpoints. If your cell E3 entry is --- (as it typically will be), enter the value '--- (with a leading apostrophe) to avoid an error.

If you use the PHStat2 Histogram & Polygons procedure, these edits and enhancements are done for you if you click the appropriate output options.

Correcting the Histogram

As you correct your frequency distribution, your histogram also changes, and the bar representing the in-error "More" group disappears. At this point, the histogram still contains the errors shown in Figure E2.10: Gaps between the bars correspond to the class intervals in the histogram, the bins are labeled with their maximum bin values and not with their midpoint values, and the secondary y-axis scale exceeds 100%.

To correct these errors, you need to first relocate your histogram to its own chart sheet in order to more easily work with the histogram. Right-click the background area of the histogram and click **Location** (97–2003) or **Move Chart** (2007) in the shortcut menu. In the dialog box that appears, select the **As new sheet** option (97–2003) or **New sheet** (2007) and click **OK**. The histogram now appears (much larger) in its own chart sheet, and you can continue with the following instructions to correct the histogram.

To eliminate the gaps between bars, right-click inside one of the histogram bars. (You will see a ToolTip that begins with **Series 'Frequency'** when your mouse is properly positioned.) Click **Format Data Series** in the shortcut menu to display the Format Data Series dialog box. If you use Excel 97–2003, click the **Options** tab, change the value of **Gap width** to **0**, and click **OK**. If you

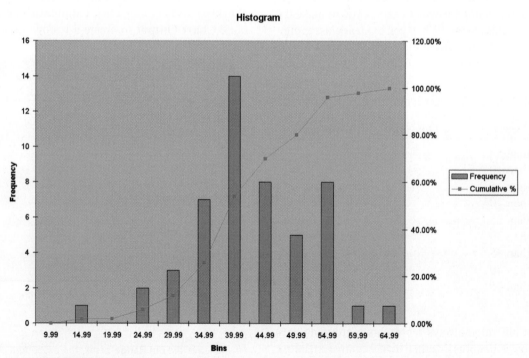

FIGURE E2.10 Histogram before applying corrections (Figure 2.8 on page 49 shows the corrected histogram.)

use Excel 2007, move the **Gap Width** slider to **No Gap** in the **Series Options** panel of this dialog box.

   To change the labels for the bins, enter midpoint values in column E. Right-click the tinted background of the chart. (You will see the ToolTip **Plot Area** when your mouse is properly positioned.) Click **Source Data** (Excel 97–2003) or **Select Data** (Excel 2007) in the shortcut menu. If you use Excel 97–2003, select the **Series** tab in the Source Data dialog box and enter the cell range of the midpoints as a formula, in the form =*SheetName*!*CellRange*, in the **Category (X) axis labels** box. Then delete the entry for the **Second category(X) axis labels** and click **OK**. If you use Excel 2007, click the **Edit** button under the **Horizontal (Categories) Axis Labels** heading in the Select Data Source dialog box. In the Axis Labels dialog box, enter the cell range of the midpoints as a formula, in the form =*SheetName*!*CellRange*, and click **OK**. (This range should start with the first midpoint value and not with the midpoint column heading). Click **OK** a second time (in the original dialog box) to complete the task.

   To rescale the secondary Y-axis, right-click on the secondary (right) Y-axis. (You will see a ToolTip that includes the words **Secondary** and **Axis** when your mouse is properly positioned.) Click **Format Axis** in the shortcut menu. If you use Excel 97–2003, change the **Maximum** in the **Scale** tab of the Format Axis dialog box to **1** and click **OK**. If you use Excel 2007, select the **Fixed** option for **Maximum** and enter **1** as the maximum value in the **Axis Options** panel of the Format Axis dialog box, and then click **OK**.

   If you use the PHStat2 Histogram & Polygons procedure, these corrections are done for you, although PHStat2 keeps the histogram on the same worksheet as the frequency distribution.

EXAMPLE Three-Year Annualized Return
for Growth Funds

To create a frequency distribution that combines the best of Tables 2.8, 2.10, and 2.13, and your own Figure 2.9 Panel A histogram (see page 49) for the three-year annualized return for growth funds, first open the `Mutual Funds.xls` workbook to the **Growth** worksheet. Column J of this worksheet contains bin values that translate the class groupings used throughout Chapter 2, thereby eliminating the need for you to do this translation yourself. (Column K contains midpoint values, used by the PHStat2 procedure.) Continue with the appropriate set of instructions.

Basic Excel Use the ToolPak Histogram procedure. Enter **H1:H839** as the **Input Range** and **J1:J10** as the **Bin Range** in the Histogram dialog box. Click **Labels**, select

the **New Worksheet Ply** option, click **Cumulative Percentage**, and click **Chart Output**. Click **OK** to create a frequency distribution and histogram together on a new worksheet. Apply the changes discussed in "Editing and Enhancing the Frequency Distribution" and "Correcting the Histogram," starting on page 86. (If you successfully make these changes, the last row of the frequency distribution will be row 11.)

PHStat2 Select **PHStat → Descriptive Statistics → Histogram & Polygons**. Enter **H1:H839** as the **Variable Cell Range**, **J1:J10** as the **Bins Cell Range** and **K1:K9** as the **Midpoints Cell Range**. Click **First cell in each range contains label** and select the **Single Group Variable** option. Enter a **Title** and click **OK**. (**Histogram** is already checked for you.)

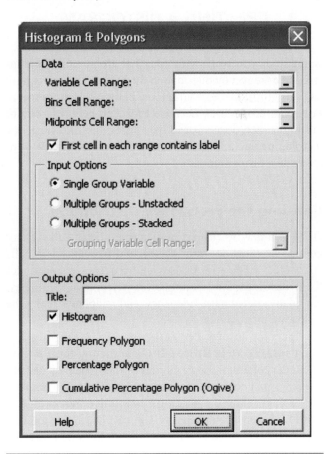

Enhancing the Histogram

You can enhance the histogram created by the ToolPak and PHStat2 procedures in several ways to improve the presentation quality of the histogram. You can change the generic title and axis labels and/or delete the cumulative percentage plot that is superimposed over the histogram. To change the generic title, click the title to make a halo appear around the title. In the formula bar, enter a better title and press the **Enter** key. Then follow a similar process to change each of the axis legends. To delete the cumulative percentage plot, click the cumulative percentage plot to highlight the plot and then press the **Delete** key. Then click the (now unnecessary) chart legend box to the right of the histogram (a halo appears around the box) and press **Delete** to eliminate this, too. Also consider removing the chart background and making other changes, if appropriate, as described in the "Additional Chart Tips" part of Section E2.2 on page 80.

> **Forum** Click the ALTERNATIVE METHODS link to learn the Excel technique you can use to create a frequency distribution that updates itself automatically when the underlying data are changed.

E2.8   CREATING A HISTOGRAM FROM SUMMARIZED DATA

Sometimes you work with data that are already summarized in a frequency distribution. In such cases, you cannot use the ToolPak Histogram or PHStat2 Histogram & Polygons procedures because those procedures require unsummarized data. Instead, you first enter the frequency distribution into a worksheet and then use the Chart Wizard to create a histogram.

Entering the Frequency Distribution

Open to a new worksheet and enter a title in cell A1 and column headings for your classes and frequencies in cells A2 and B2. Enter your classes and frequency counts under these headings. Add columns for percentage frequency, cumulative percentage frequency, and midpoints, using the following instructions.

Enter the heading **Percentage** in cell C2. Enter the formula **=B3/SUM(B:B)** in cell C3 and copy the formula down the column through the rest of the frequency distribution. Format column C for percentage display to complete the column. Enter the heading **Cumulative Percentage** in cell D2. Enter the formula **=C3** in cell D3. Enter the formula **=D3+C4** in cell D4 and copy the formula down the column through the rest of the frequency distribution. Enter the heading **Midpoints** in cell E2. Then use the cells in column E, starting with cell E3, to enter your midpoints. If your cell E3 entry is --- (as it typically will be), enter that value **'---** (with a leading apostrophe) to avoid an error.

Creating the Histogram (97–2003)

Open to the worksheet that contains your frequency distribution and use the Chart Wizard. Make these entries in the Chart Wizard dialog boxes:

Step 1   Click the **Standard Types** tab. Click **Column** as the **Chart type** and then click the first **Chart sub-type** icon, captioned **Clustered Column** when selected.

Step 2   Click the **Data Range** tab. Enter the cell range of the frequencies as the **Data range** and click the **Columns** option in the **Series in** group. Click the **Series** tab. Enter the cell range of the midpoints (as a formula in the form =*SheetName*!*CellRange*) in the **Category (X) axis labels** box.

Step 3   Click the **Titles** tab. Enter a title as the **Chart title**, **Midpoints** as the **Category (X) axis** title, and **Frequency** as the **Value (Y) axis** title. Use the formatting settings for **Axes**, **Gridlines**, **Legend**, **Data Labels**, and **Data Table** tabs that are given in the "Creating Charts (97–2003)" part of Section E2.2 on page 78.

To eliminate the gaps between the bars of the histogram the wizard created, right-click one of the histogram bars. (You will see a ToolTip that begins with **Series 'Frequency'** when your mouse is properly positioned.) Click **Format Data Series** in the shortcut menu. In the Format Data Series dialog box, click the **Options** tab, change the value of **Gap width** to **0**, and click **OK**.

Creating the Histogram (2007)

Select the cell range that is the column that contains your frequencies. Then select **Insert → Column** and click the **Clustered Column** gallery choice. Right-click the chart that appears and click **Select Data** in the shortcut menu. In the Select Data Source dialog box, click the **Edit** button under the **Horizontal (Categories) Axis Labels** heading, enter the cell range of the midpoints as a formula in the form =*SheetName*!*CellRange*, and click **OK**. Click **OK** in the Select Data Source dialog box to complete this task. (This range should start with the first midpoint value and not with the midpoint column heading). Relocate your chart to a chart sheet and customize your chart, using the instructions in "Creating Charts (2007)" in Section E.2.2 on page 79.

E2.9   CREATING POLYGONS

You create polygons by modifying a frequency distribution previously created using the instructions from Section E2.7 or Section E2.8, and then using Excel charting features. (Because charting is different in Excel 2007, this section includes passages specific to Excel 97–2003 and Excel 2007.)

The PHStat2 Histogram & Polygons procedure can create polygons for you from either an unmodified frequency distribution or unsummarized data.

Modifying the Frequency Distribution

To modify a frequency distribution for creating a polygon, open to the worksheet containing the frequency distribution. Right-click **row 3** (that is, right-click the 3 row number legend at the left of the worksheet) and click **Insert** in the shortcut menu. Enter **0** in the new cells **B3**, **C3**, and **D3**. Then enter **0** in the column B and C cells that are in the first empty row under your frequency distribution.

EXAMPLE Figure 2.12 Cumulative Percentage Polygons (Part I)

To start the process of creating your own Figure 2.12 cumulative percentage polygons for the cost of restaurant meals at city and suburban restaurants (page 52), open the `Restaurants.xls` workbook and use the appropriate set of instructions.

Basic Excel Open to the **CityFrequencies** worksheet. Right-click **row 3** (that is, right-click the 3 row number legend at the left of the worksheet) and click **Insert** in the shortcut menu. Enter **0** in the new cells **B3**, **C3**, and **D3** as well as in cells **B16** and **C16**. Open to the **SuburbanFrequencies** worksheet and make the same modifications.

PHStat2 You do not need to make any modifications to your frequency distribution if you are using the PHStat2 **Histogram & Polygons** procedure. (The procedure makes these modifications for you.)

Creating Polygons (97–2003)

With your workbook opened to the modified frequency distribution, begin the Chart Wizard and make these entries in the Chart Wizard dialog boxes:

Step 1 Click the **Standard Types** tab and then click **Line** as the **Chart type**. Click the first choice in the second row of **Chart sub-type** choices, labeled **Line with markers displayed at each data value** when selected.

Step 2 Click the **Data Range** tab. As the **Data range**, enter a cell range that contains both the leading and trailing zero entries added to the worksheet earlier. (This cell range will begin in row 3.) For a frequency polygon, enter the column B cell range that contains the zeros. For a percentage polygon, enter the column C cell range that contains the zeros. For a cumulative percentage polygon, enter the column D cell range that contains the initial zero. Click the **Columns** option in the **Series in** group. Click the **Series** tab. Enter a column E cell range that begins with cell E3 (as a formula in the form *=SheetName!CellRange*) in the

Category (X) axis labels box. For either a frequency or percentage polygon, enter the column E cell range that ends with the row that contains the trailing zero (the ending cell will be blank in column E). For a cumulative percentage polygon, enter the column E cell range that ends with the last entry in column E. Then enter a self-descriptive legend value to replace the default **Series 1** in the **Name** box.

Step 3 Click the **Titles** tab. Enter a title as the **Chart title** and appropriate values for the **Category (X) axis** and **Value (Y) axis** titles. Use the formatting settings for **Axes**, **Gridlines**, **Data Labels**, and **Data Table** tabs that are given in the "Creating Charts (97–2003)" part of Section E2.2 (see page 78). Click the **Legend** tab and click **Show legend**.

Additional data series can be added to the polygon to produce several polygons on one chart, similar to Figures 2.10 through Figures 2.13 on pages 50–52. With your workbook opened to your chart, select **Chart ➔ Add Data**. In the Add Data dialog box, enter the cell range of the new data series as a formula in the form *=Sheetname!CellRange* and click **OK**. If the Paste Special dialog box appears, select the **New series** and **Columns** options and click **OK**.

Creating Polygons (2007)

With your workbook opened to the modified frequency distribution, select **Insert ➔ Line** and click the **Line with markers** gallery choice. Right-click the chart that appears and click **Select Data** in the shortcut menu. In the Select Data Source dialog box, click the **Edit** button under the **Horizontal (Categories) Axis Labels** heading. In the Axis Labels dialog box, enter the cell range of the midpoints (not including the midpoints column heading) as a formula in the form *=SheetName!CellRange* and click **OK**. Click **OK** a second time (in the original dialog box) to complete the task.

Relocate your chart to a chart sheet and customize your chart using the instructions in "Creating Charts (2007)" in Section E.2.2 on page 79. If you plan to have more than one data series, select **Show Legend at Right** and not **None** (as Section E2.2 states) for **Legend**.

Additional data series can be added to the polygon to produce several polygons on one chart, similar to Figures 2.10 through Figures 2.13. With your workbook opened to your chart, right-click the chart and click **Select Data** in the shortcut menu. In the Edit Data Source dialog box, click **Add** and enter the cell range of the new data series as a formula in the form *=Sheetname!CellRange* and click **OK**. (This cell range should exclude the column heading cell.) Click **OK** a second time in the original dialog box to complete the task.

EXAMPLE Figure 2.12 Cumulative Percentage Polygons (Part II)

Having completed the appropriate Part I instructions (see page 89), continue with the appropriate set of instructions.

Basic Excel (97–2003) Begin the Chart Wizard. Enter **D3:D15** as the **Data Range** and click the **Columns** option in the **Series in** group in the **Data Range** tab of the Step 2 dialog box. In the **Series** tab of the same dialog box, enter **=CityFrequencies!E3:E15** as in the **Category (X) axis labels**.

After you complete the wizard, select **Chart →Add Data**. In the Add Data dialog box, enter **=SuburbanFrequencies!E3:E15** as the **Range** and click **OK**. (If the Paste Special dialog box appears, select the **New series** and **Columns** options and click **OK**.)

Basic Excel 2007 Select cell range **D3:D15** and use the preceding "Creating Polygons (2007)" instructions. Enter **=CityFrequencies!E3:E15** as the cell range for the midpoints.

PHStat2 Open to the **Data** worksheet. Because PHStat2 creates frequency distributions, histograms, and polygons in one step, you will be using a procedure similar to the one

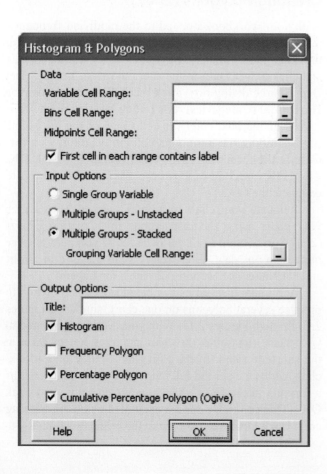

in the example for Section E2.7. Select **PHStat →Descriptive Statistics → Histogram & Polygons**. Enter **G1:G101** as the **Variable Cell Range, H1:H13** as the **Bins Cell Range**, and **I1:I12** as the **Midpoints Cell Range**. Click **First cell in each range contains label**, click **Multiple Groups - Stacked**, and enter **A1:A101** as the **Grouping Variable Cell Range**. Enter a **Title** and click **Percentage Polygon** and **Cumulative Percentage Polygon (Ogive)**. (**Histogram** is already checked for you.) Click **OK** to create the worksheets and chart sheets.

E2.10 CREATING CONTINGENCY TABLES

You use Excel PivotTable features to create a contingency table from the unsummarized data of two categorical variables. You create a contingency table by using a process almost identical to the process of creating a PivotTable summary table discussed in Section E2.1 on page 76. Because this process differs for Excel 2007, this section includes passages specific to Excel 97–2003 and Excel 2007.

The PHStat2 Two-Way Tables & Charts procedure can create a contingency table for you, and, optionally, a side-by-side chart (see Section E2.11).

Creating a Contingency Table (97–2003)

Begin with the instructions in "Starting a PivotTable (97–2003)" in Section E2.1. When you get to the Step 3 instructions, modify them as follows. In the Layout dialog box in Step 3, first drag the label of the first variable to be summarized and drop it in the ROW area. Drag a second copy of this same label and drop it in the DATA area. (The label changes to **Count of variable name.**) Then drag the label of the second variable and drop it in the COLUMN area. In the PivotTable Options dialog box, also in Step 3, verify that both **Grand total for columns** and **Grand totals for rows** are checked (they should be) and that you have entered **0** as the **For empty cells, show** value. (Excel 97 does not contain this options dialog box.)

Creating a Contingency Table (2007)

Begin with the instructions in "Starting a PivotTable (97–2003)" in Section E2.1. When you get to the instructions for using the PivotTable Field List task pane, modify them as follows. In the PivotTable Field List task pane, drag the label of the variable to be summarized and drop it in the **Row Labels** area. Drag a second copy of this same label and drop it in the Σ **Values** area. (This second label changes to **Count of variable name**.) Then drag the label of the second variable and drop it in the **Column Labels** area. When you later right-click the PivotTable, click **Table Options** in the shortcut menu. In the Total & Filters tab of the PivotTable Options dialog box, verify that both **Show grand total for columns** and **Show grand totals for rows** are checked. (Remember to also click the **Layout & Format** tab, check **For empty cells show**, and enter **0** as its value, as stated in the Section E2.1 instructions.)

EXAMPLE Table 2.14 Contingency Table

To create a PivotTable version of Table 2.14 on page 55 for fund objective and risk from your PivotTable, open the Mutual Funds.xls workbook to the **Data** worksheet and use the appropriate set of instructions.

Basic Excel 97–2003 Follow the instructions in "Creating a Contingency Table (97–2003)." In the Chart Wizard Step 2 dialog box, enter **A1:F839** as the **Range**. In the Layout dialog box of Step 3, drag the **Objective** variable label and drop it in the ROW area. Drag a second copy of this same label and drop it in the DATA area. (The second label changes to **Count of Objective** when you drop it in the DATA area.) Drag the **Risk** variable label and drop it in the COLUMN area.

When you complete the PivotTable Wizard, open to the worksheet that contains the PivotTable and click a cell outside the PivotTable. Begin the Chart Wizard and use the "Creating a Side-by-Side Chart (97–2003)" instructions of Section E2.11.

Basic Excel 2007 Follow the instructions in "Creating a Contingency Table (2007)." In the PivotTable Field List task pane, drag the **Objective** variable label and drop it in the **Row Labels** area. Drag a second copy of this same label and drop it in the Σ **Values** area. (This second label changes to **Count of variable name**.) Then drag the **Risk** variable label and drop it in the **Column Labels** area. When you complete your PivotTable, use the "Creating a Side-by-Side Chart (2007)" instructions of Section E2.11.

PHStat2 Select **PHStat → Descriptive Statistics → Two-Way Tables & Charts**. In the Two-Way Tables & Charts dialog box (see the top of the next column), enter B1:B839 as the **Row Variable Cell Range** and enter F1:F839 as the **Column Variable Cell Range**. Click **First cell in each range contains label**, enter a **Title**, and optionally click **Side-by-Side Bar Chart**. Click **OK** to produce the PivotTable and chart.

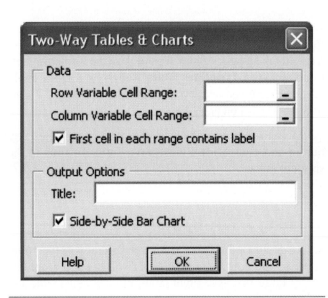

E2.11 CREATING SIDE-BY-SIDE CHARTS

You use Excel charting features to create a side-by-side chart from a contingency table of two categorical variables. Because Excel charting is different in Excel 2007, this section includes passages specific to Excel 97–2003 and Excel 2007

PHStat2 Two-Way Tables & Charts procedure creates a side-by-side chart for you when you click the Side-by-Side Chart output option.

Creating a Side-by-Side Chart (97–2003)

To create a side-by-side chart, open to the worksheet containing the contingency table. If you created a contingency table that is a PivotTable, first click a cell that is outside the PivotTable.[9] Begin the Chart Wizard and make these entries:

Step 1 Click **Bar** from the **Standard Types Chart type** box and leave the first **Chart sub-type** selected.

Step 2 If you are using a PivotTable, click the PivotTable when the **Data range** box is selected, to have Excel fill in the proper cell range. If you are using a manually entered contingency table, enter the rectangular range that excludes the total row and the total column but that includes the row and column headings.

Step 3 Click the **Titles** tab. Enter a title as the **Chart title** and appropriate values for the **Category (X) axis** and **Value (Y) axis** titles. (Unlike other charts, Excel considers the horizontal axis to be the *Value (Y) axis* and the vertical

---

[9]*If you forget to click outside the PivotTable, the Chart Wizard instantly creates a (wrong) chart. If this occurs, you can press* **Ctrl+Z** *to undo the chart.*

axis of this chart to be the *Category (X) axis*, which is different from what you might otherwise expect.) Click the **Legend** tab and click **Show legend**. Use the formatting settings for **Axes**, **Gridlines**, **Data Labels**, and **Data Table** tabs that are given in the "Creating Charts (97–2003)" part of Section E2.2 on page 78.

If field buttons appear on the chart, right-click any button and click **Hide PivotChart Field Buttons** in the shortcut menu.

Creating a Side-by-Side Chart (2007)

To create a side-by-side chart, open to the worksheet that contains the contingency table. If you created a contingency table that is a PivotTable, click a cell inside the PivotTable; otherwise, select the cell range of the contingency table, including row and column headings, but excluding the total row and total column.

Select **Insert ➔ Bar** and click the **Clustered Bar** gallery choice. If your chart contains reversed row and column variables and is not based on a PivotTable, right-click the chart and click Select Data in the shortcut menu. In the Select Data Source dialog box, click **Switch Row/Column** and then click **OK**. If your chart has reversed variables and is based on a PivotTable, you have to reorder your variables in the PivotTable in order to get the correct chart. Finish by relocating your chart to a chart sheet and customizing your chart, using the instructions in "Creating Charts (Excel 2007)" in Section E.2.2 on page 79, with this exception: After you click **Legend**, select **Show Legend at Right**.

EXAMPLE Figure 2.14 Side-by-Side Chart

If you are using PHStat2 to create your own Figure 2.14 side-by-side bar chart for fund objective and risk (page 56), first open to the **Data** worksheet of the `Mutual Funds.xls` workbook. Otherwise, first create a PivotTable version of Table 2.14, as is done in the example in Section E2.10, and open your workbook to that PivotTable. Continue by using the appropriate set of instructions.

Basic Excel 97–2003 Follow the "Creating a Side-by-Side Chart (97–2003)" instructions from this section.

Basic Excel 2007 Follow the "Creating a Side-by-Side Chart (2007)" instructions from this section.

PHStat2 Use the PHStat2 instructions for the example in Section 2.10. Click the **Side-by-Side Chart** output option before clicking **OK**.

E2.12 CREATING SCATTER PLOTS

You use Excel charting features to create scatter plots. To create a scatter plot, open to the worksheet that contains the columns for the two numerical variables you wish to analyze. Your variables should be arranged *X* variable first, then *Y* variable, reading left-to-right. (If your data are arranged first *Y* and then *X*, cut and paste the *Y* variable column so it appears to the right of the *X* variable column.) Because charting has been changed in Excel 2007, continue with the appropriate set of instructions.

You can use the Scatter Diagram output option of the PHStat2 Simple Linear Regression procedure (see the Excel Companion to Chapter 13) if you want PHStat2 to create a scatter plot for you.

Creating a Scatter Plot (97–2003)

Continue by beginning the Chart Wizard and make these entries:

Step 1 Click **XY (Scatter)** from the **Standard Types Chart type** box and leave the first **Chart sub-type** selected.

Step 2 Enter the cell range of the two variables in the **Data range** box and select the **Columns** option. If the two variables are in non-adjacent columns, first type or point to the cell range of the first variable, then type a comma, then type or point to the cell range of the second variable, and then press **Enter**. Do not make any entries in the **Series** tab of this dialog box.

Step 3 Click the **Titles** tab. Enter a title as the **Chart title** and enter appropriate values for the **Value (X) axis** and **Value (Y) axis** titles. Click, in turn, the **Axes**, **Gridlines**, **Legend**, and **Data Labels** tabs and use the formatting settings given in the "Creating Charts (97–2003)" part of Section E2.2 on page 78.

Creating a Scatter Plot (2007)

Continue by selecting the cell range of the *X* and *Y* variables. Then select **Insert ➔ Scatter** and click the **Scatter with only Markers** gallery choice. Finish by relocating your chart to a chart sheet and customizing your chart using the instructions in "Creating Charts (2007)" in Section E.2.2.

EXAMPLE Figure 2.15 Scatter Plot

To create your own Figure 2.15 scatter plot of the cost of a fast-food hamburger meal and the cost of two movie tickets (page 59), first open the `Cost of Living.xls` workbook to the **Data** worksheet and then use the following instructions.

Basic Excel 97–2003 Use the preceding "Creating a Scatter Plot (97–2003)" instructions. In the Chart Wizard Step 2 dialog box, enter **E1:E11,H1:H11** as the **Data Range** and click the **Columns** option in the **Series in** group in the **Data Range** tab.

Basic Excel 2007 Copy the cell ranges **E1:E11** and **H1:H11** to consecutive columns of a blank worksheet. (If you need to insert a new worksheet, right-click the **Data** sheet tab and select **Insert**. In the gallery that appears, click **Worksheet**.) Select the copied columns and then use the preceding "Creating a Scatter Plot (2007)" instructions.

PHStat2 Select **PHStat → Regression → Simple Linear Regression**. Enter **H1:H11** as the **Y Variable Cell Range** and **E1:E11** as the **X Variable Cell Range** . Enter a title as the **Title**, click **Scatter Diagram**, and then click **OK**. (For more information about this procedure, see the Excel Companion to Chapter 13).

E2.13 CREATING TIME-SERIES PLOTS

You use Excel charting features to create time-series plots. To create a time-series plot, open to the worksheet that contains the time variable and the numerical variable to plot. The column for your time variable should appear first, reading left-to-right. (If the column that contains the time variable appears after the column that contains the numerical variable, cut and paste the numerical variable column so it appears to the right of the time variable column.) Because charting is different in Excel 2007, continue with the appropriate set of instructions.

Creating a Time Series Plot (97–2003)

Begin the Chart Wizard and make these entries:

Step 1 Click **Line** from the **Standard Types Chart type** box and select the first **Chart sub-type** in the second row, identified as **Line with markers displayed at each data value**.

Step 2 Enter the cell range of the two variables in the **Data range** box and select the **Columns** option. If the variables are in non-adjacent columns, first type or point to the cell range of the first variable, then type a comma, then type or point to the cell range of the second variable, and then press **Enter**. Do not make any entries in the **Series** tab of this dialog box.

Step 3 Click the **Titles** tab. Enter a title as the **Chart title** and enter appropriate values for the **Value (X) axis** and **Value (Y) axis** titles. Click, in turn, the **Axes**, **Gridlines**, **Legend**, **Data Labels**, and **Data Table** tabs and adjust the formatting settings given in the "Creating Charts (97–2003)" part of Section E2.2 on page 78.

Creating a Time Series Plot (2007)

Continue by selecting the cell range of the numerical variable. Then select **Insert → Line** and click the **Line with Markers** gallery choice. Right-click the new chart and click **Select Data**. Click the **Edit** button under the **Horizontal (Categories) Axis Labels** heading in the Select Data Source dialog box. In the Axis Labels dialog box, enter the cell range of the time variable as a formula in the form =*SheetName*!*CellRange* and click **OK**. (This range should start with the first time value and not with the column heading for the time variable). Click **OK** a second time (in the original dialog box) to complete the task.

Finish by relocating your chart to a chart sheet and customizing your chart using the instructions in "Creating Charts (2007)" in Section E.2.2 on page 79.

PHStat2 does not contain a time-series plot command. PHStat2 users should use the instructions given above to create time-series plots.

EXAMPLE **Figure 2.16 Time-Series Plot**

To create your own Figure 2.16 time-series plot of the movie attendance (in billions) from 1999 to 2005 (page 60), first open the Movies.xls workbook to the **Data** worksheet and then use the appropriate set of instructions.

Basic Excel 97–2003 Use the preceding "Creating a Time-Series Plot (97–2003)" instructions. In the Chart Wizard Step 2 dialog box, enter **A1:B8** as the **Data Range** and click the **Columns** option in the **Series in** group in the **Data Range** tab.

Basic Excel 2007 Select **B1:B11** and then use the preceding "Creating a Time-Series Plot (2007)" instructions. Use =**Data!A2:A11** as the formula to enter in the Axis Labels dialog box.

CHAPTER 3

Numerical Descriptive Measures

USING STATISTICS @ Choice Is Yours, Part II

LEARNING OBJECTIVES

In this chapter, you learn:
- To describe the properties of central tendency, variation, and shape in numerical data
- To calculate descriptive summary measures for a population
- To construct and interpret a box-and-whisker plot
- To describe the covariance and the coefficient of correlation

USING STATISTICS @ Choice Is Yours, Part II

The tables and charts you prepared for the sample of 838 mutual funds has proved useful to the customers of the Choice Is Yours service. However, customers have become frustrated trying to evaluate mutual fund performance. While they know how the 838 three-year rates of return are distributed, they have no idea what a typical three-year rate of return would be for a particular category of mutual funds, such as low-risk funds, nor do they know how that typical value compares to the typical values of other categories. They also have no idea of the extent of the variability in the three-year rate of return. Are all the values relatively similar, or do they include very small and very large values? Are there a lot of small values and a few large ones, or vice versa, or are there a similar number of small and large values?

How could you help the customers get answers to these questions so that they could better evaluate the mutual funds?

The customers in the Using Statistics scenario are asking questions about numerical variables. When summarizing and describing numerical variables, you need to do more than just prepare the tables and charts discussed in Chapter 2. You need to consider the central tendency, variation, and shape of each numerical variable.

CENTRAL TENDENCY

The **central tendency** is the extent to which all the data values group around a typical or central value.

VARIATION

The **variation** is the amount of dispersion, or scattering, of values away from a central value.

SHAPE

The **shape** is the pattern of the distribution of values from the lowest value to the highest value.

This chapter discusses ways you can measure the central tendency, variation, and shape of a variable. You will also learn about the covariance and the coefficient of correlation, which help measure the strength of the association between two numerical variables. Using these measures would give the customers of the Choice Is Yours service the answers they seek.

3.1 MEASURES OF CENTRAL TENDENCY

Most sets of data show a distinct tendency to group around a central point. When people talk about an "average value" or the "middle value" or the "most frequent value," they are talking informally about the mean, median, and mode—three measures of central tendency.

The Mean

The **arithmetic mean** (typically referred to as the **mean**) is the most common measure of central tendency. The mean is the only common measure in which all the values play an equal role. The mean serves as a "balance point" in a set of data (like the fulcrum on a seesaw). You calculate the mean by adding together all the values in a data set and then dividing that sum by the *number* of values in the data set.

The symbol $\overline{X}$, called *X-bar*, is used to represent the mean of a sample. For a sample containing n values, the equation for the mean of a sample is written as

$$\overline{X} = \frac{\text{Sum of the values}}{\text{Number of values}}$$

Using the series $X_1, X_2, \ldots, X_n$ to represent the set of n values and n to represent the number of values, the equation becomes:

$$\overline{X} = \frac{X_1 + X_2 + \cdots + X_n}{n}$$

By using summation notation (discussed fully in Appendix B), you replace the numerator $X_1 + X_2 + \cdots + X_n$ by the term $\sum_{i=1}^{n} X_i$, which means sum all the X_i values from the first X value, X_1, to the last X value, X_n, to form Equation (3.1), a formal definition of the sample mean.

SAMPLE MEAN

The **sample mean** is the sum of the values divided by the number of values.

$$\overline{X} = \frac{\sum\limits_{i=1}^{n} X_i}{n} \tag{3.1}$$

where

$$\overline{X} = \text{sample mean}$$

$$n = \text{number of values or sample size}$$

$$X_i = i\text{th value of the variable } X$$

$$\sum_{i=1}^{n} X_i = \text{summation of all } X_i \text{ values in the sample}$$

Because all the values play an equal role, a mean is greatly affected by any value that is greatly different from the others in the data set. When you have such extreme values, you should avoid using the mean.

The mean can suggest a typical or central value for a data set. For example, if you knew the typical time it takes you to get ready in the morning, you might be able to better plan your morning and minimize any excessive lateness (or earliness) going to your destination. Suppose you define the time to get ready as the time (rounded to the nearest minute) from when you get out of bed to when you leave your home. You collect the times shown below for 10 consecutive work days (stored in the data file times.xls):

Day:	1	2	3	4	5	6	7	8	9	10
Time (minutes):	39	29	43	52	39	44	40	31	44	35

The mean time is 39.6 minutes, computed as follows:

$$\bar{X} = \frac{\text{Sum of the values}}{\text{Number of values}}$$

$$\bar{X} = \frac{\sum_{i=1}^{n} X_i}{n}$$

$$\bar{X} = \frac{39 + 29 + 43 + 52 + 39 + 44 + 40 + 31 + 44 + 35}{10}$$

$$\bar{X} = \frac{396}{10} = 39.6$$

Even though no one day in the sample actually had the value 39.6 minutes, allotting about 40 minutes to get ready would be a good rule for planning your mornings. The mean is a good measure of central tendency in this case because the data set does not contain any exceptionally small or large values.

Consider a case in which the value on Day 4 is 102 minutes instead of 52 minutes. This extreme value causes the mean to rise to 44.6 minutes, as follows:

$$\bar{X} = \frac{\text{Sum of the values}}{\text{Number of values}}$$

$$\bar{X} = \frac{\sum_{i=1}^{n} X_i}{n}$$

$$\bar{X} = \frac{446}{10} = 44.6$$

The one extreme value has increased the mean by more than 10%, from 39.6 to 44.6 minutes. In contrast to the original mean that was in the "middle" (that is, greater than 5 of the getting-ready times and less than the 5 other times), the new mean is greater than 9 of the 10 getting-ready times. Because of the extreme value, the mean is now a poor measure of central tendency.

EXAMPLE 3.1   **THE MEAN THREE-YEAR ANNUALIZED RETURN FOR SMALL-CAP GROWTH MUTUAL FUNDS WITH LOW RISK**

The 838 mutual funds (Mutual Funds.xls) that are part of the Using Statistics scenario (see page 96) are classified according to the category (small cap, mid cap, and large cap), the type (growth or value), and the risk level of the mutual funds (low, average, and high). You are particularly interested in small companies with a lot of growth potential. Moreover, you want to investigate only those funds with low risk. Thus, you sort the mutual fund data and locate those funds that are classified as specializing in small-cap companies, have a growth objective, and are perceived to be low risk. The following seven companies meet all these criteria:

Fund	Category	Objective	Risk	Three-Year Return
Baron Growth	Small Cap	Growth	Low	20.8
Columbia Acorn Z	Small Cap	Growth	Low	26.0
FBR Small Cap	Small Cap	Growth	Low	24.9
Perritt Micro Cap Opportunities	Small Cap	Growth	Low	29.9
Schroder Capital US Opportunities Inv	Small Cap	Growth	Low	22.3
Value Line Emerging Opportunities	Small Cap	Growth	Low	19.0
Wells Fargo Advtg Small Cap Opp Adm	Small Cap	Growth	Low	22.4

Compute the mean three-year annualized return for the small-cap growth funds with low risk.

SOLUTION The mean three-year annualized return for the small-cap growth funds with low risk is 23.61, calculated as follows:

$$\bar{X} = \frac{\text{Sum of the values}}{\text{Number of values}}$$

$$= \frac{\sum_{i=1}^{n} X_i}{n}$$

$$= \frac{165.3}{7} = 23.6143$$

The ordered array for the seven small-cap growth funds with low risk is:

19.0   20.8   22.3   22.4   24.9   26.0   29.9

Four of these returns are below the mean of 23.61, and three of them are above the mean.

The Median

The **median** is the middle value in a set of data that has been ranked from smallest to largest. Half the values are smaller than or equal to the median, and half the values are larger than or equal to the median. The median is not affected by extreme values, so you can use the median when extreme values are present.

To calculate the median for a set of data, you first rank the values from smallest to largest and then use Equation (3.2) to compute the rank of the value that is the median.

MEDIAN

$$\text{Median} = \frac{n+1}{2} \text{ ranked value} \qquad (3.2)$$

You compute the median value by following one of two rules:

- **Rule 1** If there are an *odd* number of values in the data set, the median is the middle-ranked value.
- **Rule 2** If there are an *even* number of values in the data set, then the median is the *average* of the two middle ranked values.

To compute the median for the sample of 10 times to get ready in the morning, you rank the daily times as follows:

Ranked values:

| 29 | 31 | 35 | 39 | 39 | 40 | 43 | 44 | 44 | 52 |

Ranks:

| 1 | 2 | 3 | 4 | 5 | 6 | 7 | 8 | 9 | 10 |

↑

Median = 39.5

Because the result of dividing $n + 1$ by 2 is $(10 + 1)/2 = 5.5$ for this sample of 10, you must use Rule 2 and average the fifth and sixth ranked values, 39 and 40. Therefore, the median is 39.5. The median of 39.5 means that for half the days, the time to get ready is less than or equal to 39.5 minutes, and for half the days, the time to get ready is greater than or equal to 39.5 minutes. In this case, the median time to get ready of 39.5 minutes is very close to the mean time to get ready of 39.6 minutes.

EXAMPLE 3.2

COMPUTING THE MEDIAN FROM AN ODD-SIZED SAMPLE

The 838 mutual funds (**Mutual Funds.xls**) that are part of the Using Statistics scenario (see page 96) are classified according to the category (small cap, mid cap, and large cap), the type (growth or value), and the risk level of the mutual funds (low, average, and high). Compute the median three-year annualized return for the small-cap growth funds with low risk.

SOLUTION Because the result of dividing $n + 1$ by 2 is $(7 + 1)/2 = 4$ for this sample of seven, using Rule 1, the median is the fourth ranked value. The three-year annualized returns for the seven small-cap growth funds with low risk (see page 99) are ranked from the smallest to the largest:

Ranked values:

| 19.0 | 20.8 | 22.3 | 22.4 | 24.9 | 26.0 | 29.9 |

Ranks:

| 1 | 2 | 3 | 4 | 5 | 6 | 7 |

↑

Median

The median three-year annualized return is 22.4. Half the three-year annualized returns are equal to or below 22.4, and half the returns are equal to or above 22.4.

The Mode

The **mode** is the value in a set of data that appears most frequently. Like the median and unlike the mean, extreme values do not affect the mode. Often, there is no mode or there are several modes in a set of data. For example, consider the time-to-get-ready data shown below:

| 29 | 31 | 35 | 39 | 39 | 40 | 43 | 44 | 44 | 52 |

There are two modes, 39 minutes and 44 minutes, because each of these values occurs twice.

EXAMPLE 3.3

COMPUTING THE MODE

A systems manager in charge of a company's network keeps track of the number of server failures that occur in a day. Compute the mode for the following data, which represents the number of server failures in a day for the past two weeks:

$$1 \quad 3 \quad 0 \quad 3 \quad 26 \quad 2 \quad 7 \quad 4 \quad 0 \quad 2 \quad 3 \quad 3 \quad 6 \quad 3$$

SOLUTION The ordered array for these data is

$$0 \quad 0 \quad 1 \quad 2 \quad 2 \quad 3 \quad 3 \quad 3 \quad 3 \quad 3 \quad 4 \quad 6 \quad 7 \quad 26$$

Because 3 appears five times, more times than any other value, the mode is 3. Thus, the systems manager can say that the most common occurrence is having three server failures in a day. For this data set, the median is also equal to 3, and the mean is equal to 4.5. The extreme value 26 is an outlier. For these data, the median and the mode better measure central tendency than the mean.

A set of data has no mode if none of the values is "most typical." Example 3.4 presents a data set with no mode.

EXAMPLE 3.4

DATA WITH NO MODE

Compute the mode for the three-year annualized return for the small-cap growth funds (`Mutual Funds.xls`) with low risk (see page 99).

SOLUTION The ordered array for these data is

$$19.0 \quad 20.8 \quad 22.3 \quad 22.4 \quad 24.9 \quad 26.0 \quad 29.9$$

These data have no mode. None of the values is most typical because each value appears once.

Quartiles

[1] The Q_1, median, and Q_3 are also the 25th, 50th, and 75th percentiles, respectively. Equations (3.2), (3.3), and (3.4) can be expressed generally in terms of finding percentiles: (p × 100)th percentile = p × (n + 1) ranked value.

Quartiles split a set of data into four equal parts—the **first quartile, Q_1**, divides the smallest 25.0% of the values from the other 75.0% that are larger. The **second quartile, Q_2**, is the median—50.0% of the values are smaller than the median and 50.0% are larger. The **third quartile, Q_3**, divides the smallest 75.0% of the values from the largest 25.0%. Equations (3.3) and (3.4) define the first and third quartiles.[1]

FIRST QUARTILE, Q_1

25.0% of the values are smaller than or equal to Q_1, the first quartile, and 75.0% are larger than or equal to the first quartile, Q_1.

$$Q_1 = \frac{n+1}{4} \text{ ranked value} \qquad (3.3)$$

THIRD QUARTILE, Q_3

75.0% of the values are smaller than or equal to the third quartile, Q_3, and 25.0% are larger than or equal to the third quartile, Q_3.

$$Q_3 = \frac{3(n+1)}{4} \text{ ranked value} \qquad (3.4)$$

Use the following rules to calculate the quartiles:

- **Rule 1** If the result is a whole number, then the quartile is equal to that ranked value. For example, if the sample size $n = 7$, the first quartile, Q_1, is equal to the $(7 + 1)/4 =$ second ranked value.
- **Rule 2** If the result is a fractional half (2.5, 4.5, etc.), then the quartile is equal to the average of the corresponding ranked values. For example, if the sample size $n = 9$, the first quartile, Q_1, is equal to the $(9 + 1)/4 = 2.5$ ranked value, halfway between the second ranked value and the third ranked value.
- **Rule 3** If the result is neither a whole number nor a fractional half, you round the result to the nearest integer and select that ranked value. For example, if the sample size $n = 10$, the first quartile, Q_1, is equal to the $(10 + 1)/4 = 2.75$ ranked value. Round 2.75 to 3 and use the third ranked value.

To illustrate the computation of the quartiles for the time-to-get-ready data, rank the following data from smallest to largest:

Ranked values:

29	31	35	39	39	40	43	44	44	52

Ranks:

1	2	3	4	5	6	7	8	9	10

The first quartile is the $(n + 1)/4 = (10 + 1)/4 = 2.75$ ranked value. Using Rule 3, you round up to the third ranked value. The third ranked value for the time-to-get-ready data is 35 minutes. You interpret the first quartile of 35 to mean that on 25% of the days, the time to get ready is less than or equal to 35 minutes, and on 75% of the days, the time to get ready is greater than or equal to 35 minutes.

The third quartile is the $3(n + 1)/4 = 3(10 + 1)/4 = 8.25$ ranked value. Using Rule 3 for quartiles, you round this down to the eighth ranked value. The eighth ranked value is 44 minutes. Thus, on 75% of the days, the time to get ready is less than or equal to 44 minutes, and on 25% of the days, the time to get ready is greater than or equal to 44 minutes.

EXAMPLE 3.5

COMPUTING THE QUARTILES

The 838 mutual funds (Mutual Funds.xls) that are part of the Using Statistics scenario (see page 96) are classified according to the category (small cap, mid cap, and large cap), the type (growth or value), and the risk level of the mutual funds (low, average, and high). Compute the first quartile (Q_1) and third quartile (Q_3) three-year annualized return for the small-cap growth funds with low risk.

SOLUTION Ranked from smallest to largest, the three-year annualized returns for the seven small-cap growth funds with low risk (see page 99) are:

Ranked value:

19.0	20.8	22.3	22.4	24.9	26.0	29.9

Ranks:

1	2	3	4	5	6	7

For these data

$$Q_1 = \frac{(n+1)}{4} \text{ ranked value}$$

$$= \frac{7+1}{4} \text{ ranked value} = \text{2nd ranked value}$$

Therefore, using Rule 1, Q_1 is the second ranked value. Because the second ranked value is 20.8, the first quartile, Q_1, is 20.8.

To find the third quartile, Q_3:

$$Q_3 = \frac{3(n+1)}{4} \text{ ranked value}$$

$$= \frac{3(7+1)}{4} \text{ ranked value} = \text{6th ranked value}$$

Therefore, using Rule 1, Q_3 is the sixth ranked value. Because the sixth ranked value is 26.0, Q_3 is 26.

The first quartile of 20.8 indicates that 25% of the returns are below or equal to 20.8 and 75% are greater than or equal to 20.8. The third quartile of 26.0 indicates that 75% of the returns are below or equal to 26.0 and 25% are greater than or equal to 26.0.

The Geometric Mean

The **geometric mean** measures the rate of change of a variable over time. Equation (3.5) defines the geometric mean.

GEOMETRIC MEAN

The geometric mean is the *n*th root of the product of *n* values.

$$\overline{X}_G = (X_1 \times X_2 \times \cdots \times X_n)^{1/n} \qquad (3.5)$$

The **geometric mean rate of return** measures the average percentage return of an investment over time. Equation (3.6) defines the geometric mean rate of return.

GEOMETRIC MEAN RATE OF RETURN

$$\overline{R}_G = [(1+R_1) \times (1+R_2) \times \cdots \times (1+R_n)]^{1/n} - 1 \qquad (3.6)$$

where

$$R_i \text{ is the rate of return in time period } i$$

To illustrate these measures, consider an investment of $100,000 that declined to a value of $50,000 at the end of Year 1 and then rebounded back to its original $100,000 value at the end of Year 2. The rate of return for this investment for the two-year period is 0 because the starting and ending value of the investment is unchanged. However, the arithmetic mean of the yearly rates of return of this investment is

$$\overline{X} = \frac{(-0.50) + (1.00)}{2} = 0.25, \text{ or } 25\%$$

because the rate of return for Year 1 is

$$R_1 = \left(\frac{50,000 - 100,000}{100,000} \right) = -0.50, \text{ or } -50\%$$

and the rate of return for Year 2 is

$$R_2 = \left(\frac{100,000 - 50,000}{50,000} \right) = 1.00, \text{ or } 100\%$$

Using Equation (3.6), the geometric mean rate of return for the two years is

$$\begin{aligned}
\overline{R}_G &= [(1 + R_1) \times (1 + R_2)]^{1/n} - 1 \\
&= [(1 + (-0.50)) \times (1 + (1.0))]^{1/2} - 1 \\
&= [(0.50) \times (2.0)]^{1/2} - 1 \\
&= [1.0]^{1/2} - 1 \\
&= 1 - 1 = 0
\end{aligned}$$

Thus, the geometric mean rate of return more accurately reflects the (zero) change in the value of the investment for the two-year period than does the arithmetic mean.

EXAMPLE 3.6

COMPUTING THE GEOMETRIC MEAN RATE OF RETURN

The percentage change in the Russell 2000 Index of the stock prices of 2,000 small companies was +18.33% in 2004 and +4.55% in 2005. Compute the geometric rate of return.

SOLUTION Using Equation (3.6), the geometric mean rate of return in the Russell 2000 Index for the two years is

$$\begin{aligned}
\overline{R}_G &= [(1 + R_1) \times (1 + R_2)]^{1/n} - 1 \\
&= [(1 + (0.1833)) \times (1 + (0.0455))]^{1/2} - 1 \\
&= [(1.1833) \times (1.0455)]^{1/2} - 1 \\
&= [1.23714]^{1/2} - 1 \\
&= 1.1123 - 1 = 0.1123
\end{aligned}$$

The geometric mean rate of return in the Russell 2000 Index for the two years is 11.23%.

3.2   VARIATION AND SHAPE

In addition to central tendency, every data set can be characterized by its variation and shape. Variation measures the **spread**, or **dispersion**, of values in a data set. One simple measure of variation is the range, the difference between the largest and smallest values. More commonly used in statistics are the standard deviation and variance, two measures explained later in this section. The shape of a data set represents a pattern of all the values, from the lowest to highest value. As you will learn later in this section, many data sets have a pattern that looks approximately like a bell, with a peak of values somewhere in the middle.

The Range

The **range** is the simplest numerical descriptive measure of variation in a set of data.

> **RANGE**
>
> The range is equal to the largest value minus the smallest value.
>
> $$\text{Range} = X_{\text{largest}} - X_{\text{smallest}} \qquad\qquad (3.7)$$

To determine the range of the times to get ready in the morning, you rank the data from smallest to largest:

$$29 \quad 31 \quad 35 \quad 39 \quad 39 \quad 40 \quad 43 \quad 44 \quad 44 \quad 52$$

Using Equation (3.7), the range is $52 - 29 = 23$ minutes. The range of 23 minutes indicates that the largest difference between any two days in the time to get ready in the morning is 23 minutes.

EXAMPLE 3.7

COMPUTING THE RANGE IN THE THREE-YEAR ANNUALIZED RETURNS FOR SMALL-CAP GROWTH MUTUAL FUNDS WITH LOW RISK

The 838 mutual funds (Mutual Funds.xls) that are part of the Using Statistics scenario (see page 96) are classified according to the category (small cap, mid cap, and large cap), the type (growth or value), and the risk level of the mutual funds (low, average, and high). Compute the range of the three-year annualized returns for the small-cap growth funds with low risk (see page 99).

SOLUTION Ranked from smallest to largest, the three-year annualized returns for the seven small-cap growth funds with low risk are

$$19.0 \quad 20.8 \quad 22.3 \quad 22.4 \quad 24.9 \quad 26.0 \quad 29.9$$

Therefore, using Equation (3.7), the range = $29.9 - 19.0 = 10.9$.
The largest difference between any two returns is 10.9.

The range measures the *total spread* in the set of data. Although the range is a simple measure of the total variation in the data, it does not take into account *how* the data are distributed between the smallest and largest values. In other words, the range does not indicate whether the values are evenly distributed throughout the data set, clustered near the middle, or clustered near one or both extremes. Thus, using the range as a measure of variation when at least one value is an extreme value is misleading.

The Interquartile Range

The **interquartile range** (also called **midspread**) is the difference between the *third* and *first quartiles* in a set of data.

> **INTERQUARTILE RANGE**
>
> The interquartile range is the difference between the third quartile and the first quartile.
>
> $$\text{Interquartile range} = Q_3 - Q_1 \qquad\qquad (3.8)$$

The interquartile range measures the spread in the middle 50% of the data. Therefore, it is not influenced by extreme values. To determine the interquartile range of the times to get ready

$$29 \quad 31 \quad 35 \quad 39 \quad 39 \quad 40 \quad 43 \quad 44 \quad 44 \quad 52$$

you use Equation (3.8) and the earlier results on page 102, $Q_1 = 35$ and $Q_3 = 44$:

$$\text{Interquartile range} = 44 - 35 = 9 \text{ minutes}$$

Therefore, the interquartile range in the time to get ready is 9 minutes. The interval 35 to 44 is often referred to as the *middle fifty*.

EXAMPLE 3.8

COMPUTING THE INTERQUARTILE RANGE FOR THE THREE-YEAR ANNUALIZED RETURNS FOR SMALL-CAP GROWTH MUTUAL FUNDS WITH LOW RISK

The 838 mutual funds (Mutual Funds.xls) that are part of the Using Statistics scenario (see page 96) are classified according to the category (small cap, mid cap, and large cap), the type (growth or value), and the risk level of the mutual funds (low, average, and high). Compute the interquartile range of the three-year annualized returns for the small-cap growth funds with low risk (see page 99).

SOLUTION Ranked from smallest to largest, the three-year annualized returns for the seven small-cap growth funds with low risk are

$$19.0 \quad 20.8 \quad 22.3 \quad 22.4 \quad 24.9 \quad 26.0 \quad 29.9$$

Using Equation (3.8) and the earlier results on page 103, $Q_1 = 20.8$ and $Q_3 = 26.0$:

$$\text{Interquartile range} = 26.0 - 20.8 = 5.2$$

Therefore, the interquartile range in the three-year annualized return is 5.2.

Because the interquartile range does not consider any value smaller than Q_1 or larger than Q_3, it cannot be affected by extreme values. Summary measures such as the median, Q_1, Q_3, and the interquartile range, which cannot be influenced by extreme values, are called **resistant measures**.

The Variance and the Standard Deviation

Although the range and the interquartile range are measures of variation, they do not take into consideration *how* the values distribute or cluster between the extremes. Two commonly used measures of variation that take into account how all the values in the data are distributed are the **variance** and the **standard deviation**. These statistics measure the "average" scatter around the mean—how larger values fluctuate above it and how smaller values distribute below it.

A simple measure of variation around the mean might take the difference between each value and the mean and then sum these differences. However, if you did that, you would find that because the mean is the balance point in a set of data, for *every* set of data, these differences would sum to zero. One measure of variation that differs from data set to data set *squares* the difference between each value and the mean and then sums these squared differences. In statistics, this quantity is called a **sum of squares** (or *SS*). This sum is then divided by the number of values minus 1 (for sample data) to get the sample variance (S^2). The square root of the sample variance is the sample standard deviation (S).

Because the sum of squares is a sum of squared differences that by the rules of arithmetic will always be nonnegative, *neither the variance nor the standard deviation can ever be negative*. For virtually all sets of data, the variance and standard deviation will be a positive value, although both of these statistics will be zero if there is no variation at all in a set of data and each value in the sample is the same.

For a sample containing n values, $X_1, X_2, X_3, \ldots, X_n$, the sample variance (given by the symbol S^2) is

$$S^2 = \frac{(X_1 - \overline{X})^2 + (X_2 - \overline{X})^2 + \cdots + (X_n - \overline{X})^2}{n - 1}$$

Equation (3.9) expresses the sample variance using summation notation, and Equation (3.10) expresses the sample standard deviation.

SAMPLE VARIANCE

The **sample variance** is the sum of the squared differences around the mean divided by the sample size minus one.

$$S^2 = \frac{\sum_{i=1}^{n}(X_i - \overline{X})^2}{n - 1} \tag{3.9}$$

where

$$\overline{X} = \text{mean}$$

$$n = \text{sample size}$$

$$X_i = i\text{th value of the variable } X$$

$$\sum_{i=1}^{n}(X_i - \overline{X})^2 = \text{summation of all the squared differences between the } X_i \text{ values and } \overline{X}$$

SAMPLE STANDARD DEVIATION

The **sample standard deviation** is the square root of the sum of the squared differences around the mean divided by the sample size minus one.

$$S = \sqrt{S^2} = \sqrt{\frac{\sum_{i=1}^{n}(X_i - \overline{X})^2}{n - 1}} \tag{3.10}$$

If the denominator were n instead of $n - 1$, Equation (3.9) [and the inner term in Equation (3.10)] would calculate the average of the squared differences around the mean. However, $n - 1$ is used because of certain desirable mathematical properties possessed by the statistic S^2 that make it appropriate for statistical inference (which is discussed in Chapter 7). As the sample size increases, the difference between dividing by n and by $n - 1$ becomes smaller and smaller.

You will most likely use the sample standard deviation as your measure of variation [defined in Equation (3.10)]. Unlike the sample variance, which is a squared quantity, the standard deviation is always a number that is in the same units as the original sample data. The standard deviation helps you to know how a set of data clusters or distributes around its mean. For almost all sets of data, the majority of the observed values lie within an interval of plus and minus one standard deviation above and below the mean. Therefore, knowledge of the mean and the standard deviation usually helps define where at least the majority of the data values are clustering.

To hand-calculate the sample variance, S^2, and the sample standard deviation, S:

Step 1. Compute the difference between each value and the mean.

Step 2. Square each difference.

Step 3. Add the squared differences.

Step 4. Divide this total by $n - 1$ to get the sample variance.

Step 5. Take the square root of the sample variance to get the sample standard deviation.

Table 3.1 shows the first four steps for calculating the variance and standard deviation for the getting-ready-times data with a mean ($\overline{X}$) equal to 39.6. (See page 98 for the calculation of the mean.) The second column of Table 3.1 shows step 1. The third column of Table 3.1 shows step 2. The sum of the squared differences (step 3) is shown at the bottom of Table 3.1. This total is then divided by $10 - 1 = 9$ to compute the variance (step 4).

TABLE 3.1

Computing the Variance of the Getting-Ready Times

$\overline{X} = 39.6$

Time (X)	Step 1: $(X_i - \overline{X})$	Step 2: $(X_i - \overline{X})^2$
39	−0.60	0.36
29	−10.60	112.36
43	3.40	11.56
52	12.40	153.76
39	−0.60	0.36
44	4.40	19.36
40	0.40	0.16
31	−8.60	73.96
44	4.40	19.36
35	−4.60	21.16
	Step 3: Sum:	Step 4: Divide by (n − 1):
	412.40	45.82

You can also calculate the variance by substituting values for the terms in Equation (3.9):

$$S^2 = \frac{\sum_{i=1}^{n} (X_i - \overline{X})^2}{n - 1}$$

$$= \frac{(39 - 39.6)^2 + (29 - 39.6)^2 + \cdots + (35 - 39.6)^2}{10 - 1}$$

$$= \frac{412.4}{9}$$

$$= 45.82$$

Because the variance is in squared units (in squared minutes, for these data), to compute the standard deviation, you take the square root of the variance. Using Equation (3.10) on page 107, the sample standard deviation, S, is

$$S = \sqrt{S^2} = \sqrt{\frac{\sum_{i=1}^{n}(X_i - \bar{X})^2}{n-1}} = \sqrt{45.82} = 6.77$$

This indicates that the getting-ready times in this sample are clustering within 6.77 minutes around the mean of 39.6 minutes (i.e., clustering between $\bar{X} - 1S = 32.83$ and $\bar{X} + 1S = 46.37$). In fact, 7 out of 10 getting-ready times lie within this interval.

Using the second column of Table 3.1, you can also calculate the sum of the differences between each value and the mean to be zero. For any set of data, this sum will always be zero:

$$\sum_{i=1}^{n}(X_i - \bar{X}) = 0 \text{ for all sets of data}$$

This property is one of the reasons that the mean is used as the most common measure of central tendency.

EXAMPLE 3.9

COMPUTING THE VARIANCE AND STANDARD DEVIATION OF THE THREE-YEAR ANNUALIZED RETURNS FOR SMALL-CAP GROWTH MUTUAL FUNDS WITH LOW RISK

The 838 mutual funds (Mutual Funds.xls) that are part of the Using Statistics scenario (see page 96) are classified according to the category (small cap, mid cap, and large cap), the type (growth or value), and the risk level of the mutual funds (low, average, and high). Compute the variance and standard deviation of the three-year annualized returns for the small-cap growth funds with low risk (see page 99).

SOLUTION Table 3.2 illustrates the computation of the variance and standard deviation for the three-year annualized returns for the small-cap growth funds with low risk.

TABLE 3.2

Computing the Variance of the Three-Year Annualized Returns for the Small-Cap Growth Mutual Funds with Low Risk

$\bar{X} = 23.6143$

Three-Year Annualized Return	Step 1: $(X_i - \bar{X})$	Step 2: $(X_i - \bar{X})^2$
20.8	−2.8143	7.9202
26.0	2.3857	5.6916
24.9	1.2857	1.6531
29.9	6.2857	39.5102
22.3	−1.3143	1.7273
19.0	−4.6143	21.2916
22.4	−1.2143	1.4745
	Step 3: Sum:	Step 4: Divide by $(n-1)$:
	79.2686	13.2114

Using Equation (3.9) on page 107:

$$S^2 = \frac{\sum_{i=1}^{n}(X_i - \bar{X})^2}{n-1}$$

$$= \frac{(20.8 - 23.6143)^2 + (26.0 - 23.6143)^2 + \cdots + (22.4 - 23.6143)^2}{7-1}$$

$$= \frac{79.2686}{6}$$

$$= 13.2114$$

Using Equation (3.10) on page 107, the sample standard deviation, S, is

$$S = \sqrt{S^2} = \sqrt{\frac{\sum_{i=1}^{n}(X_i - \bar{X})^2}{n-1}} = \sqrt{13.2114} = 3.635$$

The standard deviation of 3.635 indicates that the returns are clustering within 3.635 around the mean of 23.61 (i.e., clustering between $\bar{X} - 1S = 19.975$ and $\bar{X} + 1S = 27.245$). In fact, 71.4% (5 out of 7) of the three-year annualized returns lie within this interval.

The following summarizes the characteristics of the range, interquartile range, variance, and standard deviation:

- The more the data are spread out or dispersed, the larger the range, interquartile range, variance, and standard deviation.
- The more the data are concentrated or homogeneous, the smaller the range, interquartile range, variance, and standard deviation.
- If the values are all the same (so that there is no variation in the data), the range, interquartile range, variance, and standard deviation will all equal zero.
- None of the measures of variation (the range, interquartile range, standard deviation, and variance) can *ever* be negative.

The Coefficient of Variation

Unlike the previous measures of variation presented, the **coefficient of variation** is a *relative measure* of variation that is always expressed as a percentage rather than in terms of the units of the particular data. The coefficient of variation, denoted by the symbol CV, measures the scatter in the data relative to the mean.

COEFFICIENT OF VARIATION

The coefficient of variation is equal to the standard deviation divided by the mean, multiplied by 100%.

$$CV = \left(\frac{S}{\bar{X}}\right)100\% \tag{3.11}$$

where

$$S = \text{sample standard deviation}$$

$$\bar{X} = \text{sample mean}$$

For the sample of 10 getting-ready times, because $\bar{X} = 39.6$ and $S = 6.77$, the coefficient of variation is

$$CV = \left(\frac{S}{\bar{X}}\right)100\% = \left(\frac{6.77}{39.6}\right)100\% = 17.10\%$$

For the getting-ready times, the standard deviation is 17.1% of the size of the mean.

The coefficient of variation is very useful when comparing two or more sets of data that are measured in different units, as Example 3.10 illustrates.

EXAMPLE 3.10

COMPARING TWO COEFFICIENTS OF VARIATION WHEN TWO VARIABLES HAVE DIFFERENT UNITS OF MEASUREMENT

The operations manager of a package delivery service is deciding whether to purchase a new fleet of trucks. When packages are stored in the trucks in preparation for delivery, you need to consider two major constraints—the weight (in pounds) and the volume (in cubic feet) for each item.

The operations manager samples 200 packages and finds that the mean weight is 26.0 pounds, with a standard deviation of 3.9 pounds, and the mean volume is 8.8 cubic feet, with a standard deviation of 2.2 cubic feet. How can the operations manager compare the variation of the weight and the volume?

SOLUTION Because the measurement units differ for the weight and volume constraints, the operations manager should compare the relative variability in the two types of measurements.

For weight, the coefficient of variation is

$$CV_W = \left(\frac{3.9}{26.0}\right)100\% = 15.0\%$$

For volume, the coefficient of variation is

$$CV_V = \left(\frac{2.2}{8.8}\right)100\% = 25.0\%$$

Thus, relative to the mean, the package volume is much more variable than the package weight.

Z Scores

An **extreme value** or **outlier** is a value located far away from the mean. Z scores are useful in identifying outliers. The larger the Z score, the greater the distance from the value to the mean. The **Z score** is the difference between the value and the mean, divided by the standard deviation.

Z SCORES

$$Z = \frac{X - \bar{X}}{S} \tag{3.12}$$

For the time-to-get-ready data, the mean is 39.6 minutes, and the standard deviation is 6.77 minutes. The time to get ready on the first day is 39.0 minutes. You compute the Z score for Day 1 by using Equation (3.12):

$$Z = \frac{X - \bar{X}}{S}$$

$$= \frac{39.0 - 39.6}{6.77}$$

$$= -0.09$$

Table 3.3 shows the Z scores for all 10 days. The largest Z score is 1.83 for Day 4, on which the time to get ready was 52 minutes. The lowest Z score was -1.57 for Day 2, on which the time to get ready was 29 minutes. As a general rule, a Z score is considered an outlier if it is less than -3.0 or greater than $+3.0$. None of the times met that criterion to be considered outliers.

TABLE 3.3

Z Scores for the 10 Getting-Ready Times

	Time (X)	Z Score
	39	-0.09
	29	-1.57
	43	0.50
	52	1.83
	39	-0.09
	44	0.65
	40	0.06
	31	-1.27
	44	0.65
	35	-0.68
Mean	39.6	
Standard deviation	6.77	

EXAMPLE 3.11

COMPUTING THE Z SCORES OF THE THREE-YEAR ANNUALIZED RETURNS FOR SMALL-CAP GROWTH MUTUAL FUNDS WITH LOW RISK

The 838 mutual funds (Mutual Funds.xls) that are part of the Using Statistics scenario (see page 96) are classified according to the category (small cap, mid cap, and large cap), the type (growth or value), and the risk level of the mutual funds (low, average, and high). Compute the Z scores of the three-year annualized returns for the small-cap growth funds with low risk (see page 99).

SOLUTION Table 3.4 illustrates the Z scores of the three-year annualized returns for the small-cap growth funds with low risk. The largest Z score is 1.73, for an annualized return of 29.9. The lowest Z score is -1.27, for an annualized return of 19.0. There are no apparent outliers in these data because none of the Z scores are less than -3 or greater than $+3$.

TABLE 3.4

Z Scores of the Three-Year Annualized Returns for the Small-Cap Growth Mutual Funds with Low Risk

	Three-Year Return	Z Scores
	20.8	-0.77
	26.0	0.66
	24.9	0.35
	29.9	1.73
	22.3	-0.36
	19.0	-1.27
	22.4	-0.33
Mean	23.61	
Standard Deviation	3.63	

Shape

Shape is the pattern of the distribution of data values throughout the entire range of all the values. A distribution is either symmetrical or skewed. In a **symmetrical** distribution, the values below the mean are distributed exactly as the values above the mean. In this case, the low and high values balance each other out. In a **skewed** distribution, the values are not symmetrical around the mean. This skewness results in an imbalance of low values or high values.

Shape influences the relationship of the mean to the median in the following ways:

- Mean < median: negative, or left-skewed
- Mean = median: symmetric, or zero skewness
- Mean > median: positive, or right-skewed

Figure 3.1 depicts three data sets, each with a different shape.

FIGURE 3.1

A comparison of three data sets differing in shape

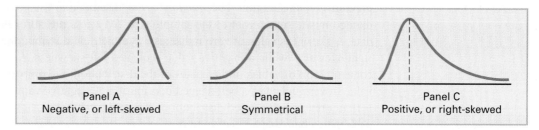

The data in Panel A are negative, or **left-skewed**. In this panel, most of the values are in the upper portion of the distribution. A long tail and distortion to the left is caused by some extremely small values. These extremely small values pull the mean downward so that the mean is less than the median.

The data in Panel B are symmetrical. Each half of the curve is a mirror image of the other half of the curve. The low and high values on the scale balance, and the mean equals the median.

The data in Panel C are positive, or **right-skewed**. In this panel, most of the values are in the lower portion of the distribution. A long tail on the right is caused by some extremely large values. These extremely large values pull the mean upward so that the mean is greater than the median.

VISUAL EXPLORATIONS Exploring Descriptive Statistics

You can use the Visual Explorations Descriptive Statistics procedure to see the effect of changing data values on measures of central tendency, variation, and shape. Open the `visual explorations.xla` add-in workbook (see Appendix D) and select **VisualExplorations → Descriptive Statistics** (Excel 97–2003) or **Add-ins → Visual Explorations → Descriptive Statistics** (Excel 2007) from the Microsoft Excel menu bar. Read the instructions in the pop-up box (see illustration below) and click **OK** to examine a dot-scale diagram for the sample of 10 getting-ready times used throughout this chapter.

Experiment by entering an extreme value such as 10 minutes into one of the tinted cells of column A. Which measures are affected by this change? Which ones are not? You can flip between the "before" and "after" diagrams by repeatedly pressing **Crtl + Z** (undo) followed by **Crtl + Y** (redo) to help see the changes the extreme value caused in the diagram.

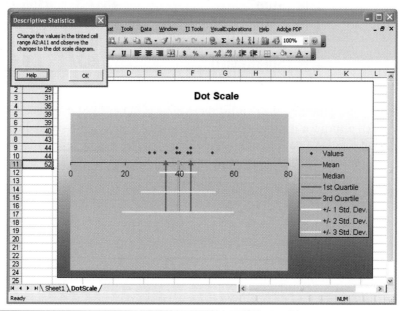

Microsoft Excel Descriptive Statistics Results

The Descriptive Statistics procedure of the ToolPak add-in (see Section E3.1) computes the mean, median, mode, standard deviation, variance, range, minimum, maximum, and count (sample size) and displays these statistics on a new worksheet. In addition, the procedure calculates and displays the standard error, the kurtosis, and skewness, three statistics not discussed previously in this section. The *standard error*, discussed in Chapter 7, is the standard deviation divided by the square root of the sample size. *Skewness* measures the lack of symmetry in the data. A skewness value of zero indicates a symmetrical distribution. A positive value indicates right skewness while a negative value indicates left skewness. *Kurtosis* measures the relative concentration of values in the center of the distribution, as compared with the tails. A kurtosis value of zero indicates a bell-shaped distribution. A negative value indicates a distribution that is flatter than a bell-shaped distribution. A positive value indicates a distribution with a sharper peak than a bell-shaped distribution.

Figure 3.2 shows the results of using the Descriptive Statistics procedure to calculate separate results for low-risk, average-risk, and high-risk mutual funds. (The procedure was used three times, and the results that appeared on three separate worksheets were consolidated on one sheet.)

FIGURE 3.2

Microsoft Excel descriptive statistics of the three-year annualized returns based on risk level

See Section E3.1 to create this.

	A	B	C	D
1	**Descriptive Statistics for 3-Year Return**			
2		**Low**	**Average**	**High Risk**
3	**Mean**	18.4101	16.9661	17.9549
4	**Standard Error**	0.3158	0.3161	0.2621
5	**Median**	17.5	16.1	17.6
6	**Mode**	14.1	15.5	16.4
7	**Standard Deviation**	4.9636	4.9478	4.8762
8	**Sample Variance**	24.6376	24.4804	23.7774
9	**Kurtosis**	0.2838	1.9893	1.1686
10	**Skewness**	0.5069	0.8118	0.7069
11	**Range**	28	35.6	33.2
12	**Minimum**	6.7	6.7	7.3
13	**Maximum**	34.7	42.3	40.5
14	**Sum**	4547.3	4156.7	6212.4
15	**Count**	247	245	346
16	**Largest(1)**	34.7	42.3	40.5
17	**Smallest(1)**	6.7	6.7	7.3

In examining the results, there appear to be slight differences in the three-year annualized return for the three risk levels. Low-risk and high-risk funds had a slightly higher mean and median than did average-risk funds. There was very little difference in the standard deviations of the three groups. Each of the risk levels showed some evidence of positive skewness.

PROBLEMS FOR SECTIONS 3.1 AND 3.2

Learning the Basics

 3.1 The following is a set of data from a sample of $n = 5$:

$$7 \quad 4 \quad 9 \quad 8 \quad 2$$

a. Compute the mean, median, and mode.
b. Compute the range, interquartile range, variance, standard deviation, and coefficient of variation.
c. Compute the Z scores. Are there any outliers?
d. Describe the shape of the data set.

 3.2 The following is a set of data from a sample of $n = 6$:

$$7 \quad 4 \quad 9 \quad 7 \quad 3 \quad 12$$

a. Compute the mean, median, and mode.
b. Compute the range, interquartile range, variance, standard deviation, and coefficient of variation.
c. Compute the Z scores. Are there any outliers?
d. Describe the shape of the data set.

 3.3 The following set of data is from a sample of $n = 7$:

$$12 \quad 7 \quad 4 \quad 9 \quad 0 \quad 7 \quad 3$$

a. Compute the mean, median, and mode.
b. Compute the range, interquartile range, variance, standard deviation, and coefficient of variation.
c. Compute the Z scores. Are there any outliers?
d. Describe the shape of the data set.

 3.4 The following is a set of data from a sample of $n = 5$:

$$7 \quad -5 \quad -8 \quad 7 \quad 9$$

a. Compute the mean, median, and mode.
b. Compute the range, interquartile range, variance, standard deviation, and coefficient of variation.
c. Compute the Z scores. Are there any outliers?
d. Describe the shape of the data set.

 3.5 Suppose the rate of return for a particular stock during the past two years was 10% and 30%. Compute the geometric mean rate of return. (*Note:* A rate of return of 10% is recorded as 0.10, and a rate of return of 30% is recorded as 0.30.)

Applying the Concepts

 3.6 The operations manager of a plant that manufactures tires wants to compare the actual inner diameters of two grades of tires, each of which is expected to be 575 millimeters. A sample of five tires of each grade was selected, and the results representing the inner diameters of the tires, ranked from smallest to largest, are as follows:

Grade X					Grade Y				
568	570	575	578	584	573	574	575	577	578

a. For each of the two grades of tires, compute the mean, median, and standard deviation.
b. Which grade of tire is providing better quality? Explain.
c. What would be the effect on your answers in (a) and (b) if the last value for grade Y were 588 instead of 578? Explain.

3.7 The data in the file **movieprices.xls** contain the price for two tickets with online service charges, large popcorn, and two medium soft drinks at a sample of six theatre chains:

$$\$36.15 \quad \$31.00 \quad \$35.05 \quad \$40.25 \quad \$33.75 \quad \$43.00$$

Source: Extracted from K. Kelly, "The Multiplex Under Siege," The Wall Street Journal, December 24–25, 2005, pp. P1, P5.

a. Compute the mean, median, first quartile, and third quartile.
b. Compute the variance, standard deviation, range, interquartile range, and coefficient of variation.
c. Are the data skewed? If so, how?
d. Based on the results of (a) through (c), what conclusions can you reach concerning the cost of going to the movies?

3.8 A total of 92,000 new single-family homes were sold in the United States during February 2006. The median price of the homes was $230,400, a decrease of 2.9% from February 2005 (U.S. Census Bureau, **www.census.gov**). Why do you think the Census Bureau refers to the median price instead of the mean price?

3.9 The data in the file **bankcost1.xls** contain the bounced check fees, in dollars, for a sample of 23 banks for direct-deposit customers who maintain a $100 balance:

$$26 \quad 28 \quad 20 \quad 20 \quad 21 \quad 22 \quad 25 \quad 25 \quad 18 \quad 25 \quad 15 \quad 20$$

$$18 \quad 20 \quad 25 \quad 25 \quad 22 \quad 30 \quad 30 \quad 30 \quad 15 \quad 20 \quad 29$$

Source: Extracted from "The New Face of Banking," June 2000. Copyright © 2000 by Consumers Union of U.S., Inc., Yonkers, NY 10703-1057.

a. Compute the mean, median, first quartile, and third quartile.
b. Compute the variance, standard deviation, range, interquartile range, coefficient of variation, and Z scores.
c. Are the data skewed? If so, how?
d. Based on the results of (a) through (c), what conclusions can you reach concerning the bounced check fees?

3.10 The data in the file coffeedrink.xls represent the calories and fat (in grams) of 16-ounce iced coffee drinks at Dunkin' Donuts and Starbucks:

Product	Calories	Fat
Dunkin' Donuts Iced Mocha Swirl latte (whole milk)	240	8.0
Starbucks Coffee Frappuccino blended coffee	260	3.5
Dunkin' Donuts Coffee Coolatta (cream)	350	22.0
Starbucks Iced Coffee Mocha Expresso (whole milk and whipped cream)	350	20.0
Starbucks Mocha Frappuccino blended coffee (whipped cream)	420	16.0
Starbucks Chocolate Brownie Frappuccino blended coffee (whipped cream)	510	22.0
Starbucks Chocolate Frappuccino Blended Crème (whipped cream)	530	19.0

Source: Extracted from "Coffee as Candy at Dunkin' Donuts and Starbucks," Consumer Reports, *June 2004, p. 9.*

a. For each variable (calories and fat), compute the mean, median, first quartile, and third quartile.
b. For each variable (calories and fat), compute the variance, standard deviation, range, interquartile range, coefficient of variation, and Z scores. Are there any outliers? Explain.
c. Are the data skewed? If so, how?
d. Based on the results of (a) through (c), what conclusions can you reach concerning the calories and fat in iced coffee drinks at Dunkin' Donuts and Starbucks?

3.11 The data in the file chicken.xls contain the total fat, in grams per serving, for a sample of 20 chicken sandwiches from fast-food chains. The data is as follows:

    7   8   4   5 16 20 20 24 19 30
   23 30 25 19 29 29 30 30 40 56

Source: Extracted from "Fast Food: Adding Health to the Menu," Consumer Reports, *September 2004, pp. 28–31.*

a. Compute the mean, median, first quartile, and third quartile.
b. Compute the variance, standard deviation, range, interquartile range, coefficient of variation, and Z scores. Are there any outliers? Explain.
c. Are the data skewed? If so, how?
d. Based on the results of (a) through (c), what conclusions can you reach concerning the total fat of chicken sandwiches?

3.12 The data in the file batterylife.xls represents the battery life (in shots) for three pixel digital cameras:

   300 180   85 170 380 460
   260   35 380 120 110 240

Source: Extracted from "Cameras: More Features in the Mix," Consumer Reports, *July 2005, pp. 14–18.*

a. Compute the mean, median, first quartile, and third quartile.
b. Compute the variance, standard deviation, range, interquartile range, coefficient of variation, and Z scores. Are there any outliers? Explain.
c. Are the data skewed? If so, how?
d. Based on the results of (a) through (c), what conclusions can you reach concerning the battery life (in shots) for three pixel digital cameras?

3.13 Is there a difference in the variation of the yields of different types of investments between banks? The data in the file bankyield.xls represents the nationwide highest yields for money market accounts and one-year CDs as of January 24, 2006:

Money Market Accounts	One-Year CD
4.55 4.50 4.40 4.38 4.38	4.94 4.90 4.85 4.85 4.85

Source: Extracted from Bankrate.com, January 24, 2006.

a. For money market accounts and one-year CDs, separately compute the variance, standard deviation, range, interquartile range, and coefficient of variation.
b. Based on the results of (a), do money market accounts or one-year CDs have more variation in the highest yields offered? Explain.

3.14 The data in the file themeparks.xls contain the starting admission price (in $) for one-day tickets to 10 theme parks in the United States:

    58   63   41   42   29   50   62   43   40   40

Source: Extracted from C. Jackson and E. Gamerman, "Rethinking the Thrill Factor," The Wall Street Journal, *April 15–16, 2006, pp. P1, P4.*

a. Compute the mean, median, first quartile, and third quartile.
b. Compute the range, variance, and standard deviation.
c. Based on the results of (a) and (b), what conclusions can you reach concerning the starting admission price for one-day tickets.
d. Suppose that the first value was 98 instead of 58. Repeat (a) through (c), using this value. Comment on the difference in the results.

3.15 A bank branch located in a commercial district of a city has developed an improved process for serving customers during the noon-to-1:00 p.m. lunch period. The waiting time, in minutes (defined as the time the customer enters the line to when he or she reaches the teller window), of a sample of 15 customers during this hour is recorded over a period of one week. The results are contained in the data file bank1.xls and are listed below:

   4.21   5.55   3.02   5.13   4.77   2.34   3.54   3.20

   4.50   6.10   0.38   5.12   6.46   6.19   3.79

a. Compute the mean, median, first quartile, and third quartile.

b. Compute the variance, standard deviation, range, interquartile range, coefficient of variation, and Z scores. Are there any outliers? Explain.

c. Are the data skewed? If so, how?

d. As a customer walks into the branch office during the lunch hour, she asks the branch manager how long she can expect to wait. The branch manager replies, "Almost certainly less than five minutes." On the basis of the results of (a) through (c), evaluate the accuracy of this statement.

3.16 Suppose that another branch, located in a residential area, is also concerned with the noon-to-1 p.m. lunch hour. The waiting time, in minutes (defined as the time the customer enters the line to when he or she reaches the teller window), of a sample of 15 customers during this hour is recorded over a period of one week. The results are contained in the data file bank2.xls and are listed below:

9.66	5.90	8.02	5.79	8.73	3.82	8.01	8.35
10.49	6.68	5.64	4.08	6.17	9.91	5.47	

a. Compute the mean, median, first quartile, and third quartile.

b. Compute the variance, standard deviation, range, interquartile range, and coefficient of variation. Are there any outliers? Explain.

c. Are the data skewed? If so, how?

d. As a customer walks into the branch office during the lunch hour, he asks the branch manager how long he can expect to wait. The branch manager replies, "Almost certainly less than five minutes." On the basis of the results of (a) through (c), evaluate the accuracy of this statement.

3.17 General Electric (GE) is one of the world's largest companies; it develops, manufactures, and markets a wide range of products, including medical diagnostic imaging devices, jet engines, lighting products, and chemicals. Through its affiliate, NBC Universal, GE produces and delivers network television and motion pictures. In 2004, GE's stock price rose 20.6%, but in 2005, the price dropped 1.4%

(Source: Extracted from **finance.yahoo.com**, *April 17, 2006).*

a. Compute the geometric mean rate of increase for the two-year period 2004–2005. (*Hint:* Denote an increase of 20.6% as $R_1 = 0.206$.)

b. If you purchased $1,000 of GE stock at the start of 2004, what was its value at the end of 2005?

c. Compare the result of (b) to that of Problem 3.18 (b).

3.18 TASER International, Inc., develops, manufactures, and sells nonlethal self-defense devices known as tasers. Marketing primarily to law enforcement, correc-

tions institutions, and the military, TASER's popularity has enjoyed a roller-coaster ride. The stock price in 2004 increased 361.4%, but in 2005, it decreased 78.0%

(Source: Extracted from **finance.yahoo.com**, *April 17, 2006).*

a. Compute the geometric mean rate of increase for the two-year period 2004–2005. (*Hint:* Denote an increase of 361.4% as $R_1 = 3.614$.)

b. If you purchased $1,000 of TASER stock at the start of 2004, what was its value at the end of 2005?

c. Compare the result of (b) to that of Problem 3.17 (b).

3.19 In 2002, all the major stock market indexes decreased dramatically as the attacks on 9/11 drove stock prices spiraling downward. Stocks soon rebounded, but what type of mean return did investors experience over the four-year period from 2002 to 2005? The data in the following table (contained in the data file indexes.xls) represent the total rate of return (in percentage) for the Dow Jones Industrial Average (DJIA), the Standard & Poor's 500 (S&P 500), and the technology-heavy NASDAQ Composite (Nasdaq).

Year	DJIA	S&P 500	NASDAQ
2005	−0.6	2.9	1.4
2004	3.4	9.1	8.6
2003	30.0	26.4	50.0
2002	−16.8	−24.2	−31.5

Source: Extracted from **finance.yahoo.com**, *April 14, 2006.*

a. Calculate the geometric mean rate of return for the DJIA, S&P 500, and Nasdaq.

b. What conclusions can you reach concerning the geometric rates of return of the three market indexes?

c. Compare the results of (b) to those of Problem 3.20 (b).

3.20 In 2002–2005 precious metals changed rapidly in value. The data in the following table (contained in the data file metals.xls) represent the total rate of return (in percentage) for platinum, gold, and silver:

Year	Platinum	Gold	Silver
2005	12.3	17.8	29.5
2004	5.7	4.6	14.2
2003	36.0	19.9	27.8
2002	24.6	25.6	3.3

Source: Extracted from **www.kitco.com**, *April 14, 2006.*

a. Calculate the geometric mean rate of return for platinum, gold, and silver.

b. What conclusions can you reach concerning the geometric rates of return of the three precious metals?

c. Compare the results of (b) to those of Problem 3.19 (b).

3.3   NUMERICAL DESCRIPTIVE MEASURES FOR A POPULATION

Sections 3.1 and 3.2 present various *statistics* that described the properties of central tendency and variation for a *sample*. If your data set represents numerical measurements for an entire *population*, you need to calculate and interpret *parameters*, summary measures for a population. In this section, you will learn about three descriptive population parameters: the population mean, population variance, and population standard deviation.

To help illustrate these parameters, first review Table 3.5, which contains the one-year return for the five largest bond funds (in terms of total assets) as of January 31, 2006. (The data are contained in the file largest bonds.xls.)

TABLE 3.5

One-Year Return for the Population Consisting of the Five Largest Bond Funds

Bond Fund	One-Year Return
Pimco:Total Rtn;Inst	2.74
Vanguard Tot Bd;Inv	1.62
American Funds Bond;A	2.25
Vanguard GNMA;Inv	2.88
Franklin CA TF Inc;A	3.66

Source: Extracted from The Wall Street Journal, *February 6, 2006, p. R6.*

The Population Mean

The **population mean** is represented by the symbol μ, the Greek lowercase letter *mu*. Equation (3.13) defines the population mean.

POPULATION MEAN

The population mean is the sum of the values in the population divided by the population size N.

$$\mu = \frac{\sum_{i=1}^{N} X_i}{N} \tag{3.13}$$

where

$$\mu = \text{population mean}$$
$$X_i = i\text{th value of the variable } X$$
$$\sum_{i=1}^{N} X_i = \text{summation of all } X_i \text{ values in the population}$$

To compute the mean one-year return for the population of bond funds given in Table 3.5, use Equation (3.13):

$$\mu = \frac{\sum_{i=1}^{N} X_i}{N} = \frac{2.74 + 1.62 + 2.25 + 2.88 + 3.66}{5} = \frac{13.15}{5} = 2.63$$

Thus, the mean percentage return for these bond funds is 2.63.

The Population Variance and Standard Deviation

The **population variance** and the **population standard deviation** measure variation in a population. Like the related sample statistics, the population standard deviation is the square root of the population variance. The symbol σ^2, the Greek lowercase letter *sigma* squared, represents the population variance, and the symbol σ, the Greek lowercase letter *sigma*, represents the population standard deviation. Equations (3.14) and (3.15) define these parameters. The denominators for the right-side terms in these equations use N and not the $(n-1)$ term that is used in the equations for the sample variance and standard deviation [see Equations (3.9) and (3.10) on page 107].

POPULATION VARIANCE

The population variance is the sum of the squared differences around the population mean divided by the population size N.

$$\sigma^2 = \frac{\sum_{i=1}^{N}(X_i - \mu)^2}{N} \tag{3.14}$$

where

$$\mu = \text{population mean}$$

$$X_i = i\text{th value of the variable } X$$

$$\sum_{i=1}^{N}(X_i - \mu)^2 = \text{summation of all the squared differences between the } X_i \text{ values and } \mu$$

POPULATION STANDARD DEVIATION

$$\sigma = \sqrt{\frac{\sum_{i=1}^{N}(X_i - \mu)^2}{N}} \tag{3.15}$$

To compute the population variance for the data of Table 3.5, you use Equation (3.14):

$$\sigma^2 = \frac{\sum_{i=1}^{N}(X_i - \mu)^2}{N}$$

$$= \frac{(2.74 - 2.63)^2 + (1.62 - 2.63)^2 + (2.25 - 2.63)^2 + (2.88 - 2.63)^2 + (3.66 - 2.63)^2}{5}$$

$$= \frac{0.0121 + 1.0201 + 0.1444 + 0.0625 + 1.0609}{5}$$

$$= \frac{2.30}{5} = 0.46$$

Thus, the variance of the one-year returns is 0.46 squared percentage return. The squared units make the variance hard to interpret. You should use the standard deviation that is expressed in the original units of the data (percentage return). From Equation (3.15),

$$\sigma = \sqrt{\sigma^2} = \sqrt{\frac{\sum_{i=1}^{N}(X_i - \mu)^2}{N}} = \sqrt{0.46} = 0.68$$

Therefore, the typical percentage return differs from the mean of 2.63 by approximately 0.68. This small amount of variation suggests that these large bond funds produce results that do not differ greatly.

The Empirical Rule

In most data sets, a large portion of the values tend to cluster somewhat near the median. In right-skewed data sets, this clustering occurs to the left of the mean—that is, at a value less than the mean. In left-skewed data sets, the values tend to cluster to the right of the mean—that is, at a value greater than the mean. In symmetrical data sets, where the median and mean are the same, the values often tend to cluster around the median and mean, producing a bell-shaped distribution. You can use the **empirical rule** to examine the variability in bell-shaped distributions:

- Approximately 68% of the values are within a distance of ±1 standard deviation from the mean.
- Approximately 95% of the values are within a distance of ±2 standard deviations from the mean.
- Approximately 99.7% are within a distance of ±3 standard deviations from the mean.

The empirical rule helps you measure how the values distribute above and below the mean and can help you identify outliers. The empirical rule implies that for bell-shaped distributions, only about 1 out of 20 values will be beyond two standard deviations from the mean in either direction. As a general rule, you can consider values not found in the interval $\mu \pm 2\sigma$ as potential outliers. The rule also implies that only about 3 in 1,000 will be beyond three standard deviations from the mean. Therefore, values not found in the interval $\mu \pm 3\sigma$ are almost always considered outliers. For heavily skewed data sets, or those not appearing bell shaped for any other reason, the Chebyshev rule discussed below should be applied instead of the empirical rule.

EXAMPLE 3.12

USING THE EMPIRICAL RULE

A population of 12-ounce cans of cola is known to have a mean fill-weight of 12.06 ounces and a standard deviation of 0.02. The population is known to be bell shaped. Describe the distribution of fill-weights. Is it very likely that a can will contain less than 12 ounces of cola?

SOLUTION

$$\mu \pm \sigma = 12.06 \pm 0.02 = (12.04, 12.08)$$

$$\mu \pm 2\sigma = 12.06 \pm 2(0.02) = (12.02, 12.10)$$

$$\mu \pm 3\sigma = 12.06 \pm 3(0.02) = (12.00, 12.12)$$

Using the empirical rule, approximately 68% of the cans will contain between 12.04 and 12.08 ounces, approximately 95% will contain between 12.02 and 12.10 ounces, and approximately 99.7% will contain between 12.00 and 12.12 ounces. Therefore, it is highly unlikely that a can will contain less than 12 ounces.

The Chebyshev Rule

The **Chebyshev rule** (reference 1) states that for any data set, regardless of shape, the percentage of values that are found within distances of k standard deviations from the mean must be at least

$$(1 - 1/k^2) \times 100\%$$

You can use this rule for any value of k greater than 1. Consider $k = 2$. The Chebyshev rule states that at least $[1 - (1/2)^2] \times 100\% = 75\%$ of the values must be found within ± 2 standard deviations of the mean.

The Chebyshev rule is very general and applies to any type of distribution. The rule indicates *at least* what percentage of the values fall within a given distance from the mean. However, if the data set is approximately bell shaped, the empirical rule will more accurately reflect the greater concentration of data close to the mean. Table 3.6 compares the Chebyshev and empirical rules.

TABLE 3.6

How Data Vary Around the Mean

| | % of Values Found in Intervals Around the Mean | |
Interval	Chebyshev (any distribution)	Empirical Rule (bell-shaped distribution)
$(\mu - \sigma, \mu + \sigma)$	At least 0%	Approximately 68%
$(\mu - 2\sigma, \mu + 2\sigma)$	At least 75%	Approximately 95%
$(\mu - 3\sigma, \mu + 3\sigma)$	At least 88.89%	Approximately 99.7%

EXAMPLE 3.13   **USING THE CHEBYSHEV RULE**

As in Example 3.12, a population of 12-ounce cans of cola is known to have a mean fill-weight of 12.06 ounces and a standard deviation of 0.02. However, the shape of the population is unknown, and you cannot assume that it is bell shaped. Describe the distribution of fill-weights. Is it very likely that a can will contain less than 12 ounces of cola?

SOLUTION

$$\mu \pm \sigma = 12.06 \pm 0.02 = (12.04, 12.08)$$

$$\mu \pm 2\sigma = 12.06 \pm 2(0.02) = (12.02, 12.10)$$

$$\mu \pm 3\sigma = 12.06 \pm 3(0.02) = (12.00, 12.12)$$

Because the distribution may be skewed, you cannot use the empirical rule. Using the Chebyshev rule, you cannot say anything about the percentage of cans containing between 12.04 and 12.08 ounces. You can state that at least 75% of the cans will contain between 12.02 and 12.10 ounces and at least 88.89% will contain between 12.00 and 12.12 ounces. Therefore, between 0 and 11.11% of the cans will contain less than 12 ounces.

You can use these two rules for understanding how data are distributed around the mean when you have sample data. In each case, you use the value you calculated for $\bar{X}$ in place of μ and the value you calculated for S in place of σ. The results you compute using the sample statistics are *approximations* because you used sample statistics ($\bar{X}$, S) and not population parameters (μ, σ).

PROBLEMS FOR SECTION 3.3

Learning the Basics

 3.21 The following is a set of data for a population with $N = 10$:

> 7 5 11 8 3 6 2 1 9 8

a. Compute the population mean.
b. Compute the population standard deviation.

 3.22 The following is a set of data for a population with $N = 10$:

> 7 5 6 6 6 4 8 6 9 3

a. Compute the population mean.
b. Compute the population standard deviation.

Applying the Concepts

3.23 The data in the file **tax.xls** represent the quarterly sales tax receipts (in thousands of dollars) submitted to the comptroller of the Village of Fair Lake for the period ending March 2006 by all 50 business establishments in that locale:

10.3	11.1	9.6	9.0	14.5
13.0	6.7	11.0	8.4	10.3
13.0	11.2	7.3	5.3	12.5
8.0	11.8	8.7	10.6	9.5
11.1	10.2	11.1	9.9	9.8
11.6	15.1	12.5	6.5	7.5
10.0	12.9	9.2	10.0	12.8
12.5	9.3	10.4	12.7	10.5
9.3	11.5	10.7	11.6	7.8
10.5	7.6	10.1	8.9	8.6

a. Compute the mean, variance, and standard deviation for this population.
b. What proportion of these businesses have quarterly sales tax receipts within ±1, ±2, or ±3 standard deviations of the mean?
c. Compare and contrast your findings with what would be expected on the basis of the empirical rule. Are you surprised at the results in (b)?

 3.24 Consider a population of 1,024 mutual funds that primarily invested in large companies. You have determined that μ, the mean one-year total percentage return achieved by all the funds, is 8.20 and that σ, the standard deviation, is 2.75. In addition, suppose you have determined that the range in the one-year total returns is from −2.0 to 17.1 and that the quartiles are 5.5 (Q_1) and 10.5 (Q_3). According to the empirical rule, what percentage of these funds is expected to be

a. within ±1 standard deviation of the mean?
b. within ±2 standard deviations of the mean?
c. According to the Chebyshev rule, what percentage of these funds are expected to be within ±1, ±2, or ±3 standard deviations of the mean?
d. According to the Chebyshev rule, at least 93.75% of these funds are expected to have one-year total returns between what two amounts?

3.25 The data in the file **stockassets.xls** represent the assets, in billions of dollars, of the five largest stock funds.

Fund	Assets
American Funds Gro; A	73.6
Vanguard 500 Index; Inv	69.4
American Funds ICA; A	67.0
American Funds Wsh; A	62.4
Fidelity Contrafund	60.1

a. Compute the mean for this population of the five largest stock funds. Interpret this parameter.
b. Compute the variance and standard deviation for this population. Interpret these parameters.
c. Is there a lot of variability in the assets of these stock funds? Explain.

3.26 The data in the file **energy.xls** contains the per capita energy consumption, in kilowatt hours, for each of the 50 states and the District of Columbia during a recent year.

a. Compute the mean, variance, and standard deviation for the population.
b. What proportion of these states has average per capita energy consumption within ±1 standard deviation of the mean, within ±2 standard deviations of the mean, and within ±3 standard deviations of the mean?
c. Compare and contrast your findings versus what would be expected based on the empirical rule. Are you surprised at the results in (b)?
d. Repeat (a) through (c) with the District of Columbia removed. How have the results changed?

3.27 Thirty companies comprise the DJIA. Just how big are these companies? One common method to measure the size of a company is to use its market capitalization, which is computed by taking the number of stock shares multiplied by the price of a share of stock. On April 4, 2006, the market capitalization of these companies ranged from Hewlett-Packard's $3.55 billion to Exxon-Mobil's $376.64 billion. The entire population of market capitalization values is recorded in the file **dowmc.xls**.
Source: Extracted from **money.cnn.com**, *April 4, 2006.*

a. Calculate the mean and standard deviation of the market capitalization for this population of 30 companies.
b. Interpret the parameters calculated in (a).

3.4   EXPLORATORY DATA ANALYSIS

Sections 3.1–3.3 discuss measures of central tendency, variation, and shape. Another way of describing numerical data is through exploratory data analysis that includes the five-number summary and the box-and-whisker plot (references 3 and 4).

The Five-Number Summary

A **five-number summary** that consists of

$$X_{\text{smallest}} \quad Q_1 \quad \text{Median} \quad Q_3 \quad X_{\text{largest}}$$

provides a way to determine the shape of a distribution. Table 3.7 explains how the relationships among the "five numbers" allows you to recognize the shape of a data set.

TABLE 3.7 Relationships Among the Five-Number Summary and the Type of Distribution

	Type of Distribution		
Comparison	**Left-Skewed**	**Symmetric**	**Right-Skewed**
The distance from X_{smallest} to the median versus the distance from the median to X_{largest}.	The distance from X_{smallest} to the median is greater than the distance from the median to X_{largest}.	Both distances are the same.	The distance from X_{smallest} to the median is less than the distance from the median to X_{largest}.
The distance from X_{smallest} to Q_1 versus the distance from Q_3 to X_{largest}.	The distance from X_{smallest} to Q_1 is greater than the distance from Q_3 to X_{largest}.	Both distances are the same.	The distance from X_{smallest} to Q_1 is less than the distance from Q_3 to X_{largest}.
The distance from Q_1 to the median versus the distance from the median to Q_3.	The distance from Q_1 to the median is greater than the distance from the median to Q_3.	Both distances are the same.	The distance from Q_1 to the median is less than the distance from the median to Q_3.

For the sample of 10 getting-ready times, the smallest value is 29 minutes and the largest value is 52 minutes (see page 100). Calculations done in Section 3.1 show that the median = 39.5, $Q_1 = 35$, and $Q_3 = 44$. Therefore, the five-number summary is

$$29 \quad 35 \quad 39.5 \quad 44 \quad 52$$

The distance from X_{smallest} to the median ($39.5 - 29 = 10.5$) is slightly less than the distance from the median to X_{largest} ($52 - 39.5 = 12.5$). The distance from X_{smallest} to Q_1 ($35 - 29 = 6$) is slightly less than the distance from Q_3 to X_{largest} ($52 - 44 = 8$). Therefore, the getting-ready times are slightly right-skewed.

EXAMPLE 3.14

COMPUTING THE FIVE-NUMBER SUMMARY OF THE THREE-YEAR ANNUALIZED RETURNS FOR SMALL-CAP GROWTH MUTUAL FUNDS WITH LOW RISK

The 838 mutual funds (Mutual Funds.xls) that are part of the Using Statistics scenario (see page 96) are classified according to the category (small cap, mid cap, and large cap), the type (growth or value), and the risk level of the mutual funds (low, average, and high). Compute the five-number summary of the three-year annualized returns for the small-cap growth funds with low risk (see page 99).

SOLUTION From previous computations for the three-year annualized returns for the small-cap growth funds with low risk (see pages 100, 102, and 103), the median = 22.4, $Q_1 = 20.8$, and $Q_3 = 26.0$. In addition, the smallest value in the data set is 19.0, and the largest value is 29.9. Therefore, the five-number summary is

$$19.0 \quad 20.8 \quad 22.4 \quad 26.0 \quad 29.9$$

The three comparisons listed in Table 3.7 are used to evaluate skewness. The distance from X_{smallest} to the median ($22.4 - 19.0 = 3.4$) is less than the distance ($29.9 - 22.4 = 7.5$) from the median to X_{largest}. The distance from X_{smallest} to Q_1 ($20.8 - 19.0 = 1.8$) is less than the distance from Q_3 to X_{largest} ($29.9 - 26.0 = 3.9$). The distance from Q_1 to the median ($22.4 - 20.8 = 1.6$) is less than the distance from the median to Q_3 ($26.0 - 22.4 = 3.6$). All three comparisons indicate a right-skewed distribution.

The Box-and-Whisker Plot

A **box-and-whisker plot** provides a graphical representation of the data based on the five-number summary. Figure 3.3 illustrates the box-and-whisker plot for the getting-ready times.

FIGURE 3.3

Box-and-whisker plot of the time to get ready

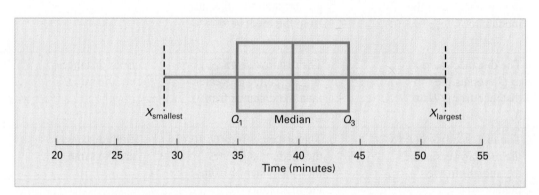

The vertical line drawn within the box represents the median. The vertical line at the left side of the box represents the location of Q_1, and the vertical line at the right side of the box represents the location of Q_3. Thus, the box contains the middle 50% of the values. The lower 25% of the data are represented by a line (i.e., a *whisker*) connecting the left side of the box to the location of the smallest value, X_{smallest}. Similarly, the upper 25% of the data are represented by a whisker connecting the right side of the box to X_{largest}.

The box-and-whisker plot of the getting-ready times in Figure 3.3 indicates very slight right-skewness because the distance between the median and the highest value is slightly greater than the distance between the lowest value and the median. Also, the right whisker is slightly longer than the left whisker.

EXAMPLE 3.15

THE BOX-AND-WHISKER PLOTS OF THE THREE-YEAR ANNUALIZED RETURNS OF LOW-, AVERAGE-, AND HIGH-RISK MUTUAL FUNDS

The 838 mutual funds (**Mutual Funds.xls**) that are part of the Using Statistics scenario (see page 96) are classified according to the risk level of the mutual funds (low, average, and high). Construct the box-and-whisker plot of the three-year annualized returns for low-risk, average-risk, and high-risk mutual funds.

SOLUTION   Figure 3.4 is a Microsoft Excel box-and-whisker plot of the three-year annualized return for low-risk, average-risk, and high-risk mutual funds. The median return and the quartiles are slightly higher for the low-risk and high-risk funds than for the average-risk funds. All three types of funds are right-skewed due to the long upper whisker.

FIGURE 3.4

Microsoft Excel box-
and-whisker plots of the
three-year annualized
return for low-risk,
average-risk, and high-
risk mutual funds

*See Section E3.4 to create
this.*

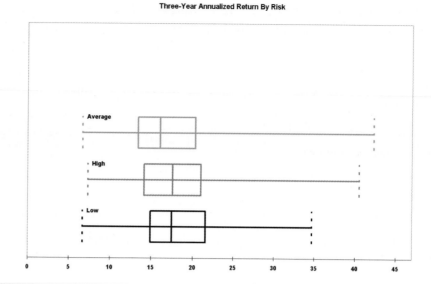

Figure 3.5 demonstrates the relationship between the box-and-whisker plot and the polygon for four different types of distributions. (*Note:* The area under each polygon is split into
quartiles corresponding to the five-number summary for the box-and-whisker plot.)

FIGURE 3.5

Box-and-whisker plots
and corresponding
polygons for four
distributions

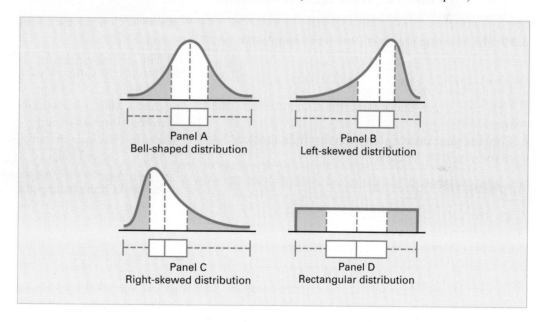

Panels A and D of Figure 3.5 are symmetrical. In these distributions, the mean and median
are equal. In addition, the length of the left whisker is equal to the length of the right whisker,
and the median line divides the box in half.

Panel B of Figure 3.5 is left-skewed. The few small values distort the mean toward the left tail.
For this left-skewed distribution, the skewness indicates that there is a heavy clustering of values at
the high end of the scale (i.e., the right side); 75% of all values are found between the left edge of
the box (Q_1) and the end of the right whisker ($X_{largest}$). Therefore, the long left whisker contains the
smallest 25% of the values, demonstrating the distortion from symmetry in this data set.

Panel C of Figure 3.5 is right-skewed. The concentration of values is on the low end of the
scale (i.e., the left side of the box-and-whisker plot). Here, 75% of all data values are found
between the beginning of the left whisker ($X_{smallest}$) and the right edge of the box (Q_3), and the
remaining 25% of the values are dispersed along the long right whisker at the upper end of the
scale.

PROBLEMS FOR SECTION 3.4

Learning the Basics

 3.28 The following is a set of data from a sample of $n = 6$:

7   4   9   7   3   12

a. List the five-number summary.
b. Construct a box-and-whisker plot and describe the shape.
c. Compare your answer in (b) with that from Problem 3.2 (d) on page 115. Discuss.

3.29 The following is a set of data from a sample of $n = 7$:

12   7   4   9   0   7   3

a. List the five-number summary.
b. Construct a box-and-whisker plot and describe the shape.
c. Compare your answer in (b) with that from Problem 3.3 (d) on page 115. Discuss.

3.30 The following is a set of data from a sample of $n = 5$:

7   −5   −8   7   9

a. List the five-number summary.
b. Construct a box-and-whisker plot and describe the shape.
c. Compare your answer in (b) with that from Problem 3.4 (d) on page 115. Discuss.

Applying the Concepts

3.31 The data file **chicken.xls** contains the total fat, in grams per serving, for a sample of 20 chicken sandwiches from fast-food chains. The data are as follows:

7   8   4   5   16   20   20   24   19   30
23   30   25   19   29   29   30   30   40   56

Source: Extracted from "Fast Food: Adding Health to the Menu," Consumer Reports, September 2004, pp. 28–31.

a. List the five-number summary.
b. Construct a box-and-whisker plot and describe the shape.

3.32 The data in the file **batterylife.xls** represent the battery life (in shots) for three pixel digital cameras:

300   180   85   170   380   460
260   35   380   120   110   240

Source: Extracted from "Cameras: More Features in the Mix," Consumer Reports, July 2005, pp. 14–18.

a. List the five-number summary.
b. Construct a box-and-whisker plot and describe the shape.

3.33 The data file **themeparks.xls** contains data on the starting admission price (in $) for one-day tickets to 10 theme parks in the United States:

58   63   41   42   29   50   62   43   40   40

Source: Extracted from C. Jackson and E. Gamerman, "Rethinking the Thrill Factor," The Wall Street Journal, April 15–16, 2006, pp. P1, P4.

a. List the five-number summary.
b. Construct a box-and-whisker plot and describe the shape of the data.

3.34 The data in the file **coffeedrink.xls** represent the calories and fat (in grams) of 16-ounce iced coffee drinks at Dunkin' Donuts and Starbucks:

Product	Calories	Fat
Dunkin' Donuts Iced Mocha Swirl latte (whole milk)	240	8.0
Starbucks Coffee Frappuccino blended coffee	260	3.5
Dunkin' Donuts Coffee Coolatta (cream)	350	22.0
Starbucks Iced Coffee Mocha Expresso (whole milk and whipped cream)	350	20.0
Starbucks Mocha Frappuccino blended coffee (whipped cream)	420	16.0
Starbucks Chocolate Brownie Frappuccino blended coffee (whipped cream)	510	22.0
Starbucks Chocolate Frappuccino Blended Crème (whipped cream)	530	19.0

Source: Extracted from "Coffee as Candy at Dunkin' Donuts and Starbucks," Consumer Reports, June 2004, p. 9.

a. For each variable (calories and fat), list the five-number summary.
b. Construct a box-and-whisker plot for calories and for fat.
c. What similarities and differences are there in the distributions for calories and for fat?

3.35 The data in the file **savings.xls** are the yields for a money market account, a one-year certificate of deposit (CD), and a five-year CD for 40 banks in South Florida as of December 20, 2005 (extracted from Bankrate.com, December 20, 2005).

a. List the five-number summary for the yield of the money market account, one-year CD, and a five-year CD.
b. Construct a box-and-whisker plot for the yield of the money market account, one-year CD, and a five-year CD.
c. What similarities and differences are there in the distributions for the yield of the money market account, one-year CD, and a five-year CD?

3.36 A bank branch located in a commercial district of a city has developed an improved process for serving customers during the noon-to-1:00 p.m. lunch period. The waiting time, in minutes (defined as the time the customer enters the line to when he or she reaches the teller window), of a sample of 15 customers during this hour is recorded over a period of one week. The results are contained in the data file bank1.xls and are listed below:

4.21   5.55   3.02   5.13   4.77   2.34   3.54   3.20
4.50   6.10   0.38   5.12   6.46   6.19   3.79

Another branch, located in a residential area, is also concerned with the noon-to-1 p.m. lunch hour. The waiting time, in minutes (defined as the time the customer enters the line to when he or she reaches the teller window), of a sample of 15 customers during this hour is recorded over a period of one week. The results are contained in the data file bank2.xls and are listed below:

9.66   5.90   8.02   5.79   8.73   3.82   8.01   8.35
10.49   6.68   5.64   4.08   6.17   9.91   5.47

a. List the five-number summaries of the waiting times at the two bank branches.
b. Construct box-and-whisker plots and describe the shape of the distribution of each for the two bank branches.
c. What similarities and differences are there in the distributions of the waiting time at the two bank branches?

3.5   THE COVARIANCE AND THE COEFFICIENT OF CORRELATION

In Section 2.5, you used scatter plots to *visually* examine the relationship between two numerical variables. This section presents two *numerical* measures that examine the relationship between two numerical variables: the covariance and the coefficient of correlation.

The Covariance

The **covariance** measures the strength of the linear relationship between two numerical variables (X and Y). Equation (3.16) defines the **sample covariance**, and Example 3.16 illustrates its use.

THE SAMPLE COVARIANCE

$$\text{cov}(X,Y) = \frac{\sum_{i=1}^{n}(X_i - \bar{X})(Y_i - \bar{Y})}{n - 1} \tag{3.16}$$

EXAMPLE 3.16

COMPUTING THE SAMPLE COVARIANCE

In Section 2.5 on page 58, you examined the relationship between the cost of a fast-food hamburger meal and the cost of two movie tickets in 10 cities around the world (extracted from K. Spors, "Keeping Up with . . . Yourself," *The Wall Street Journal*, April 11, 2005, p. R4). The data file cost of living.xls contains the complete data set. Compute the sample covariance.

SOLUTION Table 3.8 provides the cost of a fast-food hamburger meal and the cost of two movie tickets in 10 cities around the world.

TABLE 3.8

Cost of a Fast-Food Hamburger Meal and Cost of Two Movie Tickets in 10 Cities

City	Hamburger	Movie Tickets
Tokyo	5.99	32.66
London	7.62	28.41
New York	5.75	20.00
Sydney	4.45	20.71
Chicago	4.99	18.00
San Francisco	5.29	19.50
Boston	4.39	18.00
Atlanta	3.70	16.00
Toronto	4.62	18.05
Rio de Janeiro	2.99	9.90

FIGURE 3.6

Microsoft Excel worksheet for the covariance between cost of a fast-food hamburger meal and cost of two movie tickets in 10 cities

	A	B	C	
1	Covariance Analysis			
2				
3	Hamburger Meal	Movie Ticket	(X-XBar)(Y-YBar)	
4	5.99	32.66	12.67491	=(A4 - $C$16) * (B4 - $C$17)
5	7.62	28.41	21.88597	=(A5 - $C$16) * (B5 - $C$17)
6	5.75	20	-0.09483	=(A6 - $C$16) * (B6 - $C$17)
7	4.45	20.71	-0.31052	=(A7 - $C$16) * (B7 - $C$17)
8	4.99	18	-0.02335	=(A8 - $C$16) * (B8 - $C$17)
9	5.29	19.5	-0.19375	=(A9 - $C$16) * (B9 - $C$17)
10	4.39	18	1.25045	=(A10 - $C$16) * (B10 - $C$17)
11	3.7	16	5.27332	=(A11 - $C$16) * (B11 - $C$17)
12	4.62	18.05	0.74421	=(A12 - $C$16) * (B12 - $C$17)
13	2.99	9.9	20.33355	=(A13 - $C$16) * (B13 - $C$17)
14				
15		Calculations		
16		XBar	4.979	=AVERAGE(A4:A13)
17		YBar	20.123	=AVERAGE(B4:B13)
18		*n*-1	9	=COUNT(A4:A13) - 1
19		Sum	61.53993	=SUM(C4:C13)
20		Covariance	6.83777	=C19 / C18

Figure 3.6 contains a Microsoft Excel worksheet that calculates the covariance for these data. The Calculations area of Figure 3.6 breaks down Equation (3.16) into a set of smaller calculations. From cell C20, or by using Equation (3.16) directly, you find that the covariance is 6.83777:

$$\text{cov}(X,Y) = \frac{61.53993}{10 - 1}$$
$$= 6.83777$$

The covariance has a major flaw as a measure of the linear relationship between two numerical variables. Because the covariance can have any value, you are unable to determine the relative strength of the relationship. In other words, you cannot tell whether the value 6.83777 is an indication of a strong relationship or a weak relationship. To better determine the relative strength of the relationship, you need to compute the coefficient of correlation.

The Coefficient of Correlation

The **coefficient of correlation** measures the relative strength of a linear relationship between two numerical variables. The values of the coefficient of correlation range from −1 for a perfect negative correlation to +1 for a perfect positive correlation. *Perfect* means that if the points were plotted in a scatter plot, all the points could be connected with a straight line. When dealing with population data for two numerical variables, the Greek letter ρ is used as the symbol for the coefficient of correlation. Figure 3.7 illustrates three different types of association between two variables.

FIGURE 3.7

Types of association between variables

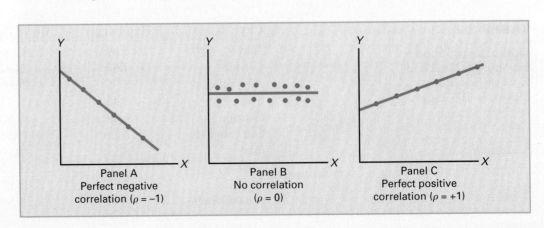

Panel A
Perfect negative correlation ($\rho = -1$)

Panel B
No correlation ($\rho = 0$)

Panel C
Perfect positive correlation ($\rho = +1$)

In Panel A of Figure 3.7, there is a perfect negative linear relationship between X and Y. Thus, the coefficient of correlation, ρ, equals -1, and when X increases, Y decreases in a perfectly predictable manner. Panel B shows a situation in which there is no relationship between X and Y. In this case, the coefficient of correlation, ρ, equals 0, and as X increases, there is no tendency for Y to increase or decrease. Panel C illustrates a perfect positive relationship where ρ equals $+1$. In this case, Y increases in a perfectly predictable manner when X increases.

When you have sample data, the sample coefficient of correlation, r, is calculated. When using sample data, you are unlikely to have a sample coefficient of exactly $+1$, 0, or -1. Figure 3.8 presents scatter plots along with their respective sample coefficients of correlation, r, for six data sets, each of which contains 100 values of X and Y.

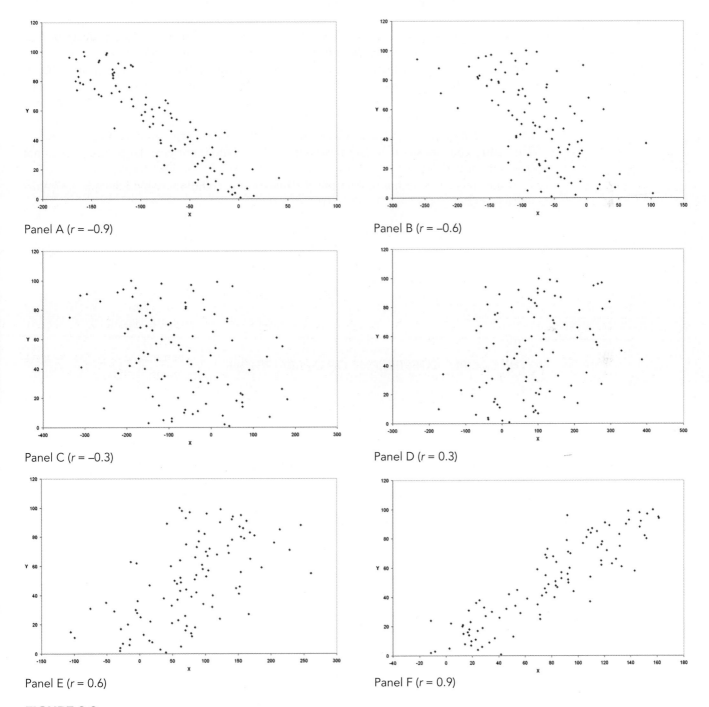

Panel A ($r = -0.9$)

Panel B ($r = -0.6$)

Panel C ($r = -0.3$)

Panel D ($r = 0.3$)

Panel E ($r = 0.6$)

Panel F ($r = 0.9$)

FIGURE 3.8

Six scatter plots created from Microsoft Excel and their sample coefficients of correlation, r

In Panel A, the coefficient of correlation, r, is −0.9. You can see that for small values of X, there is a very strong tendency for Y to be large. Likewise, the large values of X tend to be paired with small values of Y. The data do not all fall on a straight line, so the association between X and Y cannot be described as *perfect*. The data in Panel B have a coefficient of correlation equal to −0.6, and the small values of X tend to be paired with large values of Y. The linear relationship between X and Y in Panel B is not as strong as that in Panel A. Thus, the coefficient of correlation in Panel B is not as negative as that in Panel A. In Panel C, the linear relationship between X and Y is very weak, $r = -0.3$, and there is only a slight tendency for the small values of X to be paired with the larger values of Y. Panels D through F depict data sets that have positive coefficients of correlation because small values of X tend to be paired with small values of Y, and the large values of X tend to be associated with large values of Y.

In the discussion of Figure 3.8, the relationships were deliberately described as *tendencies* and not as *causes and effects*. This wording was used on purpose. Correlation alone cannot prove that there is a causation effect—that is, that the change in the value of one variable *caused* the change in the other variable. A strong correlation can be produced simply by chance, by the effect of a third variable not considered in the calculation of the correlation, or by a cause-and-effect relationship. You would need to perform additional analysis to determine which of these three situations actually produced the correlation. Therefore, you can say that causation implies correlation, but correlation alone does not imply causation.

Equation (3.17) defines the **sample coefficient of correlation**, r, and Example 3.17 illustrates its use.

THE SAMPLE COEFFICIENT OF CORRELATION

$$r = \frac{\text{cov}(X,Y)}{S_X S_Y} \tag{3.17}$$

where

$$\text{cov}(X,Y) = \frac{\sum_{i=1}^{n}(X_i - \bar{X})(Y_i - \bar{Y})}{n-1}$$

$$S_X = \sqrt{\frac{\sum_{i=1}^{n}(X_i - \bar{X})^2}{n-1}}$$

$$S_Y = \sqrt{\frac{\sum_{i=1}^{n}(Y_i - \bar{Y})^2}{n-1}}$$

EXAMPLE 3.17   COMPUTING THE SAMPLE COEFFICIENT OF CORRELATION

Consider the cost of a fast-food hamburger meal and the cost of two movie tickets in 10 cities around the world (see Table 3.8 on page 127). From Figure 3.9 and Equation (3.17), compute the sample coefficient of correlation.

SOLUTION

$$r = \frac{\text{cov}(X,Y)}{S_X S_Y}$$

$$= \frac{6.83777}{(1.2925)(6.337)}$$

$$= 0.8348$$

FIGURE 3.9

Microsoft Excel worksheet for the sample coefficient of correlation, r, between the cost of a fast-food hamburger meal and two movie tickets

See Sections E3.5 and E3.6 to create this.

	A	B	C	D	E	
1	Hamburger Meal	Movie Ticket	(X-XBar)²	(Y-YBar)²	(X-XBar)(Y-YBar)	
2	5.99	32.66	1.0221	157.1764	12.6749	
3	7.62	28.41	6.9749	68.6744	21.8860	
4	5.75	20	0.5944	0.0151	-0.0948	
5	4.45	20.71	0.2798	0.3446	-0.3105	
6	4.99	18	0.0001	4.5071	-0.0234	
7	5.29	19.5	0.0967	0.3881	-0.1938	
8	4.39	18	0.3469	4.5071	1.2504	
9	3.7	16	1.6358	16.9991	5.2733	
10	4.62	18.05	0.1289	4.2973	0.7442	
11	2.99	9.9	3.9561	104.5097	20.3335	
12		Sums:	15.03589	361.41901	61.5399	
13		:				
14				**Calculations**		
15				XBar	4.979	=AVERAGE(A2:A11)
16				YBar	20.123	=AVERAGE(B2:B11)
17				n-1	9	=COUNT(A2:A11)-1
18				Covariance	6.83777	=E12 / E17
19				Sₓ	1.2925	=SQRT(C12 / E17)
20				Sᵧ	6.3370	=SQRT(D12 / E17)
21				r	0.8348	=CORREL(A2:A11, B2:B11)

The cost of a fast-food hamburger meal and the cost of two movie tickets are positively correlated. Those cities with the lowest cost of a fast-food hamburger meal tend to be associated with the lowest cost of two movie tickets. Those cities with the highest cost of a fast-food hamburger meal tend to be associated with the highest cost of two movie tickets. This relationship is fairly strong, as indicated by a coefficient of correlation, $r = 0.8348$.

You cannot assume that having a low cost of a fast-food hamburger meal caused the low cost of two movie tickets. You can only say that this is what tended to happen in the sample.

In summary, the coefficient of correlation indicates the linear relationship, or association, between two numerical variables. When the coefficient of correlation gets closer to +1 or −1, the linear relationship between the two variables is stronger. When the coefficient of correlation is near 0, little or no linear relationship exists. The sign of the coefficient of correlation indicates whether the data are positively correlated (i.e., the larger values of X are typically paired with the larger values of Y) or negatively correlated (i.e., the larger values of X are typically paired with the smaller values of Y). The existence of a strong correlation does not imply a causation effect. It only indicates the tendencies present in the data.

PROBLEMS FOR SECTION 3.5

Learning the Basics

3.37 The following is a set of data from a sample of $n = 11$ items:

X	7	5	8	3	6	10	12	4	9	15	18
Y	21	15	24	9	18	30	36	12	27	45	54

a. Compute the covariance.
b. Compute the coefficient of correlation.
c. How strong is the relationship between X and Y? Explain.

Applying the Concepts

3.38 An article (J. Clements, "Why Investors Should Put up to 30% of Their Stock Portfolio in Foreign Funds," *The Wall Street Journal*, November 26, 2003, p. D1) that discussed investment in foreign stocks stated that the coefficient of correlation between the return on investment of U.S. stocks and international large cap stocks was 0.80, U.S. stocks and international small cap stocks was 0.53, U.S. stocks and international bonds was 0.03, U.S. stocks and emerging markets stocks was 0.71, and U.S. stocks and emerging markets debt was 0.58.

a. What conclusions can you make about the strength of the relationship between the return on investment of U. S. stocks and each of these five other types of investments?
b. Compare the results of (a) to those of Problem 3.39 (a).

3.39 An article (J. Clements, "Why Investors Should Put up to 30% of Their Stock Portfolio in Foreign Funds," *The Wall Street Journal*, November 26, 2003, p. D1) that discussed investment in foreign bonds stated that the coefficient of correlation between the return on investment of U.S. bonds and international large cap stocks was −0.13, U.S. bonds and international small cap stocks was −0.18, U.S. bonds and international bonds was 0.48, U.S. bonds and emerging markets stocks was −0.20, and U.S. bonds and emerging markets debt was 0.10.

a. What conclusions can you make about the strength of the relationship between the return on investment of U.S. bonds and each of these five other types of investments?
b. Compare the results of (a) to those of Problem 3.38 (a).

 3.40 The data in the file `coffeedrink.xls` represent the calories and fat, in grams, of 16-ounce iced coffee drinks at Dunkin' Donuts and Starbucks:

Product	Calories	Fat
Dunkin' Donuts Iced Mocha Swirl latte (whole milk)	240	8.0
Starbucks Coffee Frappuccino blended coffee	260	3.5
Dunkin' Donuts Coffee Coolatta (cream)	350	22.0
Starbucks Iced Coffee Mocha Expresso (whole milk and whipped cream)	350	20.0
Starbucks Mocha Frappuccino blended coffee (whipped cream)	420	16.0
Starbucks Chocolate Brownie Frappuccino blended coffee (whipped cream)	510	22.0
Starbucks Chocolate Frappuccino Blended Crème (whipped cream)	530	19.0

Source: Extracted from "Coffee as Candy at Dunkin' Donuts and Starbucks," Consumer Reports, June 2004, p. 9.

a. Compute the covariance.
b. Compute the coefficient of correlation.
c. Which do you think is more valuable in expressing the relationship between calories and fat—the covariance or the coefficient of correlation? Explain.
d. What conclusions can you reach about the relationship between calories and fat?

3.41 There are several methods for calculating fuel economy. The following table (contained in the file `mileage.xls`) indicates the mileage, as calculated by owners and by current government standards:

Car	Owner	Government
2005 Ford F-150	14.3	16.8
2005 Chevrolet Silverado	15.0	17.8
2002 Honda Accord LX	27.8	26.2
2002 Honda Civic	27.9	34.2
2004 Honda Civic Hybrid	48.8	47.6
2002 Ford Explorer	16.8	18.3
2005 Toyota Camry	23.7	28.5
2003 Toyota Corolla	32.8	33.1
2005 Toyota Prius	37.3	56.0

Source: Extracted from J. Healey, "Fuel Economy Calculations to be Altered," USA Today, January 11, 2006, p. 1B.

a. Compute the covariance.
b. Compute the coefficient of correlation.
c. Which do you think is more valuable in expressing the relationship between owner and current government standards mileage—the covariance or the coefficient of correlation? Explain.
d. What conclusions can you reach about the relationship between owner and current government standards mileage?

3.42 College basketball is big business, with coaches' salaries, revenues, and expenses in millions of dollars. The data file `colleges-basketball.xls` contains the coaches' salaries and revenue for college basketball at selected schools in a recent year (extracted from R. Adams, "Pay for Playoffs," *The Wall Street Journal*, March 11–12, 2006, pp. P1, P8).

a. Compute the covariance.
b. Compute the coefficient of correlation.
c. What conclusions can you reach about the relationship between a coach's salary and revenue?

3.43 College football players trying out for the NFL are given the Wonderlic standardized intelligence test. The data in the file `wonderlic.xls` contains the average Wonderlic score of football players trying out for the NFL and the graduation rate for football players at selected schools (extracted from S. Walker, "The NFL's Smartest Team," *The Wall Street Journal*, September 30, 2005, pp. W1, W10).

a. Compute the covariance.
b. Compute the coefficient of correlation.
c. What conclusions can you reach about the relationship between the average Wonderlic score and graduation rate?

3.6 PITFALLS IN NUMERICAL DESCRIPTIVE MEASURES AND ETHICAL ISSUES

In this chapter, you have studied how a set of numerical data can be characterized by various statistics that measure the properties of central tendency, variation, and shape. Your next step is analysis and interpretation of the calculated statistics. Your analysis is *objective*; your interpretation is *subjective*. You must avoid errors that may arise either in the objectivity of your analysis or in the subjectivity of your interpretation.

The analysis of the mutual funds is *objective* and reveals several impartial findings. Objectivity in data analysis means reporting the most appropriate numerical descriptive measures for a given data set. Now that you have read the chapter and have become familiar with various numerical descriptive measures and their strengths and weaknesses, how should you proceed with the objective analysis? Because the data distribute in a slightly asymmetrical manner, shouldn't you report the median in addition to the mean? Doesn't the standard deviation provide more information about the property of variation than the range? Should you describe the data set as right-skewed?

On the other hand, data interpretation is *subjective*. Different people form different conclusions when interpreting the analytical findings. Everyone sees the world from different perspectives. Thus, because data interpretation is subjective, you must do it in a fair, neutral, and clear manner.

Ethical Issues

Ethical issues are vitally important to all data analysis. As a daily consumer of information, you need to question what you read in newspapers and magazines, what you hear on the radio or television, and what you see while surfing the Internet. Over time, much skepticism has been expressed about the purpose, the focus, and the objectivity of published studies. Perhaps no comment on this topic is more telling than a quip often attributed to the famous nineteenth-century British statesman Benjamin Disraeli: "There are three kinds of lies: lies, damned lies, and statistics."

Ethical considerations arise when you are deciding what results to include in a report. You should document both good and bad results. In addition, when making oral presentations and presenting written reports, you need to give results in a fair, objective, and neutral manner. Unethical behavior occurs when you willfully choose an inappropriate summary measure (for example, the mean for a very skewed set of data) to distort the facts in order to support a particular position. In addition, unethical behavior occurs when you selectively fail to report pertinent findings because it would be detrimental to the support of a particular position.

SUMMARY

In this and the previous chapter, you studied descriptive statistics—how data are presented in tables and charts, and then summarized, described, analyzed, and interpreted. When dealing with the mutual fund data, you were able to present useful information through the use of pie charts, histograms, and other graphical methods. You explored characteristics of past performance, such as central tendency, variability, and shape, using numerical descriptive measures, such as the mean, median, quartiles, range, standard deviation, and coefficient of correlation. Table 3.9 provides a list of the numerical descriptive measures covered in this chapter.

In the next chapter, the basic principles of probability are presented in order to bridge the gap between the subject of descriptive statistics and the subject of inferential statistics.

TABLE 3.9

Summary of Numerical Descriptive Measures

Type of Analysis	Numerical Data
Describing central tendency, variation, and shape of a numerical variable	Mean, median, mode, quartiles, geometric mean, range, interquartile range, standard deviation, variance, coefficient of variation, Z scores, box-and-whisker plot (**Sections 3.1–3.4**)
Describing the relationship between two numerical variables	Covariance, coefficient of correlation (**Section 3.5**)

KEY EQUATIONS

Sample Mean

$$\bar{X} = \frac{\sum_{i=1}^{n} X_i}{n} \quad (3.1)$$

Median

$$\text{Median} = \frac{n+1}{2} \text{ ranked value} \quad (3.2)$$

First Quartile, Q_1

$$Q_1 = \frac{n+1}{4} \text{ ranked value} \quad (3.3)$$

Third Quartile, Q_3

$$Q_3 = \frac{3(n+1)}{4} \text{ ranked value} \quad (3.4)$$

Geometric Mean

$$\bar{X}_G = (X_1 \times X_2 \times \cdots \times X_n)^{1/n} \quad (3.5)$$

Geometric Mean Rate of Return

$$\bar{R}_G = [(1 + R_1) \times (1 + R_2) \times \cdots \times (1 + R_n)]^{1/n} - 1 \quad (3.6)$$

Range

$$\text{Range} = X_{\text{largest}} - X_{\text{smallest}} \quad (3.7)$$

Interquartile Range

$$\text{Interquartile range} = Q_3 - Q_1 \quad (3.8)$$

Sample Variance

$$S^2 = \frac{\sum_{i=1}^{n} (X_i - \bar{X})^2}{n-1} \quad (3.9)$$

Sample Standard Deviation

$$S = \sqrt{S^2} = \sqrt{\frac{\sum_{i=1}^{n} (X_i - \bar{X})^2}{n-1}} \quad (3.10)$$

Coefficient of Variation

$$CV = \left(\frac{S}{\bar{X}}\right)100\%$$ (3.11)

Z Scores

$$Z = \frac{X - \bar{X}}{S}$$ (3.12)

Population Mean

$$\mu = \frac{\sum_{i=1}^{N} X_i}{N}$$ (3.13)

Population Variance

$$\sigma^2 = \frac{\sum_{i=1}^{N} (X_i - \mu)^2}{N}$$ (3.14)

Population Standard Deviation

$$\sigma = \sqrt{\frac{\sum_{i=1}^{N} (X_i - \mu)^2}{N}}$$ (3.15)

Sample Covariance

$$\text{cov}(X,Y) = \frac{\sum_{i=1}^{n} (X_i - \bar{X})(Y_i - \bar{Y})}{n - 1}$$ (3.16)

Sample Coefficient of Correlation

$$r = \frac{\text{cov}(X,Y)}{S_X S_Y}$$ (3.17)

KEY TERMS

arithmetic mean   97
box-and-whisker plot   124
central tendency   96
Chebyshev rule   120
coefficient of correlation   128
coefficient of variation   110
covariance   127
dispersion   105
empirical rule   120
extreme value   111
five-number summary   123
geometric mean   103
geometric mean rate of return   103
interquartile range   106
left-skewed   113

mean   97
median   99
midspread   106
mode   100
outlier   111
population mean   118
population standard deviation   119
population variance   119
Q_1: first quartile   101
Q_2: second quartile   101
Q_3: third quartile   101
quartiles   101
range   105
resistant measure   106
right-skewed   113

sample coefficient of correlation   130
sample covariance   127
sample mean   97
sample standard deviation   107
sample variance   107
shape   96
skewed   112
spread   105
standard deviation   106
sum of squares (SS)   107
symmetrical   112
variance   106
variation   96
Z score   111

CHAPTER REVIEW PROBLEMS

Checking Your Understanding

3.44 What are the properties of a set of numerical data?

PH Grade ASSIST **3.45** What is meant by the property of central tendency?

PH Grade ASSIST **3.46** What are the differences among the mean, median, and mode, and what are the advantages and disadvantages of each?

3.47 How do you interpret the first quartile, median, and third quartile?

PH Grade ASSIST **3.48** What is meant by the property of variation?

3.49 What does the Z score measure?

PH Grade ASSIST **3.50** What are the differences among the various measures of variation, such as the range, interquartile range, variance, standard deviation, and coefficient of variation, and what are the advantages and disadvantages of each?

 3.51 How does the empirical rule help explain the ways in which the values in a set of numerical data cluster and distribute?

3.52 How do the empirical rule and the Chebychev rule differ?

3.53 What is meant by the property of shape?

3.54 How do the covariance and the coefficient of correlation differ?

Applying the Concepts

3.55 The American Society for Quality (ASQ) conducted a salary survey of all its members. ASQ members work in all areas of manufacturing and service-related institutions, with a common theme of an interest in quality. For the U.S. survey, emails were sent to 38,599 members, and 5,642 valid responses were received. The two most common job titles were manager and quality engineer. Descriptive statistics concerning salaries for these two titles are given below (Extracted from Debbie Phillips-Donaldson, "Good Year for Traditional Quality Professionals," *Quality Progress*, December, 2004, pp. 24–48). Compare the salaries of managers and quality engineers.

Title	Sample Size	Minimum	Maximum	Standard Deviation	Mean	Median
Manager	1,553	11,000	142,000	21,421	71,130	70,000
Quality Engineer	899	9,200	125,000	16,571	61,739	60,000

3.56 In New York State, savings banks are permitted to sell a form of life insurance called savings bank life insurance (SBLI). The approval process consists of underwriting, which includes a review of the application, a medical information bureau check, possible requests for additional medical information and medical exams, and a policy compilation stage during which the policy pages are generated and sent to the bank for delivery. The ability to deliver approved policies to customers in a timely manner is critical to the profitability of this service to the bank. During a period of one month, a random sample of 27 approved policies was selected, and the following total processing times in days, were recorded; the data are contained in the file insurance.xls:

73 19 16 64 28 28 31 90 60 56 31 56 22 18

45 48 17 17 17 91 92 63 50 51 69 16 17

a. Compute the mean, median, first quartile, and third quartile.
b. Compute the range, interquartile range, variance, standard deviation, and coefficient of variation.

c. Construct a box-and-whisker plot. Are the data skewed? If so, how?
d. What would you tell a customer who enters the bank to purchase this type of insurance policy and asks how long the approval process takes?

3.57 One of the major measures of the quality of service provided by any organization is the speed with which it responds to customer complaints. A large family-held department store selling furniture and flooring, including carpet, had undergone a major expansion in the past several years. In particular, the flooring department had expanded from 2 installation crews to an installation supervisor, a measurer, and 15 installation crews. A sample of 50 complaints concerning carpet installation was selected during a recent year. The data in the file furniture.xls represent the number of days between the receipt of a complaint and the resolution of the complaint:

54	5	35	137	31	27	152	2	123	81	74	27
11	19	126	110	110	29	61	35	94	31	26	5
12	4	165	32	29	28	29	26	25	1	14	13
13	10	5	27	4	52	30	22	36	26	20	23
33	68										

a. Compute the mean, median, first quartile, and third quartile.
b. Compute the range, interquartile range, variance, standard deviation, and coefficient of variation.
c. Construct a box-and-whisker plot. Are the data skewed? If so, how?
d. On the basis of the results of (a) through (c), if you had to tell the president of the company how long a customer should expect to wait to have a complaint resolved, what would you say? Explain.

3.58 A manufacturing company produces steel housings for electrical equipment. The main component part of the housing is a steel trough that is made out of a 14-gauge steel coil. It is produced using a 250-ton progressive punch press with a wipe-down operation, putting two 90-degree forms in the flat steel to make the trough. The distance from one side of the form to the other is critical because of weatherproofing in outdoor applications. The company requires that the width of the trough be between 8.31 inches and 8.61 inches. The data file trough.xls contains the widths of the troughs, in inches, for a sample of *n* = 49:

8.312 8.343 8.317 8.383 8.348 8.410 8.351 8.373 8.481 8.422

8.476 8.382 8.484 8.403 8.414 8.419 8.385 8.465 8.498 8.447

8.436 8.413 8.489 8.414 8.481 8.415 8.479 8.429 8.458 8.462

8.460 8.444 8.429 8.460 8.412 8.420 8.410 8.405 8.323 8.420

8.396 8.447 8.405 8.439 8.411 8.427 8.420 8.498 8.409

a. Calculate the mean, median, range, and standard deviation for the width. Interpret these measures of central tendency and variability.
b. List the five-number summary.
c. Construct a box-and-whisker plot and describe its shape.
d. What can you conclude about the number of troughs that will meet the company's requirement of troughs being between 8.31 and 8.61 inches wide?

3.59 The manufacturing company in Problem 3.58 also produces electric insulators. If the insulators break when in use, a short circuit is likely to occur. To test the strength of the insulators, destructive testing is carried out to determine how much force is required to break the insulators. Force is measured by observing how many pounds must be applied to the insulator before it breaks. The data from 30 insulators from this experiment are contained in the file force.xls:

1,870 1,728 1,656 1,610 1,634 1,784 1,522 1,696 1,592 1,662

1,866 1,764 1,734 1,662 1,734 1,774 1,550 1,756 1,762 1,866

1,820 1,744 1,788 1,688 1,810 1,752 1,680 1,810 1,652 1,736

a. Calculate the mean, median, range, and standard deviation for the force variable.
b. Interpret the measures of central tendency and variability in (a).
c. Construct a box-and-whisker plot and describe its shape.
d. What can you conclude about the strength of the insulators if the company requires a force measurement of at least 1,500 pounds before breakage?

3.60 Problems with a telephone line that prevent a customer from receiving or making calls are disconcerting to both the customer and the telephone company. The data contained in the file phone.xls represent samples of 20 problems reported to two different offices of a telephone company and the time to clear these problems, in minutes, from the customers' lines:

Central Office I Time to Clear Problems (minutes)

1.48 1.75 0.78 2.85 0.52 1.60 4.15 3.97 1.48 3.10
1.02 0.53 0.93 1.60 0.80 1.05 6.32 3.93 5.45 0.97

Central Office II Time to Clear Problems (minutes)

7.55 3.75 0.10 1.10 0.60 0.52 3.30 2.10 0.58 4.02
3.75 0.65 1.92 0.60 1.53 4.23 0.08 1.48 1.65 0.72

For each of the two central office locations:
a. Compute the mean, median, first quartile, and third quartile.
b. Compute the range, interquartile range, variance, standard deviation, and coefficient of variation.

c. Construct side-by-side box-and-whisker plots. Are the data skewed? If so, how?
d. On the basis of the results of (a) through (c), are there any differences between the two central offices? Explain.

3.61 In many manufacturing processes, the term *work-in-process* (often abbreviated WIP) is used. In a book manufacturing plant, the WIP represents the time it takes for sheets from a press to be folded, gathered, sewn, tipped on end sheets, and bound. The data contained in the file wip.xls represent samples of 20 books at each of two production plants and the processing time (operationally defined as the time, in days, from when the books came off the press to when they were packed in cartons) for these jobs:

Plant A

5.62 5.29 16.25 10.92 11.46 21.62 8.45 8.58 5.41 11.42
11.62 7.29 7.50 7.96 4.42 10.50 7.58 9.29 7.54 8.92

Plant B

9.54 11.46 16.62 12.62 25.75 15.41 14.29 13.13 13.71 10.04
5.75 12.46 9.17 13.21 6.00 2.33 14.25 5.37 6.25 9.71

For each of the two plants:
a. Compute the mean, median, first quartile, and third quartile.
b. Compute the range, interquartile range, variance, standard deviation, and coefficient of variation.
c. Construct side-by-side box-and-whisker plots. Are the data skewed? If so, how?
d. On the basis of the results of (a) through (c), are there any differences between the two plants? Explain.

3.62 The data contained in the file tuition2006.xls consist of the in-state tuition and fees and the out-of-state tuition and fees for four-year colleges with the highest percentage of students graduating within six years.
Source: U.S. Department of Education, 2006.

For each variable:
a. Compute the mean, median, first quartile, and third quartile.
b. Compute the range, interquartile range, variance, standard deviation, and coefficient of variation.
c. Construct a box-and-whisker plot. Are the data skewed? If so, how?
d. Compute the coefficient of correlation between the in-state tuition and fees and the out-of-state tuition and fees.
e. What conclusions can you reach concerning the in-state tuition and fees and the out-of-state tuition and fees?

3.63 A quality characteristic of interest for a tea-bag-filling process is the weight of the tea in the individual bags. If the bags are underfilled, two problems arise. First, customers may not be able to brew the tea to be as strong as they wish. Second, the company may be in violation of the truth-in-labeling laws. For this product, the label weight on the package indicates that, on average, there are 5.5 grams of tea in a bag. If the mean amount of tea in a bag exceeds the label weight, the company is giving away product. Getting an exact amount of tea in a bag is problematic because of variation in the temperature and humidity inside the factory, differences in the density of the tea, and the extremely fast filling operation of the machine (approximately 170 bags per minute). The data in the file teabags.xls shown below provide the weight, in grams, of a sample of 50 tea bags produced in one hour by a single machine:

5.65	5.44	5.42	5.40	5.53	5.34	5.54	5.45	5.52	5.41
5.57	5.40	5.53	5.54	5.55	5.62	5.56	5.46	5.44	5.51
5.47	5.40	5.47	5.61	5.53	5.32	5.67	5.29	5.49	5.55
5.77	5.57	5.42	5.58	5.58	5.50	5.32	5.50	5.53	5.58
5.61	5.45	5.44	5.25	5.56	5.63	5.50	5.57	5.67	5.36

a. Compute the mean, median, first quartile, and third quartile.
b. Compute the range, interquartile range, variance, standard deviation, and coefficient of variation.
c. Interpret the measures of central tendency and variation within the context of this problem. Why should the company producing the tea bags be concerned about the central tendency and variation?
d. Construct a box-and-whisker plot. Are the data skewed? If so, how?
e. Is the company meeting the requirement set forth on the label that, on average, there are 5.5 grams of tea in a bag? If you were in charge of this process, what changes, if any, would you try to make concerning the distribution of weights in the individual bags?

3.64 Do marketing promotions, such as bobble-head giveaways, increase attendance at Major League Baseball games? An article in the *Mid-American Journal of Business* reported on the effectiveness of marketing promotions (T. C. Boyd and T. C. Krehbiel, "An Analysis of the Effects of Specific Promotion Types on Attendance at Major League Baseball Games," *Mid-American Journal of Business*, 2006, 21, pp. 21–32). The data file royals.xls includes the following variables for the Kansas City Royals during the 2002 baseball season:
    GAME —Home games in the order in which they were played
    ATTENDANCE —Paid attendance for the game

PROMOTION—Y = a promotion was held; N = no promotion was held

a. Calculate the mean and standard deviation of attendance for the 43 games where promotions were held and for the 37 games without promotions.
b. Construct a five-number summary for the 43 games where promotions were held and for the 37 games without promotions.
c. Construct a graphical display containing two box-and-whisker plots—one for the 43 games where promotions were held and one for the 37 games without promotions.
d. Discuss the results of (a) through (c) and comment on the effectiveness of promotions at Royals' games during the 2002 season.

3.65 A study conducted by Zagat Survey concluded that many first-rate restaurants are located in hotels across the United States. Travelers can find quality food, service, and décor without leaving their hotels. The top-rated hotel restaurant is The French Room, located in The Adolphus Hotel in Dallas, Texas. The estimated price for dinner, including one drink and tip at The French Room, is $80. The highest price reported is $179 at Alain Ducasse, located in the Jumeirah Essex House in New York City (Extracted from Gary Stoller, "Top Restaurants Check into Luxury Hotels," *USA Today*, April 11, 2006, p. 5B). The file bestrest.xls contains the top 100 hotel restaurants in the United States and the variables state, city, restaurant, hotel, cost (estimated price of dinner including one drink and tip), and rating (1 to 100, with 1 the top-rated restaurant).

a. Construct the five-number summary of dinner price.
b. Construct a box-and-whisker plot of dinner price and interpret the distribution of dinner prices.
c. Calculate and interpret the correlation coefficient of the rating and dinner price.

3.66 The manufacturer of Boston and Vermont asphalt shingles provides its customers with a 20-year warranty on most of its products. To determine whether a shingle will last as long as the warranty period, accelerated-life testing is conducted at the manufacturing plant. Accelerated-life testing exposes the shingle to the stresses it would be subject to in a lifetime of normal use in a laboratory setting via an experiment that takes only a few minutes to conduct. In this test, a shingle is repeatedly scraped with a brush for a short period of time, and the shingle granules removed by the brushing are weighed (in grams). Shingles that experience low amounts of granule loss are expected to last longer in normal use than shingles that experience high amounts of granule loss. In this situation, a shingle should experience no more than 0.8 gram of granule loss if it is expected to last the length of the warranty period. The data file granule.xls contains a sample of 170 measurements made on the company's Boston shingles and 140 measurements made on Vermont shingles.

a. List the five-number summary for the Boston shingles and for the Vermont shingles.

b. Construct side-by-side box-and-whisker plots for the two brands of shingles and describe the shapes of the distributions.

c. Comment on the shingles' ability to achieve a granule loss of 0.8 gram or less.

3.67 The data in the file `states.xls` represent the results of the American Community Survey, a sampling of 700,000 households taken in each state during the 2000 U.S. Census. For each of the variables average travel-to-work time in minutes, percentage of homes with eight or more rooms, median household income, and percentage of mortgage-paying homeowners whose housing costs exceed 30% of income:

a. Compute the mean, median, first quartile, and third quartile.

b. Compute the range, interquartile range, variance, standard deviation, and coefficient of variation.

c. Construct a box-and-whisker plot. Are the data skewed? If so, how?

d. What conclusions can you reach concerning the mean travel-to-work time in minutes, percentage of homes with eight or more rooms, median household income, and percentage of mortgage-paying homeowners whose housing costs exceed 30% of income?

3.68 The economics of baseball has caused a great deal of controversy, with owners arguing that they are losing money, players arguing that owners are making money, and fans complaining about how expensive it is to attend a game and watch games on cable television. In addition to data related to team statistics for the 2001 season, the file `bb2001.xls` contains team-by-team statistics on ticket prices; the fan cost index; regular season gate receipts; local television, radio, and cable receipts; all other operating revenue; player compensation and benefits; national and other local expenses; and income from baseball operations. For each of these variables,

a. Compute the mean, median, first quartile, and third quartile.

b. Compute the range, interquartile range, variance, standard deviation, and coefficient of variation.

c. Construct a box-and-whisker plot. Are the data skewed? If so, how?

d. Compute the correlation between the number of wins and player compensation and benefits. How strong is the relationship between these two variables?

e. What conclusions can you reach concerning the regular season gate receipts; local television, radio, and cable receipts; all other operating revenue; player compensa-

tion and benefits; national and other local expenses; and income from baseball operations?

3.69 In Section 3.5 on page 131, the correlation coefficient between the cost of a fast-food hamburger meal and the cost of movie tickets in 10 different cities was computed. The data file `cost of living.xls` also includes the overall cost index, the monthly rent for a two bedroom apartment, and the costs of a cup of coffee with service, dry cleaning for a men's blazer, and toothpaste.

a. Compute the correlation coefficient between the overall cost index and the monthly rent for a two-bedroom apartment, the cost of a cup of coffee with service, the cost of a fast food hamburger meal, the cost of dry cleaning a men's blazer, the cost of toothpaste, and the cost of movie tickets. (There will be six separate correlation coefficients.)

b. What conclusions can you reach about the relationship of the overall cost index to each of these six variables?

3.70 The data in the file `chicken.xls` contains the characteristics for a sample of 20 chicken sandwiches from fast-food chains.

a. Compute the correlation coefficient between calories and carbohydrates.

b. Compute the correlation coefficient between calories and sodium.

c. Compute the correlation coefficient between calories and total fat.

d. Which variable (total fat, carbohydrates, or sodium) seems to be most closely related to calories? Explain.

3.71 The data in the file `ceo.xls` represent the total compensation (in $millions) of CEOs of the 100 largest companies, by revenue (extracted from "Special Report: Executive Compensation," *USA Today*, April 10, 2006, pp. 3B, 4B).

a. Compute the mean, median, first quartile, and third quartile.

b. Compute the range, interquartile range, variance, standard deviation, and coefficient of variation.

c. Construct a box-and-whisker plot. Are the data skewed? If so, how?

d. What conclusions can you draw concerning the total compensation (in $millions) of CEOs?

3.72 The data in the file `spending.xls` is the per capita spending, in thousands of dollars, for each state in 2004.

a. Compute the mean, median, first quartile, and third quartile.

b. Compute the range, interquartile range, variance, standard deviation, and coefficient of variation.

c. Construct side-by-side box-and-whisker plots. Are the data skewed? If so, how?

d. What conclusions can you reach concerning per capita spending, in thousands of dollars, for each state in 2004?

3.73 As an illustration of the misuse of statistics, an article by Glenn Kramon ("Coaxing the Stanford Elephant to Dance," *The New York Times* Sunday Business Section, November 11, 1990) implied that costs at Stanford Medical Center had been driven up higher than at competing institutions because the former was more likely than other organizations to treat indigent, Medicare, Medicaid, sicker, and more complex patients. The chart below was provided to compare the average 1989 to 1990 hospital charges for three medical procedures (coronary bypass, simple birth, and hip replacement) at three competing institutions (El Camino, Sequoia, and Stanford).

Suppose you were working in a medical center. Your CEO knows you are currently taking a course in statistics and calls you in to discuss this. She tells you that the article was presented in a discussion group setting as part of a meeting of regional area medical center CEOs last night and that one of them mentioned that this chart was totally meaningless and asked her opinion. She now requests that you prepare her response. You smile, take a deep breath, and reply . . .

3.74 You are planning to study for your statistics examination with a group of classmates, one of whom you particularly want to impress. This individual has volunteered to use Microsoft Excel to get the needed summary information, tables, and charts for a data set containing several numerical and categorical variables assigned by the instructor for study purposes. This person comes over to you with the printout and exclaims, "I've got it all—the means, the medians, the standard deviations, the box-and-whisker plots, the pie charts—for all our variables. The problem is, some of the output looks weird—like the box-and-whisker plots for gender and for major and the pie charts for grade point index and for height. Also, I can't understand why Professor Krehbiel said we can't get the descriptive stats for some of the variables—I got them for everything! See, the mean for height is 68.23, the mean for grade point index is 2.76, the mean for gender is 1.50, the mean for major is 4.33." What is your reply?

Report Writing Exercises

3.75 Data concerning 58 of the best-selling domestic beers in the U.S. are located in the file **domesticbeer.xls**. The values for three variables are included: percentage alcohol, number of calories per 12 ounces, and number of carbohydrates (in grams) per 12 ounces.

*Source: Extracted from **www.Beer100.com**, March 31, 2006.*

Your task is to write a report based on a complete descriptive evaluation of each of the numerical variables—percentage alcohol, number of calories per 12 ounces, and number of carbohydrates (in grams) per 12 ounces. Appended to your report should be all appropriate tables, charts, and numerical descriptive measures.

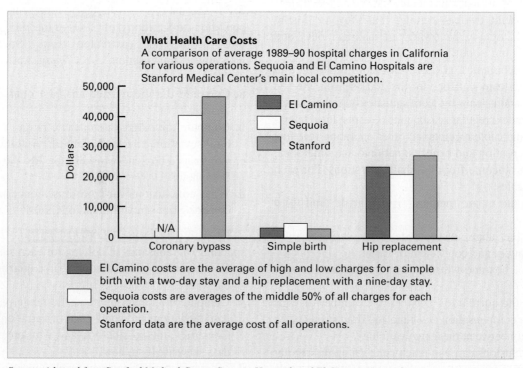

Source: Adapted from Stanford Medical Center, Sequoia Hospital, and El Camino Hospital.

Team Projects

The data file Mutual Funds.xls contains information regarding nine variables from a sample of 838 mutual funds:

Category—Type of stocks comprising the mutual fund (small cap, mid cap, large cap)

Objective—Objective of stocks comprising the mutual fund (growth or value)

Assets—In millions of dollars

Fees—Sales charges (no or yes)

Expense ratio—ratio of expenses to net assets in percentage

Risk—Risk-of-loss factor of the mutual fund (low, average, high)

2005 return—Twelve-month return in 2005

Three-year return—Annualized return, 2003–2005

Five-year return—Annualized return, 2001–2005

3.76 For expense ratio in percentage, 2005 return, three-year return, and five-year return,
a. Compute the mean, median, first quartile, and third quartile.
b. Compute the range, interquartile range, variance, standard deviation, and coefficient of variation.
c. Construct a box-and-whisker plot. Are the data skewed? If so, how?
d. What conclusions can you reach concerning these variables?

3.77 You wish to compare mutual funds that have fees to those that do not have fees. For each of these two groups, for the variables expense ratio in percentage, 2005 return, three-year return, and five-year return,
a. Compute the mean, median, first quartile, and third quartile.
b. Compute the range, interquartile range, variance, standard deviation, and coefficient of variation.
c. Construct a box-and-whisker plot. Are the data skewed? If so, how?
d. What conclusions can you reach about differences between mutual funds that have fees and those that do not have fees?

3.78 You wish to compare mutual funds that have a growth objective to those that have a value objective. For each of these two groups, for the variables expense ratio in percentage, 2005 return, three-year return, and five-year return,
a. Compute the mean, median, first quartile, and third quartile.
b. Compute the range, interquartile range, variance, standard deviation, and coefficient of variation.
c. Construct a box-and-whisker plot. Are the data skewed? If so, how?

d. What conclusions can you reach about differences between mutual funds that have a growth objective and those that have a value objective?

3.79 You wish to compare small cap, mid cap, and large cap mutual funds. For each of these three groups, for the variables expense ratio in percentage, 2005 return, three-year return, and five-year return,
a. Compute the mean, median, first quartile, and third quartile.
b. Compute the range, interquartile range, variance, standard deviation, and coefficient of variation.
c. Construct a box-and-whisker plot. Are the data skewed? If so, how?
d. What conclusions can you reach about differences between small cap, mid cap, and large cap mutual funds?

Student Survey Data Base

3.80 Problem 1.27 on page 15 describes a survey of 50 undergraduate students (see the file undergradsurvey.xls). For these data, for each numerical variable
a. Compute the mean, median, first quartile, and third quartile.
b. Compute the range, interquartile range, variance, standard deviation, and coefficient of variation.
c. Construct a box-and-whisker plot. Are the data skewed? If so, how?
d. Write a report summarizing your conclusions.

3.81 Problem 1.27 on page 15 describes a survey of 50 undergraduate students (see the file undergradsurvey.xls).
a. Select a sample of 50 undergraduate students at your school and conduct a similar survey for those students.
b. For the data collected in (a), repeat (a) through (d) of Problem 3.80.
c. Compare the results of (b) to those of Problem 3.80.

3.82 Problem 1.28 on page 15 describes a survey of 50 MBA students (see the file gradsurvey.xls). For these data, for each numerical variable,
a. Compute the mean, median, first quartile, and third quartile.
b. Compute the range, interquartile range, variance, standard deviation, and coefficient of variation.
c. Construct a box-and-whisker plot. Are the data skewed? If so, how?
d. Write a report summarizing your conclusions.

3.83 Problem 1.28 on page 15 describes a survey of 50 MBA students (see the file gradsurvey.xls).
a. Select a sample of 50 graduate students from your MBA program and conduct a similar survey for those students.
b. For the data collected in (a), repeat (a) through (d) of Problem 3.82.
c. Compare the results of (b) to those of Problem 3.82.

Managing the *Springville Herald*

For what variable in the Chapter 2 "Managing the *Springville Herald*" case (see page 73) are numerical descriptive measures needed? For the variable you identify:

1. Compute the appropriate numerical descriptive measures, and generate a box-and-whisker plot.
2. Identify another graphical display that might be useful and construct it. What conclusions can you form

from that plot that cannot be made from the box-and-whisker plot?
3. Summarize your findings in a report that can be included with the task force's study.

Web Case

Apply your knowledge about the proper use of numerical descriptive measures in this continuing Web Case from Chapter 2.

Visit EndRun Investing Services, at **www.prenhall.com/ Springville/EndRun.htm** (or open the **EndRun.htm** file in the Student CD-ROM Web Case folder) a second time and reexamine their supporting data and then answer the following:

1. Can descriptive measures be computed for any variables? How would such summary statistics support EndRun's

claims? How would those summary statistics affect your perception of EndRun's record?
2. Evaluate the methods EndRun used to summarize the results of its customer survey (see **www.prenhall.com/ Springville/ER_Survey.htm** or the **ER_Survey.htm** file on the Student CD-ROM Web Case folder. Is there anything you would do differently to summarize these results?
3. Note that the last question of the survey has fewer responses than the other questions. What factors may have limited the number of responses to that question?

REFERENCES

1. Kendall, M. G., A. Stuart, and J. K. Ord, *Kendall's Advanced Theory of Statistics, Volume 1: Distribution Theory*, 6th ed. (New York: Oxford University Press, 1994).
2. *Microsoft Excel 2007* (Redmond, WA: Microsoft Corporation, 2007).
3. Tukey, J., *Exploratory Data Analysis* (Reading, MA: Addison-Wesley, 1977).
4. Velleman, P. F., and D. C. Hoaglin, *Applications, Basics, and Computing of Exploratory Data Analysis* (Boston: Duxbury Press, 1981).

Excel Companion
to Chapter 3

This companion discusses how to compute the descriptive statistics discussed in Chapter 3. (Instructions presented in this companion apply to all Excel versions.)

E3.1 COMPUTING MEASURES OF CENTRAL TENDENCY, VARIATION, AND SHAPE

You compute measures of central tendency, variation, and shape by either using the ToolPak Descriptive Statistics procedure or by using worksheet functions.

PHStat2 does not contain a descriptive statistics procedure, although some of the descriptive statistics are computed as output options to other procedures. PHStat2 users should use one of the ways discussed below to compute descriptive statistics.

Using ToolPak Descriptive Statistics

Begin the Analysis ToolPak add-in and select **Descriptive Statistics** from the **Analysis Tools** list and then click **OK**. In the Descriptive Statistics dialog box (shown below), enter the cell range of the data as the **Input Range**. Click the **Columns** option and **Labels in first row** (for data organized according to the conventions in "Designing Effective Worksheets" in Section 1.6). Finish by clicking **New**

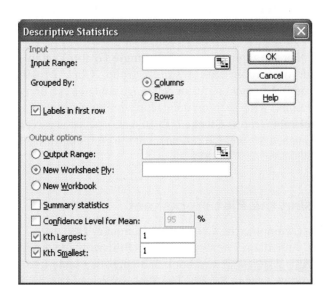

Worksheet Ply, **Summary statistics**, **Kth Largest**, and **Kth Smallest**, and then **OK**. A table of results that does not contain any formulas appears on a new worksheet.

To compute descriptive statistics for a variable by subgroups, as was done in Figure 3.2 on page 114 for the low-risk, average risk, and high-risk subgroups, first sort your data by the categorical variable to which the subgroups belong. Next, repeat the procedure for each subgroup, using the cell range of the subgroup and the New Worksheet Ply option each time. Then copy and paste the results found in the second and subsequent worksheets to this first sheet to create a multiple-column table similar to the one shown in Figure 3.2.

When you use this procedure, consider formatting the results to reduce the number of significant digits, many of which may not be accurate. For example, the procedure reported the mean for the low-risk group as 18.4101214574899, but that number has been reformatted to a more manageable 18.4101 in Figure 3.2.

Using Worksheet Functions

You use the worksheet functions SUM, COUNT, AVERAGE (for mean), MEDIAN, MODE, QUARTILE, or GEOMEAN to compute measures of central tendency and STDEV, VAR, MIN, MAX, LARGE, or SMALL to compute measures of shape and variation. For all but QUARTILE, you enter a formula in the form = *WorksheetFunction(cell range of data to be summarized)*. For QUARTILE, you enter the formula in the form =**QUARTILE***(cell range of data to be summarized, quartile number)*. Use 1 as the *quartile number* to compute the first quartile, 2 to compute the second quartile (the median), or 3 to compute the third quartile. In many Excel versions you may encounter some minor errors in results when using the QUARTILE function.

E3.2 CREATING DOT SCALE DIAGRAMS

You create dot scale diagrams by using the PHStat2 Dot Scale Diagram procedure (recommended) or by manually adjusting the **Dot Scale** worksheet of the Dot Scale.xls workbook.

Using PHStat2 Dot Scale Diagram

Open to the worksheet that contains the data to be plotted. Select **PHStat → Descriptive Statistics → Dot Scale Diagram**. In the Dot Scale Diagram dialog box (shown below) enter the cell range of the data to be plotted as the **Variable Cell Range** and click **First cell contains label**. Enter a title as the **Title** and click **OK**.

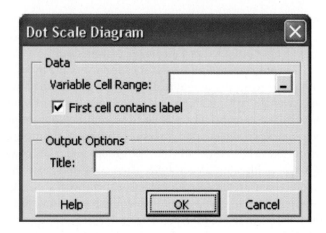

Adjusting the Dot Scale Worksheet

Open to the **DotScale** worksheet. Enter up to 20 values in the tinted cell range **A2:A21**, starting with cell A2, and not skipping any cells. As you enter each value, the dot scale diagram changes to reflect each new value.

> **Forum** Click the ALTERNATE TECHNIQUES link to learn how to modify this worksheet for sets of data that contain more than 20 values.

E3.3   COMPUTING MEASURES FOR A POPULATION

You use the worksheet functions VARP and STDEVP to compute the population variance and standard deviation. To use either function, you enter a formula in the form *=WorksheetFunction(cell range of data to be summarized)*, as shown below.

	A	B
1	**Bond Fund**	**One-Year Return**
2	Pimco:Total Rtn;Inst	2.74
3	Vanguard Tot Bd;Inv	1.62
4	American Funds Bond;A	2.25
5	Vanguard GNMA;Inv	2.88
6	Franklin CA TF Inc;A	3.66
7		
8	**Population Parameters**	
9	**Population Variance**	0.46	=VARP(B2:B6)
10	**Population Std. Deviation**	0.68	=STDEVP(B2:B6)

E3.4   CREATING BOX-AND-WHISKER PLOTS

You create box-and-whisker plots by using the PHStat2 **Box-and-Whisker Plot** procedure (recommended) or by entering a five-number summary into the Plot worksheet of the Box-and-whisker.xls workbook.

Using PHStat2 Box-and-Whisker Plot

Open to the worksheet that contains the data to be plotted. Select **PHStat → Descriptive Statistics → Box-and-Whisker Plot**. In the Box-and-Whisker Plot dialog box (shown below), enter the cell range of the data to be plotted as the **Raw Data Cell Range**. Click the appropriate option from Input Options and then enter a title as the **Title** and click **OK**.

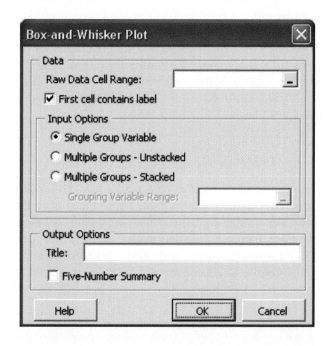

For the input option, click **Single Group Variable** if your data represents a single group. Click **Multiple Groups-Unstacked** if your cell range contains two or more columns, with each column representing a group. Click **Multiple Groups-Stacked** if you have stacked group data. (You need to enter the cell range of the grouping variable if you choose this option.)

Using the Plot Worksheet

First, compute the five-number summary (see page 123) for your data. Then open to the **Plot** worksheet of the Box-and-whisker.xls workbook and enter this table into the tinted cell range B2:B6. The Plot worksheet can display only one box-and-whisker plot at a time.

EXAMPLE Figure 3.4 Box-and-Whisker Plot

To create your own Figure 3.4 box-and-whisker plot of the three-year annualized return for low-risk, average-risk, and high-risk mutual funds, use the appropriate set of instructions.

Basic Excel You can create three separate plots that are equivalent to Figure 3.4. Open the Box-and-whisker.xls workbook and create three copies of the **Plot** worksheet. Compute the five-number summary for the low-risk, average-risk, and high-risk mutual funds (see the Data worksheet of the Mutual Funds.xls workbook). Enter each five-number summary into a different copy of the Plot worksheet.

PHStat2 Open to the Data sheet of the Mutual Funds.xls workbook. Select **PHStat → Descriptive Statistics → Box-and-Whisker Plot**. Enter **H1:H839** as the **Raw Data Cell Range** and click the **Multiple Groups–Stacked** option. This option activates the **Grouping Variable Range** box. In that box enter **F1:F839**. Enter a title as the **Title** and click **OK**.

E3.5 COMPUTING THE COVARIANCE

Open to the **Covariance** worksheet of the Covariance.xls workbook, shown in Figure 3.6 on page 128. If you want to use this worksheet with other pairs of variables, follow the instructions in the worksheet for modifying the table area. The worksheet gains its flexibility by the cell C18 formula that uses the COUNT function to determine the sample size n. This allows the worksheet to always use the proper value of $n - 1$ for the covariance calculation when you change the size of the table area.

E3.6 COMPUTING THE CORRELATION COEFFICIENT

Open the **Correlation** worksheet of the Correlation.xls workbook, shown in Figure 3.9 on page 131. If you want to use this worksheet with other pairs of variables, follow the instructions in the worksheet for modifying the table area. This worksheet shares some of the design of the covariance worksheet discussed in the previous section.

This worksheet uses the CORREL function in the formula =CORREL(A2:A11, B2:B11) in cell E21 to compute the correlation coefficient. Because the covariance, S_x, and S_Y are computed elsewhere in this worksheet, the formula =E18/(E19 * E20) could also be used to compute the correlation coefficient statistic.

CHAPTER 4

Basic Probability

USING STATISTICS @ The Consumer Electronics Company

LEARNING OBJECTIVES

In this chapter, you learn:

- Basic probability concepts
- Conditional probability
- To use Bayes' theorem to revise probabilities

USING STATISTICS @ The Consumer Electronics Company

As the marketing manager for the Consumer Electronics Company, you are analyzing the survey results of an intent-to-purchase study. This study asked the heads of 1,000 households about their intentions to purchase a big-screen television (defined as 36 inches or larger) sometime during the next 12 months. Investigations of this type are known as *intent-to-purchase studies*. As a follow-up, you plan to survey the same people 12 months later to see whether such a television was purchased. In addition, for households purchasing big-screen televisions, you would like to know whether the television they purchased was a plasma screen, whether they also purchased a digital video recorder (DVR) in the past 12 months, and whether they were satisfied with their purchase of the big-screen television.

You are expected to use the results of this survey to plan a new marketing strategy that will enhance sales and better target those households likely to purchase multiple or more expensive products. What questions can you ask in this survey? How can you express the relationships among the various intent-to-purchase responses of individual households?

In previous chapters, you learned descriptive methods to summarize categorical and numerical variables. In this chapter, you will learn about probability to answer questions such as the following:

- What is the probability that a household is planning to purchase a big-screen television in the next year?
- What is the probability that a household will actually purchase a big-screen television?
- What is the probability that a household is planning to purchase a big-screen television and actually purchases the television?
- Given that the household is planning to purchase a big-screen television, what is the probability that the purchase is made?
- Does knowledge of whether a household *plans* to purchase the television change the likelihood of predicting whether the household *will* purchase the television?
- What is the probability that a household that purchases a big-screen television will purchase a plasma-screen television?
- What is the probability that a household that purchases a big-screen television will also purchase a DVR?
- What is the probability that a household that purchases a big-screen television will be satisfied with the purchase?

With answers to questions such as these, you can begin to make decisions about your marketing strategy. Should your strategy for selling more big-screen televisions target those households that have indicated an intent to purchase? Should you concentrate on selling plasma screens? Is it likely that households that purchase televisions with plasma screens can be easily persuaded to also purchase DVRs?

The principles of probability help bridge the worlds of descriptive statistics and inferential statistics. Reading this chapter will help you learn about different types of probabilities, how to compute probability values, and then revise those values in light of new information. Probability principles are the foundation for the probability distribution, the concept of mathematical expectation, and the binomial, hypergeometric, and Poisson distributions, topics that are discussed in Chapter 5.

4.1 BASIC PROBABILITY CONCEPTS

What is meant by the word *probability*? A **probability** is the numeric value representing the chance, likelihood, or possibility a particular event will occur, such as the price of a stock increasing, a rainy day, a nonconforming unit of production, or the outcome five in a single toss of a die. In all these instances, the probability involved is a proportion or fraction whose value ranges between 0 and 1, inclusive. An event that has no chance of occurring (i.e., the **impossible event**) has a probability of 0. An event that is sure to occur (i.e., the **certain event**) has a probability of 1. There are three approaches to the subject of probability:

- *A priori* classical probability
- Empirical classical probability
- Subjective probability

In *a priori* **classical probability**, the probability of success is based on prior knowledge of the process involved. In the simplest case, where each outcome is equally likely, the chance of occurrence of the event is defined in Equation (4.1).

PROBABILITY OF OCCURRENCE

$$\text{Probability of occurrence} = \frac{X}{T} \qquad (4.1)$$

where

$$X = \text{number of ways in which the event occurs}$$

$$T = \text{total number of possible outcomes}$$

Consider a standard deck of cards that has 26 red cards and 26 black cards. The probability of selecting a black card is $26/52 = 0.50$ because there are $X = 26$ black cards and $T = 52$ total cards. What does this probability mean? If each card is replaced after it is drawn, does it mean that 1 out of the next 2 cards selected will be black? No, because you cannot say for certain what will happen on the next several selections. However, you can say that in the long run, if this selection process is continually repeated, the proportion of black cards selected will approach 0.50.

EXAMPLE 4.1

FINDING *A PRIORI* PROBABILITIES

A standard six-sided die has six faces. Each face of the die contains either one, two, three, four, five, or six dots. If you roll a die, what is the probability that you will get a face with five dots?

SOLUTION Each face is equally likely to occur. Because there are six faces, the probability of getting a face with five dots is $\frac{1}{6}$.

The preceding examples use the *a priori* classical probability approach because the number of ways the event occurs and the total number of possible outcomes are known from the composition of the deck of cards or the faces of the die.

In the **empirical classical probability** approach, the outcomes are based on observed data, not on prior knowledge of a process. Examples of this type of probability are the proportion of individuals in the Using Statistics scenario who actually purchase a big-screen television, the proportion of registered voters who prefer a certain political candidate, and the proportion of students who have part-time jobs. For example, if you take a survey of students, and 60% state that they have part-time jobs, then there is a 0.60 probability that an individual student has a part-time job.

The third approach to probability, **subjective probability**, differs from the other two approaches because subjective probability differs from person to person. For example, the development team for a new product may assign a probability of 0.6 to the chance of success for the product, while the president of the company may be less optimistic and assign a probability of 0.3. The assignment of subjective probabilities to various outcomes is usually based on a combination of an individual's past experience, personal opinion, and analysis of a particular situation. Subjective probability is especially useful in making decisions in situations in which you cannot use *a priori* classical probability or empirical classical probability.

Events and Sample Spaces

The basic elements of probability theory are the individual outcomes of a variable under study. You need the following definitions to understand probabilities.

EVENT

Each possible outcome of a variable is referred to as an **event**.
A **simple event** is described by a single characteristic.

For example, when you toss a coin, the two possible outcomes are heads and tails. Each of these represents a simple event. When you roll a standard six-sided die in which the six faces of the die contain either one, two, three, four, five, or six dots, there are six possible simple events. An event can be any one of these simple events, a set of them, or a subset of all of them. For example, the event of an *even number of dots* consists of three simple events (i.e., two, four, or six dots).

JOINT EVENT

A **joint event** is an event that has two or more characteristics.

Getting two heads on the toss of two coins is an example of a joint event because it consists of heads on the toss of the first coin and heads on the toss of the second coin.

COMPLEMENT

The **complement** of event A (represented by the symbol A') includes all events that are not part of A.

The complement of a head is a tail because that is the only event that is not a head. The complement of face five is not getting face five. Not getting face five consists of getting face one, two, three, four, or six.

SAMPLE SPACE

The collection of all the possible events is called the **sample space**.

The sample space for tossing a coin consists of heads and tails. The sample space when rolling a die consists of one, two, three, four, five, and six dots.

Example 4.2 demonstrates events and sample spaces.

EXAMPLE 4.2

EVENTS AND SAMPLE SPACES

The Using Statistics scenario on page 148 concerns the Consumer Electronics Company. Table 4.1 presents the results of the sample of 1,000 households in terms of purchase behavior for big-screen televisions.

TABLE 4.1

Purchase Behavior for Big-Screen Televisions

PLANNED TO PURCHASE	ACTUALLY PURCHASED		
	Yes	No	Total
Yes	200	50	250
No	100	650	750
Total	300	700	1,000

What is the sample space? Give examples of simple events and joint events.

SOLUTION The sample space consists of the 1,000 respondents. Simple events are "planned to purchase," "did not plan to purchase," "purchased," and "did not purchase." The complement of the event "planned to purchase" is "did not plan to purchase." The event "planned to purchase and actually purchased" is a joint event because the respondent must plan to purchase the television *and* actually purchase it.

Contingency Tables

There are several ways to present a sample space. The method used in this text is called a **contingency table** (see Section 2.4). You get the values in the cells of the table by subdividing the sample space of 1,000 households according to whether someone planned to purchase and actually purchased the big-screen television. For example, 200 of the respondents planned to purchase a big-screen television and subsequently did purchase the big-screen television.

Simple (Marginal) Probability

Now you can answer some of the questions posed in the Using Statistics scenario. Because the results are based on data collected in a survey (refer to Table 4.1 above), you can use the empirical classical probability approach.

As stated previously, the most fundamental rule for probabilities is that they range in value from 0 to 1. An impossible event has a probability of 0, and an event that is certain to occur has a probability of 1.

Simple probability refers to the probability of occurrence of a simple event, $P(A)$. A simple probability in the Using Statistics scenario is the probability of planning to purchase a big-screen television. How can you determine the probability of selecting a household that planned to purchase a big-screen television? Using Equation (4.1) on page 149:

$$\text{Probability of occurrence} = \frac{X}{T}$$

$$P(\text{Planned to purchase}) = \frac{\text{Number who planned to purchase}}{\text{Total number of households}}$$

$$= \frac{250}{1,000} = 0.25$$

Thus, there is a 0.25 (or 25%) chance that a household planned to purchase a big-screen television.

Simple probability is also called **marginal probability** because it enables you to compute the total number of successes (those who planned to purchase) from the appropriate margin of the contingency table (see Table 4.1 on page 151). Example 4.3 illustrates another application of simple probability.

EXAMPLE 4.3

COMPUTING THE PROBABILITY THAT THE BIG-SCREEN TELEVISION PURCHASED IS A PLASMA SCREEN

In the Using Statistics follow-up survey, additional questions were asked of the 300 households that actually purchased big-screen televisions. Table 4.2 indicates the consumers' responses to whether the television purchased was a plasma screen and whether they also purchased a DVR in the past 12 months.

TABLE 4.2

Purchase Behavior Regarding Plasma-Screen Televisions and DVR

| | PURCHASED DVR | | |
PURCHASED PLASMA SCREEN	Yes	No	Total
Plasma screen	38	42	80
Not plasma screen	70	150	220
Total	108	192	300

Find the probability that if a household that purchased a big-screen television is randomly selected, the television purchased is a plasma screen.

SOLUTION Using the following definitions:

A = purchased a plasma screen $\qquad B$ = purchased a DVR
A' = did not purchase a plasma screen $\qquad B'$ = did not purchase a DVR

$$P(\text{Plasma screen}) = \frac{\text{Number of plasma screen televisions}}{\text{Total number of televisions}}$$

$$= \frac{80}{300} = 0.267$$

There is a 26.7% chance that a randomly selected big-screen television purchase is a purchase of a plasma-screen television.

Joint Probability

Whereas marginal probability refers to the probability of occurrence of simple events, **joint probability** refers to the probability of an occurrence involving two or more events. An example of joint probability is the probability that you will get heads on the first toss of a coin and heads on the second toss of a coin.

Referring to Table 4.1 on page 151, those individuals who planned to purchase and actually purchased a big-screen television consist only of the outcomes in the single cell "yes—planned to purchase *and* yes—actually purchased." Because this group consists of 200 households, the probability of picking a household that planned to purchase *and* actually purchased a big-screen television is

$$P\begin{pmatrix} \text{Planned to purchase} \\ and \text{ actually purchased} \end{pmatrix} = \frac{\text{Planned to purchase } and \text{ actually purchased}}{\text{Total number of respondents}}$$

$$= \frac{200}{1,000} = 0.20$$

Example 4.4 also demonstrates how to determine joint probability.

EXAMPLE 4.4

DETERMINING THE JOINT PROBABILITY THAT A BIG-SCREEN TELEVISION CUSTOMER PURCHASED A PLASMA-SCREEN TELEVISION AND A DVR

In Table 4.2 on page 152, the purchases are cross-classified as plasma screen or not plasma screen and whether or not the household purchased a DVR. Find the probability that a randomly selected household that purchased a big-screen television also purchased a plasma-screen television and a DVR.

SOLUTION Using Equation (4.1) on page 149,

$$P(\text{Plasma screen } and \text{ DVR}) = \frac{\text{Number that purchased a plasma screen } and \text{ a DVR}}{\text{Total number of big-screen television purchasers}}$$

$$= \frac{38}{300} = 0.127$$

Therefore, there is a 12.7% chance that a randomly selected household that purchased a big-screen television purchased a plasma-screen television and a DVR.

You can view the marginal probability of a particular event by using the concept of joint probability just discussed. The marginal probability of an event consists of a set of joint probabilities. For example, if B consists of two events, B_1 and B_2, then $P(A)$, the probability of event A, consists of the joint probability of event A occurring with event B_1 and the joint probability of event A occurring with event B_2. Use Equation (4.2) to compute marginal probabilities.

MARGINAL PROBABILITY

$$P(A) = P(A \text{ and } B_1) + P(A \text{ and } B_2) + \cdots + P(A \text{ and } B_k) \qquad (4.2)$$

where $B_1, B_2, \ldots, B_k$ are k mutually exclusive and collectively exhaustive events.

Mutually exclusive events and collectively exhaustive events are defined as follows.

MUTUALLY EXCLUSIVE

Two events are **mutually exclusive** if both the events cannot occur simultaneously.

Heads and tails in a coin toss are mutually exclusive events. The result of a coin toss cannot simultaneously be a head and a tail.

COLLECTIVELY EXHAUSTIVE

A set of events is **collectively exhaustive** if one of the events must occur.

Heads and tails in a coin toss are collectively exhaustive events. One of them must occur. If heads does not occur, tails must occur. If tails does not occur, heads must occur.

Being male and being female are mutually exclusive and collectively exhaustive events. No one is both (the two are mutually exclusive), and everyone is one or the other (the two are collectively exhaustive).

You can use Equation (4.2) to compute the marginal probability of "planned to purchase" a big-screen television:

$$P(\text{Planned to purchase}) = P(\text{Planned to purchase } and \text{ purchased}) \\ + P(\text{Planned to purchase } and \text{ did not purchase})$$

$$= \frac{200}{1,000} + \frac{50}{1,000}$$

$$= \frac{250}{1,000} = 0.25$$

You get the same result if you add the number of outcomes that make up the simple event "planned to purchase."

General Addition Rule

The general addition rule allows you to find the probability of event "*A or B*." This rule considers the occurrence of either event *A* or event *B* or both *A* and *B*. How can you determine the probability that a household planned to purchase *or* actually purchased a big-screen television? The event "planned to purchase *or* actually purchased" includes all households that planned to purchase and all households that actually purchased the big-screen television. You examine each cell of the contingency table (Table 4.1 on page 151) to determine whether it is part of this event. From Table 4.1, the cell "planned to purchase *and* did not actually purchase" is part of the event because it includes respondents who planned to purchase. The cell "did not plan to purchase *and* actually purchased" is included because it contains respondents who actually purchased. Finally, the cell "planned to purchase *and* actually purchased" has both characteristics of interest. Therefore, the probability of "planned to purchase *or* actually purchased" is

$$P(\text{Planned to purchase } or \text{ actually purchased}) = P(\text{Planned to purchase } and \text{ did not actually} \\ \text{purchase}) + P(\text{Did not plan to purchase } and \\ \text{actually purchased}) + P(\text{Planned to purchase} \\ and \text{ actually purchased})$$

$$= \frac{50}{1,000} + \frac{100}{1,000} + \frac{200}{1,000} = \frac{350}{1,000} = 0.35$$

Often, it is easier to determine $P(A \text{ or } B)$, the probability of the event *A or B*, by using the **general addition rule**, defined in Equation (4.3).

> **GENERAL ADDITION RULE**
>
> The probability of *A or B* is equal to the probability of *A* plus the probability of *B* minus the probability of *A and B*.
>
> $$P(A \text{ or } B) = P(A) + P(B) - P(A \text{ and } B) \qquad (4.3)$$

Applying Equation (4.3) to the previous example produces the following result:

$P(\text{Planned to purchase } or \text{ actually purchased}) = P(\text{Planned to purchase}) + P(\text{Actually purchased})$
$$- P(\text{Planned to purchase } and \text{ actually purchased})$$

$$= \frac{250}{1,000} + \frac{300}{1,000} - \frac{200}{1,000}$$

$$= \frac{350}{1,000} = 0.35$$

The general addition rule consists of taking the probability of A and adding it to the probability of B and then subtracting the probability of the joint event A and B from this total because the joint event has already been included in computing both the probability of A and the probability of B. Referring to Table 4.1 on page 151, if the outcomes of the event "planned to purchase" are added to those of the event "actually purchased," the joint event "planned to purchase *and* actually purchased" has been included in each of these simple events. Therefore, because this joint event has been double-counted, you must subtract it to provide the correct result. Example 4.5 illustrates another application of the general addition rule.

EXAMPLE 4.5

USING THE GENERAL ADDITION RULE FOR THE HOUSEHOLDS THAT PURCHASED BIG-SCREEN TELEVISIONS

In Example 4.3 on page 152, the purchases were cross-classified as a plasma screen or not a plasma screen and whether or not the household purchased a DVR. Find the probability that among households that purchased a big-screen television, they purchased a plasma-screen television or a DVR.

SOLUTION Using Equation (4.3),

$$P(\text{Plasma screen } or \text{ DVR}) = P(\text{Plasma screen}) + P(\text{DVR}) - P(\text{Plasma screen } and \text{ DVR})$$

$$= \frac{80}{300} + \frac{108}{300} - \frac{38}{300}$$

$$= \frac{150}{300} = 0.50$$

Therefore, there is a 50.0% chance that a randomly selected household that purchased a big-screen television purchased a plasma-screen television or a DVR.

PROBLEMS FOR SECTION 4.1

Learning the Basics

 4.1 Two coins are tossed.
   a. Give an example of a simple event.
   b. Give an example of a joint event.
c. What is the complement of a head on the first toss?

4.2 An urn contains 12 red balls and 8 white balls. One ball is to be selected from the urn.
   a. Give an example of a simple event.
   b. What is the complement of a red ball?

4.3 Given the following contingency table:

	B	B'
A	10	20
A'	20	40

What is the probability of
a. event A?
b. event A'?
c. event A and B?
d. event A or B?

4.4 Given the following contingency table:

	B	B'
A	10	30
A'	25	35

What is the probability of
a. event A'?
b. event A and B?
c. event A' and B'?
d. event A' or B'?

Applying the Concepts

4.5 For each of the following, indicate whether the type of probability involved is an example of *a priori* classical probability, empirical classical probability, or subjective probability.
a. The next toss of a fair coin will land on heads.
b. Italy will win soccer's World Cup the next time the competition is held.
c. The sum of the faces of two dice will be seven.
d. The train taking a commuter to work will be more than 10 minutes late.

4.6 For each of the following, state whether the events created are mutually exclusive and collectively exhaustive. If they are not mutually exclusive and collectively exhaustive, either reword the categories to make them mutually exclusive and collectively exhaustive or explain why that would not be useful.
a. Registered voters in the United States were asked whether they registered as Republicans or Democrats.
b. Each respondent was classified by the type of car he or she drives: American, European, Japanese, or none.
c. People were asked, "Do you currently live in (i) an apartment or (ii) a house?"
d. A product was classified as defective or not defective.

4.7 The probability of each of the following events is zero. For each, state why.
a. A voter in the United States who is registered as a Republican and a Democrat

b. A product that is defective and not defective
c. An automobile that is a Ford and a Toyota

4.8 According to an Ipsos poll, the perception of unfairness in the U.S. tax code is spread fairly evenly across income groups, age groups, and education levels. In an April 2006 survey of 1,005 adults, Ipsos reported that almost 60% of all people said the code is unfair, while slightly more than 60% of those making more than $50,000 viewed the code as unfair ("People Cry Unfairness," *The Cincinnati Enquirer*, April 16, 2006, p. A8). Suppose that the following contingency table represents the specific breakdown of responses:

U.S. TAX CODE	INCOME LEVEL Less Than $50,000	More Than $50,000	Total
Fair	225	180	405
Unfair	280	320	600
Total	505	500	1,005

a. Give an example of a simple event.
b. Give an example of a joint event.
c. What is the complement of "tax code is fair"?
d. Why is "tax code is fair *and* makes less than $50,000" a joint event?

4.9 Referring to the contingency table in Problem 4.8, if a respondent is selected at random, what is the probability that he or she
a. thinks the tax code is unfair?
b. thinks the tax code is unfair and makes less than $50,000?
c. thinks the tax code is unfair or makes less than $50,000?
d. Explain the difference in the results in (b) and (c).

4.10 A yield improvement study at a semiconductor manufacturing facility provided defect data for a sample of 450 wafers. The following table presents a summary of the responses to two questions: "Was a particle found on the die that produced the wafer?" and "Is the wafer good or bad?"

QUALITY OF WAFER	CONDITION OF DIE No Particles	Particles	Totals
Good	320	14	334
Bad	80	36	116
Totals	400	50	450

Source: Extracted from S. W. Hall, "Analysis of Defectivity of Semiconductor Wafers by Contingency Table," Proceedings Institute of Environmental Sciences, *Vol. 1, 1994, pp. 177–183.*

a. Give an example of a simple event.
b. Give an example of a joint event.

c. What is the complement of a good wafer?

d. Why is a "good wafer" and a die "with particles" a joint event?

4.11 Referring to the contingency table in Problem 4.10, if a wafer is selected at random, what is the probability that

a. it was produced from a die with no particles?

b. it is a bad wafer and was produced from a die with no particles?

c. it is a bad wafer or was produced from a die with particles?

d. Explain the difference in the results in (b) and (c).

4.12 An experiment was conducted to study the choices made in mutual fund selection. Undergraduate and MBA students were presented with different S&P 500 Index funds that were identical except for fees. Suppose 100 undergraduate students and 100 MBA students were selected. Partial results are shown in the following table:

FUND	STUDENT GROUP	
	Undergraduate	MBA
Highest-cost fund	27	18
Not Highest-cost fund	73	82

Source: Extracted from J. J. Choi, D. Laibson, and B. C. Madrian, Why Does the Law of One Price Fail? *www.som.yale.edu/faculty/jjc83/fees.pdf.*

If a student is selected at random, what is the probability that he or she

a. selected the highest-cost fund?

b. selected the highest-cost fund *and* is an undergraduate?

c. selected the highest-cost fund *or* is an undergraduate?

d. Explain the difference in the results in (b) and (c).

4.13 Where people turn to for news is different for various age groups. Suppose that a study conducted on this issue (extracted from P. Johnson, "Young People Turn to the Web for News," *USA Today*, March 23, 2006, p. 9D) was based on 200 respondents who were between the ages of 36 and 50 and 200 respondents who were over age 50. Of the 200 respondents who were between the ages of 36 and 50, 82 got their news primarily from newspapers. Of the 200 respondents who were over age 50, 104 got their news primarily from newspapers. Construct a contingency table to evaluate the probabilities. If a respondent is selected at random, what is the probability that he or she

a. got news primarily from newspapers?

b. got news primarily from newspapers and is over 50 years old?

c. got news primarily from newspapers or is over 50 years old?

d. Explain the difference in the results in (b) and (c).

4.14 A sample of 500 respondents was selected in a large metropolitan area to study consumer behavior. Among the questions asked was "Do you enjoy shopping for clothing?" Of 240 males, 136 answered yes. Of 260 females, 224 answered yes. Construct a contingency table to evaluate the probabilities. What is the probability that a respondent chosen at random

a. enjoys shopping for clothing?

b. is a female and enjoys shopping for clothing?

c. is a female or enjoys shopping for clothing?

d. is a male or a female?

4.15 Each year, ratings are compiled concerning the performance of new cars during the first 90 days of use. Suppose that the cars have been categorized according to whether the car needs warranty-related repair (yes or no) and the country in which the company manufacturing the car is based (United States or not United States). Based on the data collected, the probability that the new car needs warranty repair is 0.04, the probability that the car was manufactured by a U.S.-based company is 0.60, and the probability that the new car needs a warranty repair *and* was manufactured by a U.S.-based company is 0.025. Construct a contingency table to evaluate the probabilities of a warranty-related repair. What is the probability that a new car selected at random

a. needs a warranty repair?

b. needs a warranty repair and was manufactured by a U.S.-based company?

c. needs a warranty repair or was manufactured by a U.S.-based company?

d. needs a warranty repair or was not manufactured by a U.S.-based company?

4.2 CONDITIONAL PROBABILITY

Each example in Section 4.1 involves finding the probability of an event when sampling from the entire sample space. How do you determine the probability of an event if certain information about the events involved is already known?

Computing Conditional Probabilities

Conditional probability refers to the probability of event *A*, given information about the occurrence of another event *B*.

CONDITIONAL PROBABILITY

The probability of A given B is equal to the probability of A *and* B divided by the probability of B.

$$P(A \mid B) = \frac{P(A \text{ and } B)}{P(B)} \qquad \textbf{(4.4a)}$$

The probability of B given A is equal to the probability of A *and* B divided by the probability of A.

$$P(B \mid A) = \frac{P(A \text{ and } B)}{P(A)} \qquad \textbf{(4.4b)}$$

where

$$P(A \text{ and } B) = \text{joint probability of } A \text{ and } B$$

$$P(A) = \text{marginal probability of } A$$

$$P(B) = \text{marginal probability of } B$$

Referring to the Using Statistics scenario involving the purchase of big-screen televisions, suppose you were told that a household planned to purchase a big-screen television. Now, what is the probability that the household actually purchased the television? In this example, the objective is to find P(Actual purchase | Planned to purchase). Here you are given the information that the household planned to purchase the big-screen television. Therefore, the sample space does not consist of all 1,000 households in the survey. It consists of only those households that planned to purchase the big-screen television. Of 250 such households, 200 actually purchased the big-screen television. Therefore, based on Table 4.1 on page 151, the probability that a household actually purchased the big-screen television given that he or she planned to purchase is

$$P(\text{Actually purchased} \mid \text{Planned to purchase}) = \frac{\text{Planned to purchase } and \text{ actually purchased}}{\text{Planned to purchase}}$$

$$= \frac{200}{250} = 0.80$$

You can also use Equation (4.4b) to compute this result:

$$P(B \mid A) = \frac{P(A \text{ and } B)}{P(A)}$$

where

$$A = \text{planned to purchase}$$

$$B = \text{actually purchased}$$

then

$$P(\text{Actually purchased} \mid \text{Planned to purchase}) = \frac{200/1,000}{250/1,000}$$

$$= \frac{200}{250} = 0.80$$

Example 4.6 further illustrates conditional probability.

EXAMPLE 4.6   FINDING A CONDITIONAL PROBABILITY OF PURCHASING A DVR

Table 4.2 on page 152 is a contingency table for whether the household purchased a plasma-screen television and whether the household purchased a DVR. Of the households that purchased plasma-screen televisions, what is the probability that they also purchased DVRs?

SOLUTION Because you know that the household purchased a plasma-screen television, the sample space is reduced to 80 households. Of these 80 households, 38 also purchased a DVR. Therefore, the probability that a household purchased a DVR, given that the household purchased a plasma-screen television, is:

$$P(\text{Purchased DVR} \mid \text{Purchased plasma screen}) = \frac{\text{Number purchasing plasma screen } and \text{ DVR}}{\text{Number purchasing plasma screen}}$$

$$= \frac{38}{80} = 0.475$$

If you use Equation (4.4a) on page 158:

$$A = \text{Purchased DVR} \qquad B = \text{Purchased plasma-screen television}$$

then

$$P(A \mid B) = \frac{P(A \text{ and } B)}{P(B)} = \frac{38/300}{80/300} = 0.475$$

Therefore, given that the household purchased a plasma-screen television, there is a 47.5% chance that the household also purchased a DVR. You can compare this conditional probability to the marginal probability of purchasing a DVR, which is $108/300 = 0.36$, or 36%. These results tell you that households that purchased plasma-screen televisions are more likely to purchase DVRs than are households that purchased big-screen televisions that are not plasma-screen televisions.

Decision Trees

In Table 4.1 on page 151, households are classified according to whether they planned to purchase and whether they actually purchased big-screen televisions. A **decision tree** is an alternative to the contingency table. Figure 4.1 represents the decision tree for this example.

FIGURE 4.1

Decision tree for the
Consumer Electronics
Company example

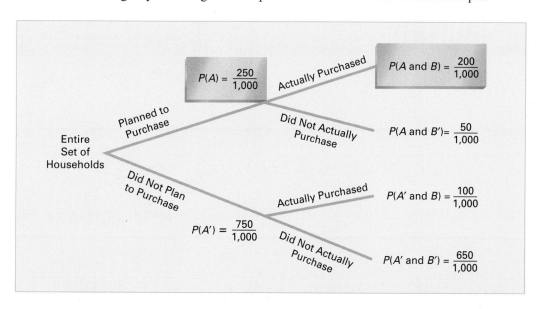

In Figure 4.1, beginning at the left with the entire set of households, there are two "branches" for whether or not the household planned to purchase a big-screen television. Each of these branches has two subbranches, corresponding to whether the household actually purchased or did not actually purchase the big-screen television. The probabilities at the end of the initial branches represent the marginal probabilities of A and A'. The probabilities at the end of each of the four subbranches represent the joint probability for each combination of events A and B. You compute the conditional probability by dividing the joint probability by the appropriate marginal probability.

For example, to compute the probability that the household actually purchased, given that the household planned to purchase the big-screen television, take P(Planned to purchase *and* actually purchased) and divide by P(Planned to purchase). From Figure 4.1:

$$P(\text{Actually purchased} \mid \text{Planned to purchase}) = \frac{200/1{,}000}{250/1{,}000}$$

$$= \frac{200}{250} = 0.80$$

Example 4.7 illustrates how to construct a decision tree.

EXAMPLE 4.7

FORMING THE DECISION TREE FOR THE HOUSEHOLDS THAT PURCHASED BIG-SCREEN TELEVISIONS

Using the cross-classified data in Table 4.2 on page 152, construct the decision tree. Use the decision tree to find the probability that a household purchased a DVR, given that the household purchased a plasma-screen television.

SOLUTION The decision tree for purchased a DVR and a plasma-screen television is displayed in Figure 4.2. Using Equation (4.4b) on page 158 and the following definitions,

$$A = \text{Purchased plasma-screen television}$$

$$B = \text{Purchased DVR}$$

$$P(B \mid A) = \frac{P(A \text{ and } B)}{P(A)} = \frac{38/300}{80/300} = 0.475$$

FIGURE 4.2

Decision tree for purchased a DVR and a plasma-screen television

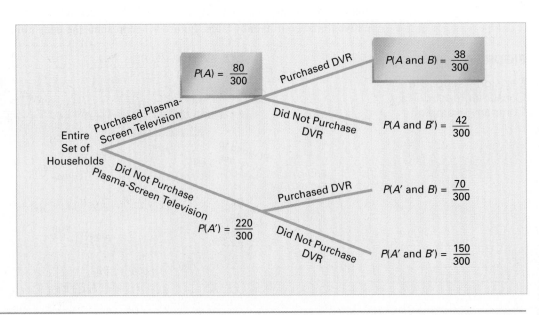

Statistical Independence

In the example concerning the purchase of big-screen televisions, the conditional probability is 200/250 = 0.80 that the selected household actually purchased the big-screen television, given that the household planned to purchase. The simple probability of selecting a household that actually purchased is 300/1,000 = 0.30. This result shows that the prior knowledge that the household planned to purchase affected the probability that the household actually purchased the television. In other words, the outcome of one event is *dependent* on the outcome of a second event.

When the outcome of one event does *not* affect the probability of occurrence of another event, the events are said to be statistically independent. **Statistical independence** can be determined by using Equation (4.5).

STATISTICAL INDEPENDENCE

Two events, A and B, are statistically independent if and only if

$$P(A \mid B) = P(A) \qquad \qquad \textbf{(4.5)}$$

where

$$P(A \mid B) = \text{conditional probability of } A \text{ given } B$$

$$P(A) = \text{marginal probability of } A$$

Example 4.8 demonstrates the use of Equation (4.5).

EXAMPLE 4.8

DETERMINING STATISTICAL INDEPENDENCE

In the follow-up survey of the 300 households that actually purchased big-screen televisions, the households were asked if they were satisfied with their purchases. Table 4.3 cross-classifies the responses to the satisfaction question with the responses to whether the television was a plasma-screen television.

TABLE 4.3

Satisfaction with Purchase of Big-Screen Televisions

	SATISFIED WITH PURCHASE?		
TYPE OF TELEVISION	**Yes**	**No**	**Total**
Plasma screen	64	16	80
Not plasma screen	176	44	220
Total	240	60	300

Determine whether being satisfied with the purchase and type of television purchased are statistically independent.

SOLUTION For these data,

$$P(\text{Satisfied} \mid \text{Plasma screen}) = \frac{64/300}{80/300} = \frac{64}{80} = 0.80$$

which is equal to

$$P(\text{Satisfied}) = \frac{240}{300} = 0.80$$

Thus, being satisfied with the purchase and type of television purchased are statistically independent. Knowledge of one event does not affect the probability of the other event.

Multiplication Rules

By manipulating the formula for conditional probability, you can determine the joint probability $P(A \text{ and } B)$ from the conditional probability of an event. The **general multiplication rule** is derived using Equation (4.4a) on page 158:

$$P(A \mid B) = \frac{P(A \text{ and } B)}{P(B)}$$

and solving for the joint probability $P(A \text{ and } B)$.

GENERAL MULTIPLICATION RULE

The probability of A and B is equal to the probability of A given B times the probability of B.

$$P(A \text{ and } B) = P(A \mid B)P(B) \qquad \textbf{(4.6)}$$

Example 4.9 demonstrates the use of the general multiplication rule.

EXAMPLE 4.9

USING THE MULTIPLICATION RULE

Consider the 80 households that purchased plasma-screen televisions. In Table 4.3 on page 161 you see that 64 households are satisfied with their purchase and 16 households are dissatisfied. Suppose two households are randomly selected from the 80 customers. Find the probability that both households are satisfied with their purchase.

SOLUTION Here you can use the multiplication rule in the following way. If:

$$A = \text{second household selected is satisfied}$$

$$B = \text{first household selected is satisfied}$$

then, using Equation (4.6),

$$P(A \text{ and } B) = P(A \mid B)P(B)$$

The probability that the first household is satisfied with the purchase is 64/80. However, the probability that the second household is also satisfied with the purchase depends on the result of the first selection. If the first household is not returned to the sample after the satisfaction level is determined (that is, sampling without replacement), the number of households remaining is 79. If the first household is satisfied, the probability that the second is also satisfied is 63/79 because 63 satisfied households remain in the sample. Therefore,

$$P(A \text{ and } B) = \left(\frac{63}{79}\right)\left(\frac{64}{80}\right) = 0.6380$$

There is a 63.80% chance that both of the households sampled will be satisfied with their purchase.

The **multiplication rule for independent events** is derived by substituting $P(A)$ for $P(A \mid B)$ in Equation (4.6).

MULTIPLICATION RULE FOR INDEPENDENT EVENTS

If A and B are statistically independent, the probability of A *and* B is equal to the probability of A times the probability of B.

$$P(A \text{ and } B) = P(A)P(B) \qquad \textbf{(4.7)}$$

If this rule holds for two events, A and B, then A and B are statistically independent. Therefore, there are two ways to determine statistical independence:

1. Events A and B are statistically independent if, and only if, $P(A \mid B) = P(A)$.
2. Events A and B are statistically independent if, and only if, $P(A \text{ and } B) = P(A)P(B)$.

Marginal Probability Using the General Multiplication Rule

In Section 4.1, marginal probability was defined using Equation (4.2) on page 153. You can state the formula for marginal probability by using the general multiplication rule. If

$$P(A) = P(A \text{ and } B_1) + P(A \text{ and } B_2) + \cdots + P(A \text{ and } B_k)$$

then, using the general multiplication rule, Equation (4.8) defines the marginal probability.

MARGINAL PROBABILITY USING THE GENERAL MULTIPLICATION RULE

$$P(A) = P(A \mid B_1)P(B_1) + P(A \mid B_2)P(B_2) + \cdots + P(A \mid B_k)P(B_k) \qquad \textbf{(4.8)}$$

where $B_1, B_2, \ldots, B_k$ are k mutually exclusive and collectively exhaustive events.

To illustrate this equation, refer to Table 4.1 on page 151. Using Equation (4.8), the probability of planning to purchase is:

$$P(A) = P(A \mid B_1)P(B_1) + P(A \mid B_2)P(B_2)$$

where

$$P(A) = \text{probability of "planned to purchase"}$$

$$P(B_1) = \text{probability of "actually purchased"}$$

$$P(B_2) = \text{probability of "did not actually purchase"}$$

$$P(A) = \left(\frac{200}{300}\right)\left(\frac{300}{1,000}\right) + \left(\frac{50}{700}\right)\left(\frac{700}{1,000}\right)$$

$$= \frac{200}{1,000} + \frac{50}{1,000} = \frac{250}{1,000} = 0.25$$

PROBLEMS FOR SECTION 4.2

Learning the Basics

 4.16 Given the following contingency table:

	B	B'
A	10	20
A'	20	40

What is the probability of
a. $A \mid B$?
b. $A \mid B'$?
c. $A' \mid B'$?
d. Are events A and B statistically independent?

4.17 Given the following contingency table:

	B	B'
A	10	30
A'	25	35

What is the probability of
a. $A \mid B$?
b. $A' \mid B'$?
c. $A \mid B'$?
d. Are events A and B statistically independent?

 4.18 If $P(A \text{ and } B) = 0.4$ and $P(B) = 0.8$, find $P(A \mid B)$.

 4.19 If $P(A) = 0.7$, $P(B) = 0.6$, and A and B are statistically independent, find $P(A \text{ and } B)$.

4.20 If $P(A) = 0.3$, $P(B) = 0.4$, and if $P(A \text{ and } B) = 0.2$, are A and B statistically independent?

Applying the Concepts

4.21 Where people turn to for news is different for various age groups. Suppose that a study conducted on this issue (extracted from P. Johnson, "Young People Turn to the Web for News," *USA Today*, March 23, 2006, p. 9D) was based on 200 respondents who were between the ages of 36 and 50 and 200 respondents who were over age 50. Of the 200 respondents who were between the ages of 36 and 50, 82 got their news primarily from newspapers. Of the 200 respondents who were over age 50, 104 got their news primarily from newspapers.
a. Given that a respondent is over age 50, what then is the probability that he or she gets news primarily from newspapers?
b. Given that a respondent gets news primarily from newspapers, what is the probability that he or she is over age 50?
c. Explain the difference in the results in (a) and (b).

d. Are the two events, whether the respondent is over age 50 and whether he or she gets news primarily from newspapers, statistically independent?

4.22 A yield improvement study at a semiconductor manufacturing facility provided defect data for a sample of 450 wafers. The following table presents a summary of the responses to two questions: "Were particles found on the die that produced the wafer?" and "Is the wafer good or bad?"

QUALITY OF WAFER	CONDITION OF DIE		
	No Particles	Particles	Totals
Good	320	14	334
Bad	80	36	116
Totals	400	50	450

Source: Extracted from S. W. Hall, "Analysis of Defectivity of Semiconductor Wafers by Contingency Table," Proceedings Institute of Environmental Sciences, Vol. 1, 1994, pp. 177–183.

a. Suppose you know that a wafer is bad. What is the probability that it was produced from a die that had particles?
b. Suppose you know that a wafer is good. What is the probability that it was produced from a die that had particles?
c. Are the two events, a good wafer and a die with no particles, statistically independent? Explain.

4.23 According to an Ipsos poll, the perception of unfairness in the U.S. tax code is spread fairly evenly across income groups, age groups, and education levels. In an April 2006 survey of 1,005 adults, Ipsos reported that almost 60% of all people said the code is unfair, while slightly more than 60% of those making more than $50,000 viewed the code as unfair ("People Cry Unfairness," *The Cincinnati Enquirer*, April 16, 2006, p. A8). Suppose that the following contingency table represents the specific breakdown of responses:

	INCOME LEVEL		
	Less Than $50,000	More Than $50,000	Total
Fair	225	180	405
Unfair	280	320	600
Total	505	500	1,005

a. Given that a respondent earns less than $50,000, what is the probability that he or she said that the tax code is fair?
b. Given that a respondent earns more than $50,000, what is the probability that he or she said that the tax code is fair?
c. Is income level statistically independent of attitude about whether the tax code is fair? Explain.

4.24 An experiment was conducted to study the choices made in mutual fund selection. Undergraduate and MBA students were presented with different S&P 500 Index funds that were identical except for fees. Suppose 100 undergraduate students and 100 MBA students were selected. Partial results are shown in the following table:

| | STUDENT GROUP | |
FUND	Undergraduate	MBA
Highest-cost fund	27	18
Not Highest-cost fund	73	82

Source: Extracted from J. J. Choi, D. Laibson, and B. C. Madrian, Why Does the Law of One Price Fail? ***www.som.yale.edu/faculty/ jjc83/fees.pdf.***

a. Given that a student is an undergraduate, what is the probability that he or she selected the highest-cost fund?
b. Given that a student selected the highest-cost fund, what is the probability that he or she is an undergraduate?
c. Explain the difference in the results in (a) and (b).
d. Are the two events "student group" and "fund selected" statistically independent? Explain.

4.25 A sample of 500 respondents was selected in a large metropolitan area to study consumer behavior, with the following results:

ENJOYS SHOPPING FOR CLOTHING	GENDER		
	Male	Female	Total
Yes	136	224	360
No	104	36	140
Total	240	260	500

a. Suppose the respondent chosen is a female. What is the probability that she does not enjoy shopping for clothing?
b. Suppose the respondent chosen enjoys shopping for clothing. What is the probability that the individual is a male?
c. Are enjoying shopping for clothing and the gender of the individual statistically independent? Explain.

4.26 Each year, ratings are compiled concerning the performance of new cars during the first 90 days of use. Suppose that the cars have been categorized according to whether the car needs warranty-related repair (yes or no) and the country in which the company manufacturing the car is based (United States or not United States). Based on the data collected, the probability that the new car needs a warranty repair is 0.04, the probability that the car is manufactured by a U.S.-based company is 0.60, and the probability that the new car needs a warranty repair *and* was manufactured by a U.S.-based company is 0.025.

a. Suppose you know that a company based in the United States manufactured a particular car. What is the probability that the car needs warranty repair?
b. Suppose you know that a company based in the United States did not manufacture a particular car. What is the probability that the car needs warranty repair?

c. Are need for warranty repair and location of the company manufacturing the car statistically independent?

4.27 In 35 of the 56 years from 1950 through 2005, the S&P 500 finished higher after the first 5 days of trading. In 30 of those 35 years, the S&P 500 finished higher for the year. Is a good first week a good omen for the upcoming year? The following table gives the first-week and annual performance over this 56-year period:

| | S&P 500's Annual Performance | |
First Week	Higher	Lower
Higher	30	5
Lower	11	10

a. If a year is selected at random, what is the probability that the S&P 500 finished higher for the year?
b. Given that the S&P 500 finished higher after the first five days of trading, what is the probability that it finished higher for the year?
c. Are the two events "first-week performance" and "annual performance" statistically independent? Explain.
d. Look up the performance after the first five days of 2006 and the 2006 annual performance of the S&P 500 at **finance.yahoo.com**. Comment on the results.

4.28 A standard deck of cards is being used to play a game. There are four suits (hearts, diamonds, clubs, and spades), each having 13 faces (ace, 2, 3, 4, 5, 6, 7, 8, 9, 10, jack, queen, and king), making a total of 52 cards. This complete deck is thoroughly mixed, and you will receive the first 2 cards from the deck without replacement.

a. What is the probability that both cards are queens?
b. What is the probability that the first card is a 10 and the second card is a 5 or 6?
c. If you were sampling with replacement, what would be the answer in (a)?
d. In the game of blackjack, the picture cards (jack, queen, king) count as 10 points, and the ace counts as either 1 or 11 points. All other cards are counted at their face value. Blackjack is achieved if 2 cards total 21 points. What is the probability of getting blackjack in this problem?

 4.29 A box of nine gloves contains two left-handed gloves and seven right-handed gloves.

a. If two gloves are randomly selected from the box without replacement, what is the probability that both gloves selected will be right-handed?
b. If two gloves are randomly selected from the box without replacement, what is the probability there will be one right-handed glove and one left-handed glove selected?
c. If three gloves are selected with replacement, what is the probability that all three will be left-handed?
d. If you were sampling with replacement, what would be the answers to (a) and (b)?

4.3   BAYES' THEOREM

Bayes' theorem is used to revise previously calculated probabilities based on new information. Developed by Thomas Bayes in the eighteenth century (see references 1, 2, and 5), Bayes' theorem is an extension of what you previously learned about conditional probability.

You can apply Bayes' theorem to the situation in which the Consumer Electronics Company is considering marketing a new model of television. In the past, 40% of the televisions introduced by the company have been successful, and 60% have been unsuccessful. Before introducing the television to the marketplace, the marketing research department conducts an extensive study and releases a report, either favorable or unfavorable. In the past, 80% of the successful televisions had received favorable market research reports, and 30% of the unsuccessful televisions had received favorable reports. For the new model of television under consideration, the marketing research department has issued a favorable report. What is the probability that the television will be successful?

Bayes' theorem is developed from the definition of conditional probability. To find the conditional probability of B given A, consider Equation (4.4b) [originally presented on page 158 and given below]:

$$P(B|A) = \frac{P(A \text{ and } B)}{P(A)} = \frac{P(A|B)P(B)}{P(A)}$$

Bayes' theorem is derived by substituting Equation (4.8) on page 163 for $P(A)$ in Equation (4.4b).

BAYES' THEOREM

$$P(B_i|A) = \frac{P(A|B_i)P(B_i)}{P(A|B_1)P(B_1) + P(A|B_2)P(B_2) + \cdots + P(A|B_k)P(B_k)} \qquad (4.9)$$

where B_i is the ith event out of k mutually exclusive and collectively exhaustive events.

To use Equation (4.9) for the television marketing example, let

event S = successful television	event F = favorable report
event S' = unsuccessful television	event F' = unfavorable report

and

$P(S) = 0.40$	$P(F \mid S) = 0.80$
$P(S') = 0.60$	$P(F \mid S') = 0.30$

Then, using Equation (4.9),

$$P(S \mid F) = \frac{P(F \mid S)P(S)}{P(F \mid S)P(S) + P(F \mid S')P(S')}$$

$$= \frac{(0.80)(0.40)}{(0.80)(0.40) + (0.30)(0.60)}$$

$$= \frac{0.32}{0.32 + 0.18} = \frac{0.32}{0.50}$$

$$= 0.64$$

The probability of a successful television, given that a favorable report was received, is 0.64. Thus, the probability of an unsuccessful television, given that a favorable report was received, is 1 − 0.64 = 0.36. Table 4.4 summarizes the computation of the probabilities, and Figure 4.3 presents the decision tree.

TABLE 4.4

Bayes' Theorem Calculations for the Television Marketing Example

Event S_i	Prior Probability $P(S_i)$	Conditional Probability $P(F \mid S_i)$	Joint Probability $P(F \mid S_i)P(S_i)$	Revised Probability $P(S_i \mid F)$
S = successful television	0.40	0.80	0.32	0.32/0.50 = 0.64 = P(S \mid F)
S′ = unsuccessful television	0.60	0.30	0.18 / 0.50	0.18/0.50 = 0.36 = P(S′ \mid F)

FIGURE 4.3

Decision tree for marketing a new television

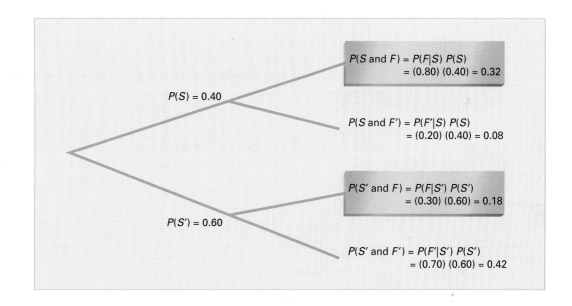

Example 4.10 applies Bayes' theorem to a medical diagnosis problem.

EXAMPLE 4.10

USING BAYES' THEOREM IN A MEDICAL DIAGNOSIS PROBLEM

The probability that a person has a certain disease is 0.03. Medical diagnostic tests are available to determine whether the person actually has the disease. If the disease is actually present, the probability that the medical diagnostic test will give a positive result (indicating that the disease is present) is 0.90. If the disease is not actually present, the probability of a positive test result (indicating that the disease is present) is 0.02. Suppose that the medical diagnostic test has given a positive result (indicating that the disease is present). What is the probability that the disease is actually present? What is the probability of a positive test result?

SOLUTION Let

event D = has disease   event T = test is positive
event D' = does not have disease   event T' = test is negative

and

$$P(D) = 0.03 \qquad P(T|D) = 0.90$$
$$P(D') = 0.97 \qquad P(T|D') = 0.02$$

Using Equation (4.9) on page 166,

$$P(D|T) = \frac{P(T|D)P(D)}{P(T|D)P(D) + P(T|D')P(D')}$$

$$= \frac{(0.90)(0.03)}{(0.90)(0.03) + (0.02)(0.97)}$$

$$= \frac{0.0270}{0.0270 + 0.0194} = \frac{0.0270}{0.0464}$$

$$= 0.582$$

The probability that the disease is actually present, given that a positive result has occurred (indicating that the disease is present), is 0.582. Table 4.5 summarizes the computation of the probabilities, and Figure 4.4 presents the decision tree.

The denominator in Bayes' theorem represents $P(T)$, the probability of a positive test result, which in this case is 0.0464, or 4.64%.

TABLE 4.5

Bayes' Theorem Calculations for the Medical Diagnosis Problem

Event D_i	Prior Probability $P(D_i)$	Conditional Probability $P(T \mid D_i)$	Joint Probability $P(T \mid D_i)P(D_i)$	Revised Probability $P(D_i \mid T)$
D = has disease	0.03	0.90	0.0270	0.0270/0.0464 = 0.582 = $P(D \mid T)$
D' = does not have disease	0.97	0.02	0.0194	0.0194/0.0464 = 0.418 = $P(D' \mid T)$
			0.0464	

FIGURE 4.4

Decision tree for the medical diagnosis problem

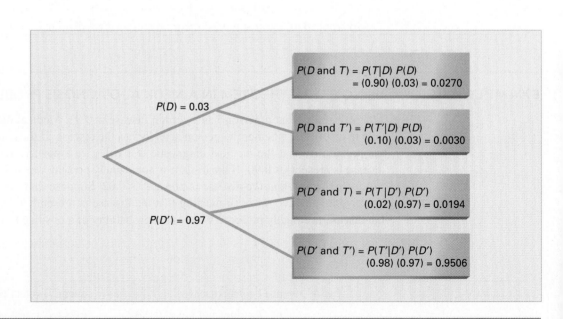

Divine Providence and Spam

You wouldn't normally think that the author of *Divine Benevolence: Or, An Attempt to Prove That the Principal End of the Divine Providence and Government Is the Happiness of His Creatures* would have anything to contribute to the discussion of probability, would you? But you might say that the author of *An Essay Towards Solving a Problem in the Doctrine of Chances* would, wouldn't you? As it turns out, both essays were written by Thomas Bayes, who was a minister and theologian by training. If you didn't guess that both essays were written by the same person, don't feel too bad because your wrong guess helps illustrate a modern-day application of Bayesian statistics—spam filters—about which you'll learn more later.

An Essay Towards Solving . . . introduced Bayes' theorem, discussed in Section 4.3. After writing the essay, Bayes put it aside, and we only know about the paper because a friend, Richard Price, published it in 1763 after Bayes' death. In Price's view, the essay proved the existence of God by showing that "the frame of the world must be the effect of wisdom and power of an intelligent cause; and thus to confirm . . . the existence of the Deity." Bayes, himself, was more modest about the essay, noting "so far as mathematics do not tend to make men more sober and rational thinkers . . . they are only to be considered as an amusement, which ought not to take us off from serious business." (By the way, Price deleted those words when he published *An Essay Towards Solving . . .*)

In spite of Price's enthusiasm, Bayes' theorem was soon dismissed by the majority of statisticians, who felt, among other reasons, that establishing the prior probabilities needed by the theorem would ultimately be nothing more than an example of setting subjective probabilities. Others, who had a more accepting view, noted that the prior probabilities would need to be constantly updated and therefore were concerned about the impossibility of keeping track of all the results that would be needed in order to constantly update those probabilities (to better reflect current experience).

While always championed by a minority of statisticians, and notably, a number of non-statisticians, Bayes' theorem remained at the fringes of respectable statistics for more than 150 years. The theorem began its long return from statistical exile when *An Essay Towards . . .* was republished in 1940, with commentary by W. Edwards Deming. (Ironically, like

Bayes' theorem, many of Deming's own ideas would also be ignored, only to be widely accepted later on, as Chapter 18 explains.) But it took the data processing power of modern computer systems to bring Bayesian statistics into the mainstream of research.

Today, applications of Bayesian statistics are making computers more "artificially intelligent." Programs that "mine" large databases, seeking to discover hidden patterns, use Bayesian techniques. Your favorite Internet search engine may use some Bayesian techniques, as well, to deliver Internet links most likely to be relevant to your search. But of all the Bayesian applications in use, the one you've most likely experienced involves spam, the unwanted junk mail that clogs your email inbox.

Return to the questions of the first paragraph concerning the titles of two essays authored by Thomas Bayes. Implicit in those questions are expectations that word frequencies vary by subject matter. A text about statistics would very likely contain the word *statistics* as well as words such as *chance*, *problem*, and *solving*. An eighteenth-century book about theology and religion would be more likely to contain the uppercase forms of *Divine* and *Providence*. Likewise, there are words very unlikely to appear in either books, such as the words *sedimentary*, *igneous*, and *metamorphic* (types of rocks), and there are words that are likely to appear in both types of books—common words such as *a, an,* and *the*.

The key words in these sentences are *likely* and *unlikely* because they suggest that we might be able to use probabilities. Of course, *likely* and *unlikely* are fuzzy concepts, and we could never be completely sure if we had classified a book correctly. After all, a book about the underground film director John Waters (of *Hairspray* fame) might talk about him traveling with the star of many of his movies, *Divine*, to see *Providence* (as in Rhode Island). Still, we would probably not mistake such a book for an eighteenth-century book on theology if we considered other words, such as *film* and *movie*, which are unlikely to be found in an eighteenth-century publication.

Classifying books into one of several categories creates complications too difficult to explain here, but what if we looked at the simpler problem of trying to classify a newly arrived email message as either spam or a legitimate message (sometimes called "ham" in this context)? More specifically, what if we

focused on all the emails sent to one address? And what if we added something to that person's email program that would track word frequencies associated with spam and ham messages in order to constantly update the prior probabilities that Bayes' theorem needs? When researchers realized all this was possible, Bayesian spam filters got their start.

These filters ask, "What is the probabilities that an email is spam, given the presence of a certain word?" Using Bayes' theorem, the filters can calculate this probabilities by multiplying the probability of finding the word in a spam email, $P(A|B)$ in Equation 4.9, by the probability that the email is spam, $P(B)$, and dividing by the probability of finding the word in an email, the denominator in Equation 4.9.

Bayesian spam filters quickly proved superior to simple keyword filters in both identifying spam and avoiding labeling a ham message as spam. Most Bayesian spam filters ignore common words found in both ham and spam emails. These filters also take shortcuts by focusing on a small set of words that have a high probability of being found in a spam email and on words that have a low probability of being found in a spam email.

As spammers (people who sent junk email) learned of these new filters, they tried to outfox them. Having learned that Bayesian filters might be assigning a high $P(A|B)$ value to words like Viagra, commonly found in early spam messages, spammers thought they could fool the filter by misspelling the word as Vi@gr@ or V1agra. What they failed to realize was that the misspelled variants were even more likely to be found in a spam message than the original word. Thus the misspelled variants made the job even easier for the Bayesian filters. Of course, through all the emails, the filters are constantly being retrained—that is, updating probabilities and noting when the user indicates a particular email marked as ham is really spam. So, the initial Vi@agr@ emails were mismarked as ham, but the filter quickly learns to treat such messages as spam. (Don't worry about filters marking a ham message as spam; most filters are set up with a bias in their probabilities that minimizes such occurrences.)

Other spammers, reading a little bit about filters, decided to add "good" words, words that would have a very low $P(A|B)$ value, or "rare" words, words not frequently encountered in emails. This, they thought, should change the result as the filter evaluated the text of an email and led the filter to enable their spam messages be viewed as

(Continued)

Divine Providence and Spam (continued)

ham messages. But these spammers overlooked the fact that the conditional probabilities are constantly updated and that words once considered "good" would be discarded by the filter as their $P(A|B)$ value increased. They also failed to realize that, as "rare" words started to show up in spam messages (and yet still rarely in ham messages), those words acted like the misspelled variants they had tried earlier.

After these attacks were beaten back by Bayesian filters, spammers apparently started learning more about Bayesian statistics. Some figured that they could "break" Bayesian filters by inserting random words in their messages. Those random words would affect the filter by causing it to see many words whose $P(A|B)$ value would be low. The Bayesian filter would begin to label many spam messages as ham and end up being of no practical use. Because the Internet still contains some Web pages and posts that triumph this approach,

we will leave it to you to figure out why this method of attack cannot succeed in the long run and why this method is not as initially successful as some would claim.

Today, spammers are still trying to outwit Bayesian filters. Some spammers have decided to eliminate all or most of the words in their messages and replace them with graphics so that Bayesian filters will have very few words with which to work. But this approach will fail too, as Bayes' filters are rewritten to consider things other than words in a message. After all, Bayes' theorem is all about events, and "graphics present with no text" is as valid an event as "*some word* present in email."

In truth, for a variety of reasons, including expediency, most email filters today use a combination of techniques that includes applying Bayesian statistics. And while the war against Bayesian filters escalates over

time, it's a war that statistics dooms spammers to lose in the long run.

You can gain a number of insights from knowing the story of Bayes' theorem and its application to the problem of email spam. You can understand better the nature of intellectual discovery, especially how fringe knowledge can become mainstream knowledge. You can see that statisticians have disagreed over important concepts as they have tried to extend the boundaries of their field, and yes, you can even reflect about the search for a proof that would confirm a benevolent Deity. If nothing else, perhaps you will begin to think how applications of statistics can show up in your life in very unexpected ways and how a knowledge of statistics is an important component of being a well-educated person.

Forum > *Click the* BAYES' THEOREM *link to continue this discussion.* < <

PROBLEMS FOR SECTION 4.3

Learning the Basics

 4.30 If $P(B) = 0.05$, $P(A \mid B) = 0.80$, $P(B') = 0.95$, and $P(A \mid B') = 0.40$, find $P(B \mid A)$.

 4.31 If $P(B) = 0.30$, $P(A \mid B) = 0.60$, $P(B') = 0.70$, and $P(A \mid B') = 0.50$, find $P(B \mid A)$.

Applying the Concepts

4.32 In Example 4.10 on page 167, suppose that the probability that a medical diagnostic test will give a positive result if the disease is not present is reduced from 0.02 to 0.01. Given this information,
a. if the medical diagnostic test has given a positive result (indicating that the disease is present), what is the probability that the disease is actually present?
b. if the medical diagnostic test has given a negative result (indicating that the disease is not present), what is the probability that the disease is not present?

 4.33 An advertising executive is studying television viewing habits of married men and women during prime-time hours. Based on past viewing records, the executive has determined that during prime time, husbands are watching television 60% of the time. When the husband is watching television, 40% of the time the wife is also watching. When the husband is not watch-

ing television, 30% of the time the wife is watching television. Find the probability that
a. if the wife is watching television, the husband is also watching television.
b. the wife is watching television in prime time.

 4.34 Olive Construction Company is determining whether it should submit a bid for a new shopping center. In the past, Olive's main competitor, Base Construction Company, has submitted bids 70% of the time. If Base Construction Company does not bid on a job, the probability that Olive Construction Company will get the job is 0.50. If Base Construction Company bids on a job, the probability that Olive Construction Company will get the job is 0.25.
a. If Olive Construction Company gets the job, what is the probability that Base Construction Company did not bid?
b. What is the probability that Olive Construction Company will get the job?

4.35 Laid-off workers who become entrepreneurs because they cannot find meaningful employment with another company are known as *entrepreneurs by necessity*. *The Wall Street Journal* reports that these entrepreneurs by necessity are less likely to grow into large businesses than are *entrepreneurs by choice* (J. Bailey, "Desire—More Than Need— Builds a Business," *The Wall Street Journal*, May 21, 2001,

p. B4). This article states that 89% of the entrepreneurs in the United States are entrepreneurs by choice and 11% are entrepreneurs by necessity. Only 2% of entrepreneurs by necessity expect their new business to employ 20 or more people within five years, while 14% of entrepreneurs by choice expect to employ at least 20 people within five years.

a. If an entrepreneur is selected at random, and that individual expects that his or her new business will employ 20 or more people within five years, what is the probability that this individual is an entrepreneur by choice?

b. Discuss several possible reasons why entrepreneurs by choice are more likely to believe that they will grow their businesses.

4.36 The editor of a textbook publishing company is trying to decide whether to publish a proposed business statistics textbook. Information on previous textbooks published indicates that 10% are huge successes, 20% are modest successes, 40% break even, and 30% are losers. However, before a publishing decision is made, the book will be reviewed. In the past, 99% of the huge successes received favorable reviews, 70% of the moderate successes received favorable reviews, 40% of the break-even books received favorable reviews, and 20% of the losers received favorable reviews.

a. If the proposed text receives a favorable review, how should the editor revise the probabilities of the various outcomes to take this information into account?

b. What proportion of textbooks receives favorable reviews?

4.37 A municipal bond service has three rating categories (A, B, and C). Suppose that in the past year, of the municipal bonds issued throughout the United States, 70% were rated A, 20% were rated B, and 10% were rated C. Of the municipal bonds rated A, 50% were issued by cities, 40% by suburbs, and 10% by rural areas. Of the municipal bonds rated B, 60% were issued by cities, 20% by suburbs, and 20% by rural areas. Of the municipal bonds rated C, 90% were issued by cities, 5% by suburbs, and 5% by rural areas.

a. If a new municipal bond is to be issued by a city, what is the probability that it will receive an A rating?

b. What proportion of municipal bonds is issued by cities?

c. What proportion of municipal bonds is issued by suburbs?

4.4   ETHICAL ISSUES AND PROBABILITY

Ethical issues can arise when any statements related to probability are presented to the public, particularly when these statements are part of an advertising campaign for a product or service. Unfortunately, many people are not comfortable with numerical concepts (see reference 4) and tend to misinterpret the meaning of the probability. In some instances, the misinterpretation is not intentional, but in other cases, advertisements may unethically try to mislead potential customers.

One example of a potentially unethical application of probability relates to advertisements for state lotteries. When purchasing a lottery ticket, the customer selects a set of numbers (such as 6) from a larger list of numbers (such as 54). Although virtually all participants know that they are unlikely to win the lottery, they also have very little idea of how unlikely it is for them to select all 6 winning numbers from the list of 54 numbers. They have even less idea of the probability of winning a consolation prize by selecting either 4 or 5 winning numbers.

Given this background, you might consider a recent commercial for a state lottery that stated, "We won't stop until we have made everyone a millionaire" to be deceptive and possibly unethical. Given the fact that the lottery brings millions of dollars into the state treasury, the state is never going to stop running it, although in our lifetime, no one can be sure of becoming a millionaire by winning the lottery.

Another example of a potentially unethical application of probability relates to an investment newsletter promising a 90% probability of a 20% annual return on investment. To make the claim in the newsletter an ethical one, the investment service needs to (a) explain the basis on which this probability estimate rests, (b) provide the probability statement in another format, such as 9 chances in 10, and (c) explain what happens to the investment in the 10% of the cases in which a 20% return is not achieved (for example, is the entire investment lost?).

PROBLEMS FOR SECTION 4.4

Applying the Concepts

4.38 Write an advertisement for the state lottery that ethically describes the probability of winning.

4.39 Write an advertisement for the investment newsletter that ethically states the probability of a 20% return.

4.5 ● (*CD-ROM Topic*) COUNTING RULES

In many instances, there are a large number of possible outcomes, and determining the exact number can be difficult. In these circumstances, rules for counting the number of possible outcomes have been developed. To study this topic, go to the section 4.5.pdf file located on the CD-ROM that accompanies this book.

S U M M A R Y

This chapter develops concepts concerning basic probability, conditional probability, and Bayes' theorem. In the next chapter, important discrete probability distributions such as the binomial, hypergeometric, and Poisson distributions are developed.

K E Y   E Q U A T I O N S

Probability of Occurrence

$$\text{Probability of occurrence} = \frac{X}{T} \quad \textbf{(4.1)}$$

Marginal Probability

$$P(A) = P(A \text{ and } B_1) + P(A \text{ and } B_2) + \cdots + P(A \text{ and } B_k) \quad \textbf{(4.2)}$$

General Addition Rule

$$P(A \text{ or } B) = P(A) + P(B) - P(A \text{ and } B) \quad \textbf{(4.3)}$$

Conditional Probability

$$P(A \mid B) = \frac{P(A \text{ and } B)}{P(B)} \quad \textbf{(4.4a)}$$

$$P(B \mid A) = \frac{P(A \text{ and } B)}{P(A)} \quad \textbf{(4.4b)}$$

Statistical Independence

$$P(A \mid B) = P(A) \quad \textbf{(4.5)}$$

General Multiplication Rule

$$P(A \text{ and } B) = P(A \mid B)P(B) \quad \textbf{(4.6)}$$

Multiplication Rule for Independent Events

$$P(A \text{ and } B) = P(A)P(B) \quad \textbf{(4.7)}$$

Marginal Probability Using the General Multiplication Rule

$$P(A) = P(A \mid B_1)P(B_1) + P(A \mid B_2)P(B_2) + \cdots + P(A \mid B_k)P(B_k) \quad \textbf{(4.8)}$$

Bayes' Theorem

$$P(B_i \mid A) = \frac{P(A \mid B_i)P(B_i)}{P(A \mid B_1)P(B_1) + P(A \mid B_2)P(B_2) + \cdots + P(A \mid B_k)P(B_k)} \quad \textbf{(4.9)}$$

K E Y   T E R M S

a priori classical probability   149
Bayes' theorem   166
certain event   149
collectively exhaustive   153
complement   150
conditional probability   157
contingency table   151
decision tree   159
empirical classical probability   149

CHAPTER REVIEW PROBLEMS

Checking Your Understanding

4.40 What are the differences between *a priori* classical probability, empirical classical probability, and subjective probability?

4.41 What is the difference between a simple event and a joint event?

4.42 How can you use the addition rule to find the probability of occurrence of event *A* or *B*?

4.43 What is the difference between mutually exclusive events and collectively exhaustive events?

4.44 How does conditional probability relate to the concept of statistical independence?

4.45 How does the multiplication rule differ for events that are and are not independent?

4.46 How can you use Bayes' theorem to revise probabilities in light of new information?

4.47 In Bayes' theorem, how does the prior probability differ from the revised probability?

Applying the Concepts

4.48 A soft drink bottling company maintains records concerning the number of unacceptable bottles of soft drink from the filling and capping machines. Based on past data, the probability that a bottle came from machine I and was nonconforming is 0.01, and the probability that a bottle came from machine II and was nonconforming is 0.005. Half the bottles are filled on machine I. The other half are filled on machine II. If a filled bottle of soft drink is randomly selected, what is the probability that
a. it is a nonconforming bottle?
b. it was filled on machine I *and* is a conforming bottle?
c. it was filled on machine I *or* is a conforming bottle?
d. Suppose you know that the bottle was filled on machine I. What is the probability that it is nonconforming?
e. Suppose you know that the bottle is nonconforming. What is the probability that it was filled on machine I?
f. Explain the difference in the answers to (d) and (e).
(*Hint:* Construct a 2 × 2 contingency table to evaluate the probabilities.)

4.49 A survey of 500 men and 500 women, designed to study financial tensions between couples, asked how likely each was to hide purchases, cash, or investments from his or her partner. The results were as follows:

| | Likely to Hide | |
Type	Men	Women
Auto-related	66	36
Cash	126	133
Clothes	62	116
Electronics	79	56
Entertainment	96	76
Food	74	94
Investments	76	52
Travel	53	39

Source: Extracted from L. Wei, "Your Money Manager as Financial Therapist," The Wall Street Journal, November 5–6, 2005, p. B4.

Construct a contingency table of likely to hide (yes or no) with gender for each type. If a respondent is chosen at random, what is the probability that
a. he or she is likely to hide a clothing purchase?
b. he or she is likely to hide investments?
c. the person is a male and is likely to hide auto-related purchases?
d. the person is a female and is likely to hide clothing purchases?
e. Given that the person hides investments, what is the probability that the person is a male?
f. Are any of the types of things that couples hide statistically independent of the gender of the respondent? Explain.

4.50 Many companies use Web sites to conduct business transactions, such as taking orders or performing financial exchanges. These sites are referred to as *transactional public Web sites*. An analysis of 490 firms listed in the Fortune 500 identified firms by their level of sales and whether the firm had a transactional public Web site (D. Young and J. Benamati, "A Cross-Industry Analysis of Large Firm Transactional Public Web Sites," *Mid-American Journal of*

Business, Vol. 19, 2004, pp. 37–46). The results of this analysis are given in the following table:

TRANSACTIONAL PUBLIC WEB SITE

SALES (IN BILLIONS OF DOLLARS)	Yes	No
Greater than $10 billion	71	88
Up to $10 billion	99	232

a. Give an example of a simple event and a joint event.
b. What is the probability that a firm in the Fortune 500 has a transactional public Web site?
c. What is the probability that a firm in the Fortune 500 has sales in excess of $10 billion and a transactional Web site?
d. Are the events "sales in excess of $10 billion" and "has a transactional public Web site" independent? Explain.

4.51 The owner of a restaurant serving Continental-style entrées was interested in studying ordering patterns of patrons for the Friday-to-Sunday weekend time period. Records were maintained that indicated the demand for dessert during the same time period. The owner decided to study two other variables, along with whether a dessert was ordered: the gender of the individual and whether a beef entrée was ordered. The results are as follows:

	GENDER		
DESSERT ORDERED	Male	Female	Total
Yes	96	40	136
No	224	240	464
Total	320	280	600

	BEEF ENTRÉE		
DESSERT ORDERED	Yes	No	Total
Yes	71	65	136
No	116	348	464
Total	187	413	600

A waiter approaches a table to take an order. What is the probability that the first customer to order at the table
a. orders a dessert?
b. orders a dessert *or* a beef entrée?
c. is a female *and* does not order a dessert?
d. is a female *or* does not order a dessert?
e. Suppose the first person that the waiter takes the dessert order from is a female. What is the probability that she does not order dessert?
f. Are gender and ordering dessert statistically independent?
g. Is ordering a beef entrée statistically independent of whether the person orders dessert?

4.52 Unsolicited commercial email messages containing product advertisements, commonly referred to as spam, are routinely deleted before being read by more than 80% of all email users. Furthermore, a small percentage of those reading the spam actually follow through and purchase items. Yet many companies use these unsolicited email advertisements because of the extremely low cost involved. Movies Unlimited, a mail-order video and DVD business in Philadelphia, is one of the more successful companies in terms of generating sales through this form of e-marketing. Ed Weiss, general manager of Movies Unlimited, estimates that somewhere from 15% to 20% of the company's email recipients read the advertisements. Moreover, approximately 15% of those who read the advertisements place orders (S. Forster, "E-Marketers Look to Polish Spam's Rusty Image," *The Wall Street Journal*, May 20, 2002, p. D2).

a. Using Mr. Weiss's lower estimate that the probability a recipient will read the advertisement is 0.15, what is the probability that a recipient will read the advertisement and place an order?
b. Movies Unlimited uses a 175,000-customer database to send email advertisements. If an email advertisement is sent to everyone in its customer database, how many customers do you expect will read the advertisement and place an order?
c. If the probability a recipient will read the advertisement is 0.20, what is the probability that a recipient will read the advertisement and place an order?
d. What is your answer to (b) if the probability that a recipient will read the advertisement is 0.20?

4.53 An experiment was conducted by James Choi, David Laibson, and Brigitte Madrian to study the choices made in fund selection. Suppose 100 undergraduate students and 100 MBA students were selected. When presented with four S&P 500 Index funds that were identical except for their fees, undergraduate and MBA students chose the funds as follows:

	STUDENT GROUP	
FUND	Undergraduate	MBA
Lowest-cost fund	19	19
Second-lowest-cost fund	37	40
Third-lowest-cost fund	17	23
Highest-cost fund	27	18

Source: Extracted from J. J. Choi, D. Laibson, and B. C. Madrian, Why Does the Law of One Price Fail? **www.som.yale.edu/faculty/jjc83/fees.pdf.**

If a student is selected at random, what is the probability that he or she
a. selected the lowest or second-lowest cost fund?
b. selected the lowest-cost fund *and* is an undergraduate?
c. selected the lowest-cost fund *or* is an undergraduate?
d. Given that the student is an undergraduate, what is the probability that he or she selected the highest-cost fund?

e. Do you think undergraduate students and graduate students differ in their fund selection? Explain.

4.54 Sport utility vehicles (SUVs), vans, and pickups are generally considered to be more prone to roll over than cars. In 1997, 24.0% of all highway fatalities involved rollovers; 15.8% of all fatalities in 1997 involved SUVs, vans, and pickups, given that the fatality involved a rollover. Given that a rollover was not involved, 5.6% of all fatalities involved SUVs, vans, and pickups (A. Wilde Mathews, "Ford Ranger, Chevy Tracker Tilt in Test," *The Wall Street Journal*, July 14, 1999, p. A2). Consider the following definitions:

A = fatality involved an SUV, van, or pickup

B = fatality involved a rollover

a. Use Bayes' theorem to find the probability that a fatality involved a rollover, given that the fatality involved an SUV, a van, or a pickup.
b. Compare the result in (a) to the probability that a fatality involved a rollover and comment on whether SUVs, vans, and pickups are generally more prone to rollover accidents than other vehicles.

4.55 Enzyme-linked immunosorbent assay (ELISA) is the most common type of screening test for detecting the HIV virus. A positive result from an ELISA indicates that the HIV virus is present. For most populations, ELISA has a high degree of sensitivity (to detect infection) and specificity (to detect noninfection). (See HIVInsite, at **HIVInsite.ucsf.edu.**) Suppose that the probability a person is infected with the HIV virus for a certain population is 0.015. If the HIV virus is actually present, the probability that the ELISA test will give a positive result is 0.995. If the HIV virus is not actually present, the probability of a positive result from an ELISA is 0.01. If the ELISA has given a positive result, use Bayes' theorem to find the probability that the HIV virus is actually present.

Team Project

The data file Mutual Funds.xls contains information regarding four categorical variables from a sample of 838 mutual funds. The variables are:

Category—Type of stocks comprising the mutual fund (small cap, mid cap, large cap)
Objective—Objective of stocks comprising the mutual fund (growth or value)
Fees—Sales charges (no or yes)
Risk—Risk-of-loss factor of the mutual fund (low, average, high)

4.56 Construct contingency tables of category and objective, category and fees, category and risk, objective and fees, and fees and risk.

a. For each of these contingency tables, compute all the conditional and marginal probabilities.
b. Based on (a), what conclusions can you reach about the independence between these variables?

Student Survey Data Base

4.57 Problem 1.27 on page 15 describes a survey of 50 undergraduate students (see the file undergradsurvey.xls). For these data, construct contingency tables of gender and major, gender and graduate school intention, gender and employment status, class and graduate school intention, class and employment status, major and graduate school intention, and major and employment status.

a. For each of these contingency tables, compute all the conditional and marginal probabilities.
b. Based on (a), what conclusions can you reach about the independence between these variables?

4.58 Problem 1.27 on page 15 describes a survey of 50 undergraduate students (see the file undergradsurvey.xls).

a. Select a sample of 50 undergraduate students at your school and conduct a similar survey for those students.
b. For these data, construct contingency tables of gender and major, gender and graduate school intention, gender and employment status, class and graduate school intention, class and employment status, major and graduate school intention, and major and employment status. For each of these contingency tables, compute all the conditional and marginal probabilities.
c. Based on (b), what conclusions can you reach about the independence between these variables?
d. Compare the results of (c) to those of Problem 4.57 (b).

4.59 Problem 1.28 on page 15 describes a survey of 50 MBA students (see the file gradsurvey.xls). For these data, construct contingency tables of gender and graduate major, gender and undergraduate major, gender and employment status, graduate major and undergraduate major, and graduate major and employment status.

a. For each of these contingency tables, compute all the conditional and marginal probabilities.
b. Based on (b), what conclusions can you reach about the independence between these variables?

4.60 Problem 1.28 on page 15 describes a survey of 50 MBA students (see the file gradsurvey.xls).

a. Select a sample of 50 MBA students from your MBA program and conduct a similar survey for those students.
b. For these data, construct contingency tables of gender and graduate major, gender and undergraduate major, gender and employment status, graduate major and undergraduate major, and graduate major and employment status. For each of these contingency tables, compute all the conditional and marginal probabilities.
c. Based on (b), what conclusions can you reach about the independence between these variables?
d. Compare the results of (c) to those of Problem 4.59 (b).

Web Case

Apply your knowledge about contingency tables and the proper application of simple and joint probabilities in this continuing Web Case from Chapter 3.

Visit the EndRun Guaranteed Investment Package (GIP) Web page, at **www.prenhall.com/Springville/ ER_Guaranteed.htm** or open this Web page file from the Student CD-ROM **Web Case** folder. Read the claims and examine the supporting data. Then answer the following:

1. How accurate is the claim of the probability of success for EndRun's GIP? In what ways is the claim misleading? How would you calculate and state the probability of having an annual rate of return not less than 15%?

2. What mistake was made in reporting the 7% probability claim? Using the table found on the "Winning Probabilities" Web page, **ER_Guaranteed3.htm**, compute the proper probabilities for the group of investors.

3. Are there any probability calculations that would be appropriate for rating an investment service? Why or why not?

REFERENCES

1. Bellhouse, D. R., "The Reverend Thomas Bayes, FRS: A Biography to Celebrate the Tercentenary of His Birth," *Statistical Science* 19 (2004), 3–43.

2. Lowd, D., and C. Meek, "Good Word Attacks on Statistical Spam Filters," presented at the Second Conference on Email and Anti-Spam, CEAS 2005.

3. *Microsoft Excel 2007* (Redmond, WA: Microsoft Corp., 2007).

4. Paulos, J. A., *Innumeracy* (New York: Hill and Wang, 1988).

5. Silberman, S., "The Quest for Meaning," *Wired 8.02*, February 2000.

Excel Companion
to Chapter 4

E4.1   COMPUTING BASIC PROBABILITIES

You compute basic probabilities by either using the PHStat2 **Simple & Joint Probabilities** procedure or by making entries in the **Probabilities** worksheet of the `Probabilities.xls` workbook.

Using PHStat2 Simple & Joint Probabilities

Open the workbook in which you want your probabilities worksheet to be placed. Select **PHStat → Probability & Prob. Distributions → Simple & Joint Probabilities** and enter event labels and counts in the tinted cells in rows 3 through 6.

Using the Probabilities Worksheet

Open to the **Probabilities** worksheet of the `Probabilities.xls` workbook. Enter event labels and counts in the tinted cells in rows 3 through 6. Figure E4.1 shows a completed work-

sheet for the data on purchase behavior for big-screen televisions from Table 4.1 on page 151. Also shown offset in Figure E4.1 are the formulas this worksheet uses to compute the various probabilities.

The worksheet also "computes" the probabilities table *labels*, using a novel application of formulas that include the ampersand (**&**) operator. For example, the cell A10 formula **="P(" & B5 & ")"** asks Excel to add the contents of B5 (**Yes**) to the label **"P("** to get **"P(Yes"** and then to **"add"** **")"** to get **"P(Yes)"** and form the formula **="P(Yes)"**. This is a novel but acceptable way of entering the label value **P(Yes)** in a cell.

E4.2   USING BAYES' THEOREM

You use Bayes' theorem by making entries in the cell range B5:C6 of the **Bayes** worksheet of the `Bayes.xls` workbook. Figure E4.2 shows a completed worksheet for the television-marketing example shown in Table 4.4 on page 167.

	A	B	C	D	E
1	Bayes Theorem Calculations				
2					
3			Probabilities		
4	Event	Prior	Conditional	Joint	Revised
5	S	0.4	0.8	0.32	0.64
6	S'	0.6	0.3	0.18	0.36
7			Total:	0.5	

Joint	Revised
=B5 * C5	=D5 / $D$7
=B6 * C6	=D6 / $D$7
=D5 + D6	

FIGURE E4.2

Bayes' theorem worksheet

	A	B	C	D	E
1	Probabilities for Purchase Behavior for Big-Screen Televisions				
2					
3	Sample Space		Actually Purchased		
4			Yes	No	Totals
5	Planned to Purchase	Yes	200	50	250
6		No	100	650	750
7		Totals	300	700	1000
8					
9	Simple Probabilities				
10	P(Yes)	0.25			
11	P(No)	0.75			
12	P(Yes)	0.30			
13	P(No)	0.70			
14					
15	Joint Probabilities				
16	P(Yes and Yes)	0.20			
17	P(Yes and No)	0.05			
18	P(No and Yes)	0.10			
19	P(No and No)	0.65			
20					
21	Addition Rule				
22	P(Yes or Yes)	0.35			
23	P(Yes or No)	0.90			
24	P(No or Yes)	0.95			
25	P(No or No)	0.80			

Simple Probabilities

="P(" & B5 & ")"	=E5 / E7
="P(" & B6 & ")"	=E6 / E7
="P(" & C4 & ")"	=C7 / E7
="P(" & D4 & ")"	=D7 / E7

Joint Probabilities

="P(" & B5 & " and " & C4 & ")"	=C5 / E7
="P(" & B5 & " and " & D4 & ")"	=D5 / E7
="P(" & B6 & " and " & C4 & ")"	=C6 / E7
="P(" & B6 & " and " & D4 & ")"	=D6 / E7

Addition Rule

="P(" & B5 & " or " & C4 & ")"	=B10 + B12 - B16
="P(" & B5 & " or " & D4 & ")"	=B10 + B13 - B17
="P(" & B6 & " or " & C4 & ")"	=B11 + B12 - B18
="P(" & B6 & " or " & D4 & ")"	=B11 + B13 - B19

FIGURE E4.1

Probabilities worksheet

CHAPTER 5

Some Important Discrete Probability Distributions

USING STATISTICS @ Saxon Home Improvement

LEARNING OBJECTIVES

In this chapter, you learn:
- The properties of a probability distribution
- To compute the expected value and variance of a probability distribution
- To calculate the covariance and understand its use in finance
- To compute probabilities from binomial, hypergeometric, and Poisson distributions
- How to use the binomial, hypergeometric, and Poisson distributions to solve business problems

USING STATISTICS @ Saxon Home Improvement

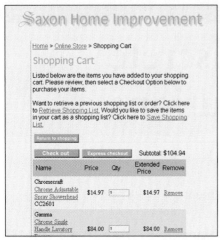

Accounting information systems collect, process, store, transform, and distribute financial information to decision makers both internal and external to a business organization (see reference 6). These systems continuously audit accounting information, looking for errors or incomplete or improbable information. For example, when customers of the Saxon Home Improvement Company submit online orders, the company's accounting information system reviews the order forms for possible mistakes. Any questionable invoices are *tagged* and included in a daily *exceptions report*. Recent data collected by the company show that the likelihood is 0.10 that an order form will be tagged. Saxon would like to determine the likelihood of finding a certain number of tagged forms in a sample of a specific size. For example, what would be the likelihood that none of the order forms are tagged in a sample of four forms? That one of the order forms is tagged?

How could the Saxon Home Improvement Company determine the solution to this type of probability problem? One way is to use a model, or small-scale representation, that approximates the process. By using such an approximation, Saxon managers could make inferences about the actual order process. Model building is a difficult task for some endeavors, and in this case, the Saxon managers can use *probability distributions*, mathematical models suited for solving the type of probability problems the managers are facing. Reading this chapter will help you learn about characteristics of a probability distribution and how to specifically apply the binomial, Poisson, and hypergeometric distributions to business problems.

5.1   THE PROBABILITY DISTRIBUTION FOR A DISCRETE RANDOM VARIABLE

In Section 1.5, a *numerical variable* was defined as a variable that yielded numerical responses, such as the number of magazines you subscribe to or your height, in inches. Numerical variables are classified as *discrete* or *continuous*. Continuous numerical variables produce outcomes that come from a measuring process (for example, your height). Discrete numerical variables produce outcomes that come from a counting process (for example, the number of magazines you subscribe to). This chapter deals with probability distributions that represent discrete numerical variables.

> **PROBABILITY DISTRIBUTION FOR A DISCRETE RANDOM VARIABLE**
>
> A **probability distribution for a discrete random variable** is a mutually exclusive listing of all possible numerical outcomes for that variable such that a particular probability of occurrence is associated with each outcome.

For example, Table 5.1 gives the distribution of the number of mortgages approved per week at the local branch office of a bank. The listing in Table 5.1 is collectively exhaustive because all possible outcomes are included. Thus, the probabilities must sum to 1. Figure 5.1 is a graphical representation of Table 5.1.

TABLE 5.1

Probability Distribution of the Number of Home Mortgages Approved per Week

Home Mortgages Approved per Week	Probability
0	0.10
1	0.10
2	0.20
3	0.30
4	0.15
5	0.10
6	0.05

FIGURE 5.1

Probability distribution of the number of home mortgages approved per week

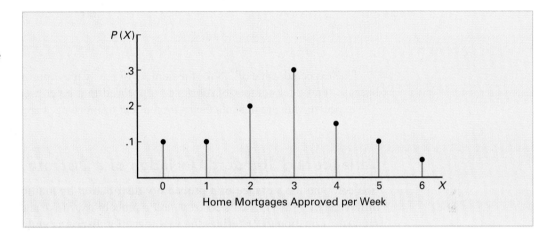

Expected Value of a Discrete Random Variable

The mean, μ, of a probability distribution is the *expected value* of its random variable. To calculate the expected value, you multiply each possible outcome, X, by its corresponding probability, P(X), and then sum these products.

EXPECTED VALUE, μ, OF A DISCRETE RANDOM VARIABLE

$$\mu = E(X) = \sum_{i=1}^{N} X_i P(X_i) \qquad (5.1)$$

where

$$X_i = \text{the } i\text{th outcome of the discrete random variable } X$$

$$P(X_i) = \text{probability of occurrence of the } i\text{th outcome of } X$$

For the probability distribution of the number of home mortgages approved per week (Table 5.1), the expected value is computed using Equation (5.1) below and is also shown in Table 5.2.

$$\mu = E(X) = \sum_{i=1}^{N} X_i P(X_i)$$

$$= (0)(0.1) + (1)(0.1) + (2)(0.2) + (3)(0.3) + (4)(0.15) + (5)(0.1) + (6)(0.05)$$

$$= 0 + 0.1 + 0.4 + 0.9 + 0.6 + 0.5 + 0.3$$

$$= 2.8$$

TABLE 5.2

Computing the
Expected Value of
the Number of Home
Mortgages Approved
per Week

Home Mortgages Approved per Week (X_i)	$P(X_i)$	$X_i P(X_i)$
0	0.10	$(0)(0.10) = 0.0$
1	0.10	$(1)(0.10) = 0.1$
2	0.20	$(2)(0.20) = 0.4$
3	0.30	$(3)(0.30) = 0.9$
4	0.15	$(4)(0.15) = 0.6$
5	0.10	$(5)(0.10) = 0.5$
6	0.05	$(6)(0.05) = 0.3$
	1.00	$\mu = E(X) = 2.8$

The expected value of 2.8 for the number of mortgages approved is not a possible outcome because the actual number of mortgages approved in a given week must be an integer value. The expected value represents the *mean* number of mortgages approved per week.

Variance and Standard Deviation of a Discrete Random Variable

You compute the variance of a probability distribution by multiplying each possible squared difference $[X_i - E(X)]^2$ by its corresponding probability, $P(X_i)$, and then summing the resulting products. Equation (5.2) defines the **variance of a discrete random variable**.

VARIANCE OF A DISCRETE RANDOM VARIABLE

$$\sigma^2 = \sum_{i=1}^{N} [X_i - E(X)]^2 P(X_i) \tag{5.2}$$

where

$$X_i = \text{the } i\text{th outcome of the discrete random variable } X$$

$$P(X_i) = \text{probability of occurrence of the } i\text{th outcome of } X$$

Equation (5.3) defines the **standard deviation of a discrete random variable**.

STANDARD DEVIATION OF A DISCRETE RANDOM VARIABLE

$$\sigma = \sqrt{\sigma^2} = \sqrt{\sum_{i=1}^{N} [X_i - E(X)]^2 P(X_i)} \tag{5.3}$$

In Table 5.3, the variance and the standard deviation of the number of home mortgages approved per week are computed using Equations (5.2) and (5.3):

TABLE 5.3

Computing the Variance and Standard Deviation of the Number of Home Mortgages Approved per Week

Home Mortgages Approved per Week (X_i)	$P(X_i)$	$X_i P(X_i)$	$[X_i - E(X)]^2 P(X_i)$
0	0.10	$(0)(0.10) = 0.0$	$(0 - 2.8)^2(0.10) = 0.784$
1	0.10	$(1)(0.10) = 0.1$	$(1 - 2.8)^2(0.10) = 0.324$
2	0.20	$(2)(0.20) = 0.4$	$(2 - 2.8)^2(0.20) = 0.128$
3	0.30	$(3)(0.30) = 0.9$	$(3 - 2.8)^2(0.30) = 0.012$
4	0.15	$(4)(0.15) = 0.6$	$(4 - 2.8)^2(0.15) = 0.216$
5	0.10	$(5)(0.10) = 0.5$	$(5 - 2.8)^2(0.10) = 0.484$
6	0.05	$(6)(0.05) = 0.3$	$(6 - 2.8)^2(0.05) = 0.512$
	1.00	$\mu = E(X) = 2.8$	$\sigma^2 = 2.46$

$$\sigma^2 = \sum_{i=1}^{N} [X_i - E(X)]^2 P(X_i)$$
$$= (0 - 2.8)^2(0.10) + (1 - 2.8)^2(0.10) + (2 - 2.8)^2(0.20) + (3 - 2.8)^2(0.30)$$
$$+ (4 - 2.8)^2(0.15) + (5 - 2.8)^2(0.10) + (6 - 2.8)^2(0.05)$$
$$= 0.784 + 0.324 + 0.128 + 0.012 + 0.216 + 0.484 + 0.512$$
$$= 2.46$$

and

$$\sigma = \sqrt{\sigma^2} = \sqrt{2.46} = 1.57$$

Thus, the mean number of mortgages approved per week is 2.8, the variance is 2.46, and the standard deviation is 1.57.

PROBLEMS FOR SECTION 5.1

Learning the Basics

 5.1 Given the following probability distributions:

Distribution A		Distribution B	
X	$P(X)$	X	$P(X)$
0	0.50	0	0.05
1	0.20	1	0.10
2	0.15	2	0.15
3	0.10	3	0.20
4	0.05	4	0.50

a. Compute the expected value for each distribution.
b. Compute the standard deviation for each distribution.
c. Compare the results of distributions *A* and *B*.

 5.2 Given the following probability distributions:

Distribution C		Distribution D	
X	$P(X)$	X	$P(X)$
0	0.20	0	0.10
1	0.20	1	0.20
2	0.20	2	0.40
3	0.20	3	0.20
4	0.20	4	0.10

a. Compute the expected value for each distribution.
b. Compute the standard deviation for each distribution.
c. Compare the results of distributions *C* and *D*.

Applying the Concepts

5.3 How many credit cards do you have in your wallet? According to a survey by Ipsos, a large survey research company, 26% of adults in the United States reported having no credit cards; 38% reported having one or two; 20% three or four; 15% five or more; and 1% reported "not sure" ("Snapshots," **usatoday.com**, April 18, 2006). Suppose that the following table contains the complete probability distribution for the number of credit cards owned by adults in the United States:

Number of Credit Cards (X)	$P(X)$
0	0.26
1	0.22
2	0.16
3	0.12
4	0.08
5	0.06
6	0.04
7	0.03
8	0.02
9	0.01

a. Compute the mean number of credit cards owned by a U.S. adult.
b. Compute the standard deviation.

 5.4 The following table contains the probability distribution for the number of traffic accidents daily in a small city:

Number of Accidents Daily (X)	$P(X)$
0	0.10
1	0.20
2	0.45
3	0.15
4	0.05
5	0.05

a. Compute the mean number of accidents per day.
b. Compute the standard deviation.

5.5 The manager of a large computer network has developed the following probability distribution of the number of interruptions per day:

Interruptions (X)	$P(X)$
0	0.32
1	0.35
2	0.18
3	0.08
4	0.04
5	0.02
6	0.01

a. Compute the expected number of interruptions per day.
b. Compute the standard deviation.

5.6 In the carnival game Under-or-Over-Seven, a pair of fair dice is rolled once, and the resulting sum determines whether the player wins or loses his or her bet. For example, the player can bet $1 that the sum will be under 7— that is, 2, 3, 4, 5, or 6. For this bet, the player loses $1 if the outcome equals or exceeds 7 and wins $1 if the result is under 7. Similarly, the player can bet $1 that the sum will be over 7—that is, 8, 9, 10, 11, or 12. Here, the player wins $1 if the result is over 7 but loses $1 if the result is 7 or under. A third method of play is to bet $1 on the outcome 7. For this bet, the player wins $4 if the result of the roll is 7 and loses $1 otherwise.

a. Construct the probability distribution representing the different outcomes that are possible for a $1 bet on being under 7.
b. Construct the probability distribution representing the different outcomes that are possible for a $1 bet on being over 7.
c. Construct the probability distribution representing the different outcomes that are possible for a $1 bet on 7.
d. Show that the expected long-run profit (or loss) to the player is the same, no matter which method of play is used.

5.2   COVARIANCE AND ITS APPLICATION IN FINANCE

In Section 5.1, the expected value, variance, and standard deviation of a discrete random variable of a probability distribution were discussed. In this section, the covariance between two variables is introduced and applied to portfolio management, a topic of great interest to financial analysts.

Covariance

The **covariance,** σ_{XY}, is a measure of the strength of the relationship between two discrete random variables, X and Y. A positive covariance indicates a positive relationship. A negative covariance indicates a negative relationship. A covariance of 0 indicates that the two variables are independent. Equation (5.4) defines the covariance.

COVARIANCE

$$\sigma_{XY} = \sum_{i=1}^{N} [X_i - E(X)][Y_i - E(Y)]P(X_iY_i) \qquad \textbf{(5.4)}$$

where

$$X = \text{discrete random variable } X$$

$$X_i = i\text{th outcome of } X$$

$$P(X_iY_i) = \text{probability of occurrence of the } i\text{th outcome of } X$$
$$\text{and the } i\text{th outcome of } Y$$

$$Y = \text{discrete random variable } Y$$

$$Y_i = i\text{th outcome of } Y$$

$$i = 1, 2, \ldots, N$$

To illustrate the covariance, suppose that you are deciding between two alternative investments for the coming year. The first investment is a mutual fund that consists of the stocks that comprise the Dow Jones Industrial Average. The second investment is a mutual fund that is expected to perform best when economic conditions are weak. Your estimate of the returns for each investment (per $1,000 investment) under three economic conditions, each with a given probability of occurrence, is summarized in Table 5.4.

TABLE 5.4

Estimated Returns for Each Investment Under Three Economic Conditions

		Investment	
$P(X_iY_i)$	**Economic Condition**	**Dow Jones Fund**	**Weak-Economy Fund**
0.2	Recession	−$100	+$200
0.5	Stable economy	+100	+50
0.3	Expanding economy	+250	−100

The expected value and standard deviation for each investment and the covariance of the two investments are computed as follows:

$$\text{Let } X = \text{Dow Jones fund, and } Y = \text{weak-economy fund}$$

$$E(X) = \mu_X = (-100)(0.2) + (100)(0.5) + (250)(0.3) = \$105$$

$$E(Y) = \mu_Y = (+200)(0.2) + (50)(0.5) + (-100)(0.3) = \$35$$

$$Var(X) = \sigma_X^2 = (-100 - 105)^2(0.2) + (100 - 105)^2(0.5) + (250 - 105)^2(0.3)$$

$$= 14,725$$

$$\sigma_X = \$121.35$$

$$Var(Y) = \sigma_Y^2 = (200 - 35)^2(0.2) + (50 - 35)^2(0.5) + (-100 - 35)^2(0.3)$$

$$= 11,025$$

$$\sigma_Y = \$105.00$$

$$\sigma_{XY} = (-100 - 105)(200 - 35)(0.2) + (100 - 105)(50 - 35)(0.5)$$
$$+ (250 - 105)(-100 - 35)(0.3)$$

$$= -6,765 - 37.5 - 5,782.5$$

$$= -12,675$$

Thus, the Dow Jones fund has a higher expected value (that is, larger expected return) than the weak-economy fund but has a higher standard deviation (that is, more risk). The covariance of −12,675 between the two investments indicates a negative relationship in which the two investments are varying in the *opposite* direction. Therefore, when the return on one investment is high, typically, the return on the other is low.

Expected Value, Variance, and Standard Deviation of the Sum of Two Random Variables

Equations (5.1)–(5.3) defined the expected value, variance, and standard deviation of a probability distribution while Equation (5.4) defines the covariance between two variables, X and Y. The **expected value of the sum of two random variables** is equal to the sum of the expected values. The **variance of the sum of two random variables** is equal to the sum of the variances plus twice the covariance. The **standard deviation of the sum of two random variables** is the square root of the variance of the sum of two random variables.

EXPECTED VALUE OF THE SUM OF TWO RANDOM VARIABLES

$$E(X + Y) = E(X) + E(Y) \qquad (5.5)$$

VARIANCE OF THE SUM OF TWO RANDOM VARIABLES

$$Var(X + Y) = \sigma^2_{X+Y} = \sigma^2_X + \sigma^2_Y + 2\sigma_{XY} \qquad (5.6)$$

STANDARD DEVIATION OF THE SUM OF TWO RANDOM VARIABLES

$$\sigma_{X+Y} = \sqrt{\sigma^2_{X+Y}} \qquad (5.7)$$

To illustrate the expected value, variance, and standard deviation of the sum of two random variables, consider the two investments previously discussed. If X = Dow Jones fund and Y = weak-economy fund, using Equations (5.5), (5.6), and (5.7),

$$E(X + Y) = E(X) + E(Y) = 105 + 35 = \$140$$

$$\sigma^2_{X+Y} = \sigma^2_X + \sigma^2_Y + 2\sigma_{XY}$$

$$= 14{,}725 + 11{,}025 + (2)(-12{,}675)$$

$$= 400$$

$$\sigma_{X+Y} = \$20$$

The expected return of the sum of the Dow Jones fund and the weak-economy fund is $140, with a standard deviation of $20. The standard deviation of the sum of the two investments is much less than the standard deviation of either single investment because there is a large negative covariance between the investments.

Portfolio Expected Return and Portfolio Risk

Now that the covariance and the expected return and standard deviation of the sum of two random variables have been defined, these concepts can be applied to the study of a group of assets referred to as a **portfolio**. Investors combine assets into portfolios to reduce their risk (see references 1 and 2). Often, the objective is to maximize the return while minimizing the risk. For such portfolios, rather than studying the sum of two random variables, each investment is weighted by the proportion of assets assigned to that investment. Equations (5.8) and (5.9) define the **portfolio expected return** and **portfolio risk**.

PORTFOLIO EXPECTED RETURN

The portfolio expected return for a two-asset investment is equal to the weight assigned to asset X multiplied by the expected return of asset X plus the weight assigned to asset Y multiplied by the expected return of asset Y.

$$E(P) = wE(X) + (1 - w)E(Y) \qquad \textbf{(5.8)}$$

where

$$E(P) = \text{portfolio expected return}$$

$$w = \text{portion of the portfolio value assigned to asset } X$$

$$(1 - w) = \text{portion of the portfolio value assigned to asset } Y$$

$$E(X) = \text{expected return of asset } X$$

$$E(Y) = \text{expected return of asset } Y$$

PORTFOLIO RISK

$$\sigma_p = \sqrt{w^2\sigma_X^2 + (1 - w)^2\sigma_Y^2 + 2w(1 - w)\sigma_{XY}} \qquad \textbf{(5.9)}$$

In the previous example, you evaluated the expected return and risk of two different investments, a Dow Jones fund and a weak-economy fund. You also computed the covariance of the two investments. Now suppose that you wish to form a portfolio of these two investments that consists of an equal investment in each of these two funds. To compute the portfolio expected return and the portfolio risk, using Equations (5.8) and (5.9), with $w = 0.50$, $E(X) = \$105$, $E(Y) = \$35$, $\sigma_X^2 = 14{,}725$, $\sigma_Y^2 = 11{,}025$, and $\sigma_{XY} = -12{,}675$,

$$E(P) = (0.5)(105) + (1 - 0.5)(35) = \$70$$

$$\sigma_p = \sqrt{(0.5)^2(14{,}725) + (1 - 0.5)^2(11{,}025) + 2(0.5)(1 - 0.5)(-12{,}675)}$$

$$= \sqrt{100} = \$10$$

Thus, the portfolio has an expected return of $70 for each $1,000 invested (a return of 7%) and has a portfolio risk of $10. The portfolio risk here is small because there is a large negative covariance between the two investments. The fact that each investment performs best under different circumstances reduces the overall risk of the portfolio.

PROBLEMS FOR SECTION 5.2

Learning the Basics

PH Grade
ASSIST
5.7 Given the following probability distributions for variables X and Y:

$P(X_iY_i)$	X	Y
0.4	100	200
0.6	200	100

Compute

a. $E(X)$ and $E(Y)$.

b. σ_X and σ_Y.

c. σ_{XY}.

d. $E(X + Y)$.

5.8 Given the following probability distributions for variables X and Y:

$P(X_iY_i)$	X	Y
0.2	−100	50
0.4	50	30
0.3	200	20
0.1	300	20

Compute
a. $E(X)$ and $E(Y)$.
b. σ_X and σ_Y.
c. σ_{XY}.
d. $E(X+Y)$.

 5.9 Two investments, X and Y, have the following characteristics:

$$E(X) = \$50, \quad E(Y) = \$100, \quad \sigma_X^2 = 9{,}000,$$

$$\sigma_Y^2 = 15{,}000, \quad \text{and } \sigma_{XY} = 7{,}500.$$

If the weight of portfolio assets assigned to investment X is 0.4, compute the
a. portfolio expected return.
b. portfolio risk.

Applying the Concepts

5.10 The process of being served at a bank consists of two independent parts—the time waiting in line and the time it takes to be served by the teller. Suppose that the time waiting in line has an expected value of 4 minutes, with a standard deviation of 1.2 minutes, and the time it takes to be served by the teller has an expected value of 5.5 minutes, with a standard deviation of 1.5 minutes. Compute the
a. expected value of the total time it takes to be served at the bank.
b. standard deviation of the total time it takes to be served at the bank.

 5.11 In the portfolio example in this section (see page 187), half the portfolio assets are invested in the Dow Jones fund and half in a weak-economy fund. Recalculate the portfolio expected return and the portfolio risk if
a. 30% of the portfolio assets are invested in the Dow Jones fund and 70% in a weak-economy fund.
b. 70% of the portfolio assets are invested in the Dow Jones fund and 30% in a weak-economy fund.
c. Which of the three investment strategies (30%, 50%, or 70% in the Dow Jones fund) would you recommend? Why?

✓SELF Test **5.12** You are trying to develop a strategy for investing in two different stocks. The anticipated annual return for a $1,000 investment in each

stock under four different economic conditions has the following probability distribution:

		Returns	
Probability	Economic Condition	Stock X	Stock Y
0.1	Recession	−$100	$50
0.3	Slow growth	0	150
0.3	Moderate growth	80	−20
0.3	Fast growth	150	−100

Compute the
a. expected return for stock X and for stock Y.
b. standard deviation for stock X and for stock Y.
c. covariance of stock X and stock Y.
d. Would you invest in stock X or stock Y? Explain.

5.13 Suppose that in Problem 5.12 you wanted to create a portfolio that consists of stock X and stock Y. Compute the portfolio expected return and portfolio risk for each of the following percentages invested in stock X:
a. 30%
b. 50%
c. 70%
d. On the basis of the results of (a) through (c), which portfolio would you recommend? Explain.

5.14 You are trying to develop a strategy for investing in two different stocks. The anticipated annual return for a $1,000 investment in each stock under four different economic conditions has the following probability distribution:

		Returns	
Probability	Economic Condition	Stock X	Stock Y
0.1	Recession	−$50	−$100
0.3	Slow growth	20	50
0.4	Moderate growth	100	130
0.2	Fast growth	150	200

Compute the
a. expected return for stock X and for stock Y.
b. standard deviation for stock X and for stock Y.
c. covariance of stock X and stock Y.
d. Would you invest in stock X or stock Y? Explain.

5.15 Suppose that in Problem 5.14 you wanted to create a portfolio that consists of stock X and stock Y. Compute the portfolio expected return and portfolio risk for each of the following percentages invested in stock X:
a. 30%
b. 50%
c. 70%
d. On the basis of the results of (a) through (c), which portfolio would you recommend? Explain.

5.16 You are trying to set up a portfolio that consists of a corporate bond fund and a common stock fund. The following information about the annual return (per $1,000) of each of these investments under different economic conditions is available, along with the probability that each of these economic conditions will occur:

Probability	Economic Conditions	Corporate Bond Fund	Common Stock Fund
0.10	Recession	−$30	−$150
0.15	Stagnation	50	−20
0.35	Slow growth	90	120
0.30	Moderate growth	100	160
0.10	High growth	110	250

Compute the
a. expected return for the corporate bond fund and for the common stock fund.

b. standard deviation for the corporate bond fund and for the common stock fund.
c. covariance of the corporate bond fund and the common stock fund.
d. Would you invest in the corporate bond fund or the common stock fund? Explain.

5.17 Suppose that in Problem 5.16 you wanted to create a portfolio that consists of a corporate bond fund and a common stock fund. Compute the portfolio expected return and portfolio risk for each of the following percentages invested in a corporate bond fund:
a. 30%
b. 50%
c. 70%
d. On the basis of the results of (a) through (c), which portfolio would you recommend? Explain.

5.3 BINOMIAL DISTRIBUTION

This section and the two that follow use mathematical models to solve business problems.

MATHEMATICAL MODEL

A **mathematical model** is a mathematical expression that represents a variable of interest.

When a mathematical expression is available, you can compute the exact probability of occurrence of any particular outcome of the variable.

The **binomial distribution** is one of the most useful mathematical models. You use the binomial distribution when the discrete variable of interest is the number of successes in a sample of n observations. The binomial distribution has four essential properties:

- The sample consists of a fixed number of observations, n.
- Each observation is classified into one of two mutually exclusive and collectively exhaustive categories, usually called *success* and *failure*.
- The probability of an observation being classified as success, p, is constant from observation to observation. Thus, the probability of an observation being classified as failure, $1 - p$, is constant over all observations.
- The outcome (i.e., success or failure) of any observation is independent of the outcome of any other observation. To ensure independence, the observations can be randomly selected either from an *infinite population without replacement* or from a *finite population with replacement*.

Returning to the Using Statistics scenario presented on page 180 concerning the accounting information system, suppose *success* is defined as a tagged order form and *failure* as any other outcome. You are interested in the number of tagged order forms in a given sample of orders.

What results can occur? If the sample contains four orders, there could be none, one, two, three, or four tagged order forms. The binomial random variable, the number of tagged order forms, cannot take on any other value because the number of tagged order forms cannot be more than the sample size, n, and cannot be less than zero. Therefore, the binomial random variable has a range from 0 to n.

Suppose that you observe the following result in a sample of four orders:

First Order	Second Order	Third Order	Fourth Order
Tagged	Tagged	Not tagged	Tagged

What is the probability of having three successes (tagged order forms) in a sample of four orders in this particular sequence? Because the historical probability of a tagged order is 0.10, the probability that each order occurs in the sequence is

First Order	Second Order	Third Order	Fourth Order
$p = 0.10$	$p = 0.10$	$1 - p = 0.90$	$p = 0.10$

Each outcome is independent of the others because the order forms were selected from an extremely large or practically infinite population without replacement. Therefore, the probability of having this particular sequence is

$$pp(1 - p)p = p^3(1 - p)^1$$
$$= (0.10)(0.10)(0.10)(0.90)$$
$$= (0.10)^3(0.90)^1$$
$$= 0.0009$$

This result indicates only the probability of three tagged order forms (successes) from a sample of four order forms in a *specific sequence*. To find the number of ways of selecting X objects from n objects, *irrespective of sequence*, you use the **rule of combinations** given in Equation (5.10).

COMBINATIONS

The number of combinations of selecting X objects out of n objects is given by

$$_nC_X = \frac{n!}{X!(n - X)!} \tag{5.10}$$

where

$$n! = (n)(n - 1) \ldots (1) \text{ is called } n \text{ factorial. By definition, } 0! = 1.$$

With $n = 4$ and $X = 3$, there are

$$_nC_X = \frac{n!}{X!(n - X)!} = \frac{4!}{3!(4 - 3)!} = \frac{4 \times 3 \times 2 \times 1}{(3 \times 2 \times 1)(1)} = 4$$

such sequences. The four possible sequences are:

Sequence 1 = *tagged, tagged, tagged, not tagged*, with probability

$ppp(1 - p) = p^3(1 - p)^1 = 0.0009$

Sequence 2 = *tagged, tagged, not tagged, tagged*, with probability

$pp(1 - p)p = p^3(1 - p)^1 = 0.0009$

Sequence 3 = *tagged, not tagged, tagged, tagged*, with probability

$p(1 - p)pp = p^3(1 - p)^1 = 0.0009$

Sequence 4 = *not tagged, tagged, tagged, tagged*, with probability

$(1 - p)ppp = p^3(1 - p)^1 = 0.0009$

Therefore, the probability of three tagged order forms is equal to

(Number of possible sequences) × (Probability of a particular sequence)

$$= (4) \times (0.0009) = 0.0036$$

You can make a similar, intuitive derivation for the other possible outcomes of the random variable—zero, one, two, and four tagged order forms. However, as n, the sample size, gets large, the computations involved in using this intuitive approach become time-consuming. A mathematical model provides a general formula for computing any binomial probability. Equation (5.11) is the mathematical model representing the binomial probability distribution for computing the number of successes, X, given the values of n and p.

BINOMIAL DISTRIBUTION

$$P(X) = \frac{n!}{X!(n-X)!} p^X (1-p)^{n-X} \qquad (5.11)$$

where

$P(X)$ = probability of X successes, given n and p

n = number of observations

p = probability of success

$1 - p$ = probability of failure

X = number of successes in the sample ($X = 0, 1, 2, \ldots, n$)

Equation (5.11) restates what you had intuitively derived. The binomial variable X can have any integer value X from 0 through n. In Equation (5.11), the product

$$p^X(1-p)^{n-X}$$

indicates the probability of exactly X successes from n observations in a *particular sequence*. The term

$$\frac{n!}{X!(n-X)!}$$

indicates *how many combinations* of the X successes from n observations are possible. Hence, given the number of observations, n, and the probability of success, p, the probability of X successes is:

$P(X)$ = (Number of possible sequences) × (Probability of a particular sequence)

$$= \frac{n!}{X!(n-X)!} p^X (1-p)^{n-X}$$

Example 5.1 illustrates the use of Equation (5.11).

EXAMPLE 5.1

DETERMINING $P(X = 3)$, GIVEN $n = 4$ AND $p = 0.1$

If the likelihood of a tagged order form is 0.1, what is the probability that there are three tagged order forms in the sample of four?

SOLUTION Using Equation (5.11), the probability of three tagged orders from a sample of four is

$$P(X = 3) = \frac{4!}{3!(4-3)!}(0.1)^3(1-0.1)^{4-3}$$

$$= \frac{4!}{3!(4-3)!}(0.1)^3(0.9)^1$$

$$= 4(0.1)(0.1)(0.1)(0.9) = 0.0036$$

Examples 5.2 and 5.3 show the computations for other values of X.

EXAMPLE 5.2

DETERMINING $P(X \geq 3)$, GIVEN $n = 4$ AND $p = 0.1$

If the likelihood of a tagged order form is 0.1, what is the probability that there are three or more (that is, at least three) tagged order forms in the sample of four?

SOLUTION In Example 5.1, you found that the probability of *exactly* three tagged order forms from a sample of four is 0.0036. To compute the probability of *at least* three tagged order forms, you need to add the probability of three tagged order forms to the probability of four tagged order forms. The probability of four tagged order forms is

$$P(X = 4) = \frac{4!}{4!(4-4)!}(0.1)^4(1-0.1)^{4-4}$$

$$= \frac{4!}{4!(0)!}(0.1)^4(0.9)^0$$

$$= 1(0.1)(0.1)(0.1)(0.1) = 0.0001$$

Thus, the probability of at least three tagged order forms is

$$P(X \geq 3) = P(X = 3) + P(X = 4)$$

$$= 0.0036 + 0.0001$$

$$= 0.0037$$

There is a 0.37% chance that there will be at least three tagged order forms in a sample of four.

EXAMPLE 5.3

DETERMINING $P(X < 3)$, GIVEN $n = 4$ AND $p = 0.1$

If the likelihood of a tagged order form is 0.1, what is the probability that there are less than three tagged order forms in the sample of four?

SOLUTION The probability that there are less than three tagged order forms is

$$P(X < 3) = P(X = 0) + P(X = 1) + P(X = 2)$$

Using Equation (5.11) on page 191, these probabilities are

$$P(X = 0) = \frac{4!}{0!(4-0)!}(0.1)^0(1-0.1)^{4-0} = 0.6561$$

$$P(X = 1) = \frac{4!}{1!(4-1)!}(0.1)^1(1-0.1)^{4-1} = 0.2916$$

$$P(X = 2) = \frac{4!}{2!(4-2)!}(0.1)^2(1-0.1)^{4-2} = 0.0486$$

Therefore, $P(X < 3) = 0.6561 + 0.2916 + 0.0486 = 0.9963$.

$P(X < 3)$ could also be calculated from its complement, $P(X \geq 3)$, as follows:

$$P(X < 3) = 1 - P(X \geq 3)$$
$$= 1 - 0.0037 = 0.9963$$

Computations such as those in Example 5.3 can become tedious, especially as n gets large. To avoid computational drudgery, you can find many binomial probabilities directly from Table E.6, a portion of which is reproduced in Table 5.5. Table E.6 provides binomial probabilities for $X = 0, 1, 2, \ldots, n$ for various selected combinations of n and p. For example, to find the probability of exactly two successes in a sample of four when the probability of success is 0.1, you first find $n = 4$ and then look in the row $X = 2$ and column $p = 0.10$. The result is 0.0486.

TABLE 5.5

Finding a Binomial Probability for $n = 4$, $X = 2$, and $p = 0.1$

				p		
n	X	0.01	0.02	....	0.10	
4	0	0.9606	0.9224	....	0.6561	
	1	0.0388	0.0753	....	0.2916	
	2	0.0006	0.0023	....	0.0486	
	3	0.0000	0.0000	....	0.0036	
	4	0.0000	0.0000	....	0.0001	

Source: Table E.6.

You can also compute the binomial probabilities given in Table E.6 by using Microsoft Excel as shown in Figure 5.2.

FIGURE 5.2

Microsoft Excel worksheet for computing binomial probabilities

See Section E5.3 to create this.

	A	B	
1	**Tagged Orders**		
2			
3	**Data**		
4	Sample size	4	
5	Probability of success	0.1	
6			
7	**Statistics**		
8	Mean	0.4	=B4 * B5
9	Variance	0.36	=B8 * (1 - B5)
10	Standard deviation	0.6	=SQRT(B9)
11			
12	**Binomial Probabilities Table**		
13	X	P(X)	
14	0	0.6561	=BINOMDIST(A14, $B$4, $B$5, FALSE)
15	1	0.2916	=BINOMDIST(A15, $B$4, $B$5, FALSE)
16	2	0.0486	=BINOMDIST(A16, $B$4, $B$5, FALSE)
17	3	0.0036	=BINOMDIST(A17, $B$4, $B$5, FALSE)
18	4	0.0001	=BINOMDIST(A18, $B$4, $B$5, FALSE)

The shape of a binomial probability distribution depends on the values of n and p. Whenever $p = 0.5$, the binomial distribution is symmetrical, regardless of how large or small the value of n. When $p \neq 0.5$, the distribution is skewed. The closer p is to 0.5 and the larger the number of observations, n, the less skewed the distribution becomes. For example, the distribution of the number of tagged order forms is highly skewed to the right because $p = 0.1$ and $n = 4$ (see Figure 5.3).

FIGURE 5.3

Microsoft Excel histogram of the binomial probability distribution with $n = 4$ and $p = 0.1$

See Section E5.6 to create this.

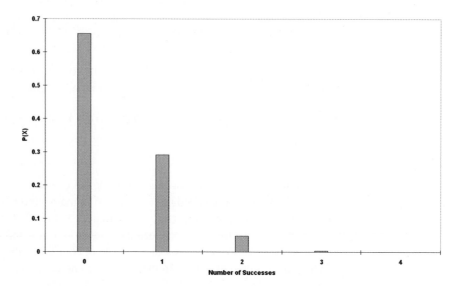

The mean of the binomial distribution is equal to the product of n and p. Instead of using Equation (5.1) on page 181 to compute the mean of the probability distribution, you use Equation (5.12) to compute the mean for variables that follow the binomial distribution.

MEAN OF THE BINOMIAL DISTRIBUTION

The mean, μ, of the binomial distribution is equal to the sample size, n, multiplied by the probability of success, p.

$$\mu = E(X) = np \qquad\qquad \textbf{(5.12)}$$

On the average, over the long run, you theoretically expect $\mu = E(X) = np = (4)(0.1) = 0.4$ tagged order form in a sample of four orders.

The standard deviation of the binomial distribution is calculated using Equation (5.13).

STANDARD DEVIATION OF THE BINOMIAL DISTRIBUTION

$$\sigma = \sqrt{\sigma^2} = \sqrt{Var(X)} = \sqrt{np(1 - p)} \qquad\qquad \textbf{(5.13)}$$

The standard deviation of the number of tagged order forms is

$$\sigma = \sqrt{4(0.1)(0.9)} = 0.60$$

You get the same result if you use Equation (5.3) on page 182.

Example 5.4 applies the binomial distribution to service at a fast-food restaurant.

EXAMPLE 5.4

COMPUTING BINOMIAL PROBABILITIES

Accuracy in taking orders at a drive-through window is an important feature for fast-food chains. Each month *QSR Magazine*, **www.qsrmagazine.com**, publishes the results of its surveys. Accuracy is measured as the percentage of orders consisting of a main item, side item, and drink (but omitting one standard item, such as a pickle) that are filled correctly. In a recent month, suppose that the percentage of correct orders of this type filled at Burger King was approximately 88%. If a sample of three orders is taken, what are the mean and standard deviation of the binomial distribution for the number of orders filled accurately? Suppose that you and two friends go to the drive-through window at Burger King, and each of you places an order of the type just mentioned. What are the probabilities that all three, that none of the three, and that at least two of the three orders will be filled accurately?

SOLUTION Because there are three orders and the probability of an accurate order is 0.88, $n = 3$ and $p = 0.88$. Using Equations (5.12) and (5.13),

$$\mu = E(X) = np = 3(0.88) = 2.64$$

$$\sigma = \sqrt{\sigma^2} = \sqrt{Var(X)} = \sqrt{np(1-p)}$$

$$= \sqrt{3(0.88)(0.12)}$$

$$= \sqrt{0.3168} = 0.563$$

Using Equation (5.11),

$$P(X = 3) = \frac{3!}{3!(3-3)!}(0.88)^3(1-0.88)^{3-3}$$

$$= \frac{3!}{3!(3-3)!}(0.88)^3(0.12)^0$$

$$= 1(0.88)(0.88)(0.88)(1) = 0.6815$$

$$P(X = 0) = \frac{3!}{0!(3-0)!}(0.88)^0(1-0.88)^{3-0}$$

$$= \frac{3!}{0!(3-0)!}(0.88)^0(0.12)^3$$

$$= 1(1)(0.12)(0.12)(0.12) = 0.0017$$

$$P(X = 2) = \frac{3!}{2!(3-2)!}(0.88)^2(1-0.88)^{3-2}$$

$$= \frac{3!}{2!(3-2)!}(0.88)^2(0.12)^1$$

$$= 3(0.88)(0.88)(0.12) = 0.2788$$

$$P(X \geq 2) = P(X = 2) + P(X = 3)$$

$$= 0.2788 + 0.6815$$

$$= 0.9603$$

The mean number of accurate orders filled in a sample of three orders is 2.64, and the standard deviation is 0.563. The probability that all three orders are filled accurately is 0.6815, or 68.15%. The probability that none of the orders are filled accurately is 0.0017, or 0.17%. The probability that at least two orders are filled accurately is 0.9603, or 96.03%.

In this section, you have been introduced to the binomial distribution. The binomial distribution is an important mathematical model in many business situations. It is also used to estimate or test hypotheses about proportions (see Chapters 8 and 9).

PROBLEMS FOR SECTION 5.3

Learning the Basics

 5.18 Determine the following:
  a. For $n = 4$ and $p = 0.12$, what is $P(X = 0)$?
  b. For $n = 10$ and $p = 0.40$, what is $P(X = 9)$?
c. For $n = 10$ and $p = 0.50$, what is $P(X = 8)$?
d. For $n = 6$ and $p = 0.83$, what is $P(X = 5)$?

5.19 If $n = 5$ and $p = 0.40$, what is the probability that
a. $X = 4$?
b. $X \leq 3$?
c. $X < 2$?
d. $X > 1$?

 5.20 Determine the mean and standard deviation of the random variable X in each of the following binomial distributions:
a. $n = 4$ and $p = 0.10$
b. $n = 4$ and $p = 0.40$
c. $n = 5$ and $p = 0.80$
d. $n = 3$ and $p = 0.50$

Applying the Concepts

5.21 The increase or decrease in the price of a stock between the beginning and the end of a trading day is assumed to be an equally likely random event. What is the probability that a stock will show an increase in its closing price on five consecutive days?

5.22 Sixty percent of Americans read their employment contracts, including the fine print ("Snapshots," **usatoday.com**, January 20, 2004). Assume that the number of employees who read every word of their contract can be modeled using the binomial distribution. For a group of five employees, what is the probability that
a. all five will have read every word of their contracts?
b. at least three will have read every word of their contracts?
c. less than two will have read every word of their contracts?
d. What are your answers in (a) through (c) if the probability is 0.80 that an employee reads every word of his or her contract?

 5.23 A student is taking a multiple-choice exam in which each question has four choices. Assuming that she has no knowledge of the correct answers to any of the questions, she has decided on a strategy in which she will place four balls (marked A, B, C, and D) into a box. She randomly selects one ball for each

question and replaces the ball in the box. The marking on the ball will determine her answer to the question. There are five multiple-choice questions on the exam. What is the probability that she will get
a. five questions correct?
b. at least four questions correct?
c. no questions correct?
d. no more than two questions correct?

 5.24 In Example 5.4 on page 195, you and two friends decided to go to Burger King. Instead, suppose that you went to McDonald's, which last month filled 90% of the orders accurately. What is the probability that
a. all three orders will be filled accurately?
b. none of the three will be filled accurately?
c. at least two of the three will be filled accurately?
d. What are the mean and standard deviation of the binomial distribution used in (a) through (c)? Interpret these values.

5.25 In April 2006, Gallup News Service reported that just 25% of U.S. adults view the country's economic outlook as positive. Gallup further reports that this pessimistic view of the economy is relatively unchanged since early 2001. During this five-year period, Gallup has surveyed more than 100,000 people (F. Newport and J. Carroll, *Public's View of Economy Has Never Recovered After Dot-Com Bust*, **galluppoll.com**, April 18, 2006.). Thus the probability that a randomly selected adult in the United States views the economic outlook as positive is 0.25.
a. You select a random sample of 10 adults in the United States. Assume that the number of the 10 adults having a positive outlook on the economy is distributed as a binomial random variable. What are the mean and standard deviation of this distribution?
b. What assumptions are necessary in (a)?

5.26 Referring to Problem 5.25, find the probability that of the 10 adults:
a. 0 have a positive outlook on the economy.
b. exactly 5 have a positive outlook on the economy.
c. 5 or less have a positive outlook on the economy.
d. 6 or more have a positive outlook on the economy.
e. If you took a random sample of 10 adults from the state of California and found that 6 had a positive outlook on the economy, what could you infer about Californians'

views of the economy compared to those in the United States as a whole?

 5.27 When a customer places an order with Rudy's On-Line Office Supplies, a computerized accounting information system (AIS) automatically checks to see if the customer has exceeded his or her credit limit. Past records indicate that the probability of customers exceeding their credit limit is 0.05. Suppose that, on a given day, 20 customers place orders. Assume that the number of customers that the AIS detects as having exceeded their credit limit is distributed as a binomial random variable.
a. What are the mean and standard deviation of the number of customers exceeding their credit limits?
b. What is the probability that 0 customers will exceed their limits?
c. What is the probability that 1 customer will exceed his or her limit?
d. What is the probability that 2 or more customers will exceed their limits?

5.28 In a survey conducted by the Society for Human Resource Management, 68% of workers said that employers have the right to monitor their telephone use. ("Snapshots," **usatoday.com**, April 18, 2006). Suppose that a random sample of 20 workers is selected, and they are asked if employers have the right to monitor telephone use. What is the probability that:
a. 5 or less of the workers agree?
b. 10 or less of the workers agree?
c. 15 or less of the workers agree?

5.29 Referring to Problem 5.28, when the same workers were asked if employers have the right to monitor their cell phone use, the percentage dropped to 52%. Suppose that the 20 workers are asked if employers have the right to monitor cell phone use. What is the probability that:
a. 5 or less of the workers agree?
b. 10 or less of the workers agree?
c. 15 or less of the workers agree?
d. Compare the results of (a) through (c) to those for Problem 5.28.

5.4   POISSON DISTRIBUTION

Many studies are based on counts of the times a particular event occurs in a given *area of opportunity*. An **area of opportunity** is a continuous unit or interval of time, volume, or such area in which more than one occurrence of an event can occur. Examples are the surface defects on a new refrigerator, the number of network failures in a day, and the number of fleas on the body of a dog. When you have situations such as these, you can use the **Poisson distribution** to calculate probabilities if

- You are interested in counting the number of times a particular event occurs in a given area of opportunity. The area of opportunity is defined by time, length, surface area, and so forth.
- The probability that an event occurs in a given area of opportunity is the same for all the areas of opportunity.
- The number of events that occur in one area of opportunity is independent of the number of events that occur in any other area of opportunity.
- The probability that two or more events will occur in an area of opportunity approaches zero as the area of opportunity becomes smaller.

Consider the number of customers arriving during the lunch hour at a bank located in the central business district in a large city. You are interested in the number of customers that arrive each minute. Does this situation match the four properties of the Poisson distribution given above? First, the *event* of interest is a customer arriving, and the *given area of opportunity* is defined as a 1-minute interval. Will zero customers arrive, one customer arrive, two customers arrive, and so on? Second, it is reasonable to assume that the probability that a customer arrives during a 1-minute interval is the same as the probability for all the other 1-minute intervals. Third, the arrival of one customer in any 1-minute interval has no effect on (that is, is statistically independent of) the arrival of any other customer in any other 1-minute interval. Finally, the probability that two or more customers will arrive in a given time period approaches zero as the time interval becomes small. For example, the probability is virtually zero that two customers will arrive in a time interval with a width of 1/100 second. Thus, you can use the Poisson distribution to determine probabilities involving the number of customers arriving at the bank in a 1-minute time interval during the lunch hour.

The Poisson distribution has one parameter, called λ (the Greek lowercase letter *lambda*), which is the mean or expected number of events per unit. The variance of a Poisson distribution is also equal to λ, and the standard deviation is equal to $\sqrt{\lambda}$. The number of events, X, of the Poisson random variable ranges from 0 to infinity (∞).

Equation (5.14) presents the mathematical expression for the Poisson distribution for computing the probability of X events, given that λ events are expected.

POISSON PROBABILITY DISTRIBUTION

$$P(X) = \frac{e^{-\lambda}\lambda^X}{X!} \qquad (5.14)$$

where

$P(X) =$ the probability of X events in an area of opportunity

$\lambda =$ expected number of events

$e =$ mathematical constant approximated by 2.71828

$X =$ number of events

To demonstrate the Poisson distribution, suppose that the mean number of customers who arrive per minute at the bank during the noon-to-1 p.m. hour is equal to 3.0. What is the probability that in a given minute, exactly two customers will arrive? And what is the probability that more than two customers will arrive in a given minute?

Using Equation (5.14) and $\lambda = 3$, the probability that in a given minute exactly two customers will arrive is

$$P(X = 2) = \frac{e^{-3.0}(3.0)^2}{2!} = \frac{9}{(2.71828)^3(2)} = 0.2240$$

To determine the probability that in any given minute more than two customers will arrive,

$$P(X > 2) = P(X = 3) + P(X = 4) + \cdots + P(X = \infty)$$

Because all the probabilities in a probability distribution must sum to 1, the terms on the right side of the equation $P(X > 2)$ also represent the complement of the probability that X is less than or equal to 2 [that is, $1 - P(X \leq 2))$]. Thus,

$$P(X > 2) = 1 - P(X \leq 2) = 1 - [P(X = 0) + P(X = 1) + P(X = 2)]$$

Now, using Equation (5.14),

$$P(X > 2) = 1 - \left[\frac{e^{-3.0}(3.0)^0}{0!} + \frac{e^{-3.0}(3.0)^1}{1!} + \frac{e^{-3.0}(3.0)^2}{2!} \right]$$

$$= 1 - [0.0498 + 0.1494 + 0.2240]$$

$$= 1 - 0.4232 = 0.5768$$

Thus, there is a 57.68% chance that more than two customers will arrive in the same minute.

To avoid computational drudgery involved in these computations, you can find Poisson probabilities directly from Table E.7, a portion of which is reproduced in Table 5.6. Table E.7 provides the probabilities that the Poisson random variable takes on values of $X = 0, 1, 2, \ldots,$

for selected values of the parameter λ. To find the probability that exactly two customers will arrive in a given minute when the mean number of customers arriving is 3.0 per minute, you can read the probability corresponding to the row $X = 2$ and column $λ = 3.0$ from the table. The result is 0.2240, as demonstrated in Table 5.6.

TABLE 5.6

Finding a Poisson Probability for λ = 3

			λ	
X	2.1	2.2	. . . .	3.0
0	.1225	.1108	. . . .	.0498
1	.2572	.2438	. . . .	.1494
2	.2700	.2681	. . . .	.2240
3	.1890	.1966	. . . .	.2240
4	.0992	.1082	. . . .	.1680
5	.0417	.0476	. . . .	.1008
6	.0146	.0174	. . . .	.0504
7	.0044	.0055	. . . .	.0216
8	.0011	.0015	. . . .	.0081
9	.0003	.0004	. . . .	.0027
10	.0001	.0001	. . . .	.0008
11	.0000	.0000	. . . .	.0002
12	.0000	.0000	. . . .	.0001

Source: Table E.7.

You can also compute the Poisson probabilities given in Table E.7 by using Microsoft Excel, as illustrated by the worksheet in Figure 5.4.

FIGURE 5.4

Microsoft Excel worksheet for computing Poisson probabilities with λ = 3

See Section E5.4 to create this.

	A	B	C	D	E
1	**Customer Arrivals Analysis**				
2					
3		**Data**			
4	**Average/Expected number of successes:**				3
5					
6	**Poisson Probabilities Table**				
7	**X**	**P(X)**			
8	0	0.049787	=POISSON(A8, $E$4, FALSE)		
9	1	0.149361	=POISSON(A9, $E$4, FALSE)		
10	2	0.224042	=POISSON(A10, $E$4, FALSE)		
11	3	0.224042	=POISSON(A11, $E$4, FALSE)		
12	4	0.168031	=POISSON(A12, $E$4, FALSE)		
13	5	0.100819	=POISSON(A13, $E$4, FALSE)		
14	6	0.050409	=POISSON(A14, $E$4, FALSE)		
15	7	0.021604	=POISSON(A15, $E$4, FALSE)		
16	8	0.008102	=POISSON(A16, $E$4, FALSE)		
17	9	0.002701	=POISSON(A17, $E$4, FALSE)		
18	10	0.000810	=POISSON(A18, $E$4, FALSE)		
19	11	0.000221	=POISSON(A19, $E$4, FALSE)		
20	12	0.000055	=POISSON(A20, $E$4, FALSE)		
21	13	0.000013	=POISSON(A21, $E$4, FALSE)		
22	14	0.000003	=POISSON(A22, $E$4, FALSE)		
23	15	0.000001	=POISSON(A23, $E$4, FALSE)		
24	16	0.000000	=POISSON(A24, $E$4, FALSE)		
25	17	0.000000	=POISSON(A25, $E$4, FALSE)		
26	18	0.000000	=POISSON(A26, $E$4, FALSE)		
27	19	0.000000	=POISSON(A27, $E$4, FALSE)		
28	20	0.000000	=POISSON(A28, $E$4, FALSE)		

EXAMPLE 5.5   **COMPUTING POISSON PROBABILITIES**

The number of work-related injuries per month in your manufacturing plant is known to follow a Poisson distribution with a mean of 2.5 work-related injuries a month. What is the probability that in a given month no work-related injuries occur? That at least one work-related injury occurs?

SOLUTION Using Equation (5.14) on page 198 with $\lambda = 2.5$ (or using Table E.7 or Microsoft Excel), the probability that in a given month no work-related injuries occur is

$$P(X = 0) = \frac{e^{-2.5}(2.5)^0}{0!} = \frac{1}{(2.71828)^{2.5}(1)} = 0.0821$$

The probability that there will be no work-related injuries in a given month is 0.0821 or 8.21%. Thus,

$$P(X \geq 1) = 1 - P(X = 0)$$
$$= 1 - 0.0821$$
$$= 0.9179$$

The probability that there will be at least one work-related injury is 0.9179 or 91.79%.

PROBLEMS FOR SECTION 5.4

Learning the Basics

  5.30 Assume a Poisson distribution.
a. If $\lambda = 2.5$, find $P(X = 2)$.
b. If $\lambda = 8.0$, find $P(X = 8)$.
c. If $\lambda = 0.5$, find $P(X = 1)$.
d. If $\lambda = 3.7$, find $P(X = 0)$.

  5.31 Assume a Poisson distribution.
a. If $\lambda = 2.0$, find $P(X \geq 2)$.
b. If $\lambda = 8.0$, find $P(X \geq 3)$.
c. If $\lambda = 0.5$, find $P(X \leq 1)$.
d. If $\lambda = 4.0$, find $P(X \geq 1)$.
e. If $\lambda = 5.0$, find $P(X \leq 3)$.

5.32 Assume a Poisson distribution with $\lambda = 5.0$. What is the probability that
a. $X = 1$?
b. $X < 1$?
c. $X > 1$?
d. $X \leq 1$?

Applying the Concepts

5.33 Assume that the number of network errors experienced in a day on a local area network (LAN) is distributed as a Poisson random variable. The mean number of network errors experienced in a day is 2.4. What is the probability that in any given day
a. zero network errors will occur?
b. exactly one network error will occur?

c. two or more network errors will occur?
d. less than three network errors will occur?

5.34 The quality control manager of Marilyn's Cookies is inspecting a batch of chocolate-chip cookies that has just been baked. If the production process is in control, the mean number of chip parts per cookie is 6.0. What is the probability that in any particular cookie being inspected
a. less than five chip parts will be found?
b. exactly five chip parts will be found?
c. five or more chip parts will be found?
d. either four or five chip parts will be found?

5.35 Refer to Problem 5.34. How many cookies in a batch of 100 should the manager expect to discard if company policy requires that all chocolate-chip cookies sold have at least four chocolate-chip parts?

5.36 The U.S. Department of Transportation maintains statistics for mishandled bags per 1,000 airline passengers. In 2005, Jet Blue had 4.06 mishandled bags per 1,000 passengers (extracted from M. Mullins, "Out of Place," *USA Today*, March 24, 2006, p. 10A). What is the probability that in the next 1,000 passengers, Jet Blue will have
a. no mishandled bags?
b. at least one mishandled bag?
c. at least two mishandled bags?
d. Compare the results in (a) through (c) to those of Delta in Problem 5.37 (a) through (c).

5.37 The U.S. Department of Transportation maintains statistics for mishandled bags per 1,000 airline passengers. In 2005, Delta had 7.09 mishandled bags per 1,000 passengers (extracted from M. Mullins, "Out of Place," *USA Today*, March 24, 2006, p. 10A). What is the probability that in the next 1,000 passengers, Delta will have
a. no mishandled bags?
b. at least one mishandled bag?
c. at least two mishandled bags?
d. Compare the results in (a) through (c) to those of Jet Blue in Problem 5.36 (a) through (c).

 5.38 Based on past experience, it is assumed that the number of flaws per foot in rolls of grade 2 paper follows a Poisson distribution with a mean of 1 flaw per 5 feet of paper (0.2 flaw per foot). What is the probability that in a
a. 1-foot roll, there will be at least 2 flaws?
b. 12-foot roll, there will be at least 1 flaw?
c. 50-foot roll, there will be greater than or equal to 5 flaws and less than or equal to 15 flaws?

5.39 J.D. Power and Associates calculates and publishes various statistics concerning car quality. The initial quality score measures the number of problems per new car sold. For 2004 model cars, the Lexus had 0.87 problems per car. Korea's Kia had 1.53 problems per car (D. Hakim, "Hyundai Near Top of a Quality Ranking," *The New York Times*, April 29, 2004, p. C8). Let the random variable X be equal to the number of problems with a newly purchased Lexus.
a. What assumptions must be made in order for X to be distributed as a Poisson random variable? Are these assumptions reasonable?
Making the assumptions as in (a), if you purchased a 2004 Lexus, what is the probability that the new car will have
b. zero problems?
c. two or less problems?
d. Give an operational definition for *problem*. Why is the operational definition important in interpreting the initial quality score?

5.40 Refer to Problem 5.39. If you purchased a 2004 Kia, what is the probability that the new car will have
a. zero problems?
b. two or less problems?
c. Compare your answers in (a) and (b) to those for the Lexus in Problem 5.39 (b) and (c).

5.41 In 2005, both Lexus and Kia improved their performance. Lexus had 0.81 problems per car, and Korea's Kia had 1.40 problems per car (S. S. Carty, "Toyota Comes Out on Top Again in Quality Study," *USA Today*, May 19, 2005, p. 3B). If you purchased a 2005 Lexus, what is the probability that the new car will have
a. zero problems?
b. two or less problems?
c. Compare your answers in (a) and (b) to those for the 2004 Lexus in Problem 5.39 (b) and (c).

5.42 Refer to Problem 5.41. If you purchased a 2005 Kia, what is the probability that the new car will have
a. zero problems?
b. two or less problems?
c. Compare your answers in (a) and (b) to those for the 2004 Kia in Problem 5.40 (a) and (b).

5.43 A toll-free phone number is available from 9 a.m. to 9 p.m. for your customers to register complaints about a product purchased from your company. Past history indicates that an average of 0.4 calls are received per minute.
a. What properties must be true about the situation described here in order to use the Poisson distribution to calculate probabilities concerning the number of phone calls received in a 1-minute period?
Assuming that this situation matches the properties discussed in (a), what is the probability that during a 1-minute period
b. zero phone calls will be received?
c. three or more phone calls will be received?
d. What is the maximum number of phone calls that will be received in a 1-minute period 99.99% of the time?

5.5   HYPERGEOMETRIC DISTRIBUTION

Both the binomial distribution and the **hypergeometric distribution** are concerned with the number of successes in a sample containing n observations. One of the differences in these two probability distributions is in the way that the samples are selected. For the binomial distribution, the sample data are selected *with* replacement from a *finite* population or *without* replacement from an *infinite* population. Thus, the probability of success, p, is constant over all observations, and the outcome of any particular observation is independent of any other. For the hypergeometric distribution, the sample data are selected *without* replacement from a *finite* population. Thus, the outcome of one observation is dependent on the outcomes of the previous observations.

Consider a population of size N. Let A represent the total number of successes in the population. The hypergeometric distribution is then used to find the probability of X successes in a sample of size n, selected without replacement. Equation (5.15) presents the mathematical expression of the hypergeometric distribution for finding X successes, given a knowledge of n, N, and A.

HYPERGEOMETRIC DISTRIBUTION

$$P(X) = \frac{\binom{A}{X}\binom{N-A}{n-X}}{\binom{N}{n}} \qquad (5.15)$$

where

$P(X) =$ the probability of X successes, given knowledge of n, N, and A

$n =$ sample size

$N =$ population size

$A =$ number of successes in the population

$N - A =$ number of failures in the population

$X =$ number of successes in the sample

$\binom{A}{X} = {}_{A}C_{X}$ (see Equation (5.10) on p. 190)

The number of successes in the sample, represented by X, cannot be greater than the number of successes in the population, A, or the sample size, n. Thus, the range of the hypergeometric random variable is limited to the sample size or to the number of successes in the population, whichever is smaller.

Equation (5.16) defines the mean of the hypergeometric distribution, and Equation (5.17) defines the standard deviation.

MEAN OF THE HYPERGEOMETRIC DISTRIBUTION

$$\mu = E(X) = \frac{nA}{N} \qquad (5.16)$$

STANDARD DEVIATION OF THE HYPERGEOMETRIC DISTRIBUTION

$$\sigma = \sqrt{\frac{nA(N-A)}{N^2}}\sqrt{\frac{N-n}{N-1}} \qquad (5.17)$$

In Equation (5.17), the expression $\sqrt{\dfrac{N-n}{N-1}}$ is a **finite population correction factor** that results from sampling without replacement from a finite population.

To illustrate the hypergeometric distribution, suppose that you are forming a team of 8 executives from different departments within your company. Your company has a total of 30 executives, and 10 of these people are from the finance department. If members of the team are to be selected at random, what is the probability that the team will contain 2 executives from the finance department? Here, the population of $N = 30$ executives within the company is finite. In addition, $A = 10$ are from the finance department. A team of $n = 8$ members is to be selected.

Using Equation (5.15),

$$P(X = 2) = \frac{\binom{10}{2}\binom{20}{6}}{\binom{30}{8}}$$

$$= \frac{\frac{10!}{2!(8)!}\frac{(20)!}{(6)!(14)!}}{\frac{30!}{8!(22)!}}$$

$$= 0.298$$

Thus, the probability that the team will contain two members from the finance department is 0.298, or 29.8%.

Such computations can become tedious, especially as N gets large. However, you can compute the probabilities by using Microsoft Excel. Figure 5.5 presents a Microsoft Excel worksheet for the team-formation example, where the number of executives from the finance department (that is, the number of successes in the sample) can be equal to 0, 1, 2, . . . , 8.

FIGURE 5.5

Microsoft Excel worksheet for the team member example

See Section E5.5 to create this.

	A	B
1	Team Formation Analysis	
2		
3	Data	
4	Sample size	8
5	No. of successes in population	10
6	Population size	30
7		
8	Hypergeometric Probabilities Table	
9	X	P(X)
10	0	0.0215 =HYPGEOMDIST(A10, $B$4, $B$5, $B$6)
11	1	0.1324 =HYPGEOMDIST(A11, $B$4, $B$5, $B$6)
12	2	0.2980 =HYPGEOMDIST(A12, $B$4, $B$5, $B$6)
13	3	0.3179 =HYPGEOMDIST(A13, $B$4, $B$5, $B$6)
14	4	0.1738 =HYPGEOMDIST(A14, $B$4, $B$5, $B$6)
15	5	0.0491 =HYPGEOMDIST(A15, $B$4, $B$5, $B$6)
16	6	0.0068 =HYPGEOMDIST(A16, $B$4, $B$5, $B$6)
17	7	0.0004 =HYPGEOMDIST(A17, $B$4, $B$5, $B$6)
18	8	0.0000 =HYPGEOMDIST(A18, $B$4, $B$5, $B$6)

PROBLEMS FOR SECTION 5.5

Learning the Basics

PH Grade ASSIST **5.44** Determine the following:
a. If $n = 4$, $N = 10$, and $A = 5$, find $P(X = 3)$.
b. If $n = 4$, $N = 6$, and $A = 3$, find $P(X = 1)$.
c. If $n = 5$, $N = 12$, and $A = 3$, find $P(X = 0)$.
d. If $n = 3$, $N = 10$, and $A = 3$, find $P(X = 3)$.

PH Grade ASSIST **5.45** Referring to Problem 5.44, compute the mean and standard deviation for the hypergeometric distributions described in (a) through (d).

Applying the Concepts

PH Grade ASSIST / SELF Test **5.46** An auditor for the Internal Revenue Service is selecting a sample of 6 tax returns for an audit. If 2 or more of these returns are "improper," the entire population of 100 tax returns will be audited. What is the probability that the entire population will be audited if the true number of improper returns in the population is
a. 25?
b. 30?
c. 5?

d. 10?

e. Discuss the differences in your results, depending on the true number of improper returns in the population.

5.47 The dean of a business school wishes to form an executive committee of 5 from among the 40 tenured faculty members at the school. The selection is to be random, and at the school there are 8 tenured faculty members in accounting. What is the probability that the committee will contain

a. none of them?

b. at least 1 of them?

c. not more than 1 of them?

d. What is your answer to (a) if the committee consists of 7 members?

5.48 From an inventory of 30 cars being shipped to a local automobile dealer, 4 are SUVs. What is the probability that if 4 cars arrive at a particular dealership,

a. all 4 are SUVs?

b. none are SUVs?

c. at least 1 is an SUV?

d. What are your answers to (a) through (c) if 6 cars being shipped are SUVs?

5.49 A state lottery is conducted in which 6 winning numbers are selected from a total of 54 numbers. What is the probability that if 6 numbers are randomly selected,

a. all 6 numbers will be winning numbers?

b. 5 numbers will be winning numbers?

c. none of the numbers will be winning numbers?

d. What are your answers to (a) through (c) if the 6 winning numbers are selected from a total of 40 numbers?

5.50 In a shipment of 15 sets of golf clubs, 3 are left-handed. If 4 sets of golf clubs are selected, what is the probability that

a. exactly 1 is left-handed?

b. at least 1 is left-handed?

c. no more than 2 are left-handed?

d. What is the mean number of left-handed sets of golf clubs that you would expect to find in the sample of 4 sets of golf clubs?

5.6   ● (*CD-ROM Topic*) USING THE POISSON DISTRIBUTION TO APPROXIMATE THE BINOMIAL DISTRIBUTION

Under certain circumstances, the Poisson distribution can be used to approximate the binomial distribution. To study this topic, go to the `section5.6.pdf` file located on the CD-ROM that accompanies this book.

SUMMARY

In this chapter, you have studied mathematical expectation, the covariance, and the development and application of the binomial, Poisson, and hypergeometric distributions. In the Using Statistics scenario, you learned how to calculate probabilities from the binomial distribution concerning the observation of tagged invoices in the accounting information system used by the Saxon Home Improvement Company. In the following chapter, you will study several important continuous distributions including the normal distribution.

To help decide what probability distribution to use for a particular situation, you need to ask the following questions:

- Is there a fixed number of observations, n, each of which is classified as success or failure? Or is there an area of opportunity? If there is a fixed number of observations, n, each of which is classified as success or failure, you use the binomial or hypergeometric distribution. If there is an area of opportunity, you use the Poisson distribution.
- In deciding whether to use the binomial or hypergeometric distribution, is the probability of success constant over all trials? If yes, you can use the binomial distribution. If no, you can use the hypergeometric distribution.

KEY EQUATIONS

Expected Value, μ, of a Discrete Random Variable

$$\mu = E(X) = \sum_{i=1}^{N} X_i P(X_i) \qquad (5.1)$$

Variance of a Discrete Random Variable

$$\sigma^2 = \sum_{i=1}^{N} [X_i - E(X)]^2 P(X_i) \qquad (5.2)$$

Standard Deviation of a Discrete Random Variable

$$\sigma = \sqrt{\sigma^2} = \sqrt{\sum_{i=1}^{N} [X_i - E(X)]^2 P(X_i)} \qquad \textbf{(5.3)}$$

Covariance

$$\sigma_{XY} = \sum_{i=1}^{N} [X_i - E(X)][Y_i - E(Y)]P(X_iY_i) \qquad \textbf{(5.4)}$$

Expected Value of the Sum of Two Random Variables

$$E(X + Y) = E(X) + E(Y) \qquad \textbf{(5.5)}$$

Variance of the Sum of Two Random Variables

$$Var(X + Y) = \sigma_{X+Y}^2 = \sigma_X^2 + \sigma_Y^2 + 2\sigma_{XY} \qquad \textbf{(5.6)}$$

Standard Deviation of the Sum of Two Random Variables

$$\sigma_{X+Y} = \sqrt{\sigma_{X+Y}^2} \qquad \textbf{(5.7)}$$

Portfolio Expected Return

$$E(P) = wE(X) + (1 - w)E(Y) \qquad \textbf{(5.8)}$$

Portfolio Risk

$$\sigma_p = \sqrt{w^2\sigma_X^2 + (1 - w)^2\sigma_Y^2 + 2w(1 - w)\sigma_{XY}} \qquad \textbf{(5.9)}$$

Combinations

$$_nC_X = \frac{n!}{X!(n - X)!} \qquad \textbf{(5.10)}$$

Binomial Distribution

$$P(X) = \frac{n!}{X!(n - X)!} p^X(1 - p)^{n-X} \qquad \textbf{(5.11)}$$

Mean of the Binomial Distribution

$$\mu = E(X) = np \qquad \textbf{(5.12)}$$

Standard Deviation of the Binomial Distribution

$$\sigma = \sqrt{\sigma^2} = \sqrt{Var(X)} = \sqrt{np(1 - p)} \qquad \textbf{(5.13)}$$

Poisson Distribution

$$P(X) = \frac{e^{-\lambda}\lambda^X}{X!} \qquad \textbf{(5.14)}$$

Hypergeometric Distribution

$$P(X) = \frac{\binom{A}{X}\binom{N - A}{n - X}}{\binom{N}{n}} \qquad \textbf{(5.15)}$$

Mean of the Hypergeometric Distribution

$$\mu = E(X) = \frac{nA}{N} \qquad \textbf{(5.16)}$$

Standard Deviation of the Hypergeometric Distribution

$$\sigma = \sqrt{\frac{nA(N - A)}{N^2}}\sqrt{\frac{N - n}{N - 1}} \qquad \textbf{(5.17)}$$

KEY TERMS

area of opportunity   197
binomial distribution   189
covariance, σ_{XY} 184
expected value of the sum of two
    random variables   186
expected value, μ, of a discrete random
    variable   181
finite population correction factor   202
hypergeometric distribution   201

mathematical model   189
Poisson distribution   197
portfolio   186
portfolio expected return   186
portfolio risk   186
probability distribution for a discrete
    random variable   180
rule of combinations   190

standard deviation of a discrete
    random variable   182
standard deviation of the sum of two
    random variables   186
variance of a discrete random
    variable   182
variance of the sum of two random
    variables   186

CHAPTER REVIEW PROBLEMS

Checking Your Understanding

5.51 What is the meaning of the expected value of a probability distribution?

5.52 What are the four properties that must be present in order to use the binomial distribution?

5.53 What are the four properties that must be present in order to use the Poisson distribution?

5.54 When do you use the hypergeometric distribution instead of the binomial distribution?

Applying the Concepts

 5.55 Event insurance allows promoters of sporting and entertainment events to protect themselves from financial losses due to uncontrollable circumstances such as rain-outs. For example, each spring, Cincinnati's Downtown Council puts on the Taste of Cincinnati. This is a rainy time of year in Cincinnati, and the chance of receiving an inch or more of rain during a spring weekend is about one out of four. An article in the *Cincinnati Enquirer*, by Jim Knippenberg ("Chicken Pox Means 3 Dog Night Remedy," *Cincinnati Enquirer*, May 28, 1997, p. E1), gave the details for an insurance policy purchased by the Downtown Council. The policy would pay $100,000 if it rained more than an inch during the weekend festival. The cost of the policy was reported to be $6,500.

a. Determine whether you believe that these dollar amounts are correct. (*Hint:* Calculate the expected value of the profit to be made by the insurance company.)

b. Assume that the dollar amounts are correct. Is this policy a good deal for Cincinnati's Downtown Council?

 5.56 Between 1872 and 2000, stock prices rose in 74% of the years (M. Hulbert, "The Stock Market Must Rise in 2002? Think Again," *The New York Times*, December 6, 2001, Business, p. 6). Based on this information, and assuming a binomial distribution, what do you think the probability is that the stock market will rise

a. next year?

b. the year after next?

c. in four of the next five years?

d. in none of the next five years?

e. For this situation, what assumption of the binomial distribution might not be valid?

5.57 The mean cost of a phone call handled by an automated customer-service system is $0.45. The mean cost of a phone call passed on to a "live" operator is $5.50. However, as more and more companies have implemented automated systems, customer annoyance with such systems has grown. Many customers are quick to leave the automated system when given an option such as "Press zero to talk to a customer-service representative." According to the Center for Client Retention, 40% of all callers to automated customer-service systems automatically opt to go to a live operator when given the chance (J. Spencer, "In Search of the Operator," *The Wall Street Journal*, May 8, 2002, p. D1).

If 10 independent callers contact an automated customer-service system, what is the probability that

a. 0 will automatically opt to talk to a live operator?

b. exactly 1 will automatically opt to talk to a live operator?

c. 2 or less will automatically opt to talk to a live operator?

d. all 10 will automatically opt to talk to a live operator?

e. If all 10 automatically opt to talk to a live operator, do you think that the 40% figure given in the article applies to this particular system? Explain.

5.58 One theory concerning the Dow Jones Industrial Average is that it is likely to increase during U.S. presidential election years. From 1964 through 2004, the Dow Jones Industrial Average increased in 9 of the 11 U.S. presidential election years. Assuming that this indicator is a random event with no predictive value, you would expect that the indicator would be correct 50% of the time.

a. What is the probability of the Dow Jones Industrial Average increasing in 9 or more of the 11 U.S. presidential election years if the true probability of an increase in the Dow Jones Industrial Average is 0.50?

b. Read Problem 5.56 and note that the Dow Jones Industrial Average increased in 74% of the years studied. What is the probability of the Dow Jones Industrial Average increasing in 9 or more of the 11 U.S. presidential election years if the probability of an increase in the Dow Jones Industrial Average is 0.74?

5.59 Priority Mail is the U.S. Postal Service's alternative to commercial express mail companies such as FedEx. An article in *The Wall Street Journal* presented some interesting conclusions comparing Priority Mail shipments with the much less expensive first-class shipments (R. Brooks, "New Data Reveal 'Priority Mail' Is Slower Than a Stamp," *The Wall Street Journal*, May 29, 2002, p. D1). When comparing shipments intended for delivery in three days, first-class deliveries failed to deliver on time 19% of the time, while Priority Mail failed 33% of the time. Note that at the time of the article, first-class deliveries started as low as $0.34, and Priority Mail started at $3.50.

If 10 items are to be shipped first-class to 10 different destinations claimed to be in a three-day delivery location, what is the probability that

a. 0 items will take more than three days?

b. exactly 1 will take more than three days?

c. 2 or more will take more than three days?

d. What are the mean and the standard deviation of the probability distribution?

5.60 Refer to Problem 5.59. If the shipments are made using Priority Mail, what is the probability that
a. 0 items will take more than three days?
b. exactly 1 will take more than three days?
c. 2 or more will take more than three days?
d. What are the mean and the standard deviation of the probability distribution?
e. Compare the results of (a) through (c) to those of Problem 5.59 (a) through (c).

5.61 Cinema advertising is increasing. Normally 60 to 90 seconds long, these advertisements are longer and more extravagant, and they tend to have more captive audiences than television advertisements. Thus, it is not surprising that the recall rates for viewers of cinema advertisements are higher than those for television advertisements. According to survey research conducted by the ComQUEST division of BBM Bureau of Measurement in Toronto, the probability a viewer will remember a cinema advertisement is 0.74, whereas the probability a viewer will remember a 30-second television advertisement is 0.37 (N. Hendley, "Cinema Advertising Comes of Age," *Marketing Magazine*, May 6, 2002, p. 16).
a. Is the 0.74 probability reported by the BBM Bureau of Measurement best classified as *a priori* classical probability, empirical classical probability, or subjective probability?
b. Suppose that 10 viewers of a cinema advertisement are randomly sampled. Consider the random variable defined by the number of viewers who recall the advertisement. What assumptions must be made in order to assume that this random variable is distributed as a binomial random variable?
c. Assuming that the number of viewers who recall the cinema advertisement is a binomial random variable, what are the mean and standard deviation of this distribution?
d. Based on your answer to (c), if none of the viewers can recall the ad, what can be inferred about the 0.74 probability given in the article?

5.62 Refer to Problem 5.61. Compute the probability that of the 10 viewers of the cinema advertisement,
a. exactly 0 can recall the advertisement.
b. all 10 can recall the advertisement.
c. more than half can recall the advertisement.
d. 8 or more can recall the advertisement.

5.63 Refer to Problem 5.61. For television advertisements, using the given probability of recall, 0.37, compute the probability that of the 10 viewers,
a. exactly 0 can recall the advertisement.
b. all 10 can recall the advertisement.
c. more than half can recall the advertisement.
d. 8 or more can recall the advertisement.
e. Compare the results of (a) through (d) to those of Problem 5.62 (a) through (d).

5.64 In a survey conducted by the Council for Marketing and Opinion Research (CMOR), a national nonprofit research industry trade group based in Cincinnati, 1,628 of 3,700 adults contacted in the United States refuse to participate in phone surveys (S. Jarvis, "CMOR Finds Survey Refusal Rate Still Rising," *Marketing News*, February 4, 2002, p. 4). Suppose that you are to randomly call 10 adults in the United States and ask them to participate in a phone survey. Using the results of the CMOR study, what is the probability that
a. all 10 will refuse?
b. exactly 5 will refuse?
c. at least 5 will refuse?
d. less than 5 will refuse?
e. less than 5 will agree to be surveyed?
f. What is the expected number of people who will refuse to participate? Explain the practical meaning of this number.

5.65 Credit card companies are increasing their revenues by raising the late fees charged to their customers. According to a study by **cardweb.com**, late fees represent the third largest revenue source for card companies, after interest charges and payments from the merchants who accept their cards. In the preceding year, 58% of all credit card customers had had to pay late fees (R. Lieber, "Credit-Card Firms Collect Record Levels of Late Fees," *The Wall Street Journal*, May 21, 2002, p. D1).
  If a random sample of 20 credit card holders is selected, what is the probability that
a. 0 had to pay a late fee?
b. no more than 5 had to pay late fees?
c. more than 10 had to pay late fees?
d. What assumptions did you have to make to answer (a) through (c)?

5.66 One of the retail industry's biggest frustrations is customers who abuse the return and exchange policies (S. Kang, "New Return Policy: Retailers Say 'No' to Serial Exchangers," *The Wall Street Journal*, November 29, 2004, pp. B1, B3). In a recent year, returns were 13% of sales in department stores. Consider a sample of 20 customers who make a purchase at a department store. Use the binomial model to answer the following questions:
a. What is the expected value, or mean, of the binomial distribution?
b. What is the standard deviation of the binomial distribution?
c. What is the probability that none of the 20 customers will make a return?
d. What is the probability that no more than 2 of the customers will make a return?
e. What is the probability that 3 or more of the customers will make a return?

5.67 Refer to Problem 5.66. In the same year, returns were 1% of sales in grocery stores.

a. What is the expected value, or mean, of the binomial distribution?

b. What is the standard deviation of the binomial distribution?

c. What is the probability that none of the 20 customers will make a return?

d. What is the probability that no more than 2 of the customers will make a return?

e. What is the probability that 3 or more of the customers will make a return?

f. Compare the results of (a) through (e) to those of Problem 5.66 (a) through (e).

5.68 One theory concerning the S&P 500 index is that if it increases during the first five trading days of the year, it is likely to increase during the entire year. From 1950 through 2005, the S&P 500 index had these early gains in 35 years. In 30 of these 35 years, the S&P 500 index increased. Assuming that this indicator is a random event with no predictive value, you would expect that the indicator would be correct 50% of the time. What is the probability of the S&P 500 index increasing in 30 or more years if the true probability of an increase in the S&P 500 index is

a. 0.50?

b. 0.70?

c. 0.90?

d. Based on the results of (a) through (c), what do you think is the probability that the S&P 500 index will increase if there is an early gain in the first five trading days of the year? Explain.

5.69 *Spurious correlation* refers to the apparent relationship between variables that either have no true relationship or are related to other variables that have not been measured. One widely publicized stock market indicator in the United States that is an example of spurious correlation is the relationship between the winner of the National Football League Super Bowl and the performance of the Dow Jones Industrial Average in that year. The indicator states that when a team representing the National Football Conference wins the Super Bowl, the Dow Jones Industrial Average will increase in that year. When a team representing the American Football Conference wins the Super Bowl, the Dow Jones Industrial Average will decline in that year. Since the first Super Bowl was held in 1967 through 2005, the indicator has been correct 32 out of 39 times. Assuming that this indicator is a random event with no predictive value, you would expect that the indicator would be correct 50% of the time.

a. What is the probability that the indicator would be correct 32 or more times in 39 years?

b. What does this tell you about the usefulness of this indicator?

5.70 Worldwide golf ball sales total more than $1 billion annually. One reason for such a large number of golf ball purchases is that golfers lose them at a rate of 4.5 per 18-hole round ("Snapshots," **usatoday.com**, January 29, 2004). Assume that the number of golf balls lost in an 18-hole round is distributed as a Poisson random variable.

a. What assumptions need to be made so that the number of golf balls lost in an 18-hole round is distributed as a Poisson random variable?

Making the assumptions given in (a), what is the probability that

b. 0 balls will be lost in an 18-hole round?

c. 5 or less balls will be lost in an 18-hole round?

d. 6 or more balls will be lost in an 18-hole round?

5.71 A study of the home pages of Fortune 500 companies reports that the mean number of bad links per home page is 0.4 and the mean number of spelling errors per home page is 0.16 (N. Tamimi, M. Rajan, and R. Sebastianella, "Benchmarking the Home Pages of 'Fortune' 500 Companies," *Quality Progress*, July 2000). Use the Poisson distribution to find the probability that a randomly selected home page will contain

a. exactly 0 bad links.

b. 5 or more bad links.

c. exactly 0 spelling errors.

d. 10 or more spelling errors.

5.72 Mega Millions is one of the most popular lottery games in the United States. Participating states in Mega Millions are Georgia, Illinois, Maryland, Massachusetts, Michigan, New Jersey, New York, Ohio, and Virginia. Rules for playing and the list of prizes are given below ("Win Megamoney Playing Ohio's Biggest Jackpot Game," Ohio Lottery Headquarters, 2002):

Rules:
- Select five numbers from a pool of numbers from 1 to 52 and one Mega Ball number from a second pool of numbers from 1 to 52.
- Each wager costs $1.

Prizes:
- Match all five numbers + Mega Ball—win jackpot (minimum of $10,000,000)
- Match all five numbers—win $175,000
- Match four numbers + Mega Ball—win $5,000
- Match four numbers—win $150
- Match three numbers + Mega Ball—win $150
- Match two numbers + Mega Ball—win $10
- Match three numbers—win $7
- Match one number + Mega Ball—win $3
- Match Mega Ball—win $2

Find the probability of winning

a. the jackpot.

b. the $175,000 prize. (Note that this requires matching all five numbers but not matching the Mega Ball.)

c. $5,000.

d. $150.

e. $10.

f. $7.

g. $3.

h. $2.

i. nothing.

j. All stores selling Mega Millions tickets are required to have a brochure that gives complete game rules and probabilities of winning each prize (the probability of having a losing ticket is not given). The slogan for all lottery games in the state of Ohio is "Play Responsibly. Odds Are, You'll Have Fun." Do you think Ohio's slogan and the requirement of making available complete game rules and probabilities of winning is an ethical approach to running the lottery system?

Managing the *Springville Herald*

The *Herald* marketing department is seeking to increase home-delivery sales through an aggressive direct-marketing campaign that includes mailings, discount coupons, and telephone solicitations. Feedback from these efforts indicates that getting their newspapers delivered early in the morning is a very important factor for both prospective as well as existing subscribers. After several brainstorming sessions, a team consisting of members from the marketing and circulation departments decided that guaranteeing newspaper delivery by a specific time could be an important selling point in retaining and getting new subscribers. The team concluded that the *Herald* should offer a guarantee that customers will receive their newspapers by a certain time or else that day's issue is free.

To assist the team in setting a guaranteed delivery time, Al Leslie, the research director, noted that the circulation department had data that showed the percentage of newspapers yet undelivered every quarter hour from 6 a.m. to 8 a.m. Jan Shapiro remembered that customers were asked on their subscription forms at what time they would be looking for their copy of the *Herald* to be delivered. These data were subsequently combined and posted on an internal *Herald* Web page. (See Circulation_Data.htm in the **HeraldCase** folder on the Student CD or go to **www.prenhall.com/HeraldCase/Circulation_Data.htm**).

EXERCISES

Review the internal data and propose a reasonable time (to the nearest quarter hour) to guarantee delivery. To help explore the effects of your choice, calculate the following probabilities:

SH5.1   If a sample of 50 customers is selected on a given day, what is the probability, given your selected delivery time, that

a. less than 3 customers will receive a free newspaper?

b. 2, 3, or 4 customers will receive a free newspaper?

c. more than 5 customers will receive a free newspaper?

SH5.2   Consider the effects of improving the newspaper delivery process so that the percentage of newspapers that go undelivered by your guaranteed delivery time decreases by 2%. If a sample of 50 customers is selected on a given day, what is the probability, given your selected delivery time (and the delivery improvement), that

a. less than 3 customers will receive a free newspaper?

b. 2, 3, or 4 customers will receive a free newspaper?

c. more than 5 customers will receive a free newspaper?

Web Case

Apply your knowledge about expected value and the covariance in this continuing Web Case from Chapters 3 and 4.

Visit the EndRun Bulls and Bears Web page, at **www.prenhall.com/Springville/ER_BullsandBears.htm** (or open the Web page file from the Student CD-ROM **Web Case** folder), read the claims, and examine the supporting data. Then answer the following:

1. Are there any "catches" about the claims the Web site makes for the rate of return of Happy Bull and Worried Bear Funds?

2. What subjective data influence the rate-of-return analyses of these funds? Could EndRun be accused of making false and misleading statements? Why or why not?

3. The expected-return analysis seems to show that the Worried Bear Fund has a greater expected return than the Happy Bull Fund. Should a rational investor then never invest in the Happy Bull Fund? Why or why not?

REFERENCES

1. Bernstein, P. L., *Against the Gods: The Remarkable Story of Risk* (New York: Wiley, 1996).
2. Emery, D. R., J. D. Finnerty, and J. D. Stowe, *Corporate Financial Management*, 3rd ed. (Upper Saddle River, NJ: Prentice Hall, 2007).
3. Kirk, R. L., ed., *Statistical Issues: A Reader for the Behavioral Sciences* (Belmont, CA: Wadsworth, 1972).
4. Levine, D. M., P. Ramsey, and R. Smidt, *Applied Statistics for Engineers and Scientists Using Microsoft Excel and Minitab* (Upper Saddle River, NJ: Prentice Hall, 2001).
5. *Microsoft Excel 2007* (Redmond, WA: Microsoft Corp., 2007).
6. Moscove, S. A., M. G. Simkin, and A. Bagranoff, *Core Concepts of Accounting Information Systems*, 8th ed. (New York: Wiley, 2003).

Excel Companion
to Chapter 5

E5.1 COMPUTING THE EXPECTED VALUE OF A DISCRETE RANDOM VARIABLE

You compute the expected value of a discrete random variable by making entries in the **Discrete** worksheet of the `Expected Value.xls` workbook. This worksheet uses the SUM and SQRT (square root) functions to calculate its statistics.

Figure E5.1 shows a completed worksheet using the mortgage probability distribution of Table 5.1 on page 181. To adapt this worksheet to other problems that have more or less than seven outcomes, first select the cell range **A5:E5**. To add table rows, right-click and select **Insert**. (If a box of options appears, click **Shift cells down** and then click **OK**.) Then, copy the formulas in cell range C4:E4 down through the new table rows and enter the new X and $P(X)$ values in columns A and B.

To delete table rows, right-click and select **Delete**. (If a box of options appears, click **Shift cells up** and then click **OK**.) Enter a corrected list of X values, starting with **1** in cell A5 in column A, and enter the new $P(X)$ values in column B.

E5.2 COMPUTING PORTFOLIO EXPECTED RETURN AND PORTFOLIO RISK

You compute the portfolio expected return and the portfolio risk of two investments by either using the PHStat2

Covariance and Portfolio Management procedure or by making entries in the `Portfolio.xls` workbook.

Using PHStat2 Covariance and Portfolio Management

Open the workbook in which you want your probabilities worksheet to be placed. Select **PHStat → Probability & Prob. Distributions → Covariance and Portfolio Management**. In the Covariance and Portfolio Management dialog box (shown below), enter a value for the **Number of Outcomes**, enter a title as the **Title**, click **Portfolio Management Analysis**, and click **OK**. In the worksheet created by PHStat2, enter the values for the probabilities and

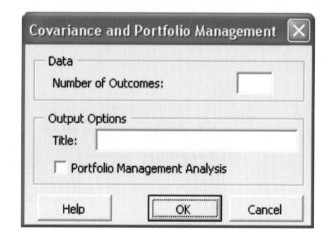

FIGURE E5.1 Discrete worksheet

outcomes in the cell range **B4:D6** and the weight (*w*) assigned to X in cell **B8**.

Using the Portfolio Worksheet

Open to the **Portfolio** worksheet of the `Portfolio.xls` workbook (see Figure E5.2). This worksheet already contains the entries for the estimated returns for the investment data of Table 5.4. To adapt this worksheet to other problems, change the probabilities and outcomes data and the **Weight Assigned to X** value. If your problem has more or fewer than three outcomes, first select row **5** and then add or delete rows one at a time by right-clicking row 5 and clicking either **Insert** or **Delete**. (If you inserted rows, you also have to copy formulas down to those new rows.)

The worksheet features the **SUMPRODUCT** function, which computes the sum of the products of corresponding elements of two cell ranges. In this worksheet, the cell range is always the set of $P(X_iY_i)$ probabilities. To compute the variance, standard deviation, and covariance, the worksheet uses a calculation area in columns F through J, shown in Figure E5.3. This area was created by entering the following row 4 formulas: F4: **=C4 - $B$11**, G4: **=D4 - $B$12**, H4: **=F4^2**, I4: **=G4^2**, and J4: **=F4*G4** and then copying them down to rows 5 and 6.

	F	G	H	I	J
1		Calculations Area			
2	For variance and standard deviation:				For covariance
3	X-mu	Y-mu	(X-mu)^2	(Y-mu)^2	(X-mu)(Y-mu)
4	-205	165	42025	27225	-33825
5	-5	15	25	225	-75
6	145	-135	21025	18225	-19575

FIGURE E5.3 Portfolio worksheet calculations area

E5.3   COMPUTING BINOMIAL PROBABILITIES

You compute binomial probabilities either by using the PHStat2 **Binomial** procedure or by making entries in the `Binomial.xls` workbook.

Using PHStat2 Binomial

Open the workbook in which you want your probabilities worksheet to be placed. Select **PHStat → Probability & Prob. Distributions → Binomial**. In the Binomial Probability Distribution dialog box (shown at the top of page 213), enter the **Sample Size**, the **Probability of Success**, and the range of the outcomes. Enter a title as the **Title**, click **Cumulative Probabilities**, and then click **OK**.

	A	B	C	D
1	**Portfolio Expected Return and Risk**			
2				
3	**Probabilities & Outcomes:**	**P**	**X**	**Y**
4		0.2	-100	200
5		0.5	100	50
6		0.3	250	-100
7				
8	**Weight Assigned to X**	0.5		
9				
10	**Statistics**			
11	E(X)	105	=SUMPRODUCT(B4:B6, C4:C6)	
12	E(Y)	35	=SUMPRODUCT(B4:B6, D4:D6)	
13	Variance(X)	14725	=SUMPRODUCT(B4:B6, H4:H6)	
14	Standard Deviation(X)	121.3466	=SQRT(B13)	
15	Variance(Y)	11025	=SUMPRODUCT(B4:B6, I4:I6)	
16	Standard Deviation(Y)	105	=SQRT(B15)	
17	Covariance(XY)	-12675	=SUMPRODUCT(B4:B6, J4:J6)	
18	Variance(X+Y)	400	=B13 + B15 + 2 * B17	
19	Standard Deviation(X+Y)	20	=SQRT(B18)	
20				
21	**Portfolio Management**			
22	Weight Assigned to X	0.5	=B8	
23	Weight Assigned to Y	0.5	=1 - B22	
24	Portfolio Expected Return	70	=B22 * B11 + B23 * B12	
25	Portfolio Risk	10	=SQRT(B22^2 * B13 + B23^2 * B15 + 2 * B22 * B23 * B17)	

FIGURE E5.2 Portfolio worksheet

You can create your version of the Binomial worksheet shown in Figure E5.4 by entering **0** as the **Outcomes From** value and **4** as the **Outcomes To** value.

Using the Binomial Worksheet

Open to the **Binomial** worksheet of the Binomial.xls workbook (see Figure E5.4). This worksheet already contains the entries for the tagged orders example of Section 5.3. To adapt this worksheet to other problems, change the **Sample size** and **Probability of success** values in cells B4 and B5. If your problem has a sample size other than 4, first select row **15** and then add or delete rows one at a time by right-clicking row 15 and clicking either **Insert** or **Delete** and adjusting the X values in column A. (If you inserted rows, you also have to copy formulas down to those new rows.)

	A	B	
1	**Tagged Orders**		
2			
3	**Data**		
4	Sample size	4	
5	Probability of success	0.1	
6			
7	**Statistics**		
8	Mean	0.4	=B4 * B5
9	Variance	0.36	=B8 * (1 - B5)
10	Standard deviation	0.6	=SQRT(B9)
11			
12	**Binomial Probabilities Table**		
13	X	P(X)	
14	0	0.6561	=BINOMDIST(A14, $B$4, $B$5, FALSE)
15	1	0.2916	=BINOMDIST(A15, $B$4, $B$5, FALSE)
16	2	0.0486	=BINOMDIST(A16, $B$4, $B$5, FALSE)
17	3	0.0036	=BINOMDIST(A17, $B$4, $B$5, FALSE)
18	4	0.0001	=BINOMDIST(A18, $B$4, $B$5, FALSE)

FIGURE E5.4 Binomial worksheet

The worksheet features the **BINOMDIST(X, n, p, cumulative)** function, in which X is the number of successes, n is the sample size, p is the probability of success, and *cumulative* is True or False. When *cumulative* is **True**, the function computes the probability of X or fewer successes; when *cumulative* is **False**, the function computes the probability of exactly X successes.

Forum Click the ALTERNATE TECHNIQUES link to learn how to create a table of cumulative probabilities, similar to the PHStat2 output option.

E5.4   COMPUTING POISSON PROBABILITIES

You compute Poisson probabilities either by using the PHStat2 **Poisson** procedure or by making entries in the Poisson.xls workbook.

Using PHStat2 Poisson

Open the workbook in which you want your probabilities worksheet to be placed. Select **PHStat → Probability & Prob. Distributions → Poisson**. In the Poisson Probability Distribution dialog box (shown below), enter the **Average/Expected No. of Successes**, enter a title as the **Title**, click **Cumulative Probabilities**, and then click **OK**.

Using the Poisson Worksheet

Open to the **Poisson** worksheet of the Poisson.xls workbook (see Figure E5.5 on page 214). This worksheet already contains the entries for the bank customer arrivals problem of Section 5.4. To adapt this worksheet to other problems, change the **Average/Expected number of successes** value in cell **E4**.

	A	B	C	D	E
1	**Customer Arrivals Analysis**				
2					
3		**Data**			
4	**Average/Expected number of successes:**				3
5					
6	**Poisson Probabilities Table**				
7	X	P(X)			
8	0	0.049787	=POISSON(A8, $E$4, FALSE)		
9	1	0.149361	=POISSON(A9, $E$4, FALSE)		
10	2	0.224042	=POISSON(A10, $E$4, FALSE)		
11	3	0.224042	=POISSON(A11, $E$4, FALSE)		
12	4	0.168031	=POISSON(A12, $E$4, FALSE)		
13	5	0.100819	=POISSON(A13, $E$4, FALSE)		
14	6	0.050409	=POISSON(A14, $E$4, FALSE)		
15	7	0.021604	=POISSON(A15, $E$4, FALSE)		
16	8	0.008102	=POISSON(A16, $E$4, FALSE)		
17	9	0.002701	=POISSON(A17, $E$4, FALSE)		
18	10	0.000810	=POISSON(A18, $E$4, FALSE)		
19	11	0.000221	=POISSON(A19, $E$4, FALSE)		
20	12	0.000055	=POISSON(A20, $E$4, FALSE)		
21	13	0.000013	=POISSON(A21, $E$4, FALSE)		
22	14	0.000003	=POISSON(A22, $E$4, FALSE)		
23	15	0.000001	=POISSON(A23, $E$4, FALSE)		
24	16	0.000000	=POISSON(A24, $E$4, FALSE)		
25	17	0.000000	=POISSON(A25, $E$4, FALSE)		
26	18	0.000000	=POISSON(A26, $E$4, FALSE)		
27	19	0.000000	=POISSON(A27, $E$4, FALSE)		
28	20	0.000000	=POISSON(A28, $E$4, FALSE)		

FIGURE E5.5 Poisson worksheet

The worksheet features the **POISSON(X, lambda, cumulative)** function, in which X is the number of successes, *lambda* is the average or expected number of successes, and *cumulative* is True or False. When *cumulative* is **True**, the function computes the probability of X or fewer successes; when *cumulative* is **False**, the function computes the probability of exactly X successes.

E5.5 COMPUTING HYPERGEOMETRIC PROBABILITIES

You compute hypergeometric probabilities either by using the PHStat2 **Hypergeometric** procedure or by making entries in the Hypergeometric.xls workbook.

Using PHStat2 Hypergeometric

Open the workbook in which you want your probabilities worksheet to be placed. Select **PHStat → Probability & Prob. Distributions → Hypergeometric**. In the Hypergeometric Probability Distribution dialog box (shown at right), enter the **Sample Size**, the **No. of Successes in Population**, and the **Population Size**. Enter a title as the **Title**, and then click **OK**.

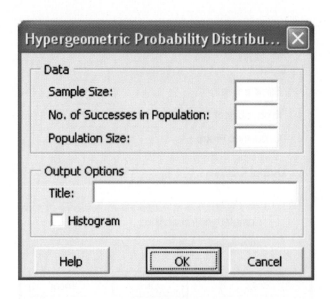

You can create your version of the Hypergeometric worksheet shown in Figure E5.6 by entering **8** as the **Sample Size, 10** as the **No. of Successes in Population**, and **30** as the **Population Size**.

Using the Hypergeometric Worksheet

Open to the **Hypergeometric** worksheet of the Hypergeometric.xls workbook (see Figure E5.6). This worksheet already contains the entries for the team formation problem of Section 5.5. To adapt this worksheet to other problems, change the **Sample size, No. of successes in population**, and **Population size** in the cell range **B4:B6**. If your problem has a sample size other than 8, first select row **11** and then add or delete rows one at a time by right-clicking and clicking either **Insert** or **Delete** and adjusting the X values in column A. (If you inserted rows, you also have to copy formulas down to those new rows.)

The worksheet features the **HYPERGEOMDIST(X, n, A, N)** function, in which X is the number of successes, n is the sample size, A is the number of successes in the population, and N is the population size.

	A	B	
1	**Team Formation Analysis**		
2			
3	**Data**		
4	Sample size	8	
5	No. of successes in population	10	
6	Population size	30	
7			
8	**Hypergeometric Probabilities Table**		
9	X	P(X)	
10	0	0.0215	=HYPGEOMDIST(A10, $B$4, $B$5, $B$6)
11	1	0.1324	=HYPGEOMDIST(A11, $B$4, $B$5, $B$6)
12	2	0.2980	=HYPGEOMDIST(A12, $B$4, $B$5, $B$6)
13	3	0.3179	=HYPGEOMDIST(A13, $B$4, $B$5, $B$6)
14	4	0.1738	=HYPGEOMDIST(A14, $B$4, $B$5, $B$6)
15	5	0.0491	=HYPGEOMDIST(A15, $B$4, $B$5, $B$6)
16	6	0.0068	=HYPGEOMDIST(A16, $B$4, $B$5, $B$6)
17	7	0.0004	=HYPGEOMDIST(A17, $B$4, $B$5, $B$6)
18	8	0.0000	=HYPGEOMDIST(A18, $B$4, $B$5, $B$6)

FIGURE E5.6 Hypergeometric worksheet

E5.6 CREATING HISTOGRAMS FOR DISCRETE PROBABILITY DISTRIBUTIONS

You can create histograms for discrete probability distributions using Excel charting features and your copy of the Binomial, Poisson, or Hypergeometric worksheets discussed in the previous three sections.

The PHStat2 Binomial, Poisson, and Hypergeometric procedures can create a histogram for you when you click the Histogram output option of those procedures.

To create a histogram, open to your discrete probability worksheet and use the appropriate set of instructions.

Creating Histograms (97–2003)

Begin the Chart Wizard (see Section E2.2) and make the following entries and choices in the step dialog boxes:

Step 1 Click the **Standard Types** tab and then click **Column** as the **Chart type**. Select the first **Chart subtype**, labeled **Clustered Column** when selected.

Step 2 Click the **Data Range** tab. Enter the cell range of the P(X) values as the **Data range** and click the **Columns** option in the **Series in** group. Click the **Series** tab. Enter the cell range of the X values as a formula in the **Category (X) axis labels** box, using the *Sheetname!CellRange* format. For the **Binomial** worksheet of Figure E5.4, enter **B14:B18** as the **Data range** and **=Binomial!A14:A18** as the **Category (X) axis labels**. For the **Poisson** worksheet of Figure E5.5, enter **B8:B28** as the **Data range** and **=Poisson!A8:A28** as the **Category (X) axis labels**. For the **Hypergeometric** worksheet of Figure E5.6, enter **B10:B18** as the **Data range** and **=Hypergeometric!A10:A18** as the **Category (X) axis labels**.

Step 3 Click the **Titles** tab. Enter a title as the **Chart title** edit box, enter **Number of Successes (X)** as the **Category**

(X) axis title, and enter **P(X)** as the **Value (Y) axis** title. Use the formatting settings for the **Axes, Gridlines, Legend, Data Labels**, and **Data Table** tabs that are given in the "Creating Charts (97–2003)" part of Section E2.2 on page 79.

Because the histogram is for a discrete probability distribution, the histogram bars should appear as spikes. To narrow the histogram bars to approximate spikes, right-click one of the histogram bars. (You will see a ToolTip that begins with "Series 'Frequency' " when your mouse is properly positioned.) Click **Format Data Series** in the shortcut menu. In the Format Data Series dialog box, click the **Options** tab, change the value of **Gap width** to **500**, and click **OK**.

Creating Histograms (2007)

Select the cell range that contains the P(X) values (exclusive of the P(X) label). Then select **Insert → Column → Clustered Column**. Right-click the chart that appears and click **Edit Data Source** in the shortcut menu. In the Edit Data Source dialog box, click the **Edit** button under the **Horizontal (Categories) Axis Labels** heading, enter the cell range of the X values (exclusive of the X label) as a formula in the form *=SheetName!CellRange*, and click **OK**. Click **OK** (in the Edit Data Source dialog box) to complete this task. Relocate your chart to a chart sheet and customize your chart by using the instructions in "Creating Charts (2007)" in Section E2.2 on page 80.

For the **Binomial** worksheet of Figure E5.4, initially select **B14:B18** and then enter **=Binomial!A14:A18** as the **Horizontal (Categories) Axis Labels**. For the **Poisson** worksheet of Figure E5.5, select **B8:B28** and then enter **=Poisson!A8:A28**. For the **Hypergeometric** worksheet of Figure E5.6, select **B10:B18** and then enter **=Hypergeometric!A10:A18**.

CHAPTER 6

The Normal Distribution and Other Continuous Distributions

USING STATISTICS @ OurCampus!

LEARNING OBJECTIVES

In this chapter, you learn:

- To compute probabilities from the normal distribution
- To use the normal probability plot to determine whether a set of data is approximately normally distributed
- To compute probabilities from the uniform distribution
- To compute probabilities from the exponential distribution

USING STATISTICS @ OurCampus!

You are a designer for the OurCampus! Web site, which targets college students. To attract and retain users, you need to make sure that the home page downloads quickly. Both the design of the home page and the load on the company's Web servers affect the download time. To check how fast the home page loads, you open a Web browser on a PC at the corporate offices of OurCampus! and measure the download time—the number of seconds that pass from first linking to the Web site until the home page is fully displayed.

Past data indicate that the mean download time is 7 seconds and that the standard deviation is 2 seconds. Approximately two-thirds of the download times are between 5 and 9 seconds, and about 95% of the download times are between 3 and 11 seconds. In other words, the download times are distributed as a bell-shaped curve, with a clustering around the mean of 7 seconds. How could you use this information to answer questions about the download times of the current home page?

In Chapter 5, Saxon Home Improvement Company managers wanted to be able to solve problems about the number of occurrences of a certain type of outcome in a given sample size. As an OurCampus! Web designer, you face a different task, one that involves a continuous measurement because a download time could be any value and not just a whole number. How can you answer questions about this *continuous numerical variable*, such as:

- What proportion of the home page downloads take more than 10 seconds?
- How many seconds elapse before 10% of the downloads are complete?
- How many seconds elapse before 99% of the downloads are complete?
- How would redesigning the home page to download faster affect the answers to these questions?

As in Chapter 5, you can use a probability distribution as a model. Reading this chapter will help you learn about characteristics of a continuous probability distribution and how to use the normal, uniform, and exponential distributions to solve business problems.

6.1 CONTINUOUS PROBABILITY DISTRIBUTIONS

A **continuous probability density function** is the mathematical expression that defines the distribution of the values for a continuous random variable. Figure 6.1 graphically displays the three continuous probability density functions discussed in this chapter.

FIGURE 6.1

Three continuous distributions

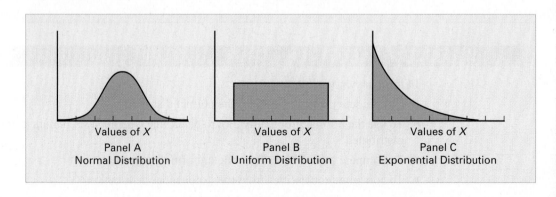

Values of X	Values of X	Values of X
Panel A	Panel B	Panel C
Normal Distribution	Uniform Distribution	Exponential Distribution

Panel A depicts a normal distribution. The normal distribution is symmetrical and bell shaped, implying that most values tend to cluster around the mean, which, due to the distribution's symmetrical shape, is equal to the median. Although the values in a normal distribution can range from negative infinity to positive infinity, the shape of the distribution makes it very unlikely that extremely large or extremely small values will occur.

Panel B depicts a uniform distribution where each value has an equal probability of occurrence anywhere in the range between the smallest value, *a*, and the largest value, *b*. Sometimes referred to as the rectangular distribution, the uniform distribution is symmetrical and therefore the mean equals the median.

Panel C illustrates an exponential distribution. This distribution is skewed to the right, making the mean larger than the median. The range for an exponential distribution is zero to positive infinity, but the distribution's shape makes the occurrence of extremely large values unlikely.

6.2   THE NORMAL DISTRIBUTION

The **normal distribution** (sometimes referred to as the *Gaussian distribution*) is the most common continuous distribution used in statistics. The normal distribution is vitally important in statistics for three main reasons:

- Numerous continuous variables common in business have distributions that closely resemble the normal distribution.
- The normal distribution can be used to approximate various discrete probability distributions.
- The normal distribution provides the basis for *classical statistical inference* because of its relationship to the *Central Limit Theorem* (which is discussed in Section 7.4).

The normal distribution is represented by the classic bell shape depicted in Panel A of Figure 6.1. In the normal distribution, you can calculate the probability that various values occur within certain ranges or intervals. However, the *exact* probability of a *particular value* from a continuous distribution such as the normal distribution is zero. This property distinguishes continuous variables, which are measured, from discrete variables, which are counted. As an example, time (in seconds) is measured and not counted. Therefore, you can determine the probability that the download time for a home page on a Web browser is between 7 and 10 seconds, or the probability that the download time is between 8 and 9 seconds, or the probability that the download time is between 7.99 and 8.01 seconds. However, the probability that the download time is *exactly* 8 seconds is zero.

The normal distribution has several important theoretical properties:

- It is bell shaped (and thus symmetrical) in its appearance.
- Its measures of central tendency (mean, median, and mode) are equal.
- Its interquartile range is equal to 1.33 standard deviations. This means that the middle 50% of the values are contained within an interval of two-thirds of a standard deviation below the mean and two-thirds of a standard deviation above the mean.
- It has an infinite range ($-\infty < X < \infty$).

In practice, many variables have distributions that closely resemble the theoretical properties of the normal distribution. The data in Table 6.1 represent the thickness (in inches) of 10,000 brass washers manufactured by a large company. The continuous variable of interest, thickness, can be approximated by the normal distribution. The measurements of the thickness of the 10,000 brass washers cluster in the interval 0.0190 to 0.0192 inch and distribute symmetrically around that grouping, forming a bell-shaped pattern.

TABLE 6.1

Thickness of 10,000
Brass Washers

Thickness (inches)	Relative Frequency
< 0.0180	48/10,000 = 0.0048
0.0180 < 0.0182	122/10,000 = 0.0122
0.0182 < 0.0184	325/10,000 = 0.0325
0.0184 < 0.0186	695/10,000 = 0.0695
0.0186 < 0.0188	1,198/10,000 = 0.1198
0.0188 < 0.0190	1,664/10,000 = 0.1664
0.0190 < 0.0192	1,896/10,000 = 0.1896
0.0192 < 0.0194	1,664/10,000 = 0.1664
0.0194 < 0.0196	1,198/10,000 = 0.1198
0.0196 < 0.0198	695/10,000 = 0.0695
0.0198 < 0.0200	325/10,000 = 0.0325
0.0200 < 0.0202	122/10,000 = 0.0122
0.0202 or above	48/10,000 = 0.0048
Total	1.0000

Figure 6.2 shows the relative frequency histogram and polygon for the distribution of the thickness of 10,000 brass washers. For these data, the first three theoretical properties of the normal distribution are approximately satisfied; however, the fourth one, having an infinite range, does not hold. The thickness of the washer cannot possibly be zero or below, nor can a washer be so thick that it becomes unusable. From Table 6.1, you see that only 48 out of every 10,000 brass washers manufactured are expected to have a thickness of 0.0202 inch or more, whereas an equal number are expected to have a thickness under 0.0180 inch. Thus, the chance of randomly getting a washer so thin or so thick is 0.0048 + 0.0048 = 0.0096, less than 1 in 100.

FIGURE 6.2

Relative frequency
histogram and polygon
of the thickness of
10,000 brass washers

*Source: Data are taken
from Table 6.1.*

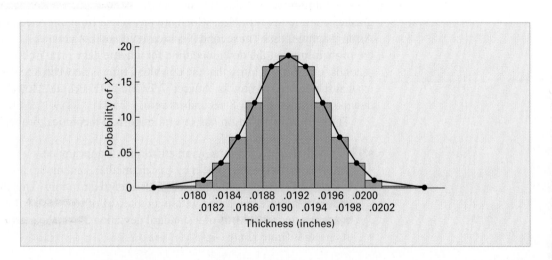

The mathematical expression representing a continuous probability density function is denoted by the symbol *f(X)*. For the normal distribution, the **normal probability density function** is given in Equation (6.1).

NORMAL PROBABILITY DENSITY FUNCTION

$$f(X) = \frac{1}{\sqrt{2\pi}\sigma} e^{-(1/2)[(X-\mu)/\sigma]^2} \tag{6.1}$$

where

> e = the mathematical constant approximated by 2.71828
>
> π = the mathematical constant approximated by 3.14159
>
> μ = the mean
>
> σ = the standard deviation
>
> X = any value of the continuous variable, where $-\infty < X < \infty$

Because e and π are mathematical constants, the probabilities of the random variable X are dependent only on the two parameters of the normal distribution—the mean, μ, and the standard deviation, σ. Every time you specify a *particular combination* of μ and σ, a *different* normal probability distribution is generated. Figure 6.3 illustrates three different normal distributions.

FIGURE 6.3

Three normal distributions

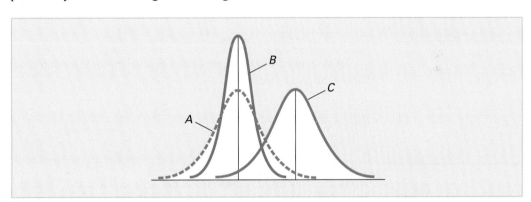

Distributions A and B have the same mean (μ) but have different standard deviations. Distributions A and C have the same standard deviation (σ) but have different means. Distributions B and C differ with respect to both μ and σ.

The mathematical expression in Equation (6.1) is computationally tedious and requires integral calculus. Fortunately, normal probability tables are available, and you can avoid the complicated computations of Equation (6.1). The first step in finding normal probabilities is to use the **transformation formula**, given in Equation (6.2), to convert any normal random variable, X, to a **standardized normal random variable**, Z.

TRANSFORMATION FORMULA

The Z value is equal to the difference between X and the mean, μ, divided by the standard deviation, σ.

$$Z = \frac{X - \mu}{\sigma} \tag{6.2}$$

Although the original data for the random variable X had mean μ and standard deviation σ, the standardized random variable, Z, will always have mean $\mu = 0$ and standard deviation $\sigma = 1$. By substituting $\mu = 0$ and $\sigma = 1$ in Equation (6.1), the probability density function of a standardized normal variable Z is given in Equation (6.3).

STANDARDIZED NORMAL PROBABILITY DENSITY FUNCTION

$$f(Z) = \frac{1}{\sqrt{2\pi}} e^{-(1/2)Z^2}$$

(6.3)

Any set of normally distributed values can be converted to its standardized form. Then you can determine the desired probabilities by using Table E.2, the **cumulative standardized normal distribution**.

To see how the transformation formula is applied and the results are used to find probabilities from Table E.2, recall from the Using Statistics scenario on page 218 that past data indicate that the time to download the Web page is normally distributed, with a mean, μ, of 7 seconds and a standard deviation, σ, of 2 seconds. From Figure 6.4, you see that every measurement, X, has a corresponding standardized measurement, Z, computed from the transformation formula [Equation (6.2)]. Therefore, a download time of 9 seconds is equivalent to 1 standardized unit (that is, 1 standard deviation above the mean) because

$$Z = \frac{9-7}{2} = +1$$

A download time of 1 second is equivalent to 3 standardized units (3 standard deviations) below the mean because

$$Z = \frac{1-7}{2} = -3$$

Thus, the standard deviation is the unit of measurement. In other words, a time of 9 seconds is 2 seconds (that is, 1 standard deviation) higher, or *slower*, than the mean time of 7 seconds. Similarly, a time of 1 second is 6 seconds (that is, 3 standard deviations) lower, or *faster*, than the mean time.

FIGURE 6.4

Transformation of scales

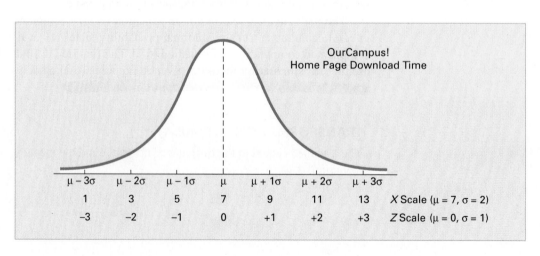

To further illustrate the transformation formula, suppose that the home page of another Web site has a download time that is normally distributed, with a mean, μ, of 4 seconds and a standard deviation, σ, of 1 second. This distribution is illustrated in Figure 6.5.

FIGURE 6.5

A different transformation of scales

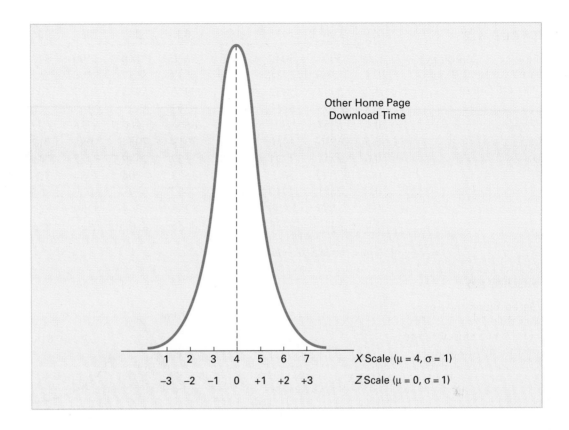

Other Home Page Download Time

X Scale ($\mu = 4$, $\sigma = 1$)

Z Scale ($\mu = 0$, $\sigma = 1$)

Comparing these results with those of the OurCampus! Web site, you see that a download time of 5 seconds is 1 standard deviation above the mean download time because

$$Z = \frac{5-4}{1} = +1$$

A time of 1 second is 3 standard deviations below the mean download time because

$$Z = \frac{1-4}{1} = -3$$

Suppose you wanted to find the probability that the download time for the OurCampus! site is less than 9 seconds. First, you use Equation (6.2) on page 221 to transform $X = 9$ to standardized Z units. Because $X = 9$ is one standard deviation above the mean, $Z = +1.00$. Next, you use Table E.2 to find the cumulative area under the normal curve less than (that is, to the left of) $Z = +1.00$. To read the probability or area under the curve less than $Z = +1.00$, you scan down the Z column from Table E.2 until you locate the Z value of interest (in 10ths) in the Z row for 1.0. Next, you read across this row until you intersect the column that contains the 100ths place of the Z value. Therefore, in the body of the table, the tabulated probability for $Z = 1.00$ corresponds to the intersection of the row $Z = 1.0$ with the column $Z = .00$, as shown in Table 6.2, which is extracted from Table E.2. This probability is 0.8413. As illustrated in Figure 6.6, there is an 84.13% chance that the download time will be less than 9 seconds.

TABLE 6.2

Finding a Cumulative Area Under the Normal Curve

Z	.00	.01	.02	.03	.04	.05	.06	.07	.08	.09
0.0	.5000	.5040	.5080	.5120	.5160	.5199	.5239	.5279	.5319	.5359
0.1	.5398	.5438	.5478	.5517	.5557	.5596	.5636	.5675	.5714	.5753
0.2	.5793	.5832	.5871	.5910	.5948	.5987	.6026	.6064	.6103	.6141
0.3	.6179	.6217	.6255	.6293	.6331	.6368	.6406	.6443	.6480	.6517
0.4	.6554	.6591	.6628	.6664	.6700	.6736	.6772	.6808	.6844	.6879
0.5	.6915	.6950	.6985	.7019	.7054	.7088	.7123	.7157	.7190	.7224
0.6	.7257	.7291	.7324	.7357	.7389	.7422	.7454	.7486	.7518	.7549
0.7	.7580	.7612	.7642	.7673	.7704	.7734	.7764	.7794	.7823	.7852
0.8	.7881	.7910	.7939	.7967	.7995	.8023	.8051	.8078	.8106	.8133
0.9	.8159	.8186	.8212	.8238	.8264	.8289	.8315	.8340	.8365	.8389
1.0	.8413	.8438	.8461	.8485	.8508	.8531	.8554	.8577	.8599	.8621

Source: Extracted from Table E.2.

FIGURE 6.6

Determining the area less than Z from a cumulative standardized normal distribution

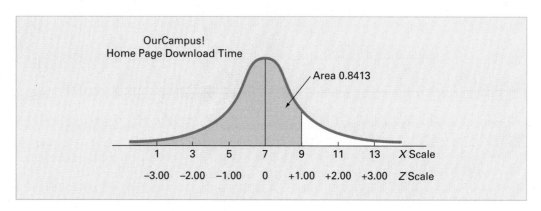

However, for the other home page, you see that a time of 5 seconds is 1 standardized unit above the mean time of 4 seconds. Thus, the probability that the download time will be less than 5 seconds is also 0.8413. Figure 6.7 shows that regardless of the value of the mean, μ, and standard deviation, σ, of a normally distributed variable, Equation (6.2) can transform the problem to Z values.

FIGURE 6.7

Demonstrating a transformation of scales for corresponding cumulative portions under two normal curves

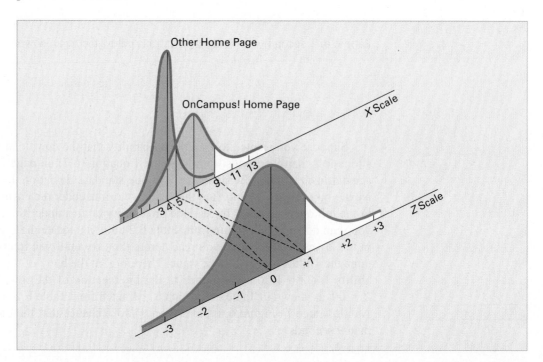

Now that you have learned to use Table E.2 with Equation (6.2), you can answer many questions related to the OurCampus! home page, using the normal distribution.

EXAMPLE 6.1

FINDING $P(X > 9)$

What is the probability that the download time will be more than 9 seconds?

SOLUTION The probability that the download time will be less than 9 seconds is 0.8413 (see Figure 6.6 on page 224). Thus, the probability that the download time will be more than 9 seconds is the *complement* of less than 9 seconds, $1 - 0.8413 = 0.1587$. Figure 6.8 illustrates this result.

FIGURE 6.8

Finding $P(X > 9)$

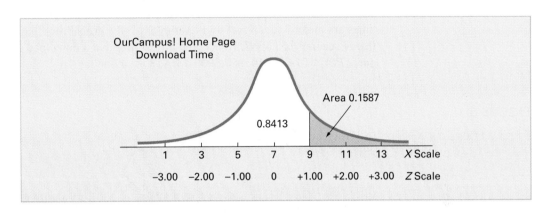

EXAMPLE 6.2

FINDING $P(7 < X < 9)$

What is the probability that the download time will be between 7 and 9 seconds?

SOLUTION From Figure 6.6 on page 224, you already determined that the probability that a download time will be less than 9 seconds is 0.8413. Now you must determine the probability that the download time will be under 7 seconds and subtract this from the probability that the download time is under 9 seconds. This is shown in Figure 6.9.

FIGURE 6.9

Finding $P(7 < X < 9)$

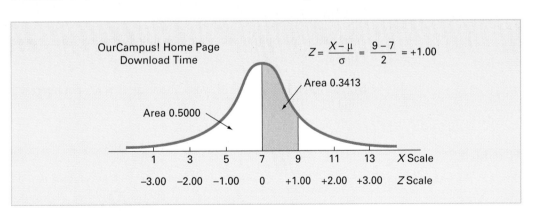

Using Equation (6.2) on page 221,

$$Z = \frac{7 - 7}{2} = 0.00$$

Using Table E.2, the area under the normal curve less than the mean of $Z = 0.00$ is 0.5000. Hence, the area under the curve between $Z = 0.00$ and $Z = 1.00$ is $0.8413 - 0.5000 = 0.3413$.

EXAMPLE 6.3

FINDING $P(X < 7$ OR $X > 9)$

What is the probability that the download time is under 7 seconds or over 9 seconds?

SOLUTION From Figure 6.9, the probability that the download time is between 7 and 9 seconds is 0.3413. The probability that the download time is under 7 seconds or over 9 seconds is its complement, $1 - 0.3413 = 0.6587$.

Another way to view this problem, however, is to separately calculate the probability of a download time of less than 7 seconds and the probability of a download time of greater than 9 seconds and then add these two probabilities together. Figure 6.10 illustrates this result. Because the mean and median are the same for normally distributed data, 50% of download times are under 7 seconds. From Example 6.1, the probability that the download time is greater than 9 seconds is 0.1587. Hence, the probability that a download time is under 7 or over 9 seconds, $P(X < 7$ or $X > 9)$, is $0.5000 + 0.1587 = 0.6587$.

FIGURE 6.10

Finding $P(X < 7$ or $X > 9)$

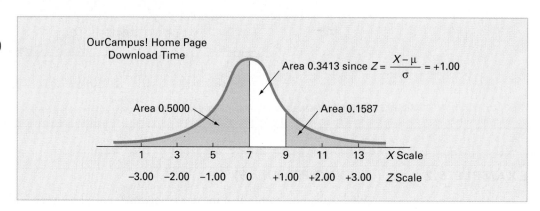

EXAMPLE 6.4

FINDING $P(5 < X < 9)$

What is the probability that the download time will be between 5 and 9 seconds—that is, $P(5 < X < 9)$?

SOLUTION In Figure 6.11, you can see that the area of interest is located between two values, 5 and 9.

FIGURE 6.11

Finding $P(5 < X < 9)$

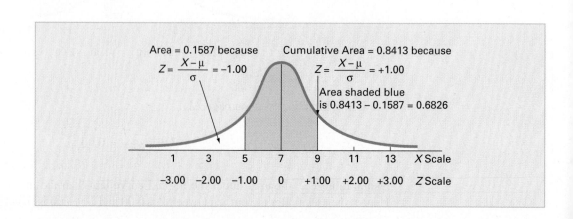

In Example 6.1 on page 225, you already found that the area under the normal curve less than 9 seconds is 0.8413. To find the area under the normal curve less than 5 seconds,

$$Z = \frac{5 - 7}{2} = -1.00$$

Using Table E.2, you look up $Z = -1.00$ and find 0.1587. Thus, the probability that the download time will be between 5 and 9 seconds is $0.8413 - 0.1587 = 0.6826$, as displayed in Figure 6.11.

The result of Example 6.4 enables you to state that for any normal distribution, 68.26% of the values will fall within ±1 standard deviation of the mean. From Figure 6.12, slightly more than 95% of the values will fall within ±2 standard deviations of the mean. Thus, 95.44% of the download times are between 3 and 11 seconds. From Figure 6.13, 99.73% of the values will fall within ±3 standard deviations above or below the mean. Thus, 99.73% of the download times are between 1 and 13 seconds. Therefore, it is unlikely (0.0027, or only 27 in 10,000) that a download time will be so fast or so slow that it will take under 1 second or more than 13 seconds. This is why 6σ (that is, 3 standard deviations above the mean to 3 standard deviations below the mean) is often used as a *practical approximation of the range* for normally distributed data.

FIGURE 6.12

Finding $P(3 < X < 11)$

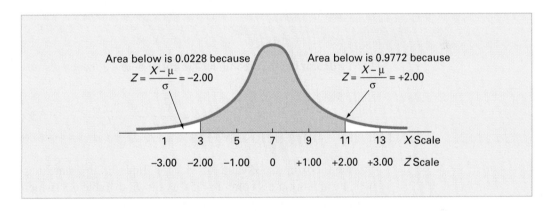

FIGURE 6.13

Finding $P(1 < X < 13)$

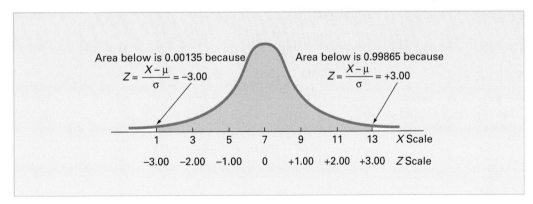

Figures 6.11, 6.12, and 6.13 illustrate how the values of a normal distribution cluster near the mean. For any normal distribution:

- Approximately 68.26% of the values fall within ±1 standard deviation of the mean.
- Approximately 95.44% of the values fall within ±2 standard deviations of the mean.
- Approximately 99.73% of the values fall within ±3 standard deviations of the mean.

This result is the justification for the empirical rule presented on page 120. The accuracy of the empirical rule improves as a data set follows the normal distribution more closely.

EXAMPLE 6.5

FINDING $P(X < 3.5)$

What is the probability that a download time will be under 3.5 seconds?

SOLUTION To calculate the probability that a download time will be under 3.5 seconds, you need to examine the shaded lower-left tail region of Figure 6.14.

FIGURE 6.14

Finding $P(X < 3.5)$

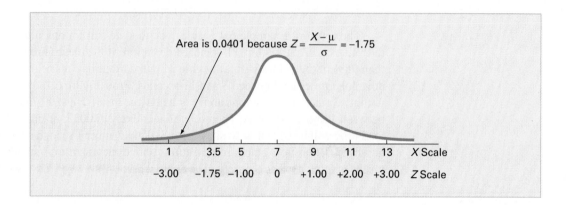

To determine the area under the curve below 3.5 seconds, you first calculate

$$Z = \frac{X - \mu}{\sigma} = \frac{3.5 - 7}{2} = -1.75$$

You then look up the Z value of -1.75 in Table E.2 by matching the appropriate Z row (-1.7) with the appropriate Z column (.05), as shown in Table 6.3 (which is extracted from Table E.2). The resulting probability or area under the curve less than -1.75 standard deviations below the mean is 0.0401.

TABLE 6.3

Finding a Cumulative Area Under the Normal Curve

Z	.00	.01	.02	.03	.04	.05	.06	.07	.08	.09
.	.	.	.	.	.	.	.	.	.	.
.	.	.	.	.	.	.	.	.	.	.
.	.	.	.	.	.	.	.	.	.	.
−1.7	.0446	.0436	.0427	.0418	.0409	.0401	.0392	.0384	.0375	.0367
−1.6	.0548	.0537	.0526	.0516	.0505	.0495	.0485	.0475	.0465	.0455

Source: Extracted from Table E.2.

Examples 6.1 through 6.5 require you to use the normal table to find an area under the normal curve that corresponds to a specific X value. There are many circumstances under which you want to find the X value that corresponds to a specific area. Examples 6.6 and 6.7 illustrate such situations.

VISUAL EXPLORATIONS Exploring the Normal Distribution

You use the Normal Distribution command of Visual Explorations to see the effects of changes in the mean and standard deviation on the area under a normal distribution curve.

Open the Visual explorations.xla add-in workbook and select **VisualExplorations → Normal** (Excel 97–2003) or **Add-Ins → Visual Explorations → Normal Distribution** (Excel 2007). You will see a normal curve for the Using Statistics home page download example and a floating control panel that allows you to adjust the shape of the curve

and the shaded area under the curve (see illustration below). Use the control panel spinner buttons to change the values for the mean, standard deviation, and X value, while noting their effects on the probability of X < = value and the corresponding shaded area under the curve (see illustration below). If you prefer, you can select the Z **Values** option button to see the normal curve labeled with Z values.

Click the **Reset** button to reset the control panel values or click **Help** for additional information about the problem. Click **Finish** when you are done exploring.

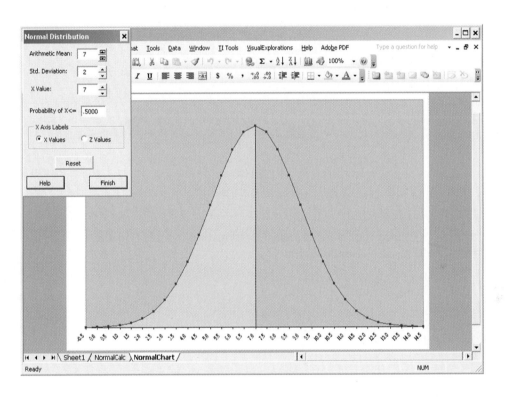

| EXAMPLE 6.6 | FINDING THE X VALUE FOR A CUMULATIVE PROBABILITY OF 0.10 |

How much time (in seconds) will elapse before 10% of the downloads are complete?

SOLUTION Because 10% of the home pages are expected to download in under X seconds, the area under the normal curve less than this value is 0.1000. Using the body of Table E.2, you search for the area or probability of 0.1000. The closest result is 0.1003, as shown in Table 6.4 (which is extracted from Table E.2).

TABLE 6.4

Finding a Z Value Corresponding to a Particular Cumulative Area (0.10) Under the Normal Curve

Z	.00	.01	.02	.03	.04	.05	.06	.07	.08	.09
.	.	.	.	.	.	.	.	.	.	.
.	.	.	.	.	.	.	.	.	.	.
.	.	.	.	.	.	.	.	.	.	.
−1.5	.0668	.0655	.0643	.0630	.0618	.0606	.0594	.0582	.0571	.0559
−1.4	.0808	.0793	.0778	.0764	.0749	.0735	.0721	.0708	.0694	.0681
−1.3	.0968	.0951	.0934	.0918	.0901	.0885	.0869	.0853	.0838	.0823
−1.2	.1151	.1131	.1112	.1093	.1075	.0156	.0138	.1020	.1003	.0985

Source: Extracted from Table E.2.

Working from this area to the margins of the table, the Z value corresponding to the particular Z row (−1.2) and Z column (.08) is −1.28 (see Figure 6.15).

FIGURE 6.15

Finding Z to determine X

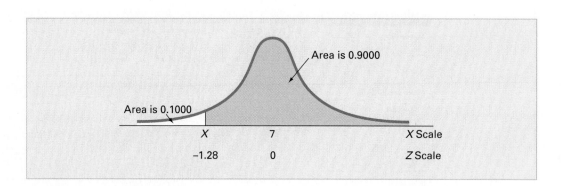

Once you find Z, use the transformation formula Equation (6.2) on page 221 to determine the X value, as follows. Let

$$Z = \frac{X - \mu}{\sigma}$$

then

$$X = \mu + Z\sigma$$

Substituting $\mu = 7$, $\sigma = 2$, and $Z = -1.28$,

$$X = 7 + (-1.28)(2) = 4.44 \text{ seconds}$$

Thus, 10% of the download times are 4.44 seconds or less.

Equation (6.4) is used for finding an X value.

FINDING AN X VALUE ASSOCIATED WITH KNOWN PROBABILITY

The X value is equal to the mean μ plus the product of the Z value and the standard deviation σ.

$$X = \mu + Z\sigma \tag{6.4}$$

To find a *particular* value associated with a known probability, follow these steps:

1. Sketch the normal curve and then place the values for the mean and X value on the X and Z scales.
2. Find the cumulative area less than X.
3. Shade the area of interest.
4. Using Table E.2, determine the Z value corresponding to the area under the normal curve less than X.
5. Using Equation (6.4), solve for X:

$$X = \mu + Z\sigma$$

EXAMPLE 6.7

FINDING THE X VALUES THAT INCLUDE 95% OF THE DOWNLOAD TIMES

What are the lower and upper values of X, symmetrically distributed around the mean, that include 95% of the download times?

SOLUTION First, you need to find the lower value of X (called X_L). Then you find the upper value of X (called X_U). Because 95% of the values are between X_L and X_U, and because X_L and X_U are equally distant from the mean, 2.5% of the values are below X_L (see Figure 6.16).

FIGURE 6.16

Finding Z to determine X_L

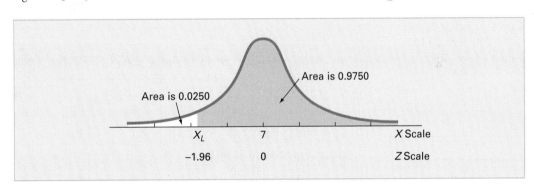

Although X_L is not known, you can find the corresponding Z value because the area under the normal curve less than this Z is 0.0250. Using the body of Table 6.5, you search for the probability 0.0250.

TABLE 6.5

Finding a Z Value Corresponding to a Cumulative Area of 0.025 Under the Normal Curve

Z	.00	.01	.02	.03	.04	.05	.06	.07	.08	.09
.	.	.	.	.	.	.	.	.	.	.
.	.	.	.	.	.	.	.	.	.	.
.	.	.	.	.	.	.	.	.	.	.
−2.0	.0228	.0222	.0217	.0212	.0207	.0202	.0197	.0192	.0188	.0183
−1.9	.0287	.0281	.0274	.0268	.0262	.0256	.0250	.0244	.0239	.0233
−1.8	.0359	.0351	.0344	.0336	.0329	.0232	.0314	.0307	.0301	.0294

Source: Extracted from Table E.2.

Working from the body of the table to the margins of the table, you see that the Z value corresponding to the particular Z row (−1.9) and Z column (.06) is −1.96.

Once you find Z, the final step is to use Equation (6.4) on page 230 as follows:

$$X = \mu + Z\sigma$$
$$= 7 + (-1.96)(2)$$
$$= 7 - 3.92$$
$$= 3.08 \text{ seconds}$$

You use a similar process to find X_U. Because only 2.5% of the home page downloads take longer than X_U seconds, 97.5% of the home page downloads take less than X_U seconds. From the symmetry of the normal distribution, the desired Z value, as shown in Figure 6.17, is +1.96 (because Z lies to the right of the standardized mean of 0). You can also extract this Z value from Table 6.6. You can see that 0.975 is the area under the normal curve less than the Z value of +1.96.

FIGURE 6.17

Finding Z to determine X_U

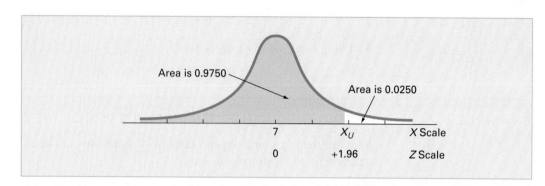

TABLE 6.6

Finding a Z Value Corresponding to a Cumulative Area of 0.975 Under the Normal Curve

Z	.00	.01	.02	.03	.04	.05	.06	.07	.08	.09
.	.	.	.	.	.	.	.	.	.	.
.	.	.	.	.	.	.	.	.	.	.
.	.	.	.	.	.	.	.	.	.	.
+1.8	.9641	.9649	.9656	.9664	.9671	.9678	.9686	.9693	.9699	.9706
+1.9	.9713	.9719	.9726	.9732	.9738	.9744	.9750	.9756	.9761	.9767
+2.0	.9772	.9778	.9783	.9788	.9793	.9798	.9803	.9808	.9812	.9817

Source: Extracted from Table E.2.

Using Equation (6.4) on page 230,

$$X = \mu + Z\sigma$$
$$= 7 + (+1.96)(2)$$
$$= 7 + 3.92$$
$$= 10.92 \text{ seconds}$$

Therefore, 95% of the download times are between 3.08 and 10.92 seconds.

You can also use Microsoft Excel to compute normal probabilities. Figure 6.18 illustrates a Microsoft Excel worksheet for Examples 6.5 and 6.6.

FIGURE 6.18

Microsoft Excel worksheet for computing normal probabilities

See Section E6.1 to create this.

	A	B	
1	**Normal Probabilities**		
2			
3	**Common Data**		
4	Mean	7	
5	Standard Deviation	2	
6			
7	**Probability for X <=**		
8	X Value	3.5	
9	Z Value	-1.75	=STANDARDIZE(B8, B4, B5)
10	P(X<=3.5)	0.0401	=NORMDIST(B8, B4, B5, TRUE)
11			
12	**Find X and Z Given Cum. Pctage.**		
13	Cumulative Percentage	10.00%	
14	Z Value	-1.2816	=NORMSINV(B13)
15	X Value	4.4369	=NORMINV(B13, B4, B5)

PROBLEMS FOR SECTION 6.2

Learning the Basics

 6.1 Given a standardized normal distribution (with a mean of 0 and a standard deviation of 1, as in Table E.2), what is the probability that
a. Z is less than 1.57?
b. Z is greater than 1.84?
c. Z is between 1.57 and 1.84?
d. Z is less than 1.57 or greater than 1.84?

 6.2 Given a standardized normal distribution (with a mean of 0 and a standard deviation of 1, as in Table E.2), what is the probability that
a. Z is between −1.57 and 1.84?
b. Z is less than −1.57 or greater than 1.84?
c. What is the value of Z if only 2.5% of all possible Z values are larger?
d. Between what two values of Z (symmetrically distributed around the mean) will 68.26% of all possible Z values be contained?

 6.3 Given a standardized normal distribution (with a mean of 0 and a standard deviation of 1, as in Table E.2), what is the probability that
a. Z is less than 1.08?
b. Z is greater than −0.21?
c. Z is less than −0.21 or greater than the mean?
d. Z is less than −0.21 or greater than 1.08?

6.4 Given a standardized normal distribution (with a mean of 0 and a standard deviation of 1, as in Table E.2), determine the following probabilities:
a. $P(Z > 1.08)$
b. $P(Z < -0.21)$
c. $P(-1.96 < Z < -0.21)$
d. What is the value of Z if only 15.87% of all possible Z values are larger?

 6.5 Given a normal distribution with $\mu = 100$ and $\sigma = 10$, what is the probability that
a. $X > 75$?
b. $X < 70$?
c. $X < 80$ or $X > 110$?
d. 80% of the values are between what two X values (symmetrically distributed around the mean)?

 6.6 Given a normal distribution with $\mu = 50$ and $\sigma = 4$, what is the probability that
a. $X > 43$?
b. $X < 42$?
c. 5% of the values are less than what X value?
d. 60% of the values are between what two X values (symmetrically distributed around the mean)?

Applying the Concepts

6.7 In a recent year, about two-thirds of U.S. households purchased ground coffee. Consider the annual ground coffee expenditures for households purchasing ground coffee, assuming that these expenditures are approximately distributed as a normal random variable with a mean of $45.16 and a standard deviation of $10.00.
a. Find the probability that a household spent less than $25.00.
b. Find the probability that a household spent more than $50.00.
c. What proportion of the households spent between $30.00 and $40.00?
d. 99% of the households spent less than what amount?

 6.8 Toby's Trucking Company determined that the distance traveled per truck per year is normally distributed, with a mean of 50.0 thousand miles and a standard deviation of 12.0 thousand miles.
a. What proportion of trucks can be expected to travel between 34.0 and 50.0 thousand miles in the year?
b. What percentage of trucks can be expected to travel either below 30.0 or above 60.0 thousand miles in the year?
c. How many miles will be traveled by at least 80% of the trucks?
d. What are your answers to (a) through (c) if the standard deviation is 10.0 thousand miles?

 6.9 The breaking strength of plastic bags used for packaging produce is normally distributed, with a mean of 5 pounds per square inch and a standard deviation of 1.5 pounds per square inch. What proportion of the bags have a breaking strength of
a. less than 3.17 pounds per square inch?
b. at least 3.6 pounds per square inch?
c. between 5 and 5.5 pounds per square inch?
d. 95% of the breaking strengths will be contained between what two values symmetrically distributed around the mean?

6.10 A set of final examination grades in an introductory statistics course is normally distributed, with a mean of 73 and a standard deviation of 8.
a. What is the probability of getting a grade below 91 on this exam?
b. What is the probability that a student scored between 65 and 89?
c. The probability is 5% that a student taking the test scores higher than what grade?
d. If the professor grades on a curve (that is, gives A's to the top 10% of the class, regardless of the score), are you

better off with a grade of 81 on this exam or a grade of 68 on a different exam, where the mean is 62 and the standard deviation is 3? Show your answer statistically and explain.

6.11 A statistical analysis of 1,000 long-distance telephone calls made from the headquarters of the Bricks and Clicks Computer Corporation indicates that the length of these calls is normally distributed, with $\mu = 240$ seconds and $\sigma = 40$ seconds.

a. What is the probability that a call lasted less than 180 seconds?
b. What is the probability that a call lasted between 180 and 300 seconds?
c. What is the probability that a call lasted between 110 and 180 seconds?
d. What is the length of a call if only 1% of all calls are shorter?

6.12 The number of shares traded daily on the New York Stock Exchange (NYSE) is referred to as the *volume* of trading. During the first three months of 2006, daily volume ranged from 1.424 billion to 2.170 billion (NYSE Group, **www.nyse.com**, April 28, 2006). Assume that the number of shares traded on the NYSE is a normally distrib-

uted random variable, with a mean of 1.8 billion and a standard deviation of 0.15 billion. For a randomly selected day, what is the probability that the volume is
a. below 1.5 billion?
b. below 1.7 billion?
c. above 2.0 billion?
d. above 2.3 billion?

6.13 Many manufacturing problems involve the matching of machine parts, such as shafts that fit into a valve hole. A particular design requires a shaft with a diameter of 22.000 mm, but shafts with diameters between 21.900 mm and 22.010 mm are acceptable. Suppose that the manufacturing process yields shafts with diameters normally distributed, with a mean of 22.002 mm and a standard deviation of 0.005 mm. For this process, what is
a. the proportion of shafts with a diameter between 21.90 mm and 22.00 mm?
b. the probability that a shaft is acceptable?
c. the diameter that will be exceeded by only 2% of the shafts?
d. What would be your answers in (a) through (c) if the standard deviation of the shaft diameters was 0.004 mm?

6.3   EVALUATING NORMALITY

As discussed in Section 6.2, many continuous variables used in business closely follow a normal distribution. This section presents two approaches for evaluating whether a set of data can be approximated by the normal distribution:

1. Compare the characteristics of the data with the theoretical properties of the normal distribution.
2. Construct a normal probability plot.

Comparing Data Characteristics to Theoretical Properties

The normal distribution has several important theoretical properties:

- It is symmetrical; thus, the mean and median are equal.
- It is bell shaped; thus, the empirical rule applies.
- The interquartile range equals 1.33 standard deviations.

In actual practice, a continuous variable may have characteristics that approximate these theoretical properties. However, many continuous variables are neither normally distributed nor approximately normally distributed. For such variables, the descriptive characteristics of the data do not match well with the properties of a normal distribution. One approach to determining whether a data set follows a normal distribution is to compare the characteristics of the data with the corresponding properties from an underlying normal distribution, as follows:

- Construct charts and observe their appearance. For small- or moderate-sized data sets, construct a stem-and-leaf display or a box-and-whisker plot. For large data sets, construct the frequency distribution and plot the histogram or polygon.
- Compute descriptive numerical measures and compare the characteristics of the data with the theoretical properties of the normal distribution. Compare the mean and median. Is the

interquartile range approximately 1.33 times the standard deviation? Is the range approximately 6 times the standard deviation?

■ Evaluate how the values in the data are distributed. Determine whether approximately two-thirds of the values lie between the mean and ±1 standard deviation. Determine whether approximately four-fifths of the values lie between the mean and ±1.28 standard deviations. Determine whether approximately 19 out of every 20 values lie between the mean ±2 standard deviations.

Do the three-year returns discussed in Chapters 2 and 3 (see the **Mutual Funds.xls** file) contain the properties of the normal distribution? Figure 6.19 displays descriptive statistics for these data, and Figure 6.20 presents a box-and-whisker plot.

FIGURE 6.19

Microsoft Excel descriptive statistics for the three-year returns

See Section E3.1 to create this.

	A	B
1	**3 Year Return**	
2		
3	**Mean**	17.8
4	**Standard Error**	0.17099
5	**Median**	17.2
6	**Mode**	15.1
7	**Standard Deviation**	4.94991
8	**Sample Variance**	24.5016
9	**Kurtosis**	1.03812
10	**Skewness**	0.66073
11	**Range**	35.6
12	**Minimum**	6.7
13	**Maximum**	42.3
14	**Sum**	14916.4
15	**Count**	838
16	**Largest(1)**	42.3
17	**Smallest(1)**	6.7
18	**Confidence Level(95.0%)**	0.33562

FIGURE 6.20

Microsoft Excel box-and-whisker plot for the three-year returns

See Section E3.4 to create this.

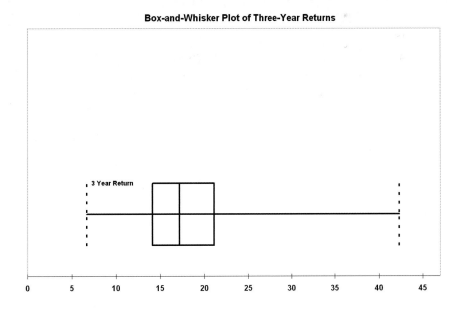

From Figures 6.19 and 6.20 and from an ordered array of the three-year returns (not shown here), you can make the following statements:

1. The mean of 17.8 is slightly higher than the median of 17.2. (In a normal distribution, the mean and median are equal.)

2. The box-and-whisker plot appears right-skewed, with an outlier at the maximum value of 42.3. (The normal distribution is symmetrical.)

3. The interquartile range of 7.0 is approximately 1.41 standard deviations. (In a normal distribution, the interquartile range is 1.33 standard deviations.)
4. The range of 35.6 is equal to 7.19 standard deviations. (In a normal distribution, the range is approximately six standard deviations.)
5. 74.2% of the returns are within ±1 standard deviation of the mean. (In a normal distribution, 68.26% of the values lie between the mean ±1 standard deviation.)
6. 83.3% of the returns are within ±1.28 standard deviations of the mean. (In a normal distribution, 80% of the values lie between the mean ±1.28 standard deviations.)

Based on these statements and the criteria given on pages 234–235, you can conclude that the three-year returns are right-skewed and are not normally distributed.

Constructing the Normal Probability Plot

A **normal probability plot** is a graphical approach for evaluating whether data are normally distributed. One common approach is called the **quantile–quantile plot**. In this method, you transform each ordered value to a Z value and then plot the data values versus the Z values. For example, if you have a sample of $n = 19$, the Z value for the smallest value corresponds to a cumulative area of $\dfrac{1}{n+1} = \dfrac{1}{19+1} = \dfrac{1}{20} = 0.05$. The Z value for a cumulative area of 0.05 (from Table E.2) is −1.65. Table 6.7 illustrates the entire set of Z values for a sample of $n = 19$.

TABLE 6.7

Ordered Values and Corresponding Z Values for a Sample of $n = 19$

Ordered Value	Z Value	Ordered Value	Z Value
1	−1.65	11	0.13
2	−1.28	12	0.25
3	−1.04	13	0.39
4	−0.84	14	0.52
5	−0.67	15	0.67
6	−0.52	16	0.84
7	−0.39	17	1.04
8	−0.25	18	1.28
9	−0.13	19	1.65
10	0.00		

The Z values are plotted on the X axis, and the corresponding values of the variable are plotted on the Y axis.

Figure 6.21 illustrates the typical shape of normal probability plots for a left-skewed distribution (Panel A), a normal distribution (Panel B), and a right-skewed distribution (Panel C). If the data are left-skewed, the curve will rise more rapidly at first and then level off. If the data are normally distributed, the points will plot along an approximately straight line. If the data are right-skewed, the data will rise more slowly at first and then rise at a faster rate for higher values of the variable being plotted.

FIGURE 6.21

Normal probability plots for a left-skewed distribution, a normal distribution, and a right-skewed distribution

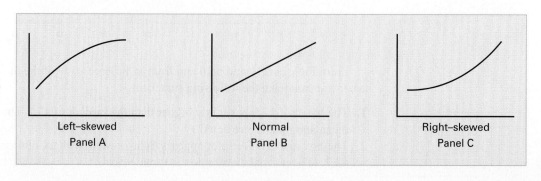

Left–skewed
Panel A

Normal
Panel B

Right–skewed
Panel C

Figure 6.22 shows a Microsoft Excel quantile–quantile normal probability plot for the three-year returns.

FIGURE 6.22

Microsoft Excel normal probability plot for three-year returns

See Section E6.2 to create this.

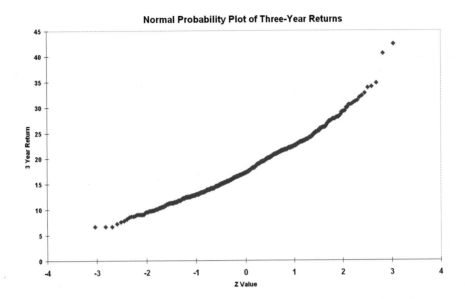

Figure 6.22 shows that the three-year returns rise more slowly at first and subsequently rise more rapidly. This occurs since the data are right-skewed. Thus, the data are not normally distributed.

PROBLEMS FOR SECTION 6.3

Learning the Basics

 6.14 Show that for a sample of $n = 39$, the smallest and largest Z values are -1.96 and $+1.96$, and the middle (that is, 20th) Z value is 0.00.

6.15 For a sample of $n = 6$, list the six Z values.

Applying the Concepts

 6.16 The data in the file chicken.xls contains the total fat, in grams per serving, for a sample of 20 chicken sandwiches from fast-food chains. The data are as follows:

7 8 4 5 16 20 20 24 19 30 23 30 25 19 29 29 30 30 40 56

Source: Extracted from "Fast Food: Adding Health to the Menu," Consumer Reports, September 2004, pp. 28–31.

Decide whether the data appear to be approximately normally distributed by
a. comparing data characteristics to theoretical properties.
b. constructing a normal probability plot.

6.17 A problem with a telephone line that prevents a customer from receiving or making calls is disconcerting to both the customer and the telephone company. The follow-

ing data (stored in the file phone.xls) represent two samples of 20 problems reported to two different offices of a telephone company. The time to clear these problems from the customers' lines is recorded, in minutes.

Central Office I Time to Clear Problems (Minutes)

1.48 1.75 0.78 2.85 0.52 1.60 4.15 3.97 1.48 3.10
1.02 0.53 0.93 1.60 0.80 1.05 6.32 3.93 5.45 0.97

Central Office II Time to Clear Problems (Minutes)

7.55 3.75 0.10 1.10 0.60 0.52 3.30 2.10 0.58 4.02
3.75 0.65 1.92 0.60 1.53 4.23 0.08 1.48 1.65 0.72

For each of the two central office locations, decide whether the data appear to be approximately normally distributed by
a. comparing data characteristics to theoretical properties.
b. constructing a normal probability plot.

6.18 Many manufacturing processes use the term *work-in-process* (often abbreviated as *WIP*). In a book manufacturing plant, the WIP represents the time it takes for sheets from a press to be folded, gathered, sewn, tipped on end sheets, and bound. The following data (stored in the file wip.xls) represent samples of 20 books at each of two production plants and the processing time (operationally defined as the time, in days, from when the books came off the press to when they were packed in cartons) for these jobs:

Plant A

5.62 5.29 16.25 10.92 11.46 21.62 8.45 8.58 5.41 11.42

11.62 7.29 7.50 7.96 4.42 10.50 7.58 9.29 7.54 18.92

Plant B

9.54 11.46 16.62 12.62 25.75 15.41 14.29 13.13 13.71 10.04

5.75 12.46 9.17 13.21 6.00 2.33 14.25 5.37 6.25 9.71

For each of the two plants, decide whether the data appear to be approximately normally distributed by
a. comparing data characteristics to theoretical properties.
b. constructing a normal probability plot.

6.19 The data in the file spending.xls represent the per capita spending, in thousands of dollars, for each state in 2004. Decide whether the data appear to be approximately normally distributed by
a. comparing data characteristics to theoretical properties.
b. constructing a normal probability plot.

6.20 One operation of a mill is to cut pieces of steel into parts that will later be used as the frame for front seats in an automotive plant. The steel is cut with a diamond saw and requires the resulting parts to be within ±0.005 inch of the length specified by the automobile company. The data come from a sample of 100 steel parts and are stored in the file steel.xls. The measurement reported is the difference, in inches, between the actual length of the steel part, as measured by a laser measurement device, and the specified length of the steel part.

Decide whether the data appear to be approximately normally distributed by
a. comparing data characteristics to theoretical properties.
b. constructing a normal probability plot.

6.21 The data in the file savings.xls are the yields for a money market account, a one-year certificate of deposit (CD), and a five-year CD for 40 banks in south Florida as of December 20, 2005 (extracted from **Bankrate.com**, December 20, 2005). For each of the three types of investments, decide whether the data appear to be approximately normally distributed by
a. comparing data characteristics to theoretical properties.
b. constructing a normal probability plot.

6.22 The following data, stored in the file utility.xls, represent the electricity costs in dollars, during July 2006 for a random sample of 50 two-bedroom apartments in a large city:

96	171	202	178	147	102	153	197	127	82
157	185	90	116	172	111	148	213	130	165
141	149	206	175	123	128	144	168	109	167
95	163	150	154	130	143	187	166	139	149
108	119	183	151	114	135	191	137	129	158

Decide whether the data appear to be approximately normally distributed by:
a. comparing data characteristics to theoretical properties.
b. constructing a normal probability plot.

6.4   THE UNIFORM DISTRIBUTION

In the **uniform distribution**, a value has the same probability of occurrence anywhere in the range between the smallest value, a, and the largest value, b. Because of its shape, the uniform distribution is sometimes called the **rectangular distribution** (see Panel B of Figure 6.1 on page 218). Equation (6.5) defines the continuous probability density function for the uniform distribution.

UNIFORM DISTRIBUTION

$$f(X) = \frac{1}{b - a} \text{ if } a \leq X \leq b \text{ and 0 elsewhere} \qquad \textbf{(6.5)}$$

where

a = the minimum value of X

b = the maximum value of X

Equation (6.6) defines the mean of the uniform distribution.

MEAN OF THE UNIFORM DISTRIBUTION

$$\mu = \frac{a + b}{2} \tag{6.6}$$

Equation (6.7) defines the variance and standard deviation of the uniform distribution.

VARIANCE AND STANDARD DEVIATION OF THE UNIFORM DISTRIBUTION

$$\sigma^2 = \frac{(b - a)^2}{12} \tag{6.7a}$$

$$\sigma = \sqrt{\frac{(b - a)^2}{12}} \tag{6.7b}$$

One of the most common uses of the uniform distribution is in the selection of random numbers. When you use simple random sampling (see Section 7.1), you assume that each value comes from a uniform distribution that has a minimum value of 0 and a maximum value of 1.

Figure 6.23 illustrates the uniform distribution with $a = 0$ and $b = 1$. The total area inside the rectangle is equal to the base (1.0) times the height (1.0). Thus, the resulting area of 1.0 satisfies the requirement that the area under any probability density function equals 1.0.

FIGURE 6.23

Probability density function for a uniform distribution with $a = 0$ and $b = 1$

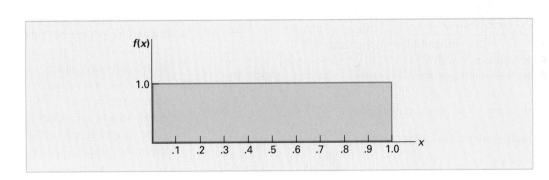

In such a distribution, what is the probability of getting a random number between 0.10 and 0.30? The area between 0.10 and 0.30, depicted in Figure 6.24, is equal to the base (which is $0.30 - 0.10 = 0.20$) times the height (1.0). Therefore,

$$P(0.10 < X < 0.30) = (\text{Base})(\text{Height}) = (0.20)(1.0) = 0.20$$

FIGURE 6.24

Finding $P(0.10 < X < 0.30)$ for a uniform distribution with $a = 0$ and $b = 1$

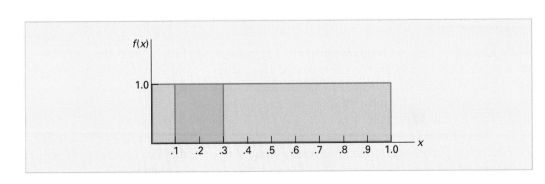

From Equations (6.6) and (6.7), the mean and standard deviation of the uniform distribution for $a = 0$ and $b = 1$ are computed as follows:

$$\mu = \frac{a + b}{2}$$

$$= \frac{0 + 1}{2} = 0.5$$

and

$$\sigma^2 = \frac{(b - a)^2}{12}$$

$$= \frac{(1 - 0)^2}{12}$$

$$= \frac{1}{12} = 0.0833$$

$$\sigma = \sqrt{0.0833} = 0.2887$$

Thus, the mean is 0.5 and the standard deviation is 0.2887.

PROBLEMS FOR SECTION 6.4

Learning the Basics

 6.23 Suppose you sample one value from a uniform distribution with $a = 0$ and $b = 10$. What is the probability that the value will be
a. between 5 and 7?
b. between 2 and 3?
c. What is the mean?
d. What is the standard deviation?

Applying the Concepts

 6.24 The time between arrivals of customers at a bank during the noon-to-1 p.m. hour has a uniform distribution between 0 to 120 seconds. What is the probability that the time between the arrival of two customers will be
a. less than 20 seconds?
b. between 10 and 30 seconds?
c. more than 35 seconds?
d. What are the mean and standard deviation of the time between arrivals?

6.25 A study of the time spent shopping in a supermarket for a market basket of 20 specific items showed an approximately uniform distribution between 20 minutes and 40 minutes. What is the probability that the shopping time will be
a. between 25 and 30 minutes?
b. less than 35 minutes?
c. What are the mean and standard deviation of the shopping time?

 6.26 The time to failure for a continuous-operation monitoring device of air quality has a uniform distribution over a 24-hour day.
a. If a failure occurs on a day when daylight is between 5:55 a.m. and 7:38 p.m., what is the probability that the failure will occur during daylight hours?
b. If the device is in secondary mode from 10 p.m. to 5 a.m., what is the probability that if a failure occurs, it will happen during secondary mode?
c. If the device has a self-checking computer chip that determines whether the device is operational every hour on the hour, what is the probability that a failure will be detected within 10 minutes of its occurrence?
d. If the device has a self-checking computer chip that determines whether the device is operational every hour on the hour, what is the probability that it will take at least 40 minutes to detect that a failure has occurred?

6.27 The scheduled commuting time on the Long Island Rail Road from Glen Cove to New York City is 65 minutes. Suppose that the actual commuting time is uniformly distributed between 64 and 74 minutes. What is the probability that the commuting time will be
a. less than 70 minutes?
b. between 65 and 70 minutes?
c. greater than 65 minutes?
d. What are the mean and standard deviation of the commuting time?

6.5   THE EXPONENTIAL DISTRIBUTION

The **exponential distribution** is a continuous distribution that is right-skewed and ranges from zero to positive infinity (see Panel C of Figure 6.1 on page 218). The exponential distribution is widely used in waiting-line (or queuing) theory to model the length of time between arrivals in processes such as customers at a bank's ATM, patients entering a hospital emergency room, and hits on a Web site.

The exponential distribution is defined by a single parameter, its mean, λ, the mean number of arrivals per unit of time. The value $1/\lambda$ is equal to the mean time between arrivals. For example, if the mean number of arrivals in a minute is $\lambda = 4$, then the mean time between arrivals is $1/\lambda = 0.25$ minutes, or 15 seconds. Equation (6.8) defines the probability that the length of time before the next arrival is less than X.

EXPONENTIAL DISTRIBUTION

$$P(\text{Arrival time} < X) = 1 - e^{-\lambda X} \qquad \textbf{(6.8)}$$

where

$e =$ the mathematical constant approximated by 2.71828

$\lambda =$ the mean number of arrivals per unit

$X =$ any value of the continuous variable where $0 < X < \infty$

To illustrate the exponential distribution, suppose that customers arrive at a bank's ATM at a rate of 20 per hour. If a customer has just arrived, what is the probability that the next customer will arrive within 6 minutes (that is, 0.1 hour)? For this example, $\lambda = 20$ and $X = 0.1$. Using Equation (6.8),

$$P(\text{Arrival time} < 0.1) = 1 - e^{-20(0.1)}$$
$$= 1 - e^{-2}$$
$$= 1 - 0.1353 = 0.8647$$

Thus, the probability that a customer will arrive within 6 minutes is 0.8647, or 86.47%. You can also use Microsoft Excel to compute this probability (see Figure 6.25).

FIGURE 6.25

Microsoft Excel worksheet for finding exponential probabilities (mean = λ)

See Section E6.3 to create this.

	A	B
1	**Exponential Probability**	
2		
3	**Data**	
4	**Mean**	20
5	**X Value**	0.1
6		
7	**Results**	
8	P(<=X)	0.8647

=EXPONDIST(B5, B4, TRUE)

EXAMPLE 6.8   COMPUTING EXPONENTIAL PROBABILITIES

In the ATM example, what is the probability that the next customer will arrive within 3 minutes (that is, 0.05 hour)?

SOLUTION For this example, $\lambda = 20$ and $X = 0.05$. Using Equation (6.8),

$$P(\text{Arrival time} < 0.05) = 1 - e^{-20(0.05)}$$

$$= 1 - e^{-1}$$

$$= 1 - 0.3679 = 0.6321$$

Thus, the probability that a customer will arrive within 3 minutes is 0.6321, or 63.21%.

PROBLEMS FOR SECTION 6.5

Learning the Basics

6.28 Given an exponential distribution with $\lambda = 10$, what is the probability that the arrival time is
a. less than $X = 0.1$?
b. greater than $X = 0.1$?
c. between $X = 0.1$ and $X = 0.2$?
d. less than $X = 0.1$ or greater than $X = 0.2$?

6.29 Given an exponential distribution with $\lambda = 30$, what is the probability that the arrival time is
a. less than $X = 0.1$?
b. greater than $X = 0.1$?
c. between $X = 0.1$ and $X = 0.2$?
d. less than $X = 0.1$ or greater than $X = 0.2$?

6.30 Given an exponential distribution with $\lambda = 20$, what is the probability that the arrival time is
a. less than $X = 4$?
b. greater than $X = 0.4$?
c. between $X = 0.4$ and $X = 0.5$?
d. less than $X = 0.4$ or greater than $X = 0.5$?

Applying the Concepts

 6.31 Autos arrive at a tollplaza located at the entrance to a bridge at the rate of 50 per minute during the 5:00–6:00 p.m. hour. If an auto has just arrived,
a. what is the probability that the next auto will arrive within 3 seconds (0.05 minute)?
b. what is the probability that the next auto will arrive within 1 second (0.0167 minute)?
c. What are your answers to (a) and (b) if the rate of arrival of autos is 60 per minute?
d. What are your answers to (a) and (b) if the rate of arrival of autos is 30 per minute?

 6.32 Customers arrive at the drive-up window of a fast-food restaurant at a rate of 2 per minute during the lunch hour.
a. What is the probability that the next customer will arrive within 1 minute?
b. What is the probability that the next customer will arrive within 5 minutes?

c. During the dinner time period, the arrival rate is 1 per minute. What are your answers to (a) and (b) for this period?

6.33 Telephone calls arrive at the information desk of a large computer software company at a rate of 15 per hour.
a. What is the probability that the next call will arrive within 3 minutes (0.05 hour)?
b. What is the probability that the next call will arrive within 15 minutes (0.25 hour)?
c. Suppose the company has just introduced an updated version of one of its software programs, and telephone calls are now arriving at a rate of 25 per hour. Given this information, redo (a) and (b).

 6.34 An on-the-job injury occurs once every 10 days on average at an automobile plant. What is the probability that the next on-the-job injury will occur within
a. 10 days?
b. 5 days?
c. 1 day?

 6.35 The time between unplanned shutdowns of a power plant has an exponential distribution with a mean of 20 days. Find the probability that the time between two unplanned shutdowns is
a. less than 14 days.
b. more than 21 days.
c. less than 7 days.

6.36 Golfers arrive at the starter's booth of a public golf course at a rate of 8 per hour during the Monday-to-Friday midweek period. If a golfer has just arrived,
a. what is the probability that the next golfer will arrive within 15 minutes (0.25 hour)?
b. what is the probability that the next golfer will arrive within 3 minutes (0.05 hour)?
c. The actual arrival rate on Fridays is 15 per hour. What are your answers to (a) and (b) for Fridays?

6.37 TrafficWeb.org claims that it can deliver 10,000 hits to a Web site in the next 60 days for only $21.95 (**www.trafficweb.org**, April 26, 2004). If this amount of

Web site traffic is experienced, then the time between hits has as a mean of 8.64 minutes (or 0.116 per minute). Assume that your Web site does get 10,000 hits in the next 60 days and that the time between hits has an exponential distribution. What is the probability that the time between two hits is

a. less than 5 minutes?
b. less than 10 minutes?
c. more than 15 minutes?
d. Do you think it is reasonable to assume that the time between hits has an exponential distribution?

6.6 ⊙ (CD-ROM Topic) THE NORMAL APPROXIMATION TO THE BINOMIAL DISTRIBUTION

In many circumstances, the normal distribution can be used to approximate the binomial distribution. For further discussion, see section 6.6.pdf on the Student CD-ROM that accompanies this text.

SUMMARY

In this chapter, you used the normal distribution in the Using Statistics scenario to study the time to download a Web page. In addition, you studied the uniform distribution, the exponential distribution, and the normal probability plot. In Chapter 7, the normal distribution is used in developing the subject of statistical inference.

KEY EQUATIONS

Normal Probability Density Function

$$f(X) = \frac{1}{\sqrt{2\pi}\sigma} e^{-(1/2)[(X-\mu)/\sigma]^2} \qquad (6.1)$$

Transformation Formula

$$Z = \frac{X - \mu}{\sigma} \qquad (6.2)$$

Standardized Normal Probability Density Function

$$f(Z) = \frac{1}{\sqrt{2\pi}} e^{-(1/2)Z^2} \qquad (6.3)$$

Finding an X Value Associated with Known Probability

$$X = \mu + Z\sigma \qquad (6.4)$$

Uniform Distribution

$$f(X) = \frac{1}{b - a} \qquad (6.5)$$

Mean of the Uniform Distribution

$$\mu = \frac{a + b}{2} \qquad (6.6)$$

Variance and Standard Deviation of the Uniform Distribution

$$\sigma^2 = \frac{(b - a)^2}{12} \qquad (6.7a)$$

$$\sigma = \sqrt{\frac{(b - a)^2}{12}} \qquad (6.7b)$$

Exponential Distribution

$$P(\text{Arrival time} < X) = 1 - e^{-\lambda X} \qquad (6.8)$$

KEY TERMS

continuous probability density function   218
cumulative standardized normal distribution   222
exponential distribution   241
normal distribution   219
normal probability density function   220
normal probability plot   236
quantile-quantile plot   236
rectangular distribution   238
standardized normal random variable   221
transformation formula   221
uniform distribution   238

CHAPTER REVIEW PROBLEMS

Checking Your Understanding

6.38 Why is it that only one normal distribution table such as Table E.2 is needed to find any probability under the normal curve?

6.39 How do you find the area between two values under the normal curve?

6.40 How do you find the X value that corresponds to a given percentile of the normal distribution?

6.41 What are some of the distinguishing properties of a normal distribution?

6.42 How does the shape of the normal distribution differ from those of the uniform and exponential distributions?

6.43 How can you use the normal probability plot to evaluate whether a set of data is normally distributed?

6.44 Under what circumstances can you use the exponential distribution?

Applying the Concepts

6.45 An industrial sewing machine uses ball bearings that are targeted to have a diameter of 0.75 inch. The lower and upper specification limits under which the ball bearings can operate are 0.74 inch and 0.76 inch, respectively. Past experience has indicated that the actual diameter of the ball bearings is approximately normally distributed, with a mean of 0.753 inch and a standard deviation of 0.004 inch. What is the probability that a ball bearing is
a. between the target and the actual mean?
b. between the lower specification limit and the target?
c. above the upper specification limit?
d. below the lower specification limit?
e. 93% of the diameters are greater than what value?

6.46 The fill amount of soft drink bottles is normally distributed, with a mean of 2.0 liters and a standard deviation of 0.05 liter. If bottles contain less than 95% of the listed net content (1.90 liters, in this case), the manufacturer may be subject to penalty by the state office of consumer affairs. Bottles that have a net content above 2.10 liters may cause excess spillage upon opening. What proportion of the bottles will contain
a. between 1.90 and 2.0 liters?
b. between 1.90 and 2.10 liters?
c. below 1.90 liters or above 2.10 liters?
d. 99% of the bottles contain at least how much soft drink?
e. 99% of the bottles contain an amount that is between which two values (symmetrically distributed) around the mean?

6.47 In an effort to reduce the number of bottles that contain less than 1.90 liters, the bottler in Problem 6.46 sets the filling machine so that the mean is 2.02 liters. Under these circumstances, what are your answers in (a) through (e)?

6.48 An orange juice producer buys all his oranges from a large orange grove. The amount of juice squeezed from each of these oranges is approximately normally distributed, with a mean of 4.70 ounces and a standard deviation of 0.40 ounce.
a. What is the probability that a randomly selected orange will contain between 4.70 and 5.00 ounces?
b. What is the probability that a randomly selected orange will contain between 5.00 and 5.50 ounces?
c. 77% of the oranges will contain at least how many ounces of juice?
d. 80% of the oranges contain between what two values (in ounces), symmetrically distributed around the population mean?

6.49 Data concerning 58 of the best-selling domestic beers in the United States are located in the file `domesticbeer.xls`. The values for three variables are included: percentage alcohol, number of calories per 12 ounces, and number of carbohydrates (in grams) per 12 ounces. For each of the three variables, decide whether the data appear to be approximately normally distributed. Support your decision through the use of appropriate statistics and graphs.

Source: Extracted from **www.Beer100.com**, *March 31, 2006.*

6.50 The evening manager of a restaurant was very concerned about the length of time some customers were waiting in line to be seated. She also had some concern about the seating times—that is, the length of time between when a customer is seated and the time he or she leaves the restaurant. Over the course of one week, 100 customers (no more than 1 per party) were randomly selected, and their waiting and seating times (in minutes) were recorded in the file `wait.xls`.
a. Think about your favorite restaurant. Do you think waiting times more closely resemble a uniform, exponential, or normal distribution?
b. Again, think about your favorite restaurant. Do you think seating times more closely resemble a uniform, exponential, or normal distribution?
c. Construct a histogram and a normal probability plot of the waiting-times. Do you think these waiting times more closely resemble a uniform, exponential, or normal distribution?
d. Construct a histogram and a normal probability plot of the seating times. Do you think these seating times more closely resemble a uniform, exponential, or normal distribution?

6.51 At the end of the first quarter of 2006, all the major stock market indexes had posted strong gains in the past 12 months. Mass Mutual Financial Group credited the increases to solid growth in corporate profits ("Market Commentary: Economic Growth Characterizes Q1 2006,"

www.massmutual.com, May 1, 2006). The mean one-year return for stocks in the S&P 500, a group of 500 very large companies, was approximately 12%. The mean one-year return for companies in the Russell 2000, a group of 2000 small companies, was approximately 26%. Historically, the one-year returns are approximately normal, the standard deviation in the S&P 500 is approximately 20%, and the standard deviation in the Russell 200 is approximately 35%.

a. What is the probability that a stock in the S&P 500 gained 25% or more in the last year? gained 50% or more?

b. What is the probability that a stock in the S&P 500 lost money in the last year? Lost 25% or more? lost 50% or more?

c. Repeat (a) and (b) for a stock in the Russell 2000.

d. Write a short summary on your findings. Be sure to include a discussion of the risks associated with a large standard deviation.

6.52 The *New York Times* reported (L. J. Flynn, "Tax Surfing," *The New York Times*, March 25, 2002, p. C10) that the mean time to download the home page for the Internal Revenue Service, **www.irs.gov**, is 0.8 second. Suppose that the download time is normally distributed with a standard deviation of 0.2 seconds. What is the probability that a download time is

a. less than 1 second?

b. between 0.5 and 1.5 seconds?

c. above 0.5 second?

d. 99% of the download times are above how many seconds?

e. 95% of the download times are between what two values, symmetrically distributed around the mean?

6.53 The same article mentioned in Problem 6.52 also reported that the mean download time for the H&R Block Web site, **www.hrblock.com**, is 2.5 seconds. Suppose that the download time is normally distributed with a standard deviation of 0.5 second. What is the probability that a download time is

a. less than 1 second?

b. between 0.5 and 1.5 seconds?

c. above 0.5 second?

d. 99% of the download times are above how many seconds?

e. Compare the results for the IRS site computed in Problem 6.52 to those of the H&R Block site.

6.54 **(Class Project)** According to Burton G. Malkiel, the daily changes in the closing price of stock follow a *random walk*—that is, these daily events are independent of each other and move upward or downward in a random manner—and can be approximated by a normal distribution. To test this theory, use either a newspaper or the Internet to select one company traded on the NYSE, one company traded on the American Stock Exchange, and one company traded "over the counter" (that is, on the NASDAQ national market) and then do the following:

1. Record the daily closing stock price of each of these companies for six consecutive weeks (so that you have 30 values per company).

2. Record the daily changes in the closing stock price of each of these companies for six consecutive weeks (so that you have 30 values per company).

For each of your six data sets, decide whether the data are approximately normally distributed by

a. examining the stem-and-leaf display, histogram or polygon, and box-and-whisker plot.

b. comparing data characteristics to theoretical properties.

c. constructing a normal probability plot.

d. Discuss the results of (a) through (c). What can you say about your three stocks with respect to daily closing prices and daily changes in closing prices? Which, if any, of the data sets are approximately normally distributed?

Note: The random-walk theory pertains to the daily changes in the closing stock price, not the daily closing stock price.

Team Projects

The data file Mutual Funds.xls contains information regarding nine variables from a sample of 838 mutual funds. The variables are:

Category—Type of stocks comprising the mutual fund (small cap, mid cap, large cap)

Objective—Objective of stocks comprising the mutual fund (growth or value)

Assets—In millions of dollars

Fees—Sales charges (no or yes)

Expense ratio—Ratio of expenses to net assets, in percentage

Risk—Risk-of-loss factor of the mutual fund (low, average, high)

2005 return—Twelve-month return in 2005

Three-year return—Annualized return, 2003–2005

Five-year return—Annualized return, 2001–2005

6.55 For the expense ratio in percentage, 2005 return, and five-year return, decide whether the data are approximately normally distributed by

a. comparing data characteristics to theoretical properties.

b. constructing a normal probability plot.

Student Survey Data Base

6.56 Problem 1.27 on page 15 describes a survey of 50 undergraduate students (see the file undergradsurvey.xls). For these data, for each numerical variable, decide whether the data are approximately normally distributed by

a. comparing data characteristics to theoretical properties.

b. constructing a normal probability plot.

6.57 Problem 1.27 on page 15 describes a survey of 50 undergraduate students (see the file undergradsurvey.xls).

a. Select a sample of 50 undergraduate students and conduct a similar survey for those students.

b. For the data collected in (a), repeat (a) and (b) of Problem 6.56.

c. Compare the results of (b) to those of Problem 6.56.

6.58 Problem 1.28 on page 15 describes a survey of 50 MBA students (see the file gradsurvey.xls). For these data, for each numerical variable, decide whether the data are approximately normally distributed by

a. comparing data characteristics to theoretical properties.

b. constructing a normal probability plot.

6.59 Problem 1.28 on page 15 describes a survey of 50 MBA students (see the file gradsurvey.xls).

a. Select a sample of 50 undergraduate students and conduct a similar survey for those students.

b. For the data collected in (a), repeat (a) and (b) of Problem 6.58.

c. Compare the results of (b) to those of Problem 6.58.

Managing the *Springville Herald*

The production department of the newspaper has embarked on a quality improvement effort. Its first project relates to the blackness of the newspaper print. Each day, a determination needs to be made concerning how black the newspaper is printed. Blackness is measured on a standard scale in which the target value is 1.0. Data collected over the past year indicate that the blackness is normally distributed, with a mean of 1.005 and a standard deviation of 0.10. Each day, one spot on the first newspaper printed is chosen, and the blackness of the spot is measured. The blackness of the newspaper is considered acceptable if the blackness of the spot is between 0.95 and 1.05.

EXERCISES

SH6.1 Assuming that the distribution has not changed from what it was in the past year, what is the probability that the blackness of the spot is
  a. less than 1.0?
  b. between 0.95 and 1.0?
  c. between 1.0 and 1.05?
  d. less than 0.95 or greater than 1.05?

SH6.2 The objective of the production team is to reduce the probability that the blackness is below 0.95 or above 1.05. Should the team focus on process improvement that lowers the mean to the target value of 1.0 or on process improvement that reduces the standard deviation to 0.075? Explain.

Web Case

Apply your knowledge about the normal distribution in this Web Case, which extends the Using Statistics scenario from this chapter.

To satisfy concerns of potential advertisers, the management of OurCampus! has undertaken a research project to learn the amount of time it takes users to download a complex video features page. The marketing department has collected data and has made some claims based on the assertion that the data follow a normal distribution. These data and conclusions can be found in a report located on the internal Web page **www.prenhall.com/Springville/Our_DownloadResearch.htm** (or in the file with the same name in the Student CD-ROM Web Case folder).

Read this marketing report and then answer the following:

1. Can the collected data be approximated by the normal distribution?

2. Review and evaluate the conclusions made by the OurCampus! marketing department. Which conclusions are correct? Which ones are incorrect?

3. If OurCampus! could improve the mean time by five minutes, how would the probabilities change?

REFERENCES

1. Gunter, B., "Q-Q Plots," *Quality Progress* (February 1994), 81–86.
2. Levine, D. M., P. Ramsey, and R. Smidt, *Applied Statistics for Engineers and Scientists Using Microsoft Excel and Minitab* (Upper Saddle River, NJ: Prentice Hall, 2001).
3 *Microsoft Excel 2007* (Redmond, WA: Microsoft Corp., 2007).

Excel Companion
to Chapter 6

E6.1 COMPUTING NORMAL PROBABILITIES

You compute normal probabilities by either using the PHStat2 Normal procedure or by making entries in the Normal.xls workbook.

Using PHStat2 Normal

Select **PHStat → Probability & Prob. Distributions → Normal**. In the Normal Probability Distribution dialog box (shown below), enter values for the mean and standard deviation. Click one or more of the input options and enter values. Enter a title as the **Title** and click **OK**.

![Normal Probability Distribution dialog box]

For Example 6.1, click **Probability for: X >** and enter **9** in its box. For Example 6.2, click **Probability for range** and enter **7** as the "from" value and **9** as the "to" value. For Example 6.5, click **Probability for: X <=** and enter **3.5**. For Example 6.6, click **X for Cumulative Percentage** and enter **10** in its box.

For problems such as Example 6.3 that require a probability of X less than a value or X greater than a value, click the first two input options and enter the tail values. Clicking all the input options creates a worksheet identical to the **Normal Expanded** worksheet described next.

Using the Normal Workbook

You open and use either the **Normal** or **Normal Expanded** worksheets of the Normal.xls workbook to compute normal probabilities. The **Normal** worksheet, shown in Figure 6.18, computes probabilities for problems similar to Examples 6.3 and 6.6. The **Normal Expanded** worksheet (see Figures E6.1 and E6.2) expands the Normal worksheet to compute all types of normal probabilities. Both worksheets use the **STANDARDIZE, NORMDIST, NORMSINV**, and **NORMINV** functions in computing normal probabilities and use the **ABS** (absolute value) function in cell E13 to compute the probability for a range as a positive value.

The **STANDARDIZE(X, mean, standard deviation)** function returns the Z value for a specific X value, mean, and standard deviation. The **NORMDIST(X, mean, standard deviation, True)** function returns the area or probability of less than a given X value for a specific mean and standard deviation. The **NORMSINV(P<X)** function returns the Z value corresponding to the probability of less than a given X. The **NORMINV(P<X, mean, standard deviation)** function returns the X value for a given probability, mean, and standard deviation.

To use either worksheet for similar probability problems, change the entries in the turquoise tinted cells to match the details of your problem. Because cells A10, A15, A17, A18, and D9 through D13 contain formulas that use the ampersand operator (see the Excel Companion to

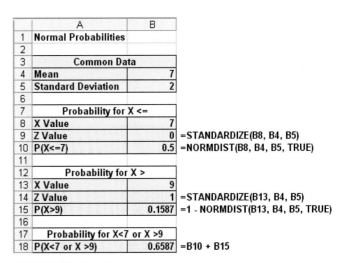

	A	B	
1	Normal Probabilities		
2			
3	**Common Data**		
4	Mean	7	
5	Standard Deviation	2	
6			
7	**Probability for X <=**		
8	X Value	7	
9	Z Value	0	=STANDARDIZE(B8, B4, B5)
10	P(X<=7)	0.5	=NORMDIST(B8, B4, B5, TRUE)
11			
12	**Probability for X >**		
13	X Value	9	
14	Z Value	1	=STANDARDIZE(B13, B4, B5)
15	P(X>9)	0.1587	=1 - NORMDIST(B13, B4, B5, TRUE)
16			
17	**Probability for X<7 or X >9**		
18	P(X<7 or X >9)	0.6587	=B10 + B15

FIGURE E6.1

Normal expanded columns A and B

Chapter 4) to create labels from the X values you enter, you do not need to edit any labels. (These nine formulas are not shown in Figures E6.1 and E6.2.)

	D	E	
1			
2			
3			
4			
5			
6	**Probability for a Range**		
7	From X Value	7	
8	To X Value	9	
9	Z Value for 7	0	=STANDARDIZE(E7, B4, B5)
10	Z Value for 9	1	=STANDARDIZE(E8, B4, B5)
11	P(X<=7)	0.5000	=NORMDIST(E7, B4, B5, TRUE)
12	P(X<=9)	0.8413	=NORMDIST(E8, B4, B5, TRUE)
13	P(7<=X<=9)	0.3413	=ABS(E12 - E11)
14			
15	**Find X and Z Given Cum. Pctage.**		
16	Cumulative Percentage	10.00%	
17	Z Value	-1.281552	=NORMSINV(E16)
18	X Value	4.436897	=NORMINV(E16, B4, B5)

FIGURE E6.2 Normal expanded columns D and E

E6.2   CREATING NORMAL PROBABILITY PLOTS

You create normal probability plots by using the PHStat2 Normal Probability Plot procedure (recommended) or by using Excel charting features with a worksheet of Z values that you create.

Using PHStat2 Normal Probability Plot

Open to the worksheet that contains the data to be plotted. Select **PHStat → Probability & Prob. Distributions → Normal Probability Plot**. In the Normal Probability Plot dialog box (shown below), enter the cell range of the data to be plotted as the **Variable Cell Range** and click **First cell contains label**. Enter a title as the **Title** and click **OK**. PHStat2 creates a chart sheet containing the plot and a worksheet of Z values on which the plot is based.

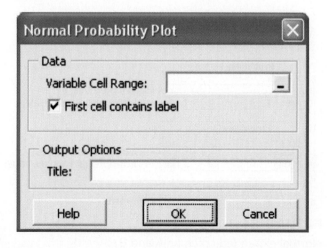

Creating a Z Values Worksheet

To use Excel charting features to create a normal probability plot, you first create a worksheet that computes Z values. This worksheet contains four columns in ascending order: rank, proportion, Z value, and the data to be evaluated for normality.

Table E6.1 shows the entries of the first three rows and the last row of the **Plot** worksheet of the Npp.xls workbook. This worksheet contains the source data for the Figure 6.22 plot of the three-year rate of returns. Column B formulas are the rank divided by $n + 1$ (839, for the sample of 838 mutual funds). Column C formulas use NORMSINV (see Section E6.1) to compute Z values based on the proportions computed in column B.

To create normal probability plots for another variable, you adjust the worksheet design by either adding or deleting rows and adjusting the divisor in the column B formulas. (The divisor should always be 1 more than the sample size.)

TABLE E6.1 Z Values Worksheet Design for Three-Year Returns Variable

	A	B	C	D
1	Rank	Proportion	Z Value	3-Year Return
2	1	=A2/839	=NORMSINV(B2)	6.7
3	2	=A3/839	=NORMSINV(B3)	6.7
⋮	⋮	⋮	⋮	⋮
839	838	=A839/839	=NORMSINV(B839)	42.3

Creating a Normal Probability Plot (97–2003)

Open to your copy of the **Z Values** worksheet. Begin the Chart Wizard and make these entries:

Step 1. Click the **Standard Types** tab and then click **XY (Scatter)** from the **Standard Types Chart type** box. Click the first **Chart sub-type**, labeled "**Scatter. Compares pairs of values**" when selected.

Step 2. Click the **Data Range** tab. Enter the columns C and D cell range as the **Data range** and click the **Columns** option in the **Series in** group.

Step 3. Click the **Titles** tab. Enter a title as the **Chart title** and enter **Z Value** as the **Category (X) axis** title. Enter a title for the **Value (Y) axis** title. Click, in turn, the **Axes, Gridlines, Data Labels**, tabs and adjust the settings, as discussed in the "Creating Charts (97–2003)" part of Section E2.2 on page 79. Click the **Legend** tab and clear **Show legend**.

Creating a Normal Probability Plot (2007)

Open to your copy of the **Z Values** worksheet. Select the columns C and D cell range that contains the Z values and the data whose normality is being tested. Click **Insert →** **X Y (Scatter) → Scatter with only Markers**. Finish by relocating your chart to a chart sheet and customizing your chart using the instructions in "Creating Charts (2007)" in Section E2.2 on page 80.

E6.3 COMPUTING EXPONENTIAL PROBABILITIES

You compute exponential probabilities by either using the PHStat2 Exponential procedure or by making entries in the **Exponential.xls** workbook.

Using PHStat2 Exponential

Open to the worksheet that contains the data to be plotted. Select **PHStat → Probability & Prob. Distributions →** **Exponential**. In the Exponential Probability Distribution dialog box (shown at right), enter values for **Mean per unit (Lambda)** and the **X Value**. Enter a title as the **Title** and click **OK**.

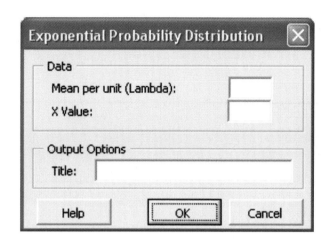

Using the Exponential Worksheet

Open to the **Exponential** worksheet of the **Exponential.xls** workbook. This worksheet (see Figure 6.25 on page 241) uses the **EXPONDIST (*X value, mean,* True)** function to compute the exponential probability for the bank ATM problem of Section 6.5. To adapt this worksheet for other problems, change the **Mean** and **X Value** values in cells B4 and B5.

CHAPTER 7

Sampling and Sampling Distributions

USING STATISTICS @ Oxford Cereals

LEARNING OBJECTIVES

In this chapter, you learn:
- To distinguish between different sampling methods
- The concept of the sampling distribution
- To compute probabilities related to the sample mean and the sample proportion
- The importance of the Central Limit Theorem

Using Statistics @ Oxford Cereals

Oxford Cereals fills thousands of boxes of cereal during an eight-hour shift. As the plant operations manager, you are responsible for monitoring the amount of cereal placed in each box. To be consistent with package labeling, boxes should contain a mean of 368 grams of cereal. Because of the speed of the process, the cereal weight varies from box to box, causing some boxes to be underfilled and others overfilled. If the process is not working properly, the mean weight in the boxes could vary too much from the label weight of 368 grams to be acceptable.

Because weighing every single box is too time-consuming, costly, and inefficient, you must take a sample of boxes. For each sample you select, you plan to weigh the individual boxes and calculate a sample mean. You need to determine the probability that such a sample mean could have been randomly selected from a population whose mean is 368 grams. Based on your analysis, you will have to decide whether to maintain, alter, or shut down the process.

In Chapter 6, you used the normal distribution to study the distribution of download times for the OurCampus! Web site. In this chapter, you need to make a decision about the cereal-filling process, based on a *sample* of cereal boxes. You will learn different methods of sampling and about *sampling distributions* and how to use them to solve business problems.

7.1   TYPES OF SAMPLING METHODS

In Section 1.3, a *sample* was defined as the portion of a population that has been selected for analysis. Rather than selecting every item in the population, statistical sampling procedures focus on collecting a small representative group of the larger population. The results of the sample are then used to estimate characteristics of the entire population. There are three main reasons for selecting a sample:

- Selecting a sample is less time-consuming than selecting every item in the population.
- Selecting a sample is less costly than selecting every item in the population.
- An analysis of a sample is less cumbersome and more practical than an analysis of the entire population.

The sampling process begins by defining the **frame**. The frame is a listing of items that make up the population. Frames are data sources such as population lists, directories, or maps. Samples are drawn from frames. Inaccurate or biased results can result if a frame excludes certain portions of the population. Using different frames to generate data can lead to opposite conclusions.

After you select a frame, you draw a sample from the frame. As illustrated in Figure 7.1, there are two kinds of samples: the nonprobability sample and the probability sample.

FIGURE 7.1

Types of samples

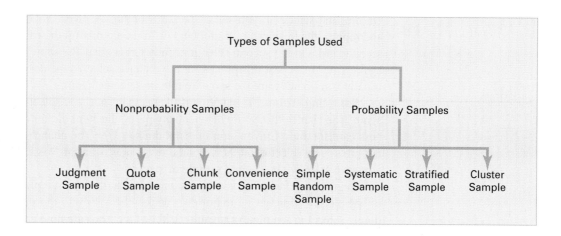

In a **nonprobability sample**, you select the items or individuals without knowing their probabilities of selection. Thus, the theory that has been developed for probability sampling cannot be applied to nonprobability samples. A common type of nonprobability sampling is **convenience sampling**. In convenience sampling, items are selected based only on the fact that they are easy, inexpensive, or convenient to sample. In many cases, participants are self-selected. For example, many companies conduct surveys by giving visitors to their Web site the opportunity to complete survey forms and submit them electronically. The responses to these surveys can provide large amounts of data quickly and inexpensively, but the sample consists of self-selected Web users (see p. 8). For many studies, only a nonprobability sample such as a judgment sample is available. In a **judgment sample**, you get the opinions of preselected experts in the subject matter. Some other common procedures of nonprobability sampling are quota sampling and chunk sampling. These are discussed in detail in specialized books on sampling methods (see reference 1).

Nonprobability samples can have certain advantages, such as convenience, speed, and low cost. However, their lack of accuracy due to selection bias and the fact that the results cannot be generalized more than offset these advantages. Therefore, you should use nonprobability sampling methods only for small-scale studies that precede larger investigations.

In a **probability sample**, you select the items based on known probabilities. Whenever possible, you should use probability sampling methods. Probability samples allow you to make unbiased inferences about the population of interest. In practice, it is often difficult or impossible to take a probability sample. However, you should work toward achieving a probability sample and acknowledge any potential biases that might exist. The four types of probability samples most commonly used are simple random, systematic, stratified, and cluster samples. These sampling methods vary in their cost, accuracy, and complexity.

Simple Random Samples

In a **simple random sample**, every item from a frame has the same chance of selection as every other item. In addition, every sample of a fixed size has the same chance of selection as every other sample of that size. Simple random sampling is the most elementary random sampling technique. It forms the basis for the other random sampling techniques.

With simple random sampling, you use n to represent the sample size and N to represent the frame size. You number every item in the frame from 1 to N. The chance that you will select any particular member of the frame on the first selection is $1/N$.

You select samples with replacement or without replacement. **Sampling with replacement** means that after you select an item, you return it to the frame, where it has the same probability of being selected again. Imagine that you have a fishbowl containing N business cards.

On the first selection, you select the card for Judy Craven. You record pertinent information and replace the business card in the bowl. You then mix up the cards in the bowl and select the second card. On the second selection, Judy Craven has the same probability of being selected again, $1/N$. You repeat this process until you have selected the desired sample size, n. However, usually you do not want the same item to be selected again.

Sampling without replacement means that once you select an item, you cannot select it again. The chance that you will select any particular item in the frame—for example, the business card for Judy Craven—on the first draw is $1/N$. The chance that you will select any card not previously selected on the second draw is now 1 out of $N - 1$. This process continues until you have selected the desired sample of size n.

Regardless of whether you have sampled with or without replacement, "fishbowl" methods of sample selection have a major drawback—the ability to thoroughly mix the cards and randomly select the sample. As a result, fishbowl methods are not very useful. You need to use less cumbersome and more scientific methods of selection.

One such method uses a **table of random numbers** (see Table E.1) for selecting the sample. A table of random numbers consists of a series of digits listed in a randomly generated sequence (see reference 8). Because the numeric system uses 10 digits (0, 1, 2, . . . , 9), the chance that you will randomly generate any particular digit is equal to the probability of generating any other digit. This probability is 1 out of 10. Hence, if you generate a sequence of 800 digits, you would expect about 80 to be the digit 0, 80 to be the digit 1, and so on. In fact, those who use tables of random numbers usually test the generated digits for randomness prior to using them. Table E.1 has met all such criteria for randomness. Because every digit or sequence of digits in the table is random, the table can be read either horizontally or vertically. The margins of the table designate row numbers and column numbers. The digits themselves are grouped into sequences of five in order to make reading the table easier.

To use such a table instead of a fishbowl for selecting the sample, you first need to assign code numbers to the individual members of the frame. Then you generate the random sample by reading the table of random numbers and selecting those individuals from the frame whose assigned code numbers match the digits found in the table. You can better understand the process of sample selection by examining Example 7.1.

EXAMPLE 7.1

SELECTING A SIMPLE RANDOM SAMPLE BY USING A TABLE OF RANDOM NUMBERS

A company wants to select a sample of 32 full-time workers from a population of 800 full-time employees in order to collect information on expenditures concerning a company-sponsored dental plan. How do you select a simple random sample?

SOLUTION The company decides to conduct an email survey. Assuming that not everyone will respond to the survey, you need to send more than 32 surveys to get the necessary 32 responses. Assuming that 8 out of 10 full-time workers will respond to such a survey (that is, a response rate of 80%), you decide to send 40 surveys.

The frame consists of a listing of the names and email addresses of all $N = 800$ full-time employees taken from the company personnel files. Thus, the frame is an accurate and complete listing of the population. To select the random sample of 40 employees from this frame, you use a table of random numbers. Because the population size (800) is a three-digit number, each assigned code number must also be three digits so that every full-time worker has an equal chance of selection. You assign a code of 001 to the first full-time employee in the population listing, a code of 002 to the second full-time employee in the population listing, and so on, until a code of 800 is assigned to the Nth full-time worker in the listing. Because $N = 800$ is the largest possible coded value, you discard all three-digit code sequences greater than 800 (that is, 801 through 999 and 000).

To select the simple random sample, you choose an arbitrary starting point from the table of random numbers. One method you can use is to close your eyes and strike the table of random numbers with a pencil. Suppose you used this procedure and you selected row 06, column 05, of Table 7.1 (which is extracted from Table E.1) as the starting point. Although you can go in any direction, in this example, you read the table from left to right, in sequences of three digits, without skipping.

TABLE 7.1

Using a Table of Random Numbers

		Column							
	Row	**00000** **12345**	**00001** **67890**	**11111** **12345**	**11112** **67890**	**22222** **12345**	**22223** **67890**	**33333** **12345**	**33334** **67890**
	01	49280	88924	35779	00283	81163	07275	89863	02348
	02	61870	41657	07468	08612	98083	97349	20775	45091
	03	43898	65923	25078	86129	78496	97653	91550	08078
	04	62993	93912	30454	84598	56095	20664	12872	64647
	05	33850	58555	51438	85507	71865	79488	76783	31708
Begin	06	97340	03364	88472	04334	63919	36394	11095	92470
selection	07	70543	29776	10087	10072	55980	64688	68239	20461
(row 06,	08	89382	93809	00796	95945	34101	81277	66090	88872
column 5)	09	37818	72142	67140	50785	22380	16703	53362	44940
	10	60430	22834	14130	96593	23298	56203	92671	15925
	11	82975	66158	84731	19436	55790	69229	28661	13675
	12	39087	71938	40355	54324	08401	26299	49420	59208
	13	55700	24586	93247	32596	11865	63397	44251	43189
	14	14756	23997	78643	75912	83832	32768	18928	57070
	15	32166	53251	70654	92827	63491	04233	33825	69662
	16	23236	73751	31888	81718	06546	83246	47651	04877
	17	45794	26926	15130	82455	78305	55058	52551	47182
	18	09893	20505	14225	68514	46427	56788	96297	78822
	19	54382	74598	91499	14523	68479	27686	46162	83554
	20	94750	89923	37089	20048	80336	94598	26940	36858
	21	70297	34135	53140	33340	42050	82341	44104	82949
	22	85157	47954	32979	26575	57600	40881	12250	73742
	23	11100	02340	12860	74697	96644	89439	28707	25815
	24	36871	50775	30592	57143	17381	68856	25853	35041
	25	23913	48357	63308	16090	51690	54607	72407	55538

Source: Partially extracted from The Rand Corporation, A Million Random Digits with 100,000 Normal Deviates *(Glencoe, IL: The Free Press, 1955) and displayed in Table E.1 in Appendix E.*

The individual with code number 003 is the first full-time employee in the sample (row 06 and columns 05–07), the second individual has code number 364 (row 06 and columns 08–10), and the third individual has code number 884. Because the highest code for any employee is 800, you discard the number 884. Individuals with code numbers 720, 433, 463, 363, 109, 592, 470, and 705 are selected third through tenth, respectively.

You continue the selection process until you get the required sample size of 40 full-time employees. During the selection process, if any three-digit coded sequence repeats, you include the employee corresponding to that coded sequence again as part of the sample if you are sampling with replacement. You discard the repeating coded sequence if you are sampling without replacement.

Systematic Samples

In a **systematic sample**, you partition the N items in the frame into n groups of k items, where

$$k = \frac{N}{n}$$

You round k to the nearest integer. To select a systematic sample, you choose the first item to be selected at random from the first k items in the frame. Then, you select the remaining $n - 1$ items by taking every kth item thereafter from the entire frame.

If the frame consists of a listing of prenumbered checks, sales receipts, or invoices, a systematic sample is faster and easier to take than a simple random sample. A systematic sample is also a convenient mechanism for collecting data from telephone books, class rosters, and consecutive items coming off an assembly line.

To take a systematic sample of $n = 40$ from the population of $N = 800$ employees, you partition the frame of 800 into 40 groups, each of which contains 20 employees. You then select a random number from the first 20 individuals and include every twentieth individual after the first selection in the sample. For example, if the first random number you select is 008, your subsequent selections are 028, 048, 068, 088, 108, . . . , 768, and 788.

Although they are simpler to use, simple random sampling and systematic sampling are generally less efficient than other, more sophisticated, probability sampling methods. Even greater possibilities for selection bias and lack of representation of the population characteristics occur when using systematic samples than with simple random samples. If there is a pattern in the frame, you could have severe selection biases. To overcome the potential problem of disproportionate representation of specific groups in a sample, you can use either stratified sampling methods or cluster sampling methods.

Stratified Samples

In a **stratified sample**, you first subdivide the N items in the frame into separate subpopulations, or **strata**. A strata is defined by some common characteristic, such as gender or year in school. You select a simple random sample within each of the strata and combine the results from the separate simple random samples. Stratified sampling is more efficient than either simple random sampling or systematic sampling because you are ensured of the representation of items across the entire population. The homogeneity of items within each stratum provides greater precision in the estimates of underlying population parameters.

EXAMPLE 7.2

SELECTING A STRATIFIED SAMPLE

A company wants to select a sample of 32 full-time workers from a population of 800 full-time employees in order to estimate expenditures from a company-sponsored dental plan. Of the full-time employees, 25% are managers and 75% are nonmanagerial workers. How do you select the stratified sample in order for the sample to represent the correct percentage of managers and nonmanagerial workers?

SOLUTION If you assume an 80% response rate, you need to send 40 surveys to get the necessary 32 responses. The frame consists of a listing of the names and email addresses of all $N = 800$ full-time employees included in the company personnel files. Because 25% of the full-time employees are managers, you first separate the population frame into two strata: a subpopulation listing of all 200 managerial-level personnel and a separate subpopulation listing of all 600 full-time nonmanagerial workers. Because the first stratum consists of a listing of 200 managers, you assign three-digit code numbers from 001 to 200. Because the second stratum contains a listing of 600 nonmanagerial workers, you assign three-digit code numbers from 001 to 600.

To collect a stratified sample proportional to the sizes of the strata, you select 25% of the overall sample from the first stratum and 75% of the overall sample from the second stratum. You take two separate simple random samples, each of which is based on a distinct random starting point from a table of random numbers (Table E.1). In the first sample, you select 10 managers from the listing of 200 in the first stratum, and in the second sample, you select 30 nonmanagerial workers from the listing of 600 in the second stratum. You then combine the results to reflect the composition of the entire company.

Cluster Samples

In a **cluster sample**, you divide the N items in the frame into several clusters so that each cluster is representative of the entire population. **Clusters** are naturally occurring designations, such as counties, election districts, city blocks, households, or sales territories. You then take a random sample of one or more clusters and study all items in each selected cluster. If clusters are large, a probability-based sample taken from a single cluster is all that is needed.

Cluster sampling is often more cost-effective than simple random sampling, particularly if the population is spread over a wide geographic region. However, cluster sampling often requires a larger sample size to produce results as precise as those from simple random sampling or stratified sampling. A detailed discussion of systematic sampling, stratified sampling, and cluster sampling procedures can be found in reference 1.

PROBLEMS FOR SECTION 7.1

Learning the Basics

 7.1 For a population containing $N = 902$ individuals, what code number would you assign for
a. the first person on the list?
b. the fortieth person on the list?
c. the last person on the list?

7.2 For a population of $N = 902$, verify that by starting in row 05, column 1 of the table of random numbers (Table E.1), you need only six rows to select a sample of $n = 60$ *without* replacement.

 7.3 Given a population of $N = 93$, starting in row 29 of the table of random numbers (Table E.1), and reading across the row, select a sample of $n = 15$
a. *without* replacement.
b. *with* replacement.

Applying the Concepts

7.4 For a study that consists of personal interviews with participants (rather than mail or phone surveys), explain why simple random sampling might be less practical than some other sampling methods.

 7.5 You want to select a random sample of $n = 1$ from a population of three items (which are called A, B, and C). The rule for selecting the sample is: Flip a coin; if it is heads, pick item A; if it is tails, flip the coin again; this time, if it is heads, choose B; if it is tails, choose C. Explain why this is a probability sample but not a simple random sample.

 7.6 A population has four members (called A, B, C, and D). You would like to select a random sample of $n = 2$, which you decide to do in the following way: Flip a coin; if it is heads, the sample will be items A and B; if it is tails, the sample will be items C and D. Although this is a random sample, it is not a simple random sample. Explain why. (If you did Problem 7.5, compare the procedure described there with the procedure described in this problem.)

7.7 The registrar of a college with a population of $N = 4,000$ full-time students is asked by the president to conduct a survey to measure satisfaction with the quality of life on campus. The table at the top of page 258 contains a breakdown of the 4,000 registered full-time students, by gender and class designation:

| | **Class Designation** | | | | |
Gender	Fr.	So.	Jr.	Sr.	Total
Female	700	520	500	480	2,200
Male	560	460	400	380	1,800
Total	1,260	980	900	860	4,000

The registrar intends to take a probability sample of $n = 200$ students and project the results from the sample to the entire population of full-time students.

a. If the frame available from the registrar's files is an alphabetical listing of the names of all $N = 4,000$ registered full-time students, what type of sample could you take? Discuss.

b. What is the advantage of selecting a simple random sample in (a)?

c. What is the advantage of selecting a systematic sample in (a)?

d. If the frame available from the registrar's files is a listing of the names of all $N = 4,000$ registered full-time students compiled from eight separate alphabetical lists, based on the gender and class designation breakdowns shown in the class designation table, what type of sample should you take? Discuss.

e. Suppose that each of the $N = 4,000$ registered full-time students lived in one of the 20 campus dormitories. Each dormitory contains four floors, with 50 beds per floor, and therefore accommodates 200 students. It is college policy to fully integrate students by gender and class designation on each floor of each dormitory. If the registrar is able to compile a frame through a listing of all student occupants on each floor within each dormitory, what type of sample should you take? Discuss.

7.8 Prenumbered sales invoices are kept in a sales journal. The invoices are numbered from 0001 to 5,000.

a. Beginning in row 16, column 1, and proceeding horizontally in Table E.1, select a simple random sample of 50 invoice numbers.

b. Select a systematic sample of 50 invoice numbers. Use the random numbers in row 20, columns 5–7, as the starting point for your selection.

c. Are the invoices selected in (a) the same as those selected in (b)? Why or why not?

 7.9 Suppose that 5,000 sales invoices are separated into four strata. Stratum 1 contains 50 invoices, stratum 2 contains 500 invoices, stratum 3 contains 1,000 invoices, and stratum 4 contains 3,450 invoices. A sample of 500 sales invoices is needed.

a. What type of sampling should you do? Why?

b. Explain how you would carry out the sampling according to the method stated in (a).

c. Why is the sampling in (a) not simple random sampling?

7.2   EVALUATING SURVEY WORTHINESS

Surveys are often used to collect samples. Nearly every day, you read or hear about survey or opinion poll results in newspapers, on the Internet, or on radio or television. To identify surveys that lack objectivity or credibility, you must critically evaluate what you read and hear by examining the worthiness of the survey. First, you must evaluate the purpose of the survey, why it was conducted, and for whom it was conducted. An opinion poll or a survey conducted to satisfy curiosity is mainly for entertainment. Its result is an end in itself rather than a means to an end. You should be skeptical of such a survey because the result should not be put to further use.

The second step in evaluating the worthiness of a survey is to determine whether it was based on a probability or nonprobability sample (as discussed in Section 7.1). You need to remember that the only way to make correct statistical inferences from a sample to a population is through the use of a probability sample. Surveys that use nonprobability sampling methods are subject to serious, perhaps unintentional, biases that may render the results meaningless, as illustrated in the following example from the 1948 U.S. presidential election.

In 1948, major pollsters predicted the outcome of the U.S. presidential election between Harry S. Truman, the incumbent president, and Thomas E. Dewey, then governor of New York, as going to Dewey. The *Chicago Tribune* was so confident of the polls' predictions that it printed its early edition based on the predictions rather than waiting for the ballots to be counted.

An embarrassed newspaper and the pollsters it had relied on had a lot of explaining to do. Why were the pollsters so wrong? Intent on discovering the source of the error, the pollsters found that their use of a nonprobability sampling method was the culprit (see reference 7). As a result, polling organizations adopted probability sampling methods for future elections.

Survey Error

Even when surveys use random probability sampling methods, they are subject to potential errors. There are four types of survey errors:

- Coverage error
- Nonresponse error
- Sampling error
- Measurement error

Good survey research design attempts to reduce or minimize these various types of survey error, often at considerable cost.

Coverage Error   The key to proper sample selection is an adequate frame. Remember, a frame is an up-to-date list of all the items from which you will select the sample. **Coverage error** occurs if certain groups of items are excluded from this frame so that they have no chance of being selected in the sample. Coverage error results in a **selection bias**. If the frame is inadequate because certain groups of items in the population were not properly included, any random probability sample selected will provide an estimate of the characteristics of the frame, not the *actual* population.

Nonresponse Error   Not everyone is willing to respond to a survey. In fact, research has shown that individuals in the upper and lower economic classes tend to respond less frequently to surveys than do people in the middle class. **Nonresponse error** arises from the failure to collect data on all items in the sample and results in a **nonresponse bias**. Because you cannot always assume that persons who do not respond to surveys are similar to those who do, you need to follow up on the nonresponses after a specified period of time. You should make several attempts to convince such individuals to complete the survey. The follow-up responses are then compared to the initial responses in order to make valid inferences from the survey (reference 1).

The mode of response you use affects the rate of response. The personal interview and the telephone interview usually produce a higher response rate than does the mail survey—but at a higher cost. The following is a famous example of coverage error and nonresponse error.

In 1936, the magazine *Literary Digest* predicted that Governor Alf Landon of Kansas would receive 57% of the votes in the U.S. presidential election and overwhelmingly defeat President Franklin D. Roosevelt's bid for a second term. However, Landon was soundly defeated when he received only 38% of the vote. Such a large error in a poll conducted by a well-known source had never occurred before. As a result, the prediction devastated the magazine's credibility with the public, eventually causing it to go bankrupt. *Literary Digest* thought it had done everything right. It had based its prediction on a huge sample size, 2.4 million respondents, out of a survey sent to 10 million registered voters. What went wrong? There are two answers: selection bias and nonresponse bias.

To understand the role of selection bias, you need some historical background. In 1936, the United States was still suffering from the Great Depression. Not accounting for this, *Literary Digest* compiled its frame from such sources as telephone books, club membership lists, magazine subscriptions, and automobile registrations (reference 2). Inadvertently, it chose a frame primarily composed of the rich and excluded the majority of the voting population, who, during the Great Depression, could not afford telephones, club memberships, magazine subscriptions, and automobiles. Thus, the 57% estimate for the Landon vote may have been very close to the frame but certainly not the total U.S. population.

Nonresponse error produced a possible bias when the huge sample of 10 million registered voters produced only 2.4 million responses. A response rate of only 24% is far too low to yield accurate estimates of the population parameters without some way of ensuring that the 7.6 million individual nonrespondents have similar opinions. However, the problem of nonresponse bias was secondary to the problem of selection bias. Even if all 10 million registered voters in the sample had responded, this would not have compensated for the fact that the composition of the frame differed substantially from that of the actual voting population.

Sampling Error   A sample is selected because it is simpler, less costly, and more efficient. However, chance dictates which individuals or items will or will not be included in the sample. **Sampling error** reflects the variation, or "chance differences," from sample to sample, based on the probability of particular individuals or items being selected in the particular samples.

When you read about the results of surveys or polls in newspapers or magazines, there is often a statement regarding a margin of error, such as "the results of this poll are expected to be within ±4 percentage points of the actual value." This margin of error is the sampling error. You can reduce sampling error by taking larger sample sizes, although this also increases the cost of conducting the survey.

Measurement Error   In the practice of good survey research, you design a questionnaire with the intention of gathering meaningful information. But you have a dilemma here: Getting meaningful measurements is often easier said than done. Consider the following proverb:

A person with one watch always knows what time it is;
A person with two watches always searches to identify the correct one;
A person with ten watches is always reminded of the difficulty in measuring time.

Unfortunately, the process of measurement is often governed by what is convenient, not what is needed. The measurements you get are often only a proxy for the ones you really desire. Much attention has been given to measurement error that occurs because of a weakness in question wording (reference 3). A question should be clear, not ambiguous. Furthermore, in order to avoid *leading questions*, you need to present them in a neutral manner.

Three sources of **measurement error** are ambiguous wording of questions, the halo effect, and respondent error. As an example of ambiguous wording, in November 1993, the U.S. Department of Labor reported that the unemployment rate in the United States had been underestimated for more than a decade because of poor questionnaire wording in the Current Population Survey. In particular, the wording had led to a significant undercount of women in the labor force. Because unemployment rates are tied to benefit programs such as state unemployment compensation, survey researchers had to rectify the situation by adjusting the questionnaire wording.

The "halo effect" occurs when the respondent feels obligated to please the interviewer. Proper interviewer training can minimize the halo effect.

Respondent error occurs as a result of an overzealous or underzealous effort by the respondent. You can minimize this error in two ways: (1) by carefully scrutinizing the data and calling back those individuals whose responses seem unusual and (2) by establishing a program of random callbacks in order to determine the reliability of the responses.

Ethical Issues

Ethical considerations arise with respect to the four types of potential errors that can occur when designing surveys that use probability samples: coverage error, nonresponse error, sampling error, and measurement error. Coverage error can result in selection bias and becomes an ethical issue if particular groups or individuals are *purposely* excluded from the frame so that the survey results are more favorable to the survey's sponsor. Nonresponse error can lead to nonresponse bias and becomes an ethical issue if the sponsor knowingly designs the survey so that particular groups or individuals are less likely than others to respond. Sampling error becomes an ethical issue if the findings are purposely presented without reference to sample size and margin of error so that the sponsor can promote a viewpoint that might otherwise be truly insignificant. Measurement error becomes an ethical issue in one of three ways: (1) a survey sponsor chooses leading questions that guide the responses in a particular direction; (2) an interviewer, through mannerisms and tone, purposely creates a halo effect or otherwise guides the responses in a particular direction; or (3) a respondent willfully provides false information.

Ethical issues also arise when the results of nonprobability samples are used to form conclusions about the entire population. When you use a nonprobability sampling method, you need to explain the sampling procedures and state that the results cannot be generalized beyond the sample.

PROBLEMS FOR SECTION 7.2

Applying the Concepts

7.10 "A survey indicates that the vast majority of college students own their own personal computers." What information would you want to know before you accepted the results of this survey?

7.11 A simple random sample of $n = 300$ full-time employees is selected from a company list containing the names of all $N = 5,000$ full-time employees in order to evaluate job satisfaction.
a. Give an example of possible coverage error.
b. Give an example of possible nonresponse error.
c. Give an example of possible sampling error.
d. Give an example of possible measurement error.

7.12 Business professor Thomas Callarman traveled to China more than a dozen times from 2000 to 2005. He warns people about believing everything they read about surveys conducted in China and gives two specific reasons. Callarman stated, "First, things are changing so rapidly that what you hear today may not be true tomorrow. Second, the people who answer the surveys may tell you what they think you want to hear, rather than what they really believe" (T. E. Callarman, "Some Thoughts on China," *Decision Line*, March, 2006, pp. 1, 43–44).
a. List the four types (or categories) of survey error discussed in this section.
b. Which categories best describe the types of survey error discussed by Professor Callarman?

7.13 The gourmet foods industry is expected to exceed $62 billion in sales by the year 2009. A survey conducted by Packaged Facts indicates that one-fifth of American adults consider themselves "gourmet consumers" ("Galloping Gourmet," *The Progressive Grocer*, January 1, 2006, pp. 80–81). What additional information would you want to know before you accepted the results of the survey?

7.14 Only 10% of Americans rated their financial situation as "excellent," according to a Gallup Poll taken April 10–13, 2006. However, 41% rated their financial situation as "good," while 37% said "only fair" and 12% "poor" (J. M. Jones, "Americans More Worried About Meeting Basic Financial Needs," *The Gallup Poll*, **galluppoll.com**, April 25, 2006). What additional information would you want to know before you accepted the results of the survey?

7.15 Researchers studied repeat purchases from two online grocers. Valid responses from 1,150 customers indicated that 28.7% placed no further orders in the following 12 months, 35.4% placed 1–10 orders, and 35.8% placed 11 or more orders (K. K. Boyer and G. T. M. Hult, "Customer Behavior in an Online Ordering Application: A Decision Scoring Model," *Decision Sciences*, December, 2005, pp. 569–598). What additional information would you want to know before you accepted the results of this study?

7.16 A study investigating the effects of CEO succession on the stock performance of large publicly held corporations also investigated the demographics of the newly announced CEOs. The mean and standard deviation of the new CEO's age were 53.3 and 5.97, respectively. The mean and standard deviation of the number of years the new CEO had been with the firm were 20.1 and 12.6, respectively. 93.6% of the new CEOs held college degrees, 30.4% held MBAs, and 3.2% held doctorates (J. C. Rhim, J. V. Peluchette, and I. Song, "Stock Market Reactions and Firm Performance Surrounding CEO Succession: Antecedents of Succession and Successor Origin," *Mid-American Journal of Business*, Spring 2006, pp. 21–30). What additional information would you want to know before you accepted the results of this study?

7.3   SAMPLING DISTRIBUTIONS

In many applications, you want to make statistical inferences that use statistics calculated from samples to estimate the values of population parameters. In the next two sections, you will learn about how the sample mean (the statistic) is used to estimate a population mean (a parameter) and how the sample proportion (the statistic) is used to estimate the population proportion (a parameter). Your main concern when making a statistical inference is drawing conclusions about a population, *not* about a sample. For example, a political pollster is interested in the sample results only as a way of estimating the actual proportion of the votes that each candidate will receive from the population of voters. Likewise, as plant operations manager for Oxford Cereals, you are only interested in using the sample mean calculated from a sample of cereal boxes for estimating the mean weight contained in a population of boxes.

In practice, you select a single random sample of a predetermined size from the population. The items included in the sample are determined through the use of a random number generator, such as a table of random numbers (see Section 7.1 and Table E.1) or by using Microsoft Excel (see pages 281–282).

Hypothetically, to use the sample statistic to estimate the population parameter, you should examine *every* possible sample of a given size that could occur. A **sampling distribution** is the distribution of the results if you actually selected all possible samples.

7.4 SAMPLING DISTRIBUTION OF THE MEAN

In Chapter 3, several measures of central tendency, including the mean, median, and mode, were discussed. Undoubtedly, the mean is the most widely used measure of central tendency. The sample mean is often used to estimate the population mean. The **sampling distribution of the mean** is the distribution of all possible sample means if you select all possible samples of a certain size.

The Unbiased Property of the Sample Mean

The sample mean is **unbiased** because the mean of all the possible sample means (of a given sample size, n) is equal to the population mean, μ. A simple example concerning a population of four administrative assistants demonstrates this property. Each assistant is asked to type the same page of a manuscript. Table 7.2 presents the number of errors. This population distribution is shown in Figure 7.2.

TABLE 7.2

Number of Errors Made by Each of Four Administrative Assistants

Administrative Assistant	Number of Errors
Ann	$X_1 = 3$
Bob	$X_2 = 2$
Carla	$X_3 = 1$
Dave	$X_4 = 4$

FIGURE 7.2

Number of errors made by a population of four administrative assistants

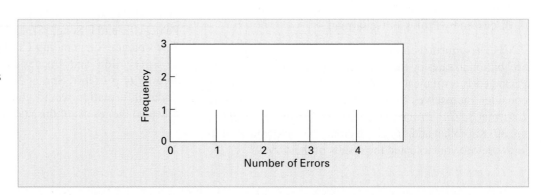

When you have the data from a population, you compute the mean by using Equation (7.1).

POPULATION MEAN

The population mean is the sum of the values in the population divided by the population size, N.

$$\mu = \frac{\sum_{i=1}^{N} X_i}{N} \tag{7.1}$$

You compute the population standard deviation, σ, using Equation (7.2):

POPULATION STANDARD DEVIATION

$$\sigma = \sqrt{\frac{\sum_{i=1}^{N}(X_i - \mu)^2}{N}}$$

(7.2)

Thus, for the data of Table 7.1,

$$\mu = \frac{3+2+1+4}{4} = 2.5 \text{ errors}$$

and

$$\sigma = \sqrt{\frac{(3-2.5)^2 + (2-2.5)^2 + (1-2.5)^2 + (4-2.5)^2}{4}} = 1.12 \text{ errors}$$

If you select samples of two administrative assistants *with* replacement from this population, there are 16 possible samples ($N^n = 4^2 = 16$). Table 7.3 lists the 16 possible sample outcomes. If you average all 16 of these sample means, the mean of these values, $\mu_{\bar{X}}$, is equal to 2.5, which is also the mean of the population μ.

TABLE 7.3

All 16 Samples of $n = 2$ Administrative Assistants from a Population of $N = 4$ Administrative Assistants When Sampling *with* Replacement

Sample	Administrative Assistants	Sample Outcomes	Sample Mean
1	Ann, Ann	3, 3	$\bar{X}_1 = 3$
2	Ann, Bob	3, 2	$\bar{X}_2 = 2.5$
3	Ann, Carla	3, 1	$\bar{X}_3 = 2$
4	Ann, Dave	3, 4	$\bar{X}_4 = 3.5$
5	Bob, Ann	2, 3	$\bar{X}_5 = 2.5$
6	Bob, Bob	2, 2	$\bar{X}_6 = 2$
7	Bob, Carla	2, 1	$\bar{X}_7 = 1.5$
8	Bob, Dave	2, 4	$\bar{X}_8 = 3$
9	Carla, Ann	1, 3	$\bar{X}_9 = 2$
10	Carla, Bob	1, 2	$\bar{X}_{10} = 1.5$
11	Carla, Carla	1, 1	$\bar{X}_{11} = 1$
12	Carla, Dave	1, 4	$\bar{X}_{12} = 2.5$
13	Dave, Ann	4, 3	$\bar{X}_{13} = 3.5$
14	Dave, Bob	4, 2	$\bar{X}_{14} = 3$
15	Dave, Carla	4, 1	$\bar{X}_{15} = 2.5$
16	Dave, Dave	4, 4	$\bar{X}_{16} = 4$
			$\mu_{\bar{X}} = 2.5$

Because the mean of the 16 sample means is equal to the population mean, the sample mean is an unbiased estimator of the population mean. Therefore, although you do not know how close the sample mean of any particular sample selected comes to the population mean, you are at least assured that the mean of all the possible sample means that could have been selected is equal to the population mean.

Standard Error of the Mean

Figure 7.3 illustrates the variation in the sample means when selecting all 16 possible samples. In this small example, although the sample means vary from sample to sample, depending on which two administrative assistants are selected, the sample means do not vary as much as the individual values in the population. That the sample means are less variable than the individual values in the population follows directly from the fact that each sample mean averages together all the values in the sample. A population consists of individual outcomes that can take on a wide range of values, from extremely small to extremely large. However, if a sample contains an extreme value, although this value will have an effect on the sample mean, the effect is reduced because the value is averaged with all the other values in the sample. As the sample size increases, the effect of a single extreme value becomes smaller because it is averaged with more values.

FIGURE 7.3

Sampling distribution of the mean, based on all possible samples containing two administrative assistants

Source: Data are from Table 7.3.

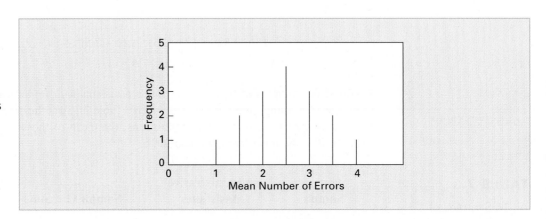

The value of the standard deviation of all possible sample means, called the **standard error of the mean**, expresses how the sample means vary from sample to sample. Equation (7.3) defines the standard error of the mean when sampling *with* replacement or *without* replacement (see page 254) from large or infinite populations.

STANDARD ERROR OF THE MEAN

The standard error of the mean, $\sigma_{\bar{X}}$, is equal to the standard deviation in the population, σ, divided by the square root of the sample size, n.

$$\sigma_{\bar{X}} = \frac{\sigma}{\sqrt{n}} \qquad (7.3)$$

Therefore, as the sample size increases, the standard error of the mean decreases by a factor equal to the square root of the sample size.

You can also use Equation (7.3) as an approximation of the standard error of the mean when the sample is selected without replacement if the sample contains less than 5% of the entire population. Example 7.3 computes the standard error of the mean for such a situation. (See the **section 7.6.pdf** file on the Student CD-ROM that accompanies this book for the case in which more than 5% of the population is contained in a sample selected without replacement.)

EXAMPLE 7.3   COMPUTING THE STANDARD ERROR OF THE MEAN

Returning to the cereal-filling process described in the Using Statistics scenario on page 252, if you randomly select a sample of 25 boxes without replacement from the thousands of boxes filled during a shift, the sample contains far less than 5% of the population. Given that the standard deviation of the cereal-filling process is 15 grams, compute the standard error of the mean.

SOLUTION Using Equation (7.3) with $n = 25$ and $\sigma = 15$, the standard error of the mean is

$$\sigma_{\overline{X}} = \frac{\sigma}{\sqrt{n}} = \frac{15}{\sqrt{25}} = \frac{15}{5} = 3$$

The variation in the sample means for samples of $n = 25$ is much less than the variation in the individual boxes of cereal (that is, $\sigma_{\overline{X}} = 3$ while $\sigma = 15$).

Sampling from Normally Distributed Populations

Now that the concept of a sampling distribution has been introduced and the standard error of the mean has been defined, what distribution will the sample mean, $\overline{X}$, follow? If you are sampling from a population that is normally distributed with mean, μ, and standard deviation, σ, regardless of the sample size, n, the sampling distribution of the mean is normally distributed, with mean, $\mu_{\overline{X}} = \mu$, and standard error of the mean, $\sigma_{\overline{X}}$.

In the simplest case, if you take samples of size $n = 1$, each possible sample mean is a single value from the population because

$$\overline{X} = \frac{\sum_{i=1}^{n} X_i}{n} = \frac{X_i}{1} = X_i$$

Therefore, if the population is normally distributed, with mean, μ, and standard deviation, σ, the sampling distribution of $\overline{X}$ for samples of $n = 1$ must also follow the normal distribution, with mean $\mu_{\overline{X}} = \mu$ and standard error of the mean $\sigma_{\overline{X}} = \sigma/\sqrt{1} = \sigma$. In addition, as the sample size increases, the sampling distribution of the mean still follows a normal distribution, with $\mu_{\overline{X}} = \mu$, but the standard error of the mean decreases, so that a larger proportion of sample means are closer to the population mean. Figure 7.4 on page 266 illustrates this reduction in variability in which 500 samples of 1, 2, 4, 8, 16, and 32 were randomly selected from a normally distributed population. From the polygons in Figure 7.4, you can see that, although the sampling distribution of the mean is approximately[1] normal for each sample size, the sample means are distributed more tightly around the population mean as the sample size increases.

To further examine the concept of the sampling distribution of the mean, consider the Using Statistics scenario described on page 252. The packaging equipment that is filling 368-gram boxes of cereal is set so that the amount of cereal in a box is normally distributed, with a mean of 368 grams. From past experience, you know the population standard deviation for this filling process is 15 grams.

If you randomly select a sample of 25 boxes from the many thousands that are filled in a day and the mean weight is computed for this sample, what type of result could you expect? For example, do you think that the sample mean could be 368 grams? 200 grams? 365 grams?

The sample acts as a miniature representation of the population, so if the values in the population are normally distributed, the values in the sample should be approximately normally distributed. Thus, if the population mean is 368 grams, the sample mean has a good chance of being close to 368 grams.

[1]Remember that "only" 500 samples out of an infinite number of samples have been selected, so that the sampling distributions shown are only approximations of the true distributions.

FIGURE 7.4

Sampling distributions of the mean from 500 samples of sizes n = 1, 2, 4, 8, 16, and 32 selected from a normal population

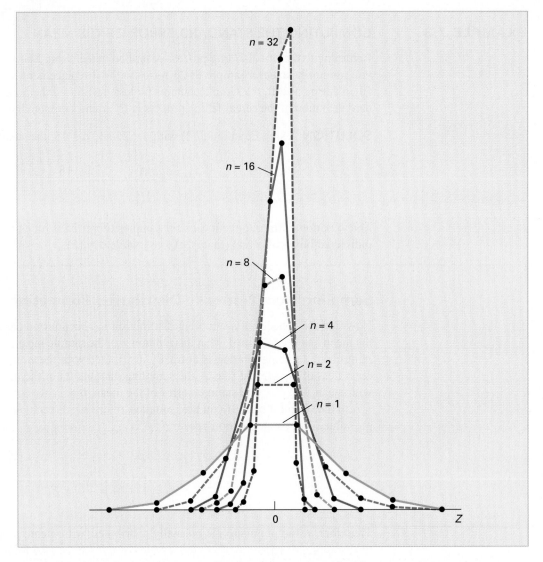

How can you determine the probability that the sample of 25 boxes will have a mean below 365 grams? From the normal distribution (Section 6.2), you know that you can find the area below any value X by converting to standardized Z values:

$$Z = \frac{X - \mu}{\sigma}$$

In the examples in Section 6.2, you studied how any single value, X, differs from the mean. Now, in this example, the value involved is a sample mean, $\overline{X}$, and you want to determine the likelihood that a sample mean is below 365. In Equation (7.4), to find the Z value, you substitute $\overline{X}$ for X, $\mu_{\overline{X}}$ for μ, and $\sigma_{\overline{X}}$ for σ.

FINDING Z FOR THE SAMPLING DISTRIBUTION OF THE MEAN

The Z value is equal to the difference between the sample mean, $\overline{X}$, and the population mean, μ, divided by the standard error of the mean, $\sigma_{\overline{X}}$.

$$Z = \frac{\overline{X} - \mu_{\overline{X}}}{\sigma_{\overline{X}}} = \frac{\overline{X} - \mu}{\dfrac{\sigma}{\sqrt{n}}} \tag{7.4}$$

To find the area below 365 grams, from Equation (7.4),

$$Z = \frac{\overline{X} - \mu_{\overline{X}}}{\sigma_{\overline{X}}} = \frac{365 - 368}{\dfrac{15}{\sqrt{25}}} = \frac{-3}{3} = -1.00$$

The area corresponding to $Z = -1.00$ in Table E.2 is 0.1587. Therefore, 15.87% of all the possible samples of 25 boxes have a sample mean below 365 grams.

The preceding statement is not the same as saying that a certain percentage of *individual* boxes will have less than 365 grams of cereal. You compute that percentage as follows:

$$Z = \frac{X - \mu}{\sigma} = \frac{365 - 368}{15} = \frac{-3}{15} = -0.20$$

The area corresponding to $Z = -0.20$ in Table E.2 is 0.4207. Therefore, 42.07% of the *individual* boxes are expected to contain less than 365 grams. Comparing these results, you see that many more *individual boxes* than *sample means* are below 365 grams. This result is explained by the fact that each sample consists of 25 different values, some small and some large. The averaging process dilutes the importance of any individual value, particularly when the sample size is large. Thus, the chance that the sample mean of 25 boxes is far away from the population mean is less than the chance that a *single* box is far away.

Examples 7.4 and 7.5 show how these results are affected by using different sample sizes.

EXAMPLE 7.4

THE EFFECT OF SAMPLE SIZE *n* ON THE COMPUTATION OF $\sigma_{\overline{X}}$

How is the standard error of the mean affected by increasing the sample size from 25 to 100 boxes?

SOLUTION If $n = 100$ boxes, then using Equation (7.3) on page 264:

$$\sigma_{\overline{X}} = \frac{\sigma}{\sqrt{n}} = \frac{15}{\sqrt{100}} = \frac{15}{10} = 1.5$$

The fourfold increase in the sample size from 25 to 100 reduces the standard error of the mean by half—from 3 grams to 1.5 grams. This demonstrates that taking a larger sample results in less variability in the sample means from sample to sample.

EXAMPLE 7.5

THE EFFECT OF SAMPLE SIZE *n* ON THE CLUSTERING OF MEANS IN THE SAMPLING DISTRIBUTION

If you select a sample of 100 boxes, what is the probability that the sample mean is below 365 grams?

SOLUTION Using Equation (7.4) on page 266,

$$Z = \frac{\overline{X} - \mu_{\overline{X}}}{\sigma_{\overline{X}}} = \frac{365 - 368}{\dfrac{15}{\sqrt{100}}} = \frac{-3}{1.5} = -2.00$$

From Table E.2, the area less than $Z = -2.00$ is 0.0228. Therefore, 2.28% of the samples of 100 boxes have means below 365 grams, as compared with 15.87% for samples of 25 boxes.

Sometimes you need to find the interval that contains a fixed proportion of the sample means. You need to determine a distance below and above the population mean containing a specific area of the normal curve. From Equation (7.4) on page 266,

$$Z = \frac{\overline{X} - \mu}{\dfrac{\sigma}{\sqrt{n}}}$$

Solving for $\overline{X}$ results in Equation (7.5).

FINDING $\overline{X}$ FOR THE SAMPLING DISTRIBUTION OF THE MEAN

$$\overline{X} = \mu + Z\frac{\sigma}{\sqrt{n}} \tag{7.5}$$

Example 7.6 illustrates the use of Equation (7.5).

EXAMPLE 7.6

DETERMINING THE INTERVAL THAT INCLUDES A FIXED PROPORTION OF THE SAMPLE MEANS

In the cereal-fill example, find an interval symmetrically distributed around the population mean that will include 95% of the sample means based on samples of 25 boxes.

SOLUTION If 95% of the sample means are in the interval, then 5% are outside the interval. Divide the 5% into two equal parts of 2.5%. The value of Z in Table E.2 corresponding to an area of 0.0250 in the lower tail of the normal curve is -1.96, and the value of Z corresponding to a cumulative area of 0.975 (that is, 0.025 in the upper tail of the normal curve) is $+1.96$. The lower value of $\overline{X}$ (called $\overline{X}_L$) and the upper value of $\overline{X}$ (called $\overline{X}_U$) are found by using Equation (7.5):

$$\overline{X}_L = 368 + (-1.96)\frac{15}{\sqrt{25}} = 368 - 5.88 = 362.12$$

$$\overline{X}_U = 368 + (1.96)\frac{15}{\sqrt{25}} = 368 + 5.88 = 373.88$$

Therefore, 95% of all sample means based on samples of 25 boxes are between 362.12 and 373.88 grams.

Sampling from Non-Normally Distributed Populations— The Central Limit Theorem

Thus far in this section, only the sampling distribution of the mean for a normally distributed population has been considered. However, in many instances, either you know that the population is not normally distributed or it is unrealistic to assume that the population is normally distributed. An important theorem in statistics, the Central Limit Theorem, deals with this situation.

THE CENTRAL LIMIT THEOREM

The **Central Limit Theorem** states that as the sample size (that is, the number of values in each sample) gets *large enough*, the sampling distribution of the mean is approximately normally distributed. This is true regardless of the shape of the distribution of the individual values in the population.

What sample size is large enough? A great deal of statistical research has gone into this issue. As a general rule, statisticians have found that for many population distributions, when the sample size is at least 30, the sampling distribution of the mean is approximately normal. However, you can apply the Central Limit Theorem for even smaller sample sizes if the population distribution is approximately bell shaped. In the uncommon case in which the distribution is extremely skewed or has more than one mode, you may need sample sizes larger than 30 to ensure normality.

Figure 7.5 illustrates the application of the Central Limit Theorem to different populations. The sampling distributions from three different continuous distributions (normal, uniform, and exponential) for varying sample sizes ($n = 2, 5, 30$) are displayed.

FIGURE 7.5

Sampling distribution of the mean for different populations for samples of $n = 2, 5,$ and 30

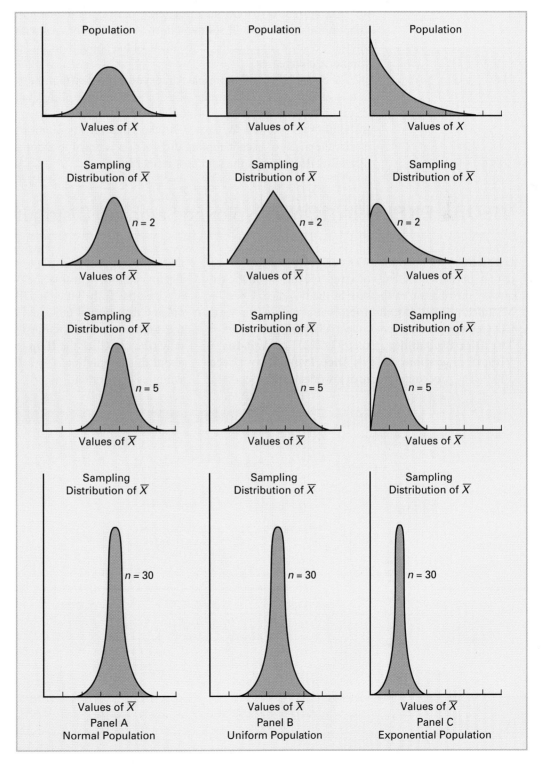

In each of the panels, because the sample mean has the property of being unbiased, the mean of any sampling distribution is always equal to the mean of the population.

Panel A of Figure 7.5 shows the sampling distribution of the mean selected from a normal population. As mentioned earlier in this section, when the population is normally distributed, the sampling distribution of the mean is normally distributed for any sample size. (You can measure the variability by using the standard error of the mean, Equation 7.3, on page 264.)

Panel B of Figure 7.5 depicts the sampling distribution from a population with a uniform (or rectangular) distribution (see Section 6.4). When samples of size $n = 2$ are selected, there is a peaking, or *central limiting*, effect already working. For $n = 5$, the sampling distribution is bell shaped and approximately normal. When $n = 30$, the sampling distribution looks very similar to a normal distribution. In general, the larger the sample size, the more closely the sampling distribution will follow a normal distribution. As with all cases, the mean of each sampling distribution is equal to the mean of the population, and the variability decreases as the sample size increases.

Panel C of Figure 7.5 presents an exponential distribution (see Section 6.5). This population is extremely right-skewed. When $n = 2$, the sampling distribution is still highly right-skewed but less so than the distribution of the population. For $n = 5$, the sampling distribution is slightly right-skewed. When $n = 30$, the sampling distribution looks approximately normal. Again, the mean of each sampling distribution is equal to the mean of the population, and the variability decreases as the sample size increases.

VISUAL EXPLORATIONS Exploring Sampling Distributions

Use the Visual Explorations **Two Dice Probability** procedure to observe the effects of simulated throws on the frequency distribution of the sum of the two dice. Open the **Visual Explorations.xla** macro workbook on the text's CD (see Appendix D) and select **VisualExplorations → Two Dice Probability** (Excel 97–2003) or **Add-Ins → VisualExplorations → Two Dice Probability** (Excel 2007). The procedure produces a worksheet that contains an empty frequency distribution table and histogram and a floating control panel (see below).

Click the **Tally** button to tally a set of throws in the frequency distribution table and histogram. Optionally, use the spinner buttons to adjust the number of throws per tally (round). Click the **Help** button for more information about this simulation. Click **Finish** when you are done with this exploration.

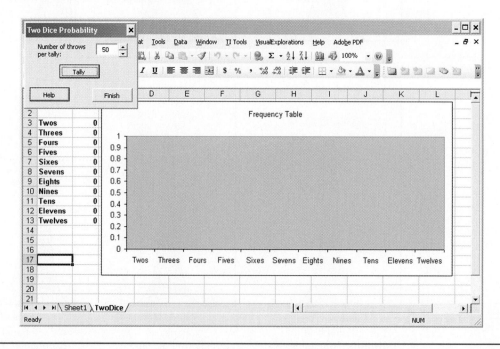

Using the results from the normal, uniform, and exponential statistical distributions, you can reach the following conclusions regarding the Central Limit Theorem:

- For most population distributions, regardless of shape, the sampling distribution of the mean is approximately normally distributed if samples of at least 30 are selected.
- If the population distribution is fairly symmetric, the sampling distribution of the mean is approximately normal for samples as small as 5.
- If the population is normally distributed, the sampling distribution of the mean is normally distributed, regardless of the sample size.

The Central Limit Theorem is of crucial importance in using statistical inference to draw conclusions about a population. It allows you to make inferences about the population mean without having to know the specific shape of the population distribution.

PROBLEMS FOR SECTION 7.4

Learning the Basics

 7.17 Given a normal distribution with $\mu = 100$ and $\sigma = 10$, if you select a sample of $n = 25$, what is the probability that $\bar{X}$ is
a. less than 95?
b. between 95 and 97.5?
c. above 102.2?
d. There is a 65% chance that $\bar{X}$ is above what value?

 7.18 Given a normal distribution with $\mu = 50$ and $\sigma = 5$, if you select a sample of $n = 100$, what is the probability that $\bar{X}$ is
a. less than 47?
b. between 47 and 49.5?
c. above 51.1?
d. There is a 35% chance that $\bar{X}$ is above what value?

Applying the Concepts

7.19 For each of the following three populations, indicate what the sampling distribution for samples of 25 would consist of:
a. Travel expense vouchers for a university in an academic year
b. Absentee records (days absent per year) in 2006 for employees of a large manufacturing company
c. Yearly sales (in gallons) of unleaded gasoline at service stations located in a particular county

7.20 The following data represent the number of days absent per year in a population of six employees of a small company:

$$1 \quad 3 \quad 6 \quad 7 \quad 9 \quad 10$$

a. Assuming that you sample without replacement, select all possible samples of $n = 2$ and construct the sampling distribution of the mean. Compute the mean of all the sample means and also compute the population mean. Are they equal? What is this property called?
b. Repeat (a) for all possible samples of $n = 3$.
c. Compare the shape of the sampling distribution of the mean in (a) and (b). Which sampling distribution has less variability? Why?
d. Assuming that you sample with replacement, repeat (a) through (c) and compare the results. Which sampling distributions have the least variability—those in (a) or (b)? Why?

 7.21 The diameter of Ping-Pong balls manufactured at a large factory is approximately normally distributed, with a mean of 1.30 inches and a standard deviation of 0.04 inch. If you select a random sample of 16 Ping-Pong balls,
a. what is the sampling distribution of the mean?
b. what is the probability that the sample mean is less than 1.28 inches?
c. what is the probability that the sample mean is between 1.31 and 1.33 inches?
d. The probability is 60% that the sample mean will be between what two values, symmetrically distributed around the population mean?

7.22 The U.S. Census Bureau announced that the median sales price of new houses sold in March 2006 was $224,200, while the mean sales price was $279,100 (**www.census.gov/newhomesales**, April 26, 2006). Assume that the standard deviation of the prices is $90,000.
a. If you select samples of $n = 2$, describe the shape of the sampling distribution of $\bar{X}$.
b. If you select samples of $n = 100$, describe the shape of the sampling distribution of $\bar{X}$.
c. If you select a random sample of $n = 100$, what is the probability that the sample mean will be less than $250,000?

7.23 Time spent using email per session is normally distributed, with $\mu = 8$ minutes and $\sigma = 2$ minutes. If you select a random sample of 25 sessions,

a. what is the probability that the sample mean is between 7.8 and 8.2 minutes?

b. what is the probability that the sample mean is between 7.5 and 8 minutes?

c. If you select a random sample of 100 sessions, what is the probability that the sample mean is between 7.8 and 8.2 minutes?

d. Explain the difference in the results of (a) and (c).

 7.24 The amount of time a bank teller spends with each customer has a population mean, μ, of 3.10 minutes and standard deviation, σ, of 0.40 minute. If you select a random sample of 16 customers,

a. what is the probability that the mean time spent per customer is at least 3 minutes?

b. there is an 85% chance that the sample mean is less than how many minutes?

c. What assumption must you make in order to solve (a) and (b)?

d. If you select a random sample of 64 customers, there is an 85% chance that the sample mean is less than how many minutes?

7.25 The *New York Times* reported (L. J. Flynn, "Tax Surfing," *The New York Times*, March 25, 2002, p. C10) that the mean time to download the home page for the Internal Revenue Service (IRS), **www.irs.gov**, was 0.8 second. Suppose that the download time was normally distributed, with a standard deviation of 0.2 second. If you select a random sample of 30 download times,

a. what is the probability that the sample mean is less than 0.75 second?

b. what is the probability that the sample mean is between 0.70 and 0.90 second?

c. the probability is 80% that the sample mean is between what two values, symmetrically distributed around the population mean?

d. the probability is 90% that the sample mean is less than what value?

7.26 The article discussed in Problem 7.25 also reported that the mean download time for the H&R Block Web site, **www.hrblock.com**, was 2.5 seconds. Suppose that the download time for the H&R Block Web site was normally distributed, with a standard deviation of 0.5 second. If you select a random sample of 30 download times,

a. what is the probability that the sample mean is less than 2.75 seconds?

b. what is the probability that the sample mean is between 2.70 and 2.90 seconds?

c. the probability is 80% that the sample mean is between what two values symmetrically distributed around the population mean?

d. the probability is 90% that the sample mean is less than what value?

7.5 SAMPLING DISTRIBUTION OF THE PROPORTION

Consider a categorical variable that has only two categories, such as the customer prefers your brand or the customer prefers the competitor's brand. Of interest is the proportion of items belonging to one of the categories—for example, the proportion of customers that prefers your brand. The population proportion, represented by π, is the proportion of items in the entire population with the characteristic of interest. The sample proportion, represented by p, is the proportion of items in the sample with the characteristic of interest. The sample proportion, a statistic, is used to estimate the population proportion, a parameter. To calculate the sample proportion, you assign the two possible outcomes scores of 1 or 0 to represent the presence or absence of the characteristic. You then sum all the 1 and 0 scores and divide by n, the sample size. For example, if, in a sample of five customers, three preferred your brand and two did not, you have three 1s and two 0s. Summing the three 1s and two 0s and dividing by the sample size of 5 gives you a sample proportion of 0.60.

SAMPLE PROPORTION

$$p = \frac{X}{n} = \frac{\text{Number of items having the characteristic of interest}}{\text{Sample size}} \qquad (7.6)$$

The sample proportion, p, takes on values between 0 and 1. If all individuals possess the characteristic, you assign each a score of 1, and p is equal to 1. If half the individuals possess the characteristic, you assign half a score of 1 and assign the other half a score of 0, and p is equal to 0.5. If none of the individuals possesses the characteristic, you assign each a score of 0, and p is equal to 0.

While the sample mean, $\overline{X}$, is an unbiased estimator of the population mean, μ, the statistic p is an unbiased estimator of the population proportion, π. By analogy to the sampling distribution of the mean, the **standard error of the proportion**, σ_p, is given in Equation (7.7).

STANDARD ERROR OF THE PROPORTION

$$\sigma_p = \sqrt{\frac{\pi(1-\pi)}{n}} \tag{7.7}$$

If you select all possible samples of a certain size, the distribution of all possible sample proportions is referred to as the **sampling distribution of the proportion**. The sampling distribution of the proportion follows the binomial distribution, as discussed in Section 5.3. However, you can use the normal distribution to approximate the binomial distribution when $n\pi$ and $n(1-\pi)$ are each at least 5 (see Section 6.6 on the CD-ROM). In most cases in which inferences are made about the proportion, the sample size is substantial enough to meet the conditions for using the normal approximation (see reference 1). Therefore, in many instances, you can use the normal distribution to estimate the sampling distribution of the proportion.

Substituting p for $\overline{X}$, π for μ, and $\sqrt{\dfrac{\pi(1-\pi)}{n}}$ for $\dfrac{\sigma}{\sqrt{n}}$ in Equation (7.4) on page 266, results in Equation (7.8).

FINDING Z FOR THE SAMPLING DISTRIBUTION OF THE PROPORTION

$$Z = \frac{p - \pi}{\sqrt{\dfrac{\pi(1-\pi)}{n}}} \tag{7.8}$$

To illustrate the sampling distribution of the proportion, suppose that the manager of the local branch of a savings bank determines that 40% of all depositors have multiple accounts at the bank. If you select a random sample of 200 depositors, the probability that the sample proportion of depositors with multiple accounts is less than 0.30 is calculated as follows: Because $n\pi = 200(0.40) = 80 \geq 5$ and $n(1-\pi) = 200(0.60) = 120 \geq 5$, the sample size is large enough to assume that the sampling distribution of the proportion is approximately normally distributed. Using Equation (7.8),

$$Z = \frac{p - \pi}{\sqrt{\dfrac{\pi(1-\pi)}{n}}}$$

$$= \frac{0.30 - 0.40}{\sqrt{\dfrac{(0.40)(0.60)}{200}}} = \frac{-0.10}{\sqrt{\dfrac{0.24}{200}}} = \frac{-0.10}{0.0346}$$

$$= -2.89$$

Using Table E.2, the area under the normal curve less than -2.89 is 0.0019. Therefore, the probability that the sample proportion is less than 0.30 is 0.0019—a highly unlikely event. This means that if the true proportion of successes in the population is 0.40, less than one-fifth of 1% of the samples of $n = 200$ would be expected to have sample proportions of less than 0.30.

PROBLEMS FOR SECTION 7.5

Learning the Basics

 7.27 In a random sample of 64 people, 48 are classified as "successful."
a. Determine the sample proportion, p, of "successful" people.
b. If the population proportion is 0.70, determine the standard error of the proportion.

 7.28 A random sample of 50 households was selected for a telephone survey. The key question asked was, "Do you or any member of your household own a cellular telephone with a built-in camera?" Of the 50 respondents, 15 said yes and 35 said no.
a. Determine the sample proportion, p, of households with cellular telephones with built-in cameras.
b. If the population proportion is 0.40, determine the standard error of the proportion.

7.29 The following data represent the responses (Y for yes and N for no) from a sample of 40 college students to the question "Do you currently own shares in any stocks?"

N N Y N N Y N Y N Y N N Y N Y Y N N N Y

N Y N N N N Y N N Y Y N N N Y N N Y N N

a. Determine the sample proportion, p, of college students who own shares of stock.
b. If the population proportion is 0.30, determine the standard error of the proportion.

Applying the Concepts

 7.30 A political pollster is conducting an analysis of sample results in order to make predictions on election night. Assuming a two-candidate election, if a specific candidate receives at least 55% of the vote in the sample, then that candidate will be forecast as the winner of the election. If you select a random sample of 100 voters, what is the probability that a candidate will be forecast as the winner when
a. the true percentage of her vote is 50.1%?
b. the true percentage of her vote is 60%?
c. the true percentage of her vote is 49% (and she will actually lose the election)?
d. If the sample size is increased to 400, what are your answers to (a) through (c)? Discuss.

 7.31 You plan to conduct a marketing experiment in which students are to taste one of two different brands of soft drink. Their task is to correctly identify the brand tasted. You select a random sample of 200 students and assume that the students have no abil-

ity to distinguish between the two brands. (Hint: If an individual has no ability to distinguish between the two soft drinks, then each brand is equally likely to be selected.)
a. What is the probability that the sample will have between 50% and 60% of the identifications correct?
b. The probability is 90% that the sample percentage is contained within what symmetrical limits of the population percentage?
c. What is the probability that the sample percentage of correct identifications is greater than 65%?
d. Which is more likely to occur—more than 60% correct identifications in the sample of 200 or more than 55% correct identifications in a sample of 1,000? Explain.

7.32 A study of women in corporate leadership was conducted by Catalyst, a New York research organization. The study concluded that slightly more than 15% of corporate officers at Fortune 500 companies are women (C. Hymowitz, "Women Put Noses to the Grindstone, and Miss Opportunities," *The Wall Street Journal*, February 3, 2004, p. B1). Suppose that you select a random sample of 200 corporate officers, and the true proportion held by women is 0.15.
a. What is the probability that in the sample, less than 15% of the corporate officers will be women?
b. What is the probability that in the sample, between 13% and 17% of the corporate officers will be women?
c. What is the probability that in the sample, between 10% and 20% of the corporate officers will be women?
d. If a sample of 100 is taken, how does this change your answers to (a) through (c)?

7.33 The NBC hit comedy *Friends* was TiVo's most popular show during the week of April 18–24, 2004. According to the Nielsen ratings, 29.7% of TiVo owners in the United States either recorded *Friends* or watched it live ("Prime-Time Nielsen Ratings," *USA Today*, April 28, 2004, p. 3D). Suppose you select a random sample of 50 TiVo owners.
a. What is the probability that more than half the people in the sample watched or recorded *Friends*?
b. What is the probability that less than 25% of the people in the sample watched or recorded *Friends*?
c. If a random sample of size 500 is taken, how does this change your answers to (a) and (b)?

7.34 According to Gallup's annual poll on personal finances, while most U.S. workers reported living comfortably now, many expected a downturn in their lifestyle when they stop working. Approximately half said they have enough money to live comfortably now and expected to do so in the future (J. M. Jones, "Only Half of Non-Retirees Expect to be Comfortable in Retirement," *The Gallup Poll*,

galluppoll.com, May 2, 2006). If you select a random sample of 200 U.S. workers,

a. what is the probability that the sample will have between 45% and 55% who say they have enough money to live comfortably now and expect to do so in the future?

b. the probability is 90% that the sample percentage will be contained within what symmetrical limits of the population percentage?

c. the probability is 95% that the sample percentage will be contained within what symmetrical limits of the population percentage?

7.35 According to the National Restaurant Association, 20% of fine-dining restaurants have instituted policies restricting the use of cell phones ("Business Bulletin," *The Wall Street Journal*, June 1, 2000, p. A1). If you select a random sample of 100 fine-dining restaurants,

a. what is the probability that the sample has between 15% and 25% that have established policies restricting cell phone use?

b. the probability is 90% that the sample percentage will be contained within what symmetrical limits of the population percentage?

c. the probability is 95% that the sample percentage will be contained within what symmetrical limits of the population percentage?

d. Suppose that in January 2007, you selected a random sample of 100 fine-dining restaurants and found that 31 had policies restricting the use of cell phones. Do you think that the population percentage has changed?

7.36 An article (P. Kitchen, "Retirement Plan: To Keep Working," *Newsday*, September 24, 2003) discussed the retirement plans of Americans ages 50 to 70 who were employed full time or part time. Twenty-nine percent of the respondents said that they did not intend to work for pay at all. If you select a random sample of 400 Americans ages 50 to 70 employed full time or part time,

a. what is the probability that the sample has between 25% and 30% who do not intend to work for pay at all?

b. If a current sample of 400 Americans ages 50 to 70 employed full time or part time has 35% who do not intend to work for pay at all, what can you infer about the population estimate of 29%? Explain.

c. If a current sample of 100 Americans ages 50 to 70 employed full time or part time has 35% who do not intend to work for pay at all, what can you infer about the population estimate of 29%? Explain.

d. Explain the difference in the results in (b) and (c).

7.37 The IRS discontinued random audits in 1988. Instead, the IRS conducts audits on returns deemed questionable by its Discriminant Function System (DFS), a complicated and highly secretive computerized analysis system. In an attempt to reduce the proportion of "no-change" audits (that is, audits that uncover that no additional taxes are due), the IRS only audits returns the DFS scores as highly questionable. The proportion of no-change audits has risen over the years and is currently approximately 0.25 (T. Herman, "Unhappy Returns: IRS Moves to Bring Back Random Audits," *The Wall Street Journal*, June 20, 2002, p. A1). Suppose that you select a random sample of 100 audits. What is the probability that the sample has

a. between 24% and 26% no-change audits?

b. between 20% and 30% no-change audits?

c. more than 30% no-change audits?

7.38 Referring to Problem 7.37, the IRS announced that it planned to resume totally random audits in 2002. Suppose that you select a random sample of 200 totally random audits and that 90% of all the returns filed would result in no-change audits. What is the probability that the sample has

a. between 89% and 91% no-change audits?

b. between 85% and 95% no-change audits?

c. more than 95% no-change audits?

7.6 ◐ (CD-ROM Topic) SAMPLING FROM FINITE POPULATIONS

In this section, sampling without replacement from finite populations is considered. For further discussion, see **section 7.6.pdf** on the Student CD-ROM that accompanies this book.

SUMMARY

In this chapter, you studied four common sampling methods—simple random, systematic, stratified, and cluster. You also studied the sampling distribution of the sample mean, the Central Limit Theorem, and the sampling distribution of the sample proportion. You learned that the sample mean is an unbiased estimator of the population mean, and the sample proportion is an unbiased estimator of the population proportion. By observing the mean weight in a sample of cereal boxes filled by Oxford Cereals, you were able to reach conclusions concerning the mean weight in the population of cereal boxes. In the next five chapters, the techniques of confidence intervals and tests of hypotheses commonly used for statistical inference are discussed.

KEY EQUATIONS

Population Mean

$$\mu = \frac{\sum\limits_{i=1}^{N} X_i}{N} \qquad (7.1)$$

Population Standard Deviation

$$\sigma = \sqrt{\frac{\sum\limits_{i=1}^{N} (X_i - \mu)^2}{N}} \qquad (7.2)$$

Standard Error of the Mean

$$\sigma_{\bar{X}} = \frac{\sigma}{\sqrt{n}} \qquad (7.3)$$

Finding Z for the Sampling Distribution of the Mean

$$Z = \frac{\bar{X} - \mu_{\bar{X}}}{\sigma_{\bar{X}}} = \frac{\bar{X} - \mu}{\dfrac{\sigma}{\sqrt{n}}} \qquad (7.4)$$

Finding $\bar{X}$ for the Sampling Distribution of the Mean

$$\bar{X} = \mu + Z \frac{\sigma}{\sqrt{n}} \qquad (7.5)$$

Sample Proportion

$$p = \frac{X}{n} \qquad (7.6)$$

Standard Error of the Proportion

$$\sigma_p = \sqrt{\frac{\pi(1 - \pi)}{n}} \qquad (7.7)$$

Finding Z for the Sampling Distribution of the Proportion

$$Z = \frac{p - \pi}{\sqrt{\dfrac{\pi(1 - \pi)}{n}}} \qquad (7.8)$$

KEY TERMS

Central Limit Theorem   268
cluster   257
cluster sample   257
convenience sampling   253
coverage error   259
frame   252
judgment sample   253
measurement error   260
nonprobability sample   253
nonresponse bias   259

nonresponse error   259
probability sample   253
sampling distribution   262
sampling distribution of the mean   262
sampling distribution of the
  proportion   273
sampling error   260
sampling with replacement   253
sampling without replacement   254
selection bias   259

simple random sample   253
standard error of the mean   264
standard error of the proportion   273
strata   256
stratified sample   256
systematic sample   256
table of random numbers   254
unbiased   262

CHAPTER REVIEW PROBLEMS

Checking Your Understanding

 7.39 Why is the sample mean an unbiased estimator of the population mean?

 7.40 Why does the standard error of the mean decrease as the sample size, n, increases?

7.41 Why does the sampling distribution of the mean follow a normal distribution for a large enough sample size, even though the population may not be normally distributed?

7.42 What is the difference between a probability distribution and a sampling distribution?

7.43 Under what circumstances does the sampling distribution of the proportion approximately follow the normal distribution?

7.44 What is the difference between probability and nonprobability sampling?

7.45 What are some potential problems with using "fish-bowl" methods to select a simple random sample?

7.46 What is the difference between sampling *with* replacement versus *without* replacement?

7.47 What is the difference between a simple random sample and a systematic sample?

 7.48 What is the difference between a simple random sample and a stratified sample?

7.49 What is the difference between a stratified sample and a cluster sample?

Applying the Concepts

7.50 An industrial sewing machine uses ball bearings that are targeted to have a diameter of 0.75 inch. The lower and upper specification limits under which the ball bearing can operate are 0.74 inch (lower) and 0.76 inch (upper). Past experience has indicated that the actual diameter of the ball bearings is approximately normally distributed, with a mean of 0.753 inch and a standard deviation of 0.004 inch. If you select a random sample of 25 ball bearings, what is the probability that the sample mean is
a. between the target and the population mean of 0.753?
b. between the lower specification limit and the target?
c. greater than the upper specification limit?
d. less than the lower specification limit?
e. The probability is 93% that the sample mean diameter will be greater than what value?

 7.51 The fill amount of bottles of a soft drink is normally distributed, with a mean of 2.0 liters and a standard deviation of 0.05 liter. If you select a random sample of 25 bottles, what is the probability that the sample mean will be
a. between 1.99 and 2.0 liters?
b. below 1.98 liters?
c. greater than 2.01 liters?
d. The probability is 99% that the sample mean will contain at least how much soft drink?
e. The probability is 99% that the sample mean will contain an amount that is between which two values (symmetrically distributed around the mean)?

 7.52 An orange juice producer buys all his oranges from a large orange grove that has one variety of orange. The amount of juice squeezed from each of these oranges is approximately normally distributed, with a mean of 4.70 ounces and a standard deviation of 0.40 ounce. Suppose that you select a sample of 25 oranges.
a. What is the probability that the sample mean will be at least 4.60 ounces?
b. The probability is 70% that the sample mean will be contained between what two values symmetrically distributed around the population mean?
c. The probability is 77% that the sample mean will be greater than what value?

7.53 In his management information systems textbook, Professor David Kroenke raises an interesting point: "If 98% of our market has Internet access, do we have a responsibility to provide non-Internet materials to that other 2%?" (D. M. Kroenke, *Using MIS*, Upper Saddle River, NJ: Prentice Hall, 2007, p. 29a.) Suppose that 98% of the customers in your market have Internet access and you select a random sample of 500 customers. What is the probability that the sample has
a. greater than 99% with Internet access?
b. between 97% and 99% with Internet access?
c. less than 97% with Internet access?

7.54 Mutual funds reported strong earnings in the first quarter of 2006. Especially strong growth occurred in mutual funds consisting of companies focusing on Latin America. This population of mutual funds earned a mean return of 15.9% in the first quarter (M. Skala, "Banking on the World," *Christian Science Monitor*, **www.csmonitor.com**, April 10, 2006.) Assume that the returns for the Latin America mutual funds were distributed as a normal random variable, with a mean of 15.9 and a standard deviation of 20. If you selected a random sample of 10 funds from this population, what is the probability that the sample would have a mean return
a. less than 0—that is, a loss?
b. between 0 and 6?
c. greater than 10?

7.55 Mutual funds reported strong earnings in the first quarter of 2006. The population of mutual funds focusing on Europe had a mean return of 13.3% during this time. Assume that the returns for the Europe mutual funds were distributed as a normal random variable, with a mean of 13.3 and a standard deviation of 12. If you select an individual fund from this population, what is the probability that it would have a return
a. less than 0—that is, a loss?
b. between 0 and 6?
c. greater than 10?
If you selected a random sample of 10 funds from this population, what is the probability that the sample would have a mean return
d. less than 0—that is, a loss?
e. between 0 and 6?
f. greater than 10?
g. Compare your results in parts (d) through (f) to (a) through (c).
h. Compare your results in parts (d) through (f) to Problem 7.54 (a) through (c).

7.56 Political polling has traditionally used telephone interviews. Researchers at Harris Black International Ltd. have argued that Internet polling is less expensive, faster, and offers higher response rates than telephone surveys. Critics are concerned about the scientific reliability of this approach (*The Wall Street Journal*, April 13, 1999). Even amid this strong criticism, Internet polling is becoming more and more common. What concerns, if any, do you have about Internet polling?

7.57 A survey sponsored by The American Dietetic Association and the agri-business giant ConAgra found that 53% of office workers take 30 minutes or less for lunch each day. Approximately 37% take 30 to 60 minutes, and 10% take more than an hour. ("Snapshots," **usatoday.com**, April 26, 2006.)

a. What additional information would you want to know before you accepted the results of the survey?

b. Discuss the four types of survey errors in the context of this survey.

c. One of the types of survey errors discussed in part (b) should have been measurement error. Explain how the root cause of measurement error in this survey could be the halo effect.

7.58 As part of a mediation process overseen by a federal judge to end a lawsuit that accuses Cincinnati, Ohio, of decades of discrimination against African Americans, surveys were done on how to improve Cincinnati police–community relations. One survey was sent to the 1,020 members of the Cincinnati police force. The survey included a cover in which the chief of police and president of the Fraternal Order of Police encouraged participation. Respondents could either return a hard copy of the survey or complete the survey online. To the researchers' dismay, only 158 surveys were completed ("Few Cops Fill Out Survey," *The Cincinnati Enquirer*, August 22, 2001, p. B3).

a. What type of errors or biases should the researchers be especially concerned with?

b. What step(s) should the researchers take to try to overcome the problems noted in (a)?

c. What could have been done differently to improve the survey's worthiness?

7.59 Connecticut shoppers spend more on women's clothing than do shoppers in any other state, according to a survey conducted by MapInfo. The mean spending per household in Connecticut was $975 annually ("Snapshots," **usatoday.com**, April 17, 2006).

a. What other information would you want to know before you accepted the results of this survey?

b. Suppose that you wished to conduct a similar survey for the geographic region you live in. Describe the population for your survey.

c. Explain how you could minimize the chance of coverage error in this type of survey.

d. Explain how you could minimize the chance of nonresponse error in this type of survey.

e. Explain how you could minimize the chance of sampling error in this type of survey.

f. Explain how you could minimize the chance of measurement error in this type of survey.

7.60 According to Dr. Sarah Beth Estes, sociology professor at the University of Cincinnati, and Dr. Jennifer Glass, sociology professor at the University of Iowa, working women who take advantage of family-friendly schedules can fall behind in wages. More specifically, the sociologists report that in a study of 300 working women who had children and returned to work and opted for flextime, telecommuting, and so on, these women had pay raises that averaged between 16% and 26% less than other workers ("Study: 'Face Time' Can Affect Moms' Raises," *The Cincinnati Enquirer*, August 28, 2001, p. A1).

a. What other information would you want to know before you accepted the results of this study?

b. If you were to perform a similar study in the geographic area where you live, define a population, frame, and sampling method you could use.

7.61 (Class Project) The table of random numbers is an example of a uniform distribution because each digit is equally likely to occur. Starting in the row corresponding to the day of the month in which you were born, use the table of random numbers (Table E.1) to take one digit at a time.

Select five different samples each of $n = 2$, $n = 5$, and $n = 10$. Compute the sample mean of each sample. Develop a frequency distribution of the sample means for the results of the entire class, based on samples of sizes $n = 2$, $n = 5$, and $n = 10$.

What can be said about the shape of the sampling distribution for each of these sample sizes?

7.62 (Class Project) Toss a coin 10 times and record the number of heads. If each student performs this experiment five times, a frequency distribution of the number of heads can be developed from the results of the entire class. Does this distribution seem to approximate the normal distribution?

7.63 (Class Project) The number of cars waiting in line at a car wash is distributed as follows:

Number of Cars	Probability
0	0.25
1	0.40
2	0.20
3	0.10
4	0.04
5	0.01

You can use the table of random numbers (Table E.1) to select samples from this distribution by assigning numbers as follows:

1. Start in the row corresponding to the day of the month in which you were born.

2. Select a two-digit random number.

3. If you select a random number from 00 to 24, record a length of 0; if from 25 to 64, record a length of 1; if from

65 to 84, record a length of 2; if from 85 to 94, record a length of 3; if from 95 to 98, record a length of 4; if 99, record a length of 5.

Select samples of $n = 2$, $n = 5$, and $n = 10$. Compute the mean for each sample. For example, if a sample of size 2 results in the random numbers 18 and 46, these would correspond to lengths of 0 and 1, respectively, producing a sample mean of 0.5. If each student selects five different samples for each sample size, a frequency distribution of the sample means (for each sample size) can be developed from the results of the entire class. What conclusions can you reach concerning the sampling distribution of the mean as the sample size is increased?

7.64 (Class Project) Using Table E.1, simulate the selection of different-colored balls from a bowl as follows:
1. Start in the row corresponding to the day of the month in which you were born.
2. Select one-digit numbers.

3. If a random digit between 0 and 6 is selected, consider the ball white; if a random digit is a 7, 8, or 9, consider the ball red.

Select samples of $n = 10$, $n = 25$, and $n = 50$ digits. In each sample, count the number of white balls and compute the proportion of white balls in the sample. If each student in the class selects five different samples for each sample size, a frequency distribution of the proportion of white balls (for each sample size) can be developed from the results of the entire class. What conclusions can you reach about the sampling distribution of the proportion as the sample size is increased?

7.65 (Class Project) Suppose that step 3 of Problem 7.64 uses the following rule: "If a random digit between 0 and 8 is selected, consider the ball to be white; if a random digit of 9 is selected, consider the ball to be red." Compare and contrast the results in this problem and those in Problem 7.64.

Managing the *Springville Herald*

Continuing its quality improvement effort first described in the Chapter 6 "Managing the *Springville Herald*" case, the production department of the newspaper has been monitoring the blackness of the newspaper print. As before, blackness is measured on a standard scale in which the target value is 1.0. Data collected over the past year indicate that the blackness is normally distributed, with a mean of 1.005 and a standard deviation of 0.10.

EXERCISE

SH7.1 Each day, 25 spots on the first newspaper printed are chosen, and the blackness of the spots is measured. Assuming that the distribution has not changed from what it was in the past year, what is the probability that the mean blackness of the spots is
a. less than 1.0?
b. between 0.95 and 1.0?
c. between 1.0 and 1.05?
d. less than 0.95 or greater than 1.05?
e. Suppose that the mean blackness of today's sample of 25 spots is 0.952. What conclusion can you make about the blackness of the newspaper based on this result? Explain.

Web Case

Apply your knowledge about sampling distributions in this Web Case, which reconsiders the Oxford Cereals Using Statistics scenario.

The advocacy group Consumers Concerned About Cereal Cheaters (CCACC) suspects that cereal companies, including Oxford Cereals, are cheating consumers by packaging cereals at less than labeled weights. Visit the organization's home page at **www.prenhall.com/Springville/ConsumersConcerned.htm** (or open the **ConsumersConcerned.htm** file in the text CD's WebCase folder), examine their claims and supporting data, and then answer the following:

1. Are the data collection procedures that the CCACC uses to form its conclusions flawed? What procedures could the group follow to make their analysis more rigorous?

2. Assume that the two samples of five cereal boxes (one sample for each of two cereal varieties) listed on the CCACC Web site were collected randomly by organization members. For each sample, do the following:

a. Calculate the sample mean.

b. Assume that the standard deviation of the process is 15 grams and a population mean of 368 grams. Calculate the percentage of all samples for each process that would have a sample mean less than the value you calculated in (a).

c. Again, assuming that the standard deviation is 15 grams, calculate the percentage of individual boxes of cereal that would have a weight less than the value you calculated in (a).

3. What, if any, conclusions can you form by using your calculations about the filling processes of the two different cereals?

4. A representative from Oxford Cereals has asked that the CCACC take down its page discussing shortages in Oxford Cereals boxes. Is that request reasonable? Why or why not?

5. Can the techniques discussed in this chapter be used to prove cheating in the manner alleged by the CCACC? Why or why not?

REFERENCES

1. Cochran, W. G., *Sampling Techniques*, 3rd ed. (New York: Wiley, 1977).

2. Crossen, C., "Deja Vu: Fiasco in 1936 Survey Brought Science to Election Polling," *The Wall Street Journal*, October 2, 2006, B1.

3. Gallup, G. H., *The Sophisticated Poll-Watcher's Guide* (Princeton, NJ: Princeton Opinion Press, 1972).

4. Goleman, D., "Pollsters Enlist Psychologists in Quest for Unbiased Results," *The New York Times*, September 7, 1993, pp. C1, C11.

5. Levine, D. M., P. Ramsey, and R. Smidt, *Applied Statistics for Engineers and Scientists Using Microsoft Excel and Minitab* (Upper Saddle River, NJ: Prentice Hall, 2001).

6. *Microsoft Excel 2007* (Redmond, WA: Microsoft Corp., 2007).

7. Mosteller, F., et al., *The Pre-Election Polls of 1948* (New York: Social Science Research Council, 1949).

8. Rand Corporation, *A Million Random Digits with 100,000 Normal Deviates* (New York: The Free Press, 1955).

Excel Companion
to Chapter 7

E7.1 CREATING SIMPLE RANDOM SAMPLES (WITHOUT REPLACEMENT)

You create simple random samples (without replacement) by using the PHStat2 Random Sample Generation procedure. (There are no basic Excel commands or features to create a simple random sample.)

Open to the worksheet that contains the data to be sampled and select **PHStat → Sampling → Random Sample Generation**. In the Random Sample Generation dialog box (shown below), enter the **Sample Size** and click **Select values from range**. Enter the cell range of the data to be sampled as the **Values Cell Range**, click **First cell contains label**, and click **OK**. A new simple random sample appears on a new worksheet.

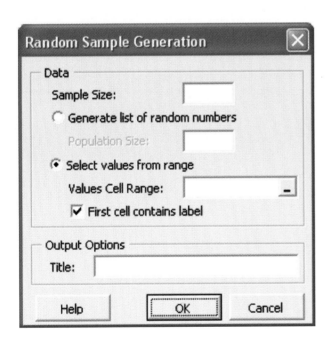

E7.2 CREATING SIMULATED SAMPLING DISTRIBUTIONS

You create simulated sampling distributions by first using the ToolPak Random Number Generation procedure to create a worksheet of all the random samples. Then you add formulas to compute the sample means and other appropriate measures for each sample. You can also use the PHStat2 Sampling

Distributions Simulation procedure, which does both of these tasks for you and optionally creates a histogram.

Using PHStat2 Sampling Distributions Simulation

Select **PHStat → Sampling → Sampling Distributions Simulation**. In the Sampling Distributions Simulation dialog box (shown below), enter values for the **Number of Samples** and the **Sample Size**. Click one of the distribution options and then enter a title as the **Title** and click **OK**. To create a histogram of the sample means, click **Histogram** before clicking OK.

If you want to use the **Discrete** option, first open to a worksheet that contains a table of X and P(X) values and then select this procedure. Then select **Discrete** and enter that table range as the **X and P(X) Values Cell Range**.

Using ToolPak Random Number Generation

Select **Tools → Data Analysis**. From the list that appears in the Data Analysis dialog box, select **Random Number**

Generation and click **OK**. In the Random Number Generation dialog box (shown below), enter the number of samples as the **Number of Variables** and enter the sample size of each sample as the **Number of Random Numbers**. Select the type of distribution from the **Distribution** drop-down list and make entries in the Parameters area, as necessary. (The contents of this area vary according to the distribution chosen.) Click **New Worksheet Ply** and then click **OK**.

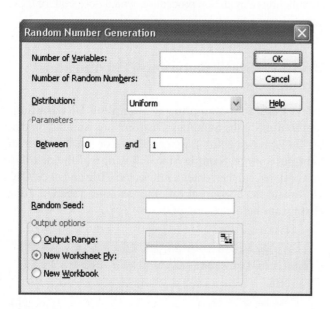

To create a histogram from the set of sample means for your simulation, enter a formula that uses the AVERAGE function in a row below the cell range that contains the samples created by the procedure. Then use the techniques for creating frequency distributions and histograms discussed in the Excel Companion to Chapter 2 to create your histogram.

EXAMPLE 100 Samples of Sample Size 30 from a Uniformly Distributed Population

Basic Excel Select **Tools → Data Analysis**. From the list that appears in the Data Analysis dialog box, select **Random Number Generation** and click **OK**. In the Random Number Generation dialog box (shown at left), enter **100** as the **Number of Variables** and enter **30** as the **Number of Random Numbers.** Select **Uniform** from the **Distribution** drop-down list, click **New Worksheet Ply**, and then click **OK**.

PHStat2 Select **PHStat → Sampling → Sampling Distributions Simulation**. In the procedure dialog box, enter **100** as the **Number of Samples** and **30** as the **Sample Size**. Click **Uniform** and then enter a title as the **Title** and click **OK**.

CHAPTER 8

Confidence Interval Estimation

USING STATISTICS @ Saxon Home Improvement

LEARNING OBJECTIVES

In this chapter, you learn:
- To construct and interpret confidence interval estimates for the mean and the proportion
- How to determine the sample size necessary to develop a confidence interval for the mean or proportion
- How to use confidence interval estimates in auditing

Using Statistics @ Saxon Home Improvement

Saxon Home Improvement distributes home improvement supplies in the northeastern United States. As a company accountant, you are responsible for the accuracy of the integrated inventory management and sales information system. You could review the contents of each and every record to check the accuracy of this system, but such a detailed review would be time-consuming and costly. A better approach would be to use statistical inference techniques to draw conclusions about the population of all records from a relatively small sample collected during an audit. At the end of each month, you could select a sample of the sales invoices to determine the following:

- The mean dollar amount listed on the sales invoices for the month.
- The total dollar amount listed on the sales invoices for the month.
- Any differences between the dollar amounts on the sales invoices and the amounts entered into the sales information system.

- The frequency of occurrence of errors that violate the internal control policy of the warehouse. Such errors include making a shipment when there is no authorized warehouse removal slip, failure to include the correct account number, and shipping the incorrect home improvement item.

How accurate are the results from the samples and how do you use this information? Are the sample sizes large enough to give you the information you need?

Statistical inference is the process of using sample results to draw conclusions about the characteristics of a population. Inferential statistics enables you to *estimate* unknown population characteristics such as a population mean or a population proportion. Two types of estimates are used to estimate population parameters: point estimates and interval estimates. A **point estimate** is the value of a single sample statistic. A **confidence interval estimate** is a range of numbers, called an interval, constructed around the point estimate. The confidence interval is constructed such that the probability that the population parameter is located somewhere within the interval is known.

Suppose you would like to estimate the mean GPA of all the students at your university. The mean GPA for all the students is an unknown population mean, denoted by μ. You select a sample of students and find that the sample mean is 2.80. The sample mean, $\overline{X} = 2.80$, is a point estimate of the population mean, μ. How accurate is 2.80? To answer this question, you must construct a confidence interval estimate.

In this chapter, you will learn how to construct and interpret confidence interval estimates. Recall that the sample mean, $\overline{X}$, is a point estimate of the population mean, μ. However, the sample mean varies from sample to sample because it depends on the items selected in the sample. By taking into account the known variability from sample to sample (see Section 7.4 on the sampling distribution of the mean), you can develop the interval estimate for the population mean. The interval constructed should have a specified confidence of correctly estimating the value of the population parameter μ. In other words, there is a specified confidence that μ is somewhere in the range of numbers defined by the interval.

Suppose that after studying this chapter, you find that a 95% confidence interval for the mean GPA at your university is ($2.75 \le \mu \le 2.85$). You can interpret this interval estimate by stating that you are 95% confident that the mean GPA at your university is between 2.75 and 2.85. There is a 5% chance that the mean GPA is below 2.75 or above 2.85.

After learning about the confidence interval for the mean, you will learn how to develop an interval estimate for the population proportion. Then you will learn how large a sample to select when constructing confidence intervals and how to perform several important estimation procedures accountants use when performing audits.

8.1 CONFIDENCE INTERVAL ESTIMATION FOR THE MEAN (σ KNOWN)

In Section 7.4, you used the Central Limit Theorem and knowledge of the population distribution to determine the percentage of sample means that fall within certain distances of the population mean. For instance, in the cereal-fill example used throughout Chapter 7 (see Example 7.6 on page 268), 95% of all sample means are between 362.12 and 373.88 grams. This statement is based on *deductive reasoning*. However, *inductive reasoning* is what you need here.

You need inductive reasoning because, in statistical inference, you use the results of a single sample to draw conclusions about the population, not vice versa. Suppose that in the cereal-fill example, you wish to estimate the unknown population mean, using the information from only a sample. Thus, rather than take $\mu \pm (1.96)(\sigma/(\sqrt{n})$ to find the upper and lower limits around μ, as in Section 7.4, you substitute the sample mean, $\overline{X}$, for the unknown μ and use $\overline{X} \pm (1.96)(\sigma/(\sqrt{n})$ as an interval to estimate the unknown μ. Although in practice you select a single sample of size n and compute the mean, $\overline{X}$, in order to understand the full meaning of the interval estimate, you need to examine a hypothetical set of all possible samples of n values.

Suppose that a sample of $n = 25$ boxes has a mean of 362.3 grams. The interval developed to estimate μ is $362.3 \pm (1.96)(15)/(\sqrt{25})$, or 362.3 ± 5.88. The estimate of μ is

$$356.42 \leq \mu \leq 368.18$$

Because the population mean, μ (equal to 368), is included within the interval, this sample results in a correct statement about μ (see Figure 8.1).

FIGURE 8.1

Confidence interval estimates for five different samples of $n = 25$ taken from a population where $\mu = 368$ and $\sigma = 15$

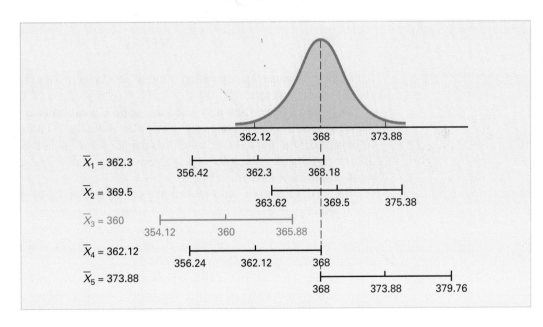

To continue this hypothetical example, suppose that for a different sample of $n = 25$ boxes, the mean is 369.5. The interval developed from this sample is

$$369.5 \pm (1.96)(15)/(\sqrt{25})$$

or 369.5 ± 5.88. The estimate is

$$363.62 \leq \mu \leq 375.38$$

Because the population mean, μ (equal to 368), is also included within this interval, this statement about μ is correct.

Now, before you begin to think that correct statements about μ are always made by developing a confidence interval estimate, suppose a third hypothetical sample of $n = 25$ boxes is selected and the sample mean is equal to 360 grams. The interval developed here is $360 \pm (1.96)(15)/(\sqrt{25})$, or 360 ± 5.88. In this case, the estimate of μ is

$$354.12 \leq \mu \leq 365.88$$

This estimate is *not* a correct statement because the population mean, μ, is not included in the interval developed from this sample (see Figure 8.1). Thus, for some samples, the interval estimate of μ is correct, but for others it is incorrect. In practice, only one sample is selected, and because the population mean is unknown, you cannot determine whether the interval estimate is correct.

To resolve this dilemma of sometimes having an interval that provides a correct estimate and sometimes having an interval that provides an incorrect estimate, you need to determine the proportion of samples producing intervals that result in correct statements about the population mean, μ. To do this, consider two other hypothetical samples: the case in which $\overline{X} = 362.12$ grams and the case in which $\overline{X} = 373.88$ grams. If $\overline{X} = 362.12$, the interval is $362.12 \pm (1.96)(15)/(\sqrt{25})$, or 362.12 ± 5.88. This leads to the following interval:

$$356.24 \leq \mu \leq 368.00$$

Because the population mean of 368 is at the upper limit of the interval, the statement is a correct one (see Figure 8.1).

When $\overline{X} = 373.88$, the interval is $373.88 \pm (1.96)(15)/(\sqrt{25})$, or 373.88 ± 5.88. The interval for the sample mean is

$$368.00 \leq \mu \leq 379.76$$

In this case, because the population mean of 368 is included at the lower limit of the interval, the statement is correct.

In Figure 8.1, you see that when the sample mean falls anywhere between 362.12 and 373.88 grams, the population mean is included *somewhere* within the interval. In Example 7.6 on page 268, you found that 95% of the sample means fall between 362.12 and 373.88 grams. Therefore, 95% of all samples of $n = 25$ boxes have sample means that include the population mean within the interval developed.

Because, in practice, you select only one sample and μ is unknown, you never know for sure whether your specific interval includes the population mean. However, if you take all possible samples of n and compute their sample means, 95% of the intervals will include the population mean, and only 5% of them will not. In other words, you have 95% confidence that the population mean is somewhere in your interval.

Consider once again, the first sample discussed in this section. A sample of $n = 25$ boxes had a sample mean of 362.3 grams. The interval constructed to estimate μ is:

$$362.3 \pm (1.96)(15)/(\sqrt{25})$$
$$362.3 \pm 5.88$$
$$356.42 \leq \mu \leq 368.18$$

The interval from 356.42 to 368.18 is referred to as a 95% confidence interval.

"I am 95% confident that the mean amount of cereal in the population of boxes is somewhere between 356.42 and 368.18 grams."

In some situations, you might want a higher degree of confidence (such as 99%) of including the population mean within the interval. In other cases, you might accept less confidence (such as 90%) of correctly estimating the population mean. In general, the **level of confidence** is symbolized by $(1 - \alpha) \times 100\%$, where α is the proportion in the tails of the distribution that is outside the confidence interval. The proportion in the upper tail of the distribution is $\alpha/2$, and the proportion in the lower tail of the distribution is $\alpha/2$. You use Equation (8.1) to construct a $(1 - \alpha) \times 100\%$ confidence interval estimate of the mean with σ known.

CONFIDENCE INTERVAL FOR THE MEAN (σ KNOWN)

$$\bar{X} \pm Z \frac{\sigma}{\sqrt{n}}$$

or

$$\bar{X} - Z \frac{\sigma}{\sqrt{n}} \leq \mu \leq \bar{X} + Z \frac{\sigma}{\sqrt{n}} \qquad \textbf{(8.1)}$$

where Z = the value corresponding to a cumulative area of $1 - \alpha/2$ from the standardized normal distribution (that is, an upper-tail probability of $\alpha/2$).

The value of Z needed for constructing a confidence interval is called the **critical value** for the distribution. 95% confidence corresponds to an α value of 0.05. The critical Z value corresponding to a cumulative area of 0.9750 is 1.96 because there is 0.025 in the upper tail of the distribution and the cumulative area less than $Z = 1.96$ is 0.975.

There is a different critical value for each level of confidence, $1 - \alpha$. A level of confidence of 95% leads to a Z value of 1.96 (see Figure 8.2). 99% confidence corresponds to an α value of 0.01. The Z value is approximately 2.58 because the upper-tail area is 0.005 and the cumulative area less than $Z = 2.58$ is 0.995 (see Figure 8.3).

FIGURE 8.2

Normal curve for determining the Z value needed for 95% confidence

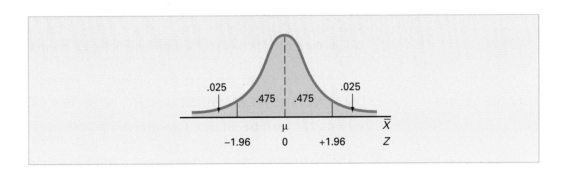

FIGURE 8.3

Normal curve for determining the Z value needed for 99% confidence

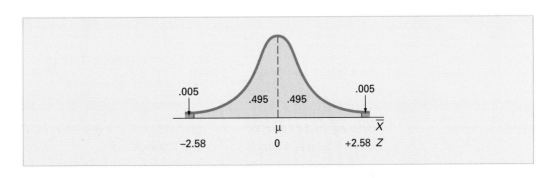

Now that various levels of confidence have been considered, why not make the confidence level as close to 100% as possible? Before doing so, you need to realize that any increase in the level of confidence is achieved only by widening (and making less precise) the confidence interval. There is no "free lunch" here. You would have more confidence that the population mean is within a broader range of values; however, this might make the interpretation of the confidence interval less useful. The trade-off between the width of the confidence interval and the level of confidence is discussed in greater depth in the context of determining the sample size in Section 8.4. Example 8.1 illustrates the application of the confidence interval estimate.

EXAMPLE 8.1

ESTIMATING THE MEAN PAPER LENGTH WITH 95% CONFIDENCE

A paper manufacturer has a production process that operates continuously throughout an entire production shift. The paper is expected to have a mean length of 11 inches, and the standard deviation of the length is 0.02 inch. At periodic intervals, a sample is selected to determine whether the mean paper length is still equal to 11 inches or whether something has gone wrong in the production process to change the length of the paper produced. You select a random sample of 100 sheets, and the mean paper length is 10.998 inches. Construct a 95% confidence interval estimate for the population mean paper length.

SOLUTION Using Equation (8.1) on page 287, with $Z = 1.96$ for 95% confidence,

$$\bar{X} \pm Z \frac{\sigma}{\sqrt{n}} = 10.998 \pm (1.96) \frac{0.02}{\sqrt{100}}$$

$$= 10.998 \pm 0.00392$$

$$10.99408 \le \mu \le 11.00192$$

Thus, with 95% confidence, you conclude that the population mean is between 10.99408 and 11.00192 inches. Because the interval includes 11, the value indicating that the production process is working properly, you have no reason to believe that anything is wrong with the production process.

To see the effect of using a 99% confidence interval, examine Example 8.2.

EXAMPLE 8.2

ESTIMATING THE MEAN PAPER LENGTH WITH 99% CONFIDENCE

Construct a 99% confidence interval estimate for the population mean paper length.

SOLUTION Using Equation (8.1) on page 287, with $Z = 2.58$ for 99% confidence,

$$\bar{X} \pm Z \frac{\sigma}{\sqrt{n}} = 10.998 \pm (2.58) \frac{0.02}{\sqrt{100}}$$

$$= 10.998 \pm 0.00516$$

$$10.99284 \le \mu \le 11.00316$$

Once again, because 11 is included within this wider interval, you have no reason to believe that anything is wrong with the production process.

As discussed in section 7.4, the sampling distribution of $\overline{X}$ is normally distributed if the population of X is a normal distribution. And, if the population of X is not a normal distribution, the Central Limit Theorem ensures that $\overline{X}$ is normally distributed when n is large. However, when dealing with a small sample size and a population of X that is not a normal distribution, the sampling distribution of $\overline{X}$ is not normally distributed and therefore the confidence interval discussed in this section is inappropriate. In practice, however, as long as the sample size is large enough and the population is not very skewed, you can use the confidence interval defined in Equation 8.1 to estimate the population mean when σ is known. To assess the assumption of normality, you can evaluate the shape of the sample data by using a histogram, stem-and-leaf display, box-and-whisker plot, or normal probability plot.

PROBLEMS FOR SECTION 8.1

Learning the Basics

 8.1 If $\overline{X} = 85$, σ = 8, and $n = 64$, construct a 95% confidence interval estimate of the population mean, μ.

 8.2 If $\overline{X} = 125$, σ = 24, and $n = 36$, construct a 99% confidence interval estimate of the population mean, μ.

8.3 A market researcher states that she has 95% confidence that the mean monthly sales of a product are between $170,000 and $200,000. Explain the meaning of this statement.

8.4 Why is it not possible in Example 8.1 on page 288 to have 100% confidence? Explain.

8.5 From the results of Example 8.1 on page 288 regarding paper production, is it true that 95% of the sample means will fall between 10.99408 and 11.00192 inches? Explain.

8.6 Is it true in Example 8.1 on page 288 that you do not know for sure whether the population mean is between 10.99408 and 11.00192 inches? Explain.

Applying the Concepts

 8.7 The manager of a paint supply store wants to estimate the actual amount of paint contained in 1-gallon cans purchased from a nationally known manufacturer. The manufacturer's specifications state that the standard deviation of the amount of paint is equal to 0.02 gallon. A random sample of 50 cans is selected, and the sample mean amount of paint per 1-gallon can is 0.995 gallon.
a. Construct a 99% confidence interval estimate of the population mean amount of paint included in a 1-gallon can.
b. On the basis of these results, do you think the manager has a right to complain to the manufacturer? Why?

c. Must you assume that the population amount of paint per can is normally distributed here? Explain.
d. Construct a 95% confidence interval estimate. How does this change your answer to (b)?

 8.8 The quality control manager at a light bulb factory needs to estimate the mean life of a large shipment of light bulbs. The standard deviation is 100 hours. A random sample of 64 light bulbs indicated a sample mean life of 350 hours.
a. Construct a 95% confidence interval estimate of the population mean life of light bulbs in this shipment.
b. Do you think that the manufacturer has the right to state that the light bulbs last an average of 400 hours? Explain.
c. Must you assume that the population of light bulb life is normally distributed? Explain.
d. Suppose that the standard deviation changes to 80 hours. What are your answers in (a) and (b)?

 8.9 The inspection division of the Lee County Weights and Measures Department wants to estimate the actual amount of soft drink in 2-liter bottles at the local bottling plant of a large nationally known soft-drink company. The bottling plant has informed the inspection division that the population standard deviation for 2-liter bottles is 0.05 liter. A random sample of 100 2-liter bottles at this bottling plant indicates a sample mean of 1.99 liters.
a. Construct a 95% confidence interval estimate of the population mean amount of soft drink in each bottle.
b. Must you assume that the population of soft-drink fill is normally distributed? Explain.
c. Explain why a value of 2.02 liters for a single bottle is not unusual, even though it is outside the confidence interval you calculated.
d. Suppose that the sample mean is 1.97 liters. What is your answer to (a)?

8.2 CONFIDENCE INTERVAL ESTIMATION FOR THE MEAN (σ UNKNOWN)

Just as the mean of the population, μ, is usually unknown, you rarely know the actual standard deviation of the population, σ. Therefore, you often need to construct a confidence interval estimate of μ, using only the sample statistics $\overline{X}$ and S.

Student's t Distribution

At the beginning of the twentieth century, William S. Gosset, a statistician for Guinness Breweries in Ireland (see reference 3) wanted to make inferences about the mean when σ was unknown. Because Guinness employees were not permitted to publish research work under their own names, Gosset adopted the pseudonym "Student." The distribution that he developed is known as **Student's t distribution** and is commonly referred to as the t distribution.

If the random variable X is normally distributed, then the following statistic has a t distribution with $n - 1$ **degrees of freedom**:

$$t = \frac{\overline{X} - \mu}{\dfrac{S}{\sqrt{n}}}$$

This expression has the same form as the Z statistic in Equation (7.4) on page 266, except that S is used to estimate the unknown σ. The concept of *degrees of freedom* is discussed further on pages 291–292.

Properties of the t Distribution

In appearance, the t distribution is very similar to the standardized normal distribution. Both distributions are bell shaped. However, the t distribution has more area in the tails and less in the center than does the standardized normal distribution (see Figure 8.4). Because S is used to estimate the unknown σ, the values of t are more variable than those for Z.

FIGURE 8.4

Standardized normal distribution and t distribution for 5 degrees of freedom

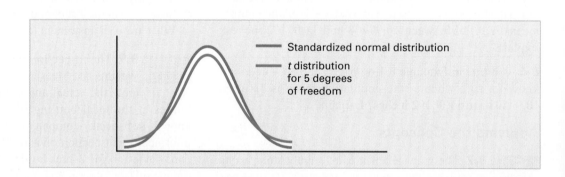

The degrees of freedom, $n - 1$, are directly related to the sample size, n. As the sample size and degrees of freedom increase, S becomes a better estimate of σ, and the t distribution gradually approaches the standardized normal distribution, until the two are virtually identical. With a sample size of about 120 or more, S estimates σ precisely enough that there is little difference between the t and Z distributions.

As stated earlier, the t distribution assumes that the random variable X is normally distributed. In practice, however, as long as the sample size is large enough and the population is not very skewed, you can use the t distribution to estimate the population mean when σ is unknown. When dealing with a small sample size and a skewed population distribution, the validity of the confidence interval is a concern. To assess the assumption of normality, you can evaluate the shape of the sample data by using a histogram, stem-and-leaf display, box-and-whisker plot, or normal probability plot.

You find the critical values of t for the appropriate degrees of freedom from the table of the t distribution (see Table E.3). The columns of the table represent the area in the upper tail of the t distribution. The rows of the table represent the degrees of freedom. The cells of the table represent the particular t value for each specific degree of freedom. For example, with 99 degrees of freedom, if you want 95% confidence, you find the appropriate value of t, as shown in Table 8.1. The 95% confidence level means that 2.5% of the values (an area of 0.025) are in each tail of the distribution. Looking in the column for an upper-tail area of 0.025 and in the row corresponding to 99 degrees of freedom gives you a critical value for t of 1.9842. Because t is a symmetrical distribution with a mean of 0, if the upper-tail value is +1.9842, the value for the lower-tail area (lower 0.025) is −1.9842. A t value of −1.9842 means that the probability that t is less than −1.9842 is 0.025, or 2.5% (see Figure 8.5). Note that for a 95% confidence interval, you will always use an upper-tail area of 0.025. Similarly, for a 99% confidence interval, use 0.005, for 98% use 0.01, 90% use 0.05, and 80% use 0.10.

TABLE 8.1

Determining the Critical Value from the t Table for an Area of 0.025 in Each Tail with 99 Degrees of Freedom

				Upper-Tail Areas		
Degrees of Freedom	**.25**	**.10**	**.05**	**.025**	**.01**	**.005**
1	1.0000	3.0777	6.3138	12.7062	31.8207	63.6574
2	0.8165	1.8856	2.9200	4.3027	6.9646	9.9248
3	0.7649	1.6377	2.3534	3.1824	4.5407	5.8409
4	0.7407	1.5332	2.1318	2.7764	3.7469	4.6041
5	0.7267	1.4759	2.0150	2.5706	3.3649	4.0322
.	.	.	.	.	.	.
.	.	.	.	.	.	.
.	.	.	.	.	.	.
96	0.6771	1.2904	1.6609	1.9850	2.3658	2.6280
97	0.6770	1.2903	1.6607	1.9847	2.3654	2.6275
98	0.6770	1.2902	1.6606	1.9845	2.3650	2.6269
99	0.6770	1.2902	1.6604	1.9842	2.3646	2.6264
100	0.6770	1.2901	1.6602	1.9840	2.3642	2.6259

Source: Extracted from Table E.3.

FIGURE 8.5

t distribution with 99 degrees of freedom

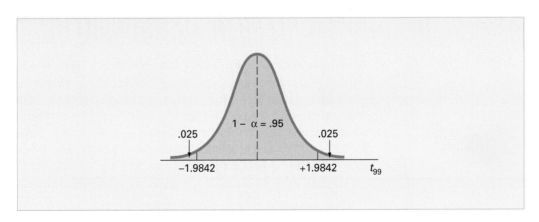

The Concept of Degrees of Freedom

In Chapter 3 you learned that the numerator of the sample variance, S^2 [see Equation (3.9) on page 107], requires the computation of

$$\sum_{i=1}^{n}(X_i - \bar{X})^2$$

In order to compute S^2, you first need to know $\overline{X}$. Therefore, only $n - 1$ of the sample values are free to vary. This means that you have $n - 1$ degrees of freedom. For example, suppose a sample of five values has a mean of 20. How many values do you need to know before you can determine the remainder of the values? The fact that $n = 5$ and $\overline{X} = 20$ also tells you that

$$\sum_{i=1}^{n} X_i = 100$$

because

$$\frac{\sum_{i=1}^{n} X_i}{n} = \overline{X}$$

Thus, when you know four of the values, the fifth one is *not* free to vary because the sum must add to 100. For example, if four of the values are 18, 24, 19, and 16, the fifth value must be 23 so that the sum equals 100.

The Confidence Interval Statement

Equation (8.2) defines the $(1 - \alpha) \times 100\%$ confidence interval estimate for the mean with σ unknown.

CONFIDENCE INTERVAL FOR THE MEAN (σ UNKNOWN)

$$\overline{X} \pm t_{n-1} \frac{S}{\sqrt{n}}$$

or

$$\overline{X} - t_{n-1} \frac{S}{\sqrt{n}} \le \mu \le \overline{X} + t_{n-1} \frac{S}{\sqrt{n}} \tag{8.2}$$

where t_{n-1} is the critical value of the t distribution, with $n - 1$ degrees of freedom for an area of $\alpha/2$ in the upper tail.

To illustrate the application of the confidence interval estimate for the mean when the standard deviation, σ, is unknown, recall the Saxon Home Improvement Company Using Statistics scenario presented on page 284. You wanted to estimate the mean dollar amount listed on the sales invoices for the month. You select a sample of 100 sales invoices from the population of sales invoices during the month, and the sample mean of the 100 sales invoices is $110.27, with a sample standard deviation of $28.95. For 95% confidence, the critical value from the t distribution (as shown in Table 8.1) is 1.9842. Using Equation (8.2),

$$\overline{X} \pm t_{n-1} \frac{S}{\sqrt{n}}$$

$$= 110.27 \pm (1.9842) \frac{28.95}{\sqrt{100}}$$

$$= 110.27 \pm 5.74$$

$$\$104.53 \le \mu \le \$116.01$$

A Microsoft Excel worksheet for these data is presented in Figure 8.6.

FIGURE 8.6

Microsoft Excel
worksheet to compute
a confidence interval
estimate for the mean
sales invoice amount
for the Saxon Home
Improvement Company

*See Section E8.2 to create
this.*

	A	B	
1	Estimate for the Mean Sales Invoice Amount		
2			
3	Data		
4	Sample Standard Deviation	28.95	
5	Sample Mean	110.27	
6	Sample Size	100	
7	Confidence Level	95%	
8			
9	Intermediate Calculations		
10	Standard Error of the Mean	2.8950	=B4/SQRT(B6)
11	Degrees of Freedom	99	=B6 - 1
12	t Value	1.9842	=TINV(1 - B7, B11)
13	Interval Half Width	5.7443	=B12 * B10
14			
15	Confidence Interval		
16	Interval Lower Limit	104.53	=B5 - B13
17	Interval Upper Limit	116.01	=B5 + B13

Thus, with 95% confidence, you conclude that the mean amount of all the sales invoices is between $104.53 and $116.01. The 95% confidence level indicates that if you selected all possible samples of 100 (something that is never done in practice), 95% of the intervals developed would include the population mean somewhere within the interval. The validity of this confidence interval estimate depends on the assumption of normality for the distribution of the amount of the sales invoices. With a sample of 100, the normality assumption is not overly restrictive, and the use of the *t* distribution is likely appropriate. Example 8.3 further illustrates how you construct the confidence interval for a mean when the population standard deviation is unknown.

EXAMPLE 8.3

ESTIMATING THE MEAN FORCE REQUIRED TO BREAK ELECTRIC INSULATORS

A manufacturing company produces electric insulators. If the insulators break when in use, a short circuit is likely. To test the strength of the insulators, you carry out destructive testing to determine how much *force* is required to break the insulators. You measure force by observing how many pounds are applied to the insulator before it breaks. Table 8.2 lists 30 values from this experiment, which are located in the file force.xls. Construct a 95% confidence interval estimate for the population mean force required to break the insulator.

TABLE 8.2

Force (in Pounds)
Required to Break
the Insulator

1,870	1,728	1,656	1,610	1,634	1,784	1,522	1,696	1,592	1,662
1,866	1,764	1,734	1,662	1,734	1,774	1,550	1,756	1,762	1,866
1,820	1,744	1,788	1,688	1,810	1,752	1,680	1,810	1,652	1,736

SOLUTION Figure 8.7 shows that the sample mean is $\overline{X}$ = 1,723.4 pounds and the sample standard deviation is S = 89.55 pounds. Using Equation (8.2) on page 292 to construct the confidence interval, you need to determine the critical value from the *t* table for an area of 0.025 in

FIGURE 8.7

Microsoft Excel
confidence interval
estimate for the mean
amount of force
required to break
electric insulators

*See Section E8.2 to create
this.*

	A	B	
1	Estimate for the Mean Amount of Force Required		
2			
3	Data		
4	Sample Standard Deviation	89.55	
5	Sample Mean	1723.4	
6	Sample Size	30	
7	Confidence Level	95%	
8			
9	Intermediate Calculations		
10	Standard Error of the Mean	16.3495	=B4/SQRT(B6)
11	Degrees of Freedom	29	=B6 - 1
12	t Value	2.0452	=TINV(1 - B7, B11)
13	Interval Half Width	33.4385	=B12 * B10
14			
15	Confidence Interval		
16	Interval Lower Limit	1689.96	=B5 - B13
17	Interval Upper Limit	1756.84	=B5 + B13

each tail, with 29 degrees of freedom. From Table E.3, you see that $t_{29} = 2.0452$. Thus, using $\overline{X} = 1,723.4$, $S = 89.55$, $n = 30$, and $t_{29} = 2.0452$,

$$\overline{X} \pm t_{n-1}\frac{S}{\sqrt{n}}$$

$$= 1,723.4 \pm (2.0452)\frac{89.55}{\sqrt{30}}$$

$$= 1,723.4 \pm 33.44$$

$$1,689.96 \leq \mu \leq 1,756.84$$

You conclude with 95% confidence that the mean breaking force required for the population of insulators is between 1,689.96 and 1,756.84 pounds. The validity of this confidence interval estimate depends on the assumption that the force required is normally distributed. Remember, however, that you can slightly relax this assumption for large sample sizes. Thus, with a sample of 30, you can use the t distribution even if the amount of force required is only slightly left skewed. From the normal probability plot displayed in Figure 8.8 or the box-and-whisker plot displayed in Figure 8.9, the amount of force required appears slightly left skewed. Thus, the t distribution is appropriate for these data.

FIGURE 8.8

Microsoft Excel normal probability plot for the amount of force required to break electric insulators

See Section E6.2 to create this.

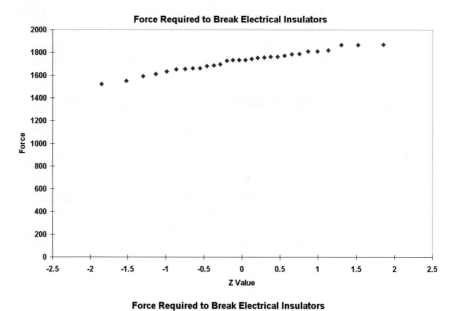

FIGURE 8.9

Microsoft Excel box-and-whisker plot for the amount of force required to break electric insulators

See Section E3.4 to create this.

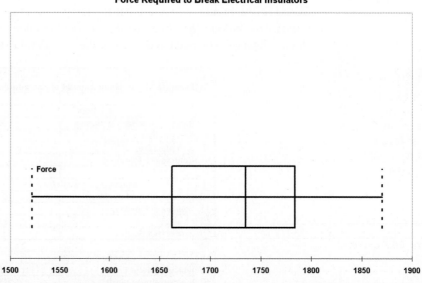

PROBLEMS FOR SECTION 8.2

Learning the Basics

 8.10 Determine the critical value of t in each of the following circumstances:

a. $1 - \alpha = 0.95$, $n = 10$
b. $1 - \alpha = 0.99$, $n = 10$
c. $1 - \alpha = 0.95$, $n = 32$
d. $1 - \alpha = 0.95$, $n = 65$
e. $1 - \alpha = 0.90$, $n = 16$

 8.11 If $\bar{X} = 75$, $S = 24$, and $n = 36$, and assuming that the population is normally distributed, construct a 95% confidence interval estimate of the population mean, μ.

 8.12 If $\bar{X} = 50$, $S = 15$, and $n = 16$, and assuming that the population is normally distributed, construct a 99% confidence interval estimate of the population mean, μ.

8.13 Construct a 95% confidence interval estimate for the population mean, based on each of the following sets of data, assuming that the population is normally distributed:

Set 1   1, 1, 1, 1, 8, 8, 8, 8
Set 2   1, 2, 3, 4, 5, 6, 7, 8

Explain why these data sets have different confidence intervals even though they have the same mean and range.

8.14 Construct a 95% confidence interval for the population mean, based on the numbers 1, 2, 3, 4, 5, 6, and 20. Change the number 20 to 7 and recalculate the confidence interval. Using these results, describe the effect of an outlier (that is, an extreme value) on the confidence interval.

Applying the Concepts

8.15 A stationery store wants to estimate the mean retail value of greeting cards that it has in its inventory. A random sample of 100 greeting cards indicates a mean value of $2.55 and a standard deviation of $0.44.

a. Assuming a normal distribution, construct a 95% confidence interval estimate of the mean value of all greeting cards in the store's inventory.

b. Suppose there were 2,500 greeting cards in the store's inventory. How are the results in (a) useful in assisting the store owner to estimate the total value of her inventory?

 8.16 Southside Hospital in Bay Shore, New York, commonly conducts stress tests to study the heart muscle after a person has a heart attack. Members of the diagnostic imaging department conducted a quality improvement project to try to reduce the turn-around time for stress tests. Turnaround time is defined as the time from when the test is ordered to when the radiologist signs off on the test results. Initially, the mean turnaround time for a stress test was 68 hours. After incorporating changes into the stress-test process, the quality improvement team collected a sample of 50 turnaround times. In this sample, the mean turnaround time was 32 hours, with a standard deviation of 9 hours (Extracted from E. Godin, D. Raven, C. Sweetapple, and F. R. Del Guidice, "Faster Test Results," *Quality Progress*, January 2004, 37(1), pp. 33–39).

a. Construct a 95% confidence interval for the population mean turnaround time.

b. Interpret the interval constructed in (a).

c. Do you think the quality improvement project was a success? Explain.

 8.17 The U.S. Department of Transportation requires tire manufacturers to provide tire performance information on the sidewall of the tire to better inform prospective customers when making purchasing decisions. One very important measure of tire performance is the tread wear index, which indicates the tire's resistance to tread wear compared with a tire graded with a base of 100. This means that a tire with a grade of 200 should last twice as long, on average, as a tire graded with a base of 100. A consumer organization wants to estimate the actual tread wear index of a brand name of tires graded 200 that are produced by a certain manufacturer. A random sample of $n = 18$ indicates a sample mean tread wear index of 195.3 and a sample standard deviation of 21.4.

a. Assuming that the population of tread wear indices is normally distributed, construct a 95% confidence interval estimate of the population mean tread wear index for tires produced by this manufacturer under this brand name.

b. Do you think that the consumer organization should accuse the manufacturer of producing tires that do not meet the performance information provided on the sidewall of the tire? Explain.

c. Explain why an observed tread wear index of 210 for a particular tire is not unusual, even though it is outside the confidence interval developed in (a).

8.18 The following data (stored in the file **bankcost1.xls**) represent the bounced check fee, in dollars, charged by a sample of 23 banks for direct-deposit customers who maintain a $100 balance:

26	28	20	20	21	22	25	25	18	25	15	20
18	20	25	25	22	30	30	30	15	20	29	

Source: Extracted from "The New Face of Banking," Consumer Reports, June 2000.

a. Construct a 95% confidence interval for the population mean bounced check fee.

b. Interpret the interval constructed in (a)

8.19 The data in the file `chicken.xls` represent the total fat, in grams per serving, for a sample of 20 chicken sandwiches from fast-food chains. The data are as follows:

```
7   8   4   5  16  20  20  24  19  30
23  30  25  19  29  29  30  30  40  56
```

*Source: Extracted from "Fast Food: Adding Health to the Menu,"
Consumer Reports, September 2004, pp. 28–31.*

a. Construct a 95% confidence interval for the population mean total fat, in grams per serving.

b. Interpret the interval constructed in (a).

8.20 One of the major measures of the quality of service provided by any organization is the speed with which it responds to customer complaints. A large family-held department store selling furniture and flooring, including carpet, had undergone a major expansion in the past several years. In particular, the flooring department had expanded from 2 installation crews to an installation supervisor, a measurer, and 15 installation crews. Last year, there were 50 complaints concerning carpet installation. The following data, in the file `furniture.xls`, represent the number of days between the receipt of a complaint and the resolution of the complaint:

```
54    5   35 137  31  27 152   2 123  81  74  27
11   19 126 110 110  29  61  35  94  31  26   5
12    4 165  32  29  28  29  26  25   1  14  13
13   10   5  27   4  52  30  22  36  26  20  23
33   68
```

a. Construct a 95% confidence interval estimate of the mean number of days between the receipt of a complaint and the resolution of the complaint.

b. What assumption must you make about the population distribution in (a)?

c. Do you think that the assumption made in (b) is seriously violated? Explain.

d. What effect might your conclusion in (c) have on the validity of the results in (a)?

8.21 In New York State, savings banks are permitted to sell a form of life insurance called savings bank life insurance (SBLI). The approval process consists of underwriting, which includes a review of the application, a medical information bureau check, possible requests for additional medical information and medical exams, and a policy com-

pilation stage in which the policy pages are generated and sent to the bank for delivery. The ability to deliver approved policies to customers in a timely manner is critical to the profitability of this service to the bank. During a period of one month, a random sample of 27 approved policies was selected, and the total processing time, in days, was as shown below and stored in the file `insurance.xls`:

```
73  19  16  64  28  28  31  90  60  56  31  56  22  18
45  48  17  17  17  91  92  63  50  51  69  16  17
```

a. Construct a 95% confidence interval estimate of the mean processing time.

b. What assumption must you make about the population distribution in (a)?

c. Do you think that the assumption made in (b) is seriously violated? Explain.

8.22 The data in the file `batterylife.xls` represent the battery life (in shots) for three-pixel digital cameras:

```
300  180  85  170  380  460  260  35  380  120  110  240
```

*Source: Extracted from "Cameras: More Features in the Mix,"
Consumer Reports, July 2005, pp. 14–18.*

a. Construct a 95% confidence interval for the population mean battery life (in shots).

b. What assumption do you need to make about the population of interest to construct the interval in (a)?

c. Given the data presented, do you think the assumption needed in (a) is valid? Explain.

8.23 One operation of a mill is to cut pieces of steel into parts that are used later in the frame for front seats in an automobile. The steel is cut with a diamond saw and requires the resulting parts to be within ± 0.005 inch of the length specified by the automobile company. The measurement reported from a sample of 100 steel parts (and stored in the file `steel.xls`) is the difference, in inches, between the actual length of the steel part, as measured by a laser measurement device, and the specified length of the steel part. For example, the first observation, -0.002, represents a steel part that is 0.002 inch shorter than the specified length.

a. Construct a 95% confidence interval estimate of the mean difference between the actual length of the steel part and the specified length of the steel part.

b. What assumption must you make about the population distribution in (a)?

c. Do you think that the assumption made in (b) is seriously violated? Explain.

d. Compare the conclusions reached in (a) with those of Problem 2.23 on page 53.

8.3   CONFIDENCE INTERVAL ESTIMATION FOR THE PROPORTION

This section extends the concept of the confidence interval to categorical data. Here you are concerned with estimating the proportion of items in a population having a certain characteristic of interest. The unknown population proportion is represented by the Greek letter π. The point estimate for π is the sample proportion, $p = X/n$, where n is the sample size and X is the number of items in the sample having the characteristic of interest. Equation (8.3) defines the confidence interval estimate for the population proportion.

CONFIDENCE INTERVAL ESTIMATE FOR THE PROPORTION

$$p \pm Z\sqrt{\frac{p(1-p)}{n}}$$

or

$$p - Z\sqrt{\frac{p(1-p)}{n}} \leq \pi \leq p + Z\sqrt{\frac{p(1-p)}{n}} \qquad (8.3)$$

where

p = Sample proportion = $\dfrac{X}{n}$ = $\dfrac{\text{Number of items having the characteristic}}{\text{Sample size}}$

π = population proportion

Z = critical value from the standardized normal distribution

n = sample size

assuming that both X and $n - X$ are greater than 5

You can use the confidence interval estimate of the proportion defined in Equation (8.3) to estimate the proportion of sales invoices that contain errors (see the Using Statistics scenario on page 284). Suppose that in a sample of 100 sales invoices, 10 contain errors. Thus, for these data, $p = X/n = 10/100 = 0.10$. Using Equation (8.3) and $Z = 1.96$ for 95% confidence,

$$p \pm Z\sqrt{\frac{p(1-p)}{n}}$$

$$= 0.10 \pm (1.96)\sqrt{\frac{(0.10)(0.90)}{100}}$$

$$= 0.10 \pm (1.96)(0.03)$$

$$= 0.10 \pm 0.0588$$

$$0.0412 \leq \pi \leq 0.1588$$

Therefore, you have 95% confidence that between 4.12% and 15.88% of all the sales invoices contain errors. Figure 8.10 shows a Microsoft Excel worksheet for these data.

FIGURE 8.10

Microsoft Excel worksheet to construct a confidence interval estimate for the proportion of sales invoices that contain errors

See Section E8.3 to create this.

	A	B	
1	Proportion of In-Error Sales Invoices		
2			
3	Data		
4	Sample Size	100	
5	Number of Successes	10	
6	Confidence Level	95%	
7			
8	Intermediate Calculations		
9	Sample Proportion	0.1	=B5/B4
10	Z Value	-1.9600	=NORMSINV((1 - B6)/2)
11	Standard Error of the Proportion	0.03	=SQRT(B9 * (1 - B9)/B4)
12	Interval Half Width	0.0588	=ABS(B10 * B11)
13			
14	Confidence Interval		
15	Interval Lower Limit	0.0412	=B9 - B12
16	Interval Upper Limit	0.1588	=B9 + B12

Example 8.4 illustrates another application of a confidence interval estimate for the proportion.

EXAMPLE 8.4

ESTIMATING THE PROPORTION OF NONCONFORMING NEWSPAPERS PRINTED

A large newspaper wants to estimate the proportion of newspapers printed that have a nonconforming attribute, such as excessive ruboff, improper page setup, missing pages, or duplicate pages. A random sample of 200 newspapers is selected from all the newspapers printed during a single day. For this sample of 200, 35 contain some type of nonconformance. Construct and interpret a 90% confidence interval for the proportion of newspapers printed during the day that have a nonconforming attribute.

SOLUTION Using Equation (8.3),

$$p = \frac{35}{200} = 0.175, \text{ and with a 90\% level of confidence } Z = 1.645$$

$$p \pm Z\sqrt{\frac{p(1-p)}{n}}$$

$$= 0.175 \pm (1.645)\sqrt{\frac{(0.175)(0.825)}{200}}$$

$$= 0.175 \pm (1.645)(0.0269)$$

$$= 0.175 \pm 0.0442$$

$$0.1308 \leq \pi \leq 0.2192$$

You conclude with 90% confidence that between 13.08% and 21.92% of the newspapers printed on that day have some type of nonconformance.

Equation (8.3) contains a Z statistic because you can use the normal distribution to approximate the binomial distribution when the sample size is sufficiently large. In Example 8.4, the confidence interval using Z provides an excellent approximation for the population proportion because both X and $n - X$ are greater than 5. However, if you do not have a sufficiently large sample size, you should use the binomial distribution rather than Equation (8.3) (see references 1, 2, and 6). The exact confidence intervals for various sample sizes and proportions of successes have been tabulated by Fisher and Yates (reference 2).

PROBLEMS FOR SECTION 8.3

Learning the Basics

 8.24 If $n = 200$ and $X = 50$, construct a 95% confidence interval estimate of the population proportion.

 8.25 If $n = 400$ and $X = 25$, construct a 99% confidence interval estimate of the population proportion.

Applying the Concepts

 8.26 The telephone company wants to estimate the proportion of households that would purchase an additional telephone line if it were made available at a substantially reduced installation cost. A random sample of 500 households is selected. The results indicate that 135 of the households would purchase the additional telephone line at a reduced installation cost.

a. Construct a 99% confidence interval estimate of the population proportion of households that would purchase the additional telephone line.

b. How would the manager in charge of promotional programs concerning residential customers use the results in (a)?

8.27 According to the Center for Work-Life Policy, a survey of 500 highly educated women who left careers for family reasons found that 66% wanted to return to work (Extracted from A. M. Chaker and H. Stout, "After Years Off, Women Struggle to Revive Careers," *The Wall Street Journal*, May 6, 2004, p. A1).

a. Construct a 95% confidence interval for the population proportion of highly educated women who left careers for family reasons who want to return to work.

b. Interpret the interval in (a).

8.28 In a survey conducted for American Express, 27% of small business owners indicated that they never check in with the office when on vacation ("Snapshots," **usatoday.com**, April 18, 2006.). The article did not disclose the sample size used in the study.

a. Suppose that the survey was based on 500 small business owners. Construct a 95% confidence interval estimate for the population proportion of small business owners who never check in with the office when on vacation.

b. Suppose that the survey was based on 1,000 small business owners. Construct a 95% confidence interval estimate for the population proportion of small business owners who never check in with the office when on vacation.

c. Discuss the effect of sample size on the confidence interval estimate.

8.29 The number of older consumers in the United States is growing, and they are becoming an even bigger economic force. Many feel overwhelmed when confronted with the task of selecting investments, banking services, health care providers, or phone service providers. A telephone survey of 1,900 older consumers found that 27% said they didn't have enough time to be good money managers (Extracted from "Seniors Confused by Financial Choices—Study," **msnbc.com**, May 6, 2004).

a. Construct a 95% confidence interval for the population proportion of older consumers who don't think they have enough time to be good money managers.

b. Interpret the interval in (a).

8.30 A survey of 705 workers (*USA Today Snapshots*, March 21, 2006, p. 1B) were asked how much they used

the Internet at work. 423 said they used it within limits, and 183 said that they did not use the Internet at work.

a. Construct a 95% confidence interval for the proportion of all workers who used the Internet within limits.

b. Construct a 95% confidence interval for the proportion of all workers who did not use the Internet at work.

8.31 When do Americans decide what to make for dinner? An online survey (N. Hellmich, "Americans Go for the Quick Fix for Dinner," *USA Today*, February 14, 2005, p. 1B) indicated that 74% of Americans decided either at the last minute or that day. Suppose that the survey was based on 500 respondents.

a. Construct a 95% confidence interval for the proportion of Americans who decided what to make for dinner either at the last minute or that day.

b. Construct a 99% confidence interval for the proportion of Americans who decided what to make for dinner either at the last minute or that day.

c. Which interval is wider? Explain why this is true.

8.32 In a survey of 894 respondents with salaries below $100,000 per year, 367 indicated that the primary reason for staying on their job was interesting job responsibilities ("What Is the Primary Reason for Staying on Your Job?" *USA Today Snapshots*, October 5, 2005, p. 1B).

a. Construct a 95% confidence interval for the proportion of all workers whose primary reason for staying on their job was interesting job responsibilities.

b. Interpret the interval constructed in (a).

8.33 A large number of companies are trying to reduce the cost of prescription drug benefits by requiring employees to purchase drugs through a mandatory mail-order program. In a survey of 600 employers, 126 indicated that they either had a mandatory mail-order program in place or were adopting one by the end of 2004 (B. Martinez, "Forcing Employees to Buy Drugs via Mail," *The Wall Street Journal*, February 18, 2004, p. 1B).

a. Construct a 95% confidence interval for the population proportion of employers who had a mandatory mail-order program in place or were adopting one by the end of 2004.

b. Construct a 99% confidence interval for the population proportion of employers who had a mandatory mail-order program in place or were adopting one by the end of 2004.

c. Interpret the intervals in (a) and (b).

d. Discuss the effect on the confidence interval estimate when you change the level of confidence.

8.4 DETERMINING SAMPLE SIZE

In each example of confidence interval estimation so far in this chapter, the sample size was reported along with the results with little discussion with regard to the width of the resulting confidence interval. In the business world, sample sizes are determined prior to data collection to ensure that the confidence interval is narrow enough to be useful in making decisions. Determining the proper sample size is a complicated procedure, subject to the constraints of budget, time, and the amount of acceptable sampling error. In the Saxon Home Improvement example, you want to estimate the mean dollar amount of the sales invoices, you must determine in advance how large a sampling error to allow in estimating the population mean. You must also determine in advance the level of confidence (that is, 90%, 95%, or 99%) to use in estimating the population parameter.

Sample Size Determination for the Mean

To develop an equation for determining the appropriate sample size needed when constructing a confidence interval estimate of the mean, recall Equation (8.1) on page 287:

$$\overline{X} \pm Z \frac{\sigma}{\sqrt{n}}$$

The amount added to or subtracted from $\overline{X}$ is equal to half the width of the interval. This quantity represents the amount of imprecision in the estimate that results from sampling error. The **sampling error**,[1] e, is defined as

$$e = Z \frac{\sigma}{\sqrt{n}}$$

Solving for n gives the sample size needed to construct the appropriate confidence interval estimate for the mean. "Appropriate" means that the resulting interval will have an acceptable amount of sampling error.

SAMPLE SIZE DETERMINATION FOR THE MEAN

The sample size, n, is equal to the product of the Z value squared and the variance, σ, squared, divided by the square of the sampling error, e,

$$n = \frac{Z^2 \sigma^2}{e^2} \tag{8.4}$$

To determine the sample size, you must know three factors:

1. The desired confidence level, which determines the value of Z, the critical value from the standardized normal distribution[2]
2. The acceptable sampling error, e
3. The standard deviation, σ

In some business-to-business relationships that require estimation of important parameters, legal contracts specify acceptable levels of sampling error and the confidence level required. For companies in the food or drug sectors, government regulations often specify sampling errors and confidence levels. In general, however, it is usually not easy to specify the two factors needed to determine the sample size. How can you determine the level of confidence and sampling error? Typically, these questions are answered only by the subject matter expert (that is, the individual most familiar with the variables under study). Although 95% is the most common confidence level used, if more confidence is desired, then 99% might be more appropriate; if less confidence is deemed acceptable, then 90% might be used. For the sampling error, you should think not of how much sampling error you would like to have (you really do not want any error) but of how much you can tolerate when drawing conclusions from the data.

In addition to specifying the confidence level and the sampling error, you need an estimate of the standard deviation. Unfortunately, you rarely know the population standard deviation, σ. In some instances, you can estimate the standard deviation from past data. In other situations, you can make an educated guess by taking into account the range and distribution of the variable. For example, if you assume a normal distribution, the range is approximately equal to 6σ (that is, $\pm3\sigma$ around the mean) so that you estimate σ as the range divided by 6. If you cannot estimate σ in this way, you can conduct a small-scale study and estimate the standard deviation from the resulting data.

To explore how to determine the sample size needed for estimating the population mean, consider again the audit at Saxon Home Improvement. In Section 8.2, you selected a sample of 100 sales invoices and constructed a 95% confidence interval estimate of the population mean sales invoice amount. How was this sample size determined? Should you have selected a different sample size?

Suppose that, after consultation with company officials, you determine that a sampling error of no more than $\pm\$5$ is desired, along with 95% confidence. Past data indicate that the standard deviation of the sales amount is approximately $25. Thus, $e = \$5$, $\sigma = \$25$, and $Z = 1.96$ (for 95% confidence). Using Equation (8.4),

$$n = \frac{Z^2\sigma^2}{e^2} = \frac{(1.96)^2(25)^2}{(5)^2}$$

$$= 96.04$$

Because the general rule is to slightly oversatisfy the criteria by rounding the sample size up to the next whole integer, you should select a sample of size 97. Thus, the sample of 100 used on page 292 is close to what is necessary to satisfy the needs of the company, based on the estimated standard deviation, desired confidence level, and sampling error. Because the calculated sample standard deviation is slightly higher than expected, $28.95 compared to $25.00, the confidence interval is slightly wider than desired. Figure 8.11 illustrates a Microsoft Excel worksheet to determine the sample size.

FIGURE 8.11

Microsoft Excel worksheet for determining sample size for estimating the mean sales invoice amount for the Saxon Home Improvement Company

See Section E8.4 to create this.

	A	B	
1	**For the Mean Sales Invoice Amount**		
2			
3	**Data**		
4	Population Standard Deviation	25	
5	Sampling Error	5	
6	Confidence Level	95%	
7			
8	Intermediate Calculations		
9	Z Value	-1.9600	=NORMSINV((1 - B6)/2)
10	Calculated Sample Size	96.0365	=((B9 * B4)/B5)^2
11			
12	Result		
13	Sample Size Needed	97	=ROUNDUP(B10, 0)

Example 8.5 illustrates another application of determining the sample size needed to develop a confidence interval estimate for the mean.

EXAMPLE 8.5

DETERMINING THE SAMPLE SIZE FOR THE MEAN

Returning to Example 8.3 on page 293, suppose you want to estimate the population mean force required to break the insulator to within ±25 pounds with 95% confidence. On the basis of a study taken the previous year, you believe that the standard deviation is 100 pounds. Find the sample size needed.

SOLUTION Using Equation (8.4) on page 300 and $e = 25$, $\sigma = 100$, and $Z = 1.96$ for 95% confidence,

$$n = \frac{Z^2\sigma^2}{e^2} = \frac{(1.96)^2(100)^2}{(25)^2}$$

$$= 61.47$$

Therefore, you should select a sample size of 62 insulators because the general rule for determining sample size is to always round up to the next integer value in order to slightly oversatisfy the criteria desired.

An actual sampling error slightly larger than 25 will result if the sample standard deviation calculated in this sample of 62 is greater than 100 and slightly smaller if the sample standard deviation is less than 100.

Sample Size Determination for the Proportion

So far in this section, you have learned how to determine the sample size needed for estimating the population mean. Now suppose that you want to determine the sample size necessary for estimating the proportion of sales invoices at Saxon Home Improvement that contain errors.

To determine the sample size needed to estimate a population proportion, π, you use a method similar to the method for a population mean. Recall that in developing the sample size for a confidence interval for the mean, the sampling error is defined by

$$e = Z\frac{\sigma}{\sqrt{n}}$$

When estimating a proportion, you replace σ with $\sqrt{\pi(1-\pi)}$. Thus, the sampling error is

$$e = Z\sqrt{\frac{\pi(1-\pi)}{n}}$$

Solving for n, you have the sample size necessary to develop a confidence interval estimate for a proportion.

SAMPLE SIZE DETERMINATION FOR THE PROPORTION

The sample size n is equal to the Z value squared times the population proportion, π, times 1 minus the population proportion, π, divided by the square of the sampling error, e,

$$n = \frac{Z^2\pi(1-\pi)}{e^2} \tag{8.5}$$

To determine the sample size, you must know three factors:

1. The desired confidence level, which determines the value of Z, the critical value from the standardized normal distribution
2. The acceptable sampling error, e
3. The population proportion, π

In practice, selecting these quantities requires some planning. Once you determine the desired level of confidence, you can find the appropriate Z value from the standardized normal distribution. The sampling error, e, indicates the amount of error that you are willing to tolerate in estimating the population proportion. The third quantity, π, is actually the population parameter that you want to estimate! Thus, how do you state a value for what you are taking a sample in order to determine?

Here you have two alternatives. In many situations, you may have past information or relevant experience that provide an educated estimate of π. Or, if you do not have past information or relevant experience, you can try to provide a value for π that would never *underestimate* the sample size needed. Referring to Equation (8.5), you can see that the quantity $\pi(1 - \pi)$ appears in the numerator. Thus, you need to determine the value of π that will make the quantity $\pi(1 - \pi)$ as large as possible. When $\pi = 0.5$, the product $\pi(1 - \pi)$ achieves its maximum result. To show this, several values of π, along with the accompanying products of $\pi(1 - \pi)$, are as follows

When $\pi = 0.9$, then $\pi(1 - \pi) = (0.9)(0.1) = 0.09$
When $\pi = 0.7$, then $\pi(1 - \pi) = (0.7)(0.3) = 0.21$
When $\pi = 0.5$, then $\pi(1 - \pi) = (0.5)(0.5) = 0.25$
When $\pi = 0.3$, then $\pi(1 - \pi) = (0.3)(0.7) = 0.21$
When $\pi = 0.1$, then $\pi(1 - \pi) = (0.1)(0.9) = 0.09$

Therefore, when you have no prior knowledge or estimate of the population proportion, π, you should use $\pi = 0.5$ for determining the sample size. This produces the largest possible sample size and results in the highest possible cost of sampling. Using $\pi = 0.5$ may overestimate the sample size needed because you use the actual sample proportion in developing the confidence interval. You will get a confidence interval narrower than originally intended if the actual sample proportion is different from 0.5. The increased precision comes at the cost of spending more time and money for an increased sample size.

Returning to the Saxon Home Improvement Using Statistics scenario, suppose that the auditing procedures require you to have 95% confidence in estimating the population proportion of sales invoices with errors to within ±0.07. The results from past months indicate that the largest proportion has been no more than 0.15. Thus, using Equation (8.5) on page 302 and $e = 0.07$, $\pi = 0.15$, and $Z = 1.96$ for 95% confidence,

$$n = \frac{Z^2\pi(1 - \pi)}{e^2}$$

$$= \frac{(1.96)^2(0.15)(0.85)}{(0.07)^2}$$

$$= 99.96$$

Because the general rule is to round the sample size up to the next whole integer to slightly oversatisfy the criteria, a sample size of 100 is needed. Thus, the sample size needed to satisfy the requirements of the company, based on the estimated proportion, desired confidence level, and sampling error, is equal to the sample size taken on page 297. The actual confidence interval is narrower than required because the sample proportion is 0.10, while 0.15 was used for π in Equation (8.5). Figure 8.12 shows a Microsoft Excel worksheet for determining sample size.

FIGURE 8.12

Microsoft Excel worksheet for determining sample size for estimating the proportion of sales invoices with errors for the Saxon Home Improvement Company

See Section E8.5 to create this.

	A	B
1	For the Proportion of In-Error Sales Invoices	
2		
3	Data	
4	Estimate of True Proportion	0.15
5	Sampling Error	0.07
6	Confidence Level	95%
7		
8	Intermediate Calculations	
9	Z Value	-1.9600
10	Calculated Sample Size	99.9563
11		
12	Result	
13	Sample Size Needed	100

=NORMSINV((1 - B6)/2)
=(B9^2 * B4 * (1 - B4))/B5^2

=ROUNDUP(B10, 0)

Example 8.6 provides a second application of determining the sample size for estimating the population proportion.

EXAMPLE 8.6

DETERMINING THE SAMPLE SIZE FOR THE POPULATION PROPORTION

You want to have 90% confidence of estimating the proportion of office workers who respond to email within an hour to within ± 0.05. Because you have not previously undertaken such a study, there is no information available from past data. Determine the sample size needed.

SOLUTION Because no information is available from past data, assume that $\pi = 0.50$. Using Equation (8.5) on page 302 and $e = 0.05$, $\pi = 0.50$, and $Z = 1.645$ for 90% confidence,

$$n = \frac{(1.645)^2 (0.50)(0.50)}{(0.05)^2}$$

$$= 270.6$$

Therefore, you need a sample of 271 office workers to estimate the population proportion to within ± 0.05 with 90% confidence.

PROBLEMS FOR SECTION 8.4

Learning the Basics

 8.34 If you want to be 95% confident of estimating the population mean to within a sampling error of ± 5 and the standard deviation is assumed to be 15, what sample size is required?

 8.35 If you want to be 99% confident of estimating the population mean to within a sampling error of ± 20 and the standard deviation is assumed to be 100, what sample size is required?

 8.36 If you want to be 99% confident of estimating the population proportion to within an error of ± 0.04, what sample size is needed?

 8.37 If you want to be 95% confident of estimating the population proportion to within an error of ± 0.02 and there is historical evidence

that the population proportion is approximately 0.40, what sample size is needed?

Applying the Concepts

 8.38 A survey is planned to determine the mean annual family medical expenses of employees of a large company. The management of the company wishes to be 95% confident that the sample mean is correct to within $\pm\$50$ of the population mean annual family medical expenses. A previous study indicates that the standard deviation is approximately $400.
a. How large a sample size is necessary?
b. If management wants to be correct to within $\pm\$25$, what sample size is necessary?

8.39 If the manager of a paint supply store wants to estimate the mean amount of paint in a 1-gallon can to within

±0.004 gallon with 95% confidence and also assumes that the standard deviation is 0.02 gallon, what sample size is needed?

8.40 If a quality control manager wants to estimate the mean life of light bulbs to within ±20 hours with 95% confidence and also assumes that the population standard deviation is 100 hours, what sample size is needed?

8.41 If the inspection division of a county weights and measures department wants to estimate the mean amount of soft-drink fill in 2-liter bottles to within ±0.01 liter with 95% confidence and also assumes that the standard deviation is 0.05 liter, what sample size is needed?

PH Grade ASSIST **8.42** A consumer group wants to estimate the mean electric bill for the month of July for single-family homes in a large city. Based on studies conducted in other cities, the standard deviation is assumed to be $25. The group wants to estimate the mean bill for July to within ±$5 with 99% confidence.
a. What sample size is needed?
b. If 95% confidence is desired, what sample size is necessary?

8.43 An advertising agency that serves a major radio station wants to estimate the mean amount of time that the station's audience spends listening to the radio daily. From past studies, the standard deviation is estimated as 45 minutes.
a. What sample size is needed if the agency wants to be 90% confident of being correct to within ±5 minutes?
b. If 99% confidence is desired, what sample size is necessary?

8.44 A growing niche in the restaurant business is gourmet-casual breakfast, lunch, and brunch. Chains in this group include Le Peep, Good Egg, Eggs & I, First Watch, and Eggs Up Grill. The mean per-person check for First Watch is approximately $7, and the mean per-person check for Eggs Up Grill is $6.50. (Extracted from J. Hayes, "Competition Heats Up as Breakfast Concepts Eye Growth," *Nation's Restaurant News*, April 24, 2006, pp. 8, 66.)
a. Assuming a standard deviation of $2.00, what sample size is needed to estimate the mean per-person check for Good Egg to within $0.25 with 95% confidence?
b. Assuming a standard deviation of $2.50, what sample size is needed to estimate the mean per-person check for Good Egg to within $0.25 with 95% confidence?
c. Assuming a standard deviation of $3.00, what sample size is needed to estimate the mean per-person check for Good Egg to within $0.25 with 95% confidence?
d. Discuss the effect of variation on selecting the sample size needed.

8.45 The U.S. Department of Transportation defines an airline flight as being "on time" if it lands less than 15 minutes after the scheduled time shown in the carrier's computerized reservation system. Cancelled and diverted flights are counted as late. A study of the 10 largest U.S. domestic airlines found Southwest Airlines to have the lowest proportion of late arrivals, at 0.1577 (Extracted from N. Tsikriktsis and J. Heineke, "The Impact of Process Variation on Customer Dissatisfaction: Evidence from the U.S. Domestic Airline Industry," *Decision Sciences*, Winter 2004, 35(1), pp. 129–142). Suppose you were asked to perform a follow-up study for Southwest Airlines in order to update the estimated proportion of late arrivals. What sample size would you use in order to estimate the population proportion to within an error of
a. ±0.06 with 95% confidence?
b. ±0.04 with 95% confidence?
c. ±0.02 with 95% confidence?

8.46 In 2005, 34% of workers reported that their jobs were more difficult, with more stress, and 37% reported that they worry about retiring comfortably. (Extracted from S. Armour, " Money Worries Hinder Job Performance," *USA Today*, October 5, 2005, p. D1). Consider a follow-up study to be conducted in the near future.
a. What sample size is needed to estimate the population proportion of workers who reported that their jobs were more difficult, with more stress, to within ±0.02 with 95% confidence?
b. What sample size is needed to estimate the population proportion of workers who worried about retiring comfortably to within ±0.02 with 95% confidence?
c. Compare the results of (a) and (b). Explain why these results differ.
d. If you were to design the follow-up study, would you use one sample and ask the respondents both questions, or would you select two separate samples? Explain the rationale behind your decision.

8.47 What proportion of people hit snags with online transactions? According to a poll conducted by Harris Interactive, 89% hit snags with online transactions ("Top Online Transaction Trouble," *USA Today Snapshots*, April 4, 2006, p. 1D).
a. To conduct a follow-up study that would provide 95% confidence that the point estimate is correct to within ±0.04 of the population proportion, how large a sample size is required?
b. To conduct a follow-up study that would provide 99% confidence that the point estimate is correct to within ±0.04 of the population proportion, how large a sample size is required?
c. To conduct a follow-up study that would provide 95% confidence that the point estimate is correct to within ±0.02 of the population proportion, how large a sample size is required?
d. To conduct a follow-up study that would provide 99% confidence that the point estimate is correct to within

±0.02 of the population proportion, how large a sample size is required?

e. Discuss the effects of changing the desired confidence level and the acceptable sampling error on sample size requirements.

8.48 A poll of 1,286 young adult cell phone users was conducted in March 2006. These cell phone users, aged 18–29, were actively engaged in multiple uses of their cell phones. The data suggest that 707 took still pictures with their phones, 604 played games, and 360 used the Internet (Extracted from "Poll: Cellphones Are Annoying but Invaluable," **usatoday.com**, April 3, 2006). Construct a 95% confidence interval estimate of the population proportion of young adults that used their cell phone to

a. take still pictures.
b. play games.
c. use the Internet.

d. You have been asked to update the results of this study. Determine the sample size necessary to estimate the population proportions in (a) through (c) to within ±0.02 with 95% confidence.

8.49 A study of 658 CEOs conducted by the Conference Board reported that 250 stated that their company's greatest concern was sustained and steady top-line growth ("CEOs' Greatest Concerns," *USA Today Snapshots*, May 8, 2006, p. 1D).

a. Construct a 95% confidence interval for the proportion of CEOs whose greatest concern was sustained and steady top-line growth.
b. Interpret the interval constructed in (a).
c. To conduct a follow-up study to estimate the population proportion of CEOs whose greatest concern was sustained and steady top-line growth to within ±0.01 with 95% confidence, how many CEOs would you survey?

8.5 APPLICATIONS OF CONFIDENCE INTERVAL ESTIMATION IN AUDITING

This chapter has focused on estimating either the population mean or the population proportion. In previous chapters, you have studied application to different business scenarios. Auditing is one of the areas in business that makes widespread use of probability sampling methods in order to construct confidence interval estimates.

AUDITING

Auditing is the collection and evaluation of evidence about information relating to an economic entity, such as a sole business proprietor, a partnership, a corporation, or a government agency, in order to determine and report on how well the information corresponds to established criteria.

Auditors rarely examine a complete population of information. Instead, they rely on estimation techniques based on the probability sampling methods you have studied in this text. The following list contains some of the reasons sampling is advantageous to examining the entire population.

- Sampling is less time consuming.
- Sampling is less costly.
- Sampling provides results that are objective and defensible. Because the sample size is based on demonstrable statistical principles, the audit is defensible before one's superiors and in a court of law.
- Sampling provides an objective way of estimating the sample size in advance.
- Sampling provides an estimate of the sampling error.
- Sampling is often more accurate for drawing conclusions about large populations than other methods. Examining large populations is time-consuming and therefore often subject to more nonsampling error than statistical sampling.
- Sampling allows auditors to combine, and then evaluate collectively, samples collected by different individuals.
- Sampling allows auditors to generalize their findings to the population with a known sampling error.

Estimating the Population Total Amount

In auditing applications, you are often more interested in developing estimates of the population **total amount** than the population mean. Equation (8.6) shows how to estimate a population total amount.

ESTIMATING THE POPULATION TOTAL

The point estimate for the population total is equal to the population size, N, times the sample mean.

$$\text{Total} = N\overline{X} \qquad (8.6)$$

Equation (8.7) defines the confidence interval estimate for the population total.

CONFIDENCE INTERVAL ESTIMATE FOR THE TOTAL

$$N\overline{X} \pm N(t_{n-1})\frac{S}{\sqrt{n}}\sqrt{\frac{N-n}{N-1}} \qquad (8.7)$$

To demonstrate the application of the confidence interval estimate for the population total amount, return to the Saxon Home Improvement Using Statistics scenario on page 284. One of the auditing tasks is to estimate the total dollar amount of all sales invoices for the month. If there are 5,000 invoices for that month and $\overline{X} = \$110.27$, then using Equation (8.6),

$$N\overline{X} = (5{,}000)(\$110.27) = \$551{,}350$$

If $n = 100$ and $S = \$28.95$, then using Equation (8.7) with $t_{99} = 1.9842$ for 95% confidence,

$$N\overline{X} \pm N(t_{n-1})\frac{S}{\sqrt{n}}\sqrt{\frac{N-n}{N-1}} = 551{,}350 \pm (5{,}000)(1.9842)\frac{28.95}{\sqrt{100}}\sqrt{\frac{5{,}000-100}{5{,}000-1}}$$

$$= 551{,}350 \pm 28{,}721.295(0.99005)$$

$$= 551{,}350 \pm 28{,}436$$

$$\$522{,}914 \le \text{Population total} \le \$579{,}786$$

Therefore, with 95% confidence, you estimate that the total amount of sales invoices is between $522,914 and $579,786. Figure 8.13 shows a Microsoft Excel worksheet for these data.

FIGURE 8.13

Microsoft Excel worksheet for the confidence interval estimate of the total amount of all invoices for the Saxon Home Improvement Company

See Section E8.6 to create this.

	A	B	
1	**Total Amount of All Sales Invoices**		
2			
3	**Data**		
4	Population Size	5000	
5	Sample Mean	110.27	
6	Sample Size	100	
7	Sample Standard Deviation	28.95	
8	Confidence Level	95%	
9			
10	**Intermediate Calculations**		
11	Population Total	551350.00	=B4 * B5
12	FPC Factor	0.9900	=SQRT((B4 - B6)/(B4 - 1))
13	Standard Error of the Total	14330.9521	=(B4 * B7 * B12)/SQRT(B6)
14	Degrees of Freedom	99	=B6 - 1
15	t Value	1.9842	=TINV(1 - B8, B14)
16	Interval Half Width	28435.72	=B15 * B13
17			
18	**Confidence Interval**		
19	Interval Lower Limit	522914.28	=B11 - B16
20	Interval Upper Limit	579785.72	=B11 + B16

Example 8.7 further illustrates the population total.

EXAMPLE 8.7

DEVELOPING A CONFIDENCE INTERVAL ESTIMATE FOR THE POPULATION TOTAL

An auditor is faced with a population of 1,000 vouchers and wants to estimate the total value of the population of vouchers. A sample of 50 vouchers is selected, with the following results:

$$\text{Mean voucher amount } (\overline{X}) = \$1,076.39$$

$$\text{Standard deviation } (S) = \$273.62$$

Construct a 95% confidence interval estimate of the total amount for the population of vouchers.

SOLUTION Using Equation (8.6) on page 307, the point estimate of the population total is

$$N\overline{X} = (1,000)(1,076.39) = \$1,076,390$$

From Equation (8.7) on page 307, a 95% confidence interval estimate of the population total amount is

$$(1,000)(1,076.39) \pm (1,000)(2.0096)\frac{273.62}{\sqrt{50}}\sqrt{\frac{1,000 - 50}{1,000 - 1}}$$

$$= 1,076,390 \pm 77,762.878 \ (0.97517)$$

$$= 1,076,390 \pm 75,832$$

$$\$1,000,558 \le \text{Population total} \le \$1,152,222$$

Therefore, with 95% confidence, you estimate that the total amount of the vouchers is between $1,000,558 and $1,152,222.

Difference Estimation

An auditor uses **difference estimation** when he or she believes that errors exist in a set of items and he or she wants to estimate the magnitude of the errors based only on a sample. The following steps are used in difference estimation:

1. Determine the sample size required.
2. Calculate the differences between the values reached during the audit and the original values recorded. The difference in value i, denoted D_i, is equal to 0 if the auditor finds that the original value is correct, is a positive value when the audited value is larger than the original value, and is negative when the audited value is smaller than the original value.
3. Compute the mean difference in the sample, $\overline{D}$, by dividing the total difference by the sample size, as shown in Equation (8.8).

MEAN DIFFERENCE

$$\overline{D} = \frac{\sum_{i=1}^{n} D_i}{n} \tag{8.8}$$

where D_i = Audited value − Original value

4. Compute the standard deviation of the differences, S_D, as shown in Equation (8.9). *Remember that any item that is not in error has a difference value of 0.*

STANDARD DEVIATION OF THE DIFFERENCE

$$S_D = \sqrt{\frac{\sum_{i=1}^{n}(D_i - \overline{D})^2}{n-1}} \qquad (8.9)$$

5. Use Equation (8.10) to construct a confidence interval estimate of the total difference in the population.

CONFIDENCE INTERVAL ESTIMATE FOR THE TOTAL DIFFERENCE

$$N\overline{D} \pm N(t_{n-1})\frac{S_D}{\sqrt{n}}\sqrt{\frac{N-n}{N-1}} \qquad (8.10)$$

The auditing procedures for Saxon Home Improvement require a 95% confidence interval estimate of the difference between the actual dollar amounts on the sales invoices and the amounts entered into the integrated inventory and sales information system. Suppose that in a sample of 100 sales invoices, you have 12 invoices in which the actual amount on the sales invoice and the amount entered into the integrated inventory management and sales information system is different. These 12 differences (stored in the file `plumbinv.xls`) are

$9.03 $7.47 $17.32 $8.30 $5.21 $10.80 $6.22 $5.63 $4.97 $7.43 $2.99 $4.63

The other 88 invoices are not in error. Their *differences* are each 0. Thus,

$$\overline{D} = \frac{\sum_{i=1}^{n}D_i}{n} = \frac{90}{100} = 0.90$$

and[3]

[3]*In the numerator, there are 100 differences. Each of the last 88 are equal to $(0 - 0.9)^2$*

$$S_D = \sqrt{\frac{\sum_{i=1}^{n}(D_i - \overline{D})^2}{n-1}}$$

$$= \sqrt{\frac{(9.03 - 0.9)^2 + (7.47 - 0.9)^2 + \cdots + (0 - 0.9)^2}{100 - 1}}$$

$$S_D = 2.752$$

Using Equation (8.10), construct the 95% confidence interval estimate for the total difference in the population of 5,000 sales invoices as follows:

$$(5,000)(0.90) \pm (5,000)(1.9842)\frac{2.752}{\sqrt{100}}\sqrt{\frac{5,000 - 100}{5,000 - 1}}$$

$$= 4,500 \pm 2,702.91$$

$$\$1,797.09 \leq \text{Total difference} \leq \$7,202.91$$

Thus, the auditor estimates with 95% confidence that the total difference between the sales invoices, as determined during the audit and the amount originally entered into the accounting system is between $1,797.09 and $7,202.91. Figure 8.14 shows an Excel worksheet for these data.

FIGURE 8.14

Microsoft Excel worksheet for the total difference between the invoice amounts found during audit and the amounts entered into the accounting system for the Saxon Home Improvement Company

See Section E8.7 to create this.

	A	B	
1	Total Difference In Actual and Entered		
2			
3	Data		
4	Population Size	5000	
5	Sample Size	100	
6	Confidence Level	95%	
7			
8	Intermediate Calculations		
9	Sum of Differences	90	=SUM(DifferencesData!A:A)
10	Average Difference in Sample	0.9	=B9/B5
11	Total Difference	4500	=B4 * B10
12	Standard Deviation of Differences	2.751797	=SQRT(E16)
13	FPC Factor	0.990049	=SQRT((B4 - B5)/(B4 - 1))
14	Standard Error of the Total Diff.	1362.206	=(B4 * B12 * B13)/SQRT(B5)
15	Degrees of Freedom	99	=B5 - 1
16	*t* Value	1.984217	=TINV(1 - B6, B15)
17	Interval Half Width	2702.913	=B16 * B14
18			
19	Confidence Interval		
20	Interval Lower Limit	1797.09	=B11 - B17
21	Interval Upper Limit	7202.91	=B11 + B17

In the previous example, all 12 differences are positive because the actual amount on the sales invoice is more than the amount entered into the accounting system. In some circumstances, you could have negative errors. Example 8.8 illustrates such a situation.

EXAMPLE 8.8

DIFFERENCE ESTIMATION

Returning to Example 8.7 on page 308, suppose that 14 vouchers in the sample of 50 vouchers contain errors. The values of the 14 errors are listed below and stored in the file **difftest.xls**. Observe that two differences are negative:

$75.41 $38.97 $108.54   −$37.18 $62.75 $118.32   −$88.84

$127.74 $55.42 $39.03 $29.41 $47.99 $28.73 $84.05

Construct a 95% confidence interval estimate of the total difference in the population of 1,000 vouchers.

SOLUTION For these data,

$$\overline{D} = \frac{\sum\limits_{i=1}^{n} D_i}{n} = \frac{690.34}{50} = 13.8068$$

and

$$S_D = \sqrt{\frac{\sum\limits_{i=1}^{n} (D_i - \overline{D})^2}{n - 1}}$$

$$= \sqrt{\frac{(75.41 - 13.8068)^2 + (38.97 - 13.8068)^2 + \cdots + (0 - 13.8068)^2}{50 - 1}}$$

$$= 37.427$$

Using Equation (8.10) on page 309, construct the confidence interval estimate for the total difference in the population as follows:

$$(1,000)(13.8068) \pm (1,000)(2.0096)\frac{37.427}{\sqrt{50}}\sqrt{\frac{1,000-50}{1,000-1}}$$

$$= 13,806.8 \pm 10,372.4$$

$$\$3,434.40 \le \text{Total difference} \le \$24,179.20$$

Therefore, with 95% confidence, you estimate that the total difference in the population of vouchers is between $3,434.40 and $24,179.20.

One-Sided Confidence Interval Estimation of the Rate of Noncompliance with Internal Controls

Organizations use internal control mechanisms to ensure that individuals act in accordance with company guidelines. For example, Saxon Home Improvement requires that an authorized warehouse-removal slip be completed before goods are removed from the warehouse. During the monthly audit of the company, the auditing team is charged with the task of estimating the proportion of times goods were removed without proper authorization. This is referred to as the *rate of noncompliance with the internal control*. To estimate the rate of noncompliance, auditors take a random sample of sales invoices and determine how often merchandise was shipped without an authorized warehouse-removal slip. The auditors then compare their results with a previously established tolerable exception rate, which is the maximum allowable proportion of items in the population not in compliance. When estimating the rate of noncompliance, it is commonplace to use a **one-sided confidence interval**. That is, the auditors estimate an upper bound on the rate of noncompliance. Equation (8.11) defines a one-sided confidence interval for a proportion.

ONE-SIDED CONFIDENCE INTERVAL FOR A PROPORTION

$$\text{Upper bound} = p + Z\sqrt{\frac{p(1-p)}{n}}\sqrt{\frac{N-n}{N-1}} \qquad (8.\text{i})$$

where Z = the value corresponding to a cumulative area of $(1-\alpha)$ from the standardized normal distribution (that is, a right-hand tail probability of α).

If the tolerable exception rate is higher than the upper bound, the auditor concludes that the company is in compliance with the internal control. If the upper bound is higher than the tolerable exception rate, the auditor concludes that the control noncompliance rate is too high. The auditor may then request a larger sample.

Suppose that in the monthly audit, you select 400 sales invoices from a population of 10,000 invoices. In the sample of 400 sales invoices, 20 are in violation of the internal control. If the tolerable exception rate for this internal control is 6%, what should you conclude? Use a 95% level of confidence.

The one-sided confidence interval is computed using $p = 20/400 = 0.05$ and $Z = 1.645$. Using Equation (8.11),

$$\text{Upper bound} = p + Z\sqrt{\frac{p(1-p)}{n}}\sqrt{\frac{N-n}{N-1}} = 0.05 + 1.645\sqrt{\frac{0.05(1-0.05)}{400}}\sqrt{\frac{10,000-400}{10,000-1}}$$

$$= 0.05 + 1.645(0.0109)(0.98) = 0.05 + 0.0176 = 0.0676$$

Thus, you have 95% confidence that the rate of noncompliance is less than 6.76%. Because the tolerable exception rate is 6%, the rate of noncompliance may be too high for this internal control. In other words, it is possible that the noncompliance rate for the population is higher than the rate deemed tolerable. Therefore, you should request a larger sample.

In many cases, the auditor is able to conclude that the rate of noncompliance with the company's internal controls is acceptable. Example 8.9 illustrates such an occurrence.

EXAMPLE 8.9

ESTIMATING THE RATE OF NONCOMPLIANCE

A large electronics firm writes 1 million checks a year. An internal control policy for the company is that the authorization to sign each check is granted only after an invoice has been initialed by an accounts payable supervisor. The company's tolerable exception rate for this control is 4%. If control deviations are found in 8 of the 400 invoices sampled, what should the auditor do? To solve this, use a 95% level of confidence.

SOLUTION The auditor constructs a 95% one-sided confidence interval for the proportion of invoices in noncompliance and compares this to the tolerable exception rate. Using Equation (8.11) on page 311, $p = 8/400 = 0.02$, and $Z = 1.645$ for 95% confidence,

$$\text{Upper bound} = p + Z\sqrt{\frac{p(1-p)}{n}}\sqrt{\frac{N-n}{N-1}} = 0.02 + 1.645\sqrt{\frac{0.02(1-0.02)}{400}}\sqrt{\frac{1,000,000-400}{1,000,000-1}}$$

$$= 0.02 + 1.645(0.007)(0.9998) = 0.02 + 0.0115 = 0.0315$$

The auditor concludes with 95% confidence that the rate of noncompliance is less than 3.15%. Because this is less than the tolerable exception rate, the auditor concludes that the internal control compliance is adequate. In other words, the auditor is more than 95% confident that the rate of noncompliance is less than 4%.

PROBLEMS FOR SECTION 8.5

Learning the Basics

8.50 A sample of 25 is selected from a population of 500 items. The sample mean is 25.7, and the sample standard deviation is 7.8. Construct a 99% confidence interval estimate of the population total.

8.51 Suppose that a sample of 200 (see the file itemerr.xls) is selected from a population of 10,000 items. Of these, 10 items are found to have errors of the following amounts:

13.76	42.87	34.65	11.09	14.54
22.87	25.52	9.81	10.03	15.49

Construct a 95% confidence interval estimate of the total difference in the population.

8.52 If $p = 0.04$, $n = 300$, and $N = 5,000$, calculate the upper bound for a one-sided confidence interval estimate of the population proportion, π, using the following levels of confidence:
a. 90%   **b.** 95%   **c.** 99%

Applying the Concepts

8.53 A stationery store wants to estimate the total retail value of the 1,000 greeting cards it has in its inventory. Construct a 95% confidence interval estimate of the population total value of all greeting cards that are in inventory if a random sample of 100 greeting cards indicates a mean value of $2.55 and a standard deviation of $0.44.

SELF Test **8.54** The personnel department of a large corporation employing 3,000 workers wants to estimate the family dental expenses of its employees to determine the feasibility of providing a dental insurance plan. A random sample of 10 employees reveals the following family dental expenses (in dollars) for the preceding year (see the dental.xls file):

110	362	246	85	510	208	173	425	316	179

Construct a 90% confidence interval estimate of the total family dental expenses for all employees in the preceding year.

8.55 A branch of a chain of large electronics stores is conducting an end-of-month inventory of the merchandise in stock. There were 1,546 items in inventory at that time. A sample of 50 items was randomly selected, and an audit was conducted, with the following results:

Value of Merchandise

$$\overline{X} = \$252.28 \qquad S = \$93.67$$

Construct a 95% confidence interval estimate of the total value of the merchandise in inventory at the end of the month.

8.56 A customer in the wholesale garment trade is often entitled to a discount for a cash payment for goods. The amount of discount varies by vendor. A sample of 150 items selected from a population of 4,000 invoices at the end of a period of time (see the discount.xls file) revealed that in 13 cases, the customer failed to take the discount to which he or she was entitled. The amounts (in dollars) of the 13 discounts that were not taken were as follows:

6.45   15.32   97.36   230.63   104.18   84.92   132.76
66.12   26.55   129.43   88.32   47.81   89.01

Construct a 99% confidence interval estimate of the population total amount of discounts not taken.

8.57 Econe Dresses is a small company that manufactures women's dresses for sale to specialty stores. It has 1,200 inventory items, and the historical cost is recorded on a first in, first out (FIFO) basis. In the past, approximately 15% of the inventory items were incorrectly priced. However, any misstatements were usually not significant. A sample of 120 items was selected (see the fifo.xls file), and the historical cost of each item was compared with the audited value. The results indicated that 15 items differed in their historical costs and audited values. These values were as follows:

Sample Number	Historical Cost ($)	Audited Value ($)	Sample Number	Historical Cost ($)	Audited Value ($)
5	261	240	60	21	210
9	87	105	73	140	152
17	201	276	86	129	112
18	121	110	95	340	216
28	315	298	96	341	402
35	411	356	107	135	97
43	249	211	119	228	220
51	216	305			

Construct a 95% confidence interval estimate of the total population difference in the historical cost and audited value.

8.58 Tom and Brent's Alpine Outfitters conduct an annual audit of its financial records. An internal control policy for the company is that a check can be issued only after the accounts payable manager initials the invoice. The tolerable exception rate for this internal control is 0.04. During an audit, a sample of 300 invoices is examined from a population of 10,000 invoices, and 11 invoices are found to violate the internal control.
a. Calculate the upper bound for a 95% one-sided confidence interval estimate for the rate of noncompliance.
b. Based on (a), what should the auditor conclude?

8.59 An internal control policy for Rhonda's Online Fashion Accessories requires a quality assurance check before a shipment is made. The tolerable exception rate for this internal control is 0.05. During an audit, 500 shipping records were sampled from a population of 5,000 shipping records, and 12 were found that violated the internal control.
a. Calculate the upper bound for a 95% one-sided confidence interval estimate for the rate of noncompliance.
b. Based on (a), what should the auditor conclude?

8.6 CONFIDENCE INTERVAL ESTIMATION AND ETHICAL ISSUES

Ethical issues relating to the selection of samples and the inferences that accompany them can occur in several ways. The major ethical issue relates to whether confidence interval estimates are provided along with the sample statistics. To provide a sample statistic without also including the confidence interval limits (typically set at 95%), the sample size used, and an interpretation of the meaning of the confidence interval in terms that a layperson can understand raises ethical issues. Failure to include a confidence interval estimate might mislead the user of the results into thinking that the point estimate is all that is needed to predict the population characteristic with certainty. Thus, it is important that you indicate the interval estimate in a prominent place in any written communication, along with a simple explanation of the meaning of the confidence interval. In addition, you should highlight the sample size.

One of the most common areas where ethical issues concerning estimation occurs is in the publication of the results of political polls. Often, the results of the polls are highlighted on the front page of the newspaper, and the sampling error involved along with the methodology used is printed on the page where the article is typically continued, often in the middle of the newspaper. To ensure an ethical presentation of statistical results, the confidence levels, sample size, and confidence limits should be made available for all surveys and other statistical studies.

8.7 ◉ (CD-ROM Topic) ESTIMATION AND SAMPLE SIZE DETERMINATION FOR FINITE POPULATIONS

In this section, confidence intervals are developed and the sample size is determined for situations in which sampling is done without replacement from a finite population. For further discussion, see section 8.7.pdf on the Student CD-ROM that accompanies this book.

SUMMARY

This chapter discusses confidence intervals for estimating the characteristics of a population, along with how you can determine the necessary sample size. You learned how an accountant at Saxon Home Improvement can use the sample data from an audit to estimate important population parameters such as the total dollar amount on invoices and the proportion of shipments made without the proper authorization. Table 8.3 provides a list of topics covered in this chapter.

TABLE 8.3

Summary of Topics in Chapter 8

Type of Analysis	Type of Data	
	Numerical	**Categorical**
Confidence interval for a population parameter	Confidence interval estimate for the mean (Sections 8.1 and 8.2)	Confidence interval estimate for the proportion (Section 8.3)
	Confidence interval estimate for the total and the mean difference (Section 8.5)	One-sided confidence interval estimate for the proportion (Section 8.5)

To determine what equation to use for a particular situation, you need to ask several questions:

- Are you developing a confidence interval or are you determining sample size?
- Do you have a numerical variable or do you have a categorical variable?

- If you have a numerical variable, do you know the population standard deviation? If you do, use the normal distribution. If you do not, use the t distribution.

The next four chapters develop a hypothesis-testing approach to making decisions about population parameters.

KEY EQUATIONS

Confidence Interval for the Mean (σ Known)

$$\bar{X} \pm Z \frac{\sigma}{\sqrt{n}}$$

or

$$\bar{X} - Z \frac{\sigma}{\sqrt{n}} \leq \mu \leq \bar{X} + Z \frac{\sigma}{\sqrt{n}} \qquad (8.1)$$

Confidence Interval for the Mean (σ Unknown)

$$\bar{X} \pm t_{n-1} \frac{S}{\sqrt{n}}$$

or

$$\bar{X} - t_{n-1} \frac{S}{\sqrt{n}} \leq \mu \leq \bar{X} + t_{n-1} \frac{S}{\sqrt{n}} \qquad (8.2)$$

Confidence Interval Estimate for the Proportion

$$p \pm Z\sqrt{\frac{p(1-p)}{n}}$$

or

$$p - Z\sqrt{\frac{p(1-p)}{n}} \leq \pi \leq p + Z\sqrt{\frac{p(1-p)}{n}} \quad \textbf{(8.3)}$$

Sample Size Determination for the Mean

$$n = \frac{Z^2\sigma^2}{e^2} \quad \textbf{(8.4)}$$

Sample Size Determination for the Proportion

$$n = \frac{Z^2\pi(1-\pi)}{e^2} \quad \textbf{(8.5)}$$

KEY TERMS

auditing   306
confidence interval estimate   284
critical value   287
degrees of freedom   290

difference estimation   308
level of confidence   287
one-sided confidence interval   311
point estimate   284

sampling error   300
Student's t distribution   290
total amount   307

CHAPTER REVIEW PROBLEMS

Checking Your Understanding

8.60 Why can you never really have 100% confidence of correctly estimating the population characteristic of interest?

8.61 When do you use the t distribution to develop the confidence interval estimate for the mean?

8.62 Why is it true that for a given sample size, n, an increase in confidence is achieved by widening (and making less precise) the confidence interval?

8.63 Under what circumstances do you use a one-sided confidence interval instead of a two-sided confidence interval?

8.64 When would you want to estimate the population total instead of the population mean?

8.65 How does difference estimation differ from estimation of the mean?

Applying the Concepts

8.66 You work in the corporate office for a nationwide convenience store franchise that operates nearly 10,000 stores. The per-store daily customer count has been steady at 900 for some time (that is, the mean number of customers in a store in one day is 900). To increase the customer count, the franchise is considering cutting coffee prices by approximately half. The 12-ounce size will now be $.59 instead of $.99, and the 16-ounce size will be $.69 instead of $1.19. Even with this reduction in price, the franchise will have a 40% gross margin on coffee. To test the new initiative, the franchise has reduced coffee prices in a sample of 34 stores, where customer counts have been running almost exactly at the national average of 900. After four weeks, the sample stores stabilize at a mean customer count of 974 and a standard deviation of 96. This increase seems like a substantial amount to you, but it also seems like a pretty small sample. Is there some way to get a feel for what the mean per-store count in all the stores will be if you cut coffee prices nationwide? Do you think reducing coffee prices is a good strategy for increasing the mean customer count?

8.67 Companies are spending more time screening applicants than in the past. A study of 102 recruiters conducted by ExecuNet found that 77 did Internet research on candidates. (Extracted from P. Kitchen, "Don't Let Any 'Digital Dirt' Bury Your Job Prospects," *Newsday*, August 21, 2005, p. A59).
a. Construct a 95% confidence interval estimate of the population proportion of recruiters who do Internet research on candidates.
b. Based on (a), is it correct to conclude that more than 70% of recruiters do Internet research on candidates?
c. Suppose that the study uses a sample size of 400 recruiters and 302 did Internet research on candidates. Construct a 95% confidence interval estimate of the population proportion of recruiters who do Internet research on candidates.
d. Based on (c), is it correct to conclude that more than 70% of recruiters do Internet research on candidates?
e. Discuss the effect of sample size on your answers to (a) through (d).

8.68 High-fructose corn syrup (HFCS) was created in the 1970s and is used today in a wide variety of foods and beverages. HFCS is cheaper than sugar and is about 75% sweeter than sucrose. Some researchers think that HFCS is linked to the growing obesity problem in the United States (Extracted from P. Lempert, "War of the Sugars," *Progressive Grocer*, April 15, 2006, p. 20). The following consumer views are from a nationwide survey of 1,114 responses:

Views on HFCS

	Yes	No
Are you concerned about consuming HFCS?	80%	20%
Do you think HFCS should be banned in food sold to schools?	88%	12%
Do you think HFCS should be banned in all foods?	56%	44%

Construct a 95% confidence interval estimate of the population proportion of people who
a. are concerned about consuming HFCS.
b. think HFCS should be banned in food sold to schools.
c. think HFCS should be banned in all foods.
d. You are in charge of a follow-up survey. Determine the sample size necessary to estimate the proportions in (a) through (c) to within ±0.02 with 95% confidence.

8.69 Starwood Hotels conducted a survey of 401 top executives who play golf (Extracted from D. Jones, "Many CEOs Bend the Rules (of Golf)," *USA Today*, June 26, 2002). Among the results were the following:
 • 329 cheat at golf.
 • 329 hate others who cheat at golf.
 • 289 believe business and golf behavior parallel.
 • 80 would let a client win to get business.
 • 40 would call in sick to play golf.
Construct a 95% confidence interval estimate for each of these questions. Based on these results, what conclusions can you reach about CEOs' attitudes toward golf?

8.70 A market researcher for a consumer electronics company wants to study the television viewing habits of residents of a particular area. A random sample of 40 respondents is selected, and each respondent is instructed to keep a detailed record of all television viewing in a particular week. The results are as follows:
 • Viewing time per week: $\bar{X} = 15.3$ hours, $S = 3.8$ hours.
 • 27 respondents watch the evening news on at least 3 weeknights.
a. Construct a 95% confidence interval estimate for the mean amount of television watched per week in this city.
b. Construct a 95% confidence interval estimate for the population proportion who watch the evening news on at least 3 weeknights per week.

Suppose that the market researcher wants to take another survey in a different city. Answer these questions:
c. What sample size is required to be 95% confident of estimating the population mean to within ±2 hours and assumes that the population standard deviation is equal to 5 hours?
d. What sample size is needed to be 95% confident of being within ±0.035 of the population proportion who watch the evening news on at least 3 weeknights if no previous estimate is available?
e. Based on (c) and (d), what sample size should the market researcher select if a single survey is being conducted?

8.71 The real estate assessor for a county government wants to study various characteristics of single-family houses in the county. A random sample of 70 houses reveals the following:
 • Heated area of the houses (in square feet): $\bar{X} = 1,759$, $S = 380$.
 • 42 houses have central air-conditioning.
a. Construct a 99% confidence interval estimate of the population mean heated area of the houses.
b. Construct a 95% confidence interval estimate of the population proportion of houses that have central air-conditioning.

8.72 The personnel director of a large corporation wishes to study absenteeism among clerical workers at the corporation's central office during the year. A random sample of 25 clerical workers reveals the following:
 • Absenteeism: $\bar{X} = 9.7$ days, $S = 4.0$ days.
 • 12 clerical workers were absent more than 10 days.
a. Construct a 95% confidence interval estimate of the mean number of absences for clerical workers during the year.
b. Construct a 95% confidence interval estimate of the population proportion of clerical workers absent more than 10 days during the year.

Suppose that the personnel director also wishes to take a survey in a branch office. Answer these questions:
c. What sample size is needed to have 95% confidence in estimating the population mean to within ±1.5 days if the population standard deviation is 4.5 days?
d. What sample size is needed to have 90% confidence in estimating the population proportion to within ±0.075 if no previous estimate is available?
e. Based on (c) and (d), what sample size is needed if a single survey is being conducted?

8.73 The market research director for Dotty's Department Store wants to study women's spending on cosmetics. A survey of the store's credit card holders is designed in order to estimate the proportion of women who purchase their cosmetics primarily from Dotty's Department Store and the mean yearly amount that women spend on cosmetics. A previous survey found that the standard deviation of the amount women spend on cosmetics in a year is approximately $18.

a. What sample size is needed to have 99% confidence of estimating the population mean to within ±$5?

b. What sample size is needed to have 90% confidence of estimating the population proportion to within ±0.045?

c. Based on the results in (a) and (b), how many of the store's credit card holders should be sampled? Explain.

8.74 The branch manager of a nationwide bookstore chain wants to study characteristics of her store's customers. She decides to focus on two variables: the amount of money spent by customers and whether the customers would consider purchasing educational DVDs relating to graduate preparation exams, such as the GMAT, GRE, or LSAT. The results from a sample of 70 customers are as follows:

- Amount spent: $\bar{X} = \$28.52$, $S = \$11.39$.
- 28 customers stated that they would consider purchasing the educational DVDs.

a. Construct a 95% confidence interval estimate of the population mean amount spent in the bookstore.

b. Construct a 90% confidence interval estimate of the population proportion of customers who would consider purchasing educational DVDs.

Assume that the branch manager of another store in the chain wants to conduct a similar survey in his store. Answer the following questions:

c. What sample size is needed to have 95% confidence of estimating the population mean amount spent in his store to within ±$2 if the standard deviation is assumed to be $10?

d. What sample size is needed to have 90% confidence of estimating the population proportion who would consider purchasing the educational DVDs to within ±0.04?

e. Based on your answers to (c) and (d), how large a sample should the manager take?

8.75 The branch manager of an outlet (Store 1) of a nationwide chain of pet supply stores wants to study characteristics of her customers. In particular, she decides to focus on two variables: the amount of money spent by customers and whether the customers own only one dog, only one cat, or more than one dog and/or cat. The results from a sample of 70 customers are as follows:

- Amount of money spent: $\bar{X} = \$21.34$, $S = \$9.22$.
- 37 customers own only a dog.
- 26 customers own only a cat.
- 7 customers own more than one dog and/or cat.

a. Construct a 95% confidence interval estimate of the population mean amount spent in the pet supply store.

b. Construct a 90% confidence interval estimate of the population proportion of customers who own only a cat.

The branch manager of another outlet (Store 2) wishes to conduct a similar survey in his store. The manager does not have access to the information generated by the manager of Store 1. Answer the following questions:

c. What sample size is needed to have 95% confidence of estimating the population mean amount spent in his store to within ±$1.50 if the standard deviation is $10?

d. What sample size is needed to have 90% confidence of estimating the population proportion of customers who own only a cat to within ±0.045?

e. Based on your answers to (c) and (d), how large a sample should the manager take?

8.76 The owner of a restaurant that serves continental food wants to study characteristics of his customers. He decides to focus on two variables: the amount of money spent by customers and whether customers order dessert. The results from a sample of 60 customers are as follows:

- Amount spent: $\bar{X} = \$38.54$, $S = \$7.26$.
- 18 customers purchased dessert.

a. Construct a 95% confidence interval estimate of the population mean amount spent per customer in the restaurant.

b. Construct a 90% confidence interval estimate of the population proportion of customers who purchase dessert.

The owner of a competing restaurant wants to conduct a similar survey in her restaurant. This owner does not have access to the information of the owner of the first restaurant. Answer the following questions:

c. What sample size is needed to have 95% confidence of estimating the population mean amount spent in her restaurant to within ±$1.50, assuming that the standard deviation is $8?

d. What sample size is needed to have 90% confidence of estimating the population proportion of customers who purchase dessert to within ±0.04?

e. Based on your answers to (c) and (d), how large a sample should the owner take?

8.77 The manufacturer of "Ice Melt" claims its product will melt snow and ice at temperatures as low as $0°$ Fahrenheit. A representative for a large chain of hardware stores is interested in testing this claim. The chain purchases a large shipment of 5-pound bags for distribution. The representative wants to know with 95% confidence, within ±0.05, what proportion of bags of Ice Melt perform the job as claimed by the manufacturer.

a. How many bags does the representative need to test? What assumption should be made concerning the population proportion? (This is called *destructive testing*; that is, the product being tested is destroyed by the test and is then unavailable to be sold.)

b. The representative tests 50 bags, and 42 of them do the job as claimed. Construct a 95% confidence interval estimate for the population proportion that will do the job as claimed.

c. How can the representative use the results of (b) to determine whether to sell the Ice Melt product?

8.78 An auditor needs to estimate the percentage of times a company fails to follow an internal control procedure. A sample of 50 from a population of 1,000 items is selected, and in 7 instances, the internal control procedure was not followed.

a. Construct a 90% one-sided confidence interval estimate of the population proportion of items in which the internal control procedure was not followed.

b. If the tolerable exception rate is 0.15, what should the auditor conclude?

8.79 An auditor for a government agency needs to evaluate payments for doctors' office visits paid by Medicare in a particular zip code during the month of June. A total of 25,056 visits occurred during June in this area. The auditor wants to estimate the total amount paid by Medicare to within ±$5 with 95% confidence. On the basis of past experience, she believes that the standard deviation is approximately $30.

a. What sample size should she select?

Using the sample size selected in (a), an audit is conducted with the following results.

Amount of Reimbursement

$$\overline{X} = \$93.70 \qquad S = \$34.55$$

In 12 of the office visits, an incorrect amount of reimbursement was provided. For the 12 office visits in which there was an incorrect reimbursement, the differences between the amount reimbursed and the amount that the auditor determined should have been reimbursed were as follows (and are stored in the file medicare.xls)

$17 $25 $14 −$10 $20 $40 $35 $30 $28 $22 $15 $5

b. Construct a 90% confidence interval estimate of the population proportion of reimbursements that contain errors.

c. Construct a 95% confidence interval estimate of the population mean reimbursement per office visit.

d. Construct a 95% confidence interval estimate of the population total amount of reimbursements for this geographic area in June.

e. Construct a 95% confidence interval estimate of the total difference between the amount reimbursed and the amount that the auditor determined should have been reimbursed.

8.80 A home furnishings store that sells bedroom furniture is conducting an end-of-month inventory of the beds (mattress, bed spring, and frame) in stock. An auditor for the store wants to estimate the mean value of the beds in stock at that time. She wants to have 99% confidence that her estimate of the mean value is correct to within ±$100. On the basis of past experience, she estimates that the standard deviation of the value of a bed is $200.

a. What sample size should she select?

b. Using the sample size selected in (a), an audit was conducted, with the following results:

$$\overline{X} = \$1,654.27 \qquad S = \$184.62$$

Construct a 99% confidence interval estimate of the total value of the beds in stock at the end of the month if there were 258 beds in stock.

8.81 A quality characteristic of interest for a tea-bag-filling process is the weight of the tea in the individual bags. In this example, the label weight on the package indicates that the mean amount is 5.5 grams of tea in a bag. If the bags are underfilled, two problems arise. First, customers may not be able to brew the tea to be as strong as they wish. Second, the company may be in violation of the truth-in-labeling laws. On the other hand, if the mean amount of tea in a bag exceeds the label weight, the company is giving away product. Getting an exact amount of tea in a bag is problematic because of variation in the temperature and humidity inside the factory, differences in the density of the tea, and the extremely fast filling operation of the machine (approximately 170 bags per minute). The following data are the weights, in grams, of a sample of 50 tea bags produced in one hour by a single machine (the data are stored in the file teabags.xls):

Weight of Tea Bags, in Grams

5.65	5.44	5.42	5.40	5.53	5.34	5.54	5.45	5.52	5.41
5.57	5.40	5.53	5.54	5.55	5.62	5.56	5.46	5.44	5.51
5.47	5.40	5.47	5.61	5.53	5.32	5.67	5.29	5.49	5.55
5.77	5.57	5.42	5.58	5.58	5.50	5.32	5.50	5.53	5.58
5.61	5.45	5.44	5.25	5.56	5.63	5.50	5.57	5.67	5.36

a. Construct a 99% confidence interval estimate of the population mean weight of the tea bags.

b. Is the company meeting the requirement set forth on the label that the mean amount of tea in a bag is 5.5 grams?

8.82 A manufacturing company produces steel housings for electrical equipment. The main component part of the housing is a steel trough that is made out of a 14-gauge steel coil. It is produced using a 250-ton progressive punch press with a wipe-down operation that puts two 90-degree forms in the flat steel to make the trough. The distance from one side of the form to the other is critical because of weather-proofing in outdoor applications. The data (stored in the file **trough.xls**) from a sample of 49 troughs follows:

Width of Trough, in Inches

8.312 8.343 8.317 8.383 8.348 8.410 8.351 8.373 8.481 8.422

8.476 8.382 8.484 8.403 8.414 8.419 8.385 8.465 8.498 8.447

8.436 8.413 8.489 8.414 8.481 8.415 8.479 8.429 8.458 8.462

8.460 8.444 8.429 8.460 8.412 8.420 8.410 8.405 8.323 8.420

8.396 8.447 8.405 8.439 8.411 8.427 8.420 8.498 8.409

a. Construct a 95% confidence interval estimate of the mean width of the troughs.

b. Interpret the interval developed in (a).

8.83 The manufacturer of Boston and Vermont asphalt shingles know that product weight is a major factor in the customer's perception of quality. The last stage of the assembly line packages the shingles before they are placed on wooden pallets. Once a pallet is full (a pallet for most brands holds 16 squares of shingles), it is weighed, and the measurement is recorded. The data file **pallet.xls** contains the weight (in pounds) from a sample of 368 pallets of Boston shingles and 330 pallets of Vermont shingles.

a. For the Boston shingles, construct a 95% confidence interval estimate of the mean weight.

b. For the Vermont shingles, construct a 95% confidence interval estimate of the mean weight.

c. Evaluate whether the assumption needed for (a) and (b) has been seriously violated.

d. Based on the results of (a) and (b), what conclusions can you reach concerning the mean weight of the Boston and Vermont shingles?

8.84 The manufacturer of Boston and Vermont asphalt shingles provides its customers with a 20-year warranty on most of its products. To determine whether a shingle will last as long as the warranty period, accelerated-life testing is conducted at the manufacturing plant. Accelerated-life testing exposes the shingle to the stresses it would be subject to in a lifetime of normal use via a laboratory experiment that takes only a few minutes to conduct. In this test, a shingle is repeatedly scraped with a brush for a short period of time, and the shingle granules removed by the brushing are weighed (in grams). Shingles that experience low amounts of granule loss are expected to last longer in normal use than shingles that experience high amounts of granule loss. In this situation, a shingle should experience no more than 0.8 grams of granule loss if it is expected to last the length of the

warranty period. The data file **granule.xls** contains a sample of 170 measurements made on the company's Boston shingles and 140 measurements made on Vermont shingles.

a. For the Boston shingles, construct a 95% confidence interval estimate of the mean granule loss.

b. For the Vermont shingles, construct a 95% confidence interval estimate of the mean granule loss.

c. Evaluate whether the assumption needed for (a) and (b) has been seriously violated.

d. Based on the results of (a) and (b), what conclusions can you reach concerning the mean granule loss of the Boston and Vermont shingles?

Report Writing Exercises

8.85 Referring to the results in Problem 8.82 on page 318 concerning the width of a steel trough, write a report that summarizes your conclusions.

Team Project

8.86 Refer to the team project on page 73 (see the **mutual funds.xls** file). Construct all appropriate confidence interval estimates of the population characteristics of low-risk, average-risk, and high-risk mutual funds. Include these estimates in a report to the vice president for research at the financial investment service.

Student Survey Database

8.87 Problem 1.27 on page 15 describes a survey of 50 undergraduate students (see the file **undergradsurvey.xls**).

a. For these data, for each variable, construct a 95% confidence interval estimate of the population characteristic.

b. Write a report that summarizes your conclusions.

8.88 Problem 1.27 on page 15 describes a survey of 50 undergraduate students (see the file **undergradsurvey.xls**).

a. Select a sample of 50 undergraduate students at your school and conduct a similar survey for those students.

b. For the data collected in (a), repeat (a) and (b) of Problem 8.87.

c. Compare the results of (b) to those of Problem 8.87.

8.89 Problem 1.28 on page 15 describes a survey of 50 MBA students (see the file **gradsurvey.xls**).

a. For these data, for each variable, construct a 95% confidence interval estimate of the population characteristic.

b. Write a report that summarizes your conclusions.

8.90 Problem 1.28 on page 15 describes a survey of 50 MBA students (see the file **gradsurvey.xls**).

a. Select a sample of 50 graduate students in your MBA program and conduct a similar survey for those students.

b. For the data collected in (a), repeat (a) and (b) of Problem 8.89.

c. Compare the results of (b) to those of Problem 8.89.

Managing the *Springville Herald*

The marketing department has been considering ways to increase the number of new subscriptions and increase the rate of retention among customers who agreed to a trial subscription. Following the suggestion of Assistant Manager Lauren Alfonso, the department staff designed a survey to help determine various characteristics of readers of the newspaper who were not home-delivery subscribers. The survey consists of the following 10 questions:

1. Do you or a member of your household ever purchase the *Springville Herald*?
    (1) Yes   (2) No
    [If the respondent answers no, the interview is terminated.]
2. Do you receive the *Springville Herald* via home delivery?
    (1) Yes   (2) No
    [If no, skip to question 4.]
3. Do you receive the *Springville Herald*:
    (1) Monday–Saturday   (2) Sunday only   (3) Every day
    [If every day, skip to question 9.]
4. How often during the Monday–Saturday period do you purchase the *Springville Herald*?
    (1) Every day (2) Most days (3) Occasionally or never
5. How often do you purchase the *Springville Herald* on Sundays?
    (1) Every Sunday   (2) 2–3 Sundays per month
    (3) No more than once a month
6. Where are you most likely to purchase the *Springville Herald*?
    (1) Convenience store   (2) Newsstand/candy store
    (3) Vending machine   (4) Supermarket   (5) Other
7. Would you consider subscribing to the *Springville Herald* for a trial period if a discount were offered?
    (1) Yes   (2) No
    [If no, skip to question 9.]
8. The *Springville Herald* currently costs $0.50 Monday–Saturday and $1.50 on Sunday, for a total of $4.50 per week. How much would you be willing to pay per week to get home delivery for a 90-day trial period?
9. Do you read a daily newspaper other than the *Springville Herald*?
    (1) Yes   (2) No
10. As an incentive for long-term subscribers, the newspaper is considering the possibility of offering a card that would provide discounts at certain restaurants in the Springville area to all subscribers who pay in advance for six months of home delivery. Would you want to get such a card under the terms of this offer?
    (1) Yes   (2) No

The group agreed to use a random-digit dialing method to poll 500 local households by telephone. Using this approach, the last four digits of a telephone number are randomly selected to go with an area code and exchange (the first 6 digits of a 10-digit telephone number). Only those pairs of area codes and exchanges that were for the Springville city area were used for this survey.

Of the 500 households selected, 94 households either refused to participate, could not be contacted after repeated attempts, or represented telephone numbers that were not in service. The summary results are as follows:

Households That Purchase the *Springville Herald*	Frequency
Yes	352
No	54

Households with Home Delivery	Frequency
Yes	136
No	216

Type of Home Delivery Subscription	Frequency
Monday–Saturday	18
Sunday only	25
7 days a week	93

Purchase Behavior of Nonsubscribers for Monday–Saturday Editions	Frequency
Every day	78
Most days	95
Occasionally or never	43

Purchase Behavior of Nonsubscribers for Sunday Editions	Frequency
Every Sunday	138
2–3 Sundays a month	54
No more than once a month	24

Nonsubscribers' Purchase Location	Frequency
Convenience store	74
Newsstand/candy store	95
Vending machine	21
Supermarket	13
Other locations	13

Would Consider Trial Subscription if Offered a Discount	Frequency
Yes	46
No	170

Rate Willing to Pay per Week (in Dollars) Data file **sh8.xls**
for a 90-Day Home-Delivery Trial Subscription

4.15	3.60	4.10	3.60	3.60	3.60	4.40	3.15	4.00	3.75	4.00
3.25	3.75	3.30	3.75	3.65	4.00	4.10	3.90	3.50	3.75	3.00
3.40	4.00	3.80	3.50	4.10	4.25	3.50	3.90	3.95	4.30	4.20
3.50	3.75	3.30	3.85	3.20	4.40	3.80	3.40	3.50	2.85	3.75
3.80	3.90									

Read a Daily Newspaper Other Than the *Springville Herald*	**Frequency**
Yes	138
No	214

Would Prepay Six Months to Receive a Restaurant Discount Card	**Frequency**
Yes	66
No	286

EXERCISES

SH8.1 Some members of the marketing department are concerned about the random-digit dialing method used to collect survey responses. Prepare a memorandum that examines the following issues:
- The advantages and disadvantages of using the random-digit dialing method.
- Possible alternative approaches for conducting the survey and their advantages and disadvantages.

SH8.2 Analyze the results of the survey of Springville households. Write a report that discusses the marketing implications of the survey results for the *Springville Herald*.

Web Case

Apply your knowledge about confidence interval estimation in this Web Case, which extends the OurCampus! Web Case from Chapter 6.

Among its other features, the OurCampus! Web site allows customers to purchase OurCampus! LifeStyles merchandise online. To handle payment processing, the management of OurCampus! has contracted with the following firms:

- PayAFriend (PAF): an online payment system with which customers and businesses such as OurCampus! register in order to exchange payments in a secure and convenient manner without the need for a credit card.
- Continental Banking Company (Conbanco): a processing services provider that allows OurCampus! customers to pay for merchandise using nationally recognized credit cards issued by a financial institution.

To reduce costs, the management is considering eliminating one of these two payment systems. However, Virginia Duffy of the sales department suspects that customers use the two forms of payment in unequal numbers and that customers display different buying behaviors when using the two forms of payment. Therefore, she would like to first determine

a. the proportion of customers using PAF and the proportion of customers using a credit card to pay for their purchases.

b. the mean purchase amount when using PAF and the mean purchase amount when using a credit card.

Assist Ms. Duffy by preparing an appropriate analysis based on a random sample of 50 transactions that she has prepared and placed in an internal file on the OurCampus! Web site, **www.prenhall.com/Springville/OurCampus_PymtSample.htm**. Summarize your findings and determine whether Ms. Duffy's conjectures about OurCampus! customer purchasing behaviors are correct. If you want the sampling error to be no more than $3 when estimating the mean purchase amount, is Ms. Duffy's sample large enough to perform a valid analysis?

REFERENCES

1. Cochran, W. G., *Sampling Techniques*, 3rd ed. (New York: Wiley, 1977).
2. Fisher, R. A., and F. Yates, *Statistical Tables for Biological, Agricultural and Medical Research*, 5th ed. (Edinburgh: Oliver & Boyd, 1957).
3. Kirk, R. E., ed., *Statistical Issues: A Reader for the Behavioral Sciences* (Belmont, CA: Wadsworth, 1972).
4. Larsen, R. L., and M. L. Marx, *An Introduction to Mathematical Statistics and Its Applications*, 4th ed. (Upper Saddle River, NJ: Prentice Hall, 2006).
5. *Microsoft Excel 2007* (Redmond, WA: Microsoft Corp., 2007).
6. Snedecor, G. W., and W. G. Cochran, *Statistical Methods*, 7th ed. (Ames, IA: Iowa State University Press, 1980).

Excel Companion
to Chapter 8

E8.1   COMPUTING THE CONFIDENCE INTERVAL ESTIMATE FOR THE MEAN (σ KNOWN)

You compute the confidence interval estimate for the mean (σ known) either by using the PHStat2 Estimate for the Mean, sigma known procedure or by making entries in the CIE sigma known.xls workbook.

Using PHStat2 Estimate for the Mean, Sigma Known

Select **PHStat → Confidence Intervals → Estimate for the Mean, sigma known**. In the Estimate for the Mean, sigma known dialog box (shown below), enter values for the **Population Standard Deviation** and the **Confidence Level**. Click one of the input options and make the required entries. Enter a title as the **Title** and click **OK**.

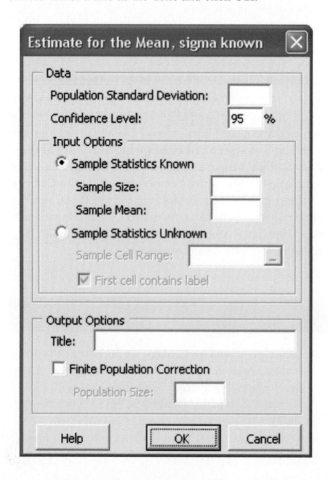

If you know the sample size and sample mean of your sample, click **Sample Statistics Known** and enter those values. Otherwise, click **Sample Statistics Unknown** and enter the cell range of your sample as the **Sample Cell Range**.

Using the CIE_SK Worksheet

Open to the **CIE_SK** worksheet of the workbook. This worksheet uses the **NORMSINV(*P<X*)** and **CONFIDENCE(1-*confidence level, population standard deviation, sample size*)** functions to compute the Z value and interval half-width for the Example 8.1 mean paper length problem on page 288. To adapt this worksheet to other problems, enter the appropriate population standard deviation, sample mean, sample size, and confidence level values in the tinted cells B4 through B7 and enter a new title in cell A1.

E8.2   COMPUTING THE CONFIDENCE INTERVAL ESTIMATE FOR THE MEAN (σ UNKNOWN)

You compute the confidence interval estimate for the mean (σ unknown) either by using the PHStat2 Estimate for the Mean, sigma unknown procedure or by making entries in the CIE sigma unknown.xls workbook.

Using PHStat2 Estimate for the Mean, Sigma Unknown

Select **PHStat → Confidence Intervals → Estimate for the Mean, sigma unknown**. In the Estimate for the Mean, sigma unknown dialog box (shown on page 323), enter a **Confidence Level** value, click one of the input options, and make the required entries. Enter a title as the **Title** and click **OK**.

If you know the sample size, sample mean, and sample standard deviation of your sample, click **Sample Statistics Known** and enter those values. Otherwise, click **Sample Statistics Unknown** and enter the cell range of your sample as the **Sample Cell Range**.

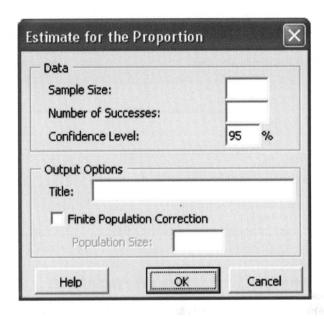

box (shown below), enter values for the **Sample Size**, the **Number of Successes**, and the **Confidence Level**. Enter a title as the **Title** and click **OK**.

Using the CIE_SU Worksheet

Open to the **CIE_SU** worksheet of the `CIE sigma unknown.xls` workbook. The worksheet (see Figure 8.6 on page 293) uses the **TINV(1-*confidence level, degrees of freedom*)** function to determine the critical value from the *t* distribution and compute the interval half-width for the Section 8.2 Saxon Home Improvement Company example. To adapt this worksheet to other problems, change the sample statistics and confidence level values in the tinted cells B4 through B7 and enter a new title in cell A1.

E8.3   COMPUTING THE CONFIDENCE INTERVAL ESTIMATE FOR THE PROPORTION

You compute the confidence interval estimate for the proportion either by using the PHStat2 Estimate for the Proportion procedure or by making entries in the `CIE Proportion.xls` workbook.

Using PHStat2 Estimate for the Proportion

Select **PHStat → Confidence Intervals → Estimate for the Proportion**. In the Estimate for the Proportion dialog

Using the CIE_P worksheet

Open to the **CIE_P** worksheet of the `CIE Proportion.xls` workbook. The worksheet (see Figure 8.10 on page 297) uses the **NORMSINV(*P<X*)** function to determine the *Z* value and uses the square root function to compute the standard error of the proportion for the Section 8.3 Saxon Home Improvement Company example. To adapt this worksheet to other problems, enter the appropriate sample size, number of successes, and confidence level values in the tinted cells B4, B5, and B6 and enter a new title in cell A1.

E8.4   COMPUTING THE SAMPLE SIZE NEEDED FOR ESTIMATING THE MEAN

You compute the sample size needed for estimating the mean either by using the PHStat2 Determination for the Mean procedure or by making entries in the `Sample Size Mean.xls` workbook.

Using PHStat2 Determination for the Mean

Select **PHStat → Sample Size → Determination for the Mean**. In the Sample Size Determination for the Mean dialog box (shown on page 324), enter values for the **Population Standard Deviation**, the **Sampling Error**, and the **Confidence Level**. Enter a title as the **Title** and click **OK**.

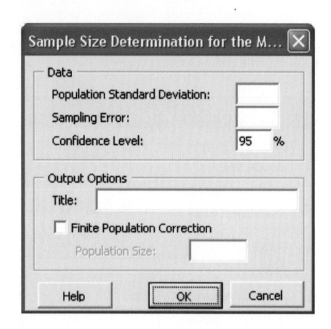

Using the SampleSize_M Worksheet

Open to the **SampleSize_M** worksheet of the `Sample Size Mean.xls` workbook. The worksheet (see Figure 8.11 on page 301) uses the **NORMSINV(P<X)** function to compute the Z value and uses the **ROUNDUP(value)** function to round up the sample size needed to the next higher integer for the Section 8.4 Saxon Home Improvement Company example. To adapt this worksheet to other problems, enter the appropriate population standard deviation, sampling error, and confidence level values in the tinted cells B4, B5, and B6 and enter a new title in cell A1.

Using the SampleSize_P Worksheet

Open to the **SampleSize_P** worksheet of the `Sample Size Proportion.xls` file. The worksheet (see Figure 8.12 on page 304) uses the **NORMSINV** and **ROUNDUP** functions, discussed in Section E8.3, for the Saxon Home Improvement Company example in Section 8.3. To adapt this worksheet to other problems, enter the appropriate estimate of true proportion, sampling error, and confidence level values in the tinted cells B4 through B6 and enter a new title in cell A1.

E8.5   COMPUTING THE SAMPLE SIZE NEEDED FOR ESTIMATING THE PROPORTION

You compute the sample size needed for estimating the proportion either by using the PHStat2 Determination for the Proportion procedure or by making entries in the `Sample Size Proportion.xls` workbook.

E8.6   COMPUTING THE CONFIDENCE INTERVAL ESTIMATE FOR THE POPULATION TOTAL

You compute the confidence interval estimate for the population total either by using the PHStat2 Estimate for the Population Total procedure or by making entries in the `CIE Total.xls` workbook.

Using PHStat2 Determination for the Proportion

Select **PHStat → Sample Size → Determination for the Proportion**. In the Sample Size Determination for the Proportion dialog box (shown at right), enter values for the **Estimate of True Proportion**, the **Sampling Error**, and the **Confidence Level**. Enter a title as the **Title** and click **OK**.

Using PHStat2 Estimate for the Population Total

Select **PHStat → Confidence Intervals → Estimate for the Population Total**. In the Estimate for the Population Total dialog box (shown on page 325), enter values for the **Population Size** and the **Confidence Level**.

Click one of the input options and make the required entries.

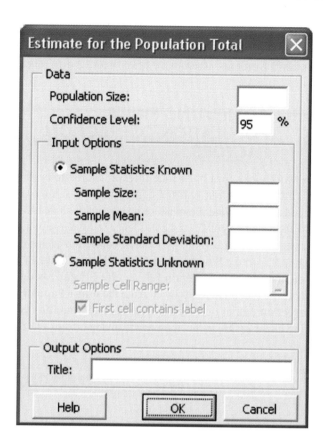

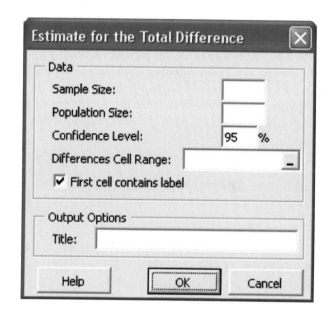

Using PHStat2 Estimate for the Total Difference

Select **PHStat → Confidence Intervals → Estimate for the Total Difference**. In the Estimate for the Total Difference dialog box (shown below), enter values for the **Sample Size**, the **Population Size**, and the **Confidence Level**. Enter the cell range of the differences as the **Differences Cell Range**. If the first cell in the column of differences contains a label, click **First cell contains label**, enter a title as the **Title**, and click **OK**.

If you know the sample size, sample mean, and sample standard deviation of your sample, click **Sample Statistics Known** and enter those values. Otherwise, click **Sample Statistics Unknown** and enter the cell range of your sample as the **Sample Cell Range**. Enter a title as the **Title** and click **OK**.

Using the CIE_T Worksheet

Open to the **CIE_T** worksheet of the CIE Total.xls workbook. This worksheet (see Figure 8.13 on page 307) uses the **TINV(1-*confidence level, degrees of freedom*)** function to determine the critical value from the *t* distribution and the interval half-width for the Section 8.5 Saxon Home Improvement Company population total example. To adapt this worksheet to other problems, enter the appropriate population size, sample mean, sample size, sample standard deviation, and confidence level values in the tinted cells B4 through B8 and enter a new title in cell A1.

E8.7 COMPUTING THE CONFIDENCE INTERVAL ESTIMATE FOR THE TOTAL DIFFERENCE

You compute the confidence interval estimate for the total difference either by using the PHStat2 Estimate for the Total Difference procedure or by making entries in the CIE Total Difference.xls workbook.

Using the CIE_TD Worksheet

Open to the **CIE_TD** worksheet of the CIE Total Difference.xls file. This worksheet (see Figure 8.14 on page 310) uses the **TINV(1-*confidence level, degrees of freedom*)** function to determine the critical value from the *t* distribution and the interval half-width for the Section 8.5 Saxon Home Improvement Company total difference example. The worksheet also contains a calculation area in cell range D9:E16, as shown in Figure E8.1, that counts and sums the differences listed on a **DifferencesData** worksheet. Figure E8.2 illustrates the first 6 of the 13 rows in the Difference Data worksheet).

	D	E	
9	Calculations Area		
10	For standard deviation of differences:		
11	Number of Differences Not = 0	12	=COUNT(DifferencesData!A:A)
12	Number of Differences = 0	88	=B5 - E11
13	SS for Differences Not = 0	678.3864	=SUM(DifferencesData!B:B)
14	SS for Differences = 0	71.28	=E12 * (-B10)^2
15	Sum of Squares	749.6664	=E13 + E14
16	Variance of Differences	7.572388	=E15/B15

FIGURE E8.1

Calculations area in the Difference Data worksheet

	A	B	
1	Differences	(D-DBar)^2)	
2	9.03	66.0969	=(A2 - CIE_TD!$B$10)^2
3	7.47	43.1649	=(A3 - CIE_TD!$B$10)^2
4	17.32	269.6164	=(A4 - CIE_TD!$B$10)^2
5	8.3	54.76	=(A5 - CIE_TD!$B$10)^2
6	5.21	18.5761	=(A6 - CIE_TD!$B$10)^2

FIGURE E8.2

DifferencesData worksheet (partial)

To adapt this worksheet to other problems, you need to change both the CIE_TD and DifferencesData worksheet. In the CIE_TD worksheet, enter the appropriate population size, sample size, and confidence level values in the tinted cells B4 through B6 and enter a new title in cell A1. In the DifferencesData worksheet, enter the differences in column A. Then adjust column B by either copying down the formula in cell B13 to all rows with difference data, if you have more than 12 differences; or by deleting unnecessary column B formulas, if you have fewer than 12 differences.

E8.8   COMPUTING FINITE POPULATION CORRECTION FACTORS

The workbooks for confidence interval estimations of the mean and proportion and for computing the sample size needed for estimating the mean or proportion include a **FPC** worksheet that calculates the confidence interval estimate or sample size, using a finite population correction factor (see Section 8.7 on the Student CD-ROM). (Open to those worksheets for further information.) If you use PHStat2, you can include these computations by clicking the **Finite Population Correction** output option and entering the **Population Size** before clicking **OK** in the appropriate dialog boxes.

CHAPTER 9

Fundamentals of Hypothesis Testing: One-Sample Tests

USING STATISTICS @ Oxford Cereals, Part II

LEARNING OBJECTIVES

In this chapter, you learn:

- The basic principles of hypothesis testing
- How to use hypothesis testing to test a mean or proportion
- The assumptions of each hypothesis-testing procedure, how to evaluate them, and the consequences if they are seriously violated
- How to avoid the pitfalls involved in hypothesis testing
- Ethical issues involved in hypothesis testing

Using Statistics @ Oxford Cereals, Part II

As in Chapter 7, you again find yourself as plant operations manager for Oxford Cereals. You are responsible for monitoring the amount in each cereal box filled. Company specifications require a mean weight of 368 grams per box. It is your responsibility to adjust the process when the mean fill weight in the population of boxes deviates from 368 grams. How can you rationally make the decision whether or not to adjust the process when it is impossible to weigh every single box as it is being filled? You begin by selecting and weighing a random sample of 25 cereal boxes. After computing a sample mean, how do you proceed?

In Chapter 7, you learned methods to determine whether a sample mean is consistent with a known population mean. In this Oxford Cereals scenario, you seek to use a sample mean to validate a claim about the population mean, a somewhat different problem. For this type of problem, you use an inferential method called **hypothesis testing**. Hypothesis testing requires that you state a claim unambiguously. In this scenario, the claim is that the population mean is 368 grams. You examine a sample statistic to see if it better supports the stated claim, called the *null hypothesis*, or the mutually exclusive alternative (for this scenario, that the population mean is not 368 grams.)

In this chapter, you will learn several applications of hypothesis testing. You will learn how to make inferences about a population parameter by *analyzing differences* between the results observed, the sample statistic, and the results you would expect to get if some underlying hypothesis were actually true. For the Oxford Cereals scenario, hypothesis testing would allow you to infer one of the following:

- The mean weight of the cereal boxes in the sample is a value consistent with what you would expect if the mean of the entire population of cereal boxes is 368 grams.
- The population mean is not equal to 368 grams because the sample mean is significantly different from 368 grams.

9.1 HYPOTHESIS-TESTING METHODOLOGY

Hypothesis testing typically begins with some theory, claim, or assertion about a particular parameter of a population. For example, your initial hypothesis about the cereal example is that the process is working properly, so the mean fill is 368 grams, and no corrective action is needed.

The Null and Alternative Hypotheses

The hypothesis that the population parameter is equal to the company specification is referred to as the null hypothesis. A **null hypothesis** is always one of status quo and is identified by the symbol H_0. Here the null hypothesis is that the filling process is working properly, and therefore the mean fill is the 368-gram specification. This is stated as

$$H_0: \mu = 368$$

Even though information is available only from the sample, the null hypothesis is written in terms of the population. Remember, your focus is on the population of all cereal boxes. The sample statistic is used to make inferences about the entire filling process. One inference may be that the results observed from the sample data indicate that the null hypothesis is false. If the null hypothesis is considered false, something else must be true.

Whenever a null hypothesis is specified, an alternative hypothesis is also specified, and it must be true if the null hypothesis is false. The **alternative hypothesis, H_1,** is the opposite of the null hypothesis, H_0. This is stated in the cereal example as

$$H_1: \mu \neq 368$$

The alternative hypothesis represents the conclusion reached by rejecting the null hypothesis. The null hypothesis is rejected when there is sufficient evidence from the sample information that the null hypothesis is false. In the cereal example, if the weights of the sampled boxes are sufficiently above or below the expected 368-gram mean specified by the company, you reject the null hypothesis in favor of the alternative hypothesis that the mean fill is different from 368 grams. You stop production and take whatever action is necessary to correct the problem. If the null hypothesis is not rejected, you should continue to believe in the status quo, that the process is working correctly and therefore no corrective action is necessary. In this second circumstance, you have not proven that the process is working correctly. Rather, you have failed to prove that it is working incorrectly, and therefore you continue your belief (although unproven) in the null hypothesis.

In the hypothesis-testing methodology, the null hypothesis is rejected when the sample evidence suggests that it is far more likely that the alternative hypothesis is true. However, failure to reject the null hypothesis is not proof that it is true. You can never prove that the null hypothesis is correct because the decision is based only on the sample information, not on the entire population. Therefore, if you fail to reject the null hypothesis, you can only conclude that there is insufficient evidence to warrant its rejection. The following key points summarize the null and alternative hypotheses:

- The null hypothesis, H_0, represents the status quo or the current belief in a situation.
- The alternative hypothesis, H_1, is the opposite of the null hypothesis and represents a research claim or specific inference you would like to prove.
- If you reject the null hypothesis, you have statistical proof that the alternative hypothesis is correct.
- If you do not reject the null hypothesis, you have failed to prove the alternative hypothesis. The failure to prove the alternative hypothesis, however, does not mean that you have proven the null hypothesis.
- The null hypothesis, H_0, always refers to a specified value of the population parameter (such as μ), not a sample statistic (such as $\overline{X}$).
- The statement of the null hypothesis always contains an equal sign regarding the specified value of the population parameter (for example, $H_0: \mu = 368$ grams).
- The statement of the alternative hypothesis never contains an equal sign regarding the specified value of the population parameter (for example, $H_1: \mu \neq 368$ grams).

EXAMPLE 9.1

THE NULL AND ALTERNATIVE HYPOTHESES

You are the manager of a fast-food restaurant. You want to determine whether the waiting time to place an order has changed in the past month from its previous population mean value of 4.5 minutes. State the null and alternative hypotheses.

SOLUTION The null hypothesis is that the population mean has not changed from its previous value of 4.5 minutes. This is stated as

$$H_0: \mu = 4.5$$

The alternative hypothesis is the opposite of the null hypothesis. Because the null hypothesis is that the population mean is 4.5 minutes, the alternative hypothesis is that the population mean is not 4.5 minutes. This is stated as

$$H_1: \mu \neq 4.5$$

The Critical Value of the Test Statistic

The logic behind the hypothesis-testing methodology is to determine how likely the null hypothesis is to be true by considering the information gathered in a sample. In the Oxford Cereal Company scenario, the null hypothesis is that the mean amount of cereal per box in the entire filling process is 368 grams (that is, the population parameter specified by the company). You select a sample of boxes from the filling process, weigh each box, and compute the sample mean. This statistic is an estimate of the corresponding parameter (the population mean, μ). Even if the null hypothesis is true, the statistic (the sample mean, $\overline{X}$) is likely to differ from the value of the parameter (the population mean, μ) because of variation due to sampling. However, you expect the sample statistic to be close to the population parameter if the null hypothesis is true. If the sample statistic is close to the population parameter, you have insufficient evidence to reject the null hypothesis. For example, if the sample mean is 367.9, you conclude that the population mean has not changed (that is, $\mu = 368$) because a sample mean of 367.9 is very close to the hypothesized value of 368. Intuitively, you think that it is likely that you could get a sample mean of 367.9 from a population whose mean is 368.

However, if there is a large difference between the value of the statistic and the hypothesized value of the population parameter, you conclude that the null hypothesis is false. For example, if the sample mean is 320, you conclude that the population mean is not 368 (that is, $\mu \neq 368$), because the sample mean is very far from the hypothesized value of 368. In such a case, you conclude that it is very unlikely to get a sample mean of 320 if the population mean is really 368. Therefore, it is more logical to conclude that the population mean is not equal to 368. Here you reject the null hypothesis.

Unfortunately, the decision-making process is not always so clear-cut. Determining what is "very close" and what is "very different" is arbitrary without clear definitions. Hypothesis-testing methodology provides clear definitions for evaluating differences. Furthermore, it enables you to quantify the decision-making process by computing the probability of getting a given sample result if the null hypothesis is true. You calculate this probability by determining the sampling distribution for the sample statistic of interest (for example, the sample mean) and then computing the particular **test statistic** based on the given sample result. Because the sampling distribution for the test statistic often follows a well-known statistical distribution, such as the standardized normal distribution or t distribution, you can use these distributions to help determine whether the null hypothesis is true.

Regions of Rejection and Nonrejection

The sampling distribution of the test statistic is divided into two regions, a **region of rejection** (sometimes called the critical region) and a **region of nonrejection** (see Figure 9.1).

If the test statistic falls into the region of nonrejection, you do not reject the null hypothesis. In the Oxford Cereals scenario, you conclude that there is insufficient evidence that the population mean fill is different from 368 grams. If the test statistic falls into the rejection region, you reject the null hypothesis. In this case, you conclude that the population mean is not 368 grams.

FIGURE 9.1

Regions of rejection and nonrejection in hypothesis testing

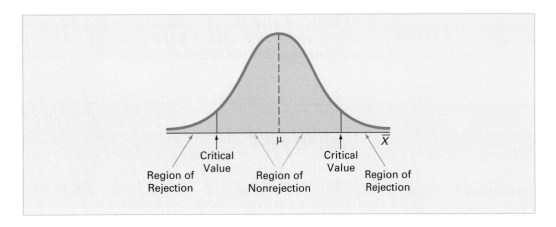

The region of rejection consists of the values of the test statistic that are unlikely to occur if the null hypothesis is true. These values are more likely to occur if the null hypothesis is false. Therefore, if a value of the test statistic falls into this *rejection region*, you reject the null hypothesis because that value is unlikely if the null hypothesis is true.

To make a decision concerning the null hypothesis, you first determine the **critical value** of the test statistic. The critical value divides the nonrejection region from the rejection region. Determining this critical value depends on the size of the rejection region. The size of the rejection region is directly related to the risks involved in using only sample evidence to make decisions about a population parameter.

Risks in Decision Making Using Hypothesis-Testing Methodology

When using a sample statistic to make decisions about a population parameter, there is a risk that you will reach an incorrect conclusion. You can make two different types of errors when applying hypothesis-testing methodology, Type I and Type II errors.

A **Type I error** occurs if you reject the null hypothesis, H_0, when it is true and should not be rejected. The probability of a Type I error occurring is α.

A **Type II error** occurs if you do not reject the null hypothesis, H_0, when it is false and should be rejected. The probability of a Type II error occurring is β.

In the Oxford Cereals scenario, you make a Type I error if you conclude that the population mean fill is *not* 368 when it *is* 368. This error causes you to adjust the filling process even though the process is working properly. You make a Type II error if you conclude that the population mean fill *is* 368 when it is *not* 368. Here, you would allow the process to continue without adjustment even though adjustments are needed.

The Level of Significance (α)   The probability of committing a Type I error, denoted by α (the lowercase Greek letter *alpha*), is referred to as the **level of significance** of the statistical test. Traditionally, you control the Type I error by deciding the risk level, α, that you are willing to have in rejecting the null hypothesis when it is true. Because you specify the level of significance before the hypothesis test is performed, the risk of committing a Type I error, α, is directly under your control. Traditionally, you select levels of 0.01, 0.05, or 0.10. The choice of a particular risk level for making a Type I error depends on the cost of making a Type I error. After you specify the value for α, you can then determine the critical values that divide the rejection and nonrejection regions. You know the size of the rejection region because α is the probability of rejection when the null hypothesis is true. From this, you can then determine the critical value or values that divide the rejection and nonrejection regions.

The Confidence Coefficient The complement of the probability of a Type I error, $(1 - \alpha)$, is called the confidence coefficient. When multiplied by 100%, the confidence coefficient yields the confidence level that was studied when constructing confidence intervals (see Section 8.1).

> The **confidence coefficient**, $(1 - \alpha)$, is the probability that you will not reject the null hypothesis, H_0, when it is true and should not be rejected. The **confidence level** of a hypothesis test is $(1 - \alpha) \times 100\%$.

In terms of hypothesis-testing methodology, the confidence coefficient represents the probability of concluding that the value of the parameter as specified in the null hypothesis is plausible when it is true. In the Oxford Cereals scenario, the confidence coefficient measures the probability of concluding that the population mean fill is 368 grams when it is actually 368 grams.

The β Risk The probability of committing a Type II error is denoted by β (the lowercase Greek letter *beta*). Unlike a Type I error, which you control by the selection of α, the probability of making a Type II error depends on the difference between the hypothesized and actual values of the population parameter. Because large differences are easier to find than small ones, if the difference between the hypothesized and actual values of the population parameter is large, β is small. For example, if the population mean is 330 grams, there is a small chance (β) that you will conclude that the mean has not changed from 368. However, if the difference between the hypothesized and actual values of the parameter is small, β is large. For example, if the population mean is actually 367 grams, there is a large chance (β) that you will conclude that the mean is still 368 grams.

The Power of a Test The complement of the probability of a Type II error, $(1 - \beta)$, is called the power of a statistical test.

> The **power of a statistical test**, $(1 - \beta)$, is the probability that you will reject the null hypothesis when it is false and should be rejected.

In the Oxford Cereals scenario, the power of the test is the probability that you will correctly conclude that the mean fill amount is not 368 grams when it actually is not 368 grams. For a detailed discussion of the power of the test, see Section 9.7 on the Student CD-ROM.

Risks in Decision Making: A Delicate Balance Table 9.1 illustrates the results of the two possible decisions (do not reject H_0 or reject H_0) that you can make in any hypothesis test. You can make a correct decision or make one of two types of errors.

TABLE 9.1

Hypothesis Testing and Decision Making

	Actual Situation	
Statistical Decision	H_0 **True**	H_0 **False**
Do not reject H_0	Correct decision Confidence = $(1 - \alpha)$	Type II error P (Type II error) = β
Reject H_0	Type I error P (Type I error) = α	Correct decision Power = $(1 - \beta)$

One way to reduce the probability of making a Type II error is by increasing the sample size. Large samples generally permit you to detect even very small differences between the hypothesized values and the population parameters. For a given level of α, increasing the sample size decreases β and therefore increases the power of the test to detect that the null hypothesis, H_0, is false. However, there is always a limit to your resources, and this affects the decision as to how large a sample you can take. Thus, for a given sample size, you must consider the trade-offs between the two possible types of errors. Because you can directly control the risk of Type I error, you can reduce this risk by selecting a smaller value for α. For example, if the negative consequences associated with making a Type I error are substantial, you could select $\alpha = 0.01$ instead of 0.05. However, when you decrease α, you increase β, so reducing the risk of a Type I error results in an increased risk of a Type II error. However, if you wish to reduce β, you could select a larger value for α. Therefore, if it is important to try to avoid a Type II error, you can select α of 0.05 or 0.10 instead of 0.01.

In the Oxford Cereals scenario, the risk of a Type I error involves concluding that the mean fill amount has changed from the hypothesized 368 grams when it actually has not changed. The risk of a Type II error involves concluding that the mean fill amount has not changed from the hypothesized 368 grams when it actually has changed. The choice of reasonable values for α and β depends on the costs inherent in each type of error. For example, if it is very costly to change the cereal-fill process, you would want to be very confident that a change is needed before making any changes. In this case, the risk of a Type I error is more important, and you would choose a small α. However, if you want to be very certain of detecting changes from a mean of 368 grams, the risk of a Type II error is more important, and you would choose a higher level of α.

PROBLEMS FOR SECTION 9.1

Learning the Basics

 9.1 You use the symbol H_0 for which hypothesis?

 9.2 You use the symbol H_1 for which hypothesis?

 9.3 What symbol do you use for the chance of committing a Type I error?

 9.4 What symbol do you use for the chance of committing a Type II error?

 9.5 What does $1 - \alpha$ represent?

9.6 What is the relationship of α to a Type I error?

9.7 What is the relationship of β to a Type II error?

9.8 How is power related to the probability of making a Type II error?

 9.9 Why is it possible to reject the null hypothesis when it is true?

 9.10 Why is it possible to not reject the null hypothesis when it is false?

9.11 For a given sample size, if α is reduced from 0.05 to 0.01, what happens to β?

9.12 For H_0: $\mu = 100$, H_1: $\mu \neq 100$, and for a sample of size n, why is β larger if the actual value of μ is 90 than if the actual value of μ is 75?

Applying the Concepts

 9.13 In the U.S. legal system, a defendant is presumed innocent until proven guilty. Consider a null hypothesis, H_0, that the defendant is innocent, and an alternative hypothesis, H_1, that the defendant is guilty. A jury has two possible decisions: Convict the defendant (that is, reject the null hypothesis) or do not convict the defendant (that is, do not reject the null hypothesis). Explain the meaning of the risks of committing either a Type I or Type II error in this example.

9.14 Suppose the defendant in Problem 9.13 is presumed guilty until proven innocent, as in some other judicial systems. How do the null and alternative hypotheses differ from those in Problem 9.13? What are the meanings of the risks of committing either a Type I or Type II error here?

9.15 The U.S. Food and Drug Administration (FDA) is responsible for approving new drugs. Many consumer groups feel that the approval process is too easy and, therefore, too many drugs are approved that are later found to be unsafe. On the other hand, a number of industry lobbyists are pushing for a more lenient approval process so that pharmaceutical companies can get new drugs approved more easily and quickly (R. Sharpe, "FDA Tries to Find Right Balance on Drug Approvals," *The Wall Street Journal*, April 20, 1999, p. A24). Consider a null hypothesis that a new, unapproved drug is unsafe and an alternative hypothesis that a new, unapproved drug is safe.

a. Explain the risks of committing a Type I or Type II error.
b. Which type of error are the consumer groups trying to avoid? Explain.
c. Which type of error are the industry lobbyists trying to avoid? Explain.
d. How would it be possible to lower the chances of both Type I and Type II errors?

9.16 As a result of complaints from both students and faculty about lateness, the registrar at a large university wants to adjust the scheduled class times to allow for adequate travel time between classes and is ready to undertake a study. Until now, the registrar has believed that there should be 20 minutes between scheduled classes. State the null hypothesis, H_0, and the alternative hypothesis, H_1.

9.17 The operations manager at a clothing factory needs to determine whether a new machine is producing a particular type of cloth according to the manufacturer's specifications, which indicate that the cloth should have a mean breaking strength of 70 pounds. State the null and alternative hypotheses.

9.18 The manager of a paint supply store wants to determine whether the amount of paint contained in 1-gallon cans purchased from a nationally known manufacturer actually averages 1 gallon. State the null and alternative hypotheses.

9.19 The quality control manager at a light bulb factory needs to determine whether the mean life of a large shipment of light bulbs is equal to the specified value of 375 hours. State the null and alternative hypotheses.

9.2 Z TEST OF HYPOTHESIS FOR THE MEAN (σ KNOWN)

Now that you have been introduced to hypothesis-testing methodology, recall that in the Using Statistics scenario on page 328, Oxford Cereals wants to determine whether the cereal-fill process is working properly (that is, whether the mean fill throughout the entire packaging process remains at the specified 368 grams, and no corrective action is needed). To evaluate the 368-gram requirement, you take a random sample of 25 boxes, weigh each box, and then evaluate the difference between the sample statistic and the hypothesized population parameter by comparing the mean weight (in grams) from the sample to the expected mean of 368 grams specified by the company. The null and alternative hypotheses are

$$H_0: \mu = 368$$

$$H_1: \mu \neq 368$$

When the standard deviation, σ, is known, you use the Z test if the population is normally distributed. If the population is not normally distributed, you can still use the Z test if the sample size is large enough for the Central Limit Theorem to take effect (see Section 7.4). Equation (9.1) defines the **Z-test statistic** for determining the difference between the sample mean, $\bar{X}$, and the population mean, μ, when the standard deviation, σ, is known.

Z TEST OF HYPOTHESIS FOR THE MEAN (σ KNOWN)

$$Z = \frac{\bar{X} - \mu}{\frac{\sigma}{\sqrt{n}}} \tag{9.1}$$

In Equation (9.1) the numerator measures how far (in an absolute sense) the observed sample mean, $\bar{X}$, is from the hypothesized mean, μ. The denominator is the standard error of the mean, so Z represents the difference between $\bar{X}$ and μ in standard error units.

The Critical Value Approach to Hypothesis Testing

The observed value of the Z test statistic, Equation (9.1), is compared to critical values. The **critical values** are expressed as standardized Z values (that is, in standard deviation units). For example, if you use a level of significance of 0.05, the size of the rejection region is 0.05. Because the rejection region is divided into the two tails of the distribution (this is called a **two-tail test**), you divide the 0.05 into two equal parts of 0.025 each. A rejection region of 0.025 in each tail of the normal distribution results in a cumulative area of 0.025 below the lower critical value and a cumulative area of 0.975 below the upper critical value. According to the cumulative standardized normal distribution table (Table E.2), the critical values that divide the rejection and nonrejection regions are -1.96 and $+1.96$. Figure 9.2 illustrates that if the mean is actually 368 grams, as H_0 claims, the values of the test statistic Z have a standardized normal distribution centered at $Z = 0$ (which corresponds to an $\overline{X}$ value of 368 grams). Values of Z greater than $+1.96$ or less than -1.96 indicate that $\overline{X}$ is so far from the hypothesized $\mu = 368$ that it is unlikely that such a value would occur if H_0 were true.

FIGURE 9.2

Testing a hypothesis about the mean (σ known) at the 0.05 level of significance

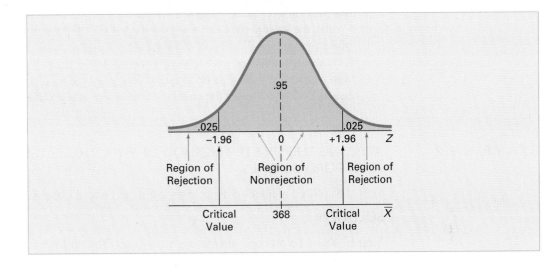

Therefore, the decision rule is

Reject H_0 if $Z > +1.96$
or if $Z < -1.96$;
otherwise, do not reject H_0.

Suppose that the sample of 25 cereal boxes indicates a sample mean, $\overline{X}$, of 372.5 grams, and the population standard deviation, σ, is assumed to be 15 grams. Using Equation (9.1) on page 334,

$$ Z = \frac{\overline{X} - \mu}{\dfrac{\sigma}{\sqrt{n}}} = \frac{372.5 - 368}{\dfrac{15}{\sqrt{25}}} = +1.50 $$

Because the test statistic $Z = +1.50$ is between -1.96 and $+1.96$, you do not reject H_0 (see Figure 9.3). You continue to believe that the mean fill amount is 368 grams. To take into account the possibility of a Type II error, you state the conclusion as "there is insufficient evidence that the mean fill is different from 368 grams."

FIGURE 9.3

Testing a hypothesis about the mean cereal weight (σ known) at 0.05 level of significance

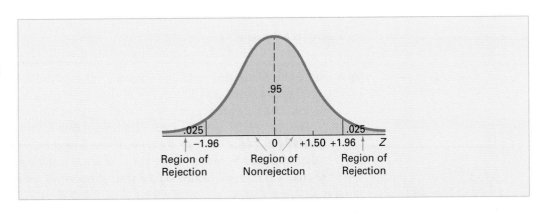

Exhibit 9.1 provides a summary of the critical value approach to hypothesis testing.

EXHIBIT 9.1   THE SIX-STEP METHOD OF HYPOTHESIS TESTING

1. State the null hypothesis, H_0, and the alternative hypothesis, H_1.
2. Choose the level of significance, α, and the sample size, n. The level of significance is based on the relative importance of the risks of committing Type I and Type II errors in the problem.
3. Determine the appropriate test statistic and sampling distribution.
4. Determine the critical values that divide the rejection and nonrejection regions.
5. Collect the sample data and compute the value of the test statistic.
6. Make the statistical decision and state the managerial conclusion. If the test statistic falls into the nonrejection region, you do not reject the null hypothesis, H_0. If the test statistic falls into the rejection region, you reject the null hypothesis. The managerial conclusion is written in the context of the real-world problem.

EXAMPLE 9.2

APPLYING THE SIX-STEP METHOD OF HYPOTHESIS TESTING AT OXFORD CEREALS

State the six-step method of hypothesis testing at Oxford Cereals.

SOLUTION

Step 1   State the null and alternative hypotheses. The null hypothesis, H_0, is always stated in statistical terms, using population parameters. In testing whether the mean fill is 368 grams, the null hypothesis states that μ equals 368. The alternative hypothesis, H_1, is also stated in statistical terms, using population parameters. Therefore, the alternative hypothesis states that μ is not equal to 368 grams.

Step 2   Choose the level of significance and the sample size. You choose the level of significance, α, according to the relative importance of the risks of committing Type I and Type II errors in the problem. The smaller the value of α, the less risk there is of making a Type I error. In this example, a Type I error is to conclude that the population mean is not 368 grams when it is 368 grams. Thus, you will take corrective action on the filling process even though the process is working properly. Here, $\alpha = 0.05$ is selected. The sample, n, is 25.

Step 3   Select the appropriate test statistic. Because σ is known from information about the filling process, you use the normal distribution and the Z test statistic.

Step 4   Determine the rejection region. Critical values for the appropriate test statistic are selected so that the rejection region contains a total area of α when H_0 is true and the nonrejection region contains a total area of $1 - \alpha$ when H_0 is true. Because $\alpha = 0.05$ in the cereal example, the critical values of the Z-test statistic are -1.96 and $+1.96$. The rejection region is therefore $Z < -1.96$ or $Z > +1.96$. The nonrejection region is $-1.96 < Z < +1.96$.

Step 5   Collect the sample data and compute the value of the test statistic. In the cereal example, $\overline{X} = 372.5$, and the value of the test statistic is $Z = +1.50$.

Step 6   State the statistical decision and the managerial conclusion. First, determine whether the test statistic has fallen into the rejection region or the nonrejection region. For the cereal example, $Z = +1.50$ is in the region of nonrejection because $-1.96 < Z = +1.50 < +1.96$. Because the test statistic falls into the nonrejection region, the statistical decision is to not reject the null hypothesis, H_0. The managerial conclusion is that insufficient evidence exists to prove that the mean fill is different from 368 grams. No corrective action on the filling process is needed.

EXAMPLE 9.3   REJECTING A NULL HYPOTHESIS

You are the manager of a fast-food restaurant. You want to determine whether the population mean waiting time to place an order has changed in the past month from its previous population mean value of 4.5 minutes. From past experience, you can assume that the population is normally distributed with a population standard deviation of 1.2 minutes. You select a sample of 25 orders during a one-hour period. The sample mean is 5.1 minutes. Use the six-step approach listed in Exhibit 9.1 to determine whether there is evidence at the 0.05 level of significance that the population mean waiting time to place an order has changed in the past month from its previous population mean value of 4.5 minutes.

SOLUTION

Step 1   The null hypothesis is that the population mean has not changed from its previous value of 4.5 minutes:

$$H_0: \mu = 4.5$$

The alternative hypothesis is the opposite of the null hypothesis. Because the null hypothesis is that the population mean is 4.5 minutes, the alternative hypothesis is that the population mean is not 4.5 minutes:

$$H_1: \mu \neq 4.5$$

Step 2   You have selected a sample of $n = 25$. The level of significance is 0.05 (that is, $\alpha = 0.05$).

Step 3   Because σ is known, you use the normal distribution and the Z test statistic.

Step 4   Because $\alpha = 0.05$, the critical values of the Z test statistic are -1.96 and $+1.96$. The rejection region is $Z < -1.96$ or $Z > +1.96$. The nonrejection region is $-1.96 < Z < +1.96$.

Step 5   You collect the sample data and compute $\overline{X} = 5.1$. Using Equation (9.1) on page 334, you compute the test statistic:

$$Z = \frac{\overline{X} - \mu}{\dfrac{\sigma}{\sqrt{n}}} = \frac{5.1 - 4.5}{\dfrac{1.2}{\sqrt{25}}} = 2.50$$

Step 6   Because $Z = 2.50 > 1.96$, you reject the null hypothesis. You conclude that there is evidence that the population mean waiting time to place an order has changed from its previous value of 4.5 minutes. The mean waiting time for customers is longer now than it was last month.

The *p*-Value Approach to Hypothesis Testing

Most modern software, including Microsoft Excel, computes the *p*-value when performing a test of hypothesis.

The ***p*-value** is the probability of getting a test statistic equal to or more extreme than the sample result, given that the null hypothesis, H_0, is true.

The *p*-value, often referred to as the *observed level of significance*, is the smallest level at which H_0 can be rejected.

The decision rules for rejecting H_0 in the *p*-value approach are

- If the *p*-value is greater than or equal to α, do not reject the null hypothesis.
- If the *p*-value is less than α, reject the null hypothesis.

Many people confuse these rules, mistakenly believing that a high *p*-value is grounds for rejection. You can avoid this confusion by remembering the following mantra:

If the *p*-value is low, then H_0 must go.

To understand the *p*-value approach, consider the Oxford Cereals scenario. You tested whether the mean fill was equal to 368 grams. The test statistic resulted in a *Z* value of +1.50, and you did not reject the null hypothesis because +1.50 was less than the upper critical value of +1.96 and more than the lower critical value of −1.96.

To use the *p*-value approach for the *two-tail test*, you find the probability of getting a test statistic *Z* that is equal to or *more extreme than* 1.50 standard deviation units from the center of a standardized normal distribution. In other words, you need to compute the probability of a *Z* value greater than +1.50, along with the probability of a *Z* value less than −1.50. Table E.2 shows that the probability of a *Z* value below −1.50 is 0.0668. The probability of a value below +1.50 is 0.9332, and the probability of a value above +1.50 is $1 - 0.9332 = 0.0668$. Therefore, the *p*-value for this two-tail test is $0.0668 + 0.0668 = 0.1336$ (see Figure 9.4). Thus, the probability of a result equal to or more extreme than the one observed is 0.1336. Because 0.1336 is greater than $\alpha = 0.05$, you do not reject the null hypothesis.

FIGURE 9.4

Finding a *p*-value for a two-tail test

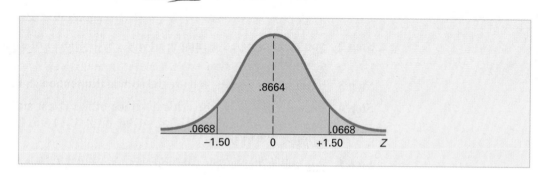

In this example, the observed sample mean is 372.5 grams, 4.5 grams above the hypothesized value, and the *p*-value is 0.1336. Thus, if the population mean is 368 grams, there is a 13.36% chance that the sample mean differs from 368 grams by more than 4.5 grams (that is, is ≥ 372.5 grams or ≤ 363.5 grams). Therefore, while 372.5 is above the hypothesized value of 368, a result as extreme as or more extreme than 372.5 is not highly unlikely when the population mean is 368.

Unless you are dealing with a test statistic that follows the normal distribution, computing the *p*-value can be very difficult. However, Microsoft Excel routinely computes the *p*-value in its hypothesis-testing procedures. Figure 9.5 displays a Microsoft Excel worksheet for the cereal-filling example discussed in this section.

FIGURE 9.5

Microsoft Excel *Z*-test results for the cereal-fill example

	A	B	
1	Cereal-Filling Process Hypothesis Test		
2			
3	Data		
4	Null Hypothesis μ=	368	
5	Level of Significance	0.05	
6	Population Standard Deviation	15	
7	Sample Size	25	
8	Sample Mean	372.5	
9			
10	Intermediate Calculations		
11	Standard Error of the Mean	3	=B6/SQRT(B7)
12	Z Test Statistic	1.5	=(B8 - B4)/B11
13			
14	Two-Tail Test		
15	Lower Critical Value	-1.9600	=NORMSINV(B5/2)
16	Upper Critical Value	1.9600	=NORMSINV(1 - B5/2)
17	p-Value	0.1336	=2 * (1 - NORMSDIST(ABS(B12)))
18	Do not reject the null hypothesis		=IF(B17 < B5, "Reject the null hypothesis", "Do not reject the null hypothesis")

Exhibit 9.2 provides a summary of the *p*-value approach for hypothesis testing.

EXHIBIT 9.2 THE FIVE-STEP *p*-VALUE APPROACH TO HYPOTHESIS TESTING

1. State the null hypothesis, H_0, and the alternative hypothesis, H_1.
2. Choose the level of significance, α, and the sample size, n. The level of significance is based on the relative importance of the risks of committing Type I and Type II errors in the problem.
3. Determine the appropriate test statistic and sampling distribution.
4. Collect the sample data, compute the value of the test statistic, and compute the *p*-value.
5. Make the statistical decision and state the managerial conclusion. If the *p*-value is greater than or equal to α, you do not reject the null hypothesis, H_0. If the *p*-value is less than α, you reject the null hypothesis. Remember the mantra: If the *p*-value is low, then H_0 must go. The managerial conclusion is written in the context of the real-world problem.

EXAMPLE 9.4

REJECTING A NULL HYPOTHESIS, USING THE *p*-VALUE APPROACH

You are the manager of a fast-food restaurant. You want to determine whether the population mean waiting time to place an order has changed in the past month from its previous value of 4.5 minutes. From past experience, you can assume that the population standard deviation is 1.2 minutes. You select a sample of 25 orders during a one-hour period. The sample mean is 5.1 minutes. Use the five-step approach of Exhibit 9.2 above to determine whether there is evidence that the population mean waiting time to place an order has changed in the past month from its previous population mean value of 4.5 minutes.

SOLUTION

Step 1 The null hypothesis is that the population mean has not changed from its previous value of 4.5 minutes:

$$H_0: \mu = 4.5$$

The alternative hypothesis is the opposite of the null hypothesis. Because the null hypothesis is that the population mean is 4.5 minutes, the alternative hypothesis is that the population mean is not 4.5 minutes:

$$H_1: \mu \neq 4.5$$

Step 2 You have selected a sample of $n = 25$. You choose a 0.05 level of significance (that is, $\alpha = 0.05$).

Step 3 Select the appropriate test statistic. Because σ is known, you use the normal distribution and the Z test statistic.

Step 4 You collect the data and compute $\overline{X} = 5.1$. Using Equation (9.1) on page 334, you compute the test statistic as follows:

$$Z = \frac{\overline{X} - \mu}{\dfrac{\sigma}{\sqrt{n}}} = \frac{5.1 - 4.5}{\dfrac{1.2}{\sqrt{25}}} = 2.50$$

To find the probability of getting a test statistic Z that is equal to or more extreme than 2.50 standard deviation units from the center of a standardized normal distribution, you compute the probability of a Z value greater than 2.50 along with the probability of a Z value less than -2.50. From Table E.2, the probability of a Z value below -2.50 is 0.0062. The probability of a value below $+2.50$ is 0.9938. Therefore, the probability of a value above $+2.50$ is $1 - 0.9938 = 0.0062$. Thus, the p-value for this two-tail test is $0.0062 + 0.0062 = 0.0124$.

Step 5 Because the p-value $= 0.0124 < \alpha = 0.05$, you reject the null hypothesis. You conclude that there is evidence that the population mean waiting time to place an order has changed from its previous population mean value of 4.5 minutes. The mean waiting time for customers is longer now than it was last month.

A Connection Between Confidence Interval Estimation and Hypothesis Testing

This chapter and Chapter 8 discuss the two major components of statistical inference: confidence interval estimation and hypothesis testing. Although they are based on the same set of concepts, they are used for different purposes. In Chapter 8, confidence intervals were used to estimate parameters. In this chapter, hypothesis testing is used for making decisions about specified values of population parameters. Hypothesis tests are used when trying to prove that a parameter is less than, more than, or not equal to a specified value. Proper interpretation of a confidence interval, however, can also indicate whether a parameter is less than, more than, or not equal to a specified value. For example, in this section, you tested whether the population mean fill amount was different from 368 grams by using Equation (9.1) on page 334:

$$Z = \frac{\overline{X} - \mu}{\dfrac{\sigma}{\sqrt{n}}}$$

Instead of testing the null hypothesis that $\mu = 368$ grams, you can reach the same conclusion by constructing a confidence interval estimate of μ. If the hypothesized value of $\mu = 368$ is contained within the interval, you do not reject the null hypothesis because 368 would not be considered an unusual value. However, if the hypothesized value does not fall into the interval, you reject the null hypothesis because "$\mu = 368$ grams" is then considered an unusual value. Using Equation (8.1) on page 287 and the following data:

$$n = 25, \ \overline{X} = 372.5 \text{ grams}, \ \sigma = 15 \text{ grams}$$

for a confidence level of 95% (corresponding to a 0.05 level of significance—that is, $\alpha = 0.05$),

$$\overline{X} \pm Z\frac{\sigma}{\sqrt{n}}$$

$$372.5 \pm (1.96)\frac{15}{\sqrt{25}}$$

$$372.5 \pm 5.88$$

so that

$$366.62 \leq \mu \leq 378.38$$

Because the interval includes the hypothesized value of 368 grams, you do not reject the null hypothesis. There is insufficient evidence that the mean fill amount over the entire filling process is not 368 grams. You reached the same decision by using two-tail hypothesis testing.

PROBLEMS FOR SECTION 9.2

Learning the Basics

 9.20 If you use a 0.05 level of significance in a (two-tail) hypothesis test, what will you decide if the computed value of the test statistic *Z* is +2.21?

 9.21 If you use a 0.10 level of significance in a (two-tail) hypothesis test, what is your decision rule for rejecting a null hypothesis that the population mean is 500 if you use the *Z* test?

 9.22 If you use a 0.01 level of significance in a (two-tail) hypothesis test, what is your decision rule for rejecting H_0: $\mu = 12.5$ if you use the *Z* test?

 9.23 What is your decision in Problem 9.22 if the computed value of the test statistic *Z* is −2.61?

 9.24 Suppose that in a two-tail hypothesis test, you compute the value of the test statistic *Z* as +2.00. What is the *p*-value?

 9.25 In Problem 9.24, what is your statistical decision if you test the null hypothesis at the 0.10 level of significance?

 9.26 Suppose that in a two-tail hypothesis test, you compute the value of the test statistic *Z* as −1.38. What is the *p*-value?

 9.27 In Problem 9.26, what is your statistical decision if you test the null hypothesis at the 0.01 level of significance?

Applying the Concepts

 9.28 The operations manager at a clothing factory needs to determine whether a new machine is producing a particular type of cloth according to the manufacturer's specifications, which indicate that the cloth should have a mean breaking strength of 70 pounds and a standard deviation of 3.5 pounds. A sample of 49 pieces of cloth reveals a sample mean breaking strength of 69.1 pounds.
a. Is there evidence that the machine is not meeting the manufacturer's specifications for mean breaking strength? (Use a 0.05 level of significance.)
b. Compute the *p*-value and interpret its meaning.
c. What is your answer in (a) if the standard deviation is 1.75 pounds?
d. What is your answer in (a) if the sample mean is 69 pounds and the standard deviation is 3.5 pounds?

9.29 The manager of a paint supply store wants to determine whether the mean amount of paint

contained in 1-gallon cans purchased from a nationally known manufacturer is actually 1 gallon. You know from the manufacturer's specifications that the standard deviation of the amount of paint is 0.02 gallon. You select a random sample of 50 cans, and the mean amount of paint per 1-gallon can is 0.995 gallon.
a. Is there evidence that the population mean amount is different from 1.0 gallon (use α = 0.01)?
b. Compute the *p*-value and interpret its meaning.
c. Construct a 99% confidence interval estimate of the population mean amount of paint.
d. Compare the results of (a) and (c). What conclusions do you reach?

9.30 The quality control manager at a light bulb factory needs to determine whether the mean life of a large shipment of light bulbs is equal to 375 hours. The population standard deviation is 100 hours. A random sample of 64 light bulbs indicates a sample mean life of 350 hours.
a. At the 0.05 level of significance, is there evidence that the population mean life is different from 375 hours?
b. Compute the *p*-value and interpret its meaning.
c. Construct a 95% confidence interval estimate of the population mean life of the light bulbs.
d. Compare the results of (a) and (c). What conclusions do you reach?

9.31 The inspection division of the Lee County Weights and Measures Department is interested in determining whether the proper amount of soft drink has been placed in 2-liter bottles at the local bottling plant of a large nationally known soft-drink company. The bottling plant has informed the inspection division that the standard deviation for 2-liter bottles is 0.05 liter. A random sample of 100 2-liter bottles selected from this bottling plant indicates a sample mean of 1.99 liters.
a. At the 0.05 level of significance, is there evidence that the population mean amount in the bottles is different from 2.0 liters?
b. Compute the *p*-value and interpret its meaning.
c. Construct a 95% confidence interval estimate of the population mean amount in the bottles.
d. Compare the results of (a) and (c). What conclusions do you reach?

9.32 A manufacturer of salad dressings uses machines to dispense liquid ingredients into bottles that move along a filling line. The machine that dispenses dressings is working properly when the mean amount dispensed is 8 ounces. The population standard deviation of the amount dispensed is 0.15 ounce. A sample of 50 bottles is selected periodically, and the filling line is stopped if there is evidence that the mean amount dispensed is different from 8 ounces. Suppose that the mean amount dispensed in a particular sample of 50 bottles is 7.983 ounces.

a. Is there evidence that the population mean amount is different from 8 ounces? (Use a 0.05 level of significance.)

b. Compute the *p*-value and interpret its meaning.

c. What is your answer in (a) if the standard deviation is 0.05 ounce?

d. What is your answer in (a) if the sample mean is 7.952 ounces and the standard deviation is 0.15 ounce?

9.33 ATMs must be stocked with enough cash to satisfy customers making withdrawals over an entire weekend. But if too much cash is unnecessarily kept in the ATMs, the bank is forgoing the opportunity of investing the money and earning interest. Suppose that at a particular branch, the population mean amount of money withdrawn from ATMs per customer transaction over the weekend is $160, with a population standard deviation of $30.

a. If a random sample of 36 customer transactions indicates that the sample mean withdrawal amount is $172, is there evidence to believe that the population mean withdrawal amount is no longer $160? (Use a 0.05 level of significance.)

b. Compute the *p*-value and interpret its meaning.

c. What is your answer in (b) if you use a 0.01 level of significance?

d. What is your answer in (b) if the standard deviation is $24 (use $\alpha = 0.05$)?

9.3   ONE-TAIL TESTS

In Section 9.2, hypothesis-testing methodology has been used to examine the question of whether the population mean amount of cereal-filled is 368 grams. The alternative hypothesis (H_1: $\mu \neq 368$) contains two possibilities: Either the mean is less than 368 grams, or the mean is more than 368 grams. For this reason, the rejection region is divided into the two tails of the sampling distribution of the mean.

In many situations, however, the alternative hypothesis focuses on a *particular direction*. One such situation occurs in the following application: A company that makes processed cheese is interested in determining whether some suppliers that provide milk for the processing operation are adding water to their milk to increase the amount supplied to the processing operation. It is known that excess water reduces the freezing point of the milk. The freezing point of natural milk is normally distributed, with a mean of −0.545° Celsius (C). The standard deviation of the freezing temperature of natural milk is known to be 0.008°C. Because the cheese company is only interested in determining whether the freezing point of the milk is less than what would be expected from natural milk, the entire rejection region is located in the lower tail of the distribution.

The Critical Value Approach

Suppose you wish to determine whether the mean freezing point of milk is less than −0.545°. To perform this one-tail hypothesis test, you use the six-step method listed in Exhibit 9.1 on page 336.

Step 1
$$H_0: \mu \geq -0.545°\text{C.}$$
$$H_1: \mu < -0.545°\text{C.}$$

The alternative hypothesis contains the statement you are trying to prove. If the conclusion of the test is "reject H_0," there is statistical proof that the mean freezing point of the milk is less than the natural freezing point of −0.545°C. If the conclusion of the test is "do not reject H_0," then there is insufficient evidence to prove that the mean freezing point is less than the natural freezing point of −0.545°C.

Step 2   You have selected a sample size of $n = 25$. You decide to use $\alpha = 0.05$.

Step 3   Because σ is known, you use the normal distribution and the Z-test statistic.

Step 4   The rejection region is entirely contained in the lower tail of the sampling distribution of the mean because you want to reject H_0 only when the sample mean is significantly less than −0.545°C. When the entire rejection region is contained in one tail of the sampling distribution of the test statistic, the test is called a **one-tail** or **directional test**. When the alternative hypothesis includes the *less than* sign, the critical value of Z must be negative. As shown in Table 9.2 and Figure 9.6, because the entire rejection region is in the lower tail of the standardized normal distribution and contains an area of 0.05, the critical value of the Z test statistic is −1.645, halfway between −1.64 and −1.65.

The decision rule is

$$\text{Reject } H_0 \text{ if } Z < -1.645;$$
$$\text{otherwise, do not reject } H_0.$$

TABLE 9.2

Finding the Critical Value of the Z Test Statistic from the Standardized Normal Distribution for a One-Tail Test with $\alpha = 0.05$

Z	.00	.01	.02	.03	.04	.05	.06	.07	.08	.09
⋮	⋮	⋮	⋮	⋮	⋮	⋮	⋮	⋮	⋮	⋮
−1.8	.0359	.0351	.0344	.0336	.0329	.0322	.0314	.0307	.0301	.0294
−1.7	.0446	.0436	.0427	.0418	.0409	.0401	.0392	.0384	.0375	.0367
−1.6	.0548	.0537	.0526	.0516	.0505	.0495	.0485	.0475	.0465	.0455

Source: Extracted from Table E.2.

FIGURE 9.6

One-tail test of hypothesis for a mean (σ known) at the 0.05 level of significance

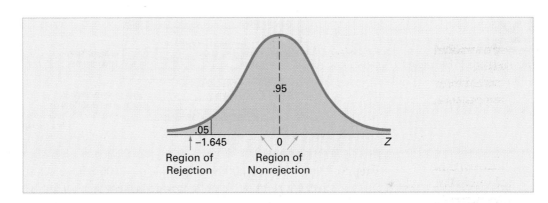

Step 5 You select a sample of 25 containers of milk and find that the sample mean freezing point equals −0.550°C. Using $n = 25$, $\overline{X} = -0.550°C$, $\sigma = 0.008°C$, and Equation (9.1) on page 334,

$$Z = \frac{\overline{X} - \mu}{\dfrac{\sigma}{\sqrt{n}}} = \frac{-0.550 - (-0.545)}{\dfrac{0.008}{\sqrt{25}}} = -3.125$$

Step 6 Because $Z = -3.125 < -1.645$, you reject the null hypothesis (see Figure 9.6). You conclude that the mean freezing point of the milk provided is below −0.545°C. The company should pursue an investigation of the milk supplier because the mean freezing point is significantly below what is expected to occur by chance.

The *p*-Value Approach

Use the five steps listed in Exhibit 9.2 on page 339 to illustrate the test from the preceding page using the *p*-value approach.

Steps 1–3 These steps are the same as in the critical value approach.

Step 4 $Z = -3.125$ (see step 5 of the critical value approach). Because the alternative hypothesis indicates a rejection region entirely in the *lower* tail of the sampling distribution of the Z test statistic, to compute the p-value, you need to find the probability that the Z value will be *less than* the test statistic of -3.125. From Table E.2, the probability that the Z value will be less than -3.125 is 0.0009 (see Figures 9.7 and 9.8).

FIGURE 9.7

Determining the p-value for a one-tail test

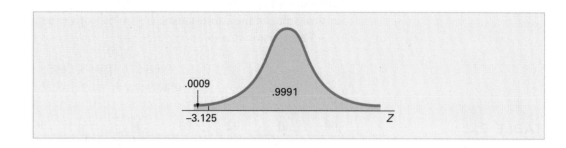

.0009 .9991

-3.125 Z

FIGURE 9.8

Microsoft Excel Z test results for the milk production example

See Section E9.1 to create this.

	A	B	
1	**Milk Production Hypothesis Test**		
2			
3	**Data**		
4	**Null Hypothesis** μ=	-0.545	
5	**Level of Significance**	0.05	
6	**Population Standard Deviation**	0.008	
7	**Sample Size**	25	
8	**Sample Mean**	-0.55	
9			
10	**Intermediate Calculations**		
11	Standard Error of the Mean	0.0016	=B6/SQRT(B7)
12	Z Test Statistic	-3.125	=(B8 - B4)/B11
13			
14	**Lower-Tail Test**		
15	**Lower Critical Value**	-1.6449	=NORMSINV(B5)
16	**p-Value**	0.0009	=NORMSDIST(B12)
17	**Reject the null hypothesis**		=IF(B16 < B5, "Reject the null hypothesis", "Do not reject the null hypothesis")

Step 5   The p-value of 0.0009 is less than $\alpha = 0.05$. You reject H_0. You conclude that the mean freezing point of the milk provided is less than $-0.545°C$. The company should pursue an investigation of the milk supplier because the mean freezing point is significantly less than what is expected to occur by chance.

EXAMPLE 9.5

A ONE-TAIL TEST FOR THE MEAN

A company that manufactures chocolate bars is particularly concerned that the mean weight of a chocolate bar not be greater than 6.03 ounces. Past experience allows you to assume that the standard deviation is 0.02 ounces. A sample of 50 chocolate bars is selected, and the sample mean is 6.034 ounces. Using the $\alpha = 0.01$ level of significance, is there evidence that the population mean weight of the chocolate bars is greater than 6.03 ounces?

SOLUTION   Using the critical value approach,

Step 1
$$H_0: \mu \leq 6.03$$
$$H_1: \mu > 6.03$$

Step 2   You have selected a sample size of $n = 50$. You decide to use $\alpha = 0.01$.

Step 3   Because σ is known, you use the normal distribution and the Z test statistic.

Step 4   The rejection region is entirely contained in the upper tail of the sampling distribution of the mean because you want to reject H_0 only when the sample mean is significantly greater than 6.03 ounces. Because the entire rejection region is in the upper tail of the standardized normal distribution and contains an area of 0.01, the critical value of the Z test statistic is 2.33.

The decision rule is

Reject H_0 if $Z > 2.33$;
otherwise, do not reject H_0.

Step 5   You select a sample of 50 chocolate bars, and the sample mean weight is 6.034 ounces. Using $n = 50$, $\bar{X} = 6.034$, $\sigma = 0.02$, and Equation (9.1) on page 334,

$$Z = \frac{\bar{X} - \mu}{\dfrac{\sigma}{\sqrt{n}}} = \frac{6.034 - 6.03}{\dfrac{0.02}{\sqrt{50}}} = 1.414$$

Step 6   Because $Z = 1.414 < 2.33$, you do not reject the null hypothesis. There is insufficient evidence to conclude that the population mean weight is greater than 6.03 ounces.

To perform one-tail tests of hypotheses, you must properly formulate H_0 and H_1. A summary of the null and alternative hypotheses for one-tail tests is as follows:

1. The null hypothesis, H_0, represents the status quo or the current belief in a situation.
2. The alternative hypothesis, H_1, is the opposite of the null hypothesis and represents a research claim or specific inference you would like to prove.
3. If you reject the null hypothesis, you have statistical proof that the alternative hypothesis is correct.
4. If you do not reject the null hypothesis, then you have failed to prove the alternative hypothesis. The failure to prove the alternative hypothesis, however, does not mean that you have proven the null hypothesis.
5. The null hypothesis (H_0) always refers to a specified value of the *population parameter* (such as μ), not to a *sample statistic* (such as $\bar{X}$).
6. The statement of the null hypothesis *always* contains an equal sign regarding the specified value of the parameter (for example, H_0: $\mu \geq -0.545°C$).
7. The statement of the alternative hypothesis *never* contains an equal sign regarding the specified value of the parameter (for example, H_1: $\mu < -0.545°C$).

PROBLEMS FOR SECTION 9.3

Learning the Basics

 9.34 In a one-tail hypothesis test where you reject H_0 only in the *upper* tail, what is the critical value of the Z test statistic at the 0.01 level of significance?

 9.35 In Problem 9.34, what is your statistical decision if the computed value of the Z test statistic is 2.39?

 9.36 In a one-tail hypothesis test where you reject H_0 only in the *lower* tail, what is the critical value of the Z test statistic at the 0.01 level of significance?

 9.37 In Problem 9.36, what is your statistical decision if the computed value of the Z test statistic is -1.15?

 9.38 Suppose that in a one-tail hypothesis test where you reject H_0 only in the *upper* tail, you compute the value of the test statistic Z to be $+2.00$. What is the p-value?

 9.39 In Problem 9.38, what is your statistical decision if you test the null hypothesis at the 0.05 level of significance?

9.40 Suppose that in a one-tail hypothesis test where you reject H_0 only in the *lower* tail, you compute the value of the test statistic Z as -1.38. What is the p-value?

9.41 In Problem 9.40, what is your statistical decision if you test the null hypothesis at the 0.01 level of significance?

9.42 In a one-tail hypothesis test where you reject H_0 only in the *lower* tail, you compute the value of the test statistic Z as $+1.38$. What is the p-value?

9.43 In Problem 9.42, what is the statistical decision if you test the null hypothesis at the 0.01 level of significance?

Applying the Concepts

 9.44 The Glen Valley Steel Company manufactures steel bars. If the production process is working properly, it turns out steel bars that are normally distributed with mean length of *at least* 2.8 feet, with a standard deviation of 0.20 foot (as determined from engineering specifications on the production equipment involved). Longer steel bars can be used or altered, but shorter bars must be scrapped. You select a sample of 25 bars, and the mean length is 2.73 feet. Do you need to adjust the production equipment?

a. If you test the null hypothesis at the 0.05 level of significance, what decision do you make using the critical value approach to hypothesis testing?
b. If you test the null hypothesis at the 0.05 level of significance, what decision do you make using the *p*-value approach to hypothesis testing?
c. Interpret the meaning of the *p*-value in this problem.
d. Compare your conclusions in (a) and (b).

9.45 You are the manager of a restaurant that delivers pizza to college dormitory rooms. You have just changed your delivery process in an effort to reduce the mean time between the order and completion of delivery from the current 25 minutes. From past experience, you can assume that the population standard deviation is 6 minutes. A sample of 36 orders using the new delivery process yields a sample mean of 22.4 minutes.

a. Using the six-step critical value approach, at the 0.05 level of significance, is there evidence that the population mean delivery time has been reduced below the previous population mean value of 25 minutes?
b. At the 0.05 level of significance, use the five-step *p*-value approach.
c. Interpret the meaning of the *p*-value in (b).
d. Compare your conclusions in (a) and (b).

9.46 Children in the United States account directly for $36 billion in sales annually. When their indirect influence over product decisions from stereos to vacations is considered, the total economic spending affected by children in the United States is $290 billion. It is estimated that by age 10, a child makes an average of more than five trips a week to a store (M. E. Goldberg, G. J. Gorn, L. A. Peracchio, and G. Bamossy, "Understanding Materialism Among Youth," *Journal of Consumer Psychology*, 2003, 13(3) pp. 278–288). Suppose that you want to prove that children in your city average more than five trips a week to a store. Let μ represent the population mean number of times children in your city make trips to a store.

a. State the null and alternative hypotheses.
b. Explain the meaning of the Type I and Type II errors in the context of this scenario.
c. Suppose that you carry out a similar study in the city in which you live. Based on past studies, you assume that the standard deviation of the number of trips to the store is 1.6. You take a sample of 100 children and find that the mean number of trips to the store is 5.47. At the 0.01 level of significance, is there evidence that the population mean number of trips to the store is greater than 5 per week?
d. Interpret the meaning of the *p*-value in (c).

9.47 The waiting time to place an order at a branch of a fast-food chain during the lunch hour has had a population mean of 3.55 minutes, with a population standard deviation of 1.1 minutes. Recently, in an effort to reduce the waiting time, the branch has experimented with a system in which there is a single waiting line. A sample of 100 customers during a recent lunch hour was selected, and their mean waiting time to place an order was 3.18 minutes. Assume that the population standard deviation of the waiting time has not changed from 1.1 minutes.

a. At the 0.05 level of significance, using the critical value approach to hypothesis testing, is there evidence that the population mean waiting time to place an order is less than 3.55 minutes?
b. At the 0.05 level of significance, using the *p*-value approach to hypothesis testing, is there evidence that the population mean waiting time to place an order is less than 3.55 minutes?
c. Interpret the meaning of the *p*-value in this problem.
d. Compare your conclusions in (a) and (b).

9.4   *t* TEST OF HYPOTHESIS FOR THE MEAN (σ UNKNOWN)

In most hypothesis-testing situations concerning the population mean μ, you do not know the population standard deviation, σ. Instead, you use the sample standard deviation, *S*. If you assume that the population is normally distributed, the sampling distribution of the mean follows a *t* distribution with $n - 1$ degrees of freedom. If the population is not normally distributed, you can still use the *t* test if the sample size is large enough for the Central Limit Theorem to take effect (see Section 7.4). Equation (9.2) defines the test statistic *t* for determining the difference between the sample mean, $\overline{X}$, and the population mean, μ, when the sample standard deviation, *S*, is used.

t TEST OF HYPOTHESIS FOR THE MEAN (σ UNKNOWN)

$$t = \frac{\overline{X} - \mu}{\dfrac{S}{\sqrt{n}}} \qquad (9.2)$$

where the test statistic *t* follows a *t* distribution having $n - 1$ degrees of freedom.

To illustrate the use of this *t* test, return to the Using Statistics scenario concerning the Saxon Home Improvement Company on page 284. Over the past five years, the mean amount per sales invoice is $120. As an accountant for the company, you need to inform the finance department if this amount changes. In other words, the hypothesis test is used to try to prove that the mean amount per sales invoice is increasing or decreasing.

The Critical Value Approach

To perform this two-tail hypothesis test, you use the six-step method listed in Exhibit 9.1 on page 336.

Step 1

$$H_0: \mu = \$120$$
$$H_1: \mu \neq \$120$$

The alternative hypothesis contains the statement you are trying to prove. If the null hypothesis is rejected, then there is statistical proof that the population mean amount per sales invoice is no longer $120. If the statistical conclusion is "do not reject H_0," then you will conclude that there is insufficient evidence to prove that the mean amount differs from the long-term mean of $120.

Step 2   You have selected a sample of $n = 12$. You decide to use $\alpha = 0.05$.

Step 3   Because σ is unknown, you use the *t* distribution and the *t* test statistic for this example. You must assume that the population of sales invoices is normally distributed. This assumption is discussed on page 346.

Step 4   For a given sample size, *n*, the test statistic *t* follows a *t* distribution with $n - 1$ degrees of freedom. The critical values of the *t* distribution with $12 - 1 = 11$ degrees of freedom are found in Table E.3, as illustrated in Table 9.3 and Figure 9.9. The alternative hypothesis, H_1, $\mu \neq \$120$ is two-tailed. Thus, the area in the rejection region of the *t* distribution's left (lower) tail is 0.025, and the area in the rejection region of the *t* distribution's right (upper) tail is also 0.025.

TABLE 9.3

Determining the Critical Value from the *t* Table for an Area of 0.025 in Each Tail with 11 Degrees of Freedom

			Upper-Tail Areas			
Degrees of Freedom	**.25**	**.10**	**.05**	**.025**	**.01**	**.005**
1	1.0000	3.0777	6.3138	12.7062	31.8207	63.6574
2	0.8165	1.8856	2.9200	4.3027	6.9646	9.9248
3	0.7649	1.6377	2.3534	3.1824	4.5407	5.8409
4	0.7407	1.5332	2.1318	2.7764	3.7469	4.6041
5	0.7267	1.4759	2.0150	2.5706	3.3649	4.0322
6	0.7176	1.4398	1.9432	2.4469	3.1427	3.7074
7	0.7111	1.4149	1.8946	2.3646	2.9980	3.4995
8	0.7064	1.3968	1.8595	2.3060	2.8965	3.3554
9	0.7027	1.3830	1.8331	2.2622	2.8214	3.2498
10	0.6998	1.3722	1.8125	2.2281	2.7638	3.1693
11	0.6974	1.3634	1.7959	2.2010	2.7181	3.1058

Source: Extracted from Table E.3.

FIGURE 9.9

Testing a hypothesis about the mean (σ unknown) at the 0.05 level of significance with 11 degrees of freedom

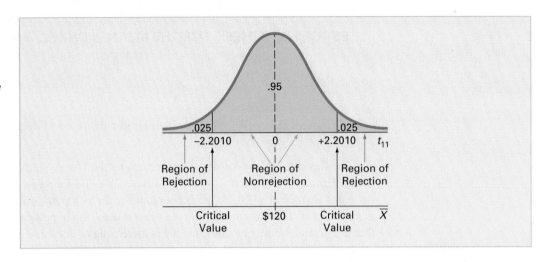

From the t table as given in Table E.3, a portion of which is shown in Table 9.3, the critical values are ± 2.2010. The decision rule is

$$\text{Reject } H_0 \text{ if } t < -t_{11} = -2.2010$$
$$\text{or if } t > t_{11} = +2.2010;$$
$$\text{otherwise, do not reject } H_0.$$

Step 5   The data in the file **invoices.xls** are the amounts (in dollars) in a random sample of 12 sales invoices.

108.98	152.22	111.45	110.59	127.46	107.26
93.32	91.97	111.56	75.71	128.58	135.11

Using Equations (3.1) and (3.10) on pages 97 and 107, or Microsoft Excel, as shown in Figure 9.10,

$$\bar{X} = \frac{\sum_{i=1}^{n} X_i}{n} = \$112.85 \quad \text{and} \quad S = \sqrt{\frac{\sum_{i=1}^{n} (X_i - \bar{X})^2}{n-1}} = \$20.80$$

From Equation (9.2) on page 347,

$$t = \frac{\bar{X} - \mu}{\frac{S}{\sqrt{n}}} = \frac{112.85 - 120}{\frac{20.80}{\sqrt{12}}} = -1.1908$$

FIGURE 9.10

Microsoft Excel results for the one-sample t test of sales invoices

See Section E9.2 to create this.

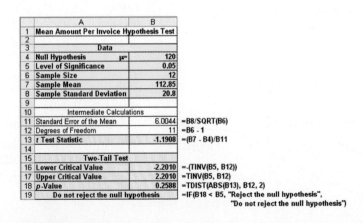

FIGURE 9.12

Microsoft Excel b...
and-whisker p...
sales invoic...

Step 6 Because $-2.2010 < t = -1.1908 < 2.2010$, you d...
evidence to conclude that the mean amount per...
should inform the finance department that the aud...
invoice has not changed.

The *p*-Value Approach 9\3

Steps 1–3 These steps are the same as in the critical value...

Step 4 From the Microsoft Excel worksheet of Figure 9.1...
0.2588 (see step 5 of the critical value approach).

Step 5 The Microsoft Excel results in Figure 9.10 give the ......-tail test as
0.2588. Because the *p*-value of 0.2588 is greater than $\alpha = 0.05$, you do not reject H_0.
The data provide insufficient evidence to conclude that the mean amount per sales
invoice differs from $120. You should inform the finance department that the audit
suggests that the mean amount per invoice has not changed. The *p*-value indicates that
if the null hypothesis is true, the probability that a sample of 12 invoices could have a
monthly mean that differs by $7.15 or more from the stated $120 is 0.2588. In other
words, if the mean amount per sales invoice is truly $120, then there is a 25.88%
chance of observing a sample mean below $112.85 or above $127.15.

In the preceding example, it is incorrect to state that there is a 25.88% chance that the null
hypothesis is true. This misinterpretation of the *p*-value is sometimes used by those not properly trained in statistics. Remember that the *p*-value is a conditional probability, calculated by
assuming that the null hypothesis is true. In general, it is proper to state the following:

> If the null hypothesis is true, there is a (*p*-value)*100% chance of observing a sample
> result at least as contradictory to the null hypothesis as the result observed.

Checking Assumptions

[1] When a large sample size
is available, S estimates σ
precisely enough that there
is little difference between
the t and Z distributions.

You use the one-sample *t* test when the population standard deviation, σ, is not known and is estimated using the sample standard deviation,[1] S. To use the one-sample *t* test, the data are assumed
to represent a random sample from a population that is normally distributed. In practice, as long
as the sample size is not very small and the population is not very skewed, the *t* distribution provides a good approximation to the sampling distribution of the mean when σ is unknown.

There are several ways to evaluate the normality assumption necessary for using the *t* test.
You can observe how closely the sample statistics match the normal distribution's theoretical
properties. You can also use a histogram, stem-and-leaf display, box-and-whisker plot, or normal probability plot. For details on evaluating normality, see Section 6.3 on page 234.

Figure 9.11 presents descriptive statistics generated by Microsoft Excel. Figure 9.12 is a
Microsoft Excel box-and-whisker plot. Figure 9.13 is a Microsoft Excel normal probability plot.

FIGURE 9.11

Microsoft Excel
descriptive statistics for
the sales invoice data

See Section E3.1 to create
this.

	A	B
1	*Invoice Amount*	
2		
3	Mean	112.8508
4	Standard Error	6.003863
5	Median	111.02
6	Mode	#N/A
7	Standard Deviation	20.79799
8	Sample Variance	432.5565
9	Kurtosis	0.172708
10	Skewness	0.133638
11	Range	76.51
12	Minimum	75.71
13	Maximum	152.22
14	Sum	1354.21
15	Count	12
16	Largest(1)	152.22
17	Smallest(1)	75.71

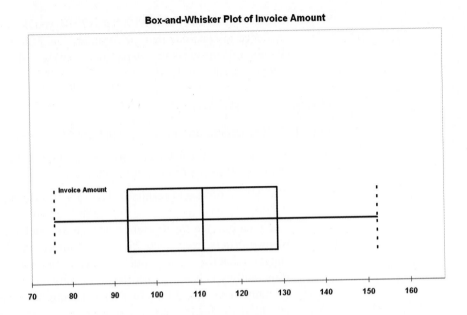

Box-and-Whisker Plot of Invoice Amount

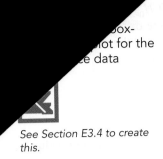

See Section E3.4 to create this.

FIGURE 9.13

Microsoft Excel normal probability plot for the sales invoice data

See Section E6.2 to create this.

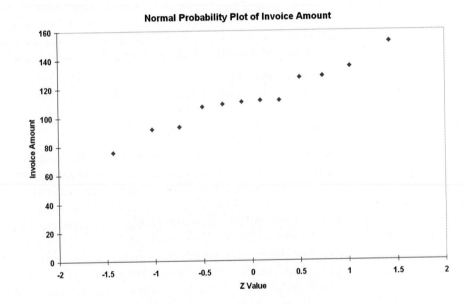

Normal Probability Plot of Invoice Amount

Because the mean is very close to the median, the points on the normal probability plot appear to be increasing approximately in a straight line, and the box-and-whisker plot appears approximately symmetrical. You can assume that the population of sales invoices is approximately normally distributed. The normality assumption is valid, and therefore the auditor's results are valid.

The *t* test is a **robust** test. It does not lose power if the shape of the population departs somewhat from a normal distribution, particularly when the sample size is large enough to enable the test statistic *t* to be influenced by the Central Limit Theorem (see Section 7.4. However, you can make erroneous conclusions and can lose statistical power if you use the *t* test incorrectly. If the sample size, *n*, is small (that is, less than 30) and you cannot easily make the assumption that the underlying population is at least approximately normally distributed, other *nonparametric* testing procedures are more appropriate (see references 1 and 2).

PROBLEMS FOR SECTION 9.4

Learning the Basics

 9.48 If, in a sample of $n = 16$ selected from a normal population, $\overline{X} = 56$ and $S = 12$, what is the value of the *t*-test statistic if you are testing the null hypothesis H_0: $\mu = 50$?

9.49 In Problem 9.48, how many degrees of freedom are there in the one-sample *t* test?

9.50 In Problems 9.48 and 9.49, what are the critical values of *t* if the level of significance, α, is 0.05 and the alternative hypothesis, H_1, is
a. $\mu \neq 50$?
b. $\mu > 50$?

9.51 In Problems 9.48, 9.49, and 9.50, what is your statistical decision if the alternative hypothesis, H_1, is
a. $\mu \neq 50$?
b. $\mu > 50$?

9.52 If, in a sample of $n = 16$ selected from a left-skewed population, $\overline{X} = 65$ and $S = 21$, would you use the *t* test to test the null hypothesis H_0: $\mu = 60$? Discuss.

9.53 If, in a sample of $n = 160$ selected from a left-skewed population, $\overline{X} = 65$ and $S = 21$, would you use the *t* test to test the null hypothesis H_0: $\mu = 60$? Discuss.

Applying the Concepts

9.54 Late payment of medical claims can add to the cost of health care. An article (M. Freudenheim, "The Check Is Not in the Mail," *The New York Times*, May 25, 2006, pp. C1, C6) reported that the mean time from the date of service to the date of payment for one insurance company was 41.4 days during a recent period. Suppose that a sample of 100 medical claims is selected during the latest time period. The sample mean time from the date of service to the date of payment was 39.6 days, and the sample standard deviation was 7.4 days.
a. Using the 0.05 level of significance, is there evidence that the population mean has changed from 41.4 days?
b. What is your answer in (a) if you use the 0.01 level of significance?
c. What is your answer in (a) if the sample mean is 38.2 days and the sample standard deviation is 10.7 days?

9.55 An article (N. Hellmich, "'Supermarket Guru' Has a Simple Mantra," *USA Today*, June 19, 2002, p. 70) claimed that the typical supermarket trip takes a mean of 22 minutes. Suppose that in an effort to test this claim, you select a sample of 50 shoppers at a local supermarket. The mean shopping time for the sample of 50 shoppers is 25.36 minutes, with a standard deviation of 7.24 minutes. Using the 0.10 level of significance, is there evidence that the mean shopping time at the local supermarket is different from the claimed value of 22 minutes?

 9.56 You are the manager of a restaurant for a fast-food franchise. Last month, the mean waiting time at the drive-through window, as measured from the time a customer places an order until the time the customer receives the order, was 3.7 minutes. The franchise helped you institute a new process intended to reduce waiting time. You select a random sample of 64 orders. The sample mean waiting time is 3.57 minutes, with a sample standard deviation of 0.8 minute. At the 0.05 level of significance, is there evidence that the population mean waiting time is now less than 3.7 minutes?

9.57 A manufacturer of chocolate candies uses machines to package candies as they move along a filling line. Although the packages are labeled as 8 ounces, the company wants the packages to contain 8.17 ounces so that virtually none of the packages contain less than 8 ounces. A sample of 50 packages is selected periodically, and the packaging process is stopped if there is evidence that the mean amount packaged is different from 8.17 ounces. Suppose that in a particular sample of 50 packages, the mean amount dispensed is 8.159 ounces, with a sample standard deviation of 0.051 ounce.
a. Is there evidence that the population mean amount is different from 8.17 ounces? (Use a 0.05 level of significance.)
b. Determine the *p*-value and interpret its meaning.

9.58 The data in the file `movieprices.xls` contains prices (in dollars) for two tickets, with online service charges, large popcorn, and two medium soft drinks at a sample of six theatre chains:

36.15   31.00   35.05   40.25   33.75   43.00

Source: Extracted from K. Kelly, "The Multiplex Under Siege," The Wall Street Journal, December 24–25, 2005, pp. P1, P5.

a. At the 0.05 level of significance, is there evidence that the mean price for two tickets, with online service charges, large popcorn, and two medium soft drinks, is different from $35?
b. Determine the *p*-value in (a) and interpret its meaning.
c. What assumption about the population distribution is needed in (a) and (b)?
d. Do you think that the assumption stated in (c) is seriously violated?

9.59 In New York State, savings banks are permitted to sell a form of life insurance called savings bank life insurance (SBLI). The approval process consists of underwriting, which includes a review of the application, a medical information bureau check, possible requests for additional medical information and medical exams, and a policy compilation stage in which the policy pages are generated and sent to the bank for delivery. The ability to deliver approved policies to customers in a timely manner is critical to the profitability of this service. During a period of one month, a random sample of 27 approved policies is selected, and the total processing time, in days, is recorded (as stored in the insurance.xls file):

```
73  19  16  64  28  28  31  90  60  56  31  56  22  18
45  48  17  17  17  91  92  63  50  51  69  16  17
```

a. In the past, the mean processing time was 45 days. At the 0.05 level of significance, is there evidence that the mean processing time has changed from 45 days?
b. What assumption about the population distribution is needed in (a)?
c. Do you think that the assumption stated in (b) is seriously violated? Explain.

9.60 The following data (see the drink.xls file) represent the amount of soft-drink filled in a sample of 50 consecutive 2-liter bottles. The results, listed horizontally in the order of being filled, were:

```
2.109 2.086 2.066 2.075 2.065 2.057 2.052 2.044 2.036 2.038
2.031 2.029 2.025 2.029 2.023 2.020 2.015 2.014 2.013 2.014
2.012 2.012 2.012 2.010 2.005 2.003 1.999 1.996 1.997 1.992
1.994 1.986 1.984 1.981 1.973 1.975 1.971 1.969 1.966 1.967
1.963 1.957 1.951 1.951 1.947 1.941 1.941 1.938 1.908 1.894
```

a. At the 0.05 level of significance, is there evidence that the mean amount of soft drink filled is different from 2.0 liters?
b. Determine the p-value in (a) and interpret its meaning.
c. Evaluate the population distribution assumption you made in (a) graphically. Are the results of (a) valid? Why?
d. Examine the values of the 50 bottles in their sequential order, as given in the problem. Is there a pattern to the results? If so, what impact might this pattern have on the validity of the results in (a)?

9.61 One of the major measures of the quality of service provided by any organization is the speed with which it responds to customer complaints. A large family-held department store selling furniture and flooring, including carpet, had undergone a major expansion in the past several years. In particular, the flooring department had expanded from 2 installation crews to an installation supervisor, a measurer, and 15 installation crews. Last year there were 50 complaints concerning carpet installation. The following data (stored in the furniture.xls file) represent the number of days between the receipt of a complaint and the resolution of the complaint:

```
54   5  35 137  31  27 152   2 123  81  74  27
11  19 126 110 110  29  61  35  94  31  26   5
12   4 165  32  29  28  29  26  25   1  14  13
13  10   5  27   4  52  30  22  36  26  20  23
33  68
```

a. The installation supervisor claims that the mean number of days between the receipt of a complaint and the resolution of the complaint is 20 days or less. At the 0.05 level of significance, is there evidence that the claim is not true (that is, that the mean number of days is greater than 20)?
b. What assumption about the population distribution must you make in (a)?
c. Do you think that the assumption made in (b) is seriously violated? Explain.
d. What effect might your conclusion in (c) have on the validity of the results in (a)?

9.62 A manufacturing company produces steel housings for electrical equipment. The main component part of the housing is a steel trough that is made out of a 14-gauge steel coil. It is produced using a 250-ton progressive punch press with a wipe-down operation that puts two 90-degree forms in the flat steel to make the trough. The distance from one side of the form to the other is critical because of weatherproofing in outdoor applications. The company requires that the width of the trough be between 8.31 inches and 8.61 inches. The data file trough.xls contains the widths of the troughs, in inches, for a sample of $n = 49$.

```
8.312 8.343 8.317 8.383 8.348 8.410 8.351 8.373 8.481 8.422
8.476 8.382 8.484 8.403 8.414 8.419 8.385 8.465 8.498 8.447
8.436 8.413 8.489 8.414 8.481 8.415 8.479 8.429 8.458 8.462
8.460 8.444 8.429 8.460 8.412 8.420 8.410 8.405 8.323 8.420
8.396 8.447 8.405 8.439 8.411 8.427 8.420 8.498 8.409
```

a. At the 0.05 level of significance, is there evidence that the mean widths of the troughs is different from 8.46 inches?
b. What assumption about the population distribution do you need to make in (a)?
c. Do you think that the assumption made in (a) has been seriously violated? Explain.

9.63 One operation of a steel mill is to cut pieces of steel into parts that are used in the frame for front seats in an automobile. The steel is cut with a diamond saw and requires the resulting parts to be within ±0.005 inch of the length specified by the automobile company. The data in the file steel.xls come from a sample of 100 steel parts. The measurement reported is the difference, in inches, between the actual length of the steel part, as measured by a laser measurement device, and the specified length of the steel part. For example, a value of −0.002 represents a steel part that is 0.002 inch shorter than the specified length.

a. At the 0.05 level of significance, is there evidence that the mean difference is not equal to 0.0 inches?

b. Determine the *p*-value in (a) and interpret its meaning.

c. What assumption about the differences between the actual length of the steel part and the specified length of the steel part must you make in (a)?

d. Evaluate the assumption in (c) graphically. Are the results of (a) valid? Why?

9.64 In Problem 3.63 on page 138, you were introduced to a tea-bag-filling operation. An important quality characteristic of interest for this process is the weight of the tea in the individual bags. The data in the file **teabags.xls** is an ordered array of the weight, in grams, of a sample of 50 tea bags produced during an eight-hour shift.

a. Is there evidence that the mean amount of tea per bag is different from 5.5 grams (use α = 0.01)?

b. Construct a 99% confidence interval estimate of the population mean amount of tea per bag. Interpret this interval.

c. Compare the conclusions reached in (a) and (b).

9.65 Although many people think they can put a meal on the table in a short period of time, a recent article reported that they end up spending about 40 minutes doing so (N. Hellmich, "Americans Go for the Quick Fix for Dinner," *USA Today*, February 14, 2006). Suppose another study is conducted to test the validity of this statement. A sample of 25 people is selected, and the length of time to prepare and cook dinner (in minutes) is recorded, with the following results (stored in the file **dinner.xls**).

44.0 51.9 49.7 40.0 55.5 33.0 43.4 41.3 45.2 40.7 41.1 49.1 30.9
45.2 55.3 52.1 55.1 38.8 43.1 39.2 58.6 49.8 43.2 47.9 46.6

a. Is there evidence that the population mean time to prepare and cook dinner is greater than 40 minutes? Use a level of significance of 0.05.

b. What assumptions are made to perform the test in (a)?

c. Do you think the assumption needed in (a) is seriously violated? Explain.

d. Determine the *p*-value and interpret its meaning.

9.5 Z TEST OF HYPOTHESIS FOR THE PROPORTION

In some situations, you want to test a hypothesis about the proportion of successes in the population, π, rather than testing the population mean. To begin, you select a random sample and compute the **sample proportion**, $p = X/n$. You then compare the value of this statistic to the hypothesized value of the parameter, π, in order to decide whether to reject the null hypothesis.

If the number of successes (X) and the number of failures ($n - X$) are each at least five, the sampling distribution of a proportion approximately follows a normal distribution. You use the **Z test for the proportion** given in Equation (9.3) to perform the hypothesis test for the difference between the sample proportion, p, and the hypothesized population proportion, π.

ONE SAMPLE Z TEST FOR THE PROPORTION

$$Z = \frac{p - \pi}{\sqrt{\dfrac{\pi(1 - \pi)}{n}}} \qquad (9.3)$$

where

$$p = \frac{X}{n} = \frac{\text{Number of successes in the sample}}{\text{Sample size}}$$

p = sample proportion of successes

π = hypothesized proportion of successes in the population

and the test statistic Z approximately follows a standardized normal distribution.

Alternatively, by multiplying the numerator and denominator by n, you can write the Z test statistic in terms of the number of successes, X, as shown in Equation (9.4).

Z TEST FOR THE PROPORTION IN TERMS OF THE NUMBER OF SUCCESSES

$$Z = \frac{X - n\pi}{\sqrt{n\pi(1 - \pi)}} \qquad (9.4)$$

To illustrate the one-sample Z test for a proportion, consider a survey of independent grocery owners. In the survey, the owners were asked to consider what they believed to be their biggest competitive threat. Some noted large-chain supermarkets, wholesale clubs, and other independent grocers. The most common response, given by 78 of the 151 owners, was that they viewed Wal-Mart as their biggest competitive threat (Extracted from J. Tarnowski and D. Chanil, "To Serve and Connect," *The Progressive Grocer*, January 1, 2006, pp. 60–65). For this survey, the null and alternative hypotheses are stated as follows:

H_0: $\pi = 0.50$ (that is, half of all independent grocery owners view Wal-Mart as their biggest competitive threat)

H_1: $\pi \neq 0.50$ (that is, either less than half or more than half of all independent grocery owners view Wal-Mart as their biggest competitive threat)

The Critical Value Approach

Because you are interested in whether the proportion of independent grocery owners who view Wal-Mart as their biggest competitive threat is 0.50, you use a two-tail test. If you select the $\alpha = 0.05$ level of significance, the rejection and nonrejection regions are set up as in Figure 9.14, and the decision rule is

Reject H_0 if $Z < -1.96$ or if $Z > +1.96$;
otherwise, do not reject H_0.

FIGURE 9.14

Two-tail test of hypothesis for the proportion at the 0.05 level of significance

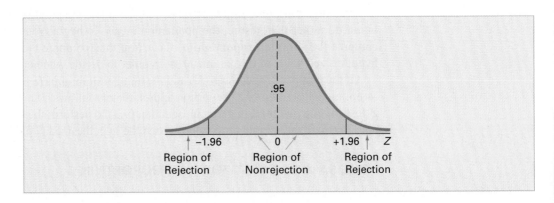

Because 78 of the 151 of independent grocery owners view Wal-Mart as their biggest competitive threat,

$$p = \frac{78}{151} = 0.5166$$

Using Equation (9.3),

$$Z = \frac{p - \pi}{\sqrt{\dfrac{\pi(1 - \pi)}{n}}} = \frac{0.5166 - 0.50}{\sqrt{\dfrac{0.50(1 - 0.50)}{151}}} = \frac{0.0166}{0.0407} = 0.4069$$

or, using Equation (9.4),

$$Z = \frac{X - n\pi}{\sqrt{n\pi(1 - \pi)}} = \frac{78 - (151)(0.50)}{\sqrt{151(0.50)(0.50)}} = \frac{2.5}{6.1441} = 0.4069$$

Because $-1.96 < Z = 0.4069 < 1.96$, you do not reject H_0. There is insufficient evidence that the proportion of independent grocery owners who view Wal-Mart as their biggest competitive threat is not 0.50. Figure 9.15 presents Microsoft Excel results for these data. In other words, the current belief that half of all independent grocers view Wal-Mart as their bigget competitive threat is not contradicted by the *Z* test.

FIGURE 9.15

Microsoft Excel results for the survey of independent grocery owners and Wal-Mart as biggest competitive threat

See Section E9.3 to create this.

	A	B
1	**Wal-Mart As Biggest Threat Hypothesis Test**	
2		
3	**Data**	
4	**Null Hypothesis** *p=*	0.5
5	**Level of Significance**	0.05
6	**Number of Successes**	78
7	**Sample Size**	151
8		
9	Intermediate Calculations	
10	Sample Proportion	0.5166 =B6/B7
11	Standard Error	0.0407 =SQRT(B4*(1 - B4)/B7)
12	**Z Test Statistic**	0.4069 =(B10 - B4)/B11
13		
14	**Two-Tail Test**	
15	**Lower Critical Value**	-1.9600 =NORMSINV(B5/2)
16	**Upper Critical Value**	1.9600 =NORMSINV(1 - B5/2)
17	*p*-Value	0.6841 =2 * (1 - NORMSDIST(ABS(B12)))
18	**Do not reject the null hypothesis**	=IF(B17 < B5, "Reject the null hypothesis", "Do not reject the null hypothesis")

The *p*-Value Approach

As an alternative to the critical value approach, you can compute the *p*-value. For this two-tail test in which the rejection region is located in the lower tail and the upper tail, you need to find the area below a *Z* value of -0.4069 and above a *Z* value of $+0.4069$. Figure 9.15 reports a *p*-value of 0.6841. Because this value is greater than the selected level of significance ($\alpha = 0.05$), you do not reject the null hypothesis.

EXAMPLE 9.6

TESTING A HYPOTHESIS FOR A PROPORTION

A fast-food chain has developed a new process to ensure that orders at the drive-through are filled correctly. The previous process filled orders correctly 85% of the time. Based on a sample of 100 orders using the new process, 94 were filled correctly. At the 0.01 level of significance, can you conclude that the new process has increased the proportion of orders filled correctly?

SOLUTION The null and alternative hypotheses are

H_0: $\pi \leq 0.85$ (that is, the proportion of orders filled correctly is less than or equal to 0.85)
H_1: $\pi > 0.85$ (that is, the proportion of orders filled correctly is greater than 0.85)

Using Equation (9.3) on page 353,

$$p = \frac{X}{n} = \frac{94}{100} = 0.94$$

$$Z = \frac{p - \pi}{\sqrt{\dfrac{\pi(1 - \pi)}{n}}} = \frac{0.94 - 0.85}{\sqrt{\dfrac{0.85(1 - 0.85)}{100}}} = \frac{0.09}{0.0357} = 2.52$$

The *p*-value for $Z > 2.52$ is 0.0059.

Using the critical value approach, you reject H_0 if $Z > 2.33$. Using the *p*-value approach, you reject H_0 if the *p*-value < 0.01. Because $Z = 2.52 > 2.33$ or the *p*-value $= 0.0059 < 0.01$, you reject H_0. You have evidence that the new process has increased the proportion of correct orders above 0.85.

PROBLEMS FOR SECTION 9.5

Learning the Basics

 9.66 If, in a random sample of 400 items, 88 are defective, what is the sample proportion of defective items?

 9.67 In Problem 9.66, if the null hypothesis is that 20% of the items in the population are defective, what is the value of the Z-test statistic?

 9.68 In Problems 9.66 and 9.67, suppose you are testing the null hypothesis H_0: $\pi = 0.20$ against the two-tail alternative hypothesis H_1: $\pi \neq 0.20$ and you choose the level of significance $\alpha = 0.05$. What is your statistical decision?

Applying the Concepts

9.69 Late payment of medical claims can add to the cost of health care. An article (M. Freudenheim, "The Check Is Not in the Mail," *The New York Times*, May 25, 2006, pp. C1, C6) reported that for one insurance company, 85.1% of the claims were paid in full when first submitted. Suppose that the insurance company developed a new payment system in an effort to increase this percentage. A sample of 200 claims processed under this system revealed that 180 of the claims were paid in full when first submitted.

a. At the 0.05 level of significance, is there evidence that the proportion of claims processed under this new system is higher than the article reported for the previous system?

b. Compute the *p*-value and interpret its meaning.

 9.70 The high cost of gasoline in the spring of 2006 had many people reconsidering their summer vacation plans. A survey of 464 Cincinnati-area adults found that 255 said that they were planning on modifying or canceling their summer travel plans because of high gas prices ("Will You Travel?" *The Cincinnati Enquirer*, May 3, 2006, p. A10.)

a. Use the six-step critical value approach to hypothesis-testing and a 0.05 level of significance to try to prove that the majority of Cincinnati-area adults were planning on modifying or canceling their summer travel plans because of high gas prices.

b. Use the five-step *p*-value approach to hypothesis testing and a 0.05 level of significance to try to prove that the majority of Cincinnati-area adults were planning on modifying or canceling their summer travel plans because of high gas prices.

c. Compare the results of (a) and (b).

9.71 A *Wall Street Journal* article suggested that age bias was a growing problem in the corporate world (C. Hymowitz, "Top Executives Chase Youthful Appearance, but Miss Real Issue," *The Wall Street Journal*, February 17, 2004, p. B1). In 2001, an estimated 78% of executives believed that age bias was a serious problem. In a 2004 study by ExecuNet, 82% of the executives surveyed considered age bias a serious problem. The sample size for the 2004 study was not disclosed. Suppose 50 executives were surveyed.

a. At the 0.05 level of significance, use the six-step critical value approach to hypothesis-testing to try to prove that the 2004 proportion of executives who believed that age bias was a serious problem was higher than the 2001 value of 0.78.

b. Use the five-step *p*-value approach. Interpret the meaning of the *p*-value.

c. Suppose that the sample size used was 1,000. Redo (a) and (b).

d. Discuss the effect that sample size had on the outcome of this analysis and, in general, the effect that sample size plays in hypothesis testing.

9.72 A *Wall Street Journal* poll ("What's News Online," *The Wall Street Journal*, March 30, 2004, p. D7) asked respondents if they trusted energy-efficiency ratings on cars and appliances; 552 responded yes, and 531 responded no.

a. At the 0.05 level of significance, use the six-step critical value approach to hypothesis-testing to try to prove that the percentage of people who trust energy-efficiency ratings differs from 50%.

b. Use the five-step *p*-value approach. Interpret the meaning of the *p*-value.

9.73 One of the biggest issues facing e-retailers is the ability to reduce the proportion of customers who cancel their transactions after they have selected their products. It has been estimated that about half of prospective customers cancel their transactions after they have selected their products (B. Tedeschi, "E-Commerce, a Cure for Abandoned Shopping Carts: A Web Checkout System That Eliminates the Need for Multiple Screens," *The New York Times*, February 14, 2005, p. C3). Suppose that a company changed its Web site so that customers could use a single-page checkout process rather than multiple pages. A sample of 500 customers who had selected their products were provided with the new checkout system. Of these 500 customers, 210 cancelled their transactions after they have selected their products.

a. At the 0.01 level of significance, is there evidence that the proportion of customers who selected products and then cancelled their transaction was less than 0.50 with the new system?

b. Suppose that a sample of 100 customers who had selected their products were provided with the new checkout system and that 42 of those customers cancelled their transactions after they had selected their products. At the 0.01 level of significance, is there evidence that the proportion of customers who selected products and then cancelled their transaction was less than 0.50 with the new system?

c. Compare the results of (a) and (b) and discuss the effect that sample size has on the outcome, and, in general, in hypothesis testing.

9.74 More professional women than ever before are forgoing motherhood because of the time constraints of their careers. However, many women still manage to find time to climb the corporate ladder *and* set time aside to have children. A survey of 187 attendees at *Fortune Magazine*'s Most Powerful Women in Business summit in March 2002 found that 133 had at least one child (C. Hymowitz, "Women

Plotting Mix of Work and Family Won't Find Perfect Plan," *The Wall Street Journal*, June 11, 2002, p. B1). Assume that the group of 187 women was a random sample from the population of all successful women executives.

a. What was the sample proportion of successful women executives who had children?

b. At the 0.05 level of significance, can you state that more than half of all successful women executives had children?

c. At the 0.05 level of significance, can you state that more than two-thirds of all successful women executives had children?

d. Do you think the random sample assumption is valid? Explain.

9.6 POTENTIAL HYPOTHESIS-TESTING PITFALLS AND ETHICAL ISSUES

To this point, you have studied the fundamental concepts of hypothesis testing. You have used hypothesis testing to analyze differences between sample estimates (that is, statistics) and hypothesized population characteristics (that is, parameters) in order to make business decisions concerning the underlying population characteristics. You have also learned how to evaluate the risks involved in making these decisions.

When planning to carry out a test of the hypothesis based on a survey, research study, or designed experiment, you must ask several questions to ensure that you use proper methodology. You need to raise and answer questions such as the following in the planning stage:

1. What is the goal of the survey, study, or experiment? How can you translate the goal into a null hypothesis and an alternative hypothesis?
2. Is the hypothesis test a two-tail test or one-tail test?
3. Can you select a random sample from the underlying population of interest?
4. What kinds of data will you collect from the sample? Are the variables numerical or categorical?
5. At what significance level, or risk of committing a Type I error, should you conduct the hypothesis test?
6. Is the intended sample size large enough to achieve the desired power of the test for the level of significance chosen?
7. What statistical test procedure should you use and why?
8. What conclusions and interpretations can you reach from the results of the hypothesis test?

Failing to consider these questions early in the planning process can lead to biased or incomplete results. Proper planning can help ensure that the statistical study will provide objective information needed to make good business decisions.

Statistical Significance Versus Practical Significance   You need to make the distinction between the existence of a statistically significant result and its practical significance in the context within a field of application. Sometimes, due to a very large sample size, you may get a result that is statistically significant but has little practical significance. For example, suppose that prior to a national marketing campaign focusing on a series of expensive television commercials, you believe that the proportion of people who recognize your brand is 0.30. At the completion of the campaign, a survey of 20,000 people indicates that 6,168 recognized your brand. A one-tail test trying to prove that the proportion is now greater than 0.30 results in a p-value of 0.0047 and the correct statistical conclusion is that the proportion of consumers recognizing your brand name has now increased. Was the campaign successful? The result of the hypothesis test indicates a statistically significant increase in brand awareness, but is this increase practically important? The population proportion is now estimated at $6,168/20,000 = 0.3084$, or 30.84%. This increase is less than 1% more than the hypothesized value of 30%. Did the large expenses associated with the marketing campaign produce a result with a meaningful increase in brand awareness? Because of the minimal real-world impact an increase of less than 1% has on the overall marketing strategy and the huge expenses associated with the marketing campaign, you should conclude that the campaign was not successful. On the other hand, if the campaign increased brand awareness by 20%, you could conclude that the campaign was successful.

Ethical Issues

You also need to distinguish between poor research methodology and unethical behavior. Ethical considerations arise when the hypothesis-testing process is manipulated. Some of the areas where ethical issues can arise include the use of human subjects in experiments, data collection method, informed consent from human subjects being "treated," the type of test (one-tail or two-tail test), the choice of the level of significance, data snooping, the cleansing and discarding of data, and the failure to report pertinent findings.

Informed Consent from Human Respondents Being "Treated"

Ethical considerations require that any individual who is to be subjected to some "treatment" in an experiment be made aware of the research endeavor and any potential behavioral or physical side effects. The person should also provide informed consent with respect to participation.

Data Collection Method—Randomization

To eliminate the possibility of potential biases in the results, you must use proper data collection methods. To draw meaningful conclusions, the data must be the outcome of a random sample from a population or from an experiment in which a **randomization** process was used. Potential respondents should not be permitted to self-select for a study, nor should they be purposely selected. Aside from the potential ethical issues that may arise, such a lack of randomization can result in serious coverage errors or selection biases that destroy the integrity of the study.

Type of Test—Two-Tail or One-Tail Test

If prior information is available that leads you to test the null hypothesis against a specifically directed alternative, then a one-tail test is more powerful than a two-tail test. However, if you are interested only in *differences* from the null hypothesis, not in the *direction* of the difference, the two-tail test is the appropriate procedure to use. For example, if previous research and statistical testing have already established the difference in a particular direction, or if an established scientific theory states that it is possible for results to occur in only one direction, then a one-tail test is appropriate. It is never appropriate to change the direction of a test after the data are collected.

Choice of Level of Significance, α

In a well-designed study, you select the level of significance, α, before data collection occurs. You cannot alter the level of significance after the fact to achieve a specific result. You should always report the *p*-value, not just the conclusions of the hypothesis test.

Data Snooping

Data snooping is never permissible. It is unethical to perform a hypothesis test on a set of data, look at the results, and then specify the level of significance or decide whether to use a one-tail or two-tail test. You must make these decisions before the data are collected in order for the conclusions to be valid. In addition, you cannot arbitrarily change or discard extreme or unusual values in order to alter the results of the hypothesis tests.

Cleansing and Discarding of Data

In the data preparation stage of editing, coding, and transcribing, you have an opportunity to review the data for any extreme or unusual values. After reviewing the data, you should construct a stem-and-leaf display and/or a box-and-whisker plot to determine whether there are possible outliers to double-check against the original data.

The process of data cleansing raises a major ethical question. Should you ever remove a value from a study? The answer is a qualified yes. If you can determine that a measurement is incomplete or grossly in error because of some equipment problem or unusual behavioral occurrence unrelated to the study, you can discard the value. Sometimes you have no choice—an individual may decide to quit a particular study he or she has been participating in before a final measurement can be made. In a well-designed experiment or study, you should decide, in advance, on all rules regarding the possible discarding of data.

Reporting of Findings   In conducting research, you should document both good and bad results. You should not just report the results of hypothesis tests that show statistical significance but omit those for which there is insufficient evidence in the findings. In instances in which there is insufficient evidence to reject H_0, you must make it clear that this does not prove that the null hypothesis is true. What the result does indicate is that with the sample size used, there is not enough information to *disprove* the null hypothesis.

Summary   To summarize, in discussing ethical issues concerning hypothesis testing, the key is *intent*. You must distinguish between poor data analysis and unethical practice. Unethical practice occurs when researchers *intentionally* create a selection bias in data collection, manipulate the treatment of human subjects without informed consent, use data snooping to select the type of test (two-tail or one-tail) and/or level of significance, hide the facts by discarding values that do not support a stated hypothesis, or fail to report pertinent findings.

9.7   ● (CD-ROM Topic) THE POWER OF A TEST

Section 9.1 defines Type I and Type II errors and the power of the test. In section 9.7.pdf on the Student CD-ROM, the power of the test is examined in greater depth.

SUMMARY

This chapter presented the foundation of hypothesis testing. You learned how to perform Z and t tests on the population mean and the Z test on the population proportion. You also learned how an operations manager of a production facility can use hypothesis testing to monitor and improve a cereal-fill process. The three chapters that follow build on the foundation of hypothesis testing discussed here.

Figure 9.16 presents a roadmap for selecting the correct one-sample hypothesis test to use.

FIGURE 9.16

Roadmap for selecting a one-sample test

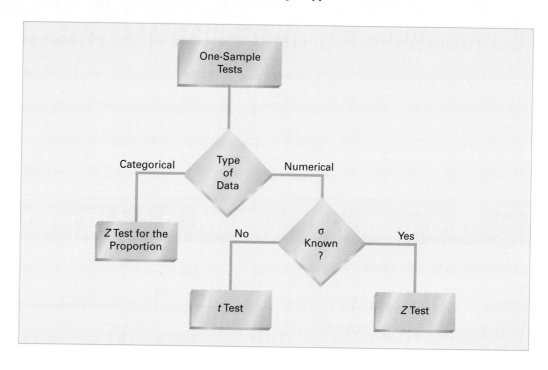

In deciding which test to use, you should ask the following questions:

- Does the test involve a numerical variable or a categorical variable? If the test involves a categorical variable, use the Z test for the proportion.

- If the test involves a numerical variable, do you know the population standard deviation? If you know the population standard deviation, use the Z test for the mean. If you do not know the population standard deviation, use the t test for the mean.

Table 9.4 provides a list of topics covered in this chapter.

TABLE 9.4

Summary of Topics in Chapter 9

Type of Analysis	Type of Data	
	Numerical	**Categorical**
Hypothesis test concerning a single parameter	Z test of hypothesis for the mean (Section 9.2) t test of hypothesis for the mean (Section 9.4)	Z test of hypothesis for the proportion (Section 9.5)

KEY EQUATIONS

Z Test of Hypothesis for the Mean (σ Known)

$$Z = \frac{\bar{X} - \mu}{\frac{\sigma}{\sqrt{n}}} \quad (9.1)$$

t Test of Hypothesis for the Mean (σ Unknown)

$$t = \frac{\bar{X} - \mu}{\frac{S}{\sqrt{n}}} \quad (9.2)$$

One Sample Z Test for the Proportion

$$Z = \frac{p - \pi}{\sqrt{\frac{\pi(1 - \pi)}{n}}} \quad (9.3)$$

Z Test for the Proportion in Terms of the Number of Successes

$$Z = \frac{X - n\pi}{\sqrt{n\pi(1 - \pi)}} \quad (9.4)$$

KEY TERMS

α (level of significance)   331
alternative hypothesis (H_1)   329
β risk   332
confidence coefficient ($1 - \alpha$)   332
confidence level   332
critical value   331
data snooping   358
directional test   343
hypothesis testing   328

level of significance (α)   331
null hypothesis (H_0)   328
one-tail test   343
p-value   337
power of a statistical test   332
randomization   358
region of nonrejection   330
region of rejection   330
robust   350

sample proportion   353
t test of hypothesis for a mean   346
test statistic   330
two-tail test   334
Type I error   331
Type II error   331
Z test of hypothesis for the mean   334
Z test for the proportion   353
Z test statistic   334

CHAPTER REVIEW PROBLEMS

Checking Your Understanding

9.75 What is the difference between a null hypothesis, H_0, and an alternative hypothesis, H_1?

9.76 What is the difference between a Type I error and a Type II error?

9.77 What is meant by the power of a test?

9.78 What is the difference between a one-tail test and a two-tail test?

9.79 What is meant by a p-value?

9.80 How can a confidence interval estimate for the population mean provide conclusions to the corresponding hypothesis test for the population mean?

9.81 What is the six-step critical value approach to hypothesis testing?

9.82 What are some of the ethical issues involved with performing a hypothesis test?

Applying the Concepts

9.83 An article in *Marketing News* (T. T. Semon, "Consider a Statistical Insignificance Test," *Marketing News*, February 1, 1999) argued that the level of significance used when comparing two products is often too low—that is, sometimes you should be using an α value greater than 0.05. Specifically, the article recounted testing the proportion of potential customers with a preference for product 1 over product 2. The null hypothesis was that the population proportion of potential customers preferring product 1 was 0.50, and the alternative hypothesis was that it was not equal to 0.50. The *p*-value for the test was 0.22. The article suggested that in some cases, this should be enough evidence to reject the null hypothesis.

a. State the null and alternative hypotheses for this example in statistical terms.

b. Explain the risks associated with Type I and Type II errors in this case.

c. What would be the consequences if you rejected the null hypothesis for a *p*-value of 0.22?

d. Why do you think the article suggested raising the value of α?

e. What would you do in this situation?

f. What is your answer in (e) if the *p*-value equals 0.12? What if it equals 0.06?

9.84 La Quinta Motor Inns developed a computer model to help predict the profitability of sites that are being considered as locations for new hotels. If the computer model predicts large profits, La Quinta buys the proposed site and builds a new hotel. If the computer model predicts small or moderate profits, La Quinta chooses not to proceed with that site (Extracted from S. E. Kimes and J. A. Fitzsimmons, "Selecting Profitable Hotel Sites at La Quinta Motor Inns," *Interfaces*, Vol. 20, March–April 1990, pp. 12–20). This decision-making procedure can be expressed in the hypothesis-testing framework. The null hypothesis is that the site is not a profitable location. The alternative hypothesis is that the site is a profitable location.

a. Explain the risks associated with committing a Type I error in this case.

b. Explain the risks associated with committing a Type II error in this case.

c. Which type of error do you think the executives at La Quinta Motor Inns are trying hard to avoid? Explain.

d. How do changes in the rejection criterion affect the probabilities of committing Type I and Type II errors?

9.85 In 2006, Visa wanted to move away from its long-running television advertising theme of "Visa, it's everywhere you want to be." During the Winter Olympics, Visa featured Olympians in commercials with a broader message, including security, check cards, and payment technologies such as contactless processing. One of the first commercials featured snowboarder Lindsey Jacobellis being coached to calm down before a big race by imagining that her Visa Check Card got stolen. A key metric for the success of television advertisements is the proportion of viewers who "like the ads a lot." Harris Ad Research Service conducted a study of 903 adults who viewed the new Visa advertisement and reported that 54 indicated that they "like the ad a lot." According to Harris, the proportion of a typical television advertisement receiving the "like the ad a lot" score is 0.21 (Extracted from T. Howard, "Visa to Change Strategies in Upcoming Ads," **usatoday.com**, January 23, 2006.).

a. Use the six-step critical value approach to hypothesis testing and a 0.05 level of significance to try to prove that the new Visa ad is less successful than a typical television advertisement.

b. Use the five-step *p*-value approach to hypothesis testing and a 0.05 level of significance to try to prove that the new Visa ad is less successful than a typical television advertisement.

c. Compare the results of (a) and (b).

9.86 The owner of a gasoline station wants to study gasoline purchasing habits by motorists at his station. He selects a random sample of 60 motorists during a certain week, with the following results:

- The amount purchased was $\overline{X} = 11.3$ gallons, $S = 3.1$ gallons.
- 11 motorists purchased premium-grade gasoline.

a. At the 0.05 level of significance, is there evidence that the mean purchase was different from 10 gallons?

b. Determine the *p*-value in (a).

c. At the 0.05 level of significance, is there evidence that fewer than 20% of all the motorists at the station purchased premium-grade gasoline?

d. What is your answer to (a) if the sample mean equals 10.3 gallons?

e. What is your answer to (c) if 7 motorists purchased premium-grade gasoline?

9.87 An auditor for a government agency is assigned the task of evaluating reimbursement for office visits to physicians paid by Medicare. The audit was conducted on a sample of 75 of the reimbursements, with the following results:

- In 12 of the office visits, an incorrect amount of reimbursement was provided.
- The amount of reimbursement was $\overline{X} = \$93.70$, $S = \$34.55$.

a. At the 0.05 level of significance, is there evidence that the mean reimbursement was less than $100?
b. At the 0.05 level of significance, is there evidence that the proportion of incorrect reimbursements in the population was greater than 0.10?
c. Discuss the underlying assumptions of the test used in (a).
d. What is your answer to (a) if the sample mean equals $90?
e. What is your answer to (b) if 15 office visits had incorrect reimbursements?

9.88 A bank branch located in a commercial district of a city has developed an improved process for serving customers during the noon-to-1:00 p.m. lunch period. The waiting time (defined as the time the customer enters the line until he or she reaches the teller window) of all customers during this hour is recorded over a period of 1 week. A random sample of 15 customers (see the data file **bank1.xls**) is selected, and the results are as follows:

4.21   5.55   3.02   5.13   4.77   2.34   3.54   3.20
4.50   6.10   0.38   5.12   6.46   6.19   3.79

a. At the 0.05 level of significance, is there evidence that the mean waiting time is less than 5 minutes?
b. What assumption must hold in order to perform the test in (a)?
c. Evaluate the assumption in (b) through a graphical approach. Discuss.
d. As a customer walks into the branch office during the lunch hour, she asks the branch manager how long she can expect to wait. The branch manager replies, "Almost certainly not longer than 5 minutes." On the basis of the results of (a), evaluate this statement.

9.89 A manufacturing company produces electrical insulators. If the insulators break when in use, a short circuit is likely to occur. To test the strength of the insulators, destructive testing is carried out to determine how much *force* is required to break the insulators. Force is measured by observing the number of pounds of force applied to the insulator before it breaks. The following data (stored in the **force.xls** file) are from 30 insulators subject to this testing:

Force (in the Number of Pounds Required to Break the Insulator)

1,870 1,728 1,656 1,610 1,634 1,784 1,522 1,696 1,592 1,662

1,866 1,764 1,734 1,662 1,734 1,774 1,550 1,756 1,762 1,866

1,820 1,744 1,788 1,688 1,810 1,752 1,680 1,810 1,652 1,736

a. At the 0.05 level of significance, is there evidence that the mean force is greater than 1,500 pounds?
b. What assumption must hold in order to perform the test in (a)?
c. Evaluate the assumption in (b) through a graphical approach. Discuss.
d. Based on (a), what can you conclude about the strength of the insulators?

9.90 An important quality characteristic used by the manufacturer of Boston and Vermont asphalt shingles is the amount of moisture the shingles contain when they are packaged. Customers may feel that they have purchased a product lacking in quality if they find moisture and wet shingles inside the packaging. In some cases, excessive moisture can cause the granules attached to the shingle for texture and coloring purposes to fall off the shingle, resulting in appearance problems. To monitor the amount of moisture present, the company conducts moisture tests. A shingle is weighed and then dried. The shingle is then reweighed, and, based on the amount of moisture taken out of the product, the pounds of moisture per 100 square feet are calculated. The company would like to show that the mean moisture content is less than 0.35 pounds per 100 square feet. The data file **moisture.xls** includes 36 measurements (in pounds per 100 square feet) for Boston shingles and 31 for Vermont shingles.

a. For the Boston shingles, is there evidence at the 0.05 level of significance that the mean moisture content is less than 0.35 pounds per 100 square feet?
b. Interpret the meaning of the *p*-value in (a).
c. For the Vermont shingles, is there evidence at the 0.05 level of significance that the mean moisture content is less than 0.35 pounds per 100 square feet?
d. Interpret the meaning of the *p*-value in (c).
e. What assumption must hold in order to perform the tests in (a) and (c)?
f. Evaluate the assumption in (e) for Boston shingles and Vermont shingles by using a graphical approach. Discuss.

9.91 Studies conducted by the manufacturer of Boston and Vermont asphalt shingles have shown product weight to be a major factor in the customer's perception of quality. Moreover, the weight represents the amount of raw materials being used and is therefore very important to the company from a cost standpoint. The last stage of the assembly line packages the shingles before the packages are placed on wooden pallets. Once a pallet is full (a pallet for most brands holds 16 squares of shingles), it is weighed, and the measurement is recorded. The data file **pallet.xls** contains the weight (in pounds) from a sample of 368 pallets of Boston shingles and 330 pallets of Vermont shingles.

a. For the Boston shingles, is there evidence that the mean weight is different from 3,150 pounds?
b. Interpret the meaning of the *p*-value in (a).
c. For the Vermont shingles, is there evidence that the mean weight is different from 3,700 pounds?
d. Interpret the meaning of the *p*-value in (c).
e. What assumption is needed for (a) and (c)?
f. Evaluate this assumption through a graphical approach. Discuss.

9.92 The manufacturer of Boston and Vermont asphalt shingles provides its customers with a 20-year warranty on most of its products. To determine whether a shingle will last as long as the warranty period, accelerated-life testing is conducted at the manufacturing plant. Accelerated-life testing exposes the shingle to the stresses it would be subject to in a lifetime of normal use in a laboratory setting via an experiment that takes only a few minutes to conduct. In this test, a shingle is repeatedly scraped with a brush for a short period of time, and the shingle granules removed by the brushing are weighed (in grams). Shingles that experience low amounts of granule loss are expected to last longer in normal use than shingles that experience high amounts of granule loss. The data file **granule.xls** contains a sample of 170 measurements made on the company's Boston shingles and 140 measurements made on Vermont shingles.

a. For the Boston shingles, is there evidence that the mean granule loss is different from 0.50 grams?

b. Interpret the meaning of the p-value in (a).

c. For the Vermont shingles, is there evidence that the mean granule loss is different from 0.50 grams?

d. Interpret the meaning of the p-value in (c).

e. What assumption is needed for (a) and (c)?

f. Evaluate this assumption through a graphical approach. Discuss.

Report Writing Exercises

9.93 Referring to the results of Problems 9.90–9.92 concerning Boston and Vermont shingles, write a report that evaluates the moisture level, weight, and granule loss of the two types of shingles.

Managing the *Springville Herald*

Continuing its monitoring of the blackness of the newspaper print, first described in the Chapter 6 Managing the *Springville Herald* case, the production department of the newspaper wants to ensure that the mean blackness of the print for all newspapers is at least 0.97 on a standard scale in which the target value is 1.0. A random sample of 50 newspapers has been selected, and the blackness of each paper has been measured (and stored in the **sh9.xls** file). Calculate the sample statistics and determine whether there is evidence that the mean blackness is less than 0.97. Write a memo to management that summarizes your conclusions.

Blackness of 50 Newspapers

0.854	1.023	1.005	1.030	1.219	0.977	1.044	0.778	1.122	1.114
1.091	1.086	1.141	0.931	0.723	0.934	1.060	1.047	0.800	0.889
1.012	0.695	0.869	0.734	1.131	0.993	0.762	0.814	1.108	0.805
1.223	1.024	0.884	0.799	0.870	0.898	0.621	0.818	1.113	1.286
1.052	0.678	1.162	0.808	1.012	0.859	0.951	1.112	1.003	0.972

Web Case

Apply your knowledge about hypothesis testing in this Web Case, which continues the cereal-fill-packaging dispute Web Case from Chapter 7.

Concerned about statements of groups such as the Consumers Concerned About Cereal Cheaters (CCACC) (see the Web Case for Chapter 7). Oxford Cereals recently conducted a public experiment concerning cereal packaging. The company claims that the results of the experiments refute the CCACC allegations that Oxford Cereals has been cheating consumers by packaging cereals at less than labeled weights. Review the Oxford Cereals' press release and supporting documents that describe the experiment at the company's Web site,

www.prenhall.com/Springville/OC_FullUp.htm, and then answer the following:

1. Are the results of the independent testing valid? Why or why not? If you were conducting the experiment, is there anything you would change?

2. Do the results support the claim that Oxford Cereals is not cheating its customers?

3. Is the claim of the Oxford Cereals CEO that many cereal boxes contain *more* than 368 grams surprising? Is it true?

4. Could there ever be a circumstance in which the results of the public experiment *and* the CCACC's results are both correct? Explain.

REFERENCES

1. Bradley, J. V., *Distribution-Free Statistical Tests* (Upper Saddle River, NJ: Prentice Hall, 1968).

2. Daniel, W., *Applied Nonparametric Statistics*, 2nd ed. (Boston: Houghton Mifflin, 1990).

3. *Microsoft Excel 2007* (Redmond, WA: Microsoft Corp., 2007).

Excel Companion
to Chapter 9

E9.1   USING THE *Z* TEST FOR THE MEAN (σ KNOWN)

You conduct a *Z* test for the mean (σ known) by either selecting the PHStat2 Z Test for the Mean, sigma known procedure or by making entries in the **Z Mean.xls** workbook.

Using PHStat2 Z Test for the Mean, Sigma Known

Select **PHStat → One-Sample Tests → Z Test for the Mean, sigma known**. In the Z Test for the Mean, sigma known, dialog box (shown below), enter values for the **Null Hypothesis**, the **Level of Significance**, and the **Population Standard Deviation**. If you know the sample size and sample mean of your sample, click **Sample**

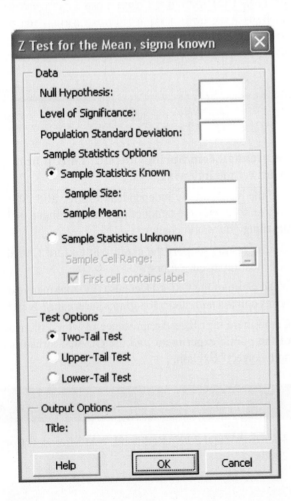

Statistics Known and enter those values. Otherwise, click **Sample Statistics Unknown** and enter the cell range of your sample as the **Sample Cell Range**. Then click one of the test options, enter a title as the **Title**, and click **OK**.

Using Z Mean.xls

You open and use either the **ZMean TT** or **ZMean_All** worksheets of the **Z Mean.xls** workbook to apply the *Z* test for the mean (σ known). These worksheets use the **NORMSINV(***P<X***)** function to determine the lower and upper critical values and use the **NORMSDIST(Z *value***)** function to compute the *p*-values from the *Z* value calculated in cell B12. The **ZMean_TT** worksheet (see Figure 9.5 on page 338) applies the two-tail *Z* test to the Example 9.2 cereal-fill example. The **ZMean_All** worksheet (see Figure E9.1) includes both the two-tail test and the upper- and lower-tail tests on one worksheet. To adapt these worksheets to other problems, change (if necessary) the null hypothesis, level of significance, population standard deviation, sample size, and sample mean values in the tinted cells B4 through B8.

If you want the ZMean_All worksheet to show only one of the single-tail tests, first make a copy of that worksheet (see the Excel Companion to Chapter 1). For a lower-tail-test-only worksheet, select and delete rows 25 through 28 and then select and delete rows 14 through 19. For an upper-tail-test-only worksheet, select and delete rows 14 through 24.

About the IF Function

Both worksheets of the **Z Mean.xls** workbook and all other hypothesis-testing worksheets presented in the rest of the book use the **IF (***comparison, what to do if comparison holds, what to do if comparison fails***)** function to suggest whether you should reject the null hypothesis. (You should always verify the results of worksheets and not blindly accept results reported by formulas containing the IF function.)

You need to supply three things when using an IF function in a formula. The comparison is an algebraic or logical comparison between two things. In Figure E9.1, the *p*-values are compared to the level of significance.

FIGURE E9.1

ZMean_All worksheet

	A	B
1	Z Test of the Hypothesis for the Mean	
2		
3	**Data**	
4	Null Hypothesis μ=	368
5	Level of Significance	0.05
6	Population Standard Deviation	15
7	Sample Size	25
8	Sample Mean	372.5
9		
10	Intermediate Calculations	
11	Standard Error of the Mean	3
12	Z Test Statistic	1.5
13		
14	**Two-Tail Test**	
15	Lower Critical Value	-1.9600
16	Upper Critical Value	1.9600
17	*p*-Value	0.1336
18	Do not reject the null hypothesis	
19		
20	**Lower-Tail Test**	
21	Lower Critical Value	-1.6449
22	*p*-Value	0.9332
23	Do not reject the null hypothesis	
24		
25	**Upper-Tail Test**	
26	Upper Critical Value	1.6449
27	*p*-Value	0.0668
28	Do not reject the null hypothesis	

Formulas (column B / A):
- Row 11: =B6/SQRT(B7)
- Row 12: =(B8 - B4)/B11
- Row 15: =NORMSINV(B5/2)
- Row 16: =NORMSINV(1 - B5/2)
- Row 17: =2 * (1 - NORMSDIST(ABS(B12)))
- Row 18: =IF(B17 < B5, "Reject the null hypothesis", "Do not reject the null hypothesis")
- Row 21: =NORMSINV(B5)
- Row 22: =NORMSDIST(B12)
- Row 23: =IF(B22 < B5, "Reject the null hypothesis", "Do not reject the null hypothesis")
- Row 26: =NORMSINV(1 - B5)
- Row 27: =1 - NORMSDIST(B12)
- Row 28: =IF(B27 < B5, "Reject the null hypothesis", "Do not reject the null hypothesis")

What to do if comparison holds/fails are either text values to display (as in Figure E9.1) or numeric values or formulas to use as the cell contents. In Figure E9.1, "Do not reject the null hypothesis" is displayed in rows 18, 23, and 28 because all three *p*-values (in cells B17, B22, and B27) are greater than the level of significance in cell B5. (By the way, text values in IF functions must be enclosed by a pair of quotation marks as they are in Figure E9.1.)

You should always enter formulas containing the IF function as a single, continuous line, even though such formulas are generally shown in this text on two physical lines (as in Figure E9.1). For the hypothesis-testing worksheets, the formulas containing the IF function have been entered into column A cells so that their text values display across columns A and B.

E9.2 USING THE *t* TEST FOR THE MEAN (σ unknown)

You conduct a *t* test for the mean (σ unknown) by either selecting the PHStat2 t Test for the Mean, sigma unknown procedure or by making entries in the T Mean.xls workbook.

Using PHStat2 *t* Test for the Mean, Sigma Unknown

Select **PHStat → One-Sample Tests → t Test for the Mean, sigma unknown**. In the t Test for the Mean, sigma unknown dialog box (shown at right), enter values for the **Null Hypothesis** and the **Level of Significance**. If you know the sample size, sample mean, and sample standard deviation, click **Sample Statistics Known** and enter those

values. Otherwise, click **Sample Statistics Unknown** and enter the cell range of your data as the **Sample Cell Range**. Then, click one of the test options, enter a title as the **Title**, and click **OK**.

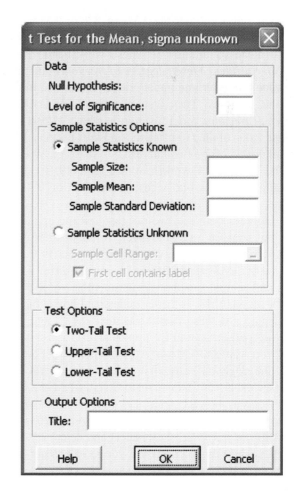

FIGURE E9.2

TMean_All worksheet

	A	B
1	t Test for the Hypothesis of the Mean	
2		
3	**Data**	
4	**Null Hypothesis** μ=	120
5	**Level of Significance**	0.05
6	**Sample Size**	12
7	**Sample Mean**	112.85
8	**Sample Standard Deviation**	20.8
9		
10	Intermediate Calculations	
11	Standard Error of the Mean	6.0044
12	Degrees of Freedom	11
13	*t* Test Statistic	-1.1908
14		
15	**Two-Tail Test**	
16	**Lower Critical Value**	-2.2010
17	**Upper Critical Value**	2.2010
18	*p*-Value	0.2588
19	Do not reject the null hypothesis	
20		
21	**Lower-Tail Test**	
22	**Lower Critical Value**	-1.7959
23	*p*-Value	0.1294
24	Do not reject the null hypothesis	
25		
26	**Upper-Tail Test**	
27	**Upper Critical Value**	1.7959
28	*p*-Value	0.8706
29	Do not reject the null hypothesis	

Formulas (column to the right of B):

- Row 11: =B8/SQRT(B6)
- Row 12: =B6 - 1
- Row 13: =(B7 - B4)/B11
- Row 16: =-(TINV(B5, B12))
- Row 17: =TINV(B5, B12)
- Row 18: =TDIST(ABS(B13), B12, 2)
- Row 19: =IF(B18 < B5, "Reject the null hypothesis", "Do not reject the null hypothesis")
- Row 22: =-(TINV(2 * B5, B12))
- Row 23: =IF(B13 < 0, E22, E23)
- Row 24: =IF(B23 < B5, "Reject the null hypothesis", "Do not reject the null hypothesis")
- Row 27: =(TINV(2 * B5, B12))
- Row 28: =IF(B13 < 0, E23, E22)
- Row 29: =IF(B28 < B5, "Reject the null hypothesis", "Do not reject the null hypothesis")

Not shown
Cell E22: =TDIST(ABS(B13), B12, 1)
Cell E23: =1 - E22

Using T Mean.xls

You open and use either the **TMean_TT** or **TMean_All** worksheets of the `T Mean.xls` workbook to apply the *t* test for the mean (σ unknown). These worksheets use the **TINV(1-*confidence level, degrees of freedom*)** function to determine the lower and upper critical values and to compute the *p*-values. They also use the **TDIST(ABS(*t*), *degrees of freedom, tails*)** function in which **ABS(*t*)** is the absolute value of the *t* test statistic and *tails* is either 1 for a one-tail test or 2 for a two-tail test.

The **TMean_TT** worksheet (see Figure 9.10 on page 348) applies the two-tail *t* test to the Section 9.4 sales invoices example. The **TMean_All** worksheet (see Figure E9.2) includes both the two-tail test and the upper- and lower-tail tests on one worksheet. To adapt these worksheets to other problems, change (if necessary) the null hypothesis, level of significance, sample size, sample mean, and sample standard deviation values in the tinted cells B4 through B8. To better understand how a message gets displayed in these worksheets, read the "About the IF Function" part of Section E9.1 on page 364.

If you want the TMean_All worksheet to show only one of the single-tail tests, first make a copy of that worksheet (see the Excel Companion to Chapter 1). For a lower-tail-test-only worksheet, select and delete rows 26 through 29 and then select and delete cell range A15:B20. For an upper-tail-test-only worksheet, select and delete cell range A15:B25. These instructions ask you to select and delete certain cell ranges in order to preserve the D20:E23 calculations area cell range (which is not shown in Figure E9.2).

E9.3   USING THE *Z* TEST FOR THE PROPORTION

You conduct a *Z* test for the proportion by either selecting the PHStat2 Z Test for the Proportion procedure or by making entries in the `Z Proportion.xls` workbook.

Using PHStat2 Z Test for the Proportion

Select **PHStat → One-Sample Tests → Z Test for the Proportion**. In the Z Test for the Proportion dialog box (shown below), enter values for the **Null Hypothesis**, the

Level of Significance, the **Number of Successes**, and the **Sample Size**. Click one of the test options, enter a title as the **Title**, and click **OK**.

Using Z Proportion.xls

You open and use either the **ZProp_TT** or **ZProp_All** worksheets of the `Z Proportion.xls` workbook to apply the Z test for the proportion. These worksheets use the **NORMSINV(P<X)** function to determine the lower and upper critical values and the **NORMSDIST(Z value)** function to compute the p-values.

The **ZProp_TT** worksheet (see Figure 9.15 on page 355) applies the two-tail Z test to the Section 9.5 competitive threat example. The **ZProp_All** worksheet (see Figure E9.3)

includes both the two-tail test and the upper- and lower-tail tests on one worksheet. To adapt these worksheet to other problems, change (if necessary) the null hypothesis, level of significance, number of successes, and sample size values in the tinted cells B4 through B8. To better understand how messages get displayed in these worksheets, read the "About the IF Function" part of Section E9.1 on page 364.

If you want the ZProp_All worksheet to show only one of the single-tail tests, first make a copy of that worksheet (see the Excel Companion to Chapter 1). For a lower-tail-test-only worksheet, select and delete rows 25 through 28 and then select and delete rows 14 through 19. For an upper-tail-test-only worksheet, select and delete rows 14 through 24.

FIGURE E9.3

ZProp_All worksheet

	A	B	
1	Wal-Mart As Biggest Threat Hypothesis Test		
2			
3	Data		
4	Null Hypothesis $p=$	0.5	
5	Level of Significance	0.05	
6	Number of Successes	78	
7	Sample Size	151	
8			
9	Intermediate Calculations		
10	Sample Proportion	0.5166	=B6/B7
11	Standard Error	0.0407	=SQRT(B4*(1 - B4)/B7)
12	Z Test Statistic	0.4069	=(B10 - B4)/B11
13			
14	Two-Tail Test		
15	Lower Critical Value	-1.9600	=NORMSINV(B5/2)
16	Upper Critical value	1.9600	=NORMSINV(1 - B5/2)
17	p-Value	0.6841	=2 * (1 - NORMSDIST(ABS(B12)))
18	Do not reject the null hypothesis		=IF(B17 < B5, "Reject the null hypothesis", "Do not reject the null hypothesis")
19			
20	Lower-Tail Test		
21	Lower Critical Value	-1.6449	=NORMSINV(B5)
22	p-Value	0.6580	=NORMSDIST(B12)
23	Do not reject the null hypothesis		=IF(B22 < B5, "Reject the null hypothesis", "Do not reject the null hypothesis")
24			
25	Upper-Tail Test		
26	Upper Critical Value	1.6449	=NORMSINV(1 - B5)
27	p-Value	0.3420	=1 - NORMSDIST(B12)
28	Do not reject the null hypothesis		=IF(B27 < B5, "Reject the null hypothesis", "Do not reject the null hypothesis")

CHAPTER 10

Two-Sample Tests

USING STATISTICS @ BLK Foods

LEARNING OBJECTIVES

In this chapter, you learn how to use hypothesis testing for comparing the difference between:

- The means of two independent populations
- The means of two related populations
- Two proportions
- The variances of two independent populations

Using Statistics @ BLK Foods

Does the type of display used in a supermarket affect the sales of products? As the regional sales manager for BLK Foods, you want to compare the sales volume of BLK cola when the product is placed in its the normal shelf location to the sales volume when the product is featured in a special end-aisle display. To test the effectiveness of the end-aisle displays, you select 20 stores from the BLK supermarket chain that all experience similar storewide sales volumes. You then randomly assign 10 of the 20 stores to group 1 and 10 to group 2. The managers of the 10 stores in group 1 place the BLK cola in the normal shelf location, alongside the other cola products. The 10 stores in group 2 use the special end-aisle promotional display. At the end of one week, the sales of BLK cola are recorded. How can you determine whether sales of BLK cola using the end-aisle displays are the same as those when the cola is placed in the normal shelf location? How can you decide if the variability in BLK cola sales from store to store is the same for the two types of displays? How could you use the answers to these questions to improve sales of BLK colas?

Hypothesis testing provides a *confirmatory* approach to data analysis. In Chapter 9, you learned a variety of commonly used hypothesis-testing procedures that relate to a single sample of data selected from a single population. In this chapter, you will learn how to extend hypothesis testing to procedures that compare statistics from two samples of data taken from two populations. One such extension would be asking, "Are the mean weekly sales of BLK cola when using an end-aisle display equal to the mean weekly sales of BLK cola when placed in the normal shelf location?"

10.1   COMPARING THE MEANS OF TWO INDEPENDENT POPULATIONS

Z Test for the Difference Between Two Means

Suppose that you take a random sample of n_1 from one population and a random sample of n_2 from a second population. The data collected in each sample are from a numerical variable. In the first population, the mean is represented by the symbol μ_1, and the standard deviation is represented by the symbol σ_1. In the second population, the mean is represented by the symbol μ_2, and the standard deviation is represented by the symbol σ_2.

The test statistic used to determine the difference between the population means is based on the difference between the sample means $(\overline{X}_1 - \overline{X}_2)$. If you assume that the samples are randomly and independently selected from populations that are normally distributed, this statistic follows the standardized normal distribution. If the populations are not normally distributed, the Z test is still appropriate if the sample sizes are large enough (typically n_1 and $n_2 \geq 30$; see the Central Limit Theorem in Section 7.4). Equation (10.1) defines the **Z test for the difference between two means**.

Z TEST FOR THE DIFFERENCE BETWEEN TWO MEANS

$$Z = \frac{(\overline{X}_1 - \overline{X}_2) - (\mu_1 - \mu_2)}{\sqrt{\dfrac{\sigma_1^2}{n_1} + \dfrac{\sigma_2^2}{n_2}}}$$

(10.1)

where

$$\bar{X}_1 = \text{mean of the sample taken from population 1}$$

$$\mu_1 = \text{mean of population 1}$$

$$\sigma_1^2 = \text{variance of population 1}$$

$$n_1 = \text{size of the sample taken from population 1}$$

$$\bar{X}_2 = \text{mean of the sample taken from population 2}$$

$$\mu_2 = \text{mean of population 2}$$

$$\sigma_2^2 = \text{variance of population 2}$$

$$n_2 = \text{size of the sample taken from population 2}$$

The test statistic Z follows a standardized normal distribution.

Pooled-Variance t Test for the Difference Between Two Means

In most cases, the variances of the two populations are not known. The only information you usually have are the sample means and the sample variances. If you assume that the samples are randomly and independently selected from populations that are normally distributed and that the population variances are equal (that is, $\sigma_1^2 = \sigma_2^2$), you can use a **pooled-variance t test** to determine whether there is a significant difference between the means of the two populations. If the populations are not normally distributed, the pooled-variance t test is still appropriate if the sample sizes are large enough (typically n_1 and $n_2 \geq 30$; see the Central Limit Theorem in Section 7.4).

To test the null hypothesis of no difference in the means of two independent populations:

$$H_0: \mu_1 = \mu_2 \text{ or } \mu_1 - \mu_2 = 0$$

against the alternative that the means are not the same:

$$H_1: \mu_1 \neq \mu_2 \text{ or } \mu_1 - \mu_2 \neq 0$$

[1]When the two sample sizes are equal (that is, $n_1 = n_2$), the equation for the pooled variance can be simplified to $S_p^2 = \dfrac{S_1^2 + S_2^2}{2}$

you use the pooled-variance t-test statistic shown in Equation (10.2). The pooled-variance t test gets its name from the fact that the test statistic pools or combines the two sample variances S_1^2 and S_2^2 to compute S_p^2, the best estimate of the variance common to both populations under the assumption that the two population variances are equal.[1]

POOLED-VARIANCE t TEST FOR THE DIFFERENCE BETWEEN TWO MEANS

$$t = \frac{(\bar{X}_1 - \bar{X}_2) - (\mu_1 - \mu_2)}{\sqrt{S_p^2 \left(\dfrac{1}{n_1} + \dfrac{1}{n_2} \right)}} \tag{10.2}$$

where

$$S_p^2 = \frac{(n_1 - 1)S_1^2 + (n_2 - 1)S_2^2}{(n_1 - 1) + (n_2 - 1)}$$

$$S_p^2 = \text{pooled variance}$$

$$\bar{X}_1 = \text{mean of the sample taken from population 1}$$

$$S_1^2 = \text{variance of the sample taken from population 1}$$

$$n_1 = \text{size of the sample taken from population 1}$$

$$\bar{X}_2 = \text{mean of the sample taken from population 2}$$

$$S_2^2 = \text{variance of the sample taken from population 2}$$

$$n_2 = \text{size of the sample taken from population 2}$$

The test statistic t follows a t distribution with $n_1 + n_2 - 2$ degrees of freedom.

The pooled-variance t-test statistic follows a t distribution with $n_1 + n_2 - 2$ degrees of freedom. For a given level of significance, α, in a two-tail test, you reject the null hypothesis if the computed t test statistic is greater than the upper-tail critical value from the t distribution or if the computed test statistic is less than the lower-tail critical value from the t distribution. Figure 10.1 displays the regions of rejection. In a one-tail test in which the rejection region is in the lower tail, you reject the null hypothesis if the computed test statistic is less than the lower-tail critical value from the t distribution. In a one-tail test in which the rejection region is in the upper tail, you reject the null hypothesis if the computed test statistic is greater than the upper-tail critical value from the t distribution.

FIGURE 10.1

Regions of rejection and nonrejection for the pooled-variance t test for the difference between the means (two-tail test)

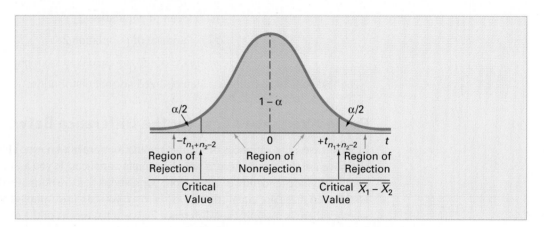

To demonstrate the use of the pooled-variance t test, return to the Using Statistics scenario on page 370. You want to determine whether the mean weekly sales of BLK cola are the same when using a normal shelf location and when using an end-aisle display. There are two populations of interest. The first population is the set of all possible weekly sales of BLK cola *if* all the BLK supermarkets used the normal shelf location. The second population is the set of all possible weekly sales of BLK cola *if* all the BLK supermarkets used the end-aisle displays. The first sample contains the weekly sales of BLK cola from the 10 stores selected to use the normal shelf location, and the second sample contains the weekly sales of BLK cola from the 10 stores selected to use the end-aisle display. Table 10.1 contains the cola sales (in number of cases) for the two samples (see the `cola.xls` file).

TABLE 10.1

Comparing BLK Cola Weekly Sales from Two Different Display Locations (in Number of Cases)

Display Location									
Normal					**End-Aisle**				
22	34	52	62	30	52	71	76	54	67
40	64	84	56	59	83	66	90	77	84

The null and alternative hypotheses are

$$H_0: \mu_1 = \mu_2 \text{ or } \mu_1 - \mu_2 = 0$$
$$H_1: \mu_1 \neq \mu_2 \text{ or } \mu_1 - \mu_2 \neq 0$$

Assuming that the samples are from underlying normal populations having equal variances, you can use the pooled-variance t test. The t test statistic follows a t distribution with $10 + 10 - 2 = 18$ degrees of freedom. Using the $\alpha = 0.05$ level of significance, you divide the rejection region into the two tails for this two-tail test (that is, two equal parts of 0.025 each). Table E.3 shows that the critical values for this two-tail test are +2.1009 and −2.1009. As shown in Figure 10.2, the decision rule is

$$\text{Reject } H_0 \text{ if } t > t_{18} = +2.1009$$
$$\text{or if } t < -t_{18} = -2.1009;$$
$$\text{otherwise, do not reject } H_0.$$

FIGURE 10.2

Two-tail test of hypothesis for the difference between the means at the 0.05 level of significance with 18 degrees of freedom

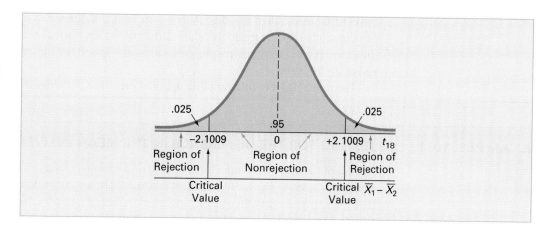

From Figure 10.3, the computed t statistic for this test is -3.0446, and the p-value is 0.0070.

FIGURE 10.3

Microsoft Excel t test results for the two display locations

See Section E10.3 to create this.

	A	B	C
1	t-Test: Two-Sample Assuming Equal Variances		
2			
3		Normal	End-Aisle
4	Mean	50.3	72
5	Variance	350.6778	157.3333
6	Observations	10	10
7	Pooled Variance	254.0056	
8	Hypothesized Mean Difference	0	
9	df	18	
10	t Stat	-3.0446	
11	P(T<=t) one-tail	0.0035	
12	t Critical one-tail	1.7341	
13	P(T<=t) two-tail	0.0070	
14	t Critical two-tail	2.1009	

Using Equation (10.2) on page 371 and the descriptive statistics provided in Figure 10.3,

$$t = \frac{(\overline{X}_1 - \overline{X}_2) - (\mu_1 - \mu_2)}{\sqrt{S_p^2\left(\dfrac{1}{n_1} + \dfrac{1}{n_2}\right)}}$$

where

$$S_p^2 = \frac{(n_1 - 1)S_1^2 + (n_2 - 1)S_2^2}{(n_1 - 1) + (n_2 - 1)}$$

$$= \frac{9(350.6778) + 9(157.3333)}{9 + 9} = 254.0056$$

Therefore,

$$t = \frac{(50.3 - 72.0) - 0.0}{\sqrt{254.0056\left(\dfrac{1}{10} + \dfrac{1}{10}\right)}} = \frac{-21.7}{\sqrt{50.801}} = -3.0446$$

You reject the null hypothesis because $t = -3.0446 < t_{18} = -2.1009$. The p-value (as computed from Microsoft Excel) is 0.0070. In other words, the probability that $t > 3.0446$ or $t < -3.0446$ is equal to 0.0070. This p-value indicates that if the population means are equal, the probability of observing a difference this large or larger in the two sample means is only 0.0070. Because the p-value is less than $\alpha = 0.05$, there is sufficient evidence to reject the null hypothesis. You can conclude that the mean sales are different for the normal shelf location and the end-aisle location. Based on these results, the sales are lower for the normal location (than for the end-aisle location).

Example 10.1 provides another application of the pooled-variance t-test.

EXAMPLE 10.1

TESTING FOR THE DIFFERENCE IN THE MEAN DELIVERY TIMES

A local pizza restaurant and a local branch of a national chain are located across the street from a college campus. The local pizza restaurant advertises that it delivers to the dormitories faster than the national chain. In order to determine whether this advertisement is valid, you and some friends have decided to order 10 pizzas from the local pizza restaurant and 10 pizzas from the national chain, all at different times. The delivery times, in minutes (see the pizzatime.xls file), are shown in Table 10.2.

TABLE 10.2

Delivery Times for Local Pizza Restaurant and National Pizza Chain

Local	Chain	Local	Chain
16.8	22.0	18.1	19.5
11.7	15.2	14.1	17.0
15.6	18.7	21.8	19.5
16.7	15.6	13.9	16.5
17.5	20.8	20.8	24.0

At the 0.05 level of significance, is there evidence that the mean delivery time for the local pizza restaurant is less than the mean delivery time for the national pizza chain?

SOLUTION Because you want to know whether the mean is *lower* for the local pizza restaurant than for the national pizza chain, you have a one-tail test with the following null and alternative hypotheses:

H_0: $\mu_1 \geq \mu_2$ (The mean delivery time for the local pizza restaurant is equal to or greater than the mean delivery time for the national pizza chain.)

H_1: $\mu_1 < \mu_2$ (The mean delivery time for the local pizza restaurant is less than the mean delivery time for the national pizza chain.)

Figure 10.4 displays Microsoft Excel results of the pooled t test for these data.

FIGURE 10.4

Microsoft Excel results of the pooled t test for the pizza delivery time data

See Section E10.3 to create this.

	A	B	C
1	t-Test: Two-Sample Assuming Equal Variances		
2			
3		Local	Chain
4	Mean	16.7	18.88
5	Variance	9.5822	8.2151
6	Observations	10	10
7	Pooled Variance	8.8987	
8	Hypothesized Mean Difference	0	
9	df	18	
10	t Stat	-1.6341	
11	P(T<=t) one-tail	0.0598	
12	t Critical one-tail	1.7341	
13	P(T<=t) two-tail	0.1196	
14	t Critical two-tail	2.1009	

Using Equation (10.2) on page 371,

$$t = \frac{(\overline{X}_1 - \overline{X}_2) - (\mu_1 - \mu_2)}{\sqrt{S_p^2\left(\dfrac{1}{n_1} + \dfrac{1}{n_2}\right)}}$$

where

$$S_p^2 = \frac{(n_1 - 1)S_1^2 + (n_2 - 1)S_2^2}{(n_1 - 1) + (n_2 - 1)}$$

$$= \frac{9(9.5822) + 9(8.2151)}{9 + 9} = 8.8987$$

Therefore,

$$t = \frac{(16.7 - 18.88) - 0.0}{\sqrt{8.8987\left(\dfrac{1}{10} + \dfrac{1}{10}\right)}} = \frac{-2.18}{\sqrt{1.7797}} = -1.6341$$

You do not reject the null hypothesis because $t = -1.6341 > t_{18} = -1.7341$. The p-value (as computed from Microsoft Excel) is 0.0598. This p-value indicates that the probability that $t < -1.6341$ is equal to 0.0598. In other words, if the population means are equal, the probability that the sample mean delivery time for the local pizza restaurant is at least 2.18 minutes faster than the national chain is 0.0598. Because the p-value is greater than $\alpha = 0.05$, there is insufficient evidence to reject the null hypothesis. Based on these results, there is insufficient evidence for the local pizza restaurant to make the advertising claim that it has a faster delivery time.

In testing for the difference between the means, you assume that the populations are normally distributed, with equal variances. For situations in which the two populations have equal variances, the pooled-variance t test is **robust** (or not sensitive) to moderate departures from the assumption of normality, provided that the sample sizes are large. In such situations, you can use the pooled-variance t test without serious effects on its power. However, if you cannot assume that the data in each group are from normally distributed populations, you have two choices. You can use a nonparametric procedure, such as the Wilcoxon rank sum test (covered in Section 12.5), that does not depend on the assumption of normality for the two populations, or you can use a normalizing transformation (see reference 5) on each of the outcomes and then use the pooled-variance t test.

To check the assumption of normality in each of the two groups, observe the box-and-whisker plot of the sales for the two display locations in Figure 10.5. There appears to be only moderate departure from normality, so the assumption of normality needed for the t test is not seriously violated.

FIGURE 10.5

Microsoft Excel box-and-whisker plot for the sales for two aisle locations

See Section E3.4 to create this.

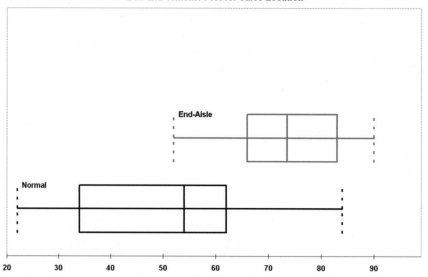

Confidence Interval Estimate of the Difference Between Two Means

Instead of, or in addition to, testing for the difference in the means of two independent populations, you can use Equation (10.3) to develop a confidence interval estimate of the difference in the means.

CONFIDENCE INTERVAL ESTIMATE OF THE DIFFERENCE BETWEEN TWO MEANS

$$(\bar{X}_1 - \bar{X}_2) \pm t_{n_1+n_2-2}\sqrt{S_p^2\left(\frac{1}{n_1} + \frac{1}{n_2}\right)} \qquad (10.3)$$

or

$$(\bar{X}_1 - \bar{X}_2) - t_{n_1+n_2-2}\sqrt{S_p^2\left(\frac{1}{n_1} + \frac{1}{n_2}\right)} \leq \mu_1 - \mu_2 \leq (\bar{X}_1 - \bar{X}_2) + t_{n_1+n_2-2}\sqrt{S_p^2\left(\frac{1}{n_1} + \frac{1}{n_2}\right)}$$

where $t_{n_1+n_2-2}$ is the critical value of the t distribution with $n_1 + n_2 - 2$ degrees of freedom for an area of $\alpha/2$ in the upper tail.

Using 95% confidence, the sample statistics reported in Figure 10.3 on page 373 and Equation (10.3),

$$\bar{X}_1 = 50.3,\ n_1 = 10,\ \bar{X}_2 = 72,\ n_2 = 10,\ S_p^2 = 254.0056,\ \text{and}\ t_{18} = 2.1009:$$

$$(50.3 - 72) \pm (2.1009)\sqrt{254.0056\left(\frac{1}{10} + \frac{1}{10}\right)}$$

$$-21.7 \pm (2.1009)(7.1275)$$

$$-21.7 \pm 14.97$$

$$-36.67 \leq \mu_1 - \mu_2 \leq -6.73$$

Therefore, you are 95% confident that the difference in mean sales between the normal shelf location and the end-aisle location is between −36.67 cases of cola and −6.73 cases of cola. In other words, the end-aisle location sells, on average, 6.73 to 36.67 cases more than the normal aisle location. From a hypothesis testing perspective, because the interval does not include zero, you reject the null hypothesis of no difference between the means of the two populations.

Separate-Variance *t* Test for the Difference Between Two Means

In testing for the difference between the means of two independent populations when the population variances are assumed to be equal, the sample variances are pooled together into a common estimate, S_p^2. However, if you cannot make this assumption, then the pooled-variance *t* test is inappropriate. In this case, it is more appropriate to use the **separate-variance *t* test** developed by Satterthwaite (see reference 4). In the Satterthwaite approximation procedure, you include the two separate sample variances in the computation of the *t*-test statistic—hence, the name separate-variance *t* test. The computations for the separate-variance *t* test are complicated but can be carried out by Microsoft Excel. Figure 10.6 presents the output from the separate-variance *t* test from Microsoft Excel for the cola data.

FIGURE 10.6

Microsoft Excel results of the separate-variance *t* test for the display location data

See Section E10.5 to create this.

	A	B	C
1	t-Test: Two-Sample Assuming Unequal Variances		
2			
3		*Normal*	*End-Aisle*
4	Mean	50.3	72
5	Variance	350.6778	157.3333
6	Observations	10	10
7	Hypothesized Mean Difference	0	
8	df	16	
9	t Stat	-3.0446	
10	P(T<=t) one-tail	0.0039	
11	t Critical one-tail	1.7459	
12	P(T<=t) two-tail	0.0077	
13	t Critical two-tail	2.1199	

In Figure 10.6, the test statistic is $t = -3.0446$ and the *p*-value is $0.0077 < 0.05$. Thus, the results for the separate-variance *t* test are almost exactly the same as those of the pooled-variance *t* test. The assumption of equality of population variances had no real effect on the results. Sometimes, however, the results from the pooled- and separate-variance *t* tests conflict because the assumption of equal variances is violated. Therefore, it is important that you evaluate the assumptions and use those results as a guide in appropriately selecting a test procedure. In Section 10.4, the *F* test is used to determine whether there is evidence of a difference in the two population variances. The results of that test can help you determine which of the *t* tests—pooled-variance or separate-variance—is more appropriate.

PROBLEMS FOR SECTION 10.1

Learning the Basics

PH Grade ASSIST **10.1** Given a sample of $n_1 = 40$ from a population with known standard deviation $\sigma_1 = 20$ and an independent sample of $n_2 = 50$ from another population with known standard deviation $\sigma_2 = 10$, what is the value of the Z test statistic for testing $H_0: \mu_1 = \mu_2$ if $\overline{X}_1 = 72$ and $\overline{X}_2 = 66$?

 10.2 What is your decision in Problem 10.1 if you are testing $H_0: \mu_1 = \mu_2$ against the two-tail alternative $H_1: \mu_1 \neq \mu_2$, using the level of significance $\alpha = 0.01$?

 10.3 What is the *p*-value in Problem 10.1 if you are testing $H_0: \mu_1 = \mu_2$ against the two-tail alternative $H_1: \mu_1 \neq \mu_2$?

10.4 Assume that you have a sample of $n_1 = 8$, with the sample mean $\overline{X}_1 = 42$ and a sample standard deviation of $S_1 = 4$, and you have an independent sample of $n_2 = 15$ from another population with a sample mean of $\overline{X}_2 = 34$ and the sample standard deviation $S_2 = 5$.

a. What is the value of the pooled-variance t-test statistic for testing $H_0: \mu_1 = \mu_2$?

b. In finding the critical value of the test statistic t, how many degrees of freedom are there?

c. Using the level of significance $\alpha = 0.01$, what is the critical value for a one-tail test of the hypothesis $H_0: \mu_1 \leq \mu_2$ against the alternative $H_1: \mu_1 > \mu_2$?

d. What is your statistical decision?

10.5 What assumptions about the two populations are necessary in Problem 10.4?

10.6 Referring to Problem 10.4, construct a 95% confidence interval estimate of the population difference between μ_1 and μ_2.

Applying the Concepts

 10.7 The operations manager at a light bulb factory wants to determine whether there is any difference in the mean life expectancy of bulbs manufactured on two different types of machines. The population standard deviation of machine I is 110 hours and of machine II is 125 hours. A random sample of 25 light bulbs from machine I indicates a sample mean of 375 hours, and a similar sample of 25 from machine II indicates a sample mean of 362 hours.

a. Using the 0.05 level of significance, is there any evidence of a difference in the mean life of bulbs produced by the two types of machines?

b. Compute the p-value in (a) and interpret its meaning.

 10.8 The purchasing director for an industrial parts factory is investigating the possibility of purchasing a new type of milling machine. She determines that the new machine will be bought if there is evidence that the parts produced have a higher mean breaking strength than those from the old machine. The population standard deviation of the breaking strength for the old machine is 10 kilograms and for the new machine is 9 kilograms. A sample of 100 parts taken from the old machine indicates a sample mean of 65 kilograms, and a similar sample of 100 from the new machine indicates a sample mean of 72 kilograms.

a. Using the 0.01 level of significance, is there evidence that the purchasing director should buy the new machine?

b. Compute the p-value in (a) and interpret its meaning.

10.9 Millions of dollars are spent each year on diet foods. Trends such as the low-fat diet or the low-carb Atkins diet have led to a host of new products. A study by Dr. Linda Stern of the Philadelphia Veterans Administration Hospital compared weight loss between obese patients on a low-fat diet and obese patients on a low-carb diet (Extracted from R. Bazell, "Study Casts Doubt on Advantages of Atkins Diet," **msnbc.com**, May 17, 2004). Let μ_1 represent the mean number of pounds obese patients on a low-fat diet lose in six months and μ_2 represent the mean number of pounds obese patients on a low-carb diet lose in six months.

a. State the null and alternative hypotheses if you want to test whether the mean weight loss between the two diets is equal.

b. In the context of this study, what is the meaning of a Type I error?

c. In the context of this study, what is the meaning of a Type II error?

d. Suppose that a sample of 100 obese patients on a low-fat diet lost a mean of 7.6 pounds in six months, with a standard deviation of 3.2 pounds, while a sample of 100 obese patients on a low-carb diet lost a mean of 6.7 pounds in six months, with a standard deviation of 3.9 pounds. Assuming that the population variances are equal and using a 0.05 level of significance, is there evidence of a difference in the mean weight loss of obese patients between the low-fat and low-carb diets?

10.10 When do children in the United States develop preferences for brand-name products? In a study reported in the *Journal of Consumer Psychology* (Extracted from G. W. Achenreiner and D. R. John, "The Meaning of Brand Names to Children: A Developmental Investigation," *Journal of Consumer Psychology*, 2003, 13(3), pp. 205–219), marketers showed children identical pictures of athletic shoes. One picture was labeled Nike, and one was labeled K-Mart. The children were asked to evaluate the shoes based on their appearance, quality, price, prestige, favorableness, and preference for owning. A score from 2 (highest product evaluation possible) to −2 (lowest product evaluation possible) was recorded for each child. The following table reports the results of the study:

Age by Brand	Sample Size	Sample Mean	Sample Standard Deviation
Age 8			
Nike	27	0.89	0.98
K-Mart	22	0.86	1.07
Age 12			
Nike	39	0.88	1.01
K-Mart	41	0.09	1.08
Age 16			
Nike	35	0.41	0.81
K-Mart	33	−0.29	0.92

a. Conduct a pooled-variance t test for the difference between two means for each of the three age groups. Use a level of significance of 0.05.

b. What assumptions are needed to conduct the tests in (a)?

c. Write a brief summary of your findings.

PH Grade ASSIST **10.11** According to a survey conducted in October 2001, consumers were trying to reduce their credit card debt (Extracted from M. Price, "Credit Debts Get Cut Down to Size," *Newsday*, November 25, 2001, p. F3). Based on a sample of 1,000 consumers in October 2001 and in October 2000, the mean credit card debt was $2,411 in October 2001 as compared to $2,814 in October 2000. Suppose that the standard deviation was $847.43 in October 2001 and $976.93 in October 2000.

a. Assuming that the population variances from both years are equal, is there evidence that the mean credit card debt was lower in October 2001 than in October 2000? (Use the $\alpha = 0.05$ level of significance.)

b. Determine the p-value in (a) and interpret its meaning.

c. Assuming that the population variances from both years are equal, construct and interpret a 95% confidence interval estimate of the difference between the population means in October 2001 and October 2000.

SELF Test **10.12** The Computer Anxiety Rating Scale (CARS) measures an individual's level of computer anxiety, on a scale from 20 (no anxiety) to 100 (highest level of anxiety). Researchers at Miami University administered CARS to 172 business students. One of the objectives of the study was to determine whether there is a difference in the level of computer anxiety experienced by female and male business students. They found the following:

	Males	Females
$\overline{X}$	40.26	36.85
S	13.35	9.42
n	100	72

Source: Extracted from T. Broome and D. Havelka, "Determinants of Computer Anxiety in Business Students," The Review of Business Information Systems, Spring 2002, 6(2), pp. 9–16.

a. At the 0.05 level of significance, is there evidence of a difference in the mean computer anxiety experienced by female and male business students?

b. Determine the p-value and interpret its meaning.

c. What assumptions do you have to make about the two populations in order to justify the use of the t test?

10.13 A company making plastic optical components was studying inconsistencies in an optical measurement called tilt. Two different types of pins used in the mold produced the following results:

	Taper Locks	Locking Pins
$\overline{X}$	1.262	0.561
S	0.297	0.307
n	20	20

Source: Extracted from J. Duncan, "Ghosts in Your Process? Who Ya Going to Call?" Quality Progress, May 2005, pp. 52–57.

a. Assuming that the population variances are equal and the populations are normally distributed, at the 0.05 level of significance, is there evidence of a difference in the means between taper locks and locking pins?

b. Repeat (a), assuming that the population variances are not equal.

c. Compare the results of (a) and (b).

10.14 A bank with a branch located in a commercial district of a city has developed an improved process for serving customers during the noon-to-1 p.m. lunch period. The waiting time (operationally defined as the time elapsed from when the customer enters the line until he or she reaches the teller window) of all customers during this hour is recorded over a period of one week. A random sample of 15 customers is selected (and stored in the file bank1.xls), and the results (in minutes) are as follows:

4.21	5.55	3.02	5.13	4.77	2.34	3.54	3.20
4.50	6.10	0.38	5.12	6.46	6.19	3.79	

Suppose that another branch, located in a residential area, is also concerned with the noon-to-1 p.m. lunch period. A random sample of 15 customers is selected (and stored in the file bank2.xls), and the results are as follows:

9.66	5.90	8.02	5.79	8.73	3.82	8.01	8.35
10.49	6.68	5.64	4.08	6.17	9.91	5.47	

a. Assuming that the population variances from both banks are equal, is there evidence of a difference in the mean waiting time between the two branches? (Use $\alpha = 0.05$.)

b. Determine the p-value in (a) and interpret its meaning.

c. What other assumption is necessary in (a)?

d. Assuming that the population variances from both branches are equal, construct and interpret a 95% confidence interval estimate of the difference between the population means in the two branches.

10.15 Repeat Problem 10.14 (a), assuming that the population variances in the two branches are not equal. Compare the results with those of Problem 10.14 (a).

10.16 A problem with a telephone line that prevents a customer from receiving or making calls is disconcerting to both the customer and the telephone company. The data in the file phone.xls represent samples of 20 problems reported to two different offices of a telephone company and the time to clear these problems (in minutes) from the customers' lines:

Central Office I Time to Clear Problems (Minutes)

1.48 1.75 0.78 2.85 0.52 1.60 4.15 3.97 1.48 3.10
1.02 0.53 0.93 1.60 0.80 1.05 6.32 3.93 5.45 0.97

Central Office II Time to Clear Problems (Minutes)

7.55 3.75 0.10 1.10 0.60 0.52 3.30 2.10 0.58 4.02
3.75 0.65 1.92 0.60 1.53 4.23 0.08 1.48 1.65 0.72

a. Assuming that the population variances from both offices are equal, is there evidence of a difference in the mean waiting times between the two offices? (Use $\alpha = 0.05$.)
b. Determine the p-value in (a) and interpret its meaning.
c. What other assumption is necessary in (a)?
d. Assuming that the population variances from both offices are equal, construct and interpret a 95% confidence interval estimate of the difference between the population means in the two offices.

10.17 Repeat Problem 10.16 (a), assuming that the population variances in the two offices are not equal. Compare the results with those of Problem 10.16 (a).

10.18 In intaglio printing, a design or figure is carved beneath the surface of hard metal or stone. Suppose that an experiment is designed to compare differences in mean surface hardness of steel plates used in intaglio printing (measured in indentation numbers), based on two different surface conditions—untreated and treated by lightly polishing with emery paper. In the experiment, 40 steel plates are randomly assigned—20 that are untreated, and 20 that are treated. The data are shown here and stored in the file intaglio.xls:

Untreated		Treated	
164.368	177.135	158.239	150.226
159.018	163.903	138.216	155.620
153.871	167.802	168.006	151.233
165.096	160.818	149.654	158.653
157.184	167.433	145.456	151.204
154.496	163.538	168.178	150.869
160.920	164.525	154.321	161.657
164.917	171.230	162.763	157.016
169.091	174.964	161.020	156.670
175.276	166.311	167.706	147.920

a. Assuming that the population variances from both conditions are equal, is there evidence of a difference in the mean surface hardness between untreated and treated steel plates? (Use $\alpha = 0.05$.)
b. Determine the p-value in (a) and interpret its meaning.
c. What other assumption is necessary in (a)?
d. Assuming that the population variances from untreated and treated steel plates are equal, construct and interpret a 95% confidence interval estimate of the

difference between the population means in the two conditions.

10.19 Repeat Problem 10.18 (a), assuming that the population variances from untreated and treated steel plates are not equal. Compare the results with those of Problem 10.18 (a).

10.20 The director of training for an electronic equipment manufacturer is interested in determining whether different training methods have an effect on the productivity of assembly-line employees. She randomly assigns 42 recently hired employees into two groups of 21. The first group receives a computer-assisted, individual-based training program, and the other receives a team-based training program. Upon completion of the training, the employees are evaluated on the time (in seconds) it takes to assemble a part. The results are in the data file training.xls.
a. Assuming that the variances in the populations of training methods are equal, is there evidence of a difference between the mean assembly times (in seconds) of employees trained in a computer-assisted, individual-based program and those trained in a team-based program? (Use a 0.05 level of significance.)
b. What other assumption is necessary in (a)?
c. Repeat (a), assuming that the population variances are not equal.
d. Compare the results of (a) and (c).
e. Assuming equal variances, construct and interpret a 95% confidence interval estimate of the difference between the population means of the two training methods.

10.21 Nondestructive evaluation is a method that is used to describe the properties of components or materials without causing any permanent physical change to the units. It includes the determination of properties of materials and the classification of flaws by size, shape, type, and location. This method is most effective for detecting surface flaws and characterizing surface properties of electrically conductive materials. Recently, data were collected that classified each component as having a flaw or not based on manual inspection and operator judgment and also reported the size of the crack in the material. Do the components classified as unflawed have a smaller mean crack size than components classified as flawed? The results in terms of crack size (in inches) are in the data file crack.xls (extracted from B. D. Olin and W. Q. Meeker, "Applications of Statistical Methods to Nondestructive Evaluation," *Technometrics*, 38, 1996, p. 101.)
a. Assuming that the population variances are equal, is there evidence that the mean crack size is smaller for the unflawed specimens than for the flawed specimens? (Use $\alpha = 0.05$.)
b. Repeat (a), assuming that the population variances are not equal.
c. Compare the results of (a) and (b).

10.2   COMPARING THE MEANS OF TWO RELATED POPULATIONS

The hypothesis-testing procedures examined in Section 10.1 enable you to make comparisons and examine differences in the means of two *independent* populations. In this section, you will learn about a procedure for analyzing the difference between the means of two populations when you collect sample data from populations that are related—that is, when results of the first population are *not* independent of the results of the second population.

There are two cases that involve related data between populations. In the first case, you take **repeated measurements** from the same set of items or individuals. In the second case, items or individuals are **matched** according to some characteristic. In either case, the variable of interest becomes the *difference between the values* rather than the *values* themselves.

The first case for analyzing related samples involves taking repeated measurements on the same items or individuals. Under the theory that the same items or individuals will behave alike if treated alike, the objective is to show that any differences between two measurements of the same items or individuals are due to different treatment conditions. For example, when performing a taste-testing experiment, you can use each person in the sample as his or her own control so that you can have *repeated measurements* on the same individual.

The second approach for analyzing related samples involves matching items or individuals according to some characteristic of interest. For example, in test marketing a product under two different advertising campaigns, a sample of test markets can be *matched* on the basis of the test market population size and/or demographic variables. By controlling these variables, you are better able to measure the effects of the two different advertising campaigns.

Regardless of whether you have matched samples or repeated measurements, the objective is to study the difference between two measurements by reducing the effect of the variability that is due to the items or individuals themselves. Table 10.3 shows the differences in the individual values for two related populations. To read this table, let $X_{11}, X_{12}, \ldots, X_{1n}$ represent the n values from a sample. And let $X_{21}, X_{22}, \ldots, X_{2n}$ represent either the corresponding n matched values from a second sample or the corresponding n repeated measurements from the initial sample. Then, $D_1, D_2, \ldots, D_n$ will represent the corresponding set of n difference *scores* such that

$$D_1 = X_{11} - X_{21}, D_2 = X_{12} - X_{22}, \ldots, \text{ and } D_n = X_{1n} - X_{2n}$$

TABLE 10.3

Determining the Difference Between Two Related Populations

Value	Group 1	Group 2	Difference
1	X_{11}	X_{21}	$D_1 = X_{11} - X_{21}$
2	X_{12}	X_{22}	$D_2 = X_{12} - X_{22}$
.	.	.	.
.	.	.	.
.	.	.	.
i	X_{1i}	X_{2i}	$D_i = X_{1i} - X_{2i}$
.	.	.	.
.	.	.	.
.	.	.	.
n	X_{1n}	X_{2n}	$D_n = X_{1n} - X_{2n}$

[2]*If the sample size is large, the Central Limit Theorem (see page 268) ensures you that the sampling distribution of $\overline{D}$ follows a normal distribution.*

To test for the mean difference between two related populations, you treat the difference scores, each D_i, as values from a single sample. If you know the population standard deviation of the difference scores, you use the Z test defined in Equation (10.4).[2] This Z test for the mean difference using samples from two related populations is equivalent to the one-sample Z test for the mean of the difference scores [see Equation (9.1) on page 334].

Z TEST FOR THE MEAN DIFFERENCE

$$Z = \frac{\overline{D} - \mu_D}{\dfrac{\sigma_D}{\sqrt{n}}} \tag{10.4}$$

where

$$\overline{D} = \frac{\displaystyle\sum_{i=1}^{n} D_i}{n}$$

μ_D = hypothesized mean difference

σ_D = population standard deviation of the difference scores

n = sample size

The test statistic Z follows a standardized normal distribution.

Paired t Test

In most cases, the population standard deviation is unknown. The only information you usually have are the sample mean and the sample standard deviation.

If you assume that the difference scores are randomly and independently selected from a population that is normally distributed, you can use the **paired t test for the mean difference in related populations** to determine whether there is a significant population mean difference. Like the one-sample t test developed in Section 9.4 [see Equation (9.2) on page 347], the t-test statistic developed here follows the t distribution, with $n - 1$ degrees of freedom. Although you must assume that the population is normally distributed, as long as the sample size is not very small and the population is not highly skewed, you can use the paired t test.

To test the null hypothesis that there is no difference in the means of two related populations:

$$H_0: \mu_D = 0 \text{ (where } \mu_D = \mu_1 - \mu_2)$$

against the alternative that the means are not the same:

$$H_1: \mu_D \neq 0$$

you compute the t test statistic using Equation (10.5).

PAIRED t TEST FOR THE MEAN DIFFERENCE

$$t = \frac{\overline{D} - \mu_D}{\dfrac{S_D}{\sqrt{n}}} \tag{10.5}$$

where

$$\overline{D} = \frac{\displaystyle\sum_{i=1}^{n} D_i}{n}$$

$$S_D = \sqrt{\frac{\displaystyle\sum_{i=1}^{n} (D_i - \overline{D})^2}{n - 1}}$$

The test statistic t follows a t distribution with $n - 1$ degrees of freedom.

For a two-tail test with a given level of significance, α, you reject the null hypothesis if the computed t test statistic is greater than the upper-tail critical value t_{n-1} from the t distribution or if the computed test statistic is less than the lower-tail critical value $-t_{n-1}$ from the t distribution. The decision rule is

$$\text{Reject } H_0 \text{ if } t > t_{n-1}$$
$$\text{or if } t < -t_{n-1};$$
$$\text{otherwise, do not reject } H_0.$$

The following example illustrates the use of the t test for the mean difference. The Automobile Assocation of America (AAA) conducted a mileage test to compare the gasoline mileage from real-life driving done by AAA members and results of city–highway driving done according to current (as of 2005) government standards (extracted from J. Healey, "Fuel Economy Calculations to Be Altered," *USA Today*, January 11, 2006, p. 1B).

What is the best way to design an experiment to compare the gasoline mileage from real-life driving done by AAA members and results of city–highway driving done according to current (as of 2005) government standards? One approach is to take two independent samples and then use the hypothesis tests discussed in Section 10.1. In this approach, you would use one set of automobiles to test the real-life driving done by AAA members. Then you would use a second set of different automobiles to test the results of city–highway driving done according to current (as of 2005) government standards.

However, because the first set of automobiles to test the real-life driving done by AAA members may get lower or higher gasoline mileage than the second set of automobiles, this is not a good approach. A better approach is to use a repeated-measurements experiment. In this experiment, you use one set of automobiles. For each automobile, you conduct a test of real-life driving done by an AAA member and a test of city–highway driving done according to current (as of 2005) government standards. Measuring the two gasoline mileages for the same automobiles serves to reduce the variability in the gasoline mileages compared with what would occur if you used two independent sets of automobiles. This approach focuses on the differences between the real-life driving done by an AAA member and the city–highway driving done according to current (as of 2005) government standards.

Table 10.4 displays results (stored in the file AAAmileage.xls) from a sample of $n = 9$ automobiles from such an experiment.

TABLE 10.4

Repeated Measurements of Gasoline Mileage for Real-Life Driving by AAA Members and City–Highway Driving Done According to Current (as of 2005) Government Standards

Model	Members	Current
2005 Ford F-150	14.3	16.8
2005 Chevrolet Silverado	15.0	17.8
2002 Honda Accord LX	27.8	26.2
2002 Honda Civic	27.9	33.2
2004 Honda Civic Hybrid	48.8	47.6
2002 Ford Explorer	16.8	18.3
2005 Toyota Camry	23.7	28.5
2003 Toyota Corolla	32.8	33.1
2005 Toyota Prius	37.3	44.0

You want to determine whether there is any difference in the mean gasoline mileage between the real-life driving done by an AAA member and the city–highway driving done according to current (as of 2005) government standards. In other words, is there evidence that the mean gasoline mileage is different between the two types of driving? Thus, the null and alternative hypotheses are

$H_0: \mu_D = 0$ (There is no difference in mean gasoline mileage between the real-life driving done by an AAA member and the city–highway driving done according to current [as of 2005] government standards.)

$H_1: \mu_D \neq 0$ (There is a difference in mean gasoline mileage between the real-life driving done by an AAA member and the city–highway driving done according to current [as of 2005] government standards.)

Choosing the level of significance of $\alpha = 0.05$ and assuming that the differences are normally distributed, you use the paired t test [Equation (10.5)]. For a sample of $n = 9$ automobiles, there are $n - 1 = 8$ degrees of freedom. Using Table E.3, the decision rule is

$$\text{Reject } H_0 \text{ if } t > t_8 = 2.3060;$$
$$\text{or if } t < -t_8 = -2.3060;$$
$$\text{otherwise, do not reject } H_0.$$

For the $n = 9$ differences (see Table 10.4), the sample mean difference is

$$\overline{D} = \frac{\sum\limits_{i=1}^{n} D_i}{n} = \frac{-21.1}{9} = -2.3444$$

and

$$S_D = \sqrt{\frac{\sum\limits_{i=1}^{n} (D_i - \overline{D})^2}{n - 1}} = 2.893575$$

From Equation (10.5) on page 382,

$$t = \frac{\overline{D} - \mu_D}{\dfrac{S_D}{\sqrt{n}}} = \frac{-2.3444 - 0}{\dfrac{2.893575}{\sqrt{9}}} = -2.4307$$

Because $t = -2.4307$ is less than -2.3060, you reject the null hypothesis, H_0 (see Figure 10.7). There is evidence of a difference in mean gasoline mileage between the real-life driving done by an AAA member and the city–highway driving done according to current (as of 2005) government standards. Real life driving results in a lower mean gasoline mileage.

FIGURE 10.7

Two-tail paired t test at the 0.05 level of significance with 8 degrees of freedom

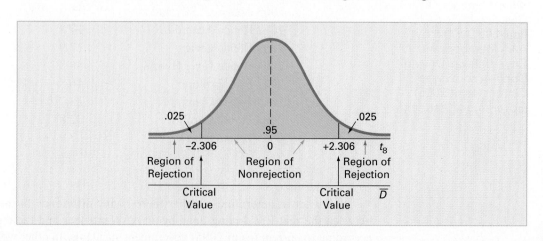

You can compute this test statistic along with the *p*-value by using Microsoft Excel (see Figure 10.8). Because the *p*-value = 0.0412 < α = 0.05, you reject H_0. The *p*-value indicates that if the two types of driving have the same mean gasoline mileage, the probability that one type of driving would have a mean that was 2.3444 miles per gallon less than the other type is 0.0412. Because this probability is less than α = 0.05, you conclude that the alternative hypothesis is true.

FIGURE 10.8

Panel A Microsoft Excel results of paired *t* test for the car mileage data

See Section E10.6 to create this worksheet.

	A	B	C
1	t-Test: Paired Two Sample for Means		
2			
3		*Members*	*Current*
4	Mean	27.1556	29.5
5	Variance	129.5528	125.0025
6	Observations	9	9
7	Pearson Correlation	0.9673	
8	Hypothesized Mean Difference	0	
9	df	8	
10	t Stat	-2.4307	
11	P(T<=t) one-tail	0.0206	
12	t Critical one-tail	1.8595	
13	P(T<=t) two-tail	0.0412	
14	t Critical two-tail	2.3060	

Panel B Microsoft Excel box-and-whisker plot for the car mileage data

See Section E3.4 to create this chart.

Box-and-Whisker Plot for Gasoline Mileage Differences

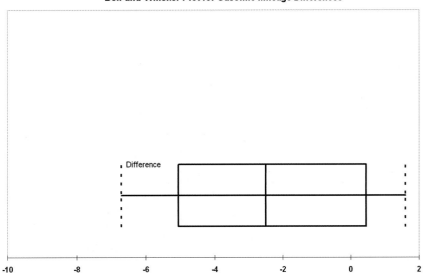

From Figure 10.8, Panel B, observe that the box-and-whisker plot shows approximate symmetry. Thus, the data do not greatly contradict the underlying assumption of normality. If an exploratory data analysis reveals that the assumption of underlying normality in the population is severely violated, then the *t* test is inappropriate. If this occurs, you can either use a *nonparametric* procedure that does not make the stringent assumption of underlying normality (see References 1 and 2) or make a data transformation (see reference 5) and then recheck the assumptions to determine whether you should use the *t* test.

EXAMPLE 10.2

PAIRED *t*-TEST OF PIZZA DELIVERY TIMES

Recall from Example 10.1 on page 374 that a local pizza restaurant located across the street from a college campus advertises that it delivers to the dormitories faster than the local branch of a national pizza chain. In order to determine whether this advertisement is valid, you and some friends have decided to order 10 pizzas from the local pizza restaurant and 10 pizzas from the national chain. In fact, each time you ordered a pizza from the local pizza restaurant, your friends ordered a pizza from the national pizza chain. Thus, you have matched data. For each of the ten times pizzas were ordered, you have one measurement from the local pizza restaurant and one from the national chain. At the 0.05 level of significance, is the mean delivery time for the local pizza restaurant less than the mean delivery time for the national pizza chain?

SOLUTION Use the paired t test to analyze the data in Table 10.5 (see the file pizzatime.xls).

TABLE 10.5

Delivery Times for Local Pizza Restaurant and National Pizza Chain

Time	Local	Chain	Difference
1	16.8	22.0	−5.2
2	11.7	15.2	−3.5
3	15.6	18.7	−3.1
4	16.7	15.6	1.1
5	17.5	20.8	−3.3
6	18.1	19.5	−1.4
7	14.1	17.0	−2.9
8	21.8	19.5	2.3
9	13.9	16.5	−2.6
10	20.8	24.0	−3.2
			−21.8

Figure 10.9 illustrates Microsoft Excel paired t test results for the pizza delivery data.

FIGURE 10.9

Microsoft Excel paired t test results for the pizza delivery data

See Section E10.6 to create this.

	A	B	C
1	t-Test: Paired Two Sample for Means		
2			
3		Local	Chain
4	Mean	16.7	18.88
5	Variance	9.5822	8.2151
6	Observations	10	10
7	Pearson Correlation	0.7141	
8	Hypothesized Mean Difference	0	
9	df	9	
10	t Stat	-3.0448	
11	P(T<=t) one-tail	0.0070	
12	t Critical one-tail	1.8331	
13	P(T<=t) two-tail	0.0139	
14	t Critical two-tail	2.2622	

The null and alternative hypotheses are

H_0: $\mu_D \geq 0$ (Mean delivery time for the local pizza restaurant is greater than or equal to the mean delivery time for the national pizza chain.)
H_1: $\mu_D < 0$ (Mean delivery time for the local pizza restaurant is less than the mean delivery time for the national pizza chain.)

Choosing the level of significance $\alpha = 0.05$ and assuming that the differences are normally distributed, you use the paired t test [Equation (10.5) on page 382]. For a sample of $n = 10$ delivery times, there are $n - 1 = 9$ degrees of freedom. Using Table E.3, the decision rule is

$$\text{Reject } H_0 \text{ if } t < t_9 = -1.8331;$$
$$\text{otherwise, do not reject } H_0.$$

For $n = 10$ differences (see Table 10.5), the sample mean difference is

$$\overline{D} = \frac{\sum_{i=1}^{n} D_i}{n} = \frac{-21.8}{10} = -2.18$$

and the sample standard deviation of the difference is

$$S_D = \sqrt{\frac{\sum_{i=1}^{n}(D_i - \overline{D})^2}{n-1}} = 2.2641$$

From Equation (10.5) on page 382,

$$t = \frac{\overline{D} - \mu_D}{\frac{S_D}{\sqrt{n}}} = \frac{-2.18 - 0}{\frac{2.2641}{\sqrt{10}}} = -3.0448$$

Because $t = -3.0448$ is less than -1.8331, you reject the null hypothesis H_0 (the p-value is $0.0070 < 0.05$). There is evidence that the mean delivery time is lower for the local pizza restaurant than for the national pizza chain.

This conclusion is different from the one you reached when you used the pooled-variance t test for these data. By pairing the delivery times, you are able to focus on the differences between the two pizza delivery services and not the variability created by ordering pizzas at different times of day. The paired t test is a more powerful statistical procedure that is better able to detect the difference between the two pizza delivery services.

Confidence Interval Estimate for the Mean Difference

Instead of, or in addition to, testing for the difference between the means of two related populations, you can use Equation 10.6 to construct a confidence interval estimate of the mean difference.

CONFIDENCE INTERVAL ESTIMATE FOR THE MEAN DIFFERENCE

$$\overline{D} \pm t_{n-1}\frac{S_D}{\sqrt{n}} \qquad\qquad (10.6)$$

or

$$\overline{D} - t_{n-1}\frac{S_D}{\sqrt{n}} \le \mu_D \le \overline{D} + t_{n-1}\frac{S_D}{\sqrt{n}}$$

Return to the example comparing gasoline mileage generated by real-life driving and by government standards. Using Equation (10.6), $\overline{D} = -2.3444$ $S_D = 2.8936$, $n = 9$, and $t = 2.306$ (for 95% confidence and $n - 1 = 8$ degrees of freedom),

$$-2.3444 \pm (2.306)\frac{2.8936}{\sqrt{9}}$$

$$-2.3444 \pm 2.2242$$

$$-4.5686 \le \mu_D \le -0.1202$$

Thus, with 95% confidence, the mean difference in gasoline mileage between the real-life driving done by an AAA member and the city–highway driving done according to current (as of 2005) government standards is between -4.5686 and -0.1202 miles per gallon. Because the interval estimate contains only values less than zero, you can conclude that there is a difference in the population means. The mean miles per gallon for the real-life driving done by an AAA member is less than the mean miles per gallon for the city–highway driving done according to current (as of 2005) government standards.

PROBLEMS FOR SECTION 10.2

Learning the Basics

10.22 An experimental design for a paired *t* test has, as a matched sample, 20 pairs of identical twins. How many degrees of freedom are there in this *t* test?

10.23 An experiment requires a measurement before and after the presentation of a stimulus to each of 15 subjects. In the analysis of the data collected from this experiment, how many degrees of freedom are there in the test?

Applying the Concepts

10.24 The September issues of monthly magazines typically carry the most advertising pages for any issue during the year. The following data (stored in the file **adpages.xls**) give the number of advertising pages in September 2004 and September 2005:

Magazine	2004	2005
Martha Stewart Living	52.14	75.25
Good Housekeeping	115.12	149.41
Parenting	123.84	158.37
Glamour (special issue)	184.78	236.00
Popular Mechanics	67.44	85.02
Ebony	122.32	141.77
Cosmopolitan (special issue)	227.35	248.60
Ladies' Home Journal	125.21	136.99
Parents	139.14	149.68
Vogue	650.63	690.55
Harper's Bazaar	261.09	274.06
Elle	342.27	346.94
Esquire	165.58	167.53
Real Simple	163.10	163.80
Men's Health	139.76	140.16
GQ	292.85	288.27
InStyle	382.96	376.00
Details	206.97	202.13

a. At the 0.05 level of significance, is there evidence of a difference in the mean number of advertising pages in September 2004 and September 2005?
b. What assumption is necessary to perform this test?
c. Determine the *p*-value in (a) and interpret its meaning.
d. Construct and interpret a 95% confidence interval estimate of the difference in the mean number of advertising pages in September 2004 and September 2005.

10.25 In industrial settings, alternative methods often exist for measuring variables of interest. The data in the file **measurement.xls** (coded to maintain confidentiality) represent measurements in-line that were collected from an analyzer during the production process and from an analytical lab (extracted from M. Leitnaker, "Comparing Measurement Processes: In-line Versus Analytical Measurements," *Quality Engineering*, 13, 2000–2001, pp. 293–298).

a. At the 0.05 level of significance, is there evidence of a difference in the mean measurements in-line and from an analytical lab?
b. What assumption is necessary to perform this test?
c. Use a graphical method to evaluate the validity of the assumption in (a).
d. Construct and interpret a 95% confidence interval estimate of the difference in the mean measurements in-line and from an analytical lab.

10.26 Can students save money by buying their textbooks at Amazon.com? To investigate this possibility, a random sample of 14 textbooks used during the 2006 summer session at Miami University was selected. The prices for these textbooks at both a local bookstore and through Amazon.com were recorded. The prices for the textbooks, including all relevant taxes and shipping, are given below (and are stored in the file **textbook.xls**):

Textbook	Book Store	Amazon
Concepts in Federal Taxation	138.21	143.95
Intermediate Accounting	151.92	152.70
The Middle East and Central Asia	52.06	53.00
West's Business Law	159.31	143.95
Leadership: Theory and Practice	49.59	48.95
Making Choices for Multicultural Education	71.74	56.95
Direct Instruction Reading	98.12	97.35
Essentials of Economics	102.12	99.60
Marriage and Family	106.92	100.98
America and Its People	100.44	95.20
Oceanography	105.18	128.95
Calculus: Early Transcendental Single Variable	115.00	133.50
Access to Health	93.47	88.60
Women and Globalization	29.54	18.48

a. At the 0.01 level of significance, is there evidence of a difference between the mean price of textbooks at the local bookstore and Amazon.com?
b. What assumption is necessary to perform this test?
c. Construct a 99% confidence interval estimate of the mean difference in price. Interpret the interval.
d. Compare the results of (a) and (c).

10.27 A newspaper article discussed the opening of a Whole Foods Market in the Time-Warner building in New York City. The following data (stored in the file **wholefoods1.xls**) compared the prices of some kitchen staples at the new Whole Foods Market and at the Fairway supermarket located about 15 blocks from the Time-Warner building:

Item	Whole Foods	Fairway
Half-gallon milk	2.19	1.35
Dozen eggs	2.39	1.69
Tropicana orange juice (64 oz.)	2.00	2.49
Head of Boston lettuce	1.98	1.29
Ground round, 1 lb.	4.99	3.69
Bumble Bee tuna, 6 oz. can	1.79	1.33
Granny Smith apples (1 lb.)	1.69	1.49
Box DeCecco linguini	1.99	1.59
Salmon steak, 1 lb.	7.99	5.99
Whole chicken, per pound	2.19	1.49

Source: Extracted from W. Grimes, "A Pleasure Palace Without the Guilt," The New York Times, February 18, 2004, pp. F1, F5.

a. At the 0.01 level of significance, is there evidence that the mean price is higher at Whole Foods Market than at the Fairway supermarket?

b. Interpret the meaning of the p-value in (a).

c. What assumption is necessary to perform the test in (a)?

10.28 Multiple myeloma, or blood plasma cancer, is characterized by increased blood vessel formulation (angiogenesis) in the bone marrow that is a prognostic factor in survival. One treatment approach used for multiple myeloma is stem cell transplantation with the patient's own stem cells. The following data (stored in the file **myeloma.xls**) represent the bone marrow microvessel density for patients who had a complete response to the stem cell transplant, as measured by blood and urine tests. The measurements were taken immediately prior to the stem cell transplant and at the time of the complete response:

Patient	Before	After
1	158	284
2	189	214
3	202	101
4	353	227
5	416	290
6	426	176
7	441	290

Source: Extracted from S. V. Rajkumar, R. Fonseca, T. E. Witzig, M. A. Gertz, and P. R. Greipp, "Bone Marrow Angiogenesis in Patients Achieving Complete Response After Stem Cell Transplantation for Multiple Myeloma," Leukemia, 1999, 13, pp. 469–472.

a. At the 0.05 level of significance, is there evidence that the mean bone marrow microvessel density is higher before the stem cell transplant than after the stem cell transplant?

b. Interpret the meaning of the p-value in (a).

c. Construct and interpret a 95% confidence interval estimate of the mean difference in bone marrow microvessel density before and after the stem cell transplant.

d. What assumption is necessary to perform the test in (a)?

10.29 Over the past year, the vice president for human resources at a large medical center has run a series of three-month workshops aimed at increasing worker motivation and performance. To check the effectiveness of the workshops, she selected a random sample of 35 employees from the personnel files and recorded their most recent annual performance ratings, along with their ratings prior to attending the workshops. The data are stored in the file **perform.xls**. The Microsoft Excel results in Panels A and B provide both descriptive and inferential information so that you can analyze the results and examine the assumptions of the hypothesis test used:

State your findings and conclusions in a report to the vice president for human resources.

	A	B
1	**Difference**	
2		
3	**Mean**	-5.2571
4	**Standard Error**	1.9478
5	**Median**	-5
6	**Mode**	-10
7	**Standard Deviation**	11.5232
8	**Sample Variance**	132.7849
9	**Kurtosis**	1.1038
10	**Skewness**	0.1103
11	**Range**	61
12	**Minimum**	-34
13	**Maximum**	27
14	**Sum**	-184
15	**Count**	35
16	**Largest(1)**	27
17	**Smallest(1)**	-34

PANEL A

	A	B	C
1	**t-Test: Paired Two Sample for Means**		
2			
3		*Before*	*After*
4	**Mean**	74.5429	79.8
5	**Variance**	80.9025	37.1647
6	**Observations**	35	35
7	**Pearson Correlation**	-0.1342	
8	**Hypothesized Mean Difference**	0	
9	**df**	34	
10	**t Stat**	-2.6990	
11	**P(T<=t) one-tail**	0.0054	
12	**t Critical one-tail**	1.6909	
13	**P(T<=t) two-tail**	0.0108	
14	**t Critical two-tail**	2.0322	

PANEL B

10.30 The data in the file concrete1.xls represent the compressive strength, in thousands of pounds per square inch (psi), of 40 samples of concrete taken two and seven days after pouring.

Source: Extracted from O. Carrillo-Gamboa and R. F. Gunst, "Measurement-Error-Model Collinearities," Technometrics, 34, 1992, pp. 454–464.

a. At the 0.01 level of significance, is there evidence that the mean strength is lower at two days than at seven days?

b. What assumption is necessary to perform this test?

c. Find the *p*-value in (a) and interpret its meaning.

10.3 COMPARING TWO POPULATION PROPORTIONS

Often, you need to make comparisons and analyze differences between two population proportions. You can perform a test for the difference between two proportions selected from independent samples by using two different methods. This section presents a procedure whose test statistic, Z, is approximated by a standardized normal distribution. In Section 12.1, a procedure whose test statistic, χ^2, is approximated by a chi-square distribution is developed. As you will see, the results from these two tests are equivalent.

Z Test for the Difference Between Two Proportions

In evaluating differences between two population proportions, you can use a **Z test for the difference between two proportions**. The test statistic Z is based on the difference between two sample proportions $(p_1 - p_2)$. This test statistic, given in Equation (10.7), approximately follows a standardized normal distribution for large enough sample sizes.

Z TEST FOR THE DIFFERENCE BETWEEN TWO PROPORTIONS

$$Z = \frac{(p_1 - p_2) - (\pi_1 - \pi_2)}{\sqrt{\bar{p}(1 - \bar{p})\left(\dfrac{1}{n_1} + \dfrac{1}{n_2}\right)}} \qquad (10.7)$$

with

$$\bar{p} = \frac{X_1 + X_2}{n_1 + n_2} \qquad p_1 = \frac{X_1}{n_1} \qquad p_2 = \frac{X_2}{n_2}$$

where

p_1 = proportion of successes in sample 1

X_1 = number of successes in sample 1

n_1 = sample size of sample 1

π_1 = proportion of successes in population 1

p_2 = proportion of successes in sample 2

X_2 = number of successes in sample 2

n_2 = sample size of sample 2

π_2 = proportion of successes in population 2

$\bar{p}$ = pooled estimate of the population proportion of successes

The test statistic Z approximately follows a standardized normal distribution.

Under the null hypothesis, you assume that the two population proportions are equal ($\pi_1 = \pi_2$). Because the pooled estimate for the population proportion is based on the null hypothesis, you combine, or pool, the two sample proportions to compute an overall estimate of the common population proportion. This estimate is equal to the number of successes in the two samples combined ($X_1 + X_2$) divided by the total sample size from the two sample groups ($n_1 + n_2$).

As shown in the following table, you can use this Z test for the difference between population proportions to determine whether there is a difference in the proportion of successes in the two groups (two-tail test) or whether one group has a higher proportion of successes than the other group (one-tail test):

Two-Tail Test	One-Tail Test	One-Tail Test
$H_0: \pi_1 = \pi_2$ $H_1: \pi_1 \neq \pi_2$	$H_0: \pi_1 \geq \pi_2$ $H_1: \pi_1 < \pi_2$	$H_0: \pi_1 \leq \pi_2$ $H_1: \pi_1 > \pi_2$

where

$$\pi_1 = \text{proportion of successes in population 1}$$

$$\pi_2 = \text{proportion of successes in population 2}$$

To test the null hypothesis that there is no difference between the proportions of two independent populations:

$$H_0: \pi_1 = \pi_2$$

against the alternative that the two population proportions are not the same:

$$H_1: \pi_1 \neq \pi_2$$

use the test statistic Z, given by Equation (10.7). For a given level of significance α, reject the null hypothesis if the computed Z test statistic is greater than the upper-tail critical value from the standardized normal distribution or if the computed test statistic is less than the lower-tail critical value from the standardized normal distribution.

To illustrate the use of the Z test for the equality of two proportions, suppose that you are the manager of T.C. Resort Properties, a collection of five upscale resort hotels located on two resort islands. On one of the islands, T.C. Resort Properties has two hotels, the Beachcomber and the Windsurfer. In tabulating the responses to the single question, "Are you likely to choose this hotel again?" 163 of 227 guests at the Beachcomber responded yes, and 154 of 262 guests at the Windsurfer responded yes. At the 0.05 level of significance, is there evidence of a significant difference in guest satisfaction (as measured by the likelihood to return to the hotel) between the two hotels?

The null and alternative hypotheses are

$$H_0: \pi_1 = \pi_2 \text{ or } \pi_1 - \pi_2 = 0$$
$$H_1: \pi_1 \neq \pi_2 \text{ or } \pi_1 - \pi_2 \neq 0$$

Using the 0.05 level of significance, the critical values are -1.96 and $+1.96$ (see Figure 10.10), and the decision rule is

Reject H_0 if $Z < -1.96$
or if $Z > +1.96$;
otherwise, do not reject H_0.

FIGURE 10.10

Regions of rejection and nonrejection when testing a hypothesis for the difference between two proportions at the 0.05 level of significance

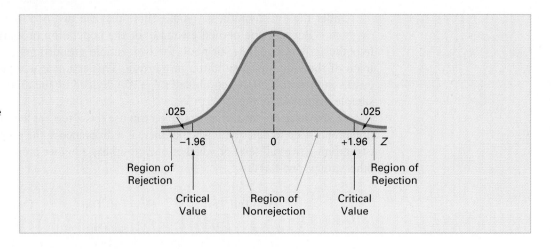

Using Equation (10.7) on page 390,

$$Z = \frac{(p_1 - p_2) - (\pi_1 - \pi_2)}{\sqrt{\bar{p}(1 - \bar{p})\left(\dfrac{1}{n_1} + \dfrac{1}{n_2}\right)}}$$

where

$$p_1 = \frac{X_1}{n_1} = \frac{163}{227} = 0.7181 \qquad p_2 = \frac{X_2}{n_2} = \frac{154}{262} = 0.5878$$

and

$$\bar{p} = \frac{X_1 + X_2}{n_1 + n_2} = \frac{163 + 154}{227 + 262} = \frac{317}{489} = 0.6483$$

so that

$$Z = \frac{(0.7181 - 0.5878) - (0)}{\sqrt{0.6483(1 - 0.6483)\left(\dfrac{1}{227} + \dfrac{1}{262}\right)}}$$

$$= \frac{0.1303}{\sqrt{(0.228)(0.0082)}}$$

$$= \frac{0.1303}{\sqrt{0.00187}}$$

$$= \frac{0.1303}{0.0432} = +3.0088$$

Using the 0.05 level of significance, reject the null hypothesis because $Z = +3.0088 > +1.96$. The p-value is 0.0026 (calculated from Table E.2 or from the Microsoft Excel results of Figure 10.11). This means that if the null hypothesis is true, the probability that a Z test statistic is less than -3.0088 is 0.0013, and, similarly, the probability that a Z test statistic is greater than $+3.0088$ is 0.0013. Thus, for this two-tail test, the p-value is $0.0013 + 0.0013 = 0.0026$. Because $0.0026 < \alpha = 0.05$, you reject the null hypothesis. There is evidence to conclude that the two hotels are significantly different with respect to guest satisfaction; a greater proportion of guests are willing to return to the Beachcomber than to the Windsurfer.

FIGURE 10.11

Microsoft Excel results for the Z test for the difference between two proportions for the hotel guest satisfaction problem

See Section E10.7 to create this.

	A	B	
1	Z Test for Differences in Two Proportions		
2			
3	**Data**		
4	Hypothesized Difference	0	
5	Level of Significance	0.05	
6	**Group 1**		
7	Number of Successes	163	
8	Sample Size	227	
9	**Group 2**		
10	Number of Successes	154	
11	Sample Size	262	
12			
13	**Intermediate Calculations**		
14	Group 1 Proportion	0.7181	=B7/B8
15	Group 2 Proportion	0.5878	=B10/B11
16	Difference in Two Proportions	0.1303	=B14 - B15
17	Average Proportion	0.6483	=(B7 + B10)/(B8 + B11)
18	Z Test Statistic	3.0088	=(B16 - B4)/SQRT(B17 * (1 - B17) * (1/B8 + 1/B11))
19			
20	**Two-Tail Test**		
21	Lower Critical Value	-1.9600	=NORMSINV(B5/2)
22	Upper Critical Value	1.9600	=NORMSINV(1 - B5/2)
23	p-Value	0.0026	=2 * (1 - NORMSDIST(ABS(B18)))
24	**Reject the null hypothesis**		=IF(B23 < B5, "Reject the null hypothesis", "Do not reject the null hypothesis")

EXAMPLE 10.3

TESTING FOR THE DIFFERENCE IN TWO PROPORTIONS

Money worries in the United States start at an early age. In a survey, 660 children (330 boys and 330 girls) ages 6 to 14 were asked the question, "Do you worry about having enough money?" Of the boys surveyed, 201 (60.9%) said yes, and 178 (53.9%) of the girls surveyed said yes (extracted from D. Haralson and K. Simmons, "Snapshots," *USA Today*, May 24, 2004, p. 1B). At the 0.05 level of significance, is the proportion of boys who worry about having enough money greater than the proportion of girls?

SOLUTION Because you want to know whether there is evidence that the proportion of boys who worry about having enough money is *greater* than the proportion of girls, you have a one-tail test. The null and alternative hypotheses are

$H_0: \pi_1 \leq \pi_2$ (The proportion of boys who worry about having enough money is less than or equal to the proportion of girls.)
$H_1: \pi_1 > \pi_2$ (The proportion of boys who worry about having enough money is greater than the proportion of girls.)

Using the 0.05 level of significance, for the one-tail test in the upper tail, the critical value is +1.645. The decision rule is

$$\text{Reject } H_0 \text{ if } Z > +1.645;$$
$$\text{otherwise, do not reject } H_0.$$

Using Equation (10.7) on page 390,

$$Z = \frac{(p_1 - p_2) - (\pi_1 - \pi_2)}{\sqrt{\bar{p}(1 - \bar{p})\left(\frac{1}{n_1} + \frac{1}{n_2}\right)}}$$

where

$$p_1 = \frac{X_1}{n_1} = \frac{201}{330} = 0.609 \qquad p_2 = \frac{X_2}{n_2} = \frac{178}{330} = 0.539$$

and

$$\bar{p} = \frac{X_1 + X_2}{n_1 + n_2} = \frac{201 + 178}{330 + 330} = \frac{379}{660} = 0.5742$$

so that

$$Z = \frac{(0.609 - 0.539) - (0)}{\sqrt{0.5742(1 - 0.5742)\left(\frac{1}{330} + \frac{1}{330}\right)}}$$

$$= \frac{0.07}{\sqrt{(0.2445)(0.00606)}}$$

$$= \frac{0.07}{\sqrt{0.00148}}$$

$$= \frac{0.07}{0.0385} = +1.818$$

Using the 0.05 level of significance, reject the null hypothesis because $Z = +1.818 > +1.645$. The p-value is 0.0344 (calculated from Table E.2). Therefore, if the null hypothesis is true, the probability that a Z test statistic is greater than $+1.818$ is 0.0344 (which is less than $\alpha = 0.05$). You conclude that there is evidence that the proportion of boys who worry about having enough money is greater than the proportion of girls.

Confidence Interval Estimate for the Difference Between Two Proportions

Instead of, or in addition to, testing for the difference between the proportions of two independent populations, you can construct a confidence interval estimate of the difference between the two proportions, using Equation (10.8).

CONFIDENCE INTERVAL ESTIMATE FOR THE DIFFERENCE BETWEEN TWO PROPORTIONS

$$(p_1 - p_2) \pm Z\sqrt{\frac{p_1(1 - p_1)}{n_1} + \frac{p_2(1 - p_2)}{n_2}} \qquad \textbf{(10.8)}$$

or

$$(p_1 - p_2) - Z\sqrt{\frac{p_1(1 - p_1)}{n_1} + \frac{p_2(1 - p_2)}{n_2}} \le (\pi_1 - \pi_2)$$

$$\le (p_1 - p_2) + Z\sqrt{\frac{p_1(1 - p_1)}{n_1} + \frac{p_2(1 - p_2)}{n_2}}$$

To construct a 95% confidence interval estimate of the population difference between the percentages of guests who would return to the Beachcomber and who would return to the Windsurfer, you use the results on page 392 or from Figure 10.11 on page 393:

$$p_1 = \frac{X_1}{n_1} = \frac{163}{227} = 0.7181 \qquad p_2 = \frac{X_2}{n_2} = \frac{154}{262} = 0.5878$$

Using Equation (10.8),

$$(0.7181 - 0.5878) \pm (1.96)\sqrt{\frac{0.7181(1 - 0.7181)}{227} + \frac{0.5878(1 - 0.5878)}{262}}$$

$$0.1303 \pm (1.96)(0.0426)$$

$$0.1303 \pm 0.0835$$

$$0.0468 \le (\pi_1 - \pi_2) \le 0.2138$$

Thus, you have 95% confidence that the difference between the population proportion of guests who would return again to the Beachcomber and the Windsurfer is between 0.0468 and 0.2138. In percentages, the difference is between 4.68% and 21.35%. Guest satisfaction is higher at the Beachcomber than at the Windsurfer.

PROBLEMS FOR SECTION 10.3

Learning the Basics

PH Grade ASSIST **10.31** Assume that $n_1 = 100$, $X_1 = 50$, $n_2 = 100$, and $X_2 = 30$.

a. At the 0.05 level of significance, is there evidence of a significant difference between the two population proportions?

b. Construct a 95% confidence interval estimate of the difference between the two population proportions.

PH Grade ASSIST **10.32** Assume that $n_1 = 100$, $X_1 = 45$, $n_2 = 50$, and $X_2 = 25$.

a. At the 0.01 level of significance, is there evidence of a significant difference between the two population proportions?

b. Construct a 99% confidence interval estimate of the difference between the two population proportions.

Applying the Concepts

PH Grade ASSIST **10.33** A sample of 500 shoppers was selected in a large metropolitan area to determine various information concerning consumer behavior. Among the questions asked was, "Do you enjoy shopping for clothing?" Of 240 males, 136 answered yes. Of 260 females, 224 answered yes.

a. Is there evidence of a significant difference between males and females in the proportion who enjoy shopping for clothing at the 0.01 level of significance?

b. Find the p-value in (a) and interpret its meaning.

c. Construct and interpret a 99% confidence interval estimate of the difference between the proportion of males and females who enjoy shopping for clothing.

d. What are your answers to (a) through (c) if 206 males enjoyed shopping for clothing?

10.34 An article referencing a survey conducted by AP-LOL Learning Services claims that parents are more confident than teachers that their schools will meet the standards set by the No Child Left Behind Act. The survey asked parents (and teachers), "How confident are you that your child's school (the school where you work) will meet the standards by the deadline." The responses to that question are given in the following table:

	Parents	Teachers
Very confident	401	162
Not very confident	684	648
Totals	1,085	810

Source: Adapted from B. Feller, "Teachers More Likely Skeptics of No Child," The Cincinnati Enquirer, April 20, 2006, p. A4.

a. Set up the null and alternative hypotheses needed to try to prove that the population proportion of parents that are very confident that their child's school will meet the standards by the deadline is greater than the population proportion of teachers that are very confident that the school where they work will meet standards by the deadline.

b. Conduct the hypothesis test defined in (a), using a 0.05 level of significance.

c. Does the result of your test in (b) make it appropriate for the article to claim that parents are more confident than teachers?

PH Grade ASSIST **10.35** The results of a study conducted as part of a yield-improvement effort at a semiconductor manufacturing facility provided defect data for a sample of 450 wafers. The following contingency table presents a summary of the responses to two questions: "Was a particle found on the die that produced the wafer?" and "Is the wafer good or bad?"

Quality of Wafer

PARTICLES	Good	Bad	Totals
Yes	14	36	50
No	320	80	400
Totals	334	116	450

Source: Extracted from S.W. Hall, "Analysis of Defectivity of Semiconductor Wafers by Contingency Table," Proceedings Institute of Environmental Sciences, Vol. 1, 1994, pp. 177–183.

a. At the 0.05 level of significance, is there evidence of a significant difference between the proportion of good and bad wafers that have particles?

b. Determine the *p*-value in (a) and interpret its meaning.

c. Construct and interpret a 95% confidence interval estimate of the difference between the population proportion of good and bad wafers that contain particles.

d. What conclusions can you reach from this analysis?

 10.36 According to an Ipsos poll, the perception of unfairness in the U.S. tax code is spread fairly evenly across income groups, age groups, and education levels. In an April 2006 survey of 1,005 adults, Ipsos reported that almost 60% of all people said the code is unfair, while slightly more that 60% of those making more than $50,000 viewed the code as unfair (Extracted from "People Cry Unfairness," *The Cincinnati Enquirer*, April 16, 2006, p. A8). Suppose that the following contingency table represents the specific breakdown of responses:

Income Level

U.S. Tax Code	Less Than $50,000	More Than $50,000	Total
Fair	225	180	405
Unfair	280	320	600
Total	505	500	1,005

a. At the 0.05 level of significance, is there evidence of a difference in the proportion of adults who think the U.S. tax code is unfair between the two income groups?

b. Find the *p*-value in (a) and interpret its meaning.

10.37 Is good gas mileage a priority for car shoppers? A survey conducted by Progressive Insurance asked this question to both men and women shopping for new cars. The data were reported as percentages, and no sample sizes were given:

Gender

GAS MILEAGE A PRIORITY?	Men	Women
Yes	76%	84%
No	24%	16%

Source: Extracted from "Snapshots," usatoday.com, June 21, 2004.

a. Assume that 50 men and 50 women were included in the survey. At the 0.05 level of significance, is there evidence of a difference in the population proportion of males and females who made gas mileage a priority?

b. Assume that 500 men and 500 women were included in the survey. At the 0.05 level of significance, is there evidence of a difference between males and females in the proportion who made gas mileage a priority?

c. Discuss the effect of sample size on the *Z* test for the difference between two proportions.

10.38 An experiment was conducted to study the choices made in mutual fund selection. Undergraduate and MBA students were presented with different S&P 500 index funds that were identical except for fees. Suppose 100 undergraduate students and 100 MBA students were selected. Partial results are shown in the following table:

	STUDENT GROUP	
FUND	Undergraduate	MBA
Highest-cost fund	27	18
Not-highest-cost fund	73	82

Source: Extracted from J. Choi, D. Laibson, and B. Madrian, "Why Does the Law of One Practice Fail? An Experiment on Mutual Funds," www.som.yale.edu/faculty/jjc83/fees.pdf.

a. At the 0.05 level of significance, is there evidence of a difference between undergraduate and MBA students in the proportion who selected the highest-cost fund?

b. Find the *p*-value in (a) and interpret its meaning.

10.39 Where people turn for news is different for various age groups (Extracted from P. Johnson, "Young People Turn to the Web for News," *USA Today*, March 23, 2006, p. 9D). Suppose that a study conducted on this issue was based on 200 respondents who were between the ages of 36 and 50 and 200 respondents who were above age 50. Of the 200 respondents who were between the ages of 36 and 50, 82 got their news primarily from newspapers. Of the 200 respondents who were above age 50, 104 got their news primarily from newspapers.

a. Is there evidence of a significant difference in the proportion who get their news primarily from newspapers between those respondents 36 to 50 years old and those above 50 years old? (Use $\alpha = 0.05$.)

b. Determine the *p*-value in (a) and interpret its meaning.

c. Construct and interpret a 95% confidence interval estimate of the difference between the population proportion of respondents who get their news primarily from newspapers between those respondents 36 to 50 years old and those above 50 years old.

10.4   *F* TEST FOR THE DIFFERENCE BETWEEN TWO VARIANCES

Often, you need to determine whether two independent populations have the same variability. This determination is made by testing variances. One important reason to test for the difference between the variances of two populations is to determine whether to use the pooled-variance *t* test (equal variance case) or the separate-variance *t* test (unequal variance case).

The test for the difference between the variances of two independent populations is based on the ratio of the two sample variances. If you assume that each population is normally distributed, then the ratio S_1^2/S_2^2 follows the **F distribution** (see Table E.5). The critical values of the *F* distribution in Table E.5 depend on two sets of degrees of freedom. The degrees of freedom in the numerator of the ratio are for the first sample, and the degrees of freedom in the denominator are for the second sample. Equation (10.9) defines the **F test statistic for testing the equality of two variances**.

F TEST STATISTIC FOR TESTING THE EQUALITY OF TWO VARIANCES

The *F*-test statistic is equal to the variance of sample 1 divided by the variance of sample 2.

$$F = \frac{S_1^2}{S_2^2} \tag{10.9}$$

where

S_1^2 = variance of sample 1

S_2^2 = variance of sample 2

n_1 = size of sample taken from population 1

n_2 = size of sample taken from population 2

$n_1 - 1$ = degrees of freedom from sample 1 (that is, the numerator degrees of freedom)

$n_2 - 1$ = degrees of freedom from sample 2 (that is, the denominator degrees of freedom)

The test statistic *F* follows an *F* distribution with $n_1 - 1$ and $n_2 - 1$ degrees of freedom.

For a given level of significance, α, to test the null hypothesis of equality of variances:

$$H_0: \sigma_1^2 = \sigma_2^2$$

against the alternative hypothesis that the two population variances are not equal:

$$H_1: \sigma_1^2 \neq \sigma_2^2$$

you reject the null hypothesis if the computed *F* test statistic is greater than the upper-tail critical value, F_U, from the *F* distribution with $n_1 - 1$ degrees of freedom in the numerator and $n_2 - 1$ degrees of freedom in the denominator, or if the computed *F* test statistic is less than the lower-tail critical value, F_L, from the *F* distribution with $n_1 - 1$ and $n_2 - 1$ degrees of freedom in the numerator and denominator, respectively. Thus, the decision rule is

Reject H_0 if $F > F_U$
or if $F < F_L$;
otherwise, do not reject H_0.

This decision rule and rejection regions are displayed in Figure 10.12.

FIGURE 10.12

Regions of rejection and nonrejection for the two-tail F test

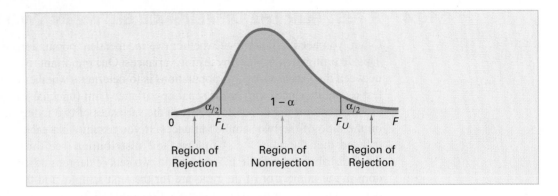

To illustrate how to use the F test to determine whether the two variances are equal, return to the Using Statistics scenario concerning the sales of BLK cola in two different aisle locations. To determine whether to use the pooled-variance *t* test or the separate-variance *t* test in Section 10.1, you can test the equality of the two population variances. The null and alternative hypotheses are

$$H_0: \sigma_1^2 = \sigma_2^2$$
$$H_1: \sigma_1^2 \neq \sigma_2^2$$

Because this is a two-tail test, the rejection region is split into the lower and upper tails of the F distribution. Using the level of significance $\alpha = 0.05$, each rejection region contains 0.025 of the distribution.

Because there are samples of 10 stores for each of the two display locations, there are $10 - 1 = 9$ degrees of freedom for group 1 and also for group 2. F_U, the upper-tail critical value of the F distribution, is found directly from Table E.5, a portion of which is presented in Table 10.6. Because there are 9 degrees of freedom in the numerator and 9 degrees of freedom in the denominator, you find the upper-tail critical value, F_U, by looking in the column labeled 9 and the row labeled 9. Thus, the upper-tail critical value of this F distribution is 4.03.

TABLE 10.6

Finding F_U, the Upper-Tail Critical Value of F with 9 and 9 Degrees of Freedom for Upper-Tail Area of 0.025

Denominator	Numerator df_1						
df_2	1	2	3	...	7	8	9
1	647.80	799.50	864.20	...	948.20	956.70	963.30
2	38.51	39.00	39.17	...	39.36	39.37	39.39
3	17.44	16.04	15.44	...	14.62	14.54	14.47
.	.	.	.		.	.	.
.	.	.	.		.	.	.
.	.	.	.		.	.	.
7	8.07	6.54	5.89	...	4.99	4.90	4.82
8	7.57	6.06	5.42	...	4.53	4.43	4.36
9	7.21	5.71	5.08	...	4.20	4.10	4.03

Source: Extracted from Table E.5.

Finding Lower-Tail Critical Values

You compute F_L, a lower-tail critical value on the F distribution with $n_1 - 1$ degrees of freedom in the numerator and $n_2 - 1$ degrees of freedom in the denominator, by taking the reciprocal of F_{U*}, an upper-tail critical value on the F distribution with degrees of freedom "switched" (that is, $n_2 - 1$ degrees of freedom in the numerator and $n_1 - 1$ degrees of freedom in the denominator). This relationship is shown in Equation (10.10).

FINDING LOWER-TAIL CRITICAL VALUES FROM THE *F* DISTRIBUTION

$$F_L = \frac{1}{F_{U*}}$$ **(10.10)**

where F_{U*} is from an *F* distribution with $n_2 - 1$ degrees of freedom in the numerator and $n_1 - 1$ degrees of freedom in the denominator.

In the cola sales example, the degrees of freedom are 9 and 9 for both the numerator sample and denominator sample, so there is no "switching" of degrees of freedom; you just take the reciprocal. Therefore, to compute the lower-tail 0.025 critical value, you need to find the upper-tail 0.025 critical value of *F* with 9 degrees of freedom in the numerator and 9 degrees of freedom in the denominator and take its reciprocal. As shown in Table 10.6 on page 398, this upper-tail value is 4.03. Using Equation (10.10),

$$F_L = \frac{1}{F_{U*}} = \frac{1}{4.03} = 0.248$$

As depicted in Figure 10.13, the decision rule is

Reject H_0 if $F > F_U = 4.03$
or if $F < F_L = 0.248$;
otherwise, do not reject H_0.

FIGURE 10.13

Regions of rejection and nonrejection for two-tail *F* test for equality of two variances at the 0.05 level of significance with 9 and 9 degrees of freedom

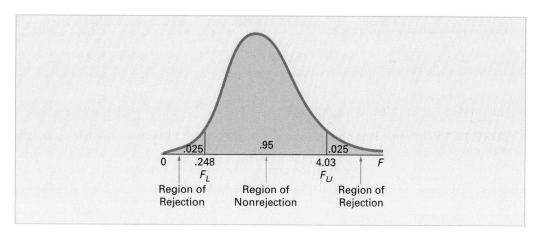

Using Equation (10.9) on page 397 and the cola sales data (see Table 10.1 on page 372), the *F* test statistic is

$$F = \frac{S_1^2}{S_2^2}$$

$$= \frac{350.6778}{157.3333} = 2.2289$$

Because $F_L = 0.248 < F = 2.2289 < F_U = 4.03$, you do not reject H_0. The *p*-value is 0.2482 for a two-tail test (twice the *p*-value for the one-tail test shown in the Microsoft Excel results in Figure 10.14). Because 0.2482 > 0.05, you conclude that there is no significant difference in the variability of the sales of cola for the two display locations.

FIGURE 10.14

Microsoft Excel *F* test
results for the BLK cola
sales data

*See Section E10.8 to create
this.*

	A	B	C
1	**F-Test Two-Sample for Variances**		
2			
3		*Normal*	*End-Aisle*
4	**Mean**	50.3	72
5	**Variance**	350.6778	157.3333
6	**Observations**	10	10
7	**df**	9	9
8	**F**	2.2289	
9	**P(F<=f) one-tail**	0.1241	
10	**F Critical one-tail**	3.1789	

In testing for a difference between two variances using the *F* test described in this section, you assume that each of the two populations is normally distributed. The *F* test is very sensitive to the normality assumption. If box-and-whisker plots or normal probability plots suggest even a mild departure from normality for either of the two populations, you should not use the *F* test. If this happens, a nonparametric approach is more appropriate (see references 1 and 2).

In testing for the equality of variances, as part of assessing the validity of the pooled-variance *t* test procedure, the *F* test is a two-tail test. However, when you are interested in the variability itself, the *F* test is often a one-tail test. Thus, in testing the equality of two variances, you can use either a two-tail or one-tail test, depending on whether you are testing whether the two population variances are *different* or whether one variance is *greater than* the other variance. Figure 10.15 illustrates the three possible situations.

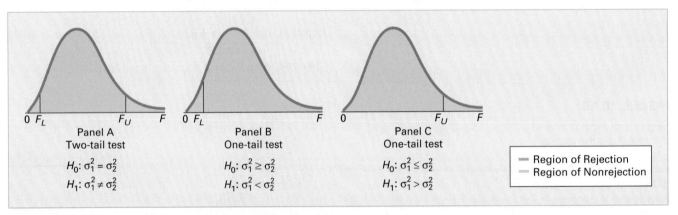

FIGURE 10.15 Determining the rejection region for testing the equality of two population variances

Often, the sample sizes in the two groups differ. Example 10.4 demonstrates how to find a lower-tail critical value from the *F* distribution in this situation.

EXAMPLE 10.4

FINDING THE LOWER-TAIL CRITICAL VALUE FROM THE *F* DISTRIBUTION IN A TWO-TAIL TEST OF A HYPOTHESIS

You select a sample of $n_1 = 8$ from a normally distributed population. The variance for this sample S_1^2 is 56.0. You select a sample of $n_2 = 10$ from a second normally distributed population (independent of the first population). The variance for this sample S_2^2 is 24.0. Using the level of significance $\alpha = 0.05$, test the null hypothesis of no difference in the two population variances against the two-tail alternative that there is evidence of a significant difference in the population variances.

SOLUTION The null and alternative hypotheses are

$$H_0: \sigma_1^2 = \sigma_2^2$$

$$H_1: \sigma_1^2 \neq \sigma_2^2$$

The *F* test statistic is given by Equation (10.9) on page 397:

$$F = \frac{S_1^2}{S_2^2}$$

You use Table E.5 to find the upper and lower critical values of the *F* distribution. With $n_1 - 1 = 7$ degrees of freedom in the numerator, $n_2 - 1 = 9$ degrees of freedom in the denominator, and $\alpha = 0.05$ split equally into the lower- and upper-tail rejection regions of 0.025 each, the upper critical value, F_U, is 4.20 (see Table 10.7).

To find the lower critical value, F_L, with 7 degrees of freedom in the numerator and 9 degrees of freedom in the denominator, you take the reciprocal of F_{U*} with degrees of freedom switched to 9 in the numerator and 7 in the denominator. Thus, from Equation (10.10) on page 399 and Table 10.7,

$$F_L = \frac{1}{F_{U*}} = \frac{1}{4.82} = 0.207$$

TABLE 10.7

Finding F_{U*} and F_L, with 7 and 9 Degrees of Freedom, Using the Level of Significance $\alpha = 0.05$

Denominator				Numerator df_1			
df_2	1	2	3	...	7	8	9
1	647.80	799.50	864.20	...	948.20	956.70	963.30
2	38.51	39.00	39.17	...	39.36	39.37	39.39
3	17.44	16.04	15.44	...	14.62	14.54	14.47
.	.	.	.			.	
.	.	.	.			.	
.	.	.	.			.	
7	8.07	6.54	5.89	...	4.99	4.90	4.82
8	7.57	6.06	5.42	...	4.53	4.43	4.36
9	7.21	5.71	5.08	...	4.20	4.10	4.03

Source: Extracted from Table E.5.

The decision rule is

$$\text{Reject } H_0 \text{ if } F > F_U = 4.20$$
$$\text{or if } F < F_L = 0.207;$$
$$\text{otherwise, do not reject } H_0.$$

From Equation (10.9) on page 397, the *F* test statistic is

$$F = \frac{S_1^2}{S_2^2}$$

$$= \frac{56.0}{24.0} = 2.33$$

Because $F_L = 0.207 < F = 2.33 < F_U = 4.20$, you do not reject H_0. Using a 0.05 level of significance, you conclude that there is no evidence of a significant difference between the variances in these two independent populations.

PROBLEMS FOR SECTION 10.4

Learning the Basics

 10.40 Determine F_U and F_L, the upper- and lower-tail critical values of F, in each of the following two-tail tests:
a. $\alpha = 0.10$, $n_1 = 16$, $n_2 = 21$
b. $\alpha = 0.05$, $n_1 = 16$, $n_2 = 21$
c. $\alpha = 0.02$, $n_1 = 16$, $n_2 = 21$
d. $\alpha = 0.01$, $n_1 = 16$, $n_2 = 21$

10.41 Determine F_U, the upper-tail critical value of F, in each of the following one-tail tests:
a. $\alpha = 0.05$, $n_1 = 16$, $n_2 = 21$
b. $\alpha = 0.025$, $n_1 = 16$, $n_2 = 21$
c. $\alpha = 0.01$, $n_1 = 16$, $n_2 = 21$
d. $\alpha = 0.005$, $n_1 = 16$, $n_2 = 21$

10.42 Determine F_L, the lower-tail critical value of F, in each of the following one-tail tests:
a. $\alpha = 0.05$, $n_1 = 16$, $n_2 = 21$
b. $\alpha = 0.025$, $n_1 = 16$, $n_2 = 21$
c. $\alpha = 0.01$, $n_1 = 16$, $n_2 = 21$
d. $\alpha = 0.005$, $n_1 = 16$, $n_2 = 21$

 10.43 The following information is available for two samples drawn from independent normally distributed populations:

$$n_1 = 25 \quad S_1^2 = 133.7 \quad n_2 = 25 \quad S_2^2 = 161.9$$

What is the value of the F test statistic if you are testing the null hypothesis H_0: $\sigma_1^2 = \sigma_2^2$?

 10.44 In Problem 10.43, how many degrees of freedom are there in the numerator and denominator of the F test?

10.45 In Problems 10.43 and 10.44, what are the critical values for F_U and F_L if the level of significance, α, is 0.05 and the alternative hypothesis is H_1: $\sigma_1^2 \neq \sigma_2^2$?

10.46 In Problems 10.43 through 10.45, what is your statistical decision?

10.47 The following information is available for two samples selected from independent but very right-skewed populations:

$$n_1 = 16 \quad S_1^2 = 47.3 \quad n_2 = 13 \quad S_2^2 = 36.4$$

Should you use the F test to test the null hypothesis of equality of variances (H_0: $\sigma_1^2 = \sigma_2^2$)? Discuss.

10.48 In Problem 10.47, assume that two samples are selected from independent normally distributed populations.
a. At the 0.05 level of significance, is there evidence of a difference between σ_1^2 and σ_2^2?
b. Suppose that you want to perform a one-tail test. At the 0.05 level of significance, what is the upper-tail critical value of the F test statistic to determine whether there is evidence that $\sigma_1^2 > \sigma_2^2$? What is your statistical decision?
c. Suppose that you want to perform a one-tail test. At the 0.05 level of significance, what is the lower-tail critical value of the F test statistic to determine whether there is evidence that $\sigma_1^2 < \sigma_2^2$? What is your statistical decision?

Applying the Concepts

 10.49 A professor in the accounting department of a business school claims that there is much more variability in the final exam scores of students taking the introductory accounting course as a requirement than for students taking the course as part of a major in accounting. Random samples of 13 non-accounting majors (group 1) and 10 accounting majors (group 2) are taken from the professor's class roster in his large lecture, and the following results are computed based on the final exam scores:

$$n_1 = 13 \quad S_1^2 = 210.2 \quad n_2 = 10 \quad S_2^2 = 36.5$$

a. At the 0.05 level of significance, is there evidence to support the professor's claim?
b. Interpret the p-value.
c. What assumption do you need to make in (a) about the two populations in order to justify your use of the F test?

 10.50 The Computer Anxiety Rating Scale (CARS) measures an individual's level of computer anxiety, on a scale from 20 (no anxiety) to 100 (highest level of anxiety). Researchers at Miami University administered CARS to 172 business students. One of the objectives of the study was to determine whether there is a difference between the level of computer anxiety experienced by female students and male students. They found the following:

	Males	Females
$\bar{X}$	40.26	36.85
S	13.35	9.42
n	100	72

Source: Extracted from T. Broome and D. Havelka, "Determinants of Computer Anxiety in Business Students," The Review of Business Information Systems, Spring 2002, 6(2), pp. 9–16.

a. At the 0.05 level of significance, is there evidence of a difference in the variability of the computer anxiety experienced by females and males?

b. Interpret the *p*-value.

c. What assumption do you need to make about the two populations in order to justify the use of the *F* test?

d. Based on (a) and (b), which *t* test defined in Section 10.1 should you use to test whether there is a significant difference in mean computer anxiety for female and male students?

10.51 A bank with a branch located in a commercial district of a city has developed an improved process for serving customers during the noon-to-1 p.m. lunch period. The waiting time (defined as the time elapsed from when the customer enters the line until he or she reaches the teller window) of all customers during this hour is recorded over a period of one week. A random sample of 15 customers is selected (and stored in the file bank1.xls), and the results (in minutes) are as follows:

4.21	5.55	3.02	5.13	4.77	2.34	3.54	3.20
4.50	6.10	0.38	5.12	6.46	6.19	3.79	

Suppose that another branch, located in a residential area, is also concerned with the noon-to-1 p.m. lunch period. A random sample of 15 customers is selected (and stored in the file bank2.xls), and the results (in minutes) are as follows:

9.66	5.90	8.02	5.79	8.73	3.82	8.01	8.35
10.49	6.68	5.64	4.08	6.17	9.91	5.47	

a. Is there evidence of a difference in the variability of the waiting time between the two branches? (Use $\alpha = 0.05$.)

b. Determine the *p*-value in (a) and interpret its meaning.

c. What assumption is necessary in (a)? Is the assumption valid for these data?

d. Based on the results of (a), is it appropriate to use the pooled-variance *t* test to compare the means of the two branches?

PH Grade ASSIST **10.52** A problem with a telephone line that prevents a customer from receiving or making calls is disconcerting to both the customer and the telephone company. The following data (stored in the file phone.xls) represent samples of 20 problems reported to two different offices of a telephone company and the time to clear these problems (in minutes) from the customers' lines:

Central Office I Time to Clear Problems (Minutes)

1.48	1.75	0.78	2.85	0.52	1.60	4.15	3.97	1.48	3.10
1.02	0.53	0.93	1.60	0.80	1.05	6.32	3.93	5.45	0.97

Central Office II Time to Clear Problems (Minutes)

7.55	3.75	0.10	1.10	0.60	0.52	3.30	2.10	0.58	4.02
3.75	0.65	1.92	0.60	1.53	4.23	0.08	1.48	1.65	0.72

a. Is there evidence of a difference in the variability of the waiting times between the two offices? (Use $\alpha = 0.05$.)

b. Determine the *p*-value in (a) and interpret its meaning.

c. What assumption is necessary in (a)? Is the assumption valid for these data?

d. Based on the results of (a), which *t* test defined in Section 10.1 should you use to compare the means of the two offices?

10.53 The director of training for a company that manufactures electronic equipment is interested in determining whether different training methods have an effect on the productivity of assembly-line employees. She randomly assigns 42 recently hired employees to two groups of 21. The first group receives a computer-assisted, individual-based training program, and the other receives a team-based training program. Upon completion of the training, the employees are evaluated on the time (in seconds) it takes to assemble a part. The results are in the data file training.xls.

a. Using a 0.05 level of significance, is there evidence of a difference between the variances in assembly times (in seconds) of employees trained in a computer-assisted, individual-based program and those trained in a team-based program?

b. On the basis of the results in (a), which *t* test defined in Section 10.1 should you use to compare the means of the two groups? Discuss.

10.54 Is there a difference in the variation of the yield of different types of investment between banks? The following data, from the file bankyield.xls, represent the nationwide highest yields for money market accounts and one-year CDs as of January 24, 2006:

Money Market Accounts	One-Year CD
4.55 4.50 4.40 4.38 4.38	4.94 4.90 4.85 4.85 4.85

Source: Extracted from Bankrate.com, January 24, 2006.

At the 0.05 level of significance, is there evidence of a difference in the variance of the yield between money market accounts and one-year CDs? Assume that the population yields are normally distributed.

SUMMARY

In this chapter, you were introduced to a variety of two-sample tests. For situations in which the samples are independent, you learned statistical test procedures for analyzing possible differences between means, variances, and proportions. In addition, you learned a test procedure that is frequently used when analyzing differences between the means of two related samples. Remember that you need to select the test that is most appropriate for a given set of conditions and to critically investigate the validity of the assumptions underlying each of the hypothesis-testing procedures.

The roadmap in Figure 10.16 illustrates the steps needed in determining which two-sample test of hypothesis to use: The following are the questions you need to consider.

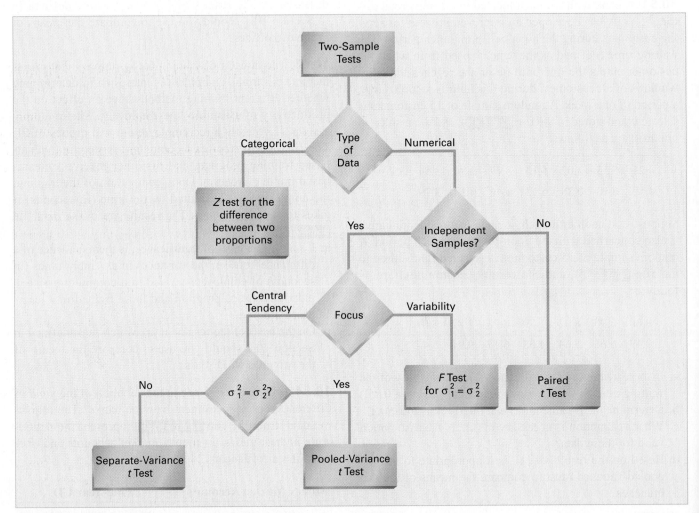

FIGURE 10.16 Roadmap for selecting a two-sample test of hypothesis

1. What type of data do you have? If you are dealing with categorical variables, use the Z test for the difference between two proportions. (This test assumes independent samples.)
2. If you have a numerical variable, determine whether you have independent samples or related samples. If you have related samples, use the paired t test.
3. If you have independent samples, is your focus on variability or central tendency? If the focus is variability, use the F test.

4. If your focus is central tendency, determine whether you can assume that the variances of the two groups are equal. (This assumption can be tested using the F test.)
5. If you can assume that the two groups have equal variances, use the pooled-variance t test. If you cannot assume that the two groups have equal variances, use the separate-variance t test.

Table 10.8 provides a list of topics covered in this chapter.

TABLE 10.8

Summary of Topics in Chapter 10

Type of Analysis	Types of Data	
	Numerical	**Categorical**
Comparing two populations	Z and t tests for the difference in the means of two independent populations (Section 10.1) Paired t test (Section 10.2) F test for differences between two variances (Section 10.4)	Z test for the difference between two proportions (Section 10.3)

KEY EQUATIONS

Z Test for the Difference Between Two Means

$$Z = \frac{(\overline{X}_1 - \overline{X}_2) - (\mu_1 - \mu_2)}{\sqrt{\dfrac{\sigma_1^2}{n_1} + \dfrac{\sigma_2^2}{n_2}}} \qquad (10.1)$$

Pooled-Variance t Test for the Difference Between Two Means

$$t = \frac{(\overline{X}_1 - \overline{X}_2) - (\mu_1 - \mu_2)}{\sqrt{S_p^2\left(\dfrac{1}{n_1} + \dfrac{1}{n_2}\right)}} \qquad (10.2)$$

Confidence Interval Estimate of the Difference in the Means of Two Independent Populations

$$(\overline{X}_1 - \overline{X}_2) \pm t_{n_1+n_2-2}\sqrt{S_p^2\left(\frac{1}{n_1} + \frac{1}{n_2}\right)} \qquad (10.3)$$

or

$$(\overline{X}_1 - \overline{X}_2) - t_{n_1+n_2-2}\sqrt{S_p^2\left(\frac{1}{n_1} + \frac{1}{n_2}\right)} \le \mu_1 - \mu_2$$

$$\le (\overline{X}_1 - \overline{X}_2) + t_{n_1+n_2-2}\sqrt{S_p^2\left(\frac{1}{n_1} + \frac{1}{n_2}\right)}$$

Z Test for the Mean Difference

$$Z = \frac{\overline{D} - \mu_D}{\dfrac{\sigma_D}{\sqrt{n}}} \qquad (10.4)$$

Paired t Test for the Mean Difference

$$t = \frac{\overline{D} - \mu_D}{\dfrac{S_D}{\sqrt{n}}} \qquad (10.5)$$

Confidence Interval Estimate for the Mean Difference

$$\overline{D} \pm t_{n-1}\frac{S_D}{\sqrt{n}} \qquad (10.6)$$

or

$$\overline{D} - t_{n-1}\frac{S_D}{\sqrt{n}} \le \mu_D \le \overline{D} + t_{n-1}\frac{S_D}{\sqrt{n}}$$

Z Test for the Difference Between Two Proportions

$$Z = \frac{(p_1 - p_2) - (\pi_1 - \pi_2)}{\sqrt{\overline{p}(1-\overline{p})\left(\dfrac{1}{n_1} + \dfrac{1}{n_2}\right)}} \qquad (10.7)$$

Confidence Interval Estimate for the Difference Between Two Proportions

$$(p_1 - p_2) \pm Z\sqrt{\frac{p_1(1-p_1)}{n_1} + \frac{p_2(1-p_2)}{n_2}} \qquad (10.8)$$

or

$$(p_1 - p_2) - Z\sqrt{\frac{p_1(1-p_1)}{n_1} + \frac{p_2(1-p_2)}{n_2}} \le (\pi_1 - \pi_2)$$

$$\le (p_1 - p_2) + Z\sqrt{\frac{p_1(1-p_1)}{n_1} + \frac{p_2(1-p_2)}{n_2}}$$

F Test Statistic for Testing the Equality of Two Variances

$$F = \frac{S_1^2}{S_2^2} \qquad (10.9)$$

Finding Lower-Tail Critical Values from the F Distribution

$$F_L = \frac{1}{F_{U*}} \qquad (10.10)$$

KEY TERMS

F distribution   397
F test statistic for testing the equality
   of two variances   397
matched   381
paired t test for the mean difference
   in related populations   382

pooled-variance t test   371
repeated measurements   381
robust   375
separate-variance t test   377

Z test for difference between
   two means   370
Z test for the difference between
   two proportions   390

CHAPTER REVIEW PROBLEMS

Checking Your Understanding

10.55 What are some of the criteria used in the selection of a particular hypothesis-testing procedure?

10.56 Under what conditions should you use the pooled-variance t test to examine possible differences in the means of two independent populations?

10.57 Under what conditions should you use the F test to examine possible differences in the variances of two independent populations?

10.58 What is the distinction between two independent populations and two related populations?

10.59 What is the distinction between repeated measurements and matched (or paired) items?

10.60 Under what conditions should you use the paired t test for the mean difference between two related populations?

10.61 Explain the similarities and differences between the test of hypothesis for the difference between the means of two independent populations and the confidence interval estimate of the difference between the means.

Applying the Concepts

10.62 A study compared music compact disc prices for Internet-based retailers and traditional brick-and-mortar retailers (Extracted from L. Zoonky and S. Gosain, "A Longitudinal Price Comparison for Music CDs in Electronic and Brick-and-Mortar Markets: Pricing Strategies in Emergent Electronic Commerce," *Journal of Business Strategies*, Spring 2002, 19(1), pp. 55–72). Before collecting the data, the researchers carefully defined several research hypotheses, including:

1. The price dispersion on the Internet is lower than the price dispersion in the brick-and-mortar market.
2. Prices in electronic markets are lower than prices in physical markets.

a. Consider research hypothesis 1. Write the null and alternative hypotheses in terms of population parameters. Carefully define the population parameters used.
b. Define a Type I and Type II error for the hypotheses in (a).

c. What type of statistical test should you use?
d. What assumptions are needed to perform the test you selected?
e. Repeat (a) through (d) for research hypothesis 2.

10.63 The pet-drug market is growing very rapidly. Before new pet drugs can be introduced into the marketplace, they must be approved by the U.S. Food and Drug Administration (FDA). In 1999, the Novartis company was trying to get Anafranil, a drug to reduce dog anxiety, approved. According to an article (E. Tanouye, "The Ow in Bowwow: With Growing Market in Pet Drugs, Makers Revamp Clinical Trials," *The Wall Street Journal*, April 13, 1999), Novartis had to find a way to translate a dog's anxiety symptoms into numbers that could be used to prove to the FDA that the drug had a statistically significant effect on the condition.

a. What is meant by the phrase *statistically significant effect*?
b. Consider an experiment in which dogs suffering from anxiety are divided into two groups. One group will be given Anafranil, and the other will be given a placebo (that is, a drug without active ingredients). How can you translate a dog's anxiety symptoms into numbers? In other words, define a continuous variable, X_1, the measurement of effectiveness of the drug Anafranil, and X_2, the measurement of the effectiveness of the placebo.
c. Building on your answer to part (b), define the null and alternative hypotheses for this study.

10.64 In response to lawsuits filed against the tobacco industry, many companies, such as Philip Morris, are running television advertisements that are supposed to educate teenagers about the dangers of smoking. Are these tobacco industry antismoking campaigns successful? Are state-sponsored antismoking commercials more effective? An article (G. Fairclough, "Philip Morris's Antismoking Campaign Draws Fire," *The Wall Street Journal*, April 6, 1999, p. B1) discussed a study in California that compared commercials made by the state of California and commercials produced by Philip Morris. Researchers showed the state ads and the Philip Morris ads to a group of California teenagers and measured the effectiveness of both. The researchers concluded that the state ads were more effective in relaying the dangers of smoking than the Philip Morris ads. The article suggests, however, that the study is not *statistically reliable* because the sample size was too small and because the study specifically selected participants who are considered more likely to start smoking than others.

a. How do you think the researchers measured effectiveness?
b. Define the null and alternative hypotheses for this study.
c. Explain the risks associated with Type I and Type II errors in this study.
d. What type of test is most appropriate in this situation?
e. What do you think is meant by the phrase *statistically reliable*?

10.65 The FedEx St. Jude Classic professional golf tournament is held each year in Memphis, Tennessee. FedEx sponsors this PGA tournament, and part of the proceeds go to the St. Jude Children's Research Hospital. In 2003, the tournament raised $679,115 for the hospital. This type of corporate sponsorship is known as *cause-related marketing*. A sample of spectators at the tournament were surveyed and asked to respond to a series of statements on a 5-point scale (1 = Strongly Disagree, 2 = Disagree, 3 = Neutral, 4 = Agree, and 5 = Strongly Agree). The following are four of the questions asked:

1. Cause-related marketing creates a positive company image.
2. I would be willing to pay more for a service that supports a cause I care about.
3. Cause-related marketing should be a standard part of a company's activities.
4. Based on its support of St. Jude, I will be more likely to use FedEx services.

For each question, the researchers tested the null hypothesis that the mean response for males and females is equal. The alternative hypothesis is that the mean response is different for males and females. The following table summarizes the results:

| | Sample Mean | | | |
| | Female | Male | | |
Question	($n_1 = 137$)	($n_2 = 305$)	t	p-Value
1	4.46	4.26	1.907	0.057
2	4.09	3.86	2.105	0.035
3	4.26	3.91	3.258	0.001
4	4.12	4.06	0.567	0.571

Source: Extracted from R. L. Irwin, T. Lachowetz, T. B. Cornwell, and J. S. Cook, "Cause-Related Sport Sponsorship: An Assessment of Spectator Beliefs, Attitudes, and Behavioral Intentions," Sport Marketing Quarterly, 2003, 12(3), pp. 131–139.

a. Interpret the results of the t test for question 1.
b. Interpret the results of the t test for question 2.
c. Interpret the results of the t test for question 3.
d. Interpret the results of the t test for question 4.
e. Write a short summary about the differences between males and females concerning their views toward cause-related sponsorship.

10.66 Two professors wanted to study how students from their two universities compared in their capabilities of using Excel spreadsheets in undergraduate information systems courses (Extracted from H. Howe, and M. G. Simkin, "Factors Affecting the Ability to Detect Spreadsheet Errors," *Decision Sciences Journal of Innovative Education*, January 2006, pp. 101–122). A comparison of the student demographics was also performed. One school is a state university in the Western United States, and the other school is a state university in the Eastern United States. The following table contains information regarding the ages of the students:

School	Sample Size	Mean Age	Standard Deviation
Western	93	23.28	6.29
Eastern	135	21.16	1.32

a. Using a 0.01 level of significance, is there evidence of a difference between the variances in age of students at the Western school and at the Eastern school?
b. Discuss the practical implications of the test performed in (a). Address, specifically, the impact equal (or unequal) variances in age has on teaching an undergraduate information systems course.
c. To test for a difference in the mean age of students, is it most appropriate to use the pooled-variance t test or the separate-variance t test?

The following table contains information regarding the years of spreadsheet usage of the students:

School	Sample Size	Mean Years	Standard Deviation
Western	93	2.6	2.4
Eastern	135	4.0	2.1

d. Using a 0.01 level of significance, is there evidence of a difference between the variances in years of spreadsheet usage of students at the Western school and at the Eastern school?
e. Based on the results of (d), use the most appropriate test to determine, at the 0.01 level of significance, whether there is evidence of a difference in the mean years of spreadsheet usage of students at the Western school and at the Eastern school?

10.67 The manager of computer operations of a large company wants to study computer usage of two departments within the company—the accounting department and the research department. A random sample of five jobs from the accounting department in the past week and six jobs from the research department in the past week are selected, and the processing time (in seconds) for each job is recorded (and stored in the `accres.xls` file):

Department	Processing Time (in Seconds)					
Accounting	9	3	8	7	12	
Research	4	13	10	9	9	6

Use a level of significance of 0.05.
a. Is there evidence that the mean processing time in the research department is greater than 6 seconds?
b. Is there evidence of a difference between the variances in the processing time of the two departments?
c. Is there evidence of a difference between the mean processing time of the accounting department and that of the research department?
d. Determine the *p*-values in (a) through (c) and interpret their meanings.
e. Construct and interpret a 95% confidence interval estimate of the difference in the mean processing times between the accounting and research departments.

10.68 A computer information systems professor is interested in studying the amount of time it takes students enrolled in the introduction to computers course to write and run a program in Visual Basic. The professor hires you to analyze the following results (in minutes) from a random sample of nine students (the data are stored in the `vb.xls` file):

$$10 \quad 13 \quad 9 \quad 15 \quad 12 \quad 13 \quad 11 \quad 13 \quad 12$$

a. At the 0.05 level of significance, is there evidence that the population mean amount is greater than 10 minutes? What will you tell the professor?
b. Suppose the computer professor, when checking her results, realizes that the fourth student needed 51 minutes rather than the recorded 15 minutes to write and run the Visual Basic program. At the 0.05 level of significance, reanalyze the question posed in (a), using the revised data. What will you tell the professor now?
c. The professor is perplexed by these paradoxical results and requests an explanation from you regarding the justification for the difference in your findings in (a) and (b). Discuss.
d. A few days later, the professor calls to tell you that the dilemma is completely resolved. The original number 15 (the fourth data value) was correct, and therefore your findings in (a) are being used in the article she is writing for a computer journal. Now she wants to hire you to compare the results from that group of introduction to computers students against those from a sample of 11 computer majors in order to determine whether there is evidence that computer majors can write a Visual Basic program in less time than introductory students. For the computer majors, the sample mean is 8.5 minutes, and the sample standard deviation is 2.0 minutes. At the 0.05 level of significance, completely analyze these data. What will you tell the professor?
e. A few days later, the professor calls again to tell you that a reviewer of her article wants her to include the *p*-value for the "correct" result in (a). In addition, the professor inquires about an unequal-variances problem, which the reviewer wants her to discuss in her article. In your own words, discuss the concept of *p*-value and describe the unequal-variances problem. Determine the *p*-value in (a) and discuss whether the unequal-variances problem had any meaning in the professor's study.

10.69 An article in *USA Today* (D. Sharp, "Cellphones Reveal Screaming Lack of Courtesy," *USA Today*, September 2001, p. 4A) reported that according to a poll, the mean talking time per month for cell phones was 372 minutes for men and 275 minutes for women, while the mean talking time per month for traditional home phones was 334 minutes for men and 510 minutes for women. Suppose that the poll was based on a sample of 100 men and 100 women, and that the standard deviation of the talking time per month for cell phones was 120 minutes for men and 100 minutes for women, while the standard deviation of the talking time per month for traditional home phones was 100 minutes for men and 150 minutes for women.
Use a level of significance of 0.05.
a. Is there evidence of a difference in the mean monthly talking time on cell phones for men and women?
b. Is there evidence of a difference in the mean monthly talking time on traditional home phones for men and women?
c. Construct and interpret a 95% confidence interval estimate of the difference in the mean monthly talking time on cell phones for men and women.
d. Construct and interpret a 95% confidence interval estimate of the difference in the mean monthly talking time on traditional home phones for men and women.
e. Is there evidence of a difference in the variance of the monthly talking time on cell phones for men and women?
f. Is there evidence of a difference in the variance of the monthly talking time on traditional home phones for men and women?
g. Based on the results of (a) through (f), what conclusions can you make concerning cell phone and traditional home phone usage between men and women?

10.70 A survey of 500 men and 500 women designed to study financial tensions between couples asked how likely they were to hide purchases, cash, or investments from their partners. The results were as follows:

Likely to Hide

Type	Men	Women
Auto-related	66	36
Cash	126	133
Clothes	62	116
Electronics	79	56
Entertainment	96	76
Food	74	94
Investments	76	52
Travel	53	39

Source: Extracted from L. Wei, "Your Money Manager as Financial Therapist," The Wall Street Journal, November 5–6, 2005, p. B4.

For *each type of purchase*, determine whether there is a difference between men and women at the 0.05 level of significance.

10.71 As more Americans use cell phones, they question where it is okay to talk on cell phones. The following is a table of results, in percentages, for 2000 and 2006 (extracted from W. Koch, "Business Put a Lid on Chatterboxes," *USA Today*, February 7, 2006, p. 3A). Suppose the survey was based on 100 respondents in 2000 and 100 respondents in 2006.

	YEAR	
OKAY TO TALK ON A CELL PHONE IN A	**2000**	**2006**
Bathroom	39	38
Movie/theater	11	2
Car	76	63
Supermarket	60	66
Public transit	52	45
Restaurant	31	21

For *each type of location*, determine whether there is a difference between 2000 and 2006 in the proportion who think it is okay to talk on a cell phone (use the 0.05 level of significance).

10.72 The lengths of life (in hours) of a sample of 40 100-watt light bulbs produced by manufacturer A and a sample of 40 100-watt light bulbs produced by manufacturer B are in the file bulbs.xls. Completely analyze the differences between the lengths of life of the bulbs produced by two manufacturers (use $\alpha = 0.05$).

10.73 The data file restaurants.xls contains the ratings for food, decor, service, and the price per person for a sample of 50 restaurants located in an urban area and 50 restaurants located in a suburban area. Completely analyze the differences between urban and suburban restaurants for the variables food rating, decor rating, service rating, and price per person, using $\alpha = 0.05$.

Source: Extracted from Zagat Survey 2002: New York City Restaurants and Zagat Survey 2001–2002: Long Island Restaurants.

10.74 Management of a hotel was concerned with increasing the return rate for hotel guests. One aspect of first impressions by guests relates to the time it takes to deliver the guest's luggage to the room after check-in to the hotel. A random sample of 20 deliveries on a particular day were selected in Wing A of the hotel, and a random sample of 20 deliveries were selected in Wing B. The results are stored in the file luggage.xls. Analyze the data and determine whether there is a difference in the mean delivery time in the two wings of the hotel (use $\alpha = 0.05$).

10.75 In manufacturing processes, the term *work-in-process* (often abbreviated *WIP*) is often used. In a book manufacturing plant, WIP represents the time it takes for sheets from a press to be folded, gathered, sewn, tipped on end sheets, and bound. The following data (stored in the file wip.xls) represent samples of 20 books at each of two production plants and the processing time (operationally defined as the time, in days, from when the books came off the press to when they were packed in cartons):

Plant A

5.62 5.29 16.25 10.92 11.46 21.62 8.45 8.58 5.41 11.42

11.62 7.29 7.50 7.96 4.42 10.50 7.58 9.29 7.54 8.92

Plant B

9.54 11.46 16.62 12.62 25.75 15.41 14.29 13.13 13.71 10.04

5.75 12.46 9.17 13.21 6.00 2.33 14.25 5.37 6.25 9.71

Completely analyze the differences between the processing times for the two plants, using $\alpha = 0.05$, and write a summary of your findings to be presented to the vice president for operations of the company.

10.76 Do marketing promotions, such as bobble-head giveaways, increase attendance at Major League Baseball games? An article reported on the effectiveness of marketing promotions (extracted from T. C. Boyd and T. C. Krehbiel, "An Analysis of Specific Promotion Types on Attendance at Major League Baseball Games," *Mid-American Journal of Business*, 2006, 21, pp. 21–32). The data file royals.xls includes the following variables for the Kansas City Royals during the 2002 baseball season:
  Game—Home games, in the order in which they were played
  Attendance—Paid attendance for the game
  Promotion—1 = if a promotion was held; 0 = if no promotion was held
a. At the 0.05 level of significance, is there evidence of a difference between the variances in the attendance at games with promotions and games without promotions?
b. Based on the result of (a), conduct the appropriate test of hypothesis to determine whether there is a difference in the mean attendance at games with promotions and games without promotions. (Use $\alpha = 0.05$.)
c. Write a brief summary of your results.

10.77 The manufacturer of Boston and Vermont asphalt shingles knows that product weight is a major factor in the customer's perception of quality. Moreover, the weight represents the amount of raw materials being used and is therefore very important to the company from a cost standpoint. The last stage of the assembly-line packages the shingles before they are placed on wooden pallets. Once a pallet is full (a pallet for most brands holds 16 squares of shingles), it is weighed, and the measurement is recorded. The data file pallet.xls contains the weight (in pounds) from a sample of 368 pallets of Boston shingles and 330 pallets of Vermont shingles. Completely analyze the differences in the weights of the Boston and Vermont shingles, using $\alpha = 0.05$.

10.78 The manufacturer of Boston and Vermont asphalt shingles provides its customers with a 20-year warranty on most of its products. To determine whether a shingle will last as long as the warranty period, accelerated-life testing is conducted at the manufacturing plant. Accelerated-life testing exposes the shingle to the stresses it would be subject to in a lifetime of normal use in a laboratory setting via an experiment that takes only a few minutes to conduct. In this test, a shingle is repeatedly scraped with a brush for a short period of time, and the shingle granules removed by the brushing are weighed (in grams). Shingles that experience low amounts of granule loss are expected to last longer in normal use than shingles that experience high amounts of granule loss. In this situation, a shingle should experience no more than 0.8 grams of granule loss if it is expected to last the length of the warranty period. The data file granule.xls contains a sample of 170 measurements made on the company's Boston shingles and 140 measurements made on Vermont shingles. Completely analyze the differences in the granule loss of the Boston and Vermont shingles, using $\alpha = 0.05$.

Report Writing Exercise

10.79 Referring to the results of Problems 10.77 and 10.78 concerning the weight and granule loss of Boston and Vermont shingles, write a report that summarizes your conclusions.

Team Project

The data file mutual funds.xls contains information regarding nine variables from a sample of 838 mutual funds. The variables are

Category—Type of stocks comprising the mutual fund (small cap, mid cap, or large cap)

Objective—Objective of stocks comprising the mutual fund (growth or value)

Assets—In millions of dollars

Fees—Sales charges (no or yes)

Expense ratio—Ratio of expenses to net assets, in percentage

2005 return—Twelve-month return in 2005

Three-year return—Annualized return, 2003–2005

Five-year return—Annualized return, 2001–2005

Risk—Risk-of-loss factor of the mutual fund (low, average, or high)

10.80 Completely analyze the difference between mutual funds without fees and mutual funds with fees in terms of 2005 return, three-year return, five-year return, and expense ratio. Write a report summarizing your findings.

10.81 Completely analyze the difference between mutual funds that have a growth objective and mutual funds that have a value objective in terms of 2005 return, three-year return, five-year return, and expense ratio. Write a report summarizing your findings.

Student Survey Data Base

10.82 Problem 1.27 on page 15 describes a survey of 50 undergraduate students (see the file undergradsurvey.xls). For these data,

a. at the 0.05 level of significance, is there evidence of a difference between males and females in grade point average, expected starting salary, salary expected in five years, age, and spending on textbooks and supplies?

b. at the 0.05 level of significance, is there evidence of a difference between those students who plan to go to graduate school and those who do not plan to go to graduate school in grade point average, expected starting salary, salary expected in five years, age, and spending on textbooks and supplies?

10.83 Problem 1.27 on page 15 describes a survey of 50 undergraduate students (see the file undergradsurvey.xls).

a. Select a sample of 50 undergraduate students at your school and conduct a similar survey for them.

b. For the data collected in (a), repeat (a) and (b) of Problem 10.82.

c. Compare the results of (b) to those of Problem 10.82.

10.84 Problem 1.28 on page 15 describes a survey of 50 MBA students (see the file gradsurvey.xls). For these data, at the 0.05 level of significance, is there evidence of a difference between males and females in age, undergraduate grade point average, graduate grade point average, GMAT score, expected salary upon graduation, salary expected in five years, and spending on textbooks and supplies?

10.85 Problem 1.28 on page 15 describes a survey of 50 MBA students (see the file gradsurvey.xls).

a. Select a sample of 50 graduate students in your MBA program and conduct a similar survey for those students.

b. For the data collected in (a), repeat Problem 10.84.

c. Compare the results of (b) to those of Problem 10.84.

Managing the *Springville Herald*

A marketing department team is charged with improving the telemarketing process in order to increase the number of home-delivery subscriptions sold. After several brainstorming sessions, it was clear that the longer a caller speaks to a respondent, the greater the chance that the caller will sell a home-delivery subscription. Therefore, the team decided to find ways to increase the length of the phone calls.

Initially, the team investigated the impact that the time of a call might have on the length of the call. Under current arrangements, calls were made in the evening hours, between 5:00 p.m. and 9:00 p.m., Monday through Friday. The team wanted to compare the length of calls made early in the evening (before 7:00 p.m.) with those made later in the evening (after 7:00 p.m.) to determine whether one of these time periods is more conducive to lengthier calls and,

correspondingly, to increased subscription sales. The team selected a sample of 30 female callers who staff the telephone bank on Wednesday evenings and randomly assigned 15 of them to the "early" group and 15 to the "later" group. The callers knew that the team was observing their efforts that evening but didn't know which calls were monitored. The callers had been trained to make their telephone presentations in a structured manner. They were to read from a script, and their greeting was personal but informal ("Hi, this is Mary Jones from the *Springville Herald*. May I speak to Bill Richards?").

Measurements were taken on the length of the call (defined as the difference, in seconds, between the time the person answered the phone and the time he or she hung up). The results (stored in the file sh10.xls) are presented in Table SH10.1.

TABLE SH10.1

Length of Calls, in Seconds, Based on Time of Call—Early Versus Late in the Evening

Time of Call		Time of Call	
Early	**Late**	**Early**	**Late**
41.3	37.1	40.6	40.7
37.5	38.9	33.3	38.0
39.3	42.2	39.6	43.6
37.4	45.7	35.7	43.8
33.6	42.4	31.3	34.9
38.5	39.0	36.8	35.7
32.6	40.9	36.3	47.4
37.3	40.5		

EXERCISES

SH10.1 Analyze the data in Table SH10.1 and write a report to the marketing department team that indicates your findings. Include an attached appendix in which you discuss the reason you selected a particular statistical test to compare the two independent groups of callers.

SH10.2 Suppose that instead of the research design described here, there were only 15 callers sampled,

and each caller was to be monitored twice in the evening—once in the early time period and once in the later time period. Suppose that in Table SH10.1, each pair of values represents a particular caller's two measurements. Reanalyze these data and write a report for presentation to the team that indicates your findings.

SH10.3 What other variables should be investigated next? Why?

Web Case

Apply your knowledge about hypothesis testing in this Web Case, which continues the cereal-fill packaging dispute Web Case from Chapters 7 and 9.

Even after the recent public experiment about cereal box weights, the Consumers Concerned About Cereal Cheaters (CCACC) remains convinced that Oxford Cereals has misled the public. The group has created and posted a document in which it claims that cereal boxes produced at Plant Number 2 in Springville weigh less than the claimed mean of 368 grams. Visit the CCACC More Cheating page at **www.prenhall.com/Springville/MoreCheating.htm** (or open this Web page file from the text CD's Web Case folder) and then answer the following:

1. Do the CCACC's results prove that there is a statistical difference in the mean weights of cereal boxes produced at Plant Numbers 1 and 2?

2. Perform the appropriate analysis to test the CCACC's hypothesis. What conclusions can you reach based on the data?

REFERENCES

1. Conover, W. J., *Practical Nonparametric Statistics*, 3rd ed. (New York: Wiley, 2000).

2. Daniel, W., *Applied Nonparametric Statistics*, 2nd ed. (Boston: Houghton Mifflin, 1990).

3. *Microsoft Excel 2007* (Redmond, WA: Microsoft Corp., 2007).

4. Satterthwaite, F. E., "An Approximate Distribution of Estimates of Variance Components," *Biometrics Bulletin*, 2(1946): 110–114.

5. Snedecor, G. W., and W. G. Cochran, *Statistical Methods*, 8th ed. (Ames, IA: Iowa State University Press, 1989).

6. Winer, B. J., D. R. Brown, and K. M. Michels, *Statistical Principles in Experimental Design*, 3rd ed. (New York: McGraw-Hill, 1989).

Excel Companion
to Chapter 10

You can use Microsoft Excel to conduct all six two-sample hypothesis tests discussed in Chapter 10. Some tests require the use of ToolPak procedure. Others require that you use PHStat2 or one of the workbooks stored on the Student CD-ROM. Some tests have Excel versions in which you can use only unsummarized data, and others have Excel versions in which you must use summarized data. (A few tests have Excel versions for either unsummarized or summarized data.)

Use Table E10.1 below to help choose the right test for your data and as a guide for the rest of this Excel Companion.

Two-Sample Data Arrangements

Unsummarized data can be entered in a **stacked** or **unstacked** arrangement. In a stacked arrangement, all the values for a variable appear in a single column, next to a column that identifies the sample or group to which individual values belong. In an unstacked arrangement, the values for the samples or groups appear in separate columns. For example, Figure E10.1 shows the stacked and unstacked versions of the cola display location sales analysis data of Table 10.1 on page 372.

	A	B
1	Group	Value
2	Normal	22
3	Normal	34
4	Normal	52
5	Normal	62
6	Normal	30
7	Normal	40
8	Normal	64
9	Normal	84
10	Normal	56
11	Normal	59
12	End-Aisle	52
13	End-Aisle	71
14	End-Aisle	76
15	End-Aisle	54
16	End-Aisle	67
17	End-Aisle	83
18	End-Aisle	66
19	End-Aisle	90
20	End-Aisle	77
21	End-Aisle	84

	A	B
1	Normal	End-Aisle
2	22	52
3	34	71
4	52	76
5	62	54
6	30	67
7	40	83
8	64	66
9	84	90
10	56	77
11	59	84

FIGURE E10.1 Stacked and unstacked data

TABLE E10.1

Two-Sample Tests in Microsoft Excel

Two-Sample Test	Unsummarized Data (Excel Companion Section)	Summarized Data (Excel Companion Section)
Z test for the difference between two means	ToolPak z-Test: Two Sample for Means (E10.1)	Z Two Means.xls or PHStat2 Z Test for Differences in Two Means (E10.2)
Pooled-variance t test for the difference between two means	ToolPak t-Test: Two-Sample Assuming Equal Variances (E10.3)	Pooled-variance T.xls or PHStat2 t Test for Differences Between Two Means (E10.4)
Separate-variance t test for the difference between two means	ToolPak t-Test: Two-Sample Assuming Unequal Variances (E10.5)	Not included
Paired t test	ToolPak t-Test: Paired Two Sample for Means (E10.6)	Not included
Z test for the difference between two proportions	Not included	Z Two Proportions.xls or PHStat2 Z Test for Differences Between Two Proportions (E10.7)
F test for the difference between two variances	ToolPak F-Test Two-Sample for Variances (E10.8)	F Two Variances.xls or PHStat2 F Test for Differences Between Two Variances (E10.9)

Specific statistical procedures or Excel worksheets for analyses involving two or more groups require that the data be arranged either as stacked or unstacked data. The two-sample hypothesis tests for unsummarized data discussed in this Excel Companion require that your data be unstacked.

If you need to change stacked data into its unstacked equivalent, you can sort the data by sample or group and then cut and paste the second sample's data to a new column. Likewise, to stack unstacked data, you can copy the data from the second sample directly below the first sample and then add a column that identifies the group.

PHStat2 can automate these tasks by using either the **Unstack Data** or **Stack Data** procedures found in the PHStat2 **Data Preparation** submenu.

E10.1 USING THE Z TEST FOR THE DIFFERENCE BETWEEN TWO MEANS (UNSUMMARIZED DATA)

For unsummarized data, you conduct a Z test for the difference between two means by selecting the ToolPak z-Test: Two Sample for Means procedure.

Open to the worksheet that contains the unsummarized data for the two samples. Select **Tools → Data Analysis**, select **z-Test: Two Sample for Means** from the **Data Analysis** list, and click **OK**. In the procedure's dialog box (shown below), enter the cell range of one sample as the **Variable 1 Range** and the cell range of the other sample as the **Variable 2 Range**. Enter the **Hypothesized Mean Difference**, the population variance of the first sample as the **Variable 1 Variance (known)**, and the population variance of the second sample as the **Variable 2 Variance (known)**. Select **Labels** and click **OK**. Results appear on a new worksheet.

E10.2 USING THE Z TEST FOR THE DIFFERENCE BETWEEN TWO MEANS (SUMMARIZED DATA)

For summarized data, you conduct a Z test for the difference between two means by either selecting the PHStat2 Z Test for Differences in Two Means procedure or by making entries in the Z Two Means.xls workbook.

Using PHStat2 Z Test for the Difference Between Two Means

Select **PHStat → Two-Sample Tests → Z Test for Differences in Two Means**. In the Z Test for the Differences in Two Means dialog box (shown below), enter the **Hypothesized Difference** and, if necessary, change the **Level of Significance**. Enter the sample size, sample mean, and population standard deviation for the population 1 sample and the population 2 sample. Click one of the test options, enter a title as the **Title**, and click **OK**.

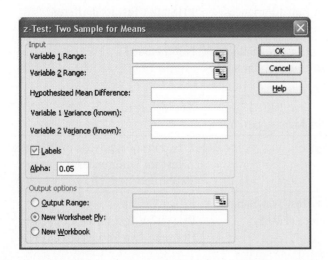

FIGURE E10.2

Z Two Means worksheet

	A	B	
1	Z Test for Differences in Two Means		
2			
3	**Data**		
4	Hypothesized Difference	0	
5	Level of Significance	0.05	
6	**Population 1 Sample**		
7	Sample Size	40	
8	Sample Mean	72	
9	Population Standard Deviation	20	
10	**Population 2 Sample**		
11	Sample Size	50	
12	Sample Mean	66	
13	Population Standard Deviation	10	
14			
15	**Intermediate Calculations**		
16	Difference in Sample Means	6	=B8 - B12
17	Standard Error of the Difference in Means	3.4641	=SQRT(((B9^ 2)/B7) + (B13^ 2)/B11)
18	Z-Test Statistic	1.7321	=(B16 - B4)/B17
19			
20	**Two-Tail Test**		
21	Lower Critical Value	-1.9600	=NORMSINV(B5/2)
22	Upper Critical Value	1.9600	=NORMSINV(1 - (B5/2))
23	*p*-Value	0.0833	=2 * (1 - NORMSDIST(ABS(B18)))
24	**Do not reject the null hypothesis**		=IF(B23 < B5, "Reject the null hypothesis", "Do not reject the null hypothesis")
25			
26	**Lower-Tail Test**		
27	Lower Critical Value	-1.6449	=NORMSINV(B5)
28	*p*-Value	0.9584	=NORMSDIST(B18)
29	**Do not reject the null hypothesis**		=IF(B28 < B5, "Reject the null hypothesis", "Do not reject the null hypothesis")
30			
31	**Upper-Tail Test**		
32	Upper Critical Value	1.6449	=NORMSINV(1 - B5)
33	*p*-Value	0.0416	=1 - NORMSDIST(B18)
34	**Reject the null hypothesis**		=IF(B33 < B5, "Reject the null hypothesis", "Do not reject the null hypothesis")

Using Z Two Means.xls

Open to the **Z Two Means** worksheet of the Z Two Means.xls workbook. This worksheet (see Figure E10.2) uses the **NORMSINV(P<X)** function to determine the lower and upper critical values and the **NORMSDIST(Z *value*)** function to compute the *p*-values from the *Z* value calculated in cell B18. The worksheet contains the entries to solve Problem 10.1 on page 377. To adapt this worksheet to other problems, change, as is necessary, the hypothesized difference and level of significance in cells B4 and B5 and the sample size, sample mean and population standard deviation of each sample in the cell range B7:B9 and B11:B13.

If you want to use this worksheet to show only one test, first make a copy of the worksheet (see the Excel Companion to Chapter 1). For a two-tail test, select and delete rows 26 through 34. For a lower-tail-test-only worksheet, select and delete rows 31 through 34 and then select and delete rows 20 through 25. For an upper-tail-test-only worksheet, select and delete rows 20 through 30.

E10.3 USING THE POOLED-VARIANCE *t* TEST (UNSUMMARIZED DATA)

For unsummarized data, you conduct a pooled-variance *t* test by selecting the ToolPak t-Test: Two-Sample Assuming Equal Variances procedure.

Open to the worksheet that contains the unsummarized data for the two samples. Select **Tools → Data Analysis**, select **t-Test: Two-Sample Assuming Equal Variances**

from the **Data Analysis** list and click **OK**. In the procedure's dialog box (shown below), enter the cell range of one sample as the **Variable 1 Range** and the cell range of the other sample as the **Variable 2 Range**. Enter the **Hypothesized Mean Difference**, click **Labels**, and click **OK**. Results appear on a new worksheet. Figure 10.3 on page 373 shows the results for the Table 10.1 BLK cola sales data.

E10.4 USING THE POOLED-VARIANCE *t* TEST (SUMMARIZED DATA)

For summarized data, you conduct a pooled-variance *t* test by either using the PHStat2 t Test for Differences in Two Means procedure or by making entries in the Pooled-Variance T.xls workbook.

Using PHStat2 *t* Test for the Differences in Two Means

Select **PHStat → Two-Sample Tests → t Test for Differences in Two Means**. In the t Test for Differences in Two Means dialog box (shown at right), enter values for the **Hypothesized Difference** and the **Level of Significance** and then enter the **Sample Size, Sample Mean**, and **Sample Standard Deviation** for the population 1 sample and the population 2 sample. Click one of the test options, enter a title as the **Title**, and click **OK**. To include a confidence interval estimate of the difference between the two means (similar to one found in the PVt worksheet described below), click **Confidence Interval Estimate** before you click **OK**.

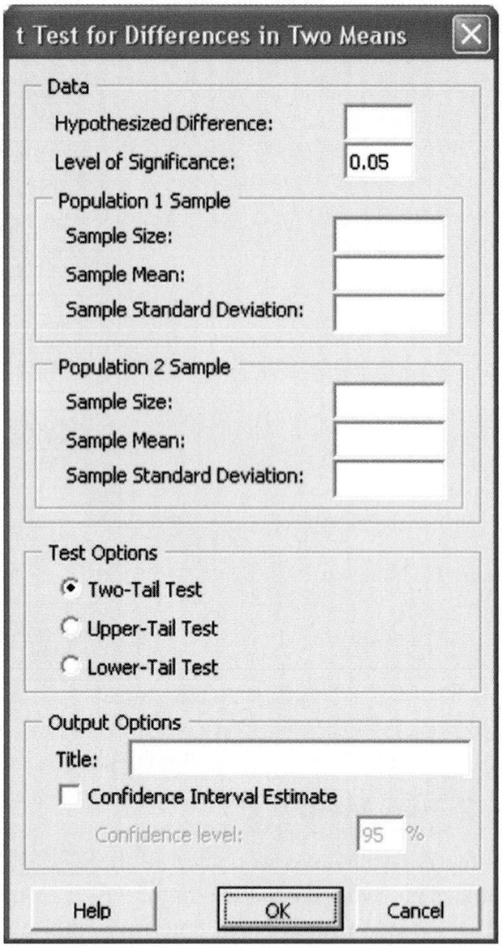

Using Pooled-Variance T.xls

Open to the **PVt** worksheet of the Pooled-Variance T.xls workbook. This worksheet (see Figure E10.3) uses the **TINV(1-*confidence level, degrees of freedom*)** function to determine the lower and upper critical values. To compute the *p*-values, this worksheet uses the **TDIST(ABS(*t*), *degrees of freedom, tails*)** function, in which **ABS(*t*)** is the absolute value of the *t* test statistic, and *tails* is either 1, for a one-tail test, or 2, for a two-tail test. The worksheet uses the IF function in cells B31 and B36 to determine which one of two values computed in a calculations area (not shown in Figure E10.3) to use.

FIGURE E10.3

PVt worksheet

	A	B	
1	Pooled-Variance t Test for Differences in Two Means		
2	(assumes equal population variances)		
3	**Data**		
4	**Hypothesized Difference**	0	
5	**Level of Significance**	0.05	
6	**Population 1 Sample**		
7	**Sample Size**	10	
8	**Sample Mean**	50.3	
9	**Sample Standard Deviation**	18.7	
10	**Population 2 Sample**		
11	**Sample Size**	10	
12	**Sample Mean**	72	
13	**Sample Standard Deviation**	12.5	
14			
15	**Intermediate Calculations**		
16	Population 1 Sample Degrees of Freedom	9	=B7 - 1
17	Population 2 Sample Degrees of Freedom	9	=B11 - 1
18	Total Degrees of Freedom	18	=B16 + B17
19	Pooled Variance	252.97	=((B16 * B9^2) + (B17 * B13^2))/B18
20	Difference in Sample Means	-21.7	=B8 - B12
21	*t* Test Statistic	-3.0508	=(B20 - B4)/SQRT(B19 * (1/B7 + 1/B11))
22			
23	**Two-Tail Test**		
24	**Lower Critical Value**	-2.1009	=-(TINV(B5, B18))
25	**Upper Critical Value**	2.1009	=TINV(B5, B18)
26	*p*-Value	0.0069	=TDIST(ABS(B21), B18, 2)
27	**Reject the null hypothesis**		=IF(B26 < B5, "Reject the null hypothesis",
28			"Do not reject the null hypothesis")
29	**Lower-Tail Test**		
30	**Lower Critical Value**	-1.7341	=-TINV(2 * B5, B18))
31	*p*-Value	0.0034	=IF(B21 < 0, E32, E33)
32	**Reject the null hypothesis**		=IF(B31 < B5, "Reject the null hypothesis",
33			"Do not reject the null hypothesis")
34	**Upper-Tail Test**		
35	**Upper Critical Value**	1.7341	=(TINV(2 * B5 ,B18))
36	*p*-Value	0.9966	=IF(B21 < 0, E33, E32)
37	**Do not reject the null hypothesis**		=IF(B36 < B5, "Reject the null hypothesis",
			"Do not reject the null hypothesis")

Not shown
Cell E32: =TDIST(ABS(B21), B18, 1)
Cell E33: =1 - E32

The worksheet contains entries based on the Table 10.1 BLK cola sales data on page 372. To adapt this worksheet to other problems, change, as necessary, the hypothesized difference, level of significance, and sample statistics of the two samples in cells B4, B5, B7:B9, and B11:B13. If you do not want to include a confidence interval estimate in your worksheet (see Figure E10.4), select and delete the cell range D3:E16.

	D	E	
1			
2			
3	**Confidence Interval Estimate**		
4	**of the Difference Between Two Means**		
5			
6	**Data**		
7	Confidence Level	95%	
8			
9	**Intermediate Calculations**		
10	Degrees of Freedom	18	=B16 + B17
11	t Value	2.1009	=TINV(1 - E7, E10)
12	Interval Half Width	14.9437	=(E11 * SQRT(B19 * (1/B7 + 1/B11)))
13			
14	**Confidence Interval**		
15	Interval Lower Limit	-36.6437	=B20 - E12
16	Interval Upper Limit	-6.7563	=B20 + E12

FIGURE E10.4 Confidence interval estimate area

E10.5 USING THE SEPARATE-VARIANCE *t* TEST FOR THE DIFFERENCE BETWEEN TWO MEANS (UNSUMMARIZED DATA)

For unsummarized data, you conduct a separate-variance *t* test for the difference between two means by selecting the ToolPak t-Test: Two-Sample Assuming Unequal Variances procedure.

Open to the worksheet that contains the unsummarized data for the two samples. Select **Tools → Data Analysis**, select **t-Test: Two-Sample Assuming Unequal Variances** from the **Data Analysis** list, and click **OK**. In the procedure's dialog box (shown below), enter the cell range of one sample as the **Variable 1 Range** and the cell range of the other sample as the **Variable 2 Range**. Enter the **Hypothesized Mean Difference**, click **Labels**, and click **OK**. Figure 10.6 on page 377 shows the results of applying this procedure to the Table 10.1 BLK cola sales data.

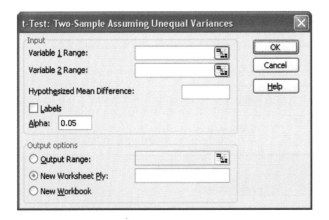

E10.6 USING THE PAIRED *t* TEST FOR THE DIFFERENCE BETWEEN TWO MEANS (UNSUMMARIZED DATA)

For unsummarized data, you conduct a paired *t* test for the difference between two means by selecting the ToolPak t-Test: Paired Two Sample for Mean procedure.

Open to the worksheet that contains the unsummarized data for the two samples. Select **Tools → Data Analysis**, select **t-Test: Paired Two Sample for Means** from the **Data Analysis** list and click **OK**. In the procedure's dialog box (shown below), enter the cell range of one sample as the **Variable 1 Range** and the cell range of the other sample as the **Variable 2 Range**. Enter the **Hypothesized Mean Difference**, click **Labels**, and click **OK**. Results appear on a new worksheet. Figure 10.8 on page 385 shows the results for the Table 10.4 car mileage data.

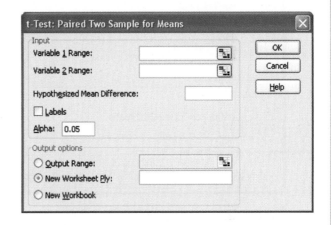

E10.7 USING THE Z TEST FOR THE DIFFERENCE BETWEEN TWO PROPORTIONS (SUMMARIZED DATA)

For summarized data, you conduct a Z test for the difference between two proportions by either selecting the PHStat2 Z Test for Differences in Two Proportions procedure or by making entries in the Z Two Proportions.xls workbook.

Using PHStat2 Z Test for Differences in Two Proportions

Select **PHStat → Two-Sample Tests → Z Test for Differences in Two Proportions**. In the Z Test for Differences in Two Proportions dialog box (shown on page 418), enter values for the **Hypothesized Difference** and the **Level of Significance**. Enter the **Number of Successes** and the **Sample Size** for the population 1 sample and the population 2 sample. Click one of the test options, enter a title as the **Title**, and click **OK**. To include a confidence interval estimate of the difference between the two proportions (similar to one shown in Figure E10.6 below), click **Confidence Interval Estimate** before you click **OK**.

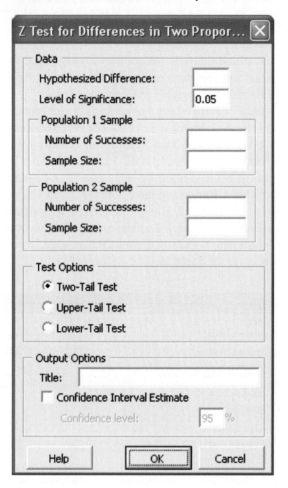

Using Z Two Proportions.xls

You open and use either the **ZTP_TT** or the **ZTP_All** worksheets of the Z Two Proportions.xls workbook to conduct a *Z* test for the difference between two proportions. These worksheets use the **NORMSINV($P<X$)** function to determine the lower and upper critical values, and the **NORMSDIST(Z *value*)** function to compute the *p*-values from the *Z* value calculated in cell B18. To better understand how a message gets displayed in these worksheets, read the "About the IF function" part of Section E9.1 on page 364.

The **ZTP_TT** worksheet (see Figure 10.11 on page 393) applies the two-tail *Z* test to the Section 10.3 hotel guest satisfaction example. The **ZTP_All** worksheet adds both the upper-tail and lower-tail test (see Figure E10.5) plus a confidence interval estimate of the difference between the two proportions (see Figure E10.6). To adapt these worksheets to other problems, change, if necessary, the hypothesized difference, level of significance, and number of successes and sample size for each sample in cells B4, B5, B7, B8, B10, and B11.

If you want the ZTP_All worksheet to show only one of the single-tail tests, first make a copy of that worksheet (see the Excel Companion to Chapter 1). For a lower-tail-test-only worksheet, select and delete rows 30 through 34 and then select and delete rows 20 through 25. For an upper-tail-test-only worksheet, select and delete rows 20 through 30. If you do not want to include a confidence interval estimate in your worksheet, delete columns D and E.

FIGURE E10.5

ZTP_All single-tail test area

FIGURE E10.6

ZTP_All confidence interval estimate area

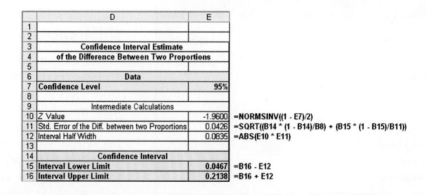

E10.8 USING THE *F* TEST FOR THE DIFFERENCE BETWEEN TWO VARIANCES (UNSUMMARIZED DATA)

For unsummarized data, you conduct an *F* test for the difference between two variances by selecting the ToolPak F Test Two-Sample for Variances procedure.

Open to the worksheet that contains the unsummarized data for the two samples. Select **Tools → Data Analysis**, select **F Test Two-Sample for Variances** from the **Data Analysis** list, and click **OK**. In the procedure's dialog box (shown below), enter the cell range of one sample as the **Variable 1 Range** and the cell range of the other sample as the **Variable 2 Range**. Click **Labels** and click **OK**. Results appear on a new worksheet. Figure 10.14 on page 400 shows results for the Table 10.1 BLK cola sales data on page 372.

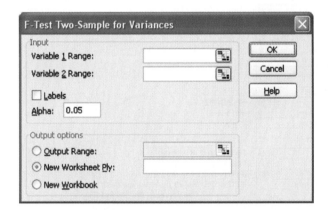

E10.9 USING THE *F* TEST FOR THE DIFFERENCE BETWEEN TWO VARIANCES (SUMMARIZED DATA)

For summarized data, you conduct an *F* test for the difference between two variances by either selecting the PHStat2 F Test for Differences in Two Variances procedure or by making entries in the F Two Variances.xls workbook.

Using PHStat2 F Test for Differences in Two Variances

Select **PHStat → Two-Sample Tests → F Test for Differences in Two Variances**. In the F Test for Differences in Two Variances dialog box (shown below), enter the **Level of Significance** and then enter the **Sample Size** and the **Sample Standard Deviation** for the population 1 sample and population 2 sample. Click one of the test options, enter a title as the **Title**, and click **OK**.

Using F Two Variances.xls

Open to the **F Two Variances** worksheet of the F Two Variances.xls workbook. This worksheet conducts an *F* test for the difference between two variances for the Section 10.4 BLK cola sales example. The worksheet (see Figure E10.7) uses the function **FINV(*upper-tailed* p-*value, numerator degrees of freedom, denominator degrees of freedom*)**, in which *upper-tailed* p-*value* is the probability that *F* will be greater than the value, to compute the upper and lower critical values and uses the function **FDIST(*F-test statistic, numerator degrees of freedom, denominator degrees of freedom*)** to compute the *p*-values.

To adapt this worksheet to other problems, change, if necessary, the level of significance and the sample statistics for the two population samples in the tinted cells B4, B6, B7, B9, and B10. If you want the worksheet to show only a single test, first make a copy of that worksheet (see the Excel Companion to Chapter 1). For a two-tail-test-only worksheet, select and delete rows 23 through 31. For a lower-tail-test-only worksheet, select and delete rows 28 through 31 and then select and delete cell range A17:B21. For an upper-tail-test-only worksheet, select and delete rows 23 through 27 and then select and delete cell range A17:B21.

FIGURE E10.7

F Two Variances worksheet

	A	B	
1	F Test for Differences in Two Variances		
2			
3	**Data**		
4	Level of Significance	0.05	
5	**Population 1 Sample**		
6	Sample Size	10	
7	Sample Standard Deviation	18.7264	
8	**Population 2 Sample**		
9	Sample Size	10	
10	Sample Standard Deviation	12.543	
11			
12	**Intermediate Calculations**		
13	*F* Test Statistic	2.2290	=B7^2/B10^2
14	Population 1 Sample Degrees of Freedom	9	=B6 - 1
15	Population 2 Sample Degrees of Freedom	9	=B9 - 1
16			
17	**Two-Tail Test**		
18	Lower Critical Value	0.2484	=FINV(1 - B4/2, B14, B15)
19	Upper Critical Value	4.0260	=FINV(B4/2, B14, B15)
20	*p*-Value	0.2482	=IF(B13 > 1, 2 * E17, 2 * E18)
21	Do not reject the null hypothesis		=IF(B20 < B5, "Reject the null hypothesis",
22			"Do not reject the null hypothesis")
23	**Lower-Tail Test**		
24	Lower Critical Value	0.3146	=FINV(1 - B4, B14, B15)
25	*p*-Value	0.8759	=E18
26	Do not reject the null hypothesis		=IF(B25 < B5, "Reject the null hypothesis",
27			"Do not reject the null hypothesis")
28	**Upper-Tail Test**		
29	Upper Critical Value	3.1789	=FINV(B4, B14, B15)
30	*p*-Value	0.1241	=E17
31	Do not reject the null hypothesis		=IF(B30 < B5, "Reject the null hypothesis",
			"Do not reject the null hypothesis")

Not shown
Cell E17: =FDIST(B13, B14, B15)
Cell E18: =1 - E17

CHAPTER 11

Analysis of Variance

USING STATISTICS @ Perfect Parachutes

LEARNING OBJECTIVES

In this chapter, you learn:

- The basic concepts of experimental design
- How to use the one-way analysis of variance to test for differences among the means of several groups
- How to use the two-way analysis of variance and interpret the interaction effect

Using Statistics @ Perfect Parachutes

You oversee production at the Perfect Parachutes Company. Parachutes are woven in your factory using a synthetic fiber purchased from one of four different suppliers. Strength of these fibers is an important characteristic that ensures quality parachutes. You need to decide whether the synthetic fibers from each of your four suppliers result in parachutes of equal strength. Furthermore, your factory uses two types of looms to produce parachutes, the *Jetta* and the *Turk*. You need to establish that the parachutes woven on both types of looms are equally strong. You also want to know if any differences in the strength of the parachute that can be attributed to the four suppliers are dependent on the type of loom used. How would you go about finding this information?

In Chapter 10, you used hypothesis testing to reach conclusions about possible differences between two populations. As a manager at Perfect Parachutes, you need to design an experiment to test the strength of parachutes woven from the synthetic fibers from the *four* suppliers. That is, you need to evaluate differences among *more than two* populations. Populations are referred to as *groups* in this chapter. This chapter begins by examining the *completely randomized design*, which has one *factor* (which supplier to use), with several groups (the four suppliers).

The completely randomized design is then extended to the *factorial design*, in which more than one factor at a time is simultaneously studied in a single experiment. For example, an experiment incorporating the four suppliers and the two types of looms would help you determine which supplier and type of loom to use in order to manufacture the strongest parachutes. Throughout the chapter, emphasis is placed on the assumptions behind the use of the various testing procedures.

11.1   THE COMPLETELY RANDOMIZED DESIGN: ONE-WAY ANALYSIS OF VARIANCE

In many situations, you need to examine differences among more than two **groups**. The groups involved can be classified according to **levels** of a **factor** of interest. For example, a factor such as baking temperature may have several groups defined by *numerical levels* such as 300°, 350°, 400°, 450°, and a factor such as preferred supplier for a parachute manufacturer may have several groups defined by *categorical levels* such as Supplier 1, Supplier 2, Supplier 3, Supplier 4. When there is a single factor, the experimental design is called a **completely randomized design**.

F Test for Differences Among More Than Two Means

When you are analyzing a numerical variable and certain assumptions are met, you use the **analysis of variance (ANOVA)** to compare the means of the groups. The ANOVA procedure used for the completely randomized design is referred to as the **one-way ANOVA**, and it is an extension of the *t* test for the difference between two means discussed in Section 10.1. Although ANOVA is an acronym for *analysis of variance*, the term is misleading because the objective is to analyze differences among the group means, *not* the variances. However, by analyzing the variation among and within the groups, you can make conclusions about possible differences in group means. In ANOVA, the total variation is subdivided into variation that is due to differences *among* the groups and variation that is due to differences *within* the groups (see Figure 11.1). **Within-group variation** is considered **random error**. **Among-group variation** is due to differences from group to group. The symbol c is used to indicate the number of groups.

FIGURE 11.1

Partitioning the total variation in a completely randomized design

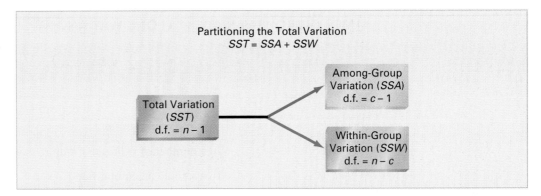

Assuming that the c groups represent populations whose values are randomly and independently selected, follow a normal distribution, and have equal variances, the null hypothesis of no differences in the population means:

$$H_0: \mu_1 = \mu_2 = \cdots = \mu_c$$

is tested against the alternative that not all the c population means are equal:

$$H_1: \text{Not all } \mu_j \text{ are equal (where } j = 1, 2, \ldots, c).$$

To perform an ANOVA test of equality of population means, you subdivide the total variation in the values into two parts—that which is due to variation among the groups and that which is due to variation within the groups. The **total variation** is represented by the **sum of squares total (SST)**. Because the population means of the c groups are assumed to be equal under the null hypothesis, you compute the total variation among all the values by summing the squared differences between each individual value and the **grand mean**, $\overline{\overline{X}}$. The grand mean is the mean of all the values in all the groups combined. Equation (11.1) shows the computation of the total variation.

TOTAL VARIATION IN ONE-WAY ANOVA

$$SST = \sum_{j=1}^{c} \sum_{i=1}^{n_j} (X_{ij} - \overline{\overline{X}})^2 \tag{11.1}$$

where

$$\overline{\overline{X}} = \frac{\displaystyle\sum_{j=1}^{c} \sum_{i=1}^{n_j} X_{ij}}{n} = \text{Grand mean}$$

$X_{ij} = i$th value in group j

$n_j =$ number of values in group j

$n =$ total number of values in all groups combined
(that is, $n = n_1 + n_2 + \cdots + n_c$)

$c =$ number of groups

You compute the among-group variation, usually called the **sum of squares among groups (SSA)**, by summing the squared differences between the sample mean of each group, $\overline{X}_j$, and the grand mean, $\overline{\overline{X}}$, weighted by the sample size, n_j, in each group. Equation (11.2) shows the computation of the among-group variation.

AMONG-GROUP VARIATION IN ONE-WAY ANOVA

$$SSA = \sum_{j=1}^{c} n_j (\overline{X}_j - \overline{\overline{X}})^2 \qquad \textbf{(11.2)}$$

where

c = number of groups

n_j = number of values in group j

$\overline{X}_j$ = sample mean of group j

$\overline{\overline{X}}$ = grand mean

The within-group variation, usually called the **sum of squares within groups (SSW)**, measures the difference between each value and the mean of its own group and sums the squares of these differences over all groups. Equation (11.3) shows the computation of the within-group variation.

WITHIN-GROUP VARIATION IN ONE-WAY ANOVA

$$SSW = \sum_{j=1}^{c} \sum_{i=1}^{n_j} (X_{ij} - \overline{X}_j)^2 \qquad \textbf{(11.3)}$$

where

X_{ij} = ith value in group j

$\overline{X}_j$ = sample mean of group j

Because you are comparing c groups, there are $c - 1$ degrees of freedom associated with the sum of squares among groups. Because each of the c groups contributes $n_j - 1$ degrees of freedom, there are $n - c$ degrees of freedom associated with the sum of squares within groups. In addition, there are $n - 1$ degrees of freedom associated with the sum of squares total because you are comparing each value, X_{ij}, to the grand mean, $\overline{\overline{X}}$, based on all n values.

If you divide each of these sums of squares by its associated degrees of freedom, you have three variances or **mean square** terms—*MSA* (mean square among), *MSW* (mean square within), and *MST* (mean square total).

MEAN SQUARES IN ONE-WAY ANOVA

$$MSA = \frac{SSA}{c - 1} \qquad \textbf{(11.4a)}$$

$$MSW = \frac{SSW}{n - c} \qquad \textbf{(11.4b)}$$

$$MST = \frac{SST}{n - 1} \qquad \textbf{(11.4c)}$$

Although you want to compare the means of the c groups to determine whether a difference exists among them, the ANOVA procedure derives its name from the fact that you are comparing variances. If the null hypothesis is true and there are no real differences in the c group means, all three mean squares (which themselves are *variances*)—*MSA, MSW,* and *MST*—provide estimates of the overall variance in the data. Thus, to test the null hypothesis:

$$H_0: \mu_1 = \mu_2 = \cdots = \mu_c$$

against the alternative:

$$H_1: \text{Not all } \mu_j \text{ are equal (where } j = 1, 2, \ldots, c)$$

you compute the **one-way ANOVA F test statistic** as the ratio of *MSA* to *MSW*, as in Equation (11.5).

ONE-WAY ANOVA F TEST STATISTIC

$$F = \frac{MSA}{MSW} \tag{11.5}$$

The F test statistic follows an **F distribution**, with $c - 1$ degrees of freedom in the numerator and $n - c$ degrees of freedom in the denominator. For a given level of significance, α, you reject the null hypothesis if the F test statistic computed in Equation (11.5) is greater than the upper-tail critical value, F_U, from the F distribution having $c - 1$ degrees of freedom in the numerator and $n - c$ in the denominator (see Table E.5). Thus, as shown in Figure 11.2, the decision rule is

$$\text{Reject } H_0 \text{ if } F > F_U;$$
$$\text{otherwise, do not reject } H_0.$$

FIGURE 11.2

Regions of rejection and nonrejection when using ANOVA

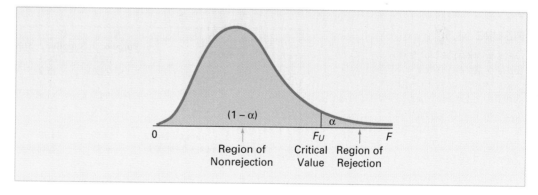

If the null hypothesis is true, the computed F statistic is expected to be approximately equal to 1 because both the numerator and denominator mean square terms are estimating the overall variance in the data. If H_0 is false (and there are real differences in the group means), the computed F statistic is expected to be substantially larger than 1 because the numerator, *MSA*, is estimating the differences among groups in addition to the overall variability in the values, while the denominator, *MSW*, is measuring only the overall variability. Thus, the ANOVA procedure provides an F test in which you reject the null hypothesis at a selected level of significance, α, only if the computed F statistic is greater than F_U, the upper-tail critical value of the F distribution having $c - 1$ and $n - c$ degrees of freedom, as illustrated in Figure 11.2.

The results of an analysis of variance are usually displayed in an **ANOVA summary table**, as shown in Table 11.1. The entries in this table include the sources of variation (that is, among-group, within-group, and total), the degrees of freedom, the sums of squares, the mean squares (that is, the variances), and the computed F statistic. In addition, Microsoft Excel includes the p-value (that is, the probability of having an F statistic as large as or larger than the one computed, given that the null hypothesis is true) in the ANOVA summary table. The p-value allows you to make direct conclusions about the null hypothesis without referring to a table of critical values of the F distribution. If the p-value is less than the chosen level of significance, α, you reject the null hypothesis.

TABLE 11.1

Analysis-of-Variance Summary Table

Source	Degrees of Freedom	Sum of Squares	Mean Square (Variance)	F
Among groups	$c - 1$	SSA	$MSA = \dfrac{SSA}{c - 1}$	$F = \dfrac{MSA}{MSW}$
Within groups	$n - c$	SSW	$MSW = \dfrac{SSW}{n - c}$	
Total	$n - 1$	SST		

To illustrate the one-way ANOVA F test, return to the Using Statistics scenario concerning Perfect Parachutes (see page 422). An experiment was conducted to determine whether any significant differences exist in the strength of parachutes woven from synthetic fibers from the different suppliers. Five parachutes were woven for each group—Supplier 1, Supplier 2, Supplier 3, and Supplier 4. The strength of the parachutes is measured by placing them in a testing device that pulls on both ends of a parachute until it tears apart. The amount of force required to tear the parachute is measured on a tensile-strength scale, where the larger the value, the stronger the parachute. The data worksheet of the `parachute.xls` workbook contains the results of this experiment (in terms of tensile strength), along with the sample mean and the sample standard deviation for each group.

FIGURE 11.3

Data worksheet of the tensile strength for parachutes woven with synthetic fibers from four different suppliers along with the sample mean and sample standard deviation

	A	B	C	D	E
1		Supplier 1	Supplier 2	Supplier 3	Supplier 4
2		18.5	26.3	20.6	25.4
3		24.0	25.3	25.2	19.9
4		17.2	24.0	20.8	22.6
5		19.9	21.2	24.7	17.5
6		18.0	24.5	22.9	20.4
7					
8	Sample Mean	19.52	24.26	22.84	21.16
9	Sample Standard Deviation	2.69	1.92	2.13	2.98

In Figure 11.3, observe that there are differences in the sample means for the four suppliers. For Supplier 1, the mean tensile strength is 19.52. For Supplier 2, the mean tensile strength is 24.26. For Supplier 3, the mean tensile strength is 22.84, and for Supplier 4, the mean tensile strength is 21.16. What you need to determine is whether these sample results are sufficiently different to conclude that the *population* means are not all equal.

In the scatter plot shown in Figure 11.4, you can visually inspect the data and see how the measurements of tensile strength distribute. You can also observe differences among the groups as well as within groups. If the sample sizes in each group were larger, you could develop stem-and-leaf displays, box-and-whisker plots, and normal probability plots.

The null hypothesis states that there is no difference in mean tensile strength among the four suppliers:

$$H_0: \mu_1 = \mu_2 = \mu_3 = \mu_4$$

FIGURE 11.4

Microsoft Excel scatter plot of tensile strengths for four different suppliers

See Section E2.12 to create this.

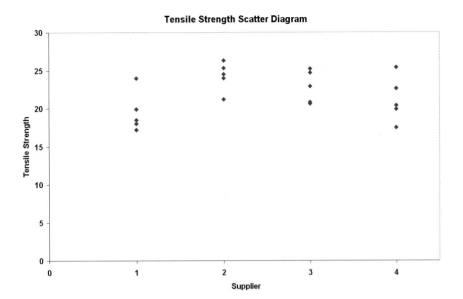

The alternative hypothesis states that at least one of the suppliers differs with respect to the mean tensile strength:

$$H_1: \text{Not all the means are equal.}$$

To construct the ANOVA summary table, you first compute the sample means in each group (see Figure 11.3 on page 426). Then you compute the grand mean by summing all 20 values and dividing by the total number of values:

$$\overline{\overline{X}} = \frac{\sum\limits_{j=1}^{c}\sum\limits_{i=1}^{n_j} X_{ij}}{n} = \frac{438.9}{20} = 21.945$$

Then, using Equations (11.1) through (11.3) on pages 423–424, you compute the sum of squares:

$$SSA = \sum_{j=1}^{c} n_j(\overline{X}_j - \overline{\overline{X}})^2 = (5)(19.52 - 21.945)^2 + (5)(24.26 - 21.945)^2$$

$$+ (5)(22.84 - 21.945)^2 + (5)(21.16 - 21.945)^2$$

$$= 63.2855$$

$$SSW = \sum_{j=1}^{c}\sum_{i=1}^{n_j} (X_{ij} - \overline{X}_j)^2$$

$$= (18.5 - 19.52)^2 + \cdots + (18 - 19.52)^2 + (26.3 - 24.26)^2 + \cdots + (24.5 - 24.26)^2$$

$$+ (20.6 - 22.84)^2 + \cdots + (22.9 - 22.84)^2 + (25.4 - 21.16)^2 + \cdots + (20.4 - 21.16)^2$$

$$= 97.5040$$

$$SST = \sum_{j=1}^{c}\sum_{i=1}^{n_j} (X_{ij} - \overline{\overline{X}})^2$$

$$= (18.5 - 21.945)^2 + (24 - 21.945)^2 + \cdots + (20.4 - 21.945)^2$$

$$= 160.7895$$

You compute the mean square terms by dividing the sum of squares by the corresponding degrees of freedom [see Equation (11.4) on page 424]. Because $c = 4$ and $n = 20$,

$$MSA = \frac{SSA}{c-1} = \frac{63.2855}{4-1} = 21.0952$$

$$MSW = \frac{SSW}{n-c} = \frac{97.5040}{20-4} = 6.0940$$

so that using Equation (11.5) on page 425,

$$F = \frac{MSA}{MSW} = \frac{21.0952}{6.0940} = 3.4616$$

For a selected level of significance, α, you find the upper-tail critical value, F_U, from the F distribution using Table E.5. A portion of Table E.5 is presented in Table 11.2. In the parachute supplier example, there are 3 degrees of freedom in the numerator and 16 degrees of freedom in the denominator. F_U, the upper-tail critical value at the 0.05 level of significance, is 3.24.

TABLE 11.2

Finding the Critical Value of F with 3 and 16 Degrees of Freedom at the 0.05 Level of Significance

Denominator, df_2	Numerator, df_1								
	1	2	**3**	4	5	6	7	8	9
.	.	.		.	.	.	.	.	.
.	.	.		.	.	.	.	.	.
.	.	.		.	.	.	.	.	.
11	4.84	3.98	3.59	3.36	3.20	3.09	3.01	2.95	2.90
12	4.75	3.89	3.49	3.26	3.11	3.00	2.91	2.85	2.80
13	4.67	3.81	3.41	3.18	3.03	2.92	2.83	2.77	2.71
14	4.60	3.74	3.34	3.11	2.96	2.85	2.76	2.70	2.65
15	4.54	3.68	3.29	3.06	2.90	2.79	2.71	2.64	2.59
16	4.49	3.63	**3.24**	3.01	2.85	2.74	2.66	2.59	2.54

Source: Extracted from Table E.5.

Because the computed test statistic $F = 3.4616$ is greater than $F_U = 3.24$, you reject the null hypothesis (see Figure 11.5). You conclude that there is a significant difference in the mean tensile strength among the four suppliers.

FIGURE 11.5

Regions of rejection and nonrejection for the one-way ANOVA at the 0.05 level of significance, with 3 and 16 degrees of freedom

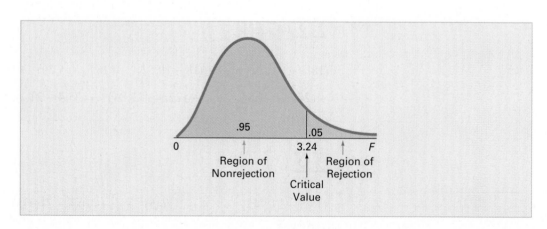

Figure 11.6 shows the Microsoft Excel ANOVA summary table and *p*-value.

FIGURE 11.6

Microsoft Excel ANOVA for the parachute example

See Section E11.1 to create this.

	A	B	C	D	E	F	G
1	**Anova: Single Factor**						
2							
3	**SUMMARY**						
4	*Groups*	*Count*	*Sum*	*Average*	*Variance*		
5	Supplier 1	5	97.6	19.52	7.237		
6	Supplier 2	5	121.3	24.26	3.683		
7	Supplier 3	5	114.2	22.84	4.553		
8	Supplier 4	5	105.8	21.16	8.903		
9							
10							
11	**ANOVA**						
12	*Source of Variation*	*SS*	*df*	*MS*	*F*	*P-value*	*F crit*
13	Between Groups	63.2855	3	21.0952	3.4616	0.0414	3.2389
14	Within Groups	97.5040	16	6.094			
15							
16	Total	160.7895	19				

The *p*-value, or probability of getting an *F* statistic of 3.4616 or larger when the null hypothesis is true, is 0.0414. Because this *p*-value is less than the specified α of 0.05, you reject the null hypothesis. The *p*-value of 0.0414 indicates that there is a 4.14% chance of observing differences this large or larger if the population means for the four suppliers are all equal.

After performing the one-way ANOVA and finding a significant difference among the suppliers, you still do not know *which* suppliers differ. All that you know is that there is sufficient evidence to state that the population means are not all the same. In other words, at least one or more population means are significantly different. To determine which suppliers differ, you can use a multiple comparison procedure such as the Tukey-Kramer procedure.

Multiple Comparisons: The Tukey-Kramer Procedure

In the Using Statistics scenario, you used the one-way ANOVA *F* test to determine that there was a difference among the suppliers. The next step is to make **multiple comparisons** to determine which suppliers are different.

Although many procedures are available (see references 5, 8, and 9), this text uses the **Tukey-Kramer multiple comparisons procedure** to determine which of the *c* means are significantly different. The Tukey-Kramer procedure enables you to simultaneously make comparisons between all pairs of groups. First, you compute the differences, $\bar{X}_j - \bar{X}_{j'}$ (where $j \neq j'$), among all $c(c-1)/2$ pairs of means. Then you compute the **critical range** for the Tukey-Kramer procedure using Equation (11.6).

CRITICAL RANGE FOR THE TUKEY-KRAMER PROCEDURE

$$\text{Critical range} = Q_U \sqrt{\frac{MSW}{2}\left(\frac{1}{n_j} + \frac{1}{n_{j'}}\right)} \qquad \textbf{(11.6)}$$

where Q_U is the upper-tail critical value from a **Studentized range distribution** having *c* degrees of freedom in the numerator and $n - c$ degrees of freedom in the denominator. (Values for the Studentized range distribution are found in Table E.9.)

If the sample sizes differ, you compute a critical range for each pairwise comparison of sample means. Finally, you compare each of the $c(c-1)/2$ pairs of means against its corresponding critical range. You declare a specific pair significantly different if the absolute difference in the sample means $\left|\bar{X}_j - \bar{X}_{j'}\right|$ is greater than the critical range.

In the parachute example, there are four suppliers. Thus, there are $4(4 − 1)/2 = 6$ pairwise comparisons. To apply the Tukey-Kramer multiple comparison procedure, you first compute the absolute mean differences for all six pairwise comparisons. *Multiple comparison* refers to the fact that you are going to simultaneously make an inference about all six of these comparisons:

1. $\left| \bar{X}_1 - \bar{X}_2 \right| = \left| 19.52 - 24.26 \right| = 4.74$

2. $\left| \bar{X}_1 - \bar{X}_3 \right| = \left| 19.52 - 22.84 \right| = 3.32$

3. $\left| \bar{X}_1 - \bar{X}_4 \right| = \left| 19.52 - 21.16 \right| = 1.64$

4. $\left| \bar{X}_2 - \bar{X}_3 \right| = \left| 24.26 - 22.84 \right| = 1.42$

5. $\left| \bar{X}_2 - \bar{X}_4 \right| = \left| 24.26 - 21.16 \right| = 3.10$

6. $\left| \bar{X}_3 - \bar{X}_4 \right| = \left| 22.84 - 21.16 \right| = 1.68$

You need to compute only one critical range because the sample sizes in the four groups are equal. From the ANOVA summary table (Figure 11.6 on page 429), $MSW = 6.094$ and $n_j = n_{j'} = 5$. From Table E.9, for $\alpha = 0.05$, $c = 4$, and $n − c = 20 − 4 = 16$, Q_U, the upper-tail critical value of the test statistic, is 4.05 (see Table 11.3).

TABLE 11.3

Finding the Studentized Range Q_U Statistic for $\alpha = 0.05$, with 4 and 16 Degrees of Freedom

Denominator Degrees of Freedom	Numerator Degrees of Freedom							
	2	3	4	5	6	7	8	9
.	.	.	.	.	.	.	.	.
.	.	.	.	.	.	.	.	.
.	.	.	.	.	.	.	.	.
11	3.11	3.82	4.26	4.57	4.82	5.03	5.20	5.35
12	3.08	3.77	4.20	4.51	4.75	4.95	5.12	5.27
13	3.06	3.73	4.15	4.45	4.69	4.88	5.05	5.19
14	3.03	3.70	4.11	4.41	4.64	4.83	4.99	5.13
15	3.01	3.67	4.08	4.37	4.60	4.78	4.94	5.08
16	3.00	3.65	4.05	4.33	4.56	4.74	4.90	5.03

Source: Extracted from Table E.9.

From Equation (11.6),

$$\text{Critical range} = 4.05 \sqrt{\left(\frac{6.094}{2} \right) \left(\frac{1}{5} + \frac{1}{5} \right)} = 4.4712$$

Because $4.74 > 4.4712$, there is a significant difference between the means of Suppliers 1 and 2. All other pairwise differences are small enough that they may be due to chance. With 95% confidence, you can conclude that parachutes woven using fiber from Supplier 1 have a lower mean tensile strength than those from Supplier 2, but there are no statistically significant differences between Suppliers 1 and 3, Suppliers 1 and 4, Suppliers 2 and 3, Suppliers 2 and 4, and Suppliers 3 and 4. Note that by using $\alpha = 0.05$, you are able to make all six of the comparisons with an overall error rate of only 5%.

These results are summarized in the Microsoft Excel results presented in Figure 11.7.

FIGURE 11.7

Microsoft Excel worksheet of the Tukey-Kramer procedure for the parachute example

See Section E11.2 to create this.

	A	B	C	D	E	F	G	H	I
1	Parachute Tensile-Strength Analysis								
2									
3		Sample	Sample			Absolute	Std. Error	Critical	
4	Group	Mean	Size		Comparison	Difference	of Difference	Range	Results
5	1	19.52	5		Group 1 to Group 2	4.74	1.10399275	4.4712	Means are different
6	2	24.26	5		Group 1 to Group 3	3.32	1.10399275	4.4712	Means are not different
7	3	22.84	5		Group 1 to Group 4	1.64	1.10399275	4.4712	Means are not different
8	4	21.16	5		Group 2 to Group 3	1.42	1.10399275	4.4712	Means are not different
9					Group 2 to Group 4	3.1	1.10399275	4.4712	Means are not different
10	Other Data				Group 3 to Group 4	1.68	1.10399275	4.4712	Means are different
11	Level of significance	0.05							
12	Numerator d.f.	4							
13	Denominator d.f.	16							
14	MSW	6.094							
15	Q Statistic	4.05							

ANOVA Assumptions

In Chapters 9 and 10, you learned about the assumptions made in the application of each hypothesis-testing procedure and the consequences of departures from these assumptions. To use the one-way ANOVA F test, you must also make certain assumptions about the data. These assumptions are

- Randomness and independence
- Normality
- Homogeneity of variance

The first assumption, **randomness and independence**, is critically important. The validity of any experiment depends on random sampling and/or the randomization process. To avoid biases in the outcomes, you need to select random samples from the c groups or randomly assign the items to the c levels of the factor. Selecting a random sample, or randomly assigning the levels, ensures that a value from one group is independent of any other value in the experiment. Departures from this assumption can seriously affect inferences from the ANOVA. These problems are discussed more thoroughly in references 5 and 8.

The second assumption, **normality**, states that the sample values in each group are from a normally distributed population. Just as in the case of the t test, the one-way ANOVA F test is fairly robust against departures from the normal distribution. As long as the distributions are not extremely different from a normal distribution, the level of significance of the ANOVA F test is usually not greatly affected, particularly for large samples. You can assess the normality of each of the c samples by constructing a normal probability plot or a box-and-whisker plot.

The third assumption, **homogeneity of variance**, states that the variances of the c groups are equal (that is, $\sigma_1^2 = \sigma_2^2 = \cdots = \sigma_c^2$). If you have equal sample sizes in each group, inferences based on the F distribution are not seriously affected by unequal variances. However, if you have unequal sample sizes, unequal variances can have a serious effect on inferences developed from the ANOVA procedure. Thus, when possible, you should have equal sample sizes in all groups. The Levene test for homogeneity of variance presented on page 432 is one method to test whether the variances of the c groups are equal.

When only the normality assumption is violated, the Kruskal-Wallis rank test, a nonparametric procedure discussed in Section 12.6, is appropriate. When only the homogeneity-of-variance assumption is violated, procedures similar to those used in the separate-variance t test of Section 10.1 are available (see references 1 and 2). When both the normality and homogeneity-of-variance assumptions have been violated, you need to use an appropriate data transformation that both normalizes the data and reduces the differences in variances (see reference 9) or use a more general nonparametric procedure (see references 2 and 3).

Levene's Test for Homogeneity of Variance

Although the one-way ANOVA F test is relatively robust with respect to the assumption of equal group variances, large differences in the group variances can seriously affect the level of significance and the power of the F test. One procedure with high statistical power is the modified **Levene test** (see references 1, 4, 6, and 8). To test for the homogeneity of variance, you use the following null hypothesis:

$$H_0: \sigma_1^2 = \sigma_2^2 = \cdots = \sigma_c^2$$

against the alternative hypothesis:

$$H_1: \text{Not all } \sigma_j^2 \text{ are equal } (j = 1, 2, 3, \ldots, c).$$

To test the null hypothesis of equal variances, you first compute the absolute value of the difference between each value and the median of the group. Then you perform a one-way ANOVA on these *absolute differences*. To illustrate the modified Levene test, return to the Using Statistics scenario concerning the tensile strength of parachutes first presented on page 422. Table 11.4 summarizes the absolute differences from the median of each supplier.

TABLE 11.4

Absolute Differences from the Median Tensile Strength for Four Suppliers

Supplier 1 (Median = 18.5)	Supplier 2 (Median = 24.5)	Supplier 3 (Median = 22.9)	Supplier 4 (Median = 20.4)
$\lvert 18.5 - 18.5 \rvert = 0.0$	$\lvert 26.3 - 24.5 \rvert = 1.8$	$\lvert 20.6 - 22.9 \rvert = 2.3$	$\lvert 25.4 - 20.4 \rvert = 5.0$
$\lvert 24.0 - 18.5 \rvert = 5.5$	$\lvert 25.3 - 24.5 \rvert = 0.8$	$\lvert 25.2 - 22.9 \rvert = 2.3$	$\lvert 19.9 - 20.4 \rvert = 0.5$
$\lvert 17.2 - 18.5 \rvert = 1.3$	$\lvert 24.0 - 24.5 \rvert = 0.5$	$\lvert 20.8 - 22.9 \rvert = 2.1$	$\lvert 22.6 - 20.4 \rvert = 2.2$
$\lvert 19.9 - 18.5 \rvert = 1.4$	$\lvert 21.2 - 24.5 \rvert = 3.3$	$\lvert 24.7 - 22.9 \rvert = 1.8$	$\lvert 17.5 - 20.4 \rvert = 2.9$
$\lvert 18.0 - 18.5 \rvert = 0.5$	$\lvert 24.5 - 24.5 \rvert = 0.0$	$\lvert 22.9 - 22.9 \rvert = 0.0$	$\lvert 20.4 - 20.4 \rvert = 0.0$

Using the absolute differences given in Table 11.4, you perform a one-way ANOVA (see Figure 11.8).

FIGURE 11.8

Microsoft Excel ANOVA of the absolute differences for the parachute data

See Section E11.3 to create this.

	A	B	C	D	E	F	G
1	Parachute Tensile-Strength Analysis						
2							
3	SUMMARY						
4	Groups	Count	Sum	Average	Variance		
5	Supplier 1	5	8.7	1.74	4.753		
6	Supplier 2	5	6.4	1.28	1.707		
7	Supplier 3	5	8.5	1.7	0.945		
8	Supplier 4	5	10.6	2.12	4.007		
9							
10							
11	ANOVA						
12	Source of Variation	SS	df	MS	F	P-value	F crit
13	Between Groups	1.77	3	0.59	0.2068	0.8902	3.2389
14	Within Groups	45.648	16	2.853			
15							
16	Total	47.418	19				

From Figure 11.8, observe that $F = 0.2068 < 3.2389$ (or the p-value $= 0.8902 > 0.05$). Thus, you do not reject H_0. There is no evidence of a significant difference among the four variances. In other words, it is reasonable to assume that the materials from the four suppliers produce parachutes with an equal amount of variability. Therefore, the homogeneity-of-variance assumption for the ANOVA procedure is justified.

EXAMPLE 11.1

ANOVA OF THE SPEED OF DRIVE-THROUGH SERVICE AT FAST-FOOD CHAINS

For fast-food restaurants, the drive-through window is an increasing source of revenue. The chain that offers the fastest service is likely to attract additional customers. In a study of drive-through times (from menu board to departure) at fast-food chains, the mean time was 150 seconds for Wendy's, 167 seconds for McDonald's, 169 seconds for Checkers, 171 seconds for Burger King, and 172 seconds for Long John Silver's (extracted from J. Ordonez, "An Efficiency Drive: Fast-Food Lanes Are Getting Even Faster," *The Wall Street Journal*, May 18, 2000, pp. A1, A10). Suppose the study was based on 20 customers for each fast-food chain and the ANOVA table given in Table 11.5 was developed.

TABLE 11.5

ANOVA Summary Table of the Speed of Drive-Through Service at Fast-Food Chains

Source	Degrees of Freedom	Sum of Squares	Mean Squares	F	p-Value
Among chains	4	6,536	1,634.0	12.51	0.0000
Within chains	95	12,407	130.6		

At the 0.05 level of significance, is there evidence of a difference in the mean drive-through times of the five chains?

SOLUTION

$H_0: \mu_1 = \mu_2 = \mu_3 = \mu_4 = \mu_5$ where 1 = Wendy's, 2 = McDonald's, 3 = Checkers, 4 = Burger King, 5 = Long John Silver's

H_1: Not all μ_j are equal   where $j = 1, 2, 3, 4, 5$

Decision rule: If p-value < 0.05, reject H_0. Because the p-value is virtually 0, which is less than $\alpha = 0.05$, reject H_0. You have sufficient evidence to conclude that the mean drive-through times of the five chains are not all equal.

To determine which of the means are significantly different from one another, use the Tukey-Kramer procedure [Equation (11.6) on page 429] to establish the critical range:

$$Q_{U(c,n-c)} = Q_{U(5,95)} \cong 3.92$$

$$\text{Critical range} = Q_{U(c,n-c)} \sqrt{\left(\frac{MSW}{2}\right)\left(\frac{1}{n_j} + \frac{1}{n_{j'}}\right)} = (3.92)\sqrt{\left(\frac{130.6}{2}\right)\left(\frac{1}{20} + \frac{1}{20}\right)}$$

$$= 10.02$$

Any observed disfference greater than 10.02 is considered significant. The mean drive-through times are different between Wendy's (mean of 150 seconds) and each of the other four chains. With 95% confidence, you can conclude that the mean drive-through time for Wendy's is faster than McDonald's, Burger King, Checkers, and Long John Silver's, but the mean drive-through times for McDonald's, Burger King, Checkers, and Long John Silver's are not statistically different.

PROBLEMS FOR SECTION 11.1

Learning the Basics

PH Grade ASSIST **11.1** An experiment has a single factor with five groups and seven values in each group.

a. How many degrees of freedom are there in determining the among-group variation?

b. How many degrees of freedom are there in determining the within-group variation?

c. How many degrees of freedom are there in determining the total variation?

PH Grade ASSIST **11.2** You are working with the same experiment as in Problem 11.1.

a. If $SSA = 60$ and $SST = 210$, what is SSW?

b. What is MSA?

c. What is MSW?

d. What is the value of the test statistic F?

PH Grade ASSIST **11.3** You are working with the same experiment as in Problems 11.1 and 11.2.

a. Construct the ANOVA summary table and fill in all values in the table.

b. At the 0.05 level of significance, what is the upper-tail critical value from the F distribution?

c. State the decision rule for testing the null hypothesis that all five groups have equal population means.

d. What is your statistical decision?

11.4 Consider an experiment with three groups, with seven values in each.

a. How many degrees of freedom are there in determining the among-group variation?

b. How many degrees of freedom are there in determining the within-group variation?

c. How many degrees of freedom are there in determining the total variation?

PH Grade ASSIST **11.5** Consider an experiment with four groups, with eight values in each. For the following ANOVA summary table, fill in all the missing results:

Source	Degrees of Freedom	Sum of Squares	Mean Square (Variance)	F
Among groups	$c - 1 = ?$	$SSA = ?$	$MSA = 80$	$F = ?$
Within groups	$n - c = ?$	$SSW = 560$	$MSW = ?$	
Total	$n - 1 = ?$	$SST = ?$		

11.6 You are working with the same experiment as in Problem 11.5.

a. At the 0.05 level of significance, state the decision rule for testing the null hypothesis that all four groups have equal population means.

b. What is your statistical decision?

c. At the 0.05 level of significance, what is the upper-tail critical value from the Studentized range distribution?

d. To perform the Tukey-Kramer procedure, what is the critical range?

Applying the Concepts

11.7 The Computer Anxiety Rating Scale (CARS) measures an individual's level of computer anxiety, on a scale from 20 (no anxiety) to 100 (highest level of anxiety). Researchers at Miami University administered CARS to 172 business students. One of the objectives of the study was to determine whether there are differences in the amount of computer anxiety experienced by students with different majors. They found the following:

Source	Degrees of Freedom	Sum of Squares	Mean Squares	F
Among majors	5	3,172		
Within majors	166	21,246		
Total	171	24,418		

Major	n	Mean
Marketing	19	44.37
Management	11	43.18
Other	14	42.21
Finance	45	41.80
Accountancy	36	37.56
MIS	47	32.21

Source: Extracted from T. Broome and D. Havelka, "Determinants of Computer Anxiety in Business Students," The Review of Business Information Systems, Spring 2002, 6(2), pp. 9–16.

a. Complete the ANOVA summary table.

b. At the 0.05 level of significance, is there evidence of a difference in the mean computer anxiety experienced by different majors?

c. If the results in (b) indicate that it is appropriate, use the Tukey-Kramer procedure to determine which majors differ in mean computer anxiety. Discuss your findings.

PH Grade ASSIST **11.8** Periodically, *The Wall Street Journal* has conducted a stock-picking contest. The last one was conducted in March 2001. In this experiment, three different methods were used to select stocks that were expected to perform well during the next five months. Four Wall Street professionals, considered experts on picking stocks, each selected one stock. Four randomly chosen readers of the *Wall Street Journal* each selected one stock. Finally, four stocks were selected by flinging darts at a table containing a list of stocks. The returns of the selected stocks for March 20, 2001, to August 31, 2001 (in percentage return), are given in the following table and stored in the file **contest2001.xls**. Note that during this period, the Dow Jones Industrial Average gained 2.4% (extracted from G. Jasen, "In Picking Stocks, Dartboard Beats the Pros," *The Wall Street Journal*, September 27, 2001, pp. C1, C10).

Experts	Readers	Darts
+39.5	−31.0	+39.0
−1.1	−20.7	+31.9
−4.5	−45.0	+14.1
−8.0	−73.3	+5.4

a. Is there evidence of a significant difference in the mean return for the three categories? (Use $\alpha = 0.05$.)
b. If appropriate, determine which categories differ in mean return.
c. Comment on the validity of the inference implied by the title of the article, which suggests that the dartboard was better than the professionals.
d. Is there evidence of a significant difference in the variation in the returns for the three categories? (Use $\alpha = 0.05$.)

11.9 A hospital conducted a study of the waiting time in its emergency room. The hospital has a main campus and three satellite locations. Management had a business objective of reducing waiting time for emergency room cases that did not require immediate attention. To study this, a random sample of 15 emergency room cases at each location were selected on a particular day, and the waiting time (measured from check-in to when the patient was called into the clinic area) was measured. The results are stored in the file **erwaiting.xls**.
a. At the 0.05 level of significance, is there evidence of a difference in the mean waiting times in the four locations?
b. If appropriate, determine which locations differ in mean waiting time.
c. At the 0.05 level of significance, is there evidence of a difference in the variation in waiting time among the four locations?

 11.10 Students in a business statistics course performed a completely randomized design to test the strength of four brands of trash bags. One-pound weights were placed into a bag, one at a time, until the bag broke. A total of 40 bags, 10 for each brand, were used. The data in the file **trashbags.xls** gives the weight (in pounds) required to break the trash bags.
a. At the 0.05 level of significance, is there evidence of a difference in the mean strength of the four brands of trash bags?

b. If appropriate, determine which brands differ in mean strength.
c. At the 0.05 level of significance, is there evidence of a difference in the variation in strength among the four brands of trash bags?
d. Which brand(s) should you buy and which brand(s) should you avoid? Explain.

11.11 The following data (stored in the file **cdyield.xls**) represent the nationwide highest yield of different types of accounts (extracted from Bankrate.com, January 24, 2006):

Money Market	6-Month CD	1-Yr CD	2.5-Yr CD	5-Yr CD
4.55	4.75	4.94	4.95	5.05
4.50	4.70	4.90	4.91	5.05
4.40	4.69	4.85	4.85	5.02
4.38	4.65	4.85	4.82	5.00
4.38	4.65	4.85	4.80	5.00

a. At the 0.05 level of significance, is there evidence of a difference in the mean yields of the different accounts?
b. If appropriate, determine which accounts differ in mean yields.
c. At the 0.05 level of significance, is there evidence of a difference in the variation in yields among the different accounts?
d. What effect does your result in (c) have on the validity of the results in (a) and (b)?

11.12 An advertising agency has been hired by a manufacturer of pens to develop an advertising campaign for the upcoming holiday season. To prepare for this project, the research director decides to initiate a study of the effect of advertising on product perception. An experiment is designed to compare five different advertisements. Advertisement *A* greatly undersells the pen's characteristics. Advertisement *B* slightly undersells the pen's characteristics. Advertisement *C* slightly oversells the pen's characteristics. Advertisement *D* greatly oversells the pen's characteristics. Advertisement *E* attempts to correctly state the pen's characteristics. A sample of 30 adult respondents, taken from a larger focus group, is randomly assigned to the five advertisements (so that there are six respondents to each). After reading the advertisement and developing a sense of "product expectation," all respondents unknowingly receive the same pen to evaluate. The respondents are permitted to test the pen and the plausibility of the advertising copy. The respondents are then asked to rate the pen from 1 to 7 on the product characteristic scales of appearance, durability, and writing performance. The *combined* scores of three ratings (appearance, durability, and writing performance) for the 30 respondents (stored in the file **pen.xls**) are as follows:

A	B	C	D	E
15	16	8	5	12
18	17	7	6	19
17	21	10	13	18
19	16	15	11	12
19	19	14	9	17
20	17	14	10	14

a. At the 0.05 level of significance, is there evidence of a difference in the mean rating of the five advertisements?

b. If appropriate, determine which advertisements differ in mean ratings.

c. At the 0.05 level of significance, is there evidence of a difference in the variation in ratings among the five advertisements?

d. Which advertisement(s) should you use and which advertisement(s) should you avoid? Explain.

11.13 The retailing manager of a supermarket chain wants to determine whether product location has any effect on the sale of pet toys. Three different aisle locations are considered: front, middle, and rear. A random sample of 18 stores is selected, with 6 stores randomly assigned to each aisle location. The size of the display area and price of the product are constant for all stores. At the end of a one-month trial period, the sales volumes (in thousands of dollars) of the product in each store were as follows (and are stored in the file locate.xls).

Aisle Location

Front	Middle	Rear
8.6	3.2	4.6
7.2	2.4	6.0
5.4	2.0	4.0
6.2	1.4	2.8
5.0	1.8	2.2
4.0	1.6	2.8

a. At the 0.05 level of significance, is there evidence of a significant difference in mean sales among the various aisle locations?

b. If appropriate, which aisle locations appear to differ significantly in mean sales?

c. At the 0.05 level of significance, is there evidence of a significant difference in the variation in sales among the various aisle locations?

d. What should the retailing manager conclude? Fully describe the retailing manager's options with respect to aisle locations.

11.14 A sporting goods manufacturing company wanted to compare the distance traveled by golf balls produced using each of four different designs. Ten balls were manufactured with each design and were brought to the local golf course for the club professional to test. The order in which the balls were hit with the same club from the first tee was randomized so that the pro did not know which type of ball was being hit. All 40 balls were hit in a short period of time, during which the environmental conditions were essentially the same. The results (distance traveled in yards) for the four designs were as follows (and are stored in the file golfball.xls):

Design

1	2	3	4
206.32	217.08	226.77	230.55
207.94	221.43	224.79	227.95
206.19	218.04	229.75	231.84
204.45	224.13	228.51	224.87
209.65	211.82	221.44	229.49
203.81	213.90	223.85	231.10
206.75	221.28	223.97	221.53
205.68	229.43	234.30	235.45
204.49	213.54	219.50	228.35
210.86	214.51	233.00	225.09

a. At the 0.05 level of significance, is there evidence of a difference in the mean distances traveled by the golf balls with different designs?

b. If the results in (a) indicate that it is appropriate, use the Tukey-Kramer procedure to determine which designs differ in mean distances.

c. What assumptions are necessary in (a)?

d. At the 0.05 level of significance, is there evidence of a difference in the variation of the distances traveled by the golf balls differing in design?

e. What golf ball design should the manufacturing manager choose? Explain.

11.2 THE FACTORIAL DESIGN: TWO-WAY ANALYSIS OF VARIANCE

In Section 11.1, you learned about the completely randomized design used for situations concerning one factor. In this section, the discussion is extended to the **two-factor factorial design**, in which two factors are simultaneously evaluated. Each factor is evaluated at two or more levels. For example, in the Using Statistics scenario, Perfect Parachutes is interested in simultaneously evaluating four suppliers and two types of looms. While discussion here is limited to two factors, you can extend factorial designs to three or more factors (see references 4, 5, 6, and 8).

Data from a two-factor factorial design are analyzed using **two-way ANOVA**. Because of the complexity of the calculations involved, you should use software such as Microsoft Excel when conducting this analysis. However, for purposes of illustration and a better conceptual understanding of two-way ANOVA, the decomposition of the total variation is presented next. The following definitions are needed to develop the two-way ANOVA procedure:

r = number of levels of factor A

c = number of levels of factor B

n' = number of values (replicates) for each cell (combination of a particular level of factor A and a particular level of factor B)

n = number of values in the entire experiment (where $n = rcn'$)

X_{ijk} = value of the kth observation for level i of factor A and level j of factor B

$$\overline{\overline{X}} = \frac{\displaystyle\sum_{i=1}^{r}\sum_{j=1}^{c}\sum_{k=1}^{n'} X_{ijk}}{rcn'} = \text{grand mean}$$

$$\overline{X}_{i..} = \frac{\displaystyle\sum_{j=1}^{c}\sum_{k=1}^{n'} X_{ijk}}{cn'} = \text{mean of the } i\text{th level of factor } A \text{ (where } i = 1, 2, \ldots, r)$$

$$\overline{X}_{.j.} = \frac{\displaystyle\sum_{i=1}^{r}\sum_{k=1}^{n'} X_{ijk}}{rn'} = \text{mean of the } j\text{th level of factor } B \text{ (where } j = 1, 2, \ldots, c)$$

$$\overline{X}_{ij.} = \frac{\displaystyle\sum_{k=1}^{n'} X_{ijk}}{n'} = \text{mean of the cell } ij, \text{ the combination of the } i\text{th level of factor } A \text{ and the } j\text{th level of factor } B$$

This text deals only with situations in which there are an equal number of **replicates** (that is, sample sizes n') for each combination of the levels of factor A with those of factor B. (See references 1 and 9 for a discussion of two-factor factorial designs with unequal sample sizes.)

Testing for Factor and Interaction Effects

There is an **interaction** between factors A and B if the effect of factor A is dependent on the level of factor B. Thus, when dividing the total variation into different sources of variation, you need to account for a possible interaction effect, as well as for factor A, factor B, and random error. To accomplish this, the total variation (SST) is subdivided into sum of squares due to factor A (or SSA), sum of squares due to factor B (or SSB), sum of squares due to the interaction effect of A and B (or $SSAB$), and sum of squares due to random error (or SSE). This decomposition of the total variation (SST) is displayed in Figure 11.9.

FIGURE 11.9

Partitioning the total variation in a two-factor factorial design

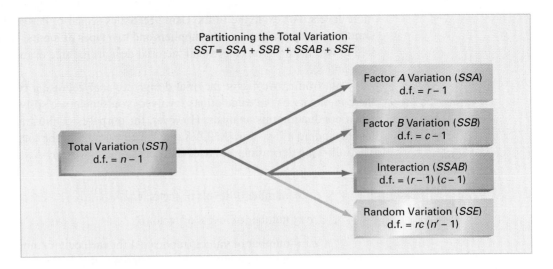

The sum of squares total (SST) represents the total variation among all the values around the grand mean. Equation (11.7) shows the computation for total variation.

TOTAL VARIATION IN TWO-WAY ANOVA

$$SST = \sum_{i=1}^{r} \sum_{j=1}^{c} \sum_{k=1}^{n'} (X_{ijk} - \bar{\bar{X}})^2 \qquad \textbf{(11.7)}$$

The **sum of squares due to factor A (SSA)** represents the differences among the various levels of factor A and the grand mean. Equation (11.8) shows the computation for factor A variation.

FACTOR A VARIATION

$$SSA = cn' \sum_{i=1}^{r} (\bar{X}_{i..} - \bar{\bar{X}})^2 \qquad \textbf{(11.8)}$$

The **sum of squares due to factor B (SSB)** represents the differences among the various levels of factor B and the grand mean. Equation (11.9) shows the computation for factor B variation.

FACTOR B VARIATION

$$SSB = rn' \sum_{j=1}^{c} (\bar{X}_{.j.} - \bar{\bar{X}})^2 \qquad \textbf{(11.9)}$$

The **sum of squares due to interaction ($SSAB$)** represents the interacting effect of specific combinations of factor A and factor B. Equation (11.10) shows the computation for interaction variation.

INTERACTION VARIATION

$$SSAB = n' \sum_{i=1}^{r} \sum_{j=1}^{c} (\bar{X}_{ij.} - \bar{X}_{i..} - \bar{X}_{.j.} + \bar{\bar{X}})^2 \qquad \textbf{(11.10)}$$

The **sum of squares error (SSE)** represents the differences among the values within each cell and the corresponding cell mean. Equation (11.11) shows the computation for random error.

RANDOM ERROR IN TWO-WAY ANOVA

$$SSE = \sum_{i=1}^{r} \sum_{j=1}^{c} \sum_{k=1}^{n'} (X_{ijk} - \bar{X}_{ij.})^2 \qquad \textbf{(11.11)}$$

Because there are r levels of factor A, there are $r - 1$ degrees of freedom associated with SSA. Similarly, because there are c levels of factor B, there are $c - 1$ degrees of freedom associated with SSB. Because there are n' replicates in each of the rc cells, there are $rc(n' - 1)$ degrees of freedom associated with the SSE term. Carrying this further, there are $n - 1$ degrees of freedom associated with the sum of squares total (SST) because you are comparing each value, X_{ijk}, to the grand mean, $\bar{\bar{X}}$, based on all n values. Therefore, because the degrees of freedom for each of the sources of variation must add to the degrees of freedom for the total variation (SST), you calculate the degrees of freedom for the interaction component ($SSAB$) by subtraction. The degrees of freedom for interaction are $(r - 1)(c - 1)$.

If you divide each of the sums of squares by its associated degrees of freedom, you have the four variances or mean square terms (that is, MSA, MSB, $MSAB$, and MSE). Equations (11.12a–d) give the mean square terms needed for the two-way ANOVA table.

MEAN SQUARES IN TWO-WAY ANOVA

$$MSA = \frac{SSA}{r - 1} \qquad \textbf{(11.12a)}$$

$$MSB = \frac{SSB}{c - 1} \qquad \textbf{(11.12b)}$$

$$MSAB = \frac{SSAB}{(r - 1)(c - 1)} \qquad \textbf{(11.12c)}$$

$$MSE = \frac{SSE}{rc(n' - 1)} \qquad \textbf{(11.12d)}$$

There are three distinct tests to perform in a two-way ANOVA:

1. To test the hypothesis of no difference due to factor A:

$$H_0: \mu_{1..} = \mu_{2..} = \cdots = \mu_{r..}$$

against the alternative:

$$H_1: \text{Not all } \mu_{i..} \text{ are equal.}$$

you use the F statistic in Equation (11.13).

F TEST FOR FACTOR A EFFECT

$$F = \frac{MSA}{MSE} \qquad \textbf{(11.13)}$$

You reject the null hypothesis at the α level of significance if

$$F = \frac{MSA}{MSE} > F_U$$

where F_U is the upper-tail critical value from an F distribution with $r - 1$ and $rc(n' - 1)$ degrees of freedom.

2. To test the hypothesis of no difference due to factor B:

$$H_0: \mu_{.1.} = \mu_{.2.} = \cdots = \mu_{.c.}$$

against the alternative:

$$H_1: \text{Not all } \mu_{j.} \text{ are equal.}$$

you use the F statistic in Equation (11.14).

F TEST FOR FACTOR B EFFECT

$$F = \frac{MSB}{MSE} \qquad \text{(11.14)}$$

You reject the null hypothesis at the α level of significance if

$$F = \frac{MSB}{MSE} > F_U$$

where F_U is the upper-tail critical value from an F distribution with $c - 1$ and $rc(n' - 1)$ degrees of freedom.

3. To test the hypothesis of no interaction of factors A and B:

$$H_0: \text{The interaction of } A \text{ and } B \text{ is equal to zero.}$$

against the alternative:

$$H_1: \text{The interaction of } A \text{ and } B \text{ is not equal to zero.}$$

you use the F statistic in Equation (11.15).

F TEST FOR INTERACTION EFFECT

$$F = \frac{MSAB}{MSE} \qquad \text{(11.15)}$$

You reject the null hypothesis at the α level of significance if

$$F = \frac{MSAB}{MSE} > F_U$$

where F_U is the upper-tail critical value from an F distribution with $(r - 1)(c - 1)$ and $rc(n' - 1)$ degrees of freedom.

Table 11.6 presents the entire two-way ANOVA table.

TABLE 11.6

Analysis-of-Variance Table for the Two-Factor Factorial Design

Source	Degrees of Freedom	Sum of Squares	Mean Square (Variance)	F
A	$r-1$	SSA	$MSA = \dfrac{SSA}{r-1}$	$F = \dfrac{MSA}{MSE}$
B	$c-1$	SSB	$MSB = \dfrac{SSB}{c-1}$	$F = \dfrac{MSB}{MSE}$
AB	$(r-1)(c-1)$	SSAB	$MSAB = \dfrac{SSAB}{(r-1)(c-1)}$	$F = \dfrac{MSAB}{MSE}$
Error	$rc(n'-1)$	SSE	$MSE = \dfrac{SSE}{rc(n'-1)}$	
Total	$n-1$	SST		

To examine a two-way ANOVA, return to the Using Statistics scenario on page 422. As production manager at Perfect Parachutes, you have decided not only to evaluate the different suppliers but also to determine whether parachutes woven on the Jetta looms are as strong as those woven on the Turk looms. In addition, you need to determine whether any differences among the four suppliers in the strength of the parachutes are dependent on the type of loom being used. Thus, you have decided to perform an experiment in which five different parachutes from each supplier are manufactured on each of the two different looms. The results are given in Table 11.7 and stored in the parachute2.xls file.

TABLE 11.7

Tensile Strengths of Parachutes Woven by Two Types of Looms, Using Synthetic Fibers from Four Suppliers

LOOM	SUPPLIER			
	1	2	3	4
Jetta	20.6	22.6	27.7	21.5
	18.0	24.6	18.6	20.0
	19.0	19.6	20.8	21.1
	21.3	23.8	25.1	23.9
	13.2	27.1	17.7	16.0
Turk	18.5	26.3	20.6	25.4
	24.0	25.3	25.2	19.9
	17.2	24.0	20.8	22.6
	19.9	21.2	24.7	17.5
	18.0	24.5	22.9	20.4

Figure 11.10 presents Microsoft Excel results.

FIGURE 11.10

Microsoft Excel
two-way ANOVA for the
parachute experiment

*See Section E11.4 to create
this.*

	A	B	C	D	E	F	G
1	**Anova: Two-Factor With Replication**						
2							
3	**SUMMARY**	**Supplier 1**	**Supplier 2**	**Supplier 3**	**Supplier 4**	**Total**	
4	*Jetta*						
5	Count	5	5	5	5	20	
6	Sum	92.1	117.7	109.9	102.5	422.2	
7	Average	18.42	23.54	21.98	20.5	21.11	
8	Variance	10.202	7.568	18.397	8.355	13.1283	
9							
10	*Turk*						
11	Count	5	5	5	5	20	
12	Sum	97.6	121.3	114.2	105.8	438.9	
13	Average	19.52	24.26	22.84	21.16	21.945	
14	Variance	7.237	3.683	4.553	8.903	8.4626	
15							
16	*Total*						
17	Count	10	10	10	10		
18	Sum	189.7	239	224.1	208.3		
19	Average	18.97	23.9	22.41	20.83		
20	Variance	8.0868	5.1444	10.4054	7.7912		
21							
22							
23	**ANOVA**						
24	*Source of Variation*	*SS*	*df*	*MS*	*F*	*P-value*	*F crit*
25	Sample	6.9723	1	6.9723	0.8096	0.3750	4.1491
26	Columns	134.3488	3	44.7829	5.1999	0.0049	2.9011
27	Interaction	0.2867	3	0.0956	0.0111	0.9984	2.9011
28	Within	275.5920	32	8.6123			
29							
30	Total	417.1998	39				

[1]*Table E.5 does not provide
the upper-tail critical values
from the F distribution with
32 degrees of freedom in
the denominator. Table E.5
gives critical values either
for F distributions with
30 degrees of freedom
in the denominator or
for F distributions with
40 degrees of freedom in
the denominator. When the
desired degrees of freedom
are not provided in the
table, you can round to the
closest value that is given or
use the p-value approach.*

In Figure 11.10, the summary tables provide the sample size, sum, mean, and variance for each combination of supplier and loom. The total columns in the first two tables provide these statistics for each loom, and the third table provides them for each supplier. In addition, in the ANOVA table, *df* represents degrees of freedom, *SS* refers to sum of squares, *MS* stands for mean squares, and *F* is the computed *F* test statistic.

To interpret the results, you start by testing whether there is an interaction effect between factor *A* (loom) and factor *B* (supplier). If the interaction effect is significant, further analysis will refer only to this interaction. If the interaction effect is not significant, you can focus on the **main effects**—potential differences in looms (factor *A*) and potential differences in suppliers (factor *B*).

Using the 0.05 level of significance, to determine whether there is evidence of an interaction effect, you reject the null hypothesis of no interaction between loom and supplier if the computed *F* value is greater than 2.92, the approximate upper-tail critical value from the *F* distribution, with 3 and 32 degrees of freedom (see Figure 11.11).[1]

Because $F = 0.0111 < F_U = 2.92$ or the *p*-value = 0.9984 > 0.05, you do not reject H_0. You conclude that there is insufficient evidence of an interaction effect between loom and supplier. You can now focus on the main effects.

FIGURE 11.11

Regions of rejection
and nonrejection
at the 0.05 level of
significance, with 3 and
32 degrees of freedom

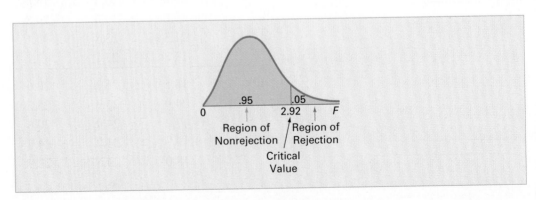

Using the 0.05 level of significance and testing for a difference between the two looms (factor A), you reject the null hypothesis if the calculated F value is greater than 4.17, the (approximate) upper-tail critical value from the F distribution with 1 and 32 degrees of freedom (see Figure 11.12). Because $F = 0.8096 < F_U = 4.17$ or the p-value $= 0.3750 > 0.05$, you do not reject H_0. You conclude that there is insufficient evidence of a difference between the two looms in terms of the mean tensile strengths of the parachutes manufactured.

FIGURE 11.12

Regions of rejection and nonrejection at the 0.05 level of significance, with 1 and 32 degrees of freedom

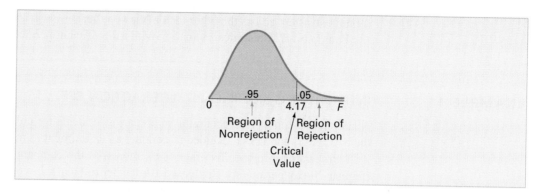

Using the 0.05 level of significance and testing for a difference among the suppliers (factor B), you reject the null hypothesis of no difference if the calculated F value exceeds 2.92, the approximate upper-tail critical value from the F, distribution with 3 degrees of freedom in the numerator and 32 degrees of freedom in the denominator (see Figure 11.11). Because $F = 5.1999 > F_U = 2.92$ or the p-value $= 0.0049 < 0.05$, reject H_0. You conclude that there is evidence of a difference among the suppliers in terms of the mean tensile strength of the parachutes.

Interpreting Interaction Effects

You can get a better understanding of the interpretation of the interaction by plotting the cell means (that is, the means of all possible factor level combinations), as shown in Figure 11.13. Figure 11.10 on page 442 provides the cell means for the loom–supplier combinations. From the plot of the mean tensile strength for each combination of loom and supplier, observe that the two lines (representing the two looms) are roughly parallel. This indicates that the *difference* between the mean tensile strength of the two looms is virtually the same for the four suppliers. In other words, there is no *interaction* between these two factors, as was clearly substantiated from the F test.

FIGURE 11.13

Microsoft Excel cell means plot of tensile strength based on loom and supplier

See Section E11.5 to create this.

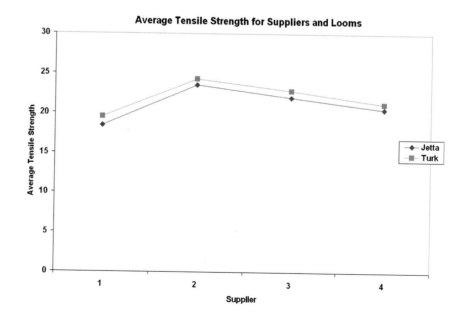

What is the interpretation if there is an interaction? In such a situation, some levels of factor A would respond better with certain levels of factor B. For example, with respect to tensile strength, suppose that some suppliers were better for the Jetta loom and other suppliers were better for the Turk loom. If this were true, the lines of Figure 11.13 would not be nearly as parallel, and the interaction effect might be statistically significant. In such a situation, the difference between the looms is no longer the same for all suppliers. Such an outcome would also complicate the interpretation of the *main effects* because differences in one factor (the loom) are not consistent across the other factor (the supplier).

Example 11.2 illustrates a situation with a significant interaction effect.

EXAMPLE 11.2

INTERPRETING SIGNIFICANT INTERACTION EFFECTS

A nationwide company specializing in preparing students for college entrance exams, such as the SAT, ACT, and LSAT, decided to conduct an experiment to investigate ways to improve its ACT Preparatory Course. Two factors of interest to the company are the length of the course (regular 30-day period or a condensed 10-day period) and the type of course (traditional classroom or online distance learning). The company randomly assigned 10 clients to each of the four cells. Table 11.8 lists the students' scores on the ACT for this two-factor design. The data are stored in the file act.xls.

What are the effects of the type of course and the length of the course on ACT scores?

TABLE 11.8

ACT Scores for Different Types and Lengths of Courses

	LENGTH OF COURSE			
TYPE OF COURSE	Condensed		Regular	
Traditional	26	18	34	28
	27	24	24	21
	25	29	35	23
	21	20	31	29
	21	28	28	26
Online	27	21	24	21
	29	32	26	19
	20	19	32	19
	24	28	20	24
	30	29	23	25

SOLUTION The cell means plot presented in Figure 11.14 illustrates a strong interaction between the type of course and the length of the course. The non-parallel lines indicate that the effect of condensing the course depends on whether the course is taught in the traditional classroom manner or via online distance learning. The online mean score is higher when the course is condensed to a 10-day period, whereas the traditional mean score is higher when the course takes place over the traditional 30-day period.

To verify the somewhat subjective analysis provided by interpreting the cell means plot, you begin by testing whether there is a statistically significant interaction between factor A (length of course) and factor B (type of course). Using a 0.05 level of significance, you reject the null hypothesis because the p-value equals $0.0184 < 0.05$ (see Figure 11.15). Thus, the hypothesis test confirms the interaction evident in the cell means plot. The existence of this significant interaction effect complicates the interpretation of the hypothesis tests concerning the two main effects. You cannot directly conclude that there is no effect with respect to length of course and type of course, even though both have p-values > 0.05. Whether condensing a

FIGURE 11.14

Microsoft Excel cell means plot of ACT scores

See Section E11.5 to create this.

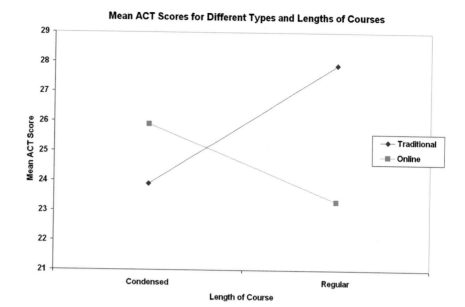

Mean ACT Scores for Different Types and Lengths of Courses

course is a good idea depends on whether the course is a traditional class or an online distance learning course. To ensure the highest mean ACT scores, the company should use the traditional approach when offering courses over a 30-day period but use the online approach when offering the condensed courses over a 10-day period.

FIGURE 11.15

Microsoft Excel two-way ANOVA for ACT scores

See Section E11.4 to create this.

	A	B	C	D	E	F	G
1	Anova: Two-Factor With Replication						
2							
3	SUMMARY	Condensed	Regular	Total			
4	Traditional						
5	Count	10	10	20			
6	Sum	239	279	518			
7	Average	23.9	27.9	25.9			
8	Variance	13.8778	20.9889	20.7263			
9							
10	Online						
11	Count	10	10	20			
12	Sum	259	233	492			
13	Average	25.9	23.3	24.6			
14	Variance	20.9889	15.5667	19.0947			
15							
16	Total						
17	Count	20	20				
18	Sum	498	512				
19	Average	24.9	25.6				
20	Variance	17.5684	22.8842				
21							
22							
23	ANOVA						
24	Source of Variation	SS	df	MS	F	P-value	F crit
25	Sample	16.9	1	16.9	0.9465	0.3371	4.1132
26	Columns	4.9	1	4.9	0.2744	0.6036	4.1132
27	Interaction	108.9	1	108.9	6.0989	0.0184	4.1132
28	Within	642.8	36	17.8556			
29							
30	Total	773.5	39				

Multiple Comparisons: The Tukey Procedure

If there is no significant interaction effect, you can determine the particular levels of the factors that are significantly different by using the **Tukey multiple comparisons procedure** (see references 8 and 9). Equation (11.16) gives the critical range for factor A.

CRITICAL RANGE FOR FACTOR A

$$\text{Critical range} = Q_U \sqrt{\frac{MSE}{cn'}} \qquad \textbf{(11.16)}$$

where Q_U is the upper-tail critical value from a Studentized range distribution having r and $rc(n' - 1)$ degrees of freedom. (Values for the Studentized range distribution are found in Table E.9.)

Equation (11.17) gives the critical range for factor B.

CRITICAL RANGE FOR FACTOR B

$$\text{Critical range} = Q_U \sqrt{\frac{MSE}{rn'}} \qquad \textbf{(11.17)}$$

where Q_U is the upper-tail critical value from a Studentized range distribution having c and $rc(n' - 1)$ degrees of freedom. (Values for the Studentized range distribution are found in Table E.9.)

To use the Tukey procedure, return to the parachute manufacturing data of Table 11.7 on page 441. In Figures 11.10 on page 442 (the ANOVA summary table provided by Microsoft Excel), only one of the main effects is significant. Using $\alpha = 0.05$, there is no evidence of a significant difference between the two looms (Jetta and Turk) that comprise factor A, but there is evidence of a significant difference among the four suppliers that comprise factor B. Thus, you can use the Tukey multiple comparisons procedure to further analyze differences between the suppliers of factor B.

Because there are four levels of factor B, there are $4(4 - 1)/2 = 6$ pairwise comparisons. Using the calculations presented in Figures 11.10, the absolute mean differences are as follows:

1. $\left| \bar{X}_{.1.} - \bar{X}_{.2.} \right| = \left| 18.97 - 23.90 \right| = 4.93$

2. $\left| \bar{X}_{.1.} - \bar{X}_{.3.} \right| = \left| 18.97 - 22.41 \right| = 3.44$

3. $\left| \bar{X}_{.1.} - \bar{X}_{.4.} \right| = \left| 18.97 - 20.83 \right| = 1.86$

4. $\left| \bar{X}_{.2.} - \bar{X}_{.3.} \right| = \left| 23.90 - 22.41 \right| = 1.49$

5. $\left| \bar{X}_{.2.} - \bar{X}_{.4.} \right| = \left| 23.90 - 20.83 \right| = 3.07$

6. $\left| \bar{X}_{.3.} - \bar{X}_{.4.} \right| = \left| 22.41 - 20.83 \right| = 1.58$

To determine the critical range, refer to Figure 11.10 to find $MSE = 8.612$, $r = 2$, $c = 4$, and $n' = 5$. From Table E.9 [for $\alpha = 0.05$, $c = 4$, and $rc(n' - 1) = 32$], Q_U, the upper-tail critical value of the test statistic with 4 and 32 degrees of freedom, is approximated as 3.84. Using Equation (11.17),

$$\text{Critical range} = 3.84 \sqrt{\frac{8.612}{10}} = 3.56$$

Because $4.93 > 3.56$, only the means of Suppliers 1 and 2 are different. You can conclude that the mean tensile strength is lower for Supplier 1 than for Supplier 2, but there are no statistically significant differences between Suppliers 1 and 3, Suppliers 1 and 4, Suppliers 2 and 3, Suppliers 2 and 4, and Suppliers 3 and 4. Note that by using $\alpha = 0.05$, you are able to make all six comparisons with an overall error rate of only 5%.

PROBLEMS FOR SECTION 11.2

Learning the Basics

 11.15 Consider a two-factor factorial design with three levels in factor A, three levels in factor B, and four replicates in each of the nine cells.
a. How many degrees of freedom are there in determining the factor A variation and the factor B variation?
b. How many degrees of freedom are there in determining the interaction variation?
c. How many degrees of freedom are there in determining the random error variation?
d. How many degrees of freedom are there in determining the total variation?

 11.16 Assume that you are working with the results from Problem 11.15.
a. If $SSA = 120$, $SSB = 110$, $SSE = 270$, and $SST = 540$, what is $SSAB$?
b. What are MSA and MSB?
c. What is $MSAB$?
d. What is MSE?

11.17 Assume that you are working with the results of Problems 11.15 and 11.16.
a. What is the value of the test statistic F for the interaction effect?
b. What is the value of the test statistic F for the factor A effect?
c. What is the value of the test statistic F for the factor B effect?
d. Form the ANOVA summary table and fill in all values in the body of the table.

 11.18 Given the results from Problems 11.15 through 11.17,
a. at the 0.05 level of significance, is there an effect due to factor A?
b. at the 0.05 level of significance, is there an effect due to factor B?
c. at the 0.05 level of significance, is there an interaction effect?

11.19 Given a two-way ANOVA with two levels for factor A, five levels for factor B, and four replicates in each of the 10 cells, with $SSA = 18$, $SSB = 64$, $SSE = 60$, and $SST = 150$,
a. form the ANOVA summary table and fill in all values in the body of the table.
b. at the 0.05 level of significance, is there an effect due to factor A?
c. at the 0.05 level of significance, is there an effect due to factor B?

d. at the 0.05 level of significance, is there an interaction effect?

 11.20 Given a two-factor factorial experiment and the ANOVA summary table that follows, fill in all the missing results:

Source	Degrees of Freedom	Sum of Squares	Mean Square (Variance)	F
Factor A	$r - 1 = 2$	$SSA = ?$	$MSA = 80$	$F = ?$
Factor B	$c - 1 = ?$	$SSB = 220$	$MSB = ?$	$F = 11.0$
AB interaction	$(r-1)(c-1) = 8$	$SSAB = ?$	$MSAB = 10$	$F = ?$
Error	$rc(n'-1) = 30$	$SSE = ?$	$MSE = ?$	
Total	$n - 1 = ?$	$SST = ?$		

 11.21 From the results of Problem 11.20,
a. at the 0.05 level of significance, is there an effect due to factor A?
b. At the 0.05 level of significance, is there an effect due to factor B?
c. At the 0.05 level of significance, is there an interaction effect?

Applying the Concepts

11.22 The effects of developer strength (factor A) and development time (factor B) on the density of photographic plate film were being studied. Two strengths and two development times were used, and four replicates in each of the four cells were evaluated. The results (with larger being best) are stored in the file photo.xls and shown in the following table:

	DEVELOPMENT TIME (MINUTES)	
DEVELOPER STRENGTH	10	14
1	0	1
	5	4
	2	3
	4	2
2	4	6
	7	7
	6	8
	5	7

At the 0.05 level of significance,
a. is there an interaction between developer strength and development time?
b. is there an effect due to developer strength?
c. is there an effect due to development time?
d. Plot the mean density of each developer strength for each development time.
e. What can you conclude about the effect of developer strength and development time on density?

11.23 A chef in a restaurant that specializes in pasta dishes was experiencing difficulty in getting brands of pasta to be *al dente*—that is, cooked enough so as not to feel starchy or hard but still feel firm when bitten into. She decided to conduct an experiment in which two brands of pasta, one American and one Italian, were cooked for either 4 or 8 minutes. The variable of interest was weight of the pasta because cooking the pasta enables it to absorb water. A pasta with a faster rate of water absorption may provide a shorter interval in which the pasta is *al dente*, thereby increasing the chance that it might be overcooked. The experiment was conducted by using 150 grams of uncooked pasta. Each trial began by bringing a pot containing 6 quarts of cold, unsalted water to a moderate boil. The 150 grams of uncooked pasta was added and then weighed after a given period of time by lifting the pasta from the pot via a built-in strainer. The results (in terms of weight in grams) for two replicates of each type of pasta and cooking time are stored in the file **pasta.xls** and are as follows:

	COOKING TIME (MINUTES)	
TYPE OF PASTA	**4**	**8**
American	265	310
	270	320
Italian	250	300
	245	305

At the 0.05 level of significance,
a. is there an interaction between type of pasta and cooking time?
b. is there an effect due to type of pasta?
c. is there an effect due to cooking time?
d. Plot the mean weight for each type of pasta for each cooking time.
e. What conclusions can you reach concerning the importance of each of these two factors on the weight of the pasta?

11.24 A student team in a business statistics course performed a factorial experiment to investigate the time required for pain-relief tablets to dissolve in a glass of water. The two factors of interest were brand name (Equate, Kroger, or Alka-Seltzer) and temperature of the water (hot or cold). The experiment consisted of four replicates for each of the six factor combinations. The following data (stored in the file **pain-relief.xls**) show the time a tablet took to dissolve (in seconds) for the 24 tablets used in the experiment:

BRAND OF PAIN-RELIEF TABLET

WATER	Equate	Kroger	Alka-Seltzer
Cold	85.87	75.98	100.11
	78.69	87.66	99.65
	76.42	85.71	100.83
	74.43	86.31	94.16
Hot	21.53	24.10	23.80
	26.26	25.83	21.29
	24.95	26.32	20.82
	21.52	22.91	23.21

At the 0.05 level of significance,
a. is there an interaction between brand of pain reliever and temperature of water?
b. is there an effect due to brand?
c. is there an effect due to the temperature of the water?
d. Plot the mean dissolving time for each brand for the two temperatures.
e. Discuss the results of (a) through (d).

11.25 Integrated circuits are manufactured on silicon wafers through a process that involves a series of steps. An experiment was carried out to study the effect of the cleansing and etching steps on the yield (coded to maintain confidentiality). The results (stored in the file **yield.xls**) are as follows:

	ETCHING STEP	
CLEANSING STEP	**New**	**Standard**
New 1	38	34
	34	19
	38	28
New 2	29	20
	35	35
	34	37
Standard	31	29
	23	32
	38	30

Source: Extracted from J. Ramirez and W. Taam, "An Autologistic Model for Integrated Circuit Manufacturing," Journal of Quality Technology, 2000, 32, pp. 254–262.

At the 0.05 level of significance,
a. is there an interaction between the cleansing step and the etching step?
b. is there an effect due to the cleansing step?
c. is there an effect due to the etching step?

d. Plot the mean yield for each cleansing step for the two etching steps.

e. Discuss the results of (a) through (d).

11.26 An experiment was conducted to study the distortion of drive gears in automobiles. Two factors were studied—the tooth size of the gear and the part positioning. The results (stored in the file `gear.xls`) are as follows: At the 0.05 level of significance,

a. is there an interaction between the tooth size and the part positioning?

b. is there an effect due to tooth size?

c. is there an effect due to the part positioning?

d. Plot the mean yield for each tooth size for the two part positions.

e. Discuss the results of (a) through (d).

	PART POSITIONING	
TOOTH SIZE	**Low**	**High**
Low	18.0	13.5
	16.5	8.5
	26.0	11.5
	22.5	16.0
	21.5	~4.5
	21.0	4.0
	30.0	1.0
	24.5	9.0
High	27.5	17.5
	19.5	11.5
	31.0	10.0
	27.0	1.0
	17.0	14.5
	14.0	3.5
	18.0	7.5
	17.5	6.5

Source: Extracted from D. R. Bingham and R. R. Sitter, "Design Issues in Fractional Factorial Split-Plot Experiments," Journal of Quality Technology, *33, 2001, pp. 2–15.*

11.3 ⊙ (*CD-ROM Topic*) THE RANDOMIZED BLOCK DESIGN

The randomized block design is an extension of the paired *t* test covered in Section 10.2 to more than two groups. For further discussion, see `section 11.3.pdf` on the Student CD-ROM that accompanies this book.

S U M M A R Y

In this chapter, various statistical procedures were used to analyze the effect of one or two factors of interest. You learned how the production manager of the Perfect Parachutes Company could use these procedures to identify the best suppliers and loom types in order to increase the strength of the parachutes. The assumptions required for using these procedures were discussed in detail. Remember that you need to critically investigate the validity of the assumptions underlying the hypothesis test procedures. Table 11.9 summarizes the topics covered in this chapter.

TABLE 11.9

Summary of Topics in Chapter 11

Type of Analysis	Type of Data Numerical
Comparing more than two groups (one factor)	One-way analysis of variance (Section 11.1)
Factorial design	Two-way analysis of variance (Section 11.2)
Comparing more than two groups (one factor with repeated measurements or matched items)	Randomized block design (Section 11.3 on the Student CD-ROM)

KEY EQUATIONS

Total Variation in One-Way ANOVA

$$SST = \sum_{j=1}^{c}\sum_{i=1}^{n_j}(X_{ij} - \bar{\bar{X}})^2 \quad \textbf{(11.1)}$$

Among-Group Variation in One-Way ANOVA

$$SSA = \sum_{j=1}^{c} n_j(\bar{X}_j - \bar{\bar{X}})^2 \quad \textbf{(11.2)}$$

Within-Group Variation in One-Way ANOVA

$$SSW = \sum_{j=1}^{c}\sum_{i=1}^{n_j}(X_{ij} - \bar{X}_j)^2 \quad \textbf{(11.3)}$$

Mean Squares in One-Way ANOVA

$$MSA = \frac{SSA}{c-1} \quad \textbf{(11.4a)}$$

$$MSW = \frac{SSW}{n-c} \quad \textbf{(11.4b)}$$

$$MST = \frac{SST}{n-1} \quad \textbf{(11.4c)}$$

One-Way ANOVA F Test Statistic

$$F = \frac{MSA}{MSW} \quad \textbf{(11.5)}$$

Critical Range for the Tukey-Kramer Procedure

$$\text{Critical range} = Q_U\sqrt{\frac{MSW}{2}\left(\frac{1}{n_j} + \frac{1}{n_{j'}}\right)} \quad \textbf{(11.6)}$$

Total Variation in Two-Way ANOVA

$$SST = \sum_{i=1}^{r}\sum_{j=1}^{c}\sum_{k=1}^{n'}(X_{ijk} - \bar{\bar{X}})^2 \quad \textbf{(11.7)}$$

Factor A Variation

$$SSA = cn'\sum_{i=1}^{r}(\bar{X}_{i..} - \bar{\bar{X}})^2 \quad \textbf{(11.8)}$$

Factor B Variation

$$SSB = rn'\sum_{j=1}^{c}(\bar{X}_{.j.} - \bar{\bar{X}})^2 \quad \textbf{(11.9)}$$

Interaction Variation

$$SSAB = n'\sum_{i=1}^{r}\sum_{j=1}^{c}(\bar{X}_{ij.} - \bar{X}_{i..} - \bar{X}_{.j.} + \bar{\bar{X}})^2 \quad \textbf{(11.10)}$$

Random Error in Two-Way ANOVA

$$SSE = \sum_{i=1}^{r}\sum_{j=1}^{c}\sum_{k=1}^{n'}(X_{ijk} - \bar{X}_{ij.})^2 \quad \textbf{(11.11)}$$

Mean Squares in Two-Way ANOVA

$$MSA = \frac{SSA}{r-1} \quad \textbf{(11.12a)}$$

$$MSB = \frac{SSB}{c-1} \quad \textbf{(11.12b)}$$

$$MSAB = \frac{SSAB}{(r-1)(c-1)} \quad \textbf{(11.12c)}$$

$$MSE = \frac{SSE}{rc(n'-1)} \quad \textbf{(11.12d)}$$

F Test for Factor A Effect

$$F = \frac{MSA}{MSE} \quad \textbf{(11.13)}$$

F Test for Factor B Effect

$$F = \frac{MSB}{MSE} \quad \textbf{(11.14)}$$

F Test for Interaction Effect

$$F = \frac{MSAB}{MSE} \quad \textbf{(11.15)}$$

Critical Range for Factor A

$$\text{Critical range} = Q_U\sqrt{\frac{MSE}{cn'}} \quad \textbf{(11.16)}$$

Critical Range for Factor B

$$\text{Critical range} = Q_U\sqrt{\frac{MSE}{rn'}} \quad \textbf{(11.17)}$$

KEY TERMS

among-group variation   423
analysis of variance (ANOVA)   422
ANOVA summary table   425
completely randomized design   422
critical range   429
F distribution   425
factor   422
grand mean, $\bar{\bar{X}}$ 423
group   422
homogeneity of variance   431
interaction   437
level   422
Levene test   432
main effect   442
mean square   424

multiple comparisons   429
normality   431
one-way ANOVA   422
one-way ANOVA F test statistic   425
random error   423
randomness and independence   431
replicate   437
Studentized range distribution   429
sum of squares among groups
   (SSA)   424
sum of squares due to factor A
   (SSA)   438
sum of squares due to factor B
   (SSB)   438

sum of squares due to interaction
   ($SSAB$)   438
sum of squares error (SSE)   439
sum of squares total (SST)   423
sum of squares within groups (SSW)
   424
total variation   423
Tukey multiple comparisons
   procedure   445
Tukey-Kramer multiple comparisons
   procedure   429
two-factor factorial design   436
two-way ANOVA   437
within-group variation   423

CHAPTER REVIEW PROBLEMS

Checking Your Understanding

11.27 In a one-way ANOVA, what is the difference between among-group variation and within-group variation?

11.28 What are the distinguishing features of the completely randomized design and two-factor factorial designs?

11.29 What are the assumptions of ANOVA?

11.30 Under what conditions should you select the one-way ANOVA F test to examine possible differences among the means of c independent groups?

11.31 When and how should you use multiple comparisons procedures for evaluating pairwise combinations of the group means?

11.32 What is the difference between the one-way ANOVA F test and the Levene test?

11.33 Under what conditions should you use the two-way ANOVA F test to examine possible differences among the means of each factor in a factorial design?

11.34 What is meant by the concept of interaction in a two-factor factorial design?

11.35 How can you determine whether there is an interaction in the two-factor factorial design?

Applying the Concepts

11.36 The operations manager for an appliance manufacturer wants to determine the optimal length of time for the washing cycle of a household clothes washer. An experiment is designed to measure the effect of detergent brand and washing cycle time on the amount of dirt removed from standard household laundry loads. Four brands of detergent (A, B, C, D) and four levels of washing cycle (18, 20, 22, and 24 minutes) are specifically selected for analysis. In order to run the experiment, 32 standard household laundry loads (having equal weight and dirt) are randomly assigned, 2 each, to the 16 detergent-washing cycle time combinations. The results, in pounds of dirt removed (stored in the `laundry.xls` file), are as follows:

DETERGENT BRAND	WASHING CYCLE TIME (IN MINUTES)			
	18	20	22	24
A	0.11	0.13	0.17	0.17
	0.09	0.13	0.19	0.18
B	0.12	0.14	0.17	0.19
	0.10	0.15	0.18	0.17
C	0.08	0.16	0.18	0.20
	0.09	0.13	0.17	0.16
D	0.11	0.12	0.16	0.15
	0.13	0.13	0.17	0.17

At the 0.05 level of significance,
a. is there an interaction between detergent and washing cycle time?
b. is there an effect due to detergent brand?

fect due to washing cycle time?

an amount of dirt removed (in pounds) for
ent brand for each washing cycle time.
ite, use the Tukey procedure to determine dif-
tween detergent brands and between washing
cycle times.

f. What washing cycle should be used for this type of household clothes washer?

g. Repeat the analysis, using washing cycle time as the only factor. Compare your results to those of (c), (e), and (f).

11.37 The quality control director for a clothing manufacturer wants to study the effect of operators and machines on the breaking strength (in pounds) of wool serge material. A batch of the material is cut into square-yard pieces, and these are randomly assigned, 3 each, to all 12 combinations of 4 operators and 3 machines chosen specifically for the experiment. The results (stored in the file breakstw.xls) are as follows:

MACHINE

OPERATOR	I	II	III
A	115	111	109
	115	108	110
	119	114	107
B	117	105	110
	114	102	113
	114	106	114
C	109	100	103
	110	103	102
	106	101	105
D	112	105	108
	115	107	111
	111	107	110

At the 0.05 level of significance,

a. is there an interaction between operator and machine?

b. is there an effect due to operator?

c. is there an effect due to machine?

d. Plot the mean breaking strength for each operator for each machine.

e. If appropriate, use the Tukey procedure to examine differences among operators and among machines.

f. What can you conclude about the effects of operators and machines on breaking strength? Explain.

g. Repeat the analysis, using machines as the only factor. Compare your results to those of (c), (e), and (f).

11.38 An operations manager wants to examine the effect of air-jet pressure (in psi) on the breaking strength of yarn. Three different levels of air-jet pressure are to be considered: 30 psi, 40 psi, and 50 psi. A random sample of 18 homogeneous filling yarns are selected from the same batch, and the yarns are randomly assigned, 6 each, to the 3 levels of air-jet pressure. The breaking strength scores are in the file yarn.xls.

a. Is there evidence of a significant difference in the variances of the breaking strengths for the three air-jet pressures? (Use $\alpha = 0.05$).

b. At the 0.05 level of significance, is there evidence of a difference among mean breaking strengths for the three air-jet pressures?

c. If appropriate, use the Tukey-Kramer procedure to determine which air-jet pressures significantly differ with respect to mean breaking strength. (Use $\alpha = 0.05$.)

d. What should the operations manager conclude?

11.39 Suppose that, when setting up his experiment in Problem 11.38, the operations manager is able to study the effect of side-to-side aspect in addition to air-jet pressure. Thus, instead of the one-factor completely randomized design in Problem 11.38, he used a two-factor factorial design, with the first factor, side-to-side aspects, having two levels (nozzle and opposite) and the second factor, air-jet pressure, having three levels (30 psi, 40 psi, and 50 psi). A sample of 18 yarns is randomly assigned, 3 to each of the 6 side-to-side aspect and pressure level combinations. The breaking-strength scores are as follows:

SIDE-TO-SIDE ASPECT	AIR-JET PRESSURE		
	30 psi	40 psi	50 psi
Nozzle	25.5	24.8	23.2
	24.9	23.7	23.7
	26.1	24.4	22.7
Opposite	24.7	23.6	22.6
	24.2	23.3	22.8
	23.6	21.4	24.9

At the 0.05 level of significance,

a. is there an interaction between side-to-side aspect and air-jet pressure?

b. is there an effect due to side-to-side aspect?

c. is there an effect due to air-jet pressure?

d. Plot the mean yarn breaking strength for the two levels of side-to-side aspect for each level of air-jet pressure.

e. If appropriate, use the Tukey procedure to study differences among the air-jet pressures.

f. On the basis of the results of (a) through (c), what conclusions can you reach concerning yarn breaking strength? Discuss.

g. Compare your results in (a) through (f) with those from the completely randomized design in Problem 11.38 (a) through (d). Discuss fully.

11.40 A hotel wanted to develop a new system for delivering room service breakfasts. In the current system, an order form is left on the bed in each room. If the customer wishes to receive a room service breakfast, he or she places the order form on the doorknob before 11 p.m. The current system includes a delivery time that provides a 15-minute interval for desired delivery time (6:30–6:45 a.m., 6:45–7:00 a.m., and so on). The new system is designed to allow the customer to request a specific delivery time. The hotel wants to measure the difference between the actual delivery time and the requested delivery time of room service orders for breakfast. (A negative time means that the order was delivered before the requested time. A positive time means that the order was delivered after the requested time.) The factors included were the menu choice (American or Continental) and the desired time period in which the order was to be delivered (Early Time Period [6:30–8:00 a.m.] or Late Time Period [8:00–9:30 a.m.]). Ten orders for each combination of menu choice and desired time period were studied on a particular day. The data (stored in the file **breakfast.xls**) are as follows:

DESIRED TIME

TYPE OF BREAKFAST	Early Time Period	Late Time Period
Continental	1.2	−2.5
	2.1	3.0
	3.3	−0.2
	4.4	1.2
	3.4	1.2
	5.3	0.7
	2.2	−1.3
	1.0	0.2
	5.4	−0.5
	1.4	3.8
American	4.4	6.0
	1.1	2.3
	4.8	4.2
	7.1	3.8
	6.7	5.5
	5.6	1.8
	9.5	5.1
	4.1	4.2
	7.9	4.9
	9.4	4.0

At the 0.05 level of significance,

a. is there an interaction between type of breakfast and desired time?

b. is there an effect due to type of breakfast?

c. is there an effect due to desired time?

d. Plot the mean delivery time difference for the two desired times for type of breakfast.

e. On the basis of the results of (a) through (d), what conclusions can you reach concerning delivery time difference? Discuss.

f. Suppose, instead, that the results are as shown below (and stored in the file **breakfast2.xls**). Repeat (a) through (e), using these data and compare the results to those of (a) through (e).

DESIRED TIME

TYPE OF BREAKFAST	Early	Late
Continental	1.2	−0.5
	2.1	5.0
	3.3	1.8
	4.4	3.2
	3.4	3.2
	5.3	2.7
	2.2	0.7
	1.0	2.2
	5.4	1.5
	1.4	5.8
American	4.4	6.0
	1.1	2.3
	4.8	4.2
	7.1	3.8
	6.7	5.5
	5.6	1.8
	9.5	5.1
	4.1	4.2
	7.9	4.9
	9.4	4.0

11.41 Modern software applications require rapid data access capabilities. An experiment was conducted to test the effect of data file size on the ability to access the files (as measured by read time, in milliseconds). Three different levels of data file size were considered: small—50,000 characters; medium—75,000 characters; or large—100,000 characters. A sample of eight files of each size was evaluated. The access read times, in milliseconds, are in the data file **access.xls**.

a. Is there evidence of a significant difference in the variance of the access read times for the three file sizes? (Use $\alpha = 0.05$).

b. At the 0.05 level of significance, is there evidence of a difference among mean access read times for the three file sizes?

c. If appropriate, use the Tukey-Kramer multiple comparisons procedure to determine which file sizes significantly differ with respect to mean access read time. (Use $\alpha = 0.05$.)

d. What conclusions can you reach?

11.42 Suppose that in Problem 11.41, when setting up the experiment, the effects of the size of the input/output buffer was studied in addition to the effects of the data file size. Thus, instead of the one-factor completely randomized design given in Problem 11.41, the experiment used a two-factor factorial design, with the first factor, buffer size, having two levels (20 kilobytes and 40 kilobytes) and the second factor, data file size, having three levels (small, medium, and large). That is, there are two factors under consideration: buffer size and data file size. A sample of four programs (replicates) were evaluated for each buffer size and data file size combination. The access read times, in milliseconds, are in the data file `access.xls`.

At the 0.05 level of significance,

a. is there an interaction between buffer size and data file size?
b. is there an effect due to buffer size?
c. is there an effect due to data file size?
d. Plot the mean access read times (in milliseconds) for the two buffer size levels for each of the three data file size levels. Describe the interaction and discuss why you can or cannot interpret the main effects in (b) and (c).
e. On the basis of the results of (a) through (d), what conclusions can you reach concerning access read times? Discuss.
f. Compare and contrast your results in (a) through (e) with those from the completely randomized design in Problem 11.41(a) through (d). Discuss fully.

11.43 A student team in a business statistics course conducted an experiment to test the download times of the three different types of computers (MAC, iMAC, and Dell) available at the university library. The students randomly selected one computer of each type. The students went to the Microsoft game Web site and clicked on the download link for the NBA game. The time (in seconds) between clicking on the link and the completion of the download was recorded. After each download, the file was deleted, and the trash folder was emptied. A total of 30 downloads were completed, in random order. Completely analyze the data shown in the following table and stored in the file `computers.xls`.

Computer

MAC	iMAC	Dell
156	160	236
166	165	238
148	184	257
160	192	242
139	197	282
151	172	253
158	189	270
167	179	256
142	200	267
219	193	259

11.44 In a second experiment performed by the team in Problem 11.43, the browser (Netscape Communicator or Internet Explorer) was added as a second factor. In this experiment, only two of the types of computers were used (MAC and Dell). Eight downloads from each of the four factor combinations were completed. Completely analyze the data shown in the following table and stored in the file `computers2.xls`.

BROWSER	COMPUTER	
	MAC	Dell
Netscape Communicator	142	284
	132	304
	125	273
	136	340
	127	326
	138	301
	147	291
	143	285
Internet Explorer	198	285
	210	292
	199	305
	202	325
	196	297
	213	301
	207	285
	201	290

Team Project

The data file `Mutual Funds.xls` contains information regarding nine variables from a sample of 838 mutual funds. The variables are

Category—Type of stocks comprising the mutual fund (small cap, mid cap, or large cap)
Objective—Objective of stocks comprising the mutual fund (growth or value)
Assets—In millions of dollars
Fees—Sales charges (no or yes)
Expense ratio—Ratio of expenses to net assets in percentage
2005 return—Twelve-month return in 2005
Three-year return—Annualized return, 2003–2005
Five-year return—Annualized return, 2001–2005
Risk—Risk-of-loss factor of the mutual fund (low, average, or high)

11.45 Completely analyze the difference between small cap, mid cap, and large cap mutual funds in terms of 2005 return, three-year return, five-year return, and expense ratio. Write a report summarizing your findings.

11.46 Completely analyze the difference between low-risk, average-risk, and high-risk mutual funds in terms of 2005 return, three-year return, five-year return, and expense ratio. Write a report summarizing your findings.

Student Survey Database

11.47 Problem 1.27 on page 15 describes a survey of 50 undergraduate students (see the file undergradsurvey.xls). For these data,
a. at the 0.05 level of significance, is there evidence of a difference based on academic major in grade point average, expected starting salary, salary expected in five years, age, and spending on textbooks and supplies?
b. at the 0.05 level of significance, is there evidence of a difference based on graduate school intention in grade point average, expected starting salary, salary expected in five years, age, and spending on textbooks and supplies?
c. at the 0.05 level of significance, is there evidence of a difference based on employment status in grade point average, expected starting salary, salary expected in five years, age, and spending on textbooks and supplies?

11.48 Problem 1.27 on page 15 describes a survey of 50 undergraduate students (see the file undergradsurvey.xls).
a. Select a sample of 50 undergraduate students at your school and conduct a similar survey for those students.
b. For the data collected in (a), repeat (a) through (c) of Problem 11.47.
c. Compare the results of (b) to those of Problem 11.47.

11.49 Problem 1.28 on page 15 describes a survey of 50 MBA students (see the file gradsurvey.xls). For these data, at the 0.05 level of significance,
a. is there evidence of a difference, based on undergraduate major, in age, undergraduate grade point average, graduate grade point average, GMAT score, expected salary upon graduation, salary expected in five years, and spending on textbooks and supplies?
b. Is there evidence of a difference, based on graduate major, in age, undergraduate grade point average, graduate grade point average, GMAT score, expected salary upon graduation, salary expected in five years, and spending on textbooks and supplies?
c. Is there evidence of a difference, based on employment status, in age, undergraduate grade point average, graduate grade point average, GMAT score, expected salary upon graduation, salary expected in five years, and spending on textbooks and supplies?

11.50 Problem 1.28 on page 15 describes a survey of 50 MBA students (see the file gradsurvey.xls).
a. Select a sample of 50 graduate students in your MBA program and conduct a similar survey for those students.
b. For the data collected in (a), repeat (a) through (c) of Problem 11.49.
c. Compare the results of (b) to those of Problem 11.49.

Managing the *Springville Herald*

Phase 1

In studying the home delivery solicitation process, the marketing department team determined that the so-called "later" calls made between 7:00 p.m. and 9:00 p.m. were significantly more conducive to lengthier calls than those made earlier in the evening (between 5:00 p.m. and 7:00 p.m.).

Knowing that the 7:00 p.m.-to-9:00 p.m. time period is superior, the team sought to investigate the effect of the type of presentation on the length of the call. A group of 24 female callers was randomly assigned, 8 each, to one of three presentation plans—structured, semistructured, and unstructured—and trained to make the telephone presentation. All calls were made between 7:00 p.m. and 9:00 p.m., the later time period, and the callers were to provide an introductory greeting that was personal but informal ("Hi, this is Mary Jones from the *Springville Herald*. May I speak to Bill Richards?"). The callers knew that the team was observing their efforts that evening but didn't know which particular calls were monitored. Measurements were taken on the length of call (defined as the difference, in seconds, between the time the person answers the phone and the time he or she hangs up). Table SH11.1 presents the results (which are stored in the file sh11-1.xls).

TABLE SH11.1 Length of Calls (in Seconds) Based on Presentation Plan

PRESENTATION PLAN		
Structured	**Semistructured**	**Unstructured**
38.8	41.8	32.9
42.1	36.4	36.1
45.2	39.1	39.2
34.8	28.7	29.3
48.3	36.4	41.9
37.8	36.1	31.7
41.1	35.8	35.2
43.6	33.7	38.1

EXERCISE

SH11.1 Analyze these data and write a report to the team that indicates your findings. Be sure to include your recommendations based on your findings. Also, include an appendix in which you discuss the reason you selected a particular statistical test to compare the three independent groups of callers.

DO NOT CONTINUE UNTIL THE PHASE 1 EXERCISE HAS BEEN COMPLETED.

Phase 2

In analyzing the data of Table SH11.1, the marketing department team observed that the structured presentation plan resulted in a significantly longer call than either the semistructured or unstructured plans. The team decided to tentatively recommend that all solicitations be completely structured calls made later in the evening, from 7:00 p.m. to 9:00 p.m. The team also decided to study the effect of two additional factors on the length of call:

- Gender of the caller: male versus female.
- Type of greeting: personal but formal (for example, "Hello, my name is Mary Jones from the *Springville Herald*. May I speak to Mr. Richards?"), personal but informal (for example, "Hi, this is Mary Jones from the *Springville Herald*. May I speak to Bill Richards?"), or impersonal (for example, "I represent the *Springville Herald* . . .").

The team acknowledged that in its previous studies, it had controlled for these variables. Only female callers were selected to participate in the studies, and they were trained to use a personal but informal greeting style. However, the team wondered if this choice of gender and greeting type was, in fact, best.

The team designed a study in which a total of 30 callers, 15 males and 15 females, were chosen to participate. The callers were randomly assigned to one of the three greeting-style training groups so that there were five callers in each of the six combinations of the two factors,

gender and greeting style (personal but formal—PF; personal but informal—PI; and impersonal). The callers knew that the team was observing their efforts that evening but didn't know which particular calls were monitored.

Measurements were taken on the length of call (defined as the difference, in seconds, between the time the person answers and the time he or she hangs up the phone). Table SH11.2 summarizes the results (which are stored in the file sh11-2.xls).

TABLE SH11.2 Length of Calls (in Seconds), Based on Gender and Type of Greeting

GENDER	GREETING		
	PF	PI	Impersonal
M	45.6	41.7	35.3
	49.0	42.8	37.7
	41.8	40.0	41.0
	35.6	39.6	28.7
	43.4	36.0	31.8
F	44.1	37.9	43.3
	40.8	41.1	40.0
	46.9	35.8	43.1
	51.8	45.3	39.6
	48.5	40.2	33.2

EXERCISES

SH11.2 Completely analyze these data and write a report to the team that indicates the importance of each of the two factors and/or the interaction between them on the length of the call. Include recommendations for future experiments to perform.

SH11.3 Do you believe the length of the telephone call is the most appropriate outcome to study? What other variables should be investigated next? Discuss.

Web Case

Apply your knowledge about ANOVA in this Web Case, which continues the cereal-fill packaging dispute Web Case from Chapters 7, 9, and 10.

After reviewing CCACC's latest posting (see Web Case for Chapter 10), Oxford Cereals is complaining that the group is guilty of using selective data. Visit the company's response page at **www.prenhall.com/Springville/OC_DataSelective.htm**, or open this Web page file from the text CD's Web case folder and then answer the following:

1. Does Oxford Cereals have a legitimate argument? Why or why not?
2. Assuming that the samples the company has posted were randomly selected, perform the appropriate analysis to resolve the ongoing weight dispute.
3. What conclusions can you reach from your results? If you were called as an expert witness, would you support the claims of the CCACC or the claims of Oxford Cereals? Explain.

REFERENCES

1. Berenson, M. L., D. M. Levine, and M. Goldstein, *Intermediate Statistical Methods and Applications: A Computer Package Approach* (Upper Saddle River, NJ: Prentice Hall, 1983).

2. Conover, W. J., *Practical Nonparametric Statistics*, 3rd ed. (New York: Wiley, 2000).

3. Daniel, W. W., *Applied Nonparametric Statistics*, 2nd ed. (Boston: PWS Kent, 1990).

4. Gitlow, H. S., and D. M. Levine, *Six Sigma for Green Belts and Champions: Foundations, DMAIC, Tools, Cases, and Certification* (Upper Saddle River, NJ: Financial Times/Prentice Hall, 2005).

5. Hicks, C. R., and K. V. Turner, *Fundamental Concepts in the Design of Experiments*, 5th ed. (New York: Oxford University Press, 1999).

6. Levine, D. M., *Statistics for Six Sigma Green Belts* (Upper Saddle River, NJ: Financial Times/Prentice Hall, 2006).

7. *Microsoft Excel 2007* (Redmond, WA: Microsoft Corp., 2003).

8. Montgomery, D. M., *Design and Analysis of Experiments*, 6th ed. (New York: Wiley, 2005).

9. Neter, J., M. H. Kutner, C. Nachtsheim, and W. Wasserman, *Applied Linear Statistical Models*, 5th ed. (New York: McGraw-Hill-Irwin, 2005).

Excel Companion
to Chapter 11

E11.1 USING THE ONE-WAY ANOVA

You conduct the One-Way ANOVA by selecting the ToolPak Anova: Single Factor procedure.

Open to a worksheet that contains unstacked multiple group data (see the Excel Companion to Chapter 10 on page 413) to be analyzed. Select **Tools → Data Analysis**, select **Anova: Single Factor** from the **Data Analysis** list, and click **OK**. In the procedure's dialog box (shown below), enter the cell range of the data as the **Input Range**, click **Columns**, check **Labels in first row**, and click **OK**. Results appear on a new worksheet.

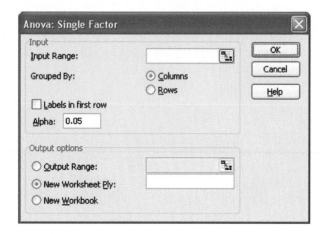

E11.2 USING THE TUKEY-KRAMER PROCEDURE

You conduct a Tukey-Kramer procedure for unstacked multiple group data by either selecting the PHStat2 Tukey-Kramer Procedure or by following a three-step process that includes making entries in the Tukey-Kramer.xls workbook.

Using PHStat2 Tukey-Kramer Procedure

Open to the worksheet that contains the unstacked multiple group data to be analyzed and select **PHStat → Multiple-Sample Tests → Tukey-Kramer Procedure**. In the Tukey-Kramer Procedure dialog box (shown at the top of the next column), enter the cell range of the data as the **Group Data Cell Range**, leave **First cells contains label** checked, enter a title as the **Title**, and click **OK**.

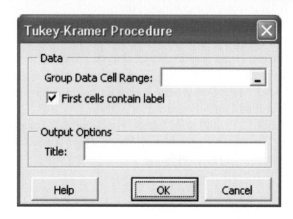

Complete the worksheet created by PHStat2 by looking up the value of Studentized Range Q statistic from Table E.9 on pages 810–811 for the desired level of significance and the numerator and denominator degrees of freedom values displayed in the worksheet.

Using Tukey-Kramer.xls

To use the Tukey-Kramer.xls workbook, first follow the instructions of Section E11.1 to create an ANOVA worksheet. Record the sample size and sample mean of each group (found in the Count and Average columns, respectively). Also record the *MSW* value, found in the cell that is the intersection of the MS column and the Within Groups row, and the denominator degrees of freedom, found in the cell that is the intersection of the df column and the Within Groups row.

Next, open the Tukey-Kramer.xls workbook and select the worksheet for your number of groups. If you have three groups, select the **TukeyKramer3** worksheet; for four groups, select the **TukeyKramer4** worksheet. (The workbook also has worksheets for five, six, and seven groups.) Enter the sample size, sample mean, denominator degrees of freedom, and *MSW* value you recorded earlier. Finally, look up the Studentized Range Q statistic from Table E.9 on pages 810–811 for the desired level of significance and the numerator and denominator degrees of freedom values displayed in the worksheet.

Figure E11.1 on page 459 shows the formulas in column F, G, and H of the TukeyKramer4 worksheet shown in Figure 11.7 on page 431. Figure E11.2 shows the formulas for column I of this worksheet. The IF comparison **B15** = "", in the cell I4 formula, holds if B15 is empty—that is, if you

	E	F	G	H
1				
2				
3		Absolute	Std. Error	Critical
4	Comparison	Difference	of Difference	Range
5	Group 1 to Group 2	=ABS(B5 - B6)	=SQRT((B14/2) * ((1/C5) + (1/C6)))	=B15 * G5
6	Group 1 to Group 3	=ABS(B5 - B7)	=SQRT((B14/2) * ((1/C5) + (1/C7)))	=B15 * G6
7	Group 1 to Group 4	=ABS(B5 - B8)	=SQRT((B14/2) * ((1/C5) + (1/C8)))	=B15 * G7
8	Group 2 to Group 3	=ABS(B6 - B7)	=SQRT((B14/2) * ((1/C6) + (1/C7)))	=B15 * G8
9	Group 2 to Group 4	=ABS(B6 - B8)	=SQRT((B14/2) * ((1/C6) + (1/C8)))	=B15 * G9
10	Group 3 to Group 4	=ABS(B7 - B8)	=SQRT((B14/2) * ((1/C7) + (1/C8)))	=B15 * G10

FIGURE E11.1

TukeyKramer4 worksheet columns F, G, and H formulas

	I
1	
2	
3	
4	=IF(B15 = "", "Results are NOT valid until Q Statistic is entered into B15", "Results")
5	=IF(F5 > H5, "Means are different", "Means are not different")
6	=IF(F6 > H6, "Means are different", "Means are not different")
7	=IF(F7 > H7, "Means are different", "Means are not different")
8	=IF(F8 > H8, "Means are different", "Means are not different")
9	=IF(F9 > H9, "Means are different", "Means are not different")
10	=IF(F10 > H10, "Means are different", "Means are not different")

FIGURE E11.2

TukeyKramer4 worksheet column I formulas

have not yet entered the Studentized Range Q statistic. If cell B15 is empty, a warning message is displayed; otherwise, the label "Results" is displayed.

E11.3 USING THE LEVENE TEST FOR HOMOGENEITY OF VARIANCE

You use the Levene test for unstacked multiple group data by either selecting the PHStat2 Levene Test procedure or by following a two-step manual process.

Using PHStat2 Levene Test

Open to the worksheet that contains the unstacked multiple group data to be analyzed and select **PHStat → Multiple-Sample Tests → Levene Test**. In the Levene Test dialog box (shown below), enter the **Level of Significance** and the cell range of the data to be analyzed as the **Sample Data Cell Range**. Leave **First cells contain label** checked, enter a title as the **Title**, and click **OK**.

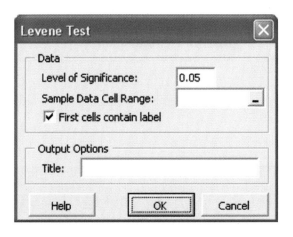

Using the Manual Process

Open to the worksheet that contains the unstacked multiple group data. Using Table 11.4 on page 432 and the **Model** worksheet of the Absolute Differences.xls workbook as your guide, add a row of formulas to determine the median for each group and then add new columns that compute the absolute differences. (The **Formulas** worksheet of this workbook displays the formulas used in the **Model** worksheet.) After you create the new columns, perform a one-way ANOVA by following the instructions in Section E11.1, using the cell range of the new absolute difference columns as the **Input Range** cell range. For example, if you were using the **Model** worksheet of the Absolute Differences.xls workbook, you would enter **F1:I6** as the **Input Range**.

E11.4 USING THE TWO-WAY ANOVA

You conduct a two-way ANOVA for a two-factor factorial design by selecting the ToolPak Anova: Two Factor With Replication procedure.

To use this ToolPak procedure, factor A data must be placed in rows, starting with row 2, and factor B data must be placed in columns, starting with column B. Enter labels for factor A in column A, starting with cell A2, and enter labels for factor B in row 1, starting with cell B1. (Cell A1 is not used by the procedure, but as a placeholder, you should enter a label that identifies factor A.) The **Data** worksheet of the Parachute2.xls workbook (shown in Figure E11.3) illustrates these rules and is one that you can use as a model for your own two-factor worksheets.

	A	B	C	D	E
1	Loom	Supplier 1	Supplier 2	Supplier 3	Supplier 4
2	Jetta	20.6	22.6	27.7	21.5
3	Jetta	18.0	24.6	18.6	20.0
4	Jetta	19.0	19.6	20.8	21.1
5	Jetta	21.3	23.8	25.1	23.9
6	Jetta	13.2	27.1	17.7	16.0
7	Turk	18.5	26.3	20.6	25.4
8	Turk	24.0	25.3	25.2	19.9
9	Turk	17.2	24.0	20.8	22.6
10	Turk	19.9	21.2	24.7	17.5
11	Turk	18.0	24.5	22.9	20.4

FIGURE E11.3

Data worksheet of the Parachute2.xls workbook

With a two-factor factorial design data worksheet opened, select **Tools → Data Analysis**. Select **Anova: Two Factor With Replication** from the **Data Analysis** list and click **OK**. In the procedure's dialog box (shown on page 460), enter the cell range of the data (including all labels) as the **Input Range**. Enter the **Rows per sample** (if you were using the Figure E11.3 worksheet, you would enter **5**), enter the **Alpha** value, and then click **OK**. Results appear on a new worksheet.

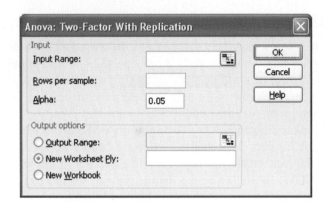

E11.5 CREATING PLOTS OF CELL MEANS

You create plots of cell means by using Excel charting features and the worksheet created by the ToolPak Anova: Two Factor With Replication procedure (see Section E11.4). Because this process differs for Excel 2007, this section includes passages specific to Excel 97-2003 and Excel 2007.

Creating a Plot (97-2003)

Open to the worksheet created by the ToolPak Anova: Two Factor With Replication procedure. Begin the Chart Wizard and make these entries:

Step 1 Click **Line** from the **Standard Types Chart type** box. Click the first choice of the second row in the **Chart sub-types** gallery, described as **Line with markers displayed at each value**.

Step 2 Click the **Data Range** tab. Enter the cell range of the means for each combination of factors (found in rows labeled "Average") as the **Data range** and select the **Rows** option. Because the means will appear in more than one area, enter the cell range using one or more commas (see Section E1.3 on page 25). For example, to enter the cell means shown in Figure 11.10 on page 442, enter **B7:E7,B13:E13** as the Data Range. Then click the **Series** tab. In the **Series** list box, select each generic Series*n* name and enter the appropriate factor *A* label in the **Name** box. For example, enter **Jetta** as the Series 1 name and **Turk** as

the Series2 name if plotting the cell means from the Figure 11.10 worksheet. Finally, enter the cell range of the factor *B* labels as the **Category (X) axis labels** (**B3:E3** for the Figure 11.10 worksheet).

Step 3 Click the **Titles** tab. Enter values for the **Chart title**, the **Category (X) axis**, and the **Value (Y) axis** title. Click the **Legend** tab and click **Show legend**. Click, in turn, the **Axes, Gridlines, Data Labels**, and **Data Table** tabs and use the formatting settings given in the "Creating Charts (97-2003)" part of Section E2.2 on page 79.

Creating a Plot (2007)

Open to the worksheet created by the ToolPak Anova: Two Factor With Replication procedure. Select the cell range of the means for each combination of factors (found in rows labeled "Average"). Because the means will appear in more than one area, select the first area, then hold down the **Ctrl** key while selecting the other areas. For example, to center the cell means shown in Figure 11.10 on page 442, select the range **B7:E7**, hold down the **Ctrl** key, and continue by selecting **B13:E13**.

With the cell means selected, select **Insert ➜ Line** and in the Line gallery select the choice labeled **Line with Markers**. Right-click the chart and click **Edit Data Source** on the shortcut menu. In the **Legend Entries (Series)** list box, do the following for each generic Series*n* name listed: (1) select the generic name, (2) click **Edit** [inside the Legend Entries (Series) dialog box], and (3) in the Edit Series dialog box that appears, enter the appropriate factor *A* label in the **Series name** box and click **OK**. For example, enter **Jetta** as the Series 1 name if plotting the cell means from the Figure 11.10 worksheet. When you are finished entering the Factor A labels, click **Edit** in the **Horizontal (Categories) Axis Labels** list box. In the Axis Labels dialog box, enter the cell range of the factor *B* labels as the **Axis Label Range** and click **OK**. Back in the Edit Data Source dialog box, click **OK**. For example, enter **Turk** as the Series2 name if plotting the cell means from the Figure 11.10 worksheet.

Finish by relocating your chart to a chart sheet. Customize your chart using the instructions in "Creating a Chart (2007)" in Section E.2.2 (see page 80), skipping the instructions given there for **Data Labels**.

CHAPTER 12

Chi-Square Tests and Nonparametric Tests

LEARNING OBJECTIVES

In this chapter, you learn:

- How and when to use the chi-square test for contingency tables
- How to use the Marascuilo procedure for determining pairwise differences when evaluating more than two proportions
- How and when to use the McNemar test
- How and when to use nonparametric tests

Using Statistics @ T.C. Resort Properties

You are the manager of T.C. Resort Properties, a collection of five upscale hotels located on two resort islands. Guests who are satisfied with the quality of services during their stay are more likely to return on a future vacation and to recommend the hotel to friends and relatives. To assess the quality of services being provided by your hotels, guests are encouraged to complete a satisfaction survey when they check out. You need to analyze the data from these surveys to determine the overall satisfaction with the services provided, the likelihood that the guests will return to the hotel, and the reasons some guests indicate that they will not return. For example, on one island, T.C. Resort Properties operates the Beachcomber and Windsurfer hotels. Is the perceived quality at the Beachcomber Hotel the same as at the Windsurfer Hotel? If a difference is present, how can you use this information to improve the overall quality of service at T.C. Resort Properties? Furthermore, if guests indicate that they are not planning to return, what are the most common reasons given for this decision? Are the reasons given unique to a certain hotel or common to all hotels operated by T.C. Resort Properties?

In the preceding three chapters, you used hypothesis-testing procedures to analyze both numerical and categorical data. Chapter 9 presented a variety of one-sample tests, and Chapter 10 developed several two-sample tests. Chapter 11 discussed the analysis of variance (ANOVA) that you use to study one or two factors of interest. This chapter extends hypothesis testing to analyze differences between population proportions based on two or more samples, as well as the hypothesis of *independence* in the joint responses to two categorical variables. The chapter concludes with nonparametric tests as alternatives to several hypothesis tests considered in Chapters 10 and 11.

12.1 CHI-SQUARE TEST FOR THE DIFFERENCE BETWEEN TWO PROPORTIONS (INDEPENDENT SAMPLES)

In Section 10.3, you studied the Z test for the difference between two proportions. In this section, the data are examined from a different perspective. The hypothesis-testing procedure uses a test statistic that is approximated by a chi-square (χ^2) distribution. The results of this χ^2 test are equivalent to those of the Z test described in Section 10.3.

If you are interested in comparing the counts of categorical responses between two independent groups, you can develop a two-way **contingency table** (see Section 2.4) to display the frequency of occurrence of successes and failures for each group. In Chapter 4, contingency tables were used to define and study probability.

To illustrate the contingency table, return to the Using Statistics scenario concerning T.C. Resort Properties. On one of the islands, T.C. Resort Properties has two hotels (the Beachcomber and the Windsurfer). In tabulating the responses to the single question "Are you likely to choose this hotel again?" 163 of 227 guests at the Beachcomber responded yes, and 154 of 262 guests at the Windsurfer responded yes. At the 0.05 level of significance, is there evidence of a significant difference in guest satisfaction (as measured by likelihood to return to the hotel) between the two hotels?

The contingency table displayed in Table 12.1 has two rows and two columns and is called a **2 × 2 contingency table**. The cells in the table indicate the frequency for each row and column combination.

TABLE 12.1

Layout of a 2×2 Contingency Table

	COLUMN VARIABLE (GROUP)		
ROW VARIABLE	**1**	**2**	**Totals**
Successes	X_1	X_2	X
Failures	$n_1 - X_1$	$n_2 - X_2$	$n - X$
Totals	n_1	n_2	n

where

$$X_1 = \text{number of successes in group 1}$$

$$X_2 = \text{number of successes in group 2}$$

$$n_1 - X_1 = \text{number of failures in group 1}$$

$$n_2 - X_2 = \text{number of failures in group 2}$$

$$X = X_1 + X_2, \text{ the total number of successes}$$

$$n - X = (n_1 - X_1) + (n_2 - X_2), \text{ the total number of failures}$$

$$n_1 = \text{sample size in group 1}$$

$$n_2 = \text{sample size in group 2}$$

$$n = n_1 + n_2 = \text{total sample size}$$

Table 12.2 contains the contingency table for the hotel guest satisfaction study. The contingency table has two rows, indicating whether the guests would return to the hotel (that is, success) or would not return to the hotel (that is, failure), and two columns, one for each hotel. The cells in the table indicate the frequency of each row and column combination. The row totals indicate the number of guests who would return to the hotel and those who would not return to the hotel. The column totals are the sample sizes for each hotel location.

TABLE 12.2

2×2 Contingency Table for the Hotel Guest Satisfaction Survey

	HOTEL		
CHOOSE HOTEL AGAIN?	**Beachcomber**	**Windsurfer**	**Total**
Yes	163	154	317
No	64	108	172
Total	227	262	489

To test whether the population proportion of guests who would return to the Beachcomber, π_1, is equal to the population proportion of guests who would return to the Windsurfer, π_2, you can use the χ^2 test for equality of proportions. To test the null hypothesis that there is no difference between the two population proportions:

$$H_0: \pi_1 = \pi_2$$

against the alternative that the two population proportions are not the same:

$$H_1: \pi_1 \neq \pi_2$$

you use the χ^2 test statistic, shown in Equation (12.1).

χ^2 TEST FOR THE DIFFERENCE BETWEEN TWO PROPORTIONS

The χ^2 test statistic is equal to the squared difference between the observed and expected frequencies, divided by the expected frequency in each cell of the table, summed over all cells of the table.

$$\chi^2 = \sum_{all\,cells} \frac{(f_o - f_e)^2}{f_e} \qquad (12.1)$$

where

f_o = **observed frequency** in a particular cell of a contingency table

f_e = **expected frequency** in a particular cell if the null hypothesis is true

The test statistic χ^2 approximately follows a chi-square distribution with 1 degree of freedom.[1]

[1]In general, in a contingency table, the degrees of freedom are equal to the (number of rows −1) times the (number of columns −1).

To compute the expected frequency, f_e, in any cell, you need to understand that if the null hypothesis is true, the proportion of successes in the two populations will be equal. Then the sample proportions you compute from each of the two groups would differ from each other only by chance. Each would provide an estimate of the common population parameter, π. A statistic that combines these two separate estimates together into one overall estimate of the population parameter provides more information than either of the two separate estimates could provide by itself. This statistic, given by the symbol $\bar{p}$ represents the estimated overall proportion of successes for the two groups combined (that is, the total number of successes divided by the total sample size). The complement of $\bar{p}$, $1 - \bar{p}$, represents the estimated overall proportion of failures in the two groups. Using the notation presented in Table 12.1 on page 463, Equation (12.2) defines $\bar{p}$.

COMPUTING THE ESTIMATED OVERALL PROPORTION

$$\bar{p} = \frac{X_1 + X_2}{n_1 + n_2} = \frac{X}{n} \qquad (12.2)$$

To compute the expected frequency, f_e, for each cell pertaining to success (that is, the cells in the first row in the contingency table), you multiply the sample size (or column total) for a group by $\bar{p}$. To compute the expected frequency, f_e, for each cell pertaining to failure (that is, the cells in the second row in the contingency table), you multiply the sample size (or column total) for a group by $(1 - \bar{p})$.

The test statistic shown in Equation (12.1) approximately follows a **chi-square distribution** (see Table E.4) with 1 degree of freedom. Using a level of significance α, you reject the null hypothesis if the computed χ^2 test statistic is greater than χ_U^2, the upper-tail critical value from the χ^2 distribution having 1 degree of freedom. Thus, the decision rule is

Reject H_0 if $\chi^2 > \chi_U^2$;

otherwise, do not reject H_0.

Figure 12.1 illustrates the decision rule.

FIGURE 12.1

Regions of rejection and nonrejection when using the chi-square test for the difference between two proportions, with level of significance α

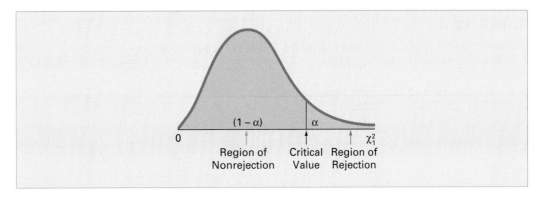

If the null hypothesis is true, the computed χ^2 statistic should be close to zero because the squared difference between what is actually observed in each cell, f_o, and what is theoretically expected, f_e, should be very small. If H_0 is false, then there are differences in the population proportions and the computed χ^2 statistic is expected to be large. However, what constitutes a large difference in a cell is relative. The same actual difference between f_o and f_e from a cell with a small number of expected frequencies contributes more to the χ^2 test statistic than a cell with a large number of expected frequencies.

To illustrate the use of the chi-square test for the difference between two proportions, return to the Using Statistics scenario concerning T.C. Resort Properties and the corresponding contingency table displayed in Table 12.2 on page 463. The null hypothesis ($H_0: \pi_1 = \pi_2$) states that there is no difference between the proportion of guests who are likely to choose either of these hotels again. To begin,

$$\bar{p} = \frac{X_1 + X_2}{n_1 + n_2} = \frac{163 + 154}{227 + 262} = \frac{317}{489} = 0.6483$$

$\bar{p}$ is the estimate of the common parameter π, the population proportion of guests who are likely to choose either of these hotels again if the null hypothesis is true. The estimated proportion of guests who are *not* likely to choose these hotels again is the complement of $\bar{p}$, $1 - 0.6483 = 0.3517$. Multiplying these two proportions by the sample size for the Beachcomber Hotel gives the number of guests expected to choose the Beachcomber again and the number not expected to choose this hotel again. In a similar manner, multiplying the two respective proportions by the Windsurfer Hotel's sample size yields the corresponding expected frequencies for that group.

EXAMPLE 12.1

COMPUTING THE EXPECTED FREQUENCIES

Compute the expected frequencies for each of the four cells of Table 12.2 on page 463.

SOLUTION

Yes—Beachcomber: $\bar{p} = 0.6483$ and $n_1 = 227$, so $f_e = 147.16$
Yes—Windsurfer: $\bar{p} = 0.6483$ and $n_2 = 262$, so $f_e = 169.84$
No—Beachcomber: $1 - \bar{p} = 0.3517$ and $n_1 = 227$, so $f_e = 79.84$
No—Windsurfer: $1 - \bar{p} = 0.3517$ and $n_2 = 262$, so $f_e = 92.16$

Table 12.3 presents these expected frequencies next to the corresponding observed frequencies.

TABLE 12.3

Comparing the Observed (f_o) and Expected (f_e) Frequencies

CHOOSE HOTEL AGAIN?	HOTEL				
	Beachcomber		Windsurfer		
	Observed	Expected	Observed	Expected	Total
Yes	163	147.16	154	169.84	317
No	64	79.84	108	92.16	172
Total	227	227.00	262	262.00	489

To test the null hypothesis that the population proportions are equal:

$$H_0: \pi_1 = \pi_2$$

against the alternative that the population proportions are not equal:

$$H_1: \pi_1 \neq \pi_2$$

you use the observed and expected frequencies from Table 12.3 to compute the χ^2 test statistic given by Equation (12.1) on page 464. Table 12.4 presents the calculations.

TABLE 12.4

Computation of χ^2 Test Statistic for the Hotel Guest Satisfaction Survey

f_o	f_e	$(f_o - f_e)$	$(f_o - f_e)^2$	$(f_o - f_e)^2/f_e$
163	147.16	15.84	250.91	1.71
154	169.84	−15.84	250.91	1.48
64	79.84	−15.84	250.91	3.14
108	92.16	15.84	250.91	2.72
				9.05

The **chi-square distribution** is a right-skewed distribution whose shape depends solely on the number of degrees of freedom. You find the critical value of the χ^2 test statistic from Table E.4, a portion of which is presented as Table 12.5.

TABLE 12.5

Finding the χ^2 Critical Value from the Chi-Square Distribution with 1 Degree of Freedom, Using the 0.05 Level of Significance

Degrees of Freedom	Upper-Tail Area						
	.995	.99	...	.05	.025	.01	.005
1			...	3.841	5.024	6.635	7.879
2	0.010	0.020	...	5.991	7.378	9.210	10.597
3	0.072	0.115	...	7.815	9.348	11.345	12.838
4	0.207	0.297	...	9.488	11.143	13.277	14.860
5	0.412	0.554	...	11.071	12.833	15.086	16.750

The values in Table 12.5 refer to selected upper-tail areas of the χ^2 distribution. A 2×2 contingency table has $(2 - 1)(2 - 1) = 1$ degree of freedom. Using $\alpha = 0.05$, with 1 degree of freedom, the critical value of χ^2 from Table 12.5 is 3.841. You reject H_0 if the computed χ^2 statistic is greater than 3.841 (see Figure 12.2). Because $9.05 > 3.841$, you reject H_0. You conclude that there is a difference in the proportion of guests who would return to the Beachcomber and the Windsurfer.

FIGURE 12.2

Regions of rejection and nonrejection when finding the χ^2 critical value with 1 degree of freedom, at the 0.05 level of significance

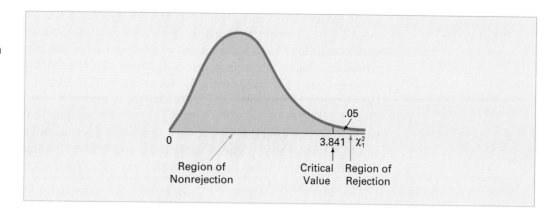

Figure 12.3 represents a Microsoft Excel worksheet for the guest satisfaction contingency table (Table 12.2 on page 463).

FIGURE 12.3

Microsoft Excel worksheet for the hotel guest satisfaction data

See Section E12.1 to create this. Figure E12.1 in that section includes the formulas for the first 15 rows of the worksheet that are the basis for computing the chi-square statistic in cell B25.

	A	B	C	D
1	**Guest Satisfaction Analysis**			
2				
3	**Observed Frequencies**			
4		**Hotel**		
5	**Choose Again?**	**Beachcomber**	**Windsurfer**	**Total**
6	Yes	163	154	317
7	No	64	108	172
8	Total	227	262	489
9				
10	**Expected Frequencies**			
11		Hotel		
12	Choose Again?	Beachcomber	Windsurfer	Total
13	Yes	147.1554	169.8446	317
14	No	79.8446	92.1554	172
15	Total	227	262	489
16				
17	**Data**			
18	Level of Significance	0.05		
19	Number of Rows	2		
20	Number of Columns	2		
21	Degrees of Freedom	1		
22				
23	**Results**			
24	Critical Value	3.8415	=CHIINV(B18, B21)	
25	Chi-Square Test Statistic	9.0526	=SUM(F13:G14)	
26	*p*-Value	0.0026	=CHIDIST(B25, B21)	
27	Reject the null hypothesis		=IF(B26 < B18, "Reject the null hypothesis", "Do not reject the null hypothesis")	
28				
29	*Expected frequency assumption*			
30	*is met.*		=IF(OR(B13 < 5, C13 < 5, B14 < 5, C14 < 5), " is violated.", " is met.")	

This worksheet includes the expected frequencies, χ^2 test statistic, degrees of freedom, and *p*-value. The χ^2 test statistic is 9.0526, which is greater than the critical value of 3.8415 (or the *p*-value = 0.0026 < 0.05), so you reject the null hypothesis that there is no difference in guest satisfaction between the two hotels. The *p*-value of 0.0026 is the probability of observing sample proportions as different as or more different than the actual difference ($0.718 - 0.588 = 0.13$ observed in the sample data), if the population proportions for the Beachcomber and Windsurfer hotels are equal. Thus, there is strong evidence to conclude that the two hotels are significantly different with respect to guest satisfaction, as measured by whether the guest is likely to return to the hotel again. An examination of Table 12.3 on page 466 indicates that a greater proportion of guests at the Beachcomber are likely to return than at the Windsurfer.

For the χ^2 test to give accurate results for a 2×2 table, you must assume that each expected frequency is at least 5. If this assumption is not satisfied, you can use alternative procedures such as Fisher's exact test (see references 1, 2, and 4).

In the hotel guest satisfaction survey, both the Z test based on the standardized normal distribution (see Section 10.3) and the χ^2 test based on the chi-square distribution provide the same conclusion. You can explain this result by the interrelationship between the standardized normal distribution and a chi-square distribution with 1 degree of freedom. For such situations, the χ^2 test statistic is the square of the Z test statistic. For instance, in the guest satisfaction study, the computed Z test statistic is +3.0088 and the computed χ^2 test statistic is 9.0526. Except for rounding error, this latter value is the square of +3.0088 [that is, $(+3.0088)^2 \cong 9.0526$]. Also, if you compare the critical values of the test statistics from the two distributions, at the 0.05 level of significance, the χ_1^2 value of 3.841 is the square of the Z value of ±1.96 (that is, $\chi_1^2 = Z^2$). Furthermore, the p-values for both tests are equal. Therefore, when testing the null hypothesis of equality of proportions:

$$H_0: \pi_1 = \pi_2$$

against the alternative that the population proportions are not equal:

$$H_1: \pi_1 \neq \pi_2$$

the Z test and the χ^2 test are equivalent methods. However, if you are interested in determining whether there is evidence of a *directional* difference, such as $\pi_1 > \pi_2$, you must use the Z test, with the entire rejection region located in one tail of the standardized normal distribution. In Section 12.2, the χ^2 test is extended to make comparisons and evaluate differences between the proportions among more than two groups. However, you cannot use the Z test if there are more than two groups.

PROBLEMS FOR SECTION 12.1

Learning the Basics

12.1 Determine the critical value of χ^2 with 1 degree of freedom in each of the following circumstances:
a. $\alpha = 0.01$, $n = 16$
b. $\alpha = 0.025$, $n = 11$
c. $\alpha = 0.05$, $n = 8$

12.2 Determine the critical value of χ^2 with 1 degree of freedom in each of the following circumstances:
a. $\alpha = 0.05$, $n = 28$
b. $\alpha = 0.025$, $n = 21$
c. $\alpha = 0.01$, $n = 5$

 12.3 Use the following contingency table:

	A	B	Total
1	20	30	50
2	30	45	75
Total	50	75	125

a. Find the expected frequency for each cell.
b. Compare the observed and expected frequencies for each cell.
c. Compute the χ^2 statistic. Is it significant at $\alpha = 0.05$?

PH Grade ASSIST **12.4** Use the following contingency table:

	A	B	Total
1	20	30	50
2	30	20	50
Total	50	50	100

a. Find the expected frequency for each cell.
b. Find the χ^2 statistic for this contingency table. Is it significant at $\alpha = 0.05$?

Applying the Concepts

12.5 A sample of 500 shoppers was selected in a large metropolitan area to determine various information concerning consumer behavior. Among the questions asked was, "Do you enjoy shopping for clothing?" The results are summarized in the following contingency table:

ENJOY SHOPPING FOR CLOTHING	GENDER		
	Male	Female	Total
Yes	136	224	360
No	104	36	140
Total	240	260	500

a. Is there evidence of a significant difference between the proportion of males and females who enjoy shopping for clothing at the 0.01 level of significance?

b. Determine the *p*-value in (a) and interpret its meaning.

c. What are your answers to (a) and (b) if 206 males enjoyed shopping for clothing and 34 did not?

d. Compare the results of (a) through (c) to those of Problem 10.33 (a) through (c) on page 395.

12.6 Is good gas mileage a priority for car shoppers? A survey conducted by Progressive Insurance asked this question of both men and women shopping for new cars. The data were reported as percentages, and no sample sizes were given:

GAS MILEAGE A PRIORITY?	GENDER	
	Men	Women
Yes	76%	84%
No	24%	16%

Source: Extracted from "Snapshots," **usatoday.com**, *June 21, 2004.*

a. Assume that 50 men and 50 women were included in the survey. At the 0.05 level of significance, is there a difference between males and females in the proportion who make gas mileage a priority?

b. Assume that 500 men and 500 women were included in the survey. At the 0.05 level of significance, is there a difference between males and females in the proportion who make gas mileage a priority?

c. Discuss the effect of sample size on the chi-square test.

12.7 The results of a yield improvement study at a semiconductor manufacturing facility provided defect data for a sample of 450 wafers. The following contingency table presents a summary of the responses to two questions: "Was a particle found on the die that produced the wafer?" and "Is the wafer good or bad?"

PARTICLES	QUALITY OF WAFER		
	Good	Bad	Totals
Yes	14	36	50
No	320	80	400
Totals	334	116	450

Source: Extracted from S. W. Hall, "Analysis of Defectivity of Semiconductor Wafers by Contingency Table," Proceedings Institute of Environmental Sciences, *Vol. 1 (1994), pp. 177–183.*

a. At the 0.05 level of significance, is there a difference between the proportion of good and bad wafers that have particles?

b. Determine the *p*-value in (a) and interpret its meaning.

c. What conclusions can you draw from this analysis?

d. Compare the results of (a) and (b) to those of Problem 10.35 on page 395.

 12.8 According to an Ipsos poll, the perception of unfairness in the U.S. tax code is spread fairly evenly across income groups, age groups, and education levels. In an April 2006 survey of 1,005 adults, Ipsos reported that almost 60% of all people said the code is unfair, while slightly more that 60% of those making more than $50,000 viewed the code as unfair (Extracted from "People Cry Unfairness," *The Cincinnati Enquirer*, April 16, 2006, p. A8). Suppose that the following contingency table represents the specific breakdown of responses:

U.S. TAX CODE	INCOME LEVEL		
	Less Than $50,000	More Than $50,000	Total
Fair	225	180	405
Unfair	280	320	600
Total	505	500	1,005

a. At the 0.05 level of significance, is there evidence of a difference in the proportion of adults who think the U.S. tax code is unfair between the two income groups?

b. Determine the *p*-value in (a) and interpret its meaning.

c. Compare the results of (a) and (b) to those of Problem 10.36 on page 396.

12.9 Where people turn to for news is different for various age groups. Suppose that a study conducted on this issue (extracted from P. Johnson, "Young People Turn to the Web for News," *USA Today*, March 23, 2006, p. 9D) was based on 200 respondents who were between the ages of 36 and 50 and 200 respondents who were above age 50. Of the 200 respondents who were between the ages of 36 and 50, 82 got their news primarily from newspapers. Of the 200 respondents who were above age 50, 104 got their news primarily from newspapers.

a. Construct a 2×2 contingency table.

b. Is there evidence of a significant difference in the proportion who get their news primarily from newspapers between those 36 to 50 years old and those above 50 years old? (Use $\alpha = 0.05$.)

c. Determine the *p*-value in (a) and interpret its meaning.

d. Compare the results of (b) and (c) to those of Problem 10.39 on page 396.

12.10 An experiment was conducted to study the choices made in mutual fund selection. Undergraduate and MBA students were presented with different S&P 500 index funds that were identical except for fees. Suppose 100 undergraduate students and 100 MBA students were selected. Partial results are shown on page 470:

	STUDENT GROUP	
FUND	**Undergraduate**	**MBA**
Highest-cost fund	27	18
Not highest-cost fund	73	82

Source: Extracted from J. Choi, D. Laibson, and B. Madrian, "Why Does the Law of One Practice Fail? An Experiment on Mutual Funds," **www.som.yale.edu/faculty/jjc83/fees.pdf**.

a. At the 0.05 level of significance, is there evidence of a difference between undergraduate and MBA students in the proportion who selected the highest-cost fund?
b. Determine the *p*-value in (a) and interpret its meaning.
c. Compare the results of (a) and (b) to those of Problem 10.38 on page 396.

12.2 CHI-SQUARE TEST FOR DIFFERENCES AMONG MORE THAN TWO PROPORTIONS

In this section, the χ^2 test is extended to compare more than two independent populations. The letter c is used to represent the number of independent populations under consideration. Thus, the contingency table now has two rows and c columns. To test the null hypothesis that there are no differences among the c population proportions:

$$H_0: \pi_1 = \pi_2 = \cdots = \pi_c$$

against the alternative that not all the c population proportions are equal:

$$H_1: \text{Not all } \pi_j \text{ are equal (where } j = 1, 2, \ldots, c)$$

you use Equation (12.1) on page 464:

$$\chi^2 = \sum_{all \text{ cells}} \frac{(f_o - f_e)^2}{f_e}$$

where

f_o = observed frequency in a particular cell of a $2 \times c$ contingency table

f_e = expected frequency in a particular cell if the null hypothesis is true

If the null hypothesis is true and the proportions are equal across all c populations, the c sample proportions should differ only by chance. In such a situation, a statistic that combines these c separate estimates into one overall estimate of the population proportion, π, provides more information than any one of the c separate estimates alone. To expand on Equation (12.2) on page 464, the statistic $\bar{p}$ in Equation (12.3) represents the estimated overall proportion for all c groups combined.

COMPUTING THE ESTIMATED OVERALL PROPORTION FOR c GROUPS

$$\bar{p} = \frac{X_1 + X_2 + \cdots + X_c}{n_1 + n_2 + \cdots + n_c} = \frac{X}{n} \tag{12.3}$$

To compute the expected frequency, f_e, for each cell in the first row in the contingency table, multiply each sample size (or column total) by $\bar{p}$. To compute the expected frequency, f_e, for each cell in the second row in the contingency table, multiply each sample size (or column total) by $(1 - \bar{p})$. The test statistic shown in Equation (12.1) on page 464 approximately follows a chi-square distribution, with degrees of freedom equal to the number of rows in the contingency table minus 1, times the number of columns in the table minus 1. For a **2 × c contingency table**, there are $c - 1$ degrees of freedom:

$$\text{Degrees of freedom} = (2 - 1)(c - 1) = c - 1$$

Using the level of significance α, you reject the null hypothesis if the computed χ^2 test statistic is greater than χ_U^2, the upper-tail critical value from a chi-square distribution having $c - 1$ degrees of freedom. Therefore, the decision rule is

$$\text{Reject } H_0 \text{ if } \chi^2 > \chi_U^2;$$

$$\text{otherwise, do not reject } H_0.$$

Figure 12.4 illustrates the decision rule.

FIGURE 12.4

Regions of rejection and nonrejection when testing for differences among c proportions using the χ^2 test

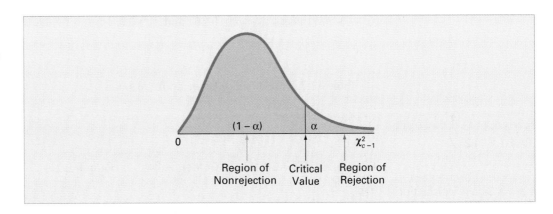

To illustrate the χ^2 test for equality of proportions when there are more than two groups, return to the Using Statistics scenario concerning T.C. Resort Properties. A similar survey was recently conducted on a different island on which T.C. Resort Properties has three different hotels. Table 12.6 presents the responses to a question concerning whether guests would be likely to choose this hotel again.

TABLE 12.6

2 × 3 Contingency Table for Guest Satisfaction Survey

	HOTEL			
CHOOSE HOTEL AGAIN	**Golden Palm**	**Palm Royale**	**Palm Princess**	**Total**
Yes	128	199	186	513
No	88	33	66	187
Total	216	232	252	700

Because the null hypothesis states that there are no differences among the three hotels in the proportion of guests who would likely return again, you use Equation (12.3) to calculate an estimate of π, the population proportion of guests who would likely return again:

$$\bar{p} = \frac{X_1 + X_2 + \cdots + X_c}{n_1 + n_2 + \cdots + n_c} = \frac{X}{n}$$

$$= \frac{(128 + 199 + 186)}{(216 + 232 + 252)} = \frac{513}{700}$$

$$= 0.733$$

The estimated overall proportion of guests who would *not* be likely to return again is the complement, $(1 - \bar{p})$, or 0.267. Multiplying these two proportions by the sample size taken at each hotel yields the expected number of guests who would and would not likely return.

EXAMPLE 12.2

COMPUTING THE EXPECTED FREQUENCIES

Compute the expected frequencies for each of the six cells in Table 12.6.

SOLUTION

Yes—Golden Palm: $\bar{p} = 0.733$ and $n_1 = 216$, so $f_e = 158.30$
Yes—Palm Royale: $\bar{p} = 0.733$ and $n_2 = 232$, so $f_e = 170.02$
Yes—Palm Princess: $\bar{p} = 0.733$ and $n_3 = 252$, so $f_e = 184.68$
No—Golden Palm: $1 - \bar{p} = 0.267$ and $n_1 = 216$, so $f_e = 57.70$
No—Palm Royale: $1 - \bar{p} = 0.267$ and $n_2 = 232$, so $f_e = 61.98$
No—Palm Princess: $1 - \bar{p} = 0.267$ and $n_3 = 252$, so $f_e = 67.32$

Table 12.7 presents these expected frequencies.

TABLE 12.7

Contingency Table of Expected Frequencies from a Guest Satisfaction Survey of Three Hotels

	HOTEL			
CHOOSE HOTEL AGAIN?	Golden Palm	Palm Royale	Palm Princess	Total
Yes	158.30	170.02	184.68	513
No	57.70	61.98	67.32	187
Total	216.00	232.00	252.00	700

To test the null hypothesis that the proportions are equal:

$$H_0: \pi_1 = \pi_2 = \pi_3$$

against the alternative that not all three proportions are equal:

$$H_1: \text{Not all } \pi_j \text{ are equal (where } j = 1, 2, 3).$$

You use the observed frequencies from Table 12.6 on page 471 and the expected frequencies from Table 12.7 to compute the χ^2 test statistic (given by Equation (12.1) on page 464) displayed in Table 12.8.

TABLE 12.8

Computation of χ^2 Test Statistic for the Guest Satisfaction Survey of Three Hotels

f_o	f_e	$(f_o - f_e)$	$(f_o - f_e)^2$	$(f_o - f_e)^2/f_e$
128	158.30	−30.30	918.09	5.80
199	170.02	28.98	839.84	4.94
186	184.68	1.32	1.74	0.01
88	57.70	30.30	918.09	15.91
33	61.98	−28.98	839.84	13.55
66	67.32	−1.32	1.74	0.02
				40.23

You use Table E.4 to find the critical value of the χ^2 test statistic. In the guest satisfaction survey, because three hotels are evaluated, there are $(2 - 1)(3 - 1) = 2$ degrees of freedom. Using $\alpha = 0.05$, the χ^2 critical value with 2 degrees of freedom is 5.991. Because the computed test statistic ($\chi^2 = 40.23$) is greater than this critical value, you reject the null hypothesis (see Figure 12.5). Microsoft Excel (see Figure 12.6) also reports the p-value. Likewise, because the p-value is approximately 0.0000, which is less than $\alpha = 0.05$, you reject the null hypothesis. Further, this p-value indicates that there is virtually no chance to see differences this large or larger among the three sample proportions, if the population proportions for the three hotels are equal. Thus, there is sufficient evidence to conclude that the hotel properties are different with respect to the proportion of guests who are likely to return.

FIGURE 12.5

Regions of rejection and nonrejection when testing for differences in three proportions at the 0.05 level of significance, with 2 degrees of freedom

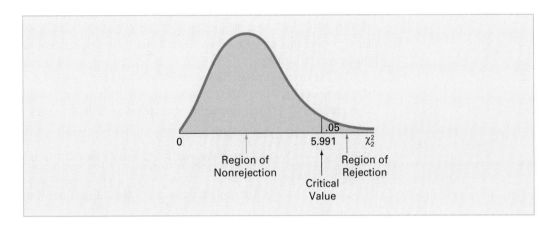

FIGURE 12.6

Microsoft Excel worksheet for the guest satisfaction data of Table 12.6

See Section E12.2 to create this.

For the χ^2 test to give accurate results when dealing with $2 \times c$ contingency tables, all expected frequencies must be large. There is much debate among statisticians about the definition of *large*. Some statisticians (see reference 5) have found that the test gives accurate results as long as all expected frequencies equal or exceed 0.5. Other statisticians, more conservative in their approach, require that no more than 20% of the cells contain expected frequencies less than 5 and no cells have expected frequencies less than 1 (see reference 3). A reasonable compromise between these points of view is to make sure that each expected frequency is at least 1. To accomplish this, you may need to collapse two or more low-expected-frequency categories into one category in the contingency table before performing the test. Such merging of categories usually results in expected frequencies sufficiently large to conduct the χ^2 test accurately. If combining categories is undesirable, alternative procedures are available (see references 1, 2 and 7).

The Marascuilo Procedure

Rejecting the null hypothesis in a χ^2 test of equality of proportions in a $2 \times c$ table only allows you to reach the conclusion that not all c population proportions are equal. But *which* of the proportions differ? Because the result of the χ^2 test for equality of proportions does not specifically answer this question, you need to use a multiple comparisons procedure such as the Marascuilo procedure.

The **Marascuilo procedure** enables you to make comparisons between all pairs of groups. First, compute the observed differences $p_j - p_{j'}$ (where $j \neq j'$) among all $c(c - 1)/2$ pairs. Then, use Equation (12.4) to compute the corresponding critical ranges for the Marascuilo procedure.

CRITICAL RANGE FOR THE MARASCUILO PROCEDURE

$$\text{Critical range} = \sqrt{\chi_U^2}\sqrt{\frac{p_j(1 - p_j)}{n_j} + \frac{p_{j'}(1 - p_{j'})}{n_{j'}}} \qquad (12.4)$$

You need to compute a different critical range for each pairwise comparison of sample proportions. In the final step, you compare each of the $c(c - 1)/2$ pairs of sample proportions against its corresponding critical range. You declare a specific pair significantly different if the absolute difference in the sample proportions $|p_j - p_{j'}|$ is greater than its critical range.

To apply the Marascuilo procedure, return to the guest satisfaction survey. Using the χ^2 test, you concluded that there was evidence of a significant difference among the population proportions. Because there are three hotels, there are $(3)(3 - 1)/2 = 3$ pairwise comparisons. From Table 12.6 on page 471, the three sample proportions are

$$p_1 = \frac{X_1}{n_1} = \frac{128}{216} = 0.593$$

$$p_2 = \frac{X_2}{n_2} = \frac{199}{232} = 0.858$$

$$p_3 = \frac{X_3}{n_3} = \frac{186}{252} = 0.738$$

Using Table E.4 and an overall level of significance of 0.05, the upper-tail critical value of the χ^2 test statistic for a chi-square distribution having $(c - 1) = 2$ degrees of freedom is 5.991. Thus,

$$\sqrt{\chi_U^2} = \sqrt{5.991} = 2.448$$

Next, you compute the three pairs of absolute differences in sample proportions and their corresponding critical ranges. If the absolute difference is greater than its critical range, the proportions are significantly different:

Absolute Difference in Proportions	Critical Range
$|p_j - p_{j'}|$	$2.448\sqrt{\dfrac{p_j(1-p_j)}{n_j} + \dfrac{p_{j'}(1-p_{j'})}{n_{j'}}}$
$|p_1 - p_2| = |0.593 - 0.858| = 0.265$	$2.448\sqrt{\dfrac{(0.593)(0.407)}{216} + \dfrac{(0.858)(0.142)}{232}} = 0.0992$
$|p_1 - p_3| = |0.593 - 0.738| = 0.145$	$2.448\sqrt{\dfrac{(0.593)(0.407)}{216} + \dfrac{(0.738)(0.262)}{252}} = 0.1063$
$|p_2 - p_3| = |0.858 - 0.738| = 0.120$	$2.448\sqrt{\dfrac{(0.858)(0.142)}{232} + \dfrac{(0.738)(0.262)}{252}} = 0.0880$

These computations are shown in worksheet format in Figure 12.7.

FIGURE 12.7

Microsoft Excel
Marascuilo procedure
worksheet

See the "Using the
Marascuilo Worksheets"
part of Section E12.2 to
learn more about this
worksheet.

	A	B	C	D
1	Marascuilo Procedure			
2	Guest Satisfaction (3-Hotels) Analysis			
3	Level of Significance	0.05		
4	Square Root of Critical Value	2.4477		
5				
6	Sample Proportions			
7	Group 1	0.5926		
8	Group 2	0.8578		
9	Group 3	0.7381		
10				
11	MARASCUILO TABLE			
12	Proportions	Absolute Differences	Critical Range	
13	Group 1 - Group 2	0.2652	0.0992	Significant
14	Group 1 - Group 3	0.1455	0.1063	Significant
15				
16	Group 2 - Group 3	0.1197	0.0880	Significant

With 95% confidence, you can conclude that guest satisfaction is higher at the Palm Royale ($p_2 = 0.858$) than at either the Golden Palm ($p_1 = 0.593$) or the Palm Princess ($p_3 = 0.738$) and that guest satisfaction is also higher at the Palm Princess than at the Golden Palm. These results clearly suggest that management should study the reasons for these differences and, in particular, should try to determine why satisfaction is significantly lower at the Golden Palm than at the other two hotels.

PROBLEMS FOR SECTION 12.2

Learning the Basics

 12.11 Consider a contingency table with two rows and five columns.
  a. Find the degrees of freedom.
b. Find the critical value for $\alpha = 0.05$.
c. Find the critical value for $\alpha = 0.01$.

12.12 Use the following contingency table:

	A	B	C	Total
1	10	30	50	90
2	40	45	50	135
Total	50	75	100	225

a. Compute the expected frequencies for each cell.
b. Compute the χ^2 statistic for this contingency table. Is it significant at $\alpha = 0.05$?
c. If appropriate, use the Marascuilo procedure and $\alpha = 0.05$ to determine which groups are different.

12.13 Use the following contingency table:

	A	B	C	Total
1	20	30	25	75
2	30	20	25	75
Total	50	50	50	150

a. Compute the expected frequencies for each cell.
b. Compute the χ^2 statistic for this contingency table. Is it significant at $\alpha = 0.05$?

c. If appropriate, use the Marascuilo procedure and α = 0.05 to determine which groups are different.

Applying the Concepts

12.14 A survey was conducted in five countries. The percentages of respondents who said that they eat out once a week or more are as follows:

Germany	10%
France	12%
United Kingdom	28%
Greece	39%
United States	57%

Source: Adapted from M. Kissel, "Americans Are Keen on Cocooning," The Wall Street Journal, July 22, 2003, p. D3.

Suppose that the survey was based on 1,000 respondents in each country.

a. At the 0.05 level of significance, determine whether there is a significant difference in the proportion of people who eat out at least once a week in the various countries.
b. Find the *p*-value in (a) and interpret its meaning.
c. If appropriate, use the Marascuilo procedure and α = 0.05 to determine which countries are different. Discuss your results.

12.15 Is the degree to which students withdraw from introductory business statistics courses the same for online courses and traditional courses taught in a classroom? Professor Constance McLaren at Indiana State University collected data for five semesters to investigate this question. The following table cross-classifies introductory business statistics students by the type of course (classroom or online) and student persistence (active, dropped, or vanished):

	STUDENT PERSISTENCE		
TYPE OF COURSE	Active	Dropped	Vanished
Classroom	127	8	4
Online	81	51	20

Source: Extracted from C. McLaren, "A Comparison of Student Persistence and Performance in Online and Classroom Business Statistics Experiences," Decision Sciences Journal of Innovative Education, Spring 2004, 2(1), pp. 1–10. Published by the Decision Sciences Institute, headquartered at Georgia State University, Atlanta, GA.

a. Is there evidence of a difference in student persistence (active, dropped, or vanished) based on type of course? (Use α = 0.05.)
b. Compute the *p*-value and interpret its meaning.
c. If appropriate, use the Marascuilo procedure and α = 0.05 to determine which groups are different.

 12.16 More shoppers do the majority of their grocery shopping on Saturday than any other day of the week. However, is the day of the week a person does the majority of grocery shopping dependent on age? A study cross-classified grocery shoppers by age and major shopping day ("Major Shopping by Day," *Progressive Grocer Annual Report*, April 30, 2002). The data were reported as percentages, and no sample sizes were given:

	AGE		
MAJOR SHOPPING DAY	Under 35	35–54	Over 54
Saturday	24%	28%	12%
A day other than Saturday	76%	72%	88%

Source: Extracted from "Major Shopping by Day," Progressive Grocer Annual Report, April 30, 2002.

Assume that 200 shoppers for each age category were surveyed.

a. Is there evidence of a significant difference among the age groups with respect to major grocery shopping day? (Use α = 0.05.)
b. Determine the *p*-value in (a) and interpret its meaning.
c. If appropriate, use the Marascuilo procedure and α = 0.05 to determine which age groups are different. Discuss your results.
d. Discuss the managerial implications of (a) and (c). How can grocery stores use this information to improve marketing and sales? Be specific.

12.17 Repeat (a) through (b) of Problem 12.16, assuming that only 50 shoppers for each age category were surveyed. Discuss the implications of sample size on the χ^2 test for differences among more than two populations.

12.18 An experiment was conducted by James Choi, David Laibson, and Brigitte Madrian to study the choices made in fund selection. When presented with four S&P 500 index funds that were identical except for their fees, undergraduate and MBA students chose the funds as follows (in percentages):

	FUND			
STUDENT GROUP	Lowest Cost	Second-Lowest Cost	Third-Lowest Cost	Highest Cost
Under-graduates	19	37	17	27
MBA	19	40	23	18

Source: Extracted from J. Choi, D. Laibson, and B. Madrian, "Why Does the Law of One Practice? An Experiment in Mutual Funds," www.som.yale.edu/faculty/jjc83/fees.pdf.

a. Determine whether there is a difference in the fund selection (lowest cost, second-lowest cost, third-lowest cost, highest cost) based on the student group. (Use $\alpha = 0.05$.)

b. Determine the *p*-value and interpret its meaning.

c. If appropriate, use the Marascuilo procedure and $\alpha = 0.05$ to determine which groups are different.

12.19 An article (Extracted from P. Kitchen, "Retirement Plan: To Keep Working," *Newsday*, September 24, 2003) discussed the results of a sample of 2,001 Americans ages 50 to 70 who were employed full time or part time. The results were as follows:

	PLANS					
GENDER	Not Work for Pay	Start Own Business	Work Full Time	Work Part Time	Don't Know	Other
Male	257	115	103	457	27	42
Female	359	87	49	436	34	35

a. Is there evidence of a significant difference among the plans for retirement with respect to gender? (Use $\alpha = 0.05$.)

b. Determine the *p*-value in (a) and interpret its meaning.

12.3 CHI-SQUARE TEST OF INDEPENDENCE

In Sections 12.1 and 12.2, you used the χ^2 test to evaluate potential differences among population proportions. For a contingency table that has *r* rows and *c* columns, you can generalize the χ^2 test as a *test of independence* for two categorical variables.

For a test of independence, the null and alternative hypotheses follow:

H_0: The two categorical variables are independent
(that is, there is no relationship between them).
H_1: The two categorical variables are dependent
(that is, there is a relationship between them).

Once again, you use Equation (12.1) on page 464 to compute the test statistic:

$$\chi^2 = \sum_{all\ cells} \frac{(f_o - f_e)^2}{f_e}$$

You reject the null hypothesis at the α level of significance if the computed value of the χ^2 test statistic is greater than χ_U^2, the upper-tail critical value from a chi-square distribution with $(r-1)(c-1)$ degrees of freedom (see Figure 12.8). Thus, the decision rule is

Reject H_0 if $\chi^2 > \chi_U^2$;

otherwise, do not reject H_0.

FIGURE 12.8

Regions of rejection and nonrejection when testing for independence in an $r \times c$ contingency table, using the χ^2 test

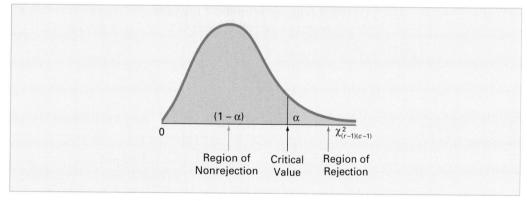

The χ^2 **test of independence** is similar to the χ^2 test for equality of proportions. The test statistics and the decision rules are the same, but the stated hypotheses and conclusions are different. For example, in the guest satisfaction survey of Sections 12.1 and 12.2, there is evidence of a significant difference between the hotels with respect to the proportion of guests who would return. From a different viewpoint, you could conclude that there is a significant relationship between the hotels and the likelihood that a guest would return. Nevertheless, there is a fundamental difference between the two types of tests. The major difference is in how the samples are selected.

In a test for equality of proportions, there is one factor of interest, with two or more levels. These levels represent samples drawn from independent populations. The categorical responses in each sample group or level are classified into two categories, such as *success* and *failure*. The objective is to make comparisons and evaluate differences between the proportions of *success* among the various levels. However, in a test for independence, there are two factors of interest, each of which has two or more levels. You select one sample and tally the joint responses to the two categorical variables into the cells of a contingency table.

To illustrate the χ^2 test for independence, suppose that in the survey on hotel guest satisfaction, a second question was asked of all respondents who indicated that they were not likely to return. These guests were asked to indicate the primary reason for their response. Table 12.9 presents the resulting 4×3 contingency table.

TABLE 12.9

Contingency Table of Primary Reason for Not Returning and Hotel

PRIMARY REASON FOR NOT RETURNING	HOTEL			
	Golden Palm	Palm Royale	Palm Princess	Total
Price	23	7	37	67
Location	39	13	8	60
Room accommodation	13	5	13	31
Other	13	8	8	29
Total	88	33	66	187

In Table 12.9, observe that of the primary reasons for not planning to return to the hotel, 67 were due to price, 60 were due to location, 31 were due to room accommodation, and 29 were due to other reasons. As in Table 12.6 on page 471, there were 88 guests in the Golden Palm, 33 guests in the Palm Royale, and 66 guests in the Palm Princess who were not planning to return. The observed frequencies in the cells of the 4×3 contingency table represent the joint tallies of the sampled guests with respect to primary reason for not returning and the hotel.

The null and alternative hypotheses are

H_0: There is no relationship between the primary reason for not returning and the hotel.
H_1: There is a relationship between the primary reason for not returning and the hotel.

To test this null hypothesis of independence against the alternative that there is a relationship between the two categorical variables, you use Equation (12.1) on page 464 to compute the test statistic:

$$\chi^2 = \sum_{all\ cells} \frac{(f_o - f_e)^2}{f_e}$$

where

f_o = observed frequency in a particular cell of the $r \times c$ contingency table

f_e = expected frequency in a particular cell if the null hypothesis of independence were true

To compute the expected frequency, f_e, in any cell, use the multiplication rule for independent events discussed on page 163 [see Equation (4.7)]. For example, under the null hypothesis of independence, the probability of responses expected in the upper-left-corner cell representing primary reason of price for the Golden Palm is the product of the two separate probabilities: $P(\text{Price})$ and $P(\text{Golden Palm})$. Here, the proportion of reasons that are due to price, $P(\text{Price})$, is $67/187 = 0.3583$, and the proportion of all responses from the Golden Palm, $P(\text{Golden Palm})$, is $88/187 = 0.4706$. If the null hypothesis is true, then the primary reason for not returning and the hotel are independent:

$$P(\text{Price } and \text{ Golden Palm}) = P(\text{Price}) \times P(\text{Golden Palm})$$

$$= (0.3583) \times (0.4706)$$

$$= 0.1686$$

The expected frequency is the product of the overall sample size, n, and this probability, $187 \times 0.1686 = 31.53$. The f_e values for the remaining cells are calculated in a similar manner (see Table 12.10).

Equation (12.5) presents a simpler way to compute the expected frequency.

COMPUTING THE EXPECTED FREQUENCY

The expected frequency in a cell is the product of its row total and column total, divided by the overall sample size.

$$f_e = \frac{\text{Row total} \times \text{Column total}}{n} \qquad (12.5)$$

where

$$\text{row total} = \text{sum of all the frequencies in the row}$$

$$\text{column total} = \text{sum of all the frequencies in the column}$$

$$n = \text{overall sample size}$$

For example, using Equation (12.5) for the upper-left-corner cell (price for the Golden Palm),

$$f_e = \frac{\text{Row total} \times \text{Column total}}{n} = \frac{(67)(88)}{187} = 31.53$$

and for the lower-right-corner cell (other reason for the Palm Princess),

$$f_e = \frac{\text{Row total} \times \text{Column total}}{n} = \frac{(29)(66)}{187} = 10.24$$

Table 12.10 lists the entire set of f_e values.

TABLE 12.10

Contingency Table of Expected Frequencies of Primary Reason for Not Returning with Hotel

PRIMARY REASON FOR NOT RETURNING	HOTEL			
	Golden Palm	Palm Royale	Palm Princess	Total
Price	31.53	11.82	23.65	67
Location	28.24	10.59	21.18	60
Room accommodation	14.59	5.47	10.94	31
Other	13.65	5.12	10.24	29
Total	88.00	33.00	66.00	187

To perform the test of independence, you use the χ^2 test statistic shown in Equation (12.1) on page 464. Here, the test statistic approximately follows a chi-square distribution, with degrees of freedom equal to the number of rows in the contingency table minus 1, times the number of columns in the table minus 1:

$$\text{Degrees of freedom} = (r - 1)(c - 1)$$
$$= (4 - 1)(3 - 1) = 6$$

Table 12.11 illustrates the computations for the χ^2 test statistic.

TABLE 12.11

Computation of χ^2 Test Statistic for the Test of Independence

Cell	f_o	f_e	$(f_o - f_e)$	$(f_o - f_e)^2$	$(f_o - f_e)^2 / f_e$
Price/Golden Palm	23	31.53	−8.53	72.76	2.31
Price/Palm Royale	7	11.82	−4.82	23.23	1.97
Price/Palm Princess	37	23.65	13.35	178.22	7.54
Location/Golden Palm	39	28.24	10.76	115.78	4.10
Location/Palm Royale	13	10.59	2.41	5.81	0.55
Location/Palm Princess	8	21.18	−13.18	173.71	8.20
Room/Golden Palm	13	14.59	−1.59	2.53	0.17
Room/Palm Royale	5	5.47	−0.47	0.22	0.04
Room/Palm Princess	13	10.94	2.06	4.24	0.39
Other/Golden Palm	13	13.65	−0.65	0.42	0.03
Other/Palm Royale	8	5.12	2.88	8.29	1.62
Other/Palm Princess	8	10.24	−2.24	5.02	0.49
					27.41

Using the level of significance $\alpha = 0.05$, the upper-tail critical value from the chi-square distribution with 6 degrees of freedom is 12.592 (see Table E.4). Because the computed test statistic $\chi^2 = 27.41 > 12.592$, you reject the null hypothesis of independence (see Figure 12.9). Similarly, you can use the Microsoft Excel worksheet in Figure 12.10. Because the p-value = 0.0001 < 0.05, you reject the null hypothesis of independence. This p-value indicates that there is virtually no chance of having a relationship this large or larger between hotels and primary reasons for not returning in a sample, if the primary reasons for not returning are independent of the specific hotels in the entire population. Thus, there is strong evidence of a relationship between primary reason for not returning and the hotel.

FIGURE 12.9

Regions of rejection and nonrejection when testing for independence in the hotel guest satisfaction survey example at the 0.05 level of significance, with 6 degrees of freedom

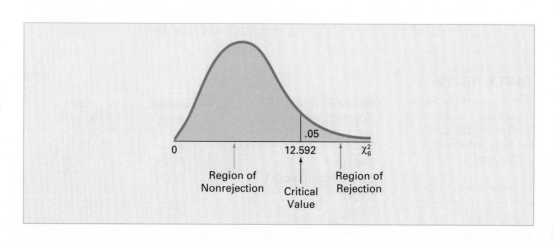

FIGURE 12.10

Microsoft Excel worksheet for the 4 × 3 contingency table for primary reason for not returning and hotel

See Section E12.3 to create this. Formulas not shown in Figure 12.10 (in rows 3 through 19) are similar to formulas shown in Figure E12.1.

	A	B	C	D	E
1	Cross-Classification Hotel Analysis				
2					
3		Observed Frequencies			
4		Hotel			
5	Reason for Not Returning	Golden Palm	Palm Royale	Palm Princess	Total
6	Price	23	7	37	67
7	Location	39	13	8	60
8	Room accommodation	13	5	13	31
9	Other	13	8	8	29
10	Total	88	33	66	187
11					
12		Expected Frequencies			
13		Hotel			
14	Reason for Not Returning	Golden Palm	Palm Royale	Palm Princess	Total
15	Price	31.5294	11.8235	23.6471	67
16	Location	28.2353	10.5882	21.1765	60
17	Room accommodation	14.5882	5.4706	10.9412	31
18	Other	13.6471	5.1176	10.2353	29
19	Total	88	33	66	187
20					
21	Data				
22	Level of Significance	0.05			
23	Number of Rows	4			
24	Number of Columns	3			
25	Degrees of Freedom	6	=(B23 - 1) * (B24 - 1)		
26					
27	Results				
28	Critical Value	12.5916	=CHIINV(B22, B25)		
29	Chi-Square Test Statistic	27.4104	=SUM(G15:I18)		
30	*p*-Value	0.0001	=CHIDIST(B29, B25)		
31	Reject the null hypothesis		=IF(B30 < B22, "Reject the null hypothesis",		
32			"Do not reject the null hypothesis")		
33	*Expected frequency assumption*		=IF(OR(B15 < 1, C15 < 1, D15 < 1, B16 < 1, C16 < 1 ,D16 < 1,		
34	*is met.*		B17 < 1, C17 < 1, D17 < 1, B18 < 1, C18 < 1, D18 < 1)		
			" is violated."," is met.")		

Examination of the observed and expected frequencies (see Table 12.11) reveals that price is underrepresented as a reason for not returning to the Golden Palm (that is, $f_o = 23$ and $f_e = 31.53$) but is overrepresented at the Palm Princess. Guests are more satisfied with the price at the Golden Palm compared to the Palm Princess. Location is overrepresented as a reason for not returning to the Golden Palm but greatly underrepresented at the Palm Princess. Thus, guests are much more satisfied with the location of the Palm Princess than that of the Golden Palm.

To ensure accurate results, all expected frequencies need to be large in order to use the χ^2 test when dealing with $r \times c$ contingency tables. As in the case of $2 \times c$ contingency tables on page 471, all expected frequencies should be at least 1. For cases in which one or more expected frequencies are less than 1, you can use the test after collapsing two or more low-frequency rows into one row (or collapsing two or more low-frequency columns into one column). Merging of rows or columns usually results in expected frequencies sufficiently large to conduct the χ^2 test accurately.

PROBLEMS FOR SECTION 12.3

Learning the Basics

 12.20 If a contingency table has three rows and four columns, how many degrees of freedom are there for the χ^2 test for independence?

 12.21 When performing a χ^2 test for independence in a contingency table with r rows and c columns, determine the upper-tail critical value of the χ^2 test statistic in each of the following circumstances:
a. $\alpha = 0.05$, $r = 4$ rows, $c = 5$ columns
b. $\alpha = 0.01$, $r = 4$ rows, $c = 5$ columns
c. $\alpha = 0.01$, $r = 4$ rows, $c = 6$ columns
d. $\alpha = 0.01$, $r = 3$ rows, $c = 6$ columns
e. $\alpha = 0.01$, $r = 6$ rows, $c = 3$ columns

Applying the Concepts

12.22 During the Vietnam War, a lottery system was instituted to choose males to be drafted into the military. Numbers representing days of the year were "randomly" selected; men born on days of the year with low numbers were drafted first; those with high numbers were not drafted. The table on page 452 shows how many low

(1–122), medium (123–244), and high (245–366) numbers were drawn for birth dates in each quarter of the year:

NUMBER SET	QUARTER OF YEAR				
	Jan.–Mar.	Apr.–Jun.	Jul.–Sep.	Oct.–Dec.	Total
Low	21	28	35	38	122
Medium	34	22	29	37	122
High	36	41	28	17	122
Total	91	91	92	92	366

a. Is there evidence that the numbers selected were significantly related to the time of year? (Use $\alpha = 0.05$.)
b. Would you conclude that the lottery drawing appears to have been random?
c. What are your answers to (a) and (b) if the frequencies are

$$23 \quad 30 \quad 32 \quad 37$$
$$27 \quad 30 \quad 34 \quad 31$$
$$41 \quad 31 \quad 26 \quad 24$$

12.23 *USA Today* reported on preferred types of office communication by different age groups ("Talking Face to Face vs. Group Meetings," *USA Today*, October 13, 2003, p. A1). Suppose the results were based on a survey of 500 respondents in each age group. The results are cross-classified in the following table:

AGE GROUP	TYPE OF COMMUNICATION PREFERRED				
	Group Meetings	Face-to-face Meetings with Individuals	Emails	Other	Total
Generation Y	180	260	50	10	500
Generation X	210	190	65	35	500
Boomer	205	195	65	35	500
Mature	200	195	50	55	500
Total	795	840	230	135	2,000

Source: Extracted from "Talking Face to Face vs. Group Meetings," USA Today, October 13, 2003, p. A1.

At the 0.05 level of significance, is there evidence of a relationship between age group and type of communication preferred?

12.24 A large corporation is interested in determining whether a relationship exists between the commuting time of its employees and the level of stress-related problems observed on the job. A study of 116 assembly-line workers reveals the following:

COMMUTING TIME	STRESS LEVEL			
	High	Moderate	Low	Total
Under 15 min.	9	5	18	32
15–45 min.	17	8	28	53
Over 45 min.	18	6	7	31
Total	44	19	53	116

a. At the 0.01 level of significance, is there evidence of a significant relationship between commuting time and stress level?
b. What is your answer to (a) if you use the 0.05 level of significance?

12.25 Where people turn to for news is different for various age groups. A study indicated where different age groups primarily get their news:

MEDIA	AGE GROUP		
	Under 36	36–50	50+
Local TV	107	119	133
National TV	73	102	127
Radio	75	97	109
Local newspaper	52	79	107
Internet	95	83	76

At the 0.05 level of significance, is there evidence of a significant relationship between the age group and where people primarily get their news? If so, explain the relationship.

12.26 *USA Today* reported on when the decision of what to have for dinner is made. Suppose the results were based on a survey of 1,000 respondents and considered whether the household included any children under 18 years old. The results were cross-classified in the following table:

WHEN DECISION MADE	TYPE OF HOUSEHOLD		
	One Adult/No Children	Adult/Children	Two or More Adults/No Children
Just before eating	162	54	154
In the afternoon	73	38	69
In the morning	59	58	53
A few days before	21	64	45
The night before	15	50	45
Always eat the same thing on this night	2	16	2
Not sure	7	6	7

Source: Extracted from "What's for Dinner," USA Today, January 10, 2000.

At the 0.05 level of significance, is there evidence of a significant relationship between when the decision is made of what to have for dinner and the type of household?

12.4   McNEMAR TEST FOR THE DIFFERENCE BETWEEN TWO PROPORTIONS (RELATED SAMPLES)

In Section 10.3, you used the Z test, and in Section 12.1, you used the chi-square test to test for the difference between two proportions. These tests require that the samples are independent from one another. However, sometimes when you are testing differences between two proportions, the data are from repeated measurements or matched samples, and therefore the samples are related. Such situations arise often in marketing when you want to determine whether there has been a change in attitude, perception, or behavior from one time period to another.

To test whether there is evidence of a difference between the proportions of two related samples, you can use the **McNemar test**. If you are doing a two-tail test, you could use a test statistic that follows a chi-square distribution or one that approximately follows the normal distribution. However, if you are carrying out a one-tail test, you need to use the test statistic that approximately follows the normal distribution.

Table 12.12 presents the 2×2 table needed for the McNemar test.

TABLE 12.12

2 × 2 Contingency Table for the McNemar Test

	CONDITION (GROUP) 2		
CONDITION (GROUP) 1	Yes	No	Totals
Yes	A	B	$A + B$
No	C	D	$C + D$
Totals	$A + C$	$B + D$	n

where

A = number of respondents who answer yes to condition 1 and yes to condition 2

B = number of respondents who answer yes to condition 1 and no to condition 2

C = number of respondents who answer no to condition 1 and yes to condition 2

D = number of respondents who answer no to condition 1 and no to condition 2

n = number of respondents in the sample

The sample proportions are

$$p_1 = \frac{A + B}{n} = \text{ proportion of respondents in the sample who answer yes to condition 1}$$

$$p_2 = \frac{A + C}{n} = \text{ proportion of respondents in the sample who answer yes to condition 2}$$

The population proportions are

π_1 = proportion in the population who would answer yes to condition 1

π_2 = proportion in the population who would answer yes to condition 2

Equation (12.6) presents the McNemar test statistic used to test H_0: $\pi_1 = \pi_2$.

McNEMAR TEST

$$Z = \frac{B - C}{\sqrt{B + C}}$$

(12.6)

where the test statistic Z is approximately normally distributed.

To illustrate the McNemar test, suppose that a consumer panel of $n = 600$ participants is selected for a marketing study and the panel members are initially asked to state their preferences for two competing cell phone providers, Sprint and Verizon. Suppose that, initially, 282 panelists say they prefer Sprint and 318 say they prefer Verizon. After exposing the entire panel to an intensive marketing campaign strategy for Verizon, suppose the same 600 panelists are again asked to state their preferences, with the following results: Of the 282 panelists who previously preferred Sprint, 246 maintain their brand loyalty, but 36 switch to Verizon. Of the 318 panelists who initially preferred Verizon, 306 remain brand loyal, but 12 switch to Sprint. The results are displayed Table 12.13.

TABLE 12.13

Brand Loyalty for Cell Phone Providers

BEFORE MARKETING CAMPAIGN	AFTER MARKETING CAMPAIGN		
	Sprint	Verizon	Total
Sprint	246	36	282
Verizon	12	306	318
Total	258	342	600

You use the McNemar test for these data because you have repeated measurements from the same set of panelists. Each panelist gave a response about whether he or she preferred Sprint or Verizon before exposure to the intensive marketing campaign and then again after exposure to the campaign.

To determine whether the intensive marketing campaign was effective, you want to investigate whether there is a difference between the population proportion who favor Verizon before the campaign, π_1, versus the proportion who favor Verizon after the campaign, π_2. The null and alternative hypotheses are

$$H_0: \pi_1 = \pi_2$$
$$H_1: \pi_1 \neq \pi_2$$

Using a 0.05 level of significance, the critical values are -1.96 and $+1.96$ (see Figure 12.11), and the decision rule is

Reject H_0 if $Z < -1.96$ or if $Z > +1.96$;

otherwise, do not reject H_0.

FIGURE 12.11

Two-tail McNemar Test at the 0.05 level of significance

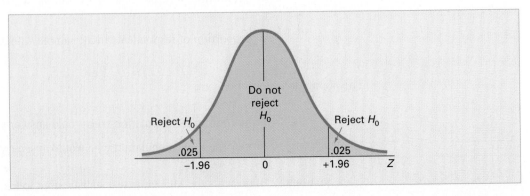

For the data in Table 12.13,

$$A = 246 \quad B = 36 \quad C = 12 \quad D = 306$$

so that

$$p_1 = \frac{A + B}{n} = \frac{246 + 36}{600} = \frac{282}{600} = 0.47 \text{ and } p_2 = \frac{A + C}{n} = \frac{246 + 12}{600} = \frac{258}{600} = 0.43$$

Using Equation (12.6),

$$Z = \frac{B - C}{\sqrt{B + C}} = \frac{36 - 12}{\sqrt{36 + 12}} = \frac{24}{\sqrt{48}} = 3.4641$$

Because $Z = 3.4641 > 1.96$, you reject H_0. Using the p-value approach (see Figure 12.12), the p-value is 0.0005. Because $0.0005 < 0.05$, you reject H_0. You can conclude that the proportion who preferred Verizon before the intensive marketing campaign is different from the proportion who prefer Verizon after exposure to the intensive marketing campaign. In fact, from Table 12.13, observe that more panelists actually preferred Verizon over Sprint after exposure to the intensive marketing campaign.

FIGURE 12.12

Microsoft Excel results for the McNemar test for brand loyalty of cell phone providers

See Section E12.4 to create this.

	A	B	C	D
1	McNemar Test			
2				
3	Observed Frequencies			
4		Column variable		
5	Row variable	Sprint	Verizon	Total
6	Sprint	246	36	282
7	Verizon	12	306	318
8	Total	258	342	600
9				
10	Data			
11	Level of Significance	0.05		
12				
13	Intermediate Calculations			
14	Numerator	24	=C6 - B7	
15	Denominator	6.9282	=SQRT(C6 + B7)	
16	Z Test Statistic	3.4641	=B14/B15	
17				
18	Two-Tail Test			
19	Lower Critical Value	-1.9600	=NORMSINV(B11/2)	
20	Upper Critical Value	1.9600	=NORMSINV(1 - B11/2)	
21	p-Value	0.0005	=2 * (1 - NORMSDIST(ABS(B16)))	
22	Reject the null hypothesis		=IF(B21 < B11, "Reject the null hypothesis", "Do not reject the null hypothesis")	

PROBLEMS FOR SECTION 12.4

Learning the Basics

12.27 Given the following table for two related samples:

	GROUP 2		
GROUP 1	Yes	No	Total
Yes	46	25	71
No	16	59	75
Total	62	84	146

a. Compute the McNemar test statistic.
b. At the 0.05 level of significance, is there evidence of a difference between group 1 and group 2?

Applying the Concepts

12.28 A market researcher wanted to determine whether the proportion of coffee drinkers who preferred Brand *A* increased as the result of an advertising campaign. A random sample of 200 coffee drinkers was selected. The results indicating preference for Brand A or Brand B prior to the beginning of the advertising campaign and after its completion are shown in the following table:

PREFERENCE PRIOR TO ADVERTISING CAMPAIGN	PREFERENCE AFTER COMPLETION OF ADVERTISING CAMPAIGN		
	Brand A	Brand B	Total
Brand A	101	9	110
Brand B	22	68	90
Total	123	77	200

a. At the 0.05 level of significance, is there evidence that the proportion of coffee drinkers who prefer Brand A is lower at the beginning of the advertising campaign than at the end of the advertising campaign?

b. Compute the p-value in (a) and interpret its meaning.

12.29 Two candidates for governor participated in a televised debate. A political pollster recorded the preferences of 500 registered voters in a random sample prior to and after the debate:

PREFERENCE PRIOR TO DEBATE	PREFERENCE AFTER DEBATE		
	Candidate A	Candidate B	Total
Candidate A	269	21	290
Candidate B	36	174	210
Total	305	195	500

a. At the 0.01 level of significance, is there evidence of a difference in the proportion of voters who favor Candidate A prior to and after the debate?

b. Compute the p-value in (a) and interpret its meaning.

12.30 A taste-testing experiment compared two brands of Chilean merlot wines. After the initial comparison, 60 preferred Brand A, and 40 preferred Brand B. The 100 respondents were then exposed to a very professional and powerful advertisement promoting Brand A. The 100 respondents were then asked to taste the two wines again and declare which brand they preferred. The results are shown in the following table.

PREFERENCE PRIOR TO ADVERTISING	PREFERENCE AFTER COMPLETION OF ADVERTISING		
	Brand A	Brand B	Total
Brand A	55	5	60
Brand B	15	25	40
Total	70	30	100

a. At the 0.05 level of significance, is there evidence that the proportion who prefer Brand A is lower before the advertising than after the advertising?

b. Compute the p-value in (a) and interpret its meaning.

12.31 The CEO of a large metropolitan health care facility would like to assess the effects of recent implementation of Six Sigma management on customer satisfaction. A random sample of 100 patients is selected from a list of thousands of patients who were at the facility the past week and also a year ago:

SATISFIED LAST YEAR	SATISFIED NOW		
	Yes	No	Total
Yes	67	5	72
No	20	8	28
Total	87	13	100

a. At the 0.05 level of significance, is there evidence that satisfaction was lower last year, prior to introduction of Six Sigma management?

b. Compute the p-value in (a) and interpret its meaning.

12.32 The personnel director of a large department store wants to reduce absenteeism among sales associates. She decides to institute an incentive plan that provides financial rewards for sales associates who are absent fewer than five days in a given calendar year. A sample of 100 sales associates selected at the end of the second year reveals the following:

YEAR 1	YEAR 2		
	<5 Days Absent	≥5 Days Absent	Total
<5 days absent	32	4	36
≥5 days absent	25	39	64
Total	57	43	100

a. At the 0.05 level of significance, is there evidence that the proportion of employees absent fewer than 5 days was lower in year 1 than in year 2?

b. Compute the p-value in (a) and interpret its meaning.

12.5   WILCOXON RANK SUM TEST: NONPARAMETRIC ANALYSIS FOR TWO INDEPENDENT POPULATIONS

"A nonparametric procedure is a statistical procedure that has (certain) desirable properties that hold under relatively mild assumptions regarding the underlying population(s) from which the data are obtained."

—Myles Hollander and Douglas A. Wolfe (reference 4, p. 1)

In Section 10.1, you used the t test for the difference between the means of two independent populations. If sample sizes are small and you cannot assume that the data in each sample are from normally distributed populations, you have two choices:

- Use the Wilcoxon rank sum test that does not depend on the assumption of normality for the two populations.
- Use the pooled-variance t test, following some *normalizing transformation* on the data (see reference 9).

This section introduces the **Wilcoxon rank sum test** for testing whether there is a difference between two medians. The Wilcoxon rank sum test is almost as powerful as the pooled-variance and separate-variance t tests under conditions appropriate to these tests and is likely to be more powerful when the assumptions of those t tests are not met. In addition, you can use the Wilcoxon rank sum test when you have only ordinal data, as often happens when dealing with studies in consumer behavior and marketing research.

To perform the Wilcoxon rank sum test, you replace the values in the two samples of size n_1 and n_2 with their combined ranks (unless the data contained the ranks initially). You begin by defining $n = n_1 + n_2$ as the total sample size. Next, you assign the ranks so that rank 1 is given to the smallest of the n combined values, rank 2 is given to the second smallest, and so on, until rank n is given to the largest. If several values are tied, you assign each the average of the ranks that otherwise would have been assigned had there been no ties.

For convenience, whenever the two sample sizes are unequal, n_1 represents the smaller sample and n_2 the larger sample. The Wilcoxon rank sum test statistic, T_1, is defined as the sum of the ranks assigned to the n_1 values in the smaller sample. (For equal samples, either sample may be selected for determining T_1.) For any integer value n, the sum of the first n consecutive integers is $n(n + 1)/2$. Therefore, the test statistic T_1 plus T_2, the sum of the ranks assigned to the n_2 items in the second sample, must equal $n(n + 1)/2$. You can use Equation (12.7) to check the accuracy of your rankings.

CHECKING THE RANKINGS

$$T_1 + T_2 = \frac{n(n + 1)}{2} \qquad\qquad (12.7)$$

The Wilcoxon rank sum test can be either a two-tail test or a one-tail test, depending on whether you are testing whether the two population medians are *different* or whether one median is *greater than* the other median:

Two-Tail Test	One-Tail Test	One-Tail Test
$H_0: M_1 = M_2$	$H_0: M_1 \geq M_2$	$H_0: M_1 \leq M_2$
$H_1: M_1 \neq M_2$	$H_1: M_1 < M_2$	$H_1: M_1 > M_2$

where

$$M_1 = \text{median of population 1}$$

$$M_2 = \text{median of population 2}$$

When both samples n_1 and n_2 are ≤ 10, you use Table E.8 to find the critical values of the test statistic T_1. For a two-tail test, you reject the null hypothesis (see Panel A of Figure 12.13) if the computed value of T_1 equals or is greater than the upper critical value, or if T_1 is less than or equal to the lower critical value. For one-tail tests having the alternative hypothesis $H_1: M_1 < M_2$, you reject the null hypothesis if the observed value of T_1 is less than or equal to the lower critical value (see Panel B of Figure 12.13). For one-tail tests having the alternative hypothesis $H_1: M_1 > M_2$, you reject the null hypothesis if the observed value of T_1 equals or is greater than the upper critical value (see Panel C of Figure 12.13).

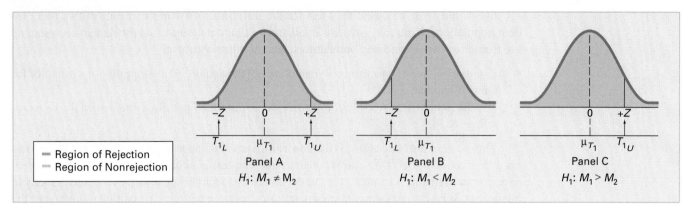

FIGURE 12.13 Regions of rejection and nonrejection using the Wilcoxon rank sum test

For large sample sizes, the test statistic T_1 is approximately normally distributed, with the mean, μ_{T_1}, equal to

$$\mu_{T_1} = \frac{n_1(n + 1)}{2}$$

and the standard deviation, σ_{T_1}, equal to

$$\sigma_{T_1} = \sqrt{\frac{n_1 n_2 (n + 1)}{12}}$$

Therefore, Equation (12.8) defines the standardized Z test statistic.

LARGE SAMPLE WILCOXON RANK SUM TEST

$$Z = \frac{T_1 - \dfrac{n_1(n + 1)}{2}}{\sqrt{\dfrac{n_1 n_2 (n + 1)}{12}}} \tag{12.8}$$

where the test statistic Z approximately follows a standardized normal distribution.

You use Equation (12.8) for testing the null hypothesis when the sample sizes are outside the range of Table E.8. Based on α, the level of significance selected, you reject the null hypothesis if the computed Z value falls in the rejection region.

To study an application of the Wilcoxon rank sum test, return to the Using Statistics scenario of Chapter 10 concerning sales of BLK cola for the two locations: normal shelf display and end-aisle location (see page 370). If you do not think that the populations are normally distributed, you can use the Wilcoxon rank sum test for evaluating possible differences in the median sales for the two display locations.[1] The data (stored in the file **cola.xls**) and the combined ranks are shown in Table 12.14.

Because you have not specified in advance which aisle location is likely to have a higher median, you use a two-tail test with the following null and alternative hypotheses:

$H_0: M_1 = M_2$ (the median sales are equal)
$H_1: M_1 \neq M_2$ (the median sales are not equal)

To perform the Wilcoxon rank sum test, you compute the rankings for the sales from the $n_1 = 10$ stores with a normal shelf display and the $n_2 = 10$ stores with an end-aisle display. Table 12.14 provides the combined rankings.

[1]To test for differences in the median sales between the two locations, you must assume that the distributions of sales in both populations are identical except for differences in location (that is, the medians).

TABLE 12.14

Forming the Combined Rankings

Sales			
Normal Display $(n_1 = 10)$	**Combined Ranking**	**End-Aisle Display** $(n_2 = 10)$	**Combined Ranking**
22	1.0	52	5.5
34	3.0	71	14.0
52	5.5	76	15.0
62	10.0	54	7.0
30	2.0	67	13.0
40	4.0	83	17.0
64	11.0	66	12.0
84	18.5	90	20.0
56	8.0	77	16.0
59	9.0	84	18.5

Source: Data are taken from Table 10.1 on page 372.

The next step is to compute T_1, the sum of the ranks assigned to the *smaller* sample. When the sample sizes are equal, as in this example, you can identify either sample as the group from which to compute T_1. Choosing the normal display as the first sample,

$$T_1 = 1 + 3 + 5.5 + 10 + 2 + 4 + 11 + 18.5 + 8 + 9 = 72$$

As a check on the ranking procedure, you compute T_2 from

$$T_2 = 5.5 + 14 + 15 + 7 + 13 + 17 + 12 + 20 + 16 + 18.5 = 138$$

and then use Equation (12.7) on page 487 to show that the sum of the first $n = 20$ integers in the combined ranking is equal to $T_1 + T_2$:

$$T_1 + T_2 = \frac{n(n + 1)}{2}$$

$$72 + 138 = \frac{20(21)}{2} = 210$$

$$210 = 210$$

To test the null hypothesis that there is no difference between the median sales of the two populations, you use Table E.8 to determine the lower- and upper-tail critical values for the test statistic T_1. From Table 12.15, a portion of Table E.8, observe that for a level of significance of 0.05, the critical values are 78 and 132. The decision rule is

Reject H_0 if $T_1 \leq 78$ or if $T_1 \geq 132$;

otherwise, do not reject H_0.

TABLE 12.15

Finding the Lower- and Upper-Tail Critical Values for the Wilcoxon Rank Sum Test Statistic, T_1, Where $n_1 = 10$, $n_2 = 10$, and $\alpha = 0.05$

n_2	α One-Tail	α Two-Tail	4	5	6	7	8	9	10
						(Lower, Upper)			
9	.05	.10	16,40	24,51	33,63	43,76	54,90	66,105	
	.025	.05	14,42	22,53	31,65	40,79	51,93	62,109	
	.01	.02	13,43	20,55	28,68	37,82	47,97	59,112	
	.005	.01	11,45	18,57	26,70	35,84	45,99	56,115	
10	.05	.10	17,43	26,54	35,67	45,81	56,96	69,111	82,128
	.025	.05	15,45	23,57	32,70	42,84	53,99	65,115	78,132
	.01	.02	13,47	21,59	29,73	39,87	49,103	61,119	74,136
	.005	.01	12,48	19,61	27,75	37,89	47,105	58,122	71,139

Source: Extracted from Table E.8.

Because the test statistic $T_1 = 72 < 78$, you reject H_0. There is evidence of a significant difference in the median sales for the two displays. Because the sum of the ranks is higher for the end-aisle display, you conclude that median sales are higher for the end-aisle display. From the Microsoft Excel worksheet in Figure 12.14, observe that the p-value is 0.0126, which is less than $\alpha = 0.05$. The p-value indicates that if the medians of the two populations are equal, the chance of finding a difference at least this large in the samples is only 0.0126.

FIGURE 12.14

Microsoft Excel
Wilcoxon rank sum test
worksheet for the BLK
cola sales example

*See Section E12.5 to create
this.*

	A	B	
1	Display Location Analysis		
2			
3	Data		
4	Level of Significance	0.05	
5			
6	Population 1 Sample		
7	Sample Size	10	
8	Sum of Ranks	72	
9	Population 2 Sample		
10	Sample Size	10	
11	Sum of Ranks	138	
12			
13	Intermediate Calculations		
14	Total Sample Size n	20	=B7 + B10
15	T1 Test Statistic	72	=IF(B7 <= B10, B8, B11)
16	T1 Mean	105	=IF(B7 <= B10, B7 * (B14 + 1)/2, B10 * (B14 + 1)/2)
17	Standard Error of T1	13.2288	=SQRT(B7 * B10 * (B14 + 1)/12)
18	Z Test Statistic	-2.4946	=(B15 - B16)/B17
19			
20	Two-Tail Test		
21	Lower Critical Value	-1.9600	=NORMSINV(B4/2)
22	Upper Critical Value	1.9600	=NORMSINV(1 - B4/2)
23	p-Value	0.0126	=2 * (1 - NORMSDIST(ABS(B18)))
24	Reject the null hypothesis		=IF(B23 < B4, "Reject the null hypothesis", "Do not reject the null hypothesis")

Table E.8 shows the lower and upper critical values of the Wilcoxon rank sum test statistic, T_1, but only for situations in which both n_1 and n_2 are less than or equal to 10. If either one or both of the sample sizes are greater than 10, you *must* use the large-sample Z approximation formula [Equation (12.8) on page 488]. However, you can also use this approximation formula for small sample sizes. To demonstrate the large-sample Z approximation formula, consider the BLK cola sales data. Using Equation (12.8),

$$Z = \frac{T_1 - \dfrac{n_1(n+1)}{2}}{\sqrt{\dfrac{n_1 n_2 (n+1)}{12}}}$$

$$= \frac{72 - \dfrac{(10)(21)}{2}}{\sqrt{\dfrac{(10)(10)(21)}{12}}}$$

$$= \frac{72 - 105}{13.2288} = -2.4946$$

Because $Z = -2.4946 < -1.96$, the critical value of Z at the 0.05 level of significance, you reject H_0.

PROBLEMS FOR SECTION 12.5

Learning the Basics

12.33 Using Table E.8, determine the lower- and upper-tail critical values for the Wilcoxon rank sum test statistic, T_1, in each of the following two-tail tests:

a. $\alpha = 0.10$, $n_1 = 6$, $n_2 = 8$
b. $\alpha = 0.05$, $n_1 = 6$, $n_2 = 8$
c. $\alpha = 0.01$, $n_1 = 6$, $n_2 = 8$
d. Given your results in (a) through (c), what do you conclude regarding the width of the region of nonrejection as the selected level of significance α gets smaller?

12.34 Using Table E.8, determine the lower-tail critical value for the Wilcoxon rank sum test statistic, T_1, in each of the following one-tail tests:
a. $\alpha = 0.05$, $n_1 = 6$, $n_2 = 8$
b. $\alpha = 0.025$, $n_1 = 6$, $n_2 = 8$
c. $\alpha = 0.01$, $n_1 = 6$, $n_2 = 8$
d. $\alpha = 0.005$, $n_1 = 6$, $n_2 = 8$

12.35 The following information is available for two samples selected from independent populations:

Sample 1: $n_1 = 7$ Assigned ranks: 4 1 8 2 5 10 11

Sample 2: $n_2 = 9$ Assigned ranks: 7 16 12 9 3 14 13 6 15

What is the value of T_1 if you are testing the null hypothesis H_0: $M_1 = M_2$?

 12.36 In Problem 12.35, what are the lower- and upper-tail critical values for the test statistic T_1 from Table E.8 if you use a 0.05 level of significance and the alternative hypothesis is H_1: $M_1 \neq M_2$?

12.37 In Problems 12.35 and 12.36, what is your statistical decision?

12.38 The following information is available for two samples selected from independent and similarly shaped right-skewed populations:

Sample 1: $n_1 = 5$ 1.1 2.3 2.9 3.6 14.7

Sample 2: $n_2 = 6$ 2.8 4.4 4.4 5.2 6.0 18.5

a. Replace the observed values with the corresponding ranks (where 1 = smallest value; $n = n_1 + n_2 = 11 = $ largest value) in the combined samples.
b. What is the value of the test statistic T_1?
c. Compute the value of T_2, the sum of the ranks in the larger sample.
d. To check the accuracy of your rankings, use Equation (12.7) on page 487 to demonstrate that

$$T_1 + T_2 = \frac{n(n+1)}{2}$$

 12.39 From Problem 12.38, at the 0.05 level of significance, determine the lower-tail critical value for the Wilcoxon rank sum test statistic, T_1, if you want to test the null hypothesis, H_0: $M_1 \geq M_2$, against the one-tail alternative, H_1: $M_1 < M_2$.

12.40 In Problems 12.38 and 12.39, what is your statistical decision?

Applying the Concepts

12.41 A vice president for marketing recruits 20 college graduates for management training. The 20 individuals are randomly assigned, 10 each, to one of two groups. A "traditional" method of training (T) is used in one group, and an "experimental" method (E) is used in the other. After the graduates spend six months on the job, the vice president ranks them on the basis of their performance, from 1 (worst) to 20 (best), with the following results (stored in the file **testrank.xls**):

T	1	2	3	5	9	10	12	13	14	15
E	4	6	7	8	11	16	17	18	19	20

Is there evidence of a difference in the median performance between the two methods? (Use $\alpha = 0.05$.)

12.42 Wine experts Gaiter and Brecher use a six-category scale when rating wines: Yech, OK, Good, Very Good, Delicious, and Delicious! (D. Gaiter and J. Brecher, "A Good U.S. Cabernet Is Hard to Find," *The Wall Street Journal*, May 19, 2006, p. W7). Suppose Gaiter and Brecher tested a random sample of eight inexpensive California Cabernets and a random sample of eight inexpensive Washington Cabernets. *Inexpensive* is defined as a suggested retail value in the United States of under $20. The data, stored in the **cabernet.xls** file, are as follows:

California—Good, Delicious, Yech, OK, OK, Very Good, Yech, OK
Washington—Very Good, OK, Delicious!, Very Good, Delicious, Good, Delicious, Delicious!

a. Are the data collected by rating wines using this scale nominal, ordinal, interval, or ratio?
b. Why is the two-sample t test defined in Section 10.1 inappropriate to test the mean rating of California Cabernets versus Washington Cabernets?
c. Is there evidence of a significance difference in the median rating of California Cabernets and Washington Cabernets? (Use $\alpha = 0.05$.)

12.43 In intaglio printing, a design or figure is carved beneath the surface of hard metal or stone. Suppose that an experiment is designed to compare differences in surface hardness of steel plates used in intaglio printing (measured in indentation numbers), based on two different surface conditions—untreated and treated by lightly polishing with emery paper. In the experiment, 40 steel plates are randomly assigned—20 that are untreated, and 20 that are treated. The data are shown in the following table and are stored in the file **intaglio.xls**:

Untreated		Treated	
164.368	177.135	158.239	150.226
159.018	163.903	138.216	155.620
153.871	167.802	168.006	151.233
165.096	160.818	149.654	158.653
157.184	167.433	145.456	151.204
154.496	163.538	168.178	150.869
160.920	164.525	154.321	161.657
164.917	171.230	162.763	157.016
169.091	174.964	161.020	156.670
175.276	166.311	167.706	147.920

a. Is there evidence of a difference in the median surface hardness between untreated and treated steel plates? (Use $\alpha = 0.05$.)

b. What assumptions must you make in (a)?

c. Compare the results of (a) with those of Problem 10.18 (a) on page 380.

 12.44 Management of a hotel was concerned with increasing the return rate for hotel guests. One aspect of first impressions by guests relates to the time it takes to deliver a guest's luggage to the room after check-in to the hotel. A random sample of 20 deliveries on a particular day were selected in Wing *A* of the hotel, and a random sample of 20 deliveries were selected in Wing *B*. The results are stored in the file luggage.xls.

a. Is there evidence of a difference in the median delivery time in the two wings of the hotel? (Use $\alpha = 0.05$.)

b. Compare the results of (a) with those of Problem 10.74 on page 409.

12.45 The director of training for an electronic equipment manufacturer wants to determine whether different training methods have an effect on the productivity of assembly-line employees. She randomly assigns 42 recently hired employees to two groups of 21. The first group receives a computer-assisted, individual-based training program, and the other group receives a team-based training program. Upon completion of the training, the employees are evaluated on the time (in seconds) it takes to assemble a part. The results are in the data file training.xls.

a. Using a 0.05 level of significance, is there evidence of a difference in the median assembly times (in seconds) between employees trained in a computer-assisted, individual-based program and those trained in a team-based program?

b. What assumptions must you make in order to do (a) of this problem?

c. Compare the results of Problem 10.20 (a) on page 380 with the results of (a) in this problem. Discuss.

12.46 Nondestructive evaluation is a method that is used to describe the properties of components or materials without causing any permanent physical change to the units. It includes the determination of properties of materials and the classification of flaws by size, shape, type, and location. This method is most effective for detecting surface flaws and characterizing surface properties of electrically conductive materials. Recently, data were collected that classified each component as having a flaw or not, based on manual inspection and operator judgment, and also reported the size of the crack in the material. Do the components classified as unflawed have a smaller median crack size than components classified as flawed? The results in terms of crack size (in inches) are in the data file

crack.xls (extracted from B. D. Olin and W. Q. Meeker, "Applications of Statistical Methods to Nondestructive Evaluation," *Technometrics*, 38, 1996, p. 101.)

Unflawed

0.003 0.004 0.012 0.014 0.021 0.023 0.024 0.030 0.034

0.041 0.041 0.042 0.043 0.045 0.057 0.063 0.074 0.076

Flawed

0.022 0.026 0.026 0.030 0.031 0.034 0.042 0.043 0.044

0.046 0.046 0.052 0.055 0.058 0.060 0.060 0.070 0.071

0.073 0.073 0.078 0.079 0.079 0.083 0.090 0.095 0.095

0.096 0.100 0.102 0.103 0.105 0.114 0.119 0.120 0.130

0.160 0.306 0.328 0.440

a. Using a 0.05 level of significance, is there evidence that the median crack size is less for unflawed components than for flawed components?

b. What assumptions must you make in (a)?

c. Compare the results of Problem 10.21 (a) on page 380 with the results of (a) in this problem. Discuss.

12.47 A bank with a branch located in a commercial district of a city has developed an improved process for serving customers during the noon-to-1 p.m. lunch period. The waiting time (defined as the time elapsed from when the customer enters the line until he or she reaches the teller window) of all customers during this hour is recorded over a period of 1 week. A random sample of 15 customers is selected (and stored in the file bank1.xls), and the results (in minutes) are as follows:

4.21	5.55	3.02	5.13	4.77	2.34	3.54	3.20
4.50	6.10	0.38	5.12	6.46	6.19	3.79	

Another branch, located in a residential area, is also concerned with the noon-to-1 p.m. lunch period. A random sample of 15 customers is selected (and stored in the file bank2.xls), and the results (in minutes) are as follows:

9.66	5.90	8.02	5.79	8.73	3.82	8.01	8.35
10.49	6.68	5.64	4.08	6.17	9.91	5.47	

a. Is there evidence of a difference in the median waiting time between the two branches? (Use $\alpha = 0.05$.)

b. What assumptions must you make in (a)?

c. Compare the results of Problem 10.14 (a) on page 379 with the results of (a) in this problem. Discuss.

12.48 A problem with a telephone line that prevents a customer from receiving or making calls is upsetting to both the customer and the telephone company. The data in the file phone.xls represent samples of 20 problems reported to two different offices of a telephone company and the time to clear these problems (in minutes) from the customers' lines:

Central Office I Time to Clear Problems (Minutes)

1.48	1.75	0.78	2.85	0.52	1.60	4.15	3.97	1.48	3.10
1.02	0.53	0.93	1.60	0.80	1.05	6.32	3.93	5.45	0.97

Central Office II Time to Clear Problems (Minutes)

7.55	3.75	0.10	1.10	0.60	0.52	3.30	2.10	0.58	4.02
3.75	0.65	1.92	0.60	1.53	4.23	0.08	1.48	1.65	0.72

a. Is there evidence of a difference in the median time to clear these problems between the two offices? (Use $\alpha = 0.05$.)

b. What assumptions must you make in (a)?

c. Compare the results of Problem 10.16 (a) on page 379 with the results of (a) in this problem. Discuss.

12.6 KRUSKAL-WALLIS RANK TEST: NONPARAMETRIC ANALYSIS FOR THE ONE-WAY ANOVA

If the normality assumption of the one-way ANOVA F test is not met, you can use the Kruskal-Wallis rank test. The Kruskal-Wallis rank test for differences among c medians (where $c > 2$) is an extension of the Wilcoxon rank sum test for two independent populations, discussed in Section 12.5. Thus, the Kruskal-Wallis test has the same power relative to the one-way ANOVA F test that the Wilcoxon rank sum test has relative to the t test.

You use the **Kruskal-Wallis rank test** to test whether c independent groups have equal medians. The null hypothesis is

$$H_0: M_1 = M_2 = \cdots = M_c$$

and the alternative hypothesis is

$$H_1: \text{Not all } M_j \text{ are equal (where } j = 1, 2, \ldots, c).$$

To use the Kruskal-Wallis rank test, you first replace the values in the c samples with their combined ranks (if necessary). Rank 1 is given to the smallest of the combined values and rank n to the largest of the combined values (where $n = n_1 + n_2 + \cdots + n_c$). If any values are tied, you assign them the mean of the ranks they would have otherwise been assigned if ties had not been present in the data.

The Kruskal-Wallis test is an alternative to the one-way ANOVA F test. Instead of comparing each of the c group means, $\bar{X}_j$, against the grand mean, $\bar{\bar{X}}$, the Kruskal-Wallis test compares the mean rank in each of the c groups against the overall mean rank, based on all n combined values. If there is a significant difference among the c groups, the mean rank differs considerably from group to group. In the process of squaring these differences, the test statistic H becomes large. If there are no differences present, the test statistic H is small because the mean of the ranks assigned in each group should be very similar from group to group.

Equation (12.9) defines the Kruskal-Wallis test statistic, H.

KRUSKAL-WALLIS RANK TEST FOR DIFFERENCES AMONG c MEDIANS

$$H = \left[\frac{12}{n(n+1)} \sum_{j=1}^{c} \frac{T_j^2}{n_j} \right] - 3(n+1) \tag{12.9}$$

where

n = total number of values over the combined samples

n_j = number of values in the jth sample ($j = 1, 2, \ldots, c$)

T_j = sum of the ranks assigned to the jth sample

T_j^2 = square of the sum of the ranks assigned to the jth sample

c = number of groups

As the sample sizes in each group get large (that is, greater than 5), you can approximate the test statistic, H, by the chi-square distribution with $c - 1$ degrees of freedom. Thus, you reject the null hypothesis if the computed value of H is greater than the χ_U^2 upper-tail critical value (see Figure 12.15). Therefore, the decision rule is

$$\text{Reject } H_0 \text{ if } H > \chi_U^2;$$

$$\text{otherwise, do not reject } H_0.$$

FIGURE 12.15

Determining the rejection region for the Kruskal-Wallis test

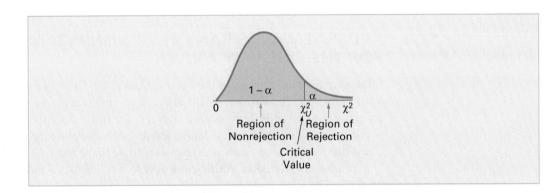

To illustrate the Kruskal-Wallis rank test for differences among c medians, return to the Using Statistics scenario from Chapter 11, concerning the strength of parachutes. If you cannot assume that the tensile strength is normally distributed in all c groups, you can use the Kruskal-Wallis rank test.

The null hypothesis is that the median tensile strengths of parachutes for the four suppliers are equal. The alternative hypothesis is that at least one of the suppliers differs from the others.

$$H_0: M_1 = M_2 = M_3 = M_4$$
$$H_1: \text{Not all } M_j \text{ are equal (where } j = 1, 2, 3, 4).$$

Table 12.16 presents the data (stored in the file **parachute.xls**), along with the corresponding ranks.

TABLE 12.16

Tensile Strength and Ranks of Parachutes Woven from Synthetic Fibers from Four Suppliers

							Supplier	
	1		2		3		4	
Amount	Rank	Amount	Rank	Amount	Rank	Amount	Rank
18.5	4	26.3	20	20.6	8	25.4	19
24.0	13.5	25.3	18	25.2	17	19.9	5.5
17.2	1	24.0	13.5	20.8	9	22.6	11
19.9	5.5	21.2	10	24.7	16	17.5	2
18.0	3	24.5	15	22.9	12	20.4	7

In converting the 20 tensile strengths to ranks, observe in Table 12.16 that the third parachute for Supplier 1 has the lowest tensile strength, 17.2. It is given a rank of 1. The fourth value for Supplier 1 and the second value for Supplier 4 each have a value of 19.9. Because they are tied for ranks 5 and 6, they are assigned the rank 5.5. Finally, the first value for Supplier 2 is the largest value, 26.3, and is assigned a rank of 20.

After all the ranks are assigned, you compute the sum of the ranks for each group:

Rank sums: $\quad T_1 = 27 \quad T_2 = 76.5 \quad T_3 = 62 \quad T_4 = 44.5$

As a check on the rankings, recall from Equation (12.7) on page 487 that for any integer n, the sum of the first n consecutive integers is $\dfrac{n(n+1)}{2}$. Therefore

$$T_1 + T_2 + T_3 + T_4 = \frac{n(n+1)}{2}$$

$$27 + 76.5 + 62 + 44.5 = \frac{(20)(21)}{2}$$

$$210 = 210$$

Using Equation (12.9) on page 493 to test the null hypothesis of equal population medians,

$$H = \left[\frac{12}{n(n+1)} \sum_{j=1}^{c} \frac{T_j^2}{n_j} \right] - 3(n+1)$$

$$= \left\{ \frac{12}{(20)(21)} \left[\frac{(27)^2}{5} + \frac{(76.5)^2}{5} + \frac{(62)^2}{5} + \frac{(44.5)^2}{5} \right] \right\} - 3(21)$$

$$= \left(\frac{12}{420} \right)(2,481.1) - 63 = 7.8886$$

The statistic H approximately follows a chi-square distribution with $c - 1$ degrees of freedom. Using a 0.05 level of significance, χ_U^2, the upper-tail critical value of the chi-square distribution with $c - 1 = 3$ degrees of freedom is 7.815 (see Table 12.17). Because the computed value of the test statistic $H = 7.8886$ is greater than the critical value, you reject the null hypothesis and conclude that not all the suppliers are the same with respect to median tensile strength. The same conclusion is reached by using the p-value approach. In Figure 12.16, observe that the p-value = 0.0484 < 0.05.

TABLE 12.17

Finding χ_U^2, the Upper-Tail Critical Value for the Kruskal-Wallis Rank Test, at the 0.05 Level of Significance with 3 Degrees of Freedom

Degrees of Freedom	Upper-Tail Area									
	.995	.99	.975	.95	.90	.75	.25	.10	.05	.025
1	—	—	0.001	0.004	0.016	0.102	1.323	2.706	3.841	5.024
2	0.010	0.020	0.051	0.103	0.211	0.575	2.773	4.605	5.991	7.378
3	0.072	0.115	0.216	0.352	0.584	1.213	4.108	6.251	7.815	9.348
4	0.207	0.297	0.484	0.711	1.064	1.923	5.385	7.779	9.488	11.143
5	0.412	0.554	0.831	1.145	1.610	2.675	6.626	9.236	11.071	12.833

Source: Extracted from Table E.4.

FIGURE 12.16

Microsoft Excel worksheet for the Kruskal-Wallis rank test for differences among the four medians in the parachute example

See Section E12.6 to create this.

	A	B	C	D	E	F	G
1	Tensile-Strength Analysis						
2							
3	Data						
4	Level of Significance	0.05					
5					Group	Sample Size	Sum of Ranks	Mean Ranks
6	Intermediate Calculations				1	5	27	5.4
7	Sum of Squared Ranks/Sample Size	2481.1			2	5	76.5	15.3
8	Sum of Sample Sizes	20			3	5	62	12.4
9	Number of Groups	4			4	5	44.5	8.9
10							
11	Test Result						
12	H Test Statistic	7.8886		=(12/(B8 * (B8 + 1))) * B7 - (3 * (B8 + 1))			
13	Critical Value	7.8147		=CHIINV(B4, B9 - 1)			
14	p-Value	0.0484		=CHIDIST(B12, B9 - 1)			
15	Reject the null hypothesis			=IF(B14 < B4, "Reject the null hypothesis",			
16				"Do not reject the null hypothesis")			
17				Also			
18				Cell B7: =(G6 * F6) + (G7 * F7) + (G8 * F8) + (G9 * F9)			
19				Cell B8: =SUM(E6:E9)			

You reject the null hypothesis and conclude that there is evidence of a significant difference among the suppliers with respect to the median tensile strength. At this point, you could simultaneously compare all pairs of suppliers to determine which ones differ (see reference 2). The following assumptions are needed to use the Kruskal-Wallis rank test:

- The c samples are randomly and independently selected from their respective populations.
- The underlying variable is continuous.
- The data provide at least a set of ranks, both within and among the c samples.
- The c populations have the same variability.
- The c populations have the same shape.

The Kruskal-Wallis procedure makes less stringent assumptions than does the F test. If you ignore the last two assumptions (variability and shape), you can still use the Kruskal-Wallis rank test to determine whether at least one of the populations differs from the other populations in some characteristic—such as central tendency, variation, or shape. However, to use the F test, you must assume that the c samples are from underlying normal populations that have equal variances.

When the more stringent assumptions of the F test hold, you should use the F test instead of the Kruskal-Wallis test because it has slightly more power to detect significant differences among groups. However, if the assumptions of the F test do not hold, you should use the Kruskal-Wallis test.

PROBLEMS FOR SECTION 12.6

Learning the Basics

12.49 What is the upper-tail critical value from the chi-square distribution if you use the Kruskal-Wallis rank test for comparing the medians in six populations at the 0.01 level of significance?

12.50 Using the results of Problem 12.49,
a. State the decision rule for testing the null hypothesis that all six groups have equal population medians.
b. What is your statistical decision if the computed value of the test statistic H is 13.77?

Applying the Concepts

12.51 Periodically, *The Wall Street Journal* has conducted a stock-picking contest. The last one was conducted in March 2001. In this experiment, three different methods were used to select stocks that were expected to perform well during the next five months. Four Wall Street professionals, considered experts on picking stocks, each selected one stock. Four randomly chosen readers of *The Wall Street Journal* each selected one stock. Finally, four stocks were selected by flinging darts at a table containing a list of stocks. The returns of the selected stocks for March 20, 2001, to August 31, 2001 (in percentage return), are given in the following table and stored in the file contest2001.xls. Note that during this period, the Dow Jones Industrial Average gained 2.4% (extracted from

G. Jasen, "In Picking Stocks, Dartboard Beats the Pros," *The Wall Street Journal*, September 27, 2001, pp. C1, C10).

Experts	Readers	Darts
+39.5	−31.0	+39.0
−1.1	−20.7	+31.9
−4.5	−45.0	+14.1
−8.0	−73.3	+5.4

a. Is there evidence of a significant difference in the median return for the three categories? (Use $\alpha = 0.05$.)
b. Compare the results of (a) with those of Problem 11.8 (a) on page 434.
c. Which assumptions do you think are more appropriate, those of Problem 11.8 (a) or those of part (a) of this problem? Explain.

12.52 A hospital conducted a study of the waiting time in its emergency room. The hospital has a main campus, along with three satellite locations. Management had a business objective of reducing waiting time for emergency room cases that did not require immediate attention. To study this, a random sample of 15 emergency room cases at each location were selected on a particular day, and the waiting time (measured from check-in to when the patient was called into the clinic area) was measured. The results are stored in the file erwaiting.xls.
a. At the 0.05 level of significance, is there evidence of a difference in the median waiting times in the four locations?

b. Compare the results of (a) with those of Problem 11.9 (a) on page 435.

12.53 The following data (stored in the file cdyield.xls) represent the nationwide highest yield of different types of accounts (extracted from Bankrate.com, January 24, 2006):

Money Market	6-Month CD	1-Yr CD	2.5-Yr CD	5-Yr CD
4.55	4.75	4.94	4.95	5.05
4.50	4.70	4.90	4.91	5.05
4.40	4.69	4.85	4.85	5.02
4.38	4.65	4.85	4.82	5.00
4.38	4.65	4.85	4.80	5.00

a. At the 0.05 level of significance, is there evidence of a difference in the median yields of the different accounts?

b. Compare the results of (a) with those of Problem 11.11 (a) on page 435.

12.54 An advertising agency has been hired by a manufacturer of pens to develop an advertising campaign for the upcoming holiday season. To prepare for this project, the research director decides to initiate a study of the effect of advertising on product perception. An experiment is designed to compare five different advertisements. Advertisement *A* greatly undersells the pen's characteristics. Advertisement *B* slightly undersells the pen's characteristics. Advertisement *C* slightly oversells the pen's characteristics. Advertisement *D* greatly oversells the pen's characteristics. Advertisement *E* attempts to correctly state the pen's characteristics. A sample of 30 adult respondents, taken from a larger focus group, is randomly assigned to the five advertisements (so that there are six respondents to each). After reading the advertisement and developing a sense of product expectation, all respondents unknowingly receive the same pen to evaluate. The respondents are permitted to test the pen and the plausibility of the advertising copy. The respondents are then asked to rate the pen from 1 to 7 on the product characteristic scales of appearance, durability, and writing performance. The *combined* scores of three ratings (appearance, durability, and writing performance) for the 30 respondents (stored in the file pen.xls) are as follows:

A	B	C	D	E
15	16	8	5	12
18	17	7	6	19
17	21	10	13	18
19	16	15	11	12
19	19	14	9	17
20	17	14	10	14

a. At the 0.05 level of significance, is there evidence of a difference in the median ratings of the five advertisements?

b. Compare the results of (a) with those of Problem 11.12 (a) on page 435.

c. Which assumptions do you think are more appropriate, those of Problem 11.12 (a) or those of part (a) of this problem? Explain.

12.55 A sporting goods manufacturing company wanted to compare the distance traveled by golf balls produced using each of four different designs. Ten balls were manufactured with each design and were brought to the local golf course for the club professional to test. The order in which the balls were hit with the same club from the first tee was randomized so that the pro did not know which type of ball was being hit. All 40 balls were hit in a short period of time, during which the environmental conditions were essentially the same. The results (distance traveled in yards) for the four designs are stored in the file golfball.xls:

a. At the 0.05 level of significance, is there evidence of a difference in the median distances traveled by the golf balls with different designs?

b. Compare the results of (a) with those of Problem 11.14 (a) on page 436.

12.56 Students in a business statistics course performed an experiment to test the strength of four brands of trash bags. One-pound weights were placed into a bag, one at a time, until the bag broke. A total of 40 bags were used (10 for each brand). The data file trashbags.xls gives the weight (in pounds) required to break the trash bags.

a. At the 0.05 level of significance, is there evidence of a difference in the median strength of the four brands of trash bags?

b. Compare the results in (a) to those in Problem 11.10 on page 435.

12.7   ☻ *(CD-ROM Topic)* CHI-SQUARE TEST FOR A VARIANCE OR STANDARD DEVIATION

When analyzing numerical data, sometimes you need to make conclusions about a population variance or standard deviation. For further discussion, see Section 12.7 on the Student CD-ROM that accompanies this book.

SUMMARY

Figure 12.17 presents a roadmap for this chapter. First, you used hypothesis testing for analyzing categorical response data from two samples (independent and related) and from more than two independent samples. In addition, the rules of probability from Section 4.2 were extended to the hypothesis of independence in the joint responses to two categorical variables. You applied these methods to the surveys conducted by T.C. Resort Properties. You concluded that a greater proportion of guests are willing to return to the Beachcomber Hotel than to the Windsurfer; that the Golden Palm, Palm Royale, and Palm Princess hotels are different with respect to the proportion of guests who are likely to return; and that the reasons given for not returning to a hotel are dependent on the hotel the guests visited. These inferences will allow T.C. Resort Properties to improve the quality of service it provides.

In addition to the chi-square tests, you also studied two nonparametric tests. You used the Wilcoxon rank sum test when the assumptions of the t test for two independent samples were violated and the Kruskal-Wallis test when the assumptions of the one-way ANOVA were violated.

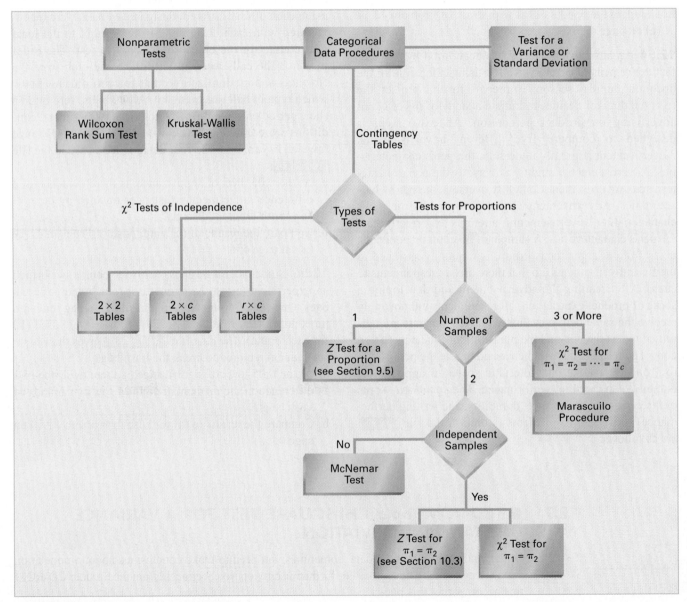

FIGURE 12.17 Roadmap of Chapter 12

KEY EQUATIONS

χ^2 Test for the Difference Between Two Proportions

$$\chi^2 = \sum_{all\ cells} \frac{(f_o - f_e)^2}{f_e} \qquad (12.1)$$

Computing the Estimated Overall Proportion

$$\bar{p} = \frac{X_1 + X_2}{n_1 + n_2} = \frac{X}{n} \qquad (12.2)$$

Computing the Estimated Overall Proportion for c Groups

$$\bar{p} = \frac{X_1 + X_2 + \cdots + X_c}{n_1 + n_2 + \cdots + n_c} = \frac{X}{n} \qquad (12.3)$$

Critical Range for the Marascuilo Procedure

$$\text{Critical range} = \sqrt{\chi^2_U} \sqrt{\frac{p_j(1 - p_j)}{n_j} + \frac{p_{j'}(1 - p_{j'})}{n_{j'}}} \qquad (12.4)$$

Computing the Expected Frequency

$$f_e = \frac{\text{Row total} \times \text{Column total}}{n} \qquad (12.5)$$

McNemar Test

$$Z = \frac{B - C}{\sqrt{B + C}} \qquad (12.6)$$

Checking the Rankings

$$T_1 + T_2 = \frac{n(n + 1)}{2} \qquad (12.7)$$

Large-Sample Wilcoxon Rank Sum Test

$$Z = \frac{T_1 - \dfrac{n_1(n + 1)}{2}}{\sqrt{\dfrac{n_1 n_2(n + 1)}{12}}} \qquad (12.8)$$

Kruskal-Wallis Rank Test for Differences Among c Medians

$$H = \left[\frac{12}{n(n + 1)} \sum_{j=1}^{c} \frac{T_j^2}{n_j} \right] - 3(n + 1) \qquad (12.9)$$

KEY TERMS

chi-square (χ^2) distribution 466
chi-square (χ^2) test of independence 477
contingency table 462

expected frequency (f_e) 464
Kruskal-Wallis rank test 493
Marascuilo procedure 474
McNemar test 483

observed frequency (f_o) 464
$2 \times c$ contingency table 471
2×2 contingency table 462
Wilcoxon rank sum test 487

CHAPTER REVIEW PROBLEMS

Checking Your Understanding

12.57 Under what conditions should you use the χ^2 test to determine whether there is a difference between the proportions of two independent populations?

12.58 Under what conditions should you use the χ^2 test to determine whether there is a difference between the proportions of more than two independent populations?

12.59 Under what conditions should you use the χ^2 test of independence?

12.60 Under what conditions should you use the McNemar test?

12.61 What is a nonparametric procedure?

12.62 Under what conditions should you use the Wilcoxon rank sum test?

12.63 Under what conditions should you use the Kruskal-Wallis rank test?

Applying the Concepts

12.64 Undergraduate students at Miami University in Oxford, Ohio, were surveyed in order to evaluate the effect of gender and price on purchasing a pizza from Pizza Hut. Students were told to suppose that they were planning on having a large two-topping pizza delivered to their residence that evening. The students had to decide between ordering from Pizza Hut at a reduced price of $8.49 (the regular price for a large two-topping pizza from the Oxford Pizza Hut at this time was $11.49) and ordering a pizza from a different pizzeria. The results from this question are summarized in the following contingency table:

	PIZZERIA		
GENDER	Pizza Hut	Other	Total
Female	4	13	17
Male	6	12	18
Total	10	25	35

The survey also evaluated purchase decisions at other prices. These results are summarized in the following contingency table:

	PRICE			
PIZZERIA	$8.49	$11.49	$14.49	Total
Pizza Hut	10	5	2	17
Other	25	23	27	75
Total	35	28	29	92

a. Using a 0.05 level of significance and using the data in the first contingency table, is there evidence of a significant relationship between a student's gender and his or her pizzeria selection?
b. What is your answer to (a) if nine of the male students selected Pizza Hut and nine selected other?
c. Using a 0.05 level of significance and using the data in the second contingency table, is there evidence of a difference in pizzeria selection based on price?
d. Determine the p-value in (c) and interpret its meaning.
e. If appropriate, use the Marascuilo procedure and $\alpha = 0.05$ to determine which prices are different in terms of pizzeria preference.

12.65 A 2004 study by the American Society for Quality investigated executives' views toward quality. Top executives were asked whether they view quality as a profession in the way law, medicine, engineering, and accounting are viewed, or whether they see practicing quality more as the ability to understand and use a variety of tools and techniques to produce a result. Table (1) provides the responses to this question, cross-classified by the type of industry with which the executive is involved. A second question asked whether the executives' companies actually measure the impact of process improvement initiatives designed to raise the quality of their products or services. Table (2) provides the results to this question.

(1) Do you believe that quality is a profession?

	Manufacturing	Service	Health Care
Yes	108	88	49
No	72	132	50

(2) Does your company measure the impact of process improvement initiatives?

	Manufacturing	Service	Health Care
Yes	132	129	54
No	48	91	46

Source: Adapted from G. Weiler, "What Do CEOs Think About Quality?" *Quality Progress*, May 2004, 37(5), pp. 52–56.

a. Is there a significant difference among the three industries with respect to the proportion of top executives who believe quality is a profession? (Use $\alpha = 0.05$.)
b. If appropriate, apply the Marascuilo procedure to (a), using $\alpha = 0.05$.
c. Is there a significant difference among the different industries with respect to the proportion of companies that measure the impact of process improvement initiatives? (Use $\alpha = 0.05$.)
d. If appropriate, apply the Marascuilo procedure to (c), using $\alpha = 0.05$.

12.66 A company is considering an organizational change by adopting the use of self-managed work teams. To assess the attitudes of employees of the company toward this change, a sample of 400 employees is selected and asked whether they favor the institution of self-managed work teams in the organization. Three responses are permitted: favor, neutral, or oppose. The results of the survey, cross-classified by type of job and attitude toward self-managed work teams, are summarized as follows:

TYPE OF JOB	SELF-MANAGED WORK TEAMS			
	Favor	Neutral	Oppose	Total
Hourly worker	108	46	71	225
Supervisor	18	12	30	60
Middle management	35	14	26	75
Upper management	24	7	9	40
Total	185	79	136	400

a. At the 0.05 level of significance, is there evidence of a relationship between attitude toward self-managed work teams and type of job?

The survey also asked respondents about their attitudes toward instituting a policy whereby an employee could take one additional vacation day per month without pay. The results, cross-classified by type of job, are shown on page 501.

TYPE OF JOB	VACATION TIME WITHOUT PAY			
	Favor	Neutral	Oppose	Total
Hourly worker	135	23	67	225
Supervisor	39	7	14	60
Middle management	47	6	22	75
Upper management	26	6	8	40
Total	247	42	111	400

b. At the 0.05 level of significance, is there evidence of a relationship between attitude toward vacation time without pay and type of job?

12.67 A company that produces and markets videotaped continuing education programs for the financial industry has traditionally mailed sample tapes that contain previews of the programs to prospective customers. Customers then agree to purchase the program tapes or return the sample tapes. A group of sales representatives studied how to increase sales and found that many prospective customers believed it was difficult to tell from a sample tape alone whether the educational programs would meet their needs. The sales representatives performed an experiment to test whether sending the complete program tapes for review by customers would increase sales. They selected 80 customers from the mailing list and randomly assigned 40 to receive the sample tapes and 40 to receive the full-program tapes for review. They then determined the number of tapes that were purchased and returned in each group. The results of the experiment are as follows:

ACTION	TYPE OF VIDEOTAPE RECEIVED		
	Sample	Full	Total
Purchased	6	14	20
Returned	34	26	60
Total	40	40	80

a. At the 0.05 level of significance, is there evidence of a difference in the proportion of tapes purchased on the basis of the type of tape sent to the customer?

b. On the basis of the results of (a), which tape do you think a representative should send in the future? Explain the rationale for your decision.

The sales representatives also wanted to determine which of three initial sales approaches result in the most sales: (1) a video sales-information tape mailed to prospective customers, (2) a personal sales call to prospective customers, and (3) a telephone call to prospective customers. A random sample of 300 prospective customers was selected, and 100 were randomly assigned to each of the three sales approaches. The results, in terms of purchases of the full-program tapes, are as follows:

ACTION	SALES APPROACH			
	Videotape	Personal Sales Call	Telephone	Total
Purchase	19	27	14	60
Don't purchase	81	73	86	240
Total	100	100	100	300

c. At the 0.05 level of significance, is there evidence of a difference in the proportion of tapes purchased on the basis of the sales strategy used?

d. If appropriate, use the Marascuilo procedure and $\alpha = 0.05$ to determine which sales approaches are different.

e. On the basis of the results of (c) and (d), which sales approach do you think a representative should use in the future? Explain the rationale for your decision.

12.68 A market researcher investigated consumer preferences for Coca-Cola and Pepsi before a taste test and after a taste test. The following table summarizes the results from a sample of 200 respondents:

PREFERENCE BEFORE TASTE TEST	PREFERENCE AFTER TASTE TEST		
	Coca-Cola	Pepsi	Total
Coca-Cola	104	6	110
Pepsi	14	76	90
Total	118	82	200

a. Is there evidence of a difference in the proportion of respondents who prefer Coca-Cola before and after the taste tests? (Use $\alpha = 0.10$.)

b. Compute the p-value and interpret its meaning.

c. Show how the following table was derived from the table above:

PREFERENCE	SOFT DRINK		
	Coca-Cola	Pepsi	Total
Before taste test	110	90	200
After taste test	118	82	200
Total	228	172	400

d. Using the second table, is there evidence of a difference in preference for Coca-Cola before and after the taste test? (Use $\alpha = 0.05$.)

e. Determine the p-value and interpret its meaning.

f. Explain the difference in the results of (a) and (d). Which method of analyzing the data should you use? Why?

12.69 A market researcher was interested in studying the effect of advertisements on brand preference of new car buyers. Prospective purchasers of new cars were first asked whether they preferred Toyota or GM and then watched video advertisements of comparable models of the two manufacturers. After viewing the ads, the prospective customers again indicated their preferences. The results are summarized in the following table:

PREFERENCE AFTER ADS

PREFERENCE BEFORE ADS	Toyota	GM	Total
Toyota	97	3	100
GM	11	89	100
Total	108	92	200

a. Is there evidence of a difference in the proportion of respondents who prefer Toyota before and after viewing the ads? (Use $\alpha = 0.05$.)
b. Compute the *p*-value and interpret its meaning.
c. Show how the following table was derived from the table above.

MANUFACTURER

PREFERENCE	Toyota	GM	Total
Before ad	100	100	200
After ad	108	92	200
Total	208	192	400

d. Using the second table, is there evidence of a difference in preference for Toyota before and after viewing the ads? (Use $\alpha = 0.05$.)
e. Determine the *p*-value and interpret its meaning.
f. Explain the difference in the results of (a) and (d). Which method of analyzing the data should you use? Why?

12.70 Researchers studied the goals and outcomes of 349 work teams from various manufacturing companies in Ohio. In the first table, teams are categorized as to whether they had specified environmental improvements as a goal and also according to one of four types of manufacturing processes that best described their workplace. The following three tables indicate different outcomes the teams accomplished, based on whether the team had specified cost cutting as one of the team goals.

ENVIRONMENTAL GOAL

TYPE OF MANUFACTURING PROCESS	Yes	No	Total
Job shop or batch	2	42	44
Repetitive batch	4	57	61
Discrete process	15	147	162
Continuous process	17	65	82
Total	38	311	349

COST-CUTTING GOAL

OUTCOME	Yes	No	Total
Improved environmental performance	77	52	129
Environmental performance not improved	91	129	220
Total	168	181	349

COST-CUTTING GOAL

OUTCOME	Yes	No	Total
Improved profitability	70	68	138
Profitability not improved	98	113	211
Total	168	181	349

COST-CUTTING GOAL

OUTCOME	Yes	No	Total
Improved morale	67	55	122
Morale not improved	101	126	227
Total	168	181	349

Source: Extracted from M. Hanna, W. Newman, and P. Johnson, "Linking Operational and Environmental Improvement Thru Employee Involvement," International Journal of Operations and Production Management, 2000, 20, pp. 148–165.

a. At the 0.05 level of significance, determine whether there is evidence of a significant relationship between the presence of environmental goals and the type of manufacturing process.
b. Determine the *p*-value in (a) and interpret its meaning.
c. At the 0.05 level of significance, is there evidence of a difference in improved environmental performance for teams with a specified goal of cutting costs?
d. Determine the *p*-value in (c) and interpret its meaning.
e. At the 0.05 level of significance, is there evidence of a difference in improved profitability for teams with a specified goal of cutting costs?
f. Determine the *p*-value in (e) and interpret its meaning.
g. At the 0.05 level of significance, is there evidence of a difference in improved morale for teams with a specified goal of cutting costs?
h. Determine the *p*-value in (g) and interpret its meaning.

Team Project

The data file Mutual Funds.xls contains information regarding nine variables from a sample of 838 mutual funds. The variables are:

Category—Type of stocks comprising the mutual fund (small cap, mid cap, or large cap)

Objective—Objective of stocks comprising the mutual fund (growth or value)

Assets—In millions of dollars

Fees—Sales charges (no or yes)

Expense ratio—Ratio of expenses to net assets in percentage

2005 return—Twelve-month return in 2005

Three-year return—Annualized return, 2003–2005

Five-year return—Annualized return, 2001–2005

Risk—Risk-of-loss factor of the mutual fund (low, average, or high)

12.71 a. Construct a 2×2 contingency table, using fees as the row variable and objective as the column variable.

b. At the 0.05 level of significance, is there evidence of a significant relationship between the objective of a mutual fund and whether there is a fee?

12.72 a. Construct a 2×3 contingency table, using fees as the row variable and risk as the column variable.

b. At the 0.05 level of significance, is there evidence of a significant relationship between the perceived risk of a mutual fund and whether there is a fee?

12.73 a. Construct a 3×2 contingency table, using risk as the row variable and objective as the column variable.

b. At the 0.05 level of significance, is there evidence of a significant relationship between the objective of a mutual fund and its perceived risk?

12.74 a. Construct a 3×3 contingency table, using risk as the row variable and category as the column variable.

b. At the 0.05 level of significance, is there evidence of a significant relationship between the category of a mutual fund and its perceived risk?

Student Survey Database

12.75 Problem 1.27 on page 15 describes a survey of 50 undergraduate students (see the file undergradsurvey.xls).

For these data, construct contingency tables, using gender, major, plans to go to graduate school, and employment status. (You need to construct six tables, taking two variables at a time.) Analyze the data at the 0.05 level of significance to determine whether any significant relationships exist among these variables.

12.76 Problem 1.27 on page 15 describes a survey of 50 undergraduate students (see the file undergradsurvey.xls).

a. Select a sample of 50 undergraduate students at your school and conduct a similar survey for those students.

b. For the data collected in (a), repeat Problem 12.75.

c. Compare the results of (b) to those of Problem 12.75.

12.77 Problem 1.28 on page 15 describes a survey of 50 MBA students (see the file gradsurvey.xls). For these data, construct contingency tables, using gender, undergraduate major, graduate major, and employment status. (You need to construct six tables, taking two variables at a time.) Analyze the data at the 0.05 level of significance to determine whether any significant relationships exist among these variables.

12.78 Problem 1.28 on page 15 describes a survey of 50 MBA students (see the file gradsurvey.xls).

a. Select a sample of 50 graduate students in your MBA program and conduct a similar survey for those students.

b. For the data collected in (a), repeat Problem 12.77.

c. Compare the results of (b) to those of Problem 12.77.

Managing the *Springville Herald*

Phase 1

Reviewing the results of its research, the marketing department concluded that a segment of Springville households might be interested in a discounted trial home subscription to the *Herald*. The team decided to test various discounts before determining the type of discount to offer during the trial period. It decided to conduct an experiment using three types of discounts plus a plan that offered no discount during the trial period:

1. No discount for the newspaper. Subscribers would pay $4.50 per week for the newspaper during the 90-day trial period.

2. Moderate discount for the newspaper. Subscribers would pay $4.00 per week for the newspaper during the 90-day trial period.

3. Substantial discount for the newspaper. Subscribers would pay $3.00 per week for the newspaper during the 90-day trial period.

4. Discount restaurant card. Subscribers would be given a card providing a discount of 15% at selected restaurants in Springville during the trial period.

Each participant in the experiment was randomly assigned to a discount plan. A random sample of 100 subscribers to each plan during the trial period was tracked to determine how many would continue to subscribe to the *Herald* after the trial period. Table SH12.1 summarizes the results.

TABLE SH12.1 Number of Subscribers Who Continue Subscriptions After Trial Period with Four Discount Plans

CONTINUE SUBSCRIPTIONS AFTER TRIAL PERIOD	DISCOUNT PLANS				
	No Discount	Moderate Discount	Substantial Discount	Restaurant Card	Total
Yes	34	37	38	61	170
No	66	63	62	39	230
Total	100	100	100	100	400

EXERCISE

SH12.1 Analyze the results of the experiment. Write a report to the team that includes your recommendation for which discount plan to use. Be prepared to discuss the limitations and assumptions of the experiment.

DO NOT CONTINUE UNTIL THE PHASE 1 EXERCISE HAS BEEN COMPLETED.

Phase 2

The marketing department team discussed the results of the survey presented in Chapter 8, on pages 320–321. The team realized that the evaluation of individual questions was providing only limited information. In order to further understand the market for home-delivery subscriptions, the data were organized in the following cross-classification tables:

READ OTHER NEWSPAPER

HOME DELIVERY	Yes	No	Total
Yes	61	75	136
No	77	139	216
Total	138	214	352

RESTAURANT CARD

HOME DELIVERY	Yes	No	Total
Yes	26	110	136
No	40	176	216
Total	66	286	352

MONDAY–SATURDAY PURCHASE BEHAVIOR

INTEREST IN TRIAL SUBSCRIPTION	Every Day	Most Days	Occasionally or Never	Total
Yes	29	14	3	46
No	49	81	40	170
Total	78	95	43	216

SUNDAY PURCHASE BEHAVIOR

INTEREST IN TRIAL SUBSCRIPTION	Every Sunday	2–3 Times/ Month	No More Than Once/ Month	Total
Yes	35	10	1	46
No	103	44	23	170
Total	138	54	24	216

INTEREST IN TRIAL SUBSCRIPTION

WHERE PURCHASED	Yes	No	Total
Convenience store	12	62	74
Newsstand/candy store	15	80	95
Vending machine	10	11	21
Supermarket	5	8	13
Other locations	4	9	13
Total	46	170	216

MONDAY–SATURDAY PURCHASE BEHAVIOR

SUNDAY PURCHASE BEHAVIOR	Every Day	Most Days	Occasionally or Never	Total
Every Sunday	55	65	18	138
2–3 times/month	19	23	12	54
Once/month	4	7	13	24
Total	78	95	43	216

EXERCISE

SH12.2 Analyze the results of the cross-classification tables. Write a report for the marketing department team and discuss the marketing implications of the results for the *Springville Herald*.

Web Case

Apply your knowledge of testing for the difference between two proportions in this Web Case, which extends the T.C. Resort Properties Using Statistics scenario of this chapter.

As T.C. Resort Properties seeks to improve its customer service, the company faces new competition from SunLow Resorts. SunLow has recently opened resort hotels on the islands where T.C. Resort Properties has its five hotels. SunLow is currently advertising that a random survey of 300 customers revealed that about 60% percent of the customers preferred its "Concierge Class" travel reward program over the T.C. Resorts "TCPass Plus" program. Visit the SunLow Web site, **www.prenhall.com/ Springville/SunLowHome.htm** (or open the Web page file in the Web Case folder on the Student CD-ROM), and examine the survey data. Then answer the following:

1. Are the claims made by SunLow valid?

2. What analyses of the survey data would lead to a more favorable impression about T.C. Resort Properties?

3. Perform one of the analyses identified in your answer to step 2.

4. Review the data about the T.C. Resorts Properties customers presented in this chapter. Are there any other factors that you might include in a future survey of travel reward programs? Explain.

REFERENCES

1. Conover, W. J., *Practical Nonparametric Statistics*, 3rd ed. (New York: Wiley, 2000).
2. Daniel, W. W., *Applied Nonparametric Statistics*, 2nd ed. (Boston: PWS Kent, 1990).
3. Dixon, W. J., and F. J. Massey, Jr., *Introduction to Statistical Analysis*, 4th ed. (New York: McGraw-Hill, 1983).
4. Hollander, M., and D. A. Wolfe, *Nonparametric Statistical Methods* 2nd ed. (New York: Wiley, 1999).
5. Lewontin, R. C., and J. Felsenstein, "Robustness of Homogeneity Tests in 2 × *n* Tables," *Biometrics* 21 (March 1965): 19–33.
6. Marascuilo, L. A., "Large-Sample Multiple Comparisons," *Psychological Bulletin* 65 (1966): 280–290.
7. Marascuilo, L. A., and M. McSweeney, *Nonparametric and Distribution-Free Methods for the Social Sciences* (Monterey, CA: Brooks/Cole, 1977).
8. *Microsoft Excel 2007* (Redmond, WA: Microsoft Corp., 2007).
9. Winer, B. J., D. R. Brown, and K. M. Michels, *Statistical Principles in Experimental Design*, 3rd ed. (New York: McGraw-Hill, 1989).

Excel Companion
to Chapter 12

E12.1 USING THE CHI-SQUARE TEST FOR THE DIFFERENCE BETWEEN TWO PROPORTIONS

You conduct a chi-square test for the difference between two proportions by either selecting the PHStat2 Chi-Square Test for Differences in Two Proportions procedure or by making entries in the `Chi-Square.xls` workbook.

Using PHStat2 Chi-Square Test for Differences in Two Proportions

Select **PHStat → Two-Sample Tests → Chi-Square Test for Differences in Two Proportions**. In the procedure's dialog box (shown below), enter the **Level of Significance**, enter a title as the **Title**, and click **OK**.

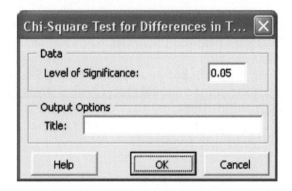

PHStat2 creates a worksheet in which you enter contingency table data, such as Table 12.2 on page 463, into the rows 4 through 7 Observed Frequencies area. (You can also enter custom row and column labels for your data.)

Before you enter contingency table data, many worksheet cells display the message #DIV/0!. This is not an error.

Using Chi-Square.xls

Open to the **ChiSquare2P** worksheet of the `Chi-Square.xls` workbook. This worksheet (see Figure 12.3 on page 467) uses the function **CHIINV(*level of significance, degrees of freedom*)** to compute the critical value and the function **CHIDIST(χ^2 *test statistic, degrees of freedom*)** to compute the *p*-value for the Section 12.1 hotel guest satisfaction example. To adapt this worksheet to other problems, enter the problem's contingency table data into the rows 4 through 7 Observed Frequencies area, edit the title in cell A1, and change the level of significance in cell B18, if necessary.

Figure E12.1 shows the cell formulas for rows 6 through 15, not shown in Figure 12.3. Formulas in cells B11, A12, A13, A14, B12, and C12 display the row and column labels entered in the Observed Frequencies area. The results of the formulas in cells F13:G14 are summed in cell B25 to compute the χ^2 test statistic. (The other formulas shown compute row or column totals or the expected frequencies.)

Not shown in Figure E12.1 is the A30 formula. This formula uses an IF function to complete the phrase "Expected frequency assumption . . . ". The *comparison* part of this IF function (see Section E9.1 on page 364), **OR(B13 < 5, C13 < 5, B14 < 5, C14 < 5)**, uses the OR function to make sure that none of the expected frequencies is less than 5, an assumption that is necessary for the chi-square test to be accurate.

	A	B	C	D	E	F	G
3		Observed Frequencies					
4		Hotel				Calculations	
5	Choose Again?	Beachcomber	Windsurfer	Total		fo-fe	
6	Yes	163	154	=SUM(B6:C6)		=B6 - B13	=C6 - C13
7	No	64	108	=SUM(B7:C7)		=B7 - B14	=C7 - C14
8	Total	=SUM(B6:B7)	=SUM(C6:C7)	=SUM(B8:C8)			
9							
10		Expected Frequencies					
11		=B4					
12	=A5	=B5	=C5	Total		(fo-fe)^2/fe	
13	=A6	=D6 * B8/D8	=D6 * C8/D8	=SUM(B13:C13)		=F6^2/B13	=G6^2/C13
14	=A7	=D7 * B8/D8	=D7 * C8/D8	=SUM(B14:C14)		=F7^2/B14	=G7^2/C14
15	Total	=SUM(B13:B14)	=SUM(C13:C14)	=SUM(B15:C15)			

FIGURE E12.1 ChiSquare2P rows 3 through 15

E12.2 USING THE CHI-SQUARE TEST FOR THE DIFFERENCES AMONG MORE THAN TWO PROPORTIONS

You conduct a chi-square test for the differences among more than two proportions by either selecting the PHStat2 Chi-Square Test procedure or by making entries in the Chi-Square Worksheets.xls workbook.

Using PHStat2 Chi-Square Test

Select **PHStat → Multiple-Sample Tests → Chi-Square Test**. In the procedure's dialog box (shown below), enter the **Level of Significance**, enter **2** as the **Number of Rows**, and enter the **Number of Columns**. Enter a title as the **Title** and click **OK**. If you want to select the Marascuilo procedure, select **Marascuilo Procedure** before clicking **OK**.

PHStat2 creates a worksheet in which you enter your $2 \times c$ contingency table data, such as Table 12.6 on page 471, in the Observed Frequencies area that begins in row 4. (You can also enter custom row and column labels for your data.) Before you enter contingency table data, many worksheet cells display the message #DIV/0!. This is not an error.

Using Chi-Square Worksheets.xls

Open the Chi-Square Worksheets.xls workbook to the worksheet that contains the appropriate $2 \times c$ observed frequency table for your problem. For example, for the guest satisfaction data in Table 12.6 on page 471 that requires a 2×3 table, open to the **ChiSquare2x3** worksheet. Worksheets with empty observed frequencies tables display the message #DIV/0! in many cells. This is not an

error, and these messages disappear when you enter your contingency table data.

All $2 \times c$ worksheets contain formulas similar to those in the ChiSquare2P worksheet discussed in Section E12.1. All worksheets have their level of significance set to 0.05, but you can change this value. The Chi-Square Worksheets.xls workbook includes the ChiSquare2x3Formulas worksheet, which allows you to examine the formulas of the ChiSquare2x3 worksheet in formatted, formulas view. You should note that the formula in cell A30 verifies whether all expected frequencies are at least 1, an assumption of the Chi-Square test.

Using the Marascuilo Worksheets

Each $2 \times c$ chi square worksheet is linked to a companion Marascuilo worksheet in the Chi-Square Worksheets.xls workbook. Marascuilo worksheet names echo the chi-square worksheet to which they are linked, so that **Marascuilo2x3** is linked to **ChiSquare2x3**. (The Marascuilo2x3 worksheet is shown in Figure 12.7 on page 475.)

The **Marascuilo2x3Formulas** worksheet allows you to examine the formulas of the Marascuilo2x3 worksheet in formatted, formulas view. If you examine this worksheet, you see that the formulas for the level of significance, the square root of the critical value, the sample proportions, and the critical range all use one or more values from the ChiSquare2x3 worksheet.

All Marascuilo worksheets compare the absolute differences and critical range values for each pair of groups and display either Significant or Not Significant in column D.

E12.3 USING THE CHI-SQUARE TEST OF INDEPENDENCE

Adapt the instructions of the previous section to the chi-square test of independence. If you use PHStat2, enter your number of rows as the **Number of Rows**. If you use the Chi-Square Worksheets.xls workbook, open to either the chi-square worksheets for 3×4, 4×3, 7×3, or 8×3, or open one of the $2 \times c$ worksheets mentioned in Section E12.2.

E12.4 USING THE McNEMAR TEST

You conduct a McNemar test by either selecting the PHStat2 McNemar Test procedure or by making entries in the McNemar.xls workbook.

Using PHStat2 McNemar Test

Select **PHStat → Two-Sample Tests → McNemar Test**. In the procedure's dialog box (see top of page 508), enter the **Level of Significance**, click a test option, enter a title as the **Title**, and click **OK**.

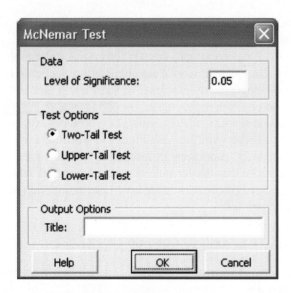

PHStat2 creates a worksheet in which you enter the observed frequencies, such as Table 12.13 on page 484, in the Observed Frequencies area that begins in row 3. (You can also enter custom row and column labels for your data.) Before you enter data, many worksheet cells display the message #DIV/0!. This is not an error.

Using McNemar.xls

You open and use either the **McNemar_TT** or the **McNemar_All** worksheets of the McNemar.xls workbook to use the McNemar test. These worksheets use the **NORMSINV(***P<X***)** function to determine the lower and upper critical values and use the **NORMSDIST(Z** *value***)** function to compute the *p*-values from the *Z* value calculated in cell B16. To understand how messages get displayed in these worksheets, read "About the IF Function" on page 364.

The **McNemar_TT** worksheet (see Figure 12.12 on page 485) uses the two-tail test for the Section 12.4 consumer preference example. The **McNemar_All** worksheet also includes the one-tail tests (these additions are shown in Figure E12.2). To adapt these worksheets to other problems, change the observed frequency table data and labels in rows 4 through 7 and (if necessary) the level of significance in cell B11.

	A	B	
24	Lower-Tail Test		
25	Lower Critical Value	-1.6449	=NORMSINV(B11)
26	p-Value	0.9997	=NORMSDIST(B16)
27	Do not reject the null hypothesis		=IF(B26 < B11, "Reject the null hypothesis",
28			"Do not reject the null hypothesis")
29	Upper-Tail Test		
30	Upper Critical Value	1.6449	=NORMSINV(1-B11)
31	p-Value	0.0003	=1 - NORMSDIST(B16)
32	Reject the null hypothesis		=IF(B31 < B11, "Reject the null hypothesis",
			"Do not reject the null hypothesis")

FIGURE E12.2 McNemar_All worksheet one-tail tests

If you want the **McNemar_All** worksheet to show only one of the one-tail tests, first make a copy of that worksheet (see the Excel Companion to Chapter 1). For a lower-tail-test-only worksheet, select and delete rows 29 through 32 and then select and delete rows 18 through 23. For an upper-tail-test-only worksheet, select and delete rows 18 through 28.

E12.5 USING THE WILCOXON RANK SUM TEST

You conduct a Wilcoxon rank sum test by either selecting the PHStat2 Wilcoxon Rank Sum Test procedure or by making entries in the Wilcoxon.xls workbook. The PHStat2 procedure uses unsummarized, unstacked data, while the workbook uses summarized data. (See "Counting and Summing Ranks" on page 509 if you have unsummarized, unstacked data and you wish to use the workbook.)

Using PHStat2 Wilcoxon Rank Sum Test

Open to the worksheet that contains the unsummarized, unstacked data for the two independent populations. Select **PHStat → Two-Sample Tests → Wilcoxon Rank Sum Test**. In the procedure's dialog box (shown below), enter the **Level of Significance** and the cell ranges for the **Population 1 Sample Cell Range** and the **Population 2 Sample Cell Range**. Click **First cells in both ranges contain label**, click a test option, enter a title as the **Title**, and click **OK**.

PHStat creates a worksheet similar to the Figure 12.14 worksheet on page 490. However, PHStat2 uses the functions **COUNTIF** and **SUMIF** in formulas in cells B7, B8, B10, and B11 to compute the sample size and sum of the ranks for each population. To learn more about these functions, read "Counting and Summing Ranks," later in this section.

Using Wilcoxon.xls

You open and use either the **Wilcoxon_TT** or the **Wilcoxon_All** worksheets of the Wilcoxon.xls workbook to use the Wilcoxon rank sum test. These worksheets use the **NORMSINV(P<X)** function to determine the lower and upper critical values and use the **NORMSDIST(Z value)** function to compute the *p*-values from the *Z* value calculated in cell B18. To understand how messages get displayed in these worksheets, read "About the IF Function" on page 364.

The **Wilcoxon_TT** worksheet (see Figure 12.14 on page 490) uses the two-tail test for the Section 12.5 BLK cola sales example. The **Wilcoxon_All** worksheet also includes the one-tail tests (these additions are shown in Figure E12.3). To adapt these worksheets to other problems, change the title in cell A1 and (if necessary) the level of significance, sample sizes, and rank sum values in the tinted cells B4, B7, B8, B10, and B11.

	A	B	
25			
26	**Lower-Tail Test**		
27	Lower Critical Value	-1.6449	=NORMSINV(B4)
28	p-Value	0.0063	=NORMSDIST(B18)
29	**Reject the null hypothesis**		=IF(B28 < B4, "Reject the null hypothesis", "Do not reject the null hypothesis")
30			
31	**Upper-Tail Test**		
32	Upper Critical Value	1.6449	=NORMSINV(1 - B4)
33	p-Value	0.9937	=1 - NORMSDIST(B18)
34	Do not reject the null hypothesis		=IF(B33 < B4, "Reject the null hypothesis", "Do not reject the null hypothesis")

FIGURE E12.3 Wilcoxon one-tail tests

If you want the Wilcoxon_All worksheet to show only one of the one-tail tests, first make a copy of that worksheet (see the Excel Companion to Chapter 1). For a lower-tail-test-only worksheet, select and delete rows 31 through 34 and then select and delete rows 20 through 25. For an upper-tail-test-only worksheet, select and delete rows 20 through 30.

Counting and Summing Ranks

If you want to use the Wilcoxon.xls workbook but have unsummarized, unstacked data, you can use the **COUNTIF (*cell range for matching, value to be matched*)** function to compute the sample size and the **SUMIF(*cell range for matching, value to be matched, cell range for summing*)** function to compute the sum of the ranks of each population.

To use these functions, first sort your unstacked data worksheet in ascending order, using the column containing the values (not the population labels). Then add a column of ranks, breaking ties by using the method stated on page 487. With your data so arranged, you can use the formula

=COUNTIF(*cell range of all population labels, "population 1 name"*) to count the sample size of the population 1 sample and the formula **=SUMIF(*cell range of all population labels, "population 1 name", cell range of all sorted values*)** to sum the ranks of the population 1 sample. (The population 1 name must appear in a set of double quotation marks.) Create another pair of formulas and use the name of the second population as the *value to be matched* to count the sample size and sum the ranks of the population 2 sample.

For example, the formulas **=COUNTIF(A1:A21, "EndAisle")** and **=SUMIF(A1:A21, "EndAisle", C1:C21)** would compute the sample size and the sum of ranks for the BLK cola end-aisle sales if placed in empty cells of the **ColaSortedStacked** worksheet of the Cola.xls workbook. The formulas **=COUNTIF(A1:A21, "Normal")** and **=SUMIF(A1:A21, "Normal", C1:C21)** would do the same things for the normal display sample.

E12.6 USING THE KRUSKAL-WALLIS RANK TEST

You conduct a Kruskal-Wallis rank test by either selecting the PHStat2 Kruskal-Wallis Rank Test procedure or by making entries in the Kruskal-Wallis Worksheets.xls workbook. The PHStat2 procedure uses unsummarized, unstacked data, while the workbook uses summarized data.

Using PHStat2 Kruskal-Wallis Rank Test

Select **PHStat → Multiple-Sample Tests → Kruskal-Wallis Rank Test**. In the procedure's dialog box (shown below), enter the **Level of Significance** and enter the cell range of the unsummarized, unstacked data as the **Sample Data Cell Range**. Click **First cells contain label**, enter a title as the **Title**, and click **OK**.

Using Kruskal-Wallis.xls

Open the `Kruskal-Wallis Worksheets.xls` workbook to the worksheet that contains the appropriate number of groups (populations) for your problem. For example, for the Section 12.6 parachute example that contains four different groups, open to the **Kruskal-Wallis4** worksheet (shown in Figure 12.16 on page 495).

Kruskal-Wallis worksheets use the function **CHIINV(*level of significance, degrees of freedom*)** to compute the critical value and the function **CHIDIST(χ^2 *test statistic, degrees of freedom*)** to com-

pute the *p*-value. When you open to a worksheet, enter the sample size, sum of ranks, and mean rank values in the tinted cells in columns E through G, the level of significance value in cell B4, and a title in cell A1 to complete the worksheet. #DIV/0! messages that may appear in several cells disappear after you enter data. This is not an error.

> **Forum** Click on the ALTERNATIVE METHODS link to learn more about how the COUNTIF and SUMIF functions (see Section E12.4) could be used with Kruskal-Wallis worksheets.

CHAPTER 13

Simple Linear Regression

USING STATISTICS @ Sunflowers Apparel

LEARNING OBJECTIVES

In this chapter, you learn:

- To use regression analysis to predict the value of a dependent variable based on an independent variable
- The meaning of the regression coefficients b_0 and b_1
- To evaluate the assumptions of regression analysis and know what to do if the assumptions are violated
- To make inferences about the slope and correlation coefficient
- To estimate mean values and predict individual values

Using Statistics @ Sunflowers Apparel

The sales for Sunflowers Apparel, a chain of upscale clothing stores for women, have increased during the past 12 years as the chain has expanded the number of stores open. Until now, Sunflowers managers selected sites based on subjective factors, such as the availability of a good lease or the perception that a location seemed ideal for an apparel store. As the new director of planning, you need to develop a systematic approach that will lead to making better decisions during the site selection process. As a starting point, you believe that the size of the store significantly contributes to store sales, and you want to use this relationship in the decision-making process. How can you use statistics so that you can forecast the annual sales of a proposed store based on the size of that store?

In this chapter and the next two chapters, you learn how **regression analysis** enables you to develop a model to predict the values of a numerical variable, based on the value of other variables.

In regression analysis, the variable you wish to predict is called the **dependent variable**. The variables used to make the prediction are called **independent variables**. In addition to predicting values of the dependent variable, regression analysis also allows you to identify the type of mathematical relationship that exists between a dependent and an independent variable, to quantify the effect that changes in the independent variable have on the dependent variable, and to identify unusual observations. For example, as the director of planning, you may wish to predict sales for a Sunflowers store, based on the size of the store. Other examples include predicting the monthly rent of an apartment, based on its size, and predicting the monthly sales of a product in a supermarket, based on the amount of shelf space devoted to the product.

This chapter discusses **simple linear regression**, in which a *single* numerical independent variable, X, is used to predict the numerical dependent variable Y, such as using the size of a store to predict the annual sales of the store. Chapters 14 and 15 discuss *multiple regression models*, which use several independent variables to predict a numerical dependent variable, Y. For example, you could use the amount of advertising expenditures, price, and the amount of shelf space devoted to a product to predict its monthly sales.

13.1 TYPES OF REGRESSION MODELS

In Section 2.5, you used a **scatter plot** (also known as a **scatter diagram**) to examine the relationship between an X variable on the horizontal axis and a Y variable on the vertical axis. The nature of the relationship between two variables can take many forms, ranging from simple to extremely complicated mathematical functions. The simplest relationship consists of a straight-line, or **linear relationship**. An example of this relationship is shown in Figure 13.1.

FIGURE 13.1

A positive straight-line relationship

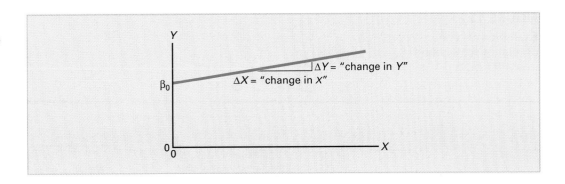

Equation (13.1) represents the straight-line (linear) model.

SIMPLE LINEAR REGRESSION MODEL

$$Y_i = \beta_0 + \beta_1 X_i + \varepsilon_i \qquad \textbf{(13.1)}$$

where

$\beta_0 = Y$ intercept for the population

$\beta_1 = $ slope for the population

$\varepsilon_i = $ random error in Y for observation i

$Y_i = $ dependent variable (sometimes referred to as the **response variable**) for observation i

$X_i = $ independent variable (sometimes referred to as the **explanatory variable**) for observation i

The portion $Y_i = \beta_0 + \beta_1 X_i$ of the simple linear regression model expressed in Equation (13.1) is a straight line. The **slope** of the line, β_1, represents the expected change in Y per unit change in X. It represents the mean amount that Y changes (either positively or negatively) for a one-unit change in X. The **Y intercept**, β_0, represents the mean value of Y when X equals 0. The last component of the model, ε_i, represents the random error in Y for each observation, i. In other words, ε_i is the vertical distance of the actual value of Y_i above or below the predicted value of Y_i on the line.

The selection of the proper mathematical model depends on the distribution of the X and Y values on the scatter plot. In Panel A of Figure 13.2 on page 514, the values of Y are generally increasing linearly as X increases. This panel is similar to Figure 13.3 on page 515, which illustrates the positive relationship between the square footage of the store and the annual sales at branches of the Sunflowers Apparel women's clothing store chain.

Panel B is an example of a negative linear relationship. As X increases, the values of Y are generally decreasing. An example of this type of relationship might be the price of a particular product and the amount of sales.

The data in Panel C show a positive curvilinear relationship between X and Y. The values of Y increase as X increases, but this increase tapers off beyond certain values of X. An example of a positive curvilinear relationship might be the age and maintenance cost of a machine. As a machine gets older, the maintenance cost may rise rapidly at first, but then level off beyond a certain number of years.

Panel D shows a U-shaped relationship between X and Y. As X increases, at first Y generally decreases; but as X continues to increase, Y not only stops decreasing but actually increases above its minimum value. An example of this type of relationship might be the number of errors per hour at a task and the number of hours worked. The number of errors per hour

FIGURE 13.2

Examples of types of relationships found in scatter plots

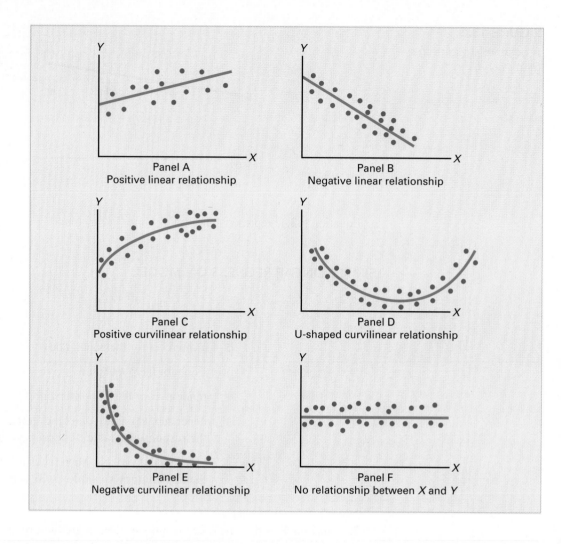

decreases as the individual becomes more proficient at the task, but then it increases beyond a certain point because of factors such as fatigue and boredom.

Panel E indicates an exponential relationship between X and Y. In this case, Y decreases very rapidly as X first increases, but then it decreases much less rapidly as X increases further. An example of an exponential relationship could be the resale value of an automobile and its age. In the first year, the resale value drops drastically from its original price; however, the resale value then decreases much less rapidly in subsequent years.

Finally, Panel F shows a set of data in which there is very little or no relationship between X and Y. High and low values of Y appear at each value of X.

In this section, a variety of different models that represent the relationship between two variables were briefly examined. Although scatter plots are useful in visually displaying the mathematical form of a relationship, more sophisticated statistical procedures are available to determine the most appropriate model for a set of variables. The rest of this chapter discusses the model used when there is a *linear* relationship between variables.

13.2 DETERMINING THE SIMPLE LINEAR REGRESSION EQUATION

In the Using Statistics scenario on page 512, the stated goal is to forecast annual sales for all new stores, based on store size. To examine the relationship between the store size in square feet and its annual sales, a sample of 14 stores was selected. Table 13.1 summarizes the results for these 14 stores, which are stored in the file site.xls.

TABLE 13.1

Square Footage (in Thousands of Square Feet) and Annual Sales (in Millions of Dollars) for a Sample of 14 Branches of Sunflowers Apparel

Store	Square Feet (Thousands)	Annual Sales (in Millions of Dollars)	Store	Square Feet (Thousands)	Annual Sales (in Millions of Dollars)
1	1.7	3.7	8	1.1	2.7
2	1.6	3.9	9	3.2	5.5
3	2.8	6.7	10	1.5	2.9
4	5.6	9.5	11	5.2	10.7
5	1.3	3.4	12	4.6	7.6
6	2.2	5.6	13	5.8	11.8
7	1.3	3.7	14	3.0	4.1

Figure 13.3 displays the scatter plot for the data in Table 13.1. Observe the increasing relationship between square feet (X) and annual sales (Y). As the size of the store increases, annual sales increase approximately as a straight line. Thus, you can assume that a straight line provides a useful mathematical model of this relationship. Now you need to determine the specific straight line that is the *best* fit to these data.

FIGURE 13.3

Microsoft Excel scatter plot for the Sunflowers Apparel data

See Section E2.12 to create this.

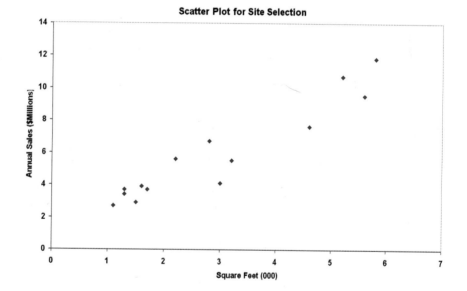

The Least-Squares Method

In the preceding section, a statistical model is hypothesized to represent the relationship between two variables, square footage and sales, in the entire population of Sunflowers Apparel stores. However, as shown in Table 13.1, the data are from only a random sample of stores. If certain assumptions are valid (see Section 13.4), you can use the sample Y intercept, b_0, and the sample slope, b_1, as estimates of the respective population parameters, β_0 and β_1. Equation (13.2) uses these estimates to form the **simple linear regression equation**. This straight line is often referred to as the **prediction line**.

SIMPLE LINEAR REGRESSION EQUATION: THE PREDICTION LINE

The predicted value of Y equals the Y intercept plus the slope times the value of X.

$$\hat{Y}_i = b_0 + b_1 X_i \qquad \textbf{(13.2)}$$

where

$$\hat{Y}_i = \text{predicted value of } Y \text{ for observation } i$$

$$X_i = \text{value of } X \text{ for observation } i$$

$$b_0 = \text{sample } Y \text{ intercept}$$

$$b_1 = \text{sample slope}$$

Equation (13.2) requires the determination of two **regression coefficients**—b_0 (the sample Y intercept) and b_1 (the sample slope). The most common approach to finding b_0 and b_1 is the method of least squares. This method minimizes the sum of the squared differences between the actual values (Y_i) and the predicted values ($\hat{Y}_i$) using the simple linear regression equation [that is, the prediction line; see Equation (13.2)]. This sum of squared differences is equal to

$$\sum_{i=1}^{n} (Y_i - \hat{Y}_i)^2$$

Because $\hat{Y}_i = b_0 + b_1 X_i$,

$$\sum_{i=1}^{n} (Y_i - \hat{Y}_i)^2 = \sum_{i=1}^{n} [Y_i - (b_0 + b_1 X_i)]^2$$

Because this equation has two unknowns, b_0 and b_1, the sum of squared differences depends on the sample Y intercept, b_0, and the sample slope, b_1. The **least-squares method** determines the values of b_0 and b_1 that minimize the sum of squared differences. Any values for b_0 and b_1 other than those determined by the least-squares method result in a greater sum of squared differences between the actual values (Y_i) and the predicted values $\hat{Y}_i$. In this book, Microsoft Excel is used to perform the computations involved in the least-squares method. For the data of Table 13.1, Figure 13.4 presents results from Microsoft Excel.

FIGURE 13.4

Microsoft Excel results for the Sunflowers Apparel data

See Section E13.1 to create this.

	A	B	C	D	E	F	G
1	Site Selection Analysis						
2							
3	Regression Statistics						
4	Multiple R	0.9509					
5	R Square	0.9042					
6	Adjusted R Square	0.8962					
7	Standard Error	0.9664 —S_{YX}					
8	Observations	14 —n					
9							
10	ANOVA						
11		df	SS	MS	F	Significance F	
12	Regression	1	SSR—105.7476	105.7476	113.2335	0.0000	
13	Residual	12	SSE—11.2067	0.9339		p-value	
14	Total	13	SST—116.9543				
15							
16		Coefficients	Standard Error	t Stat	P-value	Lower 95%	Upper 95%
17	Intercept	b_0—0.9645	0.5262	1.8329	0.0917	-0.1820	2.1110
18	Square Feet	b_1—1.6699	0.1569	10.6411	0.0000	1.3280	2.0118

To understand how the results are computed, many of the computations involved are illustrated in Examples 13.3 and 13.4 on pages 520–521 and 526–527. In Figure 13.4, observe that $b_0 = 0.9645$ and $b_1 = 1.6699$. Thus, the prediction line [see Equation (13.2) on page 515] for these data is

$$\hat{Y}_i = 0.9645 + 1.6699 X_i$$

The slope, b_1, is +1.6699. This means that for each increase of 1 unit in X, the mean value of Y is estimated to increase by 1.6699 units. In other words, for each increase of 1.0 thousand square feet in the size of the store, the mean annual sales are estimated to increase by 1.6699 millions of dollars. Thus, the slope represents the portion of the annual sales that are estimated to vary according to the size of the store.

The Y intercept, b_0, is +0.9645. The Y intercept represents the mean value of Y when X equals 0. Because the square footage of the store cannot be 0, this Y intercept has no practical interpretation. Also, the Y intercept for this example is outside the range of the observed values of the X variable, and therefore interpretations of the value of b_0 should be made cautiously. Figure 13.5 displays the actual observations and the prediction line. To illustrate a situation in which there is a direct interpretation for the Y intercept, b_0, see Example 13.1.

FIGURE 13.5

Microsoft Excel scatter plot and prediction line for Sunflowers Apparel data

See Section E13.2 to create this.

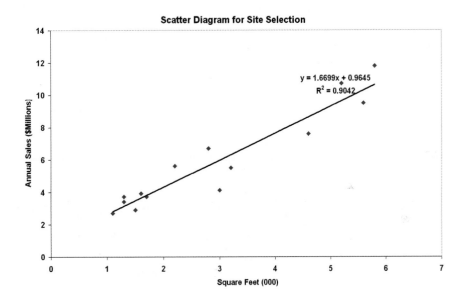

EXAMPLE 13.1

INTERPRETING THE Y INTERCEPT, b_0, AND THE SLOPE, b_1

A statistics professor wants to use the number of hours a student studies for a statistics final exam (X) to predict the final exam score (Y). A regression model was fit based on data collected for a class during the previous semester, with the following results:

$$\hat{Y}_i = 35.0 + 3X_i$$

What is the interpretation of the Y intercept, b_0, and the slope, b_1?

SOLUTION The Y intercept $b_0 = 35.0$ indicates that when the student does not study for the final exam, the mean final exam score is 35.0. The slope $b_1 = 3$ indicates that for each increase of one hour in studying time, the mean change in the final exam score is predicted to be +3.0. In other words, the final exam score is predicted to increase by 3 points for each one-hour increase in studying time.

VISUAL EXPLORATIONS Exploring Simple Linear Regression Coefficients

Use the Visual Explorations Simple Linear Regression procedure to produce a prediction line that is as close as possible to the prediction line defined by the least-squares solution. Open the `Visual Explorations.xla` add-in workbook and select **VisualExplorations → Simple Linear Regression** (Excel 97-2003) or **Add-ins → Visual Explorations → Simple Linear Regression** (Excel 2007). (See Section E1.6 to learn about using add-ins.)

When a scatter plot of the Sunflowers Apparel data of Table 13.1 on page 515 with an initial prediction line appears (shown below), click the spinner buttons to change the values for b_1, the slope of the prediction line, and b_0, the Y intercept of the prediction line.

Try to produce a prediction line that is as close as possible to the prediction line defined by the least-squares estimates, using the chart display and the Difference from Target SSE value as feedback (see page 525 for an explanation of SSE). Click **Finish** when you are done with this exploration.

At any time, click **Reset** to reset the b_1 and b_0 values, **Help** for more information, or **Solution** to reveal the prediction line defined by the least-squares method.

Using Your Own Regression Data

To use Visual Explorations to find a prediction line for your own data, open the `Visual Explorations.xla` add-in workbook and select **VisualExplorations → Simple Linear Regression with your worksheet data** (97-2003) or **Add-ins → Visual Explorations → Simple Linear Regression with your worksheet data** (2007). In the procedure's dialog box (shown below), enter your Y variable cell range as the **Y Variable Cell Range** and your X variable cell range as the **X Variable Cell Range**. Click **First cells in both ranges contain a label**, enter a title as the **Title**, and click **OK**. When the scatter plot with an initial prediction line appears, use the instructions in the first part of this section to try to produce the prediction line defined by the least-squares method.

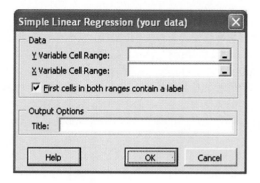

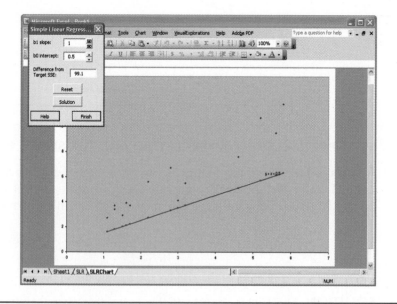

Return to the Using Statistics scenario concerning the Sunflowers Apparel stores. Example 13.2 illustrates how you use the prediction equation to predict the mean annual sales.

EXAMPLE 13.2

PREDICTING MEAN ANNUAL SALES, BASED ON SQUARE FOOTAGE

Use the prediction line to predict the mean annual sales for a store with 4,000 square feet.

SOLUTION You can determine the predicted value by substituting $X = 4$ (thousands of square feet) into the simple linear regression equation:

$$\hat{Y}_i = 0.9645 + 1.6699 X_i$$

$$\hat{Y}_i = 0.9645 + 1.6699(4) = 7.644 \text{ or } \$7,644,000$$

Thus, the predicted mean annual sales of a store with 4,000 square feet is $7,644,000.

Predictions in Regression Analysis: Interpolation Versus Extrapolation

When using a regression model for prediction purposes, you need to consider only the **relevant range** of the independent variable in making predictions. This relevant range includes all values from the smallest to the largest X used in developing the regression model. Hence, when predicting Y for a given value of X, you can interpolate within this relevant range of the X values, but you should not extrapolate beyond the range of X values. When you use the square footage to predict annual sales, the square footage (in thousands of square feet) varies from 1.1 to 5.8 (see Table 13.1 on page 515). Therefore, you should predict annual sales *only* for stores whose size is between 1.1 and 5.8 thousands of square feet. Any prediction of annual sales for stores outside this range assumes that the observed relationship between sales and store size for store sizes from 1.1 to 5.8 thousand square feet is the same as for stores outside this range. For example, you cannot extrapolate the linear relationship beyond 5,800 square feet in Example 13.2. It would be improper to use the prediction line to forecast the sales for a new store containing 8,000 square feet. It is quite possible that store size has a point of diminishing returns. If that is true, as square footage increases beyond 5,800 square feet, the effect on sales might become smaller and smaller.

Computing the Y Intercept, b_0, and the Slope, b_1

For small data sets, you can use a hand calculator to compute the least-squares regression coefficients. Equations (13.3) and (13.4) give the values of b_0 and b_1, which minimize

$$\sum_{i=1}^{n} (Y_i - \hat{Y}_i)^2 = \sum_{i=1}^{n} [Y_i - (b_0 + b_1 X_i)]^2$$

COMPUTATIONAL FORMULA FOR THE SLOPE, b_1

$$b_1 = \frac{SSXY}{SSX} \tag{13.3}$$

where

$$SSXY = \sum_{i=1}^{n} (X_i - \bar{X})(Y_i - \bar{Y}) = \sum_{i=1}^{n} X_i Y_i - \frac{\left(\sum_{i=1}^{n} X_i\right)\left(\sum_{i=1}^{n} Y_i\right)}{n}$$

$$SSX = \sum_{i=1}^{n} (X_i - \bar{X})^2 = \sum_{i=1}^{n} X_i^2 - \frac{\left(\sum_{i=1}^{n} X_i\right)^2}{n}$$

COMPUTATIONAL FORMULA FOR THE Y INTERCEPT, b_0

$$b_0 = \bar{Y} - b_1 \bar{X} \qquad \qquad (13.4)$$

where

$$\bar{Y} = \frac{\sum\limits_{i=1}^{n} Y_i}{n}$$

$$\bar{X} = \frac{\sum\limits_{i=1}^{n} X_i}{n}$$

EXAMPLE 13.3

COMPUTING THE Y INTERCEPT, b_0, AND THE SLOPE, b_1

Compute the Y intercept, b_0, and the slope, b_1, for the Sunflowers Apparel data.

SOLUTION Examining Equations (13.3) and (13.4), you see that five quantities must be calculated to determine b_1 and b_0. These are n, the sample size; $\sum\limits_{i=1}^{n} X_i$, the sum of the X values; $\sum\limits_{i=1}^{n} Y_i$, the sum of the Y values; $\sum\limits_{i=1}^{n} X_i^2$, the sum of the squared X values; and $\sum\limits_{i=1}^{n} X_i Y_i$, the sum of the product of X and Y. For the Sunflowers Apparel data, the number of square feet is used to predict the annual sales in a store. Table 13.2 presents the computations of the various sums needed for the site selection problem, plus $\sum\limits_{i=1}^{n} Y_i^2$, the sum of the squared Y values that will be used to compute SST in Section 13.3.

TABLE 13.2

Computations for the Sunflowers Apparel Data

Store	Square Feet (X)	Annual Sales (Y)	X^2	Y^2	XY
1	1.7	3.7	2.89	13.69	6.29
2	1.6	3.9	2.56	15.21	6.24
3	2.8	6.7	7.84	44.89	18.76
4	5.6	9.5	31.36	90.25	53.20
5	1.3	3.4	1.69	11.56	4.42
6	2.2	5.6	4.84	31.36	12.32
7	1.3	3.7	1.69	13.69	4.81
8	1.1	2.7	1.21	7.29	2.97
9	3.2	5.5	10.24	30.25	17.60
10	1.5	2.9	2.25	8.41	4.35
11	5.2	10.7	27.04	114.49	55.64
12	4.6	7.6	21.16	57.76	34.96
13	5.8	11.8	33.64	139.24	68.44
14	3.0	4.1	9.00	16.81	12.30
Totals	40.9	81.8	157.41	594.90	302.30

Using Equations (13.3) and (13.4), you can compute the values of b_0 and b_1:

$$b_1 = \frac{SSXY}{SSX}$$

$$SSXY = \sum_{i=1}^{n} (X_i - \overline{X})(Y_i - \overline{Y}) = \sum_{i=1}^{n} X_i Y_i - \frac{\left(\sum_{i=1}^{n} X_i\right)\left(\sum_{i=1}^{n} Y_i\right)}{n}$$

$$SSXY = 302.3 - \frac{(40.9)(81.8)}{14}$$
$$= 302.3 - 238.97285$$
$$= 63.32715$$

$$SSX = \sum_{i=1}^{n} (X_i - \overline{X})^2 = \sum_{i=1}^{n} X_i^2 - \frac{\left(\sum_{i=1}^{n} X_i\right)^2}{n}$$
$$= 157.41 - \frac{(40.9)^2}{14}$$
$$= 157.41 - 119.48642$$
$$= 37.92358$$

so that

$$b_1 = \frac{63.32715}{37.92358}$$
$$= 1.6699$$

and

$$b_0 = \overline{Y} - b_1 \overline{X}$$

$$\overline{Y} = \frac{\sum_{i=1}^{n} Y_i}{n} = \frac{81.8}{14} = 5.842857$$

$$\overline{X} = \frac{\sum_{i=1}^{n} X_i}{n} = \frac{40.9}{14} = 2.92143$$

$$b_0 = 5.842857 - (1.6699)(2.92143)$$
$$= 0.9645$$

PROBLEMS FOR SECTION 13.2

Learning the Basics

 13.1 Fitting a straight line to a set of data yields the following prediction line:

$$\hat{Y}_i = 2 + 5X_i$$

a. Interpret the meaning of the Y intercept, b_0.
b. Interpret the meaning of the slope, b_1.
c. Predict the mean value of Y for $X = 3$.

13.2 If the values of X in Problem 13.1 range from 2 to 25, should you use this model to predict the mean value of Y when X equals
a. 3?
b. −3?
c. 0?
d. 24?

 13.3 Fitting a straight line to a set of data yields the following prediction line:

$$\hat{Y}_i = 16 - 0.5X_i$$

a. Interpret the meaning of the Y intercept, b_0.
b. Interpret the meaning of the slope, b_1.
c. Predict the mean value of Y for $X = 6$.

Applying the Concepts

 13.4 The marketing manager of a large supermarket chain would like to use shelf space to predict the sales of pet food. A random sample of 12 equal-sized stores is selected, with the following results (stored in the file **petfood.xls**):

Store	Shelf Space (X) (Feet)	Weekly Sales (Y) ($)
1	5	160
2	5	220
3	5	140
4	10	190
5	10	240
6	10	260
7	15	230
8	15	270
9	15	280
10	20	260
11	20	290
12	20	310

a. Construct a scatter plot.

For these data, $b_0 = 145$ and $b_1 = 7.4$.
b. Interpret the meaning of the slope, b_1, in this problem.
c. Predict the mean weekly sales (in hundreds of dollars) of pet food for stores with 8 feet of shelf space for pet food.

13.5 Circulation is the lifeblood of the publishing business. The larger the sales of a magazine, the more it can charge advertisers. Recently, a circulation gap has appeared between the publishers' reports of magazines' newsstand sales and subsequent audits by the Audit Bureau of Circulations. The data in the file **circulation.xls** represent the reported and audited newsstand sales (in thousands) in 2001 for the following 10 magazines:

Magazine	Reported (X)	Audited (Y)
YM	621.0	299.6
CosmoGirl	359.7	207.7
Rosie	530.0	325.0
Playboy	492.1	336.3
Esquire	70.5	48.6
TeenPeople	567.0	400.3
More	125.5	91.2
Spin	50.6	39.1
Vogue	353.3	268.6
Elle	263.6	214.3

Source: Extracted from M. Rose, "In Fight for Ads, Publishers Often Overstate Their Sales," The Wall Street Journal, August 6, 2003, pp. A1, A10.

a. Construct a scatter plot.

For these data $b_0 = 26.724$ and $b_1 = 0.5719$.
b. Interpret the meaning of the slope, b_1, in this problem.
c. Predict the mean audited newsstand sales for a magazine that reports newsstand sales of 400,000.

13.6 The owner of a moving company typically has his most experienced manager predict the total number of labor hours that will be required to complete an upcoming move. This approach has proved useful in the past, but he would like to be able to develop a more accurate method of predicting labor hours by using the number of cubic feet moved. In a preliminary effort to provide a more accurate method, he has collected data for 36 moves in which the origin and destination were within the borough of Manhattan in New York City and in which the travel time was an insignificant portion of the hours worked. The data are stored in the file **moving.xls**.

a. Construct a scatter plot.
b. Assuming a linear relationship, use the least-squares method to find the regression coefficients b_0 and b_1.
c. Interpret the meaning of the slope, b_1, in this problem.
d. Predict the mean labor hours for moving 500 cubic feet.

13.7 A large mail-order house believes that there is a linear relationship between the weight of the mail it receives and the number of orders to be filled. It would like to investigate the relationship in order to predict the number of orders, based on the weight of the mail. From an operational perspective, knowledge of the number of orders will help in the planning of the order-fulfillment process. A sample of 25 mail shipments is selected that range from 200 to 700 pounds. The results (stored in the file mail.xls) are as follows:

Weight of Mail (Pounds)	Orders (Thousands)	Weight of Mail (Pounds)	Orders (Thousands)
216	6.1	432	13.6
283	9.1	409	12.8
237	7.2	553	16.5
203	7.5	572	17.1
259	6.9	506	15.0
374	11.5	528	16.2
342	10.3	501	15.8
301	9.5	628	19.0
365	9.2	677	19.4
384	10.6	602	19.1
404	12.5	630	18.0
426	12.9	652	20.2
482	14.5		

a. Construct a scatter plot.
b. Assuming a linear relationship, use the least-squares method to find the regression coefficients b_0 and b_1.
c. Interpret the meaning of the slope, b_1, in this problem.
d. Predict the mean number of orders when the weight of the mail is 500 pounds.

13.8 The value of a sports franchise is directly related to the amount of revenue that a franchise can generate. The data in the file bbrevenue.xls represent the value in 2005 (in millions of dollars) and the annual revenue (in millions of dollars) for 30 baseball franchises. Suppose you want to develop a simple linear regression model to predict franchise value based on annual revenue generated.
a. Construct a scatter plot.
b. Use the least-squares method to find the regression coefficients b_0 and b_1.
c. Interpret the meaning of b_0 and b_1 in this problem.
d. Predict the mean value of a baseball franchise that generates $150 million of annual revenue.

13.9 An agent for a residential real estate company in a large city would like to be able to predict the monthly rental cost for apartments, based on the size of the apartment, as defined by square footage. A sample of 25 apartments (stored in the file rent.xls) in a particular residential neighborhood was selected, and the information gathered revealed the following:

Apartment	Monthly Rent ($)	Size (Square Feet)	Apartment	Monthly Rent ($)	Size (Square Feet)
1	950	850	14	1,800	1,369
2	1,600	1,450	15	1,400	1,175
3	1,200	1,085	16	1,450	1,225
4	1,500	1,232	17	1,100	1,245
5	950	718	18	1,700	1,259
6	1,700	1,485	19	1,200	1,150
7	1,650	1,136	20	1,150	896
8	935	726	21	1,600	1,361
9	875	700	22	1,650	1,040
10	1,150	956	23	1,200	755
11	1,400	1,100	24	800	1,000
12	1,650	1,285	25	1,750	1,200
13	2,300	1,985			

a. Construct a scatter plot.
b. Use the least-squares method to find the regression coefficients b_0 and b_1.
c. Interpret the meaning of b_0 and b_1 in this problem.
d. Predict the mean monthly rent for an apartment that has 1,000 square feet.
e. Why would it not be appropriate to use the model to predict the monthly rent for apartments that have 500 square feet?
f. Your friends Jim and Jennifer are considering signing a lease for an apartment in this residential neighborhood. They are trying to decide between two apartments, one with 1,000 square feet for a monthly rent of $1,275 and the other with 1,200 square feet for a monthly rent of $1,425. What would you recommend to them based on (a) through (d)?

13.10 The data in the file hardness.xls provide measurements on the hardness and tensile strength for 35 specimens of die-cast aluminum. It is believed that hardness (measured in Rockwell E units) can be used to predict tensile strength (measured in thousands of pounds per square inch).
a. Construct a scatter plot.
b. Assuming a linear relationship, use the least-squares method to find the regression coefficients b_0 and b_1.
c. Interpret the meaning of the slope, b_1, in this problem.
d. Predict the mean tensile strength for die-cast aluminum that has a hardness of 30 Rockwell E units.

13.3 MEASURES OF VARIATION

When using the least-squares method to determine the regression coefficients for a set of data, you need to compute three important measures of variation. The first measure, the **total sum of squares (SST)**, is a measure of variation of the Y_i values around their mean, $\bar{Y}$. In a regression analysis, the **total variation** or total sum of squares is subdivided into **explained variation** and **unexplained variation**. The explained variation or **regression sum of squares (SSR)** is due to the relationship between X and Y, and the **unexplained variation**, or **error sum of squares (SSE)** is due to factors other than the relationship between X and Y. Figure 13.6 shows these different measures of variation.

FIGURE 13.6

Measures of variation

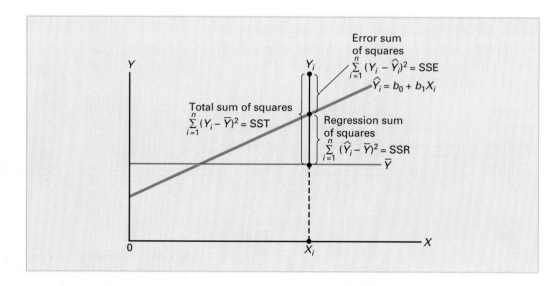

Computing the Sum of Squares

The regression sum of squares (SSR) is based on the difference between $\hat{Y}_i$ (the predicted value of Y from the prediction line) and $\bar{Y}$ (the mean value of Y). The error sum of squares (SSE) represents the part of the variation in Y that is not explained by the regression. It is based on the difference between Y_i and $\hat{Y}_i$. Equations (13.5), (13.6), (13.7), and (13.8) define these measures of variation.

MEASURES OF VARIATION IN REGRESSION

The total sum of squares is equal to the regression sum of squares plus the error sum of squares.

$$SST = SSR + SSE \qquad (13.5)$$

TOTAL SUM OF SQUARES (SST)

The total sum of squares (SST) is equal to the sum of the squared differences between each observed Y value and $\bar{Y}$, the mean value of Y.

$$SST = \text{Total sum of squares} \qquad (13.6)$$

$$= \sum_{i=1}^{n} (Y_i - \bar{Y})^2$$

REGRESSION SUM OF SQUARES (*SSR*)

The regression sum of squares (*SSR*) is equal to the sum of the squared differences between the predicted value of Y and $\overline{Y}$, the mean value of Y.

$$SSR = \text{Explained variation or regression of squares} \quad \textbf{(13.7)}$$

$$= \sum_{i=1}^{n} (\hat{Y}_i - \overline{Y})^2$$

ERROR SUM OF SQUARES (*SSE*)

The error sum of squares (*SSE*) is equal to the sum of the squared differences between the observed value of Y and the predicted value of Y.

$$SSE = \text{Unexplained variation or error sum of squares} \quad \textbf{(13.8)}$$

$$= \sum_{i=1}^{n} (Y_i - \hat{Y}_i)^2$$

Figure 13.7 shows the sum of squares area of the worksheet containing the Microsoft Excel results for the Sunflowers Apparel data. The total variation, *SST*, is equal to 116.9543. This amount is subdivided into the sum of squares explained by the regression (*SSR*), equal to 105.7476, and the sum of squares unexplained by the regression (*SSE*), equal to 11.2067. From Equation (13.5) on page 524:

$$SST = SSR + SSE$$

$$116.9543 = 105.7476 + 11.2067$$

FIGURE 13.7

Microsoft Excel sum of squares for the Sunflowers Apparel data

See Section E13.1 to create the worksheet that contains this area.

	A	B	C	D	E	F	G
10	ANOVA						
11		*df*	*SS*	*MS*	*F*	*Significance F*	
12	Regression	1	105.7476	105.7476	113.2335	0.0000	
13	Residual	12	11.2067	0.9339			
14	Total	13	116.9543				
15							
16		*Coefficients*	*Standard Error*	*t Stat*	*P-value*	*Lower 95%*	*Upper 95%*
17	Intercept	0.9645	0.5262	1.8329	0.0917	-0.1820	2.1110
18	Square Feet	1.6699	0.1569	10.6411	0.0000	1.3280	2.0118

In a data set that has a large number of significant digits, the results of a regression analysis are sometimes displayed using a numerical format known as *scientific notation*. This type of format is used to display very small or very large values. The number after the letter E represents the number of digits that the decimal point needs to be moved to the left (for a negative number) or to the right (for a positive number). For example, the number 3.7431E+02 means that the decimal point should be moved two places to the right, producing the number 374.31. The number 3.7431E-02 means that the decimal point should be moved two places to the left, producing the number 0.037431. When scientific notation is used, fewer significant digits are usually displayed, and the numbers may appear to be rounded.

The Coefficient of Determination

By themselves, SSR, SSE, and SST provide little information. However, the ratio of the regression sum of squares (SSR) to the total sum of squares (SST) measures the proportion of variation in Y that is explained by the independent variable X in the regression model. This ratio is called the **coefficient of determination**, r^2, and is defined in Equation (13.9).

COEFFICIENT OF DETERMINATION

The coefficient of determination is equal to the regression sum of squares (that is, explained variation) divided by the total sum of squares (that is, total variation).

$$r^2 = \frac{\text{Regression sum of squares}}{\text{Total sum of squares}} = \frac{SSR}{SST} \tag{13.9}$$

The coefficient of determination measures the proportion of variation in Y that is explained by the independent variable X in the regression model. For the Sunflowers Apparel data, with $SSR = 105.7476$, $SSE = 11.2067$, and $SST = 116.9543$,

$$r^2 = \frac{105.7476}{116.9543} = 0.9042$$

Therefore, 90.42% of the variation in annual sales is explained by the variability in the size of the store, as measured by the square footage. This large r^2 indicates a strong positive linear relationship between two variables because the use of a regression model has reduced the variability in predicting annual sales by 90.42%. Only 9.58% of the sample variability in annual sales is due to factors other than what is accounted for by the linear regression model that uses square footage.

Figure 13.8 presents the coefficient of determination portion of the Microsoft Excel results for the Sunflowers Apparel data.

FIGURE 13.8

Partial Microsoft Excel regression results for the Sunflowers Apparel data

See Section E13.1 to create the worksheet that contains this area.

	A	B
3	**Regression Statistics**	
4	**Multiple R**	0.9509
5	**R Square**	0.9042
6	**Adjusted R Square**	0.8962
7	**Standard Error**	S_{YX}—0.9664
8	**Observations**	14

EXAMPLE 13.4

COMPUTING THE COEFFICIENT OF DETERMINATION

Compute the coefficient of determination, r^2, for the Sunflowers Apparel data.

SOLUTION   You can compute SST, SSR, and SSE, that are defined in Equations (13.6), (13.7), and (13.8) on pages 524–525, by using Equations (13.10), (13.11), and (13.12).

COMPUTATIONAL FORMULA FOR SST

$$SST = \sum_{i=1}^{n} (Y_i - \bar{Y})^2 = \sum_{i=1}^{n} Y_i^2 - \frac{\left(\sum_{i=1}^{n} Y_i\right)^2}{n} \tag{13.10}$$

COMPUTATIONAL FORMULA FOR *SSR*

$$SSR = \sum_{i=1}^{n} (\hat{Y}_i - \overline{Y})^2 = b_0 \sum_{i=1}^{n} Y_i + b_1 \sum_{i=1}^{n} X_i Y_i - \frac{\left(\sum_{i=1}^{n} Y_i\right)^2}{n} \quad \textbf{(13.11)}$$

COMPUTATIONAL FORMULA FOR *SSE*

$$SSE = \sum_{i=1}^{n} (Y_i - \hat{Y})^2 = \sum_{i=1}^{n} Y_i^2 - b_0 \sum_{i=1}^{n} Y_i - b_1 \sum_{i=1}^{n} X_i Y_i \quad \textbf{(13.12)}$$

Using the summary results from Table 13.2 on page 520,

$$SST = \sum_{i=1}^{n} (\hat{Y}_i - \overline{Y})^2 = \sum_{i=1}^{n} Y_i^2 - \frac{\left(\sum_{i=1}^{n} Y_i\right)^2}{n}$$

$$= 594.9 - \frac{(81.8)^2}{14}$$

$$= 594.9 - 477.94571$$

$$= 116.95429$$

$$SSR = \sum_{i=1}^{n} (\hat{Y}_i - \overline{Y})^2$$

$$= b_0 \sum_{i=1}^{n} Y_i + b_1 \sum_{i=1}^{n} X_i Y_i - \frac{\left(\sum_{i=1}^{n} Y_i\right)^2}{n}$$

$$= (0.964478)(81.8) + (1.66986)(302.3) - \frac{(81.8)^2}{14}$$

$$= 105.74726$$

$$SSE = \sum_{i=1}^{n} (Y_i - \hat{Y}_i)^2$$

$$= \sum_{i=1}^{n} Y_i^2 - b_0 \sum_{i=1}^{n} Y_i - b_1 \sum_{i=1}^{n} X_i Y_i$$

$$= 594.9 - (0.964478)(81.8) - (1.66986)(302.3)$$

$$= 11.2067$$

Therefore,

$$r^2 = \frac{105.74726}{116.95429} = 0.9042$$

Standard Error of the Estimate

Although the least-squares method results in the line that fits the data with the minimum amount of error, unless all the observed data points fall on a straight line, the prediction line is not a perfect predictor. Just as all data values cannot be expected to be exactly equal to their mean, neither can they be expected to fall exactly on the prediction line. An important statistic, called the **standard error of the estimate**, measures the variability of the actual Y values from the predicted Y values in the same way that the standard deviation in Chapter 3 measures the variability of each value around the sample mean. In other words, the standard error of the estimate is the standard deviation *around* the prediction line, whereas the standard deviation in Chapter 3 is the standard deviation *around* the sample mean.

Figure 13.5 on page 517 illustrates the variability around the prediction line for the Sunflowers Apparel data. Observe that although many of the actual values of Y fall near the prediction line, none of the values are exactly on the line.

The standard error of the estimate, represented by the symbol S_{YX}, is defined in Equation (13.13).

STANDARD ERROR OF THE ESTIMATE

$$S_{YX} = \sqrt{\frac{SSE}{n-2}} = \sqrt{\frac{\sum_{i=1}^{n}(Y_i - \hat{Y}_i)^2}{n-2}} \qquad (13.13)$$

where

Y_i = actual value of Y for a given X_i

$\hat{Y}_i$ = predicted value of Y for a given X_i

SSE = error sum of squares

From Equation (13.8) and Figure 13.4 on page 516, $SSE = 11.2067$. Thus,

$$S_{YX} = \sqrt{\frac{11.2067}{14-2}} = 0.9664$$

This standard error of the estimate, equal to 0.9664 millions of dollars (that is, $966,400), is labeled Standard Error in the Microsoft Excel results shown in Figure 13.8 on page 526. The standard error of the estimate represents a measure of the variation around the prediction line. It is measured in the same units as the dependent variable Y. The interpretation of the standard error of the estimate is similar to that of the standard deviation. Just as the standard deviation measures variability around the mean, the standard error of the estimate measures variability around the prediction line. For Sunflowers Apparel, the typical difference between actual annual sales at a store and the predicted annual sales using the regression equation is approximately $966,400.

PROBLEMS FOR SECTION 13.3

Learning the Basics

 13.11 How do you interpret a coefficient of determination, r^2, equal to 0.80?

 13.12 If $SSR = 36$ and $SSE = 4$, determine SST and then compute the coefficient of determination, r^2, and interpret its meaning.

 13.13 If $SSR = 66$ and $SST = 88$, compute the coefficient of determination, r^2, and interpret its meaning.

 13.14 If $SSE = 10$ and $SSR = 30$, compute the coefficient of determination, r^2, and interpret its meaning.

13.15 If *SSR* = 120, why is it impossible for *SST* to equal 110?

Applying the Concepts

 13.16 In Problem 13.4 on page 522, the marketing manager used shelf space for pet food to predict weekly sales (stored in the file **petfood.xls**). For that data, *SSR* = 20,535 and *SST* = 30,025.
a. Determine the coefficient of determination, r^2, and interpret its meaning.
b. Determine the standard error of the estimate.
c. How useful do you think this regression model is for predicting sales?

13.17 In Problem 13.5 on page 522, you used reported magazine newsstand sales to predict audited sales (stored in the file **circulation.xls**). For that data, *SSR* = 130,301.41 and *SST* = 144,538.64.
a. Determine the coefficient of determination, r^2, and interpret its meaning.
b. Determine the standard error of the estimate.
c. How useful do you think this regression model is for predicting audited sales?

13.18 In Problem 13.6 on page 522, an owner of a moving company wanted to predict labor hours, based on the cubic feet moved (stored in the file **moving.xls**). Using the results of that problem,
a. determine the coefficient of determination, r^2, and interpret its meaning.
b. determine the standard error of the estimate.
c. How useful do you think this regression model is for predicting labor hours?

13.19 In Problem 13.7 on page 523, you used the weight of mail to predict the number of orders received (stored in the file **mail.xls**). Using the results of that problem,
a. determine the coefficient of determination, r^2, and interpret its meaning.
b. find the standard error of the estimate.
c. How useful do you think this regression model is for predicting the number of orders?

13.20 In Problem 13.8 on page 523, you used annual revenues to predict the value of a baseball franchise (stored in the file **bbrevenue.xls**). Using the results of that problem,
a. determine the coefficient of determination, r^2, and interpret its meaning.
b. determine the standard error of the estimate.
c. How useful do you think this regression model is for predicting the value of a baseball franchise?

13.21 In Problem 13.9 on page 523, an agent for a real estate company wanted to predict the monthly rent for apartments, based on the size of the apartment (stored in the file **rent.xls**). Using the results of that problem,
a. determine the coefficient of determination, r^2, and interpret its meaning.
b. determine the standard error of the estimate.
c. How useful do you think this regression model is for predicting the monthly rent?

13.22 In Problem 13.10 on page 523, you used hardness to predict the tensile strength of die-cast aluminum (stored in the file **hardness.xls**). Using the results of that problem,
a. determine the coefficient of determination, r^2, and interpret its meaning.
b. find the standard error of the estimate.
c. How useful do you think this regression model is for predicting the tensile strength of die-cast aluminum?

13.4 ASSUMPTIONS

The discussion of hypothesis testing and the analysis of variance emphasized the importance of the assumptions to the validity of any conclusions reached. The assumptions necessary for regression are similar to those of the analysis of variance because both topics fall in the general category of *linear models* (reference 4).

The four **assumptions of regression** (known by the acronym LINE) are as follows:

- **Linearity**
- **Independence of errors**
- **Normality of error**
- **Equal variance**

The first assumption, linearity, states that the relationship between variables is linear. Relationships between variables that are not linear are discussed in Chapter 15.

The second assumption, **independence of errors**, requires that the errors (ε_i) are independent of one another. This assumption is particularly important when data are collected over a period of time. In such situations, the errors for a specific time period are sometimes correlated with those of the previous time period.

The third assumption, **normality**, requires that the errors (ε_i) are normally distributed at each value of X. Like the t test and the ANOVA F test, regression analysis is fairly robust against departures from the normality assumption. As long as the distribution of the errors at each level of X is not extremely different from a normal distribution, inferences about β_0 and β_1 are not seriously affected.

The fourth assumption, **equal variance** or **homoscedasticity**, requires that the variance of the errors (ε_i) are constant for all values of X. In other words, the variability of Y values is the same when X is a low value as when X is a high value. The equal variance assumption is important when making inferences about β_0 and β_1. If there are serious departures from this assumption, you can use either data transformations or weighted least-squares methods (see reference 4).

13.5   RESIDUAL ANALYSIS

In Section 13.1, regression analysis was introduced. In Sections 13.2 and 13.3, a regression model was developed using the least-squares approach for the Sunflowers Apparel data. Is this the correct model for these data? Are the assumptions introduced in Section 13.4 valid? In this section, a graphical approach called **residual analysis** is used to evaluate the assumptions and determine whether the regression model selected is an appropriate model.

The **residual** or estimated error value, e_i, is the difference between the observed (Y_i) and predicted ($\hat{Y}_i$) values of the dependent variable for a given value of X_i. Graphically, a residual appears on a scatter plot as the vertical distance between an observed value of Y and the prediction line. Equation (13.14) defines the residual.

RESIDUAL

The residual is equal to the difference between the observed value of Y and the predicted value of Y.

$$e_i = Y_i - \hat{Y}_i \qquad \textbf{(13.14)}$$

Evaluating the Assumptions

Recall from Section 13.4 that the four assumptions of regression (known by the acronym LINE) are linearity, independence, normality, and equal variance.

Linearity   To evaluate linearity, you plot the residuals on the vertical axis against the corresponding X_i values of the independent variable on the horizontal axis. If the linear model is appropriate for the data, there is no apparent pattern in this plot. However, if the linear model is not appropriate, there is a relationship between the X_i values and the residuals, e_i. You can see such a pattern in Figure 13.9. Panel A shows a situation in which, although there is an increasing trend in Y as X increases, the relationship seems curvilinear because the upward trend decreases for increasing values of X. This quadratic effect is highlighted in Panel B, where there is a clear relationship between X_i and e_i. By plotting the residuals, the linear trend of X with Y has been removed, thereby exposing the lack of fit in the simple linear model. Thus, a quadratic model is a better fit and should be used in place of the simple linear model. (See Section 15.1 for further discussion of fitting quadratic models.)

To determine whether the simple linear regression model is appropriate, return to the evaluation of the Sunflowers Apparel data. Figure 13.10 provides the predicted and residual values of the response variable (annual sales) computed by Microsoft Excel.

FIGURE 13.9
Studying the appropriateness of the simple linear regression model

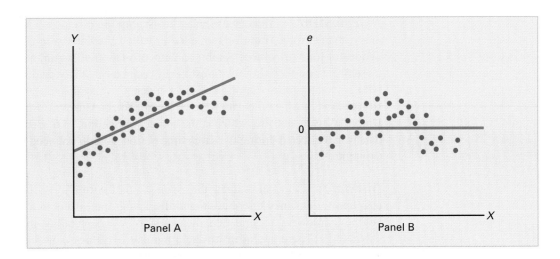

Panel A   Panel B

FIGURE 13.10
Microsoft Excel residual statistics for the Sunflowers Apparel data

See Section E13.3 to create the worksheet that contains this area.

	A	B	C
22	**RESIDUAL OUTPUT**		
23			
24	*Observation*	*Predicted Annual Sales*	*Residuals*
25	1	3.803239598	-0.103239598
26	2	3.636253367	0.263746633
27	3	5.640088147	1.059911853
28	4	10.31570263	-0.815702635
29	5	3.135294672	0.264705328
30	6	4.638170757	0.961829243
31	7	3.135294672	0.564705328
32	8	2.801322208	-0.101322208
33	9	6.308033074	-0.808033074
34	10	3.469267135	-0.569267135
35	11	9.647757708	1.052242292
36	12	8.645840318	-1.045840318
37	13	10.6496751	1.150324902
38	14	5.974060611	-1.874060611

To assess linearity, the residuals are plotted against the independent variable (store size, in thousands of square feet) in Figure 13.11. Although there is widespread scatter in the residual plot, there is no apparent pattern or relationship between the residuals and X_i. The residuals appear to be evenly spread above and below 0 for the differing values of X. You can conclude that the linear model is appropriate for the Sunflowers Apparel data.

FIGURE 13.11
Microsoft Excel plot of residuals against the square footage of a store for the Sunflowers Apparel data

See Section E2.12 to create this.

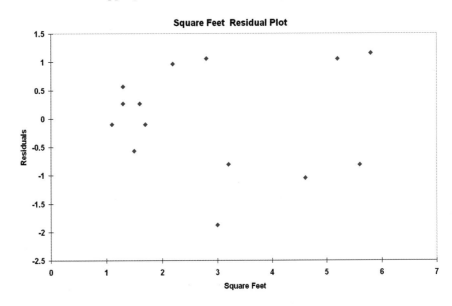

Independence You can evaluate the assumption of independence of the errors by plotting the residuals in the order or sequence in which the data were collected. Data collected over periods of time sometimes exhibit an autocorrelation effect among successive observations. In these instances, there is a relationship between consecutive residuals. If this relationship exists (which violates the assumption of independence), it is apparent in the plot of the residuals versus the time in which the data were collected. You can also test for autocorrelation by using the Durbin-Watson statistic, which is the subject of Section 13.6. Because the Sunflowers Apparel data were collected during the same time period, you do not need to evaluate the independence assumption.

Normality You can evaluate the assumption of normality in the errors by tallying the residuals into a frequency distribution and displaying the results in a histogram (see Section 2.3). For the Sunflowers Apparel data, the residuals have been tallied into a frequency distribution in Table 13.3. (There are an insufficient number of values, however, to construct a histogram.) You can also evaluate the normality assumption by comparing the actual versus theoretical values of the residuals or by constructing a normal probability plot of the residuals (see Section 6.3). Figure 13.12 is a normal probability plot of the residuals for the Sunflower Apparel data.

TABLE 13.3

Frequency Distribution of 14 Residual Values for the Sunflowers Apparel Data

Residuals	Frequency
−2.25 but less than −1.75	1
−1.75 but less than −1.25	0
−1.25 but less than −0.75	3
−0.75 but less than −0.25	1
−0.25 but less than +0.25	2
+0.25 but less than +0.75	3
+0.75 but less than +1.25	4
	14

FIGURE 13.12

Microsoft Excel normal probability plot of the residuals for the Sunflowers Apparel data

See Section E6.2 to create this.

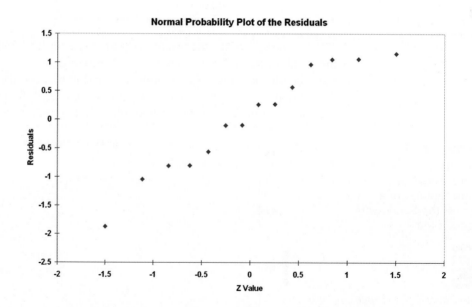

It is difficult to evaluate the normality assumption for a sample of only 14 values, regardless of whether you use a histogram, stem-and-leaf display, box-and-whisker plot, or normal probability plot. You can see from Figure 13.12 that the data do not appear to depart substantially from a normal distribution. The robustness of regression analysis with modest departures from normality enables you to conclude that you should not be overly concerned about departures from this normality assumption in the Sunflowers Apparel data.

Equal Variance   You can evaluate the assumption of equal variance from a plot of the residuals with X_i. For the Sunflowers Apparel data of Figure 13.11 on page 531, there do not appear to be major differences in the variability of the residuals for different X_i values. Thus, you can conclude that there is no apparent violation in the assumption of equal variance at each level of X.

To examine a case in which the equal variance assumption is violated, observe Figure 13.13, which is a plot of the residuals with X_i for a hypothetical set of data. In this plot, the variability of the residuals increases dramatically as X increases, demonstrating the lack of homogeneity in the variances of Y_i at each level of X. For these data, the equal variance assumption is invalid.

FIGURE 13.13

Violation of equal variance

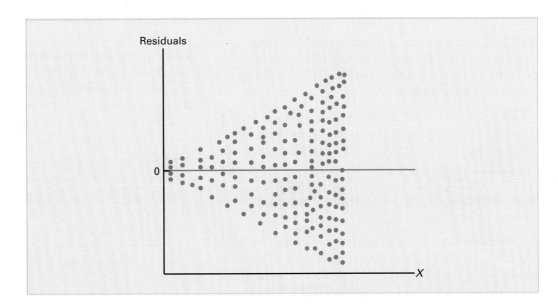

PROBLEMS FOR SECTION 13.5

Learning the Basics

13.23 The results below provide the X values, residuals, and a residual plot from a regression analysis:

X	Residuals
1	0.70
2	-0.78
3	1.03
4	0.33
5	2.39
6	-0.67
7	0.16
8	1.65
9	-1.19
10	0.84
11	0.29
12	-1.28
13	1.21
14	-0.37
15	1.02
16	-0.16
17	1.42
18	-0.71
19	-0.63
20	0.67

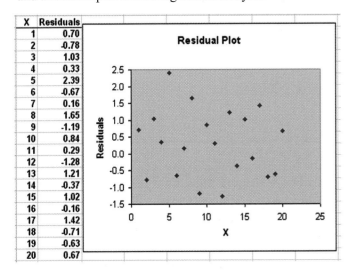

Is there any evidence of a pattern in the residuals? Explain.

13.24 The results below show the X values, residuals, and a residual plot from a regression analysis:

X	Residuals
1	0.70
2	1.58
3	1.03
4	0.33
5	-0.39
6	-0.67
7	-0.56
8	-0.65
9	-1.19
10	-0.84
11	-0.29
12	-1.28
13	-0.21
14	-0.37
15	0.22
16	-0.16
17	0.82

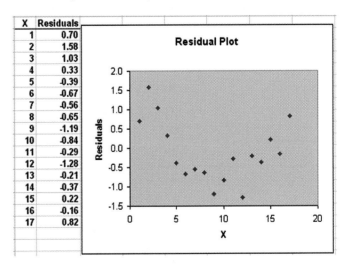

Is there any evidence of a pattern in the residuals? Explain.

Applying the Concepts

13.25 In Problem 13.5 on page 522, you used reported magazine newsstand sales to predict audited sales. The data are stored in the file `circulation.xls`. Perform a residual analysis for these data.
a. Determine the adequacy of the fit of the model.
b. Evaluate whether the assumptions of regression have been seriously violated.

 13.26 In Problem 13.4 on page 522, the marketing manager used shelf space for pet food to predict weekly sales. The data are stored in the file `petfood.xls`. Perform a residual analysis for these data.
a. Determine the adequacy of the fit of the model.
b. Evaluate whether the assumptions of regression have been seriously violated.

13.27 In Problem 13.7 on page 523, you used the weight of mail to predict the number of orders received. Perform a residual analysis for these data. The data are stored in the file `mail.xls`. Based on these results,
a. determine the adequacy of the fit of the model.
b. evaluate whether the assumptions of regression have been seriously violated.

13.28 In Problem 13.6 on page 522, the owner of a moving company wanted to predict labor hours based on the cubic feet moved. Perform a residual analysis for these data. The data are stored in the file `moving.xls`. Based on these results,
a. determine the adequacy of the fit of the model.
b. evaluate whether the assumptions of regression have been seriously violated.

13.29 In Problem 13.9 on page 523, an agent for a real estate company wanted to predict the monthly rent for apartments, based on the size of the apartments. Perform a residual analysis for these data. The data are stored in the file `rent.xls`. Based on these results,
a. determine the adequacy of the fit of the model.
b. evaluate whether the assumptions of regression have been seriously violated.

13.30 In Problem 13.8 on page 523, you used annual revenues to predict the value of a baseball franchise. The data are stored in the file `bbrevenue.xls`. Perform a residual analysis for these data. Based on these results,
a. determine the adequacy of the fit of the model.
b. evaluate whether the assumptions of regression have been seriously violated.

13.31 In Problem 13.10 on page 523, you used hardness to predict the tensile strength of die-cast aluminum. The data are stored in the file `hardness.xls`. Perform a residual analysis for these data. Based on these results,
a. determine the adequacy of the fit of the model.
b. evaluate whether the assumptions of regression have been seriously violated.

13.6 MEASURING AUTOCORRELATION: THE DURBIN-WATSON STATISTIC

One of the basic assumptions of the regression model is the independence of the errors. This assumption is sometimes violated when data are collected over sequential time periods because a residual at any one time period may tend to be similar to residuals at adjacent time periods. This pattern in the residuals is called **autocorrelation**. When a set of data has substantial autocorrelation, the validity of a regression model can be in serious doubt.

Residual Plots to Detect Autocorrelation

As mentioned in Section 13.5, one way to detect autocorrelation is to plot the residuals in time order. If a positive autocorrelation effect is present, there will be clusters of residuals with the same sign, and you will readily detect an apparent pattern. If negative autocorrelation exists, residuals will tend to jump back and forth from positive to negative to positive, and so on. This type of pattern is very rarely seen in regression analysis. Thus, the focus of this section is on positive autocorrelation. To illustrate positive autocorrelation, consider the following example.

The manager of a package delivery store wants to predict weekly sales, based on the number of customers making purchases for a period of 15 weeks. In this situation, because data are collected over a period of 15 consecutive weeks at the same store, you need to determine whether autocorrelation is present. Table 13.4 presents the data (stored in the file `custsale.xls`). Figure 13.14 illustrates Microsoft Excel results for these data.

TABLE 13.4

Customers and Sales for a Period of 15 Consecutive Weeks

Week	Customers	Sales (Thousands of Dollars)	Week	Customers	Sales (Thousands of Dollars)
1	794	9.33	9	880	12.07
2	799	8.26	10	905	12.55
3	837	7.48	11	886	11.92
4	855	9.08	12	843	10.27
5	845	9.83	13	904	11.80
6	844	10.09	14	950	12.15
7	863	11.01	15	841	9.64
8	875	11.49			

FIGURE 13.14

Microsoft Excel results for the package delivery store data of Table 13.4

See Section E13.1 to create this.

From Figure 13.14, observe that r^2 is 0.6574, indicating that 65.74% of the variation in sales is explained by variation in the number of customers. In addition, the Y intercept, b_0, is -16.0322, and the slope, b_1, is 0.0308. However, before using this model for prediction, you must undertake proper analyses of the residuals. Because the data have been collected over a consecutive period of 15 weeks, in addition to checking the linearity, normality, and equal-variance assumptions, you must investigate the independence-of-errors assumption. You can plot the residuals versus time to help you see whether a pattern exists. In Figure 13.15, you can see that the residuals tend to fluctuate up and down in a cyclical pattern. This cyclical pattern provides strong cause for concern about the autocorrelation of the residuals and, hence, a violation of the independence-of-errors assumption.

FIGURE 13.15

Microsoft Excel residual plot for the package delivery store data of Table 13.4

See Section E13.3 to create this.

The Durbin-Watson Statistic

The **Durbin-Watson statistic** is used to measure autocorrelation. This statistic measures the correlation between each residual and the residual for the time period immediately preceding the one of interest. Equation (13.15) defines the Durbin-Watson statistic.

DURBIN-WATSON STATISTIC

$$D = \frac{\sum_{i=2}^{n} (e_i - e_{i-1})^2}{\sum_{i=1}^{n} e_i^2} \qquad (13.15)$$

where

$$e_i = \text{residual at the time period } i$$

To better understand the Durbin-Watson statistic, D, you can examine Equation (13.15). The numerator, $\sum_{i=2}^{n} (e_i - e_{i-1})^2$, represents the squared difference between two successive residuals, summed from the second value to the nth value. The denominator, $\sum_{i=1}^{n} e_i^2$, represents the sum of the squared residuals. When successive residuals are positively autocorrelated, the value of D approaches 0. If the residuals are not correlated, the value of D will be close to 2. (If there is negative autocorrelation, D will be greater than 2 and could even approach its maximum value of 4.) For the package delivery store data, as shown in the Microsoft Excel results of Figure 13.16, the Durbin-Watson statistic, D, is 0.8830.

FIGURE 13.16

Microsoft Excel results of the Durbin-Watson statistic for the package delivery store data

See Section E13.4 to create this.

	A	B	
1	**Durbin-Watson Calculations**		
2			
3	Sum of Squared Difference of Residuals	10.0575	
4	Sum of Squared Residuals	11.3901	
5			
6	**Durbin-Watson Statistic**	0.8830	=B3/B4

You need to determine when the autocorrelation is large enough to make the Durbin-Watson statistic, D, fall sufficiently below 2 to conclude that there is significant positive autocorrelation. After computing D, you compare it to the critical values of the Durbin-Watson statistic found in Table E.10, a portion of which is presented in Table 13.5. The critical values depend on α, the significance level chosen, n, the sample size, and k, the number of independent variables in the model (in simple linear regression, $k = 1$).

TABLE 13.5

Finding Critical Values of the Durbin-Watson Statistic

						$\alpha = .05$					
	$k = 1$		$k = 2$		$k = 3$		$k = 4$		$k = 5$	
n	d_L	d_U	d_L	d_U	d_L	d_U	d_L	d_U	d_L	d_U
15	1.08	1.36	.95	1.54	.82	1.75	.69	1.97	.56	2.21
16	1.10	1.37	.98	1.54	.86	1.73	.74	1.93	.62	2.15
17	1.13	1.38	1.02	1.54	.90	1.71	.78	1.90	.67	2.10
18	1.16	1.39	1.05	1.53	.93	1.69	.82	1.87	.71	2.06

In Table 13.5, two values are shown for each combination of α (level of significance), n (sample size), and k (number of independent variables in the model). The first value, d_L, represents the lower critical value. If D is below d_L, you conclude that there is evidence of positive autocorrelation among the residuals. If this occurs, the least-squares method used in this chapter is inappropriate, and you should use alternative methods (see reference 4). The second value, d_U, represents the upper critical value of D, above which you would conclude that there is no evidence of positive autocorrelation among the residuals. If D is between d_L and d_U, you are unable to arrive at a definite conclusion.

For the package delivery store data, with one independent variable ($k = 1$) and 15 values ($n = 15$), $d_L = 1.08$ and $d_U = 1.36$. Because $D = 0.8830 < 1.08$, you conclude that there is positive autocorrelation among the residuals. The least-squares regression analysis of the data is inappropriate because of the presence of significant positive autocorrelation among the residuals. In other words, the independence-of-errors assumption is invalid. You need to use alternative approaches discussed in reference 4.

PROBLEMS FOR SECTION 13.6

Learning the Basics

 13.32 The residuals for 10 consecutive time periods are as follows:

Time Period	Residual	Time Period	Residual
1	−5	6	+1
2	−4	7	+2
3	−3	8	+3
4	−2	9	+4
5	−1	10	+5

a. Plot the residuals over time. What conclusion can you reach about the pattern of the residuals over time?
b. Based on (a), what conclusion can you reach about the autocorrelation of the residuals?

 13.33 The residuals for 15 consecutive time periods are as follows:

Time Period	Residual	Time Period	Residual
1	+4	9	+6
2	−6	10	−3
3	−1	11	+1
4	−5	12	+3
5	+2	13	0
6	+5	14	−4
7	−2	15	−7
8	+7		

a. Plot the residuals over time. What conclusion can you reach about the pattern of the residuals over time?

b. Compute the Durbin-Watson statistic. At the 0.05 level of significance, is there evidence of positive autocorrelation among the residuals?
c. Based on (a) and (b), what conclusion can you reach about the autocorrelation of the residuals?

Applying the Concepts

 13.34 In Problem 13.4 on page 522 concerning pet food sales, the marketing manager used shelf space for pet food to predict weekly sales.
a. Is it necessary to compute the Durbin-Watson statistic in this case? Explain.
b. Under what circumstances is it necessary to compute the Durbin-Watson statistic before proceeding with the least-squares method of regression analysis?

13.35 The owner of a single-family home in a suburban county in the northeastern United States would like to develop a model to predict electricity consumption in his all-electric house (lights, fans, heat, appliances, and so on), based on average atmospheric temperature (in degrees Fahrenheit). Monthly kilowatt usage and temperature data are available for a period of 24 consecutive months in the file elecuse.xls.
a. Assuming a linear relationship, use the least-squares method to find the regression coefficients b_0 and b_1.
b. Predict the mean kilowatt usage when the average atmospheric temperature is 50° Fahrenheit.
c. Plot the residuals versus the time period.
d. Compute the Durbin-Watson statistic. At the 0.05 level of significance, is there evidence of positive autocorrelation among the residuals?
e. Based on the results of (c) and (d), is there reason to question the validity of the model?

13.36 A mail-order catalog business that sells personal computer supplies, software, and hardware maintains a centralized warehouse for the distribution of products ordered. Management is currently examining the process of distribution from the warehouse and is interested in studying the factors that affect warehouse distribution costs. Currently, a small handling fee is added to the order, regardless of the amount of the order. Data have been collected over the past 24 months, indicating the warehouse distribution costs and the number of orders received. They are stored in the file warecost.xls. The results are as follows:

Months	Distribution Cost (Thousands of Dollars)	Number of Orders
1	52.95	4,015
2	71.66	3,806
3	85.58	5,309
4	63.69	4,262
5	72.81	4,296
6	68.44	4,097
7	52.46	3,213
8	70.77	4,809
9	82.03	5,237
10	74.39	4,732
11	70.84	4,413
12	54.08	2,921
13	62.98	3,977
14	72.30	4,428
15	58.99	3,964
16	79.38	4,582
17	94.44	5,582
18	59.74	3,450
19	90.50	5,079
20	93.24	5,735
21	69.33	4,269
22	53.71	3,708
23	89.18	5,387
24	66.80	4,161

a. Assuming a linear relationship, use the least-squares method to find the regression coefficients b_0 and b_1.
b. Predict the monthly warehouse distribution costs when the number of orders is 4,500.
c. Plot the residuals versus the time period.
d. Compute the Durbin-Watson statistic. At the 0.05 level of significance, is there evidence of positive autocorrelation among the residuals?
e. Based on the results of (c) and (d), is there reason to question the validity of the model?

13.37 A freshly brewed shot of espresso has three distinct components: the heart, body, and crema. The separation of these three components typically lasts only 10 to 20 seconds.

To use the espresso shot in making a latte, cappuccino, or other drinks, the shot must be poured into the beverage during the separation of the heart, body, and crema. If the shot is used after the separation occurs, the drink becomes excessively bitter and acidic, ruining the final drink. Thus, a longer separation time allows the drink-maker more time to pour the shot and ensure that the beverage will meet expectations. An employee at a coffee shop hypothesized that the harder the espresso grounds were tamped down into the portafilter before brewing, the longer the separation time would be. An experiment using 24 observations was conducted to test this relationship. The independent variable Tamp measures the distance, in inches, between the espresso grounds and the top of the portafilter (that is, the harder the tamp, the larger the distance). The dependent variable Time is the number of seconds the heart, body, and crema are separated (that is, the amount of time after the shot is poured before it must be used for the customer's beverage). The data are stored in the file espresso.xls:

Shot	Tamp	Time	Shot	Tamp	Time
1	0.20	14	13	0.50	18
2	0.50	14	14	0.50	13
3	0.50	18	15	0.35	19
4	0.20	16	16	0.35	19
5	0.20	16	17	0.20	17
6	0.50	13	18	0.20	18
7	0.20	12	19	0.20	15
8	0.35	15	20	0.20	16
9	0.50	9	21	0.35	18
10	0.35	15	22	0.35	16
11	0.50	11	23	0.35	14
12	0.50	16	24	0.35	16

a. Determine the prediction line, using Time as the dependent variable and Tamp as the independent variable.
b. Predict the mean separation time for a Tamp distance of 0.50 inch.
c. Plot the residuals versus the time order of experimentation. Are there any noticeable patterns?
d. Compute the Durbin-Watson statistic. At the 0.05 level of significance, is there evidence of positive autocorrelation among the residuals?
e. Based on the results of (c) and (d), is there reason to question the validity of the model?

13.38 The owner of a chain of ice cream stores would like to study the effect of atmospheric temperature on sales during the summer season. A sample of 21 consecutive days is selected, with the results stored in the data file icecream.xls.

(**Hint:** Determine which are the independent and dependent variables.)

a. Assuming a linear relationship, use the least-squares method to find the regression coefficients b_0 and b_1.
b. Predict the sales per store for a day in which the temperature is 83°F.
c. Plot the residuals versus the time period.

d. Compute the Durbin-Watson statistic. At the 0.05 level of significance, is there evidence of positive autocorrelation among the residuals?
e. Based on the results of (c) and (d), is there reason to question the validity of the model?

13.7   INFERENCES ABOUT THE SLOPE AND CORRELATION COEFFICIENT

In Sections 13.1 through 13.3, regression was used solely for descriptive purposes. You learned how the least-squares method determines the regression coefficients and how to predict Y for a given value of X. In addition, you learned how to compute and interpret the standard error of the estimate and the coefficient of determination.

When residual analysis, as discussed in Section 13.5, indicates that the assumptions of a least-squares regression model are not seriously violated and that the straight-line model is appropriate, you can make inferences about the linear relationship between the variables in the population.

t Test for the Slope

To determine the existence of a significant linear relationship between the X and Y variables, you test whether β_1 (the population slope) is equal to 0. The null and alternative hypotheses are as follows:

$$H_0: \beta_1 = 0 \text{ (There is no linear relationship.)}$$
$$H_1: \beta_1 \neq 0 \text{ (There is a linear relationship.)}$$

If you reject the null hypothesis, you conclude that there is evidence of a linear relationship. Equation (13.16) defines the test statistic.

TESTING A HYPOTHESIS FOR A POPULATION SLOPE, β_1, USING THE t TEST

The t statistic equals the difference between the sample slope and hypothesized value of the population slope divided by the standard error of the slope.

$$t = \frac{b_1 - \beta_1}{S_{b_1}} \tag{13.16}$$

where

$$S_{b_1} = \frac{S_{YX}}{\sqrt{SSX}}$$

$$SSX = \sum_{i=1}^{n} (X_i - \bar{X})^2$$

The test statistic t follows a t distribution with $n - 2$ degrees of freedom.

Return to the Using Statistics scenario concerning Sunflowers Apparel. To test whether there is a significant linear relationship between the size of the store and the annual sales at the 0.05 level of significance, refer to the Microsoft Excel worksheet for the t test presented in Figure 13.17.

FIGURE 13.17

Microsoft Excel *t* test for the slope for the Sunflowers Apparel data

	A	B	C	D	E	F	G
15							
16		Coefficients	Standard Error	t Stat	P-value	Lower 95%	Upper 95%
17	Intercept	0.9645	0.5262	1.8329	0.0917	-0.1820	2.1110
18	Square Feet	1.6699	0.1569	10.6411	0.0000	1.3280	2.0118

From Figure 13.17,

$$b_1 = +1.6699 \quad n = 14 \quad S_{b_1} = 0.1569$$

and

$$t = \frac{b_1 - \beta_1}{S_{b_1}}$$

$$= \frac{1.6699 - 0}{0.1569} = 10.6411$$

Microsoft Excel labels this *t* statistic *t* Stat (see Figure 13.17). Using the 0.05 level of significance, the critical value of *t* with $n - 2 = 12$ degrees of freedom is 2.1788. Because $t = 10.6411 > 2.1788$, you reject H_0 (see Figure 13.18). Using the *p*-value, you reject H_0 because the *p*-value is approximately 0 which is less than $\alpha = 0.05$. Hence, you can conclude that there is a significant linear relationship between mean annual sales and the size of the store.

FIGURE 13.18

Testing a hypothesis about the population slope at the 0.05 level of significance, with 12 degrees of freedom

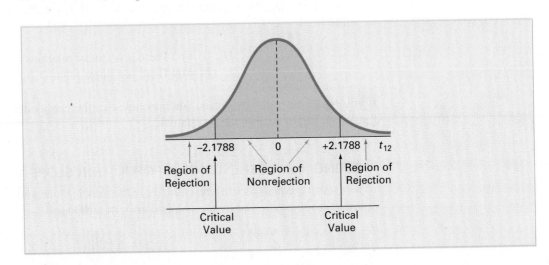

F Test for the Slope

As an alternative to the *t* test, you can use an *F* test to determine whether the slope in simple linear regression is statistically significant. In Section 10.4, you used the *F* distribution to test the ratio of two variances. Equation (13.17) defines the *F* test for the slope as the ratio of the variance that is due to the regression (*MSR*) divided by the error variance ($MSE = S_{YX}^2$).

TESTING A HYPOTHESIS FOR A POPULATION SLOPE, β_1, USING THE F TEST

The *F* statistic is equal to the regression mean square (*MSR*) divided by the error mean square (*MSE*).

$$F = \frac{MSR}{MSE} \qquad (13.17)$$

where

$$MSR = \frac{SSR}{k}$$

$$MSE = \frac{SSE}{n - k - 1}$$

k = number of independent variables in the regression model

The test statistic F follows an F distribution with k and $n - k - 1$ degrees of freedom.

Using a level of significance α, the decision rule is

$$\text{Reject } H_0 \text{ if } F > F_U;$$

otherwise, do not reject H_0.

Table 13.6 organizes the complete set of results into an ANOVA table.

TABLE 13.6
ANOVA Table for Testing the Significance of a Regression Coefficient

Source	df	Sum of Squares	Mean Square (Variance)	F
Regression	k	SSR	$MSR = \dfrac{SSR}{k}$	$F = \dfrac{MSR}{MSE}$
Error	$n - k - 1$	SSE	$MSE = \dfrac{SSE}{n - k - 1}$	
Total	$n - 1$	SST		

The completed ANOVA table is also part of the Microsoft Excel results shown in Figure 13.19. Figure 13.19 shows that the computed F statistic is 113.2335 and the p-value is approximately 0.

FIGURE 13.19
Microsoft Excel F test for the Sunflowers Apparel data

	A	B	C	D	E	F
10	ANOVA					
11		df	SS	MS	F	Significance F
12	Regression	1	105.7476	105.7476	113.2335	0.0000
13	Residual	12	11.2067	0.9339		
14	Total	13	116.9543			

See Section E13.1 to create the worksheet that contains this area.

Using a level of significance of 0.05, from Table E.5, the critical value of the F distribution, with 1 and 12 degrees of freedom, is 4.75 (see Figure 13.20). Because $F = 113.2335 > 4.75$ or because the p-value $= 0.0000 < 0.05$, you reject H_0 and conclude that the size of the store is significantly related to annual sales. Because the F test in Equation 13.17 on page 540 is equivalent to the t test on page 539, you reach the same conclusion.

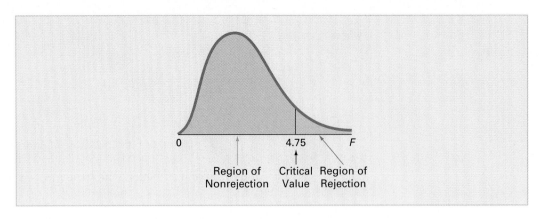

Confidence Interval Estimate of the Slope (β_1)

As an alternative to testing for the existence of a linear relationship between the variables, you can construct a confidence interval estimate of β_1 and determine whether the hypothesized value ($\beta_1 = 0$) is included in the interval. Equation (13.18) defines the confidence interval estimate of β_1.

> **CONFIDENCE INTERVAL ESTIMATE OF THE SLOPE, β_1**
>
> The confidence interval estimate for the slope can be constructed by taking the sample slope, b_1, and adding and subtracting the critical t value multiplied by the standard error of the slope.
>
> $$b_1 \pm t_{n-2}S_{b_1} \qquad\qquad (13.18)$$

From the Microsoft Excel results of Figure 13.17 on page 540,

$$b_1 = 1.6699 \quad n = 14 \quad S_{b_1} = 0.1569$$

To construct a 95% confidence interval estimate, $\alpha/2 = 0.025$, and from Table E.3, $t_{12} = 2.1788$. Thus,

$$b_1 \pm t_{n-2}S_{b_1} = 1.6699 \pm (2.1788)(0.1569)$$

$$= 1.6699 \pm 0.3419$$

$$1.3280 \leq \beta_1 \leq 2.0118$$

Therefore, you estimate with 95% confidence that the population slope is between 1.3280 and 2.0118. Because these values are above 0, you conclude that there is a significant linear relationship between annual sales and the size of the store. Had the interval included 0, you would have concluded that no significant relationship exists between the variables. The confidence interval indicates that for each increase of 1,000 square feet, mean annual sales are estimated to increase by at least $1,328,000 but no more than $2,011,800.

t Test for the Correlation Coefficient

In Section 3.5 on page 130, the strength of the relationship between two numerical variables was measured, using the **correlation coefficient**, r. You can use the correlation coefficient to determine whether there is a statistically significant linear relationship between X and Y. To do so, you hypothesize that the population correlation coefficient, ρ, is 0. Thus, the null and alternative hypotheses are

$$H_0: \rho = 0 \text{ (no correlation)}$$
$$H_1: \rho \neq 0 \text{ (correlation)}$$

Equation (13.19) defines the test statistic for determining the existence of a significant correlation.

TESTING FOR THE EXISTENCE OF CORRELATION

$$t = \frac{r - \rho}{\sqrt{\dfrac{1 - r^2}{n - 2}}} \qquad (13.19)$$

where

$$r = +\sqrt{r^2} \text{ if } b_1 > 0$$
$$r = -\sqrt{r^2} \text{ if } b_1 < 0$$

The test statistic t follows a t distribution with $n - 2$ degrees of freedom.

In the Sunflowers Apparel problem, $r^2 = 0.9042$ and $b_1 = +1.6699$ (see Figure 13.4 on page 516). Because $b_1 > 0$, the correlation coefficient for annual sales and store size is the positive square root of r^2, that is, $r^2 = +\sqrt{0.9042} = +0.9509$. Testing the null hypothesis that there is no correlation between these two variables results in the following observed t statistic:

$$t = \frac{r - 0}{\sqrt{\dfrac{1 - r^2}{n - 2}}}$$

$$= \frac{0.9509 - 0}{\sqrt{\dfrac{1 - (0.9509)^2}{14 - 2}}} = 10.6411$$

Using the 0.05 level of significance, because $t = 10.6411 > 2.1788$, you reject the null hypothesis. You conclude that there is evidence of an association between annual sales and store size. This t statistic is equivalent to the t statistic found when testing whether the population slope, β_1, is equal to zero (see Figure 13.17 on page 540).

When inferences concerning the population slope were discussed, confidence intervals and tests of hypothesis were used interchangeably. However, developing a confidence interval for the correlation coefficient is more complicated because the shape of the sampling distribution of the statistic r varies for different values of the population correlation coefficient. Methods for developing a confidence interval estimate for the correlation coefficient are presented in reference 4.

PROBLEMS FOR SECTION 13.7

Learning the Basics

13.39 You are testing the null hypothesis that there is no linear relationship between two variables, X and Y. From your sample of $n = 10$, you determine that $r = 0.80$.

a. What is the value of the t test statistic?

b. At the $\alpha = 0.05$ level of significance, what are the critical values?

c. Based on your answers to (a) and (b), what statistical decision should you make?

13.40 You are testing the null hypothesis that there is no relationship between two variables, X and Y. From your sample of $n = 18$, you determine that $b_1 = +4.5$ and $S_{b_1} = 1.5$.

a. What is the value of the t test statistic?

b. At the $\alpha = 0.05$ level of significance, what are the critical values?

c. Based on your answers to (a) and (b), what statistical decision should you make?

d. Construct a 95% confidence interval estimate of the population slope, β_1.

 13.41 You are testing the null hypothesis that there is no relationship between two variables, X and Y. From your sample of $n = 20$, you determine that $SSR = 60$ and $SSE = 40$.

a. What is the value of the F test statistic?

b. At the $\alpha = 0.05$ level of significance, what is the critical value?

c. Based on your answers to (a) and (b), what statistical decision should you make?

d. Compute the correlation coefficient by first computing r^2 and assuming that b_1 is negative.

e. At the 0.05 level of significance, is there a significant correlation between X and Y?

Applying the Concepts

 13.42 In Problem 13.4 on page 522, the marketing manager used shelf space for pet food to predict weekly sales. The data are stored in the file **petfood.xls**. From the results of that problem, $b_1 = 7.4$ and $S_{b_1} = 1.59$.

a. At the 0.05 level of significance, is there evidence of a linear relationship between shelf space and sales?

b. Construct a 95% confidence interval estimate of the population slope, β_1.

13.43 In Problem 13.5 on page 522, you used reported magazine newsstand sales to predict audited sales. The data are stored in the file **circulation.xls**. Using the results of that problem, $b_1 = 0.5719$ and $S_{b_1} = 0.0668$.

a. At the 0.05 level of significance, is there evidence of a linear relationship between reported sales and audited sales?

b. Construct a 95% confidence interval estimate of the population slope, β_1.

13.44 In Problem 13.6 on pages 522–523, the owner of a moving company wanted to predict labor hours, based on the number of cubic feet moved. The data are stored in the file **moving.xls**. Using the results of that problem,

a. at the 0.05 level of significance, is there evidence of a linear relationship between the number of cubic feet moved and labor hours?

b. construct a 95% confidence interval estimate of the population slope, β_1.

 13.45 In Problem 13.7 on page 523, you used the weight of mail to predict the number of orders received. The data are stored in the file **mail.xls**. Using the results of that problem,

a. at the 0.05 level of significance, is there evidence of a linear relationship between the weight of mail and the number of orders received?

b. construct a 95% confidence interval estimate of the population slope, β_1.

13.46 In Problem 13.8 on page 523, you used annual revenues to predict the value of a baseball franchise. The data are stored in the file **bbrevenue.xls**. Using the results of that problem,

a. at the 0.05 level of significance, is there evidence of a linear relationship between annual revenue and franchise value?

b. construct a 95% confidence interval estimate of the population slope, β_1.

13.47 In Problem 13.9 on page 523, an agent for a real estate company wanted to predict the monthly rent for apartments, based on the size of the apartment. The data are stored in the file **rent.xls**. Using the results of that problem,

a. at the 0.05 level of significance, is there evidence of a linear relationship between the size of the apartment and the monthly rent?

b. construct a 95% confidence interval estimate of the population slope, β_1.

13.48 In Problem 13.10 on page 523, you used hardness to predict the tensile strength of die-cast aluminum. The data are stored in the file **hardness.xls**. Using the results of that problem,

a. at the 0.05 level of significance, is there evidence of a linear relationship between hardness and tensile strength?

b. construct a 95% confidence interval estimate of the population slope, β_1.

13.49 The volatility of a stock is often measured by its beta value. You can estimate the beta value of a stock by developing a simple linear regression model, using the percentage weekly change in the stock as the dependent variable and the percentage weekly change in a market index as the independent variable. The S&P 500 Index is a common index to use. For example, if you wanted to estimate the beta for IBM, you could use the following model, which is sometimes referred to as a *market model*:

$$(\% \text{ weekly change in IBM}) = \beta_0 + \beta_1 (\% \text{ weekly change in } S \& P \ 500 \text{ index}) + \varepsilon$$

The least-squares regression estimate of the slope b_1 is the estimate of the beta value for IBM. A stock with a beta value of 1.0 tends to move the same as the overall market. A stock with a beta value of 1.5 tends to move 50% more than the overall market, and a stock with a beta value of 0.6

tends to move only 60% as much as the overall market. Stocks with negative beta values tend to move in a direction opposite that of the overall market. The following table gives some beta values for some widely held stocks:

Company	Ticker Symbol	Beta
AT&T	T	0.80
IBM	IBM	1.20
Disney Company	DIS	1.40
Alcoa	AA	2.26
LSI Logic	LSI	3.61

Source: Extracted from **finance.yahoo.com**, *May 31, 2006.*

a. For each of the five companies, interpret the beta value.
b. How can investors use the beta value as a guide for investing?

13.50 Index funds are mutual funds that try to mimic the movement of leading indexes, such as the S&P 500 Index, the NASDAQ 100 Index, or the Russell 2000 Index. The beta values for these funds (as described in Problem 13.49) are therefore approximately 1.0. The estimated market models for these funds are approximately

(% weekly change in index fund) = 0.0 + 1.0 (% weekly change in the index)

Leveraged index funds are designed to magnify the movement of major indexes. An article in *Mutual Funds* (L. O'Shaughnessy, "Reach for Higher Returns," *Mutual Funds*, July 1999, pp. 44–49) described some of the risks and rewards associated with these funds and gave details on some of the most popular leveraged funds, including those in the following table:

Name (Ticker Symbol)	Fund Description
Potomac Small Cap Plus (POSCX)	125% of Russell 2000 Index
Rydex "Inv" Nova (RYNVX)	150% of the S&P 500 Index
ProFund UltraOTC "Inv" (UOPIX)	Double (200%) the NASDAQ 100 Index

Thus, estimated market models for these funds are approximately

(% weekly change in POSCX) = 0.0 + 1.25 (% weekly change in the Russell 2000 Index)

(% weekly change in RYNVX) = 0.0 + 1.50 (% weekly change in the S&P 500 Index)

(% weekly change in UOPIX fund) = 0.0 + 2.0 (% weekly change in the NASDAQ 100 Index)

Thus, if the Russell 2000 Index gains 10% over a period of time, the leveraged mutual fund POSCX gains approxi-

mately 12.5%. On the downside, if the same index loses 20%, POSCX loses approximately 25%.

a. Consider the leveraged mutual fund ProFund UltraOTC "Inv" (UOPIX), whose description is 200% of the performance of the S&P 500 Index. What is its approximate market model?
b. If the NASDAQ gains 30% in a year, what return do you expect UOPIX to have?
c. If the NASDAQ loses 35% in a year, what return do you expect UOPIX to have?
d. What type of investors should be attracted to leveraged funds? What type of investors should stay away from these funds?

13.51 The data in the file `coffeedrink.xls` represent the calories and fat (in grams) of 16-ounce iced coffee drinks at Dunkin' Donuts and Starbucks:

Product	Calories	Fat
Dunkin' Donuts Iced Mocha Swirl latte (whole milk)	240	8.0
Starbucks Coffee Frappuccino blended coffee	260	3.5
Dunkin' Donuts Coffee Coolatta (cream)	350	22.0
Starbucks Iced Coffee Mocha Espresso (whole milk and whipped cream)	350	20.0
Starbucks Mocha Frappuccino blended coffee (whipped cream)	420	16.0
Starbucks Chocolate Brownie Frappuccino blended coffee (whipped cream)	510	22.0
Starbucks Chocolate Frappuccino Blended Crème (whipped cream)	530	19.0

Source: Extracted from "Coffee as Candy at Dunkin' Donuts and Starbucks," Consumer Reports, June 2004, p. 9.

a. Compute and interpret the coefficient of correlation, r.
b. At the 0.05 level of significance, is there a significant linear relationship between the calories and fat?

13.52 There are several methods for calculating fuel economy. The following table (contained in the file `mileage.xls`) indicates the mileage as calculated by owners and by current government standards:

Vehicle	Owner	Government Standards
2005 Ford F-150	14.3	16.8
2005 Chevrolet Silverado	15.0	17.8
2002 Honda Accord LX	27.8	26.2
2002 Honda Civic	27.9	34.2
2004 Honda Civic Hybrid	48.8	47.6
2002 Ford Explorer	16.8	18.3
2005 Toyota Camry	23.7	28.5
2003 Toyota Corolla	32.8	33.1
2005 Toyota Prius	37.3	56.0

a. Compute and interpret the coefficient of correlation, r.

b. At the 0.05 level of significance, is there a significant linear relationship between the mileage as calculated by owners and by current government standards?

13.53 College basketball is big business, with coaches' salaries, revenues, and expenses in millions of dollars. The data in the file colleges-basketball.xls represent the coaches' salaries and revenues for college basketball at selected schools in a recent year (extracted from R. Adams, "Pay for Playoffs," *The Wall Street Journal*, March 11–12, 2006, pp. P1, P8).

a. Compute and interpret the coefficient of correlation, r.

b. At the 0.05 level of significance, is there a significant linear relationship between a coach's salary and revenue?

13.54 College football players trying out for the NFL are given the Wonderlic standardized intelligence test. The data in the file wonderlic.xls represent the average Wonderlic scores of football players trying out for the NFL and the graduation rates for football players at selected schools (extracted from S. Walker, "The NFL's Smartest Team," *The Wall Street Journal*, September 30, 2005, pp. W1, W10).

a. Compute and interpret the coefficient of correlation, r.

b. At the 0.05 level of significance, is there a significant linear relationship between the average Wonderlic score of football players trying out for the NFL and the graduation rates for football players at selected schools?

c. What conclusions can you reach about the relationship between the average Wonderlic score of football players trying out for the NFL and the graduation rates for football players at selected schools?

13.8   ESTIMATION OF MEAN VALUES AND PREDICTION OF INDIVIDUAL VALUES

This section presents methods of making inferences about the mean of Y and predicting individual values of Y.

The Confidence Interval Estimate

In Example 13.2 on page 519, you used the prediction line to predict the value of Y for a given X. The mean annual sales for stores with 4,000 square feet was predicted to be 7.644 millions of dollars ($7,644,000). This estimate, however, is a *point estimate* of the population mean. In Chapter 8, you studied the concept of the confidence interval as an estimate of the population mean. In a similar fashion, Equation (13.20) defines the **confidence interval estimate for the mean response** for a given X.

CONFIDENCE INTERVAL ESTIMATE FOR THE MEAN OF Y

$$\hat{Y}_i \pm t_{n-2} S_{YX} \sqrt{h_i}$$

$$\hat{Y}_i - t_{n-2} S_{YX} \sqrt{h_i} \leq \mu_{Y|X=X_i} \leq \hat{Y}_i + t_{n-2} S_{YX} \sqrt{h_i} \qquad (13.20)$$

$$h_i = \frac{1}{n} + \frac{(X_i - \bar{X})^2}{SSX}$$

where

$$\hat{Y}_i = \text{predicted value of } Y;\ \hat{Y}_i = b_0 + b_1 X_i$$

$$S_{YX} = \text{standard error of the estimate}$$

$$n = \text{sample size}$$

$$X_i = \text{given value of } X$$

$$\mu_{Y|X=X_i} = \text{mean value of } Y \text{ when } X = X_i$$

$$SSX = \sum_{i=1}^{n} (X_i - \bar{X})^2$$

The width of the confidence interval in Equation (13.20) depends on several factors. For a given level of confidence, increased variation around the prediction line, as measured by the standard error of the estimate, results in a wider interval. However, as you would expect, increased sample size reduces the width of the interval. In addition, the width of the interval also varies at different values of X. When you predict Y for values of X close to $\bar{X}$, the interval is narrower than for predictions for X values more distant from $\bar{X}$.

In the Sunflowers Apparel example, suppose you want to construct a 95% confidence interval estimate of the mean annual sales for the entire population of stores that contain 4,000 square feet ($X = 4$). Using the simple linear regression equation,

$$\hat{Y}_i = 0.9645 + 1.6699 X_i$$
$$= 0.9645 + 1.6699(4) = 7.6439 \text{ (millions of dollars)}$$

Also, given the following:

$$\bar{X} = 2.9214 \qquad S_{YX} = 0.9664$$

$$SSX = \sum_{i=1}^{n} (X_i - \bar{X})^2 = 37.9236$$

From Table E.3, $t_{12} = 2.1788$. Thus,

$$\hat{Y}_i \pm t_{n-2} S_{YX} \sqrt{h_i}$$

where

$$h_i = \frac{1}{n} + \frac{(X_i - \bar{X})^2}{SSX}$$

so that

$$\hat{Y}_i \pm t_{n-2} S_{YX} \sqrt{\frac{1}{n} + \frac{(X_i - \bar{X})^2}{SSX}}$$

$$= 7.6439 \pm (2.1788)(0.9664) \sqrt{\frac{1}{14} + \frac{(4 - 2.9214)^2}{37.9236}}$$

$$= 7.6439 \pm 0.6728$$

so

$$6.9711 \leq \mu_{Y|X=4} \leq 8.3167$$

Therefore, the 95% confidence interval estimate is that the mean annual sales are between $6,971,100 and $8,316,700 for the population of stores with 4,000 square feet.

The Prediction Interval

In addition to the need for a confidence interval estimate for the mean value, you often want to predict the response for an individual value. Although the form of the prediction interval is similar to that of the confidence interval estimate of Equation (13.20), the prediction interval is predicting an individual value, not estimating a parameter. Equation (13.21) defines the **prediction interval for an individual response, Y,** at a particular value, X_i, denoted by $Y_{X=X_i}$.

PREDICTION INTERVAL FOR AN INDIVIDUAL RESPONSE, Y

$$\hat{Y}_i \pm t_{n-2} S_{YX} \sqrt{1 + h_i}$$

$$\hat{Y}_i - t_{n-2} S_{YX} \sqrt{1 + h_i} \leq Y_{X=X_i} \leq \hat{Y}_i + t_{n-2} S_{YX} \sqrt{1 + h_i}$$

(13.21)

where h_i, $\hat{Y}_i$, S_{YX}, n, and X_i are defined as in Equation (13.20) on page 546 and $Y_{X=X_i}$ is a future value of Y when $X = X_i$.

To construct a 95% prediction interval of the annual sales for an individual store that contains 4,000 square feet ($X = 4$), you first compute $\hat{Y}_i$. Using the prediction line:

$$\hat{Y}_i = 0.9645 + 1.6699 X_i$$
$$= 0.9645 + 1.6699(4)$$
$$= 7.6439 \text{ (millions of dollars)}$$

Also, given the following:

$$\bar{X} = 2.9214 \quad S_{YX} = 0.9664$$

$$SSX = \sum_{i=1}^{n} (X_i - \bar{X})^2 = 37.9236$$

From Table E.3, $t_{12} = 2.1788$. Thus,

$$\hat{Y}_i \pm t_{n-2} S_{YX} \sqrt{1 + h_i}$$

where

$$h_i = \frac{1}{n} + \frac{(X_i - \bar{X})^2}{\sum_{i=1}^{n} (X_i - \bar{X})^2}$$

so that

$$\hat{Y}_i \pm t_{n-2} S_{YX} \sqrt{1 + \frac{1}{n} + \frac{(X_i - \bar{X})^2}{SSX}}$$

$$= 7.6439 \pm (2.1788)(0.9664) \sqrt{1 + \frac{1}{14} + \frac{(4 - 2.9214)^2}{37.9236}}$$

$$= 7.6439 \pm 2.2104$$

so

$$5.4335 \leq Y_{X=4} \leq 9.8543$$

Therefore, with 95% confidence, you predict that the annual sales for an individual store with 4,000 square feet is between $5,433,500 and $9,854,300.

Figure 13.21 is a Microsoft Excel worksheet that illustrates the confidence interval estimate and the prediction interval for the Sunflowers Apparel problem. If you compare the results of the confidence interval estimate and the prediction interval, you see that the width of the prediction interval for an individual store is much wider than the confidence interval estimate for the mean. Remember that there is much more variation in predicting an individual value than in estimating a mean value.

FIGURE 13.21

Microsoft Excel confidence interval estimate and prediction interval for the Sunflowers Apparel data

See Section E13.5 to create this.

	A	B	
1	Site Selection Analysis		
2			
3	**Data**		
4	X Value	4	
5	Confidence Level	95%	
6			
7	**Intermediate Calculations**		
8	Sample Size	14	=DataCopy!F2
9	Degrees of Freedom	12	=B8 - 2
10	t Value	2.1788	=TINV(1 - B5, B9)
11	Sample Mean	2.9214	=DataCopy!F3
12	Sum of Squared Difference	37.9236	=DataCopy!F4
13	Standard Error of the Estimate	0.9664	from regression worksheet cell B7
14	h Statistic	0.1021	=1/B8 + (B4 - B11)^2/B12
15	Predicted Y (YHat)	7.6439	=DataCopy!F5
16			
17	**For Average Y**		
18	Interval Half Width	0.6728	=B10 * B13 * SQRT(B14)
19	Confidence Interval Lower Limit	6.9711	=B15 - B18
20	Confidence Interval Upper Limit	8.3167	=B15 + B18
21			
22	**For Individual Response Y**		
23	Interval Half Width	2.2104	=B10 * B13 * SQRT(1 + B14)
24	Prediction Interval Lower Limit	5.4335	=B15 - B23
25	Prediction Interval Upper Limit	9.8544	=B15 + B23

PROBLEMS FOR SECTION 13.8

Learning the Basics

 13.55 Based on a sample of $n = 20$, the least-squares method was used to develop the following prediction line: $\hat{Y}_i = 5 + 3X_i$. In addition,

$$S_{YX} = 1.0 \quad \overline{X} = 2 \quad \sum_{i=1}^{n}(X_i - \overline{X})^2 = 20$$

a. Construct a 95% confidence interval estimate of the population mean response for $X = 2$.
b. Construct a 95% prediction interval of an individual response for $X = 2$.

 13.56 Based on a sample of $n = 20$, the least-squares method was used to develop the following prediction line: $\hat{Y}_i = 5 + 3X_i$. In addition,

$$S_{YX} = 1.0 \quad \overline{X} = 2 \quad \sum_{i=1}^{n}(X_i - \overline{X})^2 = 20$$

a. Construct a 95% confidence interval estimate of the population mean response for $X = 4$.
b. Construct a 95% prediction interval of an individual response for $X = 4$.
c. Compare the results of (a) and (b) with those of Problem 13.55 (a) and (b). Which interval is wider? Why?

Applying the Concepts

13.57 In Problem 13.5 on page 522, you used reported sales to predict audited sales of magazines. The data are stored in the file **circulation.xls**. For these data $S_{YX} = 42.186$ and $h_i = 0.108$ when $X = 400$.
a. Construct a 95% confidence interval estimate of the mean audited sales for magazines that report newsstand sales of 400,000.
b. Construct a 95% prediction interval of the audited sales for an individual magazine that reports newsstand sales of 400,000.
c. Explain the difference in the results in (a) and (b).

 13.58 In Problem 13.4 on page 522, the marketing manager used shelf space for pet food to predict weekly sales. The data are stored in the file **petfood.xls**. For these data $S_{YX} = 30.81$ and $h_i = 0.1373$ when $X = 8$.
a. Construct a 95% confidence interval estimate of the mean weekly sales for all stores that have 8 feet of shelf space for pet food.
b. Construct a 95% prediction interval of the weekly sales of an individual store that has 8 feet of shelf space for pet food.
c. Explain the difference in the results in (a) and (b).

13.59 In Problem 13.7 on page 523, you used the weight of mail to predict the number of orders received. The data are stored in the file `mail.xls`.

a. Construct a 95% confidence interval estimate of the mean number of orders received for all packages with a weight of 500 pounds.

b. Construct a 95% prediction interval of the number of orders received for an individual package with a weight of 500 pounds.

c. Explain the difference in the results in (a) and (b).

13.60 In Problem 13.6 on page 522, the owner of a moving company wanted to predict labor hours based on the number of cubic feet moved. The data are stored in the file `moving.xls`.

a. Construct a 95% confidence interval estimate of the mean labor hours for all moves of 500 cubic feet.

b. Construct a 95% prediction interval of the labor hours of an individual move that has 500 cubic feet.

c. Explain the difference in the results in (a) and (b).

13.61 In Problem 13.9 on page 523, an agent for a real estate company wanted to predict the monthly rent for apartments, based on the size of the apartment. The data are stored in the file `rent.xls`.

a. Construct a 95% confidence interval estimate of the mean monthly rental for all apartments that are 1,000 square feet in size.

b. Construct a 95% prediction interval of the monthly rental of an individual apartment that is 1,000 square feet in size.

c. Explain the difference in the results in (a) and (b).

13.62 In Problem 13.8 on page 523, you predicted the value of a baseball franchise, based on current revenue. The data are stored in the file `bbrevenue.xls`.

a. Construct a 95% confidence interval estimate of the mean value of all baseball franchises that generate $150 million of annual revenue.

b. Construct a 95% prediction interval of the value of an individual baseball franchise that generates $150 million of annual revenue.

c. Explain the difference in the results in (a) and (b).

13.63 In Problem 13.10 on page 523, you used hardness to predict the tensile strength of die-cast aluminum. The data are stored in the file `hardness.xls`.

a. Construct a 95% confidence interval estimate of the mean tensile strength for all specimens with a hardness of 30 Rockwell E units.

b. Construct a 95% prediction interval of the tensile strength for an individual specimen that has a hardness of 30 Rockwell E units.

c. Explain the difference in the results in (a) and (b).

13.9   PITFALLS IN REGRESSION AND ETHICAL ISSUES

Some of the pitfalls involved in using regression analysis are as follows:

- Lacking an awareness of the assumptions of least-squares regression
- Not knowing how to evaluate the assumptions of least-squares regression
- Not knowing what the alternatives to least-squares regression are if a particular assumption is violated
- Using a regression model without knowledge of the subject matter
- Extrapolating outside the relevant range
- Concluding that a significant relationship identified in an observational study is due to a cause-and-effect relationship

The widespread availability of spreadsheet and statistical software has made regression analysis much more feasible. However, for many users, this enhanced availability of software has not been accompanied by an understanding of how to use regression analysis properly. Someone who is not familiar with either the assumptions of regression or how to evaluate the assumptions cannot be expected to know what the alternatives to least-squares regression are if a particular assumption is violated.

The data in Table 13.7 (stored in the file `anscombe.xls`) illustrate the importance of using scatter plots and residual analysis to go beyond the basic number crunching of computing the Y intercept, the slope, and r^2.

TABLE 13.7

Four Sets of Artificial
Data

Data Set A		Data Set B		Data Set C		Data Set D	
X_i	Y_i	X_i	Y_i	X_i	Y_i	X_i	Y_i
10	8.04	10	9.14	10	7.46	8	6.58
14	9.96	14	8.10	14	8.84	8	5.76
5	5.68	5	4.74	5	5.73	8	7.71
8	6.95	8	8.14	8	6.77	8	8.84
9	8.81	9	8.77	9	7.11	8	8.47
12	10.84	12	9.13	12	8.15	8	7.04
4	4.26	4	3.10	4	5.39	8	5.25
7	4.82	7	7.26	7	6.42	19	12.50
11	8.33	11	9.26	11	7.81	8	5.56
13	7.58	13	8.74	13	12.74	8	7.91
6	7.24	6	6.13	6	6.08	8	6.89

Source: Extracted from F. J. Anscombe, "Graphs in Statistical Analysis," American Statistician, *Vol. 27 (1973),
pp. 17–21.*

Anscombe (reference 1) showed that all four data sets given in Table 13.7 have the following identical results:

$$\hat{Y}_i = 3.0 + 0.5X_i$$

$$S_{YX} = 1.237$$

$$S_{b_1} = 0.118$$

$$r^2 = 0.667$$

$$SSR = \text{Explained variation} = \sum_{i=1}^{n}(\hat{Y}_i - \bar{Y})^2 = 27.51$$

$$SSE = \text{Unxplained variation} = \sum_{i=1}^{n}(Y_i - \hat{Y}_i)^2 = 13.76$$

$$SST = \text{Total variation} = \sum_{i=1}^{n}(Y_i - \bar{Y})^2 = 41.27$$

Thus, with respect to these statistics associated with a simple linear regression analysis, the four data sets are identical. Were you to stop the analysis at this point, you would fail to observe the important differences among the four data sets. By examining the scatter plots for the four data sets in Figure 13.22 on page 552, and their residual plots in Figure 13.23 on page 552, you can clearly see that each of the four data sets has a different relationship between X and Y.

From the scatter plots of Figure 13.22 and the residual plots of Figure 13.23, you see how different the data sets are. The only data set that seems to follow an approximate straight line is data set A. The residual plot for data set A does not show any obvious patterns or outlying residuals. This is certainly not true for data sets B, C, and D. The scatter plot for data set B shows that a quadratic regression model (see Section 15.1) is more appropriate. This conclusion is reinforced by the residual plot for data set B. The scatter plot and the residual plot for data set C clearly show an outlying observation. If this is the case, you may want to remove the outlier and reestimate the regression model (see reference 4). Similarly, the scatter plot for data set D represents the situation in which the model is heavily dependent on the outcome of a single response ($X_8 = 19$ and $Y_8 = 12.50$). You would have to cautiously evaluate any regression model because its regression coefficients are heavily dependent on a single observation.

FIGURE 13.22

Scatter plots for four data sets

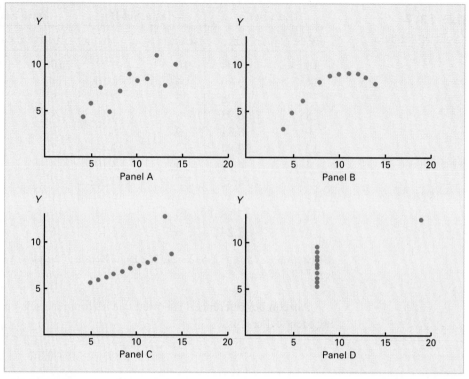

FIGURE 13.23

Residual plots for four data sets

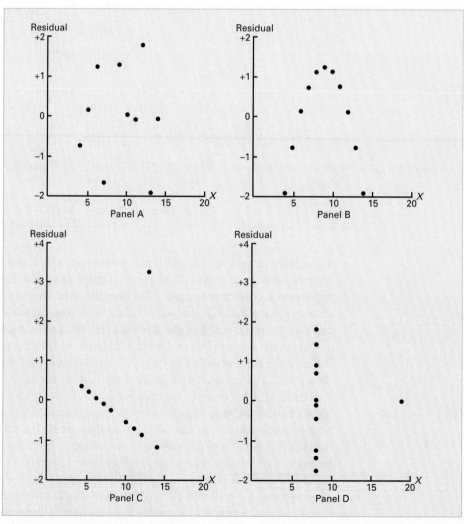

In summary, scatter plots and residual plots are of vital importance to a complete regression analysis. The information they provide is so basic to a credible analysis that you should always include these graphical methods as part of a regression analysis. Thus, a strategy that you can use to help avoid the pitfalls of regression is as follows:

1. Start with a scatter plot to observe the possible relationship between X and Y.
2. Check the assumptions of regression before moving on to using the results of the model.
3. Plot the residuals versus the independent variable to determine whether the linear model is appropriate and to check the equal-variance assumption.
4. Use a histogram, stem-and-leaf display, box-and-whisker plot, or normal probability plot of the residuals to check the normality assumption.
5. If you collected the data over time, plot the residuals versus time and use the Durbin-Watson test to check the independence assumption.
6. If there are violations of the assumptions, use alternative methods to least-squares regression or alternative least-squares models.
7. If there are no violations of the assumptions, carry out tests for the significance of the regression coefficients and develop confidence and prediction intervals.
8. Avoid making predictions and forecasts outside the relevant range of the independent variable.
9. Keep in mind that the relationships identified in observational studies may or may not be due to cause-and-effect relationships. Remember that while causation implies correlation, correlation does not imply causation.

America's Top Models

From the Author's Desktop

Perhaps you are familiar with the TV competition organized by model Tyra Banks to find "America's top model." You may be less familiar with another set of top models that are emerging from the business world.

In a *Business Week* article from its January 23, 2006, edition (S. Baker, "Why Math Will Rock Your World: More Math Geeks Are Calling the Shots in Business. Is Your Industry Next?" *Business Week*, pp. 54–62), Stephen Baker talks about how "quants" turned finance upside down and is moving on to other business fields. The name *quants* derives from the fact that "math geeks" develop models and forecasts by using "quantitative methods." These methods are built on the principles of regression analysis discussed in this chapter, although the actual models are much more complicated than the simple linear models discussed in this chapter.

Regression-based models have become the top models for many types of business analyses. Some examples include

- **Advertising and marketing** Managers use econometric models (in other words,

regression models) to determine the effect of an advertisement on sales, based on a set of factors. Also, managers use data mining to predict patterns of behavior of what customers will buy in the future, based on historic information about the consumer.

- **Finance** Any time you read about a financial "model," you should understand that some type of regression model is being used. For example, a *New York Times* article on June 18, 2006, titled "An Old Formula That Points to New Worry" by Mark Hulbert (p. BU8) discusses a market timing model that predicts the return of stocks in the next three to five years, based on the dividend yield of the stock market and the interest rate of 90-day Treasury bills.

- **Food and beverage** Believe it or not, Enologix, a California consulting company, has developed a "formula" (a regression model) that predicts a wine's quality index, based on a set of chemical compounds found in the wine (see D. Darlington, "The Chemistry of a 90+ Wine," *The New York Times Magazine*, August 7, 2005, pp. 36–39).

- **Publishing** A study of the effect of price changes at Amazon.com and BN.com on sales (again, regression analysis) found that a 1% price change at BN.com pushed sales down 4%, but it pushed sales down only 0.5% at Amazon.com. (You can download the paper at **http://gsbadg.uchicago.edu/vitae.htm**.)

- **Transportation** Farecast.com uses data mining and predictive technologies to objectively predict airfare pricing (see D. Darlin, "Airfares Made Easy (Or Easier)," *The New York Times*, July 1, 2006, pp. C1, C6).

- **Real estate** Zillow.com uses information about the features contained in a home and its location to develop estimates about the market value of the home, using a "formula" built with a proprietary algorithm.

In the article, Baker stated that statistics and probability will become core skills for businesspeople and consumers. Those who are successful will know how to use statistics, whether they are building financial models or making marketing plans. He also strongly endorsed the need for everyone in business to have knowledge of Microsoft Excel to be able to produce statistical analysis and reports.

SUMMARY

As you can see from the chapter roadmap in Figure 13.24, this chapter develops the simple linear regression model and discusses the assumptions and how to evaluate them.

Once you are assured that the model is appropriate, you can predict values by using the prediction line and test for the significance of the slope.

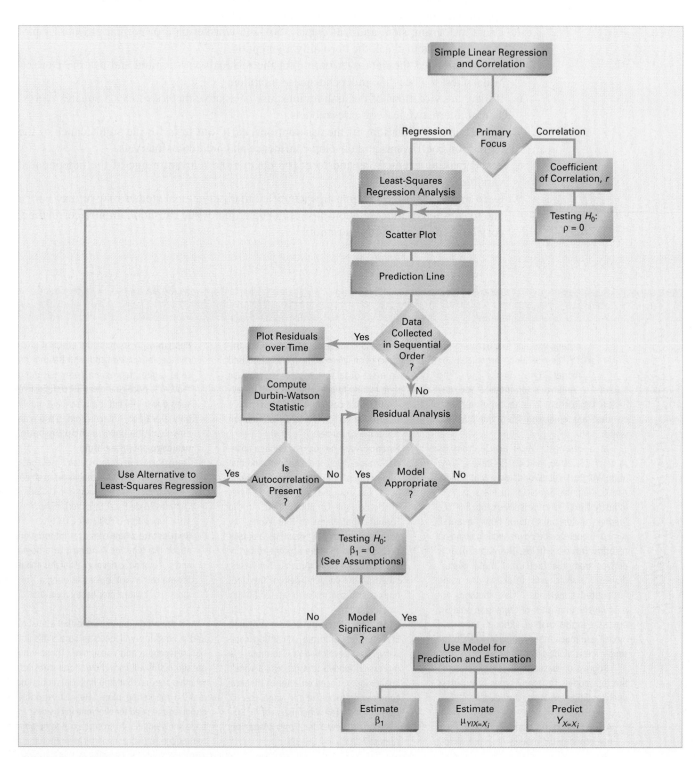

FIGURE 13.24 Roadmap for simple linear regression

You have learned how the director of planning for a chain of clothing stores can use regression analysis to investigate the relationship between the size of a store and its annual sales. You have used this analysis to make better decisions when selecting new sites for stores as well as to forecast sales for existing stores. In Chapter 14, regression analysis is extended to situations in which more than one independent variable is used to predict the value of a dependent variable.

KEY EQUATIONS

Simple Linear Regression Model

$$Y_i = \beta_0 + \beta_1 X_i + \varepsilon_i \tag{13.1}$$

Simple Linear Regression Equation: The Prediction Line

$$\hat{Y}_i = b_0 + b_1 X_i \tag{13.2}$$

Computational Formula for the Slope, b_1

$$b_1 = \frac{SSXY}{SSX} \tag{13.3}$$

Computational Formula for the Y Intercept, b_0

$$b_0 = \bar{Y} - b_1 \bar{X} \tag{13.4}$$

Measures of Variation in Regression

$$SST = SSR + SSE \tag{13.5}$$

Total Sum of Squares (SST)

$$SST = \text{Total sum of squares} = \sum_{i=1}^{n} (Y_i - \bar{Y})^2 \tag{13.6}$$

Regression Sum of Squares (SSR)

$SSR = \text{Explained variation or regression of squares}$

$$= \sum_{i=1}^{n} (\hat{Y}_i - \bar{Y})^2 \tag{13.7}$$

Error Sum of Squares (SSE)

$SSE = \text{Unexplained variation or error sum of squares}$

$$= \sum_{i=1}^{n} (Y_i - \hat{Y}_i)^2 \tag{13.8}$$

Coefficient of Determination

$$r^2 = \frac{\text{Regression sum of squares}}{\text{Total sum of squares}} = \frac{SSR}{SST} \tag{13.9}$$

Computational Formula for SST

$$SST = \sum_{i=1}^{n} (Y_i - \bar{Y})^2 = \sum_{i=1}^{n} Y_i^2 - \frac{\left(\sum_{i=1}^{n} Y_i\right)^2}{n} \tag{13.10}$$

Computational Formula for SSR

$$SSR = \sum_{i=1}^{n} (\hat{Y}_i - \bar{Y})^2$$

$$= b_0 \sum_{i=1}^{n} Y_i + b_1 \sum_{i=1}^{n} X_i Y_i - \frac{\left(\sum_{i=1}^{n} Y_i\right)^2}{n} \tag{13.11}$$

Computational Formula for SSE

$$SSE = \sum_{i=1}^{n} (Y_i - \hat{Y})^2 = \sum_{i=1}^{n} Y_i^2 - b_0 \sum_{i=1}^{n} Y_i - b_1 \sum_{i=1}^{n} X_i Y_i \tag{13.12}$$

Standard Error of the Estimate

$$S_{YX} = \sqrt{\frac{SSE}{n-2}} = \sqrt{\frac{\sum_{i=1}^{n} (Y_i - \hat{Y}_i)^2}{n-2}} \tag{13.13}$$

Residual

$$e_i = Y_i - \hat{Y}_i \tag{13.14}$$

Durbin-Watson Statistic

$$D = \frac{\sum_{i=2}^{n} (e_i - e_{i-1})^2}{\sum_{i=1}^{n} e_i^2} \tag{13.15}$$

Testing a Hypothesis for a Population Slope, β_1, Using the t Test

$$t = \frac{b_1 - \beta_1}{S_{b_1}} \tag{13.16}$$

Testing a Hypothesis for a Population Slope, β_1, Using the F Test

$$F = \frac{MSR}{MSE} \tag{13.17}$$

Confidence Interval Estimate of the Slope, β_1

$$b_1 \pm t_{n-2} S_{b_1} \tag{13.18}$$

$$b_1 - t_{n-2} S_{b_1} \le \beta_1 \le b_1 + t_{n-2} S_{b_1}$$

Testing for the Existence of Correlation

$$t = \frac{r - \rho}{\sqrt{\dfrac{1 - r^2}{n - 2}}} \qquad \text{(13.19)}$$

Confidence Interval Estimate for the Mean of Y

$$\hat{Y}_i \pm t_{n-2} S_{YX} \sqrt{h_i}$$

$$\hat{Y}_i - t_{n-2} S_{YX} \sqrt{h_i} \leq \mu_{Y|X=X_i} \leq \hat{Y}_i + t_{n-2} S_{YX} \sqrt{h_i} \qquad \text{(13.20)}$$

Prediction Interval for an Individual Response, Y

$$\hat{Y}_i \pm t_{n-2} S_{YX} \sqrt{1 + h_i} \qquad \text{(13.21)}$$

$$\hat{Y}_i - t_{n-2} S_{YX} \sqrt{1 + h_i} \leq Y_{X=X_i} \leq \hat{Y}_i + t_{n-2} S_{YX} \sqrt{1 + h_i}$$

KEY TERMS

assumptions of regression 529
autocorrelation 534
coefficient of determination 526
confidence interval estimate for the
   mean response 546
correlation coefficient 542
dependent variable 512
Durbin-Watson statistic 536
error sum of squares (*SSE*) 524
equal variance 530
explained variation 524
explanatory variable 513
homoscedasticity 530

independence of errors 529
independent variable 512
least-squares method 516
linear relationship 512
normality 530
prediction interval for an individual
   response, *Y* 547
prediction line 515
regression analysis 512
regression coefficient 516
regression sum of squares (*SSR*) 524
relevant range 519
residual 530

residual analysis 530
response variable 513
scatter diagram 512
scatter plot 512
simple linear regression 512
simple linear regression equation 515
slope 513
standard error of the estimate 528
total sum of squares (*SST*) 524
total variation 524
unexplained variation 524
Y intercept 513

CHAPTER REVIEW PROBLEMS

Checking Your Understanding

13.64 What is the interpretation of the Y intercept and the slope in the simple linear regression equation?

13.65 What is the interpretation of the coefficient of determination?

13.66 When is the unexplained variation (that is, error sum of squares) equal to 0?

13.67 When is the explained variation (that is, regression sum of squares) equal to 0?

13.68 Why should you always carry out a residual analysis as part of a regression model?

13.69 What are the assumptions of regression analysis?

13.70 How do you evaluate the assumptions of regression analysis?

13.71 When and how do you use the Durbin-Watson statistic?

13.72 What is the difference between a confidence interval estimate of the mean response, $\mu_{Y|X=X_i}$, and a prediction interval of $Y_{X=X_i}$?

Applying the Concepts

13.73 Researchers from the Lubin School of Business at Pace University in New York City conducted a study on Internet-supported courses. In one part of the study, four numerical variables were collected on 108 students in an introductory management course that met once a week for an entire semester. One variable collected was *hit consistency*. To measure hit consistency, the researchers did the following: If a student did not visit the Internet site between classes, the student was given a 0 for that time period. If a student visited the Internet site one or more times between classes, the student was given a 1 for that time period. Because there were 13 time periods, a student's score on hit consistency could range from 0 to 13.

    The other three variables included the student's course average, the student's cumulative grade point average

(GPA), and the total number of hits the student had on the Internet site supporting the course. The following table gives the correlation coefficient for all pairs of variables. Note that correlations marked with an * are statistically significant, using $\alpha = 0.001$:

Variable	Correlation
Course Average, Cumulative GPA	0.72*
Course Average, Total Hits	0.08
Course Average, Hit Consistency	0.37*
Cumulative GPA, Total Hits	0.12
Cumulative GPA, Hit Consistency	0.32*
Total Hits, Hit Consistency	0.64*

Source: Extracted from D. Baugher, A. Varanelli, and E. Weisbord, "Student Hits in an Internet-Supported Course: How Can Instructors Use Them and What Do They Mean?" Decision Sciences Journal of Innovative Education, Fall 2003, 1(2), pp. 159–179.

a. What conclusions can you reach from this correlation analysis?

b. Are you surprised by the results, or are they consistent with your own observations and experiences?

13.74 Management of a soft-drink bottling company wants to develop a method for allocating delivery costs to customers. Although one cost clearly relates to travel time within a particular route, another variable cost reflects the time required to unload the cases of soft drink at the delivery point. A sample of 20 deliveries within a territory was selected. The delivery times and the numbers of cases delivered were recorded in the delivery.xls file:

Customer	Number of Cases	Delivery Time (Minutes)	Customer	Number of Cases	Delivery Time (Minutes)
1	52	32.1	11	161	43.0
2	64	34.8	12	184	49.4
3	73	36.2	13	202	57.2
4	85	37.8	14	218	56.8
5	95	37.8	15	243	60.6
6	103	39.7	16	254	61.2
7	116	38.5	17	267	58.2
8	121	41.9	18	275	63.1
9	143	44.2	19	287	65.6
10	157	47.1	20	298	67.3

Develop a regression model to predict delivery time, based on the number of cases delivered.

a. Use the least-squares method to compute the regression coefficients b_0 and b_1.

b. Interpret the meaning of b_0 and b_1 in this problem.

c. Predict the delivery time for 150 cases of soft drink.

d. Should you use the model to predict the delivery time for a customer who is receiving 500 cases of soft drink? Why or why not?

e. Determine the coefficient of determination, r^2, and explain its meaning in this problem.

f. Perform a residual analysis. Is there any evidence of a pattern in the residuals? Explain.

g. At the 0.05 level of significance, is there evidence of a linear relationship between delivery time and the number of cases delivered?

h. Construct a 95% confidence interval estimate of the mean delivery time for 150 cases of soft drink.

i. Construct a 95% prediction interval of the delivery time for a single delivery of 150 cases of soft drink.

j. Construct a 95% confidence interval estimate of the population slope.

k. Explain how the results in (a) through (j) can help allocate delivery costs to customers.

13.75 A brokerage house wants to predict the number of trade executions per day, using the number of incoming phone calls as a predictor variable. Data were collected over a period of 35 days and are stored in the file trades.xls.

a. Use the least-squares method to compute the regression coefficients b_0 and b_1.

b. Interpret the meaning of b_0 and b_1 in this problem.

c. Predict the number of trades executed for a day in which the number of incoming calls is 2,000.

d. Should you use the model to predict the number of trades executed for a day in which the number of incoming calls is 5,000? Why or why not?

e. Determine the coefficient of determination, r^2, and explain its meaning in this problem.

f. Plot the residuals against the number of incoming calls and also against the days. Is there any evidence of a pattern in the residuals with either of these variables? Explain.

g. Determine the Durbin-Watson statistic for these data.

h. Based on the results of (f) and (g), is there reason to question the validity of the model? Explain.

i. At the 0.05 level of significance, is there evidence of a linear relationship between the volume of trade executions and the number of incoming calls?

j. Construct a 95% confidence interval estimate of the mean number of trades executed for days in which the number of incoming calls is 2,000.

k. Construct a 95% prediction interval of the number of trades executed for a particular day in which the number of incoming calls is 2,000.

l. Construct a 95% confidence interval estimate of the population slope.

m. Based on the results of (a) through (l), do you think the brokerage house should focus on a strategy of increasing the total number of incoming calls or on a strategy that relies on trading by a small number of heavy traders? Explain.

13.76 You want to develop a model to predict the selling price of homes based on assessed value. A sample of 30 recently sold single-family houses in a small city is selected to study the relationship between selling price (in thousands of dollars) and assessed value (in thousands of dollars). The houses in the city had been reassessed at full value one year prior to the study. The results are in the file house1.xls.

(**Hint:** First, determine which are the independent and dependent variables.)

a. Construct a scatter plot and, assuming a linear relationship, use the least-squares method to compute the regression coefficients b_0 and b_1.
b. Interpret the meaning of the Y intercept, b_0, and the slope, b_1, in this problem.
c. Use the prediction line developed in (a) to predict the selling price for a house whose assessed value is $170,000.
d. Determine the coefficient of determination, r^2, and interpret its meaning in this problem.
e. Perform a residual analysis on your results and determine the adequacy of the fit of the model.
f. At the 0.05 level of significance, is there evidence of a linear relationship between selling price and assessed value?
g. Construct a 95% confidence interval estimate of the mean selling price for houses with an assessed value of $170,000.
h. Construct a 95% prediction interval of the selling price of an individual house with an assessed value of $170,000.
i. Construct a 95% confidence interval estimate of the population slope.

13.77 You want to develop a model to predict the assessed value of houses, based on heating area. A sample of 15 single-family houses is selected in a city. The assessed value (in thousands of dollars) and the heating area of the houses (in thousands of square feet) are recorded, with the following results, stored in the file house2.xls:

House	Assessed Value ($000)	Heating Area of Dwelling (Thousands of Square Feet)
1	184.4	2.00
2	177.4	1.71
3	175.7	1.45
4	185.9	1.76
5	179.1	1.93
6	170.4	1.20
7	175.8	1.55
8	185.9	1.93
9	178.5	1.59
10	179.2	1.50
11	186.7	1.90
12	179.3	1.39
13	174.5	1.54
14	183.8	1.89
15	176.8	1.59

(**Hint:** First, determine which are the independent and dependent variables.)

a. Construct a scatter plot and, assuming a linear relationship, use the least-squares method to compute the regression coefficients b_0 and b_1.
b. Interpret the meaning of the Y intercept, b_0, and the slope, b_1, in this problem.
c. Use the prediction line developed in (a) to predict the assessed value for a house whose heating area is 1,750 square feet.
d. Determine the coefficient of determination, r^2, and interpret its meaning in this problem.
e. Perform a residual analysis on your results and determine the adequacy of the fit of the model.
f. At the 0.05 level of significance, is there evidence of a linear relationship between assessed value and heating area?
g. Construct a 95% confidence interval estimate of the mean assessed value for houses with a heating area of 1,750 square feet.
h. Construct a 95% prediction interval of the assessed value of an individual house with a heating area of 1,750 square feet.
i. Construct a 95% confidence interval estimate of the population slope.

13.78 The director of graduate studies at a large college of business would like to predict the grade point average (GPA) of students in an MBA program based on the Graduate Management Admission Test (GMAT) score. A sample of 20 students who had completed 2 years in the program is selected. The results are stored in the file gpigmat.xls:

Observation	GMAT Score	GPA	Observation	GMAT Score	GPA
1	688	3.72	11	567	3.07
2	647	3.44	12	542	2.86
3	652	3.21	13	551	2.91
4	608	3.29	14	573	2.79
5	680	3.91	15	536	3.00
6	617	3.28	16	639	3.55
7	557	3.02	17	619	3.47
8	599	3.13	18	694	3.60
9	616	3.45	19	718	3.88
10	594	3.33	20	759	3.76

(**Hint:** First, determine which are the independent and dependent variables.)

a. Construct a scatter plot and, assuming a linear relationship, use the least-squares method to compute the regression coefficients b_0 and b_1.
b. Interpret the meaning of the Y intercept, b_0, and the slope, b_1, in this problem.
c. Use the prediction line developed in (a) to predict the GPA for a student with a GMAT score of 600.
d. Determine the coefficient of determination, r^2, and interpret its meaning in this problem.
e. Perform a residual analysis on your results and determine the adequacy of the fit of the model.

f. At the 0.05 level of significance, is there evidence of a linear relationship between GMAT score and GPA?

g. Construct a 95% confidence interval estimate of the mean GPA of students with a GMAT score of 600.

h. Construct a 95% prediction interval of the GPA for a particular student with a GMAT score of 600.

i. Construct a 95% confidence interval estimate of the population slope.

13.79 The manager of the purchasing department of a large banking organization would like to develop a model to predict the amount of time it takes to process invoices. Data are collected from a sample of 30 days, and the number of invoices processed and completion time, in hours, is stored in the file invoice.xls.

(**Hint:** First, determine which are the independent and dependent variables.)

a. Assuming a linear relationship, use the least-squares method to compute the regression coefficients b_0 and b_1.

b. Interpret the meaning of the Y intercept, b_0, and the slope, b_1, in this problem.

c. Use the prediction line developed in (a) to predict the amount of time it would take to process 150 invoices.

d. Determine the coefficient of determination, r^2, and interpret its meaning.

e. Plot the residuals against the number of invoices processed and also against time.

f. Based on the plots in (e), does the model seem appropriate?

g. Compute the Durbin-Watson statistic and, at the 0.05 level of significance, determine whether there is any autocorrelation in the residuals.

h. Based on the results of (e) through (g), what conclusions can you reach concerning the validity of the model?

i. At the 0.05 level of significance, is there evidence of a linear relationship between the amount of time and the number of invoices processed?

j. Construct a 95% confidence interval estimate of the mean amount of time it would take to process 150 invoices.

k. Construct a 95% prediction interval of the amount of time it would take to process 150 invoices on a particular day.

13.80 On January 28, 1986, the space shuttle *Challenger* exploded, and seven astronauts were killed. Prior to the launch, the predicted atmospheric temperature was for freezing weather at the launch site. Engineers for Morton Thiokol (the manufacturer of the rocket motor) prepared charts to make the case that the launch should not take place due to the cold weather. These arguments were rejected, and the launch tragically took place. Upon investigation after the tragedy, experts agreed that the disaster occurred because of leaky rubber O-rings that did not seal properly due to the cold temperature. Data indicating the atmospheric temperature at the time of 23 previous launches and the O-ring damage index are stored in the file o-ring.xls:

Flight Number	Temperature (°F)	O-Ring Damage Index
1	66	0
2	70	4
3	69	0
5	68	0
6	67	0
7	72	0
8	73	0
9	70	0
41-B	57	4
41-C	63	2
41-D	70	4
41-G	78	0
51-A	67	0
51-B	75	0
51-C	53	11
51-D	67	0
51-F	81	0
51-G	70	0
51-I	67	0
51-J	79	0
61-A	75	4
61-B	76	0
61-C	58	4

Note: Data from flight 4 is omitted due to unknown O-ring condition.

Source: Extracted from Report of the Presidential Commission on the Space Shuttle Challenger Accident, *Washington, DC, 1986, Vol. II (H1–H3) and Vol. IV (664), and* Post Challenger Evaluation of Space Shuttle Risk Assessment and Management, *Washington, DC, 1988, pp. 135–136.*

a. Construct a scatter plot for the seven flights in which there was O-ring damage (O-ring damage index ≠ 0). What conclusions, if any, can you draw about the relationship between atmospheric temperature and O-ring damage?

b. Construct a scatter plot for all 23 flights.

c. Explain any differences in the interpretation of the relationship between atmospheric temperature and O-ring damage in (a) and (b).

d. Based on the scatter plot in (b), provide reasons why a prediction should not be made for an atmospheric temperature of 31°F, the temperature on the morning of the launch of the *Challenger*.

e. Although the assumption of a linear relationship may not be valid, fit a simple linear regression model to predict O-ring damage, based on atmospheric temperature.

f. Include the prediction line found in (e) on the scatter plot developed in (b).

g. Based on the results of (f), do you think a linear model is appropriate for these data? Explain.

h. Perform a residual analysis. What conclusions do you reach?

13.81 Crazy Dave, a well-known baseball analyst, would like to study various team statistics for the 2005 baseball season to determine which variables might be useful in predicting the number of wins achieved by teams during the season. He has decided to begin by using a team's earned run average (ERA), a measure of pitching performance, to predict the number of wins. The data for the 30 Major League Baseball teams are in the file **bb2005.xls**.

(**Hint:** First, determine which are the independent and dependent variables.)

a. Assuming a linear relationship, use the least-squares method to compute the regression coefficients b_0 and b_1.
b. Interpret the meaning of the Y intercept, b_0, and the slope, b_1, in this problem.
c. Use the prediction line developed in (a) to predict the number of wins for a team with an ERA of 4.50.
d. Compute the coefficient of determination, r^2, and interpret its meaning.
e. Perform a residual analysis on your results and determine the adequacy of the fit of the model.
f. At the 0.05 level of significance, is there evidence of a linear relationship between the number of wins and the ERA?
g. Construct a 95% confidence interval estimate of the mean number of wins expected for teams with an ERA of 4.50.
h. Construct a 95% prediction interval of the number of wins for an individual team that has an ERA of 4.50.
i. Construct a 95% confidence interval estimate of the slope.
j. The 30 teams constitute a population. In order to use statistical inference, as in (f) through (i), the data must be assumed to represent a random sample. What "population" would this sample be drawing conclusions about?
k. What other independent variables might you consider for inclusion in the model?

13.82 College football players trying out for the NFL are given the Wonderlic standardized intelligence test. The data in the file **wonderlic.xls** contains the average Wonderlic scores of football players trying out for the NFL and the graduation rates for football players at selected schools (extracted from S. Walker, "The NFL's Smartest Team," *The Wall Street Journal*, September 30, 2005, pp. W1, W10). You plan to develop a regression model to predict the Wonderlic scores for football players trying out for the NFL, based on the graduation rate of the school they attended.

a. Assuming a linear relationship, use the least-squares method to compute the regression coefficients b_0 and b_1.
b. Interpret the meaning of the Y intercept, b_0, and the slope, b_1, in this problem.
c. Use the prediction line developed in (a) to predict the Wonderlic score for football players trying out for the NFL from a school that has a graduation rate of 50%.

d. Compute the coefficient of determination, r^2, and interpret its meaning.
e. Perform a residual analysis on your results and determine the adequacy of the fit of the model.
f. At the 0.05 level of significance, is there evidence of a linear relationship between the Wonderlic score for a football player trying out for the NFL from a school and the school's graduation rate?
g. Construct a 95% confidence interval estimate of the mean Wonderlic score for football players trying out for the NFL from a school that has a graduation rate of 50%.
h. Construct a 95% prediction interval of the Wonderlic score for a football player trying out for the NFL from a school that has a graduation rate of 50%.
i. Construct a 95% confidence interval estimate of the slope.

13.83 College basketball is big business, with coaches' salaries, revenues, and expenses in millions of dollars. The data in the file **colleges-basketball.xls** contains the coaches' salaries and revenues for college basketball at selected schools in a recent year (extracted from R. Adams, "Pay for Playoffs," *The Wall Street Journal*, March 11–12, 2006, pp. P1, P8). You plan to develop a regression model to predict a coach's salary based on revenue.

a. Assuming a linear relationship, use the least-squares method to compute the regression coefficients b_0 and b_1.
b. Interpret the meaning of the Y intercept, b_0, and the slope, b_1, in this problem.
c. Use the prediction line developed in (a) to predict the coach's salary for a school that has revenue of $7 million.
d. Compute the coefficient of determination, r^2, and interpret its meaning.
e. Perform a residual analysis on your results and determine the adequacy of the fit of the model.
f. At the 0.05 level of significance, is there evidence of a linear relationship between the coach's salary for a school and revenue?
g. Construct a 95% confidence interval estimate of the mean salary of coaches at schools that have revenue of $7 million.
h. Construct a 95% prediction interval of the coach's salary for a school that has revenue of $7 million.
i. Construct a 95% confidence interval estimate of the slope.

13.84 During the fall harvest season in the United States, pumpkins are sold in large quantities at farm stands. Often, instead of weighing the pumpkins prior to sale, the farm stand operator will just place the pumpkin in the appropriate circular cutout on the counter. When asked why this was done, one farmer replied, "I can tell the weight of the pumpkin from its circumference." To determine whether this was really true, a sample of 23 pumpkins were measured for circumference and weighed, with the following results, stored in the file `pumpkin.xls`:

Circumference (cm)	Weight (Grams)	Circumference (cm)	Weight (Grams)
50	1,200	57	2,000
55	2,000	66	2,500
54	1,500	82	4,600
52	1,700	83	4,600
37	500	70	3,100
52	1,000	34	600
53	1,500	51	1,500
47	1,400	50	1,500
51	1,500	49	1,600
63	2,500	60	2,300
33	500	59	2,100
43	1,000		

a. Assuming a linear relationship, use the least-squares method to compute the regression coefficients b_0 and b_1.
b. Interpret the meaning of the slope, b_1, in this problem.
c. Predict the mean weight for a pumpkin that is 60 centimeters in circumference.
d. Do you think it is a good idea for the farmer to sell pumpkins by circumference instead of weight? Explain.
e. Determine the coefficient of determination, r^2, and interpret its meaning.
f. Perform a residual analysis for these data and determine the adequacy of the fit of the model.
g. At the 0.05 level of significance, is there evidence of a linear relationship between the circumference and the weight of a pumpkin?
h. Construct a 95% confidence interval estimate of the population slope, β_1.
i. Construct a 95% confidence interval estimate of the population mean weight for pumpkins that have a circumference of 60 centimeters.
j. Construct a 95% prediction interval of the weight for an individual pumpkin that has a circumference of 60 centimeters.

13.85 Can demographic information be helpful in predicting sales of sporting goods stores? The data stored in the file `sporting.xls` are the monthly sales totals from a random sample of 38 stores in a large chain of nationwide sporting goods stores. All stores in the franchise, and thus within the sample, are approximately the same size and carry the same merchandise. The county or, in some cases, counties in which the store draws the majority of its customers is referred to here as the customer base. For each of the 38 stores, demographic information about the customer base is provided. The data are real, but the name of the franchise is not used, at the request of the company. The variables in the data set are

Sales—Latest one-month sales total (dollars)
Age—Median age of customer base (years)
HS—Percentage of customer base with a high school diploma
College—Percentage of customer base with a college diploma
Growth—Annual population growth rate of customer base over the past 10 years
Income—Median family income of customer base (dollars)

a. Construct a scatter plot, using sales as the dependent variable and median family income as the independent variable. Discuss the scatter diagram.
b. Assuming a linear relationship, use the least-squares method to compute the regression coefficients b_0 and b_1.
c. Interpret the meaning of the Y intercept, b_0, and the slope, b_1, in this problem.
d. Compute the coefficient of determination, r^2, and interpret its meaning.
e. Perform a residual analysis on your results and determine the adequacy of the fit of the model.
f. At the 0.05 level of significance, is there evidence of a linear relationship between the independent variable and the dependent variable?
g. Construct a 95% confidence interval estimate of the slope and interpret its meaning.

13.86 For the data of Problem 13.85, repeat (a) through (g), using median age as the independent variable.

13.87 For the data of Problem 13.85, repeat (a) through (g), using high school graduation rate as the independent variable.

13.88 For the data of Problem 13.85, repeat (a) through (g), using college graduation rate as the independent variable.

13.89 For the data of Problem 13.85, repeat (a) through (g), using population growth as the independent variable.

13.90 Zagat's publishes restaurant ratings for various locations in the United States. The data file `restaurants.xls` contains the Zagat rating for food, decor, service, and the price per person for a sample of 50 restaurants located in an urban area (New York City) and 50 restaurants located in a suburb of New York City. Develop a regression model to predict the price per person, based on a variable that represents the sum of the ratings for food, decor, and service.

Source: Extracted from Zagat Survey 2002 New York City Restaurants and Zagat Survey 2001–2002, Long Island Restaurants.

a. Assuming a linear relationship, use the least-squares method to compute the regression coefficients b_0 and b_1.
b. Interpret the meaning of the Y intercept, b_0, and the slope, b_1, in this problem.
c. Use the prediction line developed in (a) to predict the price per person for a restaurant with a summated rating of 50.
d. Compute the coefficient of determination, r^2, and interpret its meaning.

e. Perform a residual analysis on your results and determine the adequacy of the fit of the model.

f. At the 0.05 level of significance, is there evidence of a linear relationship between the price per person and the summated rating?

g. Construct a 95% confidence interval estimate of the mean price per person for all restaurants with a summated rating of 50.

h. Construct a 95% prediction interval of the price per person for a restaurant with a summated rating of 50.

i. Construct a 95% confidence interval estimate of the slope.

j. How useful do you think the summated rating is as a predictor of price? Explain.

13.91 Refer to the discussion of beta values and market models in Problem 13.49 on pages 544–545. One hundred weeks of data, ending the week of May 22, 2006, for the S&P 500 and three individual stocks are included in the data file **sp500.xls**. Note that the *weekly percentage change* for both the S&P 500 and the individual stocks is measured as the percentage change from the previous week's closing value to the current week's closing value. The variables included are

  Week—Current week
  SP500—Weekly percentage change in the S&P 500 Index
  WALMART—Weekly percentage change in stock price of Wal-Mart Stores, Inc.
  TARGET—Weekly percentage change in stock price of the Target Corporation
  SARALEE—Weekly percentage change in stock price of the Sara Lee Corporation

Source: Extracted from **finance.yahoo.com**, *May 31, 2006.*

a. Estimate the market model for Wal-Mart Stores Inc. (*Hint:* Use the percentage change in the S&P 500 Index as the independent variable and the percentage change in Wal-Mart Stores, Inc.'s stock price as the dependent variable.)

b. Interpret the beta value for Wal-Mart Stores, Inc.

c. Repeat (a) and (b) for Target Corporation.

d. Repeat (a) and (b) for Sara Lee Corporation.

e. Write a brief summary of your findings.

13.92 The data file **returns.xls** contains the stock prices of four companies, collected weekly for 53 consecutive weeks, ending May 22, 2006. The variables are

  Week—Closing date for stock prices
  MSFT—Stock price of Microsoft, Inc.
  Ford—Stock price of Ford Motor Company
  GM—Stock price of General Motors, Inc.
  IAL—Stock price of International Aluminum, Inc.

Source: Extracted from **finance.yahoo.com**, *May 31, 2006.*

a. Calculate the correlation coefficient, *r*, for each pair of stocks. (There are six of them.)

b. Interpret the meaning of *r* for each pair.

c. Is it a good idea to have all the stocks in an individual's portfolio be strongly positively correlated among each other? Explain.

13.93 Is the daily performance of stocks and bonds correlated? The data file **stocks&bonds.xls** contains information concerning the closing value of the Dow Jones Industrial Average and the Vanguard Long-Term Bond Index Fund for 60 consecutive business days, ending May 30, 2006. The variables included are

  Date—Current day
  Bonds—Closing price of Vanguard Long-Term Bond Index Fund
  Stocks—Closing price of the Dow Jones Industrial Average

Source: Extracted from **finance.yahoo.com**, *May 31, 2006.*

a. Compute and interpret the correlation coefficient, *r*, for the variables Stocks and Bonds.

b. At the 0.05 level of significance, is there a relationship between these two variables? Explain.

Report Writing Exercises

13.94 In Problems 13.85–13.89 on page 561, you developed regression models to predict monthly sales at a sporting goods store. Now, write a report based on the models you developed. Append to your report all appropriate charts and statistical information.

Managing the *Springville Herald*

To ensure that as many trial subscriptions as possible are converted to regular subscriptions, the *Herald* marketing department works closely with the distribution department to accomplish a smooth initial delivery process for the trial subscription customers. To assist in this effort, the marketing department needs to accurately forecast the number of new regular subscriptions for the coming months.

A team consisting of managers from the marketing and distribution departments was convened to develop a better method of forecasting new subscriptions. Previously, after examining new subscription data for the prior three months, a group of three managers would develop a subjective forecast of the number of new subscriptions. Lauren Hall, who was recently hired by the company to provide special skills in quantitative forecasting methods, suggested that the department look for factors that might help in predicting new subscriptions.

Members of the team found that the forecasts in the past year had been particularly inaccurate because in some months, much more time was spent on telemarketing than in other months. In particular, in the past month, only 1,055 hours were completed because callers were busy during the first week of the month attending training sessions on the personal but formal greeting style and a new standard presentation guide (see "Managing the *Springville Herald*" in Chapter 11). Lauren collected data (stored in the file `sh13.xls`) for the number of new subscriptions and hours spent on telemarketing for each month for the past two years.

EXERCISES

SH13.1 What criticism can you make concerning the method of forecasting that involved taking the new subscriptions data for the prior three months as the basis for future projections?

SH13.2 What factors other than number of telemarketing hours spent might be useful in predicting the number of new subscriptions? Explain.

SH13.3 **a.** Analyze the data and develop a regression model to predict the mean number of new subscriptions for a month, based on the number of hours spent on telemarketing for new subscriptions.

b. If you expect to spend 1,200 hours on telemarketing per month, estimate the mean number of new subscriptions for the month. Indicate the assumptions on which this prediction is based. Do you think these assumptions are valid? Explain.

c. What would be the danger of predicting the number of new subscriptions for a month in which 2,000 hours were spent on telemarketing?

Web Case

Apply your knowledge of simple linear regression in this Web Case, which extends the Sunflowers Apparel Using Statistics scenario from this chapter.

Leasing agents from the Triangle Mall Management Corporation have suggested that Sunflowers consider several locations in some of Triangle's newly renovated lifestyle malls that cater to shoppers with higher-than-mean disposable income. Although the locations are smaller than the typical Sunflowers location, the leasing agents argue that higher-than-mean disposable income in the surrounding community is a better predictor of higher sales than store size. The leasing agents maintain that sample data from 14 Sunflowers stores prove that this is true.

Review the leasing agents' proposal and supporting documents that describe the data at the company's Web site,

www.prenhall.com/Springville/Triangle_Sunflower.htm, (or open this Web case file from the Student CD-ROM's Web Case folder), and then answer the following:

1. Should mean disposable income be used to predict sales based on the sample of 14 Sunflowers stores?

2. Should the management of Sunflowers accept the claims of Triangle's leasing agents? Why or why not?

3. Is it possible that the mean disposable income of the surrounding area is not an important factor in leasing new locations? Explain.

4. Are there any other factors not mentioned by the leasing agents that might be relevant to the store leasing decision?

REFERENCES

1. Anscombe, F. J., "Graphs in Statistical Analysis," *The American Statistician* 27 (1973): 17–21.
2. Hoaglin, D. C., and R. Welsch, "The Hat Matrix in Regression and ANOVA," *The American Statistician* 32 (1978): 17–22.
3. Hocking, R. R., "Developments in Linear Regression Methodology: 1959–1982," *Technometrics* 25 (1983): 219–250.
4. Kutner, M. H., C. J. Nachtsheim, J. Neter, and W. Li, *Applied Linear Statistical Models*, 5th ed. (New York: McGraw-Hill/Irwin, 2005).
5. *Microsoft Excel 2007* (Redmond, WA: Microsoft Corp., 2007).

Excel Companion
to Chapter 13

E13.1 PERFORMING SIMPLE LINEAR REGRESSION ANALYSES

You perform a simple linear regression analysis by either using the PHStat2 Simple Linear Regression procedure or by using the ToolPak Regression procedure.

Using PHStat2 Simple Linear Regression

Open to the worksheet that contains the data for the regression analysis. Select **PHStat → Regression → Simple Linear Regression**. In the procedure's dialog box (shown below), enter the cell range of the *Y* variable as the **Y Variable Cell Range** and the cell range of the *X* variable as the **X Variable Cell Range**. Click **First cells in both ranges contain label** and enter a value for the **Confidence level for regression coefficients**. Click the **Regression Statistics Table** and the **ANOVA and Coefficients Table** Regression Tool Output Options, enter a title as the **Title**, and click **OK**.

PHStat2 performs the regression analysis, using the ToolPak Regression procedure. Therefore, the worksheet produced does *not* dynamically change if you change your data. (Rerun the procedure to create revised results.) The three Output Options available in the PHStat2 dialog box enhance the ToolPak procedure and are explained in Sections E13.2, E13.4, and E13.5.

Using ToolPak Regression

Open to the worksheet that contains the data for the regression analysis. Select **Tools → Data Analysis**, select **Regression** from the Data Analysis list, and click **OK**. In the procedure's dialog box (shown below), enter the cell range of the *Y* variable data as the **Input Y Range** and enter the cell range of the *X* variable data as the **Input X Range**. Click **Labels**, click **Confidence Level** and enter a value in its box, and then click **OK**. Results appear on a new worksheet.

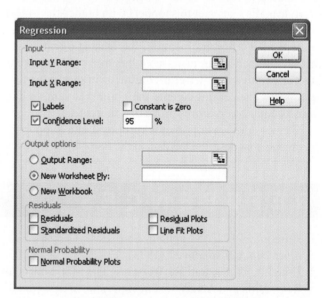

E13.2 CREATING SCATTER PLOTS AND ADDING A PREDICTION LINE

You use Excel charting features to create a scatter plot and add a prediction line to that plot. If you select the **Scatter Diagram** output option of the PHStat2 Simple Linear Regression procedure (see Section E13.1), you can skip to the "Adding a Prediction Line" section that applies to the Excel version you use.

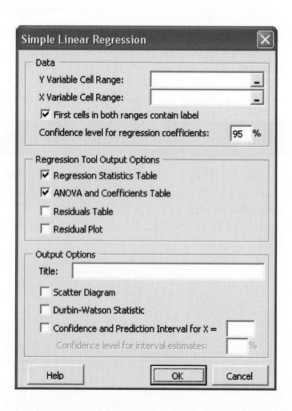

Creating a Scatter Plot

Use either the Section E2.12 instructions to create a scatter plot (see page 93) or use the Section E13.1 instructions in "Using PHStat2 Simple Linear Regression", but clicking **Scatter Diagram** before you click **OK**.

Adding a Prediction Line (97–2003)

Open to the chart sheet that contains your scatter plot and select **Chart → Add Trendline**. In the Add Trendline dialog box (see Figure E13.1), click the **Type** tab and then click **Linear**. Click the **Options** tab and select the **Automatic** option. Click **Display equation on chart** and **Display R-squared value on chart** and then click **OK**. If you have included a label as part of your data range, you will see that label displayed in place of **Series1** in this dialog box.

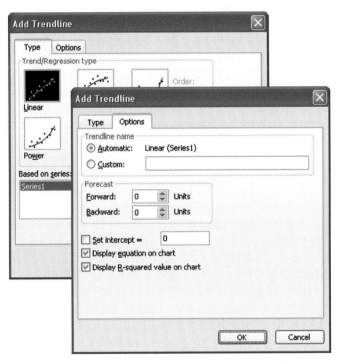

FIGURE E13.1 Add Trendline dialog box (97–2003)

Adding a Prediction Line (2007)

Open to the chart sheet that contains your scatter plot and select **Layout → Trendline** and in the Trendline gallery, select **More Trendline Options**. In the Trendline Opitions panel of the Format Trendline dialog box (see Figure E13.2), select the **Linear** option, click **Display equation on chart** and **Display R-squared value on chart**, and click **Close**.

Relocating an X Axis

If there are Y values on a residual plot or scatter plot that are less than zero, Microsoft Excel places the X axis at the point Y = 0, possibly obscuring some of the data points. To

FIGURE E13.2 Format Trendline dialog box (2007)

relocate the X axis to the bottom of the chart, open to the chart, right-click the Y **axis** and select **Format Axis** from the shortcut menu.

If you use Excel 97–2003, select the **Scale** tab in the Format Axis dialog box (see Figure E13.3), and enter the value found in the **Minimum** box (-6 in Figure E13.3) as the **Value (X) axis Crosses at** value and click **OK**. (As you enter this value, the check box for this entry is cleared automatically.)

FIGURE E13.3 Format Axis dialog box (97–2003)

If you use Excel 2007, in the Axis Options panel of the Format Axis dialog box (see Figure E13.4), select the **Axis value** option, change its default value of 0.0 (shown in Figure E13.4) to a value less than the minimum Y value, and click **Close**.

FIGURE E13.4 Format Axis dialog box (2007)

E13.3 PERFORMING RESIDUAL ANALYSES

You modify the procedures of Section E13.1 to perform a residual analysis. If you use the PHStat2 Simple Linear Regression procedure, click all the Regression Tool output options (**Regression Statistics Table, ANOVA and Coefficients Table, Residuals Table**, and **Residual Plot**). If you use the ToolPak Regression procedure, click **Residuals** and **Residual Plots** before clicking **OK**. If you need to relocate an X axis to the bottom of a residual plot, review the "Relocating an X Axis" part of Section E13.2.

E13.4 COMPUTING THE DURBIN-WATSON STATISTIC

You compute the Durbin-Watson Statistic by either using the PHStat2 Simple Linear Regression procedure or by using a several-step process that uses the Durbin-Watson.xls workbook.

Using PHStat2 Simple Linear Regression

Use the Section E13.1 instructions in "Using PHStat2 Simple Linear Regression," but clicking **Durbin-Watson Statistic** before you click **OK**. Choosing the Durbin-

Watson Statistic causes PHStat2 to create a residuals table, even if you did not check the **Residuals Table** Regression Tool output option.

The Durbin-Watson Statistic output option creates a new **Durbin-Watson** worksheet similar to the one shown in Figure 13.16 on page 536. This worksheet references cells in the regression results worksheet that is also created by the procedure. If you delete the regression results worksheet, the DurbinWatson worksheet displays an error message.

Using Durbin-Watson.xls

Open to the **DurbinWatson** worksheet of the Durbin-Watson.xls workbook. This worksheet (see Figure 13.16 on page 536) uses the **SUMXMY2 (*cell range 1, cell range 2*)** function in cell B3 to compute the sum of squared difference of the residuals, and the **SUMSQ (*residuals cell range*)** function in cell B4 to compute the sum of squared residuals for the Section 13.6 package delivery store example.

By setting *cell range 1* to the cell range of the first residual through the second-to-last residual and *cell range 2* to the cell range of the second residual through the last *residual*, you can get SUMXMY2 to compute the squared difference between two successive residuals, which is the numerator term of Equation (13.15). Because residuals appear in a regression results worksheet, cell references used in the SUMXMY2 function must refer to the regression results worksheet by name.

In the Durbin-Watson workbook, the **SLR** worksheet contains the simple linear regression analysis for the Section 13.6 package delivery example. The residuals appear in the cell range C25:C39. Therefore, cell range 1 is set to **SLR!C25:C38**, and cell range 2 is set to **SLR!C26:C39**. This makes the cell B3 formula **=SUMXMY2(SLR!C26:C39, SLR!C25:C38)**. The cell B4 formula, which also must refer to the SLR worksheet, is **=SUMSQ(SLR!C25:C39)**.

To adapt the Durbin-Watson workbook to other problems, first create a simple linear regression results worksheet that contains residual output and copy that worksheet to the Durbin-Watson workbook. Then open to the **Durbin-Watson** worksheet and edit the formulas in cells B3 and B4 so that they refer to the correct cell ranges on your regression worksheet. Finally, delete the no-longer-needed SLR worksheet.

E13.5 ESTIMATING THE MEAN OF Y AND PREDICTING Y VALUES

You compute a confidence interval estimate for the mean response and the prediction interval for an individual response either by selecting the PHStat2 Simple Linear Regression procedure or by making entries in the CIEandPIforSLR.xls workbook.

FIGURE E13.5

DataCopy worksheet (first six rows)

	A	B	C	D	E	F	
1	Square Feet	Annual Sales	(X-XBar)^2				
2	1.7	3.7	1.4919		Sample Size	14	=COUNT(B:B)
3	1.6	3.9	1.7462		Sample Mean	2.9214	=AVERAGE(A:A)
4	2.8	6.7	0.0147		Sum of Squared Difference	37.9236	=SUM(C:C)
5	5.6	9.5	7.1747		Predicted Y (YHat)	7.6439	=TREND(B2:B15, A2:A15, CIEandPI!B4)
6	1.3	3.4	2.6290				
7	2.2	5.6	0.5205				

Using PHStat2 Simple Linear Regression

Use the Section E13.1 instructions in "Using PHStat2 Simple Linear Regression", but before you click **OK**, click **Confidence and Prediction Interval for X =** and enter an *X* value in its box (see below). Then enter a value for the **Confidence level for interval estimates** and click **OK**.

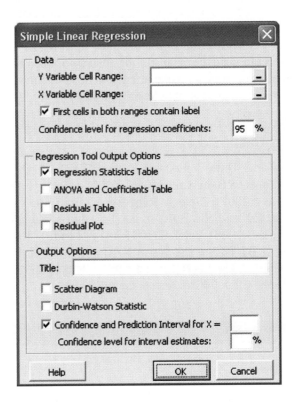

PHStat2 places the confidence interval estimate and prediction interval on a new worksheet similar to the one shown in Figure 13.21 on page 549. (PHStat2 also creates a DataCopy worksheet that is discussed in the next part of this section.)

Using CIEandPIforSLR.xls

Open to the **CIEandPI** worksheet of the CIEandPIforSLR.xls workbook. This worksheet (shown in Figure 13.21 on page 549) uses the function **TINV(1-***confidence level, degrees of freedom***)** to determine the *t* value and compute the confidence interval estimate and prediction interval for the Section 13.8 Sunflower's Apparel example.

Cells B8, B11, B12, and B15 contain formulas that reference individual cells on a **DataCopy** worksheet. This worksheet, the first six rows of which are shown in Figure E13.5, contains a copy of the regression data in columns A and B and a formula in column C that squares the difference between each *X* and $\overline{X}$. The worksheet also computes the sample size, the sample mean, the sum of the squared differences [*SSX* in Equation (13.20) on page 546], and the predicted *Y* value in cells F2, F3, F4, and F5.

The cell F5 formula uses the function **TREND (Y** *variable cell range***, X** *variable cell range***, X** *value***)** to calculate the predicted *Y* value. Because the formula uses the *X* value that has been entered on the CIEandPI worksheet, the **X** *value* in the cell F5 formula is set to **CIEandPI!B4**. Because the DataCopy and CIEandPI worksheets reference each other, you should consider these worksheets a matched pair that should not be broken up.

To adapt these worksheets to other problems, first create a simple linear regression results worksheet. Then, transfer the standard error value, always found in the regression results worksheet cell B7, to cell **B13** of the CIEandPI worksheet. Change, as is necessary, the *X* Value and the confidence level in cells B4 and B5 of the CIEandPI worksheet. Next, open to the **DataCopy** worksheet, and if your sample size is not 14, follow the instructions found in the worksheet. Enter the problem's *X* values in column A and *Y* values in column B. Finally, return to the CIEandPI worksheet to examine its updated results.

E13.6 EXAMPLE: SUNFLOWERS APPAREL DATA

This section shows you how to use PHStat2 or Basic Excel to perform a regression analysis for Sunflowers Apparel using the square footage and annual sales data stored in the site.xls workbook.

Using PHStat2

Open to the **Data** worksheet of the SITE.xls workbook. Select **PHStat → Regression → Simple Linear Regression**. In the procedure's dialog box (see Figure E13.6), enter **C1:C15** as the **Y Variable Cell Range** and **B1:B15** as the **X Variable Cell Range**. Click **First cells in both ranges**

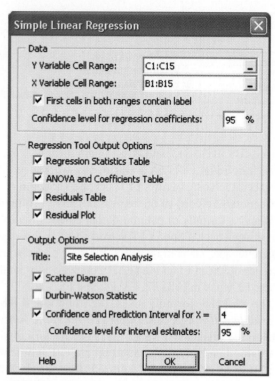

FIGURE E13.6 Completed Simple Linear Regression dialog box

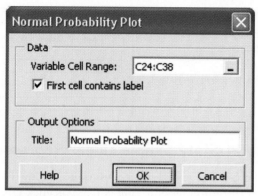

FIGURE E13.7 Completed Normal Probability Plot dialog box

contain label and enter a value for the **Confidence level for regression coefficients**. Click the **Regression Statistics Table, ANOVA and Coefficients Table**, **Residuals Table**, and **Residual Plot** Regression Tool Output Options. Enter **Site Selection Analysis** as the **Title** and click **Scatter Diagram**. Click **Confidence and Prediction Interval for X=** and enter **4** in its box. Enter **95** in the **Confidence level for interval estimates** box. Click **OK** to execute the procedure.

To evaluate the assumption of linearity, you review the **Residual Plot for X1** chart sheet. Note that there is no apparent pattern or relationship between the residuals and *X* variable.

To evaluate the normality assumption, create a normal probability plot. With your workbook open to the **SLR** worksheet, select **PHStat → Probability & Prob. Distributions → Normal Probability Plot**. In the procedure's dialog box (see Figure E13.7), enter **C24:C38** as the **Variable Cell Range** and click **First cell contains label**. Enter **Normal Probability Plot** as the **Title** and click **OK**. In the **NormalPlot** chart sheet, observe that the data do not appear to depart substantially from a normal distribution.

To evaluate the assumption of equal variances, review the **Residual Plot for X1** chart sheet. Note that there do not appear to be major differences in the variability of the residuals.

You conclude that all assumptions are valid and that you can use this simple linear regression model for the Sunflowers Apparel data. You can now open to the **SLR** worksheet to view the details of the analysis or open to the **Estimate** worksheet to make inferences about the mean of *Y* and the prediction of individual values of *Y*.

Using Basic Excel

Open to the **Data** worksheet of the **SITE.xls** workbook. Select **Tools → Data Analysis** (97–2003) or **Data → Data Analysis** (2007). Select **Regression** from the Data Analysis list, and click **OK**. In the procedure's dialog box (see Figure E13.8), enter **C1:C15** as the **Input Y Range** and enter **B1:B15** as the **Input X Range**. Click **Labels**, click **Confidence Level** and enter **95** in its box, and click **Residuals**. Click **OK** to execute the procedure.

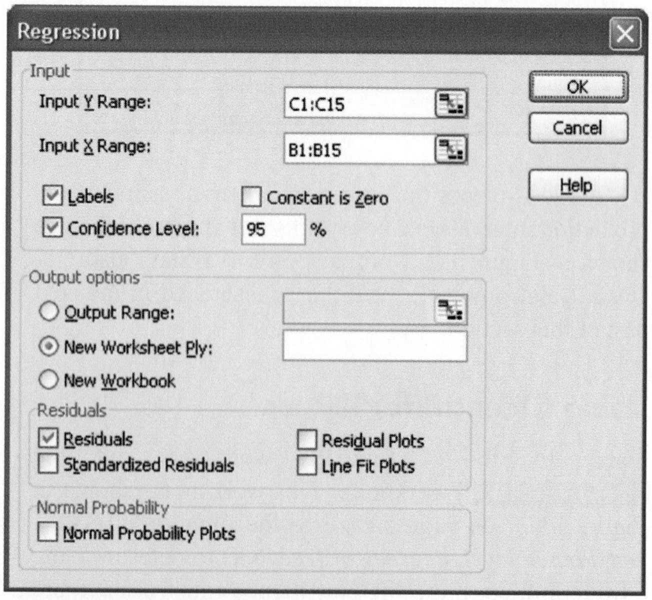

FIGURE E13.8 Completed Regression dialog box

To evaluate the assumption of linearity, you plot the residuals against the square feet (independent) variable. To simplify creating this plot, open to the Data worksheet and copy the square feet cell range B1:B15 to cell E1. Then copy the cell range of the residuals, C24:C38 on the SLR worksheet, to cell F1 of the Data worksheet. With your workbook open to the Data worksheet, use the Section E13.2 instructions on pages 564–566 to create a scatter plot. (Use **E1:F15** as the **Data range** (Excel 97–2003) or as the cell range of the *X* and *Y* variables (Excel 2007) when creating the scatter plot.) Review the scatter plot. Observe that there is no apparent pattern or relationship between the residuals and *X* variable. You conclude that the linearity assumption holds.

You now evaluate the normality assumption by creating a normal probability plot. Create a **Plot** worksheet, using the model worksheet in the NPP.xls workbook as your guide. In a new worksheet, enter **Rank** in cell A1 and then enter the series 1 through 14 in cells A2:A15. Enter **Proportion** in cell B1 and enter the formula =**A2/15** in cell B2. Next, enter **Z Value** in cell C1 and the formula =**NORMSINV(B2)** in cell C2. Copy the residuals (including their column heading) to the cell range D1:D15. Select the formulas in cell range B2:C2 and copy them down through row 15. Open to the probability plot and observe that the data do not appear to depart substantially from a normal distribution.

To evaluate the assumption of equal variance, return to the scatter plot of the residuals and the *X* variable that you already developed. Observe that there do not appear to be major differences in the variability of the residuals.

You conclude that all assumptions are valid and that you can use this simple linear regression model for the Sunflowers Apparel data. You can now evaluate the details of the regression results worksheet. If you are interested in making inferences about the mean of *Y* and the prediction of individual values of *Y*, open the CIEandPIforSLR.xls workbook. (Usually, you would have to first make adjustments to the **DataCopy** worksheet, as discussed in Section E13.5, but this workbook already contains the entries for the Sunflowers Apparel analysis.) Open to the **CIEandPI** worksheet to make inferences about the mean of *Y* and the prediction of individual values of *Y*.

CHAPTER 14

Introduction to Multiple Regression

USING STATISTICS @ OmniFoods

LEARNING OBJECTIVES

In this chapter, you learn:

- How to develop a multiple regression model
- How to interpret the regression coefficients
- How to determine which independent variables to include in the regression model
- How to determine which independent variables are most important in predicting a dependent variable
- How to use categorical variables in a regression model

Using Statistics @ OmniFoods

You are the marketing manager for OmniFoods, a large food products company. The company is planning a nationwide introduction of OmniPower, a new high-energy bar. Although originally marketed to runners, mountain climbers, and other athletes, high-energy bars are now popular with the general public. OmniFoods is anxious to capture a share of this thriving market.

Because the marketplace already contains several successful energy bars, you want to maximize the effect of your marketing plans. In particular, you need to determine the effect that price and in-store promotions will have on the sales of OmniPower before marketing the bar nationwide. You plan to use a sample of 34 stores in a supermarket chain for a test-market study of OmniPower sales. How can you extend the linear regression methods discussed in Chapter 13 to incorporate the effects of price *and* promotion into the same model? How can you use this model to improve the success of the nationwide introduction of OmniPower?

Chapter 13 focused on simple linear regression models that use *one* numerical independent variable, X, to predict the value of a numerical dependent variable, Y. Often you can make better predictions by using *more than one* independent variable. This chapter introduces you to **multiple regression models** that use two or more independent variables to predict the value of a dependent variable.

14.1 DEVELOPING A MULTIPLE REGRESSION MODEL

A sample of 34 stores in a supermarket chain is selected for a test-market study of OmniPower. All the stores selected have approximately the same monthly sales volume. Two independent variables are considered here—the price of an OmniPower bar, as measured in cents (X_1), and the monthly budget for in-store promotional expenditures, measured in dollars (X_2). In-store promotional expenditures typically include signs and displays, in-store coupons, and free samples. The dependent variable Y is the number of OmniPower bars sold in a month. Table 14.1 presents the results (stored in the file omni.xls) of the test-market study.

TABLE 14.1

Monthly OmniPower Sales, Price, and Promotional Expenditures

Store	Sales	Price	Promotion	Store	Sales	Price	Promotion
1	4,141	59	200	18	2,730	79	400
2	3,842	59	200	19	2,618	79	400
3	3,056	59	200	20	4,421	79	400
4	3,519	59	200	21	4,113	79	600
5	4,226	59	400	22	3,746	79	600
6	4,630	59	400	23	3,532	79	600
7	3,507	59	400	24	3,825	79	600
8	3,754	59	400	25	1,096	99	200
9	5,000	59	600	26	761	99	200
10	5,120	59	600	27	2,088	99	200
11	4,011	59	600	28	820	99	200
12	5,015	59	600	29	2,114	99	400
13	1,916	79	200	30	1,882	99	400
14	675	79	200	31	2,159	99	400
15	3,636	79	200	32	1,602	99	400
16	3,224	79	200	33	3,354	99	600
17	2,295	79	400	34	2,927	99	600

Interpreting the Regression Coefficients

When there are several independent variables, you can extend the simple linear regression model of Equation (13.1) on page 513 by assuming a linear relationship between each independent variable and the dependent variable. For example, with k independent variables, the multiple regression model is expressed in Equation (14.1).

MULTIPLE REGRESSION MODEL WITH k INDEPENDENT VARIABLES

$$Y_i = \beta_0 + \beta_1 X_{1i} + \beta_2 X_{2i} + \beta_3 X_{3i} + \cdots + \beta_k X_{ki} + \varepsilon_i \qquad \textbf{(14.1)}$$

where

$\beta_0 = Y$ intercept

$\beta_1 =$ slope of Y with variable X_1, holding variables $X_2, X_3, \ldots, X_k$ constant

$\beta_2 =$ slope of Y with variable X_2, holding variables $X_1, X_3, \ldots, X_k$ constant

$\beta_3 =$ slope of Y with variable X_3, holding variables $X_1, X_2, X_4, \ldots, X_k$ constant

.
.
.

$\beta_k =$ slope of Y with variable X_k, holding variables $X_1, X_2, X_3, \ldots, X_{k-1}$ constant

$\varepsilon_i =$ random error in Y for observation i

Equation (14.2) defines the multiple regression model with two independent variables.

MULTIPLE REGRESSION MODEL WITH TWO INDEPENDENT VARIABLES

$$Y_i = \beta_0 + \beta_1 X_{1i} + \beta_2 X_{2i} + \varepsilon_i \qquad \textbf{(14.2)}$$

where

$\beta_0 = Y$ intercept

$\beta_1 =$ slope of Y with variable X_1, holding variable X_2 constant

$\beta_2 =$ slope of Y with variable X_2, holding variable X_1 constant

$\varepsilon_i =$ random error in Y for observation i

Compare the multiple regression model to the simple linear regression model [Equation (13.1) on page 513]:

$$Y_i = \beta_0 + \beta_1 X_i + \varepsilon_i$$

In the simple linear regression model, the slope, β_1, represents the change in the mean of Y per unit change in X and does not take into account any other variables. In the multiple regression model with two independent variables [Equation (14.2)], the slope, β_1, represents the change in the mean of Y per unit change in X_1, taking into account the effect of X_2.

As in the case of simple linear regression, you use the sample regression coefficients (b_0, b_1, and b_2) as estimates of the population parameters (β_0, β_1, and β_2). Equation (14.3) defines the regression equation for a multiple regression model with two independent variables.

MULTIPLE REGRESSION EQUATION WITH TWO INDEPENDENT VARIABLES

$$\hat{Y}_i = b_0 + b_1 X_{1i} + b_2 X_{2i} \tag{14.3}$$

You can use Microsoft Excel to compute the values of the three regression coefficients for the OmniPower sales data (see Figure 14.1).

FIGURE 14.1

Partial Microsoft Excel results for OmniPower sales data

See Section E14.1 to create this.

	A	B	C	D	E	F	G
1	OmniPower Sales Analysis						
2							
3	*Regression Statistics*						
4	Multiple R	0.8705					
5	R Square	0.7577					
6	Adjusted R Square	0.7421					
7	Standard Error	638.0653					
8	Observations	34					
9							
10	ANOVA						
11		*df*	*SS*	*MS*	*F*	*Significance F*	
12	Regression	2	39472730.77	19736365.387	48.4771	2.86258E-10	
13	Residual	31	12620946.67	407127.312			
14	Total	33	52093677.44				
15							
16		*Coefficients*	*Standard Error*	*t Stat*	*P-value*	*Lower 95%*	*Upper 95%*
17	Intercept	5837.5208	628.1502	9.2932	1.791E-10	4556.3992	7118.6423
18	Price	-53.2173	6.8522	-7.7664	9.200E-09	-67.1925	-39.2421
19	Promotion	3.6131	0.6852	5.2728	9.822E-06	2.2155	5.0106

From Figure 14.1, the computed values of the regression coefficients are

$$b_0 = 5{,}837.5208 \quad b_1 = -53.2173 \quad b_2 = 3.6131$$

Therefore, the multiple regression equation is

$$\hat{Y}_i = 5{,}837.5208 - 53.2173 X_{1i} + 3.6131 X_{2i}$$

where

$$\hat{Y}_i = \text{predicted monthly sales of OmniPower bars for store } i$$

$$X_{1i} = \text{price of OmniPower bar (in cents) for store } i$$

$$X_{2i} = \text{monthly in-store promotional expenditures (in dollars) for store } i$$

The sample Y intercept ($b_0 = 5{,}837.5208$) estimates the number of OmniPower bars sold in a month if the price is \$0.00 and the total amount spent on promotional expenditures is also \$0.00. Because these values of price and promotion are outside the range of price and promotion used in the test-market study, and are nonsensical, the value of b_0 has no practical interpretation.

The slope of price with OmniPower sales ($b_1 = -53.2173$) indicates that, for a given amount of monthly promotional expenditures, the mean sales of OmniPower are estimated to decrease by 53.2173 bars per month for each 1-cent increase in the price. The slope of monthly promotional expenditures with OmniPower sales ($b_2 = 3.6131$) indicates that, for a given price, the mean sales of OmniPower are estimated to increase by 3.6131 bars for each additional \$1 spent on promotions. These estimates allow you to better understand the likely effect that price and promotion decisions will have in the marketplace. For example, a 10-cent decrease in price is estimated to increase mean sales by 532.173 bars, with a fixed amount of monthly promotional expenditures. A \$100 increase in promotional expenditures is estimated to increase mean sales by 361.31 bars, for a given price.

Regression coefficients in multiple regression are called **net regression coefficients**; they estimate the mean change in Y per unit change in a particular X, *holding constant the effect of the other X variables*. For example, in the study of OmniPower bar sales, for a store with a given amount of promotional expenditures, the mean sales are estimated to decrease by 53.2173 bars per month for each 1-cent increase in the price of an OmniPower bar. Another way to interpret this "net effect" is to think of two stores with an equal amount of promotional expenditures. If the first store charges 1 cent more than the other store, the net effect of this difference is that the first store is predicted to sell 53.2173 fewer bars per month than the second store. To interpret the net effect of promotional expenditures, you can consider two stores that are charging the same price. If the first store spends $1 more on promotional expenditures, the net effect of this difference is that the first store is predicted to sell 3.6131 more bars per month than the second store.

Predicting the Dependent Variable Y

You can use the multiple regression equation computed by Microsoft Excel to predict values of the dependent variable. For example, what is the predicted sales for a store charging 79 cents during a month in which promotional expenditures are $400? Using the multiple regression equation,

$$\hat{Y}_i = 5{,}837.5208 - 53.2173X_{1i} + 3.6131X_{2i}$$

with $X_{1i} = 79$ and $X_{2i} = 400$,

$$\hat{Y}_i = 5{,}837.5208 - 53.2173(79) + 3.6131(400)$$

$$= 3{,}078.57$$

Thus, your sales prediction for stores charging 79 cents and spending $400 in promotional expenditures is 3,078.57 OmniPower bars per month.

After you have predicted Y and done a residual analysis (see Section 14.3), the next step often involves a confidence interval estimate of the mean response and a prediction interval for an individual response. The computation of these intervals is too complex to do by hand, and you should use Microsoft Excel to perform the calculations. Figure 14.2 illustrates Microsoft Excel results.

FIGURE 14.2

Microsoft Excel confidence interval estimate and prediction interval for the OmniPower sales data

See Section E14.3 to create this.

	A	B	C	D
1	Confidence Interval Estimate and Prediction Interval			
2				
3	Data			
4	Confidence Level	95%		
5		1		
6	Price given value	79		
7	Promotion given value	400		
8				
9	XX	34	2646	13200
10		2646	214674	1018800
11		13200	1018800	6000000
12				
13	Inverse of XX	0.969163	-0.00941	-0.00053
14		-0.009408	0.000115	1.12E-06
15		-0.000535	1.12E-06	1.15E-06
16				
17	X'G times Inverse of XX	0.012054	0.000149	1.49E-05
18				
19	[X'G times Inverse of XX] times XG	0.029762	=MMULT(B17:D17, B5:B7)	
20	t Statistic	2.0395	=TINV(1 - B4, MR!B13)	
21	Predicted Y (YHat)	3078.57	{=MMULT(TRANSPOSE(B5:B7), MR!B17:B19)} 17:B19)}	
22				
23	For Average Predicted Y (YHat)			
24	Interval Half Width	224.50	=B20 * SQRT(B19)* MR!B7	
25	Confidence Interval Lower Limit	2854.07	=B21 - B24	
26	Confidence Interval Upper Limit	3303.08	=B21 + B24	
27				
28	For Individual Response Y			
29	Interval Half Width	1320.57	=B20 * SQRT(1 + B19)* MR!B7	
30	Prediction Interval Lower Limit	1758.01	=B21 - B29	
31	Prediction Interval Upper Limit	4399.14	=B21 + B29	

The 95% confidence interval estimate of the mean OmniPower sales for all stores charging 79 cents and spending $400 in promotional expenditures is 2,854.07 to 3,303.08 bars. The prediction interval for an individual store is 1,758.01 to 4,399.14 bars.

PROBLEMS FOR SECTION 14.1

Learning the Basics

 14.1 For this problem, use the following multiple regression equation:

$$\hat{Y}_i = 10 + 5X_{1i} + 3X_{2i}$$

a. Interpret the meaning of the slopes.
b. Interpret the meaning of the Y intercept.

 14.2 For this problem, use the following multiple regression equation:

$$\hat{Y}_i = 50 + 2X_{1i} + 7X_{2i}$$

a. Interpret the meaning of the slopes.
b. Interpret the meaning of the Y intercept.

Appying the Concepts

 14.3 A marketing analyst for a shoe manufacturer is considering the development of a new brand of running shoes. The marketing analyst wants to determine which variables to use in predicting durability (that is, the effect of long-term impact). Two independent variables under consideration are X_1 (FOREIMP), a measurement of the forefoot shock-absorbing capability, and X_2 (MIDSOLE), a measurement of the change in impact properties over time. The dependent variable Y is LTIMP, a measure of the shoe's durability after a repeated impact test. A random sample of 15 types of currently manufactured running shoes was selected for testing, with the following results:

ANOVA	df	SS	MS	F	Significance F
Regression	2	12.61020	6.30510	97.69	0.0001
Error	12	0.77453	0.06454		
Total	14	13.38473			

Variable	Coefficients	Standard Error	t Statistic	p-Value
INTERCEPT	−0.02686	0.06905	−0.39	0.7034
FOREIMP	0.79116	0.06295	12.57	0.0000
MIDSOLE	0.60484	0.07174	8.43	0.0000

a. State the multiple regression equation.
b. Interpret the meaning of the slopes in this problem.

 14.4 A mail-order catalog business selling personal computer supplies, software, and hardware maintains a centralized warehouse. Management is currently examining the process of distribution from the warehouse and wants to study the factors that affect warehouse distribution costs. Currently, a small handling fee is added to each order, regardless of the amount of the order. Data collected over the past 24 months (stored in the file **warecost.xls**) indicate the warehouse distribution costs (in thousands of dollars), the sales (in thousands of dollars), and the number of orders received.
a. State the multiple regression equation.
b. Interpret the meaning of the slopes, b_1 and b_2, in this problem.
c. Explain why the regression coefficient, b_0, has no practical meaning in the context of this problem.
d. Predict the mean monthly warehouse distribution cost when sales are $400,000 and the number of orders is 4,500.
e. Construct a 95% confidence interval estimate for the mean monthly warehouse distribution cost when sales are $400,000 and the number of orders is 4,500.
f. Construct a 95% prediction interval for the monthly warehouse distribution cost for a particular month when sales are $400,000 and the number of orders is 4,500.

 14.5 A consumer organization wants to develop a regression model to predict gasoline mileage (as measured by miles per gallon) based on the horsepower of the car's engine and the weight of the car, in pounds. A sample of 50 recent car models was selected, with the results recorded in the file **auto.xls**.
a. State the multiple regression equation.
b. Interpret the meaning of the slopes, b_1 and b_2, in this problem.
c. Explain why the regression coefficient, b_0, has no practical meaning in the context of this problem.
d. Predict the mean miles per gallon for cars that have 60 horsepower and weigh 2,000 pounds.
e. Construct a 95% confidence interval estimate for the mean miles per gallon for cars that have 60 horsepower and weigh 2,000 pounds.
f. Construct a 95% prediction interval for the miles per gallon for an individual car that has 60 horsepower and weighs 2,000 pounds.

 14.6 A consumer products company wants to measure the effectiveness of different types of advertising media in the promotion of its products. Specifically, the company is interested in the effectiveness of radio advertising and newspaper advertising (including the cost of discount coupons). A sample of 22 cities with approximately equal populations is selected for study during a test period of one month. Each city is allocated a specific expenditure level both for radio advertising and for newspaper advertising. The sales of the product (in thousands of dollars) and also the levels of media expenditure (in thousands of dollars) during the test month are recorded, with the following results stored in the file **advertise.xls**:

City	Sales ($000)	Radio Advertising ($000)	Newspaper Advertising $000)
1	973	0	40
2	1,119	0	40
3	875	25	25
4	625	25	25
5	910	30	30
6	971	30	30
7	931	35	35
8	1,177	35	35
9	882	40	25
10	982	40	25
11	1,628	45	45
12	1,577	45	45
13	1,044	50	0
14	914	50	0
15	1,329	55	25
16	1,330	55	25
17	1,405	60	30
18	1,436	60	30
19	1,521	65	35
20	1,741	65	35
21	1,866	70	40
22	1,717	70	40

a. State the multiple regression equation.
b. Interpret the meaning of the slopes, b_1 and b_2, in this problem.
c. Interpret the meaning of the regression coefficient, b_0.
d. Predict the mean sales for a city in which radio advertising is $20,000 and newspaper advertising is $20,000.
e. Construct a 95% confidence interval estimate for the mean sales for cities in which radio advertising is $20,000 and newspaper advertising is $20,000.
f. Construct a 95% prediction interval for the sales for an individual city in which radio advertising is $20,000 and newspaper advertising is $20,000.

14.7 The director of broadcasting operations for a television station wants to study the issue of standby hours (that is, hours in which unionized graphic artists at the station are paid but are not actually involved in any activity). The variables in the study include

Standby hours (Y)—Total number of standby hours in a week

Total staff present (X_1)—Weekly total of people-days
Remote hours (X_2)—Total number of hours worked by employees at locations away from the central plant
The results for a period of 26 weeks are in the data file standby.xls.
a. State the multiple regression equation.
b. Interpret the meaning of the slopes, b_1 and b_2, in this problem.
c. Explain why the regression coefficient, b_0, has no practical meaning in the context of this problem.
d. Predict the mean standby hours for a week in which the total staff present have 310 people-days and the remote hours are 400.
e. Construct a 95% confidence interval estimate for the mean standby hours for weeks in which the total staff present have 310 people-days and the remote hours are 400.
f. Construct a 95% prediction interval for the standby hours for a single week in which the total staff present have 310 people-days and the remote hours are 400.

14.8 Nassau County is located approximately 25 miles east of New York City. Until all residential property was recently reappraised, property taxes were assessed based on actual value in 1938 or when the property was built, if it was constructed after 1938. Data in the file glencove.xls include the appraised value, land area of the property in acres, and age, in years, for a sample of 30 single-family homes located in Glen Cove, a small city in Nassau County. Develop a multiple linear regression model to predict appraised value based on land area of the property and age, in years.
a. State the multiple regression equation.
b. Interpret the meaning of the slopes, b_1 and b_2, in this problem.
c. Explain why the regression coefficient, b_0, has no practical meaning in the context of this problem.
d. Predict the mean appraised value for a house that has a land area of 0.25 acres and is 45 years old.
e. Construct a 95% confidence interval estimate for the mean appraised value for houses that have a land area of 0.25 acres and are 45 years old.
f. Construct a 95% prediction interval estimate for the appraised value for an individual house that has a land area of 0.25 acres and is 45 years old.

14.2 r^2, ADJUSTED r^2, AND THE OVERALL F TEST

This section discusses three methods you can use to evaluate the overall usefulness of the multiple regression model: the coefficient of multiple determination r^2, the adjusted r^2, and the overall F test.

Coefficient of Multiple Determination

Recall from Section 13.3 that the coefficient of determination, r^2, measures the variation in Y that is explained by the independent variable X in the simple linear regression model. In multiple regression, the **coefficient of multiple determination** represents the proportion of the variation in Y that is explained by the set of independent variables. Equation (14.4) defines the coefficient of multiple determination for a multiple regression model with two or more independent variables.

COEFFICIENT OF MULTIPLE DETERMINATION

The coefficient of multiple determination is equal to the regression sum of squares (SSR) divided by the total sum of squares (SST).

$$r^2 = \frac{\text{Regression sum of squares}}{\text{Total sum of squares}} = \frac{SSR}{SST} \qquad \textbf{(14.4)}$$

where

$$SSR = \text{regression sum of squares}$$

$$SST = \text{total sum of squares}$$

In the OmniPower example, from Figure 14.1 on page 574, $SSR = 39,472,730.77$ and $SST = 52,093,677.44$. Thus,

$$r^2 = \frac{SSR}{SST} = \frac{39,472,730.77}{52,093,677.44} = 0.7577$$

The coefficient of multiple determination ($r^2 = 0.7577$) indicates that 75.77% of the variation in sales is explained by the variation in the price and in the promotional expenditures.

Adjusted r^2

When considering multiple regression models, some statisticians suggest that you should use the **adjusted r^2** to reflect both the number of independent variables in the model and the sample size. Reporting the adjusted r^2 is extremely important when you are comparing two or more regression models that predict the same dependent variable but have a different number of independent variables. Equation (14.5) defines the adjusted r^2.

ADJUSTED r^2

$$r_{\text{adj}}^2 = 1 - \left[(1 - r^2) \frac{n - 1}{n - k - 1} \right] \qquad \textbf{(14.5)}$$

where k is the number of independent variables in the regression equation.

Thus, for the OmniPower data, because $r^2 = 0.7577$, $n = 34$, and $k = 2$,

$$r_{\text{adj}}^2 = 1 - \left[(1 - r^2) \frac{34 - 1}{(34 - 2 - 1)} \right]$$

$$= 1 - \left[(1 - 0.7577) \frac{33}{31} \right]$$

$$= 1 - 0.2579$$

$$= 0.7421$$

Hence, 74.21% of the variation in sales is explained by the multiple regression model—adjusted for number of independent variables and sample size.

Test for the Significance of the Overall Multiple Regression Model

You use the **overall F test** to test whether there is a significant relationship between the dependent variable and the entire set of independent variables (the overall multiple regression model). Because there is more than one independent variable, you use the following null and alternative hypotheses:

H_0: $\beta_1 = \beta_2 = \cdots = \beta_k = 0$ (There is no linear relationship between the dependent variable and the independent variables.)

H_1: At least one $\beta_j \neq 0$, $j = 1, 2, \ldots, k$ (There is a linear relationship between the dependent variable and at least one of the independent variables.)

Equation (14.6) defines the statistic for the overall F test. Table 14.2 presents the associated ANOVA summary table.

OVERALL F TEST STATISTIC

The F statistic is equal to the regression mean square (MSR) divided by the error mean square (MSE).

$$F = \frac{MSR}{MSE} \qquad (14.6)$$

where

F = test statistic from an F distribution with k and $n - k - 1$ degrees of freedom

k = number of independent variables in the regression model

TABLE 14.2

ANOVA Summary Table for the Overall F Test

Source	Degrees of Freedom	Sum of Squares	Mean Square (Variance)	F
Regression	k	SSR	$MSR = \dfrac{SSR}{k}$	$F = \dfrac{MSR}{MSE}$
Error	$n - k - 1$	SSE	$MSE = \dfrac{SSE}{n - k - 1}$	
Total	$n - 1$	SST		

The decision rule is

Reject H_0 at the α level of significance if $F > F_{U(k,n-k-1)}$;

otherwise, do not reject H_0.

Using a 0.05 level of significance, the critical value of the F distribution with 2 and 31 degrees of freedom found from Table E.5 is approximately 3.32 (see Figure 14.3 on page 580). From Figure 14.1 on page 574, the F statistic given in the ANOVA summary table is 48.4771. Because $48.4771 > 3.32$, or because the p-value $= 0.000 < 0.05$, you reject H_0 and conclude that at least one of the independent variables (price and/or promotional expenditures) is related to sales.

FIGURE 14.3

Testing for the significance of a set of regression coefficients at the 0.05 level of significance, with 2 and 31 degrees of freedom

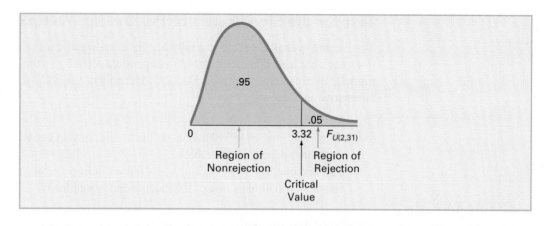

PROBLEMS FOR SECTION 14.2

Learning the Basics

14.9 The following ANOVA summary table is for a multiple regression model with two independent variables:

Source	Degrees of Freedom	Sum of Squares	Mean Squares	F
Regression	2	60		
Error	18	120		
Total	20	180		

a. Determine the regression mean square (MSR) and the mean square error (MSE).
b. Compute the F statistic.
c. Determine whether there is a significant relationship between Y and the two independent variables at the 0.05 level of significance.
d. Compute the coefficient of multiple determination, r^2, and interpret its meaning.
e. Compute the adjusted r^2.

14.10 The following ANOVA summary table is for a multiple regression model with two independent variables:

Source	Degrees of Freedom	Sum of Squares	Mean Squares	F
Regression	2	30		
Error	10	120		
Total	12	150		

a. Determine the regression mean square (MSR) and the mean square error (MSE).
b. Compute the F statistic.
c. Determine whether there is a significant relationship between Y and the two independent variables at the 0.05 level of significance.
d. Compute the coefficient of multiple determination, r^2, and interpret its meaning.
e. Compute the adjusted r^2.

Applying the Concepts

14.11 Eileen M. Van Aken and Brian M. Kleiner, professors at Virginia Polytechnic Institute and State University, investigated the factors that contribute to the effectiveness of teams ("Determinants of Effectiveness for Cross-Functional Organizational Design Teams," *Quality Management Journal*, 1997, 4, pp. 51–79). The researchers studied 34 independent variables, such as team skills, diversity, meeting frequency, and clarity in expectations. For each of the teams studied, each of the variables was given a value of 1 through 100, based on the results of interviews and survey data, where 100 represents the highest rating. The dependent variable, team performance, was also given a value of 1 through 100, with 100 representing the highest rating. Many different regression models were explored, including the following:

Model 1

$$\text{Team performance} = \beta_0 + \beta_1(\text{Team skills}) + \varepsilon,$$
$$r_{adj}^2 = 0.68$$

Model 2

$$\text{Team performance} = \beta_0 + \beta_1(\text{Clarity in expectations}) + \varepsilon,$$
$$r_{adj}^2 = 0.78$$

Model 3

$$\text{Team performance} = \beta_0 + \beta_1(\text{Team skills}) +$$
$$\beta_2(\text{Clarity in expectations}) + \varepsilon,$$
$$r_{adj}^2 = 0.97$$

a. Interpret the adjusted r^2 for each of the three models.
b. Which of these three models do you think is the best predictor of team performance?

14.12 In Problem 14.3 on page 576, you predicted the durability of a brand of running shoe, based on the forefoot shock-absorbing capability and the change in impact properties over time. The regression analysis resulted in the following ANOVA summary table:

Source	Degrees of Freedom	Sum of Squares	Mean Squares	F	Significance
Regression	2	12.61020	6.30510	97.69	0.0001
Error	12	0.77453	0.06454		
Total	14	13.38473			

a. Determine whether there is a significant relationship between durability and the two independent variables at the 0.05 level of significance.
b. Interpret the meaning of the p-value.
c. Compute the coefficient of multiple determination, r^2, and interpret its meaning.
d. Compute the adjusted r^2.

 14.13 In Problem 14.5 on page 576, you used horsepower and weight to predict gasoline mileage (see the auto.xls file). Using the results from that problem,
a. determine whether there is a significant relationship between gasoline mileage and the two independent variables (horsepower and weight) at the 0.05 level of significance.
b. interpret the meaning of the p-value.
c. compute the coefficient of multiple determination, r^2, and interpret its meaning.
d. compute the adjusted r^2.

 14.14 In Problem 14.4 on page 576, you used sales and number of orders to predict distribution costs at a mail-order catalog business (see the warecost.xls file). Using the results from that problem,
a. determine whether there is a significant relationship between distribution costs and the two independent variables (sales and number of orders) at the 0.05 level of significance.

b. interpret the meaning of the p-value.
c. compute the coefficient of multiple determination, r^2, and interpret its meaning.
d. compute the adjusted r^2.

14.15 In Problem 14.7 on page 577, you used the total staff present and remote hours to predict standby hours (see the file standby.xls). Using the results from that problem,
a. determine whether there is a significant relationship between standby hours and the two independent variables (total staff present and remote hours) at the 0.05 level of significance.
b. interpret the meaning of the p-value.
c. compute the coefficient of multiple determination, r^2, and interpret its meaning.
d. compute the adjusted r^2.

14.16 In Problem 14.6 on pages 576–577, you used radio advertising and newspaper advertising to predict sales (see the advertise.xls file). Using the results from that problem,
a. determine whether there is a significant relationship between sales and the two independent variables (radio advertising and newspaper advertising) at the 0.05 level of significance.
b. interpret the meaning of the p-value.
c. compute the coefficient of multiple determination, r^2, and interpret its meaning.
d. compute the adjusted r^2.

14.17 In Problem 14.8 on page 577, you used the land area of a property and the age of a house to predict appraised value (see the glencove.xls file). Using the results from that problem,
a. determine whether there is a significant relationship between appraised value and the two independent variables (land area of a property and age of a house) at the 0.05 level of significance.
b. interpret the meaning of the p-value.
c. compute the coefficient of multiple determination, r^2, and interpret its meaning.
d. compute the adjusted r^2.

14.3 RESIDUAL ANALYSIS FOR THE MULTIPLE REGRESSION MODEL

In Section 13.5, you used residual analysis to evaluate the appropriateness of using the simple linear regression model for a set of data. For the multiple regression model with two independent variables, you need to construct and analyze the following residual plots:

1. Residuals versus $\hat{Y}_i$
2. Residuals versus X_{1i}
3. Residuals versus X_{2i}
4. Residuals versus time

The first residual plot examines the pattern of residuals versus the predicted values of Y. If the residuals show a pattern for different predicted values of Y, there is evidence of a possible quadratic effect in at least one independent variable, a possible violation of the assumption of equal variance (see Figure 13.13 on page 533), and/or the need to transform the Y variable.

The second and third residual plots involve the independent variables. Patterns in the plot of the residuals versus an independent variable may indicate the existence of a quadratic effect and, therefore, indicate the need to add a quadratic independent variable to the multiple regression model. The fourth plot is used to investigate patterns in the residuals in order to validate the independence assumption when the data are collected in time order. Associated with this residual plot, as in Section 13.6, you can compute the Durbin-Watson statistic to determine the existence of positive autocorrelation among the residuals.

Figure 14.4 illustrates the Microsoft Excel residual plots for the OmniPower sales example. In Figure 14.4, there is very little or no pattern in the relationship between the residuals and the predicted value of Y, the value of X_1 (price), or the value of X_2 (promotional expenditures). Thus, you can conclude that the multiple regression model is appropriate for predicting sales.

FIGURE 14.4

Microsoft Excel residual plots for the OmniPower sales data: Panel *A*, residuals versus predicted *Y*; Panel *B*, residuals versus price; Panel *C*, residuals versus promotional expenditures

See Section E14.2 to create this.

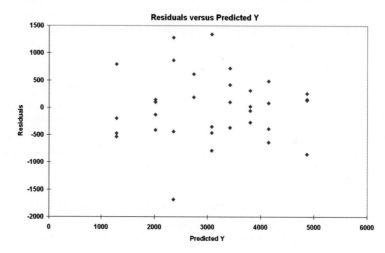

Panel A

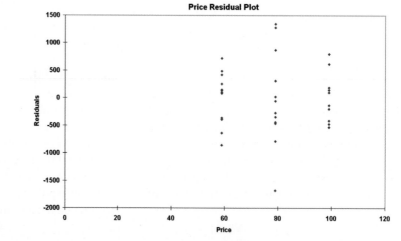

Panel B

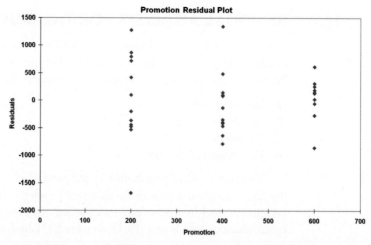

Panel C

PROBLEMS FOR SECTION 14.3

Applying the Concepts

PH Grade ASSIST **14.18** In Problem 14.4 on page 576, you used sales and number of orders to predict distribution costs at a mail-order catalog business (see the **warecost.xls** file).

a. Perform a residual analysis on your results and determine the adequacy of the model.
b. Plot the residuals against the months. Is there any evidence of a pattern in the residuals? Explain.
c. Determine the Durbin-Watson statistic.
d. At the 0.05 level of significance, is there evidence of positive autocorrelation in the residuals?

PH Grade ASSIST **14.19** In Problem 14.5 on page 576, you used horsepower and weight to predict gasoline mileage (see the **auto.xls** file). Perform a residual analysis on your results and determine the adequacy of the model.

14.20 In Problem 14.6 on pages 576–577, you used radio advertising and newspaper advertising to predict sales (see the **advertise.xls** file). Perform a residual analysis on your results and determine the adequacy of the model.

14.21 In Problem 14.7 on page 577, you used the total staff present and remote hours to predict standby hours (see the **standby.xls** file).

a. Perform a residual analysis on your results and determine the adequacy of the model.
b. Plot the residuals against the weeks. Is there evidence of a pattern in the residuals? Explain.
c. Determine the Durbin-Watson statistic.
d. At the 0.05 level of significance, is there evidence of positive autocorrelation in the residuals?

14.22 In Problem 14.8 on page 577, you used the land area of a property and the age of a house to predict appraised value (see the **glencove.xls** file). Perform a residual analysis on your results and determine the adequacy of the model.

14.4 INFERENCES CONCERNING THE POPULATION REGRESSION COEFFICIENTS

In Section 13.7, you tested the slope in a simple linear regression model to determine the significance of the relationship between X and Y. In addition, you constructed a confidence interval estimate of the population slope. This section extends those procedures to multiple regression.

Tests of Hypothesis

In a simple linear regression model, to test a hypothesis concerning the population slope, β_1, you used Equation (13.16) on page 539:

$$t = \frac{b_1 - \beta_1}{S_{b_1}}$$

Equation (14.7) generalizes this equation for multiple regression.

TESTING FOR THE SLOPE IN MULTIPLE REGRESSION

$$t = \frac{b_j - \beta_j}{S_{b_j}} \qquad (14.7)$$

where

b_j = slope of variable j with Y, holding constant the effects of all other independent variables

S_{b_j} = standard error of the regression coefficient b_j

t = test statistic for a t distribution with $n - k - 1$ degrees of freedom

k = number of independent variables in the regression equation

β_j = hypothesized value of the population slope for variable j, holding constant the effects of all other independent variables

To determine whether variable X_2 (amount of promotional expenditures) has a significant effect on sales, taking into account the price of OmniPower bars, the null and alternative hypotheses are

$$H_0: \beta_2 = 0$$
$$H_1: \beta_2 \neq 0$$

From Equation (14.7) and Figure 14.1 on page 574,

$$t = \frac{b_2 - \beta_2}{S_{b_2}}$$

$$= \frac{3.6131 - 0}{0.6852} = 5.2728$$

If you select a level of significance of 0.05, the critical values of t for 31 degrees of freedom from Table E.3 are -2.0395 and $+2.0395$ (see Figure 14.5).

FIGURE 14.5

Testing for significance of a regression coefficient at the 0.05 level of significance, with 31 degrees of freedom

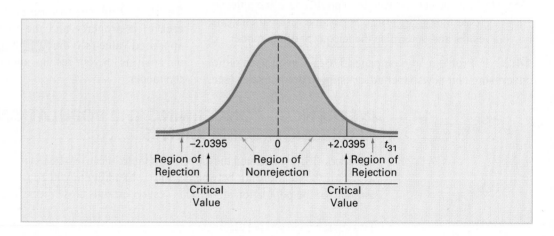

From Figure 14.1, the p-value is 0.000009822 (or 9.822E-06 in scientific notation). Because $t = 5.2728 > 2.0395$ or the p-value of 0.000009822 < 0.05, you reject H_0 and conclude that there is a significant relationship between the variable X_2 (promotional expenditures) and sales, taking into account the price, X_1. This extremely small p-value allows you to strongly reject the null hypothesis that there is no linear relationship between sales and promotional expenditures. Example 14.1 presents the test for the significance of β_1, the slope of sales with price.

EXAMPLE 14.1

TESTING FOR THE SIGNIFICANCE OF THE SLOPE OF SALES WITH PRICE

At the 0.05 level of significance, is there evidence that the slope of sales with price is different from zero?

SOLUTION From Figure 14.1 on page 574, $t = -7.7664 < -2.0395$ (the critical value for $\alpha = 0.05$) or the p-value = 0.0000000092 < 0.05. Thus, there is a significant relationship between price, X_1, and sales, taking into account the promotional expenditures, X_2.

As seen with each of the two X variables, the test of significance for a particular regression coefficient is actually a test for the significance of adding a particular variable into a regression model, given that the other variable is included. Therefore, the t test for the regression coefficient is equivalent to testing for the contribution of each independent variable.

Confidence Interval Estimation

Instead of testing the significance of a population slope, you may want to estimate the value of a population slope. Equation (14.8) defines the confidence interval estimate for a population slope in multiple regression.

CONFIDENCE INTERVAL ESTIMATE FOR THE SLOPE

$$b_j \pm t_{n-k-1} S_{b_j} \tag{14.8}$$

To construct a 95% confidence interval estimate of the population slope, β_1 (the effect of price, X_1, on sales, Y, holding constant the effect of promotional expenditures, X_2), the critical value of t at the 95% confidence level with 31 degrees of freedom is 2.0395 (see Table E.3). Then, using Equation (14.8) and Figure 14.1 on page 574,

$$b_1 \pm t_{n-k-1} S_{b_1}$$
$$-53.2173 \pm (2.0395)(6.8522)$$
$$-53.2173 \pm 13.9752$$
$$-67.1925 \le \beta_1 \le -39.2421$$

Taking into account the effect of promotional expenditures, the estimated effect of a 1-cent increase in price is to reduce mean sales by approximately 39.2 to 67.2 bars. You have 95% confidence that this interval correctly estimates the relationship between these variables. From a hypothesis-testing viewpoint, because this confidence interval does not include 0, you conclude that the regression coefficient, β_1, has a significant effect.

Example 14.2 constructs and interprets a confidence interval estimate for the slope of sales with promotional expenditures.

EXAMPLE 14.2   **CONSTRUCTING A CONFIDENCE INTERVAL ESTIMATE FOR THE SLOPE OF SALES WITH PROMOTIONAL EXPENDITURES**

Construct a 95% confidence interval estimate of the population slope of sales with promotional expenditures.

SOLUTION The critical value of t at the 95% confidence level, with 31 degrees of freedom, is 2.0395 (see Table E.3). Using Equation (14.8) and Figure 14.1 on page 574,

$$3.6131 \pm (2.0395)(0.6852)$$
$$3.6131 \pm 1.3975$$
$$2.2156 \le \beta_2 \le 5.0106$$

Thus, taking into account the effect of price, the estimated effect of each additional dollar of promotional expenditures is to increase mean sales by approximately 2.2 to 5.0 bars. You have 95% confidence that this interval correctly estimates the relationship between these variables. From a hypothesis-testing viewpoint, because this confidence interval does not include 0, you can conclude that the regression coefficient, β_2, has a significant effect.

PROBLEMS FOR SECTION 14.4

Learning the Basics

 14.23 Given the following information from a multiple regression analysis:

$$n = 25 \quad b_1 = 5 \quad b_2 = 10 \quad S_{b_1} = 2 \quad S_{b_2} = 8$$

a. Which variable has the largest slope, in units of a t statistic?
b. Construct a 95% confidence interval estimate of the population slope, β_1.
c. At the 0.05 level of significance, determine whether each independent variable makes a significant contribution to the regression model. On the basis of these results, indicate the independent variables to include in this model.

14.24 Given the following information from a multiple regression analysis:

$$n = 20 \quad b_1 = 4 \quad b_2 = 3 \quad S_{b_1} = 1.2 \quad S_{b_2} = 0.8$$

a. Which variable has the largest slope, in units of a t statistic?
b. Construct a 95% confidence interval estimate of the population slope, β_1.
c. At the 0.05 level of significance, determine whether each independent variable makes a significant contribution to the regression model. On the basis of these results, indicate the independent variables to include in this model.

Applying the Concepts

 14.25 In Problem 14.3 on page 576, you predicted the durability of a brand of running shoe, based on the forefoot shock-absorbing capability (FOREIMP) and the change in impact properties over time (MIDSOLE) for a sample of 15 pairs of shoes. Use the following results:

Variable	Coefficient	Standard Error	t Statistic	p-Value
INTERCEPT	−0.02686	0.06905	−0.39	0.7034
FOREIMP	0.79116	0.06295	12.57	0.0000
MIDSOLE	0.60484	0.07174	8.43	0.0000

a. Construct a 95% confidence interval estimate of the population slope between durability and forefoot shock-absorbing capability.
b. At the 0.05 level of significance, determine whether each independent variable makes a significant contribution to the regression model. On the basis of these results, indicate the independent variables to include in this model.

 14.26 In Problem 14.4 on page 576, you used sales and number of orders to predict distribution costs at a mail-order catalog business (see the **warecost.xls** file). Using the results from that problem,
a. construct a 95% confidence interval estimate of the population slope between distribution cost and sales.
b. at the 0.05 level of significance, determine whether each independent variable makes a significant contribution to the regression model. On the basis of these results, indicate the independent variables to include in this model.

14.27 In Problem 14.5 on page 576, you used horsepower and weight to predict gasoline mileage (see the **auto.xls** file). Using the results from that problem,
a. construct a 95% confidence interval estimate of the population slope between gasoline mileage and horsepower.
b. at the 0.05 level of significance, determine whether each independent variable makes a significant contribution to the regression model. On the basis of these results, indicate the independent variables to include in this model.

14.28 In Problem 14.6 on pages 576–577, you used radio advertising and newspaper advertising to predict sales (see the **advertise.xls** file). Using the results from that problem,
a. construct a 95% confidence interval estimate of the population slope between sales and radio advertising.
b. at the 0.05 level of significance, determine whether each independent variable makes a significant contribution to the regression model. On the basis of these results, indicate the independent variables to include in this model.

14.29 In Problem 14.7 on page 577, you used the total number of staff present and remote hours to predict standby hours (see the **standby.xls** file). Using the results from that problem,
a. construct a 95% confidence interval estimate of the population slope between standby hours and total number of staff present.
b. at the 0.05 level of significance, determine whether each independent variable makes a significant contribution to the regression model. On the basis of these results, indicate the independent variables to include in this model.

14.30 In Problem 14.8 on page 577, you used land area of a property and age of a house to predict appraised value (see the **glencove.xls** file). Using the results from that problem,
a. construct a 95% confidence interval estimate of the population slope between appraised value and land area of a property.
b. at the 0.05 level of significance, determine whether each independent variable makes a significant contribution to the regression model. On the basis of these results, indicate the independent variables to include in this model.

14.5   TESTING PORTIONS OF THE MULTIPLE REGRESSION MODEL

In developing a multiple regression model, you want to use only those independent variables that significantly reduce the error in predicting the value of a dependent variable. If an independent variable does not improve the prediction, you can delete it from the multiple regression model and use a model with fewer independent variables.

The **partial F test** is an alternative method to the t test discussed in Section 14.4 for determining the contribution of an independent variable. It involves determining the contribution to the regression sum of squares made by each independent variable after all the other independent variables have been included in the model. The new independent variable is included only if it significantly improves the model.

To conduct partial F tests for the OmniPower sales example, you need to evaluate the contribution of promotional expenditures (X_2) after price (X_1) has been included in the model, and also evaluate the contribution of price (X_1) after promotional expenditures (X_2) have been included in the model.

In general, if there are several independent variables, you determine the contribution of each independent variable by taking into account the regression sum of squares of a model that includes all independent variables except the one of interest, SSR (all variables except j). Equation (14.9) determines the contribution of variable j, assuming that all other variables are already included.

DETERMINING THE CONTRIBUTION OF AN INDEPENDENT VARIABLE TO THE REGRESSION MODEL

$SSR(X_j \mid$ All variables *except* $j)$

$\qquad = SSR$ (All variables *including* j) $- SSR$ (All variables *except* j)   **(14.9)**

If there are two independent variables, you use Equations (14.10a) and (14.10b) to determine the contribution of each.

CONTRIBUTION OF VARIABLE X_1, GIVEN THAT X_2 HAS BEEN INCLUDED

$$SSR(X_1 \mid X_2) = SSR(X_1 \text{ and } X_2) - SSR(X_2) \qquad \textbf{(14.10a)}$$

CONTRIBUTION OF VARIABLE X_2, GIVEN THAT X_1 HAS BEEN INCLUDED

$$SSR(X_2 \mid X_1) = SSR(X_1 \text{ and } X_2) - SSR(X_1) \qquad \textbf{(14.10b)}$$

The term $SSR(X_2)$ represents the sum of squares that is due to regression for a model that includes only the independent variable X_2 (promotional expenditures). Similarly, $SSR(X_1)$ represents the sum of squares that is due to regression for a model that includes only the independent variable X_1 (price). Figures 14.6 and 14.7 present Microsoft Excel results for these two models.

FIGURE 14.6

Microsoft Excel results of a simple linear regression analysis for sales and promotional expenditures, $SSR(X_2)$

See Section E13.1 to create this.

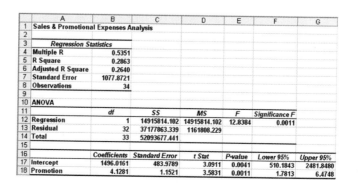

	A	B	C	D	E	F	G
1	Sales & Promotional Expenses Analysis						
2							
3	Regression Statistics						
4	Multiple R	0.5351					
5	R Square	0.2863					
6	Adjusted R Square	0.2640					
7	Standard Error	1077.8721					
8	Observations	34					
9							
10	ANOVA						
11		df	SS	MS	F	Significance F	
12	Regression	1	14915814.102	14915814.102	12.8384	0.0011	
13	Residual	32	37177863.339	1161808.229			
14	Total	33	52093677.441				
15							
16		Coefficients	Standard Error	t Stat	P-value	Lower 95%	Upper 95%
17	Intercept	1496.0161	483.9789	3.0911	0.0041	510.1843	2481.8480
18	Promotion	4.1281	1.1521	3.5831	0.0011	1.7813	6.4748

FIGURE 14.7

Microsoft Excel results of a simple linear regression model for sales and price, $SSR(X_1)$

See Section E13.1 to create this.

	A	B	C	D	E	F	G
1	Sales & Price Analysis						
2							
3	Regression Statistics						
4	Multiple R	0.7351					
5	R Square	0.5404					
6	Adjusted R Square	0.5261					
7	Standard Error	864.9457					
8	Observations	34					
9							
10	ANOVA						
11			df	SS	MS	F	Significance F
12	Regression		1	28153486.15	28153486.15	37.6318	7.35855E-07
13	Residual		32	23940191.29	748130.98		
14	Total		33	52093677.44			
15							
16			Coefficients	Standard Error	t Stat	P-value	Lower 95%	Upper 95%
17	Intercept		7512.3480	734.6189	10.2262	1.30793E-11	6015.9796	9008.7164
18	Price		-56.7138	9.2451	-6.1345	7.35855E-07	-75.5455	-37.8822

From Figure 14.6, $SSR(X_2) = 14{,}915{,}814.102$ and from Figure 14.1 on page 574, $SSR(X_1$ and $X_2) = 39{,}472{,}730.77$. Then, using Equation (14.10a),

$$SSR(X_1 \mid X_2) = SSR(X_1 \text{ and } X_2) - SSR(X_2)$$
$$= 39{,}472{,}730.77 - 14{,}915{,}814.102$$
$$= 24{,}556{,}916.67$$

To determine whether X_1 significantly improves the model after X_2 has been included, you divide the regression sum of squares into two component parts, as shown in Table 14.3.

TABLE 14.3

ANOVA Table Dividing the Regression Sum of Squares into Components to Determine the Contribution of Variable X_1

Source	Degrees of Freedom	Sum of Squares	Mean Square (Variance)	F
Regression	2	39,472,730.77	19,736,365.39	
$\left\{ \begin{matrix} X_2 \\ X_1 \mid X_2 \end{matrix} \right\}$	$\left\{ \begin{matrix} 1 \\ 1 \end{matrix} \right\}$	$\left\{ \begin{matrix} 14{,}915{,}814.10 \\ 24{,}556{,}916.67 \end{matrix} \right\}$	24,556,916.67	60.32
Error	31	12,620,946.67	407,127.31	
Total	33	52,093,677.44		

The null and alternative hypotheses to test for the contribution of X_1 to the model are

H_0: Variable X_1 does not significantly improve the model after variable X_2 has been included.
H_1: Variable X_1 significantly improves the model after variable X_2 has been included.

Equation (14.11) defines the partial F test statistic for testing the contribution of an independent variable.

PARTIAL F TEST STATISTIC

$$F = \frac{SSR(X_j \mid \text{All variables } except\ j)}{MSE} \qquad \textbf{(14.11)}$$

The partial F test statistic follows an F distribution with 1 and $n - k - 1$ degrees of freedom.

From Table 14.3,

$$F = \frac{24{,}556{,}916.67}{407{,}127.31} = 60.32$$

The partial F test statistic has 1 and $n - k - 1 = 34 - 2 - 1 = 31$ degrees of freedom. Using a level of significance of 0.05, the critical value from Table E.5 is approximately 4.17 (see Figure 14.8).

FIGURE 14.8

Testing for contribution of a regression coefficient to a multiple regression model at the 0.05 level of significance, with 1 and 31 degrees of freedom

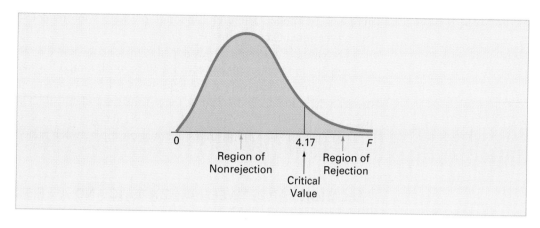

Because the partial F test statistic is greater than this critical F value (60.32 > 4.17), you reject H_0 and conclude that the addition of variable X_1 (price) significantly improves a regression model that already contains variable X_2 (promotional expenditures).

To evaluate the contribution of variable X_2 (promotional expenditures) to a model in which variable X_1 (price) has been included, you need to use Equation (14.10b). First, from Figure 14.7 on page 588, observe that $SSR(X_1) = 28,153,486.15$. Second, from Table 14.3, observe that $SSR(X_1$ and $X_2) = 39,472,730.77$. Then, using Equation (14.10b) on page 587,

$$SSR(X_2 \mid X_1) = 39,472,730.77 - 28,153,486.15 = 11,319,244.62$$

To determine whether X_2 significantly improves a model after X_1 has been included, you can divide the regression sum of squares into two component parts, as shown in Table 14.4.

TABLE 14.4

ANOVA Table Dividing the Regression Sum of Squares into Components to Determine the Contribution of Variable X_2

Source	Degrees of Freedom	Sum of Squares	Mean Square (Variance)	F
Regression	2	39,472,730.77	19,736,365.39	
$\left\{\begin{array}{c}X_1 \\ X_2 \mid X_1\end{array}\right\}$	$\left\{\begin{array}{c}1 \\ 1\end{array}\right\}$	$\left\{\begin{array}{c}28,153,486.15 \\ 11,319,244.62\end{array}\right\}$	11,319,244.62	27.80
Error	31	12,620,946.67	407,127.31	
Total	33	52,093,677.44		

The null and alternative hypotheses to test for the contribution of X_2 to the model are

H_0: Variable X_2 does not significantly improve the model after variable X_1 has been included.
H_1: Variable X_2 significantly improves the model after variable X_1 has been included.

Using Equation (14.11) and Table 14.4,

$$F = \frac{11,319,244.62}{407,127.31} = 27.80$$

In Figure 14.8 above, you can see that, using a 0.05 level of significance, the critical value of F, with 1 and 31 degrees of freedom, is approximately 4.17. Because the partial F test statistic is greater than this critical value (27.80 > 4.17), you reject H_0 and conclude that the addition of variable X_2 (promotional expenditures) significantly improves the multiple regression model already containing X_1 (price).

Thus, by testing for the contribution of each independent variable after the other has been included in the model, you determine that each of the two independent variables significantly improves the model. Therefore, the multiple regression model should include both price, X_1, and promotional expenditures, X_2.

The partial F test statistic developed in this section and the t test statistic of Equation (14.7) on page 583 are both used to determine the contribution of an independent variable to a multiple regression model. In fact, the hypothesis tests associated with these two statistics always result in the same decision (that is, the p-values are identical). The t values for the OmniPower regression model are -7.7664 and $+5.2728$, and the corresponding F values are 60.32 and 27.80. Equation (14.12) illustrates the relationship between t and F.

RELATIONSHIP BETWEEN A t STATISTIC AND AN F STATISTIC

$$t_a^2 = F_{1,a} \qquad \textbf{(14.12)}$$

where

$$a = \text{degrees of freedom}$$

Coefficients of Partial Determination

Recall from Section 14.2 that the coefficient of multiple determination, r^2, measures the proportion of the variation in Y that is explained by variation in the independent variables. Now, the contribution of each independent variable to a multiple regression model, while holding constant the other variable, is examined. The **coefficients of partial determination** ($r_{Y1.2}^2$ and $r_{Y2.1}^2$) measure the proportion of the variation in the dependent variable that is explained by each independent variable while controlling for, or holding constant, the other independent variable. Equation (14.13) defines the coefficients of partial determination for a multiple regression model with two independent variables.

COEFFICIENTS OF PARTIAL DETERMINATION FOR A MULTIPLE REGRESSION MODEL CONTAINING TWO INDEPENDENT VARIABLES

$$r_{Y1.2}^2 = \frac{SSR(X_1 \mid X_2)}{SST - SSR(X_1 \text{ and } X_2) + SSR(X_1 \mid X_2)} \qquad \textbf{(14.13a)}$$

and

$$r_{Y2.1}^2 = \frac{SSR(X_2 \mid X_1)}{SST - SSR(X_1 \text{ and } X_2) + SSR(X_2 \mid X_1)} \qquad \textbf{(14.13b)}$$

where

$SSR(X_1 \mid X_2) = $ sum of squares of the contribution of variable X_1 to the regression model, given that variable X_2 has been included in the model

$SST = $ total sum of squares for Y

$SSR(X_1 \text{ and } X_2) = $ regression sum of squares when variables X_1 and X_2 are both included in the multiple regression model

$SSR(X_2 \mid X_1) = $ sum of squares of the contribution of variable X_2 to the regression model, given that variable X_1 has been included in the model

For the OmniPower sales example,

$$r_{Y1.2}^2 = \frac{24{,}556{,}916.67}{52{,}093{,}677.44 - 39{,}472{,}730.77 + 24{,}556{,}916.67}$$

$$= 0.6605$$

$$r_{Y2.1}^2 = \frac{11{,}319{,}244.62}{52{,}093{,}677.44 - 39{,}472{,}730.77 + 11{,}319{,}244.62}$$

$$= 0.4728$$

The coefficient of partial determination of variable Y with X_1 while holding X_2 constant $(r_{Y1.2}^2)$ is 0.6605. Thus, for a given (constant) amount of promotional expenditures, 66.05% of the variation in OmniPower sales is explained by the variation in the price. The coefficient of partial determination of variable Y with X_2 while holding X_1 constant $(r_{Y2.1}^2)$ is 0.4728. Thus, for a given (constant) price, 47.28% of the variation in sales of OmniPower bars is explained by variation in the amount of promotional expenditures.

Equation (14.14) defines the coefficient of partial determination for the jth variable in a multiple regression model containing several (k) independent variables.

COEFFICIENT OF PARTIAL DETERMINATION FOR A MULTIPLE REGRESSION MODEL CONTAINING k INDEPENDENT VARIABLES

$$r_{Yj.(\text{All variables } except\, j)}^2 = \frac{SSR(X_j|\text{All variables } except\, j)}{SST - SSR(\text{All variables } including\, j) + SSR(X_j|\text{All variables } except\, j)}$$

(14.14)

PROBLEMS FOR SECTION 14.5

Learning the Basics

 14.31 The following is the ANOVA summary table for a multiple regression model with two independent variables:

Source	Degrees of Freedom	Sum of Squares	Mean Squares	F
Regression	2	60		
Error	18	120		
Total	20	180		

If $SSR(X_1) = 45$ and $SSR(X_2) = 25$,
a. determine whether there is a significant relationship between Y and each of the independent variables at the 0.05 level of significance.
b. compute the coefficients of partial determination, $r_{Y1.2}^2$ and $r_{Y2.1}^2$, and interpret their meaning.

 14.32 The following is the ANOVA summary table for a multiple regression model with two independent variables:

Source	Degrees of Freedom	Sum of Squares	Mean Squares	F
Regression	2	30		
Error	10	120		
Total	12	150		

If $SSR(X_1) = 20$ and $SSR(X_2) = 15$,
a. determine whether there is a significant relationship between Y and each of the independent variables at the 0.05 level of significance.
b. compute the coefficients of partial determination, $r_{Y1.2}^2$ and $r_{Y2.1}^2$, and interpret their meaning.

Applying the Concepts

14.33 In Problem 14.5 on page 576, you used horsepower and weight to predict gasoline mileage (see the **auto.xls** file). Using the results from that problem,
a. at the 0.05 level of significance, determine whether each independent variable makes a significant contribution to the regression model. On the basis of these results, indicate the most appropriate regression model for this set of data.

b. compute the coefficients of partial determination, $r^2_{Y1.2}$ and $r^2_{Y2.1}$, and interpret their meaning.

 14.34 In Problem 14.4 on page 576, you used sales and number of orders to predict distribution costs at a mail-order catalog business (see the **warecost.xls** file). Using the results from that problem,

a. at the 0.05 level of significance, determine whether each independent variable makes a significant contribution to the regression model. On the basis of these results, indicate the most appropriate regression model for this set of data.

b. compute the coefficients of partial determination, $r^2_{Y1.2}$ and $r^2_{Y2.1}$, and interpret their meaning.

14.35 In Problem 14.7 on page 576, you used the total staff present and remote hours to predict standby hours (see the **standby.xls** file). Using the results from that problem,

a. at the 0.05 level of significance, determine whether each independent variable makes a significant contribution to the regression model. On the basis of these results, indicate the most appropriate regression model for this set of data.

b. compute the coefficients of partial determination, $r^2_{Y1.2}$ and $r^2_{Y2.1}$, and interpret their meaning.

14.36 In Problem 14.6 on pages 576–577, you used radio advertising and newspaper advertising to predict sales (see the **advertise.xls** file). Using the results from that problem,

a. at the 0.05 level of significance, determine whether each independent variable makes a significant contribution to the regression model. On the basis of these results, indicate the most appropriate regression model for this set of data.

b. compute the coefficients of partial determination, $r^2_{Y1.2}$ and $r^2_{Y2.1}$, and interpret their meaning.

14.37 In Problem 14.8 on page 577, you used land area of a property and age of a house to predict appraised value (see the **glencove.xls** file). Using the results from that problem,

a. at the 0.05 level of significance, determine whether each independent variable makes a significant contribution to the regression model. On the basis of these results, indicate the most appropriate regression model for this set of data.

b. compute the coefficients of partial determination, $r^2_{Y1.2}$ and $r^2_{Y2.1}$, and interpret their meaning.

14.6 USING DUMMY VARIABLES AND INTERACTION TERMS IN REGRESSION MODELS

The multiple regression models discussed in Sections 14.1 through 14.5 assumed that each independent variable is numerical. However, in some situations, you might want to include categorical variables as independent variables in the regression model. For example, in Section 14.1, you used price and promotional expenditures to predict the monthly sales of OmniPower high-energy bars. In addition to these numerical independent variables, you may want to include the effect of the shelf location in the store (for example, end-aisle display or no end-aisle display) when developing a model to predict OmniPower sales.

The use of **dummy variables** allows you to include categorical independent variables as part of the regression model. If a given categorical independent variable has two categories, then you need only one dummy variable to represent the two categories. A dummy variable, X_d, is defined as

$$X_d = 0 \text{ if the observation is in category 1}$$
$$X_d = 1 \text{ if the observation is in category 2}$$

To illustrate the application of dummy variables in regression, consider a model for predicting the assessed value from a sample of 15 houses, based on the size of the house (in thousands of square feet) and whether the house has a fireplace. To include the categorical variable concerning the presence of a fireplace, the dummy variable X_2 is defined as

$$X_2 = 0 \text{ if the house does not have a fireplace}$$
$$X_2 = 1 \text{ if the house has a fireplace}$$

Table 14.5 presents the data, which are also stored in the file **house3.xls**. In the last column of Table 14.5, you can see how the categorical data are converted to numerical values.

TABLE 14.5

Predicting Assessed Value, Based on Size of House and Presence of a Fireplace

House	Y = Assessed Value ($000)	X₁ = Size of House (Thousands of Square Feet)	Fireplace	X₂= Fireplace
1	84.4	2.00	Yes	1
2	77.4	1.71	No	0
3	75.7	1.45	No	0
4	85.9	1.76	Yes	1
5	79.1	1.93	No	0
6	70.4	1.20	Yes	1
7	75.8	1.55	Yes	1
8	85.9	1.93	Yes	1
9	78.5	1.59	Yes	1
10	79.2	1.50	Yes	1
11	86.7	1.90	Yes	1
12	79.3	1.39	Yes	1
13	74.5	1.54	No	0
14	83.8	1.89	Yes	1
15	76.8	1.59	No	0

Assuming that the slope of assessed value with the size of the house is the same for houses that have and do not have a fireplace, the multiple regression model is

$$Y_i = \beta_0 + \beta_1 X_{1i} + \beta_2 X_{2i} + \varepsilon_i$$

where

Y_i = assessed value in thousands of dollars for house i

β_0 = Y intercept

X_{1i} = size of the house, in thousands of square feet, for house i

β_1 = slope of assessed value with size of the house, holding constant the presence or absence of a fireplace

X_{2i} = dummy variable representing the presence or absence of a fireplace for house i

β_2 = incremental effect of the presence of a fireplace on assessed value, holding constant the size of the house

ε_i = random error in Y for house i

Figure 14.9 illustrates the Microsoft Excel results for this model.

FIGURE 14.9

Microsoft Excel results for the regression model that includes size of the house and presence of fireplace

See Section E14.1 to create this.

	A	B	C	D	E	F	G
1	Assessed Value Analysis						
2							
3	*Regression Statistics*						
4	Multiple R	0.9006					
5	R Square	0.8111					
6	Adjusted R Square	0.7796					
7	Standard Error	2.2626					
8	Observations	15					
9							
10	ANOVA						
11		*df*	*SS*	*MS*	*F*	*Significance F*	
12	Regression	2	263.7039	131.8520	25.7557	4.54968E-05	
13	Residual	12	61.4321	5.1193			
14	Total	14	325.1360				
15							
16		*Coefficients*	*Standard Error*	*t Stat*	*P-value*	*Lower 95%*	*Upper 95%*
17	Intercept	50.0905	4.3517	11.5107	7.67943E-08	40.6090	59.5719
18	Size	16.1858	2.5744	6.2871	4.02437E-05	10.5766	21.7951
19	Fireplace	3.8530	1.2412	3.1042	0.0091	1.1486	6.5574

From Figure 14.9, the regression equation is

$$\hat{Y}_i = 50.0905 + 16.1858 X_{1i} + 3.8530 X_{2i}$$

For houses without a fireplace, you substitute $X_2 = 0$ into the regression equation:

$$\hat{Y}_i = 50.0905 + 16.1858 X_{1i} + 3.8530 X_{2i}$$
$$= 50.0905 + 16.1858 X_{1i} + 3.8530(0)$$
$$= 50.0905 + 16.1858 X_{1i}$$

For houses with a fireplace, you substitute $X_2 = 1$ into the regression equation:

$$\hat{Y}_i = 50.0905 + 16.1858 X_{1i} + 3.8530 X_{2i}$$
$$= 50.0905 + 16.1858 X_{1i} + 3.8530(1)$$
$$= 53.9435 + 16.1858 X_{1i}$$

In this model, the regression coefficients are interpreted as follows:

1. Holding constant whether a house has a fireplace, for each increase of 1.0 thousand square feet in the size of the house, the mean assessed value is estimated to increase by 16.1858 thousand dollars (that is, $16,185.80).
2. Holding constant the size of the house, the presence of a fireplace is estimated to increase the mean assessed value of the house by 3.8530 thousand dollars (or $3,853).

In Figure 14.9, the t statistic for the slope of the size of the house with assessed value is 6.2871, and the p-value is approximately 0.000; the t statistic for presence of a fireplace is 3.1042, and the p-value is 0.0091. Thus, each of the two variables makes a significant contribution to the model at a level of significance of 0.01. In addition, the coefficient of multiple determination indicates that 81.11% of the variation in assessed value is explained by variation in the size of the house and whether the house has a fireplace.

EXAMPLE 14.3

MODELING A THREE-LEVEL CATEGORICAL VARIABLE

Define a multiple regression model using sales as the dependent variable and package design and price as independent variables. Package design is a three-level categorical variable with designs A, B, or C.

SOLUTION To model a three-level categorical variable, two dummy variables are needed:

$$X_{1i} = 1 \text{ if package design A is used in observation } i; 0 \text{ otherwise}$$
$$X_{2i} = 1 \text{ if package design B is used in observation } i; 0 \text{ otherwise}$$

If observation i is for package design A, then $X_{1i} = 1$ and $X_{2i} = 0$; for package design B, then $X_{1i} = 0$ and $X_{2i} = 1$; and for package design C, then $X_{1i} = X_{2i} = 0$. A third independent variable is used for price:

$$X_{3i} = \text{price for observation } i$$

Thus, the regression model for this example is

$$Y_i = \beta_0 + \beta_1 X_{1i} + \beta_2 X_{2i} + \beta_3 X_{3i} + \varepsilon_i$$

where

Y_i = sales for observation i

β_0 = Y intercept

β_1 = difference between the mean sales of design A and the mean sales of design C, holding the price constant

β_2 = difference between the mean sales of design B and the mean sales of design C, holding the price constant

β_3 = slope of sales with price, holding the package design constant

ε_i = random error in Y for observation i

Interactions

In all the regression models discussed so far, the *effect* an independent variable has on the dependent variable was assumed to be statistically independent of the other independent variables in the model. An **interaction** occurs if the effect of an independent variable on the dependent variable is affected by the *value* of a second independent variable. For example, it is possible for advertising to have a large effect on the sales of a product when the price of a product is low. However, if the price of the product is too high, increases in advertising will not dramatically change sales. In this case, price and advertising are said to interact. In other words, you cannot make general statements about the effect of advertising on sales. The effect that advertising has on sales is *dependent* on the price. You use an **interaction term** (sometimes referred to as a **cross-product term**) to model an interaction effect in a regression model.

To illustrate the concept of interaction and use of an interaction term, return to the example concerning the assessed values of homes discussed on pages 592–594. In the regression model, you assumed that the effect the size of the home has on the assessed value is independent of whether the house has a fireplace. In other words, you assumed that the slope of assessed value with size is the same for houses with fireplaces as it is for houses without fireplaces. If these two slopes are different, an interaction between size of the home and fireplace exists.

To evaluate the possibility of an interaction, you first define an interaction term that consists of the product of the independent variable X_1 (size of house) and the dummy variable X_2 (fireplace). You then test whether this interaction variable makes a significant contribution to the regression model. If the interaction is significant, you cannot use the original model for prediction. For the data of Table 14.5 on page 593, let

$$X_3 = X_1 \times X_2$$

Figure 14.10 illustrates Microsoft Excel results for this regression model, which includes the size of the house, X_1, the presence of a fireplace, X_2, and the interaction of X_1 and X_2 (which is defined as X_3).

FIGURE 14.10

Microsoft Excel results for a regression model that includes size, presence of fireplace, and interaction of size and fireplace

See Sections E14.1 and E14.6 to create this.

	A	B	C	D	E	F	G
1	Assessed Value Analysis						
2							
3	*Regression Statistics*						
4	Multiple R	0.9179					
5	R Square	0.8426					
6	Adjusted R Square	0.7996					
7	Standard Error	2.1573					
8	Observations	15					
9							
10	ANOVA						
11		*df*	*SS*	*MS*	*F*	*Significance F*	
12	Regression	3	273.9441	91.3147	19.6215	0.0001	
13	Residual	11	51.1919	4.6538			
14	Total	14	325.1360				
15							
16		*Coefficients*	*Standard Error*	*t Stat*	*P-value*	*Lower 95%*	*Upper 95%*
17	Intercept	62.9522	9.6122	6.5492	4.13993E-05	41.7959	84.1085
18	Size	8.3624	5.8173	1.4375	0.1784	-4.4414	21.1662
19	Fireplace	-11.8404	10.6455	-1.1122	0.2898	-35.2710	11.5902
20	Size * Fireplace	9.5180	6.4165	1.4834	0.1661	-4.6046	23.6406

To test for the existence of an interaction, you use the null hypothesis H_0: $\beta_3 = 0$ versus the alternative hypothesis H_1: $\beta_3 \neq 0$. In Figure 14.10, the t statistic for the interaction of size and fireplace is 1.4834. Because the p-value = 0.1661 > 0.05, you do not reject the null hypothesis. Therefore, the interaction does not make a significant contribution to the model, given that size and presence of a fireplace are already included.

Regression models can have several numerical independent variables. Example 14.4 illustrates a regression model in which there are two numerical independent variables as well as a categorical independent variable.

EXAMPLE 14.4

STUDYING A REGRESSION MODEL THAT CONTAINS A DUMMY VARIABLE

A real estate developer wants to predict heating oil consumption in single-family houses, based on atmospheric temperature, X_1, and the amount of attic insulation, X_2. Suppose that, of 15 houses selected, houses 1, 4, 6, 7, 8, 10, and 12 are ranch-style houses. The data are stored in the file htngoil.xls. Develop and analyze an appropriate regression model, using these three independent variables, X_1, X_2, and X_3 (the dummy variable for ranch-style houses).

SOLUTION Define X_3, a dummy variable for ranch-style house, as follows:

$$X_3 = 0 \text{ if the style is not ranch}$$
$$X_3 = 1 \text{ if the style is ranch}$$

Assuming that the slope between home heating oil consumption and atmospheric temperature, X_1, and between home heating oil consumption and the amount of attic insulation, X_2, is the same for both styles of houses, the regression model is

$$Y_i = \beta_0 + \beta_1 X_{1i} + \beta_2 X_{2i} + \beta_3 X_{3i} + \varepsilon_i$$

where

Y_i = monthly heating oil consumption, in gallons, for house i

β_0 = Y intercept

β_1 = slope of heating oil consumption with atmospheric temperature, holding constant the effect of attic insulation and the style of the house

β_2 = slope of heating oil consumption with attic insulation, holding constant the effect of atmospheric temperature and the style of the house

β_3 = incremental effect of the presence of a ranch-style house, holding constant the effect of atmospheric temperature and attic insulation

ε_i = random error in Y for house i

Figure 14.11 displays Microsoft Excel results.

FIGURE 14.11

Microsoft Excel results for a regression model that includes temperature, insulation, and style for the heating oil data

	A	B	C	D	E	F	G
1	Heating Oil Consumption Analysis						
2							
3	*Regression Statistics*						
4	Multiple R	0.9942					
5	R Square	0.9884					
6	Adjusted R Square	0.9853					
7	Standard Error	15.7489					
8	Observations	15					
9							
10	ANOVA						
11		df	SS	MS	F	Significance F	
12	Regression	3	233406.9094	77802.3031	313.6822	6.21548E-11	
13	Residual	11	2728.3200	248.0291			
14	Total	14	236135.2293				
15							
16		Coefficients	Standard Error	t Stat	P-value	Lower 95%	Upper 95%
17	Intercept	592.5401	14.3370	41.3295	2.02317E-13	560.9846	624.0956
18	Temperature	-5.5251	0.2044	-27.0267	2.07188E-11	-5.9751	-5.0752
19	Insulation	-21.3761	1.4480	-14.7623	1.34816E-08	-24.5632	-18.1891
20	Ranch-style	-38.9727	8.3584	-4.6627	0.0007	-57.3695	-20.5759

From the results in Figure 14.11, the regression equation is

$$\hat{Y}_i = 592.5401 - 5.5251X_{1i} - 21.3761X_{2i} - 38.9727X_{3i}$$

For houses that are not ranch style, because $X_3 = 0$, this reduces to

$$\hat{Y}_i = 592.5401 - 5.5251X_{1i} - 21.3761X_{2i}$$

For houses that are ranch style, because $X_3 = 1$, this reduces to

$$\hat{Y}_i = 553.5674 - 5.5251X_{1i} - 21.3761X_{2i}$$

The regression coefficients are interpreted as follows:

1. Holding constant the attic insulation and the house style, for each additional 1°F increase in atmospheric temperature, you estimate that the mean oil consumption decreases by 5.5251 gallons.
2. Holding constant the atmospheric temperature and the house style, for each additional 1-inch increase in attic insulation, you estimate that the mean oil consumption decreases by 21.3761 gallons.
3. b_3 measures the effect on oil consumption of having a ranch-style house ($X_3 = 1$) compared with having a house that is not ranch style ($X_3 = 0$). Thus, with atmospheric temperature and attic insulation held constant, you estimate that the mean oil consumption is 38.9727 gallons less for a ranch-style house than for a house that is not ranch style.

The three t statistics representing the slopes for temperature, insulation, and ranch style are -27.0267, -14.7623, and -4.6627. Each of the corresponding p-values is extremely small, all being less than 0.001. Thus, each of the three variables makes a significant contribution to the model. In addition, the coefficient of multiple determination indicates that 98.84% of the variation in oil usage is explained by variation in the temperature, insulation, and whether the house is ranch style.

Before you can use the model in Example 14.4, you need to determine whether the independent variables interact with each other. In Example 14.5, three interaction terms are added to the model.

EXAMPLE 14.5   EVALUATING A REGRESSION MODEL WITH SEVERAL INTERACTIONS

For the data of Example 14.4, determine whether adding the interaction terms make a significant contribution to the regression model.

SOLUTION To evaluate possible interactions between the independent variables, three interaction terms are constructed. Let $X_4 = X_1 \times X_2$, $X_5 = X_1 \times X_3$, and $X_6 = X_2 \times X_3$. The regression model is now

$$Y_i = \beta_0 + \beta_1 X_{1i} + \beta_2 X_{2i} + \beta_3 X_{3i} + \beta_4 X_{4i} + \beta_5 X_{5i} + \beta_6 X_{6i} + \varepsilon_i$$

where X_1 is temperature, X_2 is insulation, X_3 is the dummy variable ranch style, X_4 is the interaction between temperature and insulation, X_5 is the interaction between temperature and ranch style, and X_6 is the interaction between insulation and ranch style.

To test whether the three interactions significantly improve the regression model, you use the partial F test. The null and alternative hypotheses are

H_0: $\beta_4 = \beta_5 = \beta_6 = 0$ (There are no interactions among X_1, X_2, and X_3.)
H_1: $\beta_4 \neq 0$ and/or $\beta_5 \neq 0$ and/or $\beta_6 \neq 0$ (X_1 interacts with X_2, and/or X_1 interacts with X_3, and/or X_2 interacts with X_3.)

From Figure 14.12,

$$SSR(X_1, X_2, X_3, X_4, X_5, X_6) = 234{,}510.582 \text{ with 6 degrees of freedom}$$

and from Figure 14.11 on page 596, $SSR(X_1, X_2, X_3) = 233{,}406.9094$ with 3 degrees of freedom.

FIGURE 14.12

Microsoft Excel results for a regression model that includes temperature, X_1; insulation, X_2; the dummy variable ranch style, X_3; the interaction of temperature and insulation, X_4; the interaction of temperature and ranch style, X_5; and the interaction of insulation and ranch style, X_6

	A	B	C	D	E	F	G
1	Heating Oil Consumption Analysis						
2							
3	*Regression Statistics*						
4	Multiple R	0.9966					
5	R Square	0.9931					
6	Adjusted R Square	0.9880					
7	Standard Error	14.2506					
8	Observations	15					
9							
10	ANOVA						
11		df	SS	MS	F	Significance F	
12	Regression	6	234510.582	39085.097	192.4607	3.32423E-08	
13	Residual	8	1624.647	203.081			
14	Total	14	236135.229				
15							
16		Coefficients	Standard Error	t Stat	P-value	Lower 95%	Upper 95%
17	Intercept	642.8867	26.7059	24.0728	9.45284E-09	581.3027	704.4707
18	Temperature	-6.9263	0.7531	-9.1969	1.58014E-05	-8.6629	-5.1896
19	Insulation	-27.8825	3.5801	-7.7882	5.29456E-05	-36.1383	-19.6268
20	Style	-84.6088	29.9956	-2.8207	0.0225	-153.7788	-15.4389
21	Temperature * Insulation	0.1702	0.0886	1.9204	0.0911	-0.0342	0.3746
22	Temperature * Ranch-style	0.6596	0.4617	1.4286	0.1910	-0.4051	1.7242
23	Insulation * Ranch-style	4.9870	3.5137	1.4193	0.1936	-3.1156	13.0895

Thus, $SSR(X_1, X_2, X_3, X_4, X_5, X_6) - SSR(X_1, X_2, X_3) = 234{,}510.582 - 233{,}406.9094 = 1{,}103.67$. The difference in degrees of freedom is $6 - 3 = 3$.

To use the partial F test for the simultaneous contribution of three variables to a model, you use an extension of Equation (14.11) on page 588.[1] The partial F test statistic is

$$F = \frac{[SSR(X_1, X_2, X_3, X_4, X_5, X_6) - SSR(X_1, X_2, X_3)] / 3}{MSE(X_1, X_2, X_3, X_4, X_5, X_6)} = \frac{1{,}103.67 / 3}{203.08} = 1.81$$

You compare the F test statistic of 1.81 to the critical F value for 3 and 8 degrees of freedom. Using a level of significance of 0.05, the critical F value from Table E.5 is 4.07. Because 1.81 < 4.07, you conclude that the interactions do not make a significant contribution to the model, given that the model already includes temperature, X_1; insulation, X_2; and whether the house is ranch style, X_3. Therefore, the multiple regression model using X_1, X_2, and X_3 but no interaction terms is the better model. If you rejected this null hypothesis, you would then test the contribution of each interaction separately in order to determine which interaction terms to include in the model.

[1] In general, if a model has several independent variables and you want to test whether an additional set of independent variables contribute to the model, the numerator of the F test is [SSR (for all independent variables)] – SSR (for the initial set of variables) divided by the number of independent variables whose contribution is being tested.

PROBLEMS FOR SECTION 14.6

Learning the Basics

14.38 Suppose X_1 is a numerical variable and X_2 is a dummy variable and the regression equation for a sample of $n = 20$ is

$$\hat{Y}_i = 6 + 4X_{1i} + 2X_{2i}$$

a. Interpret the meaning of the slope for variable X_1.
b. Interpret the meaning of the slope for variable X_2.
c. Suppose that the t statistic for testing the contribution of variable X_2 is 3.27. At the 0.05 level of significance, is there evidence that variable X_2 makes a significant contribution to the model?

Applying the Concepts

14.39 The chair of the accounting department wants to develop a regression model to predict the grade point average in accounting for graduating accounting majors, based on the student's SAT score and whether the student received a grade of B or higher in the introductory statistics course (0 = no and 1 = yes).
a. Explain the steps involved in developing a regression model for these data. Be sure to indicate the particular models you need to evaluate and compare.
b. Suppose the regression coefficient for the variable of whether the student received a grade of B or higher in the introductory statistics course is +0.30. How do you interpret this result?

14.40 A real estate association in a suburban community would like to study the relationship between the size of a single-family house (as measured by the number of rooms) and the selling price of the house (in thousands of dollars). Two different neighborhoods are included in the study, one on the east side of the community (=0) and the other on the west side (=1). A random sample of 20 houses was selected, with the results given in the file **neighbor.xls**.
a. State the multiple regression equation.
b. Interpret the meaning of the slopes in this problem.
c. Predict the mean selling price for a house with nine rooms that is located in an east-side neighborhood. Construct a 95% confidence interval estimate and a 95% prediction interval.
d. Perform a residual analysis on the results and determine the adequacy of the model.
e. Is there a significant relationship between selling price and the two independent variables (rooms and neighborhood) at the 0.05 level of significance?
f. At the 0.05 level of significance, determine whether each independent variable makes a contribution to the

regression model. Indicate the most appropriate regression model for this set of data.
g. Construct 95% confidence interval estimates of the population slope for the relationship between selling price and number of rooms and between selling price and neighborhood.
h. Interpret the meaning of the coefficient of multiple determination.
i. Compute the adjusted r^2.
j. Compute the coefficients of partial determination and interpret their meaning.
k. What assumption do you need to make about the slope of selling price with number of rooms?
l. Add an interaction term to the model and, at the 0.05 level of significance, determine whether it makes a significant contribution to the model.
m. On the basis of the results of (f) and (l), which model is most appropriate? Explain.

14.41 The marketing manager of a large supermarket chain would like to determine the effect of shelf space and whether the product was placed at the front or back of the aisle on the sales of pet food. A random sample of 12 equal-sized stores is selected, with the following results (stored in the file **petfood.xls**):

Store	Shelf Space (Feet)	Location	Weekly Sales (Dollars)
1	5	Back	160
2	5	Front	220
3	5	Back	140
4	10	Back	190
5	10	Back	240
6	10	Front	260
7	15	Back	230
8	15	Back	270
9	15	Front	280
10	20	Back	260
11	20	Back	290
12	20	Front	310

a. State the multiple regression equation.
b. Interpret the meaning of the slopes in this problem.
c. Predict the mean weekly sales of pet food for a store with 8 feet of shelf space situated at the back of the aisle. Construct a 95% confidence interval estimate and a 95% prediction interval.
d. Perform a residual analysis on the results and determine the adequacy of the model.

e. Is there a significant relationship between sales and the two independent variables (shelf space and aisle position) at the 0.05 level of significance?

f. At the 0.05 level of significance, determine whether each independent variable makes a contribution to the regression model. Indicate the most appropriate regression model for this set of data.

g. Construct 95% confidence interval estimates of the population slope for the relationship between sales and shelf space and between sales and aisle location.

h. Compare the slope in (b) with the slope for the simple linear regression model of Problem 13.4 on page 522. Explain the difference in the results.

i. Interpret the meaning of the coefficient of multiple determination, r^2.

j. Compute the adjusted r^2.

k. Compare r^2 with the r^2 value computed in Problem 13.16 (a) on page 529.

l. Compute the coefficients of partial determination and interpret their meaning.

m. What assumption about the slope of shelf space with sales do you need to make in this problem?

n. Add an interaction term to the model and, at the 0.05 level of significance, determine whether it makes a significant contribution to the model.

o. On the basis of the results of (f) and (n), which model is most appropriate? Explain.

14.42 In mining engineering, holes are often drilled through rock, using drill bits. As the drill hole gets deeper, additional rods are added to the drill bit to enable additional drilling to take place. It is expected that drilling time increases with depth. This increased drilling time could be caused by several factors, including the mass of the drill rods that are strung together. A key question relates to whether drilling is faster using dry drilling holes or wet drilling holes. Using dry drilling holes involves forcing compressed air down the drill rods to flush the cuttings and drive the hammer. Using wet drilling holes involves forcing water rather than air down the hole. The data file drill.xls contains measurements for a sample of 50 drill holes of the time to drill each additional 5 feet (in minutes), the depth (in feet), and whether the hole was a dry drilling hole or a wet drilling hole. Develop a model to predict additional drilling time, based on depth and type of drilling hole (dry or wet).

Source: Extracted from R. Penner and D. G. Watts, "Mining Information," The American Statistician, 45, 1991, pp. 4–9.

a. State the multiple regression equation.

b. Interpret the meaning of the slopes in this problem.

c. Predict the mean additional drilling time for a dry drilling hole at a depth of 100 feet. Construct a 95% confidence interval estimate and a 95% prediction interval.

d. Perform a residual analysis on the results and determine the adequacy of the model.

e. Is there a significant relationship between additional drilling time and the two independent variables (depth and type of drilling hole) at the 0.05 level of significance?

f. At the 0.05 level of significance, determine whether each independent variable makes a contribution to the regression model. Indicate the most appropriate regression model for this set of data.

g. Construct 95% confidence interval estimates of the population slope for the relationship between additional drilling time and depth and between additional drilling time and type of drilling hole.

h. Interpret the meaning of the coefficient of multiple determination.

i. Compute the adjusted r^2.

j. Compute the coefficients of partial determination and interpret their meaning.

k. What assumption do you need to make about the slope of additional drilling time with depth?

l. Add an interaction term to the model and, at the 0.05 level of significance, determine whether it makes a significant contribution to the model.

m. On the basis of the results of (f) and (l), which model is most appropriate? Explain.

14.43 The owner of a moving company typically has his most experienced manager predict the total number of labor hours that will be required to complete an upcoming move. This approach has proved useful in the past, but the owner would like to be able to develop a more accurate method of predicting the labor hours by using the number of cubic feet moved and whether there is an elevator in the apartment building. In a preliminary effort to provide a more accurate method, he has collected data for 36 moves in which the origin and destination were within the borough of Manhattan in New York City and the travel time was an insignificant portion of the hours worked. The data are stored in the file moving.xls.

a. State the multiple regression equation.

b. Interpret the meaning of the slopes in this problem.

c. Predict the mean labor hours for moving 500 cubic feet in an apartment building that has an elevator, and construct a 95% confidence interval estimate and a 95% prediction interval.

d. Perform a residual analysis on the results and determine the adequacy of the model.

e. Is there a significant relationship between labor hours and the two independent variables (cubic feet moved and whether there is an elevator in the apartment building) at the 0.05 level of significance?

f. At the 0.05 level of significance, determine whether each independent variable makes a contribution to the regression model. Indicate the most appropriate regression model for this set of data.

g. Construct a 95% confidence interval estimate of the population slope for the relationship between labor hours and cubic feet moved, and between labor hours and whether there is an elevator in the apartment building.

h. Interpret the meaning of the coefficient of multiple determination.

i. Compute the adjusted r^2.

j. Compute the coefficients of partial determination and interpret their meaning.

k. What assumption about the slope of labor hours with cubic feet moved do you need to make?

l. Add an interaction term to the model and, at the 0.05 level of significance, determine whether it makes a significant contribution to the model.

m. On the basis of the results of (f) and (l), which model is most appropriate? Explain.

 14.44 In Problem 14.4 on page 576, you used sales and orders to predict distribution cost (see the file **warecost.xls**). Develop a regression model to predict distribution cost that includes the sales, orders, and the interaction of sales and orders.

a. At the 0.05 level of significance, is there evidence that the interaction term makes a significant contribution to the model?

b. Which regression model is more appropriate, the one used in (a) or the one used in Problem 14.4? Explain.

14.45 Zagat's publishes restaurant ratings for various locations in the United States. The data file **restaurants.xls** contains the Zagat rating for food, décor, service, and the price per person for a sample of 50 restaurants located in an urban area (New York City) and 50 restaurants located in a suburban area (Long Island). Develop a regression model to predict the price per person based on a variable that represents the sum of the ratings for food, décor, and service and a dummy variable concerning location (New York City or Long Island).

Source: Extracted from Zagat Survey 2002 New York City Restaurants and Zagat Survey 2001–2002 Long Island Restaurants.

a. State the multiple regression equation.

b. Interpret the meaning of the slopes in this problem.

c. Predict the mean price for a restaurant with a summated rating of 60 that is located in New York City and construct a 95% confidence interval estimate and a 95% prediction interval.

d. Perform a residual analysis on the results and determine the adequacy of the model.

e. Is there a significant relationship between price and the two independent variables (summated rating and location) at the 0.05 level of significance?

f. At the 0.05 level of significance, determine whether each independent variable makes a contribution to the regression model. Indicate the most appropriate regression model for this set of data.

g. Construct a 95% confidence interval estimate of the population slope for the relationship between price and summated rating, and between price and location.

h. Compare the slope in (b) with the slope for the simple linear regression model of Problem 13.90 on page 561. Explain the difference in the results.

i. Interpret the meaning of the coefficient of multiple determination.

j. Compute the adjusted r^2.

k. Compare r^2 with the r^2 value computed in Problem 13.90 (d) on page 561.

l. Compute the coefficients of partial determination and interpret their meaning.

m. What assumption about the slope of price with summated rating do you need to make in this problem?

n. Add an interaction term to the model and, at the 0.05 level of significance, determine whether it makes a significant contribution to the model.

o. On the basis of the results of (f) and (n), which model is most appropriate? Explain.

14.46 In Problem 14.6 on pages 576–577, you used radio advertising and newspaper advertising to predict sales (see the file **advertise.xls**). Develop a regression model to predict sales that includes radio advertising, newspaper advertising, and the interaction of radio advertising and newspaper advertising.

a. At the 0.05 level of significance, is there evidence that the interaction term makes a significant contribution to the model?

b. Which regression model is more appropriate, the one used in this problem or the one used in Problem 14.6? Explain.

 14.47 In Problem 14.5 on page 576, horsepower and weight were used to predict miles per gallon (see the file **auto.xls**). Develop a regression model that includes horsepower, weight, and the interaction of horsepower and weight to predict miles per gallon.

a. At the 0.05 level of significance, is there evidence that the interaction term makes a significant contribution to the model?

b. Which regression model is more appropriate, the one used in this problem or the one used in Problem 14.5? Explain.

14.48 In Problem 14.7 on page 577, you used total staff present and remote hours to predict standby hours (see the file **standby.xls**). Develop a regression model to predict standby hours that includes total staff present, remote hours, and the interaction of total staff present and remote hours.

a. At the 0.05 level of significance, is there evidence that the interaction term makes a significant contribution to the model?

b. Which regression model is more appropriate, the one used in this problem or the one used in Problem 14.7? Explain.

14.49 The director of a training program for a large insurance company is evaluating three different methods of training underwriters. The three methods are traditional, CD-ROM based, and Web based. She divides 30 trainees into three randomly assigned groups of 10. Before the start of the training, each trainee is given a proficiency exam that measures mathematics and computer skills. At the end of the training, all students take the same end-of-training exam. The results, stored in the file **underwriting.xls** are as follows:

Proficiency Exam	End-of-Training Exam	Method
94	14	Traditional
96	19	Traditional
98	17	Traditional
100	38	Traditional
102	40	Traditional
105	26	Traditional
109	41	Traditional
110	28	Traditional
111	36	Traditional
130	66	Traditional
80	38	CD-ROM based
84	34	CD-ROM based
90	43	CD-ROM based
97	43	CD-ROM based
97	61	CD-ROM based
112	63	CD-ROM based
115	93	CD-ROM based
118	74	CD-ROM based
120	76	CD-ROM based
120	79	CD-ROM based
92	55	Web based
96	53	Web based
99	55	Web based
101	52	Web based
102	35	Web based
104	46	Web based
107	57	Web based
110	55	Web based
111	42	Web based
118	81	Web based

Develop a multiple regression model to predict the score on the end-of-training exam, based on the score on the proficiency exam and the method of training used.

a. State the multiple regression equation.

b. Interpret the meaning of the slopes in this problem.

c. Predict the mean end-of-training exam score for a student with a proficiency exam score of 100 who had Web-based training.

d. Perform a residual analysis on your results and determine the adequacy of the model.

e. Is there a significant relationship between the end-of-training exam score and the independent variables (proficiency score and training method) at the 0.05 level of significance?

f. At the 0.05 level of significance, determine whether each independent variable makes a contribution to the regression model. Indicate the most appropriate regression model for this set of data.

g. Construct 95% confidence interval estimates of the population slope for the relationship between end-of-training exam score and each independent variable.

h. Interpret the meaning of the coefficient of multiple determination.

i. Compute the adjusted r^2.

j. Compute the coefficients of partial determination and interpret their meaning.

k. What assumption about the slope of proficiency score with end-of-training exam score do you need to make in this problem?

l. Add interaction terms to the model and, at the 0.05 level of significance, determine whether any interaction terms make a significant contribution to the model.

m. On the basis of the results of (f) and (l), which model is most appropriate? Explain.

SUMMARY

In this chapter, you learned how a marketing manager can use multiple regression analysis to understand the effects of price and promotional expenses on the sales of a new product. You also learned how to include categorical independent variables and interaction terms in regression models. Figure 14.13 represents a roadmap of the chapter.

FIGURE 14.13
Roadmap for multiple regression

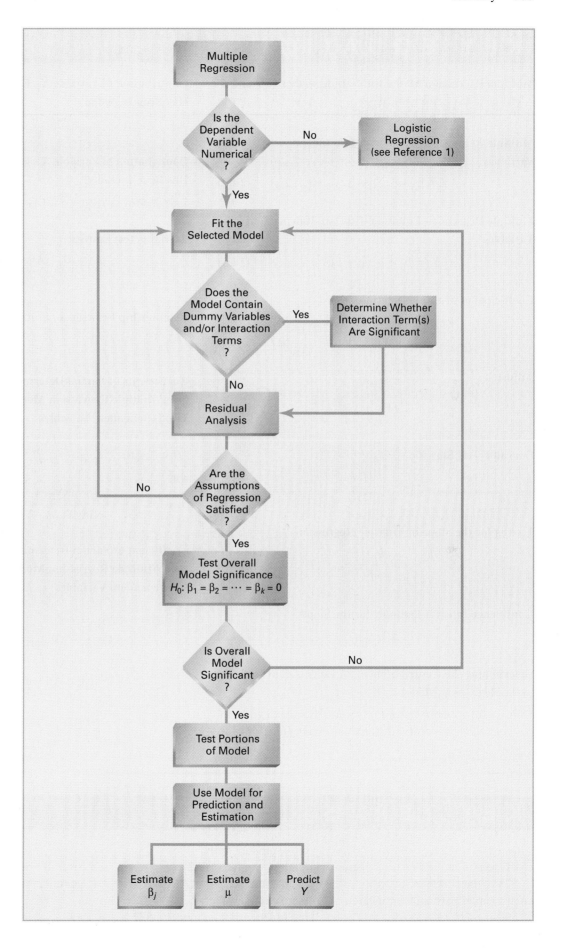

KEY EQUATIONS

Multiple Regression Model with k Independent Variables

$$Y_i = \beta_0 + \beta_1 X_{1i} + \beta_2 X_{2i} + \beta_3 X_{3i} + \cdots + \beta_k X_{ki} + \varepsilon_i \quad \text{(14.1)}$$

Multiple Regression Model with Two Independent Variables

$$Y_i = \beta_0 + \beta_1 X_{1i} + \beta_2 X_{2i} + \varepsilon_i \quad \text{(14.2)}$$

Multiple Regression Equation with Two Independent Variables

$$\hat{Y}_i = b_0 + b_1 X_{1i} + b_2 X_{2i} \quad \text{(14.3)}$$

Coefficient of Multiple Determination

$$r^2 = \frac{\text{Regression sum of squares}}{\text{Total sum of squares}} = \frac{SSR}{SST} \quad \text{(14.4)}$$

Adjusted r^2

$$r_{\text{adj}}^2 = 1 - \left[(1 - r^2) \frac{n-1}{n-k-1} \right] \quad \text{(14.5)}$$

Overall F Test Statistic

$$F = \frac{MSR}{MSE} \quad \text{(14.6)}$$

Testing for the Slope in Multiple Regression

$$t = \frac{b_j - \beta_j}{S_{b_j}} \quad \text{(14.7)}$$

Confidence Interval Estimate for the Slope

$$b_j \pm t_{n-k-1} S_{b_j} \quad \text{(14.8)}$$

Determining the Contribution of an Independent Variable to the Regression Model

$$SSR(X_j \mid \text{All variables } except\ j) = SSR \text{ (All variables } including\ j) - SSR \text{ (All variables } except\ j) \quad \text{(14.9)}$$

Contribution of Variable X_1, Given That X_2 Has Been Included

$$SSR(X_1 \mid X_2) = SSR(X_1 \text{ and } X_2) - SSR(X_2) \quad \text{(14.10a)}$$

Contribution of Variable X_2, Given That X_1 Has Been Included

$$SSR(X_2 \mid X_1) = SSR(X_1 \text{ and } X_2) - SSR(X_1) \quad \text{(14.10b)}$$

Partial F Test Statistic

$$F = \frac{SSR(X_j \mid \text{All variables } except\ j)}{MSE} \quad \text{(14.11)}$$

Relationship Between a t Statistic and an F Statistic

$$t_a^2 = F_{1,a} \quad \text{(14.12)}$$

Coefficients of Partial Determination for a Multiple Regression Model Containing Two Independent Variables

$$r_{Y1.2}^2 = \frac{SSR(X_1 \mid X_2)}{SST - SSR(X_1 \text{ and } X_2) + SSR(X_1 \mid X_2)} \quad \text{(14.13a)}$$

and

$$r_{Y2.1}^2 = \frac{SSR(X_2 \mid X_1)}{SST - SSR(X_1 \text{ and } X_2) + SSR(X_2 \mid X_1)} \quad \text{(14.13b)}$$

Coefficient of Partial Determination for a Multiple Regression Model Containing k Independent Variables

$$r_{Y_j.(\text{All variables } except\ j)}^2$$

$$= \frac{SSR(X_j \mid \text{All variables } except\ j)}{SST - SSR(\text{All variables } including\ j) + SSR(X_j \mid \text{All variables } except\ j)} \quad \text{(14.14)}$$

KEY TERMS

CHAPTER REVIEW PROBLEMS

Checking Your Understanding

14.50 How does the interpretation of the regression coefficients differ in multiple regression and simple regression?

14.51 How does testing the significance of the entire multiple regression model differ from testing the contribution of each independent variable?

14.52 How do the coefficients of partial determination differ from the coefficient of multiple determination?

14.53 Why and how do you use dummy variables?

14.54 How can you evaluate whether the slope of the response variable with an independent variable is the same for each level of the dummy variable?

14.55 Under what circumstances do you include an interaction in a regression model?

14.56 When a dummy variable is included in a regression model that has one numerical independent variable, what assumption do you need to make concerning the slope between the response variable, Y, and the numerical independent variable, X?

Applying the Concepts

14.57 Increasing customer satisfaction typically results in increased purchase behavior. For many products, there is more than one measure of customer satisfaction. In many of these instances, purchase behavior can increase dramatically with an increase in any one of the customer satisfaction measures, not necessarily all of them at the same time. Gunst and Barry ("One Way to Moderate Ceiling Effects," *Quality Progress*, October 2003, pp. 83–85) consider a product with two satisfaction measures, X_1 and X_2, that range from the lowest level of satisfaction, 1, to the highest level of satisfaction, 7. The dependent variable, Y, is a measure of purchase behavior, with the highest value generating the most sales. The following regression equation is presented:

$$\hat{Y}_i = -3.888 + 1.449X_{1i} + 1.462X_{2i} - 0.190X_{1i}X_{2i}$$

Suppose that X_1 is the perceived quality of the product and X_2 is the perceived value of the product. (*Note:* If the product is overpriced in the view of the customer, he or she perceives it to be of low value and vice versa.)

a. What is the predicted purchase behavior when $X_1 = 2$ and $X_2 = 2$?

b. What is the predicted purchase behavior when $X_1 = 2$ and $X_2 = 7$?

c. What is the predicted purchase behavior when $X_1 = 7$ and $X_2 = 2$?

d. What is the predicted purchase behavior when $X_1 = 7$ and $X_2 = 7$?

e. What is the regression equation when $X_2 = 2$? What is the slope for X_1 now?

f. What is the regression equation when $X_2 = 7$? What is the slope for X_1 now?

g. What is the regression equation when $X_1 = 2$? What is the slope for X_2 now?

h. What is the regression equation when $X_1 = 7$? What is the slope for X_2 now?

i. Discuss the implications of (a) through (h) within the context of increasing sales for this product with two customer satisfaction measures.

14.58 The owner of a moving company typically has his most experienced manager predict the total number of labor hours that will be required to complete an upcoming move. This approach has proved useful in the past, but the owner would like to be able to develop a more accurate method of predicting the labor hours by using the number of cubic feet moved and the number of pieces of large furniture. In a preliminary effort to provide a more accurate method, he has collected data for 36 moves in which the origin and destination were within the borough of Manhattan in New York City and the travel time was an insignificant portion of the hours worked. The data are stored in the file moving.xls.

a. State the multiple regression equation.

b. Interpret the meaning of the slopes in this equation.

c. Predict the mean labor hours for moving 500 cubic feet with two large pieces of furniture.

d. Perform a residual analysis on your results and determine the adequacy of the model.

e. Determine whether there is a significant relationship between labor hours and the two independent variables (the amount of cubic feet moved and the number of pieces of large furniture) at the 0.05 level of significance.

f. Determine the p-value in (e) and interpret its meaning.

g. Interpret the meaning of the coefficient of multiple determination in this problem.

h. Determine the adjusted r^2.

i. At the 0.05 level of significance, determine whether each independent variable makes a significant contribution to the regression model. Indicate the most appropriate regression model for this set of data.

j. Determine the p-values in (i) and interpret their meaning.

k. Construct a 95% confidence interval estimate of the population slope between labor hours and the number of cubic feet moved. How does the interpretation of the slope here differ from that in Problem 13.44 on page 544?

l. Compute and interpret the coefficients of partial determination.

14.59 Professional basketball has truly become a sport that generates interest among fans around the world. More and more players come from outside the United States to play in the National Basketball Association (NBA). You want to develop a regression model to predict the number of wins achieved by each NBA team, based on field goal (shots made) percentage for the team and for the opponent. The data are stored in the file **nba2006.xls**.
a. State the multiple regression equation.
b. Interpret the meaning of the slopes in this equation.
c. Predict the mean number of wins for a team that has a field goal percentage of 45% and an opponent field goal percentage of 44%.
d. Perform a residual analysis on your results and determine the adequacy of the fit of the model.
e. Is there a significant relationship between number of wins and the two independent variables (field goal percentage for the team and for the opponent) at the 0.05 level of significance?
f. Determine the p-value in (e) and interpret its meaning.
g. Interpret the meaning of the coefficient of multiple determination in this problem.
h. Determine the adjusted r^2.
i. At the 0.05 level of significance, determine whether each independent variable makes a significant contribution to the regression model. Indicate the most appropriate regression model for this set of data.
j. Determine the p-values in (i) and interpret their meaning.
k. Compute and interpret the coefficients of partial determination.

14.60 A sample of 30 recently sold single-family houses in a small city is selected. Develop a model to predict the selling price (in thousands of dollars), using the assessed value (in thousands of dollars) as well as time period (in months since reassessment). The houses in the city had been reassessed at full value one year prior to the study. The results are contained in the file **house1.xls**.
a. State the multiple regression equation.
b. Interpret the meaning of the slopes in this equation.
c. Predict the mean selling price for a house that has an assessed value of $170,000 and was sold in time period 12.
d. Perform a residual analysis on your results and determine the adequacy of the model.
e. Determine whether there is a significant relationship between selling price and the two independent variables (assessed value and time period) at the 0.05 level of significance.
f. Determine the p-value in (e) and interpret its meaning.
g. Interpret the meaning of the coefficient of multiple determination in this problem.
h. Determine the adjusted r^2.

i. At the 0.05 level of significance, determine whether each independent variable makes a significant contribution to the regression model. Indicate the most appropriate regression model for this set of data.
j. Determine the p-values in (i) and interpret their meaning.
k. Construct a 95% confidence interval estimate of the population slope between selling price and assessed value. How does the interpretation of the slope here differ from that in Problem 13.76 on page 557?
l. Compute and interpret the coefficients of partial determination.

14.61 Measuring the height of a California redwood tree is a very difficult undertaking because these trees grow to heights of over 300 feet. People familiar with these trees understand that the height of a California redwood tree is related to other characteristics of the tree, including the diameter of the tree at the breast height of a person and the thickness of the bark of the tree. The data in the file **redwood.xls** represent the height, diameter at breast height of a person, and bark thickness for a sample of 21 California redwood trees.
a. State the multiple regression equation.
b. Interpret the meaning of the slopes in this equation.
c. Predict the mean height for a tree that has a breast diameter of 25 inches and a bark thickness of 2 inches.
d. Interpret the meaning of the coefficient of multiple determination in this problem.
e. Perform a residual analysis on the results and determine the adequacy of the model.
f. Determine whether there is a significant relationship between the height of redwood trees and the two independent variables (breast diameter and the bark thickness) at the 0.05 level of significance.
g. Construct a 95% confidence interval estimate of the population slope between the height of the redwood trees and breast diameter and between the height of redwood trees and the bark thickness.
h. At the 0.05 level of significance, determine whether each independent variable makes a significant contribution to the regression model. Indicate the independent variables to include in this model.
i. Construct a 95% confidence interval estimate of the mean height for trees that have a breast diameter of 25 inches and a bark thickness of 2 inches along with a prediction interval for an individual tree.
j. Compute and interpret the coefficients of partial determination.

14.62 Develop a model to predict the assessed value (in thousands of dollars), using the size of the houses (in thousands of square feet) and the age of the houses (in years) from the following table (whose data are stored in the file **house2.xls**):

House	Assessed Value ($000)	Size of House (Thousands of Square Feet)	Age (Years)
1	184.4	2.00	3.42
2	177.4	1.71	11.50
3	175.7	1.45	8.33
4	185.9	1.76	0.00
5	179.1	1.93	7.42
6	170.4	1.20	32.00
7	175.8	1.55	16.00
8	185.9	1.93	2.00
9	178.5	1.59	1.75
10	179.2	1.50	2.75
11	186.7	1.90	0.00
12	179.3	1.39	0.00
13	174.5	1.54	12.58
14	183.8	1.89	2.75
15	176.8	1.59	7.17

a. State the multiple regression equation.
b. Interpret the meaning of the slopes in this equation.
c. Predict the mean assessed value for a house that has a size of 1,750 square feet and is 10 years old.
d. Perform a residual analysis on the results and determine the adequacy of the model.
e. Determine whether there is a significant relationship between assessed value and the two independent variables (size and age) at the 0.05 level of significance.
f. Determine the p-value in (e) and interpret its meaning.
g. Interpret the meaning of the coefficient of multiple determination in this problem.
h. Determine the adjusted r^2.
i. At the 0.05 level of significance, determine whether each independent variable makes a significant contribution to the regression model. Indicate the most appropriate regression model for this set of data.
j. Determine the p-values in (i) and interpret their meaning.
k. Construct a 95% confidence interval estimate of the population slope between assessed value and size. How does the interpretation of the slope here differ from that of Problem 13.77 on page 558?
l. Compute and interpret the coefficients of partial determination.
m. The real estate assessor's office has been publicly quoted as saying that the age of a house has no bearing on its assessed value. Based on your answers to (a) through (l), do you agree with this statement? Explain.

14.63 Crazy Dave, a well-known baseball analyst, wants to determine which variables are important in predicting a team's wins in a given season. He has collected data related to wins, earned run average (ERA), and runs scored for the 2005 season (stored in the file bb2005.xls). Develop a model to predict the number of wins based on ERA and runs scored.
a. State the multiple regression equation.

b. Interpret the meaning of the slopes in this equation.
c. Predict the mean number of wins for a team that has an ERA of 4.50 and has scored 750 runs.
d. Perform a residual analysis on the results and determine the adequacy of the model.
e. Is there a significant relationship between number of wins and the two independent variables (ERA and runs scored) at the 0.05 level of significance?
f. Determine the p-value in (e) and interpret its meaning.
g. Interpret the meaning of the coefficient of multiple determination in this problem.
h. Determine the adjusted r^2.
i. At the 0.05 level of significance, determine whether each independent variable makes a significant contribution to the regression model. Indicate the most appropriate regression model for this set of data.
j. Determine the p-values in (i) and interpret their meaning.
k. Construct a 95% confidence interval estimate of the population slope between wins and ERA.
l. Compute and interpret the coefficients of partial determination.
m. Which is more important in predicting wins—pitching, as measured by ERA, or offense, as measured by runs scored? Explain.

14.64 Referring to Problem 14.63, suppose that in addition to using ERA to predict the number of wins, Crazy Dave wants to include the league (American vs. National) as an independent variable. Develop a model to predict wins based on ERA and league.
a. State the multiple regression equation.
b. Interpret the meaning of the slopes in this problem.
c. Predict the mean number of wins for a team with an ERA of 4.50 in the American League. Construct a 95% confidence interval estimate for all teams and a 95% prediction interval for an individual team.
d. Perform a residual analysis on the results and determine the adequacy of the model.
e. Is there a significant relationship between wins and the two independent variables (ERA and league) at the 0.05 level of significance?
f. At the 0.05 level of significance, determine whether each independent variable makes a contribution to the regression model. Indicate the most appropriate regression model for this set of data.
g. Construct 95% confidence interval estimates of the population slope for the relationship between wins and ERA and between wins and league.
h. Interpret the meaning of the coefficient of multiple determination.
i. Determine the adjusted r^2.
j. Compute and interpret the coefficients of partial determination.
k. What assumption do you have to make about the slope of wins with ERA?

l. Add an interaction term to the model and, at the 0.05 level of significance, determine whether it makes a significant contribution to the model.

m. On the basis of the results of (f) and (l), which model is most appropriate? Explain.

14.65 You are a real estate broker who wants to compare property values in Glen Cove and Roslyn (which are located approximately 8 miles apart). In order to do so, you will analyze the data in the `gcroslyn.xls` file that includes samples for Glen Cove and Roslyn. Making sure to include the dummy variable for location (Glen Cove or Roslyn) in the regression model, develop a regression model to predict appraised value, based on the land area of a property, the age of a house, and location. Be sure to determine whether any interaction terms need to be included in the model.

Managing the *Springville Herald*

In its continuing study of the home-delivery subscription solicitation process, a marketing department team wants to test the effects of two types of structured sales presentations (personal formal and personal informal) and the number of hours spent on telemarketing on the number of new subscriptions. The staff has recorded these data in the file `sh14.xls` for the past 24 weeks. You can find this data set at **www.prenhall.com/HeraldCase/EffectsData.htm** and in the **EffectsData.htm** file in the **HeraldCase** folder on the Student CD-ROM that accompanies this book.

Analyze these data and develop a multiple regression model to predict the number of new subscriptions for a week, based on the number of hours spent on telemarketing and the sales presentation type. Write a report, giving detailed findings concerning the regression model used.

Web Case

Apply your knowledge of multiple regression models in this Web Case, which extends the Using Statistics OmniFoods scenario from this chapter.

To ensure a successful test marketing of its OmniPower energy bars, the OmniFoods marketing department has contracted with In-Store Placements Group (ISPG), a merchandising consultancy. ISPG will work with the grocery store chain that is conducting the test market study. Using the same 34-store sample used in the test market study, ISPG claims that the choice of shelf location and the presence of in-store OmniPower coupon dispensers each increase sale of the energy bars.

Review the ISPG claims and supporting data at the OmniFoods internal Web page, **www.prenhall.com/Springville/Omni_ISPGMemo.htm**, (or open this Web page file from the Student CD-ROM Web Case folder) and then answer the following:

1. Are the supporting data consistent with ISPG's claims? Perform an appropriate statistical analysis to confirm (or discredit) the stated relationship between sales and the two independent variables of product shelf location and the presence of in-store OmniPower coupon dispensers.

2. If you were advising OmniFoods, would you recommend using a specific shelf location and in-store coupon dispensers to sell OmniPower bars?

3. What additional data would you advise collecting in order to determine the effectiveness of the sales promotion techniques used by ISPG?

REFERENCES

1. Hosmer, D. W., and S. Lemeshow, *Applied Logistic Regression*, 2nd ed. (New York: Wiley, 2001).
2. Kutner, M., C. Nachtsheim, J. Neter, and W. Li, *Applied Linear Statistical Models*, 5th ed. (New York: McGraw-Hill/Irwin, 2005).
3. *Microsoft Excel 2007* (Redmond, WA: Microsoft Corp., 2007).

Excel Companion
to Chapter 14

E14.1 PERFORMING MULTIPLE REGRESSION ANALYSES

You perform a multiple regression analysis by either selecting the PHStat2 Multiple Regression procedure or the ToolPak Regression procedure.

Using PHStat2 Multiple Regression

Select **PHStat → Regression → Multiple Regression**. In the procedure's dialog box (shown below), enter the cell range of the *Y* variable as the **Y Variable Cell Range** and the cell range of the *X* variables as the **X Variables Cell Range**. Click **First cells in both ranges contain label** and enter a value for the **Confidence level for regression coefficients**. Click the **Regression Statistics Table** and the **ANOVA and Coefficients Table** Regression Tool Output Options, enter a title as the **Title**, and click **OK**.

PHStat2 uses the ToolPak Regression procedure to create the regression results worksheet. This worksheet does

not dynamically change, and you need to rerun the PHStat2 procedure if you change your data.

The four output options found in the PHStat2 dialog box enhance the ToolPak procedure. The Durbin-Watson statistic is discussed in Section E13.4, and the other three options are explained in Sections E14.3, E14.4, and E15.3.

Using ToolPak Regression

Open to the worksheet that contains the data for the regression analysis. Select **Tools → Data Analysis**, select **Regression** from the Data Analysis list, and click **OK**. In the procedure's dialog box (shown below), enter the cell range of the *Y* variable data as the **Input Y Range** and enter the cell range of the *X* variables data as the **Input X Range**. (The *X* variables cell range must be contiguous columns.) Click **Labels**. Click **Confidence Level**, and enter a value in its box, and then click **OK**. Results appear on a new worksheet.

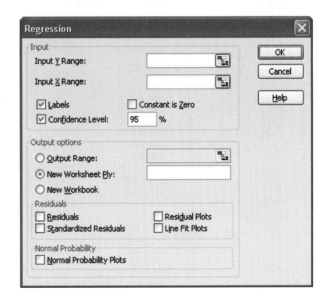

E14.2 CREATING MULTIPLE REGRESSION RESIDUAL PLOTS

You modify the instructions of Section E14.1 to create a table of residuals and then use Excel charting features to create the residual plots needed in multiple regression (see pages 581–582).

Creating a Table of Residuals

You create a table of residuals by clicking additional check boxes when you perform a multiple regression analysis. If you use the PHStat2 Multiple Regression procedure, click the **Regression Statistics Table, ANOVA and Coefficients Table, Residuals Table**, and **Residual Plots** check boxes before you click **OK**. If you use the ToolPak Regression procedure, click the **Residuals** check box before you click **OK**.

Using either one of these modifications creates a regression results worksheet that includes a residual output table that contains columns for observation number, predicted values, and residuals. Figure E14.1 shows the residual output area for the **MR** worksheet of the `Chapter 14.xls` workbook that was used to create the residual plots in Figure 14.4 on page 582 this table of residuals, you can use Excel charting features to create the four types of residual plots needed for a multiple regression residual analysis.

X_{1i}, X_{2i}, or *Observation* as your X variable values. (If you use PHStat2, the **Residual Plots** option created the residuals versus X_{1i} plot and the residuals versus X_{2i} plot for you, so you do not need to manually create these two plots.)

Recall from Section E2.12 that variables need to be arranged X variable first and then Y variable in order for the scatter plot to be correct. For the residuals versus $\hat{Y}_i$ (that is, the predicted values of Y) residual plot, this not a problem as the two exist in the proper order, in side-by-side columns, in the residual output table of the regression model worksheet. However, for the three other types of residual plots, the data for the plot is split between the regression model worksheet and the worksheet that contains the data for the model. You need to have all the data together on one worksheet (it does not matter which worksheet you use) and make sure that the column of residual values appears to the right of the column holding the X_{1i}, X_{2i} or *Observation* values.

	A	B	C
23	RESIDUAL OUTPUT		
24			
25	Observation	Predicted Sales	Residuals
26	1	3420.309524	720.6904762
27	2	3420.309524	421.6904762
28	3	3420.309524	-364.3095238
29	4	3420.309524	98.69047619
30	5	4142.921131	83.07886905
31	6	4142.921131	487.078869
32	7	4142.921131	-635.921131
33	8	4142.921131	-388.921131
34	9	4865.532738	134.4672619
35	10	4865.532738	254.4672619
36	11	4865.532738	-854.5327381
37	12	4865.532738	149.4672619
38	13	2355.962798	-439.9627976
39	14	2355.962798	-1680.962798
40	15	2355.962798	1280.037202
41	16	2355.962798	868.0372024
42	17	3078.574405	-783.5744048
43	18	3078.574405	-348.5744048
44	19	3078.574405	-460.5744048
45	20	3078.574405	1342.425595
46	21	3801.186012	311.8139881
47	22	3801.186012	-55.1860119
48	23	3801.186012	-269.1860119
49	24	3801.186012	23.8139881
50	25	1291.616071	-195.6160714
51	26	1291.616071	-530.6160714
52	27	1291.616071	796.3839286
53	28	1291.616071	-471.6160714
54	29	2014.227679	99.77232143
55	30	2014.227679	-132.2276786
56	31	2014.227679	144.7723214
57	32	2014.227679	-412.2276786
58	33	2736.839286	617.1607143
59	34	2736.839286	190.1607143

FIGURE E14.1 Creating residual plots

Use the Section E2.12 instructions, "Creating Scatter Plots," to create residual plots. Use the cell range of your residuals as the Y variable and the cell range of either $\hat{Y}_i$,

E14.3 COMPUTING THE CONFIDENCE INTERVAL ESTIMATE OF THE MEAN AND THE PREDICTION INTERVAL

You modify the instructions for using the PHStat2 Multiple Regression procedure in Section E14.1 to compute the confidence interval estimate of the mean response and prediction interval for an individual Y.

Click **Confidence Interval Estimate & Prediction Interval** and enter a value for the **Confidence level for interval estimates** (see Figure E14.2) before you click **OK** to create the confidence interval estimate and prediction interval estimate on a separate worksheet, similar to Figure 14.2 on page 575.

Alternatives to using PHStat2 are complex and beyond the scope of this textbook. However, you can open to the **CIEandPI** worksheet of the `CIEandPIforMR.xls` workbook (shown in Figure 14.2) and review its contents. This worksheet uses the function **TINV(1-*confidence level, degrees of freedom*)** to compute the t statistic in cell B20. It uses the **TRANSPOSE(*cell range*)**, **MMULT(*cell range 1, cell range 2*)**, and **MINVERSE(*cell range*)** functions to perform advanced matrix mathematics. Some formulas in the worksheet refer to cells on the **MR** regression model worksheet, while others, not shown in Figure 14.2, refer to a **DC** worksheet that contains a copy of the regression data and a column of all 1s.

Forum Click on the ADVANCED TECHNIQUES link to learn more about the techniques used in this worksheet.

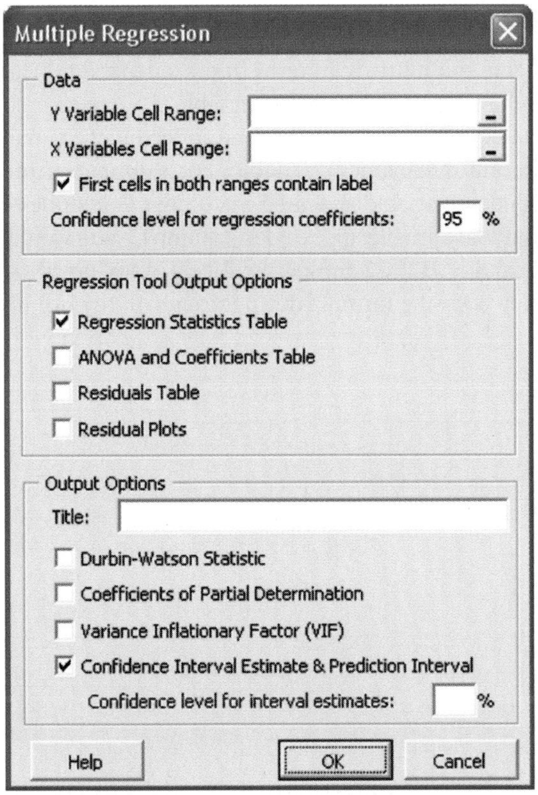

FIGURE E14.2 Dialog box after clicking the Confidence Interval Estimate & Prediction Interval output option

E14.4 COMPUTING THE COEFFICIENTS OF PARTIAL DETERMINATION

You modify the procedures of Section E14.1 to compute the coefficients of partial determination.

Using PHStat2 Multiple Regression

Use the Section E14.1 instructions in "Using PHStat2 Multiple Regression," but click the **Coefficients of Partial Determination** output option click **OK**. The coefficients of partial determination appear on a separate worksheet that is similar to Figure E14.3.

Using ToolPak Regression

If you use the ToolPak Regression procedure, use the Section E14.1 procedures to create all necessary regression results worksheets. (For example, if you have two independent variables, you need to perform a regression analysis using X_1 and X_2, X_1 alone, and X_2 alone.) Then open the

	A	B	C	D	E
1	**OmniPower Sales Analysis**				
2	**Coefficients of Partial Determination**				
3					
4	Intermediate Calculations			**Cell entries:**	
5	SSR(X1, X2)	39472730.7730		**Cell B5:**	**multiple regression worksheet cell C12 value**
6	SST	52093677.4412		**Cell B6:**	**multiple regression worksheet cell C14 value**
7	SSR(X2)	14915814.1025		**Cell B7:**	**exclude-first-X-regression worksheet cell C12 value**
8	SSR(X1)	28153486.1482		**Cell B8:**	**exclude-second-X-regression worksheet cell C12 value**
9	SSR(X1 | X2)	24556916.6706	**=B5 - B7**		
10	SSR(X2 | X1)	11319244.6249	**=B5 - B8**		
11					
12	**Coefficients**				
13	**r2 Y1.2**	**0.6605**	**=B9/(B6 - B5 + B9)**		
14	**r2 Y2.1**	**0.4728**	**=B10/(B6 - B5 + B10)**		

FIGURE E14.3 Completed CPD_2 worksheet for the Omni Power sales example

CPD.xls workbook. Copy the worksheets for all your regression models to this workbook and then open to the CPD worksheet that matches your model. (For example, if you have two independent variables, open the **CPD_2** worksheet.) Then follow the instructions on the worksheet to complete the worksheet. Some worksheet cells may display the #DIV/0! message until you are finished making your entries. This is not an error.

Figure E14.3 shows the CPD_2 worksheet completed for the OmniPower sales example.

E14.5 CREATING DUMMY VARIABLES

You use the Excel find-and-replace feature to create a dummy variable for a categorical variable. To do so, you find each categorical value and replace it with a number.

To use find-and-replace, first open the worksheet that contains your regression data. Select the (column) cell range of the categorical variable for which you are creating a dummy variable. Press **Crtl+C** to copy these values. Select the first cell of the first empty column in your worksheet and press **Crtl+V** to paste the values in this column.

Select all the newly pasted values and press **Crtl+H** to display the Find and Replace dialog box (shown below).

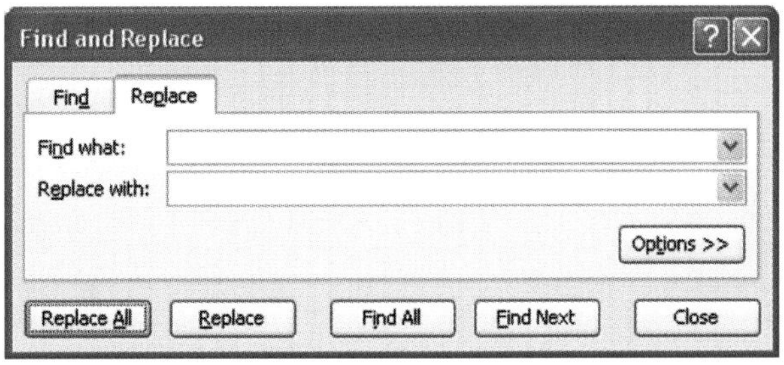

For each unique categorical value in the column,

- Enter the categorical value as the **Find what** value.
- Enter the number that will represent that categorical value as the **Replace with** value.
- Click **Replace All**.

If a message box to confirm the replacement appears, click **OK** to continue.

Click **Close** when you are finished making all replacements. If you inadvertently click the worksheet while using this dialog box, reselect all the newly pasted values before continuing to replace. When you finish, verify your work by comparing the original column of categorical values to your new column of numerical values.

E14.6 CREATING INTERACTION TERMS

To define the interaction term of an independent variable, X_1, and a second independent variable, X_2, create a column of formulas that multiply the first independent variable by the second independent variable. For example, if the first independent variable appeared in column B and the second independent variable appeared in column C, you would enter the formula **=B2*C2** in the row 2 cell of an empty column and then copy the formula down through all rows of data.

CHAPTER 15

Multiple Regression Model Building

USING STATISTICS @ WTT-TV

LEARNING OBJECTIVES

In this chapter, you learn:
- To use quadratic terms in a regression model
- To use transformed variables in a regression model
- To measure the correlation among independent variables
- To build a regression model, using either the stepwise or best-subsets approach
- To avoid the pitfalls involved in developing a multiple regression model

Using Statistics @ WTT-TV

As part of your job as the operations manager at WTT-TV, you look for ways to reduce labor expenses. Currently, the unionized graphic artists at the station receive hourly pay for a significant number of hours during which they are idle. These hours are called standby hours. You have collected data concerning standby hours and four factors that you suspect are related to the excessive number of standby hours the station is currently experiencing: the total number of staff present, remote hours, Dubner hours, and total labor hours.

You plan to build a multiple regression model to help determine which factors most heavily affect standby hours. You believe that an appropriate model will help you to predict the number of future standby hours, identify the root causes for excessive numbers of standby hours, and allow you to reduce the total number of future standby hours. How do you build the model with the most appropriate mix of independent variables? Are there statistical techniques to help you identify a "best" model without having to consider all possible models? How do you begin?

In Chapter 14, you studied multiple regression models that contained two independent variables. In this chapter, regression analysis is extended to models containing more than two independent variables. In order to help you learn to develop the best model when confronted with a large set of data (such as the one described in the Using Statistics scenario), this chapter introduces you to various topics related to model building. These topics include quadratic independent variables, transformations of either the dependent or independent variables, stepwise regression, and best subsets regression.

15.1 THE QUADRATIC REGRESSION MODEL

The simple regression model discussed in Chapter 13 and the multiple regression model discussed in Chapter 14 assumed that the relationship between Y and each independent variable is linear. However, in Section 13.1, several different types of nonlinear relationships between variables were introduced. One of the most common nonlinear relationships is a quadratic relationship between two variables in which Y increases (or decreases) at a changing rate for various values of X (see Figure 13.2, Panels C–E, on page 514). You can use the quadratic regression model defined in Equation (15.1) to analyze this type of relationship between X and Y.

> **QUADRATIC REGRESSION MODEL**
> $$Y_i = \beta_0 + \beta_1 X_{1i} + \beta_2 X_{1i}^2 + \varepsilon_i \qquad \textbf{(15.1)}$$
>
> where
>
> $\beta_0 = Y$ intercept
>
> $\beta_1 = $ coefficient of the linear effect on Y
>
> $\beta_2 = $ coefficient of the quadratic effect on Y
>
> $\varepsilon_i = $ random error in Y for observation i

This **quadratic regression model** is similar to the multiple regression model with two independent variables [see Equation (14.2) on page 573] except that the second independent variable is the square of the first independent variable. Once again, you use the sample regression coefficients (b_0, b_1, and b_2) as estimates of the population parameters (β_0, β_1, and β_2). Equation (15.2) defines the regression equation for the quadratic model with one independent variable (X_1) and a dependent variable (Y).

QUADRATIC REGRESSION EQUATION

$$\hat{Y}_i = b_0 + b_1X_{1i} + b_2X_{1i}^2$$

(15.2)

In Equation (15.2), the first regression coefficient, b_0, represents the Y intercept; the second regression coefficient, b_1, represents the linear effect; and the third regression coefficient, b_2, represents the quadratic effect.

Finding the Regression Coefficients and Predicting Y

To illustrate the quadratic regression model, consider the following experiment, conducted to study the effect of various amounts of an ingredient called fly ash on the strength of concrete. A sample of 18 specimens of 28-day-old concrete was collected, in which the percentage of fly ash in the concrete varies from 0 to 60%. Table 15.1 summarizes the data, which are stored in the file flyash.xls.

TABLE 15.1

Fly Ash Percentage and Strength of 18 Samples of 28-Day-Old Concrete

Fly Ash %	Strength (psi)	Fly Ash %	Strength (psi)
0	4,779	40	5,995
0	4,706	40	5,628
0	4,350	40	5,897
20	5,189	50	5,746
20	5,140	50	5,719
20	4,976	50	5,782
30	5,110	60	4,895
30	5,685	60	5,030
30	5,618	60	4,648

The scatter plot in Figure 15.1 can help you select the proper model for expressing the relationship between fly ash percentage and strength. Figure 15.1 indicates an initial increase in the

FIGURE 15.1

Microsoft Excel scatter plot of fly ash percentage (X) and strength (Y)

See Section E2.12 to create this.

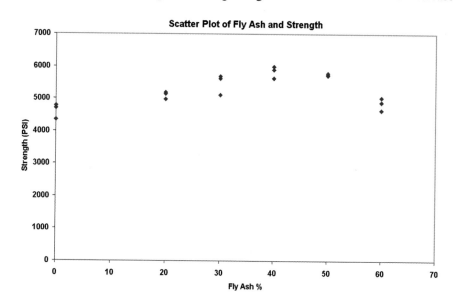

strength of the concrete as the percentage of fly ash increases. The strength appears to level off and then drop after achieving maximum strength at about 40% fly ash. Strength for 50% fly ash is slightly below strength at 40%, but strength at 60% is substantially below strength at 50%. Therefore, a quadratic model is a more appropriate choice than a linear model to estimate strength based on fly ash percentage.

Figure 15.2 shows the Excel worksheet for these data.

FIGURE 15.2

Microsoft Excel results for the concrete strength data

See Section E15.1 to create this.

	A	B	C	D	E	F	G
1	Concrete Strength Analysis						
2							
3	*Regression Statistics*						
4	Multiple R	0.8053					
5	R Square	0.6485					
6	Adjusted R Square	0.6016					
7	Standard Error	312.1129					
8	Observations	18					
9							
10	ANOVA						
11		*df*	*SS*	*MS*	*F*	*Significance F*	
12	Regression	2	2695473.49	1347736.745	13.8351	0.0004	
13	Residual	15	1461217.01	97414.4674			
14	Total	17	4156690.5				
15							
16		*Coefficients*	*Standard Error*	*t Stat*	*P-value*	*Lower 95%*	*Upper 95%*
17	Intercept	4486.3611	174.7531	25.6726	8.24736E-14	4113.8834	4858.8389
18	Fly Ash%	63.0052	12.3725	5.0923	0.0001	36.6338	89.3767
19	Fly Ash% ^2	-0.8765	0.1966	-4.4578	0.0005	-1.2955	-0.4574

From Figure 15.2,

$$b_0 = 4{,}486.3611 \quad b_1 = 63.0052 \quad b_2 = -0.8765$$

Therefore, the quadratic regression equation is

$$\hat{Y}_i = 4{,}486.3611 + 63.0052 X_{1i} - 0.8765 X_{1i}^2$$

where

$$\hat{Y}_i = \text{predicted strength for sample } i$$

$$X_{1i} = \text{percentage of fly ash for sample } i$$

Figure 15.3 plots this quadratic regression equation on the scatter plot to show the fit of the quadratic regression model to the original data.

FIGURE 15.3

Microsoft Excel scatter plot expressing the quadratic relationship between fly ash percentage and strength for the concrete data

See Section E2.12 to create this.

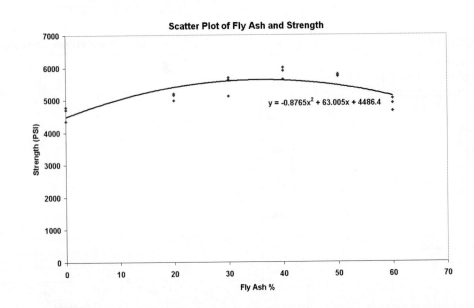

From the quadratic regression equation and Figure 15.3, the Y intercept ($b_0 = 4{,}486.3611$) is the predicted strength when the percentage of fly ash is 0. To interpret the coefficients b_1 and b_2, observe that after an initial increase, strength decreases as fly ash percentage increases. This nonlinear relationship is further demonstrated by predicting the strength for fly ash percentages of 20, 40, and 60. Using the quadratic regression equation,

$$\hat{Y}_i = 4{,}486.3611 + 63.0052 X_{1i} - 0.8765 X_{1i}^2$$

for $X_{1i} = 20$,

$$\hat{Y}_i = 4{,}486.3611 + 63.0052(20) - 0.8765(20)^2 = 5{,}395.865$$

for $X_{1i} = 40$,

$$\hat{Y}_i = 4{,}486.3611 + 63.0052(40) - 0.8765(40)^2 = 5{,}604.169$$

and for $X_{1i} = 60$,

$$\hat{Y}_i = 4{,}486.3611 + 63.0052(60) - 0.8765(60)^2 = 5{,}111.273$$

Thus, the predicted concrete strength for 40% fly ash is 208.304 psi above the predicted strength for 20% fly ash, but the predicted strength for 60% fly ash is 492.896 psi below the predicted strength for 40% fly ash.

Testing for the Significance of the Quadratic Model

After you calculate the quadratic regression equation, you can test whether there is a significant overall relationship between strength, Y, and fly ash percentage, X_1. The null and alternative hypotheses are as follows:

H_0: $\beta_1 = \beta_2 = 0$ (There is no overall relationship between X_1 and Y.)
H_1: β_1 and/or $\beta_2 \neq 0$ (There is an overall relationship between X_1 and Y.)

Equation (14.6) on page 579 defines the overall F statistic used for this test:

$$F = \frac{MSR}{MSE}$$

From the Excel results in Figure 15.2 on page 616,

$$F = \frac{MSR}{MSE} = \frac{1{,}347{,}736.745}{97{,}414.4674} = 13.8351$$

If you choose a level of significance of 0.05, from Table E.5, the critical value of the F distribution, with 2 and 15 degrees of freedom, is 3.68 (see Figure 15.4). Because $F = 13.8351 > 3.68$, or because the p-value $= 0.0004 < 0.05$, you reject the null hypothesis (H_0) and conclude that there is a significant overall relationship between strength and fly ash percentage.

FIGURE 15.4

Testing for the existence of the overall relationship at the 0.05 level of significance, with 2 and 15 degrees of freedom

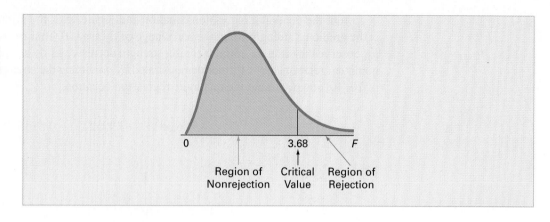

Testing the Quadratic Effect

In using a regression model to examine a relationship between two variables, you want to find not only the most accurate model but also the simplest model that expresses that relationship. Therefore, you need to examine whether there is a significant difference between the quadratic model:

$$Y_i = \beta_0 + \beta_1 X_{1i} + \beta_2 X_{1i}^2 + \varepsilon_i$$

and the linear model:

$$Y_i = \beta_0 + \beta_1 X_{1i} + \varepsilon_i$$

In Section 14.4, you used the t test to determine whether each independent variable makes a significant contribution to the regression model. To test the significance of the contribution of the quadratic effect, you use the following null and alternative hypotheses:

H_0: Including the quadratic effect does not significantly improve the model ($\beta_2 = 0$).
H_1: Including the quadratic effect significantly improves the model ($\beta_2 \neq 0$).

The standard error of each regression coefficient and its corresponding t statistic are part of the Excel results (see Figure 15.2 on page 616). Equation (14.7) on page 583 defines the t test statistic:

$$t = \frac{b_2 - \beta_2}{S_{b_2}}$$

$$= \frac{-0.8765 - 0}{0.1966} = -4.4578$$

If you select the 0.05 level of significance, then from Table E.3, the critical values for the t distribution with 15 degrees of freedom are -2.1315 and $+2.1315$ (see Figure 15.5).

FIGURE 15.5

Testing for the contribution of the quadratic effect to a regression model at the 0.05 level of significance, with 15 degrees of freedom

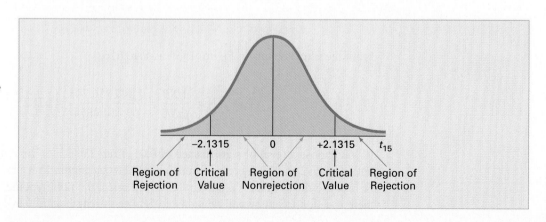

Because $t = -4.4578 < -2.1315$ or because the p-value $= 0.0005 < 0.05$, you reject H_0 and conclude that the quadratic model is significantly better than the linear model for representing the relationship between strength and fly ash percentage.

Example 15.1 provides an additional illustration of a possible quadratic effect.

EXAMPLE 15.1   STUDYING THE QUADRATIC EFFECT IN A MULTIPLE REGRESSION MODEL

A real estate developer studying the effect of atmospheric temperature and the amount of attic insulation on the amount of heating oil consumed selects a random sample of 15 single-family houses. The data, including the consumption of heating oil, are stored in the file `htngoil.xls`. Figure 15.6 shows the Excel results for a multiple regression model using the two independent variables, atmospheric temperature, and attic insulation.

FIGURE 15.6

Microsoft Excel results for the monthly consumption of heating oil

See Section E14.1 to create this.

	A	B	C	D	E	F	G
1	Heating Oil Consumption Analysis						
2							
3	*Regression Statistics*						
4	Multiple R	0.9827					
5	R Square	0.9656					
6	Adjusted R Square	0.9599					
7	Standard Error	26.0138					
8	Observations	15					
9							
10	ANOVA						
11		df	SS	MS	F	Significance F	
12	Regression	2	228014.6263	114007.3132	168.4712	1.65411E-09	
13	Residual	12	8120.6030	676.7169			
14	Total	14	236135.2293				
15							
16		Coefficients	Standard Error	t Stat	P-value	Lower 95%	Upper 95%
17	Intercept	562.1510	21.0931	26.6509	4.77868E-12	516.1931	608.1089
18	Temperature	-5.4366	0.3362	-16.1699	1.64178E-09	-6.1691	-4.7040
19	Insulation	-20.0123	2.3425	-8.5431	1.90731E-06	-25.1162	-14.9084

The residual plot for attic insulation (not shown here) contained some evidence of a quadratic effect. Thus, the real estate developer reanalyzed the data by adding a quadratic term for attic insulation to the multiple regression model. At the 0.05 level of significance, is there evidence of a significant quadratic effect for attic insulation?

SOLUTION   Figure 15.7 shows the Excel results for this regression model.

FIGURE 15.7

Microsoft Excel results for the multiple regression model with a quadratic term for attic insulation

See Section E15.1 to create this.

	A	B	C	D	E	F	G
1	Quadratic Effect for Insulation Variable?						
2							
3	*Regression Statistics*						
4	Multiple R	0.9862					
5	R Square	0.9725					
6	Adjusted R Square	0.9650					
7	Standard Error	24.2938					
8	Observations	15					
9							
10	ANOVA						
11		df	SS	MS	F	Significance F	
12	Regression	3	229643.2	76547.7215	129.7006	7.26403E-09	
13	Residual	11	6492.1	590.1877			
14	Total	14	236135.2				
15							
16		Coefficients	Standard Error	t Stat	P-value	Lower 95%	Upper 95%
17	Intercept	624.5864	42.4352	14.7186	1.39085E-08	531.1872	717.9856
18	Temperature	-5.3626	0.3171	-16.9099	3.20817E-09	-6.0606	-4.6646
19	Insulation	-44.5868	14.9547	-2.9815	0.0125	-77.5019	-11.6717
20	Insulation ^2	1.8667	1.1238	1.6611	0.1249	-0.6067	4.3401

The multiple regression equation is

$$\hat{Y}_i = 624.5864 - 5.3626X_{1i} - 44.5868X_{2i} + 1.8667X_{2i}^2$$

To test for the significance of the quadratic effect,

H_0: Including the quadratic effect does not significantly improve the model ($\beta_3 = 0$).
H_1: Including the quadratic effect significantly improves the model ($\beta_3 \neq 0$).

From Figure 15.7 and Table E.3, $-2.2010 < t = 1.661 < 2.2010$ or the p-value $= 0.1249 > 0.05$. Therefore, you do not reject the null hypothesis. You conclude that there is insufficient evidence that the quadratic effect for attic insulation is different from zero. In the interest of keeping the model as simple as possible, you should use the multiple regression equation computed in Figure 15.6:

$$\hat{Y}_i = 562.1510 - 5.4366X_{1i} - 20.0123X_{2i}$$

The Coefficient of Multiple Determination

In the multiple regression model, the coefficient of multiple determination, r^2 (see Section 14.2), represents the proportion of variation in Y that is explained by variation in the independent variables. Consider the quadratic regression model you used to predict the strength of concrete using fly ash and fly ash squared. You compute r^2 by using Equation (14.4) on page 578:

$$r^2 = \frac{SSR}{SST}$$

From Figure 15.2 on page 616,

$$SSR = 2{,}695{,}473.49 \quad SST = 4{,}156{,}690.5$$

Thus,

$$r^2 = \frac{SSR}{SST} = \frac{2{,}695{,}473.49}{4{,}156{,}690.5} = 0.6485$$

This coefficient of multiple determination indicates that 64.85% of the variation in strength is explained by the quadratic relationship between strength and the percentage of fly ash. You should also compute r^2_{adj} to account for the number of independent variables and the sample size. In the quadratic regression model, $k = 2$ because there are two independent variables, X_1 and X_1^2. Thus, using Equation (14.5) on page 578,

$$r^2_{adj} = 1 - \left[(1 - r^2)\frac{(n-1)}{(n-k-1)}\right]$$

$$= 1 - \left[(1 - 0.6485)\frac{17}{15}\right]$$

$$= 1 - 0.3984$$

$$= 0.6016$$

PROBLEMS FOR SECTION 15.1

Learning the Basics

 15.1 The following quadratic regression equation is for a sample of $n = 25$:

$$\hat{Y}_i = 5 + 3X_{1i} + 1.5X_{1i}^2$$

a. Predict the Y for $X_1 = 2$.
b. Suppose the t statistic for the quadratic regression coefficient is 2.35. At the 0.05 level of significance, is there evidence that the quadratic model is better than the linear model?

c. Suppose the t statistic for the quadratic regression coefficient is 1.17. At the 0.05 level of significance, is there evidence that the quadratic model is better than the linear model?
d. Suppose the regression coefficient for the linear effect is -3.0. Predict Y for $X_1 = 2$.

Applying the Concepts

15.2 Is the number of calories in a beer related to the number of carbohydrates and/or the percentage of alcohol in the beer? Data concerning 58 of the best-selling domestic beers in the United States are located in the file . The values for three variables are included: the number of calories per 12 ounces, the percentage alcohol, and the number of carbohydrates (in grams) per 12 ounces (extracted from **www.Beer100.com**, March 31, 2006).

a. Perform a multiple regression analysis, using calories as the dependent variable and percentage alcohol and the number of carbohydrates as the independent variables.

b. Add quadratic terms for percentage alcohol and the number of carbohydrates.

c. Which model is better, the one in (a) or (b)?

d. Write a short summary concerning the relationship between the number of calories in a beer and the percentage alcohol and number of carbohydrates.

PH Grade
ASSIST **15.3** The marketing department of a large supermarket chain wants to study the effect of price on the sales of packages of disposable razors. A sample of 15 stores with equivalent store traffic and product placement (that is, at the checkout counter) is selected. Five stores are randomly assigned to each of three price levels (79, 99, and 119 cents) for the package of razors. The number of packages sold over a full week and the price at each store are in the following table (and in the file **dispraz.xls**):

Sales	Price (Cents)	Sales	Price (Cents)
142	79	115	99
151	79	126	99
163	79	77	119
168	79	86	119
176	79	95	119
91	99	100	119
100	99	106	119
107	99		

Assume a quadratic relationship between price and sales.

a. Construct a scatter plot for price and sales.

b. State the quadratic regression equation.

c. Predict the mean weekly sales for a price per package of 79 cents.

d. Perform a residual analysis on the results and determine the adequacy of the model.

e. At the 0.05 level of significance, is there a significant quadratic relationship between weekly sales and price?

f. At the 0.05 level of significance, determine whether the quadratic model is a better fit than the linear model.

g. Interpret the meaning of the coefficient of multiple determination.

h. Compute the adjusted r^2.

✓ SELF
Test **15.4** An agronomist designed a study in which tomatoes were grown using six different amounts of fertilizer: 0, 20, 40, 60, 80, and 100 pounds per 1,000 square feet. These fertilizer application rates were then randomly assigned to plots of land. The results including the yield of tomatoes (in pounds) were as follows (see the file **tomyld2.xls**):

Plot	Fertilizer Application Rate	Yield	Plot	Fertilizer Application Rate	Yield
1	0	6	7	60	46
2	0	9	8	60	50
3	20	19	9	80	48
4	20	24	10	80	54
5	40	32	11	100	52
6	40	38	12	100	58

Assume a quadratic relationship between the fertilizer application rate and yield.

a. Construct a scatter plot for fertilizer application rate and yield.

b. State the quadratic regression equation.

c. Predict the mean yield for a plot of land fertilized with 70 pounds per 1,000 square feet.

d. Perform a residual analysis on the results and determine the adequacy of the model.

e. At the 0.05 level of significance, is there a significant overall relationship between the fertilizer application rate and tomato yield?

f. What is the p-value in (e)? Interpret its meaning.

g. At the 0.05 level of significance, determine whether there is a significant quadratic effect.

h. What is the p-value in (g)? Interpret its meaning.

i. Interpret the meaning of the coefficient of multiple determination.

j. Compute the adjusted r^2.

15.5 An auditor for a county government would like to develop a model to predict the county taxes, based on the age of single-family houses. She selects a random sample of 19 single-family houses, and the results are in the data file **taxes.xls**. Assume a quadratic relationship between age and county taxes.

a. Construct a scatter plot between age and county taxes.

b. State the quadratic regression equation.

c. Predict the mean county taxes for a house that is 20 years old.

d. Perform a residual analysis on the results and determine the adequacy of the model.

e. At the 0.05 level of significance, is there a significant overall relationship between age and county taxes?

f. What is the p-value in (e)? Interpret its meaning.

g. At the 0.05 level of significance, determine whether the quadratic model is superior to the linear model.

h. What is the p-value in (g)? Interpret its meaning.

i. Interpret the meaning of the coefficient of multiple determination.

j. Compute the adjusted r^2.

15.2   USING TRANSFORMATIONS IN REGRESSION MODELS

This section introduces regression models in which the independent variable, the dependent variable, or both are transformed in order to either overcome violations of the assumptions of regression or to make a model linear in form. Among the many transformations available (see reference 1) are the square-root transformation and transformations involving the common logarithm (base 10) and the natural logarithm (base e).[1]

[1] For more information on logarithms, see Appendix A.3.

The Square-Root Transformation

The **square-root transformation** is often used to overcome violations of the equal-variance assumption as well as to transform a model that is not linear in form into one that is linear. Equation (15.3) shows a regression model that uses a square-root transformation of the independent variable.

> **REGRESSION MODEL WITH A SQUARE-ROOT TRANSFORMATION**
>
> $$Y_i = \beta_0 + \beta_1 \sqrt{X_{1i}} + \varepsilon_i \tag{15.3}$$

Example 15.2 illustrates the use of a square-root transformation.

EXAMPLE 15.2   **USING THE SQUARE-ROOT TRANSFORMATION**

Given the following values for Y and X, use a square-root transformation for the X variable:

Y	X	Y	X
42.7	1	100.4	3
50.4	1	104.7	4
69.1	2	112.3	4
79.8	2	113.6	5
90.0	3	123.9	5

Construct a scatter plot for X and Y and for the square root of X and Y.

SOLUTION Figure 15.8, Panel A, displays the scatter plot of X and Y; Panel B shows the square root of X versus Y.

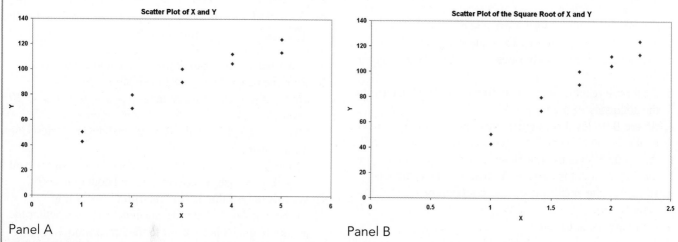

Panel A   Panel B

FIGURE 15.8 Panel A: Scatter plot of X and Y; Panel B: Scatter plot of the square root of X and Y

You can see that the square-root transformation has transformed a nonlinear relationship into a linear relationship.

The Log Transformation

The **logarithmic transformation** is often used to overcome violations to the equal-variance assumption. You can also use the logarithmic transformation to change a nonlinear model into a linear model. Equation (15.4) shows a multiplicative model.

ORIGINAL MULTIPLICATIVE MODEL

$$Y_i = \beta_0 X_{1i}^{\beta_1} X_{2i}^{\beta_2} \varepsilon_i \qquad (15.4)$$

By taking base 10 logarithms of both the dependent and independent variables, you can transform Equation (15.4) to the model shown in Equation (15.5).

TRANSFORMED MULTIPLICATIVE MODEL

$$\begin{aligned}
\log Y_i &= \log(\beta_0 X_{1i}^{\beta_1} X_{2i}^{\beta_2} \varepsilon_i) \\
&= \log \beta_0 + \log(X_{1i}^{\beta_1}) + \log(X_{2i}^{\beta_2}) + \log \varepsilon_i \qquad (15.5) \\
&= \log \beta_0 + \beta_1 \log X_{1i} + \beta_2 \log X_{2i} + \log \varepsilon_i
\end{aligned}$$

Hence, Equation (15.5) is linear in the logarithms. In a similar fashion, you can transform the exponential model shown in Equation (15.6) to linear form by taking the natural logarithm of both sides of the equation. Equation (15.7) is the transformed model.

ORIGINAL EXPONENTIAL MODEL

$$Y_i = e^{\beta_0 + \beta_1 X_{1i} + \beta_2 X_{2i}} \varepsilon_i \qquad (15.6)$$

TRANSFORMED EXPONENTIAL MODEL

$$\begin{aligned}
\ln Y_i &= \ln(e^{\beta_0 + \beta_1 X_{1i} + \beta_2 X_{2i}} \varepsilon_i) \\
&= \ln(e^{\beta_0 + \beta_1 X_{1i} + \beta_2 X_{2i}}) + \ln \varepsilon_i \qquad (15.7) \\
&= \beta_0 + \beta_1 X_{1i} + \beta_2 X_{2i} + \ln \varepsilon_i
\end{aligned}$$

EXAMPLE 15.3

USING THE NATURAL LOG TRANSFORMATION

Given the following values for Y and X, use a natural logarithm transformation for the Y variable:

Y	X	Y	X
0.7	1	4.8	3
0.5	1	12.9	4
1.6	2	11.5	4
1.8	2	32.1	5
4.2	3	33.9	5

Construct a scatter plot for X and Y and for X and the natural logarithm of Y.

SOLUTION As shown in Figure 15.9, the natural logarithm transformation has transformed a nonlinear relationship into a linear relationship.

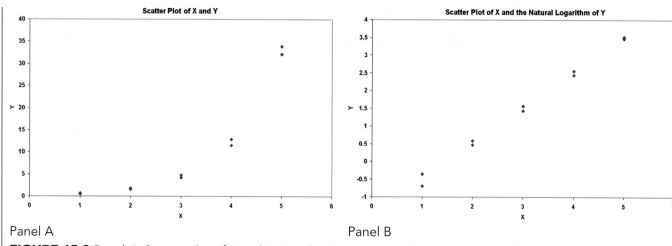

Panel A   Panel B

FIGURE 15.9 Panel *A*: Scatter plot of *X* and *Y*; Panel *B*: Scatter plot of *X* and the natural logarithm of *Y*

PROBLEMS FOR SECTION 15.2

Learning the Basics

 15.6 Consider the following regression equation:

$$\log \hat{Y}_i = \log 3.07 + 0.9 \log X_{1i} + 1.41 \log X_{2i}$$

a. Predict the value of *Y* when $X_1 = 8.5$ and $X_2 = 5.2$.
b. Interpret the meaning of the slopes.

 15.7 Consider the following regression equation:

$$\ln \hat{Y}_i = 4.62 + 0.5X_{1i} + 0.7X_{2i}$$

a. Predict the value of *Y* when $X_1 = 8.5$ and $X_2 = 5.2$.
b. Interpret the meaning of the slopes.

Applying the Concepts

 15.8 Referring to the data of Problem 15.2 on page 621 and using the file **domesticbeer.xls**, perform a square-root transformation on each of the independent variables (percentage alcohol and the number of carbohydrates). Using calories as the dependent variable and the transformed independent variables, perform a multiple regression analysis.
a. State the regression equation.
b. Perform a residual analysis of the results and determine the adequacy of the model.
c. At the 0.05 level of significance, is there a significant relationship between calories and the square root of the percentage of alcohol and the square root of the number of carbohydrates?
d. Interpret the meaning of the coefficient of determination, r^2, in this problem.
e. Compute the adjusted r^2.

f. Compare your results with those in Problem 15.2. Which model is better? Why?

15.9 Referring to the data of Problem 15.2 on pages 620–621 and using the file **domesticbeer.xls**, perform a natural logarithmic transformation of the dependent variable (calories). Using the transformed dependent variable and the percentage of alcohol and the number of carbohydrates as the independent variables, perform a multiple regression analysis.
a. State the regression equation.
b. Perform a residual analysis of the results and determine the adequacy of the fit of the model.
c. At the 0.05 level of significance, is there a significant relationship between the natural logarithm of calories and the percentage of alcohol and the number of carbohydrates?
d. Interpret the meaning of the coefficient of determination, r^2, in this problem.
e. Compute the adjusted r^2.
f. Compare your results with those in Problems 15.2 and 15.8. Which model is best? Why?

 15.10 Referring to the data of Problem 15.4 on page 621 and using the file **tomyld2.xls**, perform a natural logarithm transformation of the dependent variable (yield). Using the transformed dependent variable and the fertilizer application rate as the independent variable, perform a regression analysis.
a. State the regression equation.
b. Predict the mean yield when 55 pounds of fertilizer is applied per 1,000 square feet.
c. Perform a residual analysis of the results and determine the adequacy of the model.

d. At the 0.05 level of significance, is there a significant relationship between the natural logarithm of yield and the fertilizer application rate?

e. Interpret the meaning of the coefficient of determination, r^2, in this problem.

f. Compute the adjusted r^2.

g. Compare your results with those in Problem 15.4. Which model is better? Why?

 15.11 Referring to the data of Problem 15.4 on page 621 and using the file **tomyld2.xls**, perform a square-root transformation of the independent variable (fertilizer application rate). Using yield as the dependent variable and the transformed independent variable, perform a regression analysis.

a. State the regression equation.

b. Predict the mean yield when 55 pounds of fertilizer is applied per 1,000 square feet.

c. Perform a residual analysis of the results and determine the adequacy of the model.

d. At the 0.05 level of significance, is there a significant relationship between yield and the square root of the fertilizer application rate?

e. Interpret the meaning of the coefficient of determination, r^2, in this problem.

f. Compute the adjusted r^2.

g. Compare your results with those of Problems 15.4 and 15.10. Which model is best? Why?

15.3 COLLINEARITY

One important problem in the application of multiple regression analysis involves the possible **collinearity** of the independent variables. This condition refers to situations in which one or more of the independent variables are highly correlated with each other. In such situations, collinear variables do not provide unique information, and it becomes difficult to separate the effect of such variables on the dependent variable. When collinearity exists, the values of the regression coefficients for the correlated variables may fluctuate drastically, depending on which independent variables are included in the model.

One method of measuring collinearity is the **variance inflationary factor (VIF)** for each independent variable. Equation (15.8) defines VIF_j, the variance inflationary factor for variable j.

> **VARIANCE INFLATIONARY FACTOR**
>
> $$VIF_j = \frac{1}{1 - R_j^2} \qquad (15.8)$$
>
> where R_j^2 is the coefficient of multiple determination of independent variable X_j with all other X variables.

If there are only two independent variables, R_1^2 is the coefficient of determination between X_1 and X_2. It is identical to R_2^2, which is the coefficient of determination between X_2 and X_1. If, for example, there are three independent variables, then R_1^2 is the coefficient of multiple determination of X_1 with X_2 and X_3; R_2^2 is the coefficient of multiple determination of X_2 with X_1 and X_3; and R_3^2 is the coefficient of multiple determination of X_3 with X_1 and X_2.

If a set of independent variables is uncorrelated, each VIF_j is equal to 1. If the set is highly correlated, then a VIF_j might even exceed 10. Marquardt (see reference 2) suggests that if VIF_j is greater than 10, there is too much correlation between the variable X_j and the other independent variables. However, other statisticians suggest a more conservative criterion. Snee (see reference 4) recommends using alternatives to least-squares regression if the maximum VIF_j exceeds 5.

You need to proceed with extreme caution when using a multiple regression model that has one or more large VIF values. You can use the model to predict values of the dependent variable *only* in the case where the values of the independent variables used in the prediction are in the relevant range of the values in the data set. However, you cannot extrapolate to values of the independent variables not observed in the sample data. And because the independent variables contain overlapping information, you should always avoid interpreting the regression coefficient estimates separately since there is no way to accurately estimate the individual effects of the independent variables. One solution to the problem is to delete the variable with the largest *VIF* value. The reduced model (that is, the model with the independent variable with the largest *VIF* value deleted) is often free of collinearity problems. If you determine that all the independent variables are needed in the model, you can use methods discussed in reference 1.

In the OmniPower sales data (see Section 14.1), the correlation between the two independent variables, price and promotional expenditure, is −0.0968. Because there are only two independent variables in the model, from Equation (15.8) on page 625:

$$VIF_1 = VIF_2 = \frac{1}{1 - (-0.0968)^2}$$
$$= 1.009$$

Thus, you can conclude that there is no problem with collinearity for the OmniPower sales data.

In models containing quadratic and interaction terms, collinearity is usually present. The linear and quadratic terms of an independent variable are usually highly correlated with each other, and an interaction term is often correlated with one or both of the independent variables making up the interaction. Thus, you cannot interpret individual parameter estimates separately. You need to interpret the linear and quadratic parameter estimates together in order to understand the nonlinear relationship. Likewise, you need to interpret an interaction parameter estimate in conjunction with the two parameter estimates associated with the variables comprising the interaction. In summary, large *VIF*s in quadratic or interaction models do not necessarily mean that the model is a poor one. They do, however, require you to carefully interpret the parameter estimates.

PROBLEMS FOR SECTION 15.3

Learning the Basics

15.12 If the coefficient of determination between two independent variables is 0.20, what is the *VIF*?

15.13 If the coefficient of determination between two independent variables is 0.50, what is the *VIF*?

Applying the Concepts

15.14 Refer to Problem 14.4 on page 576. Perform a multiple regression analysis using the file **warecost.xls** and determine the *VIF* for each independent variable in the model. Is there reason to suspect the existence of collinearity?

15.15 Refer to Problem 14.5 on page 576. Perform a multiple regression analysis using the file **auto.xls** and determine the *VIF* for each inde-

pendent variable in the model. Is there reason to suspect the existence of collinearity?

15.16 Refer to Problem 14.6 on pages 576–577. Perform a multiple regression analysis using the file **advertise.xls** and determine the *VIF* for each independent variable in the model. Is there reason to suspect the existence of collinearity?

15.17 Refer to Problem 14.7 on page 577. Perform a multiple regression analysis using the file **standby.xls** and determine the *VIF* for each independent variable in the model. Is there reason to suspect the existence of collinearity?

15.18 Refer to Problem 14.8 on page 577. Perform a multiple regression analysis using the file **glencove.xls** and determine the *VIF* for each independent variable in the model. Is there reason to suspect the existence of collinearity?

15.4   MODEL BUILDING

This chapter and Chapter 14 have introduced you to many different topics in regression analysis, including quadratic terms, dummy variables, and interaction terms. In this section, you will learn a structured approach to building the most appropriate regression model. As you will see, successful model building incorporates many of the topics you have studied so far.

To begin, refer to the Using Statistics scenario introduced on page 614, in which four independent variables (total staff present, remote hours, Dubner hours, and total labor hours) are considered in developing a regression model to predict standby hours of unionized graphic artists. Table 15.2 presents the data, which are contained in standby.xls.

TABLE 15.2

Predicting Standby Hours Based on Total Staff Present, Remote Hours, Dubner Hours, and Total Labor Hours

Week	Standby Hours	Total Staff Present	Remote Hours	Dubner Hours	Total Labor Hours
1	245	338	414	323	2,001
2	177	333	598	340	2,030
3	271	358	656	340	2,226
4	211	372	631	352	2,154
5	196	339	528	380	2,078
6	135	289	409	339	2,080
7	195	334	382	331	2,073
8	118	293	399	311	1,758
9	116	325	343	328	1,624
10	147	311	338	353	1,889
11	154	304	353	518	1,988
12	146	312	289	440	2,049
13	115	283	388	276	1,796
14	161	307	402	207	1,720
15	274	322	151	287	2,056
16	245	335	228	290	1,890
17	201	350	271	355	2,187
18	183	339	440	300	2,032
19	237	327	475	284	1,856
20	175	328	347	337	2,068
21	152	319	449	279	1,813
22	188	325	336	244	1,808
23	188	322	267	253	1,834
24	197	317	235	272	1,973
25	261	315	164	223	1,839
26	232	331	270	272	1,935

Before you develop a model to predict standby hours, you need to consider the principle of parsimony.

The principle of **parsimony** is the belief that you should select the simplest model that gets the job done adequately.

Regression models with fewer independent variables are simpler and easier to interpret, particularly because they are less likely to be affected by collinearity problems (described in Section 15.3).

The selection of an appropriate model when many independent variables are under consideration involves complexities that are not present with a model that has only two independent variables. The evaluation of all possible regression models is more computationally complex.

Although you can quantitatively evaluate competing models, there may not be a *uniquely* best model but rather several *equally appropriate* models.

To begin analyzing the standby-hours data, you compute the variance inflationary factors [see Equation (15.8) on page 625] to measure the amount of collinearity among the independent variables. Figure 15.10 shows a worksheet that summarizes the *VIF* computations (Panel A), the multiple regression prediction equation worksheet using the four independent variables, and the Durbin-Watson statistic for this model (Panel B). Observe that all the *VIF* values are relatively small, ranging from a high of 1.99928 for the total labor hours to a low of 1.23325 for remote hours. Thus, on the basis of the criteria developed by Snee that all *VIF* values should be less than 5.0 (see reference 4), there is little evidence of collinearity among the set of independent variables.

Panel A

	A	B	C	D	E
1	Standby Hours Analysis				
2		Regression Statistics			
3		Total Staff and all other X	Remote and all other X	Dubner and all other X	Total Labor and all other X
4	Multiple R	0.64368	0.43490	0.56099	0.70698
5	R Square	0.41433	0.18914	0.31471	0.49982
6	Adjusted R Square	0.33446	0.07856	0.22126	0.43161
7	Standard Error	16.47151	124.93921	57.55254	114.41183
8	Observations	26	26	26	26
9	VIF	1.70743	1.23325	1.45924	1.99928

Panel B

	A	B	C	D	E	F	G
1	Standby Hours Analysis						
2							
3		Regression Statistics					
4	Multiple R	0.7894					
5	R Square	0.6231					
6	Adjusted R Square	0.5513					
7	Standard Error	31.8350					
8	Observations	26					
9							
10	ANOVA						
11			df	SS	MS	F	Significance F
12	Regression		4	35181.7937	8795.4484	8.6786	0.0003
13	Residual		21	21282.8217	1013.4677		
14	Total		25	56464.6154			
15							
16			Coefficients	Standard Error	t Stat	P-value	Lower 95%	Upper 95%
17	Intercept		-330.8318	110.8954	-2.9833	0.0071	-561.4514	-100.2123
18	Total Staff		1.2456	0.4121	3.0229	0.0065	0.3887	2.1026
19	Remote		-0.1184	0.0543	-2.1798	0.0408	-0.2314	-0.0054
20	Dubner		-0.2971	0.1179	-2.5189	0.0199	-0.5423	-0.0518
21	Total Labor		0.1305	0.0593	2.2004	0.0391	0.0072	0.2539

Durbin-Watson inset:

	A	B
1	Durbin-Watson Calculations	
2		
3	Sum of Squared Difference of Residuals	47241.6126
4	Sum of Squared Residuals	21282.8217
5		
6	Durbin-Watson Statistic	2.2197

FIGURE 15.10 Microsoft Excel regression results for predicting standby hours based on four independent variables

Panel A was created by copying and pasting results from four different regression results worksheets that were produced using instructions from Section 15.3.

Panel B is a composite of worksheets created using instructions in Sections E14.1 and E13.4.

The Stepwise Regression Approach to Model Building

You continue your analysis of the standby hours data by attempting to determine whether a subset of all independent variables yields an adequate and appropriate model. The first approach described here is **stepwise regression**, which attempts to find the "best" regression model without examining all possible models.

The first step of stepwise regression is to find the best model that uses one independent variable. The next step is to find the best of the remaining independent variables to add to the model selected in the first step. An important feature of the stepwise approach is that an independent variable that has entered into the model at an early stage may subsequently be removed after other independent variables are considered. Thus, in stepwise regression, variables are either added to or deleted from the regression model at each step of the model-building process. The partial *F*-test statistic (see Section 14.5) is used to determine whether variables are added or deleted. The stepwise procedure terminates with the selection of a best-fitting model when no additional variables can be added to or deleted from the last model evaluated.

Figure 15.11 represents Microsoft Excel stepwise regression results for the standby-hours data. For this example, a significance level of 0.05 is used to enter a variable into the model or to delete a variable from the model. The first variable entered into the model is total staff, the variable that correlates most highly with the dependent variable standby hours. Because the *p*-value of 0.0011 is less than 0.05, total staff is included in the regression model.

The next step involves selecting a second independent variable for the model. The second variable chosen is one that makes the largest contribution to the model, given that the first variable has been selected. For this model, the second variable is remote hours. Because the *p*-value of 0.0269 for remote hours is less than 0.05, remote hours is included in the regression model.

FIGURE 15.11

Microsoft Excel stepwise regression results for the standby-hours data

See Section E15.4 to create this.

	A	B	C	D	E	F	G	H
1	Stepwise Analysis for Standby Hours							
2	Table of Results for General Stepwise							
3								
4	Total Staff entered.							
5								
6			df	SS	MS	F	Significance F	
7		Regression	1	20667.3980	20667.3980	13.8563	0.0011	
8		Residual	24	35797.2174	1491.5507			
9		Total	25	56464.6154				
10								
11			Coefficients	Standard Error	t Stat	P-value	Lower 95%	Upper 95%
12		Intercept	-272.3816	124.2402	-2.1924	0.0383	-528.8008	-15.9625
13		Total Staff	1.4241	0.3826	3.7224	0.0011	0.6345	2.2136
14								
15								
16	Remote entered.							
17								
18			df	SS	MS	F	Significance F	
19		Regression	2	27662.5429	13831.2714	11.0450	0.0004	
20		Residual	23	28802.0725	1252.2640			
21		Total	25	56464.6154				
22								
23			Coefficients	Standard Error	t Stat	P-value	Lower 95%	Upper 95%
24		Intercept	-330.6748	116.4802	-2.8389	0.0093	-571.6322	-89.7175
25		Total Staff	1.7649	0.3790	4.6562	0.0001	0.9808	2.5490
26		Remote	-0.1390	0.0588	-2.3635	0.0269	-0.2606	-0.0173
27								
28								
29	No other variables could be entered into the model. Stepwise ends.							

After remote hours is entered into the model, the stepwise procedure determines whether total staff is still an important contributing variable or whether it can be eliminated from the model. Because the p-value of 0.0001 for total staff is less than 0.05, total staff remains in the regression model.

The next step involves selecting a third independent variable for the model. Because none of the other variables meets the 0.05 criterion for entry into the model, the stepwise procedure terminates with a model that includes total staff present and the number of remote hours.

This stepwise regression approach to model building was originally developed more than four decades ago, in an era in which regression analysis on mainframe computers involved the costly use of large amounts of processing time. Under such conditions, stepwise regression became widely used, although it provides a limited evaluation of alternative models. With today's extremely fast personal computers, the evaluation of many different regression models is completed quickly, at a very small cost. Thus, a more general way of evaluating alternative regression models, in this era of fast computers, is the best-subsets approach discussed next. Stepwise regression is not obsolete, however. Today, many businesses use stepwise regression as part of a research technique called **data mining**, in which huge data sets are explored to discover significant statistical relationships among a large number of variables. These data sets are so large that the best-subsets approach is impractical.

The Best-Subsets Approach to Model Building

The **best-subsets approach** evaluates all possible regression models for a given set of independent variables. Figure 15.12 on page 630 presents Microsoft Excel results of all possible regression models for the standby-hours data.

A criterion often used in model building is the adjusted r^2, which adjusts the r^2 of each model to account for the number of independent variables in the model as well as for the sample size (see Section 14.2). Because model building requires you to compare models with different numbers of independent variables, the adjusted r^2 is more appropriate than r^2.

Referring to Figure 15.12, you see that the adjusted r^2 reaches a maximum value of 0.5513 when all four independent variables plus the intercept term (for a total of five estimated parameters) are included in the model.

A second criterion often used in the evaluation of competing models is the C_p statistic developed by Mallows (see reference 1). The C_p **statistic**, defined in Equation (15.9), measures the differences between a fitted regression model and a *true* model, along with random error.

FIGURE 15.12

Microsoft Excel best-subsets regression results for the standby-hours data

See Section E15.5 to create this.

	A	B	C	D	E	F
1	Best Subsets Analysis for Standby Hours					
2						
3	Intermediate Calculations					
4	R2T	0.6231				
5	1 - R2T	0.3769				
6	n	26				
7	T	5				
8	n - T	21				
9						
10	Model	Cp	k+1	R Square	Adj. R Square	Std. Error
11	X1	13.3215	2	0.3660	0.3396	38.6206
12	X1X2	8.4193	3	0.4899	0.4456	35.3873
13	X1X2X3	7.8418	4	0.5362	0.4729	34.5029
14	X1X2X3X4	5.0000	5	0.6231	0.5513	31.8350
15	X1X2X4	9.3449	4	0.5092	0.4423	35.4921
16	X1X3	10.6486	3	0.4499	0.4021	36.7490
17	X1X3X4	7.7517	4	0.5378	0.4748	34.4426
18	X1X4	14.7982	3	0.3754	0.3211	39.1579
19	X2	33.2078	2	0.0091	-0.0322	48.2836
20	X2X3	32.3067	3	0.0612	-0.0205	48.0087
21	X2X3X4	12.1381	4	0.4591	0.3853	37.2608
22	X2X4	23.2481	3	0.2238	0.1563	43.6540
23	X3	30.3884	2	0.0597	0.0205	47.0345
24	X3X4	11.8231	3	0.4288	0.3791	37.4466
25	X4	24.1846	2	0.1710	0.1365	44.1619

C_p STATISTIC

$$C_p = \frac{(1 - R_k^2)(n - T)}{1 - R_T^2} - [n - 2(k + 1)] \tag{15.9}$$

where

k = number of independent variables included in a regression model

T = total number of parameters (including the intercept) to be estimated in the full regression model

R_k^2 = coefficient of multiple determination for a regression model that has k independent variables

R_T^2 = coefficient of multiple determination for a full regression model that contains all T estimated parameters

Using Equation (15.9) to compute C_p for the model containing total staff present and remote hours,

$$n = 26 \quad k = 2 \quad T = 4 + 1 = 5 \quad R_k^2 = 0.4899 \quad R_T^2 = 0.6231$$

so that

$$C_p = \frac{(1 - 0.4899)(26 - 5)}{1 - 0.6231} - [26 - 2(2 + 1)]$$

$$= 8.4193$$

When a regression model with k independent variables contains only random differences from a *true* model, the mean value of C_p is $k + 1$, the number of parameters. Thus, in evaluating many alternative regression models, the goal is to find models whose C_p is close to or less than $k + 1$.

In Figure 15.12, you see that only the model with all four independent variables considered contains a C_p value close to or below $k + 1$. Therefore, you should choose that model. Although it was not the case here, the C_p statistic often provides several alternative models for you to evaluate in greater depth, using other criteria, such as parsimony, interpretability, and departure from model assumptions (as evaluated by residual analysis). The model selected using stepwise regression has a C_p value of 8.4193, which is substantially above the suggested criterion of $k + 1 = 3$ for that model.

Because the data were collected in time order, you need to compute the Durbin-Watson statistic to determine whether there is autocorrelation in the residuals (see Section 13.6). From Panel B of Figure 15.10 on page 628, you see that the Durbin-Watson statistic, D, is 2.2197. Because D is greater than 2.0, there is no indication of positive correlation in the residuals.

When you have finished selecting the independent variables to include in the model, you should perform a residual analysis to evaluate the regression assumptions. Figure 15.13 presents Microsoft Excel residual plots.

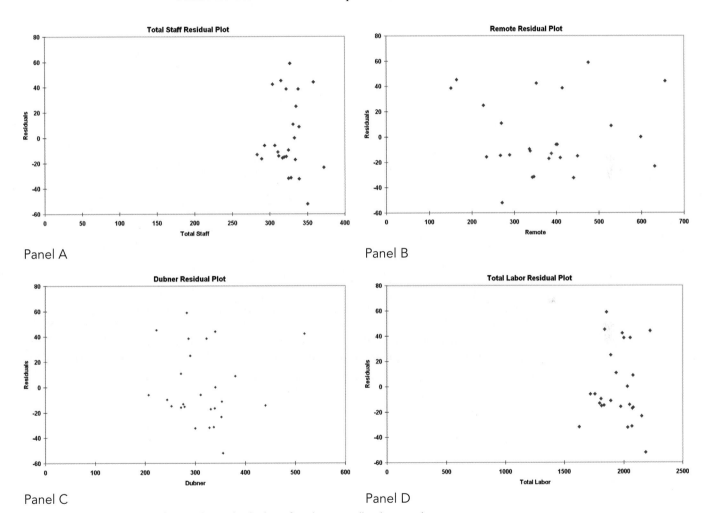

Panel A

Panel B

Panel C

Panel D

FIGURE 15.13 Microsoft Excel residual plots for the standby-hours data

See Section E2.12 to create this.

None of the residual plots versus the total staff, the remote hours, the Dubner hours, and the total labor hours reveal apparent patterns. In addition, a histogram of the residuals (not shown here) indicates only moderate departure from normality, and a plot of the residuals versus the predicted values of Y ($\hat{Y}$) (also not shown here) does not show evidence of unequal variance. Thus, from Figure 15.10 on page 628, the regression equation is

$$\hat{Y}_i = -330.8318 + 1.2456X_{1i} - 0.1184X_{2i} - 0.2971X_{3i} + 0.1305X_{4i}$$

Example 15.4 presents a situation in which there are several alternative models in which the C_p statistic is close to or less than $k + 1$.

EXAMPLE 15.4

CHOOSING AMONG ALTERNATIVE REGRESSION MODELS

Given the output in Table 15.3 from a best-subsets regression analysis of a regression model with seven independent variables, determine which regression model you would choose as the *best* model.

TABLE 15.3

Partial Output from Best-Subsets Regression

Number of Variables	r^2 (%)	Adjusted r^2 (%)	C_p	Variables Included
1	12.1	11.9	113.9	X_4
1	9.3	9.0	130.4	X_1
1	8.3	8.0	136.2	X_3
2	21.4	21.0	62.1	X_3, X_4
2	19.1	18.6	75.6	X_1, X_3
2	18.1	17.7	81.0	X_1, X_4
3	28.5	28.0	22.6	X_1, X_3, X_4
3	26.8	26.3	32.4	X_3, X_4, X_5
3	24.0	23.4	49.0	X_2, X_3, X_4
4	30.8	30.1	11.3	X_1, X_2, X_3, X_4
4	30.4	29.7	14.0	X_1, X_3, X_4, X_6
4	29.6	28.9	18.3	X_1, X_3, X_4, X_5
5	31.7	30.8	8.2	X_1, X_2, X_3, X_4, X_5
5	31.5	30.6	9.6	X_1, X_2, X_3, X_4, X_6
5	31.3	30.4	10.7	X_1, X_3, X_4, X_5, X_6
6	32.3	31.3	6.8	$X_1, X_2, X_3, X_4, X_5, X_6$
6	31.9	30.9	9.0	$X_1, X_2, X_3, X_4, X_5, X_7$
6	31.7	30.6	10.4	$X_1, X_2, X_3, X_4, X_6, X_7$
7	32.4	31.2	8.0	$X_1, X_2, X_3, X_4, X_5, X_6, X_7$

SOLUTION From Table 15.3, you need to determine which models have C_p values that are less than or close to $k + 1$. Two models meet this criterion. The model with six independent variables ($X_1, X_2, X_3, X_4, X_5, X_6$) has a C_p value of 6.8, which is less than $k + 1 = 6 + 1 = 7$, and the full model with seven independent variables ($X_1, X_2, X_3, X_4, X_5, X_6, X_7$) has a C_p value of 8.0. One way you can choose among models that meet this criterion is to determine whether the models contain a subset of variables that are common. Then you test whether the contribution of the additional variables is significant. In this case, because the models differ only by the inclusion of variable X_7 in the full model, you test whether variable X_7 makes a significant contribution to the regression model, given that the variables X_1, X_2, X_3, X_4, X_5, and X_6 are already included in the model. If the contribution is statistically significant, then you should include variable X_7 in the regression model. If variable X_7 does not make a statistically significant contribution, you should not include it in the model.

Exhibit 15.1 summarizes the steps involved in model building.

EXHIBIT 15.1 STEPS INVOLVED IN MODEL BUILDING

1. Compile a listing of all independent variables under consideration.
2. Fit a regression model that includes all the independent variables under consideration and determine the *VIF* for each independent variable. Three possible results can occur:
   a. None of the independent variables have a *VIF* > 5; in this case, proceed to step 3.
   b. One of the independent variables has a *VIF* > 5; in this case, eliminate that independent variable and proceed to step 3.
   c. More than one of the independent variables has a *VIF* > 5; in this case, eliminate the independent variable that has the highest *VIF* and repeat step 2.

3. Perform a best-subsets regression with the remaining independent variables and determine the C_p statistic and/or the adjusted r^2 for each model.
4. List all models that have C_p close to or less than $k + 1$ and/or a high adjusted r^2.
5. From those models listed in step 4, choose a best model.
6. Perform a complete analysis of the model chosen, including a residual analysis.
7. Depending on the results of the residual analysis, add quadratic terms, transform variables, and reanalyze the data.
8. Use the selected model for prediction and inference.

Figure 15.14 represents a roadmap for the steps involved in model building.

FIGURE 15.14

Roadmap for model building

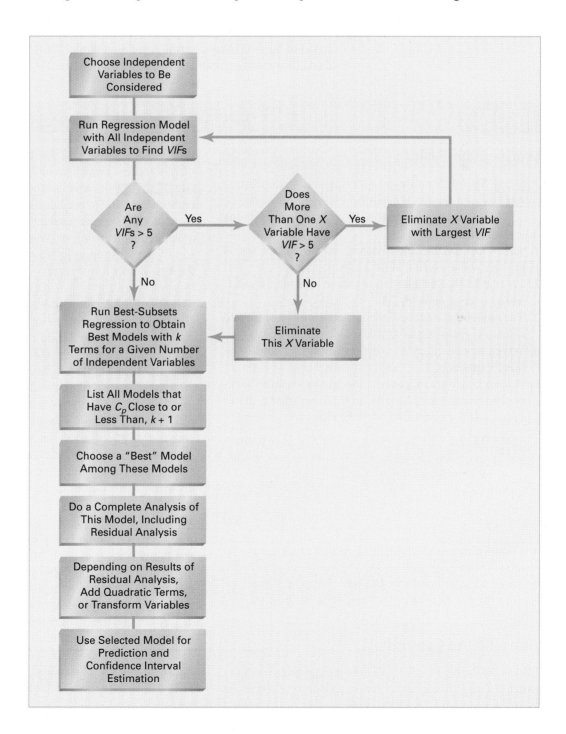

Model Validation

The final step in the model-building process is to validate the selected regression model. This step involves checking the model against data that were not part of the sample analyzed. Several ways of validating a regression model are

- Collect new data and compare the results.
- Compare the results of the regression model to previous results.
- If the data set is large, split the data into two parts and cross-validate the results.

Perhaps the best way of validating a regression model is by collecting new data. If the results with new data are consistent with the selected regression model, you have strong reason to believe that the fitted regression model is applicable in a wide set of circumstances.

If it is not possible to collect new data, you can use one of the two other approaches. In one approach, you compare your regression coefficients and predictions to previous results. If the data set is large, you can use **cross-validation**. First, you split the data into two parts. Then you use the first part of the data to develop the regression model. You then use the second part of the data to evaluate the predictive ability of the regression model.

PROBLEMS FOR SECTION 15.4

Learning the Basics

 15.19 You are considering four independent variables for inclusion in a regression model. You select a sample of 30 observations, with the following results:

1. The model that includes independent variables A and B has a C_p value equal to 4.6.
2. The model that includes independent variables A and C has a C_p value equal to 2.4.
3. The model that includes independent variables A, B, and C has a C_p value equal to 2.7.
   a. Which models meet the criterion for further consideration? Explain.
   b. How would you compare the model that contains independent variables A, B, and C to the model that contains independent variables A and B? Explain.

 15.20 You are considering six independent variables for inclusion in a regression model. You select a sample of 40 observations, with the following results:

$$n = 40 \quad k = 2 \quad T = 6 + 1 = 7 \quad R_k^2 = 0.274 \quad R_T^2 = 0.653$$

a. Compute the C_p value for this two-independent-variable model.
b. Based on your answer to (a), does this model meet the criterion for further consideration as the best model? Explain.

Applying the Concepts

15.21 In Problems 13.85–13.89 on page 561, you constructed simple linear regression models to investigate the relationship between demographic information and monthly sales for a chain of sporting goods stores (see the file **sporting.xls**). Develop the most appropriate multiple regression model to predict a store's monthly sales. Be sure to include a thorough residual analysis. In addition, provide a detailed explanation of the results, including a comparison of the most appropriate multiple regression model to the best simple linear regression model.

 15.22 You need to develop a model to predict the selling price of houses, based on assessed value, time period in which a house is sold, and whether the house is new (0 = no; 1 = yes). A sample of 30 recently sold single-family houses in a small city is selected to study the relationship between selling price and assessed value. (The houses in the city were reassessed at full value one year prior to the study.) The results are in the data file **house1.xls**. Develop the most appropriate multiple regression model to predict selling price. Be sure to perform a thorough residual analysis. In addition, provide a detailed explanation of the results.

15.23 The human resources (HR) director for a large company that produces highly technical industrial instrumentation devices is interested in using regression modeling to help in making recruiting decisions concerning sales managers. The company has 45 sales regions, each headed by a sales manager. Many of the sales managers have degrees in electrical engineering, and due to the technical nature of the product line, several company officials believe that only applicants with degrees in electrical engineering should be considered. At the time of their application, candidates are asked to take the Strong-Campbell

Interest Inventory Test and the Wonderlic Personnel Test. Due to the time and money involved with the testing, some discussion has taken place about dropping one or both of the tests. To start, the HR director gathered information on each of the 45 current sales managers, including years of selling experience, electrical engineering background, and the scores from both the Wonderlic and Strong-Campbell tests. The dependent variable was "sales index" score, which is the ratio of the regions' actual sales divided by the target sales. The target values are constructed each year by upper management, in consultation with the sales managers, and are based on past performance and market potential within each region. The data file **managers.xls** contains information on the 45 current sales managers. The variables included are

Sales—Ratio of yearly sales divided by the target sales value for that region. The target values were mutually agreed-upon "realistic expectations."

Wonder—Score from the Wonderlic Personnel Test. The higher the score, the higher the applicant's perceived ability to manage.

SC—Score on the Strong-Campbell Interest Inventory Test. The higher the score, the higher the applicant's perceived interest in sales.

Experience—Number of years of selling experience prior to becoming a sales manager.

Engineer—Dummy variable that equals 1 if the sales manager has a degree in electrical engineering and 0 otherwise.

a. Develop the most appropriate regression model to predict sales.

b. Do you think that the company should continue administering the Wonderlic and Strong-Campbell tests? Explain.

c. Do the data support the argument that electrical engineers outperform the other sales managers? Would you support the idea to hire only electrical engineers? Explain.

d. How important is prior selling experience in this case? Explain.

e. Discuss in detail how the HR director should incorporate the regression model you developed into the recruiting process.

15.5 PITFALLS IN MULTIPLE REGRESSION AND ETHICAL ISSUES

Pitfalls in Multiple Regression

Model building is an art as well as a science. Different individuals may not always agree on the best multiple regression model. Nevertheless, you should use the process described in Exhibit 15.1 on page 632. In doing so, you must avoid certain pitfalls that can interfere with the development of a useful model. Section 13.9 discussed pitfalls in simple linear regression and strategies for avoiding them. Now that you have studied a variety of multiple regression models, you need to take some additional precautions. To avoid pitfalls in multiple regression, you also need to

- Interpret the regression coefficient for a particular independent variable from a perspective in which the values of all other independent variables are held constant.
- Evaluate residual plots for each independent variable.
- Evaluate interaction and quadratic terms.
- Compute the *VIF* for each independent variable before determining which independent variables to include in the model.
- Examine several alternative models, using best-subsets regression.
- Validate the model before implementing it.

Ethical Issues

Ethical issues arise when a user who wants to make predictions manipulates the development process of the multiple regression model. The key here is intent. In addition to the situations discussed in Section 13.9, unethical behavior occurs when someone uses multiple regression analysis and *willfully fails* to remove from consideration variables that exhibit a high collinearity with other independent variables or *willfully fails* to use methods other than least-squares regression when the assumptions necessary for least-squares regression are seriously violated.

SUMMARY

In this chapter, various multiple regression topics were considered (see Figure 15.15), including quadratic regression models, transformations, collinearity, and model building. You have learned how an operations manager for a television station can build a multiple regression model as an aid in reducing labor expenses.

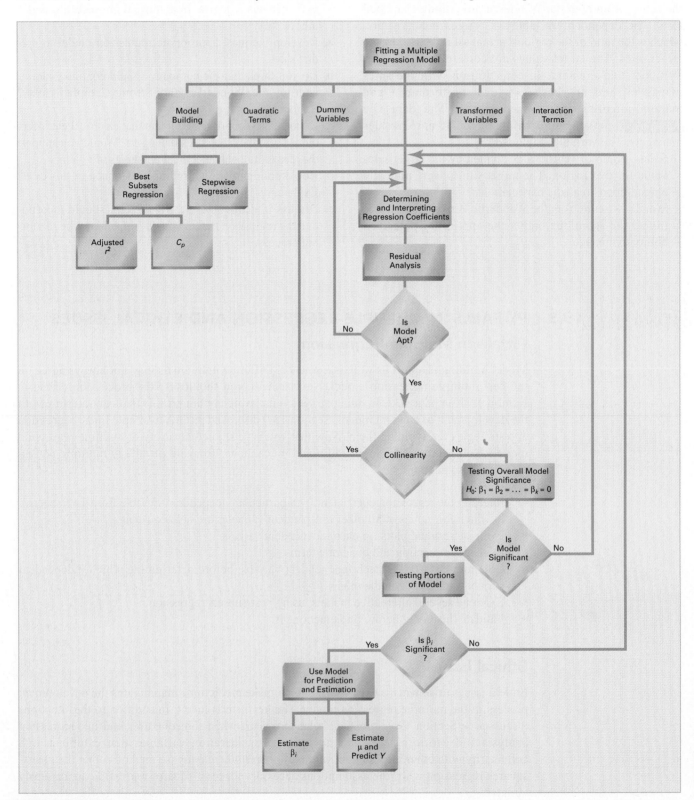

FIGURE 15.15 Roadmap for multiple regression

KEY EQUATIONS

Quadratic Regression Model

$$Y_i = \beta_0 + \beta_1 X_{1i} + \beta_2 X_{1i}^2 + \varepsilon_i \qquad \textbf{(15.1)}$$

Quadratic Regression Equation

$$\hat{Y}_i = b_0 + b_1 X_{1i} + b_2 X_{1i}^2 \qquad \textbf{(15.2)}$$

Regression Model with a Square-Root Transformation

$$Y_i = \beta_0 + \beta_1 \sqrt{X_{1i}} + \varepsilon_i \qquad \textbf{(15.3)}$$

Original Multiplicative Model

$$Y_i = \beta_0 X_{1i}^{\beta_1} X_{2i}^{\beta_2} \varepsilon_i \qquad \textbf{(15.4)}$$

Transformed Multiplicative Model

$$\log Y_i = \log(\beta_0 X_{1i}^{\beta_1} X_{2i}^{\beta_2} \varepsilon_i)$$
$$= \log \beta_0 + \log(X_{1i}^{\beta_1}) + \log(X_{2i}^{\beta_2}) + \log \varepsilon_i \qquad \textbf{(15.5)}$$
$$= \log \beta_0 + \beta_1 \log X_{1i} + \beta_2 \log X_{2i} + \log \varepsilon_i$$

Original Exponential Model

$$Y_i = e^{\beta_0 + \beta_1 X_{1i} + \beta_2 X_{2i}} \varepsilon_i \qquad \textbf{(15.6)}$$

Transformed Exponential Model

$$\ln Y_i = \ln(e^{\beta_0 + \beta_1 X_{1i} + \beta_2 X_{2i}} \varepsilon_i)$$
$$= \ln(e^{\beta_0 + \beta_1 X_{1i} + \beta_2 X_{2i}}) + \ln \varepsilon_i \qquad \textbf{(15.7)}$$
$$= \beta_0 + \beta_1 X_{1i} + \beta_2 X_{2i} + \ln \varepsilon_i$$

Variance Inflationary Factor

$$VIF_j = \frac{1}{1 - R_j^2} \qquad \textbf{(15.8)}$$

C_p Statistic

$$C_p = \frac{(1 - R_k^2)(n - T)}{1 - R_T^2} - [n - 2(k + 1)] \qquad \textbf{(15.9)}$$

KEY TERMS

best-subsets approach   629
C_p statistic   629
collinearity   625
cross-validation   634

data mining   629
logarithmic transformation   623
parsimony   627
quadratic regression model   615

square-root transformation   622
stepwise regression   628
variance inflationary factor (*VIF*)   625

CHAPTER REVIEW PROBLEMS

Checking Your Understanding

15.24 How can you evaluate whether a multiple regression model suffers from collinearity?

 15.25 What is the difference between stepwise regression and best-subsets regression?

 15.26 How do you choose among models according to the C_p statistic in best-subsets regression?

Applying the Concepts

15.27 Crazy Dave has expanded his analysis, presented in Problem 14.63 on page 607, of which variables are important in predicting a team's wins in a given baseball season. He has collected data in the file **bb2005.xls** related to wins, ERA, saves, runs scored, hits allowed, walks allowed, and errors for the 2005 season.

a. Develop the most appropriate multiple regression model to predict a team's wins. Be sure to include a thorough residual analysis. In addition, provide a detailed explanation of the results.

b. Develop the most appropriate multiple regression model to predict a team's ERA on the basis of hits allowed, walks allowed, errors, and saves. Be sure to include a thorough residual analysis. In addition, provide a detailed explanation of the results.

15.28 In the past several years, a great deal of attention has been paid to the disparity in income and player compensation among the 30 Major League Baseball teams. It is widely assumed that the teams with high player compensation and income win the most games. The data file **bb2001.xls** contains information related to regular season gate receipts, local TV and radio revenue, other local revenue, and player compensation in addition to team statistics.

a. Considering these four independent variables, develop the most appropriate multiple regression model to predict the number of wins.

b. Compare the model developed in (a) to the model developed in Problem 15.27 (a), in which on-the-field team statistics were used to predict wins. Which is a better predictor of wins—income and player compensation variables or on-the-field team statistics? Explain.

15.29 Professional basketball has truly become a sport that generates interest among fans around the world. More and more players come from outside the United States to play in the National Basketball Association (NBA). Many factors could impact the number of wins achieved by each NBA team. In addition to the number of wins, the data file NBA2006.xls contains team statistics for points per game (for team, opponent, and the difference between team and opponent), field goal (shots made) percentage (for team, opponent, and the difference between team and opponent), turnovers (losing the ball before a shot is taken) per game (for team, opponent, and the difference between team and opponent), offensive rebound percentage, and defensive rebound percentage.

a. Consider team points per game, opponent points per game, team field goal percentage, opponent field goal percentage, difference in team and opponent turnovers, offensive rebound percentage, and defensive rebound percentage as independent variables for possible inclusion in the multiple regression model. Develop the most appropriate multiple regression model to predict the number of wins.

b. Consider the difference between team points and opponent points per game, the difference between team field goal percentage and opponent field goal percentage, the difference in team and opponent turnovers, offensive rebound percentage, and defensive rebound percentage as independent variables for possible inclusion in the multiple regression model. Develop the most appropriate multiple regression model to predict the number of wins.

c. Compare the results of (a) and (b). Which model is better for predicting the number of wins? Explain.

15.30 Nassau County is located approximately 25 miles east of New York City. Until all residential property was reassessed in 2002, property taxes were assessed based on actual value in 1938 or when the property was built, if it was constructed after 1938. Data in the file glencove.xls are from a sample of 30 single-family homes located in Glen Cove. Variables included are the appraised value (in 2002), land area of the property (acres), interior size (square feet), age (years), number of rooms, number of bathrooms, and number of cars that can be parked in the garage.

a. Develop the most appropriate multiple regression model to predict appraised value.

b. Compare the results in (a) with those of Problems 15.31 (a) and 15.32 (a).

15.31 Data similar to those in Problem 15.30 are available for homes located in Roslyn and are stored in the file roslyn.xls.

a. Perform an analysis similar to that of Problem 15.30.

b. Compare the results in (a) with those of Problems 15.30 (a) and 15.32 (a).

15.32 Data similar to Problem 15.30 are available for homes located in Freeport and are stored in the file freeport.xls.

a. Perform an analysis similar to that of Problem 15.30.

b. Compare the results in (a) with those of Problems 15.30 (a) and 15.31 (a).

15.33 You are a real estate broker who wants to compare property values in Glen Cove and Roslyn (which are located approximately 8 miles apart). Use the data in the file gcroslyn.xls. Make sure to include the dummy variable for location (Glen Cove or Roslyn) in the regression model.

a. Develop the most appropriate multiple regression model to predict appraised value.

b. What conclusions can you reach concerning the differences in appraised value between Glen Cove and Roslyn?

15.34 You are a real estate broker who wants to compare property values in Glen Cove, Freeport, and Roslyn. Use the data in the file gcfreeroslyn.xls.

a. Develop the most appropriate multiple regression model to predict appraised value.

b. What conclusions can you reach concerning the differences in appraised value between Glen Cove, Freeport, and Roslyn?

PH Grade ASSIST **15.35** Over the past 30 years, public awareness and concern about air pollution have escalated dramatically. Venturi scrubbers are used for the removal of submicron particulate matter found in dust, fogs, fumes, odors, and smoke from gas streams. An experiment was conducted to determine the effect of air flow rate, water flow rate (liters/minute), recirculating water flow rate (liters/minute), and orifice size (mm) in the air side of the pneumatic nozzle on the performance of the scrubber, as measured by the number of transfer units. The results are provided in the file scrubber.xls.

Develop the most appropriate multiple regression model to predict the number of transfer units. Be sure to perform a thorough residual analysis. In addition, provide a detailed explanation of your results.

Source: Extracted from D. A. Marshall, R. J. Sumner, and C. A. Shook, "Removal of SiO₂ Particles with an Ejector Venturi Scrubber," Environmental Progress, *14, 1995, 28–32.*

15.36 A flux chamber is a Plexiglas dome about two feet in diameter that is placed over contaminated soil to sample soil gases. A study was carried out at a suspected radon hot spot to predict radon concentration (pCi/L) based on solar radiation (Ly/Day), soil temperature (°F), vapor pressure (mBar), wind speed (mph), relative humidity (%), dew point (°F), and ambient air temperature (°F). The data are contained in the radon.xls file.

Develop the most appropriate multiple regression model to predict radon concentration. Be sure to perform a thorough residual analysis. In addition, provide a detailed explanation of your results.

15.37 Oxford, Ohio, which is located 45 miles northwest of Cincinnati, is the home of Miami University. In addition to the 16,000 university students, the city has approximately 20,000 permanent residents. The data file **homes.xls** contains information on all the single-family houses sold in the city limits for one year. The variables included are

Price—Selling price of home, in dollars

Location—Rating of the location from 1 to 5, with 1 the worst and 5 the best

Condition—Rating of the condition of the home from 1 to 5, with 1 the worst and 5 the best

Bedrooms—Number of bedrooms in the home

Bathrooms—Number of bathrooms in the home

Other Rooms—Number of rooms in the home other than bedrooms and bathrooms

Perform a multiple regression analysis, using selling price as the dependent variable and the five remaining variables as independent variables.

a. State the multiple regression equation.

b. Interpret the meaning of the regression coefficients in this equation.

c. At the 0.05 level of significance, determine whether each independent variable makes a significant contribution to the regression model.

d. Determine the p-values in (c) and interpret their meaning.

e. Predict the price of a home with 3 bedrooms, 2.5 bathrooms, 4 other rooms, a location rating of 4, and a condition rating of 4. Construct a 95% confidence interval estimate and a 95% prediction interval.

f. Determine and interpret the coefficient of multiple determination.

g. Determine the adjusted r^2.

h. Do a residual analysis on the results and determine the adequacy of the model.

i. Delete any independent variables that are not making a significant contribution to the regression model, based on the best-subsets approach. Repeat (a) through (h), using this more parsimonious model. Which model do you think is better? Explain.

15.38 Many factors determine the attendance at Major League Baseball games. These factors can include when the game is played, the weather, the opponent, whether the team is having a good season, and whether a marketing promotion is held. Popular promotions during the 2002 season were the traditional hat days and poster days and the new craze, bobble-heads of star players (T. C. Boyd and T. C. Krehbiel, "An Analysis of the Effects of Specific Promotion Types on Attendance at Major League Baseball Games," *Mid-American Journal of Business*, 2006, 21, pp. 21–32). The data file **baseball.xls** includes the following variables for the 2002 Major League Baseball season:

TEAM—Kansas City Royals, Philadelphia Phillies, Chicago Cubs, or Cincinnati Reds

ATTENDANCE—Paid attendance for the game

TEMP—High temperature for the day

WIN%—Team's winning percentage at the time of the game

OPWIN%—Opponent team's winning percentage at the time of the game

WEEKEND—1 if game played on Friday, Saturday or Sunday; 0 otherwise

PROMOTION—1 if a promotion was held; 0 if no promotion was held

a. Construct a multiple regression model for the Kansas City Royals, using attendance as the dependent variable and the remaining five variables as the independent variables.

b. State the multiple regression equation.

c. Interpret the meaning of the regression coefficients.

d. At the 0.05 level of significance, determine whether each independent variable makes a significant contribution to the regression model.

e. Determine and interpret the adjusted r^2.

f. Do a residual analysis on the results and determine the adequacy of the model.

g. Based on the best-subsets approach, delete any independent variables that are not making a significant contribution to the regression model. Repeat (b) through (f), using this more parsimonious model. Which model do you think is better? Explain.

15.39 Repeat Problem 15.38 for the Philadelphia Phillies.

15.40 Repeat Problem 15.38 for the Chicago Cubs.

15.41 Repeat Problem 15.38 for the Cincinnati Reds.

15.42 Referring to Problems 15.38–15.41, in terms of increasing attendance, which team ran the most effective promotions in 2002?

15.43 Hemlock Farms is a community located in the Pocono Mountains area of eastern Pennsylvania. The data file **hemlockfarms.xls** contains information on homes that were for sale as of July 4, 2006. The variables included were

List Price—Asking price of the house

Hot Tub—Whether the house has a hot tub, with 0 = No and 1 = Yes

Rooms—Number of rooms in the house

Lake View—Whether the house has a lake view, with 0 = No and 1 = Yes

Bathrooms—Number of bathrooms

Bedrooms—Number of bedrooms

Loft/Den—Whether the house has a loft or den, with 0 = No and 1 = Yes

Finished basement—Whether the house has a finished basement, with 0 = No and 1 = Yes

Acres—Number of acres for the property

Develop the most appropriate multiple regression model to predict the asking price. Be sure to perform a thorough residual analysis. In addition, provide a detailed explanation of your results.

15.44 A headline on page 1 of *The New York Times* of March 4, 1990, read: "Wine equation puts some noses out of joint." The article explained that Professor Orley Ashenfelter, a Princeton University economist, had developed a multiple regression model to predict the quality of French Bordeaux, based on the amount of winter rain, the average temperature during the growing season, and the harvest rain. The sample multiple regression equation is

$$Q = -12.145 + 0.00117WR + 0.6164TMP - 0.00386HR$$

where

Q = logarithmic index of quality

WR = winter rain (October through March), in millimeters

TMP = average temperature during the growing season (April through September), in degrees Celsius

HR = harvest rain (August to September), in millimeters

You are at a cocktail party, sipping a glass of wine, when one of your friends mentions to you that she has read the article. She asks you to explain the meaning of the coefficients in the equation and also asks you about analyses that might have been done and were not included in the article. What is your reply?

Report Writing Exercises

15.45 In Problem 15.21 on page 634, you developed a multiple regression model to predict monthly sales at sporting goods stores for the data in the file **sporting.xls**. Your task is to write a report based on the model you developed. Append all appropriate charts and statistical information to your report.

Team Project

15.46 The data file **Mutual Funds.xls** contains information regarding nine variables from a sample of 838 mutual funds. The variables are

Category—Type of stocks comprising the mutual fund (small cap, mid cap, or large cap)

Objective—Objective of stocks comprising the mutual fund (growth or value)

Assets—In millions of dollars

Fees—Sales charges (no or yes)

Expense ratio—Ratio of expenses to net assets, in percentage

2005 return—Twelve-month return in 2005

Three-year return—Annualized return, 2003–2005

Five-year return—Annualized return, 2001–2005

Risk—Risk-of-loss factor of the mutual fund (low, average, or high)

Develop regression models to predict the 2005 return, the three-year return, and the five-year return, based on fees, expense ratio, objective, and risk. (For the purpose of this analysis, combine low risk and average risk into one category.) Be sure to perform a thorough residual analysis. In addition, provide a detailed explanation of your results. Append all appropriate charts and statistical information to your report.

The Mountain States Potato Company

Mountain States Potato Company sells a by-product of its potato-processing operation, called a filter cake, to area feedlots as cattle feed. Recently, the feedlot owners have noticed that the cattle are not gaining weight as quickly as they once were. They believe that the root cause of the problem is that the percentage of solids in the filter cake is too low.

Historically, the percentage of solids in the filter cakes ran slightly above 12%. Lately, however, the solids are running in the 11% range. What is actually affecting the solids is a mystery, but something has to be done quickly. Individuals involved in the process were asked to identify variables that might affect the percentage of solids. This review turned up the six variables (in addition to the percentage of solids) listed below in the following table. Data collected by monitoring the process several times daily for 20 days are stored in the **potato.xls** file.

Variable	Comments
SOLIDS	Percentage solids in the filter cake.
PH	Acidity. This measure of acidity indicates bacterial action in the clarifier and is controlled by

the amount of downtime in the system. As bacterial action progresses, organic acids are produced that can be measured using pH.

Variable	Comments
LOWER	Pressure of the vacuum line below the fluid line on the rotating drum.
UPPER	Pressure of the vacuum line above the fluid line on the rotating drum.
THICK	Filter cake thickness, measured on the drum.
VARIDRIV	Setting used to control the drum speed. May differ from DRUMSPD due to mechanical inefficiencies.
DRUMSPD	Speed at which the drum is rotating when collecting the filter cake. Measured with a stopwatch.

1. Thoroughly analyze the data and develop a regression model to predict the percentage of solids.
2. Write an executive summary concerning your findings to the president of the Mountain States Potato Company. Include specific recommendations on how to get the percentage of solids back above 12%.

Web Case

Apply your knowledge of multiple regression model building in this Web Case, which extends the Using Statistics scenario concerning OmniPower energy bars from Chapter 14.

Still concerned about ensuring a successful test marketing of its OmniPower energy bars, the marketing department of OmniFoods has contacted Connect2Coupons (C2C), another merchandising consultancy. C2C suggests that earlier analysis done by In-Store Placements Group (ISPG) was faulty because it did not use the correct type of data. C2C claims that its Internet-based viral marketing will have an even greater effect on OmniPower energy bar sales, as new data from the same 34-store sample will show. In response, ISPG says its earlier claims are valid and has reported to the OmniFoods marketing department that it can discern no simple relationship between C2C's viral marketing and increased OmniPower sales.

Review all these claims on the message board at the OmniFoods internal Web site, **www.prenhall.com/ Springville/Omni_OmniPowerMB.htm**, (or open this Web page file from the Student CD-ROM Web Case folder) and then answer the following:

1. Which of the claims are true? false? true but misleading? Support your answer by performing an appropriate statistical analysis.

2. If the grocery store chain allowed OmniFoods to use an unlimited number of sales techniques, which techniques should it use? Explain.

3. If the grocery store chain allowed OmniFoods to use only one sales technique, which technique should it use? Explain.

REFERENCES

1. Kutner, M., C. Nachtsheim, J. Neter, and W. Li, *Applied Linear Statistical Models*, 5th ed. (New York: McGraw-Hill/Irwin, 2005).
2. Marquardt, D. W., "You Should Standardize the Predictor Variables in Your Regression Models," discussion of "A Critique of Some Ridge Regression Methods," by G. Smith and F. Campbell, *Journal of the American Statistical Association* 75 (1980): 87–91.
3. *Microsoft Excel 2007* (Redmond, WA: Microsoft Corp., 2007).
4. Snee, R. D., "Some Aspects of Nonorthogonal Data Analysis, Part I. Developing Prediction Equations," *Journal of Quality Technology* 5 (1973): 67–79.

Excel Companion
to Chapter 15

E15.1 CREATING A QUADRATIC TERM

To create a quadratic term, open to the worksheet that contains your multiple regression data. Locate the column to the right of the column that contains the data for the linear term. If this column is not blank, select the column, right-click the column, and select **Insert** from the shortcut menu to create a (new) blank column.

In the row 1 cell of the (new or preexisting) blank column, enter a column heading. Then, starting in row 2, enter formulas in the form =*Previous Column'sCell* ^2 down the column through all the data rows. For example, if column C contains the data for your linear term and column D is blank, enter the formula =**C2^2** in cell D2 and copy the formula down through all the data rows to create the data for the quadratic term.

With your expanded regression data worksheet, perform a multiple regression analysis (see Section E14.1 on page 609) that includes both the linear and quadratic terms.

E15.2 CREATING TRANSFORMATIONS

To create transformations, enter formulas in the form =*FUNCTION*(*Previous Column's Cell*) in a blank column to the right of the column that contains the data you want to transform. If the column to the right is not blank, select the column, right-click the column, and select **Insert** from the shortcut menu to create a (new) blank column.

FUNCTION could be the SQRT (square root), LOG (common logarithm), or LN (natural logarithm) functions. For example, to create a square-root transformation in a blank column D for an independent variable in column C, enter the formula =**SQRT(C2)** in cell D2 and copy the formula down through all data rows.

E15.3 COMPUTING VARIANCE INFLATIONARY FACTORS

You compute Variance Inflationary Factors by either selecting the PHStat2 Multiple Regression procedure or the ToolPak Regression procedure.

Using PHStat2 Multiple Regression

Use the Section E14.1 instructions in "Using PHStat2 Multiple Regression", but click **Variance Inflationary**

Factor (VIF) before you click **OK** in the Multiple Regression dialog box.

Using ToolPak Regression

Perform a regression analysis for every combination of X variables. Then, in each of the regression results worksheets, enter the label **VIF** in cell **A9** and enter the formula =**1/(1-B5)** in cell **B9**.

E15.4 USING STEPWISE REGRESSION

You use a stepwise regression approach to model building by selecting the PHStat2 Stepwise Regression procedure. (There are no basic Excel commands or features to perform stepwise regression.)

Open to the worksheet that contains your multiple regression data. Select **PHStat → Regression → Stepwise Regression**. In the procedure's dialog box (shown below), enter the cell range of the Y variable as the **Y Variable Cell**

Range and the cell range of the X variables as the **X Variables Cell Range**. Click **First cells in both ranges contain label**, enter a value for the **Confidence level for regression coefficients**, and click the **p values** Stepwise Criteria option. Click the **General Stepwise** option and supply the necessary p-values. Enter a title as the **Title** and click **OK**. (The options and p-values shown in the figure on page 642 were used to create the stepwise regression worksheet shown in Figure 15.11 on page 629.)

This procedure can take a noticeable amount of time (seconds) to complete. The procedure is finished when the stepwise model worksheet includes the statement "Stepwise ends" (seen in row 29 in Figure 15.11).

E15.5 USING BEST-SUBSETS REGRESSION

You use a best-subsets approach to model building by selecting the PHStat2 Best Subsets procedure. (There are no basic Excel commands or features to perform best-subsets regression.)

Open to the worksheet that contains your multiple regression data. Select **PHStat → Regression → Best Subsets**. In the procedure's dialog box (shown below), enter the cell range of the Y variable as the **Y Variable Cell Range** and the cell range of the X variables as the **X Variables Cell Range**. Click **First cells in both ranges contain label** and enter a value for the **Confidence level for regression coefficients**. Enter a title as the **Title** and click **OK**.

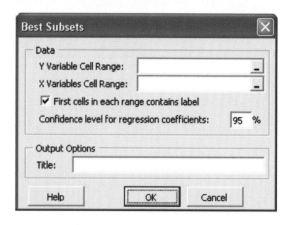

CHAPTER 16

Time-Series Forecasting and Index Numbers

USING STATISTICS @ The Principled

LEARNING OBJECTIVES

In this chapter, you learn:

- About seven different time-series forecasting models: moving averages, exponential smoothing, the linear trend, the quadratic trend, the exponential trend, the autoregressive, and the least-squares models for seasonal data.
- To choose the most appropriate time-series forecasting model
- About price indexes and the difference between aggregated and unaggregated indexes

Using Statistics @ The Principled

You are a financial analyst for The Principled, a large financial services company. You need to forecast revenues for three companies in order to better evaluate investment opportunities for your clients. To assist in the forecasting, you have collected time-series data on three companies: Wm. Wrigley Jr. Company, Cabot Corporation, and Wal-Mart. Each time series has unique characteristics due to the different types of business activities and growth patterns experienced by the three companies. You understand that you can use several different types of forecasting models. How do you decide which type of forecasting model is best for each company? How do you use the information gained from the forecasting models to evaluate investment opportunities for your clients?

In Chapters 13 through 15, you used regression analysis as a tool for model building and prediction. In this chapter, regression analysis and other statistical methodologies are applied to time-series data. A **time series** is a set of numerical data collected over time. Due to differences in the features of data for various companies such as the three companies described in the Using Statistics scenario, you need to consider several different approaches to forecasting time-series data.

This chapter begins with an introduction to the importance of business forecasting (see Section 16.1) and a description of the classical multiplicative time-series model (see Section 16.2). The coverage of forecasting *models* begins with annual time-series data. Two techniques for smoothing a series are illustrated in Section 16.3: moving averages and exponential smoothing. The analysis of annual time series continues, with the use of least-squares trend fitting and forecasting (see Section 16.4) and other more sophisticated forecasting methods (see Section 16.5). These trend-fitting and forecasting models are then extended to monthly or quarterly time series (see Section 16.7). This chapter concludes with Section 16.8 that discusses several types of index numbers.

16.1 THE IMPORTANCE OF BUSINESS FORECASTING

Forecasting is done to monitor changes that occur over time. Forecasting is commonly used in both the for-profit and not-for-profit sectors of the economy. For example, officials in government forecast unemployment, inflation, industrial production, and revenues from income taxes in order to formulate policies. Marketing executives of a retailing corporation forecast product demand, sales revenues, consumer preferences, inventory, and so on in order to make timely decisions regarding promotions and strategic planning. And the administrators of a college or university forecast student enrollment in order to plan for the construction of dormitories and other academic facilities, plan for student and faculty recruitment, and make assessments of other needs.

There are two common approaches to forecasting: *qualitative* and *quantitative*. **Qualitative forecasting methods** are especially important when historical data are unavailable. Qualitative forecasting methods are considered to be highly subjective and judgmental.

Quantitative forecasting methods make use of historical data. The goal of these methods is to use past data to predict future values. Quantitative forecasting methods are subdivided into two types: *time series* and *causal*. **Time-series forecasting methods** involve forecasting future values based entirely on the past and present values of a variable. For example, the daily closing prices of a particular stock on the New York Stock Exchange constitute a time series. Other examples of economic or business time series are the monthly publication of the consumer price index (CPI), the quarterly gross domestic product (GDP), and the annual sales revenues of a particular company.

Causal forecasting methods involve the determination of factors that relate to the variable you are trying to forecast. These include multiple regression analysis with lagged variables, econometric modeling, leading indicator analysis, diffusion indexes, and other economic barometers that are beyond the scope of this text (see references 2–4). The primary emphasis in this chapter is on time-series forecasting methods.

16.2 COMPONENT FACTORS OF THE CLASSICAL MULTIPLICATIVE TIME-SERIES MODEL

The basic assumption of time-series forecasting is that the factors that have influenced activities in the past and present will continue to do so in approximately the same way in the future. Thus, the major goals of time-series forecasting are to identify and isolate these influencing factors in order to make predictions.

To achieve these goals, many mathematical models are available to measure the fluctuations among the component factors of a time series. Perhaps the most basic is the **classical multiplicative model** for annual, quarterly, or monthly data. To demonstrate the classical multiplicative time-series model, Figure 16.1 plots the actual gross revenues for the Wm. Wrigley Jr. Company from 1984 through 2005.

FIGURE 16.1

Microsoft Excel plot of actual gross revenues (in millions of current dollars) for the Wm. Wrigley Jr. Company (1984–2005)

See Section E16.2 to create this.

A **trend** is an overall long-term upward or downward movement in a time series. From Figure 16.1, you can see that actual gross revenues have increased over the 22-year period shown. Thus, actual gross revenues for the Wrigley Company exhibit an upward trend.

Trend is not the only component factor that influences data in an annual time series. Two other factors—the cyclical component and the irregular component—are also present in the data. The **cyclical component** depicts the up-and-down swings or movements through the series. Cyclical movements vary in length, usually lasting from 2 to 10 years. They differ in intensity and are often correlated with a business cycle. In some years, the values are higher than would be predicted by a trend line (that is, they are at or near the peak of a cycle). In other years, the values are lower than would be predicted by a trend line (that is, they are at or near the bottom of a cycle). Any data that do not follow the trend modified by the cyclical component are considered part of the **irregular**, or **random, component**. When you have monthly or quarterly data, an additional component, the **seasonal component**, is considered along with the trend, cyclical, and irregular components.

Table 16.1 summarizes the four component factors that can influence an economic or business time series.

TABLE 16.1 Factors Influencing Time-Series Data

Component	Classification of Component	Definition	Reason for Influence	Duration
Trend	Systematic	Overall or persistent, long-term upward or downward pattern of movement	Changes in technology, population, wealth, value	Several years
Seasonal	Systematic	Fairly regular periodic fluctuations that occur within each 12-month period year after year	Weather conditions, social customs, religious customs, school schedules	Within 12 months (or monthly or quarterly data)
Cyclical	Systematic	Repeating up-and-down swings or movements through four phases: from peak (prosperity) to contraction (recession) to trough (depression) to expansion (recovery or growth)	Interactions of numerous combinations of factors that influence the economy	Usually 2–10 years, with differing intensity for a complete cycle
Irregular	Unsystematic	The erratic, or "residual," fluctuations in a series that exist after taking into account the systematic effects	Random variations in data due to unforeseen events, such as strikes, natural disasters, and wars	Short duration and nonrepeating

The classical multiplicative time-series model states that any value in a time series is the product of these components. When forecasting an annual time series, you do not include the seasonal component. Equation (16.1) defines Y_i, the value of an annual time series recorded in year i, as the product of the trend, cyclical, and irregular components.

CLASSICAL MULTIPLICATIVE TIME-SERIES MODEL FOR ANNUAL DATA

$$Y_i = T_i \times C_i \times I_i \qquad (16.1)$$

where

$$T_i = \text{value of the trend component in year } i$$

$$C_i = \text{value of the cyclical component in year } i$$

$$I_i = \text{value of the irregular component in year } i$$

When forecasting quarterly or monthly data, you include the seasonal component in the model. Equation (16.2) defines Y_i, a value recorded in time period i, as the product of all four components.

CLASSICAL MULTIPLICATIVE TIME-SERIES MODEL FOR DATA WITH A SEASONAL COMPONENT

$$Y_i = T_i \times S_i \times C_i \times I_i \qquad (16.2)$$

where

$$T_i, C_i, I_i = \text{value of the trend, cyclical, and irregular components in time period } i$$

$$S_i = \text{value of the seasonal component in time period } i$$

Your first step in a time-series analysis is to plot the data and observe any patterns that occur over time. You must determine whether there is a long-term upward or downward movement in the series (that is, a trend). If there is no obvious long-term upward or downward trend, then you can use the method of moving averages or the method of exponential smoothing to smooth the series and provide an overall long-term impression (see Section 16.3). If a trend is present, you can consider several time-series forecasting methods (see Sections 16.4–16.5 for forecasting annual data and Section 16.7 for forecasting monthly or quarterly time series).

16.3   SMOOTHING AN ANNUAL TIME SERIES

One of the companies of interest in the Using Statistics scenario is the Cabot Corporation. Headquartered in Boston, Massachusetts, the Cabot Corporation is a global company with businesses specializing in the manufacture and distribution of chemicals, performance materials, specialty fluids, microelectronic materials, and liquefied natural gas. The company operates 36 manufacturing facilities in 21 countries. The Cabot Corporation, **w1.cabot-corp.com**, is traded on the New York Stock Exchange with ticker symbol CBT. Revenues in 2005 were approximately $2.1 billion. Table 16.2 gives the total revenues, in millions of dollars, for 1982 to 2005 (see the file cabot.xls). Figure 16.2 presents the time-series plot.

TABLE 16.2

Revenues (in Millions of Dollars) for the Cabot Corporation from 1982 to 2005

Year	Revenue	Year	Revenue	Year	Revenue
1982	1,588	1990	1,685	1998	1,653
1983	1,558	1991	1,488	1999	1,699
1984	1,753	1992	1,562	2000	1,698
1985	1,408	1993	1,619	2001	1,523
1986	1,310	1994	1,687	2002	1,557
1987	1,424	1995	1,841	2003	1,795
1988	1,677	1996	1,865	2004	1,934
1989	1,937	1997	1,637	2005	2,125

Source: Extracted from Moody's Handbook of Common Stocks, *1992, and* Mergent's Handbook of Common Stocks, *2006.*

FIGURE 16.2

Microsoft Excel plot of revenues (in millions of dollars) for the Cabot Corporation (1982–2005)

See Section E16.2 to create this.

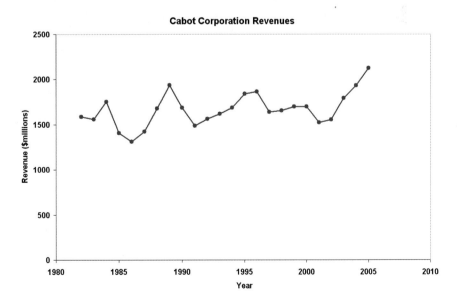

When you examine annual data, your visual impression of the long-term trend in the series is sometimes obscured by the amount of variation from year to year. Often, you cannot judge whether any long-term upward or downward trend exists in the series. To get a better overall impression of the pattern of movement in the data over time, you can use the methods of moving averages or exponential smoothing.

Moving Averages

> **Moving averages** for a chosen period of length L consist of a series of means computed over time such that each mean is calculated for a sequence of L observed values. Moving averages are represented by the symbol $MA(L)$.

To illustrate, suppose you want to compute five-year moving averages from a series that has $n = 11$ years. Because $L = 5$, the five-year moving averages consist of a series of means computed by averaging consecutive sequences of five values. You compute the first five-year moving average by summing the values for the first five years in the series and dividing by 5:

$$MA(5) = \frac{Y_1 + Y_2 + Y_3 + Y_4 + Y_5}{5}$$

You compute the second five-year moving average by summing the values of years 2 through 6 in the series and then dividing by 5:

$$MA(5) = \frac{Y_2 + Y_3 + Y_4 + Y_5 + Y_6}{5}$$

You continue this process until you have computed the last of these five-year moving averages by summing the values of the last 5 years in the series (that is, years 7 through 11) and then dividing by 5:

$$MA(5) = \frac{Y_7 + Y_8 + Y_9 + Y_{10} + Y_{11}}{5}$$

When you are dealing with annual time-series data, L, the length of the period chosen for constructing the moving averages, should be an *odd* number of years. By following this rule, you are not able to compute any moving averages for the first $(L - 1)/2$ years or the last $(L - 1)/2$ years of the series. Thus, for a five-year moving average, you cannot make computations for the first two years or the last two years of the series.

When plotting moving averages, you plot each of the computed values against the middle year of the sequence of years used to compute it. If $n = 11$ and $L = 5$, the first moving average is centered on the third year, the second moving average is centered on the fourth year, and the last moving average is centered on the ninth year. Example 16.1 illustrates the computation of five-year moving averages.

EXAMPLE 16.1

COMPUTING FIVE-YEAR MOVING AVERAGES

The following data represent total revenues (in millions of constant 1995 dollars) for a car rental agency over the 11-year period 1996 to 2006:

4.0	5.0	7.0	6.0	8.0	9.0	5.0	2.0	3.5	5.5	6.5

Compute the five-year moving averages for this annual time series.

SOLUTION To compute the five-year moving averages, you first compute the five-year moving total and then divide this total by 5. The first of the five-year moving averages is

$$MA(5) = \frac{Y_1 + Y_2 + Y_3 + Y_4 + Y_5}{5} = \frac{4.0 + 5.0 + 7.0 + 6.0 + 8.0}{5} = \frac{30.0}{5} = 6.0$$

The moving average is then centered on the middle value—the third year of this time series. To compute the second of the five-year moving averages, you compute the moving total of the second through sixth years and divide this value by 5:

$$MA(5) = \frac{Y_2 + Y_3 + Y_4 + Y_5 + Y_6}{5} = \frac{5.0 + 7.0 + 6.0 + 8.0 + 9.0}{5} = \frac{35.0}{5} = 7.0$$

This moving average is centered on the new middle value—the fourth year of the time series. The remaining moving averages are

$$MA(5) = \frac{Y_3 + Y_4 + Y_5 + Y_6 + Y_7}{5} = \frac{7.0 + 6.0 + 8.0 + 9.0 + 5.0}{5} = \frac{35.0}{5} = 7.0$$

$$MA(5) = \frac{Y_4 + Y_5 + Y_6 + Y_7 + Y_8}{5} = \frac{6.0 + 8.0 + 9.0 + 5.0 + 2.0}{5} = \frac{30.0}{5} = 6.0$$

$$MA(5) = \frac{Y_5 + Y_6 + Y_7 + Y_8 + Y_9}{5} = \frac{8.0 + 9.0 + 5.0 + 2.0 + 3.5}{5} = \frac{27.5}{5} = 5.5$$

$$MA(5) = \frac{Y_6 + Y_7 + Y_8 + Y_9 + Y_{10}}{5} = \frac{9.0 + 5.0 + 2.0 + 3.5 + 5.5}{5} = \frac{25.0}{5} = 5.0$$

$$MA(5) = \frac{Y_7 + Y_8 + Y_9 + Y_{10} + Y_{11}}{5} = \frac{5.0 + 2.0 + 3.5 + 5.5 + 6.5}{5} = \frac{22.5}{5} = 4.5$$

These moving averages are then centered on their respective middle values—the fifth, sixth, seventh, eighth, and ninth years in the time series. By using the five-year moving averages, you are unable to compute a moving average for the first two or last two values in the time series.

In practice, you should use Microsoft Excel when computing moving averages to avoid the tedious computations. Figure 16.3 presents the annual Cabot Corporation revenue data for the 24-year period from 1982 through 2005, the computations for 3- and 7-year moving averages, and a plot of the original data and the moving averages.

FIGURE 16.3

Microsoft Excel three-year and seven-year moving averages for Cabot Corporation revenues

See Section E16.1 to create this.

	A	B	C	D
1	Year	Revenue	MA 3-Year	MA 7-Year
2	1982	1588	#N/A	#N/A
3	1983	1558	1633	#N/A
4	1984	1753	1573	#N/A
5	1985	1408	1490.3	1531.1
6	1986	1310	1380.7	1581.0
7	1987	1424	1470.3	1599.1
8	1988	1677	1679.3	1561.3
9	1989	1937	1766.3	1583.3
10	1990	1685	1703.3	1627.4
11	1991	1488	1578.3	1665.0
12	1992	1562	1556.3	1688.4
13	1993	1619	1622.7	1678.1
14	1994	1687	1715.7	1671.3
15	1995	1841	1797.7	1694.9
16	1996	1865	1781.0	1714.4
17	1997	1637	1718.3	1725.7
18	1998	1653	1663.0	1702.3
19	1999	1699	1683.3	1661.7
20	2000	1698	1640.0	1651.7
21	2001	1523	1592.7	1694.1
22	2002	1557	1625.0	1761.6
23	2003	1795	1762.0	#N/A
24	2004	1934	1951.3	#N/A
25	2005	2125	#N/A	#N/A

Moving Averages for Cabot Corporation Revenue

Revenues ($millions) vs Year — Revenue, MA 3-Year, MA 7-Year

In Figure 16.3, there is no three-year moving average for the first and the last year and no seven-year moving average for the first three years and last three years. You can see that the seven-year moving averages smooth the series a great deal more than the three-year moving averages because the period is longer. Unfortunately, the longer the period, the fewer the number of moving averages you can compute. Therefore, selecting moving averages that are longer than seven years is usually undesirable because too many moving average values are missing at the beginning and end of the series. This makes it more difficult to get an overall impression of the entire series.

The selection of L, the length of the period used for constructing the averages, is highly subjective. If cyclical fluctuations are present in the data, you should choose an integer value of L that corresponds to (or is a multiple of) the estimated length of a cycle in the series. If no obvious cyclical fluctuations are present, then the most common choices are three-year, five-year, or seven-year moving averages, depending on the amount of smoothing desired and the amount of data available.

Exponential Smoothing

Exponential smoothing is another method used to smooth a time series. In addition to smoothing, you can use exponential smoothing to compute short-term (that is, one period into the future) forecasts when the presence and type of long-term trend in a time series is questionable. In this respect, exponential smoothing has a clear advantage over the method of moving averages.

The name *exponential smoothing* comes from the fact that this method consists of a series of *exponentially weighted* moving averages. The weights assigned to the values decrease so that the most recent value receives the highest weight, the previous value receives the second-highest weight, and so on, with the first value receiving the lowest weight. Throughout the series, each exponentially smoothed value depends on all previous values, which is another advantage of exponential smoothing over the method of moving averages. Although the computations involved in exponential smoothing seem formidable, you can use Microsoft Excel to perform the computations.

The equation developed for exponentially smoothing a series in any time period, i, is based on only three terms—the current value in the time series, Y_i; the previously computed exponentially smoothed value, E_{i-1}; and an assigned weight or smoothing coefficient, W.[1] You use Equation (16.3) to exponentially smooth a time series.

[1]The damping factor used by Microsoft Excel is equal to $1 - W$.

COMPUTING AN EXPONENTIALLY SMOOTHED VALUE IN TIME PERIOD i

$$E_1 = Y_1 \tag{16.3}$$

$$E_i = WY_i + (1 - W)E_{i-1} \quad i = 2, 3, 4, \ldots$$

where

E_i = value of the exponentially smoothed series being computed in time period i

E_{i-1} = value of the exponentially smoothed series already computed in time period $i - 1$

Y_i = observed value of the time series in period i

W = subjectively assigned weight or smoothing coefficient (where $0 < W < 1$). Although W can approach 1.0, in virtually all business applications, $W \leq 0.5$.

Choosing the smoothing coefficient (that is, weight) that you assign to the time series is critical. Unfortunately, this selection is somewhat subjective. If your goal is only to smooth a series by eliminating unwanted cyclical and irregular variations, you should select a small value for W (close to 0). If your goal is forecasting, you should choose a large value for W (close to 0.5). In the former case, the overall long-term tendencies of the series will be more apparent; in the latter case, future short-term directions may be more adequately predicted.

Figure 16.4 presents the Microsoft Excel exponentially smoothed values (with smoothing coefficients of $W = 0.50$ and $W = 0.25$) for annual revenue of the Cabot Corporation over the 24-year period 1982 to 2005, along with a plot of the original data and the two exponentially smoothed time series.

FIGURE 16.4

Microsoft Excel plot of exponentially smoothed series ($W = 0.50$ and $W = 0.25$) of the Cabot Corporation

See Section E16.3 to create this.

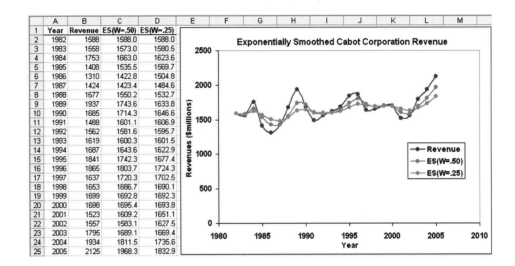

To illustrate these exponential smoothing computations for a smoothing coefficient of $W = 0.25$, you begin with the initial value $Y_{1982} = 1,588$ as the first smoothed value ($E_{1982} = 1,588$). Then, using the value of the time series for 1983 ($Y_{1983} = 1,558$), you smooth the series for 1983 by computing

$$E_{1983} = WY_{1983} + (1 - W)E_{1982}$$
$$= (0.25)(1,558) + (0.75)(1,588) = 1,580.5$$

To smooth the series for 1984:

$$E_{1984} = WY_{1984} + (1 - W)E_{1983}$$
$$= (0.25)(1,753) + (0.75)(1,580.5) = 1,623.6$$

To smooth the series for 1985:

$$E_{1985} = WY_{1985} + (1 - W)E_{1984}$$
$$= (0.25)(1,408) + (0.75)(1,623.6) = 1,569.7$$

You continue this process until you have computed the exponentially smoothed values for all 24 years in the series, as shown in Figure 16.4.

To use exponential smoothing for forecasting, you use the smoothed value in the current time period as the forecast of the value in the following period.

FORECASTING TIME PERIOD $i + 1$

$$\hat{Y}_{i+1} = E_i \qquad (16.4)$$

To forecast the revenue of Cabot Corporation during 2006, using a smoothing coefficient of $W = 0.25$, you use the smoothed value for 2005 as its estimate. Figure 16.4 shows that this value is \$1,832.9 million. (How close is this forecast? Look up Cabot Corporation's revenue in a recent *Mergent's Handbook of Common Stocks* or search the World Wide Web to find out.)

When the value for 2006 becomes available, you can use Equation (16.3) to make a forecast for 2007 by computing the smoothed value for 2006, as follows:

Current smoothed value $= (W)$(Current value) $+ (1 - W)$(previous smoothest value)

$$E_{2006} = WY_{2006} + (1 - W)E_{2005}$$

Or, in terms of forecasting, you compute the following:

New forecast $= (W)$(Current value) $+ (1 - W)$(Current forecast)

$$\hat{Y}_{2007} = WY_{2006} + (1 - W)\hat{Y}_{2006}$$

PROBLEMS FOR SECTION 16.3

Learning the Basics

16.1 If you are using exponential smoothing for forecasting an annual time series of revenues, what is your forecast for next year if the smoothed value for this year is $32.4 million?

PH Grade ASSIST   **16.2** Consider a nine-year moving average used to smooth a time series that was first recorded in 1955.
a. Which year serves as the first centered value in the smoothed series?
b. How many years of values in the series are lost when computing all the nine-year moving averages?

PH Grade ASSIST   **16.3** You are using exponential smoothing on an annual time series concerning total revenues (in millions of constant 1995 dollars). You decide to use a smoothing coefficient of $W = 0.20$ and the exponentially smoothed value for 2006 is $E_{2006} = (0.20)(12.1) + (0.80)(9.4)$.
a. What is the smoothed value of this series in 2006?
b. What is the smoothed value of this series in 2007 if the value of the series in that year is 11.5 millions of constant 1995 dollars?

Applying the Concepts

✓SELF Test   **16.4** The following data (stored in the file **movies.xls**) represent the yearly movie attendance (in billions) from 1999 to 2005:

Year	Attendance
1999	1.47
2000	1.42
2001	1.49
2002	1.63
2003	1.57
2004	1.53
2005	1.41

Source: Extracted from C. Passy, "Good Night and Good Luck," Palm Beach Post, *February 5, 2006, p. 1J).*

a. Plot the time series.
b. Fit a three-year moving average to the data and plot the results.
c. Using a smoothing coefficient of $W = 0.50$, exponentially smooth the series and plot the results.
d. Repeat (c), using $W = 0.25$.
e. Compare the results of (c) and (d).

16.5 The following data, contained in the file **deals.xls**, provides the number of mergers and acquisitions made during January 1 through January 11 of each year from 1995 to 2006 (extracted from "Back of the Envelope," *The New York Times*, January 13, 2006, p. C7):

Year	Deals	Years	Deals
1995	715	2001	1,031
1996	865	2002	893
1997	708	2003	735
1998	861	2004	759
1999	931	2005	1,013
2000	939	2006	622

a. Plot the time series.
b. Fit a three-year moving average to the data and plot the results.
c. Using a smoothing coefficient of $W = 0.50$, exponentially smooth the series and plot the results.
d. Repeat (c), using $W = 0.25$.
e. Compare the results of (c) and (d).

16.6 The NASDAQ stock market includes small- and medium-sized companies, many of which are in high-tech industries. Because of the nature of these companies, the NASDAQ tends to be more volatile than the Dow Jones Industrial Average or the S&P 500. The weekly values for the NASDAQ during the first 20 weeks of 2006 are listed in the data file **weeklyNASDAQ.xls** (extracted from **finance.yahoo.com**):

Week	NASDAQ	Week	NASDAQ
3-Jan-06	2,305.62	13-Mar-06	2,306.48
9-Jan-06	2,317.04	20-Mar-06	2,312.82
17-Jan-06	2,247.70	27-Mar-06	2,339.79
23-Jan-06	2,304.23	3-Apr-06	2,339.02
30-Jan-06	2,262.58	10-Apr-06	2,326.11
6-Feb-06	2,261.88	17-Apr-06	2,342.86
13-Feb-06	2,282.36	24-Apr-06	2,322.57
21-Feb-06	2,287.04	1-May-06	2,342.57
27-Feb-06	2,302.60	8-May-06	2,243.78
6-Mar-06	2,262.04	15-May-06	2,193.88

a. Plot the time series.

b. Fit a three-period moving average to the data and plot the results.

c. Using a smoothing coefficient of $W = 0.50$, exponentially smooth the series and plot the results.

d. Repeat (c), using $W = 0.25$.

e. What conclusions can you reach concerning the presence or absence of trends during the first 20 weeks of 2006?

16.7 The following data (in the file treasury.xls) represent the three-month Treasury bill rates in the United States from 1991 to 2005:

Year	Rate	Year	Rate
1991	5.38	1999	4.64
1992	3.43	2000	5.82
1993	3.00	2001	3.40
1994	4.25	2002	1.61
1995	5.49	2003	1.01
1996	5.01	2004	2.17
1997	5.06	2005	3.89
1998	4.78		

Source: Board of Governors of the Federal Reserve System, **federalreserve.gov***.*

a. Plot the data.

b. Fit a three-year moving average to the data and plot the results.

c. Using a smoothing coefficient of $W = 0.50$, exponentially smooth the series and plot the results.

d. What is your exponentially smoothed forecast for 2006?

e. Repeat (c) and (d), using a smoothing coefficient of $W = 0.25$.

f. Compare the results of (d) and (e).

16.8 The following data (stored in the file electricity.xls) represent the average residential prices of electricity, in cost per kilowatt hour, in the October–March winter months from 1994–1995 to 2004–2005.

Year	Cost	Year	Cost
1994–1995	8.16	2000–2001	8.11
1995–1996	8.10	2001–2002	8.37
1996–1997	8.17	2002–2003	8.20
1997–1998	8.12	2003–2004	8.49
1998–1999	7.94	2004–2005	8.78
1999–2000	7.98		

Source: Energy Information Administration, Department of Energy, **www.eia.doe.gov***.*

a. Plot the data.

b. Fit a three-year moving average to the data and plot the results.

c. Using a smoothing coefficient of $W = 0.50$, exponentially smooth the series and plot the results.

d. What is your exponentially smoothed forecast for 2005–2006?

e. Repeat (c) and (d), using a smoothing coefficient of $W = 0.25$.

f. Compare the results of (d) and (e).

16.4 LEAST-SQUARES TREND FITTING AND FORECASTING

The component factor of a time series most often studied is trend. You study trend in order to make intermediate and long-range forecasts. To get a visual impression of the overall long-term movements in a time series, you construct a time-series plot (see Figure 16.1 on page 647). If a straight-line trend adequately fits the data, the two most widely used methods of trend fitting are the methods of least squares [see Equation (16.5) and Section 13.2] and *double exponential smoothing* (see reference 1). If the time-series data indicate some long-run downward or upward quadratic movement, the two most widely used trend-fitting methods are the method of least squares [see Equation (16.6) and Section 15.1] and the method of *triple exponential smoothing* (see reference 1). When the time-series data increase at a rate such that the percentage difference from value to value is constant, an exponential trend model is appropriate [see Equation (16.7)]. The focus of this section is forecasting linear, quadratic, and exponential trends, using the method of least squares.

The Linear Trend Model

The **linear trend model**:

$$Y_i = \beta_0 + \beta_1 X_i + \varepsilon_i$$

is the simplest forecasting model. Equation (16.5) defines the linear trend forecasting equation.

LINEAR TREND FORECASTING EQUATION

$$\hat{Y}_i = b_0 + b_1 X_i \tag{16.5}$$

Recall that in linear regression analysis, you used the method of least squares to compute the sample slope, b_1, and the sample Y intercept, b_0. You then substitute the values for X into Equation (16.5) to predict Y.

When using the least-squares method for fitting trends in a time series, you can simplify the interpretation of the coefficients by coding the X values so that the first value is assigned a code value of $X = 0$. You then assign all successive values consecutively increasing integer codes: 1, 2, 3, . . . , so that the nth and last value in the series has code $n - 1$. For example, for time-series data recorded annually over 22 years, you assign the first year a coded value of 0, the second year a coded value of 1, the third year a coded value of 2, and so on, with the final (22nd) year assigned a coded value of 21.

In the Using Statistics scenario on page 646, one of the companies of interest is the Wm. Wrigley Jr. Company. Wrigley's is the world's largest manufacturer and marketer of chewing gum. Headquartered in Chicago, Illinois, Wrigley's operates factories in 12 countries and markets its products in more than 150 countries. Revenues in 2005 topped $4.1 billion (Wm. Wrigley Jr. Company, **www.wrigley.com**). Table 16.3 lists the actual gross revenues (in millions of current dollars) from 1984 to 2005 (see the file wrigley.xls). This time series is plotted in Figure 16.5 on page 657. To adjust for inflation, you use the Bureau of Labor Statistics CPI to convert (and deflate) actual gross revenue dollars into real gross revenue dollars. This adjustment is achieved by multiplying each actual gross revenue value by the corresponding quantity $\left(\frac{100}{\text{CPI}}\right)$. The revised values are real gross revenues data in millions of constant 1982 to 1984 dollars. Figure 16.5 plots the real gross revenues along with the actual gross revenues, in millions of current dollars.

TABLE 16.3

Actual Gross Revenues (in Millions of Dollars) for the Wm. Wrigley Jr. Company (1984–2005)

Year	Actual Revenue	Year	Actual Revenue
1984	591	1995	1,770
1985	620	1996	1,851
1986	699	1997	1,954
1987	781	1998	2,023
1988	891	1999	2,079
1989	993	2000	2,146
1990	1,111	2001	2,430
1991	1,149	2002	2,746
1992	1,301	2003	3,069
1993	1,440	2004	3,649
1994	1,661	2005	4,159

Source: Extracted from Moody's Handbook of Common Stocks, *1992, and* Mergent's Handbook of Common Stocks, *2006.*

FIGURE 16.5

Microsoft Excel time-series plots of actual and real gross revenues at Wm. Wrigley Jr. Company (in millions of dollars), 1984–2005

See Section E16.2 to create this.

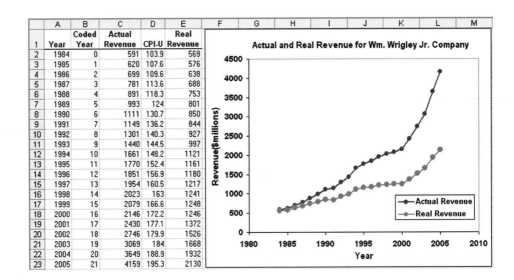

	Year	Coded Year	Actual Revenue	CPI-U	Real Revenue
2	1984	0	591	103.9	569
3	1985	1	620	107.6	576
4	1986	2	699	109.6	638
5	1987	3	781	113.6	688
6	1988	4	891	118.3	753
7	1989	5	993	124	801
8	1990	6	1111	130.7	850
9	1991	7	1149	136.2	844
10	1992	8	1301	140.3	927
11	1993	9	1440	144.5	997
12	1994	10	1661	148.2	1121
13	1995	11	1770	152.4	1161
14	1996	12	1851	156.9	1180
15	1997	13	1954	160.5	1217
16	1998	14	2023	163	1241
17	1999	15	2079	166.6	1248
18	2000	16	2146	172.2	1246
19	2001	17	2430	177.1	1372
20	2002	18	2746	179.9	1526
21	2003	19	3069	184	1668
22	2004	20	3649	188.9	1932
23	2005	21	4159	195.3	2130

Coding the consecutive X values from 0 through 21 and then using Microsoft Excel to perform a simple linear regression analysis on the adjusted time series (see Figure 16.6) results in the following linear trend forecasting equation:

$$\hat{Y}_i = 469.9158 + 62.1068X_i$$

where year zero is 1984.

FIGURE 16.6

Microsoft Excel results for a linear regression model to forecast real gross revenues (in millions of constant 1982–1984 dollars) at Wm. Wrigley Jr. Company

See Section E16.6 to create this.

	A	B	C	D	E	F	G
1	Linear Trend Model for Real Annual Gross Revenue for Wm. Wrigley Jr. Company						
2							
3	*Regression Statistics*						
4	Multiple R	0.9573					
5	R Square	0.9164					
6	Adjusted R Square	0.9122					
7	Standard Error	124.8304					
8	Observations	22					
9							
10	ANOVA						
11		*df*	*SS*	*MS*	*F*	*Significance F*	
12	Regression	1	3415597.1280	3415597.1280	219.1927	3.06194E-12	
13	Residual	20	311652.4806	15582.6240			
14	Total	21	3727249.6086				
15							
16		*Coefficients*	*Standard Error*	*t Stat*	*P-value*	*Lower 95%*	*Upper 95%*
17	Intercept	469.9158	51.4629	9.1312	1.42587E-08	362.5661	577.2655
18	Coded Year	62.1068	4.1949	14.8052	3.06194E-12	53.3563	70.8573

You interpret the regression coefficients as follows:

- The Y intercept, $b_0 = 469.9158$, is the predicted real gross revenues (in millions of constant 1982–1984 dollars) at Wm. Wrigley Jr. during the origin or base year, 1984.
- The slope, $b_1 = 62.1068$, indicates that real gross revenues are predicted to increase by 62.1068 million dollars per year.

To project the trend in the real gross revenues at Wm. Wrigley Jr. to 2006, you substitute $X_{23} = 22$, the code for 2006, into the linear trend forecasting equation:

$$\hat{Y}_i = 469.9158 + 62.1068(22) = 1{,}836.265 \text{ millions of constant 1982–1984 dollars}$$

The trend line is plotted in Figure 16.7, along with the observed values of the time series. There is a strong upward linear trend, and the adjusted r^2 is 0.9122, indicating that more than 90% of the variation in real gross revenues is explained by the linear trend over the time series. To investigate whether a different trend model might provide an even better fit, a *quadratic* trend model and an *exponential* trend model are presented next.

FIGURE 16.7

Microsoft Excel least-squares trend line for Wm. Wrigley Jr. Company real gross revenues data

See Section E16.6 to create this.

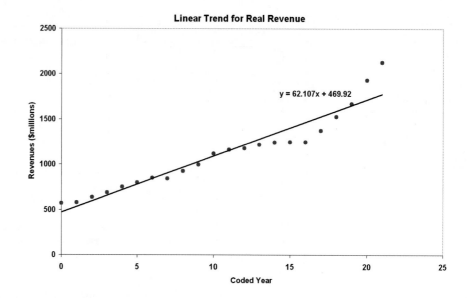

The Quadratic Trend Model

A **quadratic trend model**:

$$\hat{Y}_i = \beta_0 + \beta_1 X_i + \beta_2 X_i^2 + \varepsilon_i$$

is the simplest nonlinear model. Using the least-squares method described in Section 15.1, you can develop a quadratic trend forecasting equation, as presented in Equation (16.6).

> **QUADRATIC TREND FORECASTING EQUATION**
> $$\hat{Y}_i = b_0 + b_1 X_i + b_2 X_i^2 \qquad \textbf{(16.6)}$$
>
> where
> $$b_0 = \text{estimated } Y \text{ intercept}$$
> $$b_1 = \text{estimated } linear \text{ effect on } Y$$
> $$b_2 = \text{estimated } quadratic \text{ effect on } Y$$

Once again, you use Microsoft Excel to compute the quadratic trend forecasting equation. Figure 16.8 provides the results for the quadratic trend model used to forecast real gross revenues at the Wm. Wrigley Jr. Company.

FIGURE 16.8

Microsoft Excel results for a quadratic regression model to forecast real gross revenues at Wm. Wrigley Jr. Company

See Section E16.7 to create this.

	A	B	C	D	E	F	G
1	Quadratic Trend Model for Real Annual Gross Revenue for Wm. Wrigley Jr. Company						
2							
3	*Regression Statistics*						
4	Multiple R	0.9750					
5	R Square	0.9506					
6	Adjusted R Square	0.9454					
7	Standard Error	98.4859					
8	Observations	22					
9							
10	ANOVA						
11		df	SS	MS	F	Significance F	
12	Regression	2	3542959.4693	1771479.7346	182.6365	3.9272E-13	
13	Residual	19	184290.1393	9699.4810			
14	Total	21	3727249.6086				
15							
16		Coefficients	Standard Error	t Stat	P-value	Lower 95%	Upper 95%
17	Intercept	618.3211	57.6698	10.7217	1.6933E-09	497.6167	739.0255
18	Coded Year	17.5852	12.7243	1.3820	0.1830	-9.0472	44.2176
19	Coded Year Squared	2.1201	0.5851	3.6237	0.0018	0.8955	3.3446

In Figure 16.8,

$$\hat{Y}_i = 618.3211 + 17.5852X_i + 2.1201X_i^2$$

where year zero is 1984.

To compute a forecast using the quadratic trend equation, you substitute the appropriate coded X values into this equation. For example, to forecast the trend in real gross revenues for 2006 (that is, $X_{23} = 22$),

$$\hat{Y}_i = 618.3211 + 17.5852(22) + 2.1201(22)^2 = 2,031.324 \text{ millions of dollars}$$

Figure 16.9 plots the quadratic trend forecasting equation along with the time series for the actual data. This quadratic trend model provides a better fit (adjusted $r^2 = 0.9454$) to the time series than does the linear trend model. The t statistic for the contribution of the quadratic term to the model is 3.6237 (p-value = 0.0018).

FIGURE 16.9

Microsoft Excel fitted quadratic trend forecasting equation for the Wm. Wrigley Jr. Company

See Section E16.7 to create this.

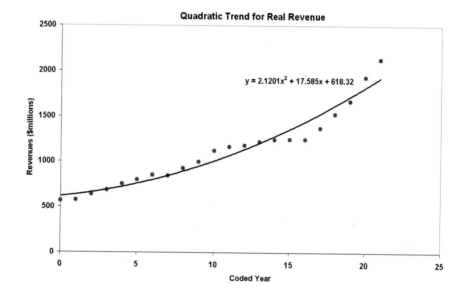

The Exponential Trend Model

When a time series increases at a rate such that the percentage difference from value to value is constant, an exponential trend is present. Equation (16.7) defines the **exponential trend model**.

EXPONENTIAL TREND MODEL

$$Y_i = \beta_0 \beta_1^{X_i} \varepsilon_i \qquad (16.7)$$

where

$$\beta_0 = Y \text{ intercept}$$

$(\beta_1 - 1) \times 100\%$ is the annual compound growth rate (in %)

[2]*Alternatively, you can use base e logarithms. For more information on logarithms, see Appendix A.*

The model in Equation (16.7) is not in the form of a linear regression model. To transform this nonlinear model to a linear model, you use a base 10 logarithm transformation.[2] Taking the logarithm of each side of Equation (16.7) results in Equation (16.8).

TRANSFORMED EXPONENTIAL TREND MODEL

$$\log(Y_i) = \log(\beta_0 \beta_1^{X_i} \varepsilon_i)$$
$$= \log(\beta_0) + \log(\beta_1^{X_i}) + \log(\varepsilon_i) \tag{16.8}$$
$$= \log(\beta_0) + X_i \log(\beta_1) + \log(\varepsilon_i)$$

Equation (16.8) is a linear model you can estimate, using the least-squares method, with $\log(Y_i)$ as the dependent variable and X_i as the independent variable. This results in Equation (16.9).

EXPONENTIAL TREND FORECASTING EQUATION

$$\log(\hat{Y}_i) = b_0 + b_1 X_i \tag{16.9a}$$

where

$$b_0 = \text{estimate of } \log(\beta_0) \text{ and thus } 10^{b_0} = \hat{\beta}_0$$
$$b_1 = \text{estimate of } \log(\beta_1) \text{ and thus } 10^{b_1} = \hat{\beta}_1$$

therefore,

$$\hat{Y}_i = \hat{\beta}_0 \hat{\beta}_1^{X_i} \tag{16.9b}$$

where

$$(\hat{\beta}_1 - 1) \times 100\% \text{ is the estimated annual compound growth rate (in \%)}$$

Figure 16.10 shows an Excel results worksheet for an exponential trend model of real gross revenues at the Wm. Wrigley Jr. Company.

FIGURE 16.10

Microsoft Excel results for an exponential regression model to forecast real gross revenues at Wm. Wrigley Jr. Company

See Section E16.8 to create this.

	A	B	C	D	E	F	G
1	Exponential Trend Model for Real Annual Gross Revenues for Wm. Wrigley Jr. Company						
2							
3	*Regression Statistics*						
4	Multiple R	0.9853					
5	R Square	0.9709					
6	Adjusted R Square	0.9694					
7	Standard Error	0.0282					
8	Observations	22					
9							
10	ANOVA						
11		*df*	*SS*	*MS*	*F*	*Significance F*	
12	Regression	1	0.5298	0.5298	666.5416	7.8607E-17	
13	Residual	20	0.0159	0.0008			
14	Total	21	0.5457				
15							
16		*Coefficients*	*Standard Error*	*t Stat*	*P-value*	*Lower 95%*	*Upper 95%*
17	Intercept	2.7647	0.0116	237.8723	5.345E-36	2.7405	2.7890
18	Coded Year	0.0245	0.0009	25.8175	7.8607E-17	0.0225	0.0264

Using Equation (16.9a) and the results from Figure 16.10,

$$\log(\hat{Y}_i) = 2.7647 + 0.0245X_i$$

where year zero is 1984.

You compute the values for $\hat{\beta}_0$ and $\hat{\beta}_1$ by taking the antilog of the regression coefficients (b_0 and b_1):

$$\hat{\beta}_0 = \text{antilog } b_0 = \text{antilog}(2.7647) = 10^{2.7647} = 581.701$$
$$\hat{\beta}_1 = \text{antilog } b_1 = \text{antilog}(0.0245) = 10^{0.0245} = 1.058$$

Thus, using Equation (16.9b), the exponential trend forecasting equation is

$$\hat{Y}_i = (581.701)(1.058)^{X_i}$$

where year zero is 1984.

The Y intercept, $\hat{\beta}_0 = 581.70^1$ millions of dollars, is the real gross revenues forecast for the base year 1984. The value $(\hat{\beta}_1 - 1) \times 100\% = 5.8\%$ is the annual compound growth rate in real gross revenues at the Wm. Wrigley Jr. Company.

For forecasting purposes, substitute the appropriate coded X values into either Equation (16.9a) or Equation (16.9b). For example, to forecast real gross revenues for 2006 (that is, $X_{23} = 22$) using Equation (16.9a),

$$\log(\hat{Y}_i) = 2.7647 + 0.0245(22) = 3.3037$$

$$\hat{Y}_i = \text{antilog}(3.3037) = 10^{3.3037} = 2,012.334 \text{ millions of dollars}$$

Figure 16.11 plots the exponential trend forecasting equation, along with the time series for the real revenue data. The adjusted r^2 for the exponential trend model (0.9694) is higher than the adjusted r^2 for the linear trend model (0.9122) or the quadratic model (0.9454).

FIGURE 16.11

Fitting an exponential trend equation using Microsoft Excel for the Wm. Wrigley Jr. Company real gross revenues data

See Section E16.8 to create this.

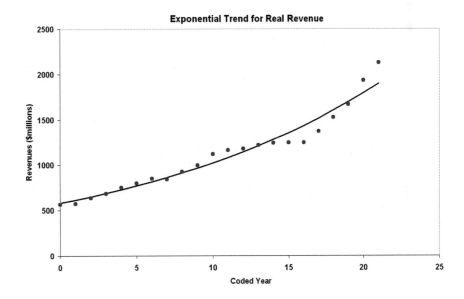

Model Selection Using First, Second, and Percentage Differences

You have used the linear, quadratic, and exponential models to forecast real gross revenues for the Wm. Wrigley Jr. Company. How can you determine which of these models is the most appropriate model? In addition to visually inspecting scatter plots and comparing adjusted r^2 values, you can compute and examine first, second, and percentage differences. The identifying features of linear, quadratic, and exponential trend models are as follows:

- If a linear trend model provides a perfect fit to a time series, then the first differences are constant. Thus, the differences between consecutive values in the series are the same throughout:

$$(Y_2 - Y_1) = (Y_3 - Y_2) = \cdots = (Y_n - Y_{n-1})$$

- If a quadratic trend model provides a perfect fit to a time series, then the second differences are constant. Thus,

$$[(Y_3 - Y_2) - (Y_2 - Y_1)] = [(Y_4 - Y_3) - (Y_3 - Y_2)] = \cdots = [(Y_n - Y_{n-1}) - (Y_{n-1} - Y_{n-2})]$$

- If an exponential trend model provides a perfect fit to a time series, then the percentage differences between consecutive values are constant. Thus,

$$\frac{Y_2 - Y_1}{Y_1} \times 100\% = \frac{Y_3 - Y_2}{Y_2} \times 100\% = \cdots = \frac{Y_n - Y_{n-1}}{Y_{n-1}} \times 100\%$$

Although you should not expect a perfectly fitting model for any particular set of time-series data, you can consider the first differences, second differences, and percentage differences for a given series as guides in choosing an appropriate model. Examples 16.2, 16.3, and 16.4 illustrate applications of linear, quadratic, and exponential trend models having perfect fits to their respective data sets.

EXAMPLE 16.2

A LINEAR TREND MODEL WITH A PERFECT FIT

The following time series represents the number of passengers per year (in millions) on ABC Airlines:

	Year									
	1997	1998	1999	2000	2001	2002	2003	2004	2005	2006
Passengers	30.0	33.0	36.0	39.0	42.0	45.0	48.0	51.0	54.0	57.0

Using first differences, show that the linear trend model provides a perfect fit to these data.

SOLUTION The following table shows the solution:

	Year									
	1997	1998	1999	2000	2001	2002	2003	2004	2005	2006
Passengers	30.0	33.0	36.0	39.0	42.0	45.0	48.0	51.0	54.0	57.0
First differences		3.0	3.0	3.0	3.0	3.0	3.0	3.0	3.0	3.0

The differences between consecutive values in the series are the same throughout. Thus, ABC Airlines is exhibiting a linear growth pattern. The number of passengers increases by 3 million per year.

EXAMPLE 16.3

A QUADRATIC TREND MODEL WITH A PERFECT FIT

The following time series represents the number of passengers per year (in millions) on XYZ Airlines:

	Year									
	1997	1998	1999	2000	2001	2002	2003	2004	2005	2006
Passengers	30.0	31.0	33.5	37.5	43.0	50.0	58.5	68.5	80.0	93.0

Using second differences, show that the quadratic trend model provides a perfect fit to these data.

SOLUTION The following table shows the solution:

	Year									
	1997	1998	1999	2000	2001	2002	2003	2004	2005	2006
Passengers	30.0	31.0	33.5	37.5	43.0	50.0	58.5	68.5	80.0	93.0
First differences		1.0	2.5	4.0	5.5	7.0	8.5	10.0	11.5	13.0
Second differences			1.5	1.5	1.5	1.5	1.5	1.5	1.5	1.5

The second differences between consecutive pairs of values in the series are the same throughout. Thus, XYZ airlines is exhibiting a quadratic growth pattern. Its rate of growth is accelerating over time.

EXAMPLE 16.4

AN EXPONENTIAL TREND MODEL WITH A PERFECT FIT

The following time series represents the number of passengers per year (in millions) for EXP Airlines:

	Year									
	1997	1998	1999	2000	2001	2002	2003	2004	2005	2006
Passengers	30.0	31.5	33.1	34.8	36.5	38.3	40.2	42.2	44.3	46.5

Using percentage differences, show that the exponential trend model provides almost a perfect fit to these data.

SOLUTION The following table shows the solution:

	Year									
	1997	1998	1999	2000	2001	2002	2003	2004	2005	2006
Passengers	30.0	31.5	33.1	34.8	36.5	38.3	40.2	42.2	44.3	46.5
First differences		1.5	1.6	1.7	1.7	1.8	1.9	2.0	2.1	2.2
Percentage differences		5.0	5.1	5.1	4.9	4.9	5.0	5.0	5.0	5.0

The percentage differences between consecutive values in the series are approximately the same throughout. Thus, EXP Airlines is exhibiting an exponential growth pattern. Its rate of growth is approximately 5% per year.

Figure 16.12 presents the first, second, and percentage differences for the real gross revenues data at Wm. Wrigley Jr. Company. Neither the first differences, second differences, nor percentage differences are constant across the series. Therefore, other models (including those considered in Section 16.5) may be more appropriate.

FIGURE 16.12

Comparing first, second, and percentage differences in real annual gross revenues (in millions of constant 1982–1984 dollars) for Wm. Wrigley Jr. Company (1984–2005)

	A	B	C	D	E
1	Year	Real Revenue	First Difference	Second Difference	Percentage Difference
2	1984	569	---	---	---
3	1985	576	7	---	1.23%
4	1986	638	62	55	10.76%
5	1987	688	50	-12	7.84%
6	1988	753	65	15	9.45%
7	1989	801	48	-17	6.37%
8	1990	850	49	1	6.12%
9	1991	844	-6	-55	-0.71%
10	1992	927	83	89	9.83%
11	1993	997	70	-13	7.55%
12	1994	1121	124	54	12.44%
13	1995	1161	40	-84	3.57%
14	1996	1180	19	-21	1.64%
15	1997	1217	37	18	3.14%
16	1998	1241	24	-13	1.97%
17	1999	1248	7	-17	0.56%
18	2000	1246	-2	-9	-0.16%
19	2001	1372	126	128	10.11%
20	2002	1526	154	28	11.22%
21	2003	1668	142	-12	9.31%
22	2004	1932	264	122	15.83%
23	2005	2130	198	-66	10.25%

PROBLEMS FOR SECTION 16.4

Learning the Basics

16.9 If using the method of least squares for fitting trends in an annual time series containing 25 consecutive yearly values,
a. what coded value do you assign to X for the first year in the series?
b. what coded value do you assign to X for the fifth year in the series?
c. what coded value do you assign to X for the most recent recorded year in the series?
d. what coded value do you assign to X if you want to project the trend and make a forecast five years beyond the last observed value?

 16.10 The linear trend forecasting equation for an annual time series containing 22 values (from 1985 to 2006) on total revenues (in millions of dollars) is

$$\hat{Y}_i = 4.0 + 1.5X_i$$

a. Interpret the Y intercept, b_0.
b. Interpret the slope, b_1.
c. What is the fitted trend value for the fifth year?
d. What is the fitted trend value for the most recent year?
e. What is the projected trend forecast three years after the last value?

16.11 The linear trend forecasting equation for an annual time series containing 42 values (from 1965 to 2006) on net sales (in billions of dollars) is

$$\hat{Y}_i = 1.2 + 0.5X_i$$

a. Interpret the Y intercept, b_0.
b. Interpret the slope, b_1.
c. What is the fitted trend value for the tenth year?
d. What is the fitted trend value for the most recent year?
e. What is the projected trend forecast two years after the last value?

Applying the Concepts

16.12 The following data (in the file **CPI-U.xls**) reflect the annual values of the CPI in the United States over the 41-year period 1965 through 2005, using 1982 through 1984 as the base period. This index measures the average change in prices over time in a fixed "market basket" of goods and services purchased by all urban consumers, including urban wage earners (that is, clerical, professional, managerial, and technical workers; self-employed individuals; and short-term workers), unemployed individuals, and retirees.

Year	CPI	Year	CPI	Year	CPI
1965	31.5	1979	72.6	1993	144.5
1966	32.4	1980	82.4	1994	148.2
1967	33.4	1981	90.9	1995	152.4
1968	34.8	1982	96.5	1996	156.9
1969	36.7	1983	99.6	1997	160.5
1970	38.8	1984	103.9	1998	163.0
1971	40.5	1985	107.6	1999	166.6
1972	41.8	1986	109.6	2000	172.2
1973	44.4	1987	113.6	2001	177.1
1974	49.3	1988	118.3	2002	179.9
1975	53.8	1989	124.0	2003	184.0
1976	56.9	1990	130.7	2004	188.9
1977	60.6	1991	136.2	2005	195.3
1978	65.2	1992	140.3		

Source: Bureau of Labor Statistics, U.S. Department of Labor, **www.bls.gov**.

a. Plot the data.
b. Describe the movement in this time series over the 41-year period.

16.13 Gross domestic product (GDP) is a major indicator of a nation's overall economic activity. It consists of personal consumption expenditures, gross domestic investment, net exports of goods and services, and government consumption expenditures. The GDP (in billions of current dollars) for the United States from 1980 to 2005 is in the data file **GDP.xls**.

Source: Bureau of Economic Analysis, U.S. Department of Commerce, **www.bea.gov**.

a. Plot the data.
b. Compute a linear trend forecasting equation and plot the trend line.
c. What are your forecasts for 2006 and 2007?
d. What conclusions can you reach concerning the trend in GDP?

16.14 The data in the file **fedrecpt.xls** represent federal receipts from 1978 through 2004, in billions of current dollars, from individual and corporate income tax, social insurance, excise tax, estate and gift tax, customs duties, and federal reserve deposits.

Source: Tax Policy Center, **www.taxpolicycenter.org**.

a. Plot the series of data.
b. Compute a linear trend forecasting equation and plot the trend line.

c. What are your forecasts of the federal receipts for 2005 and 2006?

d. What conclusions can you reach concerning the trend in federal receipts between 1978 and 2004?

16.15 The data in the file `strategic.xls` represent the amount of oil, in millions of barrels held in the U.S. strategic oil reserve, from 1981 through 2004.

Source: Energy Information Administration, U.S. Department of Energy, **www.eia.doe.gov**.

a. Plot the data.

b. Compute a linear trend forecasting equation and plot the trend line.

c. Compute a quadratic trend forecasting equation and plot the results.

d. Compute an exponential trend forecasting equation and plot the results.

e. Which model is the most appropriate?

f. Using the most appropriate model, forecast the number of barrels, in millions, for 2005. Check how accurate your forecast is by locating the true value on the Internet or in your library.

16.16 The data in the file `cocacola.xls` represent the annual net operating revenues (in billions of current dollars) at Coca-Cola Company from 1975 through 2005.

Source: Extracted from Moody's Handbook of Common Stocks, *1980, 1989, 1999, and* Mergent's Handbook of Common Stocks, *2005, and the Coca-Cola Company,* **www.cocacola.com**.

a. Plot the data.

b. Compute a linear trend forecasting equation and plot the trend line.

c. Compute a quadratic trend forecasting equation and plot the results.

d. Compute an exponential trend forecasting equation and plot the results.

e. Using the models in (b) through (d), what are your annual trend forecasts of net operating revenues for 2006 and 2007?

16.17 The data in the following table represent the closing values of the Dow Jones Industrial Average (DJIA) from 1979 through 2005 (see the file `djia.xls`):

Year	DJIA	Year	DJIA	Year	DJIA
1979	838.7	1988	2,168.6	1997	7,908.3
1980	964.0	1989	2,753.2	1998	9,181.4
1981	875.0	1990	2,633.7	1999	11,497.1
1982	1,046.5	1991	3,168.8	2000	10,788.0
1983	1,258.6	1992	3,301.1	2001	10,021.5
1984	1,211.6	1993	3,754.1	2002	8,341.6
1985	1,546.7	1994	3,834.4	2003	10,453.9
1986	1,896.0	1995	5,117.1	2004	10,788.0
1987	1,938.8	1996	6,448.3	2005	10,717.5

Source: Extracted from **finance.yahoo.com**.

a. Plot the data.

b. Compute a linear trend forecasting equation and plot the trend line.

c. Compute a quadratic trend forecasting equation and plot the results.

d. Compute an exponential trend forecasting equation and plot the results.

e. Which model is the most appropriate?

f. Using the most appropriate model, forecast the closing value for the DJIA in 2006. Discuss the accuracy of your forecast and try to explain the difference between the forecast and the actual value.

16.18 General Electric (GE) is one of the world's largest companies; it develops, manufactures, and markets a wide range of products, including medical diagnostic imaging devices, jet engines, lighting products, and chemicals. Through its affiliate NBC Universal, GE produces and delivers network television and motion pictures. The data in the file `GE.xls` represent the January 1 stock price for the 20-year period from 1987 to 2006.

Source: Extracted from **finance.yahoo.com**.

a. Plot the data.

b. Compute a linear trend forecasting equation and plot the trend line.

c. Compute a quadratic trend forecasting equation and plot the results.

d. Compute an exponential trend forecasting equation and plot the results.

e. Which model is the most appropriate?

f. Using the most appropriate model, forecast the stock price for January 1, 2007.

16.19 Although you should not expect a perfectly fitting model for any time-series data, you can consider the first differences, second differences, and percentage differences for a given series as guides in choosing an appropriate model. For this problem, use each of the time series presented in the following table and stored in the file `tsmodel1.xls`:

	Year				
	1997	**1998**	**1999**	**2000**	**2001**
Time series I	10.0	15.1	24.0	36.7	53.8
Time series II	30.0	33.1	36.4	39.9	43.9
Time series III	60.0	67.9	76.1	84.0	92.2

	Year				
	2002	**2003**	**2004**	**2005**	**2006**
Time series I	74.8	100.0	129.2	162.4	199.0
Time series II	48.2	53.2	58.2	64.5	70.7
Time series III	100.0	108.0	115.8	124.1	132.0

a. Determine the most appropriate model.
b. Compute the forecasting equation.
c. Forecast the value for 2007.

16.20 A time-series plot often helps you determine the appropriate model to use. For this problem, use each of the time-series presented in the following table and stored in the file tsmodel2.xls:

| | **Year** | | | | |
	1997	**1998**	**1999**	**2000**	**2001**
Time series I	100.0	115.2	130.1	144.9	160.0
Time series II	100.0	115.2	131.7	150.8	174.1

| | **Year** | | | | |
	2002	**2003**	**2004**	**2005**	**2006**
Time series I	175.0	189.8	204.9	219.8	235.0
Time series II	200.0	230.8	266.1	305.5	351.8

a. Plot the observed data (Y) over time (X) and plot the logarithm of the observed data ($\log Y$) over time (X) to determine whether a linear trend model or an exponential trend model is more appropriate. (*Hint:* If the plot of $\log Y$ versus X appears to be linear, an exponential trend model provides an appropriate fit.)
b. Compute the appropriate forecasting equation.
c. Forecast the value for 2007.

16.21 The data in the file oysters.xls represent the bushels of oysters harvested in Chesapeake Bay for 1990–1991 through 2003–2004 (Source: Maryland Department of Natural Resources).
a. Compare the first differences, second differences, and percentage differences to determine the most appropriate model.
b. Compute the appropriate forecasting equation.

c. Forecast the number of bushels harvested for 2004–2005 and 2005–2006.
d. What would you say about your forecasting model if you knew that in 1980–1981, 2,532,321 bushels were harvested?

16.22 Bed Bath & Beyond Inc. is a nationwide chain of retail stores that sell a wide assortment of merchandise, principally including domestics merchandise and home furnishings, as well as food, giftware, and health and beauty care items. The following data (stored in the file bedbath.xls) show the number of stores open at the end of the fiscal year from 1993 to 2006:

Year	Stores Open	Year	Stores Open
1993	38	2000	241
1994	45	2001	311
1995	61	2002	396
1996	80	2003	519
1997	108	2004	629
1998	141	2005	721
1999	186	2006	809

Source: Extracted from Bed Bath & Beyond Annual Report, 2005, May 24, 2006.

a. Plot the data.
b. Compute a linear trend forecasting equation and plot the results.
c. Compute a quadratic trend forecasting equation and plot the results.
d. Compute an exponential trend forecasting equation and plot the results.
e. Using the forecasting equations in (b) through (d), what are your annual forecasts of the number of stores open for 2007 and 2008?
f. How can you explain the differences in the three forecasts in (e)? What forecast do you think you should use? Why?

16.5 AUTOREGRESSIVE MODELING FOR TREND FITTING AND FORECASTING

[3] The exponential smoothing model described in Section 16.3 and the autoregressive models described in this section are special cases of autoregressive integrated moving average (ARIMA) models developed by Box and Jenkins (reference 2).

Frequently, the values of a time series are highly correlated with the values that precede and succeed them. This type of correlation is called autocorrelation. **Autoregressive modeling**[3] is a technique used to forecast time series with autocorrelation. A **first-order autocorrelation** refers to the association between consecutive values in a time series. A **second-order autocorrelation** refers to the relationship between values that are two periods apart. A *p*th-order **autocorrelation** refers to the correlation between values in a time series that are p periods apart. You can take into account the autocorrelation in data by using autoregressive modeling methods.

Equations (16.10), (16.11), and (16.12) define first-order, second-order, and *p*th-order autoregressive models.

FIRST-ORDER AUTOREGRESSIVE MODEL

$$Y_i = A_0 + A_1 Y_{i-1} + \delta_i \qquad (16.10)$$

SECOND-ORDER AUTOREGRESSIVE MODEL

$$Y_i = A_0 + A_1 Y_{i-1} + A_2 Y_{i-2} + \delta_i \qquad (16.11)$$

pTH-ORDER AUTOREGRESSIVE MODELS

$$Y_i = A_0 + A_1 Y_{i-1} + A_2 Y_{i-2} + \cdots + A_p Y_{i-p} + \delta_i \qquad (16.12)$$

where

Y_i = the observed value of the series at time i

Y_{i-1} = the observed value of the series at time $i - 1$

Y_{i-2} = the observed value of the series at time $i - 2$

Y_{i-p} = the observed value of the series at time $i - p$

$A_0, A_1, A_2, \ldots, A_p$ = autoregression parameters to be estimated from least-squares regression analysis

δ_i = a nonautocorrelated random error component (with mean = 0 and constant variance)

The **first-order autoregressive model** [Equation (16.10)] is similar in form to the simple linear regression model [Equation (13.1) on page 513]. The **second-order autoregressive model** [Equation (16.11)] is similar to the multiple regression model with two independent variables [Equation (14.2) on page 573]. The ***p*th-order autoregressive model** [Equation (16.12)] is similar to the multiple regression model [Equation (14.1) on page 573]. In the regression models, the regression parameters are given by the symbols $\beta_0, \beta_1, \ldots, \beta_k$, with corresponding estimates denoted by $b_0, b_1, \ldots, b_k$. In the autoregressive models, the parameters are given by the symbols $A_0, A_1, \ldots, A_p$, with corresponding estimates denoted by $a_0, a_1, \ldots, a_p$.

Selecting an appropriate autoregressive model is not easy. You must weigh the advantages that are due to simplicity against the concern of failing to take into account important autocorrelation in the data. You also must be concerned with selecting a higher-order model requiring the estimation of numerous, unnecessary parameters—especially if n, the number of values in the series, is small. The reason for this concern is that p out of n data values are lost in computing an estimate of A_p when comparing each data value with another data value, when they are p periods apart.

Examples 16.5 and 16.6 illustrate this loss of data values.

EXAMPLE 16.5

COMPARISON SCHEMA FOR A FIRST-ORDER AUTOREGRESSIVE MODEL

Consider the following series of $n = 7$ consecutive annual values:

	\multicolumn{7}{c}{**Year**}
	1	**2**	**3**	**4**	**5**	**6**	**7**
Series	31	34	37	35	36	43	40

Show the comparisons needed for a first-order autoregressive model.

SOLUTION

Year	First-Order Autoregressive Model
i	(Y_i vs. Y_{i-1})
1	31 ↔ . . .
2	34 ↔ 31
3	37 ↔ 34
4	35 ↔ 37
5	36 ↔ 35
6	43 ↔ 36
7	40 ↔ 43

Because there is no value recorded prior to Y_1, this value is lost for regression analysis. Therefore, the first-order autoregressive model is based on six pairs of values.

EXAMPLE 16.6

COMPARISON SCHEMA FOR A SECOND-ORDER AUTOREGRESSIVE MODEL

Consider the following series of $n = 7$ consecutive annual values:

	Year						
	1	2	3	4	5	6	7
Series	31	34	37	35	36	43	40

Show the comparisons needed for a second-order autoregressive model.

SOLUTION

Year	Second-Order Autoregressive Model
i	(Y_i vs. Y_{i-1} and Y_i vs. Y_{i-2})
1	31 ↔ . . . and 31 ↔ . . .
2	34 ↔ 31 and 34 ↔ . . .
3	37 ↔ 34 and 37 ↔ 31
4	35 ↔ 37 and 35 ↔ 34
5	36 ↔ 35 and 36 ↔ 37
6	43 ↔ 36 and 43 ↔ 35
7	40 ↔ 43 and 40 ↔ 36

Because there is no value recorded prior to Y_1, two values are lost for regression analysis. Therefore, the second-order autoregressive model is based on five pairs of values.

After selecting a model and using the least-squares method to compute estimates of the parameters, you need to determine the appropriateness of the model. Either you can select a particular pth-order autoregressive model based on previous experiences with similar data or, as a starting point, you can choose a model with several parameters and then eliminate the parameters that do not significantly contribute to the model. In this latter approach, you use a t test for the significance of A_p, the highest-order autoregressive parameter in the current model under consideration. The null and alternative hypotheses are

$$H_0: A_p = 0$$
$$H_1: A_p \neq 0$$

Equation (16.13) defines the test statistic.

t TEST FOR SIGNIFICANCE OF THE HIGHEST-ORDER AUTOREGRESSIVE PARAMETER, A_p

$$t = \frac{a_p - A_p}{S_{a_p}} \quad (16.13)$$

where

A_p = hypothesized value of the highest-order parameter, A_p, in the regression model

a_p = the estimate of the highest-order parameter, A_p, in the autoregressive model

S_{a_p} = the standard deviation of a_p

The test statistic t follows a t distribution having $n - 2p - 1$ degrees of freedom.[4]

[4]In addition to the degrees of freedom lost for each of the p population parameters you are estimating, p additional degrees of freedom are lost because there are p fewer comparisons to be made out of the original n values in the time series.

For a given level of significance α, you reject the null hypothesis if the computed t-test statistic is greater than the upper-tail critical value from the t distribution or if the computed test statistic is less than the lower-tail critical value from the t distribution. Thus, the decision rule is

$$\text{Reject } H_0 \text{ if } t > t_{n-2p-1} \text{ or if } t < -t_{n-2p-1};$$
$$\text{otherwise, do not reject } H_0.$$

Figure 16.13 illustrates the decision rule and regions of rejection and nonrejection.

FIGURE 16.13

Rejection regions for a two-tail test for the significance of the highest-order autoregressive parameter, A_p

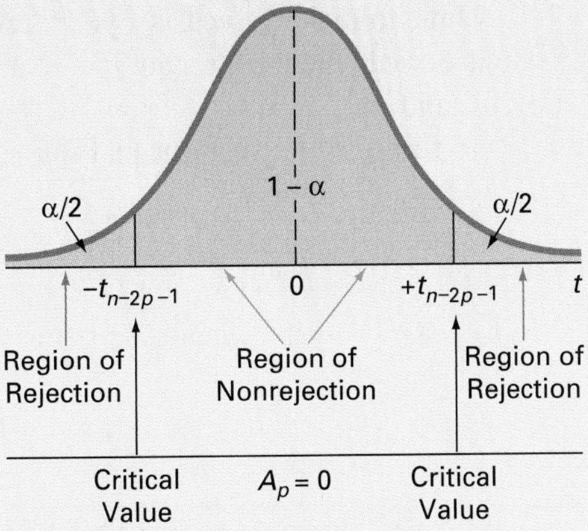

If you do not reject the null hypothesis that $A_p = 0$, you conclude that the selected model contains too many estimated parameters. You then discard the highest-order term and estimate an autoregressive model of order $p - 1$, using the least-squares method. You then repeat the test of the hypothesis that the new highest-order term is 0. This testing and modeling continues until you reject H_0. When this occurs, you know that the remaining highest-order parameter is significant, and you can use that model for forecasting purposes.

Equation (16.14) defines the fitted pth-order autoregressive equation.

FITTED pTH-ORDER AUTOREGRESSIVE EQUATION

$$\hat{Y}_i = a_0 + a_1 Y_{i-1} + a_2 Y_{i-2} + \cdots + a_p Y_{i-p} \qquad \textbf{(16.14)}$$

where

$$\hat{Y}_i = \text{fitted values of the series at time } i$$
$$Y_{i-1} = \text{observed value of the series at time } i - 1$$
$$Y_{i-2} = \text{observed value of the series at time } i - 2$$
$$Y_{i-p} = \text{observed value of the series at time } i - p$$
$$a_0, a_1, a_2, \ldots, a_p = \text{regression estimates of the parameters } A_0, A_1, A_2, \ldots, A_p$$

You use Equation (16.15) to forecast j years into the future from the current nth time period.

pTH-ORDER AUTOREGRESSIVE FORECASTING EQUATION

$$\hat{Y}_{n+j} = a_0 + a_1 \hat{Y}_{n+j-1} + a_2 \hat{Y}_{n+j-2} + \cdots + a_p \hat{Y}_{n+j-p} \qquad \textbf{(16.15)}$$

where

$$a_0, a_1, a_2, \ldots, a_p = \text{regression estimates of the parameters } A_0, A_1, A_2, \ldots, A_p$$
$$j = \text{number of years into the future}$$
$$\hat{Y}_{n+j-p} = \text{forecast of } Y_{n+j-p} \text{ from the current time period for } j - p > 0$$
$$\hat{Y}_{n+j-p} = \text{observed value for } Y_{n+j-p} \text{ for } j - p \leq 0$$

Thus, to make forecasts j years into the future, using a third-order autoregressive model, you need only the most recent $p = 3$ values (Y_n, Y_{n-1}, and Y_{n-2}) and the regression estimates a_0, a_1, a_2, and a_3.

To forecast one year ahead, Equation (16.15) becomes

$$\hat{Y}_{n+1} = a_0 + a_1 Y_n + a_2 Y_{n-1} + a_3 Y_{n-2}$$

To forecast two years ahead, Equation (16.15) becomes

$$\hat{Y}_{n+2} = a_0 + a_1 \hat{Y}_{n+1} + a_2 Y_n + a_3 Y_{n-1}$$

To forecast three years ahead, Equation (16.15) becomes

$$\hat{Y}_{n+3} = a_0 + a_1 \hat{Y}_{n+2} + a_2 \hat{Y}_{n+1} + a_3 Y_n$$

and so on.

Autoregressive modeling is a powerful forecasting technique for time series that have autocorrelation. Although slightly more complicated than other methods, the following step-by-step approach should guide you through the analysis:

1. Choose a value for p, the highest-order parameter in the autoregressive model to be evaluated, realizing that the t test for significance is based on $n - 2p - 1$ degrees of freedom.
2. Form a series of p "lagged predictor" variables such that the first variable lags by one time period, the second variable lags by two time periods, and so on and the last predictor variable lags by p time periods (see Figure 16.14).
3. Use Microsoft Excel to perform a least-squares analysis of the multiple regression model containing all p lagged predictor variables.
4. Test for the significance of A_p, the highest-order autoregressive parameter in the model.
   a. If you do not reject the null hypothesis, discard the pth variable and repeat steps 3 and 4. The test for the significance of the new highest-order parameter is based on a t distribution whose degrees of freedom are revised to correspond with the new number of predictors.
   b. If you reject the null hypothesis, select the autoregressive model with all p predictors for fitting [see Equation (16.14)] and forecasting [see Equation (16.15)].

FIGURE 16.14

Developing first-order, second-order, and third-order autoregressive models on real gross revenues for the Wm. Wrigley Jr. Company (1984–2005)

See Section E16.9 to create this.

	A	B	C	D	E
		Real			
1	Year	Revenue	Lag1	Lag2	Lag3
2	1984	569	#N/A	#N/A	#N/A
3	1985	576	569	#N/A	#N/A
4	1986	638	576	569	#N/A
5	1987	688	638	576	569
6	1988	753	688	638	576
7	1989	801	753	688	638
8	1990	850	801	753	688
9	1991	844	850	801	753
10	1992	927	844	850	801
11	1993	997	927	844	850
12	1994	1121	997	927	844
13	1995	1161	1121	997	927
14	1996	1180	1161	1121	997
15	1997	1217	1180	1161	1121
16	1998	1241	1217	1180	1161
17	1999	1248	1241	1217	1180
18	2000	1246	1248	1241	1217
19	2001	1372	1246	1248	1241
20	2002	1526	1372	1246	1248
21	2003	1668	1526	1372	1246
22	2004	1932	1668	1526	1372
23	2005	2130	1932	1668	1526

To demonstrate the autoregressive modeling approach, return to the time series concerning the real gross revenues (in millions of constant 1982 to 1984 dollars) for the Wm. Wrigley Jr. Company over the 22-year period 1984 through 2005. Figure 16.14 displays the real gross revenues and the setup for the first-order, second-order, and third-order autoregressive models. All the columns in this table are needed for fitting the third-order autoregressive model. The last column is omitted when fitting second-order autoregressive models, and the last two columns are omitted when fitting first-order autoregressive models. Thus, out of $n = 22$ values, $p = 1, 2,$ or 3 values out of $n = 22$ are lost in the comparisons needed for developing the first-order, second-order, and third-order autoregressive models.

Selecting an autoregressive model that best fits the annual time series begins with the third-order autoregressive model shown in Figure 16.15, using Microsoft Excel.

From Figure 16.15, the fitted third-order autoregressive equation is

$$\hat{Y}_i = -36.2995 + 1.5050Y_{i-1} - 0.2777Y_{i-2} - 0.1615Y_{i-3}$$

where the first year in the series is 1987.

FIGURE 16.15

Microsoft Excel results for the third-order autoregressive model for the Wm. Wrigley Jr. real gross revenues data

See Section E16.11 to create this.

	A	B	C	D	E	F	G
1	Third-Order Autoregressive Model						
2							
3	*Regression Statistics*						
4	Multiple R	0.9917					
5	R Square	0.9835					
6	Adjusted R Square	0.9802					
7	Standard Error	55.0683					
8	Observations	19					
9							
10	ANOVA						
11		*df*	*SS*	*MS*	*F*	*Significance F*	
12	Regression	3	2710252.6157	903417.5386	297.9098	1.3804E-13	
13	Residual	15	45487.8054	3032.5204			
14	Total	18	2755740.4211				
15							
16		*Coefficients*	*Standard Error*	*t Stat*	*P-value*	*Lower 95%*	*Upper 95%*
17	Intercept	-36.2995	47.8528	-0.7586	0.4599	-138.2955	65.6965
18	X Variable 1	1.5050	0.2532	5.9432	2.6960E-05	0.9652	2.0447
19	X Variable 2	-0.2777	0.5066	-0.5481	0.5917	-1.3574	0.8021
20	X Variable 3	-0.1615	0.3362	-0.4803	0.6379	-0.8782	0.5552

Next, you test for the significance of A_3, the highest-order parameter. The highest-order parameter estimate, a_3, for the fitted third-order autoregressive model is -0.1615, with a standard error of 0.3362.

To test the null hypothesis:

$$H_0: A_3 = 0$$

against the alternative hypothesis:

$$H_1: A_3 \neq 0$$

Using Equation (16.13) on page 669 and the Microsoft Excel output given in Figure 16.15,

$$t = \frac{a_3 - A_3}{S_{a_3}} = \frac{-0.1615 - 0}{0.3362} = -0.4803$$

Using a 0.05 level of significance, the two-tail t test with 15 degrees of freedom has critical values of t_{15} of ± 2.1315. Because $-2.1315 < t = -0.4803 < +2.1315$ or because the p-value $= 0.6379 > 0.05$, you do not reject H_0. You conclude that the third-order parameter of the autoregressive model is not significant and can be deleted.

Using Microsoft Excel once again (see Figure 16.16), you fit a second-order autoregressive model.

FIGURE 16.16

Microsoft Excel results for the second-order autoregressive model for the Wm. Wrigley Jr. Company real gross revenues data

See Section E16.11 to create this.

	A	B	C	D	E	F	G
1	Second-Order Autoregressive Model						
2							
3	*Regression Statistics*						
4	Multiple R	0.9920					
5	R Square	0.9841					
6	Adjusted R Square	0.9822					
7	Standard Error	53.5001					
8	Observations	20					
9							
10	ANOVA						
11		*df*	*SS*	*MS*	*F*	*Significance F*	
12	Regression	2	3012893.4938	1506446.7469	526.3128	5.1327E-16	
13	Residual	17	48658.5062	2862.2651			
14	Total	19	3061552				
15							
16		*Coefficients*	*Standard Error*	*t Stat*	*P-value*	*Lower 95%*	*Upper 95%*
17	Intercept	-21.0714	43.1389	-0.4885	0.6315	-112.0866	69.9438
18	X Variable 1	1.5511	0.2194	7.0705	1.8796E-06	1.0883	2.0140
19	X Variable 2	-0.4917	0.2470	-1.9911	0.0628	-1.0128	0.0293

The fitted second-order autoregressive equation is

$$\hat{Y}_i = -21.0714 + 1.5511 Y_{i-1} - 0.4917 Y_{i-2}$$

where the first year of the series is 1986.

From Figure 16.16, the highest-order parameter estimate is $a_2 = -0.4917$, with a standard error of 0.247.

To test the null hypothesis:

$$H_0: A_2 = 0$$

against the alternative hypothesis:

$$H_1: A_2 \neq 0$$

using Equation (16.13) on page 669,

$$t = \frac{a_2 - A_2}{S_{a_2}} = \frac{-0.4917 - 0}{0.2470} = -1.9911$$

Using the 0.05 level of significance, the two-tail t test with 17 degrees of freedom has critical values t_{17} of ± 2.1098. Because $-2.1098 < t = -1.9911 < +2.1098$ or because the p-value = $0.0628 > 0.05$, you do not reject H_0. You conclude that the second-order parameter of the autoregressive model is not significant and should be deleted from the model.

Using Microsoft Excel once again (see Figure 16.17), you fit a first-order autoregressive model.

FIGURE 16.17

Microsoft Excel results for the first-order autoregressive model for the Wm. Wrigley Jr. Company real gross revenues data

See Section E16.10 to create this.

	A	B	C	D	E	F	G
1	First-Order Autoregressive Model						
2							
3	Regression Statistics						
4	Multiple R	0.9911					
5	R Square	0.9824					
6	Adjusted R Square	0.9814					
7	Standard Error	56.2185					
8	Observations	21					
9							
10	ANOVA						
11		df	SS	MS	F	Significance F	
12	Regression	1	3345503.1055	3345503.1055	1058.5299	3.9850E-18	
13	Residual	19	60049.8469	3160.5183			
14	Total	20	3405552.9524				
15							
16		Coefficients	Standard Error	t Stat	P-value	Lower 95%	Upper 95%
17	Intercept	-55.7697	38.9911	-1.4303	0.1689	-137.3790	25.8396
18	X Variable 1	1.1211	0.0345	32.5351	3.9850E-18	1.0490	1.1933

The first-order autoregressive equation is

$$\hat{Y}_i = -55.7697 + 1.1211 Y_{i-1}$$

where the first year of the series is 1985.

From the Microsoft Excel results, the highest-order parameter estimate is $a_1 = 1.1211$ and $S_{a_1} = 0.0345$.

To test the null hypothesis:

$$H_0: A_1 = 0$$

against the alternative hypothesis:

$$H_1: A_1 \neq 0$$

using Equation (16.13) on page 669,

$$t = \frac{a_1 - A_1}{S_{a_1}} = \frac{1.1211 - 0}{0.0345} = 32.5351$$

Using the 0.05 level of significance, the two-tail t test with 19 degrees of freedom has critical values t_{19} of ± 2.0930. Because $t = 32.5351 > 2.0930$, or because the p-value $= 0.0000 < 0.05$, you reject H_0. You conclude that the first-order parameter of the autoregressive model is significant and should remain in the model. The model-building approach has led to the selection of the first-order autoregressive model as the most appropriate for the given data. Using the estimates $a_0 = -55.7697$ and $a_1 = 1.1211$, as well as the most recent data value $Y_{22} = 2,130$, the forecasts of real gross revenues at the Wm. Wrigley Jr. Company for 2006 and 2007 from Equation (16.15) on page 670 are

$$\hat{Y}_{n+j} = -55.7697 + 1.1211\hat{Y}_{n+j-1}$$

Therefore,

2006: 1 year ahead, $\hat{Y}_{23} = -55.7697 + 1.1211(2,130) = 2,332.173$ millions of dollars

2007: 2 year ahead, $\hat{Y}_{24} = -55.9697 + 1.1211(2,332.173) = 2,558.630$ millions of dollars

Figure 16.18 displays the actual value and predicted Y values from the first-order autoregressive model.

FIGURE 16.18

Microsoft Excel plot of actual and predicted real gross revenues from a first-order autoregressive model at the Wm. Wrigley Jr. Company

See Section E16.2 to create this.

PROBLEMS FOR SECTION 16.5

Learning the Basics

16.23 You are given an annual time series with 40 consecutive values and asked to fit a fifth-order autoregressive model.

a. How many comparisons are lost in the development of the autoregressive model?

b. How many parameters do you need to estimate?

c. Which of the original 40 values do you need for forecasting?

d. State the model.

e. Write an equation to indicate how you would forecast j years into the future.

16.24 A third-order autoregressive model is fitted to an annual time series with 17 values and has the following estimated parameters and standard deviations:

$$a_0 = 4.50 \qquad a_1 = 1.80 \qquad a_2 = 0.80 \qquad a_3 = 0.24$$
$$S_{a_1} = 0.50 \qquad S_{a_2} = 0.30 \qquad S_{a_3} = 0.10$$

At the 0.05 level of significance, test the appropriateness of the fitted model.

16.25 Refer to Problem 16.24. The three most recent values are

$$Y_{15} = 23 \quad Y_{16} = 28 \quad Y_{17} = 34$$

Forecast the values for the next year and the following year.

16.26 Refer to Problem 16.24. Suppose, when testing for the appropriateness of the fitted model, the standard deviations are

$$S_{a_1} = 0.45 \quad S_{a_2} = 0.35 \quad S_{a_3} = 0.15$$

a. What conclusions can you make?
b. Discuss how to proceed if forecasting is still your main objective.

Applying the Concepts

16.27 Refer to the data given in Problem 16.15 on page 665 that represent the amount of oil (in millions of barrels) held in the U.S. strategic reserve from 1981 through 2004 (see the file strategic.xls).
a. Fit a third-order autoregressive model to the amount of oil and test for the significance of the third-order autoregressive parameter. (Use $\alpha = 0.05$.)
b. If necessary, fit a second-order autoregressive model to the amount of oil and test for the significance of the second-order autoregressive parameter. (Use $\alpha = 0.05$.)
c. If necessary, fit a first-order autoregressive model to the amount of oil and test for the significance of the first-order autoregressive parameter. (Use $\alpha = 0.05$.)
d. If appropriate, forecast the barrels held in 2005.

 16.28 Refer to the data introduced in Problem 16.16 on page 665 (and stored in the file cocacola.xls) concerning annual net operating revenues (in billions of current dollars) at Coca-Cola Company over the 31-year period 1975 through 2005.
a. Fit a third-order autoregressive model to the annual net operating revenues and test for the significance of the third-order autoregressive parameter. (Use $\alpha = 0.05$.)
b. If necessary, fit a second-order autoregressive model to the annual net operating revenues and test for the significance of the second-order autoregressive parameter. (Use $\alpha = 0.05$.)
c. If necessary, fit a first-order autoregressive model to the annual net operating revenues and test for the significance of the first-order autoregressive parameter. (Use $\alpha = 0.05$.)

d. If appropriate, forecast net operating revenues for 2006 and 2007.

16.29 Refer to the data given in Problem 16.17 on page 665 that represent the closing values of the DJIA from 1979 to 2005 (stored in the file djia.xls).
a. Fit a third-order autoregressive model to the DJIA and test for the significance of the third-order autoregressive parameter. (Use $\alpha = 0.05$.)
b. If necessary, fit a second-order autoregressive model to the DJIA and test for the significance of the second-order autoregressive parameter. (Use $\alpha = 0.05$.)
c. If necessary, fit a first-order autoregressive model to the DJIA and test for the significance of the first-order autoregressive parameter. (Use $\alpha = 0.05$.)
d. If appropriate, forecast the DJIA for 2006 and 2007.

16.30 Refer to the data given in Problem 16.18 on page 665 (stored in the file GE.xls) that represent the stock prices for GE from 1987 through 2006.
a. Fit a third-order autoregressive model to the stock price and test for the significance of the third-order autoregressive parameter. (Use $\alpha = 0.05$.)
b. If necessary, fit a second-order autoregressive model to the stock price and test for the significance of the second-order autoregressive parameter. (Use $\alpha = 0.05$.)
c. If necessary, fit a first-order autoregressive model to the stock price and test for the significance of the first-order autoregressive parameter. (Use $\alpha = 0.05$.)
d. If appropriate, forecast the stock price for January 1, 2007.

16.31 Refer to the data given in Problem 16.22 on page 666 that represent the number of stores open for Bed Bath & Beyond over the 14-year period 1993 through 2006 (see the file bedbath.xls).
a. Fit a third-order autoregressive model to the number of stores and test for the significance of the third-order autoregressive parameter. (Use $\alpha = 0.05$.)
b. If necessary, fit a second-order autoregressive model to the number of stores and test for the significance of the second-order autoregressive parameter. (Use $\alpha = 0.05$.)
c. If necessary, fit a first-order autoregressive model to the number of stores and test for the significance of the first-order autoregressive parameter. (Use $\alpha = 0.05$.)
d. If appropriate, forecast the number of stores open in 2007 and 2008.

16.6 CHOOSING AN APPROPRIATE FORECASTING MODEL

In Sections 16.4 and 16.5, you studied six time-series forecasting methods: the linear trend model, the quadratic trend model, and the exponential trend model in Section 16.4; and the first-order, second-order, and pth-order autoregressive models in Section 16.5. Is there a *best* model? Among these models, which one should you select for forecasting? The following guidelines are provided for determining the adequacy of a particular forecasting model. These guidelines are based on a judgment of how well the model fits the past data of a given time series and assumes that future movements in the time series can be projected by a study of the past data:

- Perform a residual analysis.
- Measure the magnitude of the residual error through squared differences.
- Measure the magnitude of the residual error through absolute differences.
- Use the principle of parsimony.

A discussion of these guidelines follows.

Performing a Residual Analysis

Recall from Sections 13.5 and 14.3 that residuals are the differences between the observed and predicted values. After fitting a particular model to a time series, you plot the residuals over the n time periods. As shown in Panel A of Figure 16.19, if the particular model fits adequately, the residuals represent the irregular component of the time series. Therefore, they should be randomly distributed throughout the series. However, as illustrated in the three remaining panels of Figure 16.19, if the particular model does not fit adequately, the residuals may show a systematic pattern, such as a failure to account for trend (Panel B), a failure to account for cyclical variation (Panel C), or, with monthly or quarterly data, a failure to account for seasonal variation (Panel D).

FIGURE 16.19

Residual analysis for studying error patterns

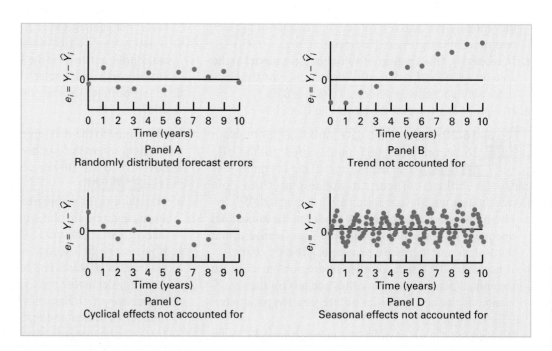

Panel A
Randomly distributed forecast errors

Panel B
Trend not accounted for

Panel C
Cyclical effects not accounted for

Panel D
Seasonal effects not accounted for

Measuring the Magnitude of the Residual Error Through Squared or Absolute Differences

If, after performing a residual analysis, you still believe that two or more models appear to fit the data adequately, you can use additional methods for model selection. Numerous measures based on the residual error are available (see references 1 and 4). However, there is no consensus among statisticians as to which particular measure is best for determining the most appropriate forecasting model.

Based on the principle of least squares, one measure that you have already used in regression analysis (see Section 13.3) is the standard error of the estimate (S_{YX}). For a particular model, this measure is based on the sum of squared differences between the actual and predicted values in a time series. If a model fits the time-series data perfectly, then the standard error of the estimate is zero. If a model fits the time-series data poorly, then S_{YX} is large. Thus, when comparing the adequacy of two or more forecasting models, you can select the model with the minimum S_{YX} as most appropriate.

However, a major drawback to using S_{YX} when comparing forecasting models is that it penalizes a model too much for a large individual forecasting error. Thus, whenever there is a large difference between even a single Y_i and $\hat{Y}_i$, the value of S_{YX} becomes magnified through the squaring process. For this reason, many statisticians prefer the **mean absolute deviation (MAD)**. Equation (16.16) defines the MAD as the mean of the absolute differences between the actual and predicted values in a time series.

MEAN ABSOLUTE DEVIATION

$$MAD = \frac{\sum_{i=1}^{n} | Y_i - \hat{Y}_i |}{n} \qquad (16.16)$$

If a model fits the time-series data perfectly, the MAD is zero. If a model fits the time-series data poorly, the MAD is large. When comparing two or more forecasting models, you can select the one with the minimum MAD as the most appropriate model.

The Principle of Parsimony

If, after performing a residual analysis and comparing the S_{YX} and MAD measures, you still believe that two or more models appear to adequately fit the data, then you can use the principle of parsimony for model selection.

The principle of **parsimony** is the belief that you should select the simplest model that gets the job done adequately.

Among the six forecasting models studied in this chapter, the least-squares linear and quadratic models and the first-order autoregressive model are regarded by most statisticians as the simplest. The second- and pth-order autoregressive models and the least-squares exponential model are considered more complex.

A Comparison of Four Forecasting Methods

Consider once again the Wm. Wrigley Jr. Company's real gross revenues data. To illustrate the model selection process, you can compare four of the forecasting models used in Sections 16.4 and 16.5: the linear model, the quadratic model, the exponential model, and the first-order autoregressive model. (There is no need to further study the second-order or third-order autoregressive model for this time series because these models did not significantly improve the fit over the simpler first-order autoregressive model.)

Figure 16.20 displays the residual plots for the four models. In drawing conclusions from these residual plots, you must use caution because there are only 22 values.

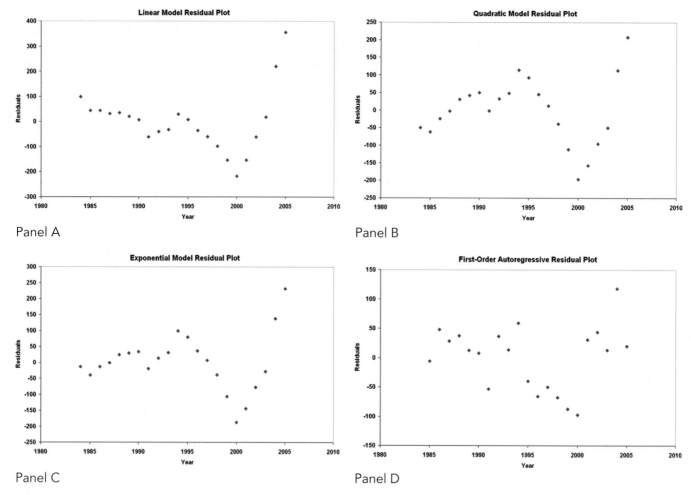

Panel A

Panel B

Panel C

Panel D

FIGURE 16.20 Microsoft Excel residual plots for four forecasting methods

See the Section E16.12 instructions to prepare the residual data. Then, see Section E2.12 to create these plots.

In Figure 16.20, observe the systematic structure of the residuals in the linear model (Panel A), quadratic model (Panel B), and exponential model (Panel C). For the autoregressive model (Panel D), the residuals appear more random.

To summarize, on the basis of the residual analysis of all four forecasting models, it appears that the first-order autoregressive model is the most appropriate, and the linear, quadratic, and exponential models are less appropriate. For further verification, you can compare the four models with respect to the magnitude of their residuals. Figure 16.21 shows the actual values (Y_i) along with the predicted values $(\hat{Y}_i)$, the residuals (e_i), the error sum of squares (SSE), the standard error of the estimate (S_{YX}), and the mean absolute deviation (MAD) for each of the four models.

For this time series, S_{YX} and MAD provide similar results. A comparison of the S_{YX} and MAD clearly indicates that the linear model provides the poorest fit. The first-order autoregressive model provides the best fit. Considering the results of the residual analysis and S_{YX} and MAD, the choice for the best model is the first-order autoregressive model.

After you select a particular forecasting model, you need to continually monitor your forecasts. If large errors occur between forecasted and actual values, the underlying structure of the time series may have changed. Remember that the forecasting methods presented in this chapter assume that the patterns inherent in the past will continue into the future. Large forecast errors are an indication that an assumption is no longer true.

FIGURE 16.21

Comparison of four forecasting methods, using S_{YX} and MAD

See Section E16.12 to create this.

	A	B	C D	E	F G	H	I J	K	L M	N
1			Linear		Quadratic		Exponential		Autoreg: First-Order	
2	Year	Actual	Predicted	Residual	Predicted	Residual	Predicted	Residual	Predicted	Residual
3	1984	569	469.916	98.900	618.321	-49.505	581.734	-12.734	#N/A	#N/A
4	1985	576	532.023	44.186	638.026	-61.818	615.438	-39.438	582.155	-6.155
5	1986	638	594.129	43.644	661.972	-24.198	651.095	-13.095	590.003	47.997
6	1987	688	656.236	31.264	690.157	-2.657	688.817	-0.817	659.513	28.487
7	1988	753	718.343	34.827	722.583	30.587	728.725	24.275	715.570	37.430
8	1989	801	780.450	20.357	759.249	41.557	770.945	30.055	788.444	12.556
9	1990	850	842.557	7.482	800.155	49.883	815.612	34.388	842.258	7.742
10	1991	844	904.663	-61.051	845.301	-1.689	862.866	-18.866	897.194	-53.194
11	1992	927	966.770	-39.471	894.688	32.611	912.858	14.142	890.467	36.533
12	1993	997	1028.877	-32.337	948.314	48.226	965.746	31.254	983.521	13.479
13	1994	1121	1090.984	29.799	1006.181	114.602	1021.698	99.302	1062.000	59.000
14	1995	1161	1153.090	8.327	1068.287	93.130	1080.892	80.108	1201.021	-40.021
15	1996	1180	1215.197	-35.465	1134.634	45.098	1143.516	36.484	1245.866	-65.866
16	1997	1217	1277.304	-59.859	1205.221	12.224	1209.768	7.232	1267.168	-50.168
17	1998	1241	1339.411	-98.306	1280.049	-38.944	1279.859	-38.859	1308.650	-67.650
18	1999	1248	1401.518	-153.618	1359.116	-111.217	1354.010	-106.010	1335.557	-87.557
19	2000	1246	1463.624	-217.399	1442.424	-196.198	1432.457	-186.457	1343.405	-97.405
20	2001	1372	1525.731	-153.625	1529.971	-157.865	1515.449	-143.449	1341.163	30.837
21	2002	1526	1587.838	-61.434	1621.759	-95.356	1603.250	-77.250	1482.425	43.575
22	2003	1668	1649.945	17.990	1717.787	-49.852	1696.138	-28.138	1655.080	12.920
23	2004	1932	1712.051	219.949	1818.055	113.945	1794.407	137.593	1814.281	117.719
24	2005	2130	1774.158	355.842	1922.564	207.436	1898.369	231.631	2110.260	19.740
25			SSE:	311652.481	SSE:	184290.139	SSE:	171194.826	SSE:	60049.847
26			S_{YX}:	124.830	S_{YX}:	98.486	S_{YX}:	92.519	S_{YX}:	56.218
27			MAD:	82.961	MAD:	71.755	MAD:	63.253	MAD:	44.573

PROBLEMS FOR SECTION 16.6

Learning the Basics

PH Grade ASSIST **16.32** The following residuals are from a linear trend model used to forecast sales:

2.0 -0.5 1.5 1.0 0.0 1.0 -3.0 1.5 -4.5 2.0 0.0 -1.0

a. Compute S_{YX} and interpret your findings.
b. Compute the MAD and interpret your findings.

PH Grade ASSIST **16.33** Refer to Problem 16.32. Suppose the first residual is 12.0 (instead of 2.0) and the last value is −11.0 (instead of −1.0).
a. Compute S_{YX} and interpret your findings
b. Compute the MAD and interpret your findings.

Applying the Concepts

16.34 Refer to the results in Problem 16.13 on page 664 (see the file).
a. Perform a residual analysis.
b. Compute the standard error of the estimate (S_{YX}).
c. Compute the MAD.
d. On the basis of (a) through (c), are you satisfied with your linear trend forecasts in Problem 16.13? Discuss.

16.35 Refer to the results in Problem 16.15 on page 665 and Problem 16.27 on page 675 concerning the number of barrels of oil in the U.S. strategic oil reserve (see the file).
a. Perform a residual analysis for each model.
b. Compute the standard error of the estimate (S_{YX}) for each model.

c. Compute the MAD for each model.
d. On the basis of (a) through (c) and the principle of parsimony, which forecasting model would you select? Discuss.

SELF Test **16.36** Refer to the results in Problem 16.16 on page 665 and Problem 16.28 on page 675 concerning annual net operating revenues at Coca-Cola (see the file).
a. Perform a residual analysis for each model.
b. Compute the standard error of the estimate (S_{YX}) for each model.
c. Compute the MAD for each model.
d. On the basis of (a) through (c) and the principle of parsimony, which forecasting model would you select? Discuss.

16.37 Refer to the results in Problem 16.17 on page 665 and Problem 16.29 on page 675 concerning the DJIA (see the file djia.xls).
a. Perform a residual analysis for each model.
b. Compute the standard error of the estimate (S_{YX}) for each model.
c. Compute the MAD for each model.
d. On the basis of (a) through (c) and the principle of parsimony, which forecasting model would you select? Discuss.

16.38 Refer to the results in Problem 16.18 on page 665 and Problem 16.30 on page 675 concerning the price per share for GE stock (see the file GE.xls).
a. Perform a residual analysis for each model.

b. Compute the standard error of the estimate (S_{YX}) for each model.

c. Compute the *MAD* for each model.

d. On the basis of (a) through (c) and the principle of parsimony, which forecasting model would you select? Discuss.

16.39 Refer to the results in Problem 16.22 on page 666 and Problem 16.31 on page 675 concerning the number

of Bed Bath & Beyond stores open (see the data file bedbath.xls).

a. Perform a residual analysis for each model.

b. Compute the standard error of the estimate (S_{YX}) for each model.

c. Compute the *MAD* for each model.

d. On the basis of (a) through (c) and the principle of parsimony, which forecasting model would you select? Discuss.

16.7 TIME-SERIES FORECASTING OF SEASONAL DATA

So far, this chapter has focused on forecasting annual data. However, numerous time series are collected quarterly or monthly, and others are collected weekly, daily, and even hourly. When a time series is collected quarterly or monthly, you must consider the impact of seasonal effects (see Table 16.1 on page 648). In this section, regression model building is used to forecast monthly or quarterly data.

One of the companies of interest in the Using Statistics scenario is Wal-Mart Stores, Inc. In 2006, Wal-Mart operated more than 6,500 Wal-Marts, Supercenters, Sam's Clubs, and Neighborhood Markets. Revenues in 2006 exceeded $312 billion (Wal-Mart Stores, Inc., **investor.walmartstores.com**). Sales for Wal-Mart are highly seasonal, and therefore you need to analyze quarterly revenue. The fiscal year for the company ends on January 31. Thus, the fourth quarter of 2006 includes November and December of 2005 and January of 2006. Table 16.4 lists the quarterly revenues, in billions of dollars, from 2000 to 2006 (see the file walmart.xls). Figure 16.22 displays the time series.

TABLE 16.4

Quarterly Revenues for Wal-Mart Stores, Inc., in Billions of Dollars (2000–2006)

Quarter	2000	2001	2002	2003	2004	2005	2006
1	34.7	43.0	48.6	55.0	56.7	64.8	71.6
2	38.2	46.1	53.3	59.7	62.6	69.7	76.8
3	40.4	45.7	51.8	58.8	62.4	68.5	75.4
4	51.4	56.6	64.2	71.1	74.5	82.2	88.6

Source: Extracted from Wal-Mart Stores, Inc., **investor.walmartstores.com**.

FIGURE 16.22

Microsoft Excel plot of quarterly revenues for Wal-Mart Stores, Inc., in billions of dollars (2000–2006)

See Section E16.13 to create this.

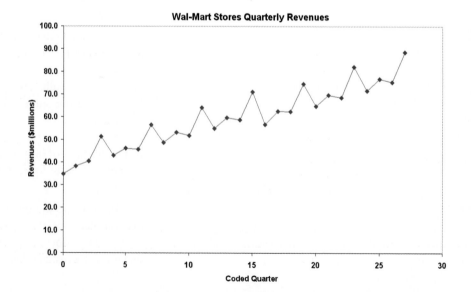

Least-Squares Forecasting with Monthly or Quarterly Data

To develop a least-squares regression model that includes trend, seasonal, cyclical, and irregular components, the approach to least-squares trend fitting in Section 16.4 is combined with the approach to model building using dummy variables (see Section 14.6) to model the seasonal component.

Equation (16.17) defines the exponential trend model for quarterly data.

EXPONENTIAL MODEL WITH QUARTERLY DATA

$$Y_i = \beta_0 \beta_1^{X_i} \beta_2^{Q_1} \beta_3^{Q_2} \beta_4^{Q_3} \varepsilon_i \qquad (16.17)$$

where

X_i = coded quarterly value, $i = 0, 1, 2, \ldots$

Q_1 = 1 if first quarter, 0 if not first quarter

Q_2 = 1 if second quarter, 0 if not second quarter

Q_3 = 1 if third quarter, 0 if not third quarter

β_0 = Y intercept

$(\beta_1 - 1) \times 100\%$ = quarterly compound growth rate (in %)

β_2 = multiplier for first quarter relative to fourth quarter

β_3 = multiplier for second quarter relative to fourth quarter

β_4 = multiplier for third quarter relative to fourth quarter

ε_i = value of the irregular component for time period i

5Alternatively, you can use base e logarithms. For more information on logarithms, see Appendix A.

The model in Equation (16.17) is not in the form of a linear regression model. To transform this nonlinear model to a linear model, you use a base 10 logarithmic transformation.[5] Taking the logarithm of each side of Equation (16.17) results in Equation (16.18).

TRANSFORMED EXPONENTIAL MODEL WITH QUARTERLY DATA

$$\log(Y_i) = \log(\beta_0 \beta_1^{X_i} \beta_2^{Q_1} \beta_3^{Q_2} \beta_4^{Q_3} \varepsilon_i)$$

$$= \log(\beta_0) + \log(\beta_1^{X_i}) + \log(\beta_2^{Q_1}) + \log(\beta_3^{Q_2}) + \log(\beta_4^{Q_3}) + \log(\varepsilon_i)$$

$$= \log(\beta_0) + X_i \log(\beta_1) + Q_1 \log(\beta_2) + Q_2 \log(\beta_3) + Q_3 \log(\beta_4) + \log(\varepsilon_i) \qquad (16.18)$$

Equation (16.18) is a linear model that you can estimate using least-squares regression. Performing the regression analysis using $\log(Y_i)$ as the dependent variable and X_i, Q_1, Q_2, and Q_3 as the independent variables results in Equation (16.19).

EXPONENTIAL GROWTH WITH QUARTERLY DATA FORECASTING EQUATION

$$\log(\hat{Y}_i) = b_0 + b_1 X_i + b_2 Q_1 + b_3 Q_2 + b_4 Q_3 \qquad (16.19)$$

where

b_0 = estimate of $\log(\beta_0)$ and thus $10^{b_0} = \hat{\beta}_0$

b_1 = estimate of $\log(\beta_1)$ and thus $10^{b_1} = \hat{\beta}_1$

b_2 = estimate of $\log(\beta_2)$ and thus $10^{b_2} = \hat{\beta}_2$

b_3 = estimate of $\log(\beta_3)$ and thus $10^{b_3} = \hat{\beta}_3$

b_4 = estimate of $\log(\beta_4)$ and thus $10^{b_4} = \hat{\beta}_4$

Equation (16.20) is used for monthly data.

EXPONENTIAL MODEL WITH MONTHLY DATA

$$Y_i = \beta_0 \beta_1^{X_i} \beta_2^{M_1} \beta_3^{M_2} \beta_4^{M_3} \beta_5^{M_4} \beta_6^{M_5} \beta_7^{M_6} \beta_8^{M_7} \beta_9^{M_8} \beta_{10}^{M_9} \beta_{11}^{M_{10}} \beta_{12}^{M_{11}} \varepsilon_i \quad \textbf{(16.20)}$$

where

$$X_i = \text{coded monthly value, } i = 0, 1, 2, \ldots$$

$$M_1 = 1 \text{ if January, 0 if not January}$$

$$M_2 = 1 \text{ if February, 0 if not February}$$

$$M_3 = 1 \text{ if March, 0 if not March}$$

$$\vdots$$

$$M_{11} = 1 \text{ if November, 0 if not November}$$

$$\beta_0 = Y \text{ intercept}$$

$$(\beta_1 - 1) \times 100\% = \text{monthly compound growth rate (in \%)}$$

$$\beta_2 = \text{multiplier for January relative to December}$$

$$\beta_3 = \text{multiplier for February relative to December}$$

$$\beta_4 = \text{multiplier for March relative to December}$$

$$\vdots$$

$$\beta_{12} = \text{multiplier for November relative to December}$$

$$\varepsilon_i = \text{value of the irregular component for time period } i$$

The model in Equation (16.20) is not in the form of a linear regression model. To transform this nonlinear model to a linear model, you can use a base 10 logarithm transformation. Taking the logarithm of each side of Equation (16.20) results in Equation (16.21).

TRANSFORMED EXPONENTIAL MODEL WITH MONTHLY DATA

$$\log(Y_i) = \log(\beta_0 \beta_1^{X_i} \beta_2^{M_1} \beta_3^{M_2} \beta_4^{M_3} \beta_5^{M_4} \beta_6^{M_5} \beta_7^{M_6} \beta_8^{M_7} \beta_9^{M_8} \beta_{10}^{M_9} \beta_{11}^{M_{10}} \beta_{12}^{M_{11}} \varepsilon_i)$$

$$= \log(\beta_0) + X_i \log(\beta_1) + M_1 \log(\beta_2) + M_2 \log(\beta_3)$$

$$+ M_3 \log(\beta_4) + M_4 \log(\beta_5) + M_5 \log(\beta_6) + M_6 \log(\beta_7)$$

$$+ M_7 \log(\beta_8) + M_8 \log(\beta_9) + M_9 \log(\beta_{10}) + M_{10} \log(\beta_{11})$$

$$+ M_{11} \log(\beta_{12}) + \log(\varepsilon_i) \quad \textbf{(16.21)}$$

Equation (16.21) is a linear model that you can estimate using the least-squares method. Performing the regression analysis using $\log(Y_i)$ as the dependent variable and $X_i, M_1, M_2, \ldots,$ and M_{11} as the independent variables results in Equation (16.22).

EXPONENTIAL GROWTH WITH MONTHLY DATA FORECASTING EQUATION

$$\log(\hat{Y}_i) = b_0 + b_1 X_i + b_2 M_1 + b_3 M_2 + b_4 M_3 + b_5 M_4 + b_6 M_5 + b_7 M_6$$
$$+ b_8 M_7 + b_9 M_8 + b_{10} M_9 + b_{11} M_{10} + b_{12} M_{11} \qquad \textbf{(16.22)}$$

where

$$b_0 = \text{estimate of } \log(\beta_0) \text{ and thus } 10^{b_0} = \hat{\beta}_0$$
$$b_1 = \text{estimate of } \log(\beta_1) \text{ and thus } 10^{b_1} = \hat{\beta}_1$$
$$b_2 = \text{estimate of } \log(\beta_2) \text{ and thus } 10^{b_2} = \hat{\beta}_2$$
$$b_3 = \text{estimate of } \log(\beta_3) \text{ and thus } 10^{b_3} = \hat{\beta}_3$$

$$\vdots$$

$$b_{12} = \text{estimate of } \log(\beta_{12}) \text{ and thus } 10^{b_{12}} = \hat{\beta}_{12}$$

Q_1, Q_2, and Q_3 are the three dummy variables needed to represent the four quarter periods in a quarterly time series. M_1, M_2, M_3, . . . , M_{11} are the 11 dummy variables needed to represent the 12 months in a monthly time series. In building the model, you use $\log(Y_i)$ instead of Y_i values and then find the regression coefficients by taking the antilog of the regression coefficients developed from Equations (16.19) and (16.22).

Although at first glance these regression models look imposing, when fitting or forecasting in any one time period, the values of all or all but one of the dummy variables in the model are set equal to zero, and the equations simplify dramatically. In establishing the dummy variables for quarterly time-series data, the fourth quarter is the base period and has a coded value of zero for each dummy variable. With a quarterly time series, Equation (16.19) reduces as follows:

For any first quarter:	$\log(\hat{Y}_i) = b_0 + b_1 X_i + b_2$
For any second quarter:	$\log(\hat{Y}_i) = b_0 + b_1 X_i + b_3$
For any third quarter:	$\log(\hat{Y}_i) = b_0 + b_1 X_i + b_4$
For any fourth quarter:	$\log(\hat{Y}_i) = b_0 + b_1 X_i$

When establishing the dummy variables for each month, December serves as the base period and has a coded value of zero for each dummy variable. For example, with a monthly time series, Equation (16.22) reduces as follows:

For any January:	$\log(\hat{Y}_i) = b_0 + b_1 X_i + b_2$
For any February:	$\log(\hat{Y}_i) = b_0 + b_1 X_i + b_3$
For any November:	$\log(\hat{Y}_i) = b_0 + b_1 X_i + b_{12}$
For any December:	$\log(\hat{Y}_i) = b_0 + b_1 X_i$

To demonstrate the process of model building and least-squares forecasting with a quarterly time series, return to the Wal-Mart revenue data (in billions of dollars) originally displayed in Table 16.4 on page 680. The data are from each quarter from the first quarter of 2000 through the last quarter of 2006. Microsoft Excel results for the quarterly exponential trend model are displayed in Figure 16.23.

FIGURE 16.23

Microsoft Excel results for fitting and forecasting with the quarterly Wal-Mart revenue data

See Section E14.1 to create this.

	A	B	C	D	E	F	G
1	Regression Analysis of Quarterly Revenue for Wal-Mart Stores 2000 - 2006						
2							
3	*Regression Statistics*						
4	Multiple R	0.9881					
5	R Square	0.9763					
6	Adjusted R Square	0.9722					
7	Standard Error	0.0172					
8	Observations	28					
9							
10	ANOVA						
11			df	SS	MS	F	Significance F
12	Regression		4	0.2820	0.0705	236.8992	2.4904E-18
13	Residual		23	0.0068	0.0003		
14	Total		27	0.2888			
15							
16		Coefficients	Standard Error	t Stat	P-value	Lower 95%	Upper 95%
17	Intercept	1.6677	0.0089	186.6163	4.3775E-38	1.6493	1.6862
18	Coded Quarter	0.0113	0.0004	27.6592	3.7316E-19	0.0104	0.0121
19	Q1	-0.0857	0.0093	-9.2171	3.4782E-09	-0.1050	-0.0665
20	Q2	-0.0609	0.0093	-6.5782	1.0343E-06	-0.0800	-0.0417
21	Q3	-0.0744	0.0092	-8.0567	3.7990E-08	-0.0934	-0.0553

From Figure 16.23, the model fits the data extremely well. The coefficient of determination $r^2 = 0.9763$ and the adjusted $r^2 = 0.9722$, and the overall F test results in an F statistic of 236.8992 (p-value = 0.000). Looking further, at the 0.05 level of significance, each regression coefficient is highly statistically significant and contributes to the classical multiplicative time-series model. Taking the antilogs of all the regression coefficients, you have the following summary:

Regression Coefficient	$b_i = \log \hat{\beta}_i$	$\hat{\beta}_i = \text{antilog}(b_i) = 10^{b_i}$
b_0: Y intercept	1.6677	46.52646
b_1: coded quarter	0.0113	1.02636
b_2: first quarter	−0.0857	0.82092
b_3: second quarter	−0.0609	0.86916
b_4: third quarter	−0.0744	0.84256

The interpretations for $\hat{\beta}_0$, $\hat{\beta}_1$, $\hat{\beta}_2$, $\hat{\beta}_3$, and $\hat{\beta}_4$ are as follows:

- The Y intercept, $\hat{\beta}_0 = 46.52646$ (in billions of dollars), is the *unadjusted* forecast for quarterly revenues in the first quarter of 2000, the initial quarter in the time series. *Unadjusted* means that the seasonal component is not incorporated in the forecast.
- The value $(\hat{\beta}_1 - 1) \times 100\% = 0.02636$, or 2.636%, is the estimated *quarterly compound growth rate* in revenues, after adjusting for the seasonal component.
- $\hat{\beta}_2 = 0.82092$ is the seasonal multiplier for the first quarter relative to the fourth quarter; it indicates that there is 17.908% less revenue for the first quarter as compared with the fourth quarter.
- $\hat{\beta}_3 = 0.86916$ is the seasonal multiplier for the second quarter relative to the fourth quarter; it indicates that there is 13.084% less revenue for the second quarter as compared with the fourth quarter.
- $\hat{\beta}_4 = 0.84256$ is the seasonal multiplier for the third quarter relative to the fourth quarter; it indicates that there is 15.744% less revenue for the third quarter than the fourth quarter. Thus, the fourth quarter, which includes the holiday shopping season, has the strongest sales.

Using the regression coefficients b_0, b_1, b_2, b_3, b_4, and Equation (16.19) on page 681, you can make forecasts for selected quarters. As an example, to predict revenues for the fourth quarter of 2006 ($X_i = 27$):

$$\log(\hat{Y}_i) = b_0 + b_1 X_i$$
$$= 1.6677 + (0.0113)(27)$$
$$= 1.9728$$

Thus,

$$\hat{Y}_i = 10^{1.9728} = 93.929$$

The predicted revenue for the fourth quarter of fiscal 2006 is \$93.929 billion. Observe that this forecast for the fourth quarter of fiscal 2006 differs markedly from the actual revenues of \$88.6 billion. Special economic circumstances may have affected these sales during the 2005 holiday season.

To make a forecast for a future time period, such as the first quarter of fiscal 2007 ($X_i = 28$, $Q_1 = 1$):

$$\log(\hat{Y}_i) = b_0 + b_1 X_i + b_2 Q_1$$
$$= 1.6677 + (0.0113)(28) + (-0.0857)(1)$$
$$= 1.8984$$

Thus,

$$\hat{Y}_i = 10^{1.8984} = 79.1407$$

The predicted revenue for the first quarter of fiscal 2007 is \$79.1407 billion.

PROBLEMS FOR SECTION 16.7

Learning the Basics

 16.40 In forecasting a monthly time series over a five-year period from January 2002 to December 2006, the exponential trend forecasting equation for January is

$$\log \hat{Y}_i = 2.0 + 0.01 X_i + 0.10 \text{ January}$$

Take the antilog of the appropriate coefficient from this equation and interpret the
a. Y intercept, $\hat{\beta}_0$.
b. monthly compound growth rate.
c. January multiplier.

16.41 In forecasting weekly time-series data, how many dummy variables are needed to account for the seasonal categorical variable week?

 16.42 In forecasting a quarterly time series over the five-year period from the first quarter of 2002 through the fourth quarter of 2006, the exponential trend forecasting equation is given by

$$\log \hat{Y}_i = 3.0 + 0.10 X_i - 0.25 Q_1 + 0.20 Q_2 + 0.15 Q_3$$

where quarter zero is first quarter of 2002. Take the antilog of the appropriate coefficient from this equation and interpret the
a. Y intercept, $\hat{\beta}_0$.
b. quarterly compound growth rate.
c. second-quarter multiplier.

 16.43 Refer to the exponential model given in Problem 16.42.
a. What is the fitted value of the series in the fourth quarter of 2004?
b. What is the fitted value of the series in the first quarter of 2005?
c. What is the forecast in the fourth quarter of 2007?
d. What is the forecast in the first quarter of 2008?

Applying the Concepts

16.44 The data given in the following table represent the S&P Composite Stock Price Index recorded at the end of each quarter from 1994 through 2005 (see the file **S&Pstkin.xls**).

| Quarter | Year | | | | | |
	1994	1995	1996	1997	1998	1999
1	445.77	500.71	645.50	757.12	1,101.75	1,286.37
2	444.27	544.75	670.63	885.14	1,133.84	1,372.71
3	462.69	584.41	687.31	947.28	1,017.01	1,282.71
4	459.27	615.93	740.74	970.43	1,229.23	1,469.25

| Quarter | Year | | | | | |
	2000	2001	2002	2003	2004	2005
1	1,498.58	1,160.33	1,147.38	848.18	1,126.21	1,180.95
2	1,454.60	1,224.38	989.81	974.51	1,140.81	1,191.33
3	1,436.51	1,040.94	815.28	995.97	1,114.58	1,228.81
4	1,320.28	1,148.08	879.28	1,111.92	1,211.92	1,248.29

Source: Extracted from **www.yahoo.com**.

a. Plot the data.

b. Develop an exponential trend forecasting equation with quarterly components.

c. What is the fitted value in the third quarter of 2005?

d. What is the fitted value in the fourth quarter of 2005?

e. What are the forecasts for all four quarters of 2006?

f. Interpret the quarterly compound growth rate.

g. Interpret the second-quarter multiplier.

16.45 Are gasoline prices higher during the height of the summer vacation season? The following table contains the mean monthly prices (in dollars per gallon) for unleaded gasoline in the United States from 2000 to 2005 (stored in the file `unleaded.xls`):

| | Year | | | | | |
Month	2000	2001	2002	2003	2004	2005
January	1.301	1.472	1.139	1.473	1.592	1.823
February	1.369	1.484	1.130	1.641	1.672	1.918
March	1.541	1.447	1.241	1.748	1.766	2.065
April	1.506	1.564	1.407	1.659	1.833	2.283
May	1.498	1.729	1.421	1.542	2.009	2.216
June	1.617	1.640	1.404	1.514	2.041	2.176
July	1.593	1.482	1.412	1.524	1.939	2.316
August	1.510	1.427	1.423	1.628	1.898	2.506
September	1.582	1.531	1.422	1.728	1.891	2.927
October	1.559	1.362	1.449	1.603	2.029	2.785
November	1.555	1.263	1.448	1.535	2.010	2.343
December	1.489	1.131	1.394	1.494	1.882	2.186

Source: Bureau of Labor Statistics, U.S. Department of Labor, **www.bls.gov**.

a. Construct a time-series plot.

b. Develop an exponential trend forecasting equation for monthly data.

c. Interpret the monthly compound growth rate.

d. Interpret the monthly multipliers.

e. Write a short summary of your findings.

 16.46 The U.S. Bureau of Labor Statistics compiles data on a wide variety of workforce issues. The data in the file `unemploy.xls` gives the monthly seasonally adjusted civilian unemployment rates for the United States from 2000 through 2005.

Source: Bureau of Labor Statistics, U.S. Department of Labor, **www.bls.gov**.

a. Plot the time-series data.

b. Develop an exponential trend forecasting equation with monthly components.

c. What is the fitted value in December 2005?

d. What are the forecasts for all 12 months of 2006?

e. Interpret the monthly compound growth rate.

f. Interpret the July multiplier.

g. Go to your library or the Internet and locate the actual unemployment rate in 2006. Discuss.

16.47 The following data (stored in the file `credit.xls`) are monthly credit card charges (in millions of dollars) for a popular credit card issued by a large bank (the name of which is not disclosed, at its request):

| | Year | | |
Month	2001	2002	2003
January	31.9	39.4	45.0
February	27.0	36.2	39.6
March	31.3	40.5	
April	31.0	44.6	
May	39.4	46.8	
June	40.7	44.7	
July	42.3	52.2	
August	49.5	54.0	
September	45.0	48.8	
October	50.0	55.8	
November	50.9	58.7	
December	58.5	63.4	

a. Construct the time-series plot.

b. Describe the monthly pattern that is evident in the data.

c. In general, would you say that the overall dollar amounts charged on the bank's credit cards is increasing or decreasing? Explain.

d. Note that December 2002 charges were more than $63 million, but those for February 2003 were less than $40 million. Was February's total close to what you would have expected?

e. Develop an exponential trend forecasting equation with monthly components.

f. Interpret the monthly compound growth rate.

g. Interpret the January multiplier.

h. What is the predicted value for March 2003?

i. What is the predicted value for April 2003?

j. How can this type of time-series forecasting benefit the bank?

16.48 The data in the file `toys-rev.xls` are quarterly revenues (in millions of dollars) for Toys Я Us from 1996 through 2005.

Source: Extracted from Standard & Poor's Stock Reports, *November 1995, November 1998, and April 2002. New York: McGraw-Hill, Inc., and Toys Я Us, Inc.,* **www.toysrus.com**.

a. Do you think that the revenues for Toys Я Us are subject to seasonal variation? Explain.

b. Plot the data. Does this chart support your answer to (a)?

c. Develop an exponential trend forecasting equation with quarterly components.

d. Interpret the quarterly compound growth rate.

e. Interpret the quarter multipliers.

f. What are the forecasts for all four quarters of 2006?

16.49 The data in the file `ford-rev.xls` are quarterly revenues (in millions of dollars) for the Ford Motor Company, from 1996 through 2005.

Source: Standard & Poor's Stock Reports, *November 2000 and April 2002. New York: McGraw-Hill, Inc., and the Ford Motor Company,* **ford.com**.

a. Do you think that the revenues for the Ford Motor Company are subject to seasonal variation? Explain.

b. Plot the data. Does this chart support your answer to (a)?

c. Develop an exponential trend forecasting equation with quarterly components.

d. Interpret the quarterly compound growth rate.

e. Interpret the quarter multipliers.

f. What are the forecasts for all four quarters of 2006?

16.8 INDEX NUMBERS

This chapter has presented various methods for forecasting time-series data. In this section, index numbers are used to compare a value of a time series relative to another value of a time series. **Index numbers** measure the value of an item (or group of items) at a particular point in time, as a percentage of the value of an item (or group of items) at another point in time. They are commonly used in business and economics as indicators of changing business or economic activity. There are many kinds of index numbers, including price indexes, quantity indexes, value indexes, and sociological indexes. In this section, only the price index is considered. In addition to allowing comparison of prices at different points in time, price indexes are also used to deflate the effect of inflation on a time series in order to compare values in real dollars instead of actual dollars.

Price Indexes

A **price index** compares the price of a commodity in a given period of time to the price paid for that commodity at a particular point of time in the past. A **simple price index** tracks the price of a single commodity. An **aggregate price index** tracks the prices for a group of commodities (called a market basket) at a given period of time to the price paid for that group of commodities at a particular point of time in the past. The **base period** is the point of time in the past against which all comparisons are made. In selecting the base period for a particular index, if possible, you select a period of economic stability rather than one at or near the peak of an expanding economy or the bottom of a recession or declining economy. In addition, the base period should be relatively recent so that comparisons are not greatly affected by changing technology and consumer attitudes and habits. Equation (16.23) defines the simple price index.

SIMPLE PRICE INDEX

$$I_i = \frac{P_i}{P_{base}} \times 100 \tag{16.23}$$

where

$$I_i = \text{price index for year } i$$

$$P_i = \text{price for year } i$$

$$P_{base} = \text{price for the base year}$$

As an example of the simple price index, consider the price per gallon of unleaded gasoline in the United States from 1980 to 2005. Table 16.5 presents the prices plus two sets of index numbers (see the file gasoline.xls). To illustrate the computation of the simple price index for 2005, using 1980 as the base year, from Equation (16.23) and Table 16.5,

$$I_{2005} = \frac{P_{2005}}{P_{1980}} \times 100 = \frac{2.30}{1.25} \times 100 = 184.0$$

TABLE 16.5

Price per Gallon of Unleaded Gasoline in the United States and Simple Price Index, with 1980 and 1995 as the Base Years (1980–2005)

Year	Gasoline Price	Price Index, 1980	Price Index, 1995
1980	1.25	100.0	108.7
1981	1.38	110.4	120.0
1982	1.30	104.0	113.0
1983	1.24	99.2	107.8
1984	1.21	96.8	105.2
1985	1.20	96.0	104.3
1986	0.93	74.4	80.9
1987	0.95	76.0	82.6
1988	0.95	76.0	82.6
1989	1.02	81.6	88.7
1990	1.16	92.8	100.9
1991	1.14	91.2	99.1
1992	1.14	91.2	99.1
1993	1.11	88.8	96.5
1994	1.11	88.8	96.5
1995	1.15	92.0	100.0
1996	1.23	98.4	107.0
1997	1.23	98.4	107.0
1998	1.06	84.8	92.2
1999	1.17	93.6	101.7
2000	1.51	120.8	131.3
2001	1.46	116.8	127.0
2002	1.36	108.8	118.3
2003	1.59	127.2	138.3
2004	1.88	150.4	163.5
2005	2.30	184.0	200.0

Source: Bureau of Labor Statistics, U.S. Department of Labor, **www.bls.gov**.

Therefore, the price per gallon of unleaded gasoline in the United States in 2005 was 84.0% higher than in 1980. An examination of the price indexes for 1980 to 2005 in Table 16.5 indicates that the price of unleaded gasoline increased in 1981 and 1982 over the base year of 1980 but then was below the 1980 price every year until 2000. Because the base period for the index numbers in Table 16.5 is 1980, you should use a base year closer to the present. The price remained fairly constant from 1990 to 1995; thus, it is appropriate to use 1995 as a base year. Equation (16.24) is used to develop index numbers with a new base.

SHIFTING THE BASE FOR A SIMPLE PRICE INDEX

$$I_{new} = \frac{I_{old}}{I_{new\,base}} \times 100 \qquad\qquad \textbf{(16.24)}$$

where

$$I_{new} = \text{new price index}$$

$$I_{old} = \text{old price index}$$

$$I_{new\,base} = \text{value of the old price index for the new base year}$$

To change the base year to 1995, $I_{new\,base} = 92.0$. Using Equation (16.24) to find the new price index for 2005,

$$I_{new} = \frac{I_{old}}{I_{new\,base}} \times 100 = \frac{184.0}{92.0} \times 100 = 200.0$$

Thus, the 2005 price for unleaded gasoline in the United States was twice the price that it was in 1995. See Table 16.5 for the complete set of price indexes.

Aggregate Price Indexes

An aggregate price index consists of a group of commodities taken together. The group of commodities under consideration is often called a *market basket*. There are two types of aggregate price indexes: unweighted aggregate price indexes and weighted aggregate price indexes. An **unweighted aggregate price index**, defined in Equation (16.25), places equal weight on all the items in the market basket.

UNWEIGHTED AGGREGATE PRICE INDEX

$$I_U^{(t)} = \frac{\sum\limits_{i=1}^{n} P_i^{(t)}}{\sum\limits_{i=1}^{n} P_i^{(0)}} \times 100 \qquad\qquad (16.25)$$

where

$$t = \text{time period } (0, 1, 2, \ldots)$$

$$i = \text{item } (1, 2, \ldots, n)$$

$$n = \text{total number of items under consideration}$$

$$\sum\limits_{i=1}^{n} P_i^{(t)} = \text{sum of the prices paid for each of the } n \text{ commodities at time period } t$$

$$\sum\limits_{i=1}^{n} P_i^{(0)} = \text{sum of the prices paid for each of the } n \text{ commodities at time period } 0$$

$$I_U^{(t)} = \text{value of the unweighted price index at time period } t$$

Table 16.6 presents the mean prices for three fruit items for selected periods from 1980 to 2005 (stored in the file fruit.xls).

TABLE 16.6

Prices (in Dollars per Pound) for Three Fruit Items

Fruit	Year					
	1980 $P_i^{(0)}$	1985 $P_i^{(1)}$	1990 $P_i^{(2)}$	1995 $P_i^{(3)}$	2000 $P_i^{(4)}$	2005 $P_i^{(5)}$
Apples	0.692	0.684	0.719	0.835	0.927	0.966
Bananas	0.342	0.367	0.463	0.490	0.509	0.838
Oranges	0.365	0.533	0.570	0.625	0.638	0.490

Source: Bureau of Labor Statistics, U.S. Department of Labor, **www.bls.gov**.

To calculate the unweighted aggregate price index for the various years, using Equation (16.25) and 1980 as the base period:

$$1980: I_U^{(0)} = \frac{\sum_{i=1}^{3} P_i^{(0)}}{\sum_{i=1}^{3} P_i^{(0)}} \times 100 = \frac{0.692 + 0.342 + 0.365}{0.692 + 0.342 + 0.365} \times 100 = \frac{1.399}{1.399} \times 100 = 100.0$$

$$1985: I_U^{(1)} = \frac{\sum_{i=1}^{3} P_i^{(1)}}{\sum_{i=1}^{3} P_i^{(0)}} \times 100 = \frac{0.684 + 0.367 + 0.533}{0.692 + 0.342 + 0.365} \times 100 = \frac{1.584}{1.399} \times 100 = 113.2$$

$$1990: I_U^{(2)} = \frac{\sum_{i=1}^{3} P_i^{(2)}}{\sum_{i=1}^{3} P_i^{(0)}} \times 100 = \frac{0.719 + 0.463 + 0.570}{0.692 + 0.342 + 0.365} \times 100 = \frac{1.752}{1.399} \times 100 = 125.2$$

$$1995: I_U^{(3)} = \frac{\sum_{i=1}^{3} P_i^{(3)}}{\sum_{i=1}^{3} P_i^{(0)}} \times 100 = \frac{0.835 + 0.490 + 0.625}{0.692 + 0.342 + 0.365} \times 100 = \frac{1.950}{1.399} \times 100 = 139.4$$

$$2000: I_U^{(4)} = \frac{\sum_{i=1}^{3} P_i^{(4)}}{\sum_{i=1}^{3} P_i^{(0)}} \times 100 = \frac{0.927 + 0.509 + 0.638}{0.692 + 0.342 + 0.365} \times 100 = \frac{2.074}{1.399} \times 100 = 148.2$$

$$2005: I_U^{(5)} = \frac{\sum_{i=1}^{3} P_i^{(5)}}{\sum_{i=1}^{3} P_i^{(0)}} \times 100 = \frac{0.966 + 0.838 + 0.490}{0.692 + 0.342 + 0.365} \times 100 = \frac{2.294}{1.399} \times 100 = 164.0$$

Thus, in 2005, the combined price of a pound of apples, a pound of bananas, and a pound of oranges was 64% more than it was in 1980.

An unweighted aggregate price index represents the changes in prices, over time, for an entire group of commodities. However, an unweighted aggregate price index has two shortcomings. First, this index considers each commodity in the group as equally important. Thus, the most expensive commodities per unit are overly influential. Second, not all the commodities are consumed at the same rate. In an unweighted index, changes in the price of the least-consumed commodities are overly influential.

Weighted Aggregate Price Indexes

Due to the shortcomings of unweighted aggregate price indexes, weighted aggregate price indexes are generally preferable. **Weighted aggregate price indexes** account for differences in the magnitude of prices per unit and differences in the consumption levels of the items in the market basket. Two types of weighted aggregate price indexes are commonly used in business and economics: the Laspeyres price index and the Paasche price index. Equation (16.26) defines the **Laspeyres price index**, which uses the consumption quantities associated with the base year in the calculation of all price indexes in the series.

LASPEYRES PRICE INDEX

$$I_L^{(t)} = \frac{\sum_{i=1}^{n} P_i^{(t)} Q_i^{(0)}}{\sum_{i=1}^{n} P_i^{(0)} Q_i^{(0)}} \times 100 \qquad \textbf{(16.26)}$$

where

t = time period (0, 1, 2, . . .)
i = item (1, 2, . . . , n)
n = total number of items under consideration
$Q_i^{(0)}$ = quantity of item i at time period 0
$I_L^{(t)}$ = value of the Laspeyres price index at time t
$P_i^{(t)}$ = price paid for commodity i at time period t
$P_i^{(0)}$ = price paid for commodity i at time period 0

Table 16.7 gives the price and per capita consumption, in pounds, for the three fruit items comprising the market basket of interest (see the file **fruit.xls**).

TABLE 16.7
Prices (in Dollars per Pound) and Quantities (Annual per Capita Consumption, in Pounds) for Three Fruit Items*

	Year					
Fruit	**1980** $P_i^{(0)}, Q_i^{(0)}$	**1985** $P_i^{(1)}, Q_i^{(1)}$	**1990** $P_i^{(2)}, Q_i^{(2)}$	**1995** $P_i^{(3)}, Q_i^{(3)}$	**2000** $P_i^{(4)}, Q_i^{(4)}$	**2005** $P_i^{(5)}, Q_i^{(5)}$
Apples	0.692, 19.2	0.684, 17.3	0.719, 19.6	0.835, 18.9	0.927, 17.5	0.966, 16.0
Bananas	0.342, 20.2	0.367, 23.5	0.463, 24.4	0.490, 27.4	0.509, 28.5	0.838, 26.8
Oranges	0.365, 14.3	0.533, 11.6	0.570, 12.4	0.625, 12.0	0.638, 11.7	0.490, 10.6

Source: Bureau of Labor Statistics, U.S. Department of Labor, **www.bls.gov**, *and Statistical Abstract of the United States, U.S. Census Bureau,* **www.census.gov**.
**The 2005 consumption values are preliminary estimates. Actual values were not available at publication time.*

Using 1980 as the base year, you calculate the Laspeyres price index for 2005 ($t = 5$) using Equation (16.26):

$$I_L^{(5)} = \frac{\sum_{i=1}^{3} P_i^{(5)} Q_i^{(0)}}{\sum_{i=1}^{3} P_i^{(0)} Q_i^{(0)}} \times 100 = \frac{(0.966 \times 19.2) + (0.838 \times 20.2) + (0.490 \times 14.3)}{(0.692 \times 19.2) + (0.342 \times 20.2) + (0.365 \times 14.3)} \times 100$$

$$= \frac{42.4818}{25.4143} \times 100 = 167.2$$

Thus, the Laspeyres price index is 167.2, indicating that the cost of purchasing these three items in 2005 was 67.2% more than in 1980. This index is more than the unweighted index, 164.0, because the least-purchased item, oranges, decreased in price over the time span while apples and bananas increased in price. In other words, in the unweighted index, the least-consumed commodity (oranges) is overly influential.

The **Paasche price index** uses the consumption quantities in the year of interest instead of using the initial quantities. Thus, the Paasche index is a more accurate reflection of total consumption costs at that point in time. However, there are two major drawbacks of the Paasche index. First, accurate consumption values for current purchases are often hard to obtain. Thus, many important indexes, such as the CPI, use the Laspeyres method. Second, if a particular product increases greatly in price compared to the other items in the market basket, consumers will avoid the high-priced item out of necessity, not because of changes in what they might prefer to purchase. Equation (16.27) defines the Paasche price index.

PAASCHE PRICE INDEX

$$I_P^{(t)} = \frac{\sum_{i=1}^{n} P_i^{(t)} Q_i^{(t)}}{\sum_{i=1}^{n} P_i^{(0)} Q_i^{(t)}} \times 100 \qquad (16.27)$$

where

t = time period (0, 1, 2, . . .)

i = item (1, 2, . . . , n)

n = total number of items under consideration

$Q_i^{(t)}$ = quantity of item i at time period t

$I_P^{(t)}$ = value of the Paasche price index at time period t

$P_i^{(t)}$ = price paid for commodity i at time period t

$P_i^{(0)}$ = price paid for commodity i at time period 0

To calculate the Paasche price index in 2005, using 1980 as a base year, you use $t = 5$ in Equation (16.29):

$$I_P^{(5)} = \frac{\sum_{i=1}^{3} P_i^{(5)} Q_i^{(5)}}{\sum_{i=1}^{3} P_i^{(0)} Q_i^{(5)}} \times 100 = \frac{(0.966 \times 16.0) + (0.838 \times 26.8) + (0.490 \times 10.6)}{(0.692 \times 16.0) + (0.342 \times 26.8) + (0.365 \times 10.6)} \times 100$$

$$= \frac{43.1084}{24.1066} \times 100 = 178.8$$

The Paasche price index for this market basket is 178.8. Thus, the cost of these three fruit items in 2000 was 78.8% higher in 2005 than in 1980, when using 2005 quantities.

Some Common Price Indexes

Various price indexes are commonly used in business and economics. The CPI is the most familiar index in the United States. This index is officially referred to as the CPI-U to reflect that it measures the prices "urban" residents are subject to, but it is commonly referred to as the CPI. The CPI, published monthly by the U.S. Bureau of Labor Statistics, is the primary measure of changes in the cost of living in the United States. The CPI is a weighted aggregate price index, using the Laspeyres method, for 400 commonly purchased food, clothing, transportation, medical, and housing items. Currently computed using 1982–1984 averages as a base year, the CPI was 195.3 in 2005. (See data file **CPI-U.xls** for a listing of the CPI-U for 1965–2005.)

An important use of the CPI is as a price deflator. The CPI is used to convert (and deflate) actual dollars into real dollars by multiplying each dollar value in a time series by the quantity (100/CPI). For example, the gross revenues of the Wm. Wrigley Jr. Company were transformed from actual revenues to real gross revenues in Figure 16.5 on page 657. This transformation allowed you to see that the increase in revenues for Wrigley's were actually *real* increases, not simply increases that could be explained by an increase in the cost of living.

Another important price index published by the U.S. Bureau of Labor Statistics is the producer price index (PPI). The PPI is a weighted aggregate price index that also uses the Laspeyres method, for prices of commodities sold by wholesalers. The PPI is considered a leading indicator of the CPI. In other words, increases in the PPI tend to precede increases in the CPI, and, similarly, decreases in the PPI tend to precede decreases in the CPI.

Financial indexes such as the DJIA Index, the S&P 500 Index, and the NASDAQ Index are price indexes for different sets of stocks in the United States. Many indexes measure the performance of international stock markets, including the Nikkei Index for Japan, the Dax 30 for Germany, and the SSE Composite for China.

PROBLEMS FOR SECTION 16.8

Learning the Basics

16.50 The simple price index for a commodity in 2006, using 1995 as the base year, is 175. Interpret this index number.

16.51 The following are prices for a commodity from 2004 to 2006:

2004: $5
2005: $8
2006: $7

a. Calculate the simple price indexes for 2004–2006, using 2004 as the base year.
b. Calculate the simple price indexes for 2004–2006, using 2005 as the base year.

 16.52 The following are prices and consumption quantities for three commodities in 1995 and 2006:

| | Year | |
| | --- | --- |
Commodity	1995 Price, Quantity	2006 Price, Quantity
A	$2, 20	$3, 21
B	$18, 3	$36, 2
C	$3, 18	$4, 23

a. Calculate the unweighted aggregate price index for 2006, using 1995 as the base year.
b. Calculate the Laspeyres aggregate price index for 2006, using 1995 as the base year.
c. Calculate the Paasche aggregate price index for 2006, using 1995 as the base year.

Applying the Concepts

16.53 The data in the file **djia.xls** represent the closing values of the DJIA from 1979 to 2005.

a. Calculate the price index for the DJIA with 1979 as the base year.
b. Shift the base of the DJIA to 1990 and recalculate the price index.
c. Compare the results of (a) and (b). Which price index do you think is more useful in understanding the changes in the DJIA? Explain.

 16.54 The data in the file **coffeeprice.xls** represent the mean price per pound of coffee in the United States from 1980 to 2006.

Source: Bureau of Labor Statistics, U.S. Department of Labor, **www.bls.gov.**

a. Calculate the simple price indexes for 1980 to 2006, using 1980 as the base year.

b. Interpret the simple price index for 2006, using 1980 as the base year.

c. Recalculate the simple price indexes found in (a), using Equation (16.24) on page 688, with 1990 as the base year.

d. Interpret the simple price index for 2006, using 1990 as the base year.

e. Would it be a good idea to use 1995 as the base year? Explain.

f. Describe the trends in coffee costs from 1980 to 2006.

16.55 The following data represent the mean prices per pound of fresh tomatoes in the United States from 1980 to 2006 (see the file tomatoes.xls):

Year	Price	Year	Price	Year	Price
1980	0.703	1989	0.797	1998	1.452
1981	0.792	1990	1.735	1999	1.904
1982	0.763	1991	0.912	2000	1.443
1983	0.726	1992	0.936	2001	1.414
1984	0.854	1993	1.141	2002	1.451
1985	0.697	1994	1.604	2003	1.711
1986	1.104	1995	1.323	2004	1.472
1987	0.943	1996	1.103	2005	1.660
1988	0.871	1997	1.213	2006	2.162

Source: Bureau of Labor Statistics, U.S. Department of Labor, **www.bls.gov**.

a. Calculate the simple price indexes for 1980 to 2006, using 1980 as the base year.

b. Interpret the simple price index for 2006, using 1980 as the base year.

c. Recalculate the simple price indexes found in (a), using Equation (16.24) on page 688, with 1990 as the base year.

d. Interpret the simple price index for 2006, using 1990 as the base year.

e. Describe the trends in the cost of fresh tomatoes from 1980 to 2006.

16.56 The data in the file energy2.xls represent the mean price for three types of energy products in the United States from 1992 to 2006. Included are electricity (dollars per 500 KWH), natural gas (dollars per 40 therms), and fuel oil (dollars per gallon).

Source: Bureau of Labor Statistics, U.S. Department of Labor, **www.bls.gov**.

a. Calculate the 1992–2006 simple price indexes for electricity, natural gas, and fuel oil, using 1992 as the base year.

b. Recalculate the price indexes in (a), using 1996 as the base year.

c. Calculate the 1992–2006 unweighted aggregate price indexes for the group of three energy items.

d. Calculate the 2006 Laspeyres price index for the group of three energy items for a family that consumed 5,000 KWH of electricity (10 units), 960 therms of natural gas (24 units), and 400 gallons of fuel oil (400 units) in 1992.

e. Calculate the 2006 Laspeyres price index for the group of three energy items for a family that consumed 6,500 KWH of electricity, 1,040 therms of natural gas, and 235 gallons of fuel oil in 1992.

16.9 PITFALLS CONCERNING TIME-SERIES FORECASTING

The value of time-series forecasting methodology, which uses past and present information as guides to the future, was recognized and most eloquently expressed more than two centuries ago by the U.S. statesman Patrick Henry, who said:

> I have but one lamp by which my feet are guided, and that is the lamp of experience. I know no way of judging the future but by the past. [Speech at Virginia Convention (Richmond), March 23, 1775]

However, critics of time-series forecasting argue that these techniques are overly naive and mechanical. They argue that a mathematical model based on the past should not be used to mechanically extrapolate trends into the future without considering personal judgments, business experiences, or changing technologies, habits, and needs (see Problem 16.69 on page 698). Thus, in recent years, econometricians have developed highly sophisticated computerized models of economic activity, incorporating such factors for forecasting purposes. Such forecasting methods, however, are beyond the scope of this text (see references 1–3).

Nevertheless, as you have seen from the preceding sections of this chapter, time-series methods provide useful guides for projecting future trends (on long- and short-term bases). If used properly and in conjunction with other forecasting methods as well as with business judgment and experience, time-series methods will continue to be useful tools for forecasting.

SUMMARY

In this chapter, you used time-series methods to develop forecasts for the Wm. Wrigley Jr. Company, Cabot Corporation, and Wal-Mart. You studied smoothing techniques, least-squares trend fitting, autoregressive models, forecasting of seasonal data, and index numbers. Figure 16.24 provides a summary chart for the time-series and index number methods discussed in this chapter.

If you are using time-series forecasting, you need to ask the following question: Is there a trend in the data? If there is no trend, then you should use moving averages or exponential smoothing. If there is a trend, then you can use

the linear, quadratic, and exponential trend models and the autoregressive model.

If you are developing index numbers, you need to ask the following question: Are you developing an aggregate index of more than one commodity? If the answer is no, then you can use a simple price index. If the answer is yes, then you need to determine whether you will develop a weighted price index. If not, you can develop an unweighted price index. If you are developing a weighted price index, you can use a Laspeyres price index or a Paasche price index.

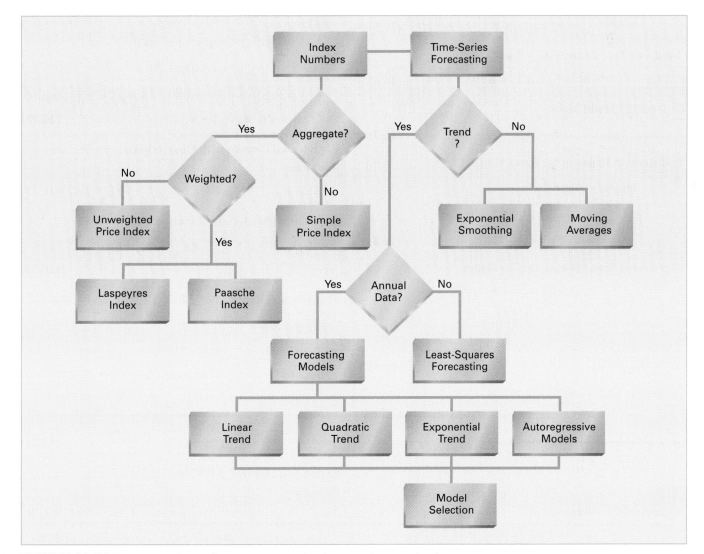

FIGURE 16.24 Summary chart of time series and index number methods

KEY EQUATIONS

Classical Multiplicative Time-Series Model for Annual Data

$$Y_i = T_i \times C_i \times I_i \qquad (16.1)$$

Classical Multiplicative Time-Series Model for Data with a Seasonal Component

$$Y_i = T_i \times S_i \times C_i \times I_i \qquad (16.2)$$

Computing an Exponentially Smoothed Value in Time Period i

$$E_1 = Y_1$$
$$E_i = WY_i + (1 - W)E_{i-1} \qquad i = 2, 3, 4, \ldots \quad (16.3)$$

Forecasting Time Period $i + 1$

$$\hat{Y}_{i+1} = E_i \qquad (16.4)$$

Linear Trend Forecasting Equation

$$\hat{Y}_i = b_0 + b_1 X_i \qquad (16.5)$$

Quadratic Trend Forecasting Equation

$$\hat{Y}_i = b_0 + b_1 X_i + b_2 X_i^2 \qquad (16.6)$$

Exponential Trend Model

$$Y_i = \beta_0 \beta_1^{X_i} \varepsilon_i \qquad (16.7)$$

Transformed Exponential Trend Model

$$\log(Y_i) = \log(\beta_0 \beta_1^{X_i} \varepsilon_i)$$
$$= \log(\beta_0) + \log(\beta_1^{X_i}) + \log(\varepsilon_i)$$
$$= \log(\beta_0) + X_i \log(\beta_1) + \log(\varepsilon_i) \quad (16.8)$$

Exponential Trend Forecasting Equation

$$\log(\hat{Y}_i) = b_0 + b_1 X_i \qquad (16.9a)$$
$$\hat{Y}_i = \hat{\beta}_0 \hat{\beta}_1^{X_i} \qquad (16.9b)$$

First-Order Autoregressive Model

$$Y_i = A_0 + A_1 Y_{i-1} + \delta_i \qquad (16.10)$$

Second-Order Autoregressive Model

$$Y_i = A_0 + A_1 Y_{i-1} + A_2 Y_{i-2} + \delta_i \qquad (16.11)$$

pth-Order Autoregressive Models

$$Y_i = A_0 + A_1 Y_{i-1} + A_2 Y_{i-2} + \cdots + A_p Y_{i-p} + \delta_i \quad (16.12)$$

t Test for Significance of the Highest-Order Autoregressive Parameter, A_p

$$t = \frac{a_p - A_p}{S_{a_p}} \qquad (16.13)$$

Fitted pth-Order Autoregressive Equation

$$\hat{Y}_i = a_0 + a_1 Y_{i-1} + a_2 Y_{i-2} + \cdots + a_p Y_{i-p} \quad (16.14)$$

pth-Order Autoregressive Forecasting Equation

$$\hat{Y}_{n+j} = a_0 + a_1 \hat{Y}_{n+j-1} + a_2 \hat{Y}_{n+j-2} + \cdots + a_p \hat{Y}_{n+j-p} \ (16.15)$$

Mean Absolute Deviation

$$MAD = \frac{\sum_{i=1}^{n} | Y_i - \hat{Y}_i |}{n} \qquad (16.16)$$

Exponential Model with Quarterly Data

$$Y_i = \beta_0 \beta_1^{X_i} \beta_2^{Q_1} \beta_3^{Q_2} \beta_4^{Q_3} \varepsilon_i \qquad (16.17)$$

Transformed Exponential Model with Quarterly Data

$$\log(Y_i) = \log(\beta_0 \beta_1^{X_i} \beta_2^{Q_1} \beta_3^{Q_2} \beta_4^{Q_3} \varepsilon_i)$$
$$= \log(\beta_0) + \log(\beta_1^{X_i}) + \log(\beta_2^{Q_1}) + \log(\beta_3^{Q_2})$$
$$+ \log(\beta_4^{Q_3}) + \log(\varepsilon_i)$$
$$= \log(\beta_0) + X_i \log(\beta_1) + Q_1 \log(\beta_2) + Q_2 \log(\beta_3)$$
$$+ Q_3 \log(\beta_4) + \log(\varepsilon_i) \qquad (16.18)$$

Exponential Growth with Quarterly Data Forecasting Equation

$$\log(\hat{Y}_i) = b_0 + b_1 X_i + b_2 Q_1 + b_3 Q_2 + b_4 Q_3 \ (16.19)$$

Exponential Model with Monthly Data

$$Y_i = \beta_0 \beta_1^{X_i} \beta_2^{M_1} \beta_3^{M_2} \beta_4^{M_3} \beta_5^{M_4} \beta_6^{M_5} \beta_7^{M_6} \beta_8^{M_7} \beta_9^{M_8} \beta_{10}^{M_9} \beta_{11}^{M_{10}} \beta_{12}^{M_{11}} \varepsilon_i$$
$$(16.20)$$

Transformed Exponential Model with Monthly Data

$$\log(Y_i) = \log(\beta_0 \beta_1^{X_i} \beta_2^{M_1} \beta_3^{M_2} \beta_4^{M_3} \beta_5^{M_4} \beta_6^{M_5} \beta_7^{M_6} \beta_8^{M_7} \beta_9^{M_8} \beta_{10}^{M_9} \beta_{11}^{M_{10}} \beta_{12}^{M_{11}} \varepsilon_i)$$
$$= \log(\beta_0) + X_i \log(\beta_1) + M_1 \log(\beta_2) + M_2 \log(\beta_3)$$
$$+ M_3 \log(\beta_4) + M_4 \log(\beta_5) + M_5 \log(\beta_6) + M_6 \log(\beta_7)$$
$$+ M_7 \log(\beta_8) + M_8 \log(\beta_9) + M_9 \log(\beta_{10}) + M_{10} \log(\beta_{11})$$
$$+ M_{11} \log(\beta_{12}) + \log(\varepsilon_i)$$
$$(16.21)$$

Exponential Growth with Monthly Data Forecasting Equation

$$\log(\hat{Y}_i) = b_0 + b_1 X_i + b_2 M_1 + b_3 M_2 + b_4 M_3 + b_5 M_4 + b_6 M_5$$
$$+ b_7 M_6 + b_8 M_7 + b_9 M_8 + b_{10} M_9 + b_{11} M_{10} + b_{12} M_{11}$$
$$(16.22)$$

Simple Price Index

$$I_i = \frac{P_i}{P_{base}} \times 100 \qquad \text{(16.23)}$$

Shifting the Base for a Simple Price Index

$$I_{new} = \frac{I_{old}}{I_{new\,base}} \times 100 \qquad \text{(16.24)}$$

Unweighted Aggregate Price Index

$$I_U^{(t)} = \frac{\sum_{i=1}^{n} P_i^{(t)}}{\sum_{i=1}^{n} P_i^{(0)}} \times 100 \qquad \text{(16.25)}$$

Laspeyres Price Index

$$I_L^{(t)} = \frac{\sum_{i=1}^{n} P_i^{(t)} Q_i^{(0)}}{\sum_{i=1}^{n} P_i^{(0)} Q_i^{(0)}} \times 100 \qquad \text{(16.26)}$$

Paasche Price Index

$$I_P^{(t)} = \frac{\sum_{i=1}^{n} P_i^{(t)} Q_i^{(t)}}{\sum_{i=1}^{n} P_i^{(0)} Q_i^{(t)}} \times 100 \qquad \text{(16.27)}$$

KEY TERMS

CHAPTER REVIEW PROBLEMS

Checking Your Understanding

16.57 What is a time series?

16.58 What are the distinguishing features among the various components of the classical multiplicative time-series model?

16.59 What is the difference between moving averages and exponential smoothing?

16.60 Under what circumstances is the exponential trend model most appropriate?

16.61 How does the least-squares linear trend forecasting model developed in this chapter differ from the least-squares linear regression model considered in Chapter 13?

16.62 How does autoregressive modeling differ from the other approaches to forecasting?

16.63 What are the different approaches to choosing an appropriate forecasting model?

16.64 What is the major difference between using S_{YX} and *MAD* for evaluating how well a particular model fits the data?

16.65 How does forecasting for monthly or quarterly data differ from forecasting for annual data?

16.66 What is an index number?

16.67 What is the difference between a simple price index and an aggregate price index?

16.68 What is the difference between a Paasche price index and a Laspeyres price index?

Applying the Concepts

16.69 The following table (stored in the file polio.xls) represents the annual incidence rates (per 100,000 persons) of reported acute poliomyelitis recorded over five-year periods from 1915 to 1955:

YEAR	1915	1920	1925	1930	1935	1940	1945	1950	1955
RATE	3.1	2.2	5.3	7.5	8.5	7.4	10.3	22.1	17.6

Source: Extracted from B. Wattenberg, ed., The Statistical History of the United States: From Colonial Times to the Present, ser. B303 (New York: Basic Books, 1976).

a. Plot the data.
b. Compute the linear trend forecasting equation and plot the trend line.
c. What are your forecasts for 1960, 1965, and 1970?
d. Using a library or the Internet, find the actually reported incidence rates of acute poliomyelitis for 1960, 1965, and 1970. Record your results.
e. Why are the forecasts you made in (c) not useful? Discuss.

16.70 The U.S. Department of Labor gathers and publishes statistics concerning the labor market. The data file workforce.xls contains the U.S. civilian noninstitutional population of people 16 years and over (in thousands) and the U.S. civilian noninstitutional workforce of people 16 years and over (in thousands) for 1984–2005. The workforce variable reports the number of people in the population who have a job or are actively looking for a job.

Year	Population	Workforce	Year	Population	Workforce
1984	176,383	113,544	1995	198,584	132,304
1985	178,206	115,461	1996	200,591	133,943
1986	180,587	117,834	1997	203,133	136,297
1987	182,753	119,865	1998	205,220	137,673
1988	184,613	121,669	1999	207,753	139,368
1989	186,393	123,869	2000	212,577	142,583
1990	189,164	125,840	2001	215,092	143,734
1991	190,925	126,346	2002	217,570	144,863
1992	192,805	128,105	2003	221,168	146,510
1993	194,838	129,200	2004	223,351	146,817
1994	196,814	131,056	2005	226,082	147,956

Source: Bureau of Labor Statistics, U.S. Department of Labor, www.bls.gov.

a. Plot the time series for the U.S. civilian noninstitutional population of people 16 years and older.
b. Compute the linear trend forecasting equation.
c. Forecast the U.S. civilian noninstitutional population of people 16 years and older for 2006 and 2007.

d. Repeat (a) through (c) for the U.S. civilian noninstitutional workforce of people 16 years and older.

16.71 The quarterly price for natural gas (dollars per 40 therms) in the United States from 1994 through 2005 is given in the data file naturalgas.xls.

Source: Bureau of Labor Statistics, U.S. Department of Labor, www.bls.gov.

a. Do you think the price for natural gas has a seasonal component?
b. Plot the time series. Does this chart support your answer in (a)?
c. Compute an exponential trend forecasting equation for quarterly data.
d. Interpret the quarterly compound growth rate.
e. Interpret the quarter multipliers. Do the multipliers support your answers to (a) and (b)?

16.72 The data in the following table (stored in the file mcdonald.xls) represent the gross revenues (in billions of current dollars) of McDonald's Corporation over the 31-year period from 1975 through 2005:

Year	Revenues	Year	Revenues	Year	Revenues
1975	1.0	1986	4.2	1997	11.4
1976	1.2	1987	4.9	1998	12.4
1977	1.4	1988	5.6	1999	13.3
1978	1.7	1989	6.1	2000	14.2
1979	1.9	1990	6.8	2001	14.9
1980	2.2	1991	6.7	2002	15.4
1981	2.5	1992	7.1	2003	17.1
1982	2.8	1993	7.4	2004	19.0
1983	3.1	1994	8.3	2005	20.5
1984	3.4	1995	9.8		
1985	3.8	1996	10.7		

Source: Extracted from Moody's Handbook of Common Stocks, 1980, 1989, and 1999, and Mergent's Handbook of Common Stocks, Spring 2002 and Spring 2006.

a. Plot the data.
b. Compute the linear trend forecasting equation.
c. Compute the quadratic trend forecasting equation.
d. Compute the exponential trend forecasting equation.
e. Find the best-fitting autoregressive model, using $\alpha = 0.05$.
f. Perform a residual analysis for each of the models in (b) through (e).
g. Compute the standard error of the estimate (S_{YX}) and the MAD for each corresponding model in (f).
h. On the basis of your results in (f) and (g), along with a consideration of the principle of parsimony, which model would you select for purposes of forecasting? Discuss.
i. Using the selected model in (h), forecast gross revenues for 2006.

16.73 The data in the file sears.xls represent the gross revenues (in billions of current dollars) of Sears, Roebuck & Company over the 30-year period from 1975 through 2004.

Source: Extracted from Moody's Handbook of Common Stocks, *1980, 1989, and 1999, and* Mergent's Handbook of Common Stocks, *Spring 2002 and Spring 2006.*

a. Plot the data.
b. Compute the linear trend forecasting equation.
c. Compute the quadratic trend forecasting equation.
d. Compute the exponential trend forecasting equation.
e. Find the best-fitting autoregressive model, using $\alpha = 0.05$.
f. Perform a residual analysis for each of the models in (b) through (e).
g. Compute the standard error of the estimate (S_{YX}) and the *MAD* for each corresponding model in (f).
h. On the basis of your results in (f) and (g), along with a consideration of the principle of parsimony, which model would you select for purposes of forecasting? Discuss.
i. Using the selected model in (h), forecast gross revenues for 2005.

16.74 Teachers' Retirement System of the City of New York offers several types of investments for its members. Among the choices are investments with fixed and variable rates of return. There are currently two categories of variable-return investments. Variable *A* consists of investments that are primarily made in stocks, and variable *B* consists of investments in corporate bonds and other types of lower-risk instruments. The following data (stored in the file trsnyc.xls) represent the value of a unit of each type of variable return investment at the beginning of each year from 1984 to 2006:

Year	A	B	Year	A	B
1984	13.111	10.342	1996	39.644	17.682
1985	13.176	11.073	1997	45.389	18.004
1986	16.526	11.925	1998	54.882	18.341
1987	18.652	12.694	1999	64.790	18.678
1988	15.564	13.352	2000	74.220	18.962
1989	20.827	13.919	2001	67.534	19.320
1990	24.738	14.557	2002	57.709	19.673
1991	22.678	15.213	2003	44.843	19.735
1992	28.549	15.883	2004	55.993	19.609
1993	29.829	16.510	2005	60.909	19.520
1994	32.199	16.970	2006	63.038	19.452
1995	30.830	17.351			

Source: Teachers' Retirement System of the City of New York, **www.trs.nyc.ny.us**.

For each of the two time series,
a. plot the data.
b. compute the linear trend forecasting equation.
c. compute the quadratic trend forecasting equation.

d. compute the exponential trend forecasting equation.
e. find the best-fitting autoregressive model, using $\alpha = 0.05$.
f. Perform a residual analysis for each of the models in (b) through (e).
g. Compute the standard error of the estimate (S_{YX}) and the *MAD* for each corresponding model in (f).
h. On the basis of your results in (f) and (g), along with a consideration of the principle of parsimony, which model would you select for purposes of forecasting? Discuss.
i. Using the selected model in (h), forecast the unit values for 2007.
j. Based on the results of (a) through (i), what investment strategy would you recommend for a member of the Teachers' Retirement System of the City of New York? Explain.

16.75 The data file basket.xls contains the prices of a basket of food items from 1992 to 2006. Included are the prices (in dollars) for a one-pound loaf of white bread, a pound of beef (ground chuck), a dozen grade A large eggs, and one pound of iceberg lettuce:

Year	Bread	Beef	Eggs	Lettuce
1992	0.726	1.926	0.933	0.573
1993	0.748	1.970	0.898	0.625
1994	0.768	1.892	0.917	0.506
1995	0.767	1.847	0.882	0.821
1996	0.860	1.799	1.155	0.769
1997	0.862	1.850	1.148	0.651
1998	0.855	1.818	1.120	1.072
1999	0.872	1.834	1.053	0.649
2000	0.907	1.903	0.975	0.748
2001	0.982	2.037	1.011	0.736
2002	1.001	2.151	0.973	1.003
2003	1.042	2.131	1.175	0.734
2004	0.946	2.585	1.573	0.876
2005	0.997	2.478	1.211	0.817
2006	1.046	2.607	1.449	0.874

Source: Bureau of Labor Statistics, U.S. Department of Labor, **www.bls.gov**.

a. Compute the 1992–2006 simple price indexes for bread, beef, eggs, and lettuce, using 1992 as the base year.
b. Recalculate the price indexes in (a), using 1996 as the base year.
c. Compute the 1992–2006 unweighted aggregate price indexes for the basket of these four food items.
d. Compute the 2006 Laspeyres price index for the basket of these four food items for a family that consumed 50 loaves of bread, 22 pounds of beef, 24 dozen eggs, and 18 pounds of lettuce in 1992.
e. Compute the 2006 Paasche price index for the basket of these four food items for a family that consumed 55 loaves of bread, 17 pounds of beef, 20 dozen eggs, and 28 pounds of lettuce in 2006.

Report Writing Exercises

16.76 As a consultant to an investment company trading in various currencies, you have been assigned the task of studying the long-term trends in the exchange rates of the Canadian dollar, the Japanese yen, and the English pound. Data have been collected for the 39-year period from 1967 to 2005 and are contained in the file **currency.xls**, where the Canadian dollar, the Japanese yen, and the English pound are expressed in units per U.S. dollar.

Develop a forecasting model for the exchange rate of each of these three currencies and provide forecasts for 2006 and 2007 for each currency. Write an executive summary for a presentation to be given to the investment company. Append to this executive summary a discussion regarding possible limitations that may exist in these models.

Managing the *Springville Herald*

As part of the continuing strategic initiative to increase home-delivery subscriptions, the circulation department is closely monitoring the number of such subscriptions. The circulation department wants to forecast future home-delivery subscriptions. To accomplish this task, the circulation department compiled the number of home-delivery subscriptions for the most recent 24-month period in the file **sh16.xls**.

EXERCISE

SH16.1 **a.** Analyze these data and develop a model to forecast home-delivery subscriptions. Present

your findings in a report that includes the assumptions of the model and its limitations. Forecast home-delivery subscriptions for the next four months.

b. Would you be willing to use the model developed to forecast home-delivery subscriptions one year into the future? Explain.

c. Compare the trend in home-delivery subscriptions to the number of new subscriptions per month provided in the data file **sh13.xls**. What explanation can you provide for any differences?

Web Case

Apply your knowledge about time-series forecasting in this Web Case, which extends the running "Managing the Springville Herald" case that appears in selected chapters of this book.

The *Springville Herald* competes for readers in the Tri-Cities area with the newer *Oxford Glen Journal* (*OGJ*). Recently, the circulation staff at the *OGJ* claimed that their newspaper's circulation and subscription base is growing faster than that of the *Herald* and that local advertisers would do better transferring their advertisements from the *Herald* to the *OGJ*. The circulation department of the *Herald* has complained to the Springville Chamber of Commerce about *OGJ*'s claims and has asked the chamber to investigate, a request that was welcomed by *OGJ*'s circulation staff.

Review the circulation dispute information collected by the Springville Chamber of Commerce about the circu-

lation dispute at the Web page, **www.prenhall.com/ Springville/SCC_CirculationDispute.htm**, (or open this Web page file from the Student CD-ROM's Web Case folder) and then answer the following:

1. Which newspaper would you say has the right to claim the fastest-growing circulation and subscription base? Support your answer by performing and summarizing an appropriate statistical analysis.

2. What is the single most positive fact about the *Herald*'s circulation and subscription base? What is the single most positive fact about the *OGJ*'s circulation and subscription base? Explain your answers.

3. What additional data would be helpful in investigating the circulation claims made by the staffs of each newspaper?

REFERENCES

1. Bowerman, B. L., R. T. O'Connell, and A. Koehler, *Forecasting, Time Series, and Regression*, 4th ed. (Belmont, CA: Duxbury Press, 2005).

2. Box, G. E. P., G. M. Jenkins, and G. C. Reinsel, *Time Series Analysis: Forecasting and Control*, 3rd ed. (Upper Saddle River, NJ: Prentice Hall, 1994).

3. Frees, E. W., *Data Analysis Using Regression Models*: *The Business Perspective* (Upper Saddle River, NJ: Prentice Hall, 1996).

4. Hanke, J. E., D. W. Wichern, and A. G. Reitsch, *Business Forecasting*, 7th ed. (Upper Saddle River, NJ: Prentice Hall, 2001).

5. *Microsoft Excel 2007* (Redmond, WA: Microsoft Corp., 2007).

Excel Companion
to Chapter 16

E16.1 COMPUTING MOVING AVERAGES

You compute moving averages by adding a column of formulas to your data worksheet. Open to the worksheet that contains time-series data. In a blank column, enter formulas that use the AVERAGE function to average values in the cell range that matches your chosen period of length L. Enter ranges such that each formula is located in the middle row of the cell range that the formula averages. Then enter the special value **#N/A** in the cells at the beginning and end of the column for which no moving average can be calculated.

For example, to create three-year and seven-year moving averages for the Cabot Corporation revenue data, open to the **Data** worksheet of the CABOT.xls workbook and make entries in the blank columns C and D. Figure E16.1 shows the entries for the first four and last four data rows of these columns and illustrates how the special value **#N/A** is used at the beginning and end of a moving average column.

	A	B	C	D
1	Year	Revenue	MA 3-Year	MA 7-Year
2	1982	1588	#N/A	#N/A
3	1983	1558	=AVERAGE(B2:B4)	#N/A
4	1984	1753	=AVERAGE(B3:B5)	#N/A
5	1985	1408	=AVERAGE(B4:B6)	=AVERAGE(B2:B8)
22	2002	1557	=AVERAGE(B21:B23)	=AVERAGE(B19:B25)
23	2003	1795	=AVERAGE(B22:B24)	#N/A
24	2004	1934	=AVERAGE(B23:B25)	#N/A
25	2005	2125	#N/A	#N/A

FIGURE E16.1 Moving averages columns (rows 6 through 21 not shown)

E16.2 CREATING TIME-SERIES PLOTS

You create time-series plots by using Excel charting features. Open to the worksheet that contains your time-series data. The column representing the time periods must be the first column of this worksheet. Then use Excel charting features to create the time-series plot.

Creating a Time-Series Plot (97–2003)

With your workbook open to the time-series data worksheet, begin the Chart Wizard and make the following entries and choices in the step dialog boxes:

Step 1   Click **XY (Scatter)** from the **Standard Types Chart type** box. Click the first choice of the third row in the **Chart sub-types** gallery, described as **Scatter with data points connected by lines**.

Step 2   Click the **Data range** tab. Enter the cell range of the data to be plotted as the **Data range** and select the **Columns** option. For example, for the modified Data worksheet shown in Figure E16.1, you would enter **A1:D25** as the **Data Range** to plot the revenues and the two moving averages on one chart.

Step 3   Click the **Titles** tab. Enter a title as the **Chart** title, and appropriate values for the **Value (Y) axis** title and **Year** as the **Value (X) axis** title. Click the **Legend** tab and click **Show legend**. Click, in turn, the **Axes, Gridlines**, and **Data Labels** tabs and use the formatting settings given in the "Creating Charts (97–2003)" part of Section E2.2 on page 79.

Creating a Time-Series Plot (2007)

With your workbook open to the time-series data worksheet, select the cell range of the original data and the moving-average data. If you were using the worksheet shown in Figure E16.1, you would select **A1:D25**. Then select **Insert → (Scatter)** and click the **Scatter with Straight Lines and Markers** gallery choice. Finish by relocating your chart to a chart sheet. Customize your chart by using the instructions in "Creating Charts (2007)" in Section E2.2 on page 80.

E16.3 CREATING EXPONENTIALLY SMOOTHED VALUES

You create exponentially smoothed values by using the ToolPak Exponential Smoothing procedure.

Open to the worksheet that contains your time-series data, with each row representing a time period. Select **Tools → Data Analysis** (97–2003) or **Data → Data Analysis** (2007) and then select **Exponential Smoothing** from the Data Analysis list and click **OK**. In the Exponential Smoothing dialog box (shown on page 703), enter the cell range of the time-series variable to be smoothed as the **Input Range**. Because the damping factor is $1 - W$, enter either **0.5** (for $W = 0.50$) or **0.75** (for $W = 0.25$) as the **damping factor**. Click **Labels**, enter the output column cell range to hold the smoothed values as the **Output Range**, and click **OK**. The column cell range should begin with row 2 so as to leave the row 1 cell blank. After the procedure creates the column, enter a column heading in the row 1 cell.

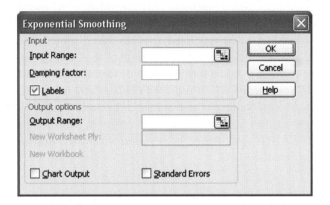

The new column contains exponentially smoothed values for each time period that are incorrectly displayed a row below their proper time periods. To adjust the column so that the exponentially smoothed values appear in the proper (same time period) rows, right-click the **row 2 cell** in that column and select **Delete** from the shortcut menu. In the Delete dialog box, select the **Shift cells up** option and click **OK**. Then copy the formula in the second-to-last cell of the column down to the last cell.

E16.4 CREATING CODED X VARIABLES

To create a coded X variable, add a new column that contains an integer series starting with zero to your time-series data. In a blank column, enter a column label in the row 1 cell and the first integer in the series in the row 2 cell. Automate the entry of the other integers by reselecting the row 2 cell and selecting **Edit → Fill → Series** (Excel 97–2003) or **Home → Fill → Series** (Excel 2007). In the Series dialog box (shown below), select the **Columns** and

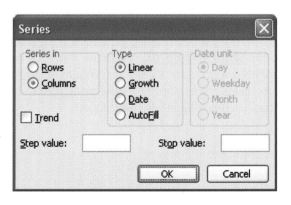

Linear options, enter the appropriate **Step value** and **Stop value**, and click **OK**. For example, enter **1** as the **Step value** and **23** as the **Stop value** to complete the 24-integer series 0 through 23.

E16.5 CREATING QUADRATIC AND EXPONENTIAL TERMS

See Sections E15.1 and E15.2 in the Excel Companion to Chapter 15 to review the methods for adding quadratic and exponential terms.

E16.6 USING LEAST-SQUARES LINEAR TREND FITTING

Use the Section E13.1 instructions, but use the cell range of the coded variable as the X variable cell range.

E16.7 USING LEAST-SQUARES QUADRATIC TREND FITTING

Use the Section E14.1 instructions, but use the cell range of the coded variable and the squared coded variable as the X variable cell range. Use the Section E15.1 instructions to create a column of squared coded variables.

E16.8 USING LEAST-SQUARES EXPONENTIAL TREND FITTING

Use the Section E13.1 instructions, but use the cell range of the log Y values as the Y variable cell range and the cell range of the coded variable as the X variable cell range.

E16.9 CREATING LAGGED INDEPENDENT VARIABLES

To create lagged independent variables, open to the worksheet that contains your time-series data. For each lagged independent variable you want to add, use a blank column and enter formulas that refer to a previous row's (that is, previous time period's) Y value. Place the special value **#N/A** (not available) in the cells in the column for which lagged values do not apply.

For example, Figure E16.2 on page 704 shows the first five rows and the last row of the worksheet shown in Figure 16.14 on page 671 that contains lagged independent variables for the first-order, second-order, and third-order autoregressive models. Because cells C2, D2, D3, E2, E3, and E4, do not have lagged values, the value **#N/A** has been entered into those cells.

	A	B	C	D	E
1	Year	Real Revenue	Lag1	Lag2	Lag3
2	1984	569	#N/A	#N/A	#N/A
3	1985	576	=B2	#N/A	#N/A
4	1986	638	=B3	=C3	#N/A
5	1987	688	=B4	=C4	=D4
23	2005	2130	=B22	=C22	=D22

FIGURE E16.2 Lagged independent variables

E16.10 CREATING FIRST-ORDER AUTOREGRESSIVE MODELS

Use the Section E13.1 instructions but use the cell range of the first-order lagged variable as the *X* variable cell range. If using PHStat2, *do not* click **First cells in both ranges contain label**. If using the ToolPak procedure, *do not* click **Labels**.

E16.11 CREATING SECOND-ORDER OR THIRD-ORDER AUTOREGRESSIVE MODELS

Use the Section E14.1 instructions but use the cell range of the lagged variables as the *X* variable cell range. Use the cell range of the first-order and second-order lagged variables for a second-order model and use the cell range of the first-order, second-order, and third-order lagged variables for the third-order model. If using PHStat2, *do not* click **First cells in both ranges contain label**. If using the ToolPak procedure, *do not* click **Labels**.

E16.12 COMPUTING THE MEAN ABSOLUTE DEVIATION (*MAD*)

For a Linear, Quadratic, or Autoregressive Model

Begin by performing a regression analysis, making sure to select the residuals check box. Then, from the regression results worksheet, copy the residual values found in column C of the Residual Output section to a blank column on the worksheet that contains the regression data. Add a column of formulas in the form ***=ABS(residual cell)*** to calculate the absolute value of the residuals. Then add a single formula in the form ***=AVERAGE(cell range of residual absolute values)*** to calculate the *MAD*.

For an Exponential Model

Begin by creating the exponential regression results worksheet with residuals. The model results will use base 10 logarithms to report predicted *Y* values and residuals. These logarithms will need to be converted to original units of the *Y* values in order to calculate the *MAD*.

To the Residual Output section of the regression model worksheet, add a column of formulas that use the **POWER(10, *LogValue*)** function to convert the predicted *Y* logarithms to the predicted *Y* values. Next, copy the original *Y* values into the cells to the right of the POWER function formulas. Add a third column of formulas in the form ***=ABS(YValueCell - PredictedYValueCell)*** to calculate the absolute value of the residuals. Then add a single formula at the end of this third column in the form ***=AVERAGE(cell range of residual absolute values)*** to calculate the *MAD*.

E16.13 CREATING DUMMY VARIABLES FOR QUARTERLY OR MONTHLY DATA

You create dummy variables for quarterly or monthly data by adding columns of formulas that use the **IF(*comparison, value if comparison is true, value to use if comparison is false*)** function.

Figure E16.3 shows the first four rows of columns F through K of a data worksheet that contains dummy variables. Columns F, G, and H contain the quarterly dummy variables Q1, Q2, and Q3 that are based on column B coded quarter values (not shown). Columns J and K contain the two monthly variables, M1 and M6, that are based on column C month values (also not shown).

	F	G	H	I	J	K
1	Q1	Q2	Q3		M1	M6
2	=IF(B2 = 1, 1, 0)	=IF(B2 = 2, 1, 0)	=IF(B2 = 3, 1, 0)		=IF(C2 ="January", 1, 0)	=IF(C2 = "June", 1, 0)
3	=IF(B3 = 1, 1, 0)	=IF(B3 = 2, 1, 0)	=IF(B3 = 3, 1, 0)		=IF(C3 ="January", 1, 0)	=IF(C3 = "June", 1, 0)
4	=IF(B4 = 1, 1, 0)	=IF(B4 = 2, 1, 0)	=IF(B4 = 3, 1, 0)		=IF(C4 ="January", 1, 0)	=IF(C4 = "June", 1, 0)

FIGURE E16.3 Dummy variables for quarterly and monthly data

E16.14 CALCULATING INDEX NUMBERS

Open the **Index Numbers.xls** workbook and explore the **Unweighted Aggregate PI** and the **Weighted Aggregate PI** worksheets for examples of how price index calculations can be computed in Microsoft Excel.

CHAPTER 17

Decision Making

USING STATISTICS @ Reliable Fund

LEARNING OBJECTIVES

In this chapter, you learn:

- To use payoff tables and decision trees to evaluate alternative courses of action
- To use several criteria to select an alternative course of action
- To use Bayes' theorem to revise probabilities in light of sample information
- About the concept of utility

Using Statistics @ Reliable Fund

As the manager of The Reliable Fund, you are responsible for purchasing and selling stocks for the fund. The investors in this mutual fund expect a large return on their investment and, at the same time, they want to minimize their risk. At the present time, you need to decide between two stocks to purchase. An economist for your company has evaluated the potential one-year returns for both stocks, under four economic conditions: recession, stability, moderate growth, and boom. She has also estimated the probability of each economic condition occurring. How can you use the information provided by the economist to determine which stock to choose in order to maximize return and minimize risk?

In Chapter 4, you studied various rules of probability and used Bayes' theorem to revise probabilities. In Chapter 5, you learned about discrete probability distributions and how to compute the expected value. In this chapter, these probability rules and probability distributions are applied to a decision-making process for evaluating alternative courses of action. In this context, you can consider the four basic features of a decision-making situation:

- *Alternative courses of action* The decision maker must have two or more possible choices to evaluate prior to selecting one course of action. For example, as a manager of a mutual fund in the Using Statistics scenario, you must decide whether to purchase stock *A* or stock *B*.
- *Events or states of the world* The decision maker must list the events that can occur and consider each event's probability of occurring. To aid in selecting which stock to purchase in the Using Statistics scenario, an economist for your company has listed four possible economic conditions and the probability of each occurring in the next year.
- *Payoffs* In order to evaluate each course of action, the decision maker must associate a value or payoff with the result of each event. In business applications, this payoff is usually expressed in terms of profits or costs, although other payoffs, such as units of satisfaction or utility, are sometimes considered. In the Using Statistics scenario, the payoff is the return on investment.
- *Decision criteria* The decision maker must determine how to select the best course of action. Section 17.2 discusses three criteria for decision making: expected monetary value, expected opportunity loss, and return-to-risk ratio.

17.1 PAYOFF TABLES AND DECISION TREES

In order to evaluate the various alternative courses of action for a complete set of events, you need to develop a payoff table or construct a decision tree. A **payoff table** contains each possible event that can occur for each alternative course of action and a value or payoff for each combination of an event and course of action. Example 17.1 discusses a payoff table for a marketing manager trying to decide whether to introduce a new model of a television set.

EXAMPLE 17.1

A PAYOFF TABLE FOR DECIDING WHETHER TO MARKET A TELEVISION SET

As the marketing manager of a consumer electronics company, you are considering whether to introduce a new television set into the market. You are aware of the risks in deciding whether to market this television set. For example, you could decide to market the television set and then, for any of a number of reasons, the introduction could turn out to be unsuccessful. Second, you could decide not to market the television set when, actually it would have been successful. There is a fixed cost of $3 million incurred prior to making a final decision to market the television set. Based on past experience, if the television set is successful, you expect to profit $45 million. If the television set is not successful, you expect to lose $36 million. Construct a payoff table for these two alternative courses of action.

SOLUTION Table 17.1 is a payoff table for the television set marketing example.

TABLE 17.1

Payoff Table for the Television Set Marketing Example (in Millions of Dollars)

EVENT, E_i	ALTERNATIVE COURSE OF ACTION	
	Market, A_1	Do Not Market, A_2
Successful television set, E_1	+45	−3
Unsuccessful television set, E_2	−36	−3

A **decision tree** is another way of representing the events for each alternative course of action. A decision tree pictorially represents the events and courses of action through a set of branches and nodes. Example 17.2 illustrates a decision tree.

EXAMPLE 17.2

A DECISION TREE FOR THE TELEVISION SET MARKETING DECISION

Given the payoff table for the television marketing example, construct a decision tree.

SOLUTION Figure 17.1 is the decision tree for the payoff table shown in Table 17.1.

FIGURE 17.1

Decision tree for the television set marketing example

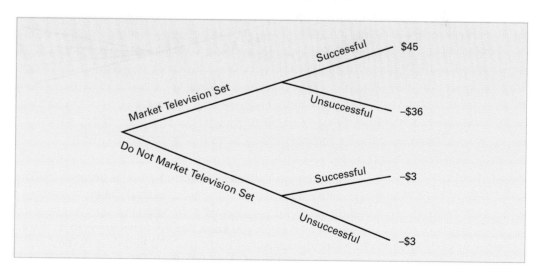

In Figure 17.1, the first set of branches relates to the two alternative courses of action: market the television set or do not market the television set. The second set of branches represents the possible events of successful television set and unsuccessful television set. These events occur for each of the alternative courses of action on the decision tree.

The decision structure for the television set marketing example contains only two possible alternative courses of action and two possible events. In general, there can be several alternative courses of action and events. As a manager of a mutual fund in the Using Statistics scenario, you need to decide between two stocks to purchase for a short-term investment of one year. An economist in the company has predicted returns for the two stocks under four economic conditions—recession, stability, moderate growth, and boom. Table 17.2 presents the predicted one-year return of a $1,000 investment in each stock under each economic condition. Figure 17.2 shows the decision tree for this payoff table. The decision (which stock to purchase) is the first branch of the tree, and the second set of branches represents the four events (the economic conditions).

TABLE 17.2

Predicted One-Year Return ($) on $1,000 Investment in Each of Two Stocks, Under Four Economic Conditions

	STOCK	
ECONOMIC CONDITION	A	B
Recession	30	−50
Stable economy	70	30
Moderate growth	100	250
Boom	150	400

FIGURE 17.2

Decision tree for the stock selection payoff table

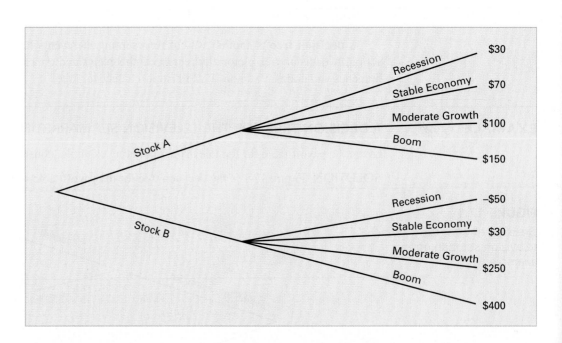

You use payoff tables and decision trees as decision-making tools to help determine the best course of action. For example, when deciding whether to market a television set, you would market it if you knew that the television set was going to be successful. Certainly, you would not market it if you knew that it was not going to be successful. For each event, you can determine the amount of profit that will be lost if the best alternative course of action is not taken. This is called opportunity loss.

The **opportunity loss** is the difference between the highest possible profit for an event and the actual profit for an action taken.

Example 17.3 illustrates the computation of opportunity loss.

EXAMPLE 17.3

FINDING OPPORTUNITY LOSS IN THE TELEVISION SET MARKETING EXAMPLE

Using the payoff table from Example 17.1 on page 707, construct an opportunity loss table.

SOLUTION For the event "successful television set," the maximum profit occurs when the product is marketed (+$45 million). The opportunity that is lost by not marketing the television set is the difference between $45 million and −$3 million, which is $48 million. If the television is unsuccessful, the best action is not to market the television set (−$3 million profit). The opportunity that is lost by making the incorrect decision of marketing the television set is −$3 − (−36) = $33 million. The opportunity loss is always a nonnegative number because it represents the difference between the profit under the best action and any other course of action that is taken for the particular event. Table 17.3 shows the complete opportunity loss table for the television set marketing example.

TABLE 17.3

Opportunity Loss Table for the Television Set Marketing Example (in Millions of Dollars)

Event	Optimum Action	Profit of Optimum Action	Alternative Course of Action	
			Market	**Do Not Market**
Successful	Market	45	45 − 45 = 0	45 − (−3) = 48
Unsuccessful	Do not market	−3	−3 − (−36) = 33	−3 − (−3) = 0

Figure 17.3 represents the Microsoft Excel opportunity loss table.

FIGURE 17.3

Microsoft Excel opportunity loss table worksheet

See Section E17.1 to create this.

	A	B	C	D	E
1	Television Marketing Opportunity Loss				
2					
3	Payoff Table:				
4		Market	Do Not Market		
5	Successful	45	-3		
6	Unsuccessful	-36	-3		
7					
8					
9	Opportunity Loss Table:				
10		Optimum	Optimum	Alternatives	
11		Action	Profit	Market	Do Not Market
12	Successful	Market	45	0	48
13	Unsuccessful	Do Not Market	-3	33	0

You can also develop an opportunity loss table for the stock selection problem in the Using Statistics scenario. Here, there are four possible events or economic conditions that will affect the one-year return for each of the two stocks. In a recession, stock *A* is best, providing a return of $30 as compared to a loss of $50 from stock *B*. In a stable economy, stock *A* again is better than stock *B* because it provides a return of $70 compared to $30 for stock *B*. However, under conditions of moderate growth or boom, stock *B* is superior to stock *A*. In a moderate growth period, stock *B* provides a return of $250 as compared to $100 from stock *A*, while in boom conditions, the difference between stocks is even greater, with stock *B* providing a return of $400 as compared to $150 for stock *A*. Table 17.4 summarizes the complete set of opportunity losses.

TABLE 17.4

Opportunity Loss Table ($) for Two Stocks Under Four Economic Conditions

Event	Optimum Action	Profit of Optimum Action	Alternative Course of Action A	Alternative Course of Action B
Recession	A	30	$30 - 30 =$ 0	$30 - (-50) = 80$
Stable economy	A	70	$70 - 70 =$ 0	$70 - 30 = 40$
Moderate growth	B	250	$250 - 100 = 150$	$250 - 250 =$ 0
Boom	B	400	$400 - 150 = 250$	$400 - 400 =$ 0

PROBLEMS FOR SECTION 17.1

Learning the Basics

 17.1 For this problem, use the following payoff table:

	ACTION	
EVENT	**A ($)**	**B ($)**
1	50	100
2	200	125

a. Construct an opportunity loss table.
b. Construct a decision tree.

 17.2 For this problem, use the following payoff table:

	ACTION	
EVENT	**A ($)**	**B ($)**
1	50	10
2	300	100
3	500	200

a. Construct an opportunity loss table.
b. Construct a decision tree.

Applying the Concepts

 17.3 A manufacturer of designer jeans must decide whether to build a large factory or a small factory in a particular location. The profit per pair of jeans manufactured is estimated as $10. A small factory will incur an annual cost of $200,000, with a production capacity of 50,000 pairs of jeans per year. A large factory will incur an annual cost of $400,000, with a production capacity of 100,000 pairs of jeans per year. Four levels of manufacturing demand are considered likely: 10,000, 20,000, 50,000, and 100,000 pairs of jeans per year.

a. Determine the payoffs for the possible levels of production for a small factory.
b. Determine the payoffs for the possible levels of production for a large factory.
c. Based on the results of (a) and (b), construct a payoff table, indicating the events and alternative courses of action.
d. Construct a decision tree.
e. Construct an opportunity loss table.

 17.4 An author is trying to choose between two publishing companies that are competing for the marketing rights to her new novel. Company *A* has offered the author $10,000 plus $2 per book sold. Company *B* has offered the author $2,000 plus $4 per book sold. The author believes that five levels of demand for the book are possible: 1,000, 2,000, 5,000, 10,000, and 50,000 books sold.

a. Compute the payoffs for each level of demand for company *A* and company *B*.
b. Construct a payoff table, indicating the events and alternative courses of action.
c. Construct a decision tree.
d. Construct an opportunity loss table.

17.5 The DellaVecchia Garden Center purchases and sells Christmas trees during the holiday season. It purchases the trees for $10 each and sells them for $20 each. Any trees not sold by Christmas day are sold for $2 each to a company that makes wood chips. The garden center estimates that four levels of demand are possible: 100, 200, 500, and 1,000 trees.

a. Compute the payoffs for purchasing 100, 200, 500, or 1,000 trees for each of the four levels of demand.
b. Construct a payoff table, indicating the events and alternative courses of action.
c. Construct a decision tree.
d. Construct an opportunity loss table.

17.2 CRITERIA FOR DECISION MAKING

After you compute the profit and opportunity loss for each event under each alternative course of action, you need to assign a probability to each event. You also need to determine the criteria for selecting the most desirable course of action. The probability assigned is based on information available from past data, from the opinions of the decision maker, or from knowledge about the probability distribution that the event may follow. Using these probabilities, along with the payoffs or opportunity losses of each event–action combination, you select the best course of action according to a particular criterion. In this section, three decision criteria are presented—expected monetary value, expected opportunity loss, and the return-to-risk ratio.

Expected Monetary Value

Equation (5.1) on page 181 was introduced to compute the expected value of a probability distribution. Now you use this equation to compute the expected monetary value for each alternative course of action. The **expected monetary value (*EMV*)** for a course of action *j* is the payoff (X_{ij}) for each combination of event *i* and action *j* multiplied by P_i, the probability of occurrence of event *i*, summed over all events [see Equation (17.1)].

EXPECTED MONETARY VALUE

$$EMV(j) = \sum_{i=1}^{N} X_{ij}P_i \qquad \textbf{(17.1)}$$

where

$EMV(j)$ = expected monetary value of action *j*

X_{ij} = payoff that occurs when course of action *j* is selected and event *i* occurs

P_i = probability of occurrence of event *i*

N = number of events

Criterion: Select the course of action with the largest *EMV*.

Example 17.4 illustrates the application of expected monetary value to the television set marketing example.

EXAMPLE 17.4

COMPUTING THE *EMV* IN THE TELEVISION SET MARKETING EXAMPLE

Returning to the payoff table for deciding whether to market a television set (Example 17.1 on page 707), suppose that the probability is 0.40 that the television set will be successful (so that the probability is 0.60 that the television will not be successful). Compute the expected monetary value for each alternative course of action and determine whether to market the television set.

SOLUTION You use Equation (17.1) to determine the expected monetary value for each alternative course of action. Table 17.5 summarizes these computations.

TABLE 17.5

Expected Monetary Value (in Millions of Dollars) for Each Alternative for the Television Set Marketing Example

		Alternative Course of Action			
Event	P_i	Market, A_1	$X_{ij}P_i$	Do Not Market, A_2	$X_{ij}P_i$
Successful	0.40	+45	45(0.4) = 18.0	−3	−3(0.4) =−1.2
Unsuccessful	0.60	−36	−36(0.6) =−21.6	−3	−3(0.6) =−1.8
			$EMV(A_1) =− 3.6$		$EMV(A_2) =−3.0$

The expected monetary value for marketing the television set is −$3.6 million, and the expected monetary value for not marketing the television set is −$3 million. Thus, if your objective is to choose the action that maximizes the expected monetary value, you would choose the action of not marketing the television set because its profit is highest (or in this case, its loss is lowest). Note, however, that if the probability that the television is successful, P_1, were slightly greater than the assumed value of 0.40, you would make a different decision. Specifically, if $P_1 = 0.41$, then $EMV(A_1) = -\$2.79$ million, $EMV(A_2) = -\$3$ million, and the best decision would be to market the television. This change in the optimal decision, when such a small change in the assumed probability of success occurs, illustrates the importance of accuracy when determining the probabilities. You need to consider the *closeness* of the decision-making criterion before making a final decision.

As a second application of expected monetary value, return to the Using Statistics scenario and the payoff table presented in Table 17.2 on page 708. Suppose the company economist assigns the following probabilities to the different economic conditions:

$$P(\text{Recession}) = 0.10$$

$$P(\text{Stable economy}) = 0.40$$

$$P(\text{Moderate growth}) = 0.30$$

$$P(\text{Boom}) = 0.20$$

Table 17.6 shows the computations of the expected monetary value for each of the two stocks.

TABLE 17.6

Expected Monetary Value ($) for Each of Two Stocks Under Four Economic Conditions

		Alternative Course of Action			
Event	P_i	A	$X_{ij}P_i$	B	$X_{ij}P_i$
Recession	0.10	30	30(0.1) = 3	−50	−50(0.1) = −5
Stable economy	0.40	70	70(0.4) = 28	30	30(0.4) = 12
Moderate growth	0.30	100	100(0.3) = 30	250	250(0.3) = 75
Boom	0.20	150	150(0.2) = 30	400	400(0.2) = 80
			$EMV(A) = 91$		$EMV(B) = 162$

Thus, the expected monetary value, or profit, for stock *A* is $91, and the expected monetary value, or profit, for stock *B* is $162. Using these results, you should choose stock *B* because the expected monetary value for stock *B* is almost twice that for stock *A*. In terms of expected rate of return on the $1,000 investment, stock *B* is 16.2% compared to 9.1% for stock *A*.

Expected Opportunity Loss

In the examples on pages 711 and 712, you learned how to use the expected monetary value criterion when making a decision. An equivalent criterion, based on opportunity losses, is introduced next. Payoffs and opportunity losses can be viewed as two sides of the same coin depending on whether you wish to view the problem in terms of *maximizing* expected monetary value or *minimizing* expected opportunity loss. The **expected opportunity loss (*EOL*)** of action j is the loss, L_{ij}, for each combination of event i and action j multiplied by P_i, the probability of occurrence of the event i, summed over all events [see Equation (17.2)].

EXPECTED OPPORTUNITY LOSS

$$EOL(j) = \sum_{i=1}^{N} L_{ij} P_i \qquad (17.2)$$

where

$$L_{ij} = \text{opportunity loss that occurs when course of action } j \text{ is selected and event } i \text{ occurs}$$

$$P_i = \text{probability of occurrence of event } i$$

Criterion: Select the course of action with the smallest *EOL*. Selecting the course of action with the smallest *EOL* is equivalent to selecting the course of action with the largest *EMV*. See Equation (17.1) on page 711.

Example 17.5 illustrates the application of expected opportunity loss for the television set marketing example.

EXAMPLE 17.5

COMPUTING THE *EOL* FOR THE TELEVISION SET MARKETING EXAMPLE

Referring to the opportunity loss table given in Table 17.3 on page 709, and assuming that the probability is 0.40 that the television set will be successful, compute the expected opportunity loss for each alternative course of action (see Table 17.7). Determine whether to market the television set.

TABLE 17.7

Expected Opportunity Loss (in Millions of Dollars) for Each Alternative for the Television Set Marketing Example

		Alternative Course of Action			
Event, E_i	P_i	Market, A_1	$L_{ij}P_i$	Do Not Market, A_2	$L_{ij}P_i$
Successful, E_1	0.40	0	0(0.4) = 0	48	48(0.4) = 19.2
Unsuccessful, E_2	0.60	33	33(0.6) = 19.8	0	0(0.6) = 0
			EOL (A_1) = 19.8		*EOL* (A_2) = 19.2

SOLUTION The expected opportunity loss is lower for not marketing the television set ($19.2 million) than for marketing the television set ($19.8 million). Therefore, using the *EOL* criterion, the optimal decision is not to market the television set. This outcome is expected because the equivalent *EMV* criterion produced the same optimal strategy. Once again, be aware that if the probability that the television set is successful, P_1, is slightly greater than the assumed value of 0.40, a different decision is made. Specifically, if $P_1 = 0.41$, then *EOL* (A_1) = $19.47 million, *EOL* ($A_2$) = $19.68 million, and the best decision is to market the television set.

The expected opportunity loss from the best decision is called the **expected value of perfect information (EVPI)**. Equation (17.3) defines the *EVPI*.

EXPECTED VALUE OF PERFECT INFORMATION

The **expected profit under certainty** represents the expected profit that you could make if you had perfect information about which event will occur.

$$EVPI = \text{Expected profit under certainty}$$
$$- \text{Expected monetary value of the best alternative} \qquad \textbf{(17.3)}$$

Example 17.6 illustrates the expected value of perfect information.

EXAMPLE 17.6

COMPUTING THE *EVPI* IN THE TELEVISION SET MARKETING EXAMPLE

Referring to the data in Example 17.5, compute the expected profit under certainty and the expected value of perfect information.

SOLUTION As the marketing manager of the consumer electronics company, if you could always predict the future, a profit of $45 million would be made for the 40% of the television sets that are successful, and a loss of $3 million would be incurred for the 60% of the television sets that are not successful. Thus,

$$\text{Expected profit under certainty} = 0.40(\$45) + 0.60(-\$3)$$
$$= \$18 - \$1.80$$
$$= \$16.2$$

The $16.2 million represents the profit you could make if you knew with *certainty* whether the television set was going to be successful. You use Equation (17.3) to compute the expected value of perfect information:

$$EVPI = \text{Expected profit under certainty} - \text{expected monetary value of the best alternative}$$
$$= \$16.2 - (-\$3) = \$19.2$$

This *EVPI* value of $19.2 million represents the maximum amount that you should be willing to pay for perfect information. Of course, you can never have perfect information, and you should never pay the entire *EVPI* for more information. Rather, the *EVPI* provides a guideline for an upper bound on how much you might consider paying for better information. The *EVPI* is also the expected opportunity loss of not marketing the television set.

Return to the Using Statistics scenario and the opportunity loss table presented in Table 17.4 on page 710. Table 17.8 presents the computations to determine the expected opportunity loss for stock *A* and stock *B*.

TABLE 17.8

Expected Opportunity Loss for Each Alternative ($) for the Stock Selection Example

Event	P_i	A	$L_{ij}P_i$	B	$L_{ij}P_i$
Recession	0.10	0	0(0.1) = 0	80	80(0.1) = 8
Stable economy	0.40	0	0(0.4) = 0	40	40(0.4) = 16
Moderate growth	0.30	150	150(0.3) = 45	0	0(0.3) = 0
Boom	0.20	250	250(0.2) = 50	0	0(0.2) = 0
			EOL (A) = 95		EOL (B) = EVPI = 24

Alternative Course of Action

The expected opportunity loss is lower for stock B than for stock A. Your optimal decision is to choose stock B, which is consistent with the decision made using expected monetary value. The expected value of perfect information is $24 (per $1,000 invested), meaning that you should be willing to pay up to $24 for perfect information.

Return-to-Risk Ratio

Unfortunately, neither the expected monetary value nor the expected opportunity loss criterion takes into account the *variability* of the payoffs for the alternative courses of action under different events. From Table 17.2 on page 708, you see that the return for stock A varies from $30 in a recession to $150 in an economic boom, while the return for stock B (the one chosen according to the expected monetary value and expected opportunity loss criteria) varies from a loss of $50 in a recession to a profit of $400 in an economic boom.

To take into account the variability of the events (in this case, the different economic conditions), you can compute the variance and standard deviation of each stock, using Equations (5.2) and (5.3) on page 182. Using the information presented in Table 17.6 on page 712, for stock A, $\mu_A = \$91$, the variance is

$$\sigma_A^2 = \sum_{i=1}^{N} (X_i - \mu)^2 P(X_i)$$

$$= (30 - 91)^2 (0.1) + (70 - 91)^2 (0.4) + (100 - 91)^2 (0.3) + (150 - 91)^2 (0.2)$$

$$= 1,269$$

and $\sigma_A = \sqrt{1,269} = \$35.62$.

For stock B, $\mu_B = \$162$, the variance is

$$\sigma_B^2 = \sum_{i=1}^{N} (X_i - \mu)^2 P(X_i)$$

$$= (-50 - 162)^2 (0.1) + (30 - 162)^2 (0.4) + (250 - 162)^2 (0.3) + (400 - 162)^2 (0.2)$$

$$= 25,116$$

and $\sigma_B = \sqrt{25,116} = \$158.48$.

Because you are comparing two sets of data with vastly different means, you should evaluate the relative risk associated with each stock. Once you compute the standard deviation of the return from each stock, you compute the coefficient of variation discussed in Section 3.2. Substituting σ for S and EMV for $\overline{X}$ in Equation (3.11) on page 110, you find that the coefficient of variation for stock A is equal to

$$CV_A = \left(\frac{\sigma_A}{EMV_A} \right) 100\%$$

$$= \left(\frac{35.62}{91} \right) 100\% = 39.1\%$$

while the coefficient of variation for stock B is equal to

$$CV_B = \left(\frac{\sigma_B}{EMV_B} \right) 100\%$$

$$= \left(\frac{158.48}{162} \right) 100\% = 97.8\%$$

Thus, there is much more variation in the return for stock B than for stock A.

When there are large differences in the amount of variability in the different events, a criterion other than *EMV* or *EOL* is needed to express the relationship between the return (as expressed by the *EMV*) and the risk (as expressed by the standard deviation). Equation (17.4) defines the **return-to-risk ratio (*RTRR*)** as the expected monetary value of action *j* divided by the standard deviation of action *j*.

RETURN-TO-RISK RATIO

$$RTRR(j) = \frac{EMV(j)}{\sigma_j} \qquad \textbf{(17.4)}$$

where

$$EMV(j) = \text{expected monetary value for alternative course of action } j$$

$$\sigma_j = \text{standard deviation for alternative course of action } j$$

Criterion: Select the course of action with the largest *RTRR*.

For each of the two stocks discussed previously, you compute the return-to-risk ratios as follows. For stock *A*, the return-to-risk ratio is equal to

$$RTRR(A) = \frac{91}{35.62} = 2.55$$

For stock *B*, the return-to-risk ratio is equal to

$$RTRR(B) = \frac{162}{158.48} = 1.02$$

Thus, relative to the risk as expressed by the standard deviation, the expected return is much higher for stock *A* than for stock *B*. Stock *A* has a smaller expected monetary value than stock *B*, but also has a much smaller risk than stock *B*. The return-to-risk ratio shows *A* to be preferable to *B*. Figure 17.4 represents Microsoft Excel results.

FIGURE 17.4

Microsoft Excel expected monetary value and standard deviation worksheet

See Section E17.2 to create this.

	A	B	C	D	E
1	Stock Selection Analysis				
2					
3	Probabilities & Payoffs Table:				
4		P	Stock A	Stock B	
5	Recession	0.1	30	-50	
6	Stable economy	0.4	70	30	
7	Moderate growth	0.3	100	250	
8	Boom	0.2	150	400	
9					
10	Statistics for:	Stock A	Stock B		
11	Expected Monetary Value		91	162	
12	Variance		1269	25116	
13	Standard Deviation		35.6230	158.4803	
14	Coefficient of Variation		0.3915	0.9783	
15	Return to Risk Ratio		2.5545	1.0222	
16					
17	Opportunity Loss Table:				
18		Optimum	Optimum	Alternatives	
19		Action	Profit	Stock A	Stock B
20	Recession	Stock A	30	0	80
21	Stable economy	Stock A	70	0	40
22	Moderate growth	Stock B	250	150	0
23	Boom	Stock B	400	250	0
24				Stock A	Stock B
25	Expected Opportunity Loss			95	24
26					EVPI

PROBLEMS FOR SECTION 17.2

Learning the Basics

PH Grade ASSIST **17.6** For the following payoff table:

	ACTION	
EVENT	A ($)	B ($)
1	50	100
2	200	125

The probability of event 1 is 0.5, and the probability of event 2 is also 0.5.

a. Compute the expected monetary value (*EMV*) for actions *A* and *B*.

b. Compute the expected opportunity loss (*EOL*) for actions *A* and *B*.

c. Explain the meaning of the expected value of perfect information (*EVPI*) in this problem.

d. Based on the results of (a) or (b), which action would you choose? Why?

e. Compute the coefficient of variation for each action.

f. Compute the return-to-risk ratio (*RTRR*) for each action.

g. Based on (e) and (f), what action would you choose? Why?

h. Compare the results of (d) and (g) and explain any differences.

PH Grade ASSIST **17.7** For the following payoff table:

	ACTION	
EVENT	A ($)	B ($)
1	50	10
2	300	100
3	500	200

The probability of event 1 is 0.8, the probability of event 2 is 0.1, and the probability of event 3 is 0.1.

a. Compute the expected monetary value (*EMV*) for actions *A* and *B*.

b. Compute the expected opportunity loss (*EOL*) for actions *A* and *B*.

c. Explain the meaning of the expected value of perfect information (*EVPI*) in this problem.

d. Based on the results of (a) or (b), which action would you choose? Why?

e. Compute the coefficient of variation for each action.

f. Compute the return-to-risk (*RTRR*) ratio for each action.

g. Based on (e) and (f), what action would you choose? Why?

h. Compare the results of (d) and (g) and explain any differences.

i. Would your answers to (d) and (g) be different if the probabilities for the three events were 0.1, 0.1, and 0.8, respectively? Discuss.

PH Grade ASSIST **17.8** For a potential investment of $1,000, if a stock has an *EMV* of $100 and a standard deviation of $25, what is the

a. rate of return?

b. coefficient of variation?

c. return-to-risk ratio?

PH Grade ASSIST **17.9** A stock has the following predicted returns under the following economic conditions:

Economic Condition	Probability	Return ($)
Recession	0.30	50
Stable economy	0.30	100
Moderate growth	0.30	120
Boom	0.10	200

Compute the

a. expected monetary value.

b. standard deviation.

c. coefficient of variation.

d. return-to-risk ratio.

PH Grade ASSIST **17.10** The following are the returns ($) for two stocks:

	A	B
Expected monetary value	90	60
Standard deviation	10	10

Which stock would you choose and why?

PH Grade ASSIST **17.11** The following are the returns ($) for two stocks:

	A	B
Expected monetary value	60	60
Standard deviation	20	10

Which stock would you choose and why?

Applying the Concepts

 17.12 A vendor at a local baseball stadium must determine whether to sell ice cream or soft drinks at today's game. The vendor believes that the profit made will depend on the weather. The payoff table (in $) is as follows:

	ACTION	
EVENT	Sell Soft Drinks	Sell Ice Cream
Cool weather	50	30
Warm weather	60	90

Based on her past experience at this time of year, the vendor estimates the probability of warm weather as 0.60.

a. Compute the expected monetary value (*EMV*) for selling soft drinks and selling ice cream.

b. Compute the expected opportunity loss (*EOL*) for selling soft drinks and selling ice cream.

c. Explain the meaning of the expected value of perfect information (*EVPI*) in this problem.

d. Based on the results of (a) or (b), would you choose to sell soft drinks or ice cream? Why?

e. Compute the coefficient of variation for selling soft drinks and for selling ice cream.

f. Compute the return-to-risk ratio (*RTRR*) for selling soft drinks and selling ice cream.

g. Based on (e) and (f), would you choose to sell soft drinks or ice cream? Why?

h. Compare the results of (d) and (g) and explain any differences.

17.13 The Islander Fishing Company purchases clams for $1.50 per pound from fishermen and sells them to various restaurants for $2.50 per pound. Any clams not sold to the restaurants by the end of the week can be sold to a local soup company for $0.50 per pound. The company can purchase 500, 1,000, or 2,000 pounds. The probabilities of various levels of demand are as follows:

Demand (Pounds)	Probability
500	0.2
1,000	0.4
2,000	0.4

a. For each possible purchase level (500, 1,000, or 2,000 pounds), compute the profit (or loss) for each level of demand.

b. Using the expected monetary value (*EMV*) criterion, determine the optimal number of pounds of clams the company should purchase from the fishermen. Discuss.

c. Compute the standard deviation for each possible purchase level.

d. Compute the expected opportunity loss (*EOL*) for purchasing 500, 1,000, and 2,000 pounds of clams.

e. Explain the meaning of the expected value of perfect information (*EVPI*) in this problem.

f. Compute the coefficient of variation for purchasing 500, 1,000, and 2,000 pounds of clams. Discuss.

g. Compute the return-to-risk ratio (*RTRR*) for purchasing 500, 1,000, and 2,000 pounds of clams. Discuss.

h. Based on (b) and (d), would you choose to purchase 500, 1,000, or 2,000 pounds of clams? Why?

i. Compare the results of (b), (d), (f), and (g) and explain any differences.

j. Suppose that clams can be sold to restaurants for $3 per pound. Repeat (a) through (h) with this selling price for clams and compare the results with those in (i).

k. What would be the effect on the results in (a) through (i) if the probability of the demand for 500, 1,000, and 2,000 clams were 0.4, 0.4, and 0.2, respectively?

PH Grade ASSIST **17.14** An investor has a certain amount of money available to invest now. Three alternative investments are available. The estimated profits ($) of each investment under each economic condition are indicated in the following payoff table:

	INVESTMENT SELECTION		
EVENT	A	B	C
Economy declines	500	−2,000	−7,000
No change	1,000	2,000	−1,000
Economy expands	2,000	5,000	20,000

Based on his own past experience, the investor assigns the following probabilities to each economic condition:

P (Economy declines) = 0.30
P (No change) = 0.50
P (Economy expands) = 0.20

a. Determine the best investment according to the expected monetary value (*EMV*) criterion. Discuss.

b. Compute the standard deviation for investments *A*, *B*, and *C*.

c. Compute the expected opportunity loss (*EOL*) for investments *A*, *B*, and *C*.

d. Explain the meaning of the expected value of perfect information (*EVPI*) in this problem.

e. Compute the coefficient of variation for investments *A*, *B*, and *C*.

f. Compute the return-to-risk ratio (*RTRR*) for investments *A*, *B*, and *C*.

g. Based on (e) and (f), would you choose investments *A*, *B*, or *C*? Why?

h. Compare the results of (a) and (g) and explain any differences.

i. Suppose the probabilities of the different economic conditions are as follows:
1. 0.1, 0.6, and 0.3
2. 0.1, 0.3, and 0.6
3. 0.4, 0.4, and 0.2
4. 0.6, 0.3, and 0.1

Repeat (a) through (h) with each of these sets of probabilities and compare the results with those originally computed in (h). Discuss.

17.15 In Problem 17.3 on page 710, you developed a payoff table for building a small factory and a large factory for manufacturing designer jeans. Given the results of that problem, suppose that the probabilities of the demand are as follows:

Demand	Probability
10,000	0.1
20,000	0.4
50,000	0.2
100,000	0.3

a. Compute the expected monetary value (*EMV*) for building a small factory and building a large factory.

b. Compute the expected opportunity loss (*EOL*) for building a small factory and building a large factory.

c. Explain the meaning of the expected value of perfect information (*EVPI*) in this problem.

d. Based on the results of (a) or (b), would you choose to build a small factory or a large factory? Why?

e. Compute the coefficient of variation for building a small factory and building a large factory.

f. Compute the return-to-risk ratio (*RTRR*) for building a small factory and building a large factory.

g. Based on (e) and (f), would you choose to build a small factory or a large factory? Why?

h. Compare the results of (d) and (g) and explain any differences.

i. Suppose that the probabilities of demand are 0.4, 0.2, 0.2, and 0.2, respectively. Repeat (a) through (h) with these probabilities and compare the results with those of (a) through (h).

 17.16 In Problem 17.4 on page 710, you developed a payoff table to assist an author in choosing between signing with company *A* or with company *B*. Given the results computed in that problem, suppose that the probabilities of the levels of demand for the novel are as follows:

Demand	Probability
1,000	0.45
2,000	0.20
5,000	0.15
10,000	0.10
50,000	0.10

a. Compute the expected monetary value (*EMV*) for signing with company *A* and with company *B*.

b. Compute the expected opportunity loss (*EOL*) for signing with company *A* and with company *B*.

c. Explain the meaning of the expected value of perfect information (*EVPI*) in this problem.

d. Based on the results of (a) or (b), if you were the author, which company would you choose to sign with, company *A* or company *B*? Why?

e. Compute the coefficient of variation for signing with company *A* and signing with company *B*.

f. Compute the return-to-risk ratio (*RTRR*) for signing with company *A* and signing with company *B*.

g. Based on (e) and (f), which company would you choose to sign with, company *A* or company *B*? Why?

h. Compare the results of (d) and (g) and explain any differences.

i. Suppose that the probabilities of demand are 0.3, 0.2, 0.2, 0.1, and 0.2, respectively. Repeat (a) through (h) with these probabilities and compare the results with those for (a) through (h).

17.17 In Problem 17.5 on page 710, you developed a payoff table for whether to purchase 100, 200, 500, or 1,000 Christmas trees. Given the results of that problem, suppose that the probabilities of the demand for the different number of trees are as follows:

Demand (Number of Trees)	Probability
100	0.20
200	0.50
500	0.20
1,000	0.10

a. Compute the expected monetary value (*EMV*) for purchasing 100, 200, 500, and 1,000 trees.

b. Compute the expected opportunity loss (*EOL*) for purchasing 100, 200, 500, and 1,000 trees.

c. Explain the meaning of the expected value of perfect information (*EVPI*) in this problem.

d. Based on the results of (a) or (b), would you choose to purchase 100, 200, 500, or 1,000 trees? Why?

e. Compute the coefficient of variation for purchasing 100, 200, 500, and 1,000 trees.

f. Compute the return-to-risk ratio (*RTRR*) for purchasing 100, 200, 500, and 1,000 trees.

g. Based on (e) and (f), would you choose to purchase 100, 200, 500, or 1,000 trees? Why?

h. Compare the results of (d) and (g) and explain any differences.

i. Suppose that the probabilities of demand are 0.4, 0.2, 0.2, and 0.2, respectively. Repeat (a) through (h) with these probabilities and compare the results with those for (a) through (h).

17.3   DECISION MAKING WITH SAMPLE INFORMATION

In Sections 17.1 and 17.2 you learned the framework for making decisions when there are several alternative courses of action. You then studied three different criteria for choosing between alternatives. For each criterion, you assigned the probabilities of the various events, using the past experience and/or the subjective judgment of the decision maker. This section introduces decision making when sample information is available to estimate probabilities. Example 17.7 illustrates decision making with sample information.

EXAMPLE 17.7

DECISION MAKING USING SAMPLE INFORMATION FOR THE TELEVISION SET MARKETING EXAMPLE

In Section 4.3 on page 166, you found that the probability of a successful television set, given that the company receives a favorable report, is 0.64. Thus, the probability of an unsuccessful television set, given that the company receives a favorable report, is $1 - 0.64 = 0.36$. Given that the company receives a favorable report, compute the expected monetary value for each alternative course of action and determine whether to market the television set.

SOLUTION You need to use the revised probabilities, not the original subjective probabilities, to compute the expected monetary value of each alternative. Table 17.9 illustrates the computations.

TABLE 17.9

Expected Monetary Value (in Millions of Dollars) Using Revised Probabilities for Each Alternative in the Television Set Marketing Example

| | | | Alternative Course of Action | | |
Event	P_i	Market, A_1	$X_{ij}P_i$	Do Not Market, A_2	$X_{ij}P_i$
Successful	0.64	+45	$45(0.64) = 28.80$	−3	$-3(0.64) = -1.92$
Unsuccessful	0.36	−36	$-36(0.36) = -12.96$	−3	$-3(0.36) = -1.08$
			$EMV(A_1) = 15.84$		$EMV(A_2) = -3.00$

See Section E17.1 to create this.

In this case, the optimal decision is to market the product because a profit of $15.84 million is expected as compared to a loss of $3 million if the television set is not marketed. This decision is different from the one considered optimal prior to the collection of the sample information in the form of the market research report. The favorable recommendation contained in the report greatly increases the probability that the television set will be successful.

Because the relative desirability of the two stocks under consideration in the Using Statistics scenario is directly affected by economic conditions, you should use a forecast of the economic conditions in the upcoming year. You can then use Bayes' theorem, introduced in Section 4.3, to revise the probabilities associated with the different economic conditions. Suppose that such a forecast can predict either an expanding economy (F_1) or a declining or stagnant economy (F_2). Past experience indicates that, when there is a recession, prior forecasts predicted an expanding economy 20% of the time. When there is a stable economy, prior forecasts predicted an expanding economy 40% of the time. When there is moderate growth, prior forecasts predicted an expanding economy 70% of the time. Finally, when there is a boom economy, prior forecasts predicted an expanding economy 90% of the time.

If the forecast is for an expanding economy, you can revise the probabilities of economic conditions by using Bayes' theorem, Equation (4.9) on page 166. Let

event E_1 = recession   event F_1 = expanding economy is predicted

event E_2 = stable economy   event F_2 = declining or stagnant economy is predicted

event E_3 = moderate growth

event E_4 = boom economy

and

$$P(E_1) = 0.10 \quad P(F_1|E_1) = 0.20$$

$$P(E_2) = 0.40 \quad P(F_1|E_2) = 0.40$$

$$P(E_3) = 0.30 \quad P(F_1|E_3) = 0.70$$

$$P(E_4) = 0.20 \quad P(F_1|E_4) = 0.90$$

Then, using Bayes' theorem

$$P(E_1|F_1) = \frac{P(F_1|E_1)P(E_1)}{P(F_1|E_1)P(E_1) + P(F_1|E_2)P(E_2) + P(F_1|E_3)P(E_3) + P(F_1|E_4)P(E_4)}$$

$$= \frac{(0.20)(0.10)}{(0.20)(0.10) + (0.40)(0.40) + (0.70)(0.30) + (0.90)(0.20)}$$

$$= \frac{0.02}{0.57} = 0.035$$

$$P(E_2|F_1) = \frac{P(F_1|E_2)P(E_2)}{P(F_1|E_1)P(E_1) + P(F_1|E_2)P(E_2) + P(F_1|E_3)P(E_3) + P(F_1|E_4)P(E_4)}$$

$$= \frac{(0.40)(0.40)}{(0.20)(0.10) + (0.40)(0.40) + (0.70)(0.30) + (0.90)(0.20)}$$

$$= \frac{0.16}{0.57} = 0.281$$

$$P(E_3|F_1) = \frac{P(F_1|E_3)P(E_3)}{P(F_1|E_1)P(E_1) + P(F_1|E_2)P(E_2) + P(F_1|E_3)P(E_3) + P(F_1|E_4)P(E_4)}$$

$$= \frac{(0.70)(0.30)}{(0.20)(0.10) + (0.40)(0.40) + (0.70)(0.30) + (0.90)(0.20)}$$

$$= \frac{0.21}{0.57} = 0.368$$

$$P(E_4|F_1) = \frac{P(F_1|E_4)P(E_4)}{P(F_1|E_1)P(E_1) + P(F_1|E_2)P(E_2) + P(F_1|E_3)P(E_3) + P(F_1|E_4)P(E_4)}$$

$$= \frac{(0.90)(0.20)}{(0.20)(0.10) + (0.40)(0.40) + (0.70)(0.30) + (0.90)(0.20)}$$

$$= \frac{0.18}{0.57} = 0.316$$

Table 17.10 summarizes the computation of these probabilities. Figure 17.5 displays the joint probabilities in a decision tree. You need to use the revised probabilities, not the original subjective probabilities, to compute the expected monetary value. Table 17.11 shows these computations.

TABLE 17.10

Bayes' Theorem Calculations for the Stock Selection Example

Event, E_i	Prior Probability, $P(E_i)$	Conditional Probability, $P(F_1|E_i)$	Joint Probability, $P(F_1|E_i)P(E_i)$	Revised Probability, $P(E_i|F_1)$
Recession, E_1	0.10	0.20	0.02	0.02/0.57 = 0.035
Stable economy, E_2	0.40	0.40	0.16	0.16/0.57 = 0.281
Moderate growth, E_3	0.30	0.70	0.21	0.21/0.57 = 0.368
Boom, E_4	0.20	0.90	0.18	0.18/0.57 = 0.316
			0.57	

FIGURE 17.5

Decision tree with joint probabilities for stock selection example

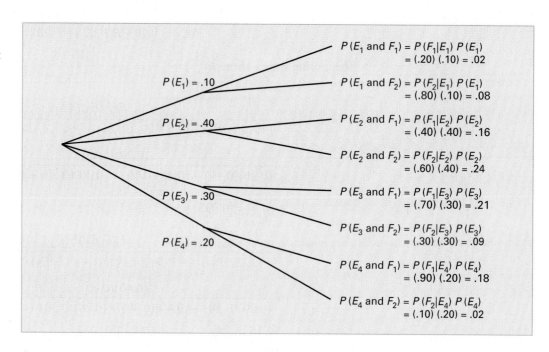

$$P(E_1 \text{ and } F_1) = P(F_1|E_1)\,P(E_1)$$
$$= (.20)\,(.10) = .02$$

$$P(E_1 \text{ and } F_2) = P(F_2|E_1)\,P(E_1)$$
$$= (.80)\,(.10) = .08$$

$$P(E_2 \text{ and } F_1) = P(F_1|E_2)\,P(E_2)$$
$$= (.40)\,(.40) = .16$$

$$P(E_2 \text{ and } F_2) = P(F_2|E_2)\,P(E_2)$$
$$= (.60)\,(.40) = .24$$

$$P(E_3 \text{ and } F_1) = P(F_1|E_3)\,P(E_3)$$
$$= (.70)\,(.30) = .21$$

$$P(E_3 \text{ and } F_2) = P(F_2|E_3)\,P(E_3)$$
$$= (.30)\,(.30) = .09$$

$$P(E_4 \text{ and } F_1) = P(F_1|E_4)\,P(E_4)$$
$$= (.90)\,(.20) = .18$$

$$P(E_4 \text{ and } F_2) = P(F_2|E_4)\,P(E_4)$$
$$= (.10)\,(.20) = .02$$

$P(E_1) = .10$

$P(E_2) = .40$

$P(E_3) = .30$

$P(E_4) = .20$

TABLE 17.11

Expected Monetary Value, Using Revised Probabilities, for Each Alternative for Each of Two Stocks Under Four Economic Conditions

Event	P_i	Alternative Courses of Action				
		A	$X_{ij}P_i$		B	$X_{ij}P_i$
Recession	0.035	30	30(0.035) = 1.05		−50	−50(0.035) = −1.75
Stable economy	0.281	70	70(0.281) = 19.67		30	30(0.281) = 8.43
Moderate growth	0.368	100	100(0.368) = 36.80		250	250(0.368) = 92.00
Boom	0.316	150	150(0.316) = 47.40		400	400(0.316) = 126.40
			EMV(A) = 104.92			EMV(B) = 225.08

Thus, the expected monetary value, or profit, for stock A is $104.92, and the expected monetary value, or profit, for stock B is $225.08. Using this criterion, you should once again choose stock B because the expected monetary value is much higher for this stock. However, you should reexamine the return-to-risk ratios in light of these revised probabilities. Using Equations (5.2) and (5.3) on page 182, for stock A because $\mu_A = \$104.92$,

$$\sigma_A^2 = \sum_{i=1}^{N}(X_i - \mu)^2 P(X_i)$$

$$= (30 - 104.92)^2(0.035) + (70 - 104.92)^2(0.281)$$

$$+ (100 - 104.92)^2(0.368) + (150 - 104.92)^2(0.316)$$

$$= 1,190.194$$

$$\sigma_A = \sqrt{1,190.194} = \$34.50.$$

For stock B, because $\mu_B = \$225.08$,

$$\sigma_B^2 = \sum_{i=1}^{N}(X_i - \mu)^2 P(X_i)$$

$$= (-50 - 225.08)^2(0.035) + (30 - 225.08)^2(0.281)$$

$$+ (250 - 225.08)^2(0.368) + (400 - 225.08)^2(0.316)$$

$$= 23,239.39$$

$$\sigma_B = \sqrt{23,239.39} = \$152.445.$$

To compute the coefficient of variation, substitute σ for S and EMV for $\overline{X}$ in Equation (3.11) on page 110,

$$CV_A = \left(\frac{\sigma_A}{EMV_A}\right)100\%$$

$$= \left(\frac{34.50}{104.92}\right)100\% = 32.88\%$$

and

$$CV_B = \left(\frac{\sigma_B}{EMV_B}\right)100\%$$

$$= \left(\frac{152.445}{225.08}\right)100\% = 67.73\%$$

Thus, there is still much more variation in the returns from stock B than from stock A. For each of these two stocks, you calculate the return-to-risk ratios as follows. For stock A, the return-to-risk ratio is equal to

$$RTRR(A) = \frac{104.92}{34.50} = 3.041$$

For stock B, the return-to-risk ratio is equal to

$$RTRR(B) = \frac{225.08}{152.445} = 1.476$$

Thus, using the return-to-risk ratio, you should select stock A. This decision is different from the one you reached when using expected monetary value (or the equivalent expected opportunity loss). What stock should you buy? Your final decision will depend on whether you believe it is more important to maximize the expected return on investment (select stock B) or to control the relative risk (select stock A).

PROBLEMS FOR SECTION 17.3

Learning the Basics

 17.18 Consider the following payoff table:

| | ACTION | |
EVENT	A ($)	B ($)
1	50	100
2	200	125

For this problem, $P(E_1) = 0.5$, $P(E_2) = 0.5$, $P(F|E_1) = 0.6$, and $P(F|E_2) = 0.4$. Suppose that you are informed that event F occurs.

a. Revise the probabilities $P(E_1)$ and $P(E_2)$ now that you know that event F has occurred.

Based on these revised probabilities, answer (b) through (i).

b. Compute the expected monetary value of action A and action B.

c. Compute the expected opportunity loss of action A and action B.

d. Explain the meaning of the expected value of perfect information ($EVPI$) in this problem.

e. On the basis of (b) or (c), which action should you choose? Why?

f. Compute the coefficient of variation for each action.

g. Compute the return-to-risk ratio ($RTRR$) for each action.

h. On the basis of (f) and (g), which action should you choose? Why?

i. Compare the results of (e) and (h), and explain any differences.

 17.19 Consider the following payoff table:

| | ACTION | |
EVENT	A ($)	B ($)
1	50	10
2	300	100
3	500	200

For this problem, $P(E_1) = 0.8$, $P(E_2) = 0.1$, $P(E_3) = 0.1$, $P(F|E_1) = 0.2$, $P(F|E_2) = 0.4$, and $P(F|E_3) = 0.4$. Suppose you are informed that event F occurs.

a. Revise the probabilities $P(E_1)$, $P(E_2)$, and $P(E_3)$ now that you know that event F has occurred.

Based on these revised probabilities, answer (b) through (i).

b. Compute the expected monetary value of action A and action B.

c. Compute the expected opportunity loss of action A and action B.

d. Explain the meaning of the expected value of perfect information ($EVPI$) in this problem.

e. On the basis of (b) and (c), which action should you choose? Why?

f. Compute the coefficient of variation for each action.

g. Compute the return-to-risk ratio ($RTRR$) for each action.

h. On the basis of (f) and (g), which action should you choose? Why?

i. Compare the results of (e) and (h) and explain any differences.

Applying the Concepts

 17.20 In Problem 17.12 on page 717, a vendor at a baseball stadium was deciding whether to sell ice cream or soft drinks at today's game. Prior to making her decision, she decides to listen to the local weather forecast. In the past, when it has been cool, the weather reporter has forecast cool weather 80% of the time. When it has been warm, the weather reporter has forecast warm weather 70% of the time. The local weather forecast is for cool weather.

a. Revise the prior probabilities now that you know that the weather forecast is for cool weather.

b. Use these revised probabilities to do Problem 17.12.

c. Compare the results in (b) to those of Problem 17.12.

17.21 In Problem 17.14 on page 718, an investor is trying to determine the optimal investment decision among three investment opportunities. Prior to making his investment decision, the investor decides to consult with his financial adviser. In the past, when the economy has declined, the financial adviser has given a rosy forecast 20% of the time (with a gloomy forecast 80% of the time). When there has been no change in the economy, the financial adviser has given a rosy forecast 40% of the time. When there has been an expanding economy, the financial adviser has given a rosy forecast 70% of the time. The financial adviser in this case gives a gloomy forecast for the economy.

a. Revise the probabilities of the investor based on this economic forecast by the financial adviser.

b. Use these revised probabilities to do Problem 17.14.

c. Compare the results in (b) to those of Problem 17.14.

17.22 In Problem 17.16 on page 719, an author is deciding which of two competing publishing companies to select to publish her new novel. Prior to making a final decision, the author decides to have an experienced reviewer examine her novel. This reviewer has an outstanding reputation for predicting the success of a novel. In the past, for novels that sold 1,000 copies, only 1% received favorable reviews. Of novels that sold 5,000 copies, 25% received favorable reviews. Of novels that sold 10,000 copies, 60% received favorable reviews. Of novels that sold 50,000 copies, 99% received favorable reviews. After examining the author's novel, the reviewer gives it an unfavorable review.

a. Revise the probabilities of the number of books sold in light of the reviewer's unfavorable review.
b. Use these revised probabilities to do Problem 17.16.
c. Compare the results in (b) to those of Problem 17.16.

17.4   UTILITY

The methods used in Sections 17.1 through 17.3 assume that each *incremental* amount of profit or loss has the same value as the previous amounts of profits attained or losses incurred. In fact, under many circumstances in the business world, this assumption of incremental changes is not valid. Most companies, as well as most individuals, make special efforts to avoid large losses. At the same time, many companies, as well as most individuals, place less value on extremely large profits as compared to initial profits. Such differential evaluation of incremental profits or losses is referred to as **utility**, a concept first discussed by Daniel Bernoulli in the eighteenth century (see reference 1). To illustrate this concept, suppose that you are faced with the following two choices:

Choice 1: A fair coin is to be tossed. If it lands on heads, you will receive $0.60; if it lands on tails, you will pay $0.40.
Choice 2: Do not play the game.

What decision should you choose? The expected value of playing this game is $(0.60)(0.50) + (-0.40)(0.50) = +\$0.10$, and the expected value of not playing the game is 0.

Most people will decide to play the game because the expected value is positive and only small amounts of money are involved. Suppose, however, that the game is formulated with a payoff of $600,000 when the coin lands on heads and a loss of $400,000 when the coin lands on tails. The expected value of playing the game is now +$100,000. With these payoffs, even though the expected value is positive, most individuals will not play the game because of the severe negative consequences of losing $400,000. Each additional dollar amount of either profit or loss does not have the same utility as the previous amount. Large negative amounts for most individuals have severely negative utility. Conversely, the extra value of each incremental dollar of profit decreases when high enough profit levels are reached. (In other words, the difference between 0 and $100,000 is much more than the difference between $1,000,000 and $1,100,000.)

An important part of the decision-making process, which is beyond the scope of this text (see references 2 and 3), is to develop a utility curve for the decision maker that represents the utility of each specified dollar amount. Figure 17.6 illustrates three types of utility curves: those of the risk averter, the risk seeker, and the risk-neutral person.

FIGURE 17.6

Three types of utility curves

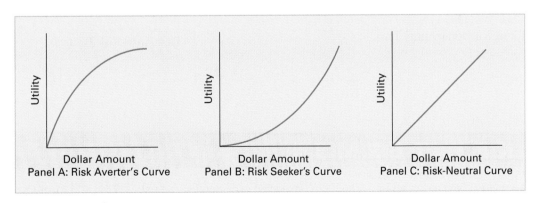

The **risk averter's curve** shows a rapid increase in utility for initial amounts of money followed by a gradual leveling off for increasing dollar amounts. This curve is appropriate for most individuals or businesses because the value of each additional dollar is not as great after large amounts of money have already been earned.

The **risk seeker's curve** represents the utility of someone who enjoys taking risks. The utility is greater for large dollar amounts. This curve represents an individual who is interested only in "striking it rich" and is willing to take large risks for the opportunity of making large profits.

The **risk-neutral curve** represents the expected monetary value approach. Each additional dollar of profit has the same value as the previous dollar.

After a utility curve is developed in a specific situation, you convert the dollar amounts to utilities. Then you compute the utility of each alternative course of action and apply the decision criteria of expected utility value, expected opportunity loss, and return-to-risk ratio to make a decision.

PROBLEMS FOR SECTION 17.4

Applying the Concepts

17.23 Do you consider yourself a risk seeker, a risk averter, or a risk-neutral person? Explain.

17.24 Refer to Problems 17.3–17.5 and 17.12–17.14 on pages 710 and 718–719, respectively. In which problems do you think the expected monetary value (risk-neutral) criterion is inappropriate? Why?

S U M M A R Y

In this chapter, you learned how to develop payoff tables and decision trees, to use various criteria to choose between alternative courses of action, and to revise probabilities in light of sample information, using Bayes' theorem. In the Using Statistics scenario, you learned how a manager of a mutual fund could use these tools to decide whether to purchase stock *A* or stock *B*. You found that stock *B* had a higher expected monetary value, a lower expected opportunity loss, but a lower return-to-risk ratio.

K E Y   E Q U A T I O N S

Expected Monetary Value

$$EMV(j) = \sum_{i=1}^{N} X_{ij}P_i \qquad (17.1)$$

Expected Opportunity Loss

$$EOL(j) = \sum_{i=1}^{N} L_{ij}P_i \qquad (17.2)$$

Expected Value of Perfect Information

$$EVPI = \text{Expected profit under certainty}$$
$$- \text{Expected monetary value of the}$$
$$\text{best alternative} \qquad (17.3)$$

Return-to-Risk Ratio

$$RTRR(j) = \frac{EMV(j)}{\sigma_j} \qquad (17.4)$$

K E Y   T E R M S

CHAPTER REVIEW PROBLEMS

Checking Your Understanding

 **17.25** What is the difference between an event and an alternative course of action?

17.26 What are the advantages and disadvantages of a payoff table as compared to a decision tree?

 17.27 How are opportunity losses computed from payoffs?

 17.28 Why can't an opportunity loss be negative?

17.29 How does expected monetary value (*EMV*) differ from expected opportunity loss (*EOL*)?

17.30 What is the meaning of the expected value of perfect information (*EVPI*)?

17.31 How does the expected value of perfect information differ from the expected profit under certainty?

17.32 What are the advantages and disadvantages of using expected monetary value (*EMV*) as compared to the return-to-risk ratio (*RTRR*)?

17.33 How is Bayes' theorem used to revise probabilities in light of the sample information?

17.34 What is the difference between a risk averter and a risk seeker?

17.35 Why should you use utilities instead of payoffs in certain circumstances?

Applying the Concepts

17.36 A supermarket chain purchases large quantities of white bread for sale during a week. The stores purchase the bread for $0.75 per loaf and sell it for $1.10 per loaf. Any loaves not sold by the end of the week can be sold to a local thrift shop for $0.40. Based on past demand, the probability of various levels of demand is as follows:

Demand (Loaves)	Probability
6,000	0.10
8,000	0.50
10,000	0.30
12,000	0.10

a. Construct the payoff table, indicating the events and alternative courses of action.
b. Construct the decision tree.
c. Compute the expected monetary value (*EMV*) for purchasing 6,000, 8,000, 10,000, and 12,000 loaves.

d. Compute the expected opportunity loss (*EOL*) for purchasing 6,000, 8,000, 10,000, and 12,000 loaves.
e. Explain the meaning of the expected value of perfect information (*EVPI*) in this problem.
f. Based on the results of (c) or (d), how many loaves would you purchase? Why?
g. Compute the coefficient of variation for each purchase level.
h. Compute the return-to-risk ratio (*RTRR*) for each purchase level.
i. Based on (g) and (h), what action would you choose? Why?
j. Compare the results of (f) and (i) and explain any differences.
k. Suppose that new information changes the probabilities associated with the demand level. Use the following probabilities to repeat (c) through (j).

Demand (Loaves)	Probability
6,000	0.30
8,000	0.40
10,000	0.20
12,000	0.10

17.37 The owner of a company that supplies home heating oil would like to determine whether to offer a solar heating installation service to its customers. The owner of the company has determined that a startup cost of $150,000 would be necessary, but a profit of $2,000 can be made on each solar heating system installed. The owner estimates the probability of various demand levels as follows:

Number of Units Installed	Probability
50	0.40
100	0.30
200	0.30

a. Construct the payoff table, indicating the events and alternative courses of action.
b. Construct the decision tree.
c. Construct the opportunity loss table.
d. Compute the expected monetary value (*EMV*) for offering this solar heating system installation service.
e. Compute the expected opportunity loss (*EOL*) for offering this solar heating system installation service.
f. Explain the meaning of the expected value of perfect information (*EVPI*) in this problem.

g. Compute the return-to-risk ratio (*RTRR*) for offering this solar heating system installation service.

h. Based on the results of (d) or (e) and (g), should the company offer this solar heating system installation service? Why?

i. How would your answers to (a) through (h) be affected if the startup cost were $200,000?

17.38 The manufacturer of a nationally distributed brand of potato chips wants to determine the feasibility of changing the product package from a cellophane bag to an unbreakable container. The product manager believes that there are three possible national market responses to a change in product package: weak, moderate, and strong. The projected payoffs, in millions of dollars, in increased or decreased profit compared to the current package are as follows:

	STRATEGY	
EVENT	**Use New Package**	**Keep Old Package**
Weak national response	−4	0
Moderate national response	1	0
Strong national response	5	0

Based on past experience, the product manager assigns the following probabilities to the different levels of national response:

P (Weak national response) = 0.30
P (Moderate national response) = 0.60
P (Strong national response) = 0.10

a. Construct the decision tree.
b. Construct the opportunity loss table.
c. Compute the expected monetary value (*EMV*) for offering this new product package.
d. Compute the expected opportunity loss (*EOL*) for offering this new product package.
e. Explain the meaning of the expected value of perfect information (*EVPI*) in this problem.
f. Compute the return-to-risk ratio (*RTRR*) for offering this new product package.
g. Based on the results of (c) or (d) and (f), should the company offer this new product package? Why?
h. What are your answers to parts (c) through (g) if the probabilities are 0.6, 0.3, and 0.1, respectively?
i. What are your answers to parts (c) through (g) if the probabilities are 0.1, 0.3, and 0.6, respectively?

Before making a final decision, the product manager would like to test market the new package in a selected city by substituting the new package for the old package. A determination is then made about whether sales have increased, decreased, or stayed the same. In previous test marketing of other products, when there was a subsequent weak national response, sales in the test city decreased 60%

of the time, stayed the same 30% of the time, and increased 10% of the time. Where there was a moderate national response, sales in the test city decreased 20% of the time, stayed the same 40% of the time, and increased 40% of the time. When there was a strong national response, sales in the test city decreased 5% of the time, stayed the same 35% of the time, and increased 60% of the time.

j. If sales in the test city stayed the same, revise the original probabilities in light of this new information.
k. Use the revised probabilities in (j) to repeat (c) through (g).
l. If sales in the test city decreased, revise the original probabilities in light of this new information.
m. Use the revised probabilities in (l) to repeat (c) through (g).

17.39 An entrepreneur wants to determine whether it would be profitable to establish a gardening service in a local suburb. The entrepreneur believes that there are four possible levels of demand for this gardening service:

Very low demand—1% of the households would use the service.

Low demand—5% of the households would use the service.

Moderate demand—10% of the households would use the service.

High demand—25% of the households would use the service.

Based on past experiences in other suburbs, the entrepreneur assigns the following probabilities to the various demand levels:

P(Very low demand) = 0.20
P(Low demand) = 0.50
P(Moderate demand) = 0.20
P(High demand) = 0.10

The entrepreneur has calculated the following profits or losses ($) of this garden service for each demand level (over a period of 1 year):

	ACTION	
DEMAND	**Provide Garden Service**	**Do Not Provide Garden Service**
Very low	−50,000	0
Low	60,000	0
Moderate	130,000	0
High	300,000	0

a. Construct a decision tree.
b. Construct an opportunity loss table.
c. Compute the expected monetary value (*EMV*) for offering this garden service.
d. Compute the expected opportunity loss (*EOL*) for offering this garden service.

e. Explain the meaning of the expected value of perfect information (*EVPI*) in this problem.
f. Compute the return-to-risk ratio (*RTRR*) for offering this garden service.
g. Based on the results of (c) or (d), and (f), should the entrepreneur offer this garden service? Why?

Before making a final decision, the entrepreneur conducts a survey to determine demand for the gardening service. A random sample of 20 households is selected, and 3 indicate that they would use this gardening service.

h. Revise the prior probabilities in light of this sample information. (*Hint:* Use the binomial distribution to determine the probability of the outcome that occurred, given a particular level of demand.)
i. Use the revised probabilities in (h) to repeat (c) through (g).

17.40 A manufacturer of a brand of inexpensive felt-tip pens maintains a production process that produces 10,000 pens per day. In order to maintain the highest quality of this product, the manufacturer guarantees free replacement of any defective pen sold. Each defective pen produced costs 20 cents for the manufacturer to replace. Based on past experience, four rates of producing defective pens are possible:

Very low—1% of the pens manufactured will be defective.

Low—5% of the pens manufactured will be defective.

Moderate—10% of the pens manufactured will be defective.

High—20% of the pens manufactured will be defective.

The manufacturer can reduce the rate of defective pens produced by having a mechanic fix the machines at the end of each day. This mechanic can reduce the rate to 1%, but his services will cost $80.

A payoff table based on the daily production of 10,000 pens, indicating the replacement costs ($) for each of the two alternatives (calling in the mechanic and not calling in the mechanic), is as follows:

	ACTION	
	Do Not Call	Call
DEFECTIVE RATE	Mechanic	Mechanic
Very low (1%)	20	100
Low (5%)	100	100
Moderate (10%)	200	100
High (20%)	400	100

Based on past experience, each defective rate is assumed to be equally likely to occur.

a. Construct a decision tree.
b. Construct an opportunity loss table.
c. Compute the expected monetary value (*EMV*) for calling and for not calling the mechanic.
d. Compute the expected opportunity loss (*EOL*) for calling and for not calling the mechanic.
e. Explain the meaning of the expected value of perfect information (*EVPI*) in this problem.
f. Compute the return-to-risk ratio (*RTRR*) for not calling the mechanic.
g. Based on the results of (c) or (d), and (f), should the company call the mechanic? Why?
h. At the end of a day's production, a sample of 15 pens is selected, and 2 are defective. Revise the prior probabilities in light of this sample information. (*Hint:* Use the binomial distribution to determine the probability of the outcome that occurred, given a particular defective rate.)
i. Use the revised probabilities in (h) to repeat (c) through (g).

Web Case

Apply your knowledge of decision-making techniques in this Web Case, which extends the EndRun Web Case from earlier chapters.

StraightArrow Banking & Investments is a Tri-Cities competitor of EndRun that is currently advertising its StraightArrow StraightDeal fund.

Visit the StraightArrow Web page at **www.prenhall.com/ Springville/SA_Home.htm** (or open the Web page file from the Student CD-ROM Web Case Folder), and examine the claims and supporting data for the fund. Compare those claims and data to the supporting data found on the EndRun Happy Bull and Worried Bear Funds Web page, **www.prenhall.com/Springville/ER_BullsandBears.htm**

(or open the Web page file from the Student CD-ROM **Web Case** folder) first discussed in the Web Case for Chapter 5. Then answer the following:

1. Is the StraightArrow StraightDeal fund a better investment than either of the EndRun funds? Support your answer by performing an appropriate analysis and summarize your results.
2. Before making a decision about which fund makes a better investment, you decide that you need a reliable forecast for the direction of the economy in the next year. After further investigation, you find that the consensus of leading economists is that the economy will be expanding in the next year. You also find out that in the past, when there has been

a recession, leading economists predicted an expanding economy 10% of the time. When there was a stable economy, they predicted an expanding economy 50% of the time, and when there was an expanding economy, they predicted an expanding economy 75% of the time. When there was a rapidly expanding economy, they predicted an expanding economy 90% of the time. Does this information change your answer to Question 1? Why or why not?

REFERENCES

1. Bernstein, P. L., *Against the Gods: The Remarkable Story of Risk* (New York: Wiley, 1996).
2. Render, B., R. M. Stair, and M. Hanna, *Quantitative Analysis for Management*, 9th ed. (Upper Saddle River, NJ: Prentice Hall, 2006).
3. Tversky, A., and D. Kahneman, "Rationale Choice and the Framing of Decisions," *Journal of Business*, 59 (1986): 251–278.

Excel Companion
to Chapter 17

E17.1 COMPUTING OPPORTUNITY LOSS

You compute opportunity loss by either selecting the PHStat2 Opportunity Loss procedure or making entries in the Opportunity Loss.xls workbook.

Using PHStat2 Opportunity Loss

Select **PHStat → Decision-Making → Opportunity Loss**. In the procedure's dialog box (shown below), enter values for both the **Number of Events** and the **Number of Alternative Actions**. Enter a title as the **Title** and click **OK**.

PHStat2 creates a worksheet in which you enter your payoff table data, such as Table 17.1 on page 707, in the Payoff Table area that begins in row 4. You can also enter custom row and column labels for your data. Before you enter your data, some worksheet cells display the message #DIV/0!. This is not an error.

Using Opportunity Loss.xls

Open to the **OLT2x2** worksheet of the Opportunity Loss.xls workbook. This worksheet (shown in Figure 17.3 on page 709) uses the **INDEX(*cell range*, 1, *column number*)** and **MATCH(*cell to be matched, cell range in which to look for a match*, 0)** functions together to display the correct alternative course of action labels for the cells in the Optimum Action column.

Figure E17.1 shows the formulas for columns B through E of the opportunity loss table. The MATCH function in the column B formulas matches the optimum profit found in column C with one of two payoff values and returns either the value 1 or 2, depending on whether the first or second payoff value matched the optimum profit. The returned value (1 or 2) is, in turn, used by INDEX as the *column number* to decide which of the two alternative course-of-action labels will be displayed in the column B cell.

	B	C	D	E
				Alternatives
10	Optimum	Optimum		
11	Action	Profit	=B4	=C4
12	=INDEX($B$4:$C$4, 1, MATCH(C12, B5:C5, 0))	=MAX(B5:C5)	=$C12 - B5	=$C12 - C5
13	=INDEX($B$4:$C$4, 1, MATCH(C13, B6:C6, 0))	=MAX(B6:C6)	=$C13 - B6	=$C13 - C6

FIGURE E17.1 Opportunity loss table, columns B through E formulas

You can modify this worksheet for other problems involving two events and two alternative courses of action by making new entries in the Payoff Table area. Although modifying the worksheet for other numbers of events and alternative courses of action is beyond the scope of this book, advanced Excel users can use the hints provided by the mix of absolute and relative cell references shown in Figure E17.1 to plan how to alter the worksheet.

E17.2 COMPUTING EXPECTED MONETARY VALUE

You compute the expected monetary value by either selecting the PHStat2 Expected Monetary Value procedure or making entries in the Expected Monetary Value.xls workbook.

Using PHStat2 Expected Monetary Value

Select **PHStat → Decision-Making → Expected Monetary Value**. In the procedure's dialog box (shown on page 732), enter values for both the **Number of Events** and the **Number of Alternative Actions**. Enter a title as the **Title**, click **Expected Opportunity Loss** and **Measures of Variation** and then click **OK**.

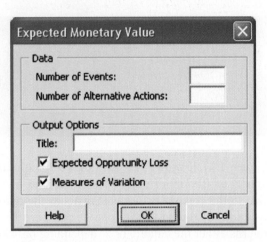

PHStat2 creates a worksheet in which you enter your custom row and column labels, probabilities and payoff table data in the area that begins in row 4. Before you enter your data, some worksheet cells display the message #DIV/0!. This is not an error.

Using Expected Monetary Value.xls

Open to the **EMV4Ex2A** worksheet of the **Expected Monetary Value.xls** workbook. This worksheet (shown in Figure 17.4 on page 716) uses the INDEX and MATCH functions in the same way that the OLT2x2 worksheet uses them (see page 716). The EMV4Ex2A worksheet uses the **SUMPRODUCT(*multiplier cell range, multiplicand cell range*)** function to compute the expected monetary value, the variance, and the expected opportunity loss

You can modify this worksheet for other problems involving four events and two alternative courses of action by making new entries in the Probabilities & Payoff Table area. Although modifying the worksheet for other numbers of events and alternative courses of action is beyond the scope of this text, advanced Excel users may benefit from studying the formulas displayed in the **EMV4Ex2AFormulas** worksheet.

CHAPTER 18

Statistical Applications in Quality Management

USING STATISTICS @ Beachcomber Hotel

LEARNING OBJECTIVES

In this chapter, you learn:
- The basic themes of quality management and Deming's 14 points
- The basic aspects of Six Sigma management
- How to construct various control charts
- Which control chart to use for a particular type of data
- How to measure the capability of a process

Using Statistics @ Beachcomber Hotel

You find yourself managing the Beachcomber Hotel, one of the resorts owned by T.C. Resort Properties (see Chapter 12). You want to continually improve the quality of service that your guests receive so that overall guest satisfaction increases. To help you achieve this improvement, T.C. Resort Properties has provided its managers with training in Six Sigma management. In order to meet the business objective of increasing the return rate of guests at your hotel, you have decided to focus on the critical first impressions of the service that your hotel provides. Is the assigned hotel room ready when a guest checks in? Are all expected amenities, such as extra towels and a complimentary guest basket, in the room when the guest first walks in? Are the video-entertainment center and high-speed Internet access working properly? And do guests receive their luggage in a reasonable amount of time?

To study these guest satisfaction issues, you have embarked on an improvement project that measures two critical-to-quality (CTQ) measurements: the readiness of the room and the time it takes to deliver luggage. You would like to learn the following:

■ Are the proportion of rooms ready and the time required to deliver luggage to the rooms acceptable?

■ Are the proportion of rooms ready and the luggage delivery time consistent from day to day, or are they increasing or decreasing?

■ On the days when the proportion of rooms that are not ready or the time to deliver luggage is greater than normal, are these due to a chance occurrences, or are there fundamental flaws in the processes used to make rooms ready and to deliver luggage?

Companies manufacturing products, as well as those providing services, such as the Beachcomber Hotel in the "Using Statistics" scenario, realize that quality is essential for survival in the global economy. Among the areas in which quality has an impact on our everyday work and personal lives are:

▪ The design, production, and reliability of our automobiles
▪ The services provided by hotels, banks, schools, retailing operations, and mail-order companies
▪ The continuous improvement in computer chips that makes for faster and more powerful computers
▪ The ever-expanding capability of communication devices such as data transmission lines, paging devices, facsimile machines, and cellular telephones
▪ The availability of new technology and equipment that has led to improved diagnosis of illnesses and the improved delivery of health care services

18.1 TOTAL QUALITY MANAGEMENT

During the past 25 years, a renewed interest in quality and productivity in the United States has occurred as a reaction to improvements of Japanese industry that began as early as 1950. Individuals such as W. Edwards Deming, Joseph Juran, and Kaoru Ishikawa developed an approach that focuses on continuous improvement of products and services through an increased emphasis on statistics, process improvement, and optimization of the total system.

This approach, widely known as **total quality management (TQM)**, is characterized by these themes:

- The primary focus is on process improvement.
- Most of the variation in a process is due to the system and not the individual.
- Teamwork is an integral part of a quality management organization.
- Customer satisfaction is a primary organizational goal.
- Organizational transformation must occur in order to implement quality management.
- Fear must be removed from organizations.
- Higher quality costs less, not more, but requires an investment in training.

In the 1980s, the federal government of the United States increased its efforts to improve quality in American business. Congress passed the Malcolm Baldrige National Improvement Act of 1987 and began awarding the Malcolm Baldrige Award to companies making the greatest strides in improving quality and customer satisfaction. W. Edwards Deming became a prominent consultant to many Fortune 500 companies, including Ford, General Motors, and Procter & Gamble. Many companies adopted some or all of **Deming's 14 points for management** listed here:

1. Create constancy of purpose for improvement of product and service.
2. Adopt the new philosophy.
3. Cease dependence on inspection to achieve quality.
4. End the practice of awarding business on the basis of price tag alone. Instead, minimize total cost by working with a single supplier.
5. Improve constantly and forever every process for planning, production, and service.
6. Institute training on the job.
7. Adopt and institute leadership.
8. Drive out fear.
9. Break down barriers between staff areas.
10. Eliminate slogans, exhortations, and targets for the workforce.
11. Eliminate numerical quotas for the workforce and numerical goals for management.
12. Remove barriers that rob people of pride of workmanship. Eliminate the annual rating or merit system.
13. Institute a vigorous program of education and self-improvement for everyone.
14. Put everyone in the company to work to accomplish the transformation.

Point 1, create constancy of purpose, refers to how an organization deals with problems that arise both at present and in the future. The focus is on the constant improvement of a product or service. This improvement process is illustrated by the **Shewhart-Deming cycle**, shown in Figure 18.1.

FIGURE 18.1

Shewhart-Deming cycle

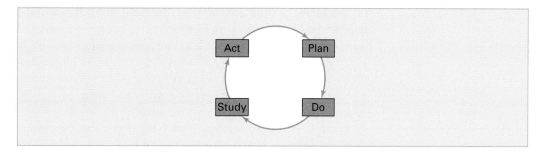

The Shewhart-Deming cycle represents a continuous cycle of "plan, do, study, and act." The first step, planning, represents the initial design phase for planning a change in a manufacturing or service process. This step involves teamwork among individuals from different areas within an organization. The second step, doing, involves implementing the change, preferably on a small scale. The third step, studying, involves analyzing the results, using statistical methods to determine what was learned. The fourth step, acting, involves the acceptance of the change, its abandonment, or further study of the change under different conditions.

Point 2, adopt the new philosophy, refers to the urgency with which companies need to realize that there is a new economic age of global competition. It is better to be proactive and change before a crisis occurs than to react to some negative experiences that may have occurred. Rather than take the approach "if it's not broke, don't fix it," it is better to continually work on improvement and avoid expensive fixes.

Point 3, cease dependence on inspection to achieve quality, implies that any inspection whose purpose is to improve quality is too late because the quality is already built into the product. It is better to focus on making it right the first time. Among the difficulties involved in inspection (besides high costs) are the failure of inspectors to agree on the operational definitions for nonconforming items and the problem of separating good and bad items. The following example illustrates the difficulties inspectors face.

Suppose your job involves proofreading the sentence in Figure 18.2, with the objective of counting the number of occurrences of the letter *F*. Perform this task and record the number of occurrences of the letter *F* that you discover.

FIGURE 18.2

An example of a proofreading process

Source: Adapted from W. W. Scherkenbach, The Deming Route to Quality and Productivity: Road Maps and Roadblocks *(Washington, DC: Ceep Press, 1986).*

FINISHED FILES ARE THE RESULT OF YEARS OF SCIENTIFIC STUDY COMBINED WITH THE EXPERIENCE OF MANY YEARS

People usually see either three Fs or six Fs. The correct number is six Fs. The number you see depends on the method you use to examine the sentence. You are likely to find three Fs if you read the sentence phonetically and six Fs if you count the number of Fs carefully. The point of the exercise is to show that if such a simple process as counting Fs leads to inconsistency of inspectors' results, what will happen when a much more complicated process fails to provide clear operational definitions? Certainly, in such situations, a large amount of variability occurs from inspector to inspector.

Point 4, end the practice of awarding business on the basis of price tag alone, implies that there is no real long-term meaning to price without knowledge of the quality of the product.

Point 5—improve constantly and forever every process for planning, production and service—reinforces the importance of the continuous focus of the Shewhart-Deming cycle and the belief that quality needs to be built in at the design stage. Attaining quality is a never-ending process in which reduction in variation translates into reduction in the financial losses resulting from products and services experiencing large fluctuations in quality.

Point 6, institute training, reflects the needs of all employees, including production workers, engineers, and managers. It is critically important for management to understand the differences between special causes and common causes of variation (see Section 18.3) so that proper action is taken in each circumstance.

Point 7, adopt and institute leadership, relates to the distinction between leadership and supervision. The aim of leadership should be to improve the system and achieve greater consistency of performance.

Points 8 through 12—drive out fear, break down barriers between staff areas, eliminate slogans, eliminate numerical quotas for the workforce and numerical goals for management, and remove barriers to pride of workmanship (including the annual rating and merit system)—are all related to the evaluation of employee performance. An emphasis on targets and exhortations may place an improper burden on the workforce. Workers cannot produce beyond what the system allows (this is clearly illustrated in Section 18.5). It is management's job to *improve* the system, not to raise the expectations on workers beyond the system's capability.

Point 13, encourage education and self-improvement for everyone, reflects the belief that the most important resource of any organization is its people. Efforts that improve the knowledge of people in the organization also serve to increase the assets of the organization. Education and self-improvement can lead to reduced turnover within an organization.

Point 14, take action to accomplish the transformation, again reflects the approach of management as a process in which one continuously strives toward improvement, in a never-ending cycle.

Although Deming's points are thought provoking, some have criticized his approach for lacking a formal, objective accountability. Many managers of large organizations, used to seeing financial analyses of policy changes, need a more prescriptive approach.

18.2 SIX SIGMA MANAGEMENT

Six Sigma management is a quality improvement system originally developed by Motorola in the mid-1980s. **Six Sigma** offers a more prescriptive and systematic approach to process improvement than TQM, and it places a higher emphasis on accountability and bottom-line results. Many companies all over the world are using Six Sigma management to improve efficiency, cut costs, eliminate defects, and reduce product variation.

The name Six Sigma comes from the fact that it is a managerial approach designed to create processes that result in no more than 3.4 defects per million.[1] One of the aspects that distinguishes Six Sigma from other approaches is a clear focus on achieving bottom-line results in a relatively short three- to six-month period of time. After seeing the huge financial successes at Motorola, GE, and other early adopters of Six Sigma, many companies worldwide have now instituted Six Sigma programs (see references 1, 9, 10, 11, 13, and 16).

To guide managers in their task of improving short- and long-term results, Six Sigma uses a five-step process known as the **DMAIC model**—named for the five steps in the process:

- **Define** The problem is defined, along with the costs, the benefits, and the impact on the customer.
- **Measure** Operational definitions for each **critical-to-quality (CTQ)** characteristic are developed. In addition, the measurement procedure is verified so that it is consistent over repeated measurements.
- **Analyze** The root causes of *why* defects occur are determined, and variables in the process causing the defects are identified. Data are collected to determine benchmark values for each process variable. This analysis often uses control charts (discussed in Sections 18.3–18.6).
- **Improve** The importance of each process variable on the CTQ characteristic is studied using designed experiments (see Chapter 11 and references 9, 10, and 13). The objective is to determine the best level for each variable.
- **Control** The objective is to maintain the benefits for the long term by avoiding potential problems that can occur when a process is changed.

Implementation of Six Sigma management requires a data-oriented approach that is heavily based on using statistical tools such as control charts and designed experiments. It also involves training everyone in the organization in the DMAIC model. For more information on Six Sigma management, see references 1, 9, 10, 11, 13, and 16.

[1] *The Six Sigma approach assumes that the process may shift as much as 1.5 standard deviations over the long term. Six standard deviations minus a 1.5 standard deviation shift produces a 4.5 standard deviation goal. The area under the normal curve outside 4.5 standard deviations is approximately 3.4 out of 1 million (0.0000034).*

18.3 THE THEORY OF CONTROL CHARTS

TQM and Six Sigma management use many different statistical tools. One tool widely used in each approach to analyze process data collected sequentially over time is the control chart.

A **control chart** monitors variation in a characteristic of a product or service over time. You can use a control chart to study past performance, to evaluate present conditions, or to predict future outcomes (see references 8, 9, and 13). Information gained from analyzing a control chart forms the basis for process improvement. Different types of control charts allow you to analyze different types of CTQ variables—for categorical variables, such as the proportion of hotel rooms that are nonconforming in terms of the availability of amenities and the working order of all appliances in the room, and continuous variables, such as the length of time required for delivering luggage to the room. In addition to providing a visual display of data representing a process, a principal focus of a control chart is the attempt to separate special causes of variation from common causes of variation.

Special causes of variation represent large fluctuations or patterns in the data that are not inherent to a process. These fluctuations are often caused by changes in the process that represent either problems to correct or opportunities to exploit. Some organizations refer to special causes of variation as **assignable causes of variation**.

Common causes of variation represent the inherent variability that exists in a process. These fluctuations consist of the numerous small causes of variability that operate randomly or by chance. Some organizations refer to common causes of variation as **chance causes of variation**.

One experiment that is useful to help you appreciate the distinction between common and special causes of variation was developed by Walter Shewhart more than 80 years ago. The experiment requires that you repeatedly write the letter A over and over again in a horizontal line across a piece of paper:

AAAAAAAAAAAAAAAAA

When you do this, you immediately notice that the As are all similar but not exactly the same. In addition, you may notice some difference in the size of the As from letter to letter. This difference is due to common cause variation. Nothing special happened that caused the differences in the size of the As. You probably would have a hard time trying to explain why the largest A is bigger than the smallest A. These types of differences almost certainly represent common cause variation. However, if you did the experiment over again but wrote half of the As with your right hand and the other half of the As with your left hand, you would almost certainly see a very big difference in the As written with each hand. In this case, which hand was used to write the As is the source of the special cause variation.

The distinction between the two causes of variation is crucial because special causes of variation are not part of a process and are correctable or exploitable without changing the system. Common causes of variation, however, can be reduced only by changing the system. Such systemic changes are the responsibility of management.

Control charts allow you to monitor a process and identify the presence or absence of special causes. By doing so, control charts help prevent two types of errors. The first type of error involves the belief that an observed value represents special cause variation when it is due to the common cause variation of the system. Treating common cause variation as special cause variation often results in overadjusting a process. This overadjustment, known as **tampering**, increases the variation in the process. The second type of error involves treating special cause variation as common cause variation. This error results in not taking immediate corrective action when necessary. Although both of these types of errors can occur even when using a control chart, they are far less likely.

To construct a control chart, you collect samples from the output of a process over time. The samples used for constructing control charts are known as **subgroups**. For each subgroup (that is, sample), you calculate the value of a statistic associated with a CTQ variable.

Commonly used statistics include the sample proportion for categorical variables (see Section 18.4) and the mean and range of a numerical variable (see Section 18.6). You then plot the values over time and add control limits to the chart. The most typical form of a control chart sets control limits that are within ±3 standard deviations[2] of the statistical measure of interest. Equation (18.1) defines, in general, the upper and lower control limits for control charts.

[2]*Recall from Section 6.2 that in the normal distribution, $\mu \pm 3\sigma$ includes almost all (99.73%) of the values in the population.*

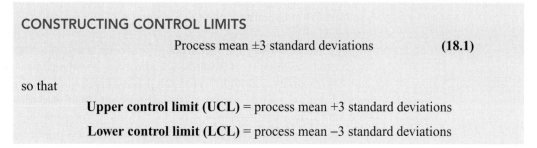

CONSTRUCTING CONTROL LIMITS

$$\text{Process mean} \pm 3 \text{ standard deviations} \qquad (18.1)$$

so that

Upper control limit (UCL) = process mean +3 standard deviations

Lower control limit (LCL) = process mean −3 standard deviations

When these control limits are set, you evaluate the control chart by trying to find any pattern that might exist in the values over time and by determining whether any points fall outside the control limits. Figure 18.3 illustrates three different situations.

FIGURE 18.3

Three control chart patterns

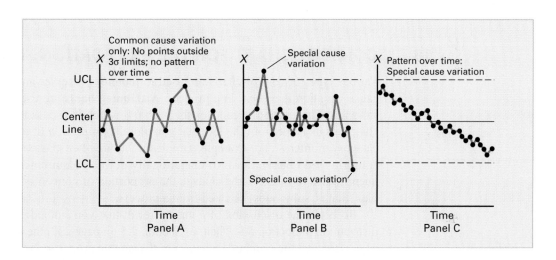

In Panel A of Figure 18.3, there is no apparent pattern in the values over time, and there are no points that fall outside the 3 standard deviation control limits. The process appears stable and contains only common cause variation. Panel B, on the contrary, contains two points that fall outside the 3 standard deviation control limits. You should investigate these points to try to determine the special causes that led to their occurrence. Although Panel C does not have any points outside the control limits, it has a series of consecutive points above the mean value (the center line) as well as a series of consecutive points below the mean value. In addition, a long-term overall downward trend is clearly visible. You should investigate the situation to try to determine what may have caused this pattern.

The detection of a trend is not always so obvious. Two other simple rules (see references 8, 9, and 13) allow you to detect a shift in the mean level of a process:

- Eight or more *consecutive points* that lie above the center line or eight or more *consecutive points* that lie below the center line
- Eight or more *consecutive points* that move upward in value or eight or more *consecutive points* that move downward in value

A process whose control chart indicates an out-of-control condition (that is, a point outside the control limits, a series of points that exhibits a trend) is said to be out of control. An **out-of-control process** contains both common causes of variation and special causes of variation.

Because special causes of variation are not part of the process design, an out-of-control process is unpredictable. When you determine that a process is out of control, you must identify the special causes of variation that are producing the out-of-control conditions. If the special causes are detrimental to the quality of the product or service, you need to implement plans to eliminate this source of variation. When a special cause increases quality, you should change the process so that the special cause is incorporated into the process design. Thus, this beneficial special cause now becomes a common cause source of variation, and the process is improved.

A process whose control chart does not indicate any out-of-control conditions is said to be in control. An **in-control process** contains only common causes of variation. Because these sources of variation are inherent to the process itself, an in-control process is predictable. In-control processes are sometimes said to be in a **state of statistical control**. When a process is in control, you must determine whether the amount of common cause variation in the process is small enough to satisfy the customers of the products or services. (In Section 18.7, you will learn statistical methods that allow you to compare common cause variation to customer expectations.) If the common cause variation is small enough to consistently satisfy the customer, you then use control charts to monitor the process on a continuing basis to make sure the process remains in control. If the common cause variation is too large, you need to alter the process itself.

18.4 CONTROL CHART FOR THE PROPORTION: THE p CHART

Various types of control charts are used to monitor processes and determine whether special cause variation is present in a process. **Attribute charts** are used for categorical or discrete variables. This section introduces the **p chart**, which is used for categorical variables. The p chart gets its name from the fact that you plot the *proportion* of items in a sample that are in a category of interest. For example, sampled items are often classified according to whether they conform or do not conform to operationally defined requirements. Thus, the p chart is frequently used to monitor and analyze the proportion of nonconforming items in repeated samples (that is, subgroups) selected from a process.

To begin the discussion of p charts, recall that you studied proportions and the binomial distribution in Section 5.3. Then, in Section 7.5 on page 232, the sample proportion is defined as $p = X/n$, and the standard deviation of the sample proportion is defined as

$$\sigma_p = \sqrt{\frac{\pi(1 - \pi)}{n}}$$

[3]In this chapter, and in quality management, the phrase "proportion of nonconforming items" is often used, although the p chart can be used to monitor any proportion of interest. Recall that in the earlier discussions of the binomial distribution, the phrase "proportion of successes" was used.

Using Equation (18.1) on page 739, control limits for the proportion of nonconforming[3] items from the sample data are established in Equation (18.2).

CONTROL LIMITS FOR THE p CHART

$$\bar{p} \pm 3\sqrt{\frac{\bar{p}(1 - \bar{p})}{\bar{n}}} \tag{18.2}$$

$$\mathrm{UCL} = \bar{p} + 3\sqrt{\frac{\bar{p}(1 - \bar{p})}{\bar{n}}}$$

$$\mathrm{LCL} = \bar{p} - 3\sqrt{\frac{\bar{p}(1 - \bar{p})}{\bar{n}}}$$

For equal n_i,

$$\bar{n} = n_i \text{ and } \bar{p} = \frac{\displaystyle\sum_{i=1}^{k} p_i}{k}$$

or in general,

$$\bar{n} = \frac{\displaystyle\sum_{i=1}^{k} n_i}{k} \text{ and } \bar{p} = \frac{\displaystyle\sum_{i=1}^{k} X_i}{\displaystyle\sum_{i=1}^{k} n_i}$$

where

X_i = number of nonconforming items in subgroup i

n_i = sample (or subgroup) size for subgroup i

$p_i = X_i/n_i$ = proportion of nonconforming items in subgroup i

k = number of subgroups selected

$\bar{n}$ = mean subgroup size

$\bar{p}$ = average proportion of nonconforming items

Any negative value for the LCL means that the LCL does not exist.

To show the application of the *p* chart, return to the Using Statistics scenario on page 734 concerning the Beachcomber Hotel. During the *Measure* phase of the Six Sigma DMAIC model, a nonconforming room was operationally defined as the absence of an amenity or an appliance not in working order upon check-in. During the *Analyze* phase of the Six Sigma DMAIC model, data on the nonconformances were collected daily from a sample of 200 rooms (see the file hotel1.xls). Table 18.1 lists the number and proportion of nonconforming rooms for each day in the four-week period.

TABLE 18.1

Nonconforming Hotel Rooms at Check-in over a 28-Day Period

Day	Rooms Studied	Rooms Not Ready	Proportion	Day	Rooms Studied	Rooms Not Ready	Proportion
1	200	16	0.080	15	200	18	0.090
2	200	7	0.035	16	200	13	0.065
3	200	21	0.105	17	200	15	0.075
4	200	17	0.085	18	200	10	0.050
5	200	25	0.125	19	200	14	0.070
6	200	19	0.095	20	200	25	0.125
7	200	16	0.080	21	200	19	0.095
8	200	15	0.075	22	200	12	0.060
9	200	11	0.055	23	200	6	0.030
10	200	12	0.060	24	200	12	0.060
11	200	22	0.110	25	200	18	0.090
12	200	20	0.100	26	200	15	0.075
13	200	17	0.085	27	200	20	0.100
14	200	26	0.130	28	200	22	0.110

For these data, $k = 28$, $\sum\limits_{i=1}^{k} p_i = 2.315$ and because the n_i are equal, $n_i = \bar{n} = 200$. Thus,

$$\bar{p} = \frac{\sum\limits_{i=1}^{k} p_i}{k} = \frac{2.315}{28} = 0.0827$$

Using Equation (18.2),

$$0.0827 \pm 3\sqrt{\frac{(0.0827)(0.9173)}{200}}$$

so that

$$UCL = 0.0827 + 0.0584 = 0.1411$$

and

$$LCL = 0.0827 - 0.0584 = 0.0243$$

Figure 18.4 displays the Microsoft Excel p chart for the data of Table 18.1. Figure 18.4 shows a process in a state of statistical control, with the individual points distributed around $\bar{p}$ without any pattern and all the points within the control limits. Thus, any improvement in the process of making rooms ready for guests in the *Improve* phase of the DMAIC model must come from the reduction of common cause variation. Such reductions require changes in the process. These changes are the responsibility of management. Remember that improvements in quality cannot occur until changes to the process itself are successfully implemented.

FIGURE 18.4

Microsoft Excel p chart for the nonconforming hotel room data

See Section E18.1 to create this.

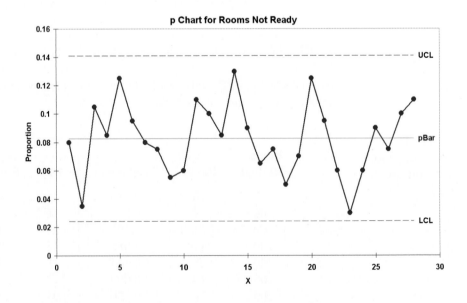

The first example illustrates a situation in which the subgroup size does not vary. As a general rule, as long as none of the subgroup sizes, n_i, differ from the mean subgroup size, $\bar{n}$, by more than ±25% of $\bar{n}$ (see reference 2), you can use Equation (18.2) on page 740 to compute the control limits for the p chart. If any subgroup size differs by more than ±25% of $\bar{n}$, you use alternative formulas for calculating the control limits (see reference 8). To illustrate the use of the p chart when the subgroup sizes are unequal, Example 18.1 studies the production of medical sponges.

EXAMPLE 18.1

USING THE *p* CHART FOR UNEQUAL SUBGROUP SIZES

Table 18.2 indicates the number of medical sponges produced daily and the number that are nonconforming for a period of 32 days (see the file `sponge.xls`). Construct a control chart for these data.

TABLE 18.2

Medical Sponges Produced and Number Nonconforming over a 32-Day Period

Day	Sponges Produced	Nonconforming Sponges	Proportion	Day	Sponges Produced	Nonconforming Sponges	Proportion
1	690	21	0.030	17	575	20	0.035
2	580	22	0.038	18	610	16	0.026
3	685	20	0.029	19	596	15	0.025
4	595	21	0.035	20	630	24	0.038
5	665	23	0.035	21	625	25	0.040
6	596	19	0.032	22	615	21	0.034
7	600	18	0.030	23	575	23	0.040
8	620	24	0.039	24	572	20	0.035
9	610	20	0.033	25	645	24	0.037
10	595	22	0.037	26	651	39	0.060
11	645	19	0.029	27	660	21	0.032
12	675	23	0.034	28	685	19	0.028
13	670	22	0.033	29	671	17	0.025
14	590	26	0.044	30	660	22	0.033
15	585	17	0.029	31	595	24	0.040
16	560	16	0.029	32	600	16	0.027

SOLUTION For these data,

$$k = 32, \quad \sum_{i=1}^{k} n_i = 19{,}926$$

$$\sum_{i=1}^{k} X_i = 679$$

Thus, using Equation (18.2) on page 740,

$$\bar{n} = \frac{19{,}926}{32} = 622.69$$

$$\bar{p} = \frac{679}{19{,}926} = 0.034$$

so that

$$0.034 \pm 3\sqrt{\frac{(0.034)(1 - 0.034)}{622.69}}$$

$$= 0.034 \pm 0.022$$

Thus,

$$\text{UCL} = 0.034 + 0.022 = 0.056$$

$$\text{LCL} = 0.034 - 0.022 = 0.012$$

Figure 18.5 displays the Microsoft Excel control chart for the sponge data. From Figure 18.5, you can see that day 26, on which there were 39 nonconforming sponges produced out of 651 sampled, is above the UCL. Management needs to determine the reason (that is, root cause) for this special cause variation and take corrective action. Once actions are taken, you can remove the data from day 26 and then construct and analyze a new control chart.

FIGURE 18.5

Microsoft Excel *p* chart for the proportion of nonconforming medical sponges

See Section E18.1 to create this.

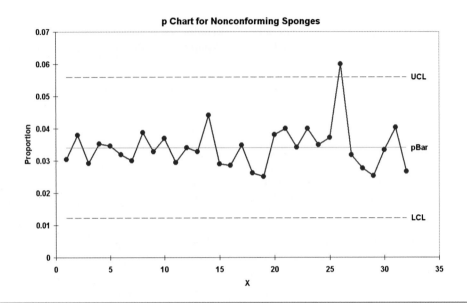

PROBLEMS FOR SECTION 18.4

Learning the Basics

PH Grade ASSIST **18.1** The following data were collected on non-conformances for a period of 10 days:

Day	Sample Size	Nonconformances
1	100	12
2	100	14
3	100	10
4	100	18
5	100	22
6	100	14
7	100	15
8	100	13
9	100	14
10	100	16

a. On what day is the proportion of nonconformances largest? smallest?
b. What are the LCL and UCL?
c. Are there any special causes of variation?

PH Grade ASSIST **18.2** The following data were collected on non-conformances for a period of 10 days:

Day	Sample Size	Nonconformances
1	111	12
2	93	14
3	105	10
4	92	18
5	117	22
6	88	14
7	117	15
8	87	13
9	119	14
10	107	16

a. On what day is the proportion of nonconformances largest? smallest?
b. What are the LCL and UCL?
c. Are there any special causes of variation?

Applying the Concepts

18.3 A medical transcription service enters medical data on patient files for hospitals. The service studied ways to improve the turnaround time (defined as the time between sending data and the time the client receives completed files). After studying the process, it was determined that turnaround time was increased by transmission errors. A transmission error was defined as data transmitted that did not go through as planned and needed to be retransmitted. Each day, a sample of 125 transmissions were randomly selected and evaluated for errors (see the file **transmit.xls**). The following table presents the number and proportion of transmissions with errors:

Day	Number of Errors	Proportion of Errors	Day	Number of Errors	Proportion of Errors
1	6	0.048	17	4	0.032
2	3	0.024	18	6	0.048
3	4	0.032	19	3	0.024
4	4	0.032	20	5	0.040
5	9	0.072	21	1	0.008
6	0	0.000	22	3	0.024
7	0	0.000	23	14	0.112
8	8	0.064	24	6	0.048
9	4	0.032	25	7	0.056
10	3	0.024	26	3	0.024
11	4	0.032	27	10	0.080
12	1	0.008	28	7	0.056
13	10	0.080	29	5	0.040
14	9	0.072	30	0	0.000
15	3	0.024	31	3	0.024
16	1	0.008			

a. Construct a *p* chart.
b. Is the process in a state of statistical control? Why?

18.4 The following data represent the findings from a study conducted at a factory that manufactures film canisters. For 32 days, 500 film canisters were sampled and inspected (see the file **canister.xls**). The following table lists the number of defective film canisters (that is, nonconforming items) for each day (that is, subgroup):

Day	Number Nonconforming	Day	Number Nonconforming
1	26	17	23
2	25	18	19
3	23	19	18
4	24	20	27
5	26	21	28
6	20	22	24
7	21	23	26
8	27	24	23
9	23	25	27
10	25	26	28
11	22	27	24
12	26	28	22
13	25	29	20
14	29	30	25
15	20	31	27
16	19	32	19

a. Construct a *p* chart.
b. Is the process in a state of statistical control? Why?

18.5 A hospital administrator is concerned with the time to process patients' medical records after discharge. She determined that all records should be processed within 5 days of discharge. Thus, any record not processed within 5 days of a patient's discharge is nonconforming. The administrator recorded the number of patients discharged and the number of records not processed within the 5-day standard for a 30-day period in the file **medrec.xls**.
a. Construct a *p* chart for these data.
b. Does the process give an out-of-control signal? Explain.
c. If the process is out of control, assume that special causes were subsequently identified and corrective action was taken to keep them from happening again. Then eliminate the data causing the out-of-control signals and recalculate the control limits.

✓ SELF Test **18.6** The bottling division of Sweet Suzy's Sugarless Cola maintains daily records of the occurrences of unacceptable cans flowing from the filling and sealing machine. The following table (whose data are stored in the file **colaspc.xls**) lists the number of cans filled and the number of nonconforming cans for one month (based on a 5-day workweek):

Day	Cans Filled	Unacceptable Cans	Day	Cans Filled	Unacceptable Cans
1	5,043	47	12	5,314	70
2	4,852	51	13	5,097	64
3	4,908	43	14	4,932	59
4	4,756	37	15	5,023	75
5	4,901	78	16	5,117	71
6	4,892	66	17	5,099	68
7	5,354	51	18	5,345	78
8	5,321	66	19	5,456	88
9	5,045	61	20	5,554	83
10	5,113	72	21	5,421	82
11	5,247	63	22	5,555	87

a. Construct a *p* chart for the proportion of unacceptable cans for the month. Does the process give an out-of-control signal?
b. If you want to develop a process for reducing the proportion of unacceptable cans, how should you proceed?

18.7 The manager of the accounting office of a large hospital is studying the problem of entering incorrect account numbers into the computer system. A subgroup of 200 account numbers is selected from each day's output, and each account number is inspected to determine whether it is a nonconforming item. The results for a period of 39 days are in the file errorspc.xls.

a. Construct a p chart for the proportion of nonconforming items. Does the process give an out-of-control signal?

b. Based on your answer to (a), if you were the manager of the accounting office, what would you do to improve the process of account number entry?

18.8 A regional manager of a telephone company is responsible for processing requests concerning additions, changes, or deletions of telephone service. She forms a service improvement team to look at the corrections in terms of central office equipment and facilities required to process the orders that are issued to service requests. Data collected over a period of 30 days are in the file telespc.xls.

a. Construct a p chart for the proportion of corrections. Does the process give an out-of-control signal?

b. What should the regional manager do to improve the processing of requests for changes in telephone service?

18.5 THE RED BEAD EXPERIMENT: UNDERSTANDING PROCESS VARIABILITY

This chapter began with a discussion of total quality management, Deming's 14 points, Six Sigma management, and definitions of common cause variation and special cause variation. Now that you have studied the p chart, this section presents a famous parable, the **red bead experiment**, to enhance your understanding of common cause and special cause variation. The red bead experiment involves the selection of beads from a box that contains 4,000 beads. Unknown to the participants in the experiment, 3,200 (80%) of the beads are white and 800 (20%) are red. You can use several different scenarios for conducting the experiment. The one used here begins with a facilitator (who will play the role of company supervisor) asking members of the audience to volunteer for the jobs of workers (at least four are needed), inspectors (two are needed), chief inspector (one is needed), and recorder (one is needed). A worker's job consists of using a paddle that has five rows of 10 bead-size holes to select 50 beads from the box of beads.

When the participants have been selected, the supervisor explains the jobs to them. The job of the workers is to produce white beads because red beads are unacceptable to the customers. Strict procedures are to be followed. Work standards call for the daily production of exactly 50 beads by each worker (a strict quota system). Management has established a standard that no more than 2 red beads (4%) per worker are to be produced on any given day. Each worker dips the paddle into the box of beads so that when it is removed, each of the 50 holes contains a bead. The worker carries the paddle to the two inspectors, who independently record the count of red beads. The chief inspector compares their counts and announces the results to the audience. The recorder writes down the number and percentage of red beads next to the name of the worker.

When all the people know their jobs, "production" can begin. Suppose that on the first "day," the number of red beads "produced" by the four workers (call them Alyson, David, Peter, and Sharyn) was 9, 12, 13, and 7, respectively. How should management react to the day's production when the standard says that no more than 2 red beads per worker should be produced? Should all the workers be reprimanded, or should only David and Peter be given a stern warning that they will be fired if they don't improve?

Suppose that production continues for an additional two days. Table 18.3 summarizes the results for all three days.

TABLE 18.3

Red Bead Experiment Results for Four Workers over Three Days

NAME	DAY 1	DAY 2	DAY 3	All Three Days
Alyson	9 (18%)	11 (22%)	6 (12%)	26 (17.33%)
David	12 (24%)	12 (24%)	8 (16%)	32 (21.33%)
Peter	13 (26%)	6 (12%)	12 (24%)	31 (20.67%)
Sharyn	7 (14%)	9 (18%)	8 (16%)	24 (16.0%)
All four workers	41	38	34	113
Mean	10.25	9.5	8.5	9.42
Percentage	20.5%	19%	17%	18.83%

From Table 18.3, on each day, some of the workers were above the mean and some below the mean. On day 1, Sharyn did best, but on day 2, Peter (who had the worst record on day 1) was best, and on day 3, Alyson was best. How can you explain all this variation? Using Equation (18.2) on page 740 to develop a *p* chart for these data,

$$k = 4 \text{ workers} \times 3 \text{ days} = 12 \quad n = 50 \quad \sum_{i=1}^{k} X_i = 113$$

Thus,

$$\bar{p} = \frac{113}{(50)(12)} = 0.1883$$

so that

$$\bar{p} \pm 3\sqrt{\frac{\bar{p}(1 - \bar{p})}{n}}$$

$$= 0.1883 \pm 3\sqrt{\frac{0.1883(1 - 0.1883)}{50}}$$

$$= 0.1883 \pm 0.1659$$

Thus,

$$\text{UCL} = 0.1883 + 0.1659 = 0.3542$$

$$\text{LCL} = 0.1883 - 0.1659 = 0.0224$$

Figure 18.6 on page 748 represents the *p* chart for the data of Table 18.3. In Figure 18.6, all the points are within the control limits, and there are no patterns in the results. The differences between the workers merely represent common cause variation inherent in a stable system.

Four morals to the parable of the red beads are

- Variation is an inherent part of any process.
- Workers work within a system over which they have little control. It is the system that primarily determines their performance.
- Only management can change the system.
- There will always be some workers above the mean and some workers below the mean.

FIGURE 18.6

p chart for the red bead experiment

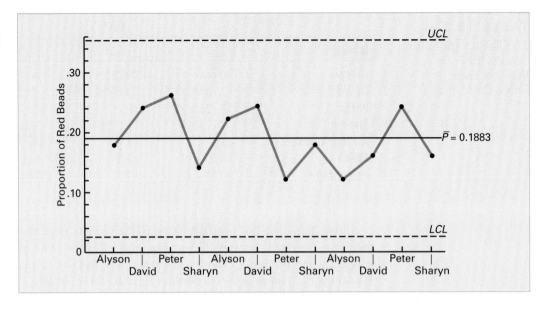

Applying the Concepts

18.9 In the red bead experiment, how do you think many managers would have reacted after day 1? day 2? day 3?

18.10 (**Class Project**) Obtain a version of the red bead experiment for your class.

a. Conduct the experiment in the same way as described in this section.
b. Remove 400 red beads from the bead box before beginning the experiment. How do your results differ from those in (a)? What does this tell you about the effect of the system on the workers?

18.6   CONTROL CHARTS FOR THE RANGE AND THE MEAN

You use **variables control charts** to monitor and analyze a process when you have numerical data. Common numerical variables include time, money, and weight. Because numerical variables provide more information than categorical data, such as the proportion of nonconforming items, variables control charts are more sensitive in detecting special cause variation than the *p* chart. Variables charts are typically used in pairs. One chart monitors the dispersion or variability in a process, and the other monitors the process mean. You must examine the chart that monitors dispersion first because if it indicates the presence of out-of-control conditions, the interpretation of the chart for the mean will be misleading. Although businesses currently use several alternative pairs of charts (see references 8, 9, and 13), this book considers only the control charts for the range and the mean.

The *R* Chart

You can use several different types of control charts to monitor the variability in a numerically measured characteristic of interest. The simplest and most common is the control chart for the range, the ***R* chart**. You use the range chart only when the sample size is 10 or less. If the sample size is greater than 10, a standard deviation chart is preferable. Because sample sizes of five or less are typically used in many applications, the standard deviation chart is not illustrated in this book. (For a discussion of standard deviation charts, see references 8, 9, and 13.) The *R* chart enables you to determine whether the variability in a process is in control or whether changes in the amount of variability are occurring over time. If the process range is in control, then the amount of variation in the process is consistent over time, and you can use the results of the R chart to develop the control limits for the mean.

To develop control limits for the range, you need an estimate of the mean range and the standard deviation of the range. As shown in Equation (18.3), these control limits depend on two constants, the d_2 **factor**, which represents the relationship between the standard deviation and the range for varying sample sizes, and the d_3 **factor**, which represents the relationship between the standard deviation and the standard error of the range for varying sample sizes. Table E.11 contains values for these factors. Equation (18.3) defines the control limits for the R chart.

CONTROL LIMITS FOR THE RANGE

$$\bar{R} \pm 3\bar{R}\frac{d_3}{d_2} \qquad (18.3)$$

$$UCL = \bar{R} + 3\bar{R}\frac{d_3}{d_2}$$

$$LCL = \bar{R} - 3\bar{R}\frac{d_3}{d_2}$$

where

$$\bar{R} = \frac{\sum_{i=1}^{k} R_i}{k}$$

You can simplify the calculations in Equation (18.3) by using the D_3 **factor**, equal to $1 - 3(d_3/d_2)$, and the D_4 **factor**, equal to $1 + 3(d_3/d_2)$, to express the control limits (see Table E.11), as shown in Equations (18.4a) and (18.4b).

CALCULATING CONTROL LIMITS FOR THE RANGE

$$UCL = D_4\bar{R} \qquad (18.4a)$$

$$LCL = D_3\bar{R} \qquad (18.4b)$$

To illustrate the R chart, return to the Using Statistics scenario concerning hotel service quality. During the *Measure* phase of the Six Sigma DMAIC model, the amount of time to deliver luggage was operationally defined as the time from when the guest completes check-in procedures to the time the luggage arrives in the guest's room. During the *Analyze* phase of the Six Sigma DMAIC model, data were recorded over a four-week period (see the file hotel2.xls). Subgroups of five deliveries were selected from the evening shift on each day. Table 18.4 on page 750 summarizes the results for all 28 days.

For the data in Table 18.4,

$$k = 28 \quad \sum_{i=1}^{k} R_i = 97.5 \quad \bar{R} = \frac{\sum_{i=1}^{k} R_i}{k} = \frac{97.5}{28} = 3.482$$

For $n = 5$, from Table E.11, $D_3 = 0$ and $D_4 = 2.114$. Then, using Equation (18.4), and $D_3 = 0$ and $D_4 = 2.114$ from Table E.11,

$$UCL = D_4\bar{R} = (2.114)(3.482) = 7.36$$

and the LCL does not exist.

TABLE 18.4

Luggage Delivery Times and Subgroup Mean and Range for 28 Days

Day	Luggage Delivery Times, in Minutes					Mean	Range
1	6.7	11.7	9.7	7.5	7.8	8.68	5.0
2	7.6	11.4	9.0	8.4	9.2	9.12	3.8
3	9.5	8.9	9.9	8.7	10.7	9.54	2.0
4	9.8	13.2	6.9	9.3	9.4	9.72	6.3
5	11.0	9.9	11.3	11.6	8.5	10.46	3.1
6	8.3	8.4	9.7	9.8	7.1	8.66	2.7
7	9.4	9.3	8.2	7.1	6.1	8.02	3.3
8	11.2	9.8	10.5	9.0	9.7	10.04	2.2
9	10.0	10.7	9.0	8.2	11.0	9.78	2.8
10	8.6	5.8	8.7	9.5	11.4	8.80	5.6
11	10.7	8.6	9.1	10.9	8.6	9.58	2.3
12	10.8	8.3	10.6	10.3	10.0	10.00	2.5
13	9.5	10.5	7.0	8.6	10.1	9.14	3.5
14	12.9	8.9	8.1	9.0	7.6	9.30	5.3
15	7.8	9.0	12.2	9.1	11.7	9.96	4.4
16	11.1	9.9	8.8	5.5	9.5	8.96	5.6
17	9.2	9.7	12.3	8.1	8.5	9.56	4.2
18	9.0	8.1	10.2	9.7	8.4	9.08	2.1
19	9.9	10.1	8.9	9.6	7.1	9.12	3.0
20	10.7	9.8	10.2	8.0	10.2	9.78	2.7
21	9.0	10.0	9.6	10.6	9.0	9.64	1.6
22	10.7	9.8	9.4	7.0	8.9	9.16	3.7
23	10.2	10.5	9.5	12.2	9.1	10.30	3.1
24	10.0	11.1	9.5	8.8	9.9	9.86	2.3
25	9.6	8.8	11.4	12.2	9.3	10.26	3.4
26	8.2	7.9	8.4	9.5	9.2	8.64	1.6
27	7.1	11.1	10.8	11.0	10.2	10.04	4.0
28	11.1	6.6	12.0	11.5	9.7	10.18	5.4
					Sums:	265.38	97.5

Figure 18.7 displays the Microsoft Excel R chart for the luggage delivery times. Figure 18.7 does not indicate any individual ranges outside the control limits or any trends.

FIGURE 18.7

Microsoft Excel R chart for the luggage delivery times

See Section E18.2 to create this.

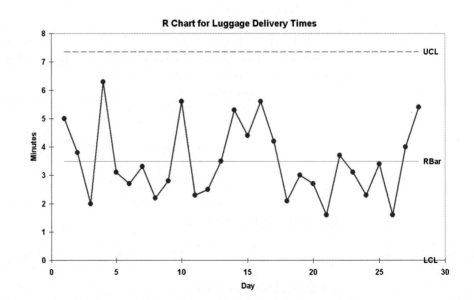

The $\bar{X}$ Chart

Now that you have determined from the control chart that the range is in control, you continue by examining the control chart for the process mean, the $\bar{X}$ **chart**.

The control chart for $\bar{X}$ uses subgroups each of size, n, for k consecutive periods of time. To compute control limits for the mean, you need to compute the mean of the subgroup means (called $\bar{\bar{X}}$) and the estimate of the standard deviation of the mean (which is called the standard error of the mean, $\sigma_{\bar{X}}$, in Chapter 7). The estimate of the standard deviation of the mean is a function of the d_2 factor, which represents the relationship between the standard deviation and the range for varying sample sizes.[4] Equations (18.5) and (18.6) define the control limits for the $\bar{X}$ chart.

[4] $\bar{R}/d_2$ is used to estimate the standard deviation of the population, and $\bar{R}/d_2\sqrt{n}$ is used to estimate the standard deviation of the mean.

CONTROL LIMITS FOR THE $\bar{X}$ CHART

$$\bar{\bar{X}} \pm 3 \frac{\bar{R}}{d_2\sqrt{n}} \qquad (18.5)$$

$$UCL = \bar{\bar{X}} + 3\frac{\bar{R}}{d_2\sqrt{n}}$$

$$LCL = \bar{\bar{X}} - 3\frac{\bar{R}}{d_2\sqrt{n}}$$

where

$$\bar{\bar{X}} = \frac{\sum_{i=1}^{k} \bar{X}_i}{k}$$

$$\bar{R} = \frac{\sum_{i=1}^{k} R_i}{k}$$

$\bar{X}_i$ = sample mean of n observations at time i

R_i = range of n observations at time i

k = number of subgroups

You can simplify the calculations in Equation (18.5) by utilizing the A_2 **factor** given in Table E.11, equal to $3/(d_2\sqrt{n})$. Equations (18.6a) and (18.6b) show the simplified control limits.

CALCULATING CONTROL LIMITS FOR THE MEAN, USING THE A_2 FACTOR

$$UCL = \bar{\bar{X}} + A_2\bar{R} \qquad (18.6a)$$

$$LCL = \bar{\bar{X}} - A_2\bar{R} \qquad (18.6b)$$

From Table 18.4 on page 750,

$$k = 28 \qquad \sum_{i=1}^{k} \bar{X}_i = 265.38 \qquad \sum_{i=1}^{k} R_i = 97.5$$

so that

$$\overline{\overline{X}} = \frac{\sum\limits_{i=1}^{k} \overline{X}_i}{k} = \frac{265.38}{28} = 9.478$$

$$\overline{R} = \frac{\sum\limits_{i=1}^{k} R_i}{k} = \frac{97.5}{28} = 3.482$$

Using Equations (18.6a) and (18.6b), and $A_2 = 0.577$, for $n = 5$, from Table E.11,

$$\text{UCL} = 9.478 + (0.577)(3.482) = 9.478 + 2.009 = 11.487$$

$$\text{LCL} = 9.478 - (0.577)(3.482) = 9.478 - 2.009 = 7.469$$

Figure 18.8 displays the Microsoft Excel $\overline{X}$ chart for the luggage delivery time data.

FIGURE 18.8

Microsoft Excel $\overline{X}$ chart for the luggage delivery times

See Section E18.2 to create this.

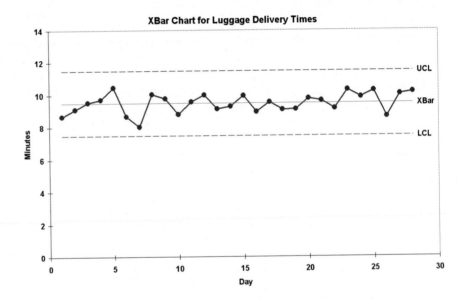

Figure 18.8 does not reveal any points outside the control limits or any trend. Although there is a considerable amount of variability among the 28 subgroup means, because both the R chart and the $\overline{X}$ chart are in control, the luggage delivery process is in a state of statistical control. If you want to reduce the variation or lower the mean delivery time, you need to change the process.

PROBLEMS FOR SECTION 18.6

Learning the Basics

18.11 For subgroups of $n = 3$, what is the value of
a. the d_2 factor?
b. the d_3 factor?
c. the D_3 factor?
d. the D_4 factor?
e. the A_2 factor?

PH Grade
ASSIST
18.12 For subgroups of $n = 4$, what is the value of
a. the d_2 factor?
b. the d_3 factor?
c. the D_3 factor?
d. the D_4 factor?
e. the A_2 factor?

18.13 The following summary of data is for subgroups of $n = 4$ for a 10-day period:

Day	Mean	Range	Day	Mean	Range
1	13.6	3.5	6	12.9	4.8
2	14.3	4.1	7	17.3	4.5
3	15.3	5.0	8	13.9	2.9
4	12.6	2.8	9	12.6	3.8
5	11.8	3.7	10	15.2	4.6

a. Compute control limits for the range.
b. Is there evidence of special cause variation in (a)?
c. Compute control limits for the mean.
d. Is there evidence of special cause variation in (c)?

Applying the Concepts

 18.14 The manager of a branch of a local bank wants to study waiting times of customers for teller service during the 12:00 noon-to-1:00 p.m. lunch hour. A subgroup of four customers is selected (one at each 15-minute interval during the hour), and the time, in minutes, is measured from the point each customer enters the line to when he or she reaches the teller window. The results over a four-week period are in the data file **banktime.xls**:

Day		Time in	Minutes	
1	7.2	8.4	7.9	4.9
2	5.6	8.7	3.3	4.2
3	5.5	7.3	3.2	6.0
4	4.4	8.0	5.4	7.4
5	9.7	4.6	4.8	5.8
6	8.3	8.9	9.1	6.2
7	4.7	6.6	5.3	5.8
8	8.8	5.5	8.4	6.9
9	5.7	4.7	4.1	4.6
10	3.7	4.0	3.0	5.2
11	2.6	3.9	5.2	4.8
12	4.6	2.7	6.3	3.4
13	4.9	6.2	7.8	8.7
14	7.1	6.3	8.2	5.5
15	7.1	5.8	6.9	7.0
16	6.7	6.9	7.0	9.4
17	5.5	6.3	3.2	4.9
18	4.9	5.1	3.2	7.6
19	7.2	8.0	4.1	5.9
20	6.1	3.4	7.2	5.9

a. Construct control charts for the range and the mean.
b. Is the process in control?

18.15 The manager of a warehouse for a local telephone company is involved in a process that receives expensive circuit boards and returns them to central stock so that they can be reused at a later date. Speedy processing of these circuit boards is critical in providing good service to customers and reducing capital expenditures. The data in the file **warehse.xls** represent the number of circuit boards processed per day by each of a subgroup of five employees over a 30-day period.
a. Construct control charts for the range and the mean.
b. Is the process in control?

18.16 An article in the *Mid-American Journal of Business* presents an analysis for a spring water bottling operation. One of the characteristics of interest is the amount of magnesium, measured in parts per million (ppm), in the water. The data in the following table (stored in the file **spwater.xls**) represent the magnesium levels from 30 subgroups of four bottles collected over a 30-hour period:

Hour	1	2	3	4
1	19.91	19.62	19.15	19.85
2	20.46	20.44	20.34	19.61
3	20.25	19.73	19.98	20.32
4	20.39	19.43	20.36	19.85
5	20.02	20.02	20.13	20.34
6	19.89	19.77	20.92	20.09
7	19.89	20.45	19.44	19.95
8	20.08	20.13	20.11	19.32
9	20.30	20.42	20.68	19.60
10	20.19	20.00	20.23	20.59
11	19.66	21.24	20.35	20.34
12	20.30	20.11	19.64	20.29
13	19.83	19.75	20.62	20.60
14	20.27	20.88	20.62	20.40
15	19.98	19.02	20.34	20.34
16	20.46	19.97	20.32	20.83
17	19.74	21.02	19.62	19.90
18	19.85	19.26	19.88	20.20
19	20.77	20.58	19.73	19.48
20	20.21	20.82	20.01	19.93
21	20.30	20.09	20.03	20.13
22	20.48	21.06	20.13	20.42
23	20.60	19.74	20.52	19.42
24	20.20	20.08	20.32	19.51
25	19.66	19.67	20.26	20.41
26	20.72	20.58	20.71	19.99
27	19.77	19.40	20.49	19.83
28	19.99	19.65	19.41	19.58
29	19.44	20.15	20.14	20.76
30	20.03	19.96	19.86	19.91

Source: Extracted from Susan K. Humphrey and Timothy C. Krehbiel, "Managing Process Capability," The Mid-American Journal of Business, 14, Fall 1999, pp. 7–12.

a. Construct a control chart for the range.
b. Construct a control chart for the mean.
c. Is the process in control?

18.17 The data in the following table (stored in the file **tensile.xls**) are the tensile strengths of bolts of cloth. The data were collected in subgroups of three bolts of cloth over a 25-hour period:

Hour	1	2	3	Hour	1	2	3
1	15.06	14.62	15.10	14	16.29	14.61	15.67
2	17.58	15.75	16.72	15	15.84	12.16	15.40
3	13.83	14.83	15.61	16	15.12	15.60	13.83
4	17.19	15.75	15.42	17	18.48	16.07	16.31
5	14.56	15.37	15.67	18	17.55	14.73	16.95
6	14.82	17.25	15.73	19	13.57	17.55	15.81
7	17.92	14.76	14.40	20	16.23	16.92	16.45
8	16.53	14.52	17.31	21	14.60	16.83	15.34
9	13.83	14.53	15.32	22	16.73	18.60	16.76
10	16.45	13.85	16.32	23	18.03	14.55	13.87
11	15.20	14.61	18.45	24	16.61	16.45	16.95
12	14.49	16.15	17.80	25	15.86	17.00	18.28
13	15.89	15.04	16.67				

a. Construct a control chart for the range.
b. Construct a control chart for the mean.
c. Is the process in control?

 18.18 The director of radiology at a large metropolitan hospital is concerned about scheduling in the radiology facilities. On a typical day, 250 patients are transported to the radiology department for treatment or diagnostic procedures. If patients do not reach the radiology unit at their scheduled times, backups occur, and other patients experience delays. The time it takes to transport patients to the radiology unit is operationally defined as the time between when the transporter is assigned to the patient and when the patient arrives at the radiology unit. A sample of $n = 4$ patients was selected each day for 20 days, and the time to transport each patient (in minutes) was determined, with the results in the data file **transport.xls**.
a. Construct control charts for the range and the mean.
b. Is the process in control?

18.19 A filling machine for a tea bag manufacturer produces approximately 170 tea bags per minute. The process manager monitors the weight of the tea placed in individual bags. A subgroup of $n = 4$ tea bags is taken every 15 min-

utes for 25 consecutive time periods. The results are given below and stored in the file **tea3.xls**:

Sample	Weight (in Grams)			
1	5.32	5.77	5.50	5.61
2	5.63	5.44	5.54	5.40
3	5.56	5.40	5.67	5.57
4	5.32	5.45	5.50	5.42
5	5.45	5.53	5.46	5.47
6	5.29	5.42	5.50	5.44
7	5.57	5.40	5.52	5.54
8	5.44	5.61	5.49	5.58
9	5.53	5.25	5.67	5.53
10	5.41	5.55	5.51	5.53
11	5.55	5.58	5.58	5.56
12	5.58	5.36	5.45	5.53
13	5.63	5.75	5.46	5.54
14	5.48	5.44	5.45	5.60
15	5.49	5.57	5.43	5.36
16	5.54	5.62	5.66	5.59
17	5.46	5.46	5.38	5.49
18	5.72	5.36	5.59	5.25
19	5.58	5.50	5.36	5.40
20	5.43	5.51	5.37	5.32
21	5.59	5.58	5.60	5.46
22	5.42	5.41	5.40	5.69
23	5.64	5.59	5.42	5.56
24	5.62	5.38	5.75	5.47
25	5.51	5.54	5.73	5.77

a. What are some of the sources of common cause variation that might be present in this process?
b. What problems might occur that would result in special causes of variation?
c. Construct control charts for the range and the mean.
d. Is the process in control?

18.20 A manufacturing company makes brackets for bookshelves. The brackets provide critical structural support and must have a 90-degree bend ±1 degree. Measurements of the bend of the brackets were taken at 18 different times. Five brackets were sampled at each time. The data are in the file **angle.xls**.
a. Construct control charts for the range and the mean.
b. Is the process in control?

18.7 PROCESS CAPABILITY

Often, it is necessary to analyze the amount of common cause variation present in an in-control process. Is the common cause variation small enough to satisfy customers with the product or service? Or is the common cause variation so large that there are too many dissatisfied customers, and a process change is needed?

Analyzing the capability of a process is a way to answer these questions. There are many methods available to analyze and report process capability (see reference 3). This section begins with a relatively simple method to estimate the percentage of products or services that will satisfy the customer. Later in the section, the use of capability indexes is introduced.

Customer Satisfaction and Specification Limits

Quality is defined by the customer. A customer who believes that a product or service has met or exceeded his or her expectations will be satisfied. The management of a company must listen to the customer and translate the customer's needs and expectations into easily measured CTQ variables. Management then sets specification limits for these CTQ variables.

> **Specification limits** are technical requirements set by management in response to customers' needs and expectations. The **upper specification limit (USL)** is the largest value a CTQ can have and still conform to customer expectations. Likewise, the **lower specification limit (LSL)** is the smallest value a CTQ can have and still conform to customer expectations.

For example, a soap manufacturer understands that customers expect their soap to produce a certain amount of lather. The customer can become dissatisfied if the soap produces too much or too little lather. Product engineers know that the level of free fatty acids in the soap controls the amount of lather. Thus, the process manager, with input from the product engineers, sets both a USL and a LSL for the amount of free fatty acids in the soap.

As an example of a case in which only a single specification limit is involved, consider the Using Statistics scenario concerning hotel service quality on page 734. Because customers want their bags delivered as quickly as possible, hotel management sets a USL for the time required for delivery. In this case, there is no LSL. As you can see in both the luggage delivery time and soap examples, specification limits are customer-driven requirements placed on a product or a service. If a process consistently meets these requirements, the process is capable of satisfying the customer.

> **Process capability** is the ability of a process to consistently meet specified customer-driven requirements.

One way to analyze the capability of a process is to estimate the percentage of products or services that are within specifications. To do this, you must have an in-control proce because an out-of-control process does not allow you to predict its capability. If you are ing with an out-of-control process, you must first identify and eliminate the special ca variation before performing a capability analysis. Out-of-control processes are unpre and, therefore, you cannot conclude that such processes are capable of meeting speci or satisfying customer expectations. In order to estimate the percentage of product within specifications, first you must estimate the mean and standard deviation of th tion of all X values, the CTQ variable of interest for the product or service. The es the mean of the population is $\overline{\overline{X}}$, the mean of all the sample means [see Equatio page 751]. The estimate of the standard deviation of the population is $\overline{R}$ divided can use the $\overline{\overline{X}}$ and $\overline{R}$ from in-control $\overline{X}$ and R charts, respectively. You need appropriate d_2 value in Table E.11.

In this book, the population of X values is assumed to be approximately nor uted. (If your data are not approximately normally distributed, see reference 3 for approach.) Assuming that the process is in control and X is approximately normas. Equation (18.7) to estimate the probability that a process outcome is within spe

ESTIMATING THE CAPABILITY OF A PROCESS

For a CTQ variable with an LSL and a USL:

P(An outcome will be within specifications) = $P(\text{LSL} < X < \text{USL})$

$$= P\left(\frac{\text{LSL} - \overline{\overline{X}}}{\overline{R} / d_2} < Z < \frac{\text{USL} - \overline{\overline{X}}}{\overline{R} / d_2}\right) \quad \textbf{(18.7a)}$$

For a CTQ variable with only a USL:

P(An outcome will be within specifications) = $P(X < \text{USL})$

$$= P\left(Z < \frac{\text{USL} - \overline{\overline{X}}}{\overline{R} / d_2}\right) \quad \textbf{(18.7b)}$$

For a CTQ variable with only an LSL:

P(An outcome will be within specifications) = $P(\text{LSL} < X)$

$$= P\left(\frac{\text{LSL} - \overline{\overline{X}}}{\overline{R} / d_2} < Z\right) \quad \textbf{(18.7c)}$$

where Z is a standardized normal random variable

In Section 18.6, you determined that the luggage delivery process was in control. Suppose that the hotel management has instituted a policy that 99% of all luggage deliveries must be completed in 14 minutes or less. From the summary computations on page 752:

$$n = 5 \quad \overline{\overline{X}} = 9.478 \quad \overline{R} = 3.482$$

and from Table E.11,

$$d_2 = 2.326$$

Using Equation (18.7b),

P(Delivery is made within specifications) = $P(X < 14)$

$$= P\left(Z < \frac{14 - 9.478}{3.482 / 2.326}\right)$$

$$= P(Z < 3.02)$$

Using Table E.2,

$$P(Z < 3.02) = 0.99874$$

Thus, you estimate that 99.874% of the luggage deliveries will be made within the specified time. The process is capable of meeting the 99% goal set forth by the hotel management.

Capability Indexes

A common approach in business is to use capability indexes to report the capability of a process. A **capability index** is an aggregate measure of a process's ability to meet specification limits. The larger the value of a capability index, the more capable the process is of meeting customer requirements. Equation (18.8) defines C_p, the most commonly used index.

C_p INDEX

$$C_p = \frac{\text{USL} - \text{LSL}}{6(\overline{R}/d_2)} \qquad (18.8)$$

$$= \frac{\text{Specification spread}}{\text{Process spread}}$$

The numerator in Equation (18.8) represents the distance between the upper and lower specification limits, referred to as the specification spread. The denominator, $6(\overline{R}/d_2)$, represents a 6 standard deviation spread in the data (the mean ± 3 standard deviations), referred to as the process spread. (Recall from Chapter 6 that approximately 99.73% of the values from a normal distribution fall in the interval from the mean ± 3 standard deviations.) You want the process spread to be small in comparison to the specification spread in order for the vast majority of the process output to fall within the specification limits. Therefore, the larger the value of C_p, the better the capability of the process.

C_p is a measure of process potential, not of actual performance, because it does not consider the current process mean. A C_p value of 1 indicates that if the process mean could be centered (that is, equal to the halfway point between the USL and LSL), approximately 99.73% of the values would be inside the specification limits. A C_p value greater than 1 indicates that a process has the potential of having more than 99.73% of its outcomes within specifications. A C_p value less than 1 indicates that the process is not very capable of meeting customer requirements, for even if the process is perfectly centered, fewer than 99.73% of the process outcomes will be within specifications. Historically, many companies required a C_p greater than or equal to 1. Now that the global economy has become more quality conscious, many companies are requiring a C_p as large as 1.33, 1.5, and for companies adopting Six Sigma management, 2.0.

To illustrate the calculation and interpretation of the C_p index, suppose a soft-drink producer bottles its beverage into 12-ounce bottles. The LSL is 11.82 ounces, and the USL is 12.18 ounces. Each hour, four bottles are selected, and the range and the mean are plotted on control charts. At the end of 24 hours, the capability of the process is studied. Suppose that the control charts indicate that the process is in control and the following summary calculations were recorded on the control charts:

$$n = 4 \qquad \overline{\overline{X}} = 12.02 \qquad \overline{R} = 0.10$$

To calculate the C_p index, assuming that the data are normally distributed, from Table E.11, $d_2 = 2.059$ for $n = 4$. Using Equation (18.8),

$$C_p = \frac{\text{USL} - \text{LSL}}{6(\overline{R}/d_2)}$$

$$= \frac{12.18 - 11.82}{6(0.10/2.059)} = 1.24$$

Because the C_p index is greater than 1, the bottling process has the potential to fill more than 99.73% of the bottles within the specification limits.

In summary, the C_p index is an aggregate measure of process potential. The larger the value of C_p, the more potential the process has of satisfying the customer. In other words, a large C_p indicates that the current amount of common cause variation is small enough to consistently produce items within specifications. For a process to reach its full potential, the process mean needs to be at or near the center of the specification limits. The following section introduces capability indexes that measure actual process performance.

CPL, CPU, and C_{pk}

To measure the capability of a process in terms of actual process performance, the most common indexes are CPL, CPU, and C_{pk}. Equation (18.9) defines the capability indexes CPL and CPU.

CPL AND CPU

$$CPL = \frac{\overline{\overline{X}} - LSL}{3(\overline{R}/d_2)} \qquad \text{(18.9a)}$$

$$CPU = \frac{USL - \overline{\overline{X}}}{3(\overline{R}/d_2)} \qquad \text{(18.9b)}$$

Because the process mean is used in the calculation of CPL and CPU, these indexes measure process performance—unlike C_p, which measures only potential. A value of CPL (or CPU) equal to 1.0 indicates that the process mean is 3 standard deviations away from the LSL (or USL). For CTQ variables with only an LSL, the CPL measures the process performance. For CTQ variables with only a USL, the CPU measures the process performance. In either case, the larger the value of the index, the greater the capability of the process.

In the Using Statistics scenario, the Beachcomber Hotel has a policy that luggage deliveries are to be made in 14 minutes or less. Thus, the CTQ variable delivery time has a USL of 14, and there is no LSL. Because you previously determined that the luggage delivery process was in control, you can now calculate the CPU. From the summary computations on page 752,

$$\overline{\overline{X}} = 9.478 \qquad \overline{R} = 3.482$$

And, from Table E.11, $d_2 = 2.326$. Then, using Equation (18.9b),

$$CPU = \frac{USL - \overline{\overline{X}}}{3(\overline{R}/d_2)} = \frac{14 - 9.478}{3(3.482/2.326)} = 1.01$$

The capability index for the luggage delivery CTQ variable is 1.01. Because this value is slightly more than 1, the USL is slightly more than 3 standard deviations above the mean. To increase CPU even farther above 1.00 and therefore increase customer satisfaction, you need to investigate changes in the luggage delivery process. To study a process that has a CPL and a CPU, see the bottling process scenario in Example 18.2.

EXAMPLE 18.2

CALCULATING CPL AND CPU FOR THE BOTTLING PROCESS

In the soft-drink bottle filling process described on page 757, the following information was provided:

$$n = 4 \qquad \overline{\overline{X}} = 12.02 \qquad \overline{R} = 0.10 \qquad LSL = 11.82 \qquad USL = 12.18 \qquad d_2 = 2.059$$

Calculate the CPL and CPU for these data.

SOLUTION You compute the capability indexes by using Equations (18.9a) and (18.9b):

$$CPL = \frac{\bar{\bar{X}} - \text{LSL}}{3(\bar{R}/d_2)}$$

$$= \frac{12.02 - 11.82}{3(0.10/2.059)} = 1.37$$

$$CPU = \frac{\text{USL} - \bar{\bar{X}}}{3(\bar{R}/d_2)}$$

$$= \frac{12.18 - 12.02}{3(0.10/2.059)} = 1.10$$

Both the *CPL* and *CPU* are greater than 1, indicating that the process mean is more than 3 standard deviations away from both the LSL and USL. Because the *CPU* is less than the *CPL*, you know that the mean is closer to the USL than the LSL.

The capability index, C_{pk}, (shown in Equation (18.10)) measures actual process performance for quality characteristics with two-sided specification limits. C_{pk} is equal to the value of either the *CPL* or *CPU*, whichever is smallest.

C_{pk}

$$C_{pk} = MIN[CPL, CPU] \qquad \qquad \textbf{(18.10)}$$

A value of 1 for C_{pk} indicates that the process mean is 3 standard deviations away from the closest specification limit. If the characteristic is normally distributed, then a value of 1 indicates that at least 99.73% of the current output is within specifications. As with all other capability indexes, the larger the value of C_{pk}, the better. Example 18.3 illustrates the use of the C_{pk} index.

EXAMPLE 18.3

CALCULATING C_{pk} FOR THE BOTTLING PROCESS

The soft-drink producer in Example 18.2 requires the bottle filling process to have a C_{pk} greater than or equal to 1. Calculate the C_{pk} index.

SOLUTION In Example 18.2, *CPL* = 1.37 and *CPU* = 1.10. Using Equation (18.10):

$$C_{pk} = MIN[CPL, \ CPU]$$

$$= MIN[1.37, \ 1.10] = 1.10$$

The C_{pk} index is greater than 1, indicating that the actual process performance exceeds the company's requirement. More than 99.73% of the bottles contain between 11.82 and 12.18 ounces.

PROBLEMS FOR SECTION 18.7

Learning the Basics

 18.21 For an in-control process with subgroup data $n = 4$, $\bar{\bar{X}} = 20$, and $\bar{R} = 2$, find the estimate of
a. the population mean of all X values.
b. the population standard deviation of all X values.

 18.22 For an in-control process with subgroup data $n = 3$, $\bar{\bar{X}} = 100$, and $\bar{R} = 3.386$, calculate the percentage of outcomes within specifications if
a. LSL = 98 and USL = 102.
b. LSL = 93 and USL = 107.5.
c. LSL = 93.8 and there is no USL.
d. USL = 110 and there is no LSL.

18.23 For an in-control process with subgroup data $n = 3$, $\bar{\bar{X}} = 100$, and $\bar{R} = 3.386$, calculate the C_p, CPL, CPU, and C_{pk} if
a. LSL = 98 and USL = 102.
b. LSL = 93 and USL = 107.5.

Applying the Concepts

 18.24 Referring to the data of Problem 18.16 on page 753, and the data file **spwater.xls**, the researchers stated, "Some of the benefits of a capable process are increased customer satisfaction, increased operating efficiencies, and reduced costs." To illustrate this point, the authors presented a capability analysis for a spring water bottling operation. One of the CTQ variables is the amount of magnesium, measured in parts per million (ppm), in the water. The LSL and USL for the level of magnesium in a bottle are 18 ppm and 22 ppm, respectively.
a. Estimate the percentage of bottles that are within specifications.
b. Calculate the C_p, CPL, CPU, and C_{pk}.

18.25 Refer to the data in Problem 18.17 on page 754 concerning the tensile strengths of bolts of cloth (see the file **tensile.xls**). There is no USL for tensile strength, and the LSL is 13.
a. Estimate the percentage of bolts that are within specifications.
b. Calculate the C_p and CPL.

 18.26 Refer to Problem 18.19 on page 754 concerning a filling machine for a tea bag manufacturer (see the file **tea3.xls**). In that problem, you should have concluded that the process is in control. The label weight for this product is 5.5 grams, the LSL is 5.2 grams, and the USL is 5.8 grams. Company policy states that at least 99% of the tea bags produced must be inside the specifications in order for the process to be considered capable.
a. Estimate the percentage of the tea bags that are inside the specification limits. Is the process capable of meeting the company policy?
b. If management implemented a new policy stating that 99.7% of all tea bags are required to be within the specifications, is this process capable of reaching that goal? Explain.

18.27 Refer to Problem 18.14 on page 753 concerning waiting time for customers at a bank (see the file **banktime.xls**). Suppose management has set a USL of 5 minutes on waiting time and specified that at least 99% of the waiting times must be less than 5 minutes in order for the process to be considered capable.
a. Estimate the percentage of the waiting times that are inside the specification limits. Is the process capable of meeting the company policy?
b. If management implemented a new policy, stating that 99.7% of all waiting times are required to be within specifications, is this process capable of reaching that goal? Explain.

SUMMARY

This chapter has introduced you to quality and productivity, including TQM, Deming's 14 points, and Six Sigma management. You have learned how to use several different types of control charts to distinguish between common causes and special causes of variation. You have learned how to measure the capability of a process by estimating the percentage of items within specifications and by calculating capability indexes. By applying these concepts to the services provided by the Beachcomber Hotel, you have learned how a manager can identify problems and continually improve service quality.

KEY EQUATIONS

Constructing Control Limits

Process mean ±3 standard deviations

Upper control limit (UCL) = process mean +3 standard deviations

Lower control limit (LCL) = process mean −3 standard deviations **(18.1)**

Control Limits for the p Chart

$$\bar{p} \pm 3\sqrt{\frac{\bar{p}(1 - \bar{p})}{\bar{n}}} \qquad (18.2)$$

$$\text{UCL} = \bar{p} + 3\sqrt{\frac{\bar{p}(1 - \bar{p})}{\bar{n}}}$$

$$\text{LCL} = \bar{p} - 3\sqrt{\frac{\bar{p}(1 - \bar{p})}{\bar{n}}}$$

Control Limits for the Range

$$\bar{R} \pm 3\bar{R}\frac{d_3}{d_2} \qquad (18.3)$$

$$\text{UCL} = \bar{R} + 3\bar{R}\frac{d_3}{d_2}$$

$$\text{LCL} = \bar{R} - 3\bar{R}\frac{d_3}{d_2}$$

Calculating Control Limits for the Range

$$\text{UCL} = D_4\bar{R} \qquad (18.4a)$$
$$\text{LCL} = D_3\bar{R} \qquad (18.4b)$$

Control Limits for the $\bar{X}$ Chart

$$\bar{\bar{X}} \pm 3\frac{\bar{R}}{d_2\sqrt{n}} \qquad (18.5)$$

$$\text{UCL} = \bar{\bar{X}} + 3\frac{\bar{R}}{d_2\sqrt{n}}$$

$$\text{LCL} = \bar{\bar{X}} - 3\frac{\bar{R}}{d_2\sqrt{n}}$$

Calculating Control Limits for the Mean, Using the A_2 Factor

$$\text{UCL} = \bar{\bar{X}} + A_2\bar{R} \qquad (18.6a)$$
$$\text{LCL} = \bar{\bar{X}} - A_2\bar{R} \qquad (18.6b)$$

Estimating the Capability of a Process

For a CTQ variable with an LSL and a USL:

$$P(\text{An outcome will be within specifications}) = P(\text{LSL} < X < \text{USL})$$

$$= P\left(\frac{\text{LSL} - \bar{\bar{X}}}{\bar{R}/d_2} < Z < \frac{\text{USL} - \bar{\bar{X}}}{\bar{R}/d_2}\right)$$

$$(18.7a)$$

For a CTQ variable with only a USL:

$$P(\text{An outcome will be within specifications}) = P(X < \text{USL})$$

$$= P\left(Z < \frac{\text{USL} - \bar{\bar{X}}}{\bar{R}/d_2}\right)$$

$$(18.7b)$$

For a CTQ variable with only an LSL:

$$P(\text{An outcome will be within specifications}) = P(\text{LSL} < X)$$

$$= P\left(\frac{\text{LSL} - \bar{\bar{X}}}{\bar{R}/d_2} < Z\right)$$

$$(18.7c)$$

The C_p Index

$$C_p = \frac{\text{USL} - \text{LSL}}{6(\bar{R}/d_2)} \qquad (18.8)$$

$$= \frac{\text{Specification spread}}{\text{Process spread}}$$

CPL and CPU

$$CPL = \frac{\bar{\bar{X}} - \text{LSL}}{3(\bar{R}/d_2)} \qquad (18.9a)$$

$$CPU = \frac{\text{USL} - \bar{\bar{X}}}{3(\bar{R}/d_2)} \qquad (18.9b)$$

C_{pk}

$$C_{pk} = MIN[CPL, CPU] \qquad (18.10)$$

KEY TERMS

A_2 factor   751
assignable causes of variation   738
attribute chart   740
capability index   757
chance causes of variation   738
common causes of variation   738
control chart   738
critical-to-quality (CTQ)   737
d_2 factor   749
d_3 factor   749
D_3 factor   749
D_4 factor   749

Deming's 14 points for management   735
DMAIC model   737
in-control process   740
lower control limit (LCL)   739
lower specification limit (LSL)   755
out-of-control process   739
p chart   740
process capability   755
R chart   748
red bead experiment   746
Shewhart-Deming cycle   735

Six Sigma management   737
special causes of variation   738
specification limit   755
state of statistical control   740
subgroup   738
tampering   738
total quality management (TQM)   735
upper control limit (UCL)   739
upper specification limit (USL)   755
variables control charts   748
$\overline{X}$ chart   751

CHAPTER REVIEW PROBLEMS

Checking Your Understanding

18.28 What is the difference between common cause variation and special cause variation?

18.29 What should you do to improve a process when special causes of variation are present?

18.30 What should you do to improve a process when only common causes of variation are present?

18.31 Under what circumstances do you use a p chart?

18.32 What is the difference between attribute control charts and variables control charts?

18.33 Why are $\overline{X}$ and R charts used together?

18.34 What principles did you learn from the red bead experiment?

18.35 What is the difference between process potential and process performance?

18.36 A company requires a C_{pk} value of 1 or larger. If a process has $C_p = 1.5$ and $C_{pk} = 0.8$, what changes should you make to the process?

18.37 Why is a capability analysis *not* performed on out-of-control processes?

Applying the Concepts

18.38 According to the American Society for Quality, customers in the United States consistently rate service quality lower than product quality (American Society for Quality, *The Quarterly Quality Report*, **www.asq.org**, May 16, 2006). For example, products in the beverage, personal care and cleaning products, and major appliances

sectors all received very high customer satisfaction ratings. At the other extreme, services provided by airlines, banks, and insurance companies all received low customer satisfaction ratings.
a. Why do you think service quality consistently rates lower than product quality?
b. What are the similarities and differences between measuring service quality and product quality?
c. Do Deming's 14 points apply to both products and services?
d. Can Six Sigma management apply to both products and services?

18.39 Six Flags Amusement Parks lost $133 million on revenue of $1.09 billion in 2005. To turn things around, Six Flags CEO Mark Shapiro is focusing on big problems (such as cutting long-term debt) and small details (such as cleaner restrooms and grounds). His attention to providing clean parks is part of his overall strategy to get entire families to enjoy their day in the park so much that they want to return (L. Petrecca, "Six Flags CEO Waves the Signal Flag for Families," **usatoday.com**, June 13, 2006). Suppose that you have been hired as a summer intern at a large amusement park. Every day, your task is to conduct 200 exit interviews in the parking lot when customers leave. You need to construct questions to address the cleanliness of the park and the customers' intent to return again. When you begin to construct a short questionnaire, you remember the control chart material you learned in a statistics course, and you decide to write questions that will provide you with data to graph on control charts. After collecting data for 30 days, you plan to construct the control charts.
a. Write a question that will allow you to control chart customers' perceptions of cleanliness of the park.

b. Give examples of common cause variation and special cause variation for the control chart.

c. If the control chart is in control, what does that indicate and what do you do next?

d. If the control chart is out of control, what does that indicate and what do you do next?

e. Repeat (a) through (d), this time addressing the customers' intent to returning to the park.

f. After the initial 30 days, assuming that the charts indicate in-control processes or that the root sources of special cause variation have been corrected, explain how the charts can be used on a daily basis to monitor and improve the quality in the park.

18.40 Researchers at Miami University in Oxford, Ohio, investigated the use of p charts to monitor the market share of a product and to document the effectiveness of marketing promotions. Market share is defined as the company's proportion of the total number of products sold in a category. If a p chart based on a company's market share indicates an in-control process, then the company's share in the marketplace is deemed to be stable and consistent over time. In the example given in the article, the RudyBird Diskette Company collected daily sales data from a nationwide retail audit service. The first 30 days of data in the accompanying table (see the file **rudybird.xls**) indicate the total number of cases of computer disks sold and the number of RudyBird diskettes sold. The final 7 days of data were taken after RudyBird launched a major in-store promotion. A control chart was used to see if the in-store promotion would result in special cause variation in the marketplace.

**Cases Sold
Before the Promotion**

Day	Total	RudyBird	Day	Total	RudyBird
1	154	35	16	177	56
2	153	43	17	143	43
3	200	44	18	200	69
4	197	56	19	134	38
5	194	54	20	192	47
6	172	38	21	155	45
7	190	43	22	135	36
8	209	62	23	189	55
9	173	53	24	184	44
10	171	39	25	170	47
11	173	44	26	178	48
12	168	37	27	167	42
13	184	45	28	204	71
14	211	58	29	183	64
15	179	35	30	169	43

**Cases Sold
After the Promotion**

Day	Total	RudyBird
31	201	92
32	177	76
33	205	85
34	199	90
35	187	77
36	168	79
37	198	97

Source: Extracted from C. T. Crespy, T. C. Krehbiel, and J. M. Stearns, "Integrating Analytic Methods into Marketing Research Education: Statistical Control Charts as an Example," Marketing Education Review, 5, Spring 1995, pp. 11–23.

a. Construct a p chart using data from the first 30 days (prior to the promotion) to monitor the market share for RudyBird Diskettes.

b. Is the market share for RudyBird in control before the start of the in-store promotion?

c. On your control chart, extend the control limits generated in (b) and plot the proportions for days 31 through 37. What effect, if any, did the in-store promotion have on RudyBird's market share?

18.41 A producer of cat food constructed control charts and analyzed several quality characteristics. One characteristic of interest is the weight of the filled cans. The LSL for weight is 2.95 pounds. The data file **catfood.xls** contains the weights of five cans tested every 15 minutes during a day's production.

a. Construct a control chart for the range.

b. Construct a control chart for the mean.

c. Is the process in control?

d. If the process is in control, estimate the percentage of the cans with weight inside the specification limits.

e. If the process is in control, calculate the *CPL*.

f. If the manufacturer requires that 99.73% of all cans be within the specification limits, comment on the capability of the process, based on your calculations in (d) and (e).

PH Grade ASSIST **18.42** A professional basketball player has embarked on a program to study his ability to shoot foul shots. On each day in which a game is not scheduled, he intends to shoot 100 foul shots. He maintains records over a period of 40 days of practice, with the following results stored in the file **foulspc.xls**:

Day	Foul Shots Made	Day	Foul Shots Made	Day	Foul Shots Made
1	73	15	73	29	76
2	75	16	76	30	80
3	69	17	69	31	78
4	72	18	68	32	83
5	77	19	72	33	84
6	71	20	70	34	81
7	68	21	64	35	86
8	70	22	67	36	85
9	67	23	72	37	86
10	74	24	70	38	87
11	75	25	74	39	85
12	72	26	76	40	85
13	70	27	75		
14	74	28	78		

a. Construct a *p* chart for the proportion of successful foul shots. Do you think that the player's foul-shooting process is in statistical control? If not, why not?

b. What if you were told that the player used a different method of shooting foul shots for the last 20 days? How might this information change your conclusions in (a)?

c. If you knew the information in (b) prior to doing (a), how might you do the analysis differently?

18.43 The manufacturer of Boston and Vermont asphalt shingles constructed control charts and analyzed several quality characteristics. One characteristic of interest is the strength of the sealant on the shingle. During each day of production, three shingles are tested for their sealant strength. (Thus, a subgroup is operationally defined as one day of production, and the sample size for each subgroup is 3.) Separate pieces are cut from the upper and lower portions of a shingle and then reassembled to simulate shingles on a roof. A timed heating process is used to simulate the sealing process. The sealed shingle pieces are pulled apart, and the amount of force (in pounds) required to break the sealant bond is measured and recorded. This variable is called the *sealant strength*. The LSL and USL for sealant strength are 1.0 and 1.5 pounds, respectively. The data file **sealant.xls** contains sealant strength measurements on 25 days of production for Boston shingles and 19 days for Vermont shingles.

For the Boston shingles,

a. construct a control chart for the range.

b. construct a control chart for the mean.

c. is the process in control?

d. if the process is in control, estimate the percentage of the shingles whose sealant strength is inside the specification limits.

e. if the process is in control, calculate the C_p, CPL, CPU, and C_{pk}.

f. if the manufacturer requires that 99.73% of all shingles be within the specification limits, comment on the capability of the process, based on your calculations in (d) and (e).

g. Repeat (a) through (f), using the 19 production days for Vermont shingles.

PH Grade ASSIST **18.44** A branch manager of a brokerage company is concerned with the number of undesirable trades made by her sales staff. A trade is considered undesirable if there is an error on the trade ticket. Trades with errors are canceled and resubmitted. The cost of correcting errors is billed to the brokerage company. The branch manager wants to know whether the proportion of undesirable trades is in a state of statistical control so she can plan the next step in a quality improvement process. Data were collected for a 30-day period, with the following results (stored in the file **trade.xls**):

Day	Undesirable Trades	Total Trades	Day	Undesirable Trades	Total Trades
1	2	74	16	3	54
2	12	85	17	12	74
3	13	114	18	11	103
4	33	136	19	11	100
5	5	97	20	14	88
6	20	115	21	4	58
7	17	108	22	10	69
8	10	76	23	19	135
9	8	69	24	1	67
10	18	98	25	11	77
11	3	104	26	12	88
12	12	98	27	4	66
13	15	105	28	11	72
14	6	98	29	13	118
15	21	204	30	15	138

a. Construct a control chart for these data.

b. Is the process in control? Explain.

c. Based on the results of (a) and (b), what should the manager do next to improve the process?

PH Grade ASSIST **18.45** The funds-transfer department of a bank is concerned with turnaround time for investigations of funds-transfer payments. A payment may involve the bank as a remitter of funds, a beneficiary of funds, or an intermediary in the payment. An investigation is initiated by a payment inquiry or a query by a party involved in the payment or any department affected by the flow of funds. When a query is received, an investigator reconstructs the transaction trail of the payment and verifies that the information is correct and that the proper payment is transmitted. The investigator then reports the results of the investigation, and the transaction is considered closed. It is important that investigations are closed rapidly, preferably within the same day. The number of new investigations and the number and proportion closed on the same day that the inquiry was made are in the file **fundtran.xls**.

a. Construct a control chart for these data.

b. Is the process in a state of statistical control? Explain.

c. Based on the results of (a) and (b), what should management do next to improve the process?

18.46 For a period of four weeks, record your pulse rate (in beats per minute) just after you get out of bed in the morning and also before you go to sleep at night. Set up $\overline{X}$ and R charts and determine whether your pulse rate is in a state of statistical control. Explain.

18.47 As chief operating officer of a local community hospital, you have just returned from a three-day seminar on quality and productivity. It is your intention to implement many of the ideas that you learned at the seminar. You have decided to maintain control charts for the upcoming month for the following variables: number of daily admissions, proportion of rework in the laboratory (based on 1,000 daily samples), and time (in hours) between receipt of a specimen at the laboratory and completion of the work (based on a subgroup of 10 specimens per day). The data collected are summarized in the file **hospadm.xls**. You are to make a presentation to the chief executive officer of the hospital and the board of directors. Prepare a report that summarizes the conclusions drawn from analyzing control charts for these variables. In addition, recommend additional variables to measure and monitor by using control charts.

18.48 (**Class Project**) Use the table of random numbers (Table E.1) to simulate the selection of different-colored balls from an urn, as follows:

1. Start in the row corresponding to the day of the month in which you were born plus the last two digits of the year in which you were born. For example, if you were born October 3, 1986, you would start in row 3 + 86 = 89. If your total exceeds 100, subtract 100 from the total.
2. Select two-digit random numbers.
3. If you select a random number from 00 to 94, consider the ball to be white; if the random number is from 95 to 99, consider the ball to be red.

Each student is to select 100 such two-digit random numbers and report the number of "red balls" in the sample. Construct a control chart for the proportion of red balls. What conclusions can you draw about the system of selecting red balls? Are all the students part of the system? Is anyone outside the system? If so, what explanation can you give for someone who has too many red balls? If a bonus were paid to the top 10% of the students (the 10% with the fewest red balls), what effect would that have on the rest of the students? Discuss.

The Harnswell Sewing Machine Company Case

Phase 1

For almost 50 years, the Harnswell Sewing Machine Company has manufactured industrial sewing machines. The company specializes in automated machines called pattern tackers that sew repetitive patterns on such mass-produced products as shoes, garments, and seat belts. Aside from the sales of machines, the company sells machine parts. Because the company's products have a reputation for being superior, Harnswell is able to command a price premium for its product line.

Recently, the operations manager, Natalie York, purchased several books relating to quality at a local bookstore. After reading them, she considered the feasibility of beginning some type of quality program at the company. At the current time, the company has no formal quality program. Parts are 100% inspected at the time of shipping to a customer or installation in a machine, yet Natalie has always wondered why inventory of certain parts (in particular, the half-inch cam rollers) invariably falls short before a full year lapses, even though 7,000 pieces have been produced for a demand of 5,000 pieces per year.

After a great deal of reflection and with some apprehension, Natalie has decided that she will approach John Harnswell, the owner of the company, about the possibility of beginning a program to improve quality in the company, starting with a trial project in the machine parts area. As she is walking to Mr. Harnswell's office for the meeting, she has second thoughts about whether this is such a good idea. After all, just last month, Mr. Harnswell told her, "Why do you need to go to graduate school for your master's degree in business? That is a waste of your time and will not be of any value to the Harnswell Company. All those professors are just up in their ivory towers and don't know a thing about running a business, like I do."

As she enters his office, Mr. Harnswell, ever courteous to her, invites Natalie to sit down across from him. "Well, what do you have on your mind this morning?" Mr. Harnswell asks her in an inquisitive tone. She begins by starting to talk about the books that she has just completed reading and about how she has some interesting ideas for making production even better than it is now and improving profits. Before she can finish, Mr. Harnswell has started to answer. "Look, my dear young lady," he says. "Everything has been fine since I started this company in 1968. I have built this company up from nothing to one that employs more than 100 people. Why do you want to make waves? Remember, if it ain't broke, don't fix it." With that he ushers her from his office with the admonishment of, "What am I going to do with you if you keep coming up with these ridiculous ideas?"

EXERCISES

HS18.1 Based on what you have read, which of Deming's 14 points of management are most lacking in the Harnswell Sewing Machine Company? Explain.

HS18.2 What changes, if any, do you think that Natalie York might be able to institute in the company? Explain.

DO NOT CONTINUE UNTIL YOU HAVE COMPLETED THE PHASE 1 EXERCISES.

Phase 2

Natalie slowly walks down the hall after leaving Mr. Harnswell's office, feeling rather downcast. He just won't listen to anyone, she thinks. As she walks, Jim Murante, the shop foreman, comes up beside her. "So," he says, "did you really think that he would listen to you? I've been here more than 25 years. The only way he listens is if he is shown something that worked after it has already been done. Let's see what we can plan together."

Natalie and Jim decide to begin by investigating the production of the cam rollers, which are precision-ground parts. The last part of the production process involves the grinding of the outer diameter. After grinding, the part mates with the cam groove of the particular sewing pattern. The half-inch rollers technically have an engineering specification for the outer diameter of the roller of 0.5075 inch (the specifications are actually metric, but in factory floor jargon, they are referred to as half-inch), plus a tolerable error of 0.0003 inch on the lower side. Thus, the outer diameter is allowed to be between 0.5072 and 0.5075 inch. Anything larger is reclassified into a different and less costly category, and anything smaller is unusable for anything other than scrap.

The grinding of the cam roller is done on a single machine with a single tool setup and no change in the grinding wheel after initial setup. The operation is done by Dave Martin, the head machinist, who has 30 years of experience in the trade and specific experience producing the cam roller part. Because production occurs in batches, Natalie and Jim sample five parts produced from each batch. Table HS18.1 presents data collected over 30 batches (stored in the file harnswell.xls).

TABLE HS18.1

Diameter of Cam Rollers (in Inches)

Batch	Cam Roller				
	1	2	3	4	5
1	.5076	.5076	.5075	.5077	.5075
2	.5075	.5077	.5076	.5076	.5075
3	.5075	.5075	.5075	.5075	.5076
4	.5075	.5076	.5074	.5076	.5073
5	.5075	.5074	.5076	.5073	.5076
6	.5076	.5075	.5076	.5075	.5075
7	.5076	.5076	.5076	.5075	.5075
8	.5075	.5076	.5076	.5075	.5074
9	.5074	.5076	.5075	.5075	.5076
10	.5076	.5077	.5075	.5075	.5075
11	.5075	.5075	.5075	.5076	.5075
12	.5075	.5076	.5075	.5077	.5075
13	.5076	.5076	.5073	.5076	.5074
14	.5075	.5076	.5074	.5076	.5075
15	.5075	.5075	.5076	.5074	.5073
16	.5075	.5074	.5076	.5075	.5075
17	.5075	.5074	.5075	.5074	.5072
18	.5075	.5075	.5076	.5075	.5076
19	.5076	.5076	.5075	.5075	.5076
20	.5075	.5074	.5077	.5076	.5074
21	.5075	.5074	.5075	.5075	.5075
22	.5076	.5076	.5075	.5076	.5074
23	.5076	.5076	.5075	.5075	.5076
24	.5075	.5076	.5075	.5076	.5075
25	.5075	.5075	.5075	.5075	.5074
26	.5077	.5076	.5076	.5074	.5075
27	.5075	.5075	.5074	.5076	.5075
28	.5077	.5076	.5075	.5075	.5076
29	.5075	.5075	.5074	.5075	.5075
30	.5076	.5075	.5075	.5076	.5075

EXERCISE

HS18.3 **a.** Is the process in control? Why?

b. What recommendations do you have for improving the process?

DO NOT CONTINUE UNTIL YOU HAVE COMPLETED THE PHASE 2 EXERCISE.

Phase 3

Natalie examines the $\bar{X}$ and R charts developed from the data presented in Table HS18.1. The R chart indicates that the process is in control, but the $\bar{X}$ chart reveals that the mean for batch 17 is outside the LCL. This immediately gives her cause for concern because low values for the roller diameter could mean that parts have to be scrapped. Natalie goes to see Jim Murante, the shop foreman, to try to find out what had happened on batch 17. Jim looks up the production records to determine when this batch was produced. "Aha!" he exclaims. "I think I've got the answer! This batch was produced on that really cold morning we had last month. I've been after Mr. Harnswell for a long time to let us install an automatic thermostat here in the shop so that the place doesn't feel so cold when we get here in the morning. All he ever tells me is that people aren't as tough as they used to be."

Natalie stands there almost in shock. She realizes that what happened is that, rather than standing idle until the environment and the equipment warmed to acceptable temperatures, the machinist opted to manufacture parts that might have to be scrapped. In fact, Natalie recalls that a major problem occurred on that same day, when several other expensive parts had to be scrapped. Natalie says to Jim, "We just have to do something. We can't let this go on now that we know what problems it is potentially causing." Natalie and Jim decide to take enough money out of petty cash to get the thermostat without having to fill out a requisition requiring Mr. Harnswell's signature. They install the thermostat and set the heating control so that the heat turns on a half hour before the shop opens each morning.

EXERCISES

HS18.4 What should Natalie now do concerning the cam roller data? Explain.

HS18.5 Explain how the actions of Natalie and Jim to avoid this particular problem in the future have resulted in quality improvement.

DO NOT CONTINUE UNTIL YOU HAVE COMPLETED THE PHASE 3 EXERCISES.

Phase 4

Because corrective action was taken to eliminate the special cause of variation, Natalie removes the data for batch 17 from the analysis. The control charts for the remaining days indicate a stable system, with only common causes of variation operating on the system. Thus, Natalie and Jim sit down with Dave Martin and several other machinists to try to determine all the possible causes for the existence of oversized and scrapped rollers. Natalie is still troubled by the data. After all, she wants to find out whether the process is giving oversizes (which are downgraded) and undersizes (which are scrapped). She thinks about which tables and charts might be most helpful.

EXERCISE

HS18.6 **a.** Construct a frequency distribution and a stem-and-leaf display of the cam roller diameters. Which one do you prefer?

b. Based on your results in (a), construct all appropriate graphs of the cam roller diameters.

c. Write a report, expressing your conclusions concerning the cam roller diameters. Be sure to discuss the diameters as they relate to the specifications.

DO NOT CONTINUE UNTIL YOU HAVE COMPLETED THE PHASE 4 EXERCISE.

Phase 5

Natalie notices immediately that the overall mean diameter with batch 17 eliminated is 0.507527, which is higher than the specification value. Thus, the mean diameter of the rollers produced is so high that they will be downgraded in value. In fact, 55 of the 150 rollers sampled (36.67%) are above the specification value. If this percentage is extrapolated to the full year's production, 36.67% of the 7,000 pieces manufactured, or 2,567, could not be sold as half-inch rollers, leaving only 4,433 available for sale. "No wonder we often have shortages that require costly emergency runs," she thinks. She also notes that not one diameter is below the lower specification of 0.5072, so not one of the rollers had to be scrapped.

Natalie realizes that there has to be a reason for all this. Along with Jim Murante, she decides to show the results to Dave Martin, the head machinist. Dave says that the results don't surprise him that much. "You know," he says, "there is only 0.0003 inch in diameter that I'm allowed in variation. If I aim for exactly halfway between 0.5072 and 0.5075, I'm afraid that I'll make a lot of short pieces that will have to be scrapped. I know from way back when I first started here that Mr. Harnswell and everybody else will come down on my head if they start seeing too many of those scraps. I figure that if I aim at 0.5075, the worst thing that will happen will be a bunch of downgrades, but I won't make any pieces that have to be scrapped."

EXERCISES

HS18.7 What approach do you think the machinist should take in terms of the diameter he should aim for? Explain.

HS18.8 What do you think that Natalie should do next? Explain.

Managing the *Springville Herald*

Phase 1

An advertising production team is charged with reducing the number and dollar amount of the advertising errors, with initial focus on the ran-in-error category. The team collects data, including the number of ads with errors, on a Monday-to-Saturday basis. Table SH18.1 includes the total number of ads and the number containing errors for a period of one month (see the data file sh18-1.xls). (Sundays are excluded because a special type of production is used for that day.)

TABLE SH18.1

Number of Ads with Errors and Daily Number of Display Ads

Day	Number of Ads with Errors	Total Number of Ads	Day	Number of Ads with Errors	Total Number of Ads
1	4	228	14	5	245
2	6	273	15	7	266
3	5	239	16	2	197
4	3	197	17	4	228
5	6	259	18	5	236
6	7	203	19	4	208
7	8	289	20	3	214
8	14	241	21	8	258
9	9	263	22	10	267
10	5	199	23	4	217
11	6	275	24	9	277
12	4	212	25	7	258
13	3	207			

EXERCISES

SH18.1 What is the first thing that the team from the advertising production department should do to reduce the number of errors? Explain.

SH18.2 **a.** Construct the appropriate control chart for these data.
   b. Is the process in a state of statistical control? Explain.
   c. What should the team recommend as the next step to improve the process?

DO NOT CONTINUE UNTIL YOU HAVE COMPLETED THE PHASE 1 EXERCISES.

Phase 2

The advertising production team examines the *p* chart developed from the data of Table SH18.1. Using the rules for determining out-of-control points, they observe that day 8 is above the UCL. Upon investigation, they determine that on that day, there was an employee from another work area assigned to the processing of the ads because several employees were out ill. The group brainstorms ways of avoiding the problem in the future and recommends that a team of people from other work areas receive training on the work done by this area. Members of this team can then cover the processing of the ads by rotating in one- or two-hour shifts.

EXERCISES

SH18.3 What should the advertising production team now do concerning the data of Table SH18.1? Explain.

SH18.4 Explain how the actions of the team to avoid this particular problem in the future have resulted in quality improvement.

SH18.5 In addition to the number of ads with errors, what other information concerning errors on a daily basis should the team collect?

DO NOT CONTINUE UNTIL YOU HAVE COMPLETED THE PHASE 2 EXERCISES.

Phase 3

A print production team also is charged with improving the quality of the *Herald*. The team has chosen the blackness of the print of the newspaper as its first project. Blackness is measured on a device that records the results on a standard scale. The blackness of the print should be approximately 1.0. The lower and upper specifications for blackness are 0.8 and 1.2, respectively. Five spots on the first newspaper printed each day are randomly selected, and the blackness of each spot is measured. Table SH18.2 presents the results for 25 days (stored in the file sh18-2.xls).

TABLE SH18.2

Newsprint Blackness for 25 Consecutive Days

Day	Spot				
	1	2	3	4	5
1	0.96	1.01	1.12	1.07	0.97
2	1.06	1.00	1.02	1.16	0.96
3	1.00	0.90	0.98	1.18	0.96
4	0.92	0.89	1.01	1.16	0.90
5	1.02	1.16	1.03	0.89	1.00
6	0.88	0.92	1.03	1.16	0.91
7	1.05	1.13	1.01	0.93	1.03
8	0.95	0.86	1.14	0.90	0.95
9	0.99	0.89	1.00	1.15	0.92
10	0.89	1.18	1.03	0.96	1.04
11	0.97	1.13	0.95	0.86	1.06
12	1.00	0.87	1.02	0.98	1.13
13	0.96	0.79	1.17	0.97	0.95
14	1.03	0.89	1.03	1.12	1.03
15	0.96	1.12	0.95	0.88	0.99
16	1.01	0.87	0.99	1.04	1.16
17	0.98	0.85	0.99	1.04	1.16
18	1.03	0.82	1.21	0.98	1.08
19	1.02	0.84	1.15	0.94	1.08
20	0.90	1.02	1.10	1.04	1.08
21	0.96	1.05	1.01	0.93	1.01
22	0.89	1.04	0.97	0.99	0.95
23	0.96	1.00	0.97	1.04	0.95
24	1.01	0.98	1.04	1.01	0.92
25	1.01	1.00	0.92	0.90	1.11

EXERCISES

SH18.6 **a.** Construct the appropriate control charts for these data.

b. Is the process in a state of statistical control? Explain.

c. Perform a capability analysis. Is the process capable of meeting the blackness specifications?

d. What should the team recommend as the next step to improve the process?

REFERENCES

1. Arndt, M., "Quality Isn't Just for Widgets," *BusinessWeek*, July 22, 2002, 72–73.
2. Automotive Industry Action Group (AIAG), *Statistical Process Control Reference Manual* (Chrysler, Ford, and General Motors Quality and Supplier Assessment Staff, 1995).
3. Bothe, D. R., *Measuring Process Capability* (New York: McGraw-Hill, 1997).
4. Deming, W. E., *The New Economics for Business, Industry, and Government* (Cambridge, MA: MIT Center for Advanced Engineering Study, 1993).
5. Deming, W. E., *Out of the Crisis* (Cambridge, MA: MIT Center for Advanced Engineering Study, 1986).
6. Friedman, T. L., *The Lexus and the Olive Tree: Understanding Globalization* (New York: Farrar, Straus and Giroux, 1999).
7. Gabor, A., *The Man Who Discovered Quality* (New York: Time Books, 1990).
8. Gitlow, H., A. Oppenheim, R. Oppenheim, and D. Levine, *Tools and Methods for the Improvement of Quality*, 3rd ed. (New York: McGraw-Hill-Irwin, 2005).

9. Gitlow, H., and D. Levine, *Six Sigma for Green Belts and Champions* (Upper Saddle River, NJ: Financial Times/ Prentice Hall, 2005).

10. Gitlow, H., D. Levine, and E. Popovich, *Design for Six Sigma for Green Belts and Champions* (Upper Saddle River, NJ: Financial Times/Prentice Hall, 2006).

11. Hahn, G. J., N. Doganaksoy, and R. Hoerl, "The Evolution of Six Sigma," *Quality Engineering*, 12 (2000): 317–326.

12. Halberstam, D., *The Reckoning* (New York: Morrow, 1986).

13. Levine, D. M., *Statistics for Six Sigma for Green Belts with Minitab and JMP* (Upper Saddle River, NJ: Financial Times/Prentice Hall, 2006).

14. *Microsoft Excel 2007* (Redmond, WA: Microsoft Corp., 2007).

15. Scherkenbach, W. W., *The Deming Route to Quality and Productivity: Road Maps and Roadblocks* (Washington, DC: CEEP Press, 1987).

16. Snee, R. D., "Impact of Six Sigma on Quality," *Quality Engineering*, 12 (2000): ix–xiv.

17. Walton, M., *The Deming Management Method* (New York: Perigee Books, 1986).

Excel Companion
to Chapter 18

E18.1 CREATING *p* CHARTS

You create *p* charts by either selecting the PHStat2 p Chart procedure or by using Excel chart features with your completed pChartData worksheet.

Using PHStat2 p Chart

Open to the worksheet that contains the data including time period, sample/subgroup size, and number of nonconformances. Select **PHStat → Control Charts → p Chart**. In the procedure's dialog box (shown below), enter the **Non-Conformances Cell Range** and click **First cell contains label**. Click one of the Sample/Subgroup Size options and make the necessary entry. Enter a title as the **Title** and click **OK**.

If the sample/subgroup size does not vary, click **Size does not vary** and enter the sample/subgroup size in its box. If the sample/subgroups size varies, click **Size varies** and enter the cell range that lists the sample/subgroup sizes for each time period.

PHStat2 creates two supporting worksheets (similar to pChartData and pCalcs worksheets explained later) as well as the chart sheet that contains the *p* chart.

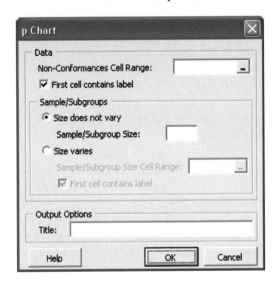

Using the p Chart.xls Workbook to Create Control Limits

To create control limits, open to the **pChartData** worksheet of the **p Chart.xls** workbook. Enter the time period

data in column A, the sample/subgroup size for each time period in column B, and the number of nonconforming items for each time period in column C. Then select the preexisting formulas in the cell range D2:G2 and copy them down through all data rows. (Before you enter your data, these cells display the message #DIV/0! This is not an error.)

The formulas that you copy are shown in Figure E18.1. The cell D2 formula computes a point to be plotted on the *p* chart. The cell E2 formula either displays the lower control limit value or displays nothing if the formula returns a value less than zero. The cell F2 formulas display the center values, and the G2 formulas display the upper control limit values. As you copy the formulas in these last three columns, the same set of three values appear in every row. This is far from being redundant: designing the worksheet to repeat the LCL, center, and UCL line for each time period simplifies creating a *p* chart. (If you do not want to create a *p* chart, you can ignore columns E through G.)

	D	E	F	G
1	*p*	LCL	Center	UCL
2	=C2/B2	=IF(pCalcs!$B$11 < 0, "", pCalcs!$B$11)	=pCalcs!$B$12	=pCalcs!$B$13

FIGURE E18.1 pChartData worksheet formulas

As you complete the pChartData worksheet, you also complete the **pCalcs** worksheet that summarizes the calculations of the control limits. You make no entries into the pCalcs worksheet; its data comes from summarizing the entries in the pChartData worksheet. Figure E18.2 shows a completed pCalcs worksheet for the *p* chart shown in Figure 18.4 on page 742.

	A	B	
1	*p* Chart		
2			
3	Intermediate Calculations		
4	Sum of Subgroup Sizes	5600	=SUM(pChartData!B:B)
5	Number of Subgroups Taken	28	=COUNT(pChartData!B:B)
6	Average Sample/Subgroup Size	200	=B4/B5
7	Average Proportion of Nonconforming Items	0.0827	=SUM(pChartData!C:C)/B4
8	Three Standard Deviations	0.0584	=3 * SQRT(B7 * (1 - B7)/B6)
9			
10	*p* Chart Control Limits		
11	Lower Control Limit	0.0243	=B7 - B8
12	Center	0.0827	=B7
13	Upper Control Limit	0.1411	=B7 + B8

FIGURE E18.2 pCalcs worksheet

Creating a *p* Chart (97–2003)

Open to your completed **pChartData** worksheet, begin the Chart Wizard, and make the following entries and choices in the step dialog boxes:

Step 1   Click **XY (Scatter)** from the **Standard Types Chart type** box and then select the first choice in the bottom row of **Chart sub-type** choices, labeled **Scatter with data points connected by lines**.

Step 2   Click the **Data Range** tab. Enter the column A cell range of your time period data, followed by the columns D through G cell range that contain the formulas as the **Data Range**. Because you are entering a data range composed of two non-adjacent areas, you must separate the two cell ranges with a comma. For example, if your pChartData worksheet contained entries in rows 2 through 29, you would enter **A1:A29,D1:G29** as the Data Range. Click the **Columns** option after you have entered the Data Range.

Step 3   Click the **Titles** tab. Enter a title as the **Chart title** and enter appropriate values for the **Value (X) axis** and **Value (Y) axis** titles. Click, in turn, the **Axes**, **Gridlines**, **Legend**, and **Data Labels** tabs and use the formatting settings given in the "Creating Charts (97–2003)" part of Section E2.2 on page 79.

At this point, the UCL, center, and LCL lines of your p chart are missing labels and are incorrectly formatted. You can correct these errors by using the following instructions.

Add Labels for the Control Chart and Center Lines Display the Drawing toolbar by selecting **View ➔ Toolbars ➔ Drawing**. For each line, click the **Text Box** icon and drag the mouse to draw a box to hold a label. (Figure E18.3 shows the Excel 2003 Text Box icon selected; the icons in other Excel versions are similar.) Type the label (UCL, pBar, or LCL). If necessary, you can adjust the size of the box by clicking and dragging one of the corner circle handles. If necessary, you can adjust the position of the box by clicking and dragging the halo around the text box.

FIGURE E18.3 Text Box icon of the Drawing toolbar (Excel 2003)

Eliminate Data Point Markers from the UCL, LCL, and Center Lines   For each line, right-click the line and select **Format Data Series** from the shortcut menu.

In the **Marker** group, select the **None** option and then click **OK**.

Reformat the UCL and LCL Lines   For each line, right-click the line and select **Format Data Series** from the shortcut menu. In the **Patterns** tab of the Format Data Series dialog box, select the first dashed line choice from the **Style drop-down** list box in the **Line** group, and click **OK**.

Reformat the Center Line   Right-click the line and select **Format Data Series** from the shortcut menu. In the **Patterns** tab of the Format Data Series dialog box, select a red color from the **Color** drop-down list in the **Line** group, select the **None** option in the **Marker** group, and click **OK**.

Creating a *p* Chart (2007)

Open to your completed **pChartData** worksheet and select column A and columns D through G data. To select these non-adjacent areas together, hold down the **Ctrl** key while selecting the ranges. Then, select **Insert ➔ (Scatter)** and in the (Scatter) gallery, select the choice labeled **Scatter with Straight Lines and Markers**. Relocate your chart to a chart sheet and customize your chart by using the instructions in "Creating Charts (2007)" in Section E.2.2 on page 80.

At this point, the UCL, center, and LCL lines of your *p* chart are missing labels and are incorrectly formatted. You can correct these errors using the following instructions.

Add Labels for the Control Chart and Center Lines For each line, click **Insert ➔ Text Box** and drag the mouse to draw a box to hold a label. Right-click in the box and select **Edit Text** from the shortcut menu. Type the label (UCL, pBar, or LCL) and click outside the text box. If necessary, you can adjust the size of the box by clicking and dragging one of the corner circle handles. If necessary, you can adjust the position of the box by clicking and dragging the box.

Reformat the UCL and LCL Lines   For each line, right-click the line and select **Format Data Series** from the shortcut menu. In the **Line Style** panel, select one of the choices from the **Dash type** drop-down list. In the **Marker Options** panel, select the **None** option and then click **Close**.

Reformat the Center Line   Right-click the line and select **Format Data Series** from the shortcut menu. In the **Line** panel, select one of the red choices from the **Color** drop-down list. In the **Marker Options** panel, select the **None** option and then click **Close**.

E18.2 CREATING *R* AND $\bar{X}$ CHARTS

You create R and $\bar{X}$ charts by either using the PHStat2 R & XBar Charts procedure or by using Excel chart features with your completed **RandXBarChart.xls** workbook.

Using PHStat2 R & $\bar{X}$ Charts

Open to the worksheet containing your data that includes the range and mean for each time period. (If you have unsummarized data for each time period, you need to compute the mean and range for each period before using this worksheet. For each time period, you can use the AVERAGE function to compute the mean. You can use the MAX and MIN functions to identify the minimum and maximum values for each time period and then compute the range by taking the difference between the MAX and MIN values.) Select **PHStat → Control Charts → R & XBar Charts**. In the procedure's dialog box (shown below), enter the **Subgroup/Sample Size** and the cell range of the **Subgroup Ranges Cell Range** and click **First cell contains label**. Click **R and XBar Charts**, enter the **Subgroup Means Cell Range** and click **First cell contains label**. Enter a title as the **Title** and click **OK**.

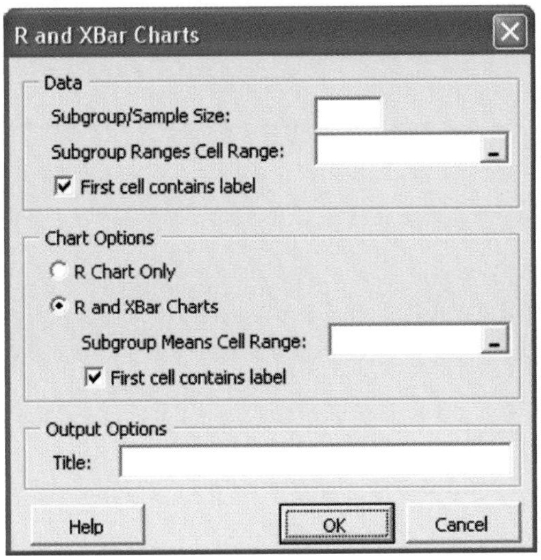

Using the RandXBarChart.xls Workbook to Create Control Limits

To compute control limits, open to the **RXChartData** worksheet of the **RandXBarChart.xls** workbook. Enter the time period, $\bar{X}$, and range data into columns A, B, and C, respectively. Then select the preexisting formulas in the cell range D2:I2 and copy them down through all data rows. (Before you enter your data, these cells display the message #DIV/0!. This is not an error.) If you have unsummarized data for each time period, you need to compute the mean and range for each period before using this worksheet using one of the techniques discussed in Section E3.1 on page 148. For each time period, place the time period and its computed mean and range in columns A through C cells of a new row of the RXChartData worksheet. If you want to use the worksheet function technique of Section E3.1, subtract the result of the MIN function from the result of the MAX function to compute the range.

The formulas that you copy compute the control limits and center lines for both the R and $\bar{X}$ chart and are similar to the formulas discussed in Section E18.1 on page 771. After you finish copying the formulas, open to the **RXCalcs** worksheet (to which the formulas refer). Enter the sample/subgroup size in cell B4. Use Table E.11 to look up the proper values for the D_3, D_4, and A_2 factors and enter those values in cells B8, B9, and B18, respectively, to complete the worksheet. Figure E18.4 shows a completed RXCalcs worksheet for the R and $\bar{X}$ charts shown in Figures 18.7 and 18.8 on pages 750 and 752.

	A	B	
1	**R and XBar Chart**		
2			
3	**Data**		
4	**Sample/Subgroup Size**	5	
5			
6	R Chart Intermediate Calculations		
7	RBar	3.4821	=AVERAGE(RXChartData!C:C)
8	D3 Factor	0	
9	D4 Factor	2.114	
10			
11	**R Chart Control Limits**		
12	**Lower Control Limit**	**0.0000**	=B8 * B7
13	**Center**	**3.4821**	=B7
14	**Upper Control Limit**	**7.3613**	=B9 * B7
15			
16	XBar Chart Intemediate Calculations		
17	Average of Subgroup Averages	9.4779	=AVERAGE(RXChartData!B:B)
18	A2 Factor	0.577	
19	A2 Factor * RBar	2.0092	=B18 * B7
20			
21	**XBar Chart Control Limits**		
22	**Lower Control Limit**	**7.4687**	=B17 - B19
23	**Center**	**9.4779**	=B17
24	**Upper Control Limit**	**11.4871**	=B17 + B19

FIGURE E18.4 RXCalcs worksheet

Creating *R* and $\bar{X}$ Charts (97–2003)

Open to your completed **RXChartData** worksheet, begin the Chart Wizard, and make the following entries and choices in the step dialog boxes:

Step 1 Click **XY (Scatter)** in the **Standard Types Chart type** box and then select the first choice in the bottom row of **Chart sub-type** choices, labeled as **Scatter with data points connected by lines**.

Step 2 Click the **Data Range** tab. To create an R chart, enter the column A cell range of your time period data followed by the columns C through F cell range that contain the formulas as the **Data Range**. To create an $\bar{X}$ chart, enter the column A and B cell range followed by the columns G through I cell range that contain the formulas as the **Data Range**. Because you are entering a data range composed of two non-adjacent areas, you must separate the two cell ranges with a comma. For example, if your RXChartData worksheet contained entries in rows 2 through 29, you would enter **A1:A29,C1:F29** if creating an *R* chart or **A1:B29,G1:I29** if creating an $\overline{X}$ chart. Click the **Columns** option after you have entered the Data Range.

Step 3   Click the **Titles** tab. Enter a title as the **Chart title** and enter appropriate values for the **Value (X) axis** and **Value (Y) axis** titles. Click, in turn, the **Axes**, **Gridlines**, **Legend**, and **Data Labels** tabs and use the formatting settings given in the "Creating Charts (97–2003)" part of Section E2.2 on page 79.

At this point, the UCL, center, and LCL lines of your *R* or $\overline{X}$ chart are missing labels and are incorrectly formatted. You can correct these errors by using the instructions in Section E18.1 on page 772.

Creating *R* and $\overline{X}$ Charts (2007)

Open to your completed **RXChartData** worksheet. To create an *R* chart, select the column A and columns C through F data. To create an $\overline{X}$ chart, select the columns A and B and columns G through I data. To select these non-adjacent areas together, hold down the **Ctrl** key while selecting the ranges. Then select **Insert → (Scatter)** gallery and in the (Scatter) gallery, select the **Scatter with Straight Lines and Markers**. Relocate your chart to a chart sheet and customize your chart by using the instructions in "Creating Charts (2007)" in Section E2.2 on page 80.

At this point, the UCL, center, and LCL lines of your R or $\overline{X}$ chart are missing labels and are incorrectly formatted. You can correct these errors by using the instructions in Section E18.1 on page 772.

APPENDICES

A. REVIEW OF ARITHMETIC, ALGEBRA, AND LOGARITHMS

A.1   RULES FOR ARITHMETIC OPERATIONS

RULE	EXAMPLE
1. $a + b = c$ and $b + a = c$	$2 + 1 = 3$ and $1 + 2 = 3$
2. $a + (b + c) = (a + b) + c$	$5 + (7 + 4) = (5 + 7) + 4 = 16$
3. $a - b = c$ but $b - a \neq c$	$9 - 7 = 2$ but $7 - 9 = -2$
4. $a \times b = b \times a$	$7 \times 6 = 6 \times 7 = 42$
5. $a \times (b + c) = (a \times b) + (a \times c)$	$2 \times (3 + 5) = (2 \times 3) + (2 \times 5) = 16$
6. $a \div b \neq b \div a$	$12 \div 3 \neq 3 \div 12$
7. $\dfrac{a + b}{c} = \dfrac{a}{c} + \dfrac{b}{c}$	$\dfrac{7 + 3}{2} = \dfrac{7}{2} + \dfrac{3}{2} = 5$
8. $\dfrac{a}{b + c} \neq \dfrac{a}{b} + \dfrac{a}{c}$	$\dfrac{3}{4 + 5} \neq \dfrac{3}{4} + \dfrac{3}{5}$
9. $\dfrac{1}{a} + \dfrac{1}{b} = \dfrac{b + a}{ab}$	$\dfrac{1}{3} + \dfrac{1}{5} = \dfrac{5 + 3}{(3)(5)} = \dfrac{8}{15}$
10. $\dfrac{a}{b} \times \dfrac{c}{d} = \dfrac{a \times c}{b \times d}$	$\dfrac{2}{3} \times \dfrac{6}{7} = \dfrac{2 \times 6}{3 \times 7} = \dfrac{12}{21}$
11. $\dfrac{a}{b} \div \dfrac{c}{d} = \dfrac{a \times d}{b \times c}$	$\dfrac{5}{8} \div \dfrac{3}{7} = \dfrac{5 \times 7}{8 \times 3} = \dfrac{35}{24}$

A.2   RULES FOR ALGEBRA: EXPONENTS AND SQUARE ROOTS

RULE	EXAMPLE
1. $X^a \times X^b = X^{a+b}$	$4^2 \times 4^3 = 4^5$
2. $(X^a)^b = X^{ab}$	$(2^2)^3 = 2^6$
3. $(X^a / X^b) = X^{a-b}$	$\dfrac{3^5}{3^3} = 3^2$
4. $\dfrac{X^a}{X^a} = X^0 = 1$	$\dfrac{3^4}{3^4} = 3^0 = 1$
5. $\sqrt{XY} = \sqrt{X}\sqrt{Y}$	$\sqrt{(25)(4)} = \sqrt{25}\sqrt{4} = 10$
6. $\sqrt{\dfrac{X}{Y}} = \dfrac{\sqrt{X}}{\sqrt{Y}}$	$\sqrt{\dfrac{16}{100}} = \dfrac{\sqrt{16}}{\sqrt{100}} = 0.40$

A.3   RULES FOR LOGARITHMS

Base 10

LOG is the symbol used for base-10 logarithms:

RULE	EXAMPLE
1. $\text{LOG}(10^A) = A$	$\text{LOG}(100) = \text{LOG}(10^2) = 2$
2. If $\text{LOG}(A) = B$, then $A = 10^B$	If $\text{LOG}(A) = 2$, then $A = 10^2 = 100$
3. $\text{LOG}(A \times B) = \text{LOG}(A) + \text{LOG}(B)$	$\text{LOG}(100) = \text{LOG}(10 \times 10)$
	$\quad = \text{LOG}(10) + \text{LOG}(10) = 1 + 1 = 2$
4. $\text{LOG}(A^B) = B \times \text{LOG}(A)$	$\text{LOG}(1000) = \text{LOG}(10^3) = 3 \times \text{LOG}(10)$
	$\quad = 3 \times 1 = 3$
5. $\text{LOG}(A/B) = \text{LOG}(A) - \text{LOG}(B)$	$\text{LOG}(100) = \text{LOG}(1000/10)$
	$\quad = \text{LOG}(1000) - \text{LOG}(10) = 3 - 1 = 2$

EXAMPLE

Take the base 10 logarithm of each side of the following equation:

$$Y = \beta_0 \beta_1^X \varepsilon$$

SOLUTION   Apply rules 3 and 4:

$$\text{LOG}(Y) = \text{LOG}(\beta_0 \beta_1^X)\varepsilon$$
$$= \text{LOG}(\beta_0) + \text{LOG}(\beta_1^X) + \text{LOG}(\varepsilon)$$
$$= \text{LOG}(\beta_0) + X \times \text{LOG}(\beta_1) + \text{LOG}(\varepsilon)$$

Base e

LN is the symbol used for base e logarithms, commonly referred to as natural logarithms. e is Euler's number, and $e \cong 2.718282$:

RULE	EXAMPLE
1. $\text{LN}(e^A) = A$	$\text{LN}(7.389056) = \text{LN}(e^2) = 2$
2. If $\text{LN}(A) = B$, then $A = e^B$	If $\text{LN}(A) = 2$, then $A = e^2 = 7.389056$
3. $\text{LN}(A \times B) = \text{LN}(A) + \text{LN}(B)$	$\text{LN}(100) = \text{LN}(10 \times 10)$
	$\quad = \text{LN}(10) + \text{LN}(10)$
	$\quad = 2.302585 + 2.302585 = 4.605170$
4. $\text{LN}(A^B) = B \times \text{LN}(A)$	$\text{LN}(1000) = \text{LN}(10^3) = 3 \times \text{LN}(10)$
	$\quad = 3 \times 2.302585 = 6.907755$
5. $\text{LN}(A/B = \text{LN}(A) - \text{LN}(B)$	$\text{LN}(100) = \text{LN}(1000/10)$
	$\quad = \text{LN}(1000) - \text{LN}(10)$
	$\quad = 6.907755 - 2.302585 = 4.605170$

EXAMPLE

Take the base e logarithm of each side of the following equation:

$$Y = \beta_0 \beta_1^X \varepsilon$$

SOLUTION   Apply rules 3 and 4:

$$\text{LN}(Y) = \text{LN}(\beta_0 \beta_1^X \varepsilon)$$
$$= \text{LN}(\beta_0) + \text{LN}(\beta_1^X) + \text{LN}(\varepsilon)$$
$$= \text{LN}(\beta_0) + X \times \text{LN}(\beta_1) + \text{LN}(\varepsilon)$$

B. SUMMATION NOTATION

The symbol Σ, the Greek capital letter sigma, is used to denote "taking the sum of." Consider a set of n values for variable X. The expression $\sum_{i=1}^{n} X_i$ means that these n values are to be added together. Thus:

$$\sum_{i=1}^{n} X_i = X_1 + X_2 + X_3 + \cdots + X_n$$

The following problem illustrates the use of summation notation. Consider five values of a variable X: $X_1 = 2$, $X_2 = 0$, $X_3 = -1$, $X_4 = 5$, and $X_5 = 7$. Thus:

$$\sum_{i=1}^{5} X_i = X_1 + X_2 + X_3 + X_4 + X_5 = 2 + 0 + (-1) + 5 + 7 = 13$$

In statistics, the squared values of a variable are often summed. Thus:

$$\sum_{i=1}^{n} X_i^2 = X_1^2 + X_2^2 + X_3^2 + \cdots + X_n^2$$

and, in the example above:

$$\sum_{i=1}^{5} X_i^2 = X_1^2 + X_2^2 + X_3^2 + X_4^2 + X_5^2$$

$$= 2^2 + 0^2 + (-1)^2 + 5^2 + 7^2$$

$$= 4 + 0 + 1 + 25 + 49$$

$$= 79$$

$\sum_{i=1}^{n} X_i^2$, the summation of the squares, is *not* the same as $\left(\sum_{i=1}^{n} X_i \right)^2$, the square of the sum:

$$\sum_{i=1}^{n} X_i^2 \neq \left(\sum_{i=1}^{n} X_i \right)^2$$

In the example given earlier, the summation of squares is equal to 79. This is not equal to the square of the sum, which is $13^2 = 169$.

Another frequently used operation involves the summation of the product. Consider two variables, X and Y, each having n values. Then:

$$\sum_{i=1}^{n} X_i Y_i = X_1 Y_1 + X_2 Y_2 + X_3 Y_3 + \cdots + X_n Y_n$$

Continuing with the previous example, suppose there is a second variable, Y, whose five values are $Y_1 = 1$, $Y_2 = 3$, $Y_3 = -2$, $Y_4 = 4$, and $Y_5 = 3$. Then,

$$\sum_{i=1}^{n} X_i Y_i = X_1 Y_1 + X_2 Y_2 + X_3 Y_3 + X_4 Y_4 + X_5 Y_5$$

$$= (2)(1) + (0)(3) + (-1)(-2) + (5)(4) + (7)(3)$$

$$= 2 + 0 + 2 + 20 + 21$$

$$= 45$$

In computing $\sum_{i=1}^{n} X_i Y_i$, realize that the first value of X is multiplied by the first value of Y, the second value of X is multiplied by the second value of Y, and so on. These cross products are then summed in order to compute the desired result. However, the summation of products is *not* equal to the product of the individual sums:

$$\sum_{i=1}^{n} X_i Y_i \neq \left(\sum_{i=1}^{n} X_i \right)\left(\sum_{i=1}^{n} Y_i \right)$$

In this example,

$$\sum_{i=1}^{5} X_i = 13$$

and

$$\sum_{i=1}^{5} Y_i = 1 + 3 + (-2) + 4 + 3 = 9$$

so that

$$\left(\sum_{i=1}^{5} X_i \right)\left(\sum_{i=1}^{5} Y_i \right) = (13)(9) = 117$$

However,

$$\sum_{i=1}^{5} X_i Y_i = 45$$

The following table summarizes these results:

VALUE	X_i	Y_i	$X_i Y_i$
1	2	1	2
2	0	3	0
3	−1	−2	2
4	5	4	20
5	7	3	21
	$\sum_{i=1}^{5} X_i = 13$	$\sum_{i=1}^{5} Y_i = 9$	$\sum_{i=1}^{5} X_i Y_i = 45$

RULE 1 The summation of the values of two variables is equal to the sum of the values of each summed variable:

$$\sum_{i=1}^{n} (X_i + Y_i) = \sum_{i=1}^{n} X_i + \sum_{i=1}^{n} Y_i$$

Thus,

$$\sum_{i=1}^{5} (X_i + Y_i) = (2 + 1) + (0 + 3) + (-1 + (-2)) + (5 + 4) + (7 + 3)$$

$$= 3 + 3 + (-3) + 9 + 10$$

$$= 22$$

$$\sum_{i=1}^{5} X_i + \sum_{i=1}^{5} Y_i = 13 + 9 = 22$$

RULE 2 The summation of a difference between the values of two variables is equal to the difference between the summed values of the variables:

$$\sum_{i=1}^{n}(X_i - Y_i) = \sum_{i=1}^{n}X_i - \sum_{i=1}^{n}Y_i$$

Thus,

$$\sum_{i=1}^{5}(X_i - Y_i) = (2 - 1) + (0 - 3) + (-1 - (-2)) + (5 - 4) + (7 - 3)$$

$$= 1 + (-3) + 1 + 1 + 4$$

$$= 4$$

$$\sum_{i=1}^{5}X_i - \sum_{i=1}^{5}Y_i = 13 - 9 = 4$$

RULE 3 The summation of a constant times a variable is equal to that constant times the summation of the values of the variable:

$$\sum_{i=1}^{n}cX_i = c\sum_{i=1}^{n}X_i$$

where c is a constant. Thus, if $c = 2$,

$$\sum_{i=1}^{5}cX_i = \sum_{i=1}^{5}2X_i = (2)(2) + (2)(0) + (2)(-1) + (2)(5) + (2)(7)$$

$$= 4 + 0 + (-2) + 10 + 14$$

$$= 26$$

$$c\sum_{i=1}^{5}X_i = 2\sum_{i=1}^{5}X_i = (2)(13) = 26$$

RULE 4 A constant summed n times will be equal to n times the value of the constant.

$$\sum_{i=1}^{n}c = nc$$

where c is a constant. Thus, if the constant $c = 2$ is summed 5 times,

$$\sum_{i=1}^{5}c = 2 + 2 + 2 + 2 + 2 = 10$$

$$nc = (5)(2) = 10$$

EXAMPLE

Suppose there are six values for the variables X and Y, such that $X_1 = 2, X_2 = 1, X_3 = 5, X_4 = -3, X_5 = 1, X_6 = -2$, and $Y_1 = 4, Y_2 = 0, Y_3 = -1, Y_4 = 2, Y_5 = 7$, and $Y_6 = -3$. Compute each of the following:

a. $\sum_{i=1}^{6}X_i$

b. $\sum_{i=1}^{6}Y_i$

c. $\sum_{i=1}^{6}X_i^2$

d. $\sum_{i=1}^{6}Y_i^2$

e. $\sum_{i=1}^{6}X_iY_i$

f. $\sum_{i=1}^{6}(X_i + Y_i)$

$$\text{g. } \sum_{i=1}^{6}(X_i - Y_i) \qquad \text{i. } \sum_{i=1}^{6}(cX_i), \text{ where } c = -1$$

$$\text{h. } \sum_{i=1}^{6}(X_i - 3Y_i + 2X_i^2) \qquad \text{j. } \sum_{i=1}^{6}(X_i - 3Y_i + c), \text{ where } c = +3$$

ANSWER
(a) 4   (b) 9   (c) 44   (d) 79   (e) 10   (f) 13   (g) −5   (h) 65   (i) −4   (j) −5

References

1. Bashaw, W. L., *Mathematics for Statistics* (New York: Wiley, 1969).
2. Lanzer, P., *Basic Math: Fractions, Decimals, Percents* (Hicksville, NY: Video Aided Instruction, 2006).
3. Levine, D., *The MBA Primer: Business Statistics* (Cincinnati, OH: Southwestern Publishing, 2000).
4. Levine, D., *Statistics* (Hicksville, NY: Video Aided Instruction, 2006).
5. Shane, H., *Algebra 1* (Hicksville, NY: Video Aided Instruction, 2006).

C. STATISTICAL SYMBOLS AND GREEK ALPHABET

C.1   STATISTICAL SYMBOLS

+ add	× multiply
− subtract	÷ divide
= equal to	≠ not equal to
≅ approximately equal to	
> greater than	< less than
≥ greater than or equal to	≤ less than or equal to

C.2   GREEK ALPHABET

GREEK LETTER		LETTER NAME	ENGLISH EQUIVALENT	GREEK LETTER		LETTER NAME	ENGLISH EQUIVALENT
A	α	Alpha	a	N	ν	Nu	n
B	β	Beta	b	Ξ	ξ	Xi	x
Γ	γ	Gamma	g	O	o	Omicron	ŏ
Δ	δ	Delta	d	Π	π	Pi	p
E	ε	Epsilon	ĕ	P	ρ	Rho	r
Z	ζ	Zeta	z	Σ	σ	Sigma	s
H	η	Eta	ē	T	τ	Tau	t
Θ	θ	Theta	th	Y	υ	Upsilon	u
I	ι	Iota	i	Φ	φ	Phi	ph
K	κ	Kappa	k	X	χ	Chi	ch
Λ	λ	Lambda	l	Ψ	ψ	Psi	ps
M	μ	Mu	m	Ω	ω	Omega	ō

D. STUDENT CD-ROM CONTENTS

D.1 CD-ROM OVERVIEW

The Student CD-ROM that is packaged with this book includes five folders that contain files that support your learning of statistics (each described separately below). For your convenience, the Student CD-ROM includes a small program that will copy the contents of folders to your system. (If you choose, you can manually explore and copy files from these folders as well.) Be sure to review the **Readme.txt** file in the root folder of the Student CD-ROM for any late-breaking changes to the contents of the CD.

Excel Data Files
Located in the **Browse** folder, the Excel Data Files folder contains the Microsoft Excel workbook files (with the extension .xls) used in the examples and problems in this text. A detailed list of the files appears in Section D.2.

Herald Case
Located in the **Browse** folder, the Herald Case folder contains the files for the "Managing the *Springville Herald*" case. (These files are also available online at the URLs listed in the case.)

Web Case
Located in the **Browse** folder, the Web Case folder contains the files for all the Web Cases that appear at the end of chapters. (These files are also available online at the URLs listed in each case.)

PHStat2
Located in the **Install** folder, the PHStat2 folder contains the setup program to install PHStat2 version 2.7 on a Windows or Vista computer. You must run the setup program successfully before you can use PHStat2 inside Microsoft Excel. (Be sure to review Section F.4 in Appendix F and the PHStat2 readme file in the PHStat2 folder before you use the setup program.)

Excel Companion Workbooks
Located in the **Browse** folder, the Microsoft Excel Companion workbooks folder contains the workbooks described and used in the Excel Companion sections. Copies of these files also appear in the Excel Data Files folder.

Visual Explorations
Located in the **Browse** folder, Visual Explorations contains the files necessary to use the add-in workbook **Visual Explorations.xla**. Before using this workbook, you should review the "Macro Security Issues" part of Section E1.6 and you may also want to consult the Appendix F FAQs.

You can open and use the **Visual Explorations.xla** file directly from the CD-ROM in Microsoft Excel. If you prefer to use Visual Explorations without the CD present, copy the files **Visual Explorations.xla** and **VEShelp.hlp** to the folder of your choice. (The Veshelp.hlp file contains the orientation and help files for this add-in.)

CD-ROM Topics
Located in the **Browse** folder, the CD-ROM Topics folder contains supplemental textbook sections in Adobe PDF files. You will need the Adobe Acrobat reader program installed on your system in order to read these sections. (In the Install folder is a version of the Adobe Reader that you can install on your system, if necessary.)

D.2 DATA FILE DESCRIPTIONS

The following presents in alphabetical order, a listing of the Excel data files that are in the Excel Data Files folder. These files are in .xls format, which can be opened in all Excel versions. Elsewhere in this book, these file names appear in this special typeface, and with the .xls extension for example as **Mutual Funds.xls**.

AAAMILEAGE Gasoline mileage from AAA members, and combined city-highway driving gasoline mileage according to current government standards (Chapter 10)

ACCESS Coded access read times (in msec), file size, programmer group, and buffer size (Chapter 11)

ACCRES Processing time, in seconds, and type of computer jobs (research = 0, accounting = 1) (Chapter 10)

ACT ACT scores for type of course (rows) and length of course (columns) (Chapter 11)

ADPAGES Magazine, ad pages in 2004, and ad pages in 2005 (Chapter 10)

ADVERTISE Sales (in thousands of dollars), radio ads (in thousands of dollars), and newspaper ads (in thousands of dollars) for 22 cities (Chapters 14, 15)

AMPHRS Capacity of batteries (Chapter 12)

ANGLE Subgroup number and angle (Chapter 18)

ANSCOMBE Data sets A, B, C, and D—each with 11 pairs of X and Y values (Chapter 13)

AUTO Miles per gallon, horsepower, and weight for a sample of 50 car models (Chapters 14, 15)

BANKCOST1 Bank names and bounced check fees (Chapters 2, 3, 8)

BANKTIME Waiting times of bank customers (Chapter 18)

BANKYIELD Yield for money market account and yield for one-year CD (Chapters 3, 10)

BANK1 Waiting time (in minutes) spent by a sample of 15 customers at a bank located in a commercial district (Chapters 3, 9, 10, 12)

BANK2 Waiting time (in minutes) spent by a sample of 15 customers at a bank located in a residential area (Chapters 3, 10, 12)

BASEBALL Team, attendance, high temperature on game day, winning percentage of home team, opponents winning percentage, game played on Friday, Saturday, or Sunday (0 = no, 1 = yes), promotion held (0 = no, 1 = yes) (Chapter 15)

BASKET Year, price of bread, beef, eggs, and lettuce (Chapter 16)

BATTERYLIFE Life of a camera battery, in number of shots (Chapters 2, 3, 8)

BB2001 Team; league (0 = American, 1 = National); wins; earned run average; runs scored; hits allowed; walks allowed; saves; errors; average ticket prices; fan cost index; regular season gate receipts; local television, radio, and cable revenues; other local operating revenues; player compensation and benefits; national and other local expenses; and income from baseball operations (Chapters 2, 13, 15)

BB2005 Team, league (0 = American, 1 = National), wins, earned run average, runs scored, hits allowed, walks allowed, saves, and errors (Chapters 13, 14, and 15)

BBREVENUE Team, value, and revenue (Chapter 13)

BEDBATH Year, coded year, and number of stores opened (Chapter 16)

BESTREST State, city, restaurant, hotel, cost (estimated price of dinner, including one drink and tip), and rating (1 to 100, with 1 the top-rated restaurant) (Chapter 3)

BREAKFAST Delivery time difference, menu choice, and desired time (Chapter 11)

BREAKFAST2 Delivery time difference, menu choice, and desired time (Chapter 11)

BREAKSTW Breaking strength for operators (rows) and machines (columns) (Chapter 11)

BUBBLEGUM Bubble diameters for four brands for six students (Chapter 11)

BULBS Length of life of 40 light bulbs from manufacturer A (= 1) and 40 light bulbs from manufacturer B (= 2) (Chapters 2, 10)

CABERNET California and Washington ratings, California and Washington rankings (Chapter 12)

CABOT Year and revenue for Cabot Corporation (Chapter 16)

CANISTER Day and number of nonconforming film canisters (Chapter 18)

CATFOOD Time period and weight of cat food (Chapter 18)

CDYIELD Yield of money market account, 6-month CD, 1-year CD, 2.5-year CD, and 5-year CD (Chapters 11, 12)

CEO Company and total compensation of CEOs (Chapters 2, 3)

CHICKEN Sandwich, calories, fat (in grams), saturated fat (in grams), carbohydrates (in grams), and sodium (in milligrams) (Chapters 2, 3, 6, 8)

CIRCUITS Thickness of semiconductor wafers, by batch and position (Chapter 11)

CIRCULATION Magazine, reported newsstand sales, and audited newsstand sales (Chapter 13)

CITYRESTAURANTS Location, food, décor, service, summated rating, coded location, and price (Chapter 2)

COCACOLA Year, coded year, and operating revenues (in billions of dollars) at Coca-Cola Company (Chapter 16)

COFFEE Rating of coffees, by expert and brand (Chapter 11)

COFFEEDRINK Product, calories, and fat in coffee drinks (Chapters 3, 13)

COFFEEPRICE Year and price per pound of coffee in the United States (Chapter 16)

COLA Sales for normal and end-aisle locations (Chapters 10, 12)

COLASPC Day, total number of cans filled, and number of unacceptable cans (over a 22-day period) (Chapter 18)

COLLEGES-BASKETBALL School, coach's salary for 2005–2006, expenses for 2004–2005, revenues for 2004–2005 (in millions of dollars), and winning percentage in 2005–2006 (Chapters 2, 3, 13)

COMPUTERS Download time of three brands of computers (Chapter 11)

COMPUTERS2 Download time, brand, and browser (Chapter 11)

CONCRETE1 Compressive strength after two days and seven days (Chapter 10)

CONCRETE2 Compressive strength after 2 days, 7 days, and 28 days (Chapter 11)

CONTEST2001 Returns for experts, readers, and dart throwers (Chapters 11, 12)

COST OF LIVING City, overall cost rating, apartment rent, and costs of a cup of coffee, a hamburger, dry cleaning a men's suit, toothpaste, and movie tickets (Chapters 2 and 3)

CPI-U Year, coded year, and value of CPI-U, the consumer price index (Chapter 16)

CRACK Type of crack and crack size (Chapters 10, 12)

CREDIT Month, coded month, credit charges (Chapter 16)

CURRENCY Year, coded year, and mean annual exchange rates (against the U.S. dollar) for the Canadian dollar, Japanese yen, and English pound (Chapter 16)

CUSTSALE Week number, number of customers, and sales (in thousands of dollars) over a period of 15 consecutive weeks (Chapter 13)

DATING Year and number of subscribers (Chapter 2)

DEALS Year and number of mergers and acquisitions from January 1 to January 11 (Chapters 2, 16)

DELIVERY Customer number, number of cases, and delivery time (Chapter 13)

DENTAL Annual family dental expenses for 10 employees (Chapter 8)

DIFFTEST Differences in the sales invoices and actual amounts from a sample of 50 vouchers (Chapter 8)

DINNER Time to prepare and cook dinner (Chapter 9)

DISCOUNT The amount of discount taken from 150 invoices (Chapter 8)

DISPRAZ Price, price squared, and sales of disposable razors in 15 stores (Chapter 15)

DJIA Year, coded year, and Dow Jones Industrial Average at the end of the year (Chapter 16)

DOMESTICBEER Brand, alcohol percentage, calories, and carbohydrates in U.S. domestic beers (Chapters 2, 3, 6, 15)

DOWMC Company, ticker symbol, and market capitalization, in billions of dollars (Chapter 3)

DRILL Time to drill additional 5 feet, depth, and type of hole (Chapter 14)

DRINK Amount of soft drink filled in a subgroup of 50 consecutive 2-liter bottles (Chapters 2, 9)

ELECTRICITY Year and cost of electricity (Chapter 16)

ELECUSE Electricity consumption (in kilowatts) and mean temperature (in degrees Fahrenheit) over a consecutive 24-month period (Chapter 13)

ENERGY State and per capita kilowatt hour use (Chapter 3)

ENERGY2 Year, price of electricity, natural gas, and fuel oil (Chapter 16)

ERRORSPC Number of nonconforming items and number of accounts processed over 39 days (Chapter 18)

ERWAITING Emergency room waiting time (in minutes) at the main facility and at satellite 1, satellite 2, and satellite 3 (Chapters 11, 12)

ESPRESSO Tamp (the distance in inches between the espresso grounds and the top of the portafilter) and time (the number of seconds the heart, body, and crema are separated) (Chapter 13)

FEDRECPT Year, coded year, and federal receipts (in billions of current dollars) (Chapter 16)

FFCHAIN Raters and restaurant ratings (Chapter 11)

FIFO Historical cost (in dollars) and audited value (in dollars) for a sample of 120 inventory items (Chapter 8)

FLYASH Fly ash percentage, fly ash percentage squared, and strength (Chapter 15)

FORCE Force required to break an insulator (Chapters 2, 3, 8, 9)

FORD-REV Quarter, coded quarter, revenue, and three dummy variables for quarters (Chapter 16)

FOULSPC Number of foul shots made and number taken over 40 days (Chapter 18)

FREEPORT Address, appraised value, property size (acres), house size, age, number of rooms, number of bathrooms, and number of cars that can be parked in the garage located in Freeport, New York (Chapter 15)

FRUIT Fruit and year, price, and quantity (Chapter 16)

FUNDTRAN Day, number of new investigations, and number of investigations closed over a 30-day period (Chapter 18)

FURNITURE Days between receipt and resolution of a sample of 50 complaints regarding purchased furniture (Chapters 2, 3, 8, 9)

GAS Week and price per gallon, in cents (Chapter 2)

GASOLINE Year, gasoline price, 1980 price index, and 1995 price index (Chapter 16)

GCFREEROSLYN Address, appraised value, location, property size (acres), house size, age, number of rooms, number of bathrooms, and number of cars that can be parked in the garage in Glen Cove, Freeport, and Roslyn, New York (Chapter 15)

GCROSLYN Address, appraised value, location, property size (acres), house size, age, number of rooms, number of bathrooms, and number of cars that can be parked in the garage in Glen Cove and Roslyn, New York (Chapter 15)

GDP Year and real gross domestic product (in billions of constant 1996 dollars) (Chapter 16)

GE Year, coded year, and stock price (Chapter 16)

GEAR Tooth size, part positioning, and gear distortion (Chapter 11)

GLENCOVE Address, appraised value, property size (acres), house size, age, number of rooms, number of bathrooms, and number of cars that can be parked in the garage in Glen Cove, New York (Chapters 14, 15)

GOLFBALL Distance for designs 1, 2, 3, and 4 (Chapters 11, 12)

GPIGMAT GMAT scores and GPI for 20 students (Chapter 13)

GRADSURVEY Gender, age (as of last birthday), height (in inches), major, current cumulative grade point average, undergraduate area of specialization, undergraduate cumulative grade point average, GMAT score, current employment status, number of different full-time jobs held in the past 10 years, expected salary upon completion of MBA (in thousands of dollars), anticipated salary after 5 years of experience after MBA (in thousands of dollars), satisfaction with student advisement services on campus, and amount spent for books and supplies this semester (Chapters 1, 2, 3, 4, 6, 8, 10, 11, 12)

GRANULE Granule loss in Boston and Vermont shingles (Chapters 3, 8, 9, 10)

HARDNESS Tensile strength and hardness of aluminum specimens (Chapter 13)

HARNSWELL Day and diameter of cam rollers (in inches) for samples of five parts produced in each of 30 batches (Chapter 18)

HEMLOCKFARMS Asking price, hot tub, rooms, lake view, bathrooms, bedrooms, loft/den, finished basement, and number of acres (Chapter 15)

HOMES Price, location, condition, bedrooms, bathrooms, and other rooms (Chapter 15)

HOSPADM Day, number of admissions, mean processing time (in hours), range of processing times, and proportion of laboratory rework (over a 30-day period) (Chapter 18)

HOTEL1 Day, number of rooms, number of nonconforming rooms per day over a 28-day period, and proportion of nonconforming items (Chapter 18)

HOTEL2 Day and delivery time for subgroups of five luggage deliveries per day over a 28-day period (Chapter 18)

HOUSE1 Selling price (in thousands of dollars), assessed value (in thousands of dollars), type (new = 0, old = 1), and time period of sale for 30 houses (Chapter 13, 14, 15)

HOUSE2 Assessed value (in thousands of dollars), size (in thousands of square feet), and age (in years) for 15 houses (Chapters 13, 14)

HOUSE3 Assessed value (in thousands of dollars), size (in thousands of square feet), and presence of a fireplace for 15 houses (Chapter 14)

HTNGOIL Monthly consumption of heating oil (in gallons), temperature (in degrees Fahrenheit), attic insulation (in inches), and style (0 = not ranch, 1 = ranch) (Chapters 14, 15)

ICECREAM Daily temperature (in degrees Fahrenheit) and sales (in thousands of dollars) for 21 days (Chapter 13)

INDEXES Year and total rate of return (in percentage) for the Dow Jones Industrial Average (DJIA), the Standards & Poor's 500 (S&P 500), and the technology-heavy NASDAQ Composite (NASDAQ) (Chapter 3)

INSURANCE Processing time for insurance policies (Chapters 3, 8, 9)

INTAGLIO Surface hardness of untreated and treated steel plates (Chapters 10, 12)

INVOICE Number of invoices processed and amount of time (in hours) for 30 days (Chapter 13)

INVOICES Amount recorded (in dollars) from a sample of 12 sales invoices (Chapter 9)

ITEMERR Amount of error (in dollars) from a sample of 200 items (Chapter 8)

KEYBOARDDEFECTS Defect and frequency (Chapter 2)

LARGESTBONDS Five-year return of bond funds (Chapter 3)

LAUNDRY Dirt (in pounds) removed for detergent brands (rows) and cycle times (columns) (Chapter 11)

LOCATE Sales volume (in thousands of dollars) for front, middle, and rear locations (Chapters 11, 12)

LUGGAGE Delivery time, in minutes, for luggage in Wing A and Wing B of a hotel (Chapters 10, 12)

MAIL Weight of mail and orders (Chapters 2, 13)

MANAGERS Sales (ratio of yearly sales divided by the target sales value for that region), score from the Wonderlic Personnel Test, score on the Strong-Campbell Interest Inventory Test, number of years of selling experience prior to becoming a sales manager, and whether the sales manager has a degree in electrical engineering (0 = no, 1 = yes) (Chapter 15)

MCDONALD Year, coded year, and annual total revenues (in billions of dollars) at McDonald's Corporation (Chapter 16)

MEASUREMENT Sample, in-line measurement, and analytical lab measurement (Chapter 10)

MEDICARE Difference in amount reimbursed and amount that should have been reimbursed for office visits (Chapter 8)

MEDREC Day, number of discharged patients, and number of records not processed for a 30-day period (Chapter 18)

METALS Year and the total rate of return (in percentage) for platinum, gold, and silver (Chapter 3)

MILEAGE Mileage of autos calculated by owner, currently, and forecasted according to government plans (Chapters 2, 3, 13)

MOISTURE Moisture content of Boston shingles and Vermont shingles (Chapter 9)

MOVIEPRICES Theatre chain and cost of two tickets, a large popcorn, and two sodas (Chapters 2, 3, 9)

MOVIES Year and movie attendance (Chapters 2 and 16)

MOVING Labor hours, cubic feet, number of large pieces of furniture, and availability of an elevator (Chapters 13 and 14)

MUSICONLINE Album/artist and prices at iTunes, Wal-Mart, MusicNow, Musicmatch, and Napster (Chapter 11)

MUTUALFUNDS Category, objective, assets, fees, expense ratio, 2005 return, three-year return, five-year return, and risk (Chapters 2, 3, 4, 6, 8, 10, 11, 12, and 16)

MYELOMA Patient, measurement before transplant, and measurement after transplant (Chapter 10)

NATURALGAS Coded quarter, price, and three dummy variables for quarters (Chapter 16)

NBA2006 Team, number of wins, points per game (for team, opponent, and the difference between team and opponent), field goal (shots made), percentage (for team, opponent, and the difference between team and opponent), turnovers (losing the ball before a shot is taken) per game (for team, opponent, and the difference between team and opponent), offensive rebound percentage, and defensive rebound percentage (Chapters 14, 15)

NEIGHBOR Selling price (in thousands of dollars), number of rooms, and neighborhood location (east = 0, west = 1) for 20 houses (Chapter 14)

OMNI Bars sold, price, and promotion expenses (Chapter 14)

O-RING Flight number, temperature, and O-ring damage index (Chapter 13)

OYSTERS Year, coded year, and number of bushels harvested (Chapter 16)

PAIN-RELIEF Temperature, brand of pain relief tablet, and time to dissolve (Chapter 11)

PALLET Weight of Boston and weight of Vermont shingles (Chapters 2, 8, 9, 10)

PARACHUTE Tensile strength of parachutes from suppliers 1, 2, 3, and 4 (Chapters 11, 12)

PARACHUTE2 Tensile strength for looms and suppliers (Chapter 11)

PASTA Weight for type of pasta (rows) and cooking time (columns) (Chapter 11)

PEN Gender, ad, and product rating (Chapters 11, 12)

PERFORM Performance rating before and after motivational training (Chapter 10)

PETFOOD Shelf space (in feet), weekly sales (in dollars), and aisle location (back = 0, front = 1) (Chapters 13, 14)

PHONE Time (in minutes) to clear telephone line problems and location (I and II) for samples of 20 customer problems reported to each of the two office locations (Chapters 3, 6, 10, 12)

PHOTO Density for developer strength (rows) and development time (columns) (Chapter 11)

PIZZATIME Time period, delivery time for local restaurant, delivery time for national chain (Chapter 10)

PLUMBINV Difference in dollars between actual amounts recorded on sales invoices and the amounts entered into the accounting system (Chapter 8)

POLIO Year and incidence rates per 100,000 persons of reported poliomyelitis (Chapter 16)

POTATO Percentage of solids content in filter cake, acidity (in pH), lower pressure, upper pressure, cake thickness, varidrive speed, and drum speed setting for 54 measurements (Chapter 15)

PRESCRIPTIONS Year and average prescription drug price (Chapter 2)

PROTEIN Calories (in grams), protein, percentage of calories from fat, percentage of calories from saturated fat, and cholesterol (in mg) for 25 popular protein foods (Chapter 2)

PUMPKIN Circumference and weight of pumpkins (Chapter 13)

RADON Solar radiation, soil temperature, vapor pressure, wind speed, relative humidity, dew point, ambient temperature, and radon concentration (Chapter 15)

RAISINS Weight of packages of raisins (Chapter 12)

REDWOOD Height, diameter, and bark thickness (Chapter 14)

RENT Monthly rental cost (in dollars) and apartment size (in square footage) for a sample of 25 apartments (Chapter 13)

RESTAURANTS Location, food rating, decor rating, service rating, summated rating, coded location (0 = urban, 1 = suburban), and price of restaurants (Chapters 2, 10, 13, 14)

RETURNS Week and stock price of Microsoft, stock price of General Motors, stock price of Ford, and stock price of International Aluminum (Chapter 13)

ROSLYN Address, appraised value, property size (acres), house size, age, number of rooms, number of bathrooms, and number of cars that can be parked in the garage in Roslyn, New York (Chapter 15)

ROYALS Game, attendance, and whether there was a promotion at Kansas City Royals games (Chapters 2 and 3)

RUDYBIRD Day, total cases sold, and cases of Rudybird sold (Chapter 18)

S&PSTKIN Coded quarters, end-of-quarter values of the quarterly Standard & Poor's Composite Stock Price Index, and three quarterly dummy variables (Chapter 16)

SAVINGS Bank, money market rate, one-year CD rate, and five-year CD rate (Chapters 2, 3, 6)

SCRUBBER Airflow, water flow, recirculating water flow, orifice diameter, and NTU (Chapter 15)

SEALANT Sample number, sealant strength for Boston shingles, and sealant strength for Vermont shingles (Chapter 18)

SEARS Year, coded year, and annual total revenues (in billions of dollars) at Sears, Roebuck & Company (Chapter 16)

SH2 Day and number of calls received at the help desk (Chapters 2, 3)

SH8 Rate ($) willing to pay for the newspaper (Chapter 8)

SH9 Blackness of newsprint (Chapter 9)

SH10 Length of early calls (in seconds), length of late calls (in seconds), and difference (in seconds) (Chapter 10)

SH11-1 Call, presentation plan (structured = 1, semi-structured = 2, unstructured = 3), and length of call (in seconds) (Chapter 11)

SH11-2 Gender of caller, type of greeting, and length of call (Chapter 11)

SH13 Hours per month spent telemarketing and number of new subscriptions per month over a 24-month period (Chapter 13)

SH14 Hours per week spent telemarketing, number of new subscriptions, and type of presentation (Chapter 14)

SH16 Month and number of home-delivery subscriptions over the most recent 24-month period (Chapter 16)

SH18-1 Day, number of ads with errors, number of ads, and number of errors over a 25-day period (Chapter 18)

SH18-2 Day and newsprint blackness measures for each of five spots made over 25 consecutive weekdays (Chapter 18)

SITE Store number, square footage (in thousands of square feet), and sales (in millions of dollars) in 14 Sunflowers Apparel stores (Chapter 13)

SP500 Week, weekly change in the S&P 500, weekly change in the price of Wal-Mart, weekly change in the price of Target, and weekly change in the price of Sara Lee (Chapter 13)

SPENDING State and per capita federal spending ($000) in 2004 (Chapters 2, 3, 6)

SPONGE Day, number of sponges produced, number of nonconforming sponges, proportion of nonconforming sponges (Chapter 18)

SPORTING Sales, age, annual population growth, income, percentage with high school diploma, and percentage with college diploma (Chapters 13, 15)

SPWATER Sample number and amount of magnesium (Chapter 18)

STANDBY Standby hours, staff, remote hours, Dubner hours, and labor hours for 26 weeks (Chapters 14, 15)

STATES State, commuting time, percentage of homes with more than eight rooms, median income, and percentage of housing that costs more than 30% of family income (Chapters 2, 3)

STEEL Error in actual length and specified length (Chapters 2, 6, 8, 9)

STOCKS&BONDS Date, closing price of Vanguard Long-Term Bond Index Fund, and closing price of the Dow Jones Industrial Average (Chapter 13)

STOCKASSETS Fund and assets, in billions of dollars (Chapter 3)

STOCKS2005 Week and closing weekly stock price for S&P, Sears, Target, and Sara Lee (Chapter 2)

STRATEGIC Year and number of barrels in U.S. strategic oil reserve (Chapter 16)

TAX Quarterly sales tax receipts (in thousands of dollars) for 50 business establishments (Chapter 3)

TAXES County taxes (in dollars) and age of house (in years) for 19 single-family houses (Chapter 15)

TEA3 Sample number and weight of tea bags (Chapter 18)

TEABAGS Weight of tea bags (Chapters 3, 8, 9)

TELESPC Number of orders and number of corrections over 30 days (Chapter 18)

TENSILE Sample number and strength (Chapter 18)

TESTRANK Rank scores for 10 people trained using a "traditional" method (Method = 0) and 10 people trained using an "experimental" method (Method = 1) (Chapter 12)

TEXTBOOK Textbook, book store price, and Amazon price (Chapter 10)

THEMEPARKS Name of location and admission price for one-day tickets (Chapter 3)

TIMES Times to get ready (Chapter 3)

TOMATOES Year and price per pound in the United States (Chapter 16)

TOMYLD2 Amount of fertilizer (in pounds per 100 square feet) and yield (in pounds) for 12 plots of land (Chapter 15)

TOYS-REV Quarter, coded quarter, revenue, and three dummy variables for quarters (Chapter 16)

TRADE Days, number of undesirable trades, and number of total trades made over a 30-day period (Chapter 18)

TRADES Day, number of incoming calls, and number of trade executions per day over a 35-day period (Chapter 13)

TRAINING Assembly time and training program (team-based = 0, individual-based = 1) (Chapters 10, 12)

TRANSMIT Day and number of errors in transmission (Chapter 18)

TRANSPORT Days and patient transport times (in minutes) for samples of four patients per day over a 30-day period (Chapter 18)

TRASHBAGS Weight required to break four brands of trash bags (Chapters 11, 12)

TREASURY Year and interest rate (Chapter 16)

TROUGH Width of trough (Chapters 2, 3, 8, 9)

TRSNYC Year, unit value of variable A, and unit value of variable B (Chapter 16)

TSMODEL1 Years, coded years, and three time series (I, II, III) (Chapter 16)

TSMODEL2 Years, coded years, and two time series (I, II) (Chapter 16)

TUITION2006 School, in-state tuition and fees, and out-of-state tuition and fees (Chapter 3)

UNDERGRADSURVEY Gender, age (*as of last birthday*), height (*in inches*), class designation, major, graduate school intention, cumulative grade point average, expected starting salary (in thousands of dollars), anticipated salary after five years of experience (in thousands of dollars), current employment status, number of campus club/group/organization/team affiliations, satisfaction with student advisement services on campus, and amount spent on books and supplies this semester (Chapters 1, 2, 3, 4, 6, 8, 10, 11, 12)

UNDERWRITING Score on proficiency exam, score on end of training exam, and training method (Chapter 14)

UNEMPLOY Year, month, and monthly unemployment rates (Chapters 2, 16)

UNLEADED Year, month, and price (Chapter 16)

UTILITY Utilities charges for 50 one-bedroom apartments (Chapters 2, 6)

VB Time (in minutes) for nine students to write and run a Visual Basic program (Chapter 10)

WAIT Waiting times and seating times, in minutes (Chapter 6)

WALMART Quarter and quarterly revenues (Chapter 16)

WARECOST Distribution cost (in thousands of dollars), sales (in thousands of dollars), and number of orders for 24 months (Chapters 13, 14, 15)

WAREHSE Number of units handled per day and employee number (Chapter 18)

WEEKLYNASDAQ Week and NASDAQ value (Chapter 16)

WHOLEFOODS1 Item, price at Whole Foods, and price at Fairway (Chapter 10)

WHOLEFOODS2 Item, price at Whole Foods, price at Gristede's, price at Fairway, and price at Stop & Shop (Chapter 11)

WIP Processing times at each of two plants (A = 1, B = 2) (Chapters 3, 6, 10)

WONDERLIC School, average Wonderlic score of football players trying out for the NFL, and graduation rate (Chapters 2, 3, 13)

WORKFORCE Year, population, and size of the workforce (Chapter 16)

WRIGLEY Year, coded year, actual revenue, consumer price index, and real revenue (Chapter 16)

YARN Breaking strength, pressure, yarn sample, and side-by-side aspect (nozzle = 1, opposite = 2) (Chapter 11)

YIELD Cleansing step, etching step, and yield (Chapter 11)

E. TABLES

E. TABLES

TABLE E.1

Table of Random Numbers

	Column							
Row	**00000 12345**	**00001 67890**	**11111 12345**	**11112 67890**	**22222 12345**	**22223 67890**	**33333 12345**	**33334 67890**
01	49280	88924	35779	00283	81163	07275	89863	02348
02	61870	41657	07468	08612	98083	97349	20775	45091
03	43898	65923	25078	86129	78496	97653	91550	08078
04	62993	93912	30454	84598	56095	20664	12872	64647
05	33850	58555	51438	85507	71865	79488	76783	31708
06	97340	03364	88472	04334	63919	36394	11095	92470
07	70543	29776	10087	10072	55980	64688	68239	20461
08	89382	93809	00796	95945	34101	81277	66090	88872
09	37818	72142	67140	50785	22380	16703	53362	44940
10	60430	22834	14130	96593	23298	56203	92671	15925
11	82975	66158	84731	19436	55790	69229	28661	13675
12	30987	71938	40355	54324	08401	26299	49420	59208
13	55700	24586	93247	32596	11865	63397	44251	43189
14	14756	23997	78643	75912	83832	32768	18928	57070
15	32166	53251	70654	92827	63491	04233	33825	69662
16	23236	73751	31888	81718	06546	83246	47651	04877
17	45794	26926	15130	82455	78305	55058	52551	47182
18	09893	20505	14225	68514	47427	56788	96297	78822
19	54382	74598	91499	14523	68479	27686	46162	83554
20	94750	89923	37089	20048	80336	94598	26940	36858
21	70297	34135	53140	33340	42050	82341	44104	82949
22	85157	47954	32979	26575	57600	40881	12250	73742
23	11100	02340	12860	74697	96644	89439	28707	25815
24	36871	50775	30592	57143	17381	68856	25853	35041
25	23913	48357	63308	16090	51690	54607	72407	55538
26	79348	36085	27973	65157	07456	22255	25626	57054
27	92074	54641	53673	54421	18130	60103	69593	49464
28	06873	21440	75593	41373	49502	17972	82578	16364
29	12478	37622	99659	31065	83613	69889	58869	29571
30	57175	55564	65411	42547	70457	03426	72937	83792
31	91616	11075	80103	07831	59309	13276	26710	73000
32	78025	73539	14621	39044	47450	03197	12787	47709
33	27587	67228	80145	10175	12822	86687	65530	49325
34	16690	20427	04251	64477	73709	73945	92396	68263
35	70183	58065	65489	31833	82093	16747	10386	59293
36	90730	35385	15679	99742	50866	78028	75573	67257
37	10934	93242	13431	24590	02770	48582	00906	58595
38	82462	30166	79613	47416	13389	80268	05085	96666
39	27463	10433	07606	16285	93699	60912	94532	95632
40	02979	52997	09079	92709	90110	47506	53693	49892
41	46888	69929	75233	52507	32097	37594	10067	67327
42	53638	83161	08289	12639	08141	12640	28437	09268
43	82433	61427	17239	89160	19666	08814	37841	12847
44	35766	31672	50082	22795	66948	65581	84393	15890
45	10853	42581	08792	13257	61973	24450	52351	16602
46	20341	27398	72906	63955	17276	10646	74692	48438
47	54458	90542	77563	51839	52901	53355	83281	19177
48	26337	66530	16687	35179	46560	00123	44546	79896
49	34314	23729	85264	05575	96855	23820	11091	79821
50	28603	10708	68933	34189	92166	15181	66628	58599

continued

TABLE E.1

Table of Random
Numbers (*Continued*)

	Column							
Row	**00000** **12345**	**00001** **67890**	**11111** **12345**	**11112** **67890**	**22222** **12345**	**22223** **67890**	**33333** **12345**	**33334** **67890**
51	66194	28926	99547	16625	45515	67953	12108	57846
52	78240	43195	24837	32511	70880	22070	52622	61881
53	00833	88000	67299	68215	11274	55624	32991	17436
54	12111	86683	61270	58036	64192	90611	15145	01748
55	47189	99951	05755	03834	43782	90599	40282	51417
56	76396	72486	62423	27618	84184	78922	73561	52818
57	46409	17469	32483	09083	76175	19985	26309	91536
58	74626	22111	87286	46772	42243	68046	44250	42439
59	34450	81974	93723	49023	58432	67083	36876	93391
60	36327	72135	33005	28701	34710	49359	50693	89311
61	74185	77536	84825	09934	99103	09325	67389	45869
62	12296	41623	62873	37943	25584	09609	63360	47270
63	90822	60280	88925	99610	42772	60561	76873	04117
64	72121	79152	96591	90305	10189	79778	68016	13747
65	95268	41377	25684	08151	61816	58555	54305	86189
66	92603	09091	75884	93424	72586	88903	30061	14457
67	18813	90291	05275	01223	79607	95426	34900	09778
68	38840	26903	28624	67157	51986	42865	14508	49315
69	05959	33836	53758	16562	41081	38012	41230	20528
70	85141	21155	99212	32685	51403	31926	69813	58781
71	75047	59643	31074	38172	03718	32119	69506	67143
72	30752	95260	68032	62871	58781	34143	68790	69766
73	22986	82575	42187	62295	84295	30634	66562	31442
74	99439	86692	90348	66036	48399	73451	26698	39437
75	20389	93029	11881	71685	65452	89047	63669	02656
76	39249	05173	68256	36359	20250	68686	05947	09335
77	96777	33605	29481	20063	09398	01843	35139	61344
78	04860	32918	10798	50492	52655	33359	94713	28393
79	41613	42375	00403	03656	77580	87772	86877	57085
80	17930	00794	53836	53692	67135	98102	61912	11246
81	24649	31845	25736	75231	83808	98917	93829	99430
82	79899	34061	54308	59358	56462	58166	97302	86828
83	76801	49594	81002	30397	52728	15101	72070	33706
84	36239	63636	38140	65731	39788	06872	38971	53363
85	07392	64449	17886	63632	53995	17574	22247	62607
86	67133	04181	33874	98835	67453	59734	76381	63455
87	77759	31504	32832	70861	15152	29733	75371	39174
88	85992	72268	42920	20810	29361	51423	90306	73574
89	79553	75952	54116	65553	47139	60579	09165	85490
90	41101	17336	48951	53674	17880	45260	08575	49321
91	36191	17095	32123	91576	84221	78902	82010	30847
92	62329	63898	23268	74283	26091	68409	69704	82267
93	14751	13151	93115	01437	56945	89661	67680	79790
94	48462	59278	44185	29616	76537	19589	83139	28454
95	29435	88105	59651	44391	74588	55114	80834	85686
96	28340	29285	12965	14821	80425	16602	44653	70467
97	02167	58940	27149	80242	10587	79786	34959	75339
98	17864	00991	39557	54981	23588	81914	37609	13128
99	79675	80605	60059	35862	00254	36546	21545	78179
100	72335	82037	92003	34100	29879	46613	89720	13274

Source: Partially extracted from the Rand Corporation, *A Million Random Digits with 100,000 Normal Deviates*
(Glencoe, IL, The Free Press, 1955).

TABLE E.2

The Cumulative Standardized Normal Distribution

Entry represents area under the cumulative standardized normal
distribution from $-\infty$ to Z

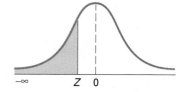

Z	0.00	0.01	0.02	0.03	0.04	0.05	0.06	0.07	0.08	0.09
−6.0	0.000000001									
−5.5	0.000000019									
−5.0	0.000000287									
−4.5	0.000003398									
−4.0	0.000031671									
−3.9	0.00005	0.00005	0.00004	0.00004	0.00004	0.00004	0.00004	0.00004	0.00003	0.00003
−3.8	0.00007	0.00007	0.00007	0.00006	0.00006	0.00006	0.00006	0.00005	0.00005	0.00005
−3.7	0.00011	0.00010	0.00010	0.00010	0.00009	0.00009	0.00008	0.00008	0.00008	0.00008
−3.6	0.00016	0.00015	0.00015	0.00014	0.00014	0.00013	0.00013	0.00012	0.00012	0.00011
−3.5	0.00023	0.00022	0.00022	0.00021	0.00020	0.00019	0.00019	0.00018	0.00017	0.00017
−3.4	0.00034	0.00032	0.00031	0.00030	0.00029	0.00028	0.00027	0.00026	0.00025	0.00024
−3.3	0.00048	0.00047	0.00045	0.00043	0.00042	0.00040	0.00039	0.00038	0.00036	0.00035
−3.2	0.00069	0.00066	0.00064	0.00062	0.00060	0.00058	0.00056	0.00054	0.00052	0.00050
−3.1	0.00097	0.00094	0.00090	0.00087	0.00084	0.00082	0.00079	0.00076	0.00074	0.00071
−3.0	0.00135	0.00131	0.00126	0.00122	0.00118	0.00114	0.00111	0.00107	0.00103	0.00100
−2.9	0.0019	0.0018	0.0018	0.0017	0.0016	0.0016	0.0015	0.0015	0.0014	0.0014
−2.8	0.0026	0.0025	0.0024	0.0023	0.0023	0.0022	0.0021	0.0021	0.0020	0.0019
−2.7	0.0035	0.0034	0.0033	0.0032	0.0031	0.0030	0.0029	0.0028	0.0027	0.0026
−2.6	0.0047	0.0045	0.0044	0.0043	0.0041	0.0040	0.0039	0.0038	0.0037	0.0036
−2.5	0.0062	0.0060	0.0059	0.0057	0.0055	0.0054	0.0052	0.0051	0.0049	0.0048
−2.4	0.0082	0.0080	0.0078	0.0075	0.0073	0.0071	0.0069	0.0068	0.0066	0.0064
−2.3	0.0107	0.0104	0.0102	0.0099	0.0096	0.0094	0.0091	0.0089	0.0087	0.0084
−2.2	0.0139	0.0136	0.0132	0.0129	0.0125	0.0122	0.0119	0.0116	0.0113	0.0110
−2.1	0.0179	0.0174	0.0170	0.0166	0.0162	0.0158	0.0154	0.0150	0.0146	0.0143
−2.0	0.0228	0.0222	0.0217	0.0212	0.0207	0.0202	0.0197	0.0192	0.0188	0.0183
−1.9	0.0287	0.0281	0.0274	0.0268	0.0262	0.0256	0.0250	0.0244	0.0239	0.0233
−1.8	0.0359	0.0351	0.0344	0.0336	0.0329	0.0322	0.0314	0.0307	0.0301	0.0294
−1.7	0.0446	0.0436	0.0427	0.0418	0.0409	0.0401	0.0392	0.0384	0.0375	0.0367
−1.6	0.0548	0.0537	0.0526	0.0516	0.0505	0.0495	0.0485	0.0475	0.0465	0.0455
−1.5	0.0668	0.0655	0.0643	0.0630	0.0618	0.0606	0.0594	0.0582	0.0571	0.0559
−1.4	0.0808	0.0793	0.0778	0.0764	0.0749	0.0735	0.0721	0.0708	0.0694	0.0681
−1.3	0.0968	0.0951	0.0934	0.0918	0.0901	0.0885	0.0869	0.0853	0.0838	0.0823
−1.2	0.1151	0.1131	0.1112	0.1093	0.1075	0.1056	0.1038	0.1020	0.1003	0.0985
−1.1	0.1357	0.1335	0.1314	0.1292	0.1271	0.1251	0.1230	0.1210	0.1190	0.1170
−1.0	0.1587	0.1562	0.1539	0.1515	0.1492	0.1469	0.1446	0.1423	0.1401	0.1379
−0.9	0.1841	0.1814	0.1788	0.1762	0.1736	0.1711	0.1685	0.1660	0.1635	0.1611
−0.8	0.2119	0.2090	0.2061	0.2033	0.2005	0.1977	0.1949	0.1922	0.1894	0.1867
−0.7	0.2420	0.2388	0.2358	0.2327	0.2296	0.2266	0.2236	0.2206	0.2177	0.2148
−0.6	0.2743	0.2709	0.2676	0.2643	0.2611	0.2578	0.2546	0.2514	0.2482	0.2451
−0.5	0.3085	0.3050	0.3015	0.2981	0.2946	0.2912	0.2877	0.2843	0.2810	0.2776
−0.4	0.3446	0.3409	0.3372	0.3336	0.3300	0.3264	0.3228	0.3192	0.3156	0.3121
−0.3	0.3821	0.3783	0.3745	0.3707	0.3669	0.3632	0.3594	0.3557	0.3520	0.3483
−0.2	0.4207	0.4168	0.4129	0.4090	0.4052	0.4013	0.3974	0.3936	0.3897	0.3859
−0.1	0.4602	0.4562	0.4522	0.4483	0.4443	0.4404	0.4364	0.4325	0.4286	0.4247
−0.0	0.5000	0.4960	0.4920	0.4880	0.4840	0.4801	0.4761	0.4721	0.4681	0.4641

continued

TABLE E.2

The Cumulative Standardized Normal Distribution (*Continued*)

Entry represents area under the cumulative standardized normal distribution from
$-\infty$ to Z

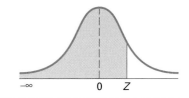

Z	0.00	0.01	0.02	0.03	0.04	0.05	0.06	0.07	0.08	0.09
0.0	0.5000	0.5040	0.5080	0.5120	0.5160	0.5199	0.5239	0.5279	0.5319	0.5359
0.1	0.5398	0.5438	0.5478	0.5517	0.5557	0.5596	0.5636	0.5675	0.5714	0.5753
0.2	0.5793	0.5832	0.5871	0.5910	0.5948	0.5987	0.6026	0.6064	0.6103	0.6141
0.3	0.6179	0.6217	0.6255	0.6293	0.6331	0.6368	0.6406	0.6443	0.6480	0.6517
0.4	0.6554	0.6591	0.6628	0.6664	0.6700	0.6736	0.6772	0.6808	0.6844	0.6879
0.5	0.6915	0.6950	0.6985	0.7019	0.7054	0.7088	0.7123	0.7157	0.7190	0.7224
0.6	0.7257	0.7291	0.7324	0.7357	0.7389	0.7422	0.7454	0.7486	0.7518	0.7549
0.7	0.7580	0.7612	0.7642	0.7673	0.7704	0.7734	0.7764	0.7794	0.7823	0.7852
0.8	0.7881	0.7910	0.7939	0.7967	0.7995	0.8023	0.8051	0.8078	0.8106	0.8133
0.9	0.8159	0.8186	0.8212	0.8238	0.8264	0.8289	0.8315	0.8340	0.8365	0.8389
1.0	0.8413	0.8438	0.8461	0.8485	0.8508	0.8531	0.8554	0.8577	0.8599	0.8621
1.1	0.8643	0.8665	0.8686	0.8708	0.8729	0.8749	0.8770	0.8790	0.8810	0.8830
1.2	0.8849	0.8869	0.8888	0.8907	0.8925	0.8944	0.8962	0.8980	0.8997	0.9015
1.3	0.9032	0.9049	0.9066	0.9082	0.9099	0.9115	0.9131	0.9147	0.9162	0.9177
1.4	0.9192	0.9207	0.9222	0.9236	0.9251	0.9265	0.9279	0.9292	0.9306	0.9319
1.5	0.9332	0.9345	0.9357	0.9370	0.9382	0.9394	0.9406	0.9418	0.9429	0.9441
1.6	0.9452	0.9463	0.9474	0.9484	0.9495	0.9505	0.9515	0.9525	0.9535	0.9545
1.7	0.9554	0.9564	0.9573	0.9582	0.9591	0.9599	0.9608	0.9616	0.9625	0.9633
1.8	0.9641	0.9649	0.9656	0.9664	0.9671	0.9678	0.9686	0.9693	0.9699	0.9706
1.9	0.9713	0.9719	0.9726	0.9732	0.9738	0.9744	0.9750	0.9756	0.9761	0.9767
2.0	0.9772	0.9778	0.9783	0.9788	0.9793	0.9798	0.9803	0.9808	0.9812	0.9817
2.1	0.9821	0.9826	0.9830	0.9834	0.9838	0.9842	0.9846	0.9850	0.9854	0.9857
2.2	0.9861	0.9864	0.9868	0.9871	0.9875	0.9878	0.9881	0.9884	0.9887	0.9890
2.3	0.9893	0.9896	0.9898	0.9901	0.9904	0.9906	0.9909	0.9911	0.9913	0.9916
2.4	0.9918	0.9920	0.9922	0.9925	0.9927	0.9929	0.9931	0.9932	0.9934	0.9936
2.5	0.9938	0.9940	0.9941	0.9943	0.9945	0.9946	0.9948	0.9949	0.9951	0.9952
2.6	0.9953	0.9955	0.9956	0.9957	0.9959	0.9960	0.9961	0.9962	0.9963	0.9964
2.7	0.9965	0.9966	0.9967	0.9968	0.9969	0.9970	0.9971	0.9972	0.9973	0.9974
2.8	0.9974	0.9975	0.9976	0.9977	0.9977	0.9978	0.9979	0.9979	0.9980	0.9981
2.9	0.9981	0.9982	0.9982	0.9983	0.9984	0.9984	0.9985	0.9985	0.9986	0.9986
3.0	0.99865	0.99869	0.99874	0.99878	0.99882	0.99886	0.99889	0.99893	0.99897	0.99900
3.1	0.99903	0.99906	0.99910	0.99913	0.99916	0.99918	0.99921	0.99924	0.99926	0.99929
3.2	0.99931	0.99934	0.99936	0.99938	0.99940	0.99942	0.99944	0.99946	0.99948	0.99950
3.3	0.99952	0.99953	0.99955	0.99957	0.99958	0.99960	0.99961	0.99962	0.99964	0.99965
3.4	0.99966	0.99968	0.99969	0.99970	0.99971	0.99972	0.99973	0.99974	0.99975	0.99976
3.5	0.99977	0.99978	0.99978	0.99979	0.99980	0.99981	0.99981	0.99982	0.99983	0.99983
3.6	0.99984	0.99985	0.99985	0.99986	0.99986	0.99987	0.99987	0.99988	0.99988	0.99989
3.7	0.99989	0.99990	0.99990	0.99990	0.99991	0.99991	0.99992	0.99992	0.99992	0.99992
3.8	0.99993	0.99993	0.99993	0.99994	0.99994	0.99994	0.99994	0.99995	0.99995	0.99995
3.9	0.99995	0.99995	0.99996	0.99996	0.99996	0.99996	0.99996	0.99996	0.99997	0.99997
4.0	0.999968329									
4.5	0.999996602									
5.0	0.999999713									
5.5	0.999999981									
6.0	0.999999999									

TABLE E.3
Critical Values of *t*

For a particular number of degrees of freedom, entry represents the
critical value of *t* corresponding to a specified upper-tail area (α)

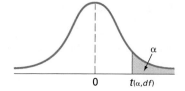

			Upper-Tail Areas			
Degrees of Freedom	0.25	0.10	0.05	0.025	0.01	0.005
1	1.0000	3.0777	6.3138	12.7062	31.8207	63.6574
2	0.8165	1.8856	2.9200	4.3027	6.9646	9.9248
3	0.7649	1.6377	2.3534	3.1824	4.5407	5.8409
4	0.7407	1.5332	2.1318	2.7764	3.7469	4.6041
5	0.7267	1.4759	2.0150	2.5706	3.3649	4.0322
6	0.7176	1.4398	1.9432	2.4469	3.1427	3.7074
7	0.7111	1.4149	1.8946	2.3646	2.9980	3.4995
8	0.7064	1.3968	1.8595	2.2060	2.8965	3.3554
9	0.7027	1.3830	1.8331	2.2622	2.8214	3.2498
10	0.6998	1.3722	1.8125	2.2281	2.7638	3.1693
11	0.6974	1.3634	1.7959	2.2010	2.7181	3.1058
12	0.6955	1.3562	1.7823	2.1788	2.6810	3.0545
13	0.6938	1.3502	1.7709	2.1604	2.6503	3.0123
14	0.6924	1.3450	1.7613	2.1448	2.6245	2.9768
15	0.6912	1.3406	1.7531	2.1315	2.6025	2.9467
16	0.6901	1.3368	1.7459	2.1199	2.5835	2.9208
17	0.6892	1.3334	1.7396	2.1098	2.5669	2.8982
18	0.6884	1.3304	1.7341	2.1009	2.5524	2.8784
19	0.6876	1.3277	1.7291	2.0930	2.5395	2.8609
20	0.6870	1.3253	1.7247	2.0860	2.5280	2.8453
21	0.6864	1.3232	1.7207	2.0796	2.5177	2.8314
22	0.6858	1.3212	1.7171	2.0739	2.5083	2.8188
23	0.6853	1.3195	1.7139	2.0687	2.4999	2.8073
24	0.6848	1.3178	1.7109	2.0639	2.4922	2.7969
25	0.6844	1.3163	1.7081	2.0595	2.4851	2.7874
26	0.6840	1.3150	1.7056	2.0555	2.4786	2.7787
27	0.6837	1.3137	1.7033	2.0518	2.4727	2.7707
28	0.6834	1.3125	1.7011	2.0484	2.4671	2.7633
29	0.6830	1.3114	1.6991	2.0452	2.4620	2.7564
30	0.6828	1.3104	1.6973	2.0423	2.4573	2.7500
31	0.6825	1.3095	1.6955	2.0395	2.4528	2.7440
32	0.6822	1.3086	1.6939	2.0369	2.4487	2.7385
33	0.6820	1.3077	1.6924	2.0345	2.4448	2.7333
34	0.6818	1.3070	1.6909	2.0322	2.4411	2.7284
35	0.6816	1.3062	1.6896	2.0301	2.4377	2.7238
36	0.6814	1.3055	1.6883	2.0281	2.4345	2.7195
37	0.6812	1.3049	1.6871	2.0262	2.4314	2.7154
38	0.6810	1.3042	1.6860	2.0244	2.4286	2.7116
39	0.6808	1.3036	1.6849	2.0227	2.4258	2.7079
40	0.6807	1.3031	1.6839	2.0211	2.4233	2.7045
41	0.6805	1.3025	1.6829	2.0195	2.4208	2.7012
42	0.6804	1.3020	1.6820	2.0181	2.4185	2.6981
43	0.6802	1.3016	1.6811	2.0167	2.4163	2.6951
44	0.6801	1.3011	1.6802	2.0154	2.4141	2.6923
45	0.6800	1.3006	1.6794	2.0141	2.4121	2.6896
46	0.6799	1.3022	1.6787	2.0129	2.4102	2.6870
47	0.6797	1.2998	1.6779	2.0117	2.4083	2.6846
48	0.6796	1.2994	1.6772	2.0106	2.4066	2.6822

continued

TABLE E.3

Critical Values of *t*
(*Continued*)

Degrees of Freedom	Upper-Tail Areas					
	0.25	0.10	0.05	0.025	0.01	0.005
49	0.6795	1.2991	1.6766	2.0096	2.4049	2.6800
50	0.6794	1.2987	1.6759	2.0086	2.4033	2.6778
51	0.6793	1.2984	1.6753	2.0076	2.4017	2.6757
52	0.6792	1.2980	1.6747	2.0066	2.4002	2.6737
53	0.6791	1.2977	1.6741	2.0057	2.3988	2.6718
54	0.6791	1.2974	1.6736	2.0049	2.3974	2.6700
55	0.6790	1.2971	1.6730	2.0040	2.3961	2.6682
56	0.6789	1.2969	1.6725	2.0032	2.3948	2.6665
57	0.6788	1.2966	1.6720	2.0025	2.3936	2.6649
58	0.6787	1.2963	1.6716	2.0017	2.3924	2.6633
59	0.6787	1.2961	1.6711	2.0010	2.3912	2.6618
60	0.6786	1.2958	1.6706	2.0003	2.3901	2.6603
61	0.6785	1.2956	1.6702	1.9996	2.3890	2.6589
62	0.6785	1.2954	1.6698	1.9990	2.3880	2.6575
63	0.6784	1.2951	1.6694	1.9983	2.3870	2.6561
64	0.6783	1.2949	1.6690	1.9977	2.3860	2.6549
65	0.6783	1.2947	1.6686	1.9971	2.3851	2.6536
66	0.6782	1.2945	1.6683	1.9966	2.3842	2.6524
67	0.6782	1.2943	1.6679	1.9960	2.3833	2.6512
68	0.6781	1.2941	1.6676	1.9955	2.3824	2.6501
69	0.6781	1.2939	1.6672	1.9949	2.3816	2.6490
70	0.6780	1.2938	1.6669	1.9944	2.3808	2.6479
71	0.6780	1.2936	1.6666	1.9939	2.3800	2.6469
72	0.6779	1.2934	1.6663	1.9935	2.3793	2.6459
73	0.6779	1.2933	1.6660	1.9930	2.3785	2.6449
74	0.6778	1.2931	1.6657	1.9925	2.3778	2.6439
75	0.6778	1.2929	1.6654	1.9921	2.3771	2.6430
76	0.6777	1.2928	1.6652	1.9917	2.3764	2.6421
77	0.6777	1.2926	1.6649	1.9913	2.3758	2.6412
78	0.6776	1.2925	1.6646	1.9908	2.3751	2.6403
79	0.6776	1.2924	1.6644	1.9905	2.3745	2.6395
80	0.6776	1.2922	1.6641	1.9901	2.3739	2.6387
81	0.6775	1.2921	1.6639	1.9897	2.3733	2.6379
82	0.6775	1.2920	1.6636	1.9893	2.3727	2.6371
83	0.6775	1.2918	1.6634	1.9890	2.3721	2.6364
84	0.6774	1.2917	1.6632	1.9886	2.3716	2.6356
85	0.6774	1.2916	1.6630	1.9883	2.3710	2.6349
86	0.6774	1.2915	1.6628	1.9879	2.3705	2.6342
87	0.6773	1.2914	1.6626	1.9876	2.3700	2.6335
88	0.6773	1.2912	1.6624	1.9873	2.3695	2.6329
89	0.6773	1.2911	1.6622	1.9870	2.3690	2.6322
90	0.6772	1.2910	1.6620	1.9867	2.3685	2.6316
91	0.6772	1.2909	1.6618	1.9864	2.3680	2.6309
92	0.6772	1.2908	1.6616	1.9861	2.3676	2.6303
93	0.6771	1.2907	1.6614	1.9858	2.3671	2.6297
94	0.6771	1.2906	1.6612	1.9855	2.3667	2.6291
95	0.6771	1.2905	1.6611	1.9853	2.3662	2.6286
96	0.6771	1.2904	1.6609	1.9850	2.3658	2.6280
97	0.6770	1.2903	1.6607	1.9847	2.3654	2.6275
98	0.6770	1.2902	1.6606	1.9845	2.3650	2.6269
99	0.6770	1.2902	1.6604	1.9842	2.3646	2.6264
100	0.6770	1.2901	1.6602	1.9840	2.3642	2.6259
110	0.6767	1.2893	1.6588	1.9818	2.3607	2.6213
120	0.6765	1.2886	1.6577	1.9799	2.3578	2.6174
∞	0.6745	1.2816	1.6449	1.9600	2.3263	2.5758

TABLE E.4

Critical Values of χ^2

For a particular number of degrees of freedom, entry represents the critical value of χ^2 corresponding to a specified upper-tail area (α).

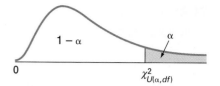

Degrees of Freedom	Upper-Tail Areas (α)											
	0.995	0.99	0.975	0.95	0.90	0.75	0.25	0.10	0.05	0.025	0.01	0.005
1			0.001	0.004	0.016	0.102	1.323	2.706	3.841	5.024	6.635	7.879
2	0.010	0.020	0.051	0.103	0.211	0.575	2.773	4.605	5.991	7.378	9.210	10.597
3	0.072	0.115	0.216	0.352	0.584	1.213	4.108	6.251	7.815	9.348	11.345	12.838
4	0.207	0.297	0.484	0.711	1.064	1.923	5.385	7.779	9.488	11.143	13.277	14.860
5	0.412	0.554	0.831	1.145	1.610	2.675	6.626	9.236	11.071	12.833	15.086	16.750
6	0.676	0.872	1.237	1.635	2.204	3.455	7.841	10.645	12.592	14.449	16.812	18.458
7	0.989	1.239	1.690	2.167	2.833	4.255	9.037	12.017	14.067	16.013	18.475	20.278
8	1.344	1.646	2.180	2.733	3.490	5.071	10.219	13.362	15.507	17.535	20.090	21.955
9	1.735	2.088	2.700	3.325	4.168	5.899	11.389	14.684	16.919	19.023	21.666	23.589
10	2.156	2.558	3.247	3.940	4.865	6.737	12.549	15.987	18.307	20.483	23.209	25.188
11	2.603	3.053	3.816	4.575	5.578	7.584	13.701	17.275	19.675	21.920	24.725	26.757
12	3.074	3.571	4.404	5.226	6.304	8.438	14.845	18.549	21.026	23.337	26.217	28.299
13	3.565	4.107	5.009	5.892	7.042	9.299	15.984	19.812	22.362	24.736	27.688	29.819
14	4.075	4.660	5.629	6.571	7.790	10.165	17.117	21.064	23.685	26.119	29.141	31.319
15	4.601	5.229	6.262	7.261	8.547	11.037	18.245	22.307	24.996	27.488	30.578	32.801
16	5.142	5.812	6.908	7.962	9.312	11.912	19.369	23.542	26.296	28.845	32.000	34.267
17	5.697	6.408	7.564	8.672	10.085	12.792	20.489	24.769	27.587	30.191	33.409	35.718
18	6.265	7.015	8.231	9.390	10.865	13.675	21.605	25.989	28.869	31.526	34.805	37.156
19	6.844	7.633	8.907	10.117	11.651	14.562	22.718	27.204	30.144	32.852	36.191	38.582
20	7.434	8.260	9.591	10.851	12.443	15.452	23.828	28.412	31.410	34.170	37.566	39.997
21	8.034	8.897	10.283	11.591	13.240	16.344	24.935	29.615	32.671	35.479	38.932	41.401
22	8.643	9.542	10.982	12.338	14.042	17.240	26.039	30.813	33.924	36.781	40.289	42.796
23	9.260	10.196	11.689	13.091	14.848	18.137	27.141	32.007	35.172	38.076	41.638	44.181
24	9.886	10.856	12.401	13.848	15.659	19.037	28.241	33.196	36.415	39.364	42.980	45.559
25	10.520	11.524	13.120	14.611	16.473	19.939	29.339	34.382	37.652	40.646	44.314	46.928
26	11.160	12.198	13.844	15.379	17.292	20.843	30.435	35.563	38.885	41.923	45.642	48.290
27	11.808	12.879	14.573	16.151	18.114	21.749	31.528	36.741	40.113	43.194	46.963	49.645
28	12.461	13.565	15.308	16.928	18.939	22.657	32.620	37.916	41.337	44.461	48.278	50.993
29	13.121	14.257	16.047	17.708	19.768	23.567	33.711	39.087	42.557	45.722	49.588	52.336
30	13.787	14.954	16.791	18.493	20.599	24.478	34.800	40.256	43.773	46.979	50.892	53.672

For larger values of degrees of freedom (df) the expression $Z = \sqrt{2\chi^2} - \sqrt{2(df) - 1}$ may be used and the resulting upper-tail area can be found from the cumulative standardized normal distribution (Table E.2).

TABLE E.5

Critical Values of F

For a particular combination of numerator and denominator degrees of freedom, entry represents the critical values of F corresponding to a specified upper-tail area (α).

$\alpha = 0.05$

$F_{U(\alpha, df_1, df_2)}$

	Numerator, df_1																		
Denominator, df_2	1	2	3	4	5	6	7	8	9	10	12	15	20	24	30	40	60	120	∞
1	161.40	199.50	215.70	224.60	230.20	234.00	236.80	238.90	240.50	241.90	243.90	245.90	248.00	249.10	250.10	251.10	252.20	253.30	254.30
2	18.51	19.00	19.16	19.25	19.30	19.33	19.35	19.37	19.38	19.40	19.41	19.43	19.45	19.45	19.46	19.47	19.48	19.49	19.50
3	10.13	9.55	9.28	9.12	9.01	8.94	8.89	8.85	8.81	8.79	8.74	8.70	8.66	8.64	8.62	8.59	8.57	8.55	8.53
4	7.71	6.94	6.59	6.39	6.26	6.16	6.09	6.04	6.00	5.96	5.91	5.86	5.80	5.77	5.75	5.72	5.69	5.66	5.63
5	6.61	5.79	5.41	5.19	5.05	4.95	4.88	4.82	4.77	4.74	4.68	4.62	4.56	4.53	4.50	4.46	4.43	4.40	4.36
6	5.99	5.14	4.76	4.53	4.39	4.28	4.21	4.15	4.10	4.06	4.00	3.94	3.87	3.84	3.81	3.77	3.74	3.70	3.67
7	5.59	4.74	4.35	4.12	3.97	3.87	3.79	3.73	3.68	3.64	3.57	3.51	3.44	3.41	3.38	3.34	3.30	3.27	3.23
8	5.32	4.46	4.07	3.84	3.69	3.58	3.50	3.44	3.39	3.35	3.28	3.22	3.15	3.12	3.08	3.04	3.01	2.97	2.93
9	5.12	4.26	3.86	3.63	3.48	3.37	3.29	3.23	3.18	3.14	3.07	3.01	2.94	2.90	2.86	2.83	2.79	2.75	2.71
10	4.96	4.10	3.71	3.48	3.33	3.22	3.14	3.07	3.02	2.98	2.91	2.85	2.77	2.74	2.70	2.66	2.62	2.58	2.54
11	4.84	3.98	3.59	3.36	3.20	3.09	3.01	2.95	2.90	2.85	2.79	2.72	2.65	2.61	2.57	2.53	2.49	2.45	2.40
12	4.75	3.89	3.49	3.26	3.11	3.00	2.91	2.85	2.80	2.75	2.69	2.62	2.54	2.51	2.47	2.43	2.38	2.34	2.30
13	4.67	3.81	3.41	3.18	3.03	2.92	2.83	2.77	2.71	2.67	2.60	2.53	2.46	2.42	2.38	2.34	2.30	2.25	2.21
14	4.60	3.74	3.34	3.11	2.96	2.85	2.76	2.70	2.65	2.60	2.53	2.46	2.39	2.35	2.31	2.27	2.22	2.18	2.13
15	4.54	3.68	3.29	3.06	2.90	2.79	2.71	2.64	2.59	2.54	2.48	2.40	2.33	2.29	2.25	2.20	2.16	2.11	2.07
16	4.49	3.63	3.24	3.01	2.85	2.74	2.66	2.59	2.54	2.49	2.42	2.35	2.28	2.24	2.19	2.15	2.11	2.06	2.01
17	4.45	3.59	3.20	2.96	2.81	2.70	2.61	2.55	2.49	2.45	2.38	2.31	2.23	2.19	2.15	2.10	2.06	2.01	1.96
18	4.41	3.55	3.16	2.93	2.77	2.66	2.58	2.51	2.46	2.41	2.34	2.27	2.19	2.15	2.11	2.06	2.02	1.97	1.92
19	4.38	3.52	3.13	2.90	2.74	2.63	2.54	2.48	2.42	2.38	2.31	2.23	2.16	2.11	2.07	2.03	1.98	1.93	1.88
20	4.35	3.49	3.10	2.87	2.71	2.60	2.51	2.45	2.39	2.35	2.28	2.20	2.12	2.08	2.04	1.99	1.95	1.90	1.84
21	4.32	3.47	3.07	2.84	2.68	2.57	2.49	2.42	2.37	2.32	2.25	2.18	2.10	2.05	2.01	1.96	1.92	1.87	1.81
22	4.30	3.44	3.05	2.82	2.66	2.55	2.46	2.40	2.34	2.30	2.23	2.15	2.07	2.03	1.98	1.91	1.89	1.84	1.78
23	4.28	3.42	3.03	2.80	2.64	2.53	2.44	2.37	2.32	2.27	2.20	2.13	2.05	2.01	1.96	1.91	1.86	1.81	1.76
24	4.26	3.40	3.01	2.78	2.62	2.51	2.42	2.36	2.30	2.25	2.18	2.11	2.03	1.98	1.94	1.89	1.84	1.79	1.73
25	4.24	3.39	2.99	2.76	2.60	2.49	2.40	2.34	2.28	2.24	2.16	2.09	2.01	1.96	1.92	1.87	1.82	1.77	1.71
26	4.23	3.37	2.98	2.74	2.59	2.47	2.39	2.32	2.27	2.22	2.15	2.07	1.99	1.95	1.90	1.85	1.80	1.75	1.69
27	4.21	3.35	2.96	2.73	2.57	2.46	2.37	2.31	2.25	2.20	2.13	2.06	1.97	1.93	1.88	1.84	1.79	1.73	1.67
28	4.20	3.34	2.95	2.71	2.56	2.45	2.36	2.29	2.24	2.19	2.12	2.04	1.96	1.91	1.87	1.82	1.77	1.71	1.65
29	4.18	3.33	2.93	2.70	2.55	2.43	2.35	2.28	2.22	2.18	2.10	2.03	1.94	1.90	1.85	1.81	1.75	1.70	1.64
30	4.17	3.32	2.92	2.69	2.53	2.42	2.33	2.27	2.21	2.16	2.09	2.01	1.93	1.89	1.84	1.79	1.74	1.68	1.62
40	4.08	3.23	2.84	2.61	2.45	2.34	2.25	2.18	2.12	2.08	2.00	1.92	1.84	1.79	1.74	1.69	1.64	1.58	1.51
60	4.00	3.15	2.76	2.53	2.37	2.25	2.17	2.10	2.04	1.99	1.92	1.84	1.75	1.70	1.65	1.59	1.53	1.47	1.39
120	3.92	3.07	2.68	2.45	2.29	2.17	2.09	2.02	1.96	1.91	1.83	1.75	1.66	1.61	1.55	1.50	1.43	1.35	1.25
∞	3.84	3.00	2.60	2.37	2.21	2.10	2.01	1.94	1.88	1.83	1.75	1.67	1.57	1.52	1.46	1.39	1.32	1.22	1.00

continued

TABLE E.5
Critical Values of F *(Continued)*

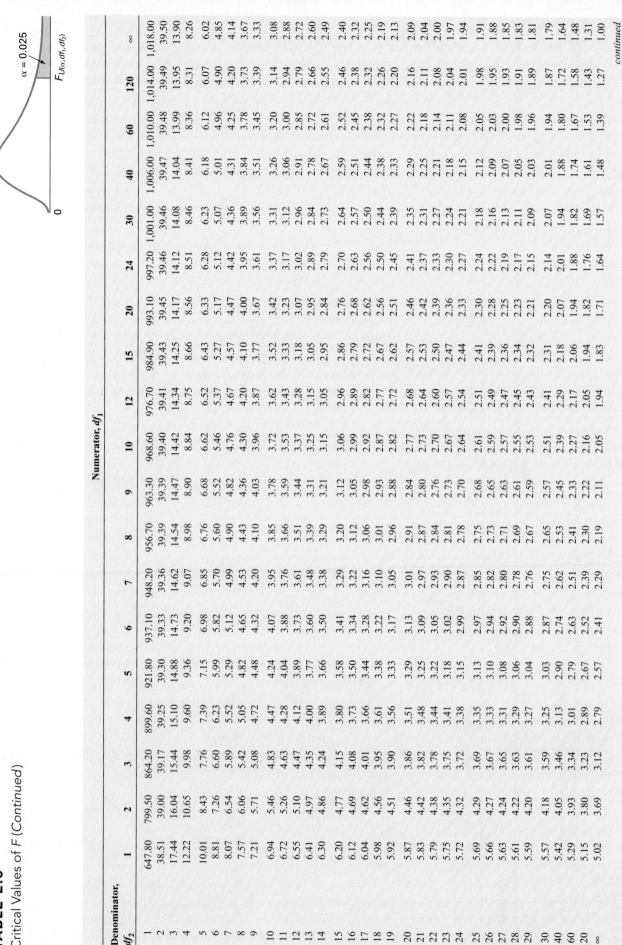

$\alpha = 0.025$

$F_{U(\alpha, df_1, df_2)}$

Numerator, df_1

Denominator, df_2	1	2	3	4	5	6	7	8	9	10	12	15	20	24	30	40	60	120	∞
1	647.80	799.50	864.20	899.60	921.80	937.10	948.20	956.70	963.30	968.60	976.70	984.90	993.10	997.20	1,001.00	1,006.00	1,010.00	1,014.00	1,018.00
2	38.51	39.00	39.17	39.25	39.30	39.33	39.36	39.39	39.39	39.40	39.41	39.43	39.45	39.46	39.46	39.47	39.48	39.49	39.50
3	17.44	16.04	15.44	15.10	14.88	14.73	14.62	14.54	14.47	14.42	14.34	14.25	14.17	14.12	14.08	14.04	13.99	13.95	13.90
4	12.22	10.65	9.98	9.60	9.36	9.20	9.07	8.98	8.90	8.84	8.75	8.66	8.56	8.51	8.46	8.41	8.36	8.31	8.26
5	10.01	8.43	7.76	7.39	7.15	6.98	6.85	6.76	6.68	6.62	6.52	6.43	6.33	6.28	6.23	6.18	6.12	6.07	6.02
6	8.81	7.26	6.60	6.23	5.99	5.82	5.70	5.60	5.52	5.46	5.37	5.27	5.17	5.12	5.07	5.01	4.96	4.90	4.85
7	8.07	6.54	5.89	5.52	5.29	5.12	4.99	4.90	4.82	4.76	4.67	4.57	4.47	4.42	4.36	4.31	4.25	4.20	4.14
8	7.57	6.06	5.42	5.05	4.82	4.65	4.53	4.43	4.36	4.30	4.20	4.10	4.00	3.95	3.89	3.84	3.78	3.73	3.67
9	7.21	5.71	5.08	4.72	4.48	4.32	4.20	4.10	4.03	3.96	3.87	3.77	3.67	3.61	3.56	3.51	3.45	3.39	3.33
10	6.94	5.46	4.83	4.47	4.24	4.07	3.95	3.85	3.78	3.72	3.62	3.52	3.42	3.37	3.31	3.26	3.20	3.14	3.08
11	6.72	5.26	4.63	4.28	4.04	3.88	3.76	3.66	3.59	3.53	3.43	3.33	3.23	3.17	3.12	3.06	3.00	2.94	2.88
12	6.55	5.10	4.47	4.12	3.89	3.73	3.61	3.51	3.44	3.37	3.28	3.18	3.07	3.02	2.96	2.91	2.85	2.79	2.72
13	6.41	4.97	4.35	4.00	3.77	3.60	3.48	3.39	3.31	3.25	3.15	3.05	2.95	2.89	2.84	2.78	2.72	2.66	2.60
14	6.30	4.86	4.24	3.89	3.66	3.50	3.38	3.29	3.21	3.15	3.05	2.95	2.84	2.79	2.73	2.67	2.61	2.55	2.49
15	6.20	4.77	4.15	3.80	3.58	3.41	3.29	3.20	3.12	3.06	2.96	2.86	2.76	2.70	2.64	2.59	2.52	2.46	2.40
16	6.12	4.69	4.08	3.73	3.50	3.34	3.22	3.12	3.05	2.99	2.89	2.79	2.68	2.63	2.57	2.51	2.45	2.38	2.32
17	6.04	4.62	4.01	3.66	3.44	3.28	3.16	3.06	2.98	2.92	2.82	2.72	2.62	2.56	2.50	2.44	2.38	2.32	2.25
18	5.98	4.56	3.95	3.61	3.38	3.22	3.10	3.01	2.93	2.87	2.77	2.67	2.56	2.50	2.44	2.38	2.32	2.26	2.19
19	5.92	4.51	3.90	3.56	3.33	3.17	3.05	2.96	2.88	2.82	2.72	2.62	2.51	2.45	2.39	2.33	2.27	2.20	2.13
20	5.87	4.46	3.86	3.51	3.29	3.13	3.01	2.91	2.84	2.77	2.68	2.57	2.46	2.41	2.35	2.29	2.22	2.16	2.09
21	5.83	4.42	3.82	3.48	3.25	3.09	2.97	2.87	2.80	2.73	2.64	2.53	2.42	2.37	2.31	2.25	2.18	2.11	2.04
22	5.79	4.38	3.78	3.44	3.22	3.05	2.93	2.84	2.76	2.70	2.60	2.50	2.39	2.33	2.27	2.21	2.14	2.08	2.00
23	5.75	4.35	3.75	3.41	3.18	3.02	2.90	2.81	2.73	2.67	2.57	2.47	2.36	2.30	2.24	2.18	2.11	2.04	1.97
24	5.72	4.32	3.72	3.38	3.15	2.99	2.87	2.78	2.70	2.64	2.54	2.44	2.33	2.27	2.21	2.15	2.08	2.01	1.94
25	5.69	4.29	3.69	3.35	3.13	2.97	2.85	2.75	2.68	2.61	2.51	2.41	2.30	2.24	2.18	2.12	2.05	1.98	1.91
26	5.66	4.27	3.67	3.33	3.10	2.94	2.82	2.73	2.65	2.59	2.49	2.39	2.28	2.22	2.16	2.09	2.03	1.95	1.88
27	5.63	4.24	3.65	3.31	3.08	2.92	2.80	2.71	2.63	2.57	2.47	2.36	2.25	2.19	2.13	2.07	2.00	1.93	1.85
28	5.61	4.22	3.63	3.29	3.06	2.90	2.78	2.69	2.61	2.55	2.45	2.34	2.23	2.17	2.11	2.05	1.98	1.91	1.83
29	5.59	4.20	3.61	3.27	3.04	2.88	2.76	2.67	2.59	2.53	2.43	2.32	2.21	2.15	2.09	2.03	1.96	1.89	1.81
30	5.57	4.18	3.59	3.25	3.03	2.87	2.75	2.65	2.57	2.51	2.41	2.31	2.20	2.14	2.07	2.01	1.94	1.87	1.79
40	5.42	4.05	3.46	3.13	2.90	2.74	2.62	2.53	2.45	2.39	2.29	2.18	2.07	2.01	1.94	1.88	1.80	1.72	1.64
60	5.29	3.93	3.34	3.01	2.79	2.63	2.51	2.41	2.33	2.27	2.17	2.06	1.94	1.88	1.82	1.74	1.67	1.58	1.48
120	5.15	3.80	3.23	2.89	2.67	2.52	2.39	2.30	2.22	2.16	2.05	1.94	1.82	1.76	1.69	1.61	1.53	1.43	1.31
∞	5.02	3.69	3.12	2.79	2.57	2.41	2.29	2.19	2.11	2.05	1.94	1.83	1.71	1.64	1.57	1.48	1.39	1.27	1.00

continued

TABLE E.5

Critical Values of F (Continued)

$\alpha = 0.01$

$F_{U(\alpha, df_1, df_2)}$

	Numerator, df_1																		
Denominator, df_2	1	2	3	4	5	6	7	8	9	10	12	15	20	24	30	40	60	120	∞
1	4,052.00	4,999.50	5,403.00	5,625.00	5,764.00	5,859.00	5,928.00	5,982.00	6,022.00	6,056.00	6,106.00	6,157.00	6,209.00	6,235.00	6,261.00	6,287.00	6,313.00	6,339.00	6,366.00
2	98.50	99.00	99.17	99.25	99.30	99.33	99.36	99.37	99.39	99.40	99.42	99.43	44.45	99.46	99.47	99.47	99.48	99.49	99.50
3	34.12	30.82	29.46	28.71	28.24	27.91	27.67	27.49	27.35	27.23	27.05	26.87	26.69	26.60	26.50	26.41	26.32	26.22	26.13
4	21.20	18.00	16.69	15.98	15.52	15.21	14.98	14.80	14.66	14.55	14.37	14.20	14.02	13.93	13.84	13.75	13.65	13.56	13.46
5	16.26	13.27	12.06	11.39	10.97	10.67	10.46	10.29	10.16	10.05	9.89	9.72	9.55	9.47	9.38	9.29	9.20	9.11	9.02
6	13.75	10.92	9.78	9.15	8.75	8.47	8.26	8.10	7.98	7.87	7.72	7.56	7.40	7.31	7.23	7.14	7.06	6.97	6.88
7	12.25	9.55	8.45	7.85	7.46	7.19	6.99	6.84	6.72	6.62	6.47	6.31	6.16	6.07	5.99	5.91	5.82	5.74	5.65
8	11.26	8.65	7.59	7.01	6.63	6.37	6.18	6.03	5.91	5.81	5.67	5.52	5.36	5.28	5.20	5.12	5.03	4.95	4.86
9	10.56	8.02	6.99	6.42	6.06	5.80	5.61	5.47	5.35	5.26	5.11	4.96	4.81	4.73	4.65	4.57	4.48	4.40	4.31
10	10.04	7.56	6.55	5.99	5.64	5.39	5.20	5.06	4.94	4.85	4.71	4.56	4.41	4.33	4.25	4.17	4.08	4.00	3.91
11	9.65	7.21	6.22	5.67	5.32	5.07	4.89	4.74	4.63	4.54	4.40	4.25	4.10	4.02	3.94	3.86	3.78	3.69	3.60
12	9.33	6.93	5.95	5.41	5.06	4.82	4.64	4.50	4.39	4.30	4.16	4.01	3.86	3.78	3.70	3.62	3.54	3.45	3.36
13	9.07	6.70	5.74	5.21	4.86	4.62	4.44	4.30	4.19	4.10	3.96	3.82	3.66	3.59	3.51	3.43	3.34	3.25	3.17
14	8.86	6.51	5.56	5.04	4.69	4.46	4.28	4.14	4.03	3.94	3.80	3.66	3.51	3.43	3.35	3.27	3.18	3.09	3.00
15	8.68	6.36	5.42	4.89	4.56	4.32	4.14	4.00	3.89	3.80	3.67	3.52	3.37	3.29	3.21	3.13	3.05	2.96	2.87
16	8.53	6.23	5.29	4.77	4.44	4.20	4.03	3.89	3.78	3.69	3.55	3.41	3.26	3.18	3.10	3.02	2.93	2.81	2.75
17	8.40	6.11	5.18	4.67	4.34	4.10	3.93	3.79	3.68	3.59	3.46	3.31	3.16	3.08	3.00	2.92	2.83	2.75	2.65
18	8.29	6.01	5.09	4.58	4.25	4.01	3.84	3.71	3.60	3.51	3.37	3.23	3.08	3.00	2.92	2.84	2.75	2.66	2.57
19	8.18	5.93	5.01	4.50	4.17	3.94	3.77	3.63	3.52	3.43	3.30	3.15	3.00	2.92	2.84	2.76	2.67	2.58	2.49
20	8.10	5.85	4.94	4.43	4.10	3.87	3.70	3.56	3.46	3.37	3.23	3.09	2.94	2.86	2.78	2.69	2.61	2.52	2.42
21	8.02	5.78	4.87	4.37	4.04	3.81	3.64	3.51	3.40	3.31	3.17	3.03	2.88	2.80	2.72	2.64	2.55	2.46	2.36
22	7.95	5.72	4.82	4.31	3.99	3.76	3.59	3.45	3.35	3.26	3.12	2.98	2.83	2.75	2.67	2.58	2.50	2.40	2.31
23	7.88	5.66	4.76	4.26	3.94	3.71	3.54	3.41	3.30	3.21	3.07	2.93	2.78	2.70	2.62	2.54	2.45	2.35	2.26
24	7.82	5.61	4.72	4.22	3.90	3.67	3.50	3.36	3.26	3.17	3.03	2.89	2.74	2.66	2.58	2.49	2.40	2.31	2.21
25	7.77	5.57	4.68	4.18	3.85	3.63	3.46	3.32	3.22	3.13	2.99	2.85	2.70	2.62	2.54	2.45	2.36	2.27	2.17
26	7.72	5.53	4.64	4.14	3.82	3.59	3.42	3.29	3.18	3.09	2.96	2.81	2.66	2.58	2.50	2.42	2.33	2.23	2.13
27	7.68	5.49	4.60	4.11	3.78	3.56	3.39	3.26	3.15	3.06	2.93	2.78	2.63	2.55	2.47	2.38	2.29	2.20	2.10
28	7.64	5.45	4.57	4.07	3.75	3.53	3.36	3.23	3.12	3.03	2.90	2.75	2.60	2.52	2.44	2.35	2.26	2.17	2.06
29	7.60	5.42	4.54	4.04	3.73	3.50	3.33	3.20	3.09	3.00	2.87	2.73	2.57	2.49	2.41	2.33	2.23	2.14	2.03
30	7.56	5.39	4.51	4.02	3.70	3.47	3.30	3.17	3.07	2.98	2.84	2.70	2.55	2.47	2.39	2.30	2.21	2.11	2.01
40	7.31	5.18	4.31	3.83	3.51	3.29	3.12	2.99	2.89	2.80	2.66	2.52	2.37	2.29	2.20	2.11	2.02	1.92	1.80
60	7.08	4.98	4.13	3.65	3.34	3.12	2.95	2.82	2.72	2.63	2.50	2.35	2.20	2.12	2.03	1.94	1.84	1.73	1.60
120	6.85	4.79	3.95	3.48	3.17	2.96	2.79	2.66	2.56	2.47	2.34	2.19	2.03	1.95	1.86	1.76	1.66	1.53	1.38
∞	6.63	4.61	3.78	3.32	3.02	2.80	2.64	2.51	2.41	2.32	2.18	2.04	1.88	1.79	1.70	1.59	1.47	1.32	1.00

continued

TABLE E.5

Critical Values of F (Continued)

$\alpha = 0.005$

$F_{U(\alpha, df_1, df_2)}$

									Numerator, df_1										
Denominator, df_2	1	2	3	4	5	6	7	8	9	10	12	15	20	24	30	40	60	120	∞
1	16,211.00	20,000.00	21,615.00	22,500.00	23,056.00	23,437.00	23,715.00	23,925.00	24,091.00	24,224.00	24,426.00	24,630.00	24,836.00	24,910.00	25,044.00	25,148.00	25,253.00	25,359.00	25,465.00
2	198.50	199.00	199.20	199.20	199.30	199.30	199.40	199.40	199.40	199.40	199.40	199.40	199.40	199.50	199.50	199.50	199.50	199.50	199.50
3	55.55	49.80	47.47	46.19	45.39	44.84	44.43	44.13	43.88	43.69	43.39	43.08	42.78	42.62	42.47	42.31	42.15	41.99	41.83
4	31.33	26.28	24.26	23.15	22.46	21.97	21.62	21.35	21.14	20.97	20.70	20.44	20.17	20.03	19.89	19.75	19.61	19.47	19.32
5	22.78	18.31	16.53	15.56	14.94	14.51	14.20	13.96	13.77	13.62	13.38	13.15	12.90	12.78	12.66	12.53	12.40	12.27	12.11
6	18.63	14.54	12.92	12.03	11.46	11.07	10.79	10.57	10.39	10.25	10.03	9.81	9.59	9.47	9.36	9.24	9.12	9.00	8.88
7	16.24	12.40	10.88	10.05	9.52	9.16	8.89	8.68	8.51	8.38	8.18	7.97	7.75	7.65	7.53	7.42	7.31	7.19	7.08
8	14.69	11.04	9.60	8.81	8.30	7.95	7.69	7.50	7.34	7.21	7.01	6.81	6.61	6.50	6.40	6.29	6.18	6.06	5.95
9	13.61	10.11	8.72	7.96	7.47	7.13	6.88	6.69	6.54	6.42	6.23	6.03	5.83	5.73	5.62	5.52	5.41	5.30	5.19
10	12.83	9.43	8.08	7.34	6.87	6.54	6.30	6.12	5.97	5.85	5.66	5.47	5.27	5.17	5.07	4.97	4.86	4.75	4.61
11	12.23	8.91	7.60	6.88	6.42	6.10	5.86	5.68	5.54	5.42	5.24	5.05	4.86	4.75	4.65	4.55	4.44	4.34	4.23
12	11.75	8.51	7.23	6.52	6.07	5.76	5.52	5.35	5.20	5.09	4.91	4.72	4.53	4.43	4.33	4.23	4.12	4.01	3.90
13	11.37	8.19	6.93	6.23	5.79	5.48	5.25	5.08	4.94	4.82	4.64	4.46	4.27	4.17	4.07	3.97	3.87	3.76	3.65
14	11.06	7.92	6.68	6.00	5.56	5.26	5.03	4.86	4.72	4.60	4.43	4.25	4.06	3.96	3.86	3.76	3.66	3.55	3.41
15	10.80	7.70	6.48	5.80	5.37	5.07	4.85	4.67	4.54	4.42	4.25	4.07	3.88	3.79	3.69	3.58	3.48	3.37	3.26
16	10.58	7.51	6.30	5.64	5.21	4.91	4.69	4.52	4.38	4.27	4.10	3.92	3.73	3.64	3.54	3.44	3.33	3.22	3.11
17	10.38	7.35	6.16	5.50	5.07	4.78	4.56	4.39	4.25	4.14	3.97	3.79	3.61	3.51	3.41	3.31	3.21	3.10	2.98
18	10.22	7.21	6.03	5.37	4.96	4.66	4.44	4.28	4.14	4.03	3.86	3.68	3.50	3.40	3.30	3.20	3.10	2.99	2.87
19	10.07	7.09	5.92	5.27	4.85	4.56	4.34	4.18	4.04	3.93	3.76	3.59	3.40	3.31	3.21	3.11	3.00	2.89	2.78
20	9.94	6.99	5.82	5.17	4.76	4.47	4.26	4.09	3.96	3.85	3.68	3.50	3.32	3.22	3.12	3.02	2.92	2.81	2.69
21	9.83	6.89	5.73	5.09	4.68	4.39	4.18	4.02	3.88	3.77	3.60	3.43	3.24	3.15	3.05	2.95	2.84	2.73	2.61
22	9.73	6.81	5.65	5.02	4.61	4.32	4.11	3.94	3.81	3.70	3.54	3.36	3.18	3.08	2.98	2.88	2.77	2.66	2.55
23	9.63	6.73	5.58	4.95	4.54	4.26	4.05	3.88	3.75	3.64	3.47	3.30	3.12	3.02	2.92	2.82	2.71	2.60	2.48
24	9.55	6.66	5.52	4.89	4.49	4.20	3.99	3.83	3.69	3.59	3.42	3.25	3.06	2.97	2.87	2.77	2.66	2.55	2.43
25	9.48	6.60	5.46	4.84	4.43	4.15	3.94	3.78	3.64	3.54	3.37	3.20	3.01	2.92	2.82	2.72	2.61	2.50	2.38
26	9.41	6.54	5.41	4.79	4.38	4.10	3.89	3.73	3.60	3.49	3.33	3.15	2.97	2.87	2.77	2.67	2.56	2.45	2.33
27	9.34	6.49	5.36	4.74	4.34	4.06	3.85	3.69	3.56	3.45	3.28	3.11	2.93	2.83	2.73	2.63	2.52	2.41	2.29
28	9.28	6.44	5.32	4.70	4.30	4.02	3.81	3.65	3.52	3.41	3.25	3.07	2.89	2.79	2.69	2.59	2.48	2.37	2.25
29	9.23	6.40	5.28	4.66	4.26	3.98	3.77	3.61	3.48	3.38	3.21	3.04	2.86	2.76	2.66	2.56	2.45	2.33	2.21
30	9.18	6.35	5.24	4.62	4.23	3.95	3.74	3.58	3.45	3.34	3.18	3.01	2.82	2.73	2.63	2.52	2.42	2.30	2.18
40	8.83	6.07	4.98	4.37	3.99	3.71	3.51	3.35	3.22	3.12	2.95	2.78	2.60	2.50	2.40	2.30	2.18	2.06	1.93
60	8.49	5.79	4.73	4.14	3.76	3.49	3.29	3.13	3.01	2.90	2.74	2.57	2.39	2.29	2.19	2.08	1.96	1.83	1.69
120	8.18	5.54	4.50	3.92	3.55	3.28	3.09	2.93	2.81	2.71	2.54	2.37	2.19	2.09	1.98	1.87	1.75	1.61	1.43
∞	7.88	5.30	4.28	3.72	3.35	3.09	2.90	2.74	2.62	2.52	2.36	2.19	2.00	1.90	1.79	1.67	1.53	1.36	1.00

TABLE E.6

TABLE OF BINOMIAL PROBABILITIES
(BEGINS ON THE FOLLOWING PAGE)

TABLE E.6
Table of Binomial Probabilities

For a given combination of n and p, entry indicates the probability of obtaining a specified value of X. To locate entry, **when $p \leq .50$**, read p across the top heading and both n and X down the left margin; **when $p \geq .50$**, read p across the bottom heading and both n and X up the right margin.

n	X	0.01	0.02	0.03	0.04	0.05	0.06	0.07	0.08	0.09	0.10	0.15	0.20	0.25	0.30	0.35	0.40	0.45	0.50	X	n
2	0	0.9801	0.9604	0.9409	0.9216	0.9025	0.8836	0.8649	0.8464	0.8281	0.8100	0.7225	0.6400	0.5625	0.4900	0.4225	0.3600	0.3025	0.2500	2	
	1	0.0198	0.0392	0.0582	0.0768	0.0950	0.1128	0.1302	0.1472	0.1638	0.1800	0.2550	0.3200	0.3750	0.4200	0.4550	0.4800	0.4950	0.5000	1	
	2	0.0001	0.0004	0.0009	0.0016	0.0025	0.0036	0.0049	0.0064	0.0081	0.0100	0.0225	0.0400	0.0625	0.0900	0.1225	0.1600	0.2025	0.2500	0	2
3	0	0.9703	0.9412	0.9127	0.8847	0.8574	0.8306	0.8044	0.7787	0.7536	0.7290	0.6141	0.5120	0.4219	0.3430	0.2746	0.2160	0.1664	0.1250	3	
	1	0.0294	0.0576	0.0847	0.1106	0.1354	0.1590	0.1816	0.2031	0.2236	0.2430	0.3251	0.3840	0.4219	0.4410	0.4436	0.4320	0.4084	0.3750	2	
	2	0.0003	0.0012	0.0026	0.0046	0.0071	0.0102	0.0137	0.0177	0.0221	0.0270	0.0574	0.0960	0.1406	0.1890	0.2389	0.2880	0.3341	0.3750	1	
	3	0.0000	0.0000	0.0000	0.0001	0.0001	0.0002	0.0003	0.0005	0.0007	0.0010	0.0034	0.0080	0.0156	0.0270	0.0429	0.0640	0.0911	0.1250	0	3
4	0	0.9606	0.9224	0.8853	0.8493	0.8145	0.7807	0.7481	0.7164	0.6857	0.6561	0.5220	0.4096	0.3164	0.2401	0.1785	0.1296	0.0915	0.0625	4	
	1	0.0388	0.0753	0.1095	0.1416	0.1715	0.1993	0.2252	0.2492	0.2713	0.2916	0.3685	0.4096	0.4219	0.4116	0.3845	0.3456	0.2995	0.2500	3	
	2	0.0006	0.0023	0.0051	0.0088	0.0135	0.0191	0.0254	0.0325	0.0402	0.0486	0.0975	0.1536	0.2109	0.2646	0.3105	0.3456	0.3675	0.3750	2	
	3	0.0000	0.0000	0.0001	0.0002	0.0005	0.0008	0.0013	0.0019	0.0027	0.0036	0.0115	0.0256	0.0469	0.0756	0.1115	0.1536	0.2005	0.2500	1	
	4	0.0000	0.0000	0.0000	0.0000	0.0000	0.0000	0.0000	0.0000	0.0001	0.0001	0.0005	0.0016	0.0039	0.0081	0.0150	0.0256	0.0410	0.0625	0	4
5	0	0.9510	0.9039	0.8587	0.8154	0.7738	0.7339	0.6957	0.6591	0.6240	0.5905	0.4437	0.3277	0.2373	0.1681	0.1160	0.0778	0.0503	0.0312	5	
	1	0.0480	0.0922	0.1328	0.1699	0.2036	0.2342	0.2618	0.2866	0.3086	0.3280	0.3915	0.4096	0.3955	0.3601	0.3124	0.2592	0.2059	0.1562	4	
	2	0.0010	0.0038	0.0082	0.0142	0.0214	0.0299	0.0394	0.0498	0.0610	0.0729	0.1382	0.2048	0.2637	0.3087	0.3364	0.3456	0.3369	0.3125	3	
	3	0.0000	0.0001	0.0003	0.0006	0.0011	0.0019	0.0030	0.0043	0.0060	0.0081	0.0244	0.0512	0.0879	0.1323	0.1811	0.2304	0.2757	0.3125	2	
	4	0.0000	0.0000	0.0000	0.0000	0.0000	0.0001	0.0001	0.0002	0.0003	0.0004	0.0022	0.0064	0.0146	0.0283	0.0488	0.0768	0.1128	0.1562	1	
	5	—	0.0000	0.0000	0.0000	0.0000	0.0000	0.0000	0.0000	0.0000	0.0000	0.0001	0.0003	0.0010	0.0024	0.0053	0.0102	0.0185	0.0312	0	5
6	0	0.9415	0.8858	0.8330	0.7828	0.7351	0.6899	0.6470	0.6064	0.5679	0.5314	0.3771	0.2621	0.1780	0.1176	0.0754	0.0467	0.0277	0.0156	6	
	1	0.0571	0.1085	0.1546	0.1957	0.2321	0.2642	0.2922	0.3164	0.3370	0.3543	0.3993	0.3932	0.3560	0.3025	0.2437	0.1866	0.1359	0.0937	5	
	2	0.0014	0.0055	0.0120	0.0204	0.0305	0.0422	0.0550	0.0688	0.0833	0.0984	0.1762	0.2458	0.2966	0.3241	0.3280	0.3110	0.2780	0.2344	4	
	3	0.0000	0.0002	0.0005	0.0011	0.0021	0.0036	0.0055	0.0080	0.0110	0.0146	0.0415	0.0819	0.1318	0.1852	0.2355	0.2765	0.3032	0.3125	3	
	4	—	0.0000	0.0000	0.0000	0.0001	0.0002	0.0003	0.0005	0.0008	0.0012	0.0055	0.0154	0.0330	0.0595	0.0951	0.1372	0.1861	0.2344	2	
	5	—	—	0.0000	0.0000	0.0000	0.0000	0.0000	0.0000	0.0000	0.0001	0.0004	0.0015	0.0044	0.0102	0.0205	0.0369	0.0609	0.0937	1	
	6	—	—	—	0.0000	0.0000	—	0.0000	0.0000	—	0.0000	0.0000	0.0001	0.0002	0.0007	0.0018	0.0041	0.0083	0.0156	0	6

n	X	0.50	0.55	0.60	0.65	0.70	0.75	0.80	0.85	0.90	0.91	0.92	0.93	0.94	0.95	0.96	0.97	0.98	0.99
7	7	0.0078	0.0152	0.0280	0.0490	0.0824	0.1335	0.2097	0.3206	0.4783	0.5168	0.5578	0.6017	0.6485	0.6983	0.7514	0.8080	0.8681	0.9321
	6	0.0547	0.0872	0.1306	0.1848	0.2471	0.3115	0.3670	0.3960	0.3720	0.3578	0.3396	0.3170	0.2897	0.2573	0.2192	0.1749	0.1240	0.0659
	5	0.1641	0.2140	0.2613	0.2985	0.3177	0.3115	0.2753	0.2097	0.1240	0.1061	0.0886	0.0716	0.0555	0.0406	0.0274	0.0162	0.0076	0.0020
	4	0.2734	0.2918	0.2903	0.2679	0.2269	0.1730	0.1147	0.0617	0.0230	0.0175	0.0128	0.0090	0.0059	0.0036	0.0019	0.0008	0.0003	0.0000
	3	0.2734	0.2388	0.1935	0.1442	0.0972	0.0577	0.0287	0.0109	0.0026	0.0017	0.0011	0.0007	0.0004	0.0002	0.0001	0.0000	—	—
	2	0.1641	0.1172	0.0774	0.0466	0.0250	0.0115	0.0043	0.0012	0.0002	0.0001	0.0001	0.0000	0.0000	0.0000	0.0000	—	—	—
	1	0.0547	0.0320	0.0172	0.0084	0.0036	0.0013	0.0004	0.0001	0.0000	0.0000	0.0000	—	—	—	—	—	—	—
	0	0.0078	0.0037	0.0016	0.0006	0.0002	0.0001	0.0000	0.0000	—	—	—	—	—	—	—	—	—	—
8	8	0.0039	0.0084	0.0168	0.0319	0.0576	0.1001	0.1678	0.2725	0.4305	0.4703	0.5132	0.5596	0.6096	0.6634	0.7214	0.7837	0.8508	0.9227
	7	0.0312	0.0548	0.0896	0.1373	0.1977	0.2670	0.3355	0.3847	0.3826	0.3721	0.3570	0.3370	0.3113	0.2793	0.2405	0.1939	0.1389	0.0746
	6	0.1094	0.1569	0.2090	0.2587	0.2965	0.3115	0.2936	0.2376	0.1488	0.1288	0.1087	0.0888	0.0695	0.0515	0.0351	0.0210	0.0099	0.0026
	5	0.2187	0.2568	0.2787	0.2786	0.2541	0.2076	0.1468	0.0839	0.0331	0.0255	0.0189	0.0134	0.0089	0.0054	0.0029	0.0013	0.0004	0.0001
	4	0.2734	0.2627	0.2322	0.1875	0.1361	0.0865	0.0459	0.0185	0.0046	0.0031	0.0021	0.0013	0.0007	0.0004	0.0002	0.0001	0.0000	0.0000
	3	0.2187	0.1719	0.1239	0.0808	0.0467	0.0231	0.0092	0.0026	0.0004	0.0002	0.0001	0.0001	0.0000	0.0000	0.0000	0.0000	—	—
	2	0.1094	0.0703	0.0413	0.0217	0.0100	0.0038	0.0011	0.0002	0.0000	0.0000	0.0000	0.0000	—	—	—	—	—	—
	1	0.0312	0.0164	0.0079	0.0033	0.0012	0.0004	0.0001	0.0000	—	—	—	—	—	—	—	—	—	—
	0	0.0039	0.0017	0.0007	0.0002	0.0001	0.0000	0.0000	—	—	—	—	—	—	—	—	—	—	—
9	9	0.0020	0.0046	0.0101	0.0207	0.0404	0.0751	0.1342	0.2316	0.3874	0.4279	0.4722	0.5204	0.5730	0.6302	0.6925	0.7602	0.8337	0.9135
	8	0.0176	0.0339	0.0605	0.1004	0.1556	0.2253	0.3020	0.3679	0.3874	0.3809	0.3695	0.3525	0.3292	0.2985	0.2597	0.2116	0.1531	0.0830
	7	0.0703	0.1110	0.1612	0.2162	0.2668	0.3003	0.3020	0.2597	0.1722	0.1507	0.1285	0.1061	0.0840	0.0629	0.0433	0.0262	0.0125	0.0034
	6	0.1641	0.2119	0.2508	0.2716	0.2668	0.2336	0.1762	0.1069	0.0446	0.0348	0.0261	0.0186	0.0125	0.0077	0.0042	0.0019	0.0006	0.0001
	5	0.2461	0.2600	0.2508	0.2194	0.1715	0.1168	0.0661	0.0283	0.0074	0.0052	0.0034	0.0021	0.0012	0.0006	0.0003	0.0001	0.0000	0.0000
	4	0.2461	0.2128	0.1672	0.1181	0.0735	0.0389	0.0165	0.0050	0.0008	0.0005	0.0003	0.0002	0.0001	0.0000	0.0000	0.0000	—	—
	3	0.1641	0.1160	0.0743	0.0424	0.0210	0.0087	0.0028	0.0006	0.0001	0.0000	0.0000	0.0000	0.0000	—	—	—	—	—
	2	0.0703	0.0407	0.0212	0.0098	0.0039	0.0012	0.0003	0.0000	0.0000	—	—	—	—	—	—	—	—	—
	1	0.0176	0.0083	0.0035	0.0013	0.0004	0.0001	0.0000	—	—	—	—	—	—	—	—	—	—	—
	0	0.0020	0.0008	0.0003	0.0001	0.0000	0.0000	—	—	—	—	—	—	—	—	—	—	—	—
10	10	0.0010	0.0025	0.0060	0.0135	0.0282	0.0563	0.1074	0.1969	0.3487	0.3894	0.4344	0.4840	0.5386	0.5987	0.6648	0.7374	0.8171	0.9044
	9	0.0098	0.0207	0.0403	0.0725	0.1211	0.1877	0.2684	0.3474	0.3874	0.3851	0.3777	0.3643	0.3438	0.3151	0.2770	0.2281	0.1667	0.0914
	8	0.0439	0.0763	0.1209	0.1757	0.2335	0.2816	0.3020	0.2759	0.1937	0.1714	0.1478	0.1234	0.0988	0.0746	0.0519	0.0317	0.0153	0.0042
	7	0.1172	0.1665	0.2150	0.2522	0.2668	0.2503	0.2013	0.1298	0.0574	0.0452	0.0343	0.0248	0.0168	0.0105	0.0058	0.0026	0.0008	0.0001
	6	0.2051	0.2384	0.2508	0.2377	0.2001	0.1460	0.0881	0.0401	0.0112	0.0078	0.0052	0.0033	0.0019	0.0010	0.0004	0.0001	0.0000	0.0000
	5	0.2461	0.2340	0.2007	0.1536	0.1029	0.0584	0.0264	0.0085	0.0015	0.0009	0.0005	0.0003	0.0001	0.0001	0.0000	0.0000	—	—
	4	0.2051	0.1596	0.1115	0.0689	0.0368	0.0162	0.0055	0.0012	0.0001	0.0001	0.0000	0.0000	0.0000	0.0000	—	—	—	—
	3	0.1172	0.0746	0.0425	0.0212	0.0090	0.0031	0.0008	0.0001	0.0000	0.0000	—	—	—	—	—	—	—	—
	2	0.0439	0.0229	0.0106	0.0043	0.0014	0.0004	0.0001	0.0000	—	—	—	—	—	—	—	—	—	—
	1	0.0098	0.0042	0.0016	0.0005	0.0001	0.0000	0.0000	—	—	—	—	—	—	—	—	—	—	—
	0	0.0010	0.0003	0.0001	0.0000	0.0000	0.0000	—	—	—	—	—	—	—	—	—	—	—	—
n	X	0.50	0.55	0.60	0.65	0.70	0.75	0.80	0.85	0.90	0.91	0.92	0.93	0.94	0.95	0.96	0.97	0.98	0.99

continued

TABLE E.6
Table of Binomial Probabilities (Continued)

p

n	X	0.01	0.02	0.03	0.04	0.05	0.06	0.07	0.08	0.09	0.10	0.15	0.20	0.25	0.30	0.35	0.40	0.45	0.50	X	n
20	0	0.8179	0.6676	0.5438	0.4420	0.3585	0.2901	0.2342	0.1887	0.1516	0.1216	0.0388	0.0115	0.0032	0.0008	0.0002	0.0000	0.0000	—	20	
	1	0.1652	0.2725	0.3364	0.3683	0.3774	0.3703	0.3526	0.3282	0.3000	0.2702	0.1368	0.0576	0.0211	0.0068	0.0020	0.0005	0.0001	0.0000	19	
	2	0.0159	0.0528	0.0988	0.1458	0.1887	0.2246	0.2521	0.2711	0.2818	0.2852	0.2293	0.1369	0.0669	0.0278	0.0100	0.0031	0.0008	0.0002	18	
	3	0.0010	0.0065	0.0183	0.0364	0.0596	0.0860	0.1139	0.1414	0.1672	0.1901	0.2428	0.2054	0.1339	0.0716	0.0323	0.0123	0.0040	0.0011	17	
	4	0.0000	0.0006	0.0024	0.0065	0.0133	0.0233	0.0364	0.0523	0.0703	0.0898	0.1821	0.2182	0.1897	0.1304	0.0738	0.0350	0.0139	0.0046	16	
	5	—	0.0000	0.0002	0.0009	0.0022	0.0048	0.0088	0.0145	0.0222	0.0319	0.1028	0.1746	0.2023	0.1789	0.1272	0.0746	0.0365	0.0148	15	
	6	—	—	0.0000	0.0001	0.0003	0.0008	0.0017	0.0032	0.0055	0.0089	0.0454	0.1091	0.1686	0.1916	0.1712	0.1244	0.0746	0.0370	14	
	7	—	—	—	0.0000	0.0000	0.0001	0.0002	0.0005	0.0011	0.0020	0.0160	0.0545	0.1124	0.1643	0.1844	0.1659	0.1221	0.0739	13	
	8	—	—	—	—	—	0.0000	0.0000	0.0001	0.0002	0.0004	0.0046	0.0222	0.0609	0.1144	0.1614	0.1797	0.1623	0.1201	12	
	9	—	—	—	—	—	—	—	0.0000	0.0000	0.0001	0.0011	0.0074	0.0271	0.0654	0.1158	0.1597	0.1771	0.1602	11	
	10	—	—	—	—	—	—	—	—	—	0.0000	0.0002	0.0020	0.0099	0.0308	0.0686	0.1171	0.1593	0.1762	10	
	11	—	—	—	—	—	—	—	—	—	—	0.0000	0.0005	0.0030	0.0120	0.0336	0.0710	0.1185	0.1602	9	
	12	—	—	—	—	—	—	—	—	—	—	—	0.0001	0.0008	0.0039	0.0136	0.0355	0.0727	0.1201	8	
	13	—	—	—	—	—	—	—	—	—	—	—	0.0000	0.0002	0.0010	0.0045	0.0146	0.0366	0.0739	7	
	14	—	—	—	—	—	—	—	—	—	—	—	—	0.0000	0.0002	0.0012	0.0049	0.0150	0.0370	6	
	15	—	—	—	—	—	—	—	—	—	—	—	—	—	0.0000	0.0003	0.0013	0.0049	0.0148	5	
	16	—	—	—	—	—	—	—	—	—	—	—	—	—	—	0.0000	0.0003	0.0013	0.0046	4	
	17	—	—	—	—	—	—	—	—	—	—	—	—	—	—	—	0.0000	0.0002	0.0011	3	
	18	—	—	—	—	—	—	—	—	—	—	—	—	—	—	—	—	0.0000	0.0002	2	
	19	—	—	—	—	—	—	—	—	—	—	—	—	—	—	—	—	—	0.0000	1	
		—	—	—	—	—	—	—	—	—	—	—	—	—	—	—	—	—	—	0	20
n	X	0.99	0.98	0.97	0.96	0.95	0.94	0.93	0.92	0.91	0.90	0.85	0.80	0.75	0.70	0.65	0.60	0.55	0.50	X	n

TABLE E.7

Table of Poisson Probabilities

For a given value of λ, entry indicates the probability of a specified value of X.

					λ					
X	0.1	0.2	0.3	0.4	0.5	0.6	0.7	0.8	0.9	1.0
0	0.9048	0.8187	0.7408	0.6703	0.6065	0.5488	0.4966	0.4493	0.4066	0.3679
1	0.0905	0.1637	0.2222	0.2681	0.3033	0.3293	0.3476	0.3595	0.3659	0.3679
2	0.0045	0.0164	0.0333	0.0536	0.0758	0.0988	0.1217	0.1438	0.1647	0.1839
3	0.0002	0.0011	0.0033	0.0072	0.0126	0.0198	0.0284	0.0383	0.0494	0.0613
4	0.0000	0.0001	0.0003	0.0007	0.0016	0.0030	0.0050	0.0077	0.0111	0.0153
5	0.0000	0.0000	0.0000	0.0001	0.0002	0.0004	0.0007	0.0012	0.0020	0.0031
6	0.0000	0.0000	0.0000	0.0000	0.0000	0.0000	0.0001	0.0002	0.0003	0.0005
7	0.0000	0.0000	0.0000	0.0000	0.0000	0.0000	0.0000	0.0000	0.0000	0.0001

					λ					
X	1.1	1.2	1.3	1.4	1.5	1.6	1.7	1.8	1.9	2.0
0	0.3329	0.3012	0.2725	0.2466	0.2231	0.2019	0.1827	0.1653	0.1496	0.1353
1	0.3662	0.3614	0.3543	0.3452	0.3347	0.3230	0.3106	0.2975	0.2842	0.2707
2	0.2014	0.2169	0.2303	0.2417	0.2510	0.2584	0.2640	0.2678	0.2700	0.2707
3	0.0738	0.0867	0.0998	0.1128	0.1255	0.1378	0.1496	0.1607	0.1710	0.1804
4	0.0203	0.0260	0.0324	0.0395	0.0471	0.0551	0.0636	0.0723	0.0812	0.0902
5	0.0045	0.0062	0.0084	0.0111	0.0141	0.0176	0.0216	0.0260	0.0309	0.0361
6	0.0008	0.0012	0.0018	0.0026	0.0035	0.0047	0.0061	0.0078	0.0098	0.0120
7	0.0001	0.0002	0.0003	0.0005	0.0008	0.0011	0.0015	0.0020	0.0027	0.0034
8	0.0000	0.0000	0.0001	0.0001	0.0001	0.0002	0.0003	0.0005	0.0006	0.0009
9	0.0000	0.0000	0.0000	0.0000	0.0000	0.0000	0.0001	0.0001	0.0001	0.0002

					λ					
X	2.1	2.2	2.3	2.4	2.5	2.6	2.7	2.8	2.9	3.0
0	0.1225	0.1108	0.1003	0.0907	0.0821	0.0743	0.0672	0.0608	0.0550	0.0498
1	0.2572	0.2438	0.2306	0.2177	0.2052	0.1931	0.1815	0.1703	0.1596	0.1494
2	0.2700	0.2681	0.2652	0.2613	0.2565	0.2510	0.2450	0.2384	0.2314	0.2240
3	0.1890	0.1966	0.2033	0.2090	0.2138	0.2176	0.2205	0.2225	0.2237	0.2240
4	0.0992	0.1082	0.1169	0.1254	0.1336	0.1414	0.1488	0.1557	0.1622	0.1680
5	0.0417	0.0476	0.0538	0.0602	0.0668	0.0735	0.0804	0.0872	0.0940	0.1008
6	0.0146	0.0174	0.0206	0.0241	0.0278	0.0319	0.0362	0.0407	0.0455	0.0504
7	0.0044	0.0055	0.0068	0.0083	0.0099	0.0118	0.0139	0.0163	0.0188	0.0216
8	0.0011	0.0015	0.0019	0.0025	0.0031	0.0038	0.0047	0.0057	0.0068	0.0081
9	0.0003	0.0004	0.0005	0.0007	0.0009	0.0011	0.0014	0.0018	0.0022	0.0027
10	0.0001	0.0001	0.0001	0.0002	0.0002	0.0003	0.0004	0.0005	0.0006	0.0008
11	0.0000	0.0000	0.0000	0.0000	0.0000	0.0001	0.0001	0.0001	0.0002	0.0002
12	0.0000	0.0000	0.0000	0.0000	0.0000	0.0000	0.0000	0.0000	0.0000	0.0001

					λ					
X	3.1	3.2	3.3	3.4	3.5	3.6	3.7	3.8	3.9	4.0
0	0.0450	0.0408	0.0369	0.0334	0.0302	0.0273	0.0247	0.0224	0.0202	0.0183
1	0.1397	0.1340	0.1217	0.1135	0.1057	0.0984	0.0915	0.0850	0.0789	0.0733
2	0.2165	0.2087	0.2008	0.1929	0.1850	0.1771	0.1692	0.1615	0.1539	0.1465
3	0.2237	0.2226	0.2209	0.2186	0.2158	0.2125	0.2087	0.2046	0.2001	0.1954
4	0.1734	0.1781	0.1823	0.1858	0.1888	0.1912	0.1931	0.1944	0.1951	0.1954
5	0.1075	0.1140	0.1203	0.1264	0.1322	0.1377	0.1429	0.1477	0.1522	0.1563
6	0.0555	0.0608	0.0662	0.0716	0.0771	0.0826	0.0881	0.0936	0.0989	0.1042
7	0.0246	0.0278	0.0312	0.0348	0.0385	0.0425	0.0466	0.0508	0.0551	0.0595
8	0.0095	0.0111	0.0129	0.0148	0.0169	0.0191	0.0215	0.0241	0.0269	0.0298
9	0.0033	0.0040	0.0047	0.0056	0.0066	0.0076	0.0089	0.0102	0.0116	0.0132
10	0.0010	0.0013	0.0016	0.0019	0.0023	0.0028	0.0033	0.0039	0.0045	0.0053
11	0.0003	0.0004	0.0005	0.0006	0.0007	0.0009	0.0011	0.0013	0.0016	0.0019
12	0.0001	0.0001	0.0001	0.0002	0.0002	0.0003	0.0003	0.0004	0.0005	0.0006
13	0.0000	0.0000	0.0000	0.0000	0.0001	0.0001	0.0001	0.0001	0.0002	0.0002
14	0.0000	0.0000	0.0000	0.0000	0.0000	0.0000	0.0000	0.0000	0.0000	0.0001

continued

TABLE E.7

Table of Poisson
Probabilities
(*Continued*)

					λ					
X	4.1	4.2	4.3	4.4	4.5	4.6	4.7	4.8	4.9	5.0
0	0.0166	0.0150	0.0136	0.0123	0.0111	0.0101	0.0091	0.0082	0.0074	0.0067
1	0.0679	0.0630	0.0583	0.0540	0.0500	0.0462	0.0427	0.0395	0.0365	0.0337
2	0.1393	0.1323	0.1254	0.1188	0.1125	0.1063	0.1005	0.0948	0.0894	0.0842
3	0.1904	0.1852	0.1798	0.1743	0.1687	0.1631	0.1574	0.1517	0.1460	0.1404
4	0.1951	0.1944	0.1933	0.1917	0.1898	0.1875	0.1849	0.1820	0.1789	0.1755
5	0.1600	0.1633	0.1662	0.1687	0.1708	0.1725	0.1738	0.1747	0.1753	0.1755
6	0.1093	0.1143	0.1191	0.1237	0.1281	0.1323	0.1362	0.1398	0.1432	0.1462
7	0.0640	0.0686	0.0732	0.0778	0.0824	0.0869	0.0914	0.0959	0.1002	0.1044
8	0.0328	0.0360	0.0393	0.0428	0.0463	0.0500	0.0537	0.0575	0.0614	0.0653
9	0.0150	0.0168	0.0188	0.0209	0.0232	0.0255	0.0280	0.0307	0.0334	0.0363
10	0.0061	0.0071	0.0081	0.0092	0.0104	0.0118	0.0132	0.0147	0.0164	0.0181
11	0.0023	0.0027	0.0032	0.0037	0.0043	0.0049	0.0056	0.0064	0.0073	0.0082
12	0.0008	0.0009	0.0011	0.0014	0.0016	0.0019	0.0022	0.0026	0.0030	0.0034
13	0.0002	0.0003	0.0004	0.0005	0.0006	0.0007	0.0008	0.0009	0.0011	0.0013
14	0.0001	0.0001	0.0001	0.0001	0.0002	0.0002	0.0003	0.0003	0.0004	0.0005
15	0.0000	0.0000	0.0000	0.0000	0.0001	0.0001	0.0001	0.0001	0.0001	0.0002

					λ					
X	5.1	5.2	5.3	5.4	5.5	5.6	5.7	5.8	5.9	6.0
0	0.0061	0.0055	0.0050	0.0045	0.0041	0.0037	0.0033	0.0030	0.0027	0.0025
1	0.0311	0.0287	0.0265	0.0244	0.0225	0.0207	0.0191	0.0176	0.0162	0.0149
2	0.0793	0.0746	0.0701	0.0659	0.0618	0.0580	0.0544	0.0509	0.0477	0.0446
3	0.1348	0.1293	0.1239	0.1185	0.1133	0.1082	0.1033	0.0985	0.0938	0.0892
4	0.1719	0.1681	0.1641	0.1600	0.1558	0.1515	0.1472	0.1428	0.1383	0.1339
5	0.1753	0.1748	0.1740	0.1728	0.1714	0.1697	0.1678	0.1656	0.1632	0.1606
6	0.1490	0.1515	0.1537	0.1555	0.1571	0.1584	0.1594	0.1601	0.1605	0.1606
7	0.1086	0.1125	0.1163	0.1200	0.1234	0.1267	0.1298	0.1326	0.1353	0.1377
8	0.0692	0.0731	0.0771	0.0810	0.0849	0.0887	0.0925	0.0962	0.0998	0.1033
9	0.0392	0.0423	0.0454	0.0486	0.0519	0.0552	0.0586	0.0620	0.0654	0.0688
10	0.0200	0.0220	0.0241	0.0262	0.0285	0.0309	0.0334	0.0359	0.0386	0.0413
11	0.0093	0.0104	0.0116	0.0129	0.0143	0.0157	0.0173	0.0190	0.0207	0.0225
12	0.0039	0.0045	0.0051	0.0058	0.0065	0.0073	0.0082	0.0092	0.0102	0.0113
13	0.0015	0.0018	0.0021	0.0024	0.0028	0.0032	0.0036	0.0041	0.0046	0.0052
14	0.0006	0.0007	0.0008	0.0009	0.0011	0.0013	0.0015	0.0017	0.0019	0.0022
15	0.0002	0.0002	0.0003	0.0003	0.0004	0.0005	0.0006	0.0007	0.0008	0.0009
16	0.0001	0.0001	0.0001	0.0001	0.0001	0.0002	0.0002	0.0002	0.0003	0.0003
17	0.0000	0.0000	0.0000	0.0000	0.0000	0.0000	0.0001	0.0001	0.0001	0.0001

					λ					
X	6.1	6.2	6.3	6.4	6.5	6.6	6.7	6.8	6.9	7.0
0	0.0022	0.0020	0.0018	0.0017	0.0015	0.0014	0.0012	0.0011	0.0010	0.0009
1	0.0137	0.0126	0.0116	0.0106	0.0098	0.0090	0.0082	0.0076	0.0070	0.0064
2	0.0417	0.0390	0.0364	0.0340	0.0318	0.0296	0.0276	0.0258	0.0240	0.0223
3	0.0848	0.0806	0.0765	0.0726	0.0688	0.0652	0.0617	0.0584	0.0552	0.0521
4	0.1294	0.1249	0.1205	0.1162	0.1118	0.1076	0.1034	0.0992	0.0952	0.0912
5	0.1579	0.1549	0.1519	0.1487	0.1454	0.1420	0.1385	0.1349	0.1314	0.1277
6	0.1605	0.1601	0.1595	0.1586	0.1575	0.1562	0.1546	0.1529	0.1511	0.1490
7	0.1399	0.1418	0.1435	0.1450	0.1462	0.1472	0.1480	0.1486	0.1489	0.1490
8	0.1066	0.1099	0.1130	0.1160	0.1188	0.1215	0.1240	0.1263	0.1284	0.1304
9	0.0723	0.0757	0.0791	0.0825	0.0858	0.0891	0.0923	0.0954	0.0985	0.1014
10	0.0441	0.0469	0.0498	0.0528	0.0558	0.0588	0.0618	0.0649	0.0679	0.0710
11	0.0245	0.0265	0.0285	0.0307	0.0330	0.0353	0.0377	0.0401	0.0426	0.0452
12	0.0124	0.0137	0.0150	0.0164	0.0179	0.0194	0.0210	0.0277	0.0245	0.0264
13	0.0058	0.0065	0.0073	0.0081	0.0089	0.0098	0.0108	0.0119	0.0130	0.0142
14	0.0025	0.0029	0.0033	0.0037	0.0041	0.0046	0.0052	0.0058	0.0064	0.0071

continued

TABLE E.7

Table of Poisson Probabilities (*Continued*)

	λ									
X	6.1	6.2	6.3	6.4	6.5	6.6	6.7	6.8	6.9	7.0
15	0.0010	0.0012	0.0014	0.0016	0.0018	0.0020	0.0023	0.0026	0.0029	0.0033
16	0.0004	0.0005	0.0005	0.0006	0.0007	0.0008	0.0010	0.0011	0.0013	0.0014
17	0.0001	0.0002	0.0002	0.0002	0.0003	0.0003	0.0004	0.0004	0.0005	0.0006
18	0.0000	0.0001	0.0001	0.0001	0.0001	0.0001	0.0001	0.0002	0.0002	0.0002
19	0.0000	0.0000	0.0000	0.0000	0.0000	0.0000	0.0000	0.0001	0.0001	0.0001

	λ									
X	7.1	7.2	7.3	7.4	7.5	7.6	7.7	7.8	7.9	8.0
0	0.0008	0.0007	0.0007	0.0006	0.0006	0.0005	0.0005	0.0004	0.0004	0.0003
1	0.0059	0.0054	0.0049	0.0045	0.0041	0.0038	0.0035	0.0032	0.0029	0.0027
2	0.0208	0.0194	0.0180	0.0167	0.0156	0.0145	0.0134	0.0125	0.0116	0.0107
3	0.0492	0.0464	0.0438	0.0413	0.0389	0.0366	0.0345	0.0324	0.0305	0.0286
4	0.0874	0.0836	0.0799	0.0764	0.0729	0.0696	0.0663	0.0632	0.0602	0.0573
5	0.1241	0.1204	0.1167	0.1130	0.1094	0.1057	0.1021	0.0986	0.0951	0.0916
6	0.1468	0.1445	0.1420	0.1394	0.1367	0.1339	0.1311	0.1282	0.1252	0.1221
7	0.1489	0.1486	0.1481	0.1474	0.1465	0.1454	0.1442	0.1428	0.1413	0.1396
8	0.1321	0.1337	0.1351	0.1363	0.1373	0.1382	0.1388	0.1392	0.1395	0.1396
9	0.1042	0.1070	0.1096	0.1121	0.1144	0.1167	0.1187	0.1207	0.1224	0.1241
10	0.0740	0.0770	0.0800	0.0829	0.0858	0.0887	0.0914	0.0941	0.0967	0.0993
11	0.0478	0.0504	0.0531	0.0558	0.0585	0.0613	0.0640	0.0667	0.0695	0.0722
12	0.0283	0.0303	0.0323	0.0344	0.0366	0.0388	0.0411	0.0434	0.0457	0.0481
13	0.0154	0.0168	0.0181	0.0196	0.0211	0.0227	0.0243	0.0260	0.0278	0.0296
14	0.0078	0.0086	0.0095	0.0104	0.0113	0.0123	0.0134	0.0145	0.0157	0.0169
15	0.0037	0.0041	0.0046	0.0051	0.0057	0.0062	0.0069	0.0075	0.0083	0.0090
16	0.0016	0.0019	0.0021	0.0024	0.0026	0.0030	0.0033	0.0037	0.0041	0.0045
17	0.0007	0.0008	0.0009	0.0010	0.0012	0.0013	0.0015	0.0017	0.0019	0.0021
18	0.0003	0.0003	0.0004	0.0004	0.0005	0.0006	0.0006	0.0007	0.0008	0.0009
19	0.0001	0.0001	0.0001	0.0002	0.0002	0.0002	0.0003	0.0003	0.0003	0.0004
20	0.0000	0.0000	0.0001	0.0001	0.0001	0.0001	0.0001	0.0001	0.0001	0.0002
21	0.0000	0.0000	0.0000	0.0000	0.0000	0.0000	0.0000	0.0000	0.0001	0.0001

	λ									
X	8.1	8.2	8.3	8.4	8.5	8.6	8.7	8.8	8.9	9.0
0	0.0003	0.0003	0.0002	0.0002	0.0002	0.0002	0.0002	0.0002	0.0001	0.0001
1	0.0025	0.0023	0.0021	0.0019	0.0017	0.0016	0.0014	0.0013	0.0012	0.0011
2	0.0100	0.0092	0.0086	0.0079	0.0074	0.0068	0.0063	0.0058	0.0054	0.0050
3	0.0269	0.0252	0.0237	0.0222	0.0208	0.0195	0.0183	0.0171	0.0160	0.0150
4	0.0544	0.0517	0.0491	0.0466	0.0443	0.0420	0.0398	0.0377	0.0357	0.0337
5	0.0882	0.0849	0.0816	0.0784	0.0752	0.0722	0.0692	0.0663	0.0635	0.0607
6	0.1191	0.1160	0.1128	0.1097	0.1066	0.1034	0.1003	0.0972	0.0941	0.0911
7	0.1378	0.1358	0.1338	0.1317	0.1294	0.1271	0.1247	0.1222	0.1197	0.1171
8	0.1395	0.1392	0.1388	0.1382	0.1375	0.1366	0.1356	0.1344	0.1332	0.1318
9	0.1256	0.1269	0.1280	0.1290	0.1299	0.1306	0.1311	0.1315	0.1317	0.1318
10	0.1017	0.1040	0.1063	0.1084	0.1104	0.1123	0.1140	0.1157	0.1172	0.1186
11	0.0749	0.0776	0.0802	0.0828	0.0853	0.0878	0.0902	0.0925	0.0948	0.0970
12	0.0505	0.0530	0.0555	0.0579	0.0604	0.0629	0.0654	0.0679	0.0703	0.0728
13	0.0315	0.0334	0.0354	0.0374	0.0395	0.0416	0.0438	0.0459	0.0481	0.0504
14	0.0182	0.0196	0.0210	0.0225	0.0240	0.0256	0.0272	0.0289	0.0306	0.0324
15	0.0098	0.0107	0.0116	0.0126	0.0136	0.0147	0.0158	0.0169	0.0182	0.0194
16	0.0050	0.0055	0.0060	0.0066	0.0072	0.0079	0.0086	0.0093	0.0101	0.0109
17	0.0024	0.0026	0.0029	0.0033	0.0036	0.0040	0.0044	0.0048	0.0053	0.0058
18	0.0011	0.0012	0.0014	0.0015	0.0017	0.0019	0.0021	0.0024	0.0026	0.0029
19	0.0005	0.0005	0.0006	0.0007	0.0008	0.0009	0.0010	0.0011	0.0012	0.0014
20	0.0002	0.0002	0.0002	0.0003	0.0003	0.0004	0.0004	0.0005	0.0005	0.0006
21	0.0001	0.0001	0.0001	0.0001	0.0001	0.0002	0.0002	0.0002	0.0002	0.0003
22	0.0000	0.0000	0.0000	0.0000	0.0001	0.0001	0.0001	0.0001	0.0001	0.0001

continued

TABLE E.7

Table of Poisson
Probabilities
(*Continued*)

					λ					
X	9.1	9.2	9.3	9.4	9.5	9.6	9.7	9.8	9.9	10
0	0.0001	0.0001	0.0001	0.0001	0.0001	0.0001	0.0001	0.0001	0.0001	0.0000
1	0.0010	0.0009	0.0009	0.0008	0.0007	0.0007	0.0006	0.0005	0.0005	0.0005
2	0.0046	0.0043	0.0040	0.0037	0.0034	0.0031	0.0029	0.0027	0.0025	0.0023
3	0.0140	0.0131	0.0123	0.0115	0.0107	0.0100	0.0093	0.0087	0.0081	0.0076
4	0.0319	0.0302	0.0285	0.0269	0.0254	0.0240	0.0226	0.0213	0.0201	0.0189
5	0.0581	0.0555	0.0530	0.0506	0.0483	0.0460	0.0439	0.0418	0.0398	0.0378
6	0.0881	0.0851	0.0822	0.0793	0.0764	0.0736	0.0709	0.0682	0.0656	0.0631
7	0.1145	0.1118	0.1091	0.1064	0.1037	0.1010	0.0982	0.0955	0.0928	0.0901
8	0.1302	0.1286	0.1269	0.1251	0.1232	0.1212	0.1191	0.1170	0.1148	0.1126
9	0.1317	0.1315	0.1311	0.1306	0.1300	0.1293	0.1284	0.1274	0.1263	0.1251
10	0.1198	0.1210	0.1219	0.1228	0.1235	0.1241	0.1245	0.1249	0.1250	0.1251
11	0.0991	0.1012	0.1031	0.1049	0.1067	0.1083	0.1098	0.1112	0.1125	0.1137
12	0.0752	0.0776	0.0799	0.0822	0.0844	0.0866	0.0888	0.0908	0.0928	0.0948
13	0.0526	0.0549	0.0572	0.0594	0.0617	0.0640	0.0662	0.0685	0.0707	0.0729
14	0.0342	0.0361	0.0380	0.0399	0.0419	0.0439	0.0459	0.0479	0.0500	0.0521
15	0.0208	0.0221	0.0235	0.0250	0.0265	0.0281	0.0297	0.0313	0.0330	0.0347
16	0.0118	0.0127	0.0137	0.0147	0.0157	0.0168	0.0180	0.0192	0.0204	0.0217
17	0.0063	0.0069	0.0075	0.0081	0.0088	0.0095	0.0103	0.0111	0.0119	0.0128
18	0.0032	0.0035	0.0039	0.0042	0.0046	0.0051	0.0055	0.0060	0.0065	0.0071
19	0.0015	0.0017	0.0019	0.0021	0.0023	0.0026	0.0028	0.0031	0.0034	0.0037
20	0.0007	0.0008	0.0009	0.0010	0.0011	0.0012	0.0014	0.0015	0.0017	0.0019
21	0.0003	0.0003	0.0004	0.0004	0.0005	0.0006	0.0006	0.0007	0.0008	0.0009
22	0.0001	0.0001	0.0002	0.0002	0.0002	0.0002	0.0003	0.0003	0.0004	0.0004
23	0.0000	0.0001	0.0001	0.0001	0.0001	0.0001	0.0001	0.0001	0.0002	0.0002
24	0.0000	0.0000	0.0000	0.0000	0.0000	0.0000	0.0000	0.0001	0.0001	0.0001

X	λ = 20	*X*	λ = 20	*X*	λ = 20	*X*	λ = 20
0	0.0000	10	0.0058	20	0.0888	30	0.0083
1	0.0000	11	0.0106	21	0.0846	31	0.0054
2	0.0000	12	0.0176	22	0.0769	32	0.0034
3	0.0000	13	0.0271	23	0.0669	33	0.0020
4	0.0000	14	0.0387	24	0.0557	34	0.0012
5	0.0001	15	0.0516	25	0.0446	35	0.0007
6	0.0002	16	0.0646	26	0.0343	36	0.0004
7	0.0005	17	0.0760	27	0.0254	37	0.0002
8	0.0013	18	0.0844	28	0.0181	38	0.0001
9	0.0029	19	0.0888	29	0.0125	39	0.0001

TABLE E.8

Lower and Upper Critical Values, T_1, of Wilcoxon Rank Sum Test

n_2	One-tail	Two-tail	4	5	6	7	8	9	10
		α				n_1			
4	0.05	0.10	11,25						
	0.025	0.05	10,26						
	0.01	0.02	—,—						
	0.005	0.01	—,—						
5	0.05	0.10	12,28	19,36					
	0.025	0.05	11,29	17,38					
	0.01	0.02	10,30	16,39					
	0.005	0.01	—,—	15,40					
6	0.05	0.10	13,31	20,40	28,50				
	0.025	0.05	12,32	18,42	26,52				
	0.01	0.02	11,33	17,43	24,54				
	0.005	0.01	10,34	16,44	23,55				
7	0.05	0.10	14,34	21,44	29,55	39,66			
	0.025	0.05	13,35	20,45	27,57	36,69			
	0.01	0.02	11,37	18,47	25,59	34,71			
	0.005	0.01	10,38	16,49	24,60	32,73			
8	0.05	0.10	15,37	23,47	31,59	41,71	51,85		
	0.025	0.05	14,38	21,49	29,61	38,74	49,87		
	0.01	0.02	12,40	19,51	27,63	35,77	45,91		
	0.005	0.01	11,41	17,53	25,65	34,78	43,93		
9	0.05	0.10	16,40	24,51	33,63	43,76	54,90	66,105	
	0.025	0.05	14,42	22,53	31,65	40,79	51,93	62,109	
	0.01	0.02	13,43	20,55	28,68	37,82	47,97	59,112	
	0.005	0.01	11,45	18,57	26,70	35,84	45,99	56,115	
10	0.05	0.10	17,43	26,54	35,67	45,81	56,96	69,111	82,128
	0.025	0.05	15,45	23,57	32,70	42,84	53,99	65,115	78,132
	0.01	0.02	13,47	21,59	29,73	39,87	49,103	61,119	74,136
	0.005	0.01	12,48	19,61	27,75	37,89	47,105	58,122	71,139

Source: Adapted from Table 1 of F. Wilcoxon and R. A. Wilcox, *Some Rapid Approximate Statistical Procedures* (Pearl River, NY: Lederle Laboratories, 1964), with permission of the American Cyanamid Company.

TABLE E.9

Critical Values of the Studentized Range, Q

Upper 5% Points ($\alpha = 0.05$)

Numerator, df

Denominator, df	2	3	4	5	6	7	8	9	10	11	12	13	14	15	16	17	18	19	20
1	18.00	27.00	32.80	37.10	40.40	43.10	45.40	47.40	49.10	50.60	52.00	53.20	54.30	55.40	56.30	57.20	58.00	58.80	59.60
2	6.09	8.30	9.80	10.90	11.70	12.40	13.00	13.50	14.00	14.40	14.70	15.10	15.40	15.70	15.90	16.10	16.40	16.60	16.80
3	4.50	5.91	6.82	7.50	8.04	8.48	8.85	9.18	9.46	9.72	9.95	10.15	10.35	10.52	10.69	10.84	10.98	11.11	11.24
4	3.93	5.04	5.76	6.29	6.71	7.05	7.35	7.60	7.83	8.03	8.21	8.37	8.52	8.66	8.79	8.91	9.03	9.13	9.23
5	3.64	4.60	5.22	5.67	6.03	6.33	6.58	6.80	6.99	7.17	7.32	7.47	7.60	7.72	7.83	7.93	8.03	8.12	8.21
6	3.46	4.34	4.90	5.31	5.63	5.89	6.12	6.32	6.49	6.65	6.79	6.92	7.03	7.14	7.24	7.34	7.43	7.51	7.59
7	3.34	4.16	4.68	5.06	5.36	5.61	5.82	6.00	6.16	6.30	6.43	6.55	6.66	6.76	6.85	6.94	7.02	7.09	7.17
8	3.26	4.04	4.53	4.89	5.17	5.40	5.60	5.77	5.92	6.05	6.18	6.29	6.39	6.48	6.57	6.65	6.73	6.80	6.87
9	3.20	3.95	4.42	4.76	5.02	5.24	5.43	5.60	5.74	5.87	5.98	6.09	6.19	6.28	6.36	6.44	6.51	6.58	6.64
10	3.15	3.88	4.33	4.65	4.91	5.12	5.30	5.46	5.60	5.72	5.83	5.93	6.03	6.11	6.20	6.27	6.34	6.40	6.47
11	3.11	3.82	4.26	4.57	4.82	5.03	5.20	5.35	5.49	5.61	5.71	5.81	5.90	5.99	6.06	6.14	6.20	6.26	6.33
12	3.08	3.77	4.20	4.51	4.75	4.95	5.12	5.27	5.40	5.51	5.62	5.71	5.80	5.88	5.95	6.03	6.09	6.15	6.21
13	3.06	3.73	4.15	4.45	4.69	4.88	5.05	5.19	5.32	5.43	5.53	5.63	5.71	5.79	5.86	5.93	6.00	6.05	6.11
14	3.03	3.70	4.11	4.41	4.64	4.83	4.99	5.13	5.25	5.36	5.46	5.55	5.64	5.72	5.79	5.85	5.92	5.97	6.03
15	3.01	3.67	4.08	4.37	4.60	4.78	4.94	5.08	5.20	5.31	5.40	5.49	5.58	5.65	5.72	5.79	5.85	5.90	5.96
16	3.00	3.65	4.05	4.33	4.56	4.74	4.90	5.03	5.15	5.26	5.35	5.44	5.52	5.59	5.66	5.72	5.79	5.84	5.90
17	2.98	3.63	4.02	4.30	4.52	4.71	4.86	4.99	5.11	5.21	5.31	5.39	5.47	5.55	5.61	5.68	5.74	5.79	5.84
18	2.97	3.61	4.00	4.28	4.49	4.67	4.82	4.96	5.07	5.17	5.27	5.35	5.43	5.50	5.57	5.63	5.69	5.74	5.79
19	2.96	3.59	3.98	4.25	4.47	4.65	4.79	4.92	5.04	5.14	5.23	5.32	5.39	5.46	5.53	5.59	5.65	5.70	5.75
20	2.95	3.58	3.96	4.23	4.45	4.62	4.77	4.90	5.01	5.11	5.20	5.28	5.36	5.43	5.49	5.55	5.61	5.66	5.71
24	2.92	3.53	3.90	4.17	4.37	4.54	4.68	4.81	4.92	5.01	5.10	5.18	5.25	5.32	5.38	5.44	5.50	5.54	5.59
30	2.89	3.49	3.84	4.10	4.30	4.46	4.60	4.72	4.83	4.92	5.00	5.08	5.15	5.21	5.27	5.33	5.38	5.43	5.48
40	2.86	3.44	3.79	4.04	4.23	4.39	4.52	4.63	4.74	4.82	4.91	4.98	5.05	5.11	5.16	5.22	5.27	5.31	5.36
60	2.83	3.40	3.74	3.98	4.16	4.31	4.44	4.55	4.65	4.73	4.81	4.88	4.94	5.00	5.06	5.11	5.16	5.20	5.24
120	2.80	3.36	3.69	3.92	4.10	4.24	4.36	4.48	4.56	4.64	4.72	4.78	4.84	4.90	4.95	5.00	5.05	5.09	5.13
∞	2.77	3.31	3.63	3.86	4.03	4.17	4.29	4.39	4.47	4.55	4.62	4.68	4.74	4.80	4.85	4.89	4.93	4.97	5.01

continued

Upper 1% Points ($\alpha = 0.01$)

Denominator, df	Numerator, df																		
	2	3	4	5	6	7	8	9	10	11	12	13	14	15	16	17	18	19	20
1	90.00	135.00	164.00	186.00	202.00	216.00	227.00	237.00	246.00	253.00	260.00	266.00	272.00	277.00	282.00	286.00	290.00	294.00	298.00
2	14.00	19.00	22.30	24.70	26.60	28.20	29.50	30.70	31.70	32.60	33.40	34.10	34.80	35.40	36.00	36.50	37.00	37.50	37.90
3	8.26	10.60	12.20	13.30	14.20	15.00	15.60	16.20	16.70	17.10	17.50	17.90	18.20	18.50	18.80	19.10	19.30	19.50	19.80
4	6.51	8.12	9.17	9.96	10.60	11.10	11.50	11.90	12.30	12.60	12.80	13.10	13.30	13.50	13.70	13.90	14.10	14.20	14.40
5	5.70	6.97	7.80	8.42	8.91	9.32	9.67	9.97	10.24	10.48	10.70	10.89	11.08	11.24	11.40	11.55	11.68	11.81	11.93
6	5.24	6.33	7.03	7.56	7.97	8.32	8.61	8.87	9.10	9.30	9.49	9.65	9.81	9.95	10.08	10.21	10.32	10.43	10.54
7	4.95	5.92	6.54	7.01	7.37	7.68	7.94	8.17	8.37	8.55	8.71	8.86	9.00	9.12	9.24	9.35	9.46	9.55	9.65
8	4.74	5.63	6.20	6.63	6.96	7.24	7.47	7.68	7.87	8.03	8.18	8.31	8.44	8.55	8.66	8.76	8.85	8.94	9.03
9	4.60	5.43	5.96	6.35	6.66	6.91	7.13	7.32	7.49	7.65	7.78	7.91	8.03	8.13	8.23	8.32	8.41	8.49	8.57
10	4.48	5.27	5.77	6.14	6.43	6.67	6.87	7.05	7.21	7.36	7.48	7.60	7.71	7.81	7.91	7.99	8.07	8.15	8.22
11	4.39	5.14	5.62	5.97	6.26	6.48	6.67	6.84	6.99	7.13	7.25	7.36	7.46	7.56	7.65	7.73	7.81	7.88	7.95
12	4.32	5.04	5.50	5.84	6.10	6.32	6.51	6.67	6.81	6.94	7.06	7.17	7.26	7.36	7.44	7.52	7.59	7.66	7.73
13	4.26	4.96	5.40	5.73	5.98	6.19	6.37	6.53	6.67	6.79	6.90	7.01	7.10	7.19	7.27	7.34	7.42	7.48	7.55
14	4.21	4.89	5.32	5.63	5.88	6.08	6.26	6.41	6.54	6.66	6.77	6.87	6.96	7.05	7.12	7.20	7.27	7.33	7.39
15	4.17	4.83	5.25	5.56	5.80	5.99	6.16	6.31	6.44	6.55	6.66	6.76	6.84	6.93	7.00	7.07	7.14	7.20	7.26
16	4.13	4.78	5.19	5.49	5.72	5.92	6.08	6.22	6.35	6.46	6.56	6.66	6.74	6.82	6.90	6.97	7.03	7.09	7.15
17	4.10	4.74	5.14	5.43	5.66	5.85	6.01	6.15	6.27	6.38	6.48	6.57	6.66	6.73	6.80	6.87	6.94	7.00	7.05
18	4.07	4.70	5.09	5.38	5.60	5.79	5.94	6.08	6.20	6.31	6.41	6.50	6.58	6.65	6.72	6.79	6.85	6.91	6.96
19	4.05	4.67	5.05	5.33	5.55	5.73	5.89	6.02	6.14	6.25	6.34	6.43	6.51	6.58	6.65	6.72	6.78	6.84	6.89
20	4.02	4.64	5.02	5.29	5.51	5.69	5.84	5.97	6.09	6.19	6.29	6.37	6.45	6.52	6.59	6.65	6.71	6.76	6.82
24	3.96	4.54	4.91	5.17	5.37	5.54	5.69	5.81	5.92	6.02	6.11	6.19	6.26	6.33	6.39	6.45	6.51	6.56	6.61
30	3.89	4.45	4.80	5.05	5.24	5.40	5.54	5.65	5.76	5.85	5.93	6.01	6.08	6.14	6.20	6.26	6.31	6.36	6.41
40	3.82	4.37	4.70	4.93	5.11	5.27	5.39	5.50	5.60	5.69	5.77	5.84	5.90	5.96	6.02	6.07	6.12	6.17	6.21
60	3.76	4.28	4.60	4.82	4.99	5.13	5.25	5.36	5.45	5.53	5.60	5.67	5.73	5.79	5.84	5.89	5.93	5.98	6.02
120	3.70	4.20	4.50	4.71	4.87	5.01	5.12	5.21	5.30	5.38	5.44	5.51	5.56	5.61	5.66	5.71	5.75	5.79	5.83
∞	3.64	4.12	4.40	4.60	4.76	4.88	4.99	5.08	5.16	5.23	5.29	5.35	5.40	5.45	5.49	5.54	5.57	5.61	5.65

Source: Reprinted from E. S. Pearson and H. O. Hartley, eds., Table 29 of *Biometrika Tables for Statisticians, Vol. 1*, 3rd ed., 1966, by permission of the *Biometrika* Trustees, London.

TABLE E.10

Critical Values d_L and d_U of the Durbin-Watson Statistic, D (Critical Values Are One Sided)[a]

	α = 0.05										α = 0.01									
	k = 1		k = 2		k = 3		k = 4		k = 5		k = 1		k = 2		k = 3		k = 4		k = 5	
n	d_L	d_U	d_L	d_U	d_L	d_U	d_L	d_U	d_L	d_U	d_L	d_U	d_L	d_U	d_L	d_U	d_L	d_U	d_L	d_U
15	1.08	1.36	.95	1.54	.82	1.75	.69	1.97	.56	2.21	.81	1.07	.70	1.25	.59	1.46	.49	1.70	.39	1.96
16	1.10	1.37	.98	1.54	.86	1.73	.74	1.93	.62	2.15	.84	1.09	.74	1.25	.63	1.44	.53	1.66	.44	1.90
17	1.13	1.38	1.02	1.54	.90	1.71	.78	1.90	.67	2.10	.87	1.10	.77	1.25	.67	1.43	.57	1.63	.48	1.85
18	1.16	1.39	1.05	1.53	.93	1.69	.82	1.87	.71	2.06	.90	1.12	.80	1.26	.71	1.42	.61	1.60	.52	1.80
19	1.18	1.40	1.08	1.53	.97	1.68	.86	1.85	.75	2.02	.93	1.13	.83	1.26	.74	1.41	.65	1.58	.56	1.77
20	1.20	1.41	1.10	1.54	1.00	1.68	.90	1.83	.79	1.99	.95	1.15	.86	1.27	.77	1.41	.68	1.57	.60	1.74
21	1.22	1.42	1.13	1.54	1.03	1.67	.93	1.81	.83	1.96	.97	1.16	.89	1.27	.80	1.41	.72	1.55	.63	1.71
22	1.24	1.43	1.15	1.54	1.05	1.66	.96	1.80	.86	1.94	1.00	1.17	.91	1.28	.83	1.40	.75	1.54	.66	1.69
23	1.26	1.44	1.17	1.54	1.08	1.66	.99	1.79	.90	1.92	1.02	1.19	.94	1.29	.86	1.40	.77	1.53	.70	1.67
24	1.27	1.45	1.19	1.55	1.10	1.66	1.01	1.78	.93	1.90	1.04	1.20	.96	1.30	.88	1.41	.80	1.53	.72	1.66
25	1.29	1.45	1.21	1.55	1.12	1.66	1.04	1.77	.95	1.89	1.05	1.21	.98	1.30	.90	1.41	.83	1.52	.75	1.65
26	1.30	1.46	1.22	1.55	1.14	1.65	1.06	1.76	.98	1.88	1.07	1.22	1.00	1.31	.93	1.41	.85	1.52	.78	1.64
27	1.32	1.47	1.24	1.56	1.16	1.65	1.08	1.76	1.01	1.86	1.09	1.23	1.02	1.32	.95	1.41	.88	1.51	.81	1.63
28	1.33	1.48	1.26	1.56	1.18	1.65	1.10	1.75	1.03	1.85	1.10	1.24	1.04	1.32	.97	1.41	.90	1.51	.83	1.62
29	1.34	1.48	1.27	1.56	1.20	1.65	1.12	1.74	1.05	1.84	1.12	1.25	1.05	1.33	.99	1.42	.92	1.51	.85	1.61
30	1.35	1.49	1.28	1.57	1.21	1.65	1.14	1.74	1.07	1.83	1.13	1.26	1.07	1.34	1.01	1.42	.94	1.51	.88	1.61
31	1.36	1.50	1.30	1.57	1.23	1.65	1.16	1.74	1.09	1.83	1.15	1.27	1.08	1.34	1.02	1.42	.96	1.51	.90	1.60
32	1.37	1.50	1.31	1.57	1.24	1.65	1.18	1.73	1.11	1.82	1.16	1.28	1.10	1.35	1.04	1.43	.98	1.51	.92	1.60
33	1.38	1.51	1.32	1.58	1.26	1.65	1.19	1.73	1.13	1.81	1.17	1.29	1.11	1.36	1.05	1.43	1.00	1.51	.94	1.59
34	1.39	1.51	1.33	1.58	1.27	1.65	1.21	1.73	1.15	1.81	1.18	1.30	1.13	1.36	1.07	1.43	1.01	1.51	.95	1.59
35	1.40	1.52	1.34	1.58	1.28	1.65	1.22	1.73	1.16	1.80	1.19	1.31	1.14	1.37	1.08	1.44	1.03	1.51	.97	1.59
36	1.41	1.52	1.35	1.59	1.29	1.65	1.24	1.73	1.18	1.80	1.21	1.32	1.15	1.38	1.10	1.44	1.04	1.51	.99	1.59
37	1.42	1.53	1.36	1.59	1.31	1.66	1.25	1.72	1.19	1.80	1.22	1.32	1.16	1.38	1.11	1.45	1.06	1.51	1.00	1.59
38	1.43	1.54	1.37	1.59	1.32	1.66	1.26	1.72	1.21	1.79	1.23	1.33	1.18	1.39	1.12	1.45	1.07	1.52	1.02	1.58
39	1.43	1.54	1.38	1.60	1.33	1.66	1.27	1.72	1.22	1.79	1.24	1.34	1.19	1.39	1.14	1.45	1.09	1.52	1.03	1.58
40	1.44	1.54	1.39	1.60	1.34	1.66	1.29	1.72	1.23	1.79	1.25	1.34	1.20	1.40	1.15	1.46	1.10	1.52	1.05	1.58
45	1.48	1.57	1.43	1.62	1.38	1.67	1.34	1.72	1.29	1.78	1.29	1.38	1.24	1.42	1.20	1.48	1.16	1.53	1.11	1.58
50	1.50	1.59	1.46	1.63	1.42	1.67	1.38	1.72	1.34	1.77	1.32	1.40	1.28	1.45	1.24	1.49	1.20	1.54	1.16	1.59
55	1.53	1.60	1.49	1.64	1.45	1.68	1.41	1.72	1.38	1.77	1.36	1.43	1.32	1.47	1.28	1.51	1.25	1.55	1.21	1.59
60	1.55	1.62	1.51	1.65	1.48	1.69	1.44	1.73	1.41	1.77	1.38	1.45	1.35	1.48	1.32	1.52	1.28	1.56	1.25	1.60
65	1.57	1.63	1.54	1.66	1.50	1.70	1.47	1.73	1.44	1.77	1.41	1.47	1.38	1.50	1.35	1.53	1.31	1.57	1.28	1.61
70	1.58	1.64	1.55	1.67	1.52	1.70	1.49	1.74	1.46	1.77	1.43	1.49	1.40	1.52	1.37	1.55	1.34	1.58	1.31	1.61
75	1.60	1.65	1.57	1.68	1.54	1.71	1.51	1.74	1.49	1.77	1.45	1.50	1.42	1.53	1.39	1.56	1.37	1.59	1.34	1.62
80	1.61	1.66	1.59	1.69	1.56	1.72	1.53	1.74	1.51	1.77	1.47	1.52	1.44	1.54	1.42	1.57	1.39	1.60	1.36	1.62
85	1.62	1.67	1.60	1.70	1.57	1.72	1.55	1.75	1.52	1.77	1.48	1.53	1.46	1.55	1.43	1.58	1.41	1.60	1.39	1.63
90	1.63	1.68	1.61	1.70	1.59	1.73	1.57	1.75	1.54	1.78	1.50	1.54	1.47	1.56	1.45	1.59	1.43	1.61	1.41	1.64
95	1.64	1.69	1.62	1.71	1.60	1.73	1.58	1.75	1.56	1.78	1.51	1.55	1.49	1.57	1.47	1.60	1.45	1.62	1.42	1.64
100	1.65	1.69	1.63	1.72	1.61	1.74	1.59	1.76	1.57	1.78	1.52	1.56	1.50	1.58	1.48	1.60	1.46	1.63	1.44	1.65

[a] n = number of observations; k = number of independent variables.

Source: This table is reproduced from Biometrika, 41 (1951): pp. 173 and 175, with the permission of the Biometrika Trustees.

TABLE E.11
Control Chart Factors

Number of Observations in Sample	d_2	d_3	D_3	D_4	A_2
2	1.128	0.853	0	3.267	1.880
3	1.693	0.888	0	2.575	1.023
4	2.059	0.880	0	2.282	0.729
5	2.326	0.864	0	2.114	0.577
6	2.534	0.848	0	2.004	0.483
7	2.704	0.833	0.076	1.924	0.419
8	2.847	0.820	0.136	1.864	0.373
9	2.970	0.808	0.184	1.816	0.337
10	3.078	0.797	0.223	1.777	0.308
11	3.173	0.787	0.256	1.744	0.285
12	3.258	0.778	0.283	1.717	0.266
13	3.336	0.770	0.307	1.693	0.249
14	3.407	0.763	0.328	1.672	0.235
15	3.472	0.756	0.347	1.653	0.223
16	3.532	0.750	0.363	1.637	0.212
17	3.588	0.744	0.378	1.622	0.203
18	3.640	0.739	0.391	1.609	0.194
19	3.689	0.733	0.404	1.596	0.187
20	3.735	0.729	0.415	1.585	0.180
21	3.778	0.724	0.425	1.575	0.173
22	3.819	0.720	0.435	1.565	0.167
23	3.858	0.716	0.443	1.557	0.162
24	3.895	0.712	0.452	1.548	0.157
25	3.931	0.708	0.459	1.541	0.153

Source: Reprinted from ASTM-STP 15D by kind permission of the American Society for Testing and Materials.

F. MICROSOFT EXCEL AND PHSTAT2 FAQS

Use this appendix to find answers to the most frequently asked questions about using the resources on the Student CD-ROM and using Microsoft Excel and PHStat2.

F.1 STUDENT CD-ROM FAQS

What textbook materials will I find on the Student CD-ROM?

You will find the Excel workbooks (as .xls files) used in examples or named in problems, the CD-ROM sections (as .PDF files), several Excel add-in workbooks (as .xla files), and programs that set up and install the Adobe Reader and PHStat2 programs on Windows PCs.

Does the Student CD-ROM contain Microsoft Excel?

No, the Student CD-ROM does not contain Microsoft Excel. If your computer did not come with Microsoft Excel or Office, you can acquire a copy of Microsoft Office and install Excel on your computer.

Can I copy the Excel workbook files to my local hard disk or other storage device?

Yes, you can, and you are encouraged to do so. If you open and use a workbook file directly from the Student CD-ROM, Microsoft Excel labels that file as being a "read-only" file and will force you to save the file under a different name if you make changes to the file.

F.2 GENERAL COMPUTING FAQS

My computer came with Microsoft Works. Can I use that program instead of using Microsoft Excel?

No, the spreadsheet component of Microsoft Works does not contain the functionality of Microsoft Excel and cannot be used with this text.

Do I need the latest version of Microsoft Excel in order to use this book?

No, you can use this book with all Excel versions supported by Microsoft. This includes (as of the date of the printing of this book) Excel 97, Excel 2000, Excel 2002 (sometimes identified as Excel XP), Excel 2003, and Excel 2007.

How can I determine which version of Microsoft Excel is installed on my computer?

Open Microsoft Excel. If your Excel window looks like Figure E1.2 on page 20, you have Excel 2007. Otherwise, select **Help → About Microsoft Excel**. In the dialog box

that appears, the first line states the version number and build number as well as the names of the service release (SR) or service pack (SP) updates that have been applied.

Should I update my copy of Excel using the security updates available on the Microsoft Web site?

Absolutely yes! You should visit the Microsoft Office Web site and apply any updates that are available for your version of Excel before you begin using this book. Then, you should periodically revisit the Web site to check for new updates that may have been added since your last visit.

Can I use an Apple Mac running Mac OS on which Microsoft Excel has been installed with the Excel data files on the Student CD-ROM?

Yes, you can. However, you will *not* be able to use PHStat2, which is designed for Microsoft Windows. (There is no Mac version of PHStat2 available.)

F.3 MICROSOFT EXCEL FAQS

Will I need access to my original Microsoft Office/Excel CDs or DVD?

Yes, you may need to use the original program discs if the Analysis ToolPak (referred to as the "ToolPak" in this book) has not been installed on your system.

How can I tell if the ToolPak has been installed? What Microsoft Office security settings should I use? How do I change Office security settings?

The answers to these related questions are discussed as part of Section E1.6, "Add-ins: Making Things Easier for You," which begins on page 28.

Are there any special procedures for using the Visual Explorations add-in workbook (Visual Explorations.xla)?

No, you can open and immediately use this workbook, provided that you have adjusted your Office security settings using the Section E1.6 instructions. With the wrong security settings in effect, Visual Explorations (and PHStat2, also) will not open in Excel.

In Excel 97–2003, how can I turn toolbars such as the Standard and Formatting toolbars shown in Figure E1.1 on page 19, on and off?

Select **View → Toolbars** and select the toolbars you want displayed.

For Excel 2007, how can I configure the Excel window to look similar to Figure E1.2 on page 20?

Right-click the title bar of the Excel 2007 window and on the shortcut menu that appears, uncheck, if checked, **Minimize the Ribbon**. You can also review this setting by clicking the drop-down arrow to the immediate right of the Quick Access toolbar.

For Excel 97–2003, how can I specify the custom settings that you recommend?

First select **Tools → Customize**. In the Customize dialog box, clear (uncheck) the **Menus show recently used commands first** check box if it is checked and click the **Close** button. Then select **Tools → Options**. In the Options dialog box, click the **Calculation** tab and verify that the **Automatic** option button of the Calculation group has been selected. Click the **Edit** tab and verify that all check boxes *except* the **Fixed decimal, Provide feedback with Animation**, and **Enable automatic percent entry** have been selected. (Excel 97 does not contain an Automatic percent entry check box.) Click the **General** tab and verify that the **R1C1 reference style** check box is cleared (that is, unchecked) and, if using Excel 97, check the **Macro virus protection** check box. Enter **3** as the number of **Sheets in new workbook**, select **Arial** from the **Standard font** list box, and select **10** from the **Size** drop-down list box. Click **OK** to finish the customization.

For Excel 2007, how can I specify the custom settings that you recommend?

First, click **Office Button** and then click **Excel Options**. In the left panel of Excel Options, click **Formulas**. In the Formulas right pane, click **Automatic** under **Workbook Calculation** and verify that all check boxes are checked except **Enable iterative calculation, R1C1 reference style**, and **Formulas referring to cells**. Click **OK** to finish the customization.

F.4 PHSTAT2 FAQS

What is PHStat2?

PHStat2 is software that makes operating Microsoft Excel as distraction free as possible. As a student studying statistics, you can focus mainly on learning statistics and not worry about having to fully master Excel first. When PHStat2 is combined with the Analysis ToolPak add-in, just about all statistical methods taught in an introductory statistics course can be illustrated using Microsoft Excel.

I do not want to use an add-in that will not be available in my business environment. Any comments?

Chapter 1 talks about these issues in detail. To summarize those pages, PHStat2 helps you learn Microsoft Excel, and using PHStat2 will not leave you any less equipped to work with Microsoft Excel in a setting where it is not available.

What do I need to do in order to begin using PHStat2?

You need to run the PHStat2 setup program (setup.exe) that is on the Student CD-ROM. If you are using Windows 2000, Windows XP, or Windows Vista, you must have logged in to Windows using an account that has administrator or software-installing privileges. (Student and faculty accounts to log in to networked computers in academic settings typically do not have this privilege. If you have such an account, ask your network or lab technician for assistance.)

What are the technical requirements for setting up and adding PHStat2 to my system?

If your system can run Microsoft Excel, it can also run PHStat2. You need approximately 10 MB hard disk free space during the setup process and up to 3 MB hard disk space after program setup.

Are updates to PHStat2 available?

Yes, minor updates to resolve issues as they are identified are available for free download from the PHStat2 Web site (**www.prenhall.com/phstat**). When you visit that Web site, link to the page that applies to your version of PHStat2 (the Student CD-ROM contains Version 2.7).

How can I identify which version of PHStat2 I have?

Open Microsoft Excel with PHStat2 and select **Help for PHStat** from the PHStat menu. A dialog box will display your current XLA and DLL version numbers. The XLA version number identifies the version of PHStat2 you have.

Where can I get help setting up PHStat2?

First, carefully review the Student CD-ROM readme file for PHStat2. If your problem is unresolved, visit the PHStat2 Web site for further information. If your problem is still unresolved, contact Pearson Education technical support by following the appropriate link on the PHStat2 Web site.

F.5 EXCEL 2007 ISSUES FAQS

I do not see the menu for an add-in workbook that I opened, where is it?

Unlike earlier versions of Excel that allowed add-ins to add menus to the menu bar, Excel 2007 places all add-in menus under the Add-ins tab. If you click Add-ins, you find the menus of all properly loaded add-ins.

What does "Compatibility Mode" mean?

When you see "Compatibility Mode" in the title bar, Excel 2007 is telling you that you are using a workbook compatible with earlier Excel versions. When you save such a workbook, Excel 2007 will automatically use the .xls file format of earlier versions.

How can I update an older workbook to the Excel 2007 .xlsx format?

The simplest way is to open the workbook file and click **Office Button → Convert**. Then save your file (click **Office Button → Save**).

You can also open the workbook file and click **Office Button → Save As** and select **Excel Workbook** (*.xlsx) from the **Save as type** list in the Save As dialog box.

Self-Test Solutions and Answers to Selected Even-Numbered Problems

The following represent worked-out solutions to Self-Test Problems and brief answers to most of the even-numbered problems in the text. For more detailed solutions, including explanations, interpretations, and Excel output, see the *Student Solutions Manual*.

CHAPTER 1

1.2 Small, medium, and large sizes imply order but do not specify how much more soft drink is added at increasing levels.

1.4 (a) The number of telephones is a numerical variable that is discrete because the variable is counted. It is ratio scaled because it has a true zero point. **(b)** The length of the longest long-distance call is a numerical variable that is continuous because any value within a range of values can occur. It is ratio scaled because it has a true zero point. **(c)** Whether there is a cell phone in the household is a categorical variable because the answer can be only yes or no. This also makes it a nominal-scaled variable. **(d)** Same answer as in (c).

1.6 (a) Categorical, nominal scale. **(b)** Numerical, continuous, ratio scale. **(c)** Numerical, discrete, ratio scale. **(d)** Numerical, discrete, ratio scale.

1.8 (a) Numerical, continuous, ratio scale. **(b)** Numerical, discrete, ratio scale. **(c)** Numerical, continuous, ratio scale. **(d)** Categorical, nominal scale.

1.10 The underlying variable, ability of the students, may be continuous, but the measuring device, the test, does not have enough precision to distinguish between the two students.

1.24 (a) A primary data source collected through a survey was used in this study. **(b)** Deciding what to make for dinner at home at the last minute. **(c)** The amount of time to prepare dinner.

1.26 (a) Cat owner households in the United States. **(b)** 1. Categorical. 2. Categorical. 3. Numerical, discrete. 4. Categorical.

CHAPTER 2

2.4 (b) The Pareto diagram is best for portraying these data because it not only sorts the frequencies in descending order, it also provides the cumulative polygon on the same scale. **(c)** You can conclude that "labor" and "lost business/revenue" make up about half of the costs.

2.6 (b) 88%. **(d)** The Pareto diagram allows you to see which sources account for most of the electricity.

2.8 (b) The bar chart is more suitable if the purpose is to compare the categories. The pie chart is more suitable if the main objective is to investigate the portion of the whole that is in a particular category.

2.10 (b) Rooms dirty, rooms not stocked, and rooms need maintenance have the largest number of complaints, so focusing on these categories can reduce the number of complaints the most.

2.12 Stem-and-leaf display of finance scores:

```
5 | 34
6 | 9
7 | 4
8 | 0
9 | 38
  | n = 7
```

2.14 50 74 74 76 81 89 92

2.16 (a) Ordered array:

$15 $15 $18 $18 $20 $20 $20 $20 $20 $21 $22 $22
$25 $25 $25 $25 $25 $26 $28 $29 $30 $30 $30

(b) Stem-and-leaf display:

```
1 | 5 5 8 8
2 | 0 0 0 0 1 2 2 5 5 5 5 5 6 8 9
3 | 0 0 0
```

(c) The stem-and-leaf display provides more information because it not only orders values from the smallest to the largest into stems and leaves, it also conveys information on how the values distribute and cluster in the data set. **(d)** The bounced check fees seem to be concentrated around $20 and $25 because there are five occurences of each of the two values in the sample of 23 banks.

2.18 (a) Ordered array:

4 5 7 8 16 19 19 20 20 23 24 25 29 29 30 30 30 30 40 56

(b) Stem-and-leaf display for fat stem, 10 unit:

```
0 | 4 5 7 8
1 | 6 9 9
2 | 0 0 3 4 5 9 9
3 | 0 0 0 0
4 | 0
5 | 6
```

(c) The stem-and-leaf display conveys more information than the ordered array. You can also obtain a sense of the distribution of the data from the stem-and-leaf display.

2.20 (a) 10 but less than 20, 20 but less than 30, 30 but less than 40, 40 but less than 50, 50 but less than 60, 60 but less than 70, 70 but less than 80, 80 but less than 90, 90 but less than 100. **(b)** 10. **(c)** 15, 25, 35, 45, 55, 65, 75, 85, 95.

2.22 (a)

Electricity Costs	Frequency	Percentage
$80 up to $100	4	8%
$100 up to $120	7	14
$120 up to $140	9	18
$140 up to $160	13	26
$160 up to $180	9	18
$180 up to $200	5	10
$200 up to $220	3	6

(c)

Electricity Costs	Frequency	Percentage	Cumulative %
$ 99	4	8.00%	8.00%
$119	7	14.00	22.00
$139	9	18.00	40.00
$159	13	26.00	66.00
$179	9	18.00	84.00
$199	5	10.00	94.00
$219	3	6.00	100.00

(d) The majority of utility charges are clustered between $120 and $180.

2.24 (a)

Width	Frequency	Percentage
8.310–8.329	3	6.12%
8.330–8.349	2	4.08
8.350–8.369	1	2.04
8.370–8.389	4	8.16
8.390–8.409	5	10.20
8.410–8.429	16	31.65
8.430–8.449	5	10.20
8.450–8.469	5	10.20
8.470–8.489	6	12.24
8.490–8.509	2	4.08

(d) All the troughs will meet the company's requirements of between 8.31 and 8.61 inches wide.

2.26 (a)

Bulb Life (hrs)	Percentage, Mfgr A	Percentage, Mfgr B
650–749	7.5%	0.0%
750–849	12.5	5.0
850–949	50.0	20.0
950–1049	22.5	40.0
1050–1149	7.5	22.5
1150–1249	0.0	12.5

(c)

Bulb Life (hrs)	Percentage Less Than, Mfgr A	Percentage Less Than, Mfgr B
650–749	7.5%	0.0%
750–849	20.0	5.0
850–949	70.0	25.0
950–1049	92.5	65.0
1050–1149	100.0	87.5
1150–1249	100.0	100.0

(d) Manufacturer B produces bulbs with longer lives than Manufacturer A. The cumulative percentage for Manufacturer B shows 65% of its bulbs lasted less than 1,050 hours, contrasted with 70% of Manufacturer A's bulbs, which lasted less than 950 hours. None of Manufacturer A's bulbs lasted more than 1,149 hours, but 12.5% of Manufacturer B's bulbs lasted between 1,150 and 1,249 hours. At the same time, 7.5% of Manufacturer A's bulbs lasted less than 750 hours, while all of Manufacturer B's bulbs lasted at least 750 hours.

2.28 (a) Table of frequencies for all student responses:

GENDER	STUDENT MAJOR CATEGORIES			
	A	C	M	Totals
Male	14	9	2	25
Female	6	6	3	15
Totals	20	15	5	40

(b) Table of percentages based on overall student responses:

GENDER	STUDENT MAJOR CATEGORIES			
	A	C	M	Totals
Male	35.0%	22.5%	5.0%	62.5%
Female	15.0	15.0	7.5	37.5
Totals	50.0	37.5	12.5	100.0

(c) Table based on row percentages:

GENDER	STUDENT MAJOR CATEGORIES			
	A	C	M	Totals
Male	56.0%	36.0%	8.0%	100.0%
Female	40.0	40.0	20.0	100.0
Totals	50.0	37.5	12.5	100.0

(d) Table based on column percentages:

GENDER	STUDENT MAJOR CATEGORIES			
	A	C	M	Totals
Male	70.0%	60.0%	40.0%	62.5%
Female	30.0	40.0	60.0	37.5
Totals	100.0	100.0	100.0	100.0

2.30 (a) Contingency table:

QUALITY	CONDITION OF DIE		
	No Particles	Particles	Totals
Good	320	14	334
Bad	80	36	116
Totals	400	50	450

Table of total percentages:

QUALITY	CONDITION OF DIE		
	No Particles	Particles	Totals
Good	71%	3%	74%
Bad	18	8	26
Totals	89	11	100

Table of row percentages:

QUALITY	CONDITION OF DIE		
	No Particles	Particles	Totals
Good	96%	4%	100%
Bad	69	31	100
Totals	89	11	100

Table of column percentages:

	CONDITION OF DIE		
QUALITY	No Particles	Particles	Totals
Good	80%	28%	74%
Bad	20	72	26
Totals	100	100	100

(c) The data suggest that there is some association between condition of the die and the quality of wafer because more good wafers are produced when no particles are found in the die, and more bad wafers are produced when there are particles found in the die.

2.32 (a) Table of row percentages:

	GENDER		
ENJOY SHOPPING FOR CLOTHING	Male	Female	Total
Yes	38%	62%	100%
No	74	26	100
Total	48	52	100

Table of column percentages:

	GENDER		
ENJOY SHOPPING FOR CLOTHING	Male	Female	Total
Yes	57%	86%	72%
No	43	14	28
Total	100	100	100

Table of total percentages:

	GENDER		
ENJOY SHOPPING FOR CLOTHING	Male	Female	Total
Yes	27%	45%	72%
No	21	7	28
Total	48	52	100

(c) The percentage that enjoys shopping for clothing is higher among females than among males.

2.34 (b) The number of MBA and undergraduate students who choose the lowest-cost fund and the second-lowest-cost fund is about the same. More MBA students chose the third-lowest cost fund while more undergraduate students chose the highest cost fund.

2.36 (b) Yes, there is a strong positive relationship between X and Y. As X increases, so does Y.

2.38 (b) There is a positive relationship between owner mileage and current government standard mileage.

2.40 (b) There appears to be a positive relationship between the coach's salary and revenue. **(c)** Yes, this is borne out by the data.

2.42 (b) The unemployment rate appeared to be trending upward from January 2001 to around January 2002. It stayed at around 6% until October 2003 and then trended downward until December 2005.

2.44 (b) The average price of prescription drugs has been rising since 2000. **(c)** The predicted average price for 2005 was around $70.

2.62 (c) The publisher gets the largest portion (64.8%) of the revenue. About half (32.2%) of the revenue received by the publisher covers manufacturing costs. The publisher's marketing and promotion account for the next largest share of the revenue, at 15.4%. Author, bookstore employee salaries and benefits, and publisher administrative costs and taxes each accounts for around 10% of the revenue, while the publisher after-tax profit, bookstore operations, bookstore pretax profit, and freight constitute the "trivial few" allocations of the revenue. Yes, the bookstore gets twice the revenue of the authors.

2.64 (b) In 2005, the United States relied on petroleum heavily, followed by coal and natural gas as major sources of energy, while renewable fuels accounted for less than 4% of the total consumption. Wood accounted for more than half of the renewable energy consumption.

2.66 (a) There is no particular pattern to the deaths due to terrorism on U.S. soil between 1990 and 2001. There are exceptionally high death counts in 1995 and 2001 due to the Oklahoma City bombing and the September 11 attacks. **(c)** The Pareto diagram is best to portray these data because it not only sorts the frequencies in descending order, it also provides the cumulative polygon on the same scale. The labels in the pie chart become cluttered because there are too many categories in the causes of death. **(d)** The major causes of death in the United States in 2000 were heart disease followed by cancer. These two accounted for more than 70% of the total deaths.

2.68 (a)

	GENDER		
DESSERT ORDERED	Male	Female	Total
Yes	71%	29%	100%
No	48	52	100
Total	53	47	100

	GENDER		
DESSERT ORDERED	Male	Female	Total
Yes	30%	14%	23%
No	70	86	77
Total	100	100	100

	BEEF ENTRÉE		
DESSERT ORDERED	Yes	No	Total
Yes	52%	48%	100%
No	25	75	100
Total	31	69	100

	BEEF ENTRÉE		
DESSERT ORDERED	Yes	No	Total
Yes	38%	16%	23%
No	62	84	77
Total	100	100	100

	BEEF ENTRÉE		
DESSERT ORDERED	Yes	No	Total
Yes	12%	11%	23%
No	19	58	77
Total	31	69	100

(b) If the owner is interested in finding out the percentage of males and females who order dessert or the percentage of those who order a beef entrée and a dessert among all patrons, the table of total percentages is most informative. If the owner is interested in the effect of gender on ordering of dessert or the effect of ordering a beef entrée on the ordering of dessert, the table of column percentages will be most informative. Because dessert is usually ordered after the main entrée, and the owner has no direct control over the gender of patrons, the table of row percentages is not very useful here. **(c)** 30% of the men ordered desserts, compared to 14% of the women; men are more than twice as likely to order desserts as women. Almost 38% of the patrons ordering a beef entrée ordered dessert, compared to 16% of patrons ordering all other entrees. Patrons ordering beef are more than 2.3 times as likely to order dessert as patrons ordering any other entrée.

2.70 (a) 23575R15 accounts for over 80% of the warranty claims. **(b)** Tread separation accounts for the majority (70%) of the warranty claims. **(c)** Tread separation accounts for more than 70% of the warranty claims among the ATX model. **(d)** The number of claims is evenly distributed among the three incidents; other/unknown incidents account for almost 40% of the claims, tread separation accounts for about 35% of the claims, and blowout accounts for about 25% of the claims.

2.72 (c) More than 80% of the 58 domestic beers have less than 5.2% alcohol content, with their alcohol content scattered around 4.7%, while fewer than 10% have more than 5.7% alcohol content. The number of calories scatters around 149, and about half (27 out of 58) of the domestic beers have between 10 and 14 grams of carbohydrates. There appears to be a positive relationship between the alcohol content and the number of calories and between calories and carbohydrates.

2.74 (c) In general, five-year CDs have the highest yields, followed by one-year CDs and then money market accounts. The yields from five-year CDs are approximately distributed around 4%; there are a few one-year CDs with very low yields of around 2.4%, and the rest have higher yields, in the neighborhood of 3.4%; a few (2 out of 40) money market accounts have yields higher than 2%, but most of them have yields lower than 1.8%.

The money market accounts and one-year CDs have yields that are positively related. One-year CDs and five-year CDs also have yields that are positively related. The yields of money market accounts are also positively related to the yields of five-year CDs. So banks that have a high yield in one of the money market accounts, one-year CDs, or five-year CDs also tend to have higher yields on the others.

2.76 (a)

Frequencies (Boston)

Weight (Boston)	Frequency	Percentage
3,015 but less than 3,050	2	0.54%
3,050 but less than 3,085	44	11.96
3,085 but less than 3,120	122	33.15
3,120 but less than 3,155	131	35.60
3,155 but less than 3,190	58	15.76
3,190 but less than 3,225	7	1.90
3,225 but less than 3,260	3	0.82
3,260 but less than 3,295	1	0.27

(b)

Frequencies (Vermont)

Weight (Vermont)	Frequency	Percentage
3,550 but less than 3,600	4	1.21%
3,600 but less than 3,650	31	9.39
3,650 but less than 3,700	115	34.85
3,700 but less than 3,750	131	39.70
3,750 but less than 3,800	36	10.91
3,800 but less than 3,850	12	3.64
3,850 but less than 3,900	1	0.30

(d) 0.54% of the Boston shingles pallets are underweight, while 0.27% are overweight. 1.21% of the Vermont shingles pallets are underweight, while 3.94% are overweight.

2.78 (a), (c)

Calories	Frequency	Percentage	Percentage Less Than
50 but less than 100	3	12%	12%
100 but less than 150	3	12	24
150 but less than 200	9	36	60
200 but less than 250	6	24	84
250 but less than 300	3	12	96
300 but less than 350	0	0	96
350 but less than 400	1	4	100

Protein	Frequency	Percentage	Percentage Less Than
16 but less than 20	1	4%	4%
20 but less than 24	5	20	24
24 but less than 28	8	32	56
28 but less than 32	9	36	92
32 but less than 36	2	8	100

Calories from Fat	Frequency	Percentage	Percentage Less Than
0% but less than 10%	3	12%	12%
10% but less than 20%	4	16	28
20% but less than 30%	2	8	36
30% but less than 40%	5	20	56
40% but less than 50%	3	12	68
50% but less than 60%	5	20	88
60% but less than 70%	2	8	96
70% but less than 80%	1	4	100

Calories from Saturated Fat	Frequency	Percentage	Percentage Less Than
0% but less than 5%	6	24%	24%
5% but less than 10%	2	8	32
10% but less than 15%	5	20	52
15% but less than 20%	5	20	72
20% but less than 25%	5	20	92
25% but less than 30%	2	8	100

Cholesterol	Frequency	Percentage	Percentage Less Than
0 but less than 50	2	8%	8%
50 but less than 100	17	68	76
100 but less than 150	4	16	92
150 but less than 200	1	4	96
200 but less than 250	0	0	96
250 but less than 300	0	0	96
300 but less than 350	0	0	96
350 but less than 400	0	0	96
400 but less than 450	0	0	96
450 but less than 500	1	4	100

(d) The sampled fresh red meats, poultry, and fish vary from 98 to 397 calories per serving, with the highest concentration between 150 to 200 calories. One protein source, spareribs, with 397 calories, is more than 100 calories beyond the next highest caloric food. The protein content of the sampled foods varies from 16 to 33 grams, with 68% of the data values falling between 24 and 32 grams. Spareribs and fried liver are both very different from other foods sampled—the former on calories and the latter on cholesterol content.

2.80 (a), (c)

Average Ticket $	Frequency	Percentage	Cumulative %
6 but less than 12	3	10.00%	10.00%
12 but less than 18	12	40.00	50.00
18 but less than 24	11	36.67	86.67
24 but less than 30	3	10.00	96.67
30 but less than 36	0	0.00	96.67
36 but less than 42	1	3.33	100.00

Fan Cost Index	Frequency	Percentage	Cumulative %
80 but less than 105	2	6.67%	6.67%
105 but less than 130	7	23.33	30.00
130 but less than 155	10	33.33	63.33
155 but less than 180	9	30.00	93.33
180 but less than 205	1	3.33	96.67
205 but less than 230	1	3.33	100.00

Regular Season Game Receipts ($millions)	Frequency	Percentage	Cumulative %
5 but less than 20	5	16.67%	16.67%
20 but less than 35	7	23.33	40.00
35 but less than 50	5	16.67	56.67
50 but less than 65	6	20.00	76.67
65 but less than 80	5	16.67	93.33
80 but less than 95	1	3.33	96.67
95 but less than 110	1	3.33	100.00

Local TV, Radio, and Cable ($millions)	Frequency	Percentage	Cumulative %
0 but less than 10	7	23.33%	23.33%
10 but less than 20	12	40.00	63.33
20 but less than 30	6	20.00	83.33
30 but less than 40	3	10.00	93.33
40 but less than 50	1	3.33	96.67
50 but less than 60	1	3.33	100.00

Other Local Operating Revenue ($millions)	Frequency	Percentage	Cumulative %
0 but less than 10	6	20.00%	20.00%
10 but less than 20	3	10.00	30.00
20 but less than 30	8	26.67	56.67
30 but less than 40	8	26.67	83.33
40 but less than 50	3	10.00	93.33
50 but less than 60	1	3.33	96.67
60 but less than 70	1	3.33	100.00

Player Compensation and Benefits ($millions)	Frequency	Percentage	Cumulative %
30 but less than 45	5	16.67%	16.67%
45 but less than 60	8	26.67	43.33
60 but less than 75	4	13.33	56.67
75 but less than 90	5	16.67	73.33
90 but less than 105	5	16.67	90.00
105 but less than 120	3	10.00	100.00

National and Other Local Expenses ($millions)	Frequency	Percentage	Cumulative %
30 but less than 40	4	13.33%	13.33%
40 but less than 50	10	33.33	46.67
50 but less than 60	9	30.00	76.67
60 but less than 70	2	6.67	83.33
70 but less than 80	3	10.00	93.33
80 but less than 90	2	6.67	100.00

Income from Baseball Operations ($millions)	Frequency	Percentage	Cumulative %
−60 but less than −45	2	6.67%	6.67%
−45 but less than −30	2	6.67	13.33
−30 but less than −15	8	26.67	40.00
−15 but less than 0	8	26.67	66.67
0 but less than 15	7	23.33	90.00
15 but less than 30	1	3.33	93.33
30 but less than 45	2	6.67	100.00

(d) There appears to be a weak positive linear relationship between number of wins and player compensation and benefits.

2.82 (c) Total fat seems to be most closely related to calories because the points in the scatter plot are closer to the imaginary line that passes through the data points.

2.84 (b) There is a downward trend in the amount filled. **(c)** The amount filled in the next bottle will most likely be below 1.894 liter. **(d)** The scatter plot of the amount of soft drink filled against time reveals the trend of the data, while a histogram only provides information on the distribution of the data.

CHAPTER 3

3.2 (a) Mean = 7, median = 7, mode = 7. **(b)** Range = 9, interquartile range = 5, $S^2 = 10.8$, $S = 3.286$, $CV = 46.943\%$. **(c)** Z scores: 0, −0.913, 0.609, 0, −1.217, 1.521. None of the Z scores is larger than 3.0 or smaller than −3.0. There is no outlier. **(d)** Symmetric because mean = median.

3.4 (a) Mean = 2, median = 7, mode = 7. **(b)** Range = 17, interquartile range = 14.5, $S^2 = 62$, $S = 7.874$, $CV = 393.7\%$. **(d)** Left skewed because mean < median.

3.6 (a)

	Grade X	Grade Y
Mean	575	575.4
Median	575	575
Standard deviation	6.40	2.07

(b) If quality is measured by central tendency, Grade X tires provide slightly better quality because X's mean and median are both equal to the expected value, 575 mm. If, however, quality is measured by consistency, Grade Y provides better quality because, even though Y's mean is only slightly larger than the mean for Grade X, Y's standard deviation is much smaller. The range in values for Grade Y is 5 mm compared to the range in values for Grade X, which is 16 mm.

(c)

	Grade X	Grade Y, Altered
Mean	575	577.4
Median	575	575
Standard deviation	6.40	6.11

When the fifth Y tire measures 588 mm rather than 578 mm, Y's mean inner diameter becomes 577.4 mm, which is larger than X's mean inner diameter, and Y's standard deviation increases from 2.07 mm to 6.11 mm. In this case, X's tires are providing better quality in terms of the mean inner diameter, with only slightly more variation among the tires than Y's.

3.8 The article reports the median home price and not the mean home price because the median is a better measure of central tendency in the presence of some extremely expensive homes that drive the mean home price upward.

3.10 (a) Calories: mean = 380, median = 350, 1st quartile = 260, 3rd quartile = 510. Fat: mean = 15.79, median = 19, 1st quartile = 8, 3rd quartile = 22. **(b)** Calories: variance = 12,800, standard deviation = 113.14, range = 290, interquartile range = 250, CV = 29.77%. None of the Z scores are less than −3 or greater than 3. There is no outlier in calories. Fat: variance = 52.82, standard deviation = 7.27, range = 18.5, interquartile range = 14, CV = 46.04%. None of the Z scores are less than −3 or greater than 3. There is no outlier in fat. **(c)** Calories are slightly right-skewed, while fat is slightly left-skewed. **(d)** The mean calories are 380, while the middle ranked calories is 350. The average scatter of calories around the mean is 113.14. The middle 50% of the calories are scattered over 250, while the difference between the highest and the lowest calories is 290. The mean fat is 15.79 grams, while the middle-ranked fat is 19 grams. The average scatter of fat around the mean is 7.27 grams. 50% of the values are scattered over 14 grams, while the difference between the highest and the lowest fat is 18.5 grams.

3.12 (a) Mean = 226.67, median = 210, first quartile = 110, third quartile = 380. **(b)** Variance = 17756.06, standard deviation = 133.25, range = 425, interquartile range = 270, CV = 58.79%. There is no outlier because none of the Z scores has an absolute value that is greater than 3.0. **(c)** The data appear to be skewed to the right because the mean is greater than the median.

3.14 (a) Mean = 46.8, median = 42.5, first quartile = 40, third quartile = 58. **(b)** Range = 34, variance = 123.29, standard deviation = 11.10. **(c)** The admission price for one-day tickets is slightly skewed to the right because the mean is slightly greater than the median. **(d) (a)** Mean = 50.8, median = 42.5, first quartile = 40, third quartile = 62. **(b)** Range = 69, variance = 382.84, standard deviation = 19.57. **(c)** The admission price for one-day tickets is skewed to the right because the mean is much greater than the median due to the much higher price of the first observation, at $98.

3.16 (a) Mean = 7.11, median = 6.68, Q_1 = 5.64, Q_3 = 8.73. **(b)** Variance = 4.336, standard deviation = 2.082, range = 6.67, interquartile range = 3.09, CV = 29.27%. **(c)** Because the mean is greater than the median, the distribution is right-skewed. **(d)** The mean and median are both greater than 5 minutes. The distribution is right-skewed, meaning that

there are some unusually high values. Further, 13 of the 15 bank customers sampled (or 86.7%) had waiting times greater than 5 minutes. So the customer is likely to experience a waiting time in excess of 5 minutes. The manager overstated the bank's service record in responding that the customer would "almost certainly" not wait longer than 5 minutes for service.

3.18 (a) $\overline{R}_G = ((1 + 3.614)(1 - 0.78))^{1/2} - 1 = 0.751\%$
(b) $P_{2004} = \$1,000$; $P_{2005} = 3.614(P_{2004}) + P_{2004} = \$4,614$; $P_{2006} = -0.78(P_{2005}) + P_{2005} = \$1,015.08$
Its value at the end of 2005 will be $1,015.08. **(c)** The geometric mean rate of return is 0.751%, which is lower than the 9.047% in Problem 3.17 (c), and, hence, the value of the stock at the end of 2005 is lower than that in Problem 3.17 (c).

3.20 (a)

Year	Platinum	Gold	Silver
2005	12.3	17.8	29.5
2004	5.7	4.6	14.2
2003	36.0	19.9	27.8
2002	24.6	25.6	3.3
Geometric mean	19.09%	16.71%	18.21%

(b) Platinum has the highest rate of return over the four years, while gold has the lowest rate of return. **(c)** In general, investing in precious metals yielded much higher rate of returns than investing in the stock market over the four-year period.

3.22 (a) Population mean, $\mu = 6$. **(b)** Population standard deviation, $\sigma = 1.673$, population variance, $\sigma^2 = 2.8$.

3.24 (a) 68%. **(b)** 95%. **(c)** Not calculable, 75%, 88.89%. **(d)** $\mu - 4\sigma$ to $\mu + 4\sigma$ or −2.8 to 19.2.

3.26 (a) Mean = 12,999.2158, variance = 14,959,700.52, standard deviation = 3,867.7772. **(b)** 64.71%, 98.04%, and 100% of these states have mean per capita energy consumption within 1, 2, and 3 standard deviation of the mean, respectively. **(c)** This is consistent with the 68%, 95%, and 99.7%, according to the empirical rule. **(d) (a)** Mean = 12,857.7402, variance = 14,238,110.67, standard deviation = 3,773.3421. **(b)** 66%, 98%, and 100% of these states have a mean per capita energy consumption within 1, 2, and 3 standard deviations of the mean, respectively. **(c)** This is consistent with the 68%, 95%, and 99.7% according to the empirical rule.

3.28 (a) 3, 4, 7, 9, 12. **(b)** The distances between the median and the extremes are close, 4 and 5, but the differences in the sizes of the whiskers are different (1 on the left and 3 on the right), so this distribution is slightly right-skewed. **(c)** In 3.2 (d), because mean = median, the distribution was said to be symmetric. The box part of the graph is symmetric, but the whiskers show right skewness.

3.30 (a) −8, −6.5, 7, 8, 9. **(b)** The shape is left-skewed. **(c)** This is consistent with the answer in 3.4 (d).

3.32 (a) Five-number summary: 35 110 210 380 460. **(b)** The distribution is slightly skewed to the right.

3.34 (a) Five-number summary for calories: 240 260 350 510 530. Five-number summary for fat: 3.5 8 19 22 22.

3.36 (a) Commercial district five-number summary: 0.38 3.2 4.5 5.55 6.46. Residential area five-number summary: 3.82 5.64 6.68 8.73 10.49. **(b)** Commercial district: The distribution is skewed to the left. Residential area: The distribution is skewed slightly to the right. **(c)** The central tendency of the waiting times for the bank branch located in the commercial district of a city is lower than that of the branch located in the residential area. There are a few longer than normal waiting times for the branch located in the residential area whereas there are a few exceptionally short waiting times for the branch located in the commercial area.

3.38 (a) You can say that there is a strong positive linear relationship between the return on investment of U.S. stocks and the international large cap stocks, U.S. stocks, and emerging market stocks; a moderate positive linear relationship between U.S. stocks and international small cap stocks, U.S. stocks, and emerging market debt stocks; and a very weak positive linear relationship between U.S. stocks and international bonds. **(b)** In general, there is a positive linear relationship between the return on investment of U.S. stocks and international stocks, U.S. bonds and international bonds, U.S. stocks and emerging market debt, and there is a very weak negative linear relationship, if any, between the return on investment of U.S. bonds and international stocks.

3.40 (a) $cov(X, Y) = 591.667$. **(b)** $r = 0.7196$. **(c)** The correlation coefficient is more valuable for expressing the relationship between calories and fat because it does not depend on the units used to measure calories and fat. **(d)** There is a strong positive linear relationship between calories and fat.

3.42 (a) $cov(X,Y) = 1.2132$ **(b)** $S_X^2 = 0.1944$, $S_Y^2 = 20.4054$

$$r = \frac{cov(X, Y)}{S_X S_Y} = \frac{1.2132}{(0.4409)(4.5172)} = 0.6092$$

(c) There is a moderate positive linear relationship between the coach's salary and revenue.

3.56 (a) Mean = 43.89, median = 45, 1st quartile = 18, 3rd quartile = 63. **(b)** Range = 76, interquartile range = 45, variance = 639.2564, standard deviation = 25.28, $CV = 57.61\%$. **(c)** The distribution is skewed to the right because there are a few policies that require an exceptionally long period to be approved. **(d)** The mean approval process takes 43.89 days, with 50% of the policies being approved in less than 45 days. 50% of the applications are approved in between 18 and 63 days. About 67% of the applications are approved in between 18.6 and 69.2 days.

3.58 (a) Mean = 8.421, median = 8.42, range = 0.186, $S = 0.0461$. The mean and median width are both 8.42 inches. The range of the widths is 0.186 inches, and the average scatter around the mean is 0.0461 inches. **(b)** 8.312, 8.404, 8.42, 8.459, 8.498. **(c)** Even though mean = median, the left whisker is slightly longer so the distribution is slightly left-skewed. **(d)** All the troughs in this sample meet the specifications.

3.60 (a) Office I: mean = 2.214, median = 1.54; Office II: mean = 2.011, median = 1.505; Office I: $Q_1 = 0.93$, $Q_3 = 3.93$; Office II: $Q_1 = 0.6$, $Q_3 = 3.75$. **(b)** Office I: range = 5.80, Interquartile range = 3.00, $S^2 = 2.952$, $S = 1.718$, $CV = 77.597\%$; Office II: range = 7.47, Interquartile range = 3.15, $S^2 = 3.579$, $S = 1.892$, $CV = 94.04\%$. **(c)** Yes, they are both right-skewed. **(d)** Office II has more variability in times to clear

problems, with a wider range and a larger standard deviation. Office II has a lower mean time to clear problems.

3.62 (a), (b)
Excel output:

	In-State Tuition/Fees	Out-of State Tuition/Fees
Mean	6841.815534	17167.71
Median	6340	16340
Mode	7062	14901
Standard Deviation	2212.221516	4274.009
Sample Variance	4893924.034	18267150
Kurtosis	4.295740452	−0.33509
Skewness	1.350377978	0.524429
Range	14466	20007
Minimum	3094	8965
Maximum	17560	28972
Sum	704707	1768274
Count	103	103
First Quartile	5378	13928
Third Quartile	8143	20134
Interquartile Range	2765	6206
Coefficient of Variation	32.33%	24.90%

(c) Both in-state and out-of-state tuition and fees are right skewed.
(d) $r = \dfrac{cov(X, Y)}{S_X S_Y} = 0.4911$ **(e)** Both in-state and out-of-state tuition and fees are right-skewed due to the outliers in the right tails. There is a moderate positive linear relationship between in-state and out-of-state tuition and fees. Those schools with high in-state tuition and fees tend to also have high out-of-state tuition and fees.

3.64 (a) With promotion: mean = 20,748.93, standard deviation = 8,109.50; without promotion: mean = 13,935.70, standard deviation = 4,437.92. **(b)** With promotion: minimum = 10,470, 1st quartile = 14,905, median = 19,775, 3rd quartile = 24,456, maximum = 40,605. Without promotion: minimum = 9,555, 1st quartile = 11,779, median = 12,952, 3rd quartile = 14,367, maximum = 28,834. **(d)** The mean attendance is 6,813 more when there is a promotion than when there is not, and the variation in attendance when there is a promotion is larger than that when there is no promotion. Many factors can cause variation in the paid attendance. Some of them are weather condition, times, day of the game, and the visiting team.

3.66 (a) Boston: 0.04, 0.17, 0.23, 0.32, 0.98; Vermont: 0.02, 0.13, 0.20, 0.28, 0.83. **(b)** Both distributions are right-skewed. **(c)** Both sets of shingles did quite well in achieving a granule loss of 0.8 grams or less. The Boston shingles had only two data points greater than 0.8 grams. The next highest to these was 0.6 grams. These two data points can be considered outliers. Only 1.176% of the shingles failed the specification. In the Vermont shingles, only one data point was greater than 0.8 grams. The next highest was 0.58 grams. Thus, only 0.714% of the shingles failed to meet the specification.

3.68 (a), (b)

	Mean	Median	Q_1	Q_3
Average Ticket $	18.1333	17.83	15.20	20.84
Fan Cost Index	144.5737	143.475	124.25	160.76
Reg. Season $	46.1367	47.55	30.20	62.10
Local TV, Radio, Cable	19.0467	16.35	10.90	23.60
Other Local Revenue	27.5933	29.05	13.90	37.00
Player Comp.	71.3567	70.80	49.40	92.80
National and local expenses	54.6467	50.50	46.90	58.50
Income from baseball operations	−8.3733	−8.35	−18.50	1.90

	Variance	Standard Deviation	Range	Interquartile Range	CV
Average Ticket $	35.9797	5.9983	33.07	5.64	33.08%
Fan Cost Index	843.4552	29.0423	143.84	36.51	20.09%
Reg. Season $	512.5445	22.6394	91.60	31.90	49.07%
Local TV, Radio, Cable	151.0184	12.2890	56.30	12.70	64.52%
Other Local Revenue	234.6186	15.3173	58.70	23.10	55.51%
Player Comp.	663.8405	25.7651	88.00	43.40	36.11%
National and local expenses	176.4081	13.2819	49.20	11.60	24.3%
Income from baseball operations	428.1531	20.6919	93.80	20.40	−247.12%

(c) Average ticket prices, local TV, radio and cable receipts, and national and other local expenses are skewed to the right; fan cost index is slightly skewed to the right; all other variables are approximately symmetrical. **(d)** $r = 0.3985$. There is a moderate positive linear relationship between the number of wins and player compensation and benefits.

3.70 (a) 0.80. **(b)** 0.53. **(c)** 0.92. **(d)** Total fat seems to be most closely related to calories because it has the highest correlation coefficient with calories.

3.72 (a) Mean = 7.5273, median = 7.263, first quartile = 6.353, third quartile = 8.248. **(b)** Range = 7.416, interquartile range = 1.895, variance = 2.6609, standard deviation = 1.6312, $CV = 21.67\%$. **(c)** The data are skewed to the right. **(d)** The per capita spending by the 50 states is right-skewed because a few states spend a lot more than the rest.

CHAPTER 4

4.2 (a) Simple events include selecting a red ball. **(b)** Selecting a white ball.

4.4 (a) 60/100 = 3/5 = 0.6. **(b)** 10/100 = 1/10 = 0.1. **(c)** 35/100 = 7/20 = 0.35. **(d)** 9/10 = 0.9.

4.6 (a) Mutually exclusive, not collectively exhaustive. **(b)** Not mutually exclusive, not collectively exhaustive. **(c)** Mutually exclusive, not collectively exhaustive. **(d)** Mutually exclusive, collectively exhaustive.

4.8 (a) "Makes less than $50,000." **(b)** "Makes less than $50,000 and tax code is unfair." **(c)** The complement of "tax code is fair" is "tax code is

unfair." **(d)** "Tax code is fair and makes less than $50,000" is a joint event because it consists of two characteristics or attributes.

4.10 (a) "A wafer is good." **(b)** "A wafer is good and no particle was found on the die." **(c)** "Bad wafer." **(d)** A wafer that is a "good wafer" and was produced by a die "with particles" is a joint event because it consists of two characteristics.

4.12 (a) P(Selected the highest-cost fund) = (27+18)/200 = 0.225. **(b)** P(Selected the highest-cost fund and is an undergraduate) = 27/200 = 0.135. **(c)** P(Selected the highest-cost fund or is an undergraduate) = (45+100–27)/200 = 0.59. **(d)** The probability of "selected the highest cost fund or is an undergraduate" includes the probability of "selected the highest cost fund," plus the probability of "undergraduate minus the joint probability of highest cost fund and undergraduate."

4.14 (a) 360/500 = 18/25 = 0.72. **(b)** 224/500 = 56/125 = 0.448. **(c)** 396/500 = 99/125 = 0.792. **(d)** 500/500 = 1.00.

4.16 (a) 10/30 = 1/3 = 0.33. **(b)** 20/60 = 1/3 = 0.33. **(c)** 40/60 = 2/3 = 0.67. **(d)** Since $P(A \mid B) = P(A) = 1/3$, events A and B are statistically independent.

4.18 $\frac{1}{2} = 0.5$

4.20 Since $P(A \text{ and } B) = 0.20$ and $P(A)\,P(B) = 0.12$, events A and B are not statistically independent.

4.22 (a) 36/116 = 0.3103. **(b)** 14/334 = 0.0419. **(c)** 320/334 = 0.9581 $P(\text{No particles}) = 400/450 = 0.8889$. Since $P(\text{No particles} \mid \text{Good}) \neq P(\text{No particles})$, "a good wafer" and "a die with no particle" are not statistically independent.

4.24 (a) P(Selected the highest cost fund | Is an undergraduate) = 27/100 = 0.27. **(b)** P(Is an undergraduate | Selected the highest cost fund) = 27/(27+18) = 0.6. **(c)** The conditional events are reversed. **(d)** Since P(Selected the highest-cost fund | Is an undergraduate) = 0.27 is not equal to P(Selected the highest-cost fund) = 0.225, the two events "student group" and "fund selected" are not statistically independent.

4.26 (a) 0.025/0.6 = 0.0417. **(b)** 0.015/0.4 = 0.0375. **(c)** Since P(Needs warranty repair | Manufacturer based in U.S.) = 0.0417 and P(Needs warranty repair) = 0.04, the two events are not statistically independent.

4.28 (a) 0.0045. **(b)** 0.012. **(c)** 0.0059. **(d)** 0.0483.

4.30 0.095.

4.32 (a) 0.736. **(b)** 0.997.

4.34 (a) 0.4615. **(b)** 0.325.

4.36 (a) P(Huge success | Favorable review) = 0.099/0.459 = 0.2157; P(Moderate success | Favorable review) = 0.14/0.459 = 0.3050; P(Break even | Favorable review) = 0.16/0.459 = 0.3486; P(Loser | Favorable review) = 0.06/0.459 = 0.1307. **(b)** P(Favorable review) = 0.459.

4.48 (a) 0.015. **(b)** 0.49. **(c)** 0.995. **(d)** 0.02. **(e)** 0.6667. **(f)** The conditions are switched. Part (d) answers $P(A \mid B)$ and part (e) answers $P(B \mid A)$.

4.50 (a) A simple event can be "a firm that has a transactional public Web site" and a joint event can be "a firm that has a transactional public Web site and has sales greater than $10 billion." **(b)** 0.3469. **(c)** 0.1449. **(d)** Since $P(\text{Transactional public Web site}) \times P(\text{Sales in excess of } \$10 \text{ billion}) \neq P(\text{Transactional public Web site and sales in excess of } \$10 \text{ billion})$, the two events "sales in excess of ten billion dollars" and "has a transactional public Web site" are not independent.

4.52 (a) 0.0225. **(b)** $3{,}937.5 \cong 3{,}938$ can be expected to read the advertisement and place an order. **(c)** 0.03. **(d)** 5,250 can be expected to read the advertisement and place an order.

4.54 (a) 0.4712. **(b)** Since the probability that a fatality involved a rollover, given that the fatality involved an SUV, a van, or a pickup is 0.4712, which is almost twice the probability that a fatality involved a rollover with any vehicle type, at 0.24, SUVs, vans, and pickups are generally more prone to rollover accidents.

CHAPTER 5

5.2 (a) C: $\mu = 2$, D: $\mu = 2$. **(b)** C: $\sigma = 1.414$, D: $\sigma = 1.095$. **(c)** Distribution C is uniform and symmetric; Distribution D is symmetric and has a single mode.

5.4 (a) $\mu = 2$. **(b)** $\sigma = 1.183$.

5.6 (a)

X	P(X)
$-1	21/36
$+1	15/36

(b)

X	P(X)
$-1	21/36
$+1	15/36

(c)

X	P(X)
$-1	30/36
$+4	6/36

(d) $-0.167 for each method of play.

5.8 (a) 90; 30. **(b)** 126.10, 10.95. **(c)** $-1,300$. **(d)** 120.

5.10 (a) 9.5 minutes. **(b)** 1.9209 minutes.

5.12

$X*P(X)$	$Y*P(Y)$	$(X-\mu_X)^2*P(X)$	$(Y-\mu_Y)^2*P(Y)$	$(X-\mu_X)(Y-\mu_Y)*P(XY)$
-10	5	2,528.1	129.6	-572.4
0	45	1,044.3	5,548.8	$-2,407.2$
24	-6	132.3	346.8	-214.2
45	-30	2,484.3	3,898.8	$-3,112.2$

(a) $E(X) = \mu_X = \sum_{i-1}^{N} X_i P(X_i) = 59$, $E(Y) = \mu_Y = \sum_{i-1}^{N} Y_i P(Y_i) = 14$

(b) $\sigma_X = \sqrt{\sum_{i-1}^{N} [X_i - E(X)]^2 P(X_i)} = 78.6702$

$\sigma_Y = \sqrt{\sum_{i=1}^{N} [Y_i - E(Y)]^2 P(Y_i)} = 99.62$

(c) $\sigma_{XY} = \sum_{i=1}^{N} [X_i - E(X)][Y_i - E(Y)]P(X_i Y_i) = -6{,}306$

(d) Stock X gives the investor a lower standard deviation while yielding a higher expected return, so the investor should select stock X.

5.14 (a) $71; $97. **(b)** 61.88, 84.27. **(c)** 5,113. **(d)** Risk-averse investors would invest in stock X, while risk takers would invest in stock Y.

5.16 (a) $E(X) = \$77$, $E(Y) = \$97$. **(b)** $\sigma_X = 39.76$, $\sigma_Y = 108.95$. **(c)** $\sigma_{XY} = 4161$. **(d)** Common stock fund gives the investor a higher expected return than corporate bond fund but also has a standard deviation more than 2.5 times higher than that for corporate bond fund. An investor should carefully weigh the increased risk.

5.18 (a) 0.5997. **(b)** 0.0016. **(c)** 0.0439. **(d)** 0.4018.

5.20

	Mean	Standard Deviation
(a)	0.40	0.600
(b)	1.60	0.980
(c)	4.00	0.894
(d)	1.50	0.866

5.22 (a) 0.0778. **(b)** 0.6826. **(c)** 0.0870. **(d)(a)** $P(X = 5) = 0.3277$. **(b)** $P(X \ge 3) = 0.9421$. **(c)** $P(X < 2) = 0.0067$.

5.24 Given $p = 0.90$ and $n = 3$,

(a) $P(X = 3) = \dfrac{n!}{X!(n-x)!} p^X (1-p)^{n-X} = \dfrac{3!}{3!\,0!}(0.9)^3(0.1)^0 = 0.729$.

(b) $P(X = 0) = \dfrac{n!}{X!(n-x)!} p^X (1-p)^{n-X} = \dfrac{3!}{0!\,3!}(0.9)^0(0.1)^3 = 0.001$.

(c) $P(X \ge 2) = P(X = 2) + P(X = 3) = \dfrac{3!}{2!\,1!}(0.9)^2(0.1)^1 + \dfrac{3!}{3!\,0!}(0.9)^3(0.1)^0$

$= 0.972$

(d) $E(X) = np = 3(0.9) = 2.7$ $\sigma_X = \sqrt{np(1-p)} = \sqrt{3(0.9)(0.1)} = 0.5196$.

5.26 (a) $P(X = 0) = 0.0563$. **(b)** $P(X = 5) = 0.0584$. **(c)** $P(X \le 5) = 0.9803$. **(d)** $P(X \ge 6) = 0.0197$. **(e)** You could infer that Californians' view of the economy is very likely to be different from the United States as a whole because the probability of seeing all 6 in the random sample of 10 having a positive outlook is only 1.622%, which is not a very likely event, if their view is the same as the United States as a whole.

5.28 (a) $P(X \le 5) = .00009919$. **(b)** $P(X \le 10) = 0.0719$. **(c)** $P(X \le 15) = 0.8173$.

5.30 (a) 0.2565. **(b)** 0.1396. **(c)** 0.3033. **(d)** 0.0247.

5.32 (a) 0.0337. **(b)** 0.0067. **(c)** 0.9596. **(d)** 0.0404.

5.34 (a)

$P(X < 5) = P(X = 0) + P(X = 1) + P(X = 2) + P(X = 3) + P(X = 4)$

$= \dfrac{e^{-6}(6)^0}{0!} + \dfrac{e^{-6}(6)^1}{1!} + \dfrac{e^{-6}(6)^2}{2!} + \dfrac{e^{-6}(6)^3}{3!} + \dfrac{e^{-6}(6)^4}{4!}$

$= 0.002479 + 0.014873 + 0.044618 + 0.089235 + 0.133853$

$= 0.2851$.

(b) $P(X = 5) = \dfrac{e^{-6}(6)^5}{5!} = 0.1606$.

(c) $P(X \ge 5) = 1 - P(X < 5) = 1 - 0.2851 = 0.7149$.

(d) $P(X = 4 \text{ or } X = 5) = P(X = 4) + P(X = 5) = \dfrac{e^{-6}(6)^4}{4!} + \dfrac{e^{-6}(6)^5}{5!}$

$= 0.2945$.

5.36 $\lambda = 4.06$. **(a)** $P(X = 0) = 0.0172$. **(b)** $P(X \geq 1) = 0.9828$.
(c) $P(X \geq 2) = 0.9127$.

5.38 (a) 0.0176. **(b)** 0.9093. **(c)** 0.9220.

5.40 (a) $\lambda = 1.53$, $P(X = 0) = 0.2165$. **(b)** $P(X \leq 2) = 0.8013$. **(c)** Because Kia had a higher mean rate of problems per car, the probability of a randomly selected Kia having no more than two problems is lower than that with a randomly chosen Lexus. Likewise, the probability of a randomly selected Kia having zero problems is lower than that with a randomly chosen Lexus.

5.42 (a) $\lambda = 1.40$, $P(X = 0) = 0.2466$. **(b)** $P(X \leq 2) = 0.8335$. **(c)** Because Kia had a lower mean rate of problems per car in 2005 compared to 2004, the probability of a randomly selected Kia having zero problems and the probability of no more than two problems are both higher than their values in 2004.

5.44 (a) 0.238. **(b)** 0.2. **(c)** 0.1591. **(d)** 0.0083.

5.46 (a) If $n = 6$, $A = 25$, and $N = 100$,

$$P(X \geq 2) = 1 - [P(X = 0) + P(X = 1)]$$

$$= 1 - \left[\frac{\binom{25}{0}\binom{100-25}{6-0}}{\binom{100}{6}} + \frac{\binom{25}{1}\binom{100-25}{6-1}}{\binom{100}{6}} \right]$$

$$= 1 - [0.1689 + 0.3620] = 0.4691$$

(b) If $n = 6$, $A = 30$, and $N = 100$,

$$P(X \geq 2) = 1 - [P(X = 0) + P(X = 1)]$$

$$= 1 - \left[\frac{\binom{30}{0}\binom{100-30}{6-0}}{\binom{100}{6}} + \frac{\binom{30}{1}\binom{100-30}{6-1}}{\binom{100}{6}} \right]$$

$$= 1 - [0.1100 + 0.3046] = 0.5854$$

(c) If $n = 6$, $A = 5$, and $N = 100$,

$$P(X \geq 2) = 1 - [P(X = 0) + P(X = 1)]$$

$$= 1 - \left[\frac{\binom{5}{0}\binom{100-5}{6-0}}{\binom{100}{6}} + \frac{\binom{5}{1}\binom{100-5}{6-1}}{\binom{100}{6}} \right]$$

$$= 1 - [0.7291 + 0.2430] = 0.0279$$

(d) If $n = 6$, $A = 10$, and $N = 100$,

$$P(X \geq 2) = 1 - [P(X = 0) + P(X = 1)]$$

$$= 1 - \left[\frac{\binom{10}{0}\binom{100-10}{6-0}}{\binom{100}{6}} + \frac{\binom{10}{1}\binom{100-10}{6-1}}{\binom{100}{6}} \right]$$

$$= 1 - [0.5223 + 0.3687] = 0.1090$$

(e) The probability that the entire group will be audited is very sensitive to the true number of improper returns in the population. If the true number is very low ($A = 5$), the probability is very low (0.0279). When the true number is increased by a factor of 6 ($A = 30$), the probability the group will be audited increases by a factor of almost 21 (0.5854).

5.48 (a) $P(X = 4) = 0.00003649$. **(b)** $P(X = 0) = 0.5455$.
(c) $P(X \geq 1) = 0.4545$. **(d)** $n = 6$. **(a)** $P(X = 4) = 0.0005$.
(b) $P(X = 0) = 0.3877$. **(c)** $P(X \geq 1) = 0.6123$.

5.50 (a) $P(X = 1) = 0.4835$. **(b)** $P(X \geq 1) = 0.6374$. **(c)** $P(X \leq 2) = 0.9912$.
(d) $\mu = n \times (A/N) = 0.8$.

5.56 (a) 0.74. **(b)** 0.74. **(c)** 0.3898. **(d)** 0.0012. **(e)** The assumption of independence may not be true.

5.58 (a) If $p = 0.50$ and $n = 11$, $P(X \geq 9) = 0.0327$. **(b)** If $p = 0.74$ and $n = 11$, $P(X = 9) = 0.2474$ and $P(X \geq 9) = 0.4247$.

5.60 (a) 0.018228. **(b)** 0.089782. **(c)** 0.89199. **(d)** Mean = 3.3, standard deviation = 1.486943.

5.62 (a) 0.0000. **(b)** 0.04924. **(c)** 0.909646. **(d)** 0.49578.

5.64 (a) 0.0003. **(b)** 0.2289. **(c)** 0.4696. **(d)** 0.5304. **(e)** 0.469581.
(f) 4.4, so about 4 people on average will refuse to participate.

5.66 (a) $\mu = np = 2.6$. **(b)** $\sigma = \sqrt{np(1 - p)} = 1.5040$.
(c) $P(X = 0) = 0.0617$. **(d)** $P(X \leq 2) = 0.5080$. **(e)** $P(X \geq 3) = 0.4920$.

5.68 (a) If $p = 0.50$ and $n = 35$, $P(X \geq 30) = 0.0000112$.
(b) If $p = 0.70$ and $n = 35$, $P(X \geq 30) = 0.0269$. **(c)** If $p = 0.90$ and $n = 35$, $P(X \geq 30) = 0.8684$. **(d)** Based on the results in (a)–(c), the probability that the Standard & Poor's 500 index will increase if there is an early gain in the first five trading days of the year is very likely to be close to 0.90 because that yields a probability of 86.84% that at least 30 of the 35 years the Standard & Poor's 500 index will increase the entire year.

5.70 (a) The assumptions needed are (i) the probability that a golfer loses a golf ball in a given interval is constant, (ii) the probability that a golfer loses more than one golf ball approaches 0 as the interval gets smaller, (iii) the probability that a golfer loses a golf ball is independent from interval to interval. **(b)** 0.0111. **(c)** 0.70293. **(d)** 0.29707.

5.72 (a) Virtually zero. **(b)** 0.00000037737. **(c)** 0.00000173886.
(d) 0.000168669. **(e)** 0.0011998. **(f)** 0.00407937. **(g)** 0.006598978.
(h) 0.0113502. **(i)** 0.976601.

CHAPTER 6

6.2 (a) 0.9089. **(b)** 0.0911. **(c)** +1.96. **(d)** −1.00 and +1.00.

6.4 (a) 0.1401. **(b)** 0.4168. **(c)** 0.3918. **(d)** +1.00.

6.6 (a) 0.9599. **(b)** 0.0228. **(c)** 43.42. **(d)** 46.64 and 53.36.

6.8 (a) $P(34 < X < 50) = P(-1.33 < Z < 0) = 0.4082$. **(b)** $P(X < 30) + P(X > 60) = P(Z < -1.67) + P(Z > 0.83) = 0.0475 + (1.0 - 0.7967) = 0.2508$.

(c) $P(Z < -0.84) \cong 0.20$, $Z = -0.84 = \dfrac{X - 50}{12}$. $X = 50 - 0.84(12) = 39.92$ thousand miles, or 39,920 miles.

(d) The smaller standard deviation makes the Z values larger.

(a) $P(34 < X < 50) = P(-1.60 < Z < 0) = 0.4452$.

(b) $P(X < 30) + P(X > 60) = P(Z < -2.00) + P(Z > 1.00) = 0.0228 + (1.0 - 0.8413) = 0.1815$.

(c) $X = 50 - 0.84(10) = 41.6$ thousand miles, or 41,600 miles.

6.10 (a) 0.9878. **(b)** 0.8185. **(c)** 86.16%. **(d)** Option 1: Since your score of 81% on this exam represents a Z score of 1.00, which is below the minimum Z score of 1.28, you will not earn an A grade on the exam under this grading option. Option 2: Since your score of 68% on this exam represents a Z score of 2.00, which is well above the minimum Z score of 1.28, you will earn an A grade on the exam under this grading option. You should prefer Option 2.

6.12 (a) $P(X < 1.5) = P(Z < -2) = 0.0228.$ **(b)** $P(X < 1.7) = P(Z < -0.6667) = 0.2525.$ **(c)** $P(X > 2.0) = P(Z > 1.3333) = 0.0912.$ **(d)** $P(X > 2.3) = P(Z > 3.3333) = 0.0004.$

6.14 With 39 values, the smallest of the standard normal quantile values covers an area under the normal curve of 0.025. The corresponding Z value is −1.96. The middle (20th) value has a cumulative area of 0.50 and a corresponding Z value of 0.0. The largest of the standard normal quantile values covers an area under the normal curve of 0.975, and its corresponding Z value is +1.96.

6.16 (a) Mean = 23.2, median = 23.5, range = 52, standard deviation = 12.3868, $6(S_X) = 6(12.3868) = 74.3205$, interquartile range = 14, $1.33(S_X) = 1.33(12.3868) = 16.4744$. The mean is almost equal to the median; the range is smaller than 6 times the standard deviation, and the interquartile range is slightly smaller than 1.33 times the standard deviation. The data appear to be approximately normally distributed but slightly skewed to the right. **(b)** The normal probability plot suggests that the data are skewed to the right.

6.18 (a)   **Plant A:** $\overline{X} = 9.382$ $S = 3.998$
Five-number summary: 4.42   7.29   8.515   11.42   21.62

The distribution is right-skewed since the mean is greater than the median.

      Plant B: $\overline{X} = 11.354$ $S = 5.126$
Five-number summary: 2.33   6.25   11.96   14.25   25.75

Although the results are inconsistent due to an extreme value in the sample, since the mean is less than the median, we can say that the data for Plant B is left-skewed. **(b)** The normal probability plot for Plant A is right-skewed. Except for the extreme value, the normal probability plot for Plant B is left-skewed.

6.20 (a) Interquartile range = 0.0025; $S_X = 0.0017$; range = 0.008; $1.33(S_X) = 0.0023$; $6(S_X) = 0.0102$. Since the interquartile range is close to $1.33(S_X)$ and the range is also close to $6(S_X)$, the data appear to be approximately normally distributed. **(b)** The normal probability plot suggests that the data appear to be approximately normally distributed.

6.22 (a) Five-number summary: 82 127 148.5 168 213; mean = 147.06; mode = 130; range = 131; interquartile range = 41; standard deviation = 31.69. The mean is very close to the median. The five-number summary suggests that the distribution is approximately symmetrical around the median. The interquartile range is very close to 1.33 times the standard deviation. The range is about $50 below 6 times the standard deviation. In general, the distribution of the data appears to closely resemble a normal distribution. **(b)** The normal probability plot confirms that the data appear to be approximately normally distributed.

6.24 (a) 0.1667. **(b)** 0.1667. **(c)** 0.7083. **(d)** Mean = 60, standard deviation = 34.641.

6.26 (a) $P(5{:}55 \text{ a.m.} < X < 7{:}38 \text{ p.m.}) = P(355 < X < 1{,}178) = (1178 - 355)/(1440) = 0.5715.$ **(b)** $P(10 \text{ p.m.} < X < 5 \text{ a.m.}) = P(1{,}320 < X < 1{,}440) + P(0 < X < 300) = (1{,}440 - 1{,}320)/1{,}440 + (300)/1{,}440 = 0.2917.$ **(c)** Let X be duration between the occurrence of a failure and its detection, $a = 0$, $b = 60$, $P(0 < X < 10) = 10/60 = 0.1667.$ **(d)** $P(40 < X < 60) = (60 - 40)/60 = 0.3333.$

6.28 (a) 0.6321. **(b)** 0.3679. **(c)** 0.2326. **(d)** 0.7674.

6.30 (a) Approximately 1.0. **(b)** 0.0003. **(c)** 0.00029. **(d)** 0.99971.

6.32 (a) 0.864665. **(b)** 0.99996. **(c)** 0.6321, 0.9933.

6.34 (a) 0.6321. **(b)** 0.3935. **(c)** 0.0952.

6.36 (a) 0.8647. **(b)** 0.3297. **(c)** 0.9765, 0.5276.

6.46 (a) 0.4772. **(b)** 0.9544. **(c)** 0.0456. **(d)** 1.8835. **(e)** 1.8710 and 2.1290.

6.48 (a) 0.2734. **(b)** 0.2038. **(c)** 4.404 ounces. **(d)** 4.188 ounces and 5.212 ounces.

6.50 (a) Waiting time will more closely resemble an exponential distribution. **(b)** Seating time will more closely resemble a normal distribution. **(c)** Both the histogram and normal probability plot suggest that waiting time more closely resembles an exponential distribution. **(d)** Both the histogram and normal probability plot suggest that seating time more closely resembles a normal distribution.

6.52 (a) 0.8413. **(b)** 0.9330. **(c)** 0.9332. **(d)** 0.3347. **(e)** 0.4080 and 1.1920.

CHAPTER 7

7.2 Sample without replacement: Read from left to right in three-digit sequences and continue unfinished sequences from the end of the row to the beginning of the next row:

Row 05: 338 505 855 551 438 855 077 186 579 488 767 833 170
Rows 05–06: 897
Row 06: 340 033 648 847 204 334 639 193 639 411 095 924
Rows 06–07: 707
Row 07: 054 329 776 100 871 007 255 980 646 886 823 920 461
Row 08: 893 829 380 900 796 959 453 410 181 277 660 908 887
Rows 08–09: 237
Row 09: 818 721 426 714 050 785 223 801 670 353 362 449
Rows 09–10: 406

Note: All sequences above 902 and duplicates are discarded.

7.4 A simple random sample would be less practical for personal interviews because of travel costs (unless interviewees are paid to go to a central interviewing location).

7.6 Here all members of the population are equally likely to be selected, and the sample selection mechanism is based on chance. But selection of two elements is not independent; for example, if A is in the sample, we know that B is also and that C and D are not.

7.8 (a)

Row 16: 2323 6737 5131 8888 1718 0654 6832 4647 6510 4877
Row 17: 4579 4269 2615 1308 2455 7830 5550 5852 5514 7182
Row 18: 0989 3205 0514 2256 8514 4642 7567 8896 2977 8822
Row 19: 5438 2745 9891 4991 4523 6847 9276 8646 1628 3554
Row 20: 9475 0899 2337 0892 0048 8033 6945 9826 9403 6858
Row 21: 7029 7341 3553 1403 3340 4205 0823 4144 1048 2949
Row 22: 8515 7479 5432 9792 6575 5760 0408 8112 2507 3742
Row 23: 1110 0023 4012 8607 4697 9664 4894 3928 7072 5815
Row 24: 3687 1507 7530 5925 7143 1738 1688 5625 8533 5041
Row 25: 2391 3483 5763 3081 6090 5169 0546

Note: All sequences above 5,000 are discarded. There were no repeating sequences.

(b)

189	189	289	389	489	589	689	789	889	989
1089	1189	1289	1389	1489	1589	1689	1789	1889	1989
2089	2189	2289	2389	2489	2589	2689	2789	2889	2989
3089	3189	3289	3389	3489	3589	3689	3789	3889	3989
4089	4189	4289	4389	4489	4589	4689	4789	4889	4989

(c) With the single exception of invoice #0989, the invoices selected in the simple random sample are not the same as those selected in the systematic sample. It would be highly unlikely that a simple random sample would select the same units as a systematic sample.

7.10 Before accepting the results of a survey of college students, you might want to know, for example:

Who funded the survey? Why was it conducted?

What was the population from which the sample was selected?

What sampling design was used?

What mode of response was used: a personal interview, a telephone interview, or a mail survey? Were interviewers trained? Were survey questions field-tested?

What questions were asked? Were they clear, accurate, unbiased, and valid?

What operational definition of "vast majority" was used?

What was the response rate?

What was the sample size?

7.12 (a) The four types of survey errors are: coverage error, nonresponse error, sampling error, and measurement error. **(b)** When people who answer the survey tell you what they think you want to hear, rather than what they really believe, it introduces the halo effect, which is a source of measurement error. Also, every survey will have sampling error that reflects the chance differences from sample to sample, based on the probability of particular individuals being selected in the particular sample.

7.14 Before accepting the results of the survey, you might want to know, for example:

Who funded the study? Why was it conducted?

What was the population from which the sample was selected?

What sampling design was used?

What mode of response was used: a personal interview, a telephone interview, or a mail survey? Were interviewers trained? Were survey questions field-tested?

What other questions were asked? Were they clear, accurate, unbiased, and valid?

What was the response rate?

What was the margin of error?

What was the sample size?

What was the frame being used?

7.16 Before accepting the results of the survey, you might want to know, for example:

Who funded the study? Why was it conducted?

What was the population from which the sample was selected?

What was the frame being used?

What sampling design was used?

What mode of response was used: a personal interview, a telephone interview, or a mail survey? Were interviewers trained? Were survey questions field-tested?

What other questions were asked? Were they clear, accurate, unbiased, and valid?

What was the response rate?

What was the margin of error?

What was the sample size?

7.18 (a) Virtually zero. **(b)** 0.1587. **(c)** 0.0139. **(d)** 50.195.

7.20 (a) Both means are equal to 6. This property is called unbiasedness. **(c)** The distribution for $n = 3$ has less variability. The larger sample size has resulted in sample means being closer to μ.

7.22 (a) When $n = 2$, the shape of the sampling distribution of $\bar{X}$ should closely resemble the shape of the distribution of the population from which the sample is selected. Since the mean is larger than the median, the distribution of the sales price of new houses is skewed to the right, and so is the sampling distribution of $\bar{X}$. **(b)** When $n = 100$, the sampling distribution of $\bar{X}$ should be very close to a normal distribution due to the Central Limit Theorem. **(c)** When $n = 100$, the sample mean should be close to the population mean. $P(\bar{X} < 250,000) = P(Z < (250,000 - 279,100)/(90,000/\sqrt{100})) = P(Z < -3.2333) = 0.0062$.

7.24 (a) $P(\bar{X} > 3) = P(Z > -1.00) = 1.0 - 0.1587 = 0.8413$. **(b)** $P(Z < 1.04) = 0.85$ $\bar{X} = 3.10 + 1.04(0.1) = 3.204$. **(c)** To be able to use the standardized normal distribution as an approximation for the area under the curve, you must assume that the population is approximately symmetrical. **(d)** $P(Z < 1.04) = 0.85$ $\bar{X} = 3.10 + 1.04(0.05) = 3.152$.

7.26 (a) 0.9969. **(b)** 0.0142. **(c)** 2.3830 and 2.6170. **(d)** 2.6170. *Note:* These answers are computed using Microsoft Excel. They may be slightly different when Table E.2 is used.

7.28 (a) 0.30. **(b)** 0.0693.

7.30 (a) $\pi = 0.501$, $\sigma_P = \sqrt{\dfrac{\pi(1-\pi)}{n}} = \sqrt{\dfrac{0.501(1-0.501)}{100}} = 0.05$

$P(p > 0.55) = P(Z > 0.98) = 1.0 - 0.8365 = 0.1635$

(b) $\pi = 0.60$, $\sigma_P = \sqrt{\dfrac{\pi(1-\pi)}{n}} = \sqrt{\dfrac{0.6(1-0.6)}{100}} = 0.04899$

$P(p > 0.55) = P(Z > -1.021) = 1.0 - 0.1539 = 0.8461$

(c) $\pi = 0.49$, $\sigma_P = \sqrt{\dfrac{\pi(1-\pi)}{n}} = \sqrt{\dfrac{0.49(1-0.49)}{100}} = 0.05$

$P(p > 0.55) = P(Z > 1.20) = 1.0 - 0.8849 = 0.1151$.

(d) Increasing the sample size by a factor of 4 decreases the standard error by a factor of 2.
(a) $P(p > 0.55) = P(Z > 1.96) = 1.0 - 0.9750 = 0.0250$.
(b) $P(p > 0.55) = P(Z > -2.04) = 1.0 - 0.0207 = 0.9793$.
(c) $P(p > 0.55) = P(Z > 2.40) = 1.0 - 0.9918 = 0.0082$.

7.32 (a) 0.50. **(b)** 0.5717. **(c)** 0.9523. **(d) (a)** 0.50. **(b)** 0.4246. **(c)** 0.8386.

7.34 (a) Since $n = 200$, which is quite large, we use the sample proportion to approximate the population proportion and, hence, $\pi = 0.50$.

$$\mu_P = \pi = 0.5, \quad \sigma_P = \sqrt{\dfrac{\pi(1-\pi)}{n}} = \sqrt{\dfrac{0.5(0.5)}{200}} = .0354$$

$P(0.45 < p < 0.55) = P(-1.4142 < Z < 1.4142) = 0.8427$.

(b) $P(A < p < B) = P(-1.6449 < Z < 1.6449) = 0.90$. $A = 0.50 - 1.6449(0.0354) = 0.4418$. $B = 0.50 + 1.6449(0.0354) = 0.5582$. The probability is 90% that the sample percentage will be contained within 5.8% symmetrically around the population percentage. **(c)** $P(A < p < B) = P(-1.96 < Z < +1.96) = 0.95$. $A = 0.50 - 1.96(0.0354) = 0.4307$. $B = 0.50 + 1.96(0.0354) = 0.5694$. The probability is 95% that the sample percentage will be contained within 6.94% symmetrically around the population percentage.

7.36 (a) 0.6314. **(b)** 0.0041. **(c)** $P(p > .35) = P(Z > 1.3223) = 0.0930$. If the population proportion is 29%, the proportion of the samples with 35% or more who do not intend to work for pay at all is 9.3%, an unlikely occurrence. Hence, the population estimate of 29% is likely to be an underestimation. **(d)** When the sample size is smaller in (c) compared to (b), the standard error of the sampling distribution of the sample proportion is larger.

7.38 (a) 0.3626. **(b)** 0.9816. **(c)** 0.0092. *Note:* These answers are computed using Microsoft Excel. They may be slightly different when Table E.2 is used.

7.50 (a) 0.4999. **(b)** 0.00009. **(c)** 0. **(d)** 0. **(e)** 0.7518.

7.52 (a) 0.8944. **(b)** 4.617, 4.783. **(c)** 4.641.

7.54 (a) $\sigma_{\overline{X}} = \dfrac{\sigma}{\sqrt{n}} = \dfrac{20}{\sqrt{10}} = 6.3246\ P(\overline{X} < 0) = P(Z < 2.514) = 0.00597$.

(b) $P(0 < \overline{X} < 6) = P(-2.514 < Z < -1.565) = 0.0528$

(c) $P(\overline{X} > 10) = P(Z > -0.9329) = 0.8246$.

7.56 Even though Internet polling is less expensive and faster and offers higher response rates than telephone surveys, it may lead to more coverage error since a greater proportion of the population may have telephones than have Internet access. It may also lead to nonresponse bias since a certain class and/or age group of people may not use the Internet or may use the Internet less frequently than others. Due to these errors, the data collected are not appropriate for making inferences about the general population.

7.58 (a) With a response rate of only 15.5%, nonresponse error should be the major cause of concern in this study. Measurement error is a possibility also. **(b)** The researchers should follow up with the nonrespondents. **(c)** The step mentioned in (b) could have been followed to increase the response rate to the survey, thus increasing its worthiness.

7.60 (a) What was the comparison group of "other workers"? Were they another sample? Where did they come from? Were they truly comparable? What was the sampling scheme? What was the population from which the sample was selected? How was salary measured? What was the mode of response? What was the response rate? **(b)** Various answers are possible.

CHAPTER 8

8.2 $114.68 \le \mu \le 135.32$

8.4 In order to have 100% certainty, the entire population would have to be sampled.

8.6 Yes, it is true since 5% of intervals will not include the true mean.

8.8 (a) $\overline{X} \pm Z \dfrac{\sigma}{\sqrt{n}} = 350 \pm 1.96 \dfrac{100}{\sqrt{64}}$; $325.50 \le \mu \le 374.50$.
(b) No. The manufacturer cannot support a claim that the bulbs have a mean of 400 hours. Based on the data from the sample, a mean of 400 hours would represent a distance of 4 standard deviations above the sample mean of 350 hours. **(c)** No. Since σ is known and $n = 64$, from the

Central Limit Theorem, you know that the sampling distribution of $\overline{X}$ is approximately normal. **(d)** The confidence interval is narrower, based on a population standard deviation of 80 hours rather than the original standard deviation of 100 hours.

(a) $\overline{X} \pm Z \dfrac{\sigma}{\sqrt{n}} = 350 \pm 1.96 \dfrac{80}{\sqrt{64}}$, $330.4 \le \mu \le 369.6$. **(b)** Based on the smaller standard deviation, a mean of 400 hours would represent a distance of 5 standard deviations above the sample mean of 350 hours. No, the manufacturer cannot support a claim that the bulbs have a mean life of 400 hours.

8.10 (a) 2.2622. **(b)** 3.2498. **(c)** 2.0395. **(d)** 1.9977. **(e)** 1.7531.

8.12 $38.95 \le \mu \le 61.05$.

8.14 $-0.12 \le \mu \le 11.84$, $2.00 \le \mu \le 6.00$. The presence of the outlier increases the sample mean and greatly inflates the sample standard deviation.

8.16 (a) $29.44 \le \mu \le 34.56$. **(b)** The quality improvement team can be 95% confident that the population mean turnaround time is between 29.44 hours and 34.56 hours. **(c)** The project was a success because the initial turnaround time of 68 hours does not fall into the interval.

8.18 (a) $\$21.01 \le \mu \le \$24.99$. **(b)** You can be 95% confident that the population mean bounced-check fee is between $21.01 and $24.99.

8.20 (a) $31.12 \le \mu \le 54.96$. **(b)** The number of days is approximately normally distributed. **(c)** Yes, the outliers skew the data. **(d)** Since the sample size is fairly large, at $n = 50$, the use of the t distribution is appropriate.

8.22 (a) $142.00 \le \mu \le 311.33$. **(b)** The population distribution needs to be normally distributed. **(c)** Both the normal probability plot and the box-and-whisker plot show that the distribution for battery life is approximately normally distributed.

8.24 $0.19 \le \pi \le 0.31$.

8.26 (a) $p = \dfrac{X}{n} = \dfrac{135}{500} = 0.27$

$p \pm Z \sqrt{\dfrac{p(1-p)}{n}} = 0.27 \pm 2.58 \sqrt{\dfrac{0.27(0.73)}{500}}$ $0.2189 \le \pi \le 0.3211$.

(b) The manager in charge of promotional programs concerning residential customers can infer that the proportion of households that would purchase an additional telephone line if it were made available at a substantially reduced installation cost is somewhere between 0.22 and 0.32, with 99% confidence.

8.28 (a) $0.2311 \le \pi \le 0.3089$. **(b)** $0.2425 \le \pi \le 0.2975$. **(c)** The larger the sample size, the narrower is the confidence interval, holding everything else constant.

8.30 (a) $0.5638 \le \pi \le 0.6362$. **(b)** $0.2272 \le \pi \le 0.2920$.

8.32 (a) $0.3783 \le \pi \le 0.4427$. **(b)** You can be 95% confident that the population proportion of all workers whose primary reason for staying on their job is interesting job responsibilities is somewhere between 0.3783 and 0.4427.

8.34 $n = 35$.

8.36 $n = 1,041$.

8.38 (a) $n = \dfrac{Z^2 \sigma^2}{e^2} = \dfrac{(1.96^2)(400^2)}{50^2} = 245.86$

Use $n = 246$.

(b) $n = \dfrac{Z^2 \sigma^2}{e^2} = \dfrac{(1.96^2)(400^2)}{25^2} = 983.41$

Use $n = 984$.

8.40 $n = 97$.

8.42 (a) $n = 167$. **(b)** $n = 97$.

8.44 (a) $n = 246$. **(b)** $n = 385$. **(c)** $n = 554$.

8.46 (a) $n = 2{,}156$. **(b)** $n = 2{,}239$. **(c)** The sample size is larger in (b) than in (a) because the estimate of the true proportion is closer to 0.5 in (b) than in (a). **(d)** If you were to design the follow-up study, you would use one sample and ask the respondents both questions rather than selecting two separate samples because it costs more to select two samples than one.

8.48 (a) $p = 0.5498$; $0.5226 \leq \pi \leq 0.5770$. **(b)** $p = 0.4697$; $0.4424 \leq \pi \leq 0.4970$. **(c)** $p = 0.2799$; $0.2554 \leq 0.3045$ **(d) (a)** $n = 2{,}378$ **(b)** $= 2{,}393$ **(c)** $= 1{,}936$

8.50 $\$10{,}721.53 \leq$ Total $\leq \$14{,}978.47$.

8.52 (a) 0.054. **(b)** 0.0586. **(c)** 0.066.

8.54 $\$543{,}176.96 \leq$ Total $\leq \$1{,}025{,}224.04$.

8.56 $\$5{,}443 \leq$ Total difference $\leq \$54{,}229$.

8.58 (a) 0.0542. **(b)** Since the upper bound is higher than the tolerable exception rate of 0.04, the auditor should request a larger sample.

8.66 $940.50 \leq \mu \leq 1007.50$. Based on the evidence gathered from the sample of 34 stores, the 95% confidence interval for the mean per-store count in all of the franchise's stores is from 940.50 to 1,007.50. With a 95% level of confidence, the franchise can conclude that the mean per-store count in all its stores is somewhere between 940.50 and 1,007.50, which is larger than the original average of 900 mean per-store count before the price reduction. Hence, reducing coffee prices is a good strategy to increase the mean customer count.

8.68 (a) $p = 0.80$, $0.7765 \leq \pi \leq 0.8235$. **(b)** $p = 0.88$, $0.8609 \leq \pi \leq 0.8991$. **(c)** $p = 0.56$, $0.5309 \leq \pi \leq 0.5891$. **(d) (a)** $n = 1{,}537$. **(b)** $n = 1{,}015$. **(c)** $n = 2{,}366$.

8.70 (a) $14.085 \leq \mu \leq 16.515$. **(b)** $0.530 \leq \pi \leq 0.820$. **(c)** $n = 25$. **(d)** $n = 784$. **(e)** If a single sample were to be selected for both purposes, the larger of the two sample sizes ($n = 784$) should be used.

8.72 (a) $8.049 \leq \mu \leq 11.351$. **(b)** $0.284 \leq \pi \leq 0.676$. **(c)** $n = 35$. **(d)** $n = 121$. **(e)** If a single sample were to be selected for both purposes, the larger of the two sample sizes ($n = 121$) should be used.

8.74 (a) $\$25.80 \leq \mu \leq \$31.24$. **(b)** $0.3037 \leq \pi \leq 0.4963$. **(c)** $n = 97$. **(d)** $n = 423$. **(e)** If a single sample were to be selected for both purposes, the larger of the two sample sizes ($n = 423$) should be used.

8.76 (a) $\$36.66 \leq \mu \leq \$40.42$. **(b)** $0.2027 \leq \pi \leq 0.3973$. **(c)** $n = 110$. **(d)** $n = 423$. **(e)** If a single sample were to be selected for both purposes, the larger of the two sample sizes ($n = 423$) should be used.

8.78 (a) $\pi \leq 0.2013$. **(b)** Since the upper bound is higher than the tolerable exception rate of 0.15, the auditor should request a larger sample.

8.80 (a) $n = 27$. **(b)** $\$402{,}652.53 \leq$ Population total $\leq \$450{,}950.79$.

8.82 (a) $8.41 \leq \mu \leq 8.43$. **(b)** With 95% confidence, the population mean width of troughs is somewhere between 8.41 and 8.43 inches.

8.84 (a) $0.2425 \leq \mu \leq 0.2856$. **(b)** $0.1975 \leq \mu \leq 0.2385$. **(c)** The amounts of granule loss for both brands are skewed to the right. **(d)** Since the two confidence intervals do not overlap, you can conclude that the mean granule loss of Boston shingles is higher than that of Vermont shingles.

CHAPTER 9

9.2 H_1 denotes the alternative hypothesis.

9.4 β.

9.6 α is the probability of making a Type I error.

9.8 The power of the test is $1 - \beta$.

9.10 It is possible to not reject a null hypothesis when it is false since it is possible for a sample mean to fall in the nonrejection region even if the null hypothesis is false.

9.12 All else being equal, the closer the population mean is to the hypothesized mean, the larger β will be.

9.14 H_0: Defendant is guilty; H_1: Defendant is innocent. A Type I error would be not convicting a guilty person. A Type II error would be convicting an innocent person.

9.16 H_0: $\mu = 20$ minutes. 20 minutes is adequate travel time between classes.
H_1: $\mu \neq 20$ minutes. 20 minutes is not adequate travel time between classes.

9.18 H_0: $\mu = 1.00$. The mean amount of paint per one-gallon can is one gallon.
H_1: $\mu \neq 1.00$. The mean amount of paint per one-gallon can differs from one gallon.

9.20 Since $Z = +2.21 > 1.96$, reject H_0.

9.22 Reject H_0 if $Z < -2.58$ or if $Z > 2.58$.

9.24 p-value $= 0.0456$.

9.26 p-value $= 0.1676$.

9.28 (a) H_0: $\mu = 70$ pounds; H_1: $\mu \neq 70$ pounds.
Decision rule: Reject H_0 if $Z < -1.96$ or $Z > +1.96$.

Test statistic: $Z = \dfrac{\bar{X} - \mu}{\sigma / \sqrt{n}} = \dfrac{69.1 - 70}{3.5 / \sqrt{49}} = -1.80$

Decision: Since $-1.96 < Z = -1.80 < 1.96$, do not reject H_0. There is insufficient evidence to conclude that the cloth has a mean breaking strength that differs from 70 pounds. **(b)** p-value $= 2(0.0359) = 0.0718$. Interpretation: The probability of getting a sample of 49 pieces that yield a mean strength that is farther away from the hypothesized population mean than this sample is 0.0718, or 7.18%.
(c) Decision rule: Reject H_0 if $Z < -1.96$ or $Z > +1.96$.

Test statistic: $Z = \dfrac{\bar{X} - \mu}{\sigma / \sqrt{n}} = \dfrac{69.1 - 70}{1.75 / \sqrt{49}} = -3.60$.

Decision: Since $Z = -3.60 < -1.96$, reject H_0. There is enough evidence to conclude that the cloth has a mean breaking strength that differs from 70 pounds. **(d)** Decision rule: Reject H_0 if $Z < -1.96$ or

$Z > +1.96$. Test statistic: $Z = \dfrac{\bar{X} - \mu}{\sigma / \sqrt{n}} = \dfrac{69 - 70}{3.5 / \sqrt{49}} = -2.00$.

Decision: Since $Z = -2.00 < -1.96$, reject H_0. There is enough evidence to conclude that the cloth has a mean breaking strength that differs from 70 pounds.

9.30 (a) Since $Z = -2.00 < -1.96$, reject H_0. **(b)** p-value $= 0.0456$. **(c)** $325.5 \le \mu \le 374.5$. **(d)** The conclusions are the same.

9.32 (a) Since $-1.96 < Z = -0.80 < 1.96$, do not reject H_0. **(b)** p-value $= 0.4238$. **(c)** Since $Z = -2.40 < -1.96$, reject H_0. **(d)** Since $Z = -2.26 < -1.96$, reject H_0.

9.34 $Z = +2.33$.

9.36 $Z = -2.33$.

9.38 p-value $= 0.0228$.

9.40 p-value $= 0.0838$.

9.42 p-value $= 0.9162$.

9.44 (a) Since $Z = -1.75 < -1.645$, reject H_0. **(b)** p-value $= 0.0401 < 0.05$, reject H_0. **(c)** The probability of getting a sample mean of 2.73 feet or less if the population mean is 2.8 feet is 0.0401. **(d)** They are the same.

9.46 (a) H_0: $\mu \le 5$; H_1: $\mu > 5$. **(b)** A Type I error occurs when you conclude that children take a mean of more than five trips a week to the store when in fact they take a mean of no more than five trips a week to the store. A Type II error occurs when you conclude that children take a mean of no more than five trips a week to the store when in fact they take a mean of more than five trips a week to the store. **(c)** Since $Z_{calc} = 2.9375 > 2.3263$ or the p-value of 0.0017 is less than 0.01, reject H_0. There is enough evidence to conclude the population mean number of trips to the store is greater than five per week. **(d)** The probability that the sample mean is 5.47 trips or more when the null hypothesis is true is 0.0017.

9.48 $t = 2.00$.

9.50 (a) $t = \pm 2.1315$. **(b)** $t = +1.7531$.

9.52 No, you should not use a t test since the original population is left-skewed and the sample size is not large enough for the t test to be valid.

9.54 (a) Since $t = -2.4324 < -1.9842$, reject H_0. There is enough evidence to conclude that the population mean has changed from 41.4 days. **(b)** Since $t = -2.4324 > -2.6264$, do not reject H_0. There is not enough evidence to conclude that the population mean has changed from 41.4 days.

(c) Since $t = -2.9907 < -1.9842$, reject H_0. There is enough evidence to conclude that the population mean has changed from 41.4 days.

9.56 Since $t = -1.30 > -1.6694$ and the p-value of $0.0992 > 0.05$, do not reject H_0. There is not enough evidence to conclude that the mean waiting time is less than 3.7 minutes.

9.58 Since $t = 0.8556 < 2.5706$, do not reject H_0. There is not enough evidence to conclude that the mean price for two tickets, with online service charges, large popcorn, and two medium soft drinks, is different from \$35. **(b)** The p-value is 0.4313. If the population mean is \$35, the probability of observing a sample of six theater chains that will result in a sample mean farther away from the hypothesized value than this sample is 0.4313. **(c)** That the distribution of prices is normally distributed. **(d)** With a small sample size, it is difficult to evaluate the assumption of normality. However, the distribution may be symmetric since the mean and the median are close in value.

9.60 (a) Since $-2.0096 < t = 0.114 < 2.0096$, do not reject H_0. **(b)** p-value $= 0.9095$. **(c)** Yes, the data appear to have met the normality assumption. **(d)** The amount of fill is decreasing over time. Therefore, the t test is invalid.

9.62 (a) Since $t = -5.9355 < -2.0106$, reject H_0. There is enough evidence to conclude that mean widths of the troughs is different from 8.46 inches. **(b)** That the population distribution is normal. **(c)** Although the distribution of the widths is left-skewed, the large sample size means that the validity of the t test is not seriously affected.

9.64 (a) Since $-2.68 < t = 0.094 < 2.68$, do not reject H_0. **(b)** $5.462 \le \mu \le 5.542$. **(c)** The conclusions are the same.

9.66 $p = 0.22$.

9.68 Do not reject H_0.

9.70 (a) H_0: $\pi \le 0.5$ H_1: $\pi > 0.5$ Decision rule: If $Z > 1.6449$, reject H_0.

Test statistic: $Z = \dfrac{p - \pi}{\sqrt{\dfrac{\pi(1 - \pi)}{n}}} = \dfrac{0.5496 - 0.5}{\sqrt{\dfrac{0.5(1 - 0.5)}{464}}} = 2.1355$

Decision: Since $Z = 2.1355 > 1.6449$, reject H_0. There is enough evidence to show that the majority of Cincinnati-area adults were planning on modifying or canceling their summer travel plans because of high gas prices. **(b)** H_0: $\pi \le 0.5$ H_1: $\pi > 0.5$ Decision rule: If p-value < 0.05, reject H_0. p-value $= 0.0164$ Decision: Since p-value $= 0.0164 < 0.05$, reject H_0. There is enough evidence to show that the majority of Cincinnati-area adults were planning on modifying or canceling their summer travel plans because of high gas prices. **(c)** The conclusions from (a) and (b) are the same as they should be.

9.72 (a) Since $-1.96 < Z = 0.6381 < 1.96$, do not reject H_0 and conclude that there is not enough evidence to show that the percentage of people who trust energy-efficiency ratings differs from 50%. **(b)** p-value $= 0.5234$. Since the p-value of $0.5234 > 0.05$, do not reject H_0.

9.74 (a) $p = 0.7112$. **(b)** Since $Z = 5.7771 > 1.6449$, reject H_0. There is enough evidence to conclude that more than half of all successful women executives have children. **(c)** Since $Z_{calc} = 1.2927 < 1.6449$, do not reject H_0. There is not enough evidence to conclude that more than two-thirds of all successful women executives have children. **(d)** The random sample assumption is not likely to be valid because the criteria used in defining "successful women executives" is very likely to be quite different than those used in defining the "most powerful women in business" who attended the summit.

9.84 (a) Buying a site that is not profitable. **(b)** Not buying a profitable site. **(c)** Type I. **(d)** If the executives adopt a less stringent rejection criterion by buying sites for which the computer model predicts moderate or large profit, the probability of committing a Type I error will increase. Many more of the sites the computer model predicts that will generate moderate profit may end up not being profitable at all. On the other hand, the less stringent rejection criterion will lower the probability of committing a Type II error since more potentially profitable sites will be purchased.

9.86 (a) Since $t = 3.248 > 2.0010$, reject H_0. **(b)** p-value $= 0.0019$. **(c)** Since $Z = -0.32 > -1.645$, do not reject H_0. **(d)** Since $-2.0010 < t = 0.75 < 2.0010$, do not reject H_0. **(e)** Since $t = -1.61 > -1.645$, do not reject H_0.

9.88 (a) Since $t = -1.69 > -1.7613$, do not reject H_0. **(b)** The data are from a population that is normally distributed.

9.90 (a) Since $t = -1.47 > -1.6896$, do not reject H_0. **(b)** p-value $= 0.0748$. **(c)** Since $t = -3.10 < -1.6973$, reject H_0. **(d)** p-value $= 0.0021$. **(e)** The data in the population are assumed to be normally distributed.

9.92 (a) $t = -21.61$, reject H_0. **(b)** p-value $= 0.0000$. **(c)** $t = -27.19$, reject H_0. **(d)** p-value $= 0.0000$.

CHAPTER 10

10.2 Since $-2.58 \le Z = 1.73 \le 2.58$, do not reject H_0.

10.4 (a) $t = 3.8959$. **(b)** $df = 21$. **(c)** 2.5177. **(d)** Since $Z = 3.8959 > 2.5177$, reject H_0.

10.6 $3.73 \le \mu_1 - \mu_2 \le 12.27$.

10.8 (a) Since $Z = 5.20 > 2.33$, reject H_0. **(b)** p-value < 0.00003.

10.10 (a) Since $-2.0117 < t = 0.1023 < 2.0117$, do not reject H_0. There is no evidence of a difference in the two means for the age 8 group. Since $t = 3.375 > 1.9908$, reject H_0. There is evidence of a difference in the two means for the age 12 group. Since $t = 3.3349 > 1.9966$, reject H_0. There is evidence of a difference in the two means for the age 16 group. **(b)** The test results show that children in the United States begin to develop preferences for brand name products as early as age 12.

10.12 (a) H_0: $\mu_1 = \mu_2$, where Populations: $1 =$ Males, $2 =$ Females

$$H_1: \mu_1 \ne \mu_2$$

Decision rule: $df = 170$. If $t < -1.974$ or $t > 1.974$, reject H_0.
Test statistic:

$$S_p^2 = \frac{(n_1 - 1)(S_1^2) + (n_2 - 1)(S_2^2)}{(n_1 - 1) + (n_2 - 1)}$$

$$= \frac{(99)(13.35^2) + (71)(9.42^2)}{99 + 71} = 140.8489$$

$$t = \frac{(\bar{X}_1 - \bar{X}_2) - (\mu_1 - \mu_2)}{\sqrt{S_p^2\left(\frac{1}{n_1} + \frac{1}{n_2}\right)}}$$

$$= \frac{(40.26 - 36.85) - 0}{\sqrt{140.8489\left(\frac{1}{100} + \frac{1}{72}\right)}} = 1.859$$

Decision: Since $-1.974 < t = 1.859 < 1.974$, do not reject H_0. There is not enough evidence to conclude that the mean computer anxiety experienced by males and females is different. **(b)** p-value $= 0.0648$. **(c)** In order to use the pooled-variance t test, you need to assume that the populations are normally distributed with equal variances.

10.14 (a) Since $-4.1343 < -2.0484$, reject H_0. **(b)** p-value $= 0.0003$. **(c)** The original populations of waiting times are approximately normally distributed. **(d)** $-4.2292 \le \mu_1 - \mu_2 \le -1.4268$.

10.16 (a) Since $-2.024 < t = 0.354 < 2.024$ or p-value $= 0.725 > 0.05$, do not reject the null hypothesis. There is not enough evidence to conclude that the mean time to clear problems in the two offices is different. **(b)** p-value $= 0.725$. The probability that a sample will yield a t test statistic more extreme than 0.3544 is 0.725 if the mean waiting time between Office 1 and Office 2 is the same. **(c)** You need to assume that the two populations are normally distributed. **(d)** $-0.9543 \le \mu_1 - \mu_2 \le 1.3593$.

10.18 (a) Since $t = 4.10 > 2.024$, reject H_0. There is evidence of a difference in the mean surface hardness between untreated and treated steel plates. **(b)** p-value $= 0.0002$. The probability that two samples have a mean difference of 9.3634 or more is 0.02% if there is no difference in the mean surface hardness between untreated and treated steel plates. **(c)** You need to assume that the population distribution of hardness of both untreated and treated steel plates is normally distributed. **(d)** $4.7447 \le \mu_1 - \mu_2 \le 13.9821$.

10.20 (a) Since $t = -2.1522 < -2.0211$, reject H_0. There is enough evidence to conclude that the mean assembly times, in seconds, are different between employees trained in a computer-assisted, individual-based program and those trained in a team-based program. **(b)** You must assume that each of the two independent populations is normally distributed. **(c)** Since $t = -2.152 < -2.052$ or p-value $= 0.041 < 0.05$, reject H_0. **(d)** The results in (a) and (c) are the same. **(e)** $-4.52 \le \mu_1 - \mu_2 \le -0.14$. You are 95% confident that the difference between the population means of the two training methods is between -4.52 and -0.14.

10.22 $df = 19$.

10.24 (a) H_0: $\mu_D = 0$ vs. H_1: $\mu_D \ne 0$
Excel Output:

	2004	2005
Mean	211.0132	214.1688
Variance	17525.43	17600.33
Observations	25	25
Pearson Correlation	0.979899	
Hypothesized Mean Difference	0	
df	24	
t Stat	−0.59375	
P(T<=t) one-tail	0.279118	
t Critical one-tail	1.710882	
P(T<=t) two-tail	0.558237	
t Critical two-tail	2.063899	

Test statistic: $t = \dfrac{\bar{D} - \mu_D}{\dfrac{S_D}{\sqrt{n}}} = -0.5937$

Decision: Since $-2.0639 < t = -0.5937 < 2.0639$, do not reject H_0. There is not enough evidence to conclude that there is a difference in the mean number of advertising pages in September 2004 and September 2005. **(b)** You must assume that the distribution of the differences between the mean measurements is approximately normal. **(c)** p-value $= 0.5582$. The probability of obtaining a mean difference in advertising pages in September 2004 and September 2005 that gives rise to a test statistic that deviates from 0 by 0.5937 or more in either direction is 0.5582 if the mean difference in the advertising pages in September 2004 and September 2005 is zero.

(d) $\bar{D} \pm t\dfrac{S_D}{\sqrt{n}} = -3.16 \pm 2.0639\dfrac{26.5736}{\sqrt{25}}$. $-14.12 \le \mu_D \le 7.81$.

You are 95% confident that the mean difference in advertising pages in September 2004 and September 2005 is somewhere between -14.12 and 7.81.

10.26 (a) Since $-3.0123 < t = 0.2758 < 3.0123$, do not reject H_0. There is not enough evidence to conclude that there is a difference between the mean price of textbooks at the local bookstore and Amazon.com. **(b)** You must assume that the distribution of the differences between the measurements is approximately normal. **(c)** $-8.12 \le \mu_D \le 9.76$. You are 99% confident that the mean difference between the mean price of textbooks at the local bookstore and Amazon.com is somewhere between -8.12 and 9.76. **(d)** The results in (a) and (c) are the same. The hypothesized value of 0 for the difference in the mean price of textbooks between the local bookstore and Amazon.com is inside the 99% confidence interval.

10.28 (a) Since $t = 1.8425 < 1.943$, do not reject H_0. There is not enough evidence to conclude that the mean bone marrow microvessel density is higher before the stem cell transplant than after the stem cell transplant. **(b)** p-value $= 0.0575$. The probability that the t statistic for the mean difference in density is 1.8425 or more is 5.75% if the mean density is not higher before the stem cell transplant than after the stem cell transplant. **(c)** $-28.26 \leq \mu_D \leq 200.55$. You are 95% confident that the mean difference in bone marrow microvessel density before and after the stem cell transplant is somewhere between -28.26 and 200.55.

10.30 (a) Since $t = -9.3721 < -2.4258$, reject H_0. **(b)** The population of differences in strength is approximately normally distributed. **(c)** $p = 0.000$.

10.32 (a) Since $-2.58 \leq Z = -0.58 \leq 2.58$, do not reject H_0. **(b)** $-0.273 \leq \pi_1 - \pi_2 \leq 0.173$.

10.34 (a) $H_0: \pi_1 \leq \pi_2$. $H_1: \pi_1 > \pi_2$. Population 1 = parents, 2 = teachers. **(b)** Since $Z = 7.9918 > 1.6449$, reject H_0. There is sufficient evidence to conclude that the population proportion of parents that are very confident that their child's school will meet the standards by the deadline is greater than the population proportion of teachers that are very confident that the school where they work will meet standards by the deadline. **(c)** Yes, the result in (b) makes it appropriate for the article to claim that parents are more confident.

10.36 (a) $H_0: \pi_1 = \pi_2$. $H_1: \pi_1 \neq \pi_2$. Decision rule: If $|Z| > 1.96$, reject H_0.

Test statistic:

$$\bar{p} = \frac{X_2 + X_2}{n_1 + n_2} = \frac{280 + 320}{505 + 500} = 0.5970$$

$$Z = \frac{(p_1 - p_2) - (\pi_1 - \pi_2)}{\sqrt{\bar{p}(1-\bar{p})\left(\dfrac{1}{n_1} + \dfrac{1}{n_2}\right)}} = \frac{(0.5545 - 0.64) - 0}{\sqrt{0.5970(1 - 0.5970)\left(\dfrac{1}{505} + \dfrac{1}{500}\right)}}$$

$$= -2.7644$$

Decision: Since $Z = -2.7644 < -1.6449$, reject H_0. There is sufficient evidence to conclude that there is a difference in the proportion of adults who think the U.S. tax code is unfair between the two income groups. **(b)** p-value $= 0.0057$. The probability of obtaining a difference in proportions that gives rise to a test statistic that deviates from 0 by 2.7644 or more in either direction is 0.0057 if there is no difference in the proportion of adults who think the U.S. tax code is unfair between the two income groups.

10.38 (a) Since $-1.96 < Z = 1.5240 < 1.96$, do not reject H_0. There is insufficient evidence of a difference between undergraduate and MBA students in the proportion who selected the highest-cost fund. **(b)** p-value $= 0.1275$. The probability of obtaining a difference in proportions that gives rise to a test statistic that deviates from 0 by 1.5240 or more in either direction is 0.1275 if there is no difference between undergraduate and MBA students in the proportion who selected the highest-cost fund.

10.40 (a) $F_U = 2.20$, $F_L = \dfrac{1}{2.33} = 0.43$.

(b) $F_U = 2.57$, $F_L = \dfrac{1}{2.76} = 0.36$. **(c)** $F_U = 3.09$, $F_L = \dfrac{1}{3.37} = 0.30$.

(d) $F_U = 3.50$, $F_L = \dfrac{1}{3.88} = 0.26$.

10.42 (a) 0.429. **(b)** 0.362. **(c)** 0.297. **(d)** 0.258.

10.44 $df_{numerator} = 24$, $df_{denominator} = 24$.

10.46 Since $0.4405 < F = 0.8258 < 2.27$, do not reject H_0.

10.48 (a) Since $0.3378 < F = 1.2995 < 3.18$, do not reject H_0. **(b)** Since $F = 1.2995 < 2.62$, do not reject H_0. **(c)** Since $F = 1.2995 > 0.4032$, do not reject H_0.

10.50 (a) $H_0: \sigma_1^2 = \sigma_2^2$. $H_0: \sigma_1^2 \neq \sigma_2^2$.
Decision rule: If $F > 1.556$ or $F < 0.653$, reject H_0.

Test statistic: $F = \dfrac{S_1^2}{S_2^2} = \dfrac{(13.35)^2}{(9.42)^2} = 2.008$.

Decision: Since $F = 2.008 > 1.556$, reject H_0. There is enough evidence to conclude that the two population variances are different. **(b)** p-value $= 0.0022$. **(c)** The test assumes that each of the two populations is normally distributed. **(d)** Based on (a) and (b), a separate-variance t test should be used.

10.52 (a) Since $0.3958 < F = 0.8248 < 2.5265$, do not reject H_0. **(b)** 0.6789. **(c)** The test assumes that the populations of times are approximately normally distributed. **(d)** The pooled t-test or a separate-variance t test.

10.54 Since $9.6045 < F = 3.6647 < F_L = 0.1041$, do not reject H_0. There is not enough evidence to conclude that there is a difference in the variance of the yield between money market accounts and one-year CDs.

10.62 (a) $H_0: \sigma_1^2 \geq \sigma_2^2$ and $H_0: \sigma_1^2 < \sigma_2^2$.
(b) Type I error: Rejecting the null hypothesis that the price variance on the Internet is no lower than the price variance in the brick-and-mortar market when the price variance on the Internet is no lower than the price variance in the brick-and-mortar market. Type II error: Failing to reject the null hypothesis that price variance on the Internet is no lower than the price variance in the brick-and-mortar market when the price variance on the Internet is lower than the price variance in the brick-and-mortar market. **(c)** An F test for differences in two variances can be used. **(d)** You need to assume that each of the two populations is normally distributed. **(e) (a)** $H_0: \mu_1 \geq \mu_2$ and $H_1: \mu_1 < \mu_2$.
(b) Type I error: Rejecting the null hypothesis that the mean price in the electronic market is no lower than the mean price in the physical market when the mean price in the electronic market is no lower than the mean price in the physical market. Type II error: Failing to reject the null hypothesis that the mean price in the electronic market is no lower than the mean price in the physical market when the mean price in the electronic market is lower than the mean price in the physical market. **(c)** A pooled t test or a separate-variances t test for the difference in the means can be used. **(d)** You must assume that the distribution of the prices in the electronic market and in the physical market are approximately normally distributed.

10.64 (a) The researchers can ask the teenagers, after viewing each ad, to rate the dangers of smoking, using a scale from 0 to 10, with 10 representing the most dangerous.
(b) $H_0: \mu_T \geq \mu_S$. $H_1: \mu_T < \mu_S$. **(c)** Type I error is the error made by concluding that ads produced by the state are more effective than those produced by Philip Morris while it is not true. The risk of Type I error here is that teenagers can miss the opportunity from the better ads produced by Philip Morris to recognize the true dangers of smoking and the additional expenses the state will have to incur to produce and run the ads. Type II error is the error made by concluding that ads produced by Philip Morris is no less effective than those produced by the state while ads produced by the state are more effective. The risk of Type II error here is that more teenagers will miss the opportunity to recognize the true dangers of smoking from the ads produced by the state. **(d)** Since both ads are shown to the same group of teenagers, a paired t test for the mean difference is most appropriate. **(e)** Statistically reliable here means the conclusions drawn from the test are reliable because all the assumptions needed for the test to be valid are fulfilled.

10.66 (a) Since $F = 22.7067 > F_U = 1.6275$, reject H_0. There is enough evidence to conclude that there is a difference between the variances in age of students at the Western school and at the Eastern school. **(b)** Since there is a difference between the variances in age of students at the Western school and at the Eastern school, schools should take that into account when designing their curriculum to accommodate the larger variance in age of students in the state university in the Western United States. **(c)** It is more appropriate to use a separate-variance t test. **(d)** Since $1.6275 < F = 1.3061 < 0.6024$, do not reject H_0. There is not enough evidence to conclude that there is a difference between the variances in years of spreadsheet usage of students at the Western school and at the Eastern school. **(e)** Using the pooled t test, since $t = -4.6640 < -2.5978$, reject H_0. There is enough evidence of a difference in the mean years of spreadsheet usage of students at the Western school and at the Eastern school.

10.68 (a) Since $t = 3.3282 > 1.8595$, reject H_0. There is enough evidence to conclude that the introductory computer students required more than a mean of 10 minutes to write and run a program in Visual Basic. **(b)** Since $t = 1.3636 < 1.8595$, do not reject H_0. There is not enough evidence to conclude that the introductory computer students required more than a mean of 10 minutes to write and run a program in Visual Basic. **(c)** Although the mean time necessary to complete the assignment increased from 12 to 16 minutes as a result of the increase in one data value, the standard deviation went from 1.8 to 13.2, which reduced the t value. **(d)** Since $0.2328 < F = 0.8125 < 3.8549$, do not reject H_0. There is not enough evidence to conclude that the population variances are different for the Introduction to Computers students and computer majors. Hence, the pooled-variance t test is a valid test to determine whether computer majors can write a Visual Basic program in less time than introductory students, assuming that the distributions of the time needed to write a Visual Basic program for both the Introduction to Computers students and the computer majors are approximately normally distributed. Since $t = 4.0666 > 1.7341$, reject H_0. There is enough evidence that the mean time is higher for Introduction to Computers students than for computer majors. **(e)** p-value = 0.000362. If the true population mean amount of time needed for Introduction to Computer students to write a Visual Basic program is no more than 10 minutes, the probability of observing a sample mean greater than the 12 minutes in the current sample is 0.0362%. Hence, at a 5% level of significance, you can conclude that the population mean amount of time needed for Introduction to Computer students to write a Visual Basic program is more than 10 minutes. As illustrated in part (d), in which there is not enough evidence to conclude that the population variances are different for the Introduction to Computers students and computer majors, the pooled-variance t test performed is a valid test to determine whether computer majors can write a Visual Basic program in less time than introductory students, assuming that the distribution of the time needed to write a Visual Basic program for both the Introduction to Computers students and the computer majors are approximately normally distributed.

10.70 Population 1 is men and population 2 is women. Auto-related: Since $Z = 3.1346 > 1.96$, reject H_0. There is sufficient evidence to conclude that there is a difference between men and women. Cash: Since $-1.96 < Z = -0.5053 < 1.96$, do not reject H_0. There is insufficient evidence to conclude that there is a difference between men and women. Clothes: Since $Z = -4.4642 < -1.96$, reject H_0. There is sufficient evidence to conclude that there is a difference between men and women. Electronics: Since $Z = 2.1284 > 1.96$, reject H_0. There is sufficient evidence to conclude that there is a difference between men and women. Entertainment: Since $-1.96 < Z = 1.6759 < 1.96$, do not reject H_0. There is insufficient evidence to conclude that there is a difference

between men and women. Food: Since $-1.96 < Z = -1.6917 < 1.96$, do not reject H_0. There is insufficient evidence to conclude that there is a difference between men and women.
Investments: Since $Z = 2.2717 > 1.96$, reject H_0. There is sufficient evidence to conclude that there is a difference between men and women. Travel: Since $-1.96 < Z = 1.5318 < 1.96$, do not reject H_0. There is insufficient evidence to conclude that there is a difference between men and women.

10.72 From the box-and-whisker plot and the summary statistics, both distributions are approximately normally distributed. $0.5289 < F = 0.947 < 1.89$. There is insufficient evidence to conclude that the two population variances are significantly different at the 5% level of significance. $t = -5.084 < -1.99$. At the 5% level of significance, there is sufficient evidence to reject the null hypothesis of no difference in the mean life of the bulbs between the two manufacturers. You can conclude that there is a significant difference in the mean life of the bulbs between the two manufacturers.

10.74 Since $F_L = 0.3958 < F = 0.9345 < F_U = 2.5265$, do not reject H_0. There is not enough evidence to conclude that there is a difference between the variances in Wing A and Wing B. Hence, a pooled-variance t test is more appropriate for determining whether there is a difference in the mean delivery time in the two wings of the hotel. Since $t = 5.1615 > 2.0244$, reject H_0. There is enough evidence of a difference in the mean delivery time in the two wings of the hotel.

10.76 (a) Since $F = 3.339 > 1.9096$ or p-value = 0.000361 < 0.05, reject H_0. There is evidence of a difference between the variances in the attendance at games with promotions and games without promotions. **(b)** Since the variances cannot be assumed to be equal, you should use a separate-variance t test for the difference in two means. Since $t = 4.745 > 1.996$ or since the p-value is approximately zero, you reject H_0. **(c)** There is evidence that there is a difference in the mean attendance at games with promotions and games without promotions at the 5% level of significance.

10.78 The normal probability plots suggest that the two populations are not normally distributed. An F test is inappropriate for testing the difference in two variances. The sample variances for Boston and Vermont shingles are 0.0203 and 0.015, respectively, which are not very different. It appears that a pooled-variance t test is appropriate for testing the difference in means. Since $t = 3.015 > 1.967$ or the p-value = 0.0028 < α = 0.05, reject H_0. There is sufficient evidence to conclude that there is a difference in the mean granule loss of Boston and Vermont shingles.

CHAPTER 11

11.2 (a) $SSW = 150$. **(b)** $MSA = 15$. **(c)** $MSW = 5$. **(d)** $F = 3$.

11.4 (a) 2. **(b)** 18. **(c)** 20.

11.6 (a) Reject H_0 if $F > 2.95$; otherwise, do not reject H_0. **(b)** Since $F = 4 > 2.95$, reject H_0. **(c)** The table does not have 28 degrees of freedom in the denominator, so use the next larger critical value, $Q_U = 3.90$. **(d)** Critical range = 6.166.

11.8 (a) Since $F = 10.99 > F = 4.26$, reject H_0. **(b)** Critical range = 40.39. The experts and darts are not different from each other, but they are both different from the readers. **(c)** It is not valid to infer that the dartboard is better than the professionals since their means are not significantly different. **(d)** Since $F = 0.101 < 4.26$, do not reject H_0. There is no evidence of a significant difference in the variation in the return for the three categories.

11.10 (a) $H_0: \mu_A = \mu_B = \mu_C = \mu_D$ and H_1: At least one mean is different.

$$MSA = \frac{SSA}{c-1} = \frac{1986.475}{3} = 662.1583$$

$$MSW = \frac{SSW}{n-c} = \frac{495.5}{36} = 13.76389$$

$$F = \frac{MSA}{MSW} = \frac{662.1583}{13.76389} = 48.1084$$

$$F_{\alpha, c-1, n-c} = F_{0.05, 3, 36} = 2.8663$$

Since the p-value is approximately zero and $F = 48.1084 > 2.8663$, reject H_0. There is sufficient evidence of a difference in the mean strength of the four brands of trash bags.

(b) Critical range $= Q_u \sqrt{\frac{MSW}{2}\left(\frac{1}{n_j}+\frac{1}{n_{j'}}\right)} = 3.79 \sqrt{\frac{13.7639}{2}\left(\frac{1}{10}+\frac{1}{10}\right)}$

$$= 4.446$$

From the Tukey-Kramer procedure, there is a difference in mean strength between Kroger and Tuffstuff, Glad and Tuffstuff, and Hefty and Tuffstuff.

(c) ANOVA output for Levene's test for homogeneity of variance:

$$MSA = \frac{SSA}{c-1} = \frac{24.075}{3} = 8.025$$

$$MSW = \frac{SSW}{n-c} = \frac{198.2}{36} = 5.5056$$

$$F = \frac{MSA}{MSW} = \frac{8.025}{5.5056} = 1.4576$$

$$F_{\alpha, c-1, n-c} = F_{0.05, 3, 36} = 2.8663$$

Since the p-value $= 0.2423 > 0.05$ and $F = 1.458 < 2.866$, do not reject H_0. There is insufficient evidence to conclude that the variances in strength among the four brands of trash bags are different. **(d)** From the results in (a) and (b), Tuffstuff has the lowest mean strength and should be avoided.

11.12 (a) Since $F = 12.56 > F_{0.05, 4, 25} = 2.76$, reject H_0. **(b)** Critical range $= 4.67$. Advertisements A and B are different from Advertisements C and D. Advertisement E is only different from Advertisement D. **(c)** Since $F = 1.927 < 2.76$, do not reject H_0. There is no evidence of a significant difference in the variation in the ratings among the five advertisements. **(d)** The advertisement underselling the pen's characteristics had the highest mean ratings, and the advertisements overselling the pen's characteristics had the lowest mean ratings. Therefore, use an advertisement that undersells the pen's characteristics and avoid advertisements that oversell the pen's characteristics.

11.14 (a) Since $F = 53.03 > F_{0.05, 3, 30} = 2.92$, reject H_0. **(b)** Critical range $= 5.27$ (using 30 degrees of freedom). Designs 3 and 4 are different from Designs 1 and 2. Designs 1 and 2 are different from each other. **(c)** The assumptions are that the samples are randomly and independently selected (or randomly assigned), the original populations of distances are approximately normally distributed, and the variances are equal. **(d)** Since $F = 2.093 < F_{3, 30} = 2.92$, do not reject H_0. There is no evidence of a significant difference in the variation in the distance among the four designs. **(e)** The manager should choose Design 3 or 4.

11.16 (a) 40. **(b)** 60 and 55. **(c)** 10. **(d)** 10.

11.18 (a) Since $F = 6.00 > 3.35$, reject H_0. **(b)** Since $F = 5.50 > F = 3.35$, reject H_0. **(c)** Since $F = 1.00 < F = 2.73$, do not reject H_0.

11.20 df B $= 4$, df total $= 44$, $SSA = 160$, $SSAB = 80$, $SSE = 150$, $SST = 610$, $MSB = 55$, $MSE = 5$, $F_A = 16$, $F_{AB} = 2$.

11.22 (a) Since $F = 1.37 < F = 4.75$, do not reject H_0. **(b)** Since $F = 23.58 > F_{0.05, 1, 12} = 4.75$, reject H_0. **(c)** Since $F = 0.70 < F_{0.05, 1, 12} = 4.75$, do not reject H_0. **(e)** Developer strength has a significant effect on density, but development time does not.

11.24 (a) H_0: There is no interaction between brand and water temperature. H_1: There is an interaction between brand and water temperature.

$$MSAB = \frac{SSAB}{(r-1)(c-1)} = \frac{506.3104}{(1)(2)} = 253.1552$$

$$F = \frac{MSAB}{MSE} = \frac{253.1552}{12.2199} = 20.7167$$

Since $F = 20.7167 > 3.555$ or the p-value $= 0.0000214 < 0.05$, reject H_0. There is evidence of interaction between brand of pain reliever and temperature of the water. **(b)** Since there is an interaction between brand and the temperature of the water, it is inappropriate to analyze the main effect due to brand. **(c)** Since there is an interaction between brand and the temperature of the water, it is an inappropriate to analyze the main effect due to water temperature. **(e)** The difference in the mean time a tablet took to dissolve in cold and hot water depends on the brand, with Alka-Seltzer having the largest difference and Equate with the smallest difference.

11.26 (a) Since $F = 0.43 < F_{0.05, 1, 28} = 4.20$, do not reject H_0. **(b)** Since $F = 0.02 < F_{0.05, 1, 28} = 4.20$, do not reject H_0. **(c)** Since $F = 45.47 > F_{0.05, 1, 28} = 4.20$, reject H_0. **(e)** Only part positioning has a significant effect on distortion.

11.36 (a) Since $F = 1.485 < F_{0.05, 9, 16} = 2.54$, do not reject H_0. **(b)** Since $F = 0.79 < F_{0.05, 3, 16} = 3.24$, do not reject H_0. **(c)** Since $F = 52.07 > F_{0.05, 3, 16} = 3.24$, reject H_0. **(e)** Critical range $= 0.0189$. Washing cycles for 22 and 24 minutes are not different with respect to dirt removal, but they are both different from 18- and 20-minute cycles. **(f)** 22 minutes. (24 minutes was not different, but 22 does just as well and would use less energy.) **(g)** The results are the same.

11.38 (a) Since $F = 0.075 < F_{0.05, 2, 15} = 3.68$, do not reject H_0. **(b)** Since $F = 4.09 > F_{0.05, 2, 15} = 3.68$, reject H_0. **(c)** Critical range $= 1.489$. Breaking strength is significantly different between 30 and 50 psi.

11.40 Since $F = 0.1899 < = 4.1132$, do not reject H_0. There is insufficient evidence to conclude that there is any interaction between type of breakfast and desired time. **(b)** Since $F = 30.4434 > 4.1132$, reject H_0. There is sufficient evidence to conclude that there is an effect that is due to type of breakfast. **(c)** Since $F = 12.4441 > 4.1132$, reject H_0. There is sufficient evidence to conclude that there is an effect that is due to desired time. **(e)** At the 5% level of significance, both the type of breakfast ordered and the desired time have an effect on delivery time difference. There is no interaction between the type of breakfast ordered and the desired time.
(f) (a) $F = 1.4611 < 4.1132$, do not reject H_0. There is insufficient evidence to conclude that there is any interaction between type of breakfast and desired time. **(b)** Since $F = 15.0000 > 4.1132$, reject H_0. There is sufficient evidence to conclude that there is an effect that is due to type of breakfast. **(c)** Since $F = 3.5458 < 4.1132$, do not reject H_0.

There is insufficient evidence to conclude that there is an effect due to desired time. **(e)** At the 5% level of significance, only the type of breakfast ordered has an effect on delivery time difference. There is no interaction between the type of breakfast ordered and the desired time.

11.42 (a) Since $F = 4.0835 > 3.55$, reject H_0. There is sufficient evidence to conclude that there is an interaction between buffer size and data file size. **(b)** and **(c)** You cannot directly conclude that there is a significant difference in mean read times due to buffer size or file size (main effects) because the mean read times for different buffer sizes are different for different sizes of files. **(e)** Conclusions about the relative speed of the buffers or file sizes cannot be drawn because buffers and file sizes interact. **(f)** In the completely randomized design, there is not enough evidence of a difference between mean access read times for the three file sizes. In the two-factor factorial design, there is significant interaction between buffer size and data file size.

11.44

ANOVA

Source of Variation	SS	df	MS	F	p-value	F crit
Sample (Browser)	8192	1	8192	41.75787	5.33E-07	4.195982
Columns (Computer)	133644.5	1	133644.5	681.239	3.4E-21	4.195982
Interaction	9800	1	9800	49.95449	1.09E-07	4.195982
Within	5493	28	196.1786			
Total	157129.5	31				

Since the p-value for the interaction is virtually zero, reject H_0. There is sufficient evidence to conclude that there is an interaction between browser and the type of computer. The existence of an interaction effect complicates the interpretation of the main effects. You cannot directly conclude that there is a significant difference between the mean download times of different browsers because the difference is not the same over all the computers. Likewise, you cannot directly conclude that there is a significant difference between the mean download times of different computers because the difference is not the same over the two browsers. It appears that the Dell performs the same, regardless of browser type, and that the Mac performs faster with Netscape than it does with Internet Explorer.

CHAPTER 12

12.2 (a) For $df = 1$ and $\alpha = 0.05$, $\chi^2 = 3.841$. **(b)** For $df = 1$ and $\alpha = 0.025$, $\chi^2 = 5.024$. **(c)** For $df = 1$ and $\alpha = 0.01$, $\chi^2 = 6.635$.

12.4 (a) All $f_e = 25$. **(b)** Since $\chi^2 = 4.00 > 3.841$, reject H_0.

12.6 (a) Since $\chi^2 = 1.0 < 3.841$, do not reject H_0. There is not enough evidence to conclude that there is a significant difference between males and females in the proportion who make gas mileage a priority. **(b)** Since $\chi^2 = 10.0 > 3.841$, reject H_0. There is enough evidence to conclude that there is a significant difference between males and females in the proportion who make gas mileage a priority. **(c)** The larger sample size in (b) increases the difference between the observed and expected frequencies and, hence, results in a larger test statistic value.

12.8 (a) $H_0: \pi_1 = \pi_2$. $H_1: \pi_1 \neq \pi_2$.

Observed Frequencies

	Column variable		
Row variable	Less Than $50,000	More Than $50,000	Total
Fair	225	180	405
Unfair	280	320	600
Total	505	500	1005

Expected Frequencies

	Column variable		
Row variable	Less Than $50,000	More Than $50,000	Total
Fair	203.5075	201.4925	405
Unfair	301.4925	298.5075	600
Total	505	500	1005

Data	
Level of Significance	0.05
Number of Rows	2
Number of Columns	2
Degrees of Freedom	1
Results	
Critical Value	3.841459
Chi-Square Test Statistic	7.64198
p-Value	0.005703
Reject the null hypothesis	

Decision rule: $df = 1$. If $\chi^2 > 3.841$, reject H_0.

Test statistic: $\chi^2 = \sum_{\text{all cells}} \frac{(f_0 - f_e)^2}{f_e} = 7.642$.

Decision: Since $\chi^2 = 7.642 > 3.841$, reject H_0. There is enough evidence to conclude that there is a significant difference in the proportion of adults who think the U.S. tax code is unfair between the two income groups. **(b)** p-value is 0.0057. The probability of obtaining a test statistic of 7.642 or larger when the null hypothesis is true is 0.0057. **(c)** The results of (a) and (b) are exactly the same as those of Problem 10.36. The χ^2 in (a) and the Z in Problem 10.36 (a) satisfy the relationship that $\chi^2 = 7.642 = Z^2 = (-2.7644)^2$, and the p-value in Problem 10.36 (b) is exactly the same as the p-value obtained in (b).

12.10 (a) Since $\chi^2 = 2.3226 < 3.841$, do not reject H_0. There is not enough evidence to conclude that there is a significant difference between undergraduate and MBA students in the proportion who selected the highest-cost fund. **(b)** p-value = 0.1275. The probability of obtaining a test statistic of 2.3226 or larger when the null hypothesis is true is 0.1275. **(c)** The results of (a) and (b) are exactly the same as those of Problem 10.38. The χ^2 in (a) and the Z in Problem 10.38 (a) satisfy the relationship that $\chi^2 = 2.3226 = Z^2 = (1.5240)^2$, and the p-value in Problem 10.38 (b) is exactly the same as the p-value obtained in (b).

12.12 (a) The expected frequencies for the first row are 20, 30, and 40. The expected frequencies for the second row are 30, 45, and 60. **(b)** Since $\chi^2 = 12.5 > 5.991$, reject H_0. **(c)** A vs. B: $0.20 > 0.196$; therefore, A and B are different. A vs. C: $0.30 > 0.185$; therefore, A and C are different. B vs. C: $0.10 < 0.185$; therefore, B and C are not different.

12.14 Since the calculated test statistic $742.3961 > 9.4877$, reject H_0 and conclude that there is a difference in the proportion of people who eat out at least once a week in the various countries. **(b)** p-value is virtually zero. The probability of a test statistic greater than 742.3961 or more is approximately zero if there is no difference in the proportion of people who eat out at least once a week in the various countries. **(c)** At the 5% level of significance, there is no significant difference between the proportions in Germany and France, while there is a significant difference between all the remaining pairs of countries.

12.16 (a) H_0: $\pi_1 = \pi_2 = \pi_3$. H_1: At least one proportion differs.

f_0	f_e	$(f_0 - f_e)$	$(f_0 - f_e)^2/f_e$
48	42.667	5.333	0.667
152	157.333	−5.333	0.181
56	42.667	13.333	4.167
144	157.333	−13.333	1.130
24	42.667	−18.667	8.167
176	157.333	18.667	2.215
			16.5254

Decision rule: $df = (c - 1) = (3 - 1) = 2$. If $\chi^2 > 5.9915$, reject H_0.

Test statistic: $\chi^2 = \sum_{\text{all cells}} \dfrac{(f_0 - f_e)^2}{f_e} = 16.5254$

Decision: Since $\chi^2 = 16.5254 > 5.9915$, reject H_0. There is a significant difference in the age groups with respect to major grocery shopping day. **(b)** p-value = 0.0003. The probability that the test statistic is greater than or equal to 16.5254 is 0.03%, if the null hypothesis is true.

(c)	Pairwise Comparisons	Critical Range	$\left| p_j - p_{j'} \right|$
	1 to 2	0.1073	0.04
	2 to 3	0.0959	0.16*
	1 to 3	0.0929	0.12*

There is a significant difference between the 35–54 and over-54 groups, and between the under 35 and over 54 groups. **(d)** The stores can use this information to target their marketing on the specific groups of shoppers on Saturday and the days other than Saturday.

12.18 (a) Since $\chi^2 = 2.817 < 7.815$, do not reject H_0. There is no evidence of a difference in fund selection based on student group. **(b)** p-value = 0.4207 **(c)** The Marascuilo procedure is not appropriate since there is no evidence of a difference among the groups.

12.20 $df = (r - 1)(c - 1) = (3 - 1)(4 - 1) = 6$.

12.22 (a) and **(b)** Since $\chi^2 = 20.680 > 12.592$, reject H_0. There is evidence of a relationship between the quarter of the year in which draft-aged men were born and the numbers assigned. It appears that the results of the lottery drawing are different from what would be expected if the lottery were random. **(c)** Since $\chi^2 = 9.803 < 12.592$, do not reject H_0. There is not enough evidence to conclude there is any relationship between the quarter of the year in which draft-aged men were born and the numbers assigned as their draft eligibilities during the Vietnam War. It appears that the results of the lottery drawing are consistent with what would be expected if the lottery were random.

12.24 (a) H_0: There is no relationship between the commuting time of company employees and the level of stress-related problems observed on the job. H_1: There is a relationship between the commuting time of company employees and the level of stress-related problems observed on the job.

f_0	f_e	$(f_0 - f_e)$	$(f_0 - f_e)^2/f_e$
9	12.1379	−3.1379	0.8112
17	20.1034	−3.1034	0.4791
18	11.7586	6.2414	3.3129
5	5.2414	−0.2414	0.0111
8	8.6810	−0.6810	0.0534
6	5.0776	0.9224	0.1676
18	14.6207	3.3793	0.7811
28	24.2155	3.7845	0.5915
7	14.1638	−7.1638	3.6233
			9.8311

(a) Decision rule: If $\chi^2 > 13.277$, reject H_0.

Test statistic: $\chi^2 = \sum_{\text{all cells}} \dfrac{(f_0 - f_e)^2}{f_e} = 9.8311$.

Decision: Since the $\chi^2 = 9.8311 < 13.277$, do not reject H_0. There is not enough evidence to conclude that there is a relationship between the commuting time of company employees and the level of stress-related problems observed on the job. **(b)** Since $\chi^2 = 9.831 > 9.488$, reject H_0. There is enough evidence at the 0.05 level to conclude that there is a relationship.

12.26 Since $\chi^2 = 129.520 > 21.026$, reject H_0. There is a relationship between when the decision is made of what to have for dinner and the type of household.

12.28 (a) H_0: $\pi_1 \geq \pi_2$ and H_1: $\pi_1 < \pi_2$, where 1 = beginning, 2 = end. Decision rule: If $Z < -1.645$, reject H_0.

Test statistic: $Z = \dfrac{B - C}{\sqrt{B + C}} = \dfrac{9 - 22}{\sqrt{9 + 22}} = -2.3349$

Decision: Since $Z = -2.3349 < -1.645$, reject H_0. There is evidence that the proportion of coffee drinkers who prefer Brand A is lower at the beginning of the advertising campaign than at the end of the advertising campaign. **(b)** p-value = 0.0098. The probability of a test statistic smaller than -2.3349 is 0.98% if the proportion of coffee drinkers who prefer Brand A is not lower at the beginning of the advertising campaign than at the end of the advertising campaign.

12.30 (a) Since $Z = -2.2361 < -1.645$, reject H_0. There is evidence that the proportion who prefer Brand A is lower before the advertising than after the advertising. **(b)** p-value = 0.0127. The probability of a test statistic less than -2.2361 is 1.27% if the proportion who prefer Brand A is not lower before the advertising than after the advertising.

12.32 (a) Since $Z = -3.8996 < -1.645$, reject H_0. There is evidence that the proportion of employees absent fewer than five days was lower in Year 1 than in Year 2. **(b)** The p-value is virtually zero. The probability of a test statistic smaller than -3.8996 is essentially zero if the proportion of employees absent fewer than five days was not lower in Year 1 than in Year 2.

12.34 (a) 31. **(b)** 29. **(c)** 27. **(d)** 25.

12.36 40 and 79.

12.38 (a) The ranks for Sample 1 are 1, 2, 4, 5, and 10. The ranks for Sample 2 are 3, 6.5, 6.5, 8, 9, and 11. **(b)** 22. **(c)** 44.

12.40 Decision: Since $T_1 = 22 > 20$, do not reject H_0.

12.42 (a) The data are ordinal. **(b)** The two-sample t test is inappropriate because the data can only be placed in ranked order. **(c)** Since $Z = -2.2054 < -1.96$, reject H_0. There is evidence of a significance difference in the median rating of California Cabernets and Washington Cabernets.

12.44 (a) $H_0: M_1 = M_2$ where Populations: 1 = Wing A, 2 = Wing B $H_1: M_1 \neq M_2$

Data	
Level of Significance	0.05
Population 1 Sample	
Sample Size	20
Sum of Ranks	561
Population 2 Sample	
Sample Size	20
Sum of Ranks	259
Intermediate Calculations	
Total Sample Size n	40
T1 Test Statistic	561
T1 Mean	410
Standard Error of T1	36.96846
Z Test Statistic	4.084563
Two-Tailed Test	
Lower Critical Value	−1.95996
Upper Critical Value	1.959964
p-value	4.42E-05
Reject the null hypothesis	

$$\mu_{T_1} = \frac{n_1(n+1)}{2} = \frac{20(40+1)}{2} = 410$$

$$\sigma_{T_1} = \sqrt{\frac{n_1 n_2 (n+1)}{12}} = \sqrt{\frac{20(20)(40+1)}{12}} = 36.9685$$

$$Z = \frac{T_1 - \mu_{T_1}}{\sigma_{T_1}} = \frac{561 - 410}{36.9685} = 4.0846$$

Decision: Since $Z = 4.0846 > 1.96$, reject H_0. There is enough evidence of a difference in the median delivery time in the two wings of the hotel. **(b)** The results of (a) are consistent with the results of Problem 10.74.

12.46 (a) Since $Z = -4.118 < -1.645$, reject H_0. There is enough evidence to conclude that the median crack size is less for the unflawed sample than for the flawed sample. **(b)** You must assume approximately equal variability in the two populations. **(c)** Using both the pooled-variance t test and the separate-variance t test allowed you to reject the null hypothesis and conclude in Problem 10.21 that the mean crack size is

less for the unflawed sample than for the flawed sample. In this test, using the Wilcoxon rank sum test with large-sample Z-approximation also allowed you to reject the null hypothesis and conclude that the median crack size is less for the unflawed sample than for the flawed sample.

12.48 (a) Since $-1.96 < Z = 0.6627 < 1.96$, do not reject H_0. There is not enough evidence to conclude that the median time to clear these problems between the two offices is different. **(b)** You must assume approximately equal variability in the two populations. **(c)** Using both the pooled-variance t test and the separate-variance t test, you do not reject the null hypothesis and conclude in Problem 10.16 that there is not enough evidence to show that the mean time to clear problems between the two offices is different. In this test, using the Wilcoxon rank sum test with large-sample Z approximation, you also do not reject the null hypothesis and conclude that there is not enough evidence to show that the median time to clear problems between the two offices is different.

12.50 (a) Decision rule: If $H > \chi_U^2 = 15.086$, reject H_0. **(b)** Decision: Since $H = 13.77 < 15.086$, do not reject H_0.

12.52 (a) $H = 13.517 > 7.815$, p-value $= 0.0036 < 0.05$, reject H_0. There is sufficient evidence of a difference in the median waiting time in the four locations. **(b)** The results are consistent with those of Problem 11.9.

12.54 (a) $H = 19.3269 > 9.488$, reject H_0. There is evidence of a difference in the median ratings of the ads. **(b)** The results are consistent with those of Problem 11.12. **(c)** Since the combined scores are not true continuous variables, the nonparametric Kruskal-Wallis rank test is more appropriate, since it does not require the scores to be normally distributed.

12.56 (a) Since $H = 22.26 > 7.815$ or the p-value is approximately zero, reject H_0. There is sufficient evidence of a difference in the median strength of the four brands of trash bags. **(b)** The results are the same.

12.64 (a) Since $\chi^2 = 0.412 < 3.841$, do not reject H_0. There is not enough evidence to conclude that there is a relationship between a student's gender and pizzeria selection. **(b)** Since $\chi^2 = 2.624 < 3.841$, do not reject H_0. There is not enough evidence to conclude that there is a relationship between a student's gender and pizzeria selection. **(c)** Since $\chi^2 = 4.956 < 5.991$, do not reject H_0. There is not enough evidence to conclude that there is a relationship between price and pizzeria selection. **(d)** p-value $= 0.0839$. The probability of a sample that gives a test statistic equal to or greater than 4.956 is 8.39% if the null hypothesis of no relationship between price and pizzeria selection is true. **(e)** Since there is no evidence that price and pizzeria selection are related, it is inappropriate to determine which prices are different in terms of pizzeria preference.

12.66 (a) Since $\chi^2 = 11.895 < 12.592$, do not reject H_0. There is not enough evidence to conclude that there is a relationship between the attitudes of employees toward the use of self-managed work teams and employee job classification. **(b)** Since $\chi^2 = 3.294 < 12.592$, do not reject H_0. There is not enough evidence to conclude that there is a relationship between the attitudes of employees toward vacation time without pay and employee job classification.

12.68 (a) Since $Z = -1.7889 < -1.645$, reject H_0. There is enough evidence of a difference in the proportion of respondents who prefer Coca-Cola before and after viewing the ads. **(b)** p-value $= 0.0736$. The probability of a test statistic that differs from 0 by 1.7889 or more in either direction is 7.36% if there is not a difference in the proportion of respondents who prefer Coca-Cola before and after viewing the ads. **(c)** The frequencies in the second table are computed from the row and column totals of the first table. **(d)** Since the calculated test statistic is $0.6528 < 3.8415$, do not reject H_0 and conclude that there is not a significant difference in preference for Coca-Cola before and after viewing the ads. **(e)** p-value = 0.4191. The probability of a test statistic larger than 0.6528 is 41.91% if there is not a significant difference in preference for Coca-Cola before and after viewing the ads. **(f)** The McNemar test performed using the information in the first table takes into consideration the fact that the same set of respondents are surveyed before and after viewing the ads while the chi-square test performed using the information in the second table ignores this fact. The McNemar test should be used because of the related samples (before–after comparison).

12.70 (a) Since $\chi^2 = 11.635 > 7.815$, reject H_0. There is enough evidence to conclude that there is a relationship between the presence of environmental goals and the type of manufacturing process. **(b)** p-value = 0.00874. The probability of obtaining a data set which gives rise to a test statistic of 11.635 or more is 0.00874 if there is no relationship between the presence of environmental goals and the type of manufacturing process. **(c)** Since $\chi^2 = 10.94 > 3.841$, reject H_0. There is enough evidence to conclude that there is a difference in improved environmental performance for teams with a specified goal of cutting costs. **(d)** p-value = 0.000941. The probability of obtaining a data set which gives rise to a test statistic of 10.94 or more is 0.000941 if there is no difference in improved environmental performance for teams with a specified goal of cutting costs. **(e)** Since $\chi^2 = 0.612 < 3.841$, do not reject H_0. There is not enough evidence to conclude that there is a difference in improved profitability for teams with a specified goal of cutting costs. **(f)** p-value = 0.4341. The probability of obtaining a data set which gives rise to a test statistic of 0.612 or more is 0.4341 if there is no difference in improved profitability for teams with a specified goal of cutting costs. **(g)** $\chi^2 = 3.454 < 3.841$, do not reject H_0. There is not enough evidence to conclude that there is a difference in improved morale for teams with a specified goal of cutting costs. **(h)** p-value = 0.063. The probability of obtaining a data set which gives rise to a test statistic of 3.454 or more is 0.063 if there is no difference in improved morale for teams with a specified goal of cutting costs.

CHAPTER 13

13.2 (a) Yes. **(b)** No. **(c)** No. **(d)** Yes.

13.4 (b)
$$b_1 = \frac{SSXY}{SSX} = \frac{2,775}{375} = 7.4$$

$$b_0 = \bar{Y} - b_1\bar{X} = 237.5 - 7.4(12.5) = 145$$

For each increase in shelf space of an additional foot, weekly sales are estimated to increase by \$7.40.
(c) $\hat{Y} = 145 + 7.4X = 145 + 7.4(8) = 204.2$, or \$204.20.

13.6 (b) $b_0 = -2.37$, $b_1 = 0.0501$. **(c)** For every cubic foot increase in the amount moved, mean labor hours are estimated to increase by 0.0501. **(d)** 22.67 labor hours.

13.8 (b) $b_0 = -368.2846$, $b_1 = 4.7306$. **(c)** For each additional million-dollar increase in revenue, the mean annual value will increase by an estimated \$4.7306 million. Literal interpretation of b_0 is not meaningful because an operating franchise cannot have zero revenue. **(d)** \$341.3027 million.

13.10 (b) $b_0 = 6.048$, $b_1 = 2.019$. **(c)** For every one Rockwell E unit increase in hardness, the mean tensile strength is estimated to increase by 2,019 psi. **(d)** 66.62 or 66,620 psi.

13.12 $r^2 = 0.90$. 90% of the variation in the dependent variable can be explained by the variation in the independent variable.

13.14 $r^2 = 0.75$. 75% of the variation in the dependent variable can be explained by the variation in the independent variable.

13.16 (a) $r^2 = \dfrac{SSR}{SST} = \dfrac{20,535}{30,025} = 0.684$. 68.4% of the variation in sales can be explained by the variation in shelf space.

(b) $S_{YX} = \sqrt{\dfrac{SSE}{n-2}} = \sqrt{\dfrac{\displaystyle\sum_{i-1}^{n}(Y_i - \hat{Y}_i)^2}{n-2}} = \sqrt{\dfrac{9490}{10}} = 30.8058$.

(c) Based on (a) and (b), the model should be very useful for predicting sales.

13.18 (a) $r^2 = 0.8892$. 88.92% of the variation in labor hours can be explained by the variation in cubic feet moved. **(b)** $S_{YX} = 5.0314$. **(c)** Based on (a) and (b), the model should be very useful for predicting the labor hours.

13.20 (a) $r^2 = 0.9334$. 93.34% of the variation in value of a baseball franchise can be explained by the variation in its annual revenue. **(b)** $S_{YX} = 42.4335$. **(c)** Based on (a) and (b), the model should be very useful for predicting the value of a baseball franchise.

13.22 (a) $r^2 = 0.4613$. 46.13% of the variation in the tensile strength can be explained by the variation in the hardness. **(b)** $S_{YX} = 9.0616$. **(c)** Based on (a) and (b), the model is only marginally useful for predicting tensile strength.

13.24 A residual analysis of the data indicates a pattern, with sizable clusters of consecutive residuals that are either all positive or all negative. This pattern indicates a violation of the assumption of linearity. A quadratic model should be investigated.

13.26 (a) There does not appear to be a pattern in the residual plot. **(b)** The assumptions of regression do not appear to be seriously violated.

13.28 (a) Based on the residual plot, there appears to be a nonlinear pattern in the residuals. A quadratic model should be investigated. **(b)** The assumptions of normality and equal variance do not appear to be seriously violated.

13.30 (a) Based on the residual plot, there appears to be a nonlinear pattern in the residuals. A quadratic model should be investigated. **(b)** There is some right-skewness in the residuals and some violation of the equal-variance assumption.

13.32 (a) An increasing linear relationship exists. **(b)** There is evidence of a strong positive autocorrelation among the residuals.

13.34 (a) No, because the data were not collected over time. **(b)** If a single store had been selected, then studied over a period of time, you would compute the Durbin-Watson statistic.

13.36 (a) $b_1 = \dfrac{SSXY}{SSX} = \dfrac{201399.05}{12495626} = 0.0161$.

$b_0 = \bar{Y} - b_1\bar{X} = 71.2621 - 0.0161\,(4393) = 0.458$. **(b)** $\hat{Y} = 0.458 + 0.0161X = 0.458 + 0.0161(4500) = 72.908$, or \$72,908. **(c)** There is no evidence of a pattern in the residuals over time.

(d) $D = \dfrac{\displaystyle\sum_{i=2}^{n}(e_i - e_{i-1})^2}{\displaystyle\sum_{i=1}^{n}e_i^2} = \dfrac{1243.2244}{599.0683} = 2.08 > 1.45$. There is no evidence of positive autocorrelation among the residuals. **(e)** Based on a residual analysis, the model appears to be adequate.

13.38 (a) $b_0 = -2.535$, $b_1 = .06073$. **(b)** \$2,505.40. **(d)** $D = 1.64 > d_U = 1.42$, so there is no evidence of positive autocorrelation among the residuals. **(e)** The plot shows some nonlinear pattern, suggesting that a nonlinear model might be better. Otherwise, the model appears to be adequate.

13.40 (a) 3.00. **(b)** $t_{16} = \pm 2.1199$. **(c)** Reject H_0. There is evidence that the fitted linear regression model is useful. **(d)** $1.32 \leq \beta_1 \leq 7.68$.

13.42 (a) $t = \dfrac{b_1 - \beta_1}{S_{b_1}} = \dfrac{7.4}{1.59} = 4.65 > t_{10} = 2.2281$ with 10 degrees of freedom for $\alpha = 0.05$. Reject H_0. There is evidence that the fitted linear regression model is useful. **(b)** $b_1 \pm t_{n-2} \, S_{b_1} = 7.4 \pm 2.2281(1.59)$ $3.86 \leq \beta_1 \leq 10.94$

13.44 (a) $t = 16.52 > 2.0322$; reject H_0. **(b)** $0.0439 \leq \beta_1 \leq 0.0562$.

13.46 (a) Since the p-value is approximately zero, reject H_0 at the 5% level of significance. There is evidence of a linear relationship between annual revenue and franchise value. **(b)** $3.7888 \leq \beta_1 \leq 4.5906$.

13.48 (a) The p-value is virtually $0 < 0.05$; reject H_0. **(b)** $1.246 \leq \beta_1 \leq 2.792$.

13.50 (b) If the S&P gains 30% in a year, the UOPIX is expected to gain an estimated 60%. **(c)** If the S&P loses 35% in a year, the UOPIX is expected to lose an estimated 70%.

13.52 (a) $r = 0.8935$. There appears to be a strong positive linear relationship between the mileage as calculated by owners and by current government standards. **(b)** $t = 5.2639 > 2.3646$, p-value $= 0.0012 < 0.05$. Reject H_0. At the 0.05 level of significance, there is a significant linear relationship between the mileage as calculated by owners and by current government standards.

13.54 (a) $r = 0.5497$. There appears to be a moderate positive linear relationship between the average Wonderlic score of football players trying out for the NFL and the graduation rate for football players at selected schools. **(b)** $t = 3.9485$, p-value $= 0.0004 < 0.05$. Reject H_0. At the 0.05 level of significance, there is a significant linear relationship between the average Wonderlic score of football players trying out for the NFL and the graduation rate for football players at selected schools. **(c)** There is a significant linear relationship between the average Wonderlic score of football players trying out for the NFL and the graduation rate for football players at selected schools, but the positive linear relationship is only moderate.

13.56 (a) $15.95 \leq \mu_{Y|X=4} \leq 18.05$. **(b)** $14.651 \leq Y_{X=4} \leq 19.349$.

13.58 (a) $\hat{Y} \pm t_{n-2} S_{YX} \sqrt{h_i}$

$$= 204.2 \pm 2.2281 \, (30.81)\sqrt{0.1373}$$
$$178.76 \leq \mu_{Y|X=8} \leq 229.64$$

(b) $\hat{Y} \pm t_{n-2} S_{YX} \sqrt{1 + h_i}$

$$= 204.2 \pm 2.2281 \, (30.81)\sqrt{1 + 0.1373}$$
$$131.00 \leq Y_{X=8} \leq 277.40$$

(c) Part (b) provides a prediction interval for the individual response given a specific value of the independent variable, and part (a) provides an interval estimate for the mean value, given a specific value of the independent variable. Since there is much more variation in predicting an individual value than in estimating a mean value, a prediction interval is wider than a confidence interval estimate.

13.60 (a) $20.799 \leq \mu_{Y|X=500} \leq 24.542$. **(b)** $12.276 \leq Y_{X=500} \leq 33.065$.

13.62 (a) $367.0757 \leq \mu_{Y|X=150} \leq 397.3254$. **(b)** $311.3562 \leq Y_{X=150} \leq 453.0448$.

13.74 (a) $b_0 = 24.84$, $b_1 = 0.14$. **(b)** For each additional case, the predicted mean delivery time is estimated to increase by 0.14 minutes. **(c)** 45.84. **(d)** No, 500 is outside the relevant range of the data used to fit the regression equation. **(e)** $r^2 = 0.972$. **(f)** There is no obvious pattern in the residuals, so the assumptions of regression are met. The model appears to be adequate. **(g)** $t = 24.88 > 2.1009$; reject H_0. **(h)** $44.88 \leq \mu_{Y|X=150} \leq 46.80$. **(i)** $41.56 \leq Y_{X=150} \leq 50.12$. **(j)** $0.128 \leq \beta_1 \leq 0.152$.

13.76 (a) $b_0 = -122.3439$, $b_1 = 1.7817$. **(b)** For each additional thousand dollars in assessed value, the estimated mean selling price of a house increases by \$1.7817 thousand. The estimated mean selling price of a house with a 0 assessed value is \$$-122.3439$ thousand. However, this interpretation is not meaningful in the current setting since the assessed value is very unlikely to be 0 for a house. **(c)** $\hat{Y} = -122.3439 + 1.78171X = -122.3439 + 1.78171(170) = 180.5475$ thousand dollars. **(d)** $r^2 = 0.9256$. So 92.56% of the variation in selling price can be explained by the variation in assessed value. **(e)** Neither the residual plot nor the normal probability plot reveal any potential violation of the linearity, equal variance and normality assumptions. **(f)** $t = 18.6648 > 2.0484$, p-value is virtually zero. Since p-value < 0.05, reject H_0. There is evidence of a linear relationship between selling price and assessed value. **(g)** $178.7066 \leq \mu_{Y|X=170} \leq 182.3884$. **(h)** $173.1953 \leq Y_{X=170} \leq 187.8998$. **(i)** $1.5862 \leq \beta_1 \leq 1.9773$.

13.78 (a) $b_0 = 0.30$, $b_1 = 0.00487$. **(b)** For each additional point on the GMAT score, the predicted mean GPI is estimated to increase by 0.00487. **(c)** 3.2225. **(d)** $r^2 = 0.798$. **(e)** There is no obvious pattern in the residuals, so the assumptions of regression are met. The model appears to be adequate. **(f)** $t = 8.43 > 2.1009$; reject H_0. **(g)** $3.144 \leq \mu_{Y|X=600} \leq 3.301$. **(h)** $2.886 \leq Y_{X=600} \leq 3.559$. **(i)** $.00366 \leq \beta_1 \leq .00608$.

13.80 (a) There is no clear relationship shown on the scatterplot. **(c)** Looking at all 23 flights, when the temperature is lower, there is likely to be some O-ring damage, particularly if the temperature is below 60 degrees. **(d)** 31 degrees is outside the relevant range, so a prediction should not be made. **(e)** Predicted $Y = 18.036 - 0.240X$, where $X =$ temperature and $Y =$ O-ring damage. **(g)** A nonlinear model would be more appropriate. **(h)** The appearance on the residual plot of a nonlinear pattern indicates a nonlinear model would be better.

13.82 (a) $b_0 = 14.6816$, $b_1 = 0.1135$. **(b)** For each additional percentage increase in graduation rate, the estimated mean average Wonderlic score increases by 0.1135. The estimated mean average Wonderlic score is 14.6816 for a school that has a 0% graduation rate. However, this interpretation is not meaningful in the current setting since graduation rate is very unlikely to be 0% for any school. **(c)** $\hat{Y} = 14.6816 + 0.11347X = 14.6816 + 0.11347(50) = 20.4$. **(d)** $r^2 = 0.3022$. So 30.22% of the variation in average Wonderlic score can be explained by the variation in graduation rate. **(e)** Neither the residual plot nor the normal probability plot reveal any potential violation of the linearity, equal variance, and normality assumptions. **(f)** $t = 3.9485 > 2.0281$, p-value $= 0.0004$. Since p-value < 0.05, reject H_0. There is evidence of a linear relationship between the average Wonderlic score for football players trying out for the NFL from a school and the graduation rate. **(g)** $19.6 \leq \mu_{Y|X=50} \leq 21.1$. **(h)** $15.9 \leq Y_{X=50} \leq 24.8$. **(i)** $0.0552 \leq \beta_1 \leq 0.1718$.

13.84 (a) $b_0 = -2629.222$, $b_1 = 82.472$. **(b)** For each additional centimeter in circumference, the mean weight is estimated to increase by 82.472 grams. **(c)** 2,319.08 grams. **(e)** $r^2 = 0.937$. **(f)** There appears to be a nonlinear relationship between circumference and weight. **(g)** p-value is virtually $0 < 0.05$; reject H_0. **(h)** $72.7875 \leq \beta_1 \leq 92.156$. **(i)** $2186.959 \leq \mu_{Y|X=60} \leq 2451.202$. **(j)** $1726.551 \leq Y_{X=60} \leq 2911.610$.

13.86 (b) $\hat{Y} = 931,626.16 + 21,782.76X$. **(c)** $b_1 = 21,782.76$ means that as the median age of the customer base increases by one year, the latest one-month mean sales total is estimated to increase by $21,782.76. **(d)** $r^2 = 0.0017$. Only 0.17% of the total variation in the franchise's latest one-month sales total can be explained by using the median age of customer base. **(e)** The residuals are very evenly spread out across different range of median age. **(f)** Since $-2.4926 < t = 0.2482 < 2.4926$, do not reject H_0. There is not enough evidence to conclude that there is a linear relationship between the one-month sales total and the median age of the customer base. **(g)** $-156,181.50 \le \beta_1 \le 199,747.02$.

13.88 (a) There is a positive linear relationship between total sales and the percentage of customer base with a college diploma. **(b)** $\hat{Y} = 789,847.38 + 35,854.15X$. **(c)** $b_1 = 35,854.15$ means that for each increase of one percent of the customer base having received a college diploma, the latest one-month mean sales total is estimated to increase by $35,854.15. **(d)** $r^2 = 0.1036$. So 10.36% of the total variation in the franchise's latest one-month sales total can be explained by the percentage of the customer base with a college diploma. **(e)** The residuals are quite evenly spread out around zero. **(f)** Since $t = 2.0392 > 2.0281$, reject H_0. There is enough evidence to conclude that there is a linear relationship between one-month sales total and percentage of customer base with a college diploma. **(g)** $b_1 \pm t_{n-2} S_{b_1} = 35,854.15 \pm 2.0281(17,582.269)$ $195.75 \le \beta_1 \le 71,512.60$.

13.90 (a) $b_0 = -13.6561$, $b_1 = 0.8923$. **(b)** For each additional unit increase in summated rating, the mean price per person is estimated to increase by $0.89. Since no restaurant will receive a summated rating of 0, it is inappropriate to interpret the Y intercept. **(c)** $31.01. **(d)** $r^2 = 0.4246$. **(e)** There is no obvious pattern in the residuals so the assumptions of regression are met. The model appears to be adequate. **(f)** The p-value is virtually $0 < 0.05$; reject H_0. **(g)** $29.07 \le \mu_{Y|X=50} \le 32.94$. **(h)** $16.95 \le Y_{X=50} \le 45.06$. **(i)** $0.6848 \le \beta_1 \le 1.1017$.

13.92 (a) Correlation of Microsoft and Ford is -0.07176, Microsoft and GM is -0.39235, Microsoft and IAL is 0.06686, Ford and GM is 0.860418, Ford and IAL is -0.91585, and GM and IAL is -0.83584. **(b)** There is a strong negative linear relationship between the stock price of Ford Motor Company and International Aluminum, a strong negative linear relationship between the stock price of General Motors and International Aluminum, a strong positive linear relationship between Ford Motor Company and General Motors, Inc., a moderately weak negative linear relationship between the stock price of General Motors and Microsoft, Inc., and almost no linear relationship between the stock price of Microsoft and Ford Motor Company and between Microsoft and International Aluminum. **(c)** It is not a good idea to have all the stocks in an individual's portfolio be strongly positively correlated among each other because the portfolio risk can be reduced if some of the stocks are negatively correlated.

CHAPTER 14

14.2 (a) For each one-unit increase in X_1, you estimate that Y will decrease 2 units, holding X_2 constant. For each one-unit increase in X_2, you estimate that Y will increase 7 units, holding X_1 constant. **(b)** The Y-intercept equal to 50 estimates the predicted value of Y when both X_1 and X_2 are zero.

14.4 (a) $\hat{Y} = -2.72825 + 0.047114X_1 + 0.011947X_2$. **(b)** For a given number of orders, for each increase of $1,000 in sales, mean distribution cost is estimated to increase by $47.114. For a given amount of sales, for each increase of one order, mean distribution cost is estimated to increase

by $11.95. **(c)** The interpretation of b_0 has no practical meaning here because it would represent the estimated distribution cost when there were no sales and no orders. **(d)** $\hat{Y} = -2.72825 + 0.047114(400) + 0.011947(4500) = 69.878$ or $69,878. **(e)** $66,419.93 \le \mu_{Y|X} \le 73,337.01$. **(f)** $59,380.61 \le Y_X \le 80,376.33$.

14.6 (a) $\hat{Y} = 156.4 + 13.081X_1 + 16.795X_2$. **(b)** For a given amount of newspaper advertising, each increase by $1,000 in radio advertising is estimated to result in a mean increase in sales of $13,081. For a given amount of radio advertising, each increase by $1,000 in newspaper advertising is estimated to result in a mean increase in sales of $16,795. **(c)** When there is no money spent on radio advertising and newspaper advertising, the estimated mean sales is $156,430.44. **(d)** $\hat{Y} = 156.4 + 13.081(20) + 16.795(20) = 753.95$ or $753,950. **(e)** $623,038.31 \le \mu_{Y|X} \le 884,860.93$. **(f)** $396,522.63 \le Y_X \le 1,111,376.60$.

14.8 (a) $\hat{Y} = 400.8057 + 456.4485X_1 - 2.4708X_2$, where $X_1 = $ land, $X_2 = $ age. **(b)** For a given age, each increase by one acre in land area is estimated to result in a mean increase in appraised value by $456.45 thousands. For a given acreage, each increase of one year in age is estimated to result in the mean decrease in appraised value by $2.47 thousands. **(c)** The interpretation of b_0 has no practical meaning here because it would represent the estimated appraised value of a new house that has no land area. **(d)** $\hat{Y} = 400.8057 + 456.4485(0.25) - 2.4708(45) = $403.73 thousands. **(e)** $372.7370 \le \mu_{Y|X} \le 434.7243$. **(f)** $235.1964 \le Y_X \le 572.2649$.

14.10 (a) $MSR = 15$, $MSE = 12$. **(b)** 1.25. **(c)** $F = 1.25 < 4.10$; do not reject H_0. **(d)** 0.20. **(e)** 0.04.

14.12 (a) $F = 97.69 > F_{U(2,15-2-1)} = 3.89$. Reject H_0. There is evidence of a significant linear relationship with at least one of the independent variables. **(b)** The p-value is 0.0001. **(c)** $r^2 = 0.9421$. 94.21% of the variation in the long-term ability to absorb shock can be explained by variation in forefoot absorbing capability and variation in midsole impact. **(d)** $r^2_{adj} = 0.93245$.

14.14 (a) $F = 74.13 > 3.467$; reject H_0. **(b)** p-value = 0. **(c)** $r^2 = 0.8759$. 87.59% of the variation in distribution cost can be explained by variation in sales and variation in number of orders. **(d)** $r^2_{adj} = 0.8641$.

14.16 (a) $F = 40.16 > F_{U(2,22-2-1)} = 3.522$. Reject H_0. There is evidence of a significant linear relationship. **(b)** The p-value is less than 0.001. **(c)** $r^2 = 0.8087$. 80.87% of the variation in sales can be explained by variation in radio advertising and variation in newspaper advertising. **(d)** $r^2_{adj} = 0.7886$.

14.18 (a) Based on a residual analysis, the model appears to be adequate. **(b)** There is no evidence of a pattern in the residuals versus time. **(c)** $D = \dfrac{1,077.0956}{477.0430} = 2.26$. **(d)** $D = 2.26 > 1.55$. There is no evidence of positive autocorrelation in the residuals.

14.20 There appears to be a quadratic relationship in the plot of the residuals against both radio and newspaper advertising. Thus, quadratic terms for each of these explanatory variables should be considered for inclusion in the model.

14.22 There is no particular pattern in the residual plots, and the model appears to be adequate.

14.24 (a) Variable X_2 has a larger slope in terms of the t statistic of 3.75 than variable X_1, which has a smaller slope in terms of the t statistic of 3.33. **(b)** $1.46824 \le \beta_1 \le 6.53176$. **(c)** For X_1: $t = 4/1.2 = 3.33 > 2.1098$, with 17 degrees of freedom for $\alpha = 0.05$. Reject H_0. There is evidence that X_1 contributes to a model already containing X_2. For X_2: $t = 3/0.8 = 3.75 > 2.1098$, with 17 degrees of freedom for $\alpha = 0.05$. Reject H_0. There is evidence that X_2 contributes to a model already containing X_1. Both X_1 and X_2 should be included in the model.

14.26 (a) 95% confidence interval on β_1: $b_1 \pm t_{n-k-1} S_{b_1}$, 0.0471 ± 2.0796 0.0203, $0.00488 \leq \beta_1 \leq 0.08932$. **(b)** For X_1: $t = b_1/S_{b_1} = 0.0471/0.0203 = 2.32 > 2.0796$. Reject H_0. There is evidence that X_1 contributes to a model already containing X_2. For X_2: $t = b_2/S_{b_2} = 0.01195/0.00225 = 5.31 > 2.0796$. Reject H_0. There is evidence that X_2 contributes to a model already containing X_1. Both X_1 (sales) and X_2 (orders) should be included in the model.

14.28 (a) $9.398 \leq \beta_1 \leq 16.763$. **(b)** For X_1: $t = 7.43 > 2.093$. Reject H_0. There is evidence that X_1 contributes to a model already containing X_2. For X_2: $t = 5.67 > 2.093$. Reject H_0. There is evidence that X_2 contributes to a model already containing X_1. Both X_1 (radio advertising) and X_2 (newspaper advertising) should be included in the model.

14.30 (a) $227.5865 \leq \beta_1 \leq 685.3104$. **(b)** For X_1: $t = 4.0922$ and p-value = 0.0003. Since p-value < 0.05, reject H_0. There is evidence that X_1 contributes to a model already containing X_2. For X_2: $t = -3.6295$ and p-value = 0.0012. Since p-value < 0.05, reject H_0. There is evidence that X_2 contributes to a model already containing X_1. Both X_1 (land area) and X_2 (age) should be included in the model.

14.32 (a) For X_1: $F = 1.25 < 4.96$; do not reject H_0. For X_2: $F = 0.833 < 4.96$; do not reject H_0. **(b)** 0.1111, 0.0769.

14.34 (a) For X_1: $SSR(X_1|X_2) = SSR(X_1 \text{ and } X_2) - SSR(X_2) = 3,368.087 - 3,246.062 = 122.025$,

$$F = \frac{SSR(X_2 \mid X_1)}{MSE} = \frac{122.025}{477.043 / 21} = 5.37 > 4.325.$$

Reject H_0. There is evidence that X_1 contributes to a model already containing X_2. For X_2: $SSR(X_2|X_1) = SSR(X_1 \text{ and } X_2) - SSR(X_1) = 3,368.087 - 2,726.822 = 641.265$,

$$F = \frac{SSR(X_2 \mid X_1)}{MSE} = \frac{641.265}{477.043 / 21} = 28.23 > 4.325. \text{ Reject } H_0.$$

There is evidence that X_2 contributes to a model already containing X_1. Since both X_1 and X_2 make a significant contribution to the model in the presence of the other variable, both variables should be included in the model. **(b)** $r^2_{Y1.2} = \dfrac{SSR(X_1 \mid X_2)}{SST - SSR(X_1 \text{ and } X_2) + SSR(X_1 \mid X_2)}$

$$= \frac{122.025}{3,845.13 - 3,368.087 + 122.025} = 0.2037.$$

Holding constant the effect of the number of orders, 20.37% of the variation in distribution cost can be explained by the variation in sales.

$$r^2_{Y2.1} = \frac{SSR(X_2 \mid X_1)}{SST - SSR(X_1 \text{ and } X_2) + SSR(X_2 \mid X_1)}$$

$$= \frac{641.265}{3,845.13 - 3,368.087 + 641.265} = 0.5734$$

Holding constant the effect of sales, 57.34% of the variation in distribution cost can be explained by the variation in the number of orders.

14.36 (a) For X_1: $F = 55.28 > 4.381$. Reject H_0. There is evidence that X_1 contributes to a model already containing X_2. For X_2: $F = 32.12 > 4.381$. Reject H_0. There is evidence that X_2 contributes to a model already containing X_1. Since both X_1 and X_2 make a significant contribution to the model in the presence of the other variable, both variables should be included in the model. **(b)** $r^2_{Y1.2} = 0.7442$. Holding constant the effect of newspaper advertising, 74.42% of the variation in sales can be explained by the variation in radio advertising. $r^2_{Y2.1} = 0.6283$. Holding constant the effect of radio advertising, 62.83% of the variation in sales can be explained by the variation in newspaper advertising.

14.40 (a) $\hat{Y} = 243.7371 + 9.2189X_1 + 12.6967X_2$, where $X_1 =$ number of rooms and $X_2 =$ neighborhood (east = 0). **(b)** Holding constant the effect of neighborhood, for each additional room, the selling price is estimated to increase by a mean of 9.2189 thousands of dollars, or \$9218.9. For a given number of rooms, a west neighborhood is estimated to increase the mean selling price over an east neighborhood by 12.6967 thousands of dollars, or \$12,696.7. **(c)** $\hat{Y} = 243.7371 + 9.2189(9) + 12.6967(0) = 326.7076$, or \$326,707.6. \$309,560.04 $\leq Y_X \leq$ \$343,855.1. \$321,471.44 $\leq \mu_{Y|X} \leq$ \$331,943.71. **(d)** Based on a residual analysis, the model appears to be adequate. **(e)** $F = 55.39$, the p-value is virtually 0. Since p-value < 0.05, reject H_0. There is evidence of a significant relationship between selling price and the two independent variables (rooms and neighborhood). **(f)** For X_1: $t = 8.9537$, the p-value is virtually 0. Reject H_0. Number of rooms makes a significant contribution and should be included in the model. For X_2: $t = 3.5913$, p-value = 0.0023 < 0.05. Reject H_0. Neighborhood makes a significant contribution and should be included in the model. Based on these results, the regression model with the two independent variables should be used. **(g)** $7.0466 \leq \beta_1 \leq 11.3913$, $5.2378 \leq \beta_2 \leq 20.1557$. **(h)** $r^2 = 0.867$. 86.7% of the variation in selling price can be explained by variation in number of rooms and variation in neighborhood. **(i)** $r^2_{adj} = 0.851$. **(j)** $r^2_{Y1.2} = 0.825$. Holding constant the effect of neighborhood, 82.5% of the variation in selling price can be explained by variation in number of rooms. $r^2_{Y2.1} = 0.431$. Holding constant the effect of number of rooms, 43.1% of the variation in selling price can be explained by variation in neighborhood. **(k)** The slope of selling price with number of rooms is the same, regardless of whether the house is located in an east or west neighborhood. **(l)** $\hat{Y} = 253.95 + 8.032X_1 - 5.90X_2 + 2.089X_1X_2$. For X_1X_2, p-value = 0.330. Do not reject H_0. There is no evidence that the interaction term makes a contribution to the model. **(m)** The model in (a) should be used.

14.42 (a) Predicted time = 8.01 + 0.00523 Depth − 2.105 Dry. **(b)** Holding constant the effect of type of drilling, for each foot increase in depth of the hole, the mean drilling time is estimated to increase by 0.0052 minutes. For a given depth, a dry drilling hole is estimated to reduce the mean drilling time over wet drilling by 2.1052 minutes. **(c)** 6.428 minutes, $6.210 \leq \mu_{Y|X} \leq 6.646$, $4.923 \leq Y_X \leq 7.932$. **(d)** The model appears to be adequate. **(e)** $F = 111.11 > 3.09$; reject H_0. **(f)** $t = 5.03 > 1.9847$; reject H_0. $t = -14.03 < -1.9847$; reject H_0. Include both variables. **(g)** $0.0032 \leq \beta_1 \leq 0.0073$, $-2.403 \leq \beta_2 \leq -1.808$. **(h)** 69.6% of the variation in drill time is explained by the variation of depth and variation in type of drilling. **(i)** 69.0%. **(j)** 0.207, 0.670. **(k)** The slope of the additional drilling time with the depth of the hole is the same, regardless of the type of drilling method used. **(l)** The p-value of the interaction term = 0.462 > 0.05, so the term is not significant and should not be included in the model. **(m)** The model in part (a) should be used.

14.44 (a) $\hat{Y} = 31.5594 + 0.0296X_1 + 0.0041X_2 + 0.000017159X_1X_2$, where $X_1 =$ sales, $X_2 =$ orders, p-value = 0.3249 > 0.05. Do not reject H_0.

There is not enough evidence that the interaction term makes a contribution to the model. **(b)** Since there is not enough evidence of any interaction effect between sales and orders, the model in Problem 14.4 should be used.

14.46 (a) The *p*-value of the interaction term = 0.002 < .05, so the term is significant and should be included in the model. **(b)** Use the model developed in this problem.

14.48 (a) For X_1X_2, *p*-value = 0.2353 > 0.05. Do not reject H_0. There is not enough evidence that the interaction term makes a contribution to the model. **(b)** Since there is not enough evidence of an interaction effect between total staff present and remote hours, the model in Problem 14.7 should be used.

14.58 (a) $\hat{Y} = -3.9152 + 0.0319X_1 + 4.2228X_2$, where X_1 = number of cubic feet moved and X_2 = number of pieces of large furniture. **(b)** Holding constant the number of pieces of large furniture, for each additional cubic feet moved, the mean labor hours are estimated to increase by 0.0319. Holding constant the amount of cubic feet moved, for each additional piece of large furniture, the mean labor hours are estimated to increase by 4.2228. **(c)**

$$\hat{Y} = -3.9152 + 0.0319(500) + 4.2228(2) = 20.4926$$

(d) Based on a residual analysis, the errors appear to be normally distributed. The equal-variance assumption might be violated because the variances appear to be larger around the center region of both independent variables. There might also be violation of the linearity assumption. A model with quadratic terms for both independent variables might be fitted. **(e)** $F = 228.80$, *p*-value is virtually 0. Since *p*-value < 0.05, reject H_0. There is evidence of a significant relationship between labor hours and the two independent variables (the amount of cubic feet moved and the number of pieces of large furniture). **(f)** The *p*-value is virtually 0. The probability of obtaining a test statistic of 228.80 or greater is virtually 0 if there is no significant relationship between labor hours and the two independent variables (the amount of cubic feet moved and the number of pieces of large furniture). **(g)** $r^2 = 0.9327$. 93.27% of the variation in labor hours can be explained by variation in the amount of cubic feet moved and the number of pieces of large furniture. **(h)** $r^2_{adj} = 0.9287$. **(i)** For X_1: $t = 6.9339$, the *p*-value is virtually 0. Reject H_0. The amount of cubic feet moved makes a significant contribution and should be included in the model. For X_2: $t = 4.6192$, the *p*-value is virtually 0. Reject H_0. The number of pieces of large furniture makes a significant contribution and should be included in the model. Based on these results, the regression model with the two independent variables should be used. **(j)** For X_1: $t = 6.9339$, the *p*-value is virtually 0. The probability of obtaining a sample that will yield a test statistic farther away than 6.9339 is virtually 0 if the number of cubic feet moved does not make a significant contribution holding the effect of the number of pieces of large furniture constant. For X_2: $t = 4.6192$, the *p*-value is virtually 0. The probability of obtaining a sample that will yield a test statistic farther away than 4.6192 is virtually 0 if the number of pieces of large furniture does not make a significant contribution holding the effect of the amount of cubic feet moved constant. **(k)** $0.0226 \le \beta_1 \le 0.0413$. We are 95% confident that the mean labor hours will increase by somewhere between 0.0226 and 0.0413 for each additional cubic foot moved, holding constant the number of pieces of large furniture. In Problem 13.44, we are 95% confident that the mean labor hours will increase by somewhere between 0.0439 and 0.0562 for each additional cubic foot moved regardless of the number of pieces of large furniture. **(l)** $r^2_{Y1.2} = 0.5930$. Holding constant the effect of the number of pieces of large furniture,

59.3% of the variation in labor hours can be explained by variation in the amount of cubic feet moved. $r^2_{Y2.1} = 0.3927$. Holding constant the effect of the amount of cubic feet moved, 39.27% of the variation in labor hours can be explained by variation in the number of pieces of large furniture.

14.60 (a) $\hat{Y} = -120.0483 + 1.7506X_1 + 0.3680X_2$, where X_1 = assessed value and X_2 = time period. **(b)** Holding constant the time period, for each additional thousand dollars of assessed value, the mean selling price is estimated to increase by 1.7507 thousand dollars. Holding constant the assessed value, for each additional month since assessment, the mean selling price is estimated to increase by 0.3680 thousand dollars. **(c)** $\hat{Y} = -120.0483 + 1.7506(170) + 0.3680(12) = 181.9692$ thousand dollars. **(d)** Based on a residual analysis, the model appears to be adequate. **(e)** $F = 223.46$, the *p*-value is virtually 0. Since *p*-value < 0.05, reject H_0. There is evidence of a significant relationship between selling price and the two independent variables (assessed value and time period). **(f)** The *p*-value is virtually 0. The probability of obtaining a test statistic of 223.46 or greater is virtually 0 if there is no significant relationship between selling price and the two independent variables (assessed value and time period). **(g)** $r^2 = 0.9430$. 94.30% of the variation in selling price can be explained by variation in assessed value and time period. **(h)** $r^2_{adj} = 0.9388$. **(i)** For X_1: $t = 20.4137$, the *p*-value is virtually 0. Reject H_0. The assessed value makes a significant contribution and should be included in the model. For X_2: $t = 2.8734$, *p*-value = $0.0078 < 0.05$. Reject H_0. The time period makes a significant contribution and should be included in the model. Based on these results, the regression model with the two independent variables should be used. **(j)** For X_1: $t = 20.4137$, the *p*-value is virtually 0. The probability of obtaining a sample that will yield a test statistic farther away than 20.4137 is virtually 0 if the assessed value does not make a significant contribution holding time period constant. For X_2: $t = 2.8734$, the *p*-value is virtually 0. The probability of obtaining a sample that will yield a test statistic farther away than 2.8734 is virtually 0 if the time period does not make a significant contribution holding the effect of the assessed value constant. **(k)** $1.5746 \le \beta_1 \le 1.9266$. We are 95% confident that the mean selling price will increase by an amount somewhere between \$1.5746 thousand and \$1.9266 thousand for each additional thousand-dollar increase in assessed value, holding constant the time period. In Problem 13.76, we are 95% confident that the mean selling price will increase by an amount somewhere between \$1.5862 thousand and \$1.9773 thousand for each additional thousand-dollar increase in assessed value regardless of the time period. **(l)** $r^2_{Y1.2} = 0.9392$. Holding constant the effect of the time period, 93.92% of the variation in selling price can be explained by variation in the assessed value. $r^2_{Y2.1} = 0.2342$. Holding constant the effect of the assessed value, 23.42% of the variation in selling price can be explained by variation in the time period.

14.62 (a) $\hat{Y} = 163.7751 + 10.7252X_1 - 0.2843X_2$, where X_1 = size and X_2 = age. **(b)** Holding age constant for each additional thousand square feet, the mean assessed value is estimated to increase by \$10.7252 thousand. Holding constant the size, for each additional year, the mean assessed value is estimated to decrease by \$0.2843 thousand. **(c)** $\hat{Y} = 163.7751 + 10.7252(1.75) - 0.2843(10) = 179.7017$ thousand dollars. **(d)** Based on a residual analysis, the errors appear to be normally distributed. The equal-variance assumption appears to be valid. There might also be violation of the linearity assumption for age. You may want to include a quadratic term for age in the model. **(e)** $F = 28.58$, *p*-value = 2.72776×10^{-5}. Since *p*-value < 0.05, reject H_0. There is evidence of a significant relationship between assessed value and the two independent variables (size and age). **(f)** *p*-value = 0.0000272776. The probability of obtaining a test statistic of 28.58 or greater is virtually 0 if there is no significant relationship between assessed value and the two independent variables (size and age). **(g)** $r^2 = 0.8265$. 82.65% of the variation in assessed value can be explained by variation in size and age. **(h)** $r^2_{adj} = 0.7976$. **(i)** For X_1: $t = 3.5581$, p-value $= 0.0039 < 0.05$. Reject H_0. The size of a house makes a significant contribution and should be included in the model. For X_2: $t = -3.4002$, p-value $= 0.0053 < 0.05$. Reject H_0. The age of a house makes a significant contribution and should be included in the model. Based on these results, the regression model with the two independent variables should be used. **(j)** For X_1: p-value $= 0.0039$. The probability of obtaining a sample that will yield a test statistic farther away than 3.5581 is 0.0039 if the size of a house does not make a significant contribution holding age constant. For X_2: p-value $= 0.0053$. The probability of obtaining a sample that will yield a test statistic farther away than -3.4002 is 0.0053 if the age of a house does not make a significant contribution, holding the effect of the size constant. **(k)** $4.1575 \le \beta_1 \le 17.2928$. We are 95% confident that the mean assessed value will increase by an amount somewhere between \$4.1575 thousand and \$17.2928 thousand for each additional thousand-square-foot increase in the size of a house, holding constant the age. In Problem 13.77, we are 95% confident that the mean assessed value will increase by an amount somewhere between \$9.4695 thousand and \$23.7972 thousand for each additional thousand-square-foot increase in heating area regardless of the age. **(l)** $r^2_{Y1.2} = 0.5134$. Holding constant the effect of age, 51.34% of the variation in assessed value can be explained by variation in the size. $r^2_{Y2.1} = 0.4907$. Holding constant the effect of the size, 49.07% of the variation in assessed value can be explained by variation in the age. **(m)** Based on your answers to (a) through (l), the age of a house does have an effect on its assessed value.

14.64 (a) $\hat{Y} = 146.0959 - 14.1276X_1 - 5.7491X_2$, where $X_1 =$ ERA and $X_2 =$ League (American $= 0$). **(b)** Holding constant the effect of the league, for each additional ERA, the mean number of wins is estimated to decrease by 14.1276. For a given ERA, a team in the National League is estimated to have a mean of 5.7491 fewer wins than a team in the American League. **(c)** $\hat{Y} = 146.0959 - 14.1276(4.5) - 5.7491(0) = 82.5216$ wins. **(d)** Based on a residual analysis, the errors appear to be right-skewed. The equal-variance and linearity assumptions appear to be valid. **(e)** $F = 26.37$, p-value $= 24.47667 \times 10^{-7}$. Since p-value < 0.05, reject H_0. There is evidence of a significant relationship between wins and the two independent variables (ERA and league). **(f)** For X_1: $t = -7.2404$, the p-value is virtually 0. Reject H_0. ERA makes a significant contribution and should be included in the model. For X_2: $t = -2.33$, p-value $= 0.0275 < 0.05$. Reject H_0. The league makes a significant contribution and should be included in the model. Based on these results, the regression model with the two independent variables should be used. **(g)** $-18.1312 \le \beta_1 \le -10.1241$. $-10.8119 \le \beta_2 \le -0.6863$. **(h)** $r^2 = 0.6614$. So 66.14% of the variation in the number of wins can be explained by ERA and league. **(i)** $r^2_{adj} = 0.6363$. **(j)** $r^2_{Y1.2} = 0.6601$. Holding constant the effect of league, 66.01% of the variation in the number of wins can be explained by variation in ERA. $r^2_{Y2.1} = 0.1674$. Holding constant the effect of ERA, 16.74% of the variation in the number of wins can be explained by the league a team plays in. **(k)** The slope of the number of wins with ERA is the same, regardless of whether the team belongs to the American or the National League. **(l)** $\hat{Y} = 152.0064 - 15.4246X_1 - 19.1124X_2 + 3.0526X_1X_2$. For X_1X_2, the p-value is 0.4497. Do not reject H_0. There is no evidence that the interaction term makes a contribution to the model. **(m)** The model in (a) should be used.

CHAPTER 15

15.2 (a) $\hat{Y} = -26.4007 + 3.7629X_1 + 26.5186X_2$, where $X_1 =$ carbohydrates and $X_2 =$ alcohol. **(b)** $\hat{Y} = 160.9443 + 5.7315X_1 - 0.0751X_1^2 - 53.4892X_2 + 7.9535X_2^2$, where $X_1 =$ carbohydrates and $X_2 =$ alcohol. **(c)** Carbohydrates: $t = -1.52$; p-value $= 0.1332 > 0.05$. Alcohol: $t = 2.0543$;

p-value $= 0.0449 < 0.05$. The quadratic term for alcohol improves the model, but the quadratic term for carbohydrates does not.

15.4 (b) Predicted yield $= 6.643 + 0.895$ AmtFert $- 0.00411$ AmtFert^2. **(c)** 49.168 pounds. **(d)** The model appears to be adequate. **(e)** $F = 157.32 > 4.26$; reject H_0. **(f)** p-value $= 0 < .05$, so the model is significant. **(g)** $t = -4.27 < -2.2622$; reject H_0. There is a significant quadratic effect. **(h)** p-value $= 0.002 < .05$, so the quadratic term is significant. **(i)** 97.2% of the variation in yield can be explained by the quadratic model. **(j)** 96.6%.

15.6 (a) 215.37. **(b)** For each additional unit of the logarithm of X_1, the logarithm of Y is estimated to increase by 0.9 units, holding all other variables constant. For each additional unit of the logarithm of X_2, the logarithm of Y is estimated to increase by 1.41 units, holding all other variables constant.

15.8 (a) $\hat{Y} = -184.6439 + 115.5693\sqrt{X_1} + 22.8081\sqrt{X_2}$, where $X_1 =$ alcohol and $X_2 =$ carbohydrates. **(b)** The residual plot suggests that the errors are right-skewed. The residual plots from the square-root transformation of carbohydrates and alcohol suggest some violation of the equal-variance assumption. **(c)** $F = 288.0536$, the p-value is virtually 0. Reject H_0. There is evidence of a relationship between calories and the square root of alcohol and/or the square root of carbohydrates. $t = 10.0878$, the p-value is virtually 0. Since the p-value < 0.05, reject H_0. There is a significant relationship between calories and the square root of percent alcohol. $t = 11.7751$, the p-value is virtually 0. Since the p-value < 0.05, reject H_0. There is a significant relationship between calories and the square root of the number of carbohydrates. **(d)** $r^2 = 0.9129$. 91.29% of the variation in the number of calories can be explained by variation in the percent alcohol and the variation in the number of carbohydrates. **(e)** $r^2_{adj} = 0.9097$. **(f)** The model in Problem 15.2 (b), which includes both the quadratic terms in alcohol and carbohydrates, is slightly better for prediction purpose since it has the highest adjusted r^2, of 0.92.

15.10 (a) Predicted ln(Yield) $= 2.475 + 0.0185$ AmtFert. **(b)** 32.95 pounds. **(c)** A quadratic pattern exists, so the model is not adequate. **(d)** $t = 6.11 > 2.2281$; reject H_0. **(e)** 78.9%. **(f)** 76.8%. **(g)** Choose the model from Problem 15.4. That model has a much higher adjusted r^2 of 96.6%.

15.12 1.25.

15.14 $R_1^2 = 0.64$, $VIF_1 = \dfrac{1}{1 - 0.64} = 2.778$, $R_2^2 = 0.64$, $VIF_2 = \dfrac{1}{1 - 0.64} = 2.778$. There is no evidence of collinearity.

15.16 $VIF = 1.0 < 5$. There is no evidence of collinearity.

15.18 $VIF = 1.0428$. There is no evidence of collinearity.

15.20 (a) 35.04. **(b)** $C_p > 3$. This does not meet the criterion for consideration of a good model.

15.22 Let $Y =$ selling price, $X_1 =$ assessed value, $X_2 =$ time period, and $X_3 =$ whether house was new ($0 =$ no, $1 =$ yes). Based on a full regression model involving all of the variables, all the VIF values (1.3, 1.0, and 1.3, respectively) are less than 5. There is no reason to suspect the existence of collinearity.

Based on a best-subsets regression and examination of the resulting C_p values, the best models appear to be a model with variables X_1 and X_2, which has $C_p = 2.8$, and the full regression model, which has $C_p = 4.0$. Based on a regression analysis with all the original variables, variable X_3 fails to make a significant contribution to the model at the 0.05 level. Thus, the best model is the model using the assessed value (X_1) and time (X_2) as the independent variables. A residual analysis shows no strong patterns. The final model is $\hat{Y} = -44.9882 + 1.7506X_1 + 0.3680X_2$, $r^2 = 0.9430$, $r^2_{adj} = 0.9388$. Overall significance of the model: $F = 223.4575$, $p < 0.001$. Each independent variable is significant at the 0.05 level.

15.28 (a) The most appropriate model includes only gate receipts as an independent variable. $\hat{Y} = 69.0198 + 0.2582X$; $r^2 = 0.202$.

15.30 (a) Best model: predicted Appraised Value = $136.794 + 276.0876$ Land $+ 0.1288$ House Size(sq ft) $- 1.3989$ Age.

15.32 (a) Predicted Appraised Value = $110.27 + 0.0821$ House Size(sq ft).

15.34 Let Y = appraised value, X_1 = land area, X_2 = interior size, X_3 = age, X_4 = number of rooms, X_5 = number of bathrooms, X_6 = garage size, $X_7 = 1$ if Glen Cove and 0 otherwise, and $X_8 = 1$ if Roslyn and 0 otherwise. **(a)** All *VIF*s are less than 5 in a full regression model involving all of the variables: There is no reason to suspect collinearity between any pair of variables. The following is the multiple regression model that has the smallest C_p (9.0) and the highest adjusted r^2 (0.891):

Appraised Value = $49.4 + 343$ Land (acres) $+ 0.115$ House Size (sq ft)

$- 0.585$ Age $- 8.24$ Rooms $+ 26.9$ Baths $+ 5.0$ Garage $+ 56.4$ Glen Cove

$+ 210$ Roslyn

The individual t test for the significance of each independent variable at the 5% level of significance concludes that only X_1, X_2, X_5, X_7, and X_8 are significant individually. This subset, however, is not chosen when the C_p criterion is used. The following is the multiple regression output for the model chosen by stepwise regression:

Appraised Value = $23.4 + 347$ Land (acres) $+ 0.106$ House Size (sq ft)

$- 0.792$ Age $+ 26.4$ Baths $+ 57.7$ Glen Cove $+ 213$ Roslyn

This model has a C_p value of 7.7 and an adjusted r^2 of 89.0. All the variables are significant individually at 5% level of significance. Combining the stepwise regression and the best subset regression results along with the individual t test results, the most appropriate multiple regression model for predicting the appraised value is

$$\hat{Y} = 23.40 + 347.02X_1 + 0.10614X_2 - 0.7921X_3$$
$$+26.38X_5 + 57.74X_7 + 213.46X_8$$

(b) The estimated mean appraised value in Glen Cove is 57.74 thousand dollars above Freeport for two otherwise identical properties. The estimated mean appraised value in Roslyn is 213.46 thousand dollars above Freeport for two otherwise identical properties.

15.36 Explanation: Remove vapor pressure, air temperature, soil radiation, and wind speed due to *VIF* > 5. After removing insignificant variables, the model has the single independent variable, dew point, and a coefficient of determination of only 10%.

15.38 (a) Let X_1 = Temp, X_2 = Win%, X_3 = OpWin%, X_4 = Weekend, X_5 = Promotion. **(b)** $\hat{Y} = -3,862.481 + 51.703X_1 + 21.108X_2 + 11.345X_3 + 367.538X_4 + 6,927.882X_5$. **(c)** Intercept: Since all the non-dummy independent variables cannot have zero values, the intercept cannot be interpreted. Temp: As the high temperature increases by 1 degree, the mean paid attendance is estimated to increase by 51.70, taking into consideration all the other independent variables included in the model. Win%: As the winning percentage of the team improves by 1%, the mean paid attendance is estimated to increase by 21.11, taking into consideration all the other independent variables included in the model. OpWin%: As the opponent team's winning percentage at the time of the game improves by 1%, the mean paid attendance is estimated to increase

by 11.35, taking into consideration all the other independent variables included in the model. Weekend: The mean paid attendance of a game played on a weekend is estimated to be 367.54 higher than when the game is played on a weekday, taking into consideration all the other independent variables included in the model. Promotion: The mean paid attendance on a promotion day is estimated to be 6,927.88 higher than when there is no promotion, taking into consideration all the other independent variables included in the model. **(d)** At a 0.05 level of significance, the independent variable that makes a significant contribution to the regression model individually is the promotion dummy variable. **(e)** Adjusted $r^2 = 0.2538$. 25.38% of the variation in attendance can be explained by the 5 independent variables after adjusting for the number of independent variables and the sample size. **(f)** The residual plots of temperature, team's winning percentage, and opponent team's winning percentage reveal potential violation of the equal-variance assumption. The normal probability plot also reveals non-normality in the residuals. **(g)** With all the 5 independent variables in the model: None of the *VIF* is > 5. Based on the smallest C_p value and the highest adjusted r^2, the best model includes win percentage, opponent's win percentage, and promotion. Since only X_5 makes a significant contribution to the regression model at the 5% level of significance, the more parsimonious model includes only X_5. **(b)** $\hat{Y} = 13,935.703 + 6,813.228X_5$. **(c)** Intercept: The estimated mean paid attendance on non-promotion days is 13,935.70. Promotion: The estimated mean paid attendance on promotion days will be 6,813.23 higher than when there is no promotion. **(d)** At the 0.05 level of significance, promotion makes a significant contribution to the regression model. **(e)** $r^2 = 0.2101$. So 21.02% of the variation in attendance can be explained by promotion. **(f)** The residual plot reveals non-normality in the residuals.

15.40 (a) Let X_1 = Temp, X_2 = Win%, X_3 = OpWin%, X_4 = Weekend, X_5 = Promotion. **(b)** $\hat{Y} = 10,682.455 + 82.205X_1 + 26.263X_2 + 7.367X_3 + 3,369.908X_4 + 3,129.013X_5$. **(c)** Intercept: Since all the non-dummy independent variables cannot have zero values, the intercept cannot be interpreted. Temp: As the high temperature increases by one degree, the mean paid attendance is estimated to increase by 82.21, taking into consideration all the other independent variables included in the model. Win%: As the winning percentage of the team improves by 1%, the mean paid attendance is estimated to increase by 26.26, taking into consideration all the other independent variables included in the model. OpWin%: As the opponent team's winning percentage at the time of the game increases by 1%, the mean paid attendance is estimated to increase by 7.37, taking into consideration all the other independent variables included in the model. Weekend: The mean paid attendance of a game played on a weekend is estimated to be 3,369.91 higher than when the game is played on a weekday, taking into consideration all the other independent variables included in the model. Promotion: The mean paid attendance on a promotion day is estimated to be 3,129.01 higher than when there is no promotion, taking into consideration all the other independent variables included in the model. **(d)** At the 0.05 level of significance, the independent variables that make a significant contribution to the regression model individually are temperature, team's winning percentage, and the weekend and promotion dummy variables. **(e)** Adjusted $r^2 = 0.3504$. So 35.04% of the variation in attendance can be explained by the five independent variables after adjusting for the number of independent variables and the sample size. **(f)** The residual plots of temperature, team's winning percentage, and opponent team's winning percentage do not show serious departure from the equal-variance assumption. The normal probability plot of the residuals does not show evidence of serious departure from normality. **(g)** With all the five independent variables in the model: None of the *VIF*s is > 5. Based on the smallest C_p value and the highest adjusted r^2, the best model is the full model that includes all the independent variables. Since only X_3 does not make significant contribution to the regression model at 5% level of significance, the more parsimonious model includes X_1, X_2, X_4, and X_5. **(b)** $\hat{Y} = 14{,}965.626 + 88.888X_1 + 23.269X_2 + 3{,}562.425X_4 + 3{,}029.087X_5$. **(c)** Intercept: Since all the non-dummy independent variables cannot have zero values, the intercept cannot be interpreted. Temp: As the high temperature increases by 1 degree, the mean paid attendance is estimated to increase by 88.89, taking into consideration all the other independent variables included in the model. Win%: As the winning percentage of the team increases by 1%, the mean paid attendance is estimated to increase by 23.27, taking into consideration all the other independent variables included in the model. Weekend: The mean paid attendance of a game played on a weekend is estimated to be 3,562.53 higher than when the game is played on a weekday, taking into consideration all the other independent variables included in the model. Promotion: The mean paid attendance on a promotion day is estimated to be 3,029.09 higher than when there is no promotion, taking into consideration all the other independent variables included in the model. **(d)** At the 0.05 level of significance, temperature and the weekend and promotion dummy variables make a significant contribution to the regression model individually. **(e)** Adjusted $r^2 = 0.3457$. So 34.57% of the variation in attendance can be explained by the four independent variables after adjusting for the number of independent variables and the sample size. **(f)** The residual plots of temperature and team's winning percentage do not show serious departure from the equal-variance assumption. The normal probability plot of the residuals also does not show evidence of serious departure from normality.

15.42 The Philadelphia Phillies ran the most effective promotions in 2002. An estimated additional 11,184.54 fans attended on days when a promotion was held.

CHAPTER 16

16.2 (a) 1959. **(b)** The first four years and the last four years.

16.4 (b), (c), and (d)

Year	Attendance	MA(3)	ES (W = 0.5)	ES (W = 0.25)
1999	1.47		1.4700	1.4700
2000	1.42	1.4600	1.4450	1.4575
2001	1.49	1.5133	1.4675	1.4656
2002	1.63	1.5633	1.5488	1.5067
2003	1.57	1.5767	1.5594	1.5225
2004	1.53	1.5033	1.5447	1.5244
2005	1.41		1.4773	1.4958

16.6 (b), (c), and (d)

Week	Nasdaq	MA (3)	ES(W = 0.50)	ES(W = 0.25)
3-Jan-06	2305.62	#N/A	2305.62	2305.62
9-Jan-06	2317.04	2290.12	2311.33	2308.48
17-Jan-06	2247.70	2289.66	2279.52	2293.28
23-Jan-06	2304.23	2271.50	2291.87	2296.02
30-Jan-06	2262.58	2276.23	2277.23	2287.66
6-Feb-06	2261.88	2268.94	2269.55	2281.21
13-Feb-06	2282.36	2277.09	2275.96	2281.50
21-Feb-06	2287.04	2290.67	2281.50	2282.89
27-Feb-06	2302.60	2283.89	2292.05	2287.81
6-Mar-06	2262.04	2290.37	2277.04	2281.37
13-Mar-06	2306.48	2293.78	2291.76	2287.65

Week	Nasdaq	MA (3)	ES(W = 0.50)	ES(W = 0.25)
20-Mar-06	2312.82	2319.70	2302.29	2293.94
27-Mar-06	2339.79	2330.54	2321.04	2305.40
3-Apr-06	2339.02	2334.97	2330.03	2313.81
10-Apr-06	2326.11	2336.00	2328.07	2316.88
17-Apr-06	2342.86	2330.51	2335.47	2323.38
24-Apr-06	2322.57	2336.00	2329.02	2323.18
1-May-06	2342.57	2302.97	2335.79	2328.02
8-May-06	2243.78	2260.08	2289.79	2306.96
15-May-06	2193.88	#N/A	2241.83	2278.69

(e) There appears to be very little trend in the first 20 weeks of 2006.

16.8 (b), (c), and (e)

Year	Cost	MA(3)	ES (W = 0.5)	ES (W = 0.25)
1994–1995	8.16		8.16	8.16
1995–1996	8.10	8.14	8.13	8.15
1996–1997	8.17	8.13	8.15	8.15
1997–1998	8.12	8.08	8.14	8.14
1998–1999	7.94	8.01	8.04	8.09
1999–2000	7.98	8.01	8.01	8.06
2000–2001	8.11	8.15	8.06	8.08
2001–2002	8.37	8.23	8.21	8.15
2002–2003	8.20	8.35	8.21	8.16
2003–2004	8.49	8.49	8.35	8.24
2004–2005	8.78		8.56	8.38

(d) $W = 0.5$: $\hat{Y}_{2005–2006} = E_{2004–2005} = 8.56$. **(e)** $W = 0.25$ $\hat{Y}_{2005–2006} = E_{2004–2005} = 8.38$. **(f)** The exponentially smoothed forecast for 2005–2006 with $W = 0.5$ is higher than that with $W = 0.25$.

16.10 (a) The Y intercept $b_0 = 4.0$ is the fitted trend value reflecting the real total revenues (in millions of dollars) during the origin or base year 1985. **(b)** The slope $b_1 = 1.5$ indicates that the real total revenues are increasing at an estimated rate of $1.5 million per year. **(c)** Year is 1989, $X = 1989 - 1985 = 4$ $\hat{Y}_5 = 4.0 + 1.5(4) = 10.0$ million dollars. **(d)** Year is 2006, $X = 2006 - 1985 = 21$, $\hat{Y}_{20} = 4.0 + 1.5(21) = 35.5$ million dollars. **(e)** Year is 2009, $X = 2009 - 1985 = 24$ $\hat{Y}_{23} = 4.0 + 1.5(24) = 40$ million dollars.

16.12 (b) There was an upward trend in the CPI in the United States over the 41-year period. The rate of increase became faster in the late 1970s and mid-1980s, but the rate of increase tapered off in the early 1980s and early 1990s.

16.14 (b) $\hat{Y} = 317.7193 + 64.3897X$, where $X =$ years relative to 1978. **(c)** $2,056.2407 billion for 2005 and $2,120.6304 billion for 2006. **(d)** There was an upward trend in federal receipts between 1978 and 2004. The trend appears to be nonlinear. A quadratic trend or exponential trend model could be explored.

16.16 (b) Linear trend: $\hat{Y} = 1.1556 + 0.7273X$, where X is relative to 1975. **(c)** Quadratic trend: $\hat{Y} = 2.1731 + 0.5168X + 0.0070X^2$, where X is relative to 1975. **(d)** Exponential trend: $\log_{10} \hat{Y} = 0.5452 + 0.0304X$, where X is relative to 1975. **(e)** Linear trend: $23.7006 billion for 2006 and $24.4279 billion for 2007. Quadratic trend: $24.9356 billion for 2006 and $25.8944 billion for 2007. Exponential trend: $30.8320 billion for 2006 and $33.0711 billion for 2007.

16.18 (b) Linear trend: $\hat{Y} = -3.2919 + 2.2245X$, where X is relative to 1987. **(c)** Quadratic trend: $\hat{Y} = -2.8475 + 2.0764X + 0.0078X^2$, where X is relative to 1987. **(d)** Exponential trend: $\log_{10}\hat{Y} = 0.3318 + 0.0752X$, where X is relative to 1987. **(e)** Investigating the first, second, and percentage differences suggests that the linear and quadratic trend models have about the same fit, while the exponential trend model seems to fit the early years' data better. **(f)** Using the exponential trend model, the prediction for January 1, 2007, is 68.6460.

16.20 (a) For Time Series I, the graph of Y vs. X appears to be more linear than the graph of log Y vs. X, so a linear model appears to be more appropriate. For Time Series II, the graph of log Y vs. X appears to be more linear than the graph of Y vs. X, so an exponential model appears to be more appropriate. **(b)** Time Series I: $\hat{Y} = 100.082 + 14.9752X$, where X = years relative to 1997. Time Series II: $\hat{Y} = 99.704(1.1501)^X$, where X = years relative to 1997. **(c)** Forecasts for the year 2007: Time Series I: 249.834, Time Series II: 403.709.

16.22 (b) Linear trend: $\hat{Y} = -88.9143 + 60.7670X$, where X is relative to 1993. **(c)** Quadratic trend: $\hat{Y} = 44.2107 - 5.7955X + 5.1202X^2$, where X is relative to 1993. **(d)** Exponential trend: $\log_{10}\hat{Y} = 1.5906 + 0.1083X$, where X is relative to 1993. **(e)** Linear trend: $\hat{Y}_{2007} = -88.9143 + 60.7670(14) = 761.82 = 762$ stores, $\hat{Y}_{2008} = -88.9143 + 60.7670(15) = 822.59 = 822$ stores. Quadratic trend: $\hat{Y}_{2007} = 44.2107 - 5.7955(14) + 5.1202(14)^2 = 966.63 = 967$ stores, $\hat{Y}_{2008} = 44.2107 - 5.7955(15) + 5.1202(15)^2 = 1109.32 = 1109$ stores. Exponential trend: 2007: $\log_{10}\hat{Y} = 1.5906 + 0.1083(14) = 1,278.79$ stores. 2008: $\log_{10}\hat{Y} = 1.5906 + 0.1083(15) = 1,640.97$ stores. **(f)** Both the quadratic trend model and the exponential trend model are capable of capturing the increasing rate of growth of the number of stores open. The rate of growth estimated by the exponential trend model is the highest, followed by the quadratic trend model, and finally the linear trend model. The quadratic trend model appears to be tracking the growth rate of the real data more closely than the exponential trend model, so it should be used to forecast the number of stores open for 2007 and 2008.

16.24 $t = 2.40 > 2.2281$; reject H_0.

16.26 (a) $t = 1.60 < 2.2281$; do not reject H_0.

16.28 (a)

	Coefficients	Standard Error	t Stat	p-Value
Intercept	0.466403278	0.306356098	1.522422045	0.14097168
YLag1	1.317428641	0.20587346	6.399215533	1.28746E-06
YLag2	−0.332888609	0.332080298	−1.002434084	0.326134451
YLag3	0.017904368	0.206925767	0.086525562	0.931766483

Since the p-value = 0.9318 > 0.05 level of significance, the third order term can be dropped.

(b)

	Coefficients	Standard Error	t Stat	p-Value
Intercept	0.457509354	0.273531737	1.672600622	0.106398594
YLag1	1.312968152	0.18697971	7.02198195	1.86248E-07
YLag2	−0.310579599	0.189251728	−1.641092544	0.112821589

Since the p-value = 0.1128 > 0.05 level of significance, the second order term can be dropped.

(c)

	Coefficients	Standard Error	t Stat	p-Value
Intercept	0.548034694	0.252114387	2.173754149	0.038334876
YLag1	1.010712337	0.018891696	53.50034886	9.62708E-30

Since the p-value is virtually 0, the first-order term cannot be dropped. **(d)** The most appropriate model for forecasting is the first-order autoregressive model: $\hat{Y}_i = 0.5480 + 1.0107Y_{i-1}$. The forecasts are 23.8955 for 2006 and 24.6995 for 2007.

16.30 (a) Since the p-value = 0.4933 > 0.05 level of significance, the third-order term can be dropped. **(b)** Since the p-value = 0.1447 > 0.05 level of significance, the second-order term can be dropped. **(c)** Since the p-value is virtually 0, the first-order term cannot be dropped. **(d)** The most appropriate model for forecasting is the first-order autoregressive model. $\hat{Y}_i = 2.9753 + 0.9255\,\hat{Y}_{i-1}$ The forecast is 35.1734 for 2007.

16.32 (a) 2.121. **(b)** 1.50.

16.34 (a) The residuals in the linear trend model show strings of consecutive positive and negative values. **(b)** $S_{YX} = 343.7342$. **(c)** $MAD = 267.1189$. **(d)** The residuals in the linear trend model show strings of consecutive positive and negative values. The linear trend model is inadequate in capturing the nonlinear trend.

16.36 (a) The residuals in the three trend models show strings of consecutive positive and negative values. The autoregressive model performs well for the historical data and has a fairly random pattern of residuals. The autoregressive model also has the smallest values in MAD and S_{YX}. **(b)** $S_{YX} = 1.3476$ for linear, 1.266 for quadratic, 2.181 for exponential, and 0.66 for first-order autoregressive. **(c)** $MAD = 1.073$ for linear, 0.95 for quadratic, 1.446 for exponential, and 0.468 for first-order autoregressive. **(d)** The autoregressive model would be the best model for forecasting.

16.38 (a) The residuals in the linear and quadratic trend models show strings of consecutive positive and negative values. The exponential trend model and the autoregressive model perform well for the historical data and have a fairly random pattern of residuals. **(b)** $S_{YX} = 7.6494$ for linear, 7.8672 for quadratic, 10.9752 for exponential, and 6.0344 for first-order autoregressive. **(c)** $MAD = 5.6777$ for linear, 5.6278 for quadratic, 6.7902 for exponential, and 4.3166 for first-order autoregressive. **(d)** Since the autoregressive model has the smallest values in MAD and S_{YX}, the autoregressive model would be the best model for forecasting.

16.40 (a) $\log\hat{\beta}_0 = 2$, $\hat{\beta}_0 = 10^2 = 100$. This is the fitted value for January 2000 prior to adjustment with the January multiplier. **(b)** $\log\hat{\beta}_1 = 0.01$, $\hat{\beta}_1 = 10^{0.01} = 1.0233$. The estimated average monthly compound growth rate is $(\hat{\beta}_1 - 1)100\% = 2.33\%$. **(c)** $\log\hat{\beta}_2 = 0.1$, $\hat{\beta}_2 = 10^{0.1} = 1.2589$. The January values in the time series are estimated to have a mean 25.89% higher than the December values.

16.42 (a) $\log\hat{\beta}_0 = 3.0$, $\hat{\beta}_0 = 10^{3.0} = 1,000$. This is the fitted value for January 2002 prior to adjustment by the quarterly multiplier. **(b)** $\log\hat{\beta}_1 = 0.1$, $\hat{\beta}_1 = 10^{0.1} = 1.2589$. The estimated average quarterly compound growth rate is $(\hat{\beta}_1 - 1)100\% = 25.89\%$. **(c)** $\log\hat{\beta}_3 = 0.2$, $\hat{\beta}_3 = 10^{0.2} = 1.5849$. The second-quarter values in the time series are estimated to have a mean 58.49% higher than the fourth-quarter values.

16.44 (b) $\log_{10}\hat{Y} = 2.8008 + 0.0077X - 0.0081Q_1 - 0.0011Q_2 - 0.0201Q_3$. **(c)** $\hat{Y}_{47} = 1362.3019$. **(d)** $\hat{Y}_{48} = 1452.4343$. **(e)** 2006: $\hat{Y}_{49} = 1450.9373$; $\hat{Y}_{50} = 1500.8344$; $\hat{Y}_{51} = 1462.2459$; $\hat{Y}_{52} = 1558.9907$. **(f)** The estimated quarterly compound growth rate is 1.79%. **(g)** The second-quarter values in the time series are estimated to have a mean 0.26% below the fourth-quarter values.

16.46 (b)

$$\log \hat{Y} = 0.6443 + 0.00178X + 0.00507M_1 + 0.00776M_2 + 0.00304M_3$$
$$+ 0.00034M_4 + 0.00187M_5 + 0.00429M_6 + 0.00164M_7$$
$$+ 0.00099M_8 - 5.20067 \times 10^{-5}M_9 - 0.00171M_{10} + 0.00194M_{11}$$

(c) $\hat{Y}_{72} = 5.90\%$. **(d)** Forecasts for all 12 months of 2006 are 5.991%, 6.053%, 6.012%, 6.0%, 6.046%, 6.104%, 6.092%, 6.108%, 6.118%, 6.12%, 6.197%, and 6.195%.
(e) $\log_{10}\hat{\beta}_1 = 0.00178$, $\hat{\beta}_1 = 10^{0.00178} = 1.0041$. The estimated quarterly compound growth rate is $(\hat{\beta}_1 - 1)100\% = 0.41\%$.
(f) $\log_{10}\hat{\beta}_8 = 0.00164$. $\hat{\beta}_8 = 10^{0.00164} = 1.0038$. $(\hat{\beta}_8 - 1)100\% = 0.38\%$. The July values in the time series are estimated to have a mean 0.38% above the December values.

16.48 (a) The retail industry is heavily subject to seasonal variation due to the holiday seasons, and so are the revenues for Toys Я Us.
(b) There is an obvious seasonal effect in the time series.
(c) $\log_{10}\hat{Y} = 3.6435 + 0.0020X - 0.3789Q_1 - 0.3846Q_2 - 0.3525Q_3$.
(d) The estimated quarterly compound growth rate is 0.46%
(e) $\log_{10}\hat{\beta}_2 = -0.3789$. $\hat{\beta}_2 = 10^{-0.3789} = 0.4179$.
$(\hat{\beta}_2 - 1)\,100\% = -58.21\%$. The first-quarter values in the time series are estimated to have a mean 58.21% below the fourth-quarter values. $\log_{10}\hat{\beta}_3 = -0.3846$. $\hat{\beta}_3 = 10^{-0.3846} = 0.4124$. $(\hat{\beta}_3 - 1)100\% = -58.76\%$. The second-quarter values in the time series are estimated to have a mean 58.76% below the fourth-quarter values. $\log_{10}\hat{\beta}_4 = -0.3525$. $\hat{\beta}_4 = 10^{-0.3525} = 0.4441$. $(\hat{\beta}_4 - 1)100\% = -55.59\%$. The third-quarter values in the time series are estimated to have a mean 55.59% below the fourth-quarter values. **(f)** Forecasts for 2006: $\hat{Y}_{41} = \$2,209.4155$ millions; $\hat{Y}_{42} = \$2,190.6572$ millions; $\hat{Y}_{43} = \$2,369.9104$ millions; $\hat{Y}_{44} = \$5,360.4578$ millions.

16.50 The price of the commodity in 2006 was 75% higher than in 1995.

16.52 (a) 186.96. **(b)** 162.16. **(c)** 154.42.

16.54 (a) and (c)

Year	Price	Price Index (base = 1980)	Price Index (base = 1990)	Year	Price	Price Index (base = 1980)	Price Index (base = 1990)
1980	3.208	100.00	109.98	1994	2.53	78.87	86.73
1981	2.777	86.56	95.20	1995	4.398	137.09	150.77
1982	2.475	77.15	84.85	1996	3.577	111.50	122.63
1983	2.528	78.80	86.66	1997	3.3	102.87	113.13
1984	2.495	77.77	85.53	1998	4.025	125.47	137.98
1985	2.585	80.58	88.62	1999	3.435	107.08	117.76
1986	2.737	85.32	93.83	2000	3.54	110.35	121.36
1987	3.192	99.50	109.43	2001	3.224	100.50	110.52
1988	2.635	82.14	90.33	2002	2.936	91.52	100.65
1989	2.964	92.39	101.61	2003	2.999	93.49	102.81
1990	2.917	90.93	100.00	2004	2.892	90.15	99.14
1991	2.945	91.80	100.96	2005	3.049	95.04	104.53
1992	2.668	83.17	91.46	2006	3.232	100.75	110.80
1993	2.352	73.32	80.63				

(b) The price of coffee in 2006 was 0.75% higher than it was in 1980.
(d) The price of coffee in 2006 was 10.80% higher than it was in 1990.
(e) It would not be a good idea to use 1995 as the base year because that was when the coffee price was at its peak. **(f)** There was a slight upward trend in coffee costs from 1980 to 2006, with a prominent cyclical component.

16.56 (a)

Year	Electricity	Natural Gas	Fuel Oil	Electricity Price Index (base = 1992)	Natural Gas Price Index (base = 1992)	Fuel Oil Price Index (base = 1992)
1992	44.501	26.376	0.985	100.00	100.00	100.00
1993	16.959	28.749	0.969	38.11	109.00	98.38
1994	48.200	30.236	0.919	108.31	114.63	93.30
1995	48.874	29.872	0.913	109.83	113.25	92.69
1996	48.538	29.570	1.007	109.07	112.11	102.23
1997	49.245	32.904	1.136	110.66	124.75	115.33
1998	46.401	31.438	0.966	104.27	119.19	98.07
1999	45.061	30.699	0.834	101.26	116.39	84.67
2000	45.207	31.664	1.189	101.59	120.05	120.71
2001	47.472	49.734	1.509	106.68	188.56	153.20
2002	47.868	36.316	1.123	107.57	137.69	114.01
2003	47.663	40.227	1.396	107.11	152.51	141.73
2004	49.159	46.048	1.508	110.47	174.58	153.10
2005	50.847	50.932	1.859	114.26	193.10	188.73
2006	57.223	66.402	2.418	128.59	251.75	245.48

(b)

Year	Electricity	Natural Gas	Fuel Oil	Electricity Price Index (base = 1996)	Natural Gas Price Index (base = 1996)	Fuel Oil Price Index (base = 1996)
1992	44.501	26.376	0.985	91.68	89.20	97.82
1993	16.959	28.749	0.969	34.94	97.22	96.23
1994	48.200	30.236	0.919	99.30	102.25	91.26
1995	48.874	29.872	0.913	100.69	101.02	90.67
1996	48.538	29.570	1.007	100.00	100.00	100.00
1997	49.245	32.904	1.136	101.46	111.27	112.81
1998	46.401	31.438	0.966	95.60	106.32	95.93
1999	45.061	30.699	0.834	92.84	103.82	82.82
2000	45.207	31.664	1.189	93.14	107.08	118.07
2001	47.472	49.734	1.509	97.80	168.19	149.85
2002	47.868	36.316	1.123	98.62	122.81	111.52
2003	47.663	40.227	1.396	98.20	136.04	138.63
2004	49.159	46.048	1.508	101.28	155.73	149.75
2005	50.847	50.932	1.859	104.76	172.24	184.61
2006	57.223	66.402	2.418	117.89	224.56	240.12

(c)

Year	Electricity	Natural Gas	Fuel Oil	Unweighted
1992	44.501	26.376	0.985	100.00
1993	16.959	28.749	0.969	64.95
1994	48.200	30.236	0.919	110.43
1995	48.874	29.872	0.913	110.85
1996	48.538	29.570	1.007	110.09
1997	49.245	32.904	1.136	115.90
1998	46.401	31.438	0.966	109.66
1999	45.061	30.699	0.834	106.58
2000	45.207	31.664	1.189	108.62
2001	47.472	49.734	1.509	137.37
2002	47.868	36.316	1.123	118.71
2003	47.663	40.227	1.396	124.25
2004	49.159	46.048	1.508	134.58
2005	50.847	50.932	1.859	144.22
2006	57.223	66.402	2.418	175.40

(d) 212.84 **(e)** 203.15.

16.70 (b) Linear trend: $\hat{Y} = 174778.8261 + 2335.3845X$, where X is relative to 1984. **(c)** 2006: 226,157.2857 thousands. 2007: 228,492.6702 thousands. **(d) (b)** Linear trend: $\hat{Y} = 114660.249 + 1655.0282X$, where X is relative to 1984. **(c)** 2006: 151,070.8701 thousands. 2007: 152,725.8984 thousands.

16.72 (b) Linear trend: $\hat{Y} = -1.3448 + 0.6075X$, where X is relative to 1975. **(c)** Quadratic trend: $\hat{Y} = 1.3856 + 0.0426X + 0.0188X^2$, where X is relative to 1975. **(d)** Exponential trend: $\log_{10} \hat{Y} = 0.1305 + 0.0414X$, where X is relative to 1975. **(e)** AR(3): $\hat{Y}_i = 0.1545 + 1.3742Y_{i-1} - 0.6504Y_{i-2} + 0.3444Y_{i-3}$. Test of A_3: p-value = 0.1373 > 0.05. Do not reject H_0 that $A_3 = 0$. Third-order term can be deleted. AR(2): $\hat{Y}_i = 0.1096 + 1.3021Y_{i-1} - 0.2490Y_{i-2}$. Test of A_2: p-value = 0.2341 > 0.05. Do not reject H_0 that $A_2 = 0$. Second-order term can be deleted. AR(1): $\hat{Y}_i = 0.1349 + 1.0702Y_{i-1}$. Test of A_1: p-value is virtually 0. Reject H_0 that $A_1 = 0$. A first-order autoregressive model is appropriate. **(f)** The residuals in the first three models show strings of consecutive positive and negative values. The autoregressive model performs well for the historical data and has a fairly random pattern of residuals. **(g)** S_{YX} is 1.4471 for the linear model, 0.4064 for the quadratic model, 1.0848 for the exponential model, and 0.3149 for the first-order autoregressive model. MAD is 1.1324 for the linear model, 0.2868 for the quadratic model, 0.6795 for the exponential model, and 0.2013 for the first-order autoregressive model. **(h)** The autoregressive model is the best model for forecasting because it has the smallest values in the standard error of the estimate and MAD. **(i)** 22.0729 billions.

16.74 (b) Variable A: $\hat{Y} = 9.5933 + 2.6679X$, where X = years relative to 1984. Variable B: $\hat{Y} = 11.7531 + 0.4286X$, where X = years relative to 1984. **(c)** Variable A: $\hat{Y} = 7.2475 + 3.3381X - 0.0305X^2$, where X = years relative to 1984. Variable B: $\hat{Y} = 10.2405 + 0.8608X - 0.0196X^2$, where X = years relative to 1984. **(d)** Variable A: $\log_{10} \hat{Y} = 1.1535 + 0.0341X$, where X = years relative to 1984. Variable B: $\log_{10} \hat{Y} = 1.0762 + 0.0121X$, where X = years relative to 1984. **(e)** Variable A: AR(3): $\hat{Y}_i = 5.0878 + 1.2279Y_{i-1} - 0.4156Y_{i-2} + 0.1066Y_{i-3}$. Test of A_3: p-value = 0.6698 > 0.05. Do not reject H_0 that $A_3 = 0$. Third-order term can be deleted. AR(2): $\hat{Y}_i = 5.0802 + 1.2000Y_{i-1} - 0.2860Y_{i-2}$. Test of A_2: p-value = 0.2149 > 0.05. Do not reject H_0 that $A_2 = 0$. Second-order term can be deleted. AR(1): $\hat{Y}_i = 4.4815 + 0.9415Y_{i-1}$. Test of A_1: p-value is virtually 0. Reject H_0 that $A_1 = 0$. A first-order autoregressive model is

appropriate. Variable B: AR(3): $\hat{Y}_i = 0.6661 + 2.0036Y_{i-1} - 1.4453Y_{i-2} + 0.4099Y_{i-3}$. Test of A_3: p-value = 0.0814 > 0.05. Do not reject H_0 that $A_3 = 0$. Third-order term can be deleted. AR(2): $\hat{Y}_i = 0.6289 + 1.6647Y_{i-1} - 0.6968Y_{i-2}$. Test of A_2: p-value = 0.0002 < 0.05. Reject H_0 that $A_2 = 0$. A second-order autoregressive model is appropriate. **(f)** Variable A: The residuals in the linear and quadratic trend models show strings of consecutive positive and negative values. There is no apparent pattern in the residuals of the exponential trend and autoregressive AR(1) model. Variable B: The residuals in the linear and exponential trend models show strings of consecutive positive and negative values. There is no apparent pattern in the residuals of the quadratic trend and autoregressive AR(2) model. **(g)** Variable A: S_{YX} is 8.3169 for the linear model, 8.4253 for the quadratic model, 10.4911 for the exponential model, and 6.4149 for the first-order autoregressive model. MAD is 5.7332 for the linear model, 5.9146 for the quadratic model, 6.8875 for the exponential model, and 4.9098 for the first-order autoregressive model. Variable B: S_{YX} is 0.8166 for the linear model, 0.1296 for the quadratic model, 1.0870 for the exponential model, and 0.0898 for the second-order autoregressive model. MAD is 0.6530 for the linear model, 0.0947 for the quadratic model, 0.8556 for the exponential model, and 0.0679 for the second-order autoregressive model. **(h)** The autoregressive model, AR(1), has the smallest values in the standard error of the estimate and MAD. Thus, the autoregressive model would probably be the best model for forecasting Variable A. The autoregressive model, AR(2), has the smallest values in the standard error of the estimate and MAD. Thus, the autoregressive model would probably be the best model for forecasting Variable B. **(i)** Variable A: 63.8349, Variable B: 19.4091. **(j)** You would recommend Variable A, which consists of investments that are primarily made in stocks, for a member of Teachers Retirement System of New York City because it had a higher return than Variable B over the past 23-year period.

CHAPTER 17

17.2

Event	A	B
1	0	40
2	0	200
3	0	300

17.4 (a) and **(b)** Payoff table:

	Action	
Event	**Company A**	**Company B**
1	$10,000 + $2 × 1,000 = $12,000	$2,000 + $4 × 1,000 = $6,000
2	$10,000 + $2 × 2,000 = $14,000	$2,000 + $4 × 2,000 = $10,000
3	$10,000 + $2 × 5,000 = $20,000	$2,000 + $4 × 5,000 = $22,000
4	$10,000 + $2 × 10,000 = $30,000	$2,000 + $4 × 10,000 = $42,000
5	$10,000 + $2 × 50,000 = $110,000	$2,000 + $4 × 50,000 = $202,000

(d) Opportunity loss table:

			Alternative Courses of Action	
Event	**Optimum Action**	**Profit of Optimum Action**	**A**	**B**
1	A	12,000	0	6,000
2	A	14,000	0	4,000
3	B	22,000	2,000	0
4	B	42,000	12,000	0
5	B	202,000	92,000	0

17.6 (a) 125, 112.5. **(b)** 25, 37.5. **(d)** Action A. **(e)** 60%, 11.11%. **(f)** 1.667, 9.0. **(g)** Action B.

17.8 (a) 10%. **(b)** 25%. **(c)** 4.0.

17.10 Stock A. It has a higher expected value and an equal standard deviation.

17.12 (a) EMV(Soft drinks) = $50(0.4) + 60(0.6) = 56$, EMV(Ice cream) = $30(0.4) + 90(0.6) = 66$. **(b)** EOL(Soft drinks) = $0(0.4) + 30(0.6) = 18$, EOL(Ice cream) = $20(0.4) + 0(0.6) = 8$. **(c)** $EVPI$ is the maximum amount of money the vendor is willing to pay for information about which event will occur. **(d)** Based on (a) and (b), choose to sell ice cream because you will earn a higher expected monetary value and incur a lower opportunity loss than choosing to sell soft drinks. **(e)** CV(Soft drinks) = $\frac{4.899}{56} \times 100\%$ = 8.7488%, CV(Ice cream) = $\frac{29.394}{66} \times 100\%$ = 44.536%. **(f)** Return-to-risk ratio for soft drinks = $\frac{56}{4.899}$ = 11.431, Return-to-risk ratio for ice cream = $\frac{66}{29.394}$ = 2.245. **(g)** Choose to sell soft drinks. **(h)** There are no differences.

17.14 (a) 1,050, 1,400, 1,400. **(b)** 522.02, 2498.00, 9656.09. **(c)** 4,100, 3,750, 3,750. **(d)** $EVPI$ = 3,750. **(e)** 49.72%, 178.43%, 689.72%. **(f)** 2.01, .56, .14.

17.16 (a) 25,200, 32,400. **(b)** 10,700, 3,500. **(c)** $EVPI$ = 3,500. **(d)** Sign with company B. **(e)** 114.25%, 177.73%. **(f)** 0.875, 0.563. **(g)** sign with company B if not risk averse.

17.18 (a) $P(E_1 \mid F) = .6$, $P(E_2 \mid F) = .4$. **(b)** 110, 110. **(c)** 30, 30. **(d)** $EVPI$ = 30. **(e)** Choose either one. **(f)** 66.8%, 11.1%. **(g)** 1.497, 8.981. **(h)** Action B.

17.20 P(Forecast cool | Cool weather) = 0.80, P(Forecast warm | Warm weather) = 0.70.
(a) Revised probabilities: P(Cool | Forecast cool) = $\frac{0.32}{0.5}$ = 0.64 P(Warm | Forecast cool) = $\frac{0.18}{0.5}$ = 0.36. **(b)** EMV(Soft drinks) = $50(0.64) + 60(0.36) = 53.6$, EMV(Ice cream) = $30(0.64) + 90(0.36) = 51.6$, EOL(Soft drinks) = $0(0.64) + 30(0.36) = 10.8$, EOL(Ice cream) = $20(0.64) + 0(0.36) = 12.8$, EMV with perfect information = $50(0.64) + 90(0.36) = 64.4$, $EVPI = EMV$, perfect information $- EMV_A = 64.4 - 53.6 = 10.8$. The vendor should not be willing to pay more than $10.80 for a perfect forecast of the weather. The vendor should sell soft drinks to maximize value and minimize loss. CV(Soft drinks) = $\frac{4.8}{53.6}$ 100% = 8.96%, CV(Ice cream) = $\frac{28.8}{51.6}$ 100% = 55.81%, Return-to-risk ratio for soft drinks = $\frac{53.6}{4.8}$ = 11.1667, Return-to-risk ratio for ice cream = $\frac{51.6}{28.8}$ = 1.7917. Based on these revised probabilities, the vendor's decision changes because of the increased likelihood of cool weather given a forecast for cool. Under these conditions, she should sell soft drinks to maximize the expected monetary value and minimize her expected opportunity loss.

17.22 (a) 0.5590, 0.2484, 0.1412, 0.0502, 0.0013. **(b)** EMV: 14,658.60, 11,315.4; EOL: 1004.4, 4347.6; CV: 38.42%, 99.55%; $RTRR$: 2.603, 1.005. **(c)** Under new circumstances, sign with Company A.

17.36 (c) 2,100, 2,660, 2,520, 1,960. **(d)** 980, 420, 560, 1,120. **(e)** $EVPI$ = $420. **(f)** Buy 8,000 loaves. **(g)** 0%, 15.79%, 35.57%, 57.14%. **(h)** Undefined, 6.333, 2.811, 1.750. **(i)** Buy 8,000 loaves. **(k) (c)** 2,100, 2,380, 2,100, 1,540. **(d)** 700, 490, 770, 1,330. **(e)** $EVPI$ = $490. **(f)** Buy 8,000 loaves. **(g)** 0%, 26.96%, 51.64%, 85.76%. **(h)** Undefined, 3.7097, 1.9365, 1.1660. **(i)** Buy 8,000 loaves.

17.38 (c) –$100,000 **(d)** 1,200,000, 1,100,000. **(e)** $EVPI$ = $1,100,000. **(f)** –.0356, undefined. **(g)** Continue using old packaging. **(h) (c)** –1,600,0000, 0. **(d)** 2,400,000, 800,000. **(e)** $EVPI$ = $800,000. **(f)** –.5101, undefined. **(g)** Continue using old packaging. **(j)** .2466, .6575, .0959. **(k) (c)** 150,600, 0. **(d)** 986,400, 1,137,000. **(e)** $EVPI$ = $986,400. **(f)** .0570, undefined. **(g)** Use new packaging. **(l)** .5902, .3934, .0164. **(m) (c)** –1,885,400, 0. **(d)** 2,360,800, 475,400. **(e)** $EVPI$ = $475,400. **(f)** –.7288, undefined. **(g)** Use old packaging.

17.40 (c) 180, 100. **(d)** 20, 100. **(e)** $EVPI$ = $20. **(f)** 1.2665, undefined. **(g)** Call the mechanic. **(h)** 0.0143, 0.2100, 0.4159, 0.3598. **(i) (c)** 248.386, 100. **(d)** 1.144, 149.53. **(e)** $EVPI$ = 1.144. **(f)** 2.055, undefined. **(g)** Call the mechanic. **(h)** 0.0143, 0.2100, 0.4159, 0.3598. **(i)** 248.386, 100 call the mechanic.

CHAPTER 18

18.2 (a) Day 4, Day 3. **(b)** LCL = 0.0397, UCL = 0.2460. **(c)** No, proportions are within control limits.

18.4 (a) $n = 500$, $\bar{p} = 761/16000 = 0.0476$

$$UCL = \bar{p} + 3\sqrt{\frac{\bar{p}(1 - \bar{p})}{n}}$$

$$= 0.0476 + 3\sqrt{\frac{0.0476(1 - 0.0476)}{500}} = 0.0761$$

$$LCL = \bar{p} - 3\sqrt{\frac{\bar{p}(1 - \bar{p})}{n}}$$

$$= 0.0476 - 3\sqrt{\frac{0.0476(1 - 0.0476)}{500}} = 0.0190$$

(b) Since the individual points are distributed around $\bar{p}$ without any pattern and all the points are within the control limits, the process is in a state of statistical control.

18.6 (a) UCL = 0.0176, LCL = 0.0082. The proportion of unacceptable cans is below the LCL on Day 4. There is evidence of a pattern over time since the last eight points are all above the mean and most of the earlier points are below the mean. Therefore, this process is out of control.

18.8 (a) UCL = 0.1431, LCL = 0.0752. Days 9, 26, and 30 are above the UCL. Therefore, this process is out of control.

18.12 (a) $d_2 = 2.059$. **(b)** $d_3 = 0.880$. **(c)** $D_3 = 0$. **(d)** $D_4 = 2.282$. **(e)** $A_2 = 0.729$.

18.14 (a) $\bar{R} = \frac{\sum_{i=1}^{k} R_i}{k} = 3.275$, $\bar{\bar{X}} = \frac{\sum_{i=1}^{k} \bar{X}_i}{k} = 5.941$.
R chart: $UCL = D_4\bar{R} = 2.282(3.275) = 7.4736$. LCL does not exist.
$\bar{X}$ chart: $UCL = \bar{\bar{X}} + A_2\bar{R} = 5.9413 + 0.729(3.275) = 8.3287$.
$LCL = \bar{\bar{X}} - A_2\bar{R} = 5.9413 - 0.729(3.275) = 3.5538$. **(b)** The process appears to be in control since there are no points outside the control limits and there is no evidence of a pattern in the range chart, and there are no points outside the control limits and there is no evidence of a pattern in the $\bar{X}$ chart.

18.16 (a) $\bar{R} = 0.8794$, LCL does not exist, UCL = 2.0068. **(b)** $\bar{\bar{X}} = 20.1065$, LCL = 19.4654, UCL = 20.7475. **(c)** The process is in control.

18.18 (a) $\bar{R} = 8.145$, LCL does not exist, UCL = 18.5869; $\bar{\bar{X}} = 18.12$, UCL = 24.0577, LCL = 12.1823. **(b)** There are no sample ranges outside the control limits and there does not appear to be a pattern in the range chart. The mean is above the UCL on Day 15 and below the LCL on Day 16. Therefore, the process is not in control.

18.20 (a) $\overline{R}$ = 0.3022, LCL does not exist, UCL = 0.6389; $\overline{\overline{X}}$ = 90.1312, UCL = 90.3060, LCL = 89.9573. **(b)** On Days 5 and 6, the sample ranges were above the UCL. The mean chart may be erroneous since the range is out of control. The process is out of control.

18.22 (a) $P(98 < X < 102) = P(-1 < Z < 1) = 0.6826$. **(b)** $P(93 < X < 107.5) = P(-3.5 < Z < 3.75) = 0.99968$. **(c)** $P(X > 93.8) = P(Z > -3.1) = 0.99903$. **(d)** $P(X < 110) = P(Z < 5) = 0.999999713$.

18.24 (a) $P(18 < X < 22)$

$$= P\left(\frac{18 - 20.1065}{0.8794/2.059} < Z < \frac{22 - 20.1065}{0.8794/2.059}\right)$$

$$= P(-4.932 < Z < 4.4335) = 0.9999$$

(b)

$$C_p = \frac{(USL - LSL)}{6(\overline{R}/d_2)} = \frac{(22 - 18)}{6(0.8794/2.059)}$$

$$= 1.56$$

$$CPL = \frac{(\overline{\overline{X}} - LSL)}{3(\overline{R}/d_2)} = \frac{(20.1065 - 18)}{3(0.8794/2.059)}$$

$$= 1.644$$

$$CPU = \frac{(USL - \overline{\overline{X}})}{3(\overline{R}/d_2)} = \frac{22 - 20.1065)}{3(0.8794/2.059)}$$

$$= 1.477$$

$$C_{pk} = \min(CPL, CPU) = 1.477$$

18.26 $\overline{R}$ = 0.2248, $\overline{\overline{X}}$ = 5.509, $n = 4$, $d_2 = 2.059$. **(a)** $P(5.2 < X < 5.8) = P(-2.83 < Z < 2.67) = 0.9962 - 0.0023 = 0.9939$. **(b)** Since only 99.39% of the tea bags are within the specification limits, this process is not capable of meeting the goal of 99.7%.

18.38 (a) The main reason that service quality is lower than product quality is because the former involves human interaction, which is prone to variation. Also, the most critical aspects of a service are often timeliness and professionalism, and customers can always perceive that the service could be done quicker and with greater professionalism. For products, customers often cannot perceive a better or more ideal product than the one they are getting. For example, a new laptop is better and contains more interesting features than any laptop the owner has ever imagined. **(b)** Both services and products are the results of processes. However, measuring services is often harder because of the dynamic variation due to the human interaction between the service provider and the customer. Product quality is often a straightforward measurement of a static physical characteristic like the amount of sugar in a can of soda. Categorical data are also more common in service quality. **(c)** Yes. **(d)** Yes.

18.40 (a) $\overline{p}$ = 0.2702, LCL = 0.1700, UCL = 0.3703. **(b)** Yes, RudyBird's market share is in control before the in-store promotion. **(c)** All seven days of the in-store promotion are above the UCL. The promotion increased market share.

18.42 (a) $\overline{p}$ = 0.75175, LCL = 0.62215, UCL = 0.88135. Although none of the points are outside the control limits, there is a clear pattern over time, with the last 13 points above the center line. Therefore, this process is not in control. **(b)** Since the increasing trend begins around Day 20, this change in method would be the assignable cause. **(c)** The control chart would have been developed using the first 20 days and then, a different control chart would be used for the final twenty points since they represent a different process.

18.44 (a) $\overline{p}$ = 0.1198, LCL = 0.0205, UCL = 0.2191. **(b)** Day 4 is above the UCL and Day 24 is below the LCL; therefore, the process is out of control. **(c)** Special causes of variation should be investigated to improve the process. Next, the process should be improved to decrease the proportion of undesirable trades.

Index

SITE LICENSE AGREEMENT AND LIMITED WARRANTY

READ THIS LICENSE CAREFULLY BEFORE USING THIS PACKAGE. BY USING THIS PACKAGE, YOU ARE AGREEING TO THE TERMS AND CONDITIONS OF THIS LICENSE. IF YOU DO NOT AGREE, DO NOT USE THE PACKAGE. PROMPTLY RETURN THE UNUSED PACKAGE AND ALL ACCOMPANYING ITEMS TO THE PLACE YOU OBTAINED. *THESE TERMS APPLY TO ALL LICENSED SOFTWARE ON THE DISK EXCEPT THAT THE TERMS FOR USE OF ANY SHAREWARE OR FREEWARE ON THE DISKETTES ARE AS SET FORTH IN THE ELECTRONIC LICENSE LOCATED ON THE DISK:*

1. GRANT OF LICENSE and OWNERSHIP: The enclosed computer programs and data ("Software") are licensed, not sold, to you by Prentice-Hall, Inc. ("We" or the "Company") in consideration of your purchase or adoption of the accompanying Company textbooks and/or other materials, and your agreement to these terms. We reserve any rights not granted to you. You own only the disk(s) but we and/or licensors own the Software itself. This license allows you to install, use, and display the enclosed copy of the Software on individual computers in the computer lab designated for use by any students of a course requiring the accompanying Company textbook and only for the as long as such textbook is a required text for such course, at a single campus or branch or geographic location of an educational institution, for academic use only, so long as you comply with the terms of this Agreement..

2. RESTRICTIONS: You may not transfer or distribute the Software or documentation to anyone else. Except for backup, you may not copy the documentation or the Software. You may not reverse engineer, disassemble, decompile, modify, adapt, translate, or create derivative works based on the Software or the Documentation. You may be held legally responsible for any copying or copyright infringement that is caused by your failure to abide by the terms of these restrictions.

3. TERMINATION: This license is effective until terminated. This license will terminate automatically without notice from the Company if you fail to comply with any provisions or limitations of this license. Upon termination, you shall destroy the Documentation and all copies of the Software. All provisions of this Agreement as to limitation and disclaimer of warranties, limitation of liability, remedies or damages, and our ownership rights shall survive termination.

4. LIMITED WARRANTY AND DISCLAIMER OF WARRANTY: Company warrants that for a period of 60 days from the date you purchase this Software (or purchase or adopt the accompanying textbook), the Software, when properly installed and used in accordance with the Documentation, will operate in substantial conformity with the description of the Software set forth in the Documentation, and that for a period of 30 days the disk(s) on which the Software is delivered shall be free from defects in materials and workmanship under normal use. The Company does not warrant that the Software will meet your requirements or that the operation of the Software will be uninterrupted or error-free. Your only remedy and the Company's only obligation under these limited warranties is, at the Company's option, return of the disk for a refund of any amounts paid for it by you or replacement of the disk. THIS LIMITED WARRANTY IS THE ONLY WARRANTY PROVIDED BY THE COMPANY AND ITS LICENSORS, AND THE COMPANY AND ITS LICENSORS DISCLAIM ALL OTHER WARRANTIES, EXPRESS OR IMPLIED, INCLUDING WITHOUT LIMITATION, THE IMPLIED WARRANTIES OF MERCHANTABILITY AND FITNESS FOR A PARTICULAR PURPOSE. THE COMPANY DOES NOT WARRANT, GUARANTEE OR MAKE ANY REPRESENTATION REGARDING THE ACCURACY, RELIABILITY, CURRENTNESS, USE, OR RESULTS OF USE, OF THE SOFTWARE.

5. LIMITATION OF REMEDIES AND DAMAGES: IN NO EVENT, SHALL THE COMPANY OR ITS EMPLOYEES, AGENTS, LICENSORS, OR CONTRACTORS BE LIABLE FOR ANY INCIDENTAL, INDIRECT, SPECIAL, OR CONSEQUENTIAL DAMAGES ARISING OUT OF OR IN CONNECTION WITH THIS LICENSE OR THE SOFTWARE, INCLUDING FOR LOSS OF USE, LOSS OF DATA, LOSS OF INCOME OR PROFIT, OR OTHER LOSSES, SUSTAINED AS A RESULT OF INJURY TO ANY PERSON, OR LOSS OF OR DAMAGE TO PROPERTY, OR CLAIMS OF THIRD PARTIES, EVEN IF THE COMPANY OR AN AUTHORIZED REPRESENTATIVE OF THE COMPANY HAS BEEN ADVISED OF THE POSSIBILITY OF SUCH DAMAGES. IN NO EVENT SHALL THE LIABILITY OF THE COMPANY FOR DAMAGES WITH RESPECT TO THE SOFTWARE EXCEED THE AMOUNTS ACTUALLY PAID BY YOU, IF ANY, FOR THE SOFTWARE OR THE ACCOMPANYING TEXTBOOK. SOME JURISDICTIONS DO NOT ALLOW THE LIMITATION OF LIABILITY IN CERTAIN CIRCUMSTANCES, THE ABOVE LIMITATIONS MAY NOT ALWAYS APPLY.

6. GENERAL: THIS AGREEMENT SHALL BE CONSTRUED IN ACCORDANCE WITH THE LAWS OF THE UNITED STATES OF AMERICA AND THE STATE OF NEW YORK, APPLICABLE TO CONTRACTS MADE IN NEW YORK, AND SHALL BENEFIT THE COMPANY, ITS AFFILIATES AND ASSIGNEES. This Agreement is the complete and exclusive statement of the agreement between you and the Company and supersedes all proposals, prior agreements, oral or written, and any other communications between you and the company or any of its representatives relating to the subject matter. If you are a U.S. Government user, this Software is licensed with "restricted rights" as set forth in subparagraphs (a)-(d) of the Commercial Computer-Restricted Rights clause at FAR 52.227-19 or in subparagraphs (c)(1)(ii) of the Rights in Technical Data and Computer Software clause at DFARS 252.227-7013, and similar clauses, as applicable.

Should you have any questions concerning this agreement or if you wish to contact the Company for any reason, please contact in writing:

Director, Media Production
Pearson Education
1 Lake Street
Upper Saddle River, NJ 07458